MANU / THE BIODIVERSITY OF SOUTHEASTERN PERU
LA BIODIVERSIDAD DEL SURESTE DEL PERÚ

Printed in Peru by Editorial Horizonte
Av. Nicolás de Piérola 995, Lima 1. Tel. 511-4279364. Fax: 511-4274341

ISBN 1-56098-710-3
Library of Congress Catalog information is available

Cover photographs: Chip Clark, National Museum of Natural History
Cover design and copy editor: Juan Damonte

MANU

The Biodiversity of Southeastern Peru

La Biodiversidad del Sureste del Perú

Edited by

Don E. Wilson
Abelardo Sandoval

1846–1996
Smithsonian
Institution

NATIONAL MUSEUM of
NATURAL HISTORY
SMITHSONIAN INSTITUTION

editorial
horizonte

MANU

The Biodiversity of Southeastern Peru	*La Biodiversidad del Sureste del Perú*

Edited by

Don E. Wilson
Abelardo Sandoval

15❋ 1846–1996
Smithsonian Institution

NATIONAL MUSEUM of NATURAL HISTORY
SMITHSONIAN INSTITUTION

editorial horizonte

Contents

8

Introduction

The Manu Biosphere Reserve in southeastern Peru is one of the richest regions in the world, with high habitat variability and enormous diversity of living organisms. Located in a remote area of the eastern Andean cordillera, this neotropical region has been the focus of considerable research on the flora and fauna in recent years. John Terborgh of Duke University and his colleagues have used their research station at Cocha Cashu to study tropical ecology and animal behavior for more than two decades. Those studies, published in a variety of outlets and widely disseminated, have contributed enormously to our understanding of tropical ecosystems. However, Cocha Cashu's location, deep within the core of the National Park, argued against the type of intense collecting activity necessary to document the tremendous biodiversity of the region.

In 1987, Terry Erwin of the Smithsonian Institution's National Museum of Natural History, initiated the Biological Diversity of Latin America (BIOLAT) program, to develop strategies for measuring and understanding biodiversity in the tropics. One of the first sites chosen for intensive inventory work was the Manu Biosphere Reserve, and a new field station was developed at Pakitza, a guard station on the boundary of the National Park. This allowed development of the intensive sampling and monitoring programs necessary to document the region's biodiversity.

Together with local Peruvian institutions and agencies, including the Dirección General de Forestal y Fauna del Ministerio de Agricultura (DGFF), the Asociación Peruana para la Conservación de la Naturaleza (APECO), and the Museo de Historia Natural de la Universidad Nacional Mayor de San Marcos among many others, the BIOLAT Program developed two parallel components for approaching important biodiversity issues: research and education. Research was oriented to the inventory, mapping, and taxonomy of flora and fauna, including the establishment of 1-ha permanent vegetation plots. Workshops, short courses, seminars, and lectures given by national and foreign scientists were the educational mechanisms, oriented towards "how to do it".

Studies were designed to present preliminary results at the end of the first five years. Thus, initial stages of research were originally planned to inventory various

11

important components of the flora and fauna. Manuscripts documenting preliminary results on various groups were published in a series of over one hundred scientific contributions (see Appendix 1). To supplement and summarize much of this information, we invited all participants in the program to contribute to the present volume.

Studies of biodiversity in Manu focused on species-level inventory, and a sampling scheme was developed in conjunction with the Smithsonian Institution/ Man and the Biosphere SI/MAB program. The focal point for many groups of plants and invertebrates was a series of 1-ha plots established to encompass the variety of habitats available at the site. For many other groups, including vertebrates, a variety of sampling schemes were used to develop checklists and to begin to document diversity. One important outgrowth of this effort was a major effort to develop standardized sampling schemes for various groups of organisms. Subsequently, Mercedes Foster of the National Biological Service, established a publication series that will produce handbooks documenting these techniques (Heyer, et al., 1994).

THE NATURAL SETTING

The natural history of the Manu region is known primarily from local investigations developed mainly at Cocha Cashu and Pakitza. Recent satellite imagery also is providing insights for studies of river and forest dynamics. An initial description of the natural history of the Pakitza site, particularly from an entomological perpective, was provided by BIOLAT Contribution # 13 (Erwin, 1991).

Location. The Manu National Park was created by the Peruvian government in 1973 for the purpose of preserving its flora and fauna. In 1977, this area became the Manu Biosphere Reserve which includes the Manu National Park, the Manu Reserve Zone and the buffer zone of surrounding territories. It covers an area of approximately 1,532,806 ha, located in the drainage of the Alto Madre de Dios river with coordinates ranging from 71°10'-72°25'W and 11°16'-13°11'S, along the eastern andean cordillera, with an elevational range of 300-4000 meters above sea level. It is shared by the departments of Cusco and Madre de Dios, in southeastern Peru.

The Manu river, a tributary of the Madre de Dios river, is the Reserve's main avenue, ranging in altitude from 310 m at Boca Manu to 400 m at Tayacome. The BIOLAT station at Pakitza is at 356 m, with tertiary soils mainly identified as clayish with some lime and sandy areas. Several terraces of various width, low altitude, and flat surfaces can be observed when one travels up river. The history of forests in the Manu basin can be reconstructed from the river profiles, as sequential forest growth is evident at various locations. Major topographic features of this ecosystem include beaches along the river, **cochas** or lakes of fluvial origins,

LOCATION OF STUDY AREA
MANU BIODIVERSITY PLOTS

Manu River

Panagua R.

Pakitza Station

B

C

A

Río Alto Madre de Dios

Manu
Diamante

Shintuya
Salvación
Pilcopata

Acjanaco
Paucartambo
Cusco

PERU

LIMA

CUSCO

Lago
Titicaca

MANU BIOSPHERE RESERVE

A   National Park
B   Reserve
C   Cultural Zone

forest terraces, and riverine or creekside riparian habitats. The latter's main feature is the presence of occasional pebbles visible during the dry season (May - September). In the rainy season (October - April) the Manu river and its tributaries reach high water levels up to 15 m above dry season lows.

Three main tributaries frame the BIOLAT sudy area in the Manu basin, Pachija, Fortaleza, and Pinquén. Mostly known as *quebradas*, these tributaries have been the focus of faunal, floral, and chemical analyses. Currently, the species list of Manu river fauna is one of the most complete for southeastern Peru.

A second area of BIOLAT studies includes the transect from Cusco to Atalaya. Encompassing elevations between 4000 and 500 m, it stretches from paramo and cloud forest to premontane tropical humid forest. Collections made along this transect help to define distributional limits for a variety of groups with detailed information from the lowland Pakitza site.

There are two ways of reaching Pakitza from Lima, Peru's capital city. Flying from Lima to Puerto Maldonado is the most common and time-efficient route, and the one favored by most BIOLAT scientists. It involves a one-and-a-half hour flight and two days of river-travel by small boat along the lower Madre de Dios and Manu rivers. The other travel alternative is a flight from Lima to Cusco, overland from Cusco to Atalaya on a dirt road so narrow as to be limited to alternate one-way traffic on alternate days, and a two-day boat trip along the alto Madre de Dios and Manu rivers. Initially, BIOLAT participants used the second option extensively, involving considerable time and high costs, but necessary for logistical preparations and transportation of field supplies and equipment. As a result, the Cusco-Atalaya option became one of the most important areas for sampling biodiversity at a variety of altitudinal zones and microhabitats.

THE CULTURAL SETTING

The region has been inhabited since prehistoric times. Archaeological remains such as ceramics suggest that the region was occupied at least from the begining of the current era. These early human inhabitants were mainly located along the rivers, upper terraces, and *cochas,* or lakes resulting from the natural enclosure of a river meander. A preliminary ceramic analysis shows a variety of patterned physical attributes suggesting a marked range of domestic use, and therefore, some economic activities. Site location and ceramic variation through time indicate the seasonally continuous use of the region by various ethnic populations.

Early written sources indicate that the Manu region was the setting of at least eight ethnic groups distributed between the lower and upper sections of the Manu river (Alvarez, 1899). The region was referred to as one of the most dangerous due to the inhabitants' behavior. Currently, three ethnic groups showing strong historical continuity can be identified: Machiguengas, Piros, and Yaminahuas. Their material cultures indicate that they survived the external inter-ethnic conflict as well as considerable environmental pressure. Ethnohistorical and ethnographic records, and current archaeological research in Manu show that these inhabitants occupied the region since prehistoric times, and the density and distribution of their sporadic settlements are expressions of their nomadic economy.

Current local inhabitants referred to them as conflicting groups due to territoriality and differential access to subsistence resources. Thus, hunters and fishermen today have to constantly define their territories due to the changing fluctuations of the river and riverine courses, during and after each rainy season. Preference of specific resources for fishing and hunting instruments, and the heterogeneity of food preparation and comsumption, are distinctive indicators of ethnic differentiation (Chiriff, 1975; Parker et al., 1983). Each of these groups has developed particular adaptive responses and cultural patterns by confronting the diversity of environmental limitations and accessibility to resources (Bunker, 1980). Most importantly, populations like these have provided first-hand methodological tools in the formulation and understanding of socio-economic processes of archeological societies in the Amazonian ecosystem.

It is unfortunate however, that wood and rubber exploitation, and modern fluvial traffic have contributed to the depopulation of streamside areas mainly along the Manu and Madre de Dios rivers. Furthermore, local development policies have dictated that native populations move *terra dentro*, in an unknown direction.

On the opposite bank of the river from the BIOLAT Pakitza station, three native women of unknown origins settled and built a typical residential hut. They seemed to be related by the maternal line. Their language could not be understood by any member of the local native groups. It is believed they were expelled from their own group located in *terra dentro*, far away from the river. Local natives suggest that reasons for their expulsion could be 1) the breaking of a tribal norm, or 2) the carrying of incurable deseases. However, other informants (Piro and Machiguenga) suggested that these women escaped from a tribal group representing descendants of the ancient Amarakaeris, locally known as Mashcos, due to their physical defects. This argument is based on the possibility that one of them was born with brain damage, suggesting unexplainable "divine punishment", which the Mashcos eliminate with the individual's death. Whatever the explanation, there is little doubt that these Mashco-piro women are expressions of the multi-ethnic composition of the region.

Hunting, fishing and small scale horticulture are the population's main subsistence activities. Mammals such as tapir, fishes as zúngaro, and slash-and-burn agriculture for corn and manioc are critical ingredients for an efficient subsistence economy (Bunker, 1980; Fearnside, 1986). Outside intervention has allowed the Manu river to gradually become the main connecting route with other ecosystems in the upper and lower lands. This activity has stimulated constant social and economic interactions, thus producing visible changes in the traditional structure of the current local ethnic groups.

ORGANIZATION

This volume is divided into three sections:

1- General floristics provides descriptions, explanations and applications of the plot and mapping methodologies.

2- The Flora section presents a variety of results mostly dealing with inventory and floristic composition, including checklists and diversity of various plant groups.

3 - The Fauna section is subdivided into vertebrate and invertebrate studies. All of the vertebrate groups are covered, including ichthyology, herpetology, ornithology, and mammalogy. Invertebrate groups include lepidoptera, homoptera, aracnidae, hymenoptera, carabidae, trichoptera, odonata, and parasitology. The contributions on vertebrate parasites are grouped with the Vertebrate papers.

ACKNOWLEDGEMENTS

The research summarized here has enjoyed the support of many organizations and individuals during the past decade. The Smithsonian Institution, through the National Museum of Natural History and many of its resident curators, research scientists, students, and fellows, provided much of the financial and personnel support for the project. Collaborators in Peru include the Museo de Historia Natural de la Universidad Nacional mayor de San Marcos, the Dirección General de Forestal y Fauna del Ministerio de Agricultura (DGFF), the Asociación Peruana para la Conservación de la Naturaleza (APECO), and the Fundación Peruana para la Conservación de la Naturaleza (FPCN). Participating researchers and students came from many additional Universities, Museums, and agencies, both within Peru, and from several foreign countries in addition to the United States.

The editors are particularly indebted to Terry Erwin, who provided the initial intellectual stimulus for the entire biodiversity effort documented in this volume. His foresight and organizational skills laid the foundation for a variety of research and training programs that continue in various forms today. Marsha Sitnik, Program Administrator for the Office of Biodiversity Programs, has provided administrative support for the program since its inception. Her efficiency and "can-do" attitude have impressed hundreds of participants over the years, and we are very grateful for her efforts. Judy Sansburry has provided the financial and accounting support for the program for many years, and her timely attention to detail and willingness to extend her job description and working hours are greatly appreciated. Francisco Dallmeier, Director of the SI/MAB program, was instrumental in the early development of the program, ongoing research efforts on the plots, and evolution of the training program to its current highly acclaimed version of Measuring and Monitoring Biodiversity. He and his staff provided constant support over the years, and we extend *abrazos* and *gracias*.

Many others in the Office of Biodiversity Programs, including Dorothy Caesar, Argelis Román, and Meridel Jellifer, have also provided ongoing support. George Venable of the NMNH Department of Entomology, has been a stalwart of the program over the years, providing both mapping and graphics support. Other members of the Museum of Natural History, too numerous to mention individually, have also contributed to the development of the volume in various ways. Additional acknowledgements can be found in the individual contributions.

Similarly, the list of individuals in Peru who have made continuous and noteworthy contributions to the effort over the years is long indeed. Gerardo Lamas, Hernán Ortega, and César Ascorra of the Museo Nacional in Lima have been stalwarts of the program from the beginning and we are grateful indeed for their continuing efforts.

Finally, we would like to thank all of the hundreds of participants in the program over the years, and in particular those who elected to contribute to the present volume. We hope this initial peek into the magnificent biodiversity of the region will spur additional efforts to document and understand the overwhelmingly complex, yet critically important tropical ecosystems of the world.

REFERENCES

Alvarez Maldonado, J. 1899. *Relación de la jornada y descubrimiento del río Manu por Juan Alvarez Maldonado en 1567.* Luis Ulloa, Sevilla.

Bunker, Stephen G. 1980. Forces of destruction in Amazonia. *Environment 22 (7):14-20, 34-43.*

Chiriff, Alberto 1975. Ocupación territorial de la Amazonía y marginación de la población nativa. *América Indígena 35(2):265-295.*

Erwin, T. L. 1990. Natural history of the carabid beetles at the BIOLAT Biologica Station, Río Manu, Pakitza, Perú. Revista Peruana de Entomología. Volume 33, Diciembre 1990:1-85

Fearnside, Philip M. 1986. *Human carrying capacity of the Brazilian rainforest.* New York, Columbia University Press.

Heyer, W. R., M. A. Donnelly, R. W. McDiarmid, L. C. Hayek, and M. S. Foster. 1994. *Measuring and Monitoring Biological Diversity: Standard methods for Amphibians.* Smithsonian Institution Press, Washington, D.C. 364 pp.

APPENDIX

NATIONAL MUSEUM OF NATURAL HISTORY — SMITHSONIAN
INSTITUTION
OFFICE OF BIODIVERSITY PROGRAMS
BIOLOGICAL DIVERSITY IN LATIN AMERICA (BIOLAT) PROJECT

CONTRIBUTION SERIES

1. **Vari, Richard P. and D.J. Siebert.** A new, unusually sexually dimorphic species of *Bryconamericus* (Pisces: Ostariophysi: Characidae) from the Peruvian Amazon. Proceedings of the Biological Society of Washington, Volume 103(3): 516-524 (1990).

2. **Saravia, Gladys and Amnon Freidberg.** Comportamiento de oviposición de *Anastrepha striata* (Diptera, Tephritidae) en Pakitza (Manu- Perú). Revista Peruana de Entomología, 31: 91-93 (1988), Lima, Perú

3. **Rocha Olivio, Omar.** Adición de Especies a la Avifauna de la Reserva de la Biósfera "Estación Biológica Beni", Bolivia. Ecología en Bolivia. Fauna Boliviana 4, 12: 13-15 (1988).

4. **de Pinna, Mario C.C. and Wayne C. Starnes.** A new genus and species of Sarcoglanidinae from the Rio Mamore, Amazon Basin, with comments on subfamilial phylogeny (Teleostei, Trichomycteridae). Journal of the Zoological Society of London. 222: 75-88 (1990).

5. **Erwin, Terry L.** Establishing a Tropical Species Co-occurrence Database. Part 1: A Plan for Developing consistent Biotic Inventories in Temperate and Tropical Habitats. Memorias del Museo de Historia Natural, No. 20, pp. 1-16 (1991), Lima, Perú

6. **Erwin, Terry L. and David L. Pearson.** Establishing a Tropical Species Co-occurrence Database. Part 3: An integrated approach toward understanding biological diversity. Memorias del Museo de Historia Natural, No. 20, pp. 17-36 (1991).

7. **Erwin, Terry L. and Margo Kabel.** Establishing a Tropical Species Co-occurrence Database. Part 2: An automated system for mapping dominant vegetation. Memorias del Museo de Historia Natural, No. 20, pp. 37-45 (1991), Lima, Perú.

8. **Wilson, Don E. and Jorge A. Salazar.** Los Murciélagos de la Reserva de la Biósfera Estación Biológica Beni, Bolivia. Ecología en Bolivia, Número 13: 47-56 (1989).

9. **Ascorra, C.F., D.E. Wilson, and C.O. Handley, Jr.** Geographic distribution of *Molossops neglectus* Williams and Genoways (Chiroptera: Molossidae). Journal of Mammalogy 72(4) (1991).

10. **Coddington, Jonathan A., Charles E. Griswold, Diana Silva Dávila, Efraín Peñaranda, and Scott F. Larcher.** Designing and testing sampling protocols to estimate biodiversity in tropical ecosystems.

DUDDLEY, E.C. (Ed.) The Unity of Evolutionary Biology, Proceedings of the Fourth International Congress of Systematic and Evolutionary Biology, Portland, Oregon, 1991, pp. 44-60. Critical Issues in Biodiversity Symposium.

11. Servat, Grace and David Pearson. Natural History Notes and Records for Seven Poorly Known Bird Species from Amazonian Peru. Bulletin British Ornithologist Club 111(2): 92-95, 1991

12. Lamas, Gerardo, Robert K. Robbins, and Donald J. Harvey. A Preliminary Survey of the Butterfly Fauna of Pakitza, Parque Nacional del Manu, Perú, with an estimate of its Species Richness. Publicaciones del Museo de Historia Natural, Serie Zoología, UNMSM (A) 40: 1-19 (1991).

14. Gelhaus, J.K. and Chen W. Young. The Immature Instars and Biology of the Crane Fly Genus *Brachypremna* Osten Sacken (Diptera: Tipulidae). Proc. Ent. Soc. Wash. 93:613-621, 1991

15. Spangler, Paul and Santiago. Ecuador. (In Prep)

16. Servat, Grace. A new method for studies of Arthropod weight from stomach contents of birds and other vertebrates. Journal of Field Ornithology. (In Press)

17. Morales, Víctor R. Estudio de la vocalización de algunas ranas dardovenenoso (Dendrobatidae, *Dendrobates*) en el Perú. Acta Zoologica Lilloana 41: 107-119. (1991)

18. Erwin, Terry L. An Evolutionary Basis for Conservation Strategies. Science, 1991, 253:750-752.

19. Ascorra, César F. and Don E. Wilson. Bat Frugivory and Seed Dispersal in the Amazon, Loreto, Peru. Publicaciones del Museo de Historia Natural, Universidad Nacional Mayor de San Marcos (A) 43: 1-6 (1992).

20. Ascorra, César, D.E. Wilson, and A.L. Gardner. Geographic distribution of *Micronycteris schmidtorum* Sanforn (Chiroptera: Phyllostomidae). Proceedings of the Biological Society of Washington. 104(2) (1991).

21. Ascorra, C.F., D.E. Wilson, and M. Romo. Lista anotada de los quirópteros del Parque Nacional Manu, Perú. Publicaciones del Museo de Historia Natural, UNMSM, Serie A Zoología 42:1-14 (1991).

22. Coddington, Jonathan and Herbert W. Levi. Systematics and Evolution of Spiders (Araneae). Annual Review of Ecology and Systematics. 22: 565-592 (1991)

23. Mazer, Susan. Seed and Litter Accumulation. Biotropica. (In Prep)

24. Robbins, Robert K. Comparison of Butterfly Diversity in the Neotropical and Oriental Regions. Journal of the Lepidopterists' Society. 46(4) 298-300 (1992).

25. Cocroft, Rex and Michael Pogue. Structure and Function of Communication Signals in a Neotropical Cicada, *Fidicina mannifera* (Fabricius) (Homoptera: Cicadidae). (In Prep)

26. Morales, Víctor R. Dos especies nuevas de *Dendrobates* (Anura: Dendrobatidae) para el Perú. Caribbean Journal of Science Vol. 28, No. 3-4, 191-199 (1992).

27. Morales, Víctor R., R.W. McDiarmid and R. Altig. The microhylid frogs of the Zona Reservada del Manu, with description of a new species (In Prep).

28. Morales, Víctor R. & R.W. McDiarmid. Systematic resolution and distribution of *Micrurus annellatus bolivianus* Roze (Reptilia, Elapidae). (In Prep).

29. **Lim, Burton K. and Don E. Wilson.** Taxonomic status of *Artibeus amplus* (Chiroptera: Phyllostomidae) in northern South America. Journal of Mammalogy 74(3):763-768, 1993

30. **Dallmeier, F., R. Foster, C. Romano, R. Rice and M. Kabel.** 1991 User's guide to the Beni Biosphere Reserve Biodiversity Plots, Vol. I. Smithsonian Institution, Washington, D.C. 134 p.

31. **Dallmeier, F., R. Foster, C. Romano, R. Rice and M. Kabel.** 1991 User's guide to the Beni Biosphere Reserve Biodiversity Plots, Vol. II. Smithsonian Institution, Washington, D.C. 131 p.

32. **Dallmeier, F., R. Foster, C. Romano, R. Rice and M. Kabel.** 1991. Field guide to the Beni Biosphere Reserve Biodiversity Plot 01. Smithsonian Institution, Washington, D.C. 58pp.

33. **Dallmeier, F., R. Foster, C. Romano, R. Rice and M. Kabel.** 1991. Field guide to the Beni Biosphere Reserve Biodiversity Plot 02. Smithsonian Institution, Washington, D.C. 58pp.

34. **Dallmeier, F., R. Foster, C. Romano, R. Rice and M. Kabel.** 1991. Field guide to the Beni Biosphere Reserve Biodiversity Plot 03. Smithsonian Institution, Washington, D.C. 58pp.

35. **Dallmeier, F., R. Foster, C. Romano, R. Rice and M. Kabel.** 1991. Field guide to the Beni Biosphere Reserve Biodiversity Plot 04. Smithsonian Institution, Washington, D.C. 58pp.

36. **Dallmeier, F., Margo Kabel and Richard Rice.** Methods for long-term biodiversity inventory plots in protected tropical forest. Francisco Dallmeier, Editor, UNESCO, MAB Digest, 1992: 11-45.

37. **Córdova, J.H. and Descailleaux, J.** Tres homocariotipos y un híbrido en poblaciones naturales de *Bufo marinus* (L) en Perú. Theorema (In Press)

38. **Córdova, J.H. and Descailleaux, J.** Evolución cariotípica del género *Bufo* (Amphibia: Anura) en el PerúTheorema. (In Press)

39. **Ascorra, César F. and Solari, Sergio A.** Adiciones a la Fauna Conocida de Quirópteros del Parque Nacional Manu, Perú. Publ. Mus. Hist. Nat. UNMSM. (In Press)

40. **Ramírez, Rina.** Acerca de *Plekocheilus* (Eurytus) floccosus (Spix, 1827) (Mollusca, Orthalicidae: Bulimulinae) en el Perú.» Publ. Mus. Hist. Nat. UNMSM (a) 34:1-8 (1990)

41. **Ramírez, Rina.** Primer registro de los Géneros *Adelopoma* Doering, 1884, *Caeciliodes* Ferussac, 1814, *Pupisoma* Stoliczka 1873 *Omalonyx* D'Orbigny, 1841 (Mollusca, Gastropoda) para el Perú. Publ. Mus. Hist. Nat. UNMSM (A) 41:1-8 (1991)

42. **Servat, Grace.** Estudio del Comportamiento en Lek de *Phaethornis ruber* (Aves: Trochilidae) en la Amazonía Peruana (Thesis - UNMSM). (In prep.)

43. **Servat, Grace.** An annotated list of birds of the Biological Station at Pakitza, Peru. (This volume)

44. **Don E. Wilson, César F. Ascorra, and Sergio Solari.** Bats as indicators of habitat disturbance. (This volume)

45. **Dallmeier, F., R. Foster, R. Rice and M. Kabel.** 1992 User's guide to the Manu Biosphere Reserve Biodiversity Plots, Vol. I. Smithsonian Institution, Washington, D.C.

46. **Dallmeier, F., R. Foster, R. Rice and M. Kabel.** 1992 User's guide to the Manu Biosphere Reserve Biodiversity Plots, Vol. II. Smithsonian Institution, Washington, D.C.

47. **Dallmeier, F., R. Foster, R. Rice and M. Kabel.** 1992 Field guide to the Manu Biosphere Reserve Biodiversity Plot 01. Smithsonian Institution, Washington, D.C.

48. **Dallmeier, F., R. Foster, R. Rice and M. Kabel.** 1992 Field guide to the Manu Biosphere Reserve Biodiversity Plot 02. Smithsonian Institution, Washington, D.C.

49. **Dallmeier, F., R. Foster, R. Rice and M. Kabel.** 1992 Field guide to the Manu Biosphere Reserve Biodiversity Plot 03. Smithsonian Institution, Washington, D.C.

50. **Dallmeier, F., R. Foster, R. Rice and M. Kabel.** 1992 Field guide to the Manu Biosphere Reserve Biodiversity Plot 04. Smithsonian Institution, Washington, D.C.

51. **Lamas, G., O.H. Mielke, and R.K. Robbins.** The Ahrenholz Technique for Attracting Tropical Skippers (Herperiidae). Journal of the Lepidopterists' Society. 47(1) 80-82 (1993).

52. **Robbins, Robert K.** Comparison of Neotropical and Oriental Butterfly Diversity. Journal of the Lepidoptera Society. (In Press).

53. **Pearson, David L.** Tiger Beetles as Indicators for Biodiversity Patterns in Amazonia. Research and Exploration 8(1), pp. 116-117. 1992.

54. **Silva, Diana and Jonathan Coddington.** Spiders of Pakitza (Madre de Dios, Peru): species richness and notes on community structure. (This volume)

55. **Heyer, W. Ronald**

56. **Louton, Jerry, Jon Gelhaus and Raymond Bouchard.** The aquatic fauna of water-filled bamboo (Poaceae: Bambusoideae: Guadua) internodes in a Peruvian lowland tropical forest. Biotropica (submitted).

57. **Cambra, Roberto A., and Diómedes Quintero A.** Studies on TIMULLA Ashmead (HYMENOPTERA: Mutillidae): New distribution records and synonimies, and descriptions of previously unknown allotypes. Pan-Pacific Entomologist, Vol. 69 (4): 299-313 (1993).

58. **Erwin, Terry,** *Agra*, arboreal beetles of Neotropical forests: *rufoaenea* and *quararibea* group systematics (Carabidae). In press.

59. **Burnham, Robyn.** Reconstructing Richness in the Plant Fossil Record. Palaios, 1993, V. 8, p. 376-384

60. **Brown, Brian V. and D. H. Feener.** Life History and immature stages of *Rhyncophoromyia maculineura*, an ant-parasitizing phorid fly (Diptera: Phoridae) from Peru. Journal of Natural History, 27, pp. 429-434 (1993).

61. **Pearson, David L. and Fabio Cassola.** World-Wide Species Richness Patterns of Tiger Beetles (Coleoptera: Cicindelidae): Indicator Taxon for Bio-

diversity and Conservation Studies. Conservation Biology, Vol. 6, No. 3, (1992).

62. Servat, Grace. First Record of *Capsiempis flaveola* (Yellow- tyrannulet) for Peru. Wilson Bulletin.

63. Servat, Grace. Comportamiento de Forrajeo y Uso de Recursos en Leks de *Phaethornis ruber*.

64. Servat, Grace. A Checklist of Birds of the Pacaya Samiria National Reserve.

65. Guerrero, Ricardo. Notas sobre Streblidae (Diptera: Pupipara) de Venezuela. II. El Género *Xenotrichobius* Wenzel, 1976, con descripción de dos especies nuevas. Mitteilungen der Munchner Entomologischen Gesellschaft.

66. Guerrero, Ricardo. Catálogo de los Streblidae (Diptera: Pupipara) parásitos de Murciélagos (Mammalia: Chiroptera) del Nuevo Mundo. I. Clave para los Géneros y Nycterophiliinae. Acta Biológica Venezuelica.

67. Guerrero, Ricardo. Catálogo de los Streblidae (Diptera: Pupipara) parásitos de Murciélagos (Mammalia: Chiroptera) del Nuevo Mundo. II. Los grupos: *pallidus, caecus, major, uniformism* y *longipes* del Género *Trichobius* Gervais, 1844. Acta Biológica Venezuelica.

68. Guerrero, Ricardo. Catálogo de los Streblidae (Diptera: Pupipara) parásitos de Murciélagos (Mammalia: Chiroptera) del Nuevo Mundo. III. Los grupos: *dugesii, dunni* y *phyllostomae* del Género *Trichobius* Gervais, 1844. Acta Biológica Venezuelica.

69. Guerrero, Ricardo. Catálogo de los Streblidae (Diptera: Pupipara) parásitos de Murciélagos (Mammalia: Chiroptera) del Nuevo Mundo. IV. Trichobiinae con alas funcionales. Boletín de Entomología de Venezuela.

70. Guerrero, Ricardo. Catálogo de los Streblidae (Diptera: Pupipara) parásitos de Murciélagos (Mammalia: Chiroptera) del Nuevo Mundo. V. Trichobiinae Apteros y braquípteros. Boletín de Entomología de Venezuela.

71. Guerrero, Ricardo. Catálogo de los Streblidae (Diptera: Pupipara) parásitos de Murciélagos (Mammalia: Chiroptera) del Nuevo Mundo. VI. Streblinae. Boletín de Entomología de Venezuela.

72. Gelhaus, Jon and chen W. Young. The pupae of the crane fly genus *Leptotarsus* (Diptera: Tipulidae) in the New World, with discussion of the monophyly of the genus Guerin-Meneville from Ecuador. Annals of the Carnegie Museum. (In press).

73. Morales, Víctor and Roy W. McDiarmid. Annotated checklist of the amphibians and reptiles of Pakitza, Manu National Park Reserve Zone, with Comments on the Herpetofauna of Madre de Dios. (This volume)

74. Erwin, Terry L. Arboreal beetles of tropical forests: The xystosomi group, subtribe xystomina (coleóptera: carabidae: bembidiini). Part I. Character analysis, taxonomy, and distribution. The Canadian Entomologist 126: 549-666 (1994).

75. Burnham, Robyn. Patterns in tropical leaf litter and implications for angiosperm paleobotany. Review of Paleobotany and Palynology, 81 (1994) 99-113.

76. Pearson, David. Tiger Beetles of Pakitza, Madre de Dios: Identification, Natural History and a Comparison to the Peruvian Fauna (Coleoptera: cicindelidae). Revista de la Pontifícia Universidad Católica del Ecuador. March/June 1995, 27(1-2):1-28.

77. Lamas, Gerardo. *Pieris guarani* Kohler, 1923, descrita de Argentina, es una especie Africana (Lepidoptera, Pieridae). Revista Peruana de Entomología, 1993, vol. 35:11-12. Diciembre 1992 (Junio 1993). Lima, Perú.

78. Venable, George and T. L. Erwin. Mapping of the Biodiversity Site at Pakitza. (This volume).

79. Brown, Brian V. Life history parameters and new host records of phorid (diptera: phoridae) parasitoids of fireflies (coleoptera: lampyridae). **The Coleopterists Bulletin.** 48(2):145-147, 1994

80. Studier, Eugene H., Steven V. Sevick, and Don E. Wilson. Proximate, caloric, nitrogen, and mineral composition of bodies of some tropical bats. Comparative Biochemistry and physiology, 109A: 601-610.

81. Pacheco, Víctor.

82. Studier, Eugene H., Steven H. Sevick, Deanne Ripley, and Don E. Wilson. Mineral and Nitrogen Concentrations in Feces of Some Neotropical Bats. Journal of Mammalogy, 75(3):674-680, 1994.

83. Coddington, Jonathan

84. Guerrero, Ricardo. The *Basilia junquiensis* species-group (Diptera: Nycteribiidae) with description of a new species from Pakitza, Peru. (This volume)

85. Guerrero, Ricardo. *Amblyopinodes amazonicus* new species (Coleoptera: Staphyliniidae) a parasite of rodents from Pakitza, Peru. (This volume)

86. Studier, Eugene H., Steven H. Sevick, Don E. Wilson and Anne P. Brooke. Concentrations of Minerals and Nitrogen in Milk of *Carollia* and other Bats. Journal of Mammalogy, 76(4):1186-1189

87. Medina C. Mirian, Robert K. Robbins, and Gerardo Lamas. Vertical stratification of flight by ithomiinae butterflies (lepidoptera: nymphalidae) at Pakitza, Manu National Park, Peru (This volume).

88. Burns, John. Genitalia at the generic level: *Atrytone* restricted, *Anatrytone* resurrected, new genus *Quasimellana* -and yes! we have no *Mellanas* (Hesperiidae). Journal of Lepidopterists' Society 48(4), 1994, 273-337. BDP/ROF support

89. Spangler, Paul and Silvia Santiago. A new species and new records from Colombia of the water beetle genus Onychelmis hinton (coleoptera: elmidae: elminae). Proc. Entomol. Soc. Wash. 93(2), 1991, pp. 495-498

90. Núñez, Verónica, Giovanni Onore y David L. Pearson. Escarabajos tigre del Ecuador (Coleoptera: Cicindelidae), Lista de Especies y Clave para Géneros. Revista de la Pontificia Universidad Católica del Ecuador. Diciembre, 1994, vol. 22, páginas 57-67.

91. Erwin, Terry L. Natural history of the carabid beetles at the BIOLAT Biological Station, Río Manu, Pakitza, Peru. Supplement I. Additional records. (This volume)

92. Robbins, Robert K., Gerardo Lamas, Olaf H.H. Mielke, Donald J. Harvey, and Mirna M. Casagrande. Taxonomic composition and ecological structure of the species-rich butterfly community at Pakitza, Parque Nacional del Manu, Peru. (This volume)

93. Burnham, Robin J. Diversity of Tropical Forest Leaf Litter from Pakitza, Peru. (This volume).

THESIS

Ramírez, Rina L.

1994 A GENERIC ANALYSIS OF THE FAMILY SYSTROPHIIDAE (MOLLUSCA: GASTROPODA): TAXOOMIC, PHYLOGENY AND BIOGEOGRAPHY). Submitted to the Department of Systematics and Ecology and the Faculty of the Graduate School of the University of Kansas, in partial fulfillment of the requirements for the degree of Master of Arts.

General Floristics

Mapping of the Biodiversity Site at Pakitza

George L. Venable and Terry L. Erwin

Department of Entomology, National Museum of Natural History,
Smithsonian Institution, Washington, DC 20560, U.S.A.

ABSTRACT

A description is given of the methods and technology used to map the biodiversity research site at Pakitza, Perú. This site has been a primary prototype for developing and testing mapping techniques, integrating computer graphics and database software and establishing standards by which other sites could be mapped for future comparison and documentation. The techniques described were conceived and begun at Tambopata, Perú, and were also used at Beni, Bolivia. Procedures used in creating the various types of maps and support graphics are defined with relation to the actual mapping process. Descriptions of various techniques, computer hardware, and software used in the production of graphic documentation is delineated.

> *Imagination is more important than knowledge.*
> *Albert Einstein*

INTRODUCTION

The biodiversity site at Pakitza contains more than 48 kilometers of well marked and documented trails forming a network to provide access to established research zones and other areas of interest. Of the ten established zones, and two proposed research zones representing various forest types (Erwin 1991), four have been mapped to record the location of all trees measuring ≥10cm in diameter. Tree plot documents produced in this project show the location of trees within a plot, including the family, genus and species of each tree that could be identified, as well as other pertinent information about the zone or individual plots. Highly detailed maps of the Pakitza site depicting trails, vegetation, location of research zones and other pertinent information have also been produced.

We intend to demonstrate the relevance of computer graphics in documenting research sites. The technology and its application are not only important for publication purposes, but can facilitate in-field research by providing immediate information feedback for ground truthing, planning and analysis, both on-site and in the laboratory. It is also our intention to make recommendations regarding the use of this technology in future mapping projects.

HISTORY

The process developed for mapping of biodiversity research sites began at the Tambopata, Perú site, in 1982. As fogging and collection data began to accumulate, it became apparent that much of this information would require preparation as visual information for publication, and that some fundamental standards should be developed. In 1984, Erwin and Maber, working on an idea that small detailed maps of specific research areas would be helpful in the field, developed a concept for producing maps of tree locations within the research zones (MABERCARDS), (Erwin 1985). The plan was to record and identify all trees that measured ≥10cm at breast height (1.3m) in each plot within a research zone, and produce a map of these trees to determine species distribution, growth and loss of trees. These tree locality maps would additionally serve as locators for other researchers, providing XY coordinates for accurately mapping of other data within the zones. The production of trail maps for the zones followed as a logical consequence to provide overall site and location maps, other areas of geographical interest, and guides for our use and that of future researchers.

The task of creating these maps and other graphic support for this project was given to GLV in support of TLE's research. Knowing this to be a lengthy project, and having just begun experimenting with computer graphics using a Macintosh computer, GLV decided that the mapping was an appropriate exercise to attempt to see what could be accomplished using this medium. Previously, all support graphics had been laboriously executed in the traditional manner using pen and ink or other media to prepare them as camera ready art, which was very time consuming. The rapid introduction and development of desktop computer graphics hardware and software allowed increasingly viable and varied solutions to old and new problems. In retrospect, the use of the computer not only changed the process of graphic representation dramatically and irrevocably for biodiversity mapping, but how we visualize and process information in other areas of research as well.

Even at the beginning of this project in 1984, using a personal Macintosh, the quite primitive graphics software available at the time and a dot matrix printer, the process of creating initial maps of fogging locations began to accelerate dramatically. Combining these efforts with some minor handwork, acceptable output was obtained for publication purposes. While these early efforts were very crude compared to the graphics being produced today, they demonstrated that the technology and the process were workable, allowing easy modification and manipulation of illustrations for publication, as well as providing a graphic database archive that could be used for other purposes.

In 1986, a "state of the art" Macintosh system and software for the purpose of creating computer generated support graphics was installed in the Department of Entomology. With this enhanced computer capability, the Biodiversity mapping project was able to reach greater levels of refinement and sophistication. Using advanced Computer Aided Design (CAD), graphing and other software, it was possible to create maps with a high degree of accuracy and functionality in less than half the time they required using traditional methods of pen and ink.

DEVELOPING ZONE AND TREE MAPS

Inventory zones in previously selected forest types are established using standard surveying instruments and procedures (Fig. 1) (Erwin 1985). Once the zones have been determined, each tree in the zone ≥10cm in diameter is identified with an aluminum tag on which the zone, plot, and tree number are permanently recorded. The location of the trees is determined using a triangulation process (Fig. 2). The location, diameter and tree identity information, including family, genus and species if known, are entered into a database (Fig. 3). It is from this database that XY coordinates of the trees were initially extrapolated for the purposes of creating computer generated maps using an in-house developed application written in Basic (Erwin & Kabel 1991).

This early effort created relatively crude bitmaps produced on a small inkjet printer, which were used for

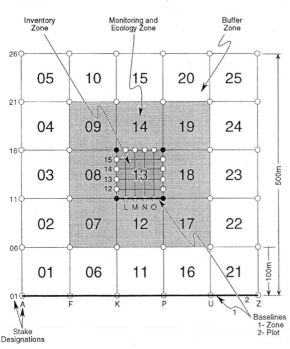

Fig. 1.– *Inventory and monitoring plots with labeled components and code numbers of hectares and quads.*

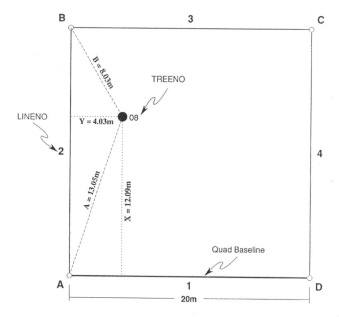

Fig. 2.– *Quad showing LINENO, measurements A and B used for data entry.*

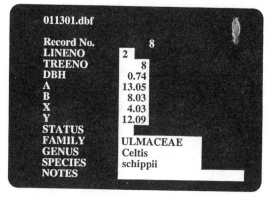

Fig. 3.– *Data screen for a single mapped tree species.*

ground truthing and record purposes (Erwin and Kabel 1991). In the beginning, GLV used these rough maps and the coordinate data produced in the field as a reference to create tree distribution maps in my original graphics software. Since there were no functional charting software applications at this time, the XY coordinates had to be positioned on the plot using a grid system. Tree symbols and other data were inserted individually by hand using MacDraw, an object-oriented drawing application. However, the result was much superior to the bitmaps, and suitable for publication.

As charting software became available, it became evident that the process could be drastically speeded up through its use. In 1987, working with Linda Sims, S.I. Entomology, the data were transferred, and accessed using Microsoft Excel, a spreadsheet application that recognized and allowed manipulation of Dbase tab-delimited files. The use of this application permitted easy sorting, editing and formatting of the information, along with the ability to import other data and add to, or modify original files. An example of one of these data files is shown in Table 1.

Once the data has been properly sorted, categorized and appended, it was imported into charting software to create XY scatter diagrams. Current charting software[1] has the capability of creating detailed scatter diagrams of the spreadsheet data as a chart picture (Fig. 4), in effect, a tree map that requires minimal editing that can be saved in a file format suitable for importing into page layout software[2], the final step in producing the Tree Maps or MABERCARDS (Erwin & Venable, in prep).

---

1. The original charting software used was Cricket Graph, which was adequate at the time, but had limited graphics enhancement capabilities. Acquisition of Delta Graph, and currently DeltaGraph Pro, has virtually eliminated the need to import the results into drawing software for enhancement. DeltaGraph Pro allows full control over all atributes of a plot. Style templates can be easily created for defining the size and type of symbols used, as well as other elements of the plot, and graphic tools allow further anhancement. This adds a great deal of automation and speed to what once was a tedious, and somewhat error prone procedure.

Table 1. Tree data sorted by dbh prior to plotting the tree locations in the charting software

LINENO	TREENO	DBH	A	B	X	Y	ZONE
2	04	0.11	9.760	10.54	02.03	10.40	011301
2	05	0.11	11.20	09.65	03.13	09.19	011301
2	03	0.14	14.00	07.37	03.73	06.43	011301
4	14	0.14	05.06	15.84	17.25	04.33	011301
4	15	0.14	02.32	20.07	17.61	03.25	011301
4	17	0.14	06.72	20.95	13.21	00.11	011301
1	19	0.14	15.03	12.30	09.33	08.13	011301
4	16	0.16	05.42	19.22	14.69	01.44	011301
2	02	0.17	14.30	05.64	00.95	05.65	011301
4	18	0.17	10.56	16.52	11.17	05.94	011301
2	01	0.19	16.88	03.30	01.42	03.08	011301
3	11	0.21	04.00	16.37	16.36	18.09	011301
2	07	0.31	17.22	02.65	02.65	19.08	011301
4	13	0.32	10.78	09.85	16.88	10.49	011301
3	09	0.33	07.90	12.36	12.30	17.61	011301
3	10	0.48	07.99	12.78	12.54	16.51	011301
1	20	0.66	11.64	13.03	10.88	12.25	011301
2	06	0.72	19.40	01.15	00.30	18.52	011301
2	08	0.74	13.05	08.03	04.03	12.09	011301
3	12	0.83	16.23	04.07	17.29	16.42	011301

Once imported into the page layout template, the list of the family, genus and species names, a quad map, site description, and other graphic enhancements were added. Final publication was accomplished on a standard 300 dpi laser printer. Maps for use in the field were laminated in plastic, a process that had to be contracted out. Laminating was costly and added additional time to production, so a simpler method of inserting the pages in vinyl document protectors, and binding the pages together as a volume in a plastic cover was adopted. While not as moisture resistant as lamination, it has proven to be serviceable in the field, allows convenient updates, and speedier production at less cost. The style of presentation has been changed as well, and can still be laminated if necessary, (Fig. 5).

---

2. The application Ready, Set, Go has been used as the page layout software from the inception of the project. It has been more than adequate for this project, and offers many design and typographical features. Other desktop publishing applications would serve just as well as they offer equal if not more advanced features.

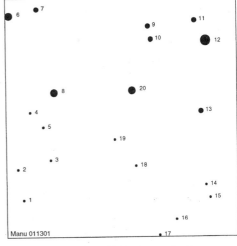

Fig. 4.– A chart picture from DeltaGrap Pro showing a completed scatter diagram representation of a tree map. Tree numbers and size of tree symbols are plotted automatically.

George L. Venable and Terry L. Erwin

DEVELOPMENT OF SITE AND TRAIL MAPS

The original base map of Pakitza is based on a 1959 map of the area, prepared by the Peruvian military. The scale is indeterminate and it contains limited geographical detail. The Manu river channel has changed considerably since the creation of this map, dramatically in one location. Subsequent acquisition of a

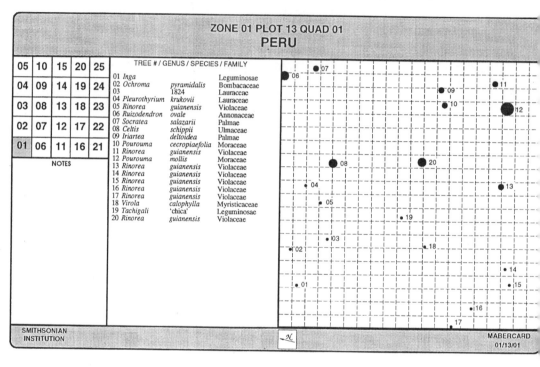

Fig. 5.– *Page from current style of Tree Map volume, which can be folded, trimmed and laminated if necessary for extreme conditions.*

photocopy of a satellite (SPOT) image of the area taken in October of 1989, has allowed some updating of the river channel, however absolute scale is difficult to determine and small estuaries are not visible. Acquisition of current satellite images, and Global Positioning System (GPS) data would simplify editing and improving the accuracy of this map. Limited funds precluded the use of existing satellite data at the time this project was begun. Consequently, we determined that absolute accuracy was not of paramount importance since our primary purpose was to show relative position, rather than detailed accuracy. In recent months, detailed imaging of the Manu river basin has been accomplished, and would be used to make any corrections to existing maps were it determined necessary.

Trail mapping evolved in much the same way as the tree maps, however because they came later much of the earlier problems with software and output had been solved. Trail maps for Tambopata were crude and simple, whereas the maps

34

for Pakitza were much more sophisticated, benefiting from being produced on a more sophisticated graphics system and laser printer, providing greater capabilities and higher output resolution.

Trail mapping was done primarily to provide a record of trails as they were developed, and as a guide showing access to the various research zones. Each trail was mapped using the "compass and chain[3] " method of mapping. Using a metric tape, "the chain," to establish distance and a hand-held compass for direction, each trail was mapped starting from camp or a branching point on an existing trail. The process is relatively simple and consists of extending the tape along a relatively unobstructed line of sight on the trail and recording distance and compass degree (Fig. 6). At Pakitza, the trails are often winding and bordered by dense vegetation, limiting the line of sight. This required sighting and measuring many short segments to ensure a comfortable degree of accuracy. At each 50 meter increment a permanent marker in the form of a white plastic stake is driven into the ground. Trail identification information is recorded with an indelible marker on the flat top surface of the stake. Using the trail Tachigali for example, the beginning of the trail is 0. The first stake at 50m would be marked T-01, the next T-02, etc. Numerical progression is always away from the trail head, i.e., base camp. In this

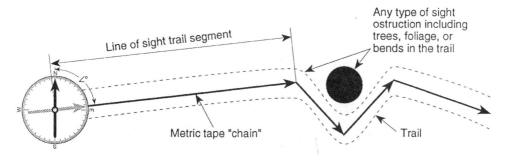

Fig. 6.– *Diagrammatic representation of the "Compass and Chain" method of mapping. Measurements and compass headings are taken along an unobstructed line of sight. Distance and compass readings are entered in a data sheet, from which the map is created in the CAD application.*

manner one will always know if they are heading away from or to the trail head. These stakes are also used as convenient locators for recording the location of collection sites.

Since CAD software is used for mapping, and is not true mapping or Geographical Information System (GIS) software, compass degrees must be converted to polar

---

3. The method is called "compass and chain" because originally an actual metal chain of measured length was used.. A foresters metric tape was used for our measurements. This method does have some degree of error, usually caused by individual variations in its use. Persons using this method should be trained in the proper use of a compass. Incorrect compass readings, or lack of care in taking readings from the tape, causes severe errors in both direction and length when mapping a trail. Electronic distance finders were tested, and while more accurate in totally unobstructed areas, they were found to be generally unreliable in areas of dense vegetation as was often the case a Pakitza. one could never be sure the reading was correct or being affected by large leaves along the trail.

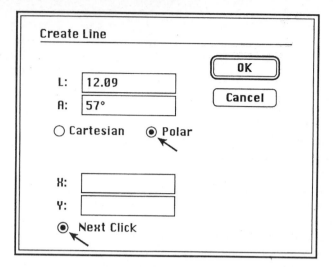

Create Line

L: `12.09`

A: `57°`

○ Cartesian ● Polar

X: `　`

Y: `　`

● Next Click

OK

Cancel

Fig. 7.– Dialog box in CAD software. Length of line, L:, is in meters, and angle, A:, is from converted compass degree in the Excel spreadsheet, entered as a Polar Coordinate. The "Next Click" option is chosen so that by placing the cursor on the end of the preceeding line entry, the line segment can be positioned properly. This is aided by a "Snap-to" function in the CAD application.

coordinates for input. This sounds complex, but is easily accomplished. Data for each trail was first entered in an Excel spreadsheet, then modified using a simple formula to convert the compass coordinates to polar coordinates that are subsequently used to correctly plot trails in the CAD application[4].

CAD software was chosen because it is generally less expensive than GIS systems that have only recently become available for the Macintosh. It also offered superior drawing tools such as bezier curves, which most mapping or GIS applications did not at the time we began this project. This was important for smooth output, and easier editing of the maps. Another consideration is that CAD could be used for other graphic needs and GIS software generally was suitable only for mapping applications.

Even considering the functionality of CAD software, creating base and trail maps can be an extremely time-intensive exercise. Rivers and streams originally digitized from old maps using a graphics tablet were edited to make corrections in areas where changes had been noted. Trails were plotted one measured increment at a time. A measured increment might be anywhere from 1-50m in length, and most often were in the 10 to 15m range, slowing the process considerably. Polar coordinates from the spreadsheet and the length of the increments had to be entered into a dialog box in the application one at a time. The use of a macro utility automated data input to a great degree. (Fig. 7) A "snap-to" function allowed accurate placement of each line segment. At each 50 meter segment, a small circle representing a trail stake was inserted in the line segment. At each 250 meter segment a stake number was inserted in order not to clutter the map with too many identifiers. Each trail was then placed on a separate layer in the CAD file for selective or collective viewing.

To date, approximately 48 kilometers of trails giving access to all research zones from the base camp have been developed and mapped at the Pakitza site. Primary trails were initially developed to create access to potential research zones and later, to interconnect all zones. (Fig. 8).

---

4   Most CAD software uses polar coordinates for determining degrees, because they are generally used for engineering and architectural drawing. This means that 0° in CAD polar coordinates is in the equivalent position of 3 o'clock much like a protractor, not at 12 o'clock, where 0° or North on a compass is located. Consequently, all compass degrees must be converted by subtracting 90° ffrom the actual compass direction recorded to create an accurate map using polar coordinates. The Excel formula is: =Sum(Cell Location-90). The CAD application used in the production of these maps was MiniCad+4. Mini Cad is a very powerful 2D-3D features-packed application that permits the user to work at any scale.

ig. 8.– *Site map of Pakitza, Perú, showing the Manu River, estuaries (so far as they have been mapped), primary and secondary trails, zones, and other geographical points of interest.*

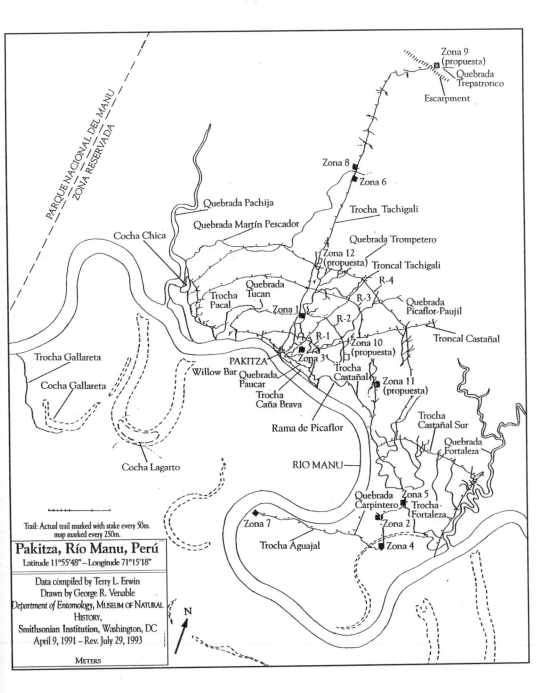

Secondary trails allow access to much more of the research area than primary trails, providing easier egress from one area to the next. They are also used in determining distribution of vegetation as well as locating other potential research areas. To date, 15 forest types including 2 species of bamboo have been mapped. An example of a forest-type distribution map is shown in Fig. 9.

In October of 1991, GLV was fortunate to have the use of a Macintosh computer in the field[5]. The results were dramatic, both in terms of time saving, accuracy and convenience. GLV was able to map a trail, input the data, output the trail map, do a ground check and make any corrections necessary by the next day: A significant improvement over previous experiences at Tambopata, Beni and Pakitza of bringing handwritten notes back to the museum to be processed, and then having to wait until someone returned to the site to verify the data. The result was a saving of months in possible delays of being able to produce finished maps.

HARDWARE AND SOFTWARE

The hardware and software listed is that which is being used currently. Over the period of the last nine years there has been an exponential explosion of technology and many upgrades to both hardware and software has been made.

Hardware Desktop system: Apple Macintosh IIfx with 8mb RAM, 210mb internal storage, FD/HD floppy drive, 800K floppy drive, Apple 8/24/GC graphics acceleration card, 20mb Bernoulli and 44mb Syquest removable media; Microtek flatbed 600dpi scanner; Wacom pressure sensitive digitizing tablet; Apple IIg Laserprinter. Field system: Apple Macintosh Portable with 2mb RAM, 40mb internal storage, FD/HD floppy drive, and an Apple StyleWriter inkjet printer.

Software: Microsoft Excel (Spreadsheet); DeltaGraph Professional (Charting & Graphing); MiniCad+4 (Computer Aided Design); Ready, Set, Go (Page Layout). A number of utility applications have been used to accelerate and facilitate automation and functionality of both hardware and software; the most used and useful has been QuicKeys (Macro Utility).

CONCLUSION

There is no doubt in the authors' minds that the use of the computer in the creation of reference maps for the Pakitza site has not only saved time, it has

---

5. Through the courtesy of Apple Computer, Inc., and Falcon Microsystems, Inc., GLV was loaned an Apple Macintosh Portable computer and an Apple Style Writer printer, respectively, for the purpose exploring the practicality of creating maps in the field. Primary power sources for these two devices was a generator, and a solar panel collector. This reduced the need to rely solely on battery power, and allowed the recharging of batteries.

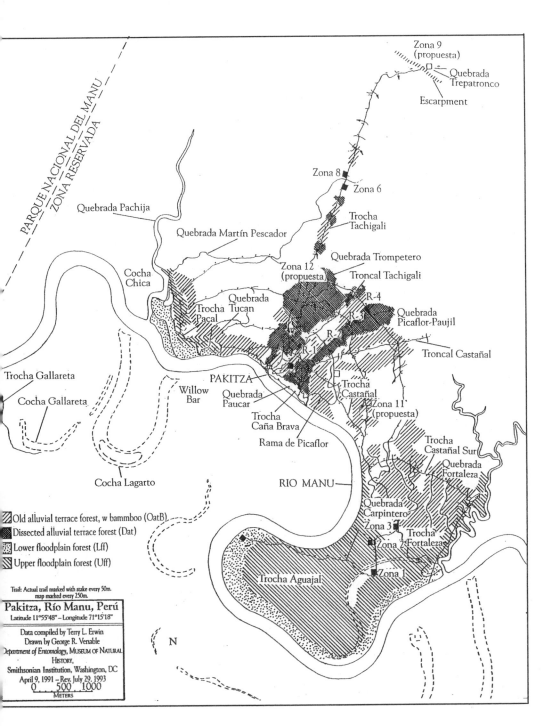

Zona 9
(propuesta)

Quebrada
Trepatronco

Escarpment

PARQUE NACIONAL DEL MANU
ZONA RESERVADA

Zona 8 ■
Zona 6

Quebrada Pachija

Trocha
Tachigali

Quebrada Martín Pescador

Quebrada Trompetero

Cocha
Chica

Zona 12
(propuesta)

Troncal Tachigali

R-4

Quebrada
Trocha Tucan
Pacal

Quebrada
Picaflor-Paujil

R-3

R-2

R-1

Troncal Castañal

Trocha Gallareta

PAKITZA

Willow
Bar

Quebrada
Paucar

Trocha
Castañal

Cocha Gallareta

Zona 11
(propuesta)

Trocha
Caña Brava

Rama de Picaflor

Trocha
Castañal Sur

Quebrada
Fortaleza

Cocha Lagarto

RIO MANU

Quebrada
Carpintero

Zona 3

Trocha
Fortaleza

▨ Old alluvial terrace forest, w bammmbo (OatB)
■ Dissected alluvial terrace forest (Dat)
▧ Lower floodplain forest (Lff)
▨ Upper floodplain forest (Uff)

Zona 2

Zona 1

Trocha Aguajal

Trail: Actual trail marked with stake every 50m.
map marked every 250m.

Pakitza, Río Manu, Perú
Latitude 11°55'48" – Longitude 71°15'18"

Data compiled by Terry L. Erwin
Drawn by George R. Venable
Department of Entomology, MUSEUM OF NATURAL
HISTORY,
Smithsonian Institution, Washington, DC
April 9, 1991 – Rev. July 29, 1993

N

0   500   1000
METERS

Fig. 9.–   Pakitza site map showing the distribution of 4 primary vegetation types . In all, 15
types of vegetation have been incorporated in the Pakitza map. Layering capabilities allow
placing different types of vegetation on separate layers so that they can be shown or hidden
selectively, for display, analysis, or publication

probably made the mapping process feasible in the first place. Considering the amount of time that would have been required to plot the data and illustrate the maps by hand using traditional pen and ink methods would have made them prohibitively expensive and virtually un-editable in any practical sense.

The expense of the computer graphics system has proven to be money well invested. The system has allowed us to modify our methods, adapt to new ideas, and more easily extract information for other purposes. In fact, the use of the computer has generated many new ideas for data usage that may well never have been considered otherwise.

The fact that an illustrator, versed in computer graphics techniques and possessing a scientific background, participated in the field studies was an added benefit. Data given to an illustrator in the laboratory is just that — data. It is difficult at best to envision the diversity of a site such as Pakitza, and not think of it as a large flat area covered with trees. Even with the most fervent imagination, one cannot begin to imagine what a tropical rainforest is like with only temperate forests as a reference. The visualization capabilities of an accomplished scientific illustrator help researchers envision their data in ways they may never think to approach it. Combining the skills of a scientific illustrator with field experience has, in our case, led to the solution of many logistic and collecting problems. It seems apparent why many early explorers, and current researchers have included scientific illustrators, cartographers, and photographers in their expeditions.

In this case, GLV wasable to draw field experience at Tambopata, Beni, and Pakitza to appreciate the requests of various researchers for graphics support and information about those sites. GLV knows Pakitza intimately, having walked all the trails, several of them many times, and worked in all the zones while mapping them during my two visits there.

The original intent of creating the maps was to better document insect/tree coexistence. The adoption of the mapping project by the BIOLAT program turned the maps into both a learning and general research tool — both the field maps generated and used by researchers and students during BIOLAT on-site workshops, and the final publishable versions. The quad maps can be used to monitor the phenology or natural history of tree species or individual trees or to teach tropical botany by adding in other plants in the understory. Patterns showing distribution of families, genera or species could be graphically represented. Taxa can be color keyed on the maps to illustrate distribution patterns. Several taxa could be displayed at once using preselected layered sets. It is obvious to us that this is just a beginning, and that other uses will be forthcoming.

Development in the following areas; GIS, GPS, image technology, satellite and cellular communications, and incorporation of high definition output devices, will change much of the way we collect, record, transmit, visualize, store and utilize data.

Consider the following scenario: A researcher/illustrator with a laptop computer equipped with an internal GPS, cellular modem, communications and GIS software, could go to any site in the world and have immediate access to maps and other information of the area. This technology could let them know their location to within a few meters. They could in effect create an overlay map as they explored a trail or uncharted area. This map could then be edited or annotated with pertinent data, and transmitted immediately to the home office or base station via satellite, whereupon it could be uploaded to a master database. This information could then be accessed, analyzed, or further enhanced at the home base for a multitude of purposes. In addition to text and graphics links, the technology would provide voice and, quite possibly, visual links with both stations, so that one never need be out of contact. Star Wars? We they not. The technology is here, now! Some still in its infancy, but much is currently available off the shelf. Who, in 1984, would have imagined when they bought a 128K Macintosh with only two software programs available for it, that we would be able to do what we can today?

Given our claim that essential scientific research is important, then to ignore current technology in this era of Global Biodiversity awareness does not make sense. It would not only hinder progress and the potential of discovery, but might well result in the loss of valuable data about vanishing biological resources.

RECOMMENDATION

It is our recommendation that Biolat and other biodiversity inventory programs invest heavily in this technology. It may be the only way to cope with the mountains of data we are collecting and it is providing better tools daily. Future efforts should use the guidelines we have set for Pakitza, and continue making recommendations to improve the process.

Acquisition of portable graphics systems for use in the field and desktop systems for use in the laboratory should be a top priority. They are a necessity not a luxury, because they allow constant monitoring and updating of information as well as timely production of essential graphic support. As computer platforms, GIS and other software are further developed and integrated into other developing technologies, there is no reason to believe that what is currently being done could not be further automated and simplified. While GLV has been a great advocate of the Apple Macintosh system, other graphics systems are rapidly approaching the ease of use and functionality of the Macintosh. The platform is irrelevant, the philosophy and technology are not.

High resolution devices for input and output, i.e., digital cameras, pre-press quality scanners, photographic image setters, electrostatic plotters, large format ink jet or dye sublimation printers, and appropriate software should be considered in the production of professional high-quality graphics from the data being collected and created on the computer. This equipment is extremely expensive, and it has been mentioned that much of it is prohibitively so for most institutions. However, the average laser printer does not provide the level of quality needed for professional publication. Sharing resources or selective outsourcing would allow many to incorporate high quality images in their publications, reducing or eliminating the need to acquire this expensive equipment.

Incorporation of appropriate storage media for archiving of data, i.e., Optical disk and CD ROM and other developing technologies should be considered for storing the mountains of data that is being acquired.

Expand the educational outreach of our programs. The incorporation of multimedia and developing technologies in our publication efforts should be explored. It is important that the information we have accumulated is distributed in a manner that can be easily accessed by all, but more importantly, those who need it and those who can provide support are made aware of it (Erwin & Pearson, 1991).

Lastly, but most importantly, we must use our imagination, for without it, all the knowledge we collect is just data and of little value to anyone.

ACKNOWLEDGEMENTS

We warmly thank all of those individuals who offered encouragement and suggestions during the development phase of this project. We thank the following for their specific contributions: Linda Sims, Steve Maber, Daniel Moreno and Irv Pogue. Funding for this project was provided by the Smithsonian Institution's Department of Entomology, and BIOLAT Program. This is paper # 78 in the BIOLAT Series.

LITERATURE CITED

Erwin, T.L. 1985. Tambopata Reserved Zone, Madre de Dios, Peru: History and Description of the Reserve. Revista Peruana de Entomología 27: 1-8.

Erwin, T.L. 1991. Establishing a Tropical Species Co-occurrence Database Part 1: A plan for developing consistent biotic inventories in temperate and tropical habitats. Memorias del Museo de Historia Natural, U.N.M.S.M. (Lima) 20: 1-16.

Erwin, T.L. & M. Kabel 1991. Establishing a Tropical Species Co-occurrence Database Part 2: An automated system for mapping dominant vegetation. Memorias del Museo de Historia Natural, U.N.M.S.M. (Lima) 20: 17-36.

Erwin, T.L. & D. Pearson. 1991. Establishing a Tropical Species Co-occurrence Database Part 3: An integrated approach toward understanding biological diversity. Memorias del Museo de Historia Natural, U.N.M.S.M. (Lima) 20: 37-45.

Erwin, T.L. & G.L. Venable (in prep). Establishing a Tropical Species Co-occurrence Database Part 6: MABERCARDs and other graphic presentations.

From The Forest to The User: a Methodology Update

Francisco Dallmeier

James A. Comiskey

Smithsonian/MAB Biodiversity Program 1100 Jefferson Drive S.W. Suite 3123
Washington, D.C. 20560, USA

ABSTRACT

Accessible, accurate information is a key ingredient in devising sound strategies for managing natural resources. This premise is reflected in the Smithsonian Institution/Man and the Biosphere (SI/MAB) biodiversity program, which combines long-term monitoring and data collection with a tailored, computerized data management system. The goal is to provide timely information for other researchers and decision makers concerned with the fate of temperate and tropical forest ecosystems. The program's protocol has been refined during the six years since the establishment of SI/MAB's first permanent research plots in Bolivia and Peru. It makes possible the cross-referencing and dissemination of valuable data, assisting in the important task of increasing our knowledge and understanding of forest dynamics and leading to more informed policies regarding forest ecosystems.

INTRODUCTION

The Smithsonian Institution's Man and the Biosphere (SI/MAB) biodiversity monitoring program is designed to: (1) develop guidelines for implementing forest biodiversity monitoring programs in a network of forested areas; (2) train in-country individuals in all aspects related to the monitoring program; and (3) create a data management system that readily exchanges information for use in comparative and time series analyses (Fig. 1; SI/MAB Biodiversity News 1991, 1992, 1994, 1995).

Since 1987, SI/MAB has developed a protocol for forest plot studies at research sites in Beni, Bolivia; Manu, Peru; Guatopo, Venezuela; Kwakwani, Guyana; Luquillo, Puerto Rico; and St. John, U.S. Virgin Islands. The protocol allows consistent documentation and publication of field results and monitoring procedures in "User's" and "Field" guides as well as other reports. The methodology is comparable to other permanent plot studies (e.g., Balslev et al., 1987; Foster and Brokaw, 1982; Foster and Hubbell, 1990; Reilly et al., 1990; Alder and Synnott, 1992).

The SI/MAB Biological Monitoring Database (BioMon) arose from the need for a flexible database to manage the information coming from the international network of biodiversity research sites. The priority was to provide a speedy turn-around between the gathering of data in the field and publication of the information for use in conservation management. SI/MAB has found that efficient data management is key to a successful, long-term forest biodiversity monitoring program.

One purpose of the guides is to get up–to–date, detailed biological data from the forest plots into the hands of other researchers, managers, and support personnel so that they might conduct more effective studies, training, and forest monitoring programs. SI/MAB work from 1987 to 1993 has yielded close to 250,000 independent observations, sufficient to begin in-depth analysis of forest diversity and dynamics.

THE SI/MAB APPROACH

SI/MAB has made many improvements in its monitoring program and information system since establishing its first research plots at Manu in Peru, and Beni in Bolivia. Greater field efficiency and refined data handling now ensures the prompt production of basic information for each site. The following sections of this paper describe the monitoring process, data management system, and products.

PLOT SELECTION AND ESTABLISHEMENT

Selection of the plot site is essential to the value of the research and should be based on the following criteria: (1) the area should contain species representative and endemic to the ecosystem; (2) common or dominant species should be represented; (3) the plot must be located within one vegetation type to give a true representation of the areas diversity (Dallmeier, in press). The botanist's job is essential in determining the initial siting of the plot aided by cartographic information, remote sensing photographs, and field verification techniques such as vegetation transects. One-hectare plots provide sufficient information to study the dynamics of most tropical forests; larger areas are required to analyze the spatial distributions of the trees, but this requires a higher cost and time investment. The results from a one-hectare plot may also be used to decide whether a larger plot size, such a 50-hectare plot, is necessary to elucidate the dynamics of the forest (Foster and Brokaw, 1982; Hubbell and Foster, 1983).

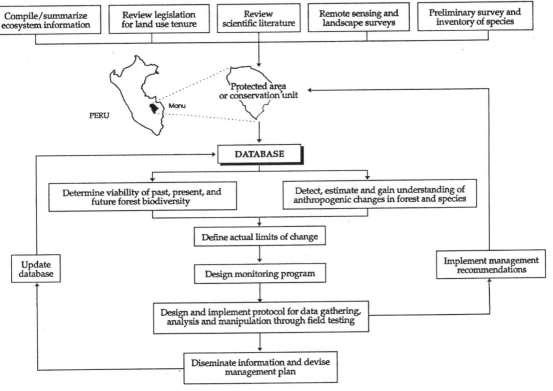

PERU — Manu

Protected area or conservation unit

DATABASE

Determine viability of past, present, and future forest biodiversity

Detect, estimate and gain understanding of anthropogenic changes in forest and species

Define actual limits of change

Update database

Design monitoring program

Implement management recommendations

Design and implement protocol for data gathering, analysis and manipulation through field testing

Diseminate information and devise management plan

Fig. 1.– *SI/MAB steps in Monitoring Biodiversity*

The forest plots are established according to Dallmeier (1992). At most new sites, professional survey or topography teams delineate a one-hectare plot (100 X 100 meters), and divide it into 25 quadrats, each 20 x 20 meters in size (Fig. 2 i & ii). The quadrats may be further divided into 16 subquadrats, each 5 X 5 meters. Close supervision is needed to ensure the least disturbance to the vegetation when the plots are set. The survey team also takes level measurements at each of the quadrat corners, producing a detailed topographic map of the plot. Exact coordinates are determined with the aid of a geoposition system (GPS). The boundaries of the quadrats are demarcated with string, to be removed later, making orientation easier within the plot.

FIELD MEASUREMENTS

Tree tagging and identification begin after the corner stakes of the quadrats are set and the strings tied. The process includes locating, measuring, marking, and mapping all trees with a diameter at breast height (DBH) ≥ 10 cm (4 cm at the dry forest site in the Virgin Islands). Diameter tape is used to measure DBH, avoiding any protrusions on the trunk. When trees below 10 cm are included in the census, they are measured with calipers. An average from three caliper readings is recorded, and a note is made of the measurement method. Where multiple stems occur on a censused tree, all individual stem diameters ≥ 1 cm are measured. The point of measurement is marked using paint. Trees are tagged with an aluminum label facing toward the base line of the plot and set with a nail 20

45

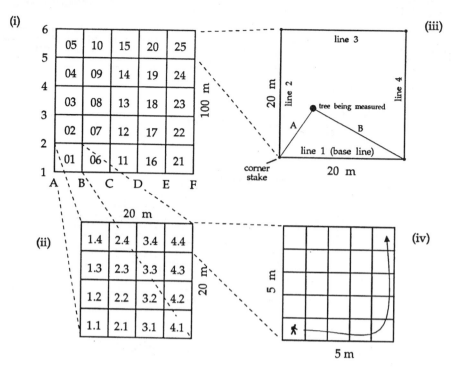

Fig. 2.– *i. One-hectare plot divided into 25 quadrats. ii. One 20 x 20 m quadrat divided into 16 subquadrats. iii. Quadrat mapping by triangulation. iv. Visual mapping of subquadrat.*

cm above the point of measurement. The nails thus serve as a general guide for future measurements.

Trees are tagged with an individual number consisting of a sequence of three double digits. Using (01-24-09) as an example, the first two numbers (01) to the one-hectare plot, the second pair (24) identifies the 20 X 20 meter quadrat. The last two numbers (09) represent an individual tree within the quadrat. No other tree receives this number. In each quadrat the tree numbers start at one and continue until the last tree is labeled.

Two mapping methods are used by SI/MAB: Quadrat mapping by a team of three people; two stand at ends of the quadrat baseline, while the third moves to each tree being measured. Electronic range finders measure the distance, to the nearest 0.5 m, from the tree to two adjacent corners. The A and B values recorded are later used, along with the diameter, to calculate the exact position of the tree, (Fig. 2 iii). Where a smaller minimum DBH is used, as in the Virgin Islands Biosphere reserve, trees are mapped by subquadrats. This provides a faster, more reliable method for the increased number of qualifying trees. Again, string is used to demarcate the boundaries of the subquadrats. A field worker can then visually locate the positions of the trees and record them on preprinted gridded forms (Fig. 2 iv), by walking around the subquadrat and gradually closing in on the center. This method is very accurate in the small subquadrats, and allows one person to map up to 200 stems per day.

VOUCHER SPECIMEN COLLECTION

Voucher specimens of the tree species occurring in the plot are the most valuable information for further study of forest biodiversity. A minimum of five herbarium specimens are always collected; most are sterile. The botanists collect and identify the specimens, assisted by two or three experienced tree climbers who go after the more inaccessible samples. Field specimens are held together with flagging tape labeled with the three double digit tree number. The samples are sorted at the base camp, trimmed, and placed between absorbent paper. The tree number, as well as the botanists' collection number, identify the samples, which are stacked and bundled, placed in plastic bags, and preserved with a solution of 50% ethanol so that they will not decompose during the trip to the herbarium.

On arrival at the herbarium, the samples are placed in driers separated by corrugated plates. They should be fully dry within two days, at which point they are sent to the respective specialists for initial identification or to confirm field identification. The final stage of the process is to mount and make high resolution photocopies of the specimens.

DATA MANAGEMENT

Guiding principles in designing BioMon were modularity, ease of use, and compatibility — all aimed at facilitating quick and accurate analysis in the field and cross-site comparisons. Off-the-shelf software was incorporated, creating a link between the physical gathering of data and its management that is made available to other researchers. Statistics, graphics, and publishing packages have been incorporated into the system to aid in data analysis and presentation.

"User friendly" menus mean inexperienced users need only minimal training to operate the system (Comiskey et al., 1995). BioMon was developed with the field work in mind, where researchers and students may manipulate more than 20,000 independent forest observations per hectare over 3 to 5 days. Field and office modules are the two main components of the system (Fig. 3). Their structures are similar, but not their intents and capabilities. The field module manages information for a specific site; the office based module manages and analyzes data for all the sites, allowing the production of diverse publications, (see Comiskey et al., 1995, for more on BioMon structure). A series of linked tables provides the framework of the database. Information from the tables is made available through forms that can be called up on the screen (Figs. 4 and 5).

In the field: The field mapping teams use a different pre-printed data sheet for each quadrat to record each tree's position, DBH, and height, as well as pertinent notes about any tree or quadrat (Appendix 1). After the mapping teams complete data collection, botanists and voucher collectors record the identities of the trees on the sheets, normally using six-letter codes for the different species mapped in the plot. Information from the finished sheet is then entered into BioMon by data

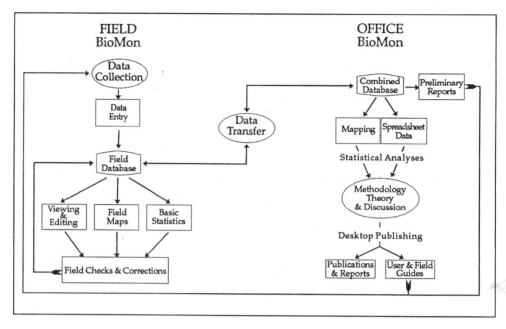

Fig. 3.– SI/MAB Data Management System (Modified from Comiskey et al.)

entry teams. For subquadrat mapping, the sheets are placed on a small digitizing tablet that allows the calculation of the X and Y coordinates to be transferred directly to the database. This procedure further reduces data entry errors and increases the speed and efficiency of data management. BioMon generates a map of each quadrat, which field personnel use to verify, on site, the correct location of the measured trees.

BioMon's database application language made it possible to create data validity checks used during data entry and editing, thus enhancing the integrity of the data. Once the data has been entered, it can easily be viewed and edited; more information can be added or corrections made. Sections of the data may also be printed, providing a hard copy of the database content and aiding in data verification.

In the office: Once in the office, data management proceeds in the office module. Information from each forest site is stored in its own directory in a series of tables with identical structures so that cross-site comparisons can be made. Data collected and entered on portable computers in the field can be downloaded via a network connection or from the backup diskettes. The office module is an extension of the field module, accommodating database management as well as statistical manipulation, map creation, and publication development. SI/MAB is automating the movement of data between the modules as much as possible to improve efficiency and consistency in the production of the users' and field guides.

INFORMATION PRODUCTS

There are three different types of information available for users at different times: field reports, user's and field guides, and scientific publications. These levels of information are produced at different time scales after the completion of the field work.

BioMon allows the production of complete field reports at each one-hectare plot as soon as data entry and verification is completed. The re-

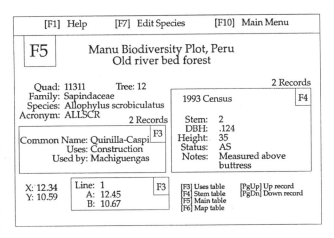

Fig. 4.– Data entry form

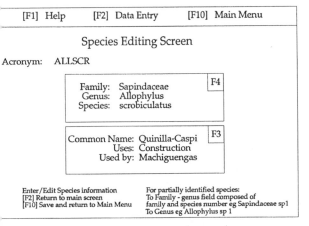

Fig. 5.– Species edit form

ports provide feedback to make on-the-spot decisions as to whether additional information from the field is needed. They also provide immediate information on tree species composition, structure, and diversity (Appendices 2 to 4).

SI/MAB's "User's" and "Field" guides are handbooks containing complete sets of the existing data at each research site for immediate use by other researchers or, in some cases, by forestry managers and decision makers (Dallmeier et al. 1993 a and b; Dallmeier et al. 1991 a and b; Dallmeier et al. 1991 a and b). The guides — usually 150 to 200 pages in length and contain information on two one-hectare plots — are produced 6 to 8 weeks after field work ends. They hold details about the history of the research site and its topography, soil, and vegetation as well as maps and spread sheets for each quadrat or subquadrat (Appendices 5 to 7). The field guide is a condensed plastic bound version of the Users' guide for easy use in the field. The guides also present a mini-herbarium, consisting of high resolution photocopies of the tree species measured in each plot.

As more plot data are accumulated during monitoring, additional publications are prepared concerning forest composition, structure, diversity, and dynamics (eg. Dallmeier et al. (this volume), Comiskey et al., 1995).

THE USER

The information obtained from the plots provide an initial inventory, floristic composition and diversity of species diversity at the site. Over time the dynamic nature of the forest is revealed allowing the users of the data to make informed decisions on the management of the area. At Manu the data collected by SI/MAB (Dallmeier et al., this volume) has provided an initial inventory of the Pakitsa area, and over time is providing information on the natural changes in the forest. At the Beni Biosphere Reserve data from the plots is being used to understand the dynamic nature of the forest/savannah transition zone (Dallmeier et al., 1991). The information will be applied to the restoration and preservation of degraded forest areas, and may prove to be an indicator of global climatic change at this unstable transition zone.

At St. John, the plot is providing information on the regeneration of dry Caribbean forest in an area previously subjected to intensive land use (Dallmeier et al., 1993). This information can then be used to help the restoration of other degraded dry forests throughout the Caribbean. At Kwakwani, Guyana, monitoring plots have provided the initial information to assist in restoration of areas degraded through deforestation and mining (Comiskey et al., 1994).

CONCLUSION

SI/MAB believes its monitoring program and data manipulating system, through their capacity for quick turnovers of large amounts of accurate information, are critical for forest conservation and management purposes. We recommend their adoption in forest biodiversity networks of 10 to 50 one-hectare plots per conservation unit. If this can be accomplished at 100 sites by the turn of the century, we should have adequate information on forest biodiversity to support sound forest management strategies.

ACKNOWLEDGEMENTS

We deeply appreciate the invaluable advice and assistance of Leonard Hirsch throughout the design and implementation of BioMon. Our thanks go to Deanne Kloepfer for her editorial comments and to Margo Kabel, who has been of great assistance since the beginning of the project. We would also like to the thank the anonymous reviewers for their comments.

REFERENCES

Alder, D., and T.J. Synnott. 1992. Permanent sample plot techniques for mixed tropical forest. Tropical Forestry Papers 25. Oxford Forestry Institute. 124pp.

Balslev, H., J. Luteyn, B. Ollgaard, and L. B. Holm-Nielsen. 1987. Composition and structure of adjacent unflooded and floodplain forest in Amazonian Ecuador. Opera Bot. 92: 37-57.

Comiskey, J.A., G. Aymard, F. Dallmeier. 1994. Structure and composition of lowland mixed forest in the Kwakwani region of Guyana. Biollania 10:13-28.

Comiskey, J.A., G. Ayzanoa, F. Dallmeier. 1995. A data management system for monitoring forest dynamics. Journal of Tropical Forest Science. 7(3): 419-427

Dallmeier, F. 1992. Long-term monitoring of biological diversity in tropical forest areas: methods for establishment and inventory of permanent plots. MAB Digest 11. UNESCO, Paris. 72pp.

_____. In press. Monitoring protected areas: the role of the biodiverstiy physician. IUCN National Park Congress. 1992.

Dallmeier, F., J. Comiskey, and G. Ray. 1993. User's guide to the Virgin Islands Biosphere Reserve biodiversity plot 1, U.S. Virgin Islands. Smithsonian Institution, Washington, D.C. 300pp.

Dallmeier, F., R. Foster, and J. Comiskey. 1993a. User's guide to the Manu Biosphere Reserve biodiversity plots, Peru. Vol. I and II. Smithsonian Institution, Washington, D.C. 300pp.

_____. 1993b. Field guide to the Manu Biosphere Reserve Biodiversity Plots, Vol. I, II, III, IV Smithsonian Institution, Washington, D.C. 100pp.

Dallmeier F., R. B. Foster, and M. Kabel. Structure, Composition and Diversity of four forests in the Pakitsa, Manu Biosphere Reserve, Peru. (This volume)

Dallmeier F., R. Foster, C. Romano, R. Rice, and M. Kabel. 1991a User's guide to the Beni Biosphere Reserve biodiversity plots, Vol. I and II. Smithsonian Institution, Washington, D.C. 250pp.

_____. 1991b. Field guide to the Beni Biosphere Reserve Biodiversity Plots, Vol. I, II, III, IV. Smithsonian Institution, Washington, DC. 22pp.

Dallmeier F., M. Kabel, C. Taylor, C. Romano, and R. Rice. 1991a. User's guide to the Bisley biodiversity plots, Luquillo Biosphere Reserve, Puerto Rico. Smithsonian Institution, Washington, D.C. 110pp.

_____. 1991b. Field guide to the Bisley biodiversity plots, Luquillo Biosphere Reserve, Perto Rico. Smithsonian Institution, Washington, D.C. 56pp.

Foster, R. B. and N. V. L. Brokaw. 1982. Structure and history of the vegetation on Barro Colorado Island. In E. G. Leigh, Jr., A. S. Rand, and D. M. Windsor (eds.), The Ecology of a Tropical Forest: Seasonal Rhythms and Long-term Changes. Smithsonian Institution Press, Washington D.C., pp.67-81.

Foster, R. B., and S. P. Hubbell. 1990. The Floristic composition of the Barro Colorado Island Forest. In A. H. Gentry (ed.), Four Neotropical Rainforests. Yale University Press. pp. 85-98.

Hubbell, S.P., and R.B. Foster. 1983. Diversity of canopy trees in a neotropical forest and impications for conservation. In: Sutton, S.L., T.C. Whitmore, and A.C. Chadwick (Eds.), Tropical rain forest: ecology and management. Blackwell Scientific Publications. Oxford. pp 25-41.

Reilly, A. E., J. E. Earhart, & G. T. Prance. 1990. Tropical Secondary Forests in the U.S. Virgin Islands: A Comparative Quantitative Ecological Inventory. Advances in Economic Botany (8) 189-198.

SI/MAB Biodiversity News. 1991. Smithsonian Institution/Man and the Biosphere Biological Diversity Program. Smithsonian Institution, Washington, DC. (Summer) 14pp.

SI/MAB Biodiversity News. 1992. Smithsonian Institution/Man and the Biosphere Biological Diversity Program. Smithsonian Institution, Washington, DC. (Winter) 16pp.

SI/MAB Biodiversity News. 1994. Smithsonian Institution/Man and the Biosphere Biological Diversity Program. Smithsonian Institution, Washington, DC. (Spring) 16pp.

Appendix 1.- Sample field form

MANU BIODIVERSITY CENSUS
1993
FIELD DATA SHEET
PLOT:_____ QUADRAT_____

NAME: DATE:

Smithsonian/MAB Biological Diversity Program
1100 Jefferson Drive, SW, Suite 3123
Washinghton, D.C. 20560

Tree#	Species	Line	A	B	DBH	Height	Field Notes
1							
2							
3							
4							
5							
6							
7							
8							
9							
10							
11							
12							
13							
14							
15							
16							
17							
18							
19							
20							
21							
22							
23							
24							
25							
26							
27							
28							
29							
30							

Apendix 2.- **Sample statiscal calculations by species**

	Number of Trees	Number of Stems	Average DBH(m)stem	Basal Area	Relative Density	Relative Dominance	Relative Frequency
			Old river bed forest, Manu 1993				
Laetia corymbulosa	214	230	.16	5.35	30.88	18.66	7.42
Allophylus scrobiculatus	86	88	.20	3.03	12.41	10.57	7.77
Calophyllum brasiliense	49	49	.21	3.09	7.07	10.79	7.77
Inga nitida	59	95	.14	1.66	8.51	5.79	6.01
Luehea cymulosa	7	8	.49	3.79	1.01	13.22	2.12
Trichilia pleeana	34	34	.19	1.11	4.91	3.88	6.71
Xylopia ligustrifolia	24	24	.26	1.44	3.46	5.01	4.24
Ficus insipida	4	4	.75	2.29	.58	7.98	1.06
Pithecellobium latifolium	16	31	.14	.58	2.31	2.01	4.59
Undetermined spp.	18	20	.17	.57	2.60	2.00	3.18
Annona hypoglauca	19	28	.13	.36	2.74	1.24	3.53
Astrocaryum chonta	18	18	.18	.3	2.60	1.85	2.47
Brosimum lactescens #1	11	11	.22	.47	1.59	1.64	3.53
Calycophyllum spruceanum	9	9	.20	.30	1.30	1.04	2.47
Euterpe precatoria	10	10	.14	.16	1.44	.54	2.83
Inga sp.	9	12	.14	.19	1.30	.66	2.12
Genipa americana	7	7	.18	.23	1.01	.80	1.77
Licania britteniana	5	5	.24	.39	.72	1.36	1.41
Sloanea guianensis	4	4	.30	.40	.58	1.39	1.41
Triplaris americana	6	6	.14	.10	.87	.34	1.77
Ficus trigona	5	10	.19	.33	.72	1.15	1.06
Otoba parvifolia	5	5	.23	.28	.72	.98	1.06
Terminalia oblonga	3	3	.22	.14	.43	.48	1.06
Spondias mombin	3	3	.20	.10	.43	.36	1.06
Unonopsis floribunda	3	3	.12	.03	.43	.12	1.06
Pseudolmedia laevis	3	3	.22	.3	.43	.44	.71
Allophylus sp.	3	3	.29	.20	.43	.71	.35
Garcinia brasiliense cf.	2	2	.20	.06	.29	.22	.71
Iriarte deltoidea	3	3	.22	.12	.43	.43	.35
Cecropia latiloba	2	2	.19	.06	.29	.21	.71
Pterocarpus rohrii aff.	2	2	.17	.05	.29	.16	.71
Andira inermis	2	2	.16	.04	.29	.15	.71
Sapium ixiamasense	2	2	.13	.03	.29	.10	.71
Cedrela fissilis	2	2	.13	.03	.29	.10	.71
Sapium marmieri	2	2	.13	.03	.29	.09	.71
Calatola venezuelana	2	2	.13	.03	.29	.09	.71
Theobroma cacao	2	2	.13	.03	.29	.09	.71
Myrtaceae sp.	2	2	.10	.02	.29	.06	.71
Guazuma crinita	1	1	.39	.12	.14	.41	.35
TOTAL:	748	842	30.01				100.00

Appendix 3.- Sample statistical calculations by family

| | Old river bed forest, Manu 1993 | | | | | | |
	Number of Trees	Number of Stems	Average DBH(m)/stem	Basal Area	Relative Density	Relative Dominance	Relative Frequency
Flacourtiaceae	225	242	.15	5.52	30.08	18.38	8.64
Sapindaceae	93	95	.20	3.36	12.43	11.18	9.47
Leguminosae-Mim	98	155	.14	2.78	13.10	9.27	8.64
Guttiferae	53	53	.20	3.18	7.09	10.59	9.05
Moraceae	33	38	.26	3.53	4.41	11.77	8.23
Annonaceae	58	67	.18	2.19	7.75	7.30	9.05
Meliaceae	40	40	.19	1.28	5.35	4.27	7.82
Tiliaceae	7	8	.49	3.79	.94	12.62	2.47
Palmae	35	35	.17	.87	4.68	2.89	4.53
Rubiaceae	18	18	.18	.55	2.41	1.84	4.94
Undetermined family	21	23	.17	.65	2.81	2.17	3.70
Polygonaceae	11	11	.13	.16	1.47	.55	3.29
Chrysobalanaceae	5	5	.24	.39	.67	1.30	1.65
Elaeocarpaceae	4	4	.30	.40	.53	1.33	1.65
Sterculiaceae	6	7	.21	.29	.80	.95	1.65
Leguminosae-Pap	5	5	.19	.16	.67	.55	2.06
Myristicaceae	6	6	.21	.29	.80	.98	1.23
Euphorbiaceae	4	4	.13	.06	.53	.18	1.65
Combretaceae	3	3	.22	.14	.40	.46	1.23
Anacardiaceae	3	3	.20	.10	.40	.34	1.23
Myrtaceae	3	3	.10	.02	.40	.08	1.23
Lauraceae	2	2	.15	.04	.27	.12	.82
Nyctaginaceae	2	2	.15	.04	.27	.12	.82
Sapotaceae	2	2	.13	.03	.27	.09	.82
Icacinaceae	2	2	.13	.03	.27	.09	.82
Ebenaceae	1	1	.30	.07	.13	.23	.41
Bombacaceae	2	2	.11	.02	.27	.06	.41
Caricaceae	1	1	.19	.03	.13	.09	.41
Apocynaceae	1	1	.13	.01	.13	.05	.41
Capparidaceae	1	1	.12	.01	.13	.04	.41
Malpighiaceae	1	1	.10	.01	.13	.03	.41
TOTAL:	748	842	30.01				100.00

Appendix 4.- **Sample species distribution map**

Old river bed forest, Manu 1993
Laetia corymbulosa
(Flacourteaceae)

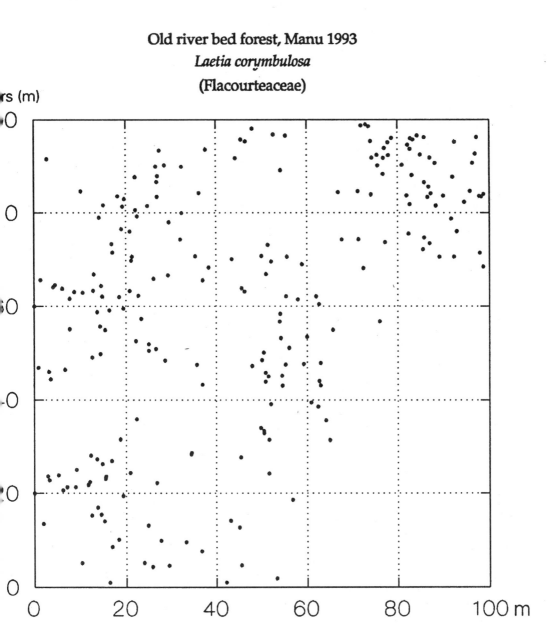

Francisco Dallmeier and James A. Comiskey

Appendix 5.- Sample subquadrat map from St. John use'r guide

St. JOHN BIODIVERSITY PLOTS, U.S. VIRGIN ISLANDS
SMITHSONIAN/MAB BIODIVERSITY PROGRAM
PLOT 01 - QUADRAT 01 SUB-QUAD 1 - 1992 CENSUS

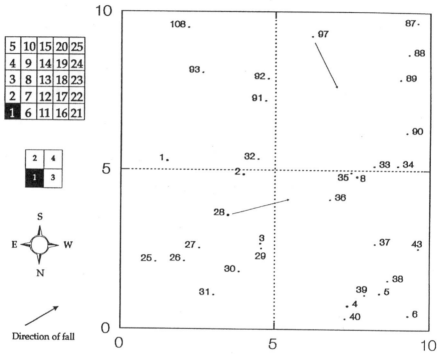

1 *Tabebuia heterophylla* **(Bignoniaceae)** TABHET
2 *Tabebuia heterophylla* **(Bignoniaceae)** TABHET
3 *Bourreria succulenta* **(Boraginaceae)** BOUSUC
4 *Tabebuia heterophylla* **(Bignoniaceae)** TABHET
5 *Bursera simaruba* **(Burseraceae)** BURSIM
6 *Bursera simaruba* **(Burseraceae)** BURSIM
8 *Maytenus elliptica* **(Celastraceae)** MAYELL
25 *Myrciaria floribunda* **(Myrtaceae)** MYRFLO
26 *Myrciaria floribunda* **(Myrtaceae)** MYRFLO
27 *Myrciaria floribunda* **(Myrtaceae)** MYRFLO
28 *Guettarda parviflora* **(Rubiaceae)** GUEPAR
29 *Amyris elemifera* **(Rutaceae)** AMYELE
30 *Sabinea florida* **(Fabaceae)** SABFLO
31 *Myrciaria floribunda* **(Myrtaceae)** MYRFLO
32 *Myrciaria floribunda* **(Myrtaceae)** MYRFLO
33 *Krugiodendron ferreum* **(Rhamnaceae)** KRUFER
34 *Myrciaria floribunda* **(Myrtaceae)** MYRFLO

35 *Sabinea florida* **(Fabaceae)** SABFLO
36 *Myrciaria floribunda* **(Myrtaceae)** MYRFLO
37 *Myrciaria floribunda* **(Myrtaceae)** MYRFLO
38 *Myrciaria floribunda* **(Myrtaceae)** MYRFLO
39 *Guapira fragrans* **(Nyctaginaceae)** GUAFRA
40 *Myrciaria floribunda* **(Myrtaceae)** MYRFLO
43 *Myrciaria floribunda* **(Myrtaceae)** MYRFLO
87 *Amyris elemifera* **(Rutaceae)** AMYELE
88 *Amyris elemifera* **(Rutaceae)** AMYELE
89 *Capparis indica* **(Capparidaceae)** CAPIND
90 *Myrciaria floribunda* **(Myrtaceae)** MYRFLO
91 *Myrciaria floribunda* **(Myrtaceae)** MYRFLO
92 *Myrciaria floribunda* **(Myrtaceae)** MYRFLO
93 *Amyris elemifera* **(Rutaceae)** AMYELE
97 *Erythroxylum brevipes* **(Erythroxylaceae)** ERYBRE
108 *Myrciaria floribunda* **(Myrtaceae)** MYRFLO

Appendix 6.- **Sample quadrat map from Manu user's guide**

MANU BIODIVERSITY PLOTS, PERU
SMITHSONIAN/MAB BIODIVERSITY PROGRAM
PLOT   0413 - QUADRAT   01 - 1991 CENSUS

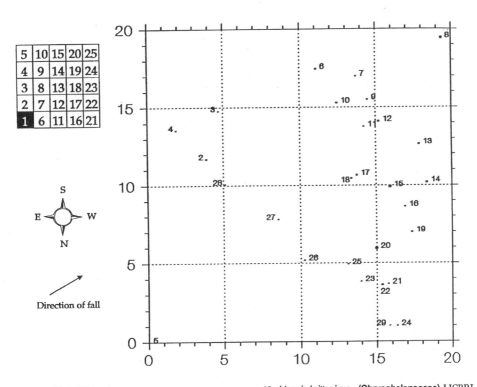

5	10	15	20	25
4	9	14	19	24
3	8	13	18	23
2	7	12	17	22
1	6	11	16	21

Direction of fall

1	*Undetermined sp.*
2	*Inga nitida* **(Leguminosae-Mim)** INGNIT
3	*Annona hypoglauca* **(Annonaceae)** ANNHYP
4	*Laetia corymbulosa* **(Flacourtiaceae)** LAECOR
5	*Undetermined sp.*
6	*Calophyllum brasiliense* **(Guttiferae)** CALBRA
7	*Laetia corymbulosa* **(Flacourtiaceae)** LAECOR
8	*Laetia corymbulosa* **(Flacourtiaceae)** LAECOR
9	*Laetia corymbulosa* **(Flacourtiaceae)** LAECOR
10	*Laetia corymbulosa* **(Flacourtiaceae)** LAECOR
11	*Inga nitida* **(Leguminosae-Mim)** INGNIT
12	*Laetia corymbulosa* **(Flacourtiaceae)** LAECOR
13	*Allophylus scrobiculatus* **(Sapindaceae)** ALLSCR
14	*Laetia corymbulosa* **(Flacourtiaceae)** LAECOR
15	*Calophyllum brasiliense* **(Guttiferae)** CALBRA
16	*Laetia corymbulosa* **(Flacourtiaceae)** LAECOR
17	*Inga punctata* **(Leguminosae-Mim)** INGPUN
18	*Licania britteniana* **(Chrysobalanaceae)** LICBRI
19	*Allophylus scrobiculatus* **(Sapindaceae)**
20	*Trichilia pleeana* **(Meliaceae)** TRIPLE
21	*Pithecellobium latifolium* **(Leguminosae-Mim)** PITLAT
22	*Inga nitida* **(Leguminosae-Mim)** INGNIT
23	*Pithecellobium latifolium* **(Leguminosae-Mim)** PITLAT
24	*Laetia corymbulosa* **(Flacourtiaceae)** LAECOR
25	*Allophylus scrobiculatus* **(Sapindaceae)** ALLSCR
26	*Laetia corymbulosa* **(Flacourtiaceae)** LAECOR
27	*Calophyllum brasiliense* **(Guttiferae)** CALBRA
28	*Annona hypoglauca* **(Annonaceae)** ANNHYP
29	*Inga nitida* **(Leguminosae-Mim)** INGNIT

Appendix 7.- **Sample spread sheet from Manu user's guide.**

									STATUS
MANU BIODIVERSITY PLOTS, PERU SMITHSONIAN/MAB BIODIVERSITY PROGRAM PLOT 0413-QUADRAT 01-1991 CENSUS									
TREE	STEM	GENUS	SPECIES	COMMON NAME	ACRONYM	X	Y	DBH	STATUS NOTES
1	1								NL
2	1	Inga	nitida	Shimbillo	INGNIT	3.88	11.68	.164	AS
2	2	Inga	nitida	Shimbillo	INGNIT	3.88	11.68	.152	AS
3	1	Annona	hypoglauca	Sacha anona	ANNHYP	4.70	14.76	.118	AS
4	1	Laetia	corymbulosa	Temareo	LAECOR	1.89	13.55	.083	AS
4	2	Laetia	corymbulosa	Temareo	LAECOR	1.89	13.55	.055	AS
4	3	Laetia	corymbulosa	Temareo	LAECOR	1.89	13.55	.130	AS
4	4	Laetia	corymbulosa	Temareo	LAECOR	1.89	13.55	.100	AS
5	1					0.00	0.00		NL
6	1	Calophyllum	brasiliense	Lagarto caspi	CALBRA	11.08	17.46	.204	AS
7	1	Laetia	corymbulosa	Temareo	LAECOR	13.71	17.00	.141	AS
8	1	Laetia	corymbulosa	Temareo	LAECOR	19.34	19.42	.300	AS
9	1	Laetia	corymbulosa	Temareo	LAECOR	14.47	15.50	.153	AS
10	1	Laetia	corymbulosa	Temareo	LAECOR	12.43	15.29	.230	AS
11	1	Inga	nitida	Shimbillo	INGNIT	14.21	13.77	.121	AS
11	2	Inga	nitida	Shimbillo	INGNIT	14.21	13.77	.119	AS
11	3	Inga	nitida	Shimbillo	INGNIT	14.21	13.77	.093	AS
11	4	Inga	nitida	Shimbillo	INGNIT	14.21	13.77	.070	AS
12	1	Laetia	corymbulosa	Temareo	LAECOR	15.19	14.10	.184	AS
13	1	Allophylus	scrobiculatus	Quinilla-caspi	ALLSCR	17.83	12.65	.208	AS
14	1	Laetia	corymbulosa	Temareo	LAECOR	18.33	10.21	.258	AS
15	1	Calophyllum	brasiliense	Largarto caspi	CALBRA	15.89	9.93	.351	AS
16	1	Laetia	corymbulosa	Temareo	LAECOR	16.88	8.64	.178	AS
17	1	Inga	punctata	Shimbillo	INGPUN	13.73	10.66	.189	AS
18	1	Licania	britteniana	Apacharama	LICBRI	13.36	10.46	.183	AS
19	1	Allophylus	scrobiculatus	Quinilla-caspi	ALLSCR	17.32	6.98	.157	AS
20	1	Trichilia	pleeana	Uchamullaca	TRIPLE	14.99	5.94	.347	AS
21	1	Pithecellobium	latifolium	Nina caspi	PITLAT	15.74	3.67	.122	AS
21	2	Pithecellobium	latifolium	Nina caspi	PITLAT	15.74	3.67	.103	AS
21	3	Pithecellobium	latifolium	Nina caspi	PITLAT	15.74	3.67	.100	AS
21	4	Pithecellobium	latifolium	Nina caspi	PITLAT	15.74	3.67	.060	AS

STATUS CODES
AS = Alive standing   AF = Alive fallen   AB = Alive broken
DS = Dead standing   DF = Dead fallen   DB = Dead broken   NL = Not located

Flora

Floristic Composition, Diversity, Mortality and Recruitment on Different Substrates: Lowland Tropical Forest, Pakitza, Río Manu, Peru

Francisco Dallmeier

Smithsonian/MAB Biodiversity Program
Smithsonian Institution, Washington, D.C. 20560 USA

Margo Kabel

Smithsonian Institution, Washington, D.C. 20560 USA

Robin B. Foster

Smithsonian Tropical Research Institute
Apartado 2072, Balboa, Panama
and Botany Department, Field Museum
Chicago, IL 60605-2496 USA

ABSTRACT

Monitoring biological composition is a basic step in determining the forces that shape and change ecosystem equilibrium. At its research sites in Latin America and the southeastern United States, the Smithsonian Institution/Man and the Biosphere Biological Diversity Program (SI/MAB) is engaged in long-term monitoring of many aspects of tropical and temperate forest ecosystems. The goal is to understand more about forest dynamics and thus aid in making sound decisions regarding conservation and use of forest ecosystems.

SI/MAB's research plots in the Upper Amazon lowland forest at Pakitsa in the Manu Biosphere Reserve, Peru, were among the first established, and they continue to provide data essential to the goal of the program. This paper summarizes information from the Pakitsa study plots related to floristic composition, diversity, mortality and recruitment -important keys to knowledge about ecosystem change. The data clearly show that monitoring, conducted over three to five-year intervals, yields detailed data that are useful in understanding differences in composition and dynamics between habitats in the Manu ecosystem.

INTRODUCTION

In 1987, the Smithsonian Institution/Man and the Biosphere Biological Diversity Program (SI/MAB), in cooperation with the Biodiversity in Latin America Program (BIOLAT), established four research plots at Manu National Park in the Manu Biosphere Reserve of Peru. The plots, in the immediate vicinity of the park's Pakitsa ranger and biological station, have served as a cornerstone of SI/MAB's long-term biodiversity monitoring effort in tropical and temperate forest ecosystems. Our Manu studies have yielded the impetus for numerous improvements in research and training methods at all SI/ MAB sites.

The richness of species diversity in tropical forests has been discussed extensively in the literature (Ashton 1969; Janzen 1970; Connell 1971, 1980; Hubbell and Foster 1986, 1990, Dallmeier and Devlin 1992). Research indicates Manu Biosphere Reserve holds one of the highest levels of biological diversity in the world (Gentry 1990). Much of this diversity has yet to be recorded despite years of on-going work. More than 1,147 species of vascular plants have been collected in an area of the park that is just 5 square kilometers in size, and it is estimated that rest of the reserve contains 5 to 10 times that number of species.

The Pakitsa station in the park is surrounded by a diversity of plant communities. That is a major reason SI/MAB located its four research plots near Pakitsa. The area is very suitable for studying and comparing composition and changes on differing substrates of a lowland tropical flood plain from high terrace to low inundated terrace, and from well-drained slopes to swamps.

This paper summarizes data from our work on four, one-hectare plots, with the following questions in mind. What are the dominant tree species in each habitat sample? How different is the floristic composition among plots? Are there significant differences in tree size and the number of multiple stems in the four plots? Does recruitment balance mortality for each site? Is recruitment replacing the same species suffering mortality?

SITE DESCRIPTION

The Manu National Park was established in 1973 and accepted by UNESCO as a biosphere reserve in 1977. It is located in the Upper Amazon Basin of southeastern Peru, northeast of the ancient Incan capital of Cuzco, in the provinces of Manu and Paucartambo of the Madre de Dios and Cuzco departments (11°19' 13°02'S – 71°07' 72°26'W) (Fig.1). The divide between the Rio Madeira drainage toward the south and the main Amazon drainage to the north, borders the reserve to the north and east.

The reserve contains more than 1,880,000 hectares of land. It contains the entire drainage system of the Rio Manu, and large parts of the Rio Alto Madre de Dios drainage. It is extraordinary because it contains most of the vegetation types of south-eastern Peru. It stretches from the alpine grasslands of the Andes Mountains at 4000 meters, down the steep slopes and deep river canyons, to the lowland rainforest regions of the Amazon plain at 240 meters. Mean annual temperatures range from 24°C in lowland forests to 5°C in the upper elevations, and annual rainfall ranges from 1500 to over 3000 millimeters.

PLOT DESCRIPTIONS

Two of the SI/MAB plots are located in an area of ancient alluvial terraces (Plots 1 and 3); and two in the recent floodplain of the Rio Manu (Plots 2 and 4). Each plot is located on a different substrate, affording the opportunity to study a variety of species associations or communities (Dallmeier et al. 1993a,b).

ANCIENT ALLUVIAL TERRACE AREA

Erosional slope and stream bottom of dissected terrace: natural regeneration forest of mixed age -

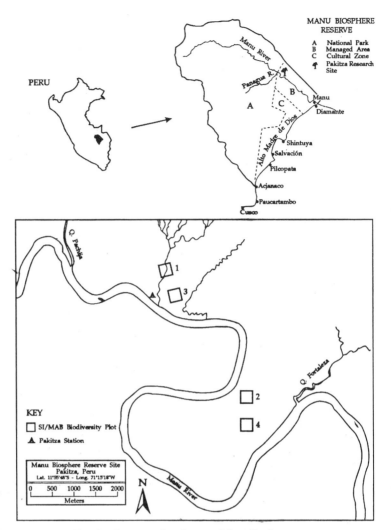

Fig. 1.– Location of study area, Manu Biodiversity

Plot 1. This plot is situated at an elevation approximately 10 - 30 meters above the Manu River. It is topographically diverse ranging from the top edge of a terrace down across the small (10 m wide) floodplain of the Pakitsa main stream. This is the stream derived from the erosion of the terrace, mainly by a process of lateral slumping of the terrace into the stream bottom. The irregularity of the slopes reflect the cut and mound formation by the slumps on the clayey soils, and secondary erosion by branch streamlets. On the sandier soils the slope is more gradual. Plot 1 contains several areas of wet seeps where the water emerges from the slope at the transition to the denser alluvial strata deeper in the terrace. (Fig. 2).

Except for the gradual sandier slopes, the forest is mostly in a state of regeneration and has a very irregular canopy. Within plot 1 there are lateral slumps of different ages and most of the forest is much less than 200 years old. Some of the discontinuity in the canopy is from the recent fall of several large trees in the

63

northern portion of the plot. The largest canopy trees include successional species such as B*rosimum alicastrum, Sclerolobium bracteosum* and *Cecropia tessmanii.* The common sub-canopy trees are *Rinorea guianensis, Iriartea deltoidea, Sagotia racemosa* and *Socratea salazarii.* The low understory of the forest is occupied principally by saplings of tree species rather than shrubs.

Fig. 2.– Physiographic configuration of SI/MAB plots 1, 2, 3, and 4, Manu Biosphere Reserve, Peru.

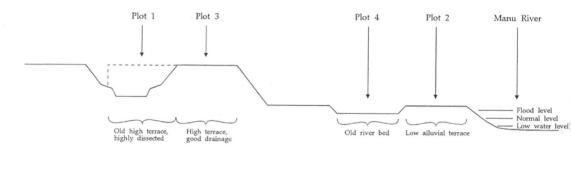

Sandy terrace: bamboo-dominated, old, second-growth forest - Plot 3.

This plot is located on a high, well-drained sandy terrace that overlooks the river (Fig. 2). A depression along the baseline north of the plot collects water during the rainy season. The position of the plot near the bluff probably exposes it to much more wind than is received by terrace sites further from the river.

The abundance of ceramic fragments on the terraces close to the river, the dominance of bamboo only on terraces that are near the river, the abundance of second-growth species in this forest, and the observation that current indigenous groups put their settlements on terraces near the river, all argue that this is second-growth forest from previous human clearing. Judging from the size and species of trees, it was probably a clearing (with a few isolated trees left standing — e.g. Dipteryx) between 100 and 200 years ago. In terms of floristic composition it is somewhat different from the typical terraces more remote from the river.

The 30 meter-high canopy is discontinuous with only a few widely-spaced large trees (e.g. *Cedrelinga catenaeformis, Erisma uncinatum, Dipteryx micrantha, Jacaranda copaia, Qualea grandiflora,* and *Tachigali polyphylla*). When the plot was established in 1987, a large successional tree, *Pourouma minor,* was common; now only a few individuals of this species remain. The understory and gaps are dominated by the bamboo *Guadua weberbaueri*, but this species has stem diameters of less than 10 cm. Common subcanopy species are: *Euterpe precatoria*, *Socratea exorrhiza*, *Lindackeria paludosa*, *Virola calophylla*, *Siparuna decipiens*.

RECENT ALLUVIAL FLOODPLAIN AREA

High floodplain: old-growth forest - Plot 2

This plot is located on the recent floodplain within a large meander of the Manu river (Fig. 2). It is a relatively high but flooded terrace with good drainage and is inundated only in very exceptional floods (Fig. 2). Bordering the west side of the plot near the center of the meander is a shallow depression formed when the river abandoned its channel and took a different course. The forest on the plot is probably several hundred years old, and that in the adjacent depression is probably less than 100 years.

The Plot 2 forest has a mostly closed, homogeneous canopy about 40 meters high with a few emergents, such as *Ceiba samauma*, *Copaifera reticulata*, *Apuleia leiocarpa*, *Poulsenia armata*, and along the edge of the depression *Calycophyllum spruceanum*. The understory is dominated by *Astrocaryum chonta*, *Iriartea deltoidea*, and *Otoba parvifolia*. The most common shrub is *Rinorea viridifolia*, and the fern, *Tectaria incisa* is a common herb.

Abandoned river-meander depression: swamp forest bordering on high floodplain - Plot 4. This plot is located in a depression on an abandoned river bed of the Rio Manu. This area may have been a «cocha» (ox-bow lake) after the river changed course, then rapidly silted in. The area is mostly flat and is seasonally flooded. Even in the dry season the soil remains moist. The southeastern corner of the plot corresponds to the old river bank and levee, a couple of meters higher and well-drained (Fig. 2). The heterogeneous forest has an open canopy, few lianas and isolated crowns of emergent *Calophyllum brasiliensis* and an occasional large *Ficus*. The understory consists mostly of three species (*Laetia corymbulosa*, *Trichilia pleeana* and *Allophylus scrobiculatus*) — small-crowned trees with straight trunks. The lowest stratum consists of trees that have multiple trunks and/or aerial roots (*Inga dumosa*, *Annona hypoglauca*, and *Ficus trigona*). At 1-2 m there is dominance by large herbaceous species of *Heliconia*, *Costus* and *Renealmia* and shrubs of *Tabernaemontana siphilitica*.

METHODS

At all SI/MAB biodiversity research sites, sampling methods and formulas used to calculate basal area, relative density, relative basal area and relative frequency follow those described by Dallmeier (1992) and Dallmeier and Comiskey (this volume). A zone of 25 hectares is established that allows for simultaneous study of a number of features (*e.g.*, nutrient dynamics, invertebrate diversity, forest

Francisco Dallmeier, Margo Kabel and Robin B. Foster

regeneration). The zone also provides the framework for the consistency needed in comparing data collected at different sites.

Within the zone, monitoring of botanical diversity occurs on smaller research plots in the center of the zone, each normally one-hectare in size. More plots can be added as necessary. The number of small plots that can be monitored with accuracy for plant and animal species is determined by the time and resources available. Site-specific data garnered from the plots are excellent educational tools for future researchers and reserve managers. SI/MAB analyzes tree diversity and floristic composition data and incorporates the information and results into users' manuals and field guides within a few months after the plots are established.

Table 1.- Structural Characteristics of the Pakitsa Forest Plots for 1991

	Plot 1	Plot 2	Plot 3	Plot 4
Number of individuals	550	610	443	688
Number of families	43	45	40	31
Number of genera	105	108	90	55
Number of species	148	157	122	73
Number of trees/species	3.72	3.89	3.63	9.42
Total basal area (m^3)	27.85	37.20	22.53	29.98

RESULTS

Table 1 and appendices 1, 2, 3, and 4, summarize basic data for SI/MAB's four Pakitsa plots. Differences and similarities, evident from the tables, are described in more detail below, along with additional findings of the monitoring process.

Stream-Bottom & Slope - Plot 1

In this plot, 550 live individuals were recorded, representing 148 species in 43 families. *Rinorea guianensis* is the most abundant tree, with 165 trees comprising 30 percent of the total population of the plot. Also abundant were the palms *Iriartea deltoidea, Socratea salazarii,* and *Astrocaryum chonta* as well as *Pseudolmedia laevis* and *Sagotia racemosa.* Basal area was factored with abundance to determine relative basal area of tree species in the plot. The most common species in plot 1 (Fig. 3a) were *Rinorea guianensis, Iriartea deltoidea, Ficus mathewsii, Brosimum alicastrum* and *Apeiba membranacea.* Eighty-four species (57 percent of all species), including *Ficus mathewsii* are represented in the plot by a single tree. Eleven families are represented by a single individual (Fig. 4a).

Sandy terrace with bamboo - Plot 3

Plot 3 contains 443 live trees representing 122 species in 40 families. The palms *Euterpe precatoria* and *Socratea exorrhiza* are the most abundant species, each contributing 21 individuals, or 10 percent, to the total population (Fig. 3c). Other abundant species are *Siparuna decipiens, Lindackeria paludosa, Mabea maynensis* and *Virola calophylla*, which together comprise 61 trees or 14 percent of the total. In contrast, species with high relative basal area values in this plot are *Cedrelinga catenaeformis, Parkia multijuga,*

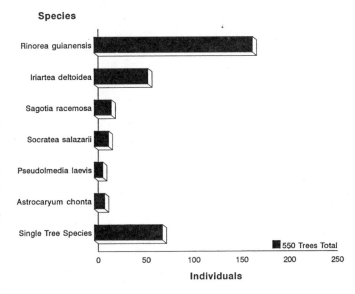

Species

Fig. 3a.– Species in plot 1 with more than 10 individuals.

Aspidosperma vargasii, Tachigali polyphylla, and *Pourouma minor.* In this plot, the dominant species are all represented by relatively few, large individuals. Fifty-six species or 46 percent of all species are represented by a single tree. This is a somewhat lower percentage of single tree species as found in plot 1. Five of the 40 families, representing less than one percent of all individuals, have only one representative (Fig. 4b).

High-floodplain old-growth - Plot 2.

With 610 live trees of 157 species in 45 families, this is the most diverse area of the four Manu plots. The five most abundant species are *Astrocaryum chonta, Iriartea deltoidea, Otoba parvifolia, Quararibea wittii* and *Guarea macrophylla* (Fig. 3c). Together they account for 218 trees or 36 percent of the 610 trees recorded in the plot. The species with the highest relative basal area values are *Copaifera reticulata, Iriartea deltoidea, Vitex cymosa, Ceiba samuama,* and *Pseudolmedia laevis.* Of the dominant species, Ceiba, Vitex and Copaifera are represented by 2 or fewer trees in this plot. Seventy-seven species (50 percent) have only

Fig. 3b.– Species in plot 3 with more than 10 individuals.

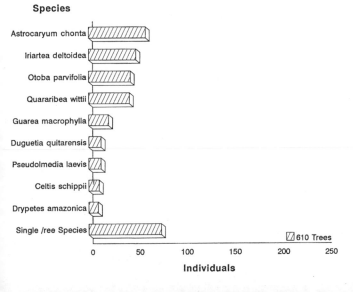

Species

67

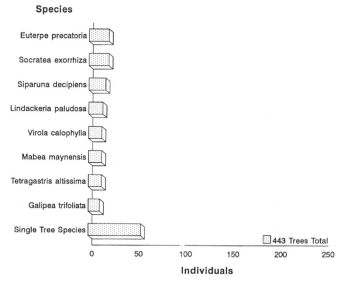

Fig. 3c.– *Species in plot 2 with more than 10 individuals*

one representative in plot 2 (Fig. 3c). This is the highest percentage of species with single individuals of the 4 plots. Palmae has more individuals than any other family, but 87 percent are of just two species, *Astrocaryum chonta* and *Iriartea deltoidea*. Six families are represented by one individual, making up less than one percent of the total number (Fig. 4c).

Abandoned Riverbed Swamp Forest - Plot 4

Of 688 live trees on this plot, 31 percent are of one species, *Laetia corymbulosa*. The most abundant species, in order, are *Allophylus scrobiculatus*, *Inga dumosa*, *Calophyllum brasiliensis* and *Trichilia pleeana*, accounting for 63 percent of the total number of trees. The list of species with the highest relative basal area are similar to the most abundant species: *Laetia corymbulosa, Calophyllum brasiliense, Luehea cymulosa, Allophylus scrobiculatus,* and *Ficus insipida.*

The 73 tree species found in this plot occur in 31 families. Thirty-one species (44 percent) are represented by a single tree (Fig. 3d). The Flacourtiaceae are represented by three species: 211 individuals of *Laetia corymbulosa*, a single *Banara guianensis*, and unidentified Flacourtiaceae species. Mimosoid Legumes, mainly *Inga*, comprise 12 percent of the individuals, and the Sapindaceae is represented on the plot by only two species (86 individuals are of one species, *Allophylus scrobiculatus*), constituting 13 percent of the trees recorded.

Size Class Distributions and Occurrence of Multiple Stemmed Trees

Under the SI/MAB research protocol (Dallmeier, 1992; Dallmeier

Fig. 3d.– *Species in plot 4 with more than 10 individuals*

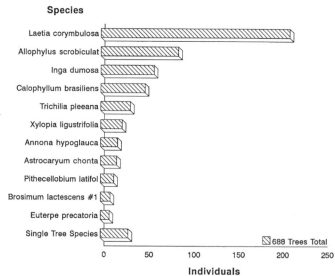

and Comiskey in this volume), any tree with one stem at least 10 cm in diameter at breast height (DBH), is tagged, identified and included in the map of the plot. The diameters of all other stems of the same tree are also measured at breast height, down to 1 cm dbh.

Plot 1 contains 550 live trees and only 11 multistemmed trees, primarily *Rinorea guianensis* (Appendix 1). The average DBH for live stems in Plot

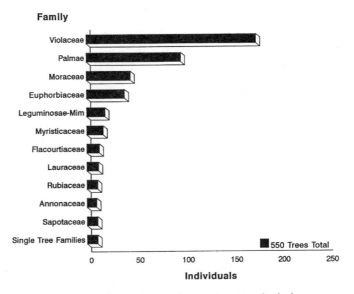

Fig. 4a.– *Families in plot 1 with more than 10 individuals.*

1 is 21 cm. Fifty-five percent of the trees in plot 1 are in the 10 to 20 cm size-class (Fig. 6a). This is 10-19 percent fewer trees in this size-class than in the other plots. There were 17 trees (3%) larger than 50 cm and 2 trees larger than 1m dbh (Fig. 6a).

Plot 3 contains the fewest live trees (443) and just one multi-stemmed individual *Lindackeria paludosa* (Appendix 3). The average live stem dbh in the plot is 21 cm; 65 percent of the live trees are less than 20 cm dbh, while 11 percent are between 30 and 50 cm dbh (Fig. 6a). Only 2 trees in this plot exceeded 1 meter in dbh.

Of 610 live trees in plot 2, only one species, The*obroma cacao* was recorded with multiple stems (Appendix 2). The average dbh of live trees in plot 2 was 22 cm. Sixty five percent of live trees had a dbh less than 20 cm, and 30 percent were between 20 and 50 cm dbh (Fig. 6b). Six trees were also recorded with a dbh larger than one meter in dbh.

Fig. 4b.– *Families in plot 2 with more than 10 individuals*

Six hundred and eighty eight live trees, 49 of them with additional 96 stems were recorded in plot 4 (Appendix 4). The

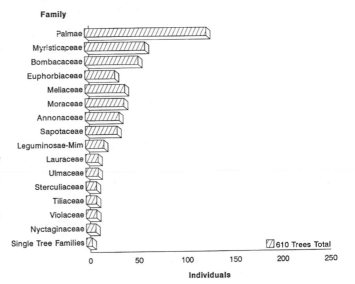

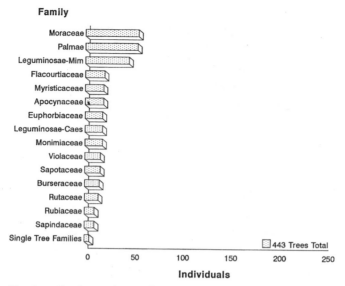

Family

Fig. 4c.– Families in plot 3 with more than 10 individuals

plot also has a large number of small trees and relatively few large emergents. Twenty two of these trees (45%) are of the species Inga *dumosa*. In addition, there are 7 multi-stemmed *Laetia corymbulosa* and five *Pithecellobium latifolium*, two *Allophylus scrobiculatus*, and one *Ficus trigona*. Fully 72 percent of the trees are less than 20 cm dbh, and only six percent are larger than 29 cm dbh (Fig. 6b). The average dbh of live trees in this plot is 18 cm, which is the smallest of the four plots.

Species Diversity and Distribution

Three hundred and forty species and 2,291 live trees 10 cm dbh and larger were recorded in our four plots. The number of species varied considerably among plots, ranging from a low of 73 in plot 4 to a high of 157 in plot 2. Although one might expect a larger number of species to occur in plots with more individuals, this was not the case in our sample. In fact, plot 4 which had the largest number of trees (688) had the fewest species (73 species).

All four plots had a large number of species represented by a single individual, ranging from 84 in plot 1 to 31 in plot 4. The proportion of single indivi-

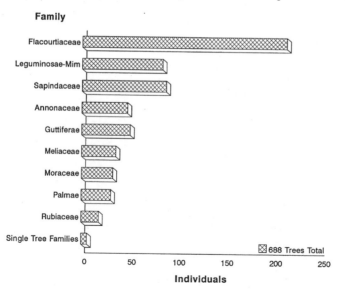

Family

Fig. 4d.– Families in plot 4 with more than 10 individuals

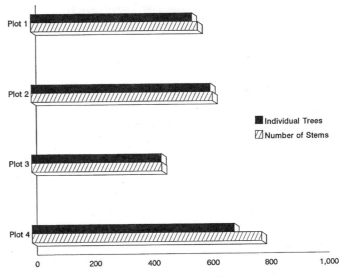

Fig. 5.– *Number of trees and stems per plot*

dual species, which varied from 44-57%, was relatively constant across the plots, despite the nearly two-fold difference in the total number of species per plot.

Plot locations were purposely chosen to vary in terms of slope, aspect and elevation to capture a range of distinct forest communities. As a result, there was a very low degree of overlap in the species composition of the plots. Of the 340 total species recorded, 210 species, or 64% are found in only one of the four plots. Twenty-five percent (82 species) were found in two plots, while 9% (50 species) were found in three plots. Just 3% (8 species) were found in all four plots. These 8 generalists species included several palms (*Astrocaryum chonta, Iriartea deltoidea, Euterpe precatoria*) as well as *Inga sp.1, Cecropia engleriana, Brosimum lactescens, Inga calantha* cf. and *Pseudolmedia laevis*.

MORTALITY AND RECRUITMENT

Mortality and recruitment over the four-year period 1987 to 1991 are summarized in Ta-ble 3 and discussed below.

Alluvial Terrace Plots. In Plot 1, 58 trees died during the study period, while 34 matured to at least 10 cm dbh. Of the trees that died, 39 fell, the larger among them *Pourouma mollis*, bringing down smaller trees in the process. The average dbh of dead trees was 25 cm compared to an average dbh of 21 cm for live trees (Ta-

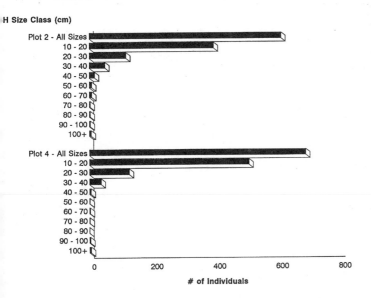

Fig. 6a.– *Size class distribution for plots 1 and 3, 1991.*

71

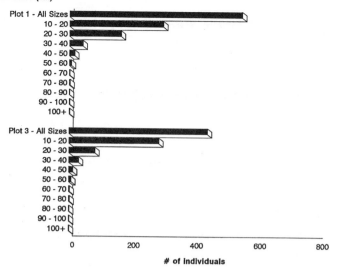

DBH Size Class (cm)

Plot 1 - All Sizes
10 - 20
20 - 30
30 - 40
40 - 50
50 - 60
60 - 70
70 - 80
80 - 90
90 - 100
100+

Plot 3 - All Sizes
10 - 20
20 - 30
30 - 40
40 - 50
50 - 60
60 - 70
70 - 80
80 - 90
90 - 100
100+

0   200   400   600   800

# of individuals

Fig. 6b.— Size class distribution for plots 2 and 4, 1991.

ble 2). The relatively large average dbh of dead trees may be due to the recent fall of several large trees in this plot; primarily *Rinorea guianensis* and *Tachigali varquerii*.

The most abundant dead tree families (in order) are Violaceae, Moraceae, Leguminosae, Palmae, and Euphorbiaceae. This mirrors the composition of live tree families. The most abundant new tree families are Violaceae, Palmae, Moraceae, Euphorbiaceae and Leguminosae.

Even with the significant amount of recruitment and mortality in this plot, no plant families were totally lost nor were any new ones gained. At the species level, *Ficus paraensis* (a strangler), *Endlicheria sp.*, *Rinorea sp.*, and *Micropholis guyanensis* were added by reaching 10 cm dbh. Seven species of trees are no longer represented in the plot; *Acacia sp.1*, *Cecropia sciadophylla*, *Couratari macrosperma*, *Inga capitata*, *Ochroma pyramidalis*, *Sapium ixiamasense* and *Tachigali varquerii* (which is monocarpic and died after setting fruit). There was a net loss of 3 spp, or 2 % of total species in the plot.

In Plot 3, 97 trees died, and 16 grew to the minimum size for monitoring. Forty-seven of the dead trees fell, while 50 remain standing. One factor contributing to this high mortality rate may be the location of this plot on a high bluff where it is exposed to more wind than sites further from the river. More significantly, high mor-

Table 2.- Tree Mortality by DBH Size Class

Size Class (cm)	Originally in plot (1987)	Dead after 4 years (1991)	Mortality/ year (%)
Plot 1 - Total	575	58	2.5
10 - 20	309	34	2.8
20 - 30	174	15	2.2
30 +	92	9	2.4
Plot 2 - Total	648	53	2.0
10 - 20	418	38	2.3
20 - 30	130	13	2.5
30 +	100	2	0.5
Plot 3 - Total	537	97	4.5
10 - 20	353	65	4.6
20 - 30	103	18	4.4
30 +	81	14	4.3
Plot 4 - Total	661	51	1.9
10 - 20	480	41	2.1
20 - 30	126	6	1.2
30 +	55	4	1.8
Totals all plots	2421	259	2.7

tality and low recruitment may be due to a large population of bamboo that has invaded the area. Bamboos can sup-press tree regeneration for many years until they flower and die (Terborgh 1992). Until the bamboos complete their life cycle, we predict that mortality will continue and eventually outweigh recruitment.

The average dbh of the live trees is very close to that of dead trees (21 cm and 20 cm). The most abundant dead trees by family are Palmae, Myristicaceae, Moraceae, Flacourtiaceae and Leguminosae, almost identical to the most abundant live tree families. The most abundant new trees by family are Palmae, Leguminosae, Rutaceae, Myristicaceae and Euphorbiaceae.

Table 3.- Status of Trees in Pakitsa Plots 1987-1991				
	Plot 1	Plot 2	Plot 3	Plot 4
# Trees 1987	575	648	537	661
Mortality	58	53	97	51
Ingrowth	34	26	16	104
Net Change	-24[1]	-27[2]	-81[3]	+53[4]
Avg. ann. mort.	2.5	2.0	4.5	1.9
Avg. lifespan (yrs)	40	50	22	53

[1] One tree not located
[2] 11 trees not located
[3] Five trees not located, eight decreased in dbh below 10 cm.
[4] 20 trees not located, 6 decreased in dbh below 10 cm.

A total of six species were lost from the plot, *Endlicheria williamsii*, *Siparuna bifida c.c.*, *Pourocema cecropiifolia*, *Neea sp.*, and an unidentified species. Three new species have been added to the plot, *Cabralea cangerana*, *Myrcia splendens*, and *Pseudima frutescens*. This is a change in species of -.5%

Floodplain plots. Tree mortality has far outpaced new growth in Plot 2 since the first inventory in 1987. Only 26 trees have been added, while 53 have died. This probably reflects the maturation and disintegration of this phase in floodplain forest succession (Foster 1992b). About twice the number of trees died as were added, a ratio similar to observations by Terborgh (1992) in Manu's Cocha Cashu area over a 10-year period. Sixty-six percent of the dead trees remain standing.

The low recruitment numbers may be related to the fact that most trees in the plot still stand after they died. This creates much smaller light gaps for new growth to enjoy. Also, standing dead trees do not provide the feast of nutrients in the form of decaying

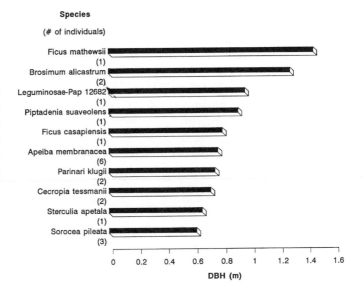

Species

(# of individuals)

Ficus mathewsii (1)
Brosimum alicastrum (2)
Leguminosae-Pap 12682 (1)
Piptadenia suaveolens (1)
Ficus casapiensis (1)
Apeiba membranacea (6)
Parinari klugii (2)
Cecropia tessmanii (2)
Sterculia apetala (1)
Sorocea pileata (3)

0   0.2   0.4   0.6   0.8   1   1.2   1.4   1.6

DBH (m)

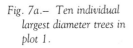

Fig. 7a.– Ten individual largest diameter trees in plot 1.

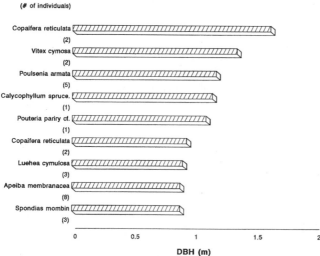

Species

(# of individuals)

Copaifera reticulata (2)
Vitex cymosa (2)
Poulsenia armata (5)
Calycophyllum spruce. (1)
Pouteria pariry cf. (1)
Copaifera reticulata (2)
Luehea cymulosa (3)
Apeiba membranacea (8)
Spondias mombin (3)

DBH (m)

Fig. 7b.– Ten individual largest diameter trees in plot 2.

twigs and branches for emerging vegetation that are available to plants when a tree falls. A simpler explanation is that recruits have not had time to respond to the mortality.

The most common dead tree species are Palmae, Myristicaceae, Meliaceae, and Euphorbiaceae. Palmae, Myristicaceae, and Rutaceae are the main recruits. Five species and two families were lost in this plot; *Apeiba hybrid, Clarisia racemosa, Inga calantha* cf. *Piper variegatum, Caryocar anygdaliforme.* The two families lost were Caryocaraceae and Piperaceae. The four new species were added to the plot were an *Inga* sp., *Eugenia muricata, Symphonia globulifera* and *Leonia glycycarpa.* This is a loss in species diversity of 0.6%. The average dbh of dead trees is 17 cm dbh compared to 22 cm for live trees. Two trees were not located in the plot, both single representatives of species. If indeed they have died, this would suppose a lose of diversity of 1.9%

Plot 4, the inundation forest on the old Manu riverbed, shows a very high rate of new growth over mortality. One hundred and four trees have been added since 1987, 51 have died. Half of the dead trees remain standing. The average dbh of dead trees is 16 cm and live trees is 18 cm. Plot 4 is the only SI/MAB plot at Manu that has gained more species than it lost. Eleven species and one family (Malpighiaceae) are new to the plot. The species are *Unonopsis matthewsii, Nectandra longifolia, Byrsonima arthropoda, Trichilia pachypoda, Cecropia sp.1, Ficus sp.1, Sorocea pileata, Guapira 11345, Coccoloba densifrons, Chrysophyllum argenteum* and Myrtaceae sp. Two species, *Guarea*

Fig. 7c.– Ten individual largest diameter trees in plot 3.

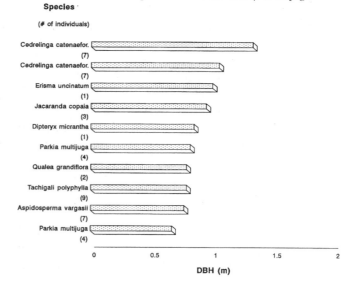

Species

(# of individuals)

Cedrelinga catenaefor. (7)
Cedrelinga catenaefor. (7)
Erisma uncinatum (1)
Jacaranda copaia (3)
Dipteryx micrantha (1)
Parkia multijuga (4)
Qualea grandiflora (2)
Tachigali polyphylla (9)
Aspidosperma vargasii (7)
Parkia multijuga (4)

DBH (m)

74

macrophylla and an unidentified species are no
longer represented. The
overall increase in spe-
cies in this plot is 14
percent.

DISCUSSION

With only four hec-
tares inventoried to
date, it is clear that the
tree species density of
the Pakitsa site is high
with up to 157 species
per hectare. Still, this

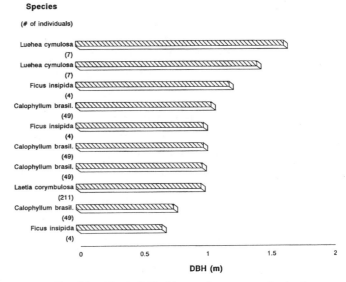

Fig. 7d.— *Ten individual largest diameter trees in plot 4.*

does not match the 200 species per hectare found up river at Cocha Cashu (Gentry
and Terborgh 1992) or the 270 species per hectare found in the Atlantic forest
of Bahia, Brazil (Brooke 1993). The species diversity on a larger scale of the forests
surrounding Pakitza may be higher than these initial numbers suggest, however.
As noted, the square one-hectare plots were purposely located within four distinct,
but relatively homoge-
neous vegetation types.
In contrast, the one-hec-
tare plots in Cocha Cas-
hu and Bahia were both
long and narrow and pur-
posely oriented along a
habitat gradient. Mo-
reover, the 340 species
found in our 4 ha sample
is higher than the num-
ber found in an inven-
tory of 50 hectares in
Panama (303) (Hubbell
and Foster, 1986).

Table 4.- *Number of Species Present in Pakitsa Plots 1987-1991*

Number of Species	Plot 1	Plot 2	Plot 3	Plot 4
1987	151	158	124	64
1991	168	157[1]	122	73[2]
Net Change	-3	-1	-2	+9
% Chg species	-2.0	-0.6	-1.6	+14.1

[1] Two sole representatives of two species not located
[2] One sole representative of a species not located

The mortality rates for trees in the four plots range from 2 to 5 percent per year
over the four-year study period. Mortality is substantially higher than that
recorded from same-sized plots at Cocha Cashu (Gentry and Terborgh, 1992), or
north of Manaus, Brazil (Rankin de Merona et al., 1992). Where annual mortality
rates held between 1 and 2 percent. Comparison with the site at Cocha Cashu is
particularly interesting as it is only 25 Km from Pakitza. The Cocha Cashu

75

inventories were done 10 years apart, with no intermediate tally. It is possible that mortality rates at SI/MAB's plots may drop to a level similar to that of Cocha Cashu when we reach over 10th year inventory. Lieberman et. al. (1985) recorded stem mortality rates at La Selva, Costa Rica over 16 years, from 1969 to 1985, showing mortality during the first 12 years between 1.8 and 2.4 percent. However, all plots experienced higher mortality rates during the second 3-year census period (2.1 to 2.6 percent).

Clearly tree mortality is highly variable across sites and over time at the same site. The advantage of long term plots censused over small intervals (3 to 5 years) is that the differences in mortality can be tracked with a higher degree of accuracy, yielding more data useful to this important study.

ACKNOWLEDGEMENTS

We extend our gratitude to the BIOLAT Program for initial support for this study. Hamilton Beltrán for leading the team in the 1991 recensus, and assistance in making field collections in 1989. Thanks also to Severo Baldeón for assistance in making field collections in 1988, also to Abelardo Sandoval for providing great organizational skills and hard work in the field. Special thanks to James Comiskey for his intense work in the data management and interpretation. We would also like to thank Richard Rice for his advice, and to Zenith Batista and Maria Lucia Kawasaki for assistance in management of the plant collections at Field Museum. Thanks to Susan Mazer, Claudia Sobrevilla, Deanne Kloepfer as well as the anonymous reviewers for their comments that much improved the manuscript.

BIBLIOGRAPHY

Ashton, P.S. 1969. Speciation among tropical forest trees: some deductions in light of recent evidence. Biological Journal of the Linnean Society 1:155-96 .

Brooke, J. 1993. Brazilian rain forest yields most diversity for species of trees. New York Times Environment. March 30.

Connell, J.H. 1971. On the role of natural enemies in preventing competitive exclusion in some marine animals and rain forest trees. In: den Boer, P.J. and G.R. Gradwell (eds.). Dynamics of populations, pp, 298-312. Proc. Advanced Study Inst., Osterbeek Wageningen, Neth. Centre Agric. Publ. Doc.

_____. 1980. Diversity and the coevolution of competitors, or the ghost of competition past. Oikos 35:131-8.

Dallmeier, F. and J.A. Comiskey. From the forest to the user: a methodology update (this volume).

Dallmeier, F. 1992. Long-term monitoring of biological diversity in tropical forest areas: method s for establishment and inventory of permanent plots. MAB Digest 11. UNESCO, Paris.

Dallmeier, F., and F. Devlin. 1992. Forest diversity in Latin America: Reversing the losses? J. Tropical Forest Science 5(2):232-270.

Dallmeier, F., R. Foster, J. Comiskey. 1993a. User's guide to the Manu Biosphere Reserve biodiversity plots, Vol. I and II. Smithsonian Institution, Washington, DC.

_____ . 1993b. User's guide to the Manu Biosphere Reserve biodiversity plots, Vol. III and IV. Smithsonian Institution, Washington, DC.

Foster, R. 1992a. The floristic composition of the Rio Manu flood-plain forest. In: Gentry A.L.(ed.). Four Neotropical Rainforests. Yale University Press, New Haven and London.

_____. 1992b. Long Term change in the successional forest community of the Rio Manu floodplain. In: Gentry, A.L. (ed.). Four Neotropical Rainforests. Yale University Press, New Haven and London.

Gentry, A.H. 1990. Four neotropical rainforests. Yale University Press. New Haven.

Gentry, A.L. and J. Terborgh. 1992. Composition and dynamics of the Cocha Cashu 'mature' floodplain forest. In: Gentry, A.L. (ed.). Four Neotropical Rainforests. Yale University Press, New Haven and London.

Hubbell, S.P. and R.B. Foster. 1986. Biology, change and history and the structure of the tropical rain forest tree communities. In: Diamond, J. and T.J. Case (eds.). Community Ecology. Harper and Row, New York, NY.

_____. 1990. The fate of juvenile trees in a neotropical forest: implications for the natural maintenance of tropical tree diversity. In: Bawa, K.S. and M. Hadley (eds.). Reproductive ecology and tropical forest plants. UNESCO, Paris, Parthenon Publishing Group, Carnforth, Lanes, UK and Park Ridge, NJ.

Janzen, D.H. 1970. Herbivores and the number of trees in tropical forests. American Naturalist 104: 501-528.

Lieberman D., M. Lieberman, R. Peralta, and G.S. Hartshorn. 1985. Mortality patterns and stand turnover rates in a wet tropical forest in Costa Rica. J. Ecology 73:915-924.

Rankin-de-Merona, J.M., R. W. Hutchings, and T.E. Lovejoy. 1992. Tree mortality and recruitment vera five-year period in undisturbed upland rain forest of the central Amazon. In: Gentry, A.L. (ed.). Four Neotropical Rain forests. Yale University Press, New Haven and London.

Terborgh, J. 1992. Diversity and the rain forest. Scientific American Library, New York, N Y .

Appendix 1.- Mixed age regeneration forest (Plot 1) statistics.

Species	Number of Trees	Number of Stems	Average DBH(m)stem	Basal Area	Relative Density	Relative Basal Area	Relative Frequency
Rinorea guianensis	165	182	.178	5,281	30.00	18.96	7.44
Iriartea deltoidea	56	56	.236	2.557	10.18	9.18	6.25
Ficus mathewsii	1	1	1.450	1.651	.18	5.93	.30
Brosimum alicastrum	2	2	.800	1.367	.36	4.91	.60
Apeiba membranacea	6	6	.369	.814	1.09	2.92	1.79
Leguminosae sp 12682	1	1	.960	.724	.18	2.60	.30
Piptadenia suaveolens	1	1	.905	.643	.18	2.31	.30
Cecropia tessmanii	2	2	.574	.552	.36	1.98	.60
Sagotia racemosa	18	18	.181	.529	3.27	1.90	2.98
Ficus casapiensis#2	1	1	.800	.503	.18	1.80	.30
Mauritia flexuosa	4	4	.384	.497	.73	1.78	.89
Sorocea pileata	3	3	.426	.472	.55	1.70	.89
Parinari klugii	2	2	.473	.472	.36	1.69	.60
Tachigali polyphylla	7	7	.268	.438	1.27	1.57	1.79
Inga sp.	8	8	.208	.405	1.45	1.46	1.79
Sapium marmieri	3	3	.363	.380	.55	1.36	.89
Sterculia apetala	1	1	.660	.342	.18	1.23	.30
Tetragastris altissima	5	5	.273	.339	.91	1.22	.89
Pseudolmedia laevis	9	9	.199	.320	1.64	1.15	2.38
Unknown species	8	8	.205	.317	1.45	1.14	1.49
Apeiba «hybrid»	3	3	.308	.271	.55	.97	.60
Socratea salazarii	13	13	.134	.268	2.36	.96	2.98
Manilkara inundata	1	1	.575	.260	.18	.93	.30
Swartzia 12799	1	1	.572	.257	.18	.92	.30
Mabea maynensis	6	6	.220	.255	1.09	.92	1.79
Chimarrhis 1818	5	5	.253	.254	.91	.91	1.19
Clarisia racemosa	3	3	.292	.251	.55	.90	.89
Astrocaryum chonta	11	11	.164	.249	2.00	.89	2.08
Scheelea cephalotes	3	3	.310	.229	.55	.82	.89
Parkia velutina	1	1	.518	.211	.18	.76	.30
Virola duckei	1	1	.514	.207	.18	.74	.30
Bixa platycarpa	2	2	.349	.191	.36	.68	.60
Sapotaceae sp 6523	1	1	.485	.185	.18	.66	.30
Otoba parvifolia	7	7	.168	.183	1.27	.66	1.49
Hyeronima alchorneoides	1	1	.464	.169	.18	.61	.30
Sloanea sinemariensis	1	1	.460	.166	.18	.60	.30
Pourouma cecropiifolia	2	2	.297	.163	.36	.59	.60
Neoraputia paraensis	5	5	.180	.158	.91	.57	1.19
Zanthoxylum 1873	1	1	.442	.153	.18	.55	.30
Brosimum guianense	1	1	.419	.138	.18	.50	.30
Virola flexuosa	1	1	.418	.137	.18	.49	.30
Pouteria procera	1	1	.417	.137	.18	.49	.30
Inga 1817	1	1	.412	.133	.18	.48	.30
Alchornea glandulosa	3	3	.218	.133	.55	.48	.60
Jessenia bataua	3	3	.230	.127	.55	.46	.89
Aspidosperma vargasii	1	1	.400	.126	.18	.45	.30
Pseudolmedia laevigata	2	2	.266	.123	.36	.44	.60
Pleurothyrium krukovii	8	9	.129	.121	1.45	.44	.60
Rubiaceae «big fuzzy»	2	2	.268	.118	.36	.42	.60
Virola mollissima	2	2	.247	.113	.36	.40	.60
Pourouma mollis	2	2	.248	.111	.36	.40	.60

Appendix 1. Mixed age regeneration forest (Plot 1) statistics (cont...)

Species	Number of Trees	Number of Stems	Average DBH(m)stem	Basal Area	Relative Density	Relative Basal Area	Relative Frequency
Virola calophylla	6	6	.143	.105	1.09	.38	1.79
Aniba 1877	1	1	.357	.100	.18	.36	.30
Inga thibaudiana	3	3	.203	.098	.55	.35	.89
Castilla ulei	4	4	.167	.097	.73	.35	1.19
Cecropia engleriana	2	2	.247	.096	.36	.34	.60
Terminalia oblonga	3	3	.195	.094	.55	.34	.60
Ruizodendron ovale	1	2	.244	.094	.18	.34	.30
Ficus maxima	1	1	.338	.090	.18	.32	.30
Vismia sprucei	2	2	.235	.087	.36	.31	.60
Euterpe precatoria	5	5	.145	.087	.91	.31	1.19
Jacaratia digitata	2	2	.235	.086	.36	.31	.30
Sapotaceae sp 1825	1	1	.330	.086	.18	.31	.30
Alseis blackiana cf.	2	2	.228	.082	.36	.29	.60
Lunania parviflora	7	7	.118	.077	1.27	.28	1.49
Brosimum lactescens #1	4	4	.153	.074	.73	.27	1.19
Celtis schippii	3	3	.167	.073	.55	.26	.89
Coccoloba mollis	1	1	.304	.073	.18	.26	.30
Turpinia occidentalis	2	2	.206	.069	.36	.25	.60
Leonia glycycarpa #2	2	2	.195	.060	.36	.22	.60
Lecointea amazonica	1	1	.276	.060	.18	.21	.30
Poulsenia armata	1	1	.272	.058	.18	.21	.30
Rinoreocarpus ulei	3	3	.155	.058	.55	.21	.89
Theobroma cacao	3	3	.155	.057	.55	.20	.89
Guapira 11340	2	2	.186	.055	.36	.20	.60
Burseraceae sp 1	1	1	.264	.055	.18	.20	.30
Glycydendron amazonicum	1	1	.263	.054	.18	.20	.30
Unonopsis floribunda	3	3	.151	.054	.55	.19	.89
Croton matourensis	2	2	.182	.053	.36	.19	.60
Caryocar amygdaliforme	1	1	.250	.049	.18	.18	.30
Drypetes 1813	1	1	.248	.048	.18	.17	.30
Rinorea lindeniana	4	4	.121	.046	.73	.17	.60
Porcelia nitida	1	1	.232	.042	.18	.15	.30
Inga striata cf.	1	1	.230	.042	.18	.15	.30
Socratea exorrhiza	2	2	.160	.041	.36	.15	.60
Himatanthus sucuuba	1	1	.221	.038	.18	.14	.30
Drypetes amazonica	2	2	.155	.038	.36	.14	.60
Macrocnemum roseum	2	2	.151	.038	.36	.14	.60
Oxandra mediocris	2	2	.153	.037	.36	.13	.60
Perebea guianensis	1	1	.217	.037	.18	.13	.30
Metrododorea flavida	2	2	.153	.037	.36	.13	.60
Sapotaceae sp	1	1	.215	.036	.18	.13	.30
Leguminosae sp 1	1	1	.213	.036	.18	.13	.30
Xylosma 1816	1	1	.212	.035	.18	.13	.30
Quaribea ochrocalyx	1	1	.211	.035	.18	.13	.30
Heisteria ovata	1	1	.208	.034	.18	.12	.30
Urera caracasana	2	2	.146	.034	.36	.12	.60
Tabernaemontana psychotriifolia	1	1	.206	.033	.18	.12	.30
Inga acreana cf	1	1	.204	.033	.18	.12	.30
Siparuna decipiens	2	2	.143	.032	.36	.11	.60
Glycydendron 1819	1	1	.191	.029	.18	.10	.30
Terminalia amazonica	1	1	.185	.027	.18	.10	.30

Appendix 1.- Mixed age regeneration forest (Plot 1) statistics (cont...)

Species	Number of Trees	Number of Stems	Average DBH(m)stem	Basal Area	Relative Density	Relative Basal Area	Relative Frequency
Neea 11941	2	2	.129	.027	.36	.10	.60
Lindackeria paludosa	2	2	.128	.026	.36	.09	.30
Pseudobombax septenatum	1	1	.182	.026	.18	.09	.30
Micropholis melinoniana	2	2	.127	.026	.36	.09	.60
Sapium aereum	1	1	.175	.024	.18	.09	.30
Pouteria ephendrantha	1	1	.166	.022	.18	.08	.30
Jacaranda copaia	1	1	.164	.021	.18	.08	.30
Vismia gracilis	1	1	.162	.021	.18	.07	.30
Tapura juruana	1	1	.160	.020	.18	.07	.30
Chrysophyllum venezuelanense	1	1	.158	.020	.18	.07	.30
Cordia 1835	1	1	.156	.019	.18	.07	.30
Pouteria tarapotensis	1	1	.150	.018	.18	.06	.30
Margaritaria nobilis	1	1	.146	.017	.18	.06	.30
Myrtaceae sp.	1	1	.146	.017	.18	.06	.30
Pourouma minor	1	1	.143	.016	.18	.06	.30
Cordia nodosa	2	2	.100	.016	.36	.06	.60
Nectandra cuspidata	1	1	.141	.016	.18	.06	.30
Ampelocera edentula	1	1	.140	.015	.18	.06	.30
Chrysochlamys ulei	1	1	.135	.014	.18	.05	.30
Tapirira peckoltiana cf.	1	1	.133	.014	.18	.05	.30
Trema micrantha	1	1	.133	.014	.18	.05	.30
Inga chartacea	1	1	.130	.013	.18	.05	.30
Trichilia poeppigi	1	1	.130	.013	.18	.05	.30
Lacistema aggregatum	1	1	.127	.013	.18	.05	.30
Parkia nitida	1	1	.126	.012	.18	.04	.30
Rollinia pittieri	1	1	.126	.012	.18	.04	.30
Neea 1851	1	1	.123	.012	.18	.04	.30
Sloanea fragrans	1	1	.123	.012	.18	.04	.30
Duguetia quitarensis	1	1	.122	.012	.18	.04	.30
Inga calantha cf.	1	1	.120	.011	.18	.04	.30
Miconia 1839	1	1	.120	.011	.18	.04	.30
Endlicheria tessmannii	1	1	.114	.010	.18	.04	.30
Miconia 1855	1	1	.113	.010	.18	.04	.30
Neea comun	1	1	.113	.010	.18	.04	.30
Trattinnickia peruviana	1	1	.113	.010	.18	.04	.30
Gustavia hexapetala	1	1	.110	.010	.18	.03	.30
Pourouma guianensis	1	1	.110	.010	.18	.03	.30
Xylopia benthamii	1	1	.109	.009	.18	.03	.30
Ficus paraensis	1	1	.105	.009	.18	.03	.30
Galipea trifoliata	1	1	.105	.009	.18	.03	.30
Rinorea sp 1	1	1	.104	.008	.18	.03	.30
Endlicheria x	1	1	.103	.008	.18	.03	.30
Maquira calophylla	1	1	.103	.008	.18	.03	.30
Casearia obovalis cf.	1	1	.101	.008	.18	.03	.30
Tetrathylacium macrophyllum	1	1	.101	.008	.18	.03	.30
Micropholis guyanensis	1	1	.100	.008	.18	.03	.30
TOTAL	550	569		27.853			

Appendix 2.- High floodplain old-growth forest (Plot 2) statistics.

Species	Number of Trees	Number of Stems	Average DBH(m)stem	Basal Area	Relative Density	Relative Basal Area	Relative Frequency
Copaifera reticulata	2	2	1.288	2.782	.33	7.48	.44
Iriartea deltoidea	50	50	.240	2.394	8.20	6.44	4.44
Vitex cymosa	2	2	1.071	1.925	.33	5.18	.44
Ceiba samauma	1	1	1.550	1.887	.16	5.07	.22
Pseudolmedia laevis	13	13	.374	1.712	2.13	4.60	2.00
Poulsenia armata	5	5	.461	1.435	.82	3.86	1.11
Luehea cymulosa	3	3	.711	1.336	.49	3.59	.67
Quararibea wittii	43	43	.180	1.196	7.05	3.22	3.78
Apeiba membranacea	8	8	.341	1.151	1.31	3.10	1.78
Astrocaryum chonta	60	60	.153	1.131	9.84	3.04	4.89
Manilkara inundata	9	9	.328	1.077	1.48	2.90	1.56
Calycophyllum spruceanum	1	1	1.150	1.039	.16	2.79	.22
Spondias mombin	3	3	.631	1.030	.49	2.77	.67
Otoba parvifolia	44	44	.158	1.010	7.21	2.72	4.67
Pouteria pariry cf.	1	1	1.100	.950	.16	2.55	.22
Matisia cordata	7	7	.362	.942	1.15	2.53	1.56
Brosimum lactescens #2	5	5	.418	.711	.82	1.91	1.11
Scheelea cephalotes	9	9	.311	.695	1.48	1.87	1.78
Apuleia leiocarpa	1	1	.850	.567	.16	1.53	.22
Celtis schippii	11	11	.228	.513	1.80	1.38	2.00
Virola duckei	7	7	.269	.497	1.15	1.34	1.11
Guarea macrophylla	21	21	.158	.444	3.44	1.19	3.11
Tapura juruana	4	4	.327	.397	.66	1.07	.67
Brosimum alicastrum	3	3	.317	.383	.49	1.03	.67
Pouteria torta	6	6	.267	.376	.98	1.01	1.11
Pouteria ephendrantha	1	1	.670	.353	.16	.95	.22
Matayba 971	1	1	.664	.346	.16	.93	.22
Cecropia tessmanii	1	1	.661	.343	.16	.92	.22
Trichilia pleeana	8	8	.207	.330	1.31	.89	1.56
Inga capitata	10	10	.184	.311	1.64	.84	1.33
Jacaratia digitata	4	4	.275	.296	.66	.80	.67
Hirtella triandra	8	8	.194	.286	1.31	.77	1.56
Theobroma cacao	7	14	.141	.271	1.15	.73	1.56
Pourouma cecropiifolia	4	4	.275	.263	.66	.71	.89
Aspidosperma vargasii	1	1	.514	.207	.16	.56	.22
Pterocarpus rohrii aff	2	2	.318	.207	.33	.56	.44
Inga 1997	1	1	.503	.199	.16	.53	.22
Mabea maynensis	3	3	.261	.183	.49	.49	.67
Sapium marmieri	4	4	.219	.174	.66	.47	.44
Duguetia quitarensis	13	13	.129	.174	2.13	.47	2.22
Zizphus cinnamomum	2	2	.289	.171	.33	.46	.44
Pouteria macrophylla	2	2	.294	.167	.33	.45	.44
Unknown species	4	4	.209	.160	.66	.43	.89
Turpinia occidentalis	7	7	.164	.158	1.15	.42	1.33
Sterculia apetala	1	1	.440	.152	.16	.41	.22
Hirtella excelsa	1	1	.434	.148	.16	.40	.22
Tetragastris altissima	3	3	.240	.145	.49	.39	.44
Drypetes amazonica	10	10	.133	.142	1.64	.38	2.22
Gustavia hexapetala	3	3	.211	.140	.49	.38	.67
Glycydendron amazonicum	1	1	.418	.137	.16	.37	.22
Sloanea fragrans	2	2	.260	.131	.33	.35	.44

Appendix 2.- High floodplain old-growth forest (Plot 2) statistics (cont...)

Species	Number of Trees	Number of Stems	Average DBH(m)stem	Basal Area	Relative Density	Relative Basal Area	Relative Frequency
Guapira 11345	2	2	.272	.125	.33	.34	.44
Nectandra pulverulenta	3	3	.222	.122	.49	.33	.67
Iryanthera juruensis	9	9	.129	.121	1.48	.33	2.00
Urera caracasana	2	2	.238	.118	.33	.32	.44
Brosimum guianense	3	3	.215	.112	.49	.30	.67
Pouteria procera	6	6	.149	.111	.98	.30	1.11
Batocarpus amazonicus	2	2	.240	.110	.33	.29	.44
Calyptranthes densiflora	2	2	.239	.107	.33	.29	.44
Ruizodendron ovale	3	3	.196	.106	.49	.28	.67
Croton tessmannii	2	2	.237	.094	.33	.25	.44
Neea 5451	4	4	.170	.093	.66	.25	.67
Drypetes 1813	1	1	.340	.091	.16	.24	.22
Rinorea viridifolia	8	8	.119	.090	1.31	.24	.89
Unknown species 1	2	2	.238	.089	.33	.24	.44
Pleurothyrium krukovii	7	7	.125	.087	1.15	.23	1.56
Euterpe precatoria	4	4	.163	.087	.66	.23	.89
Pausandra trianae	8	8	.114	.084	1.31	.22	1.56
Andira inermis	2	2	.218	.081	.33	.22	.44
Endlicheria 1993	1	1	.303	.072	.16	.19	.22
Triplaris americana	3	3	.169	.069	.49	.19	.67
Guatteria «acutissima»	1	1	.285	.064	.16	.17	.22
Jessenia bataua	1	1	.282	.062	.16	.17	.22
Coccoloba williamsii	3	3	.152	.059	.49	.16	.67
Sorocea pileata	1	1	.266	.056	.16	.15	.22
Virola calophylla	2	2	.178	.055	.33	.15	.44
Leonia glycycarpa #2	1	1	.258	.052	.16	.14	.22
Psidium acutangulum	1	1	.253	.050	.16	.14	.22
Aniba 12054	1	1	.252	.050	.16	.13	.22
Guapira 11340	3	3	.142	.050	.49	.13	.67
Unonopsis floribunda	3	3	.133	.046	.49	.12	.67
Ampelocera edentula	2	2	.170	.045	.33	.12	.44
Oxandra mediocris	4	4	.119	.045	.66	.12	.67
Unonopsis mathewsii	2	2	.157	.041	.33	.11	.22
Sterculia 12769	1	1	.223	.039	.16	.10	.22
Quararibea ochrocalyx	3	3	.127	.039	.49	.10	.67
Trichilia pachypoda cf	2	2	.154	.039	.33	.10	.44
Matayba 12764	2	2	.151	.036	.33	.10	.44
Enterolobiu cyclocarpum	1	1	.210	.035	.16	.09	.22
Malmea dielsiana	2	2	.146	.033	.33	.09	.44
Duguetia spixiana	3	3	.118	.033	.49	.09	.67
Trichilia elegans	2	2	.142	.032	.33	.09	.44
Ficus perezarbelaezii	1	1	.200	.031	.16	.08	.22
Guarea kunthiana	1	1	.200	.031	.16	.08	.22
Guazuma crinita	1	1	.199	.031	.16	.08	.22
Eschweilera coriacea	1	1	.194	.030	.16	.08	.22
Huertea glandulosa	1	1	.190	.028	.16	.08	.22
Inga 1983	1	1	.190	.028	.16	.08	.22
Leguminosae 1958	1	1	.190	.028	.16	.08	.22
Trichilia rubra	2	2	.133	.028	.33	.07	.44
Himatanthus sucuuba	1	1	.188	.028	.16	.07	.22
Astronium graveolens	1	1	.185	.027	.16	.07	.22
Inga chartacea	1	1	.185	.027	.16	.07	.22
Trichilia poeppigi	3	3	.106	.026	.49	.07	.67

Appendix 2.- High floodplain old-growth forest (Plot 2) statistics (cont...)

Species	Number of Trees	Number of Stems	Average DBH(m)stem	Basal Area	Relative Density	Relative Basal Area	Relative Frequency
Inga marginata	1	1	.183	.026	.16	.07	.22
Cecropia engleriana	1	1	.180	.025	.16	.07	.22
Sloanea 2034	2	2	.127	.025	.33	.07	.44
Lonchocarpus spiciflorus	2	2	.124	.024	.33	.06	.44
Ecclinusa guyanensis	1	1	.173	.024	.16	.06	.22
Xylopia ligustrifolia	1	1	.169	.022	.16	.06	.22
Sapium ixiamasense	1	1	.164	.021	.16	.06	.22
Acalypha mapirensis	1	1	.162	.021	.16	.06	.22
Faramea occidentalis	2	2	.112	.020	.33	.05	.44
Cordia nodosa	2	2	.110	.019	.33	.05	.44
Inga acreana cf.	1	1	.154	.019	.16	.05	.22
Inga ciliata	1	1	.153	.018	.16	.05	.22
Malmea diclina	2	2	.108	.018	.33	.05	.44
Pouteria caimito	1	1	.152	.018	.16	.05	.22
Terminalia amazonica	1	1	.152	.018	.16	.05	.22
Capparis «macrophylla»	1	1	.150	.018	.16	.05	.2
Oenocarpus mapora	2	2	.106	.018	.33	.05	.44
Micropholis egensis	1	1	.148	.017	.16	.05	.22
Tetrathylacium macrophyllum	1	1	.145	.017	.16	.04	.22
Clarisia biflora	1	1	.144	.016	.16	.04	.22
Dyospyros subrotata	1	1	.144	.016	.16	.04	.22
Cheilochinium cognatum	1	1	.138	.015	.16	.04	.22
Rubiaceae 2041	1	1	.134	.014	.16	.04	.22
Sarcaulus brasiliensis	1	1	.132	.014	.16	.04	.22
Trichilia pallida	1	1	.131	.013	.16	.04	.22
Trigynaea duckei	1	1	.131	.013	.16	.04	.22
Chorisia insignis	1	1	.130	.013	.16	.04	.22
Leonia glycycarpa	1	1	.129	.013	.16	.04	.22
Pouteria sp.,	1	1	.126	.012	.16	.03	.22
Nectandra longifolia	1	1	.123	.012	.16	.03	.22
Pouteria 1999	1	1	.123	.012	.16	.03	.22
Heisteria acuminata	1	1	.122	.012	.16	.03	.22
Inga 1975	1	1	.122	.012	.16	.03	.22
Capparis nitida	1	1	.120	.011	.16	.03	.22
Dipteryx micrantha	1	1	.120	.011	.16	.03	.22
Micropholis melinoniana	1	1	.120	.011	.16	.03	.22
Neea 11941	1	1	.119	.011	.16	.03	.22
Chrysochlamys ulei	1	1	.114	.010	.16	.03	.22
Lunania parviflora	1	1	.114	.010	.16	.03	.22
Trichilia maynasiana	1	1	.114	.010	.16	.03	.22
Allophylus divaricatus	1	1	.113	.010	.16	.03	.22
Picramnia 12766	1	1	.112	.010	.16	.03	.22
Symphonia globulifera	1	1	.111	.010	.16	.03	.22
Theobroma speciosum	1	1	.110	.010	.16	.03	.22
Eugenia myrobalana	1	1	.106	.009	.16	.02	.22
Pouteria durlandii	1	1	.106	.009	.16	.02	.22
Inga sp.	1	1	.104	.008	.16	.02	.22
Abuta grandifolia	1	1	.103	.008	.16	.02	.22
Leonia glycycarpa #1	1	1	.101	.008	.16	.02	.22
Eugenia muricata	1	1	.100	.008	.16	.02	.22
Minquartia guianensis	1	1	.100	.008	.16	.02	.22
TOTAL	610	617		37.198			

Appendix 3.- **Old second-growth forest (Plot 3) statistics.**

Species	Number of Trees	Number of Stems	Average DBH(m)stem	Basal Area	Relative Density	Relative Basal Area	Relative Frequency
Cedrelinga catenaeformis	7	7	.492	2.422	1.58	10.75	1.65
Parkia multijuga	4	4	.650	1.367	.90	6.07	1.10
Aspidosperma vargasii	7	7	.373	1.052	1.58	4.67	1.37
Tachigali polyphylla	9	9	.264	.840	2.03	3.73	2.20
Pourouma minor	9	9	.309	.821	2.03	3.64	1.92
Jacaranda copaia	3	3	.490	.818	.68	3.63	.82
Erisma uncinatum	1	1	.997	.781	.23	3.47	.27
Pourouma guianensis	8	8	.316	.728	1.81	3.23	1.92
Inga acreana cf.	8	8	.296	.673	1.81	2.99	1.65
Inga thibaudiana	9	9	.267	.603	2.03	2.68	1.92
Tetragastris altissima	14	14	.220	.601	3.16	2.67	2.47
Dipteryx micrantha	1	1	.850	.567	.23	2.52	.27
Qualea grandiflora	2	2	.493	.522	.45	2.32	.55
Parkia nitida	7	7	.273	.476	1.58	2.11	1.65
Euterpe precatoria	21	21	.163	.450	4.74	2.00	3.57
Tabernaemontana psychotriifolia	9	9	.224	.432	2.03	1.92	1.65
Socratea exorrhiza	21	21	.155	.415	4.74	1.84	3.02
Pseudolmedia laevigata	4	4	.329	.363	.90	1.61	.55
Toulicia reticulata	8	8	.203	.356	1.81	1.58	1.92
Mabea maynensis	14	14	.173	.351	3.16	1.56	3.02
Guapira 11340	6	6	.261	.348	1.31	1.54	1.37
Clarisia racemosa	2	2	.403	.327	.45	1.45	.55
Manilkara inundata	4	4	.241	.307	.90	1.36	1.10
Lindackeria paludosa	15	16	.145	.275	3.39	1.22	2.75
Virola calophylla	14	14	.144	.262	3.16	1.16	3.30
Cedrela fissilis	2	2	.334	.255	.45	1.13	.55
Siparuna decipiens	18	18	.130	.250	4.06	1.11	3.02
Senna silvestris	4	4	.260	.220	.90	.98	1.10
Inga nobilis	2	2	.328	.192	.45	.85	.55
Brosimum lactescens #1	6	6	.170	.191	1.35	.85	1.65
Unknown species	7	7	.168	.177	1.58	.79	1.92
Pseudolmedia murure	9	9	.152	.175	2.03	.78	1.65
Ampelocera edentula	2	2	.310	.175	.45	.78	.55
Apeiba membranacea	4	4	.217	.161	.90	.71	1.10
Capirona decorticans	5	5	.195	.156	1.13	.69	1.10
Galipea trifoliata	12	13	.120	.155	2.71	.69	2.20
Aniba 1877	3	3	.231	.136	.68	.61	.82
Vitex cymosa	3	3	.221	.134	.68	.60	.55
Cordia 12752	4	4	.193	.134	.90	.59	.82
Rinorea guianensis	5	5	.176	.132	1.13	.59	1.10
Inga densiflora cf.	3	3	.232	.129	.68	.57	.82
Pithecellobium corymbosum	5	5	.157	.119	1.13	.53	1.10
Inga capitacellobium	3	3	.215	.117	.68	.52	.82
Miconia argyrophylla	6	6	.150	.109	1.35	.48	1.65
Byrsonima 12596	1	1	.365	.105	.23	.46	.27
Theobroma speciosum	3	3	.210	.104	.68	.46	.82
Simarouba amara	1	1	.350	.096	.23	.43	.27
Alchornea glandulosa	3	3	.190	.095	.68	.42	.55
Pseudolmedia laevis	5	5	.145	.092	1.13	.41	1.37
Maquira calophylla	3	3	.193	.092	.68	.41	.55

Appendix 3.- Old second-growth forest (Plot 3) statistics.(cont...)

Species	Number of Trees	Number of Stems	Average DBH(m)stem	Basal Area	Relative Density	Relative Basal Area	Relative Frequency
Micropholis guyanensis	6	6	.134	.087	1.35	.38	1.65
Perebea 12696	1	1	.331	.086	.23	.38	.27
Socratea salazarii	9	9	.109	.083	2.03	.37	1.92
Tachigali vazquezii	5	5	.143	.083	1.13	.37	.82
Leonia glycycarpa #2	3	3	.169	.081	.68	.36	.82
Casearia arborea	2	2	.226	.081	.45	.36	.55
Pourouma mollis	2	2	.206	.079	.45	.35	.55
Virola duckei	1	1	.315	.078	.23	.35	.27
Sapotaceae sp 1825	1	1	.312	.076	.23	.34	.27
Huberodendron swietenioides	3	3	.176	.075	.68	.34	.82
Pithecellobium basijugum	2	2	.203	.072	.45	.32	.55
Inga alba	1	1	.300	.071	.23	.31	.27
Iriartea deltoidea	1	1	.294	.068	.23	.30	.27
Rubiaceae 12708	1	1	.290	.066	.23	.29	.27
Tabebuia serratifolia	1	1	.284	.063	.23	.28	.27
Cecropia sciadophylla	1	1	.277	.060	.23	.27	.27
Dussia tessmannii	1	1	.275	.059	.23	.26	.27
Trichilia solitudinus	1	1	.275	.059	.23	.26	.27
Rinoreocarpus ulei	5	5	.122	.059	1.13	.26	1.37
Symphonia globulifera	3	3	.145	.054	.68	.24	.82
Enterolobium cyclocarpum	1	1	.247	.048	.23	.21	.27
Jessenia bataua	1	1	.245	.047	.23	.21	.27
Castilla ulei	1	1	.241	.046	.23	.20	.27
Anaxagorea brevipes	2	2	.165	.044	.45	.19	.55
Iryanthera juruensis	4	4	.117	.043	.90	.19	1.10
Rubiaceae 12724	2	2	.163	.042	.45	.19	.55
Pouteria sp.	2	2	.156	.041	.45	.18	.55
Brosimum guianense	1	1	.226	.040	.23	.18	.27
Cecropia engleriana	1	1	.225	.040	.23	.18	.27
Unknown family sp 2	1	1	.220	.038	.23	.17	.27
Rinorea apiculata	3	3	.124	.037	.68	.16	.55
Mayna parvifolia	2	2	.144	.033	.45	.15	.55
Licania hypoleuca	2	2	.139	.032	.45	.14	.55
Licania silvae	1	1	.201	.032	.23	.14	.27
Sapotaceae 12751	3	3	.116	.032	.68	.14	.82
Aspidosperma megaphyllum	1	1	.200	.031	.23	.14	.27
Astrocaryum chonta	1	1	.200	.031	.23	.14	.27
Cordia nodosa	3	3	.110	.029	.68	.13	.82
Couratari guianensis	1	1	.185	.027	.23	.12	.27
Sapindaceae 12713	1	1	.183	.026	.23	.12	.27
Myrcia sylvatica	1	1	.181	.026	.23	.11	.27
Eschweilera 12697	1	1	.179	.025	.23	.11	.27
Perebea guianensis	1	1	.179	.025	.23	.11	.27
Myrtaceae sp.	2	2	.122	.023	.45	.10	.27
Laetia procera	1	1	.171	.023	.23	.10	.27
Quararibea ochrocalyx	1	1	.170	.023	.23	.10	.27
Aspidosperma 13158	1	1	.165	.021	.23	.09	.27
Eugenia sp 1	1	1	.164	.021	.23	.09	.27

Appendix 3.- Old second-growth forest (Plot 3) statistics (cont...)

Species	Number of Trees	Number of Stems	Average DBH(m)stem	Basal Area	Relative Density	Relative Basal Area	Relative Frequency
Duguetia 12711	1	1	.163	.021	.23	.09	.27
Endlicheria tessmannii	1	1	.158	.020	.23	.09	.27
Andira inermis	1	1	.157	.019	.23	.09	.27
Sloanea sinemariensis	1	1	.156	.019	.23	.08	.27
Gustavia hexapetala	1	1	.152	.018	.23	.08	.27
Neoraputia paraensis	1	1	.150	.018	.23	.08	.27
Drypetes 1813	1	1	.142	.016	.23	.07	.27
Unknown family sp 1	1	1	.130	.013	.23	.06	.27
Trattinnickia 12703	1	1	.127	.013	.23	.06	.27
Brosimum lactescens	1	1	.125	.012	.23	.05	.27
Rudgea 12710	1	1	.125	.012	.23	.05	.27
Terminalia amazonica	1	1	.125	.012	.23	.05	.27
Garcinia acuminata	1	1	.119	.011	.23	.05	.27
Metrododorea flavida	1	1	.119	.011	.23	.05	.27
Calycophyllum acreanum	1	1	.115	.010	.23	.05	.27
Inga sp.	1	1	.115	.010	.23	.05	.27
Quiina macrophylla	1	1	.111	.010	.23	.04	.27
Moraceae sp.	1	1	.105	.009	.23	.04	.27
Pseudima frutescens	1	1	.105	.009	.23	.04	.27
Tabebuia impetiginosa	1	1	.103	.008	.23	.04	.27
Myrcia splendens	1	1	.102	.008	.23	.04	.27
Cabralea cangerana	1	1	.100	.008	.23	.03	.27
Himatanthus sucuuba	1	1	.100	.008	.23	.03	.27
Oenocarpus mapora	1	1	.100	.008	.23	.03	.27
TOTAL	443	445	22.530				

Appendix 4.- Swamp forest (Plot 4) statistics

Species	Number of Trees	Number of Stems	Average DBH(m)stem	Basal Area	Relative Density	Relative Basal Area	Relative Frequency
Laetia corymbulosa	211	227	.157	5.323	30.67	17.76	7.45
Calophyllum brasiliense	49	50	.233	4.147	7.12	13.83	7.80
Luehea cymulosa	7	9	.504	4.062	1.02	13.55	2.13
Allophylus scrobiculatus	86	88	.196	3.027	12.50	10.10	7.80
Ficus insipida	4	4	.752	2.286	.58	7.63	1.06
Inga dumosa	59	99	.140	1.675	8.58	5.59	6.03
Xylopia ligustrifolia	24	24	.262	1.435	3.49	4.79	4.26
Trichilia pleeana	33	33	.190	1.105	4.80	3.69	6.74
Pithecellobium latifolium	15	30	.139	.568	2.18	1.89	4.26
Unknown species	17	19	.178	.567	2.47	1.89	3.19
Astrocaryum chonta	18	18	.185	.529	2.62	1.77	2.48

Appendix 4. Swamp forest (Plot 4)statistics (cont...)

Species	Number of Trees	Number of Stems	Average DBH(m)stem	Basal Area	Relative Density	Relative Basal Area	Relative Frequency
Brosimum lactescens #1	11	11	.224	.469	1.60	1.56	3.55
Sloanea guianensis	4	4	.296	.399	.58	1.33	1.42
Licania britteniana	5	5	.242	.390	.73	1.30	1.42
Annona hypoglauca	19	28	.125	.355	2.76	1.19	3.55
Ficus trigona	5	10	.186	.331	.73	1.10	1.06
Calycophyllum spruceanum	9	9	.197	.299	1.31	1.00	2.48
Otoba parvifolia	5	5	.228	.280	.73	.93	1.06
Genipa americana	7	7	.178	.229	1.02	.76	1.77
Allophylus sp.	3	3	.292	.203	.44	.68	.35
Inga sp.	9	12	.141	.200	1.31	.67	2.13
Euterpe precatoria	10	10	.140	.156	1.45	.52	2.84
Terminalia oblonga	3	3	.218	.138	.44	.46	1.06
Pseudolmedia laevis	3	3	.220	.126	.44	.42	.71
Iriartea deltoidea	3	3	.223	.123	.44	.41	.35
Guazuma crinita	1	1	.389	.119	.15	.40	.35
Triplaris americana	7	7	.142	.113	1.02	.38	1.77
Spondias mombin	3	3	.198	.103	.44	.34	1.06
Ficus casapiensis #2	1	1	.345	.093	.15	.31	.35
Lonchocarpus spiciflorus	1	1	.309	.075	.15	.25	.35
Dyospyros subrotata	1	1	.296	.069	.15	.23	.35
Garcinia brasilense cf	2	2	.197	.064	.29	.21	.71
Inga ruiziana	1	1	.281	.062	.15	.21	.35
Cecropia latiloba	2	2	.191	.059	.29	.20	.71
Ficus killipii	2	2	.177	.050	.29	.17	.35
Ficus sp.	1	1	.248	.048	.15	.16	.35
Pterocarpus rhorii aff	2	2	.171	.046	.29	.15	.71
Andira inermis	2	2	.161	.043	.29	.14	.71
Unonopsis floribunda	3	3	.117	.033	.44	.11	1.06
Sapium ixiamasense	2	2	.134	.029	.29	.10	.71
Cedrela fissilis	2	2	.135	.029	.29	.10	.71
Inga punctata	1	1	.189	.028	.15	.09	.35
Jacaratia digitata	1	1	.185	.027	.15	.09	.35
Sapium marmieri	2	2	.130	.027	.29	.09	.71
Calatola venazuelana	2	2	.130	.026	.29	.09	.71
Theobroma cacao	2	2	.129	.026	.29	.09	.71
Myrtaceae sp.	3	3	.101	.024	.44	.08	1.06
Cecropia engleriana	1	1	.173	.024	.15	.08	.35
Cecropia sp.	1	1	.172	.023	.15	.08	.35
Lauraceae sp.	1	1	.161	.020	.15	.07	.35
Flacourtiaceae sp 1	1	1	.160	.020	.15	.07	.35
Oxandra mediocris	1	1	.157	.019	.15	.06	.35
Banara guianensis	1	2	.108	.019	.15	.06	.35
Ceiba samauma	2	2	.108	.018	.29	.06	.35
Guapira 11345	1	1	.151	.018	.15	.06	.35
Neea sp.	1	1	.149	.017	.15	.06	.35
Pouteria sp.	1	1	.149	.017	.15	.06	.35
Poulsenia armata	1	1	.144	.016	.15	.05	.35
Faramea occidentalis	1	1	.140	.015	.15	.05	.35
Nectandra longifolia	1	1	.140	.015	.15	.05	.35
Trichilia pachypoda cf	1	1	.140	.015	.15	.05	.35
Himatanthus sucuuba	1	1	.132	.014	.15	.05	.35

Appendix 4. Swamp forest (Plot 4)statistics (cont...)

Species	Number of Trees	Number of Stems	Average DBH(m)stem	Basal Area	Relative Density	Relative Basal Area	Relative Frequency
Unonopsis mathewsii	1	1	.129	.013	.15	.04	.35
Salacia macrantha	1	1	.123	.012	.15	.04	.35
Capparis «macrophylla»	1	1	.122	.012	.15	.04	.35
Chrysophyllum argenteum	1	1	.115	.010	.15	.03	.35
Coccoloba densifrons	1	1	.110	.010	.15	.03	.35
Ixora peruviana	1	1	.110	.010	.15	.03	.35
Coccoloba williamsii	1	1	.104	.008	.15	.03	.35
Byrsonima arthropoda	1	1	.103	.008	.15	.03	.35
Sorocea pileata	1	1	.101	.008	.15	.03	.35
TOTAL	668	784	29.976				

Floristic Composition, Soil Quality, Litter Accumulation, and Decomposition in Terra Firme and Floodplain Habitats near Pakitza, Peru

Susan J. Mazer

Department of Ecology, Evolution and Marine Biology
University of California
Santa Barbara, CA 93106 Phone: 805-893-8011 FAX: 805-893-4724

ABSTRACT

The Manu River drainage in southeastern Peru supports tropical rainforest of high angiosperm tree species diversity, both within and among terra firme and floodplain habitats. This study detected several ecological correlates of floristic variation between one-hectare plots in terra firme and floodplain habitats in the vicinity of Pakitza, Peru (Manu National Park Headquarters). Four one-hectare plots are compared floristically, and a total of six one-hectare plots are evaluated with respect to the environments that they provide for dispersed seeds. Three of these hectares are terra firme sites elevated above the level of the Manu River floodplain; three hectares are floodplain sites subject to periodic or occasional flooding. The absolute and relative abundances of the 10 most numerous families and species (trees > 10 cm dbh) in each hectare are compared among plots and habitats, and "generalist" and "specialist" taxa are identified. The six one-hectare plots and the two habitat types they represent are compared with respect to several soil attributes that influence the type of microhabitat they provide to a seed or seedling: total nitrogen, phosphorous, potassium, magnesium, calcium, sodium, pH, and soil texture. Floodplain sites are relatively rich in exchangeable cations (calcium and magnesium), nitrogen, phosphorous, and potassium; terra firme sites are nutrient-poor, acidic, and relatively sandy. Finally, each site was sampled after each of three 10- to 13-month intervals to measure total litter accumulation and relative litter decomposition rates, suggesting strong differences between habitats with respect to litter quality. While terra firme and floodplain sites accumulate similar quantities of litter (represented by litter particles greater than 0.30 mm) over these 10 - 13-month intervals, floodplain sites appear to be characterized by more rapid rates of litter break-down. Floristic differences between sites and/or between habitat types may in part be due to species-specific tolerances of the distinct soil and litter environments they provide. The results also suggest the possibility that habitats differ intrinsically with respect to the risk

89

of decomposition faced by a newly dispersed seed. If so, this may impose a selective regime that is habitat-specific, possibly contributing to the observed floristic differences among sites.

INTRODUCTION

The high species diversity of plants in tropical rainforests has been well-documented by biosystematists. The factors that contribute, however, to the origin or maintenance of this high species diversity within and among geographically proximate sites and habitats are not well-understood. Many ecological and evolutionary mechanisms have been suggested to promote and to maintain the diversity of plant species in tropical rainforests. These processes generally (but not universally) require large- or small-scale spatial or temporal environmental heterogeneity.

Given environmental heterogeneity in time and/or space, many attributes of plant taxa may promote temporal and geographic florisitic changes in tropical rainforest communities. These attributes include: species-specific germination requirements (often related to seed mass); species-specific edaphic and hydrologic preferences and tolerances; specialized abilities to tolerate shade or sunlight as seeds and seedlings; interspecific variation in the ability to tolerate or to repel habitat-specific herbivores; density-dependent susceptibility to herbivores or pathogens; interspecific variation in the ability to colonize new habitats; differences among species in flowering phenology; and high levels of resource partitioning (Janzen, 1970; Grubb, 1988; Connell, 1978; Connell, et al., 1984; Gentry, 1981; Clark and Clark, 1984; Mazer, 1989; Condit, et al., 1992).

Similarly, historical events or relatively permanent ecological properties of sites or habitat types may contribute to the ecological and/or evolutionary development of floristic differences among them. Such properties include but are not limited to: the frequency of and nature of physical disturbances; the frequency and duration of flooding; successional stage; derivation from ancient refugia; restricted seed dispersal; geographically restricted pollinators or seed dispersers; and habitat-specific environmental conditions (e.g., topography, slope, aspect, light quality, soil quality and texture, litter quality) or selective regimes that may result in the differential invasion and colonization by distinct taxa or in the evolution of specialized life history or reproductive traits (Federov, 1966; Ashton, 1969; Prance, 1973, 1982; Gentry, 1982a, 1982b, 1986; Foster et al., 1986; Salo, et al., 1986; Denslow, 1987; Räsänen, et al., 1987; Salo, 1987; Barik, et al., 1992). The purpose of the present study was to seek evidence for some of these habitat-specific environmental conditions that may contribute to the generation of floristic variation from hectare to hectare in the rainforest of Manu National Park.

The Manu River drainage (Madre de Dios Province, Peru) supports a region of remarkably high plant diversity, both within and among habitat types (Foster *et. al*, 1986; Foster 1990). Over 2,874 species, 1,006 genera, and 153 families have been identified in the vicinity of the Manu River, with 1,215 species, 515 genera, and 107 families occupying "forest" habitat (Foster, 1990). The present study is an effort to detect and to characterize ecological correlates of high inter-site floristic diversity within this "forest" category. Six one-hectare sites are evaluated with respect to the environments that they provide for dispersed seeds and germinating seedlings. Three of these sites are terra firme sites unaffected by periodic fluctuations in the level of the Manu River; the remaining three occur on the floodplain and are subject to periodic or occasional flooding during the rainy season, particularly in wet years (December -April, which may receive over 200 mm of rain per month; Erwin, 1990). Five of these one-hectare sites (2 terra firme and 3 floodplain) have been taxonomically inventoried since 1987 by botanists sponsored by the Smithsonian Institution's BioDiversity Program. I selected a third terra firme site to provide an equal number of one-hectare sites from each of these two habitat types to be sampled for soil and litter quality.

In this chapter, I provide a brief summary of the floristic differences between these sites (additional comparative floristic analyses are reported elsewhere in this volume by Dallmeier, Kabel and Foster). Then I describe each of these six sites (or plots) and the two habitat types they represent with respect to several soil and litter attributes that influence the type of microhabitat they provide to a dispersed seed or seedling. Finally, for the six sites, which were sampled after each of three 10-to 13-month intervals, I provide measures of leaf litter accumulation and relative litter decomposition rate.

I suggest that floristic differences between sites or between habitat types (i.e., terra firme vs. floodplain) may in part be due to the distinct soil and litter environments they provide. Given that a species' ability to become established in a new locality depends on its ability to tolerate the habitat's substrate, it may be useful to seek inter-site variation in substrate quality as one step toward identifying the ecological factors that contribute to strong floristic differences between habitat types and between sites within habitat types. While taxa currently dominating a habitat as adult trees are not necessarily tolerant of its current substrate as seeds and seedlings, large and persistent differences between the substrates of distinct habitats may endure across generations and reflect the qualities favored or tolerated by their dominant species. Consequently, measures of the quality of a habitat's substrate provide general information concerning how it is experienced by the seeds or seedlings adapted to it.

The questions addressed in the current manuscript are the following:

(1) What are the dominant families and species of trees greater than 10 centimeters dbh in each site and habitat type? Is there overlap among sites or between habitats with respect to the identity of the most numerous taxa? Are there "generalist" taxa that dominate both terra firme and floodplain sites, or are most dominant taxa "specialists" restricted to one habitat type?

(2) Among one-hectare plots within a habitat or among habitat types, do the relative abundances of these dominant taxa differ? Are there differences among sites in the degree to which a few taxa dominate the flora?

(3) Do plots and habitat types differ with respect to: soil nutrients, exchangeable cations, pH, soil texture, or the presence of nitrogen and phosphorous in fine particles of decomposing litter?

(4) Do plots and habitat types differ with respect to the absolute accumulation of leaf litter or the cumulative apparent rate of decomposition of leaf litter over the course of many months?

(5) Is the accumulation of leaf litter correlated with soil quality?

(6) Is soil quality related to the rate of decomposition of accumulated leaf litter? A positive association between soil nutrient richness and decomposition rate could be the result of at least three non-mutually exclusive processes. First, if nutrient-rich soils support higher levels of microorganismal or arthropod detritivore activity than nutrient-poor soils, this may contribute directly to higher rates of litter decomposition in the former. Second, nutrients may accumulate relatively rapidly in soils in which a high rate of litter decomposition is caused by a high level of detritivore activity that occurs for reasons unrelated to initial soil quality. Third, nutrient-rich soils (e.g., floodplain soils that receive nutrient-bearing sediments from higher elevations) may promote rapid plant growth. Rapid plant growth may allow and/or require (in an evolutionary sense) the production of "inexpensive" leaves with few secondary compounds that function to repel herbivores or pathogens. Such leaves may decompose rapidly following abscission, resulting in a correlation among sites between soil quality and the rate of leaf decomposition.

METHODS

LOCATION AND DESCRIPTION OF ONE-HECTARE PLOTS

Five of the six one-hectare plots evaluated in this study are referred to as and located within the "Zones" described by Erwin, 1990: Zones 2, 4, and 7 (floodplain forest) and Zones 1 and 3 (terra firme forest) (See Figure 1). The sixth hectare, established simply to provide a third hectare in the terra firme forest, is identified here as Zone Tachigali. Coincidentally, this hectare corresponds to Zone 12 as described by Erwin (1990). Each one-hectare plot used in the present study occurs in the center of a 25-hectare area in which each of the hectares has been assigned a number (Figures 1 and 2). Within Zones 1, 3, and 4, the inventoried hectare is the central hectare, #13. Within Zone 2, the central hectare (#13) includes a forested area and a low-lying flooded depression; consequently, it was necessary to use part of hectare #13 and part of the adjacent hectare #18 to include a floristically homogeneous one-hectare site. Within Zone 7, hectare #5 (the most distant from the riverbank) was inventoried and sampled. Each one-hectare plot is divided into 25 numbered quadrats that measure 20 meters x 20 meters (Figure 3). Brief descriptions of each one-hectare site follow:

TERRA FIRME SITES

Zone 1: This one-hectare plot occurs on an alluvial terrace approximately one kilometer north of the Pakitza encampment. The hectare is crossed at its eastern edge by a stream that continues to flow throughout the dry season and into which smaller tributaries flow during the rainy season after traversing the hectare. The western bank of the stream is quite steep and topographically uneven, while the eastern bank is relatively flat and uniform. *Rinoria guianensis* (Violaceae) is the dominant tree species of this hectare, accounting for over 30% of all individual

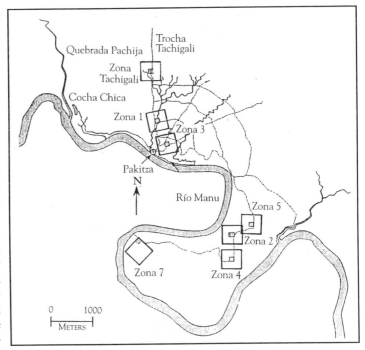

Fig. 1.– Location of one-hectare plots evaluated in the present study for soil quality, litter accumulation, and litter decomposition rates. Large squares represent 25-hectare zones in which the one-hectare plots are located. The shaded small squares within each 25-hectare area indicate the locations of the one-hectare sites of the present study. Each one-hectare plot is referred to by the name of the Zone in which it is located.

trees greater than 10 cm dbh. As in all of the terra firme or ancient alluvial sites, the soil of this plot is relatively sandy (see soil analyses below); these sites do not receive annual or periodic alluvial deposits from the Manu River.

Zone 3: This site lies approximately 0.75 km to the south of Zone 1, also on an old alluvial terrace. It differs from Zone 1 in three major ways. First, it is topo-

Fig. 2.– *Numbering system within each 25-hectare zone. Within Zones 1,3, and 4, the central hectare (#13) was inventoried and sampled for soil quality and litter accumulation. Within Zone 2, part of hectare #13 and part of the adjacent hectare #18 were used to include a homogeneous vegetation sample. In Zone 7, a hectare at one corner of the zone (#5) was inventoried. A one-hectare site in Zone Tachigali was set up specifically to provide a third terra firme plot sampled for soil quality and litter accumulation; it does not represent a 25-hectare zone established by or inventoried by the Smithsonian's Biodiversity Program.*

25-hectare Zone

1	6	11	16	21
2	7	12	17	22
3	8	13	18	23
4	9	14	19	24
5	10	15	20	25

100 meters

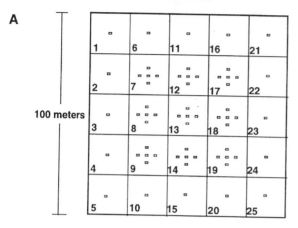

Sites of Soil Samples and Placement of Litter Traps in

Zones 1, 2, 3, 4, and Zone Tachigali

1 Hectare

A

100 meters

Placement of Litter Traps in Zone 7

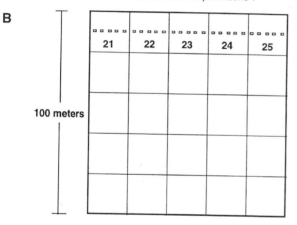

B

100 meters

Fig. 3.– *Position of soil samples and litter traps within one-hectare zones. See text for descriptions of dates and precise locations of each sample.*

graphically level. Second, it has been heavily invaded by bamboo (*Guadua* sp.), the stems of which are less than 10 cm dbh, and are therefore not included in the taxonomic inventories. Third, the most common tree species is not nearly as abundant as is *R. guianensis* in Zone 1. In Zone 3, the most common tree species is *Euterpe precatoria* (Pal-mae), which accounts for only 4% of the trees in this hectare.

Zone Tachigali: This site is located on Trocha Tachigali, 2300 meters north of Pakitza. It represents the highest and presumably the oldest of the terra firme sites in this study. It is characterized by the presence of a common understory perennial species of *Monotagma* (Marantaceae). As it was not included among the terra firme sites taxonomically inventoried by BIOLAT, the floristic composition of this Zone is not described here.

Floodplain Sites

Zone 2: This site is located 4 kilometers downriver from Pakitza and approximately 0.5 km southeast of the riverbank. It is described as an "upper floodplain forest" by Erwin (1990). This type of forest receives periodic deposits of alluvium during cycles of extreme flooding which may occur at intervals of many years or decades. One expected consequence of this periodic flooding is increased soil richness relative to terra firme sites. The most common tree species in this Zone are the palms *Astrocaryum chonta* (9.8% of all individuals) and *Iriartea deltoidea* (8.4%).

Zone 4: This site is 0.75 kilometers directly south of Zone 2. The site is not strictly assignable to the floodplain habitat; it lies on the margin of an old oxbow lake and contains soil with a much higher clay content than either Zone 2 or Zone 7 (see soil analyses below). However, since water may rise to a depth of over one meter during the rainy season in this hectare (water marks are clearly visible on most trees in October), it is included as a representative of the flooded habitats.

Table 1. Mean values (± standard deviation) of soil pH, nutrients, exchangeable cations, and texture for samples from each of six one-hectare Zones.

Within each column of data, values that do not share any superscripts are significantly different (p<0.05), as detected by a Scheffe F-test following a one-way ANOVA on natural-log transformed pH and nutrient values, and on arcsin-transformed proportions for sand, silt and clay components. The tests for significant effects of Zone on the proportion of sand, silt and clay cannot truly be considered to be independent tests because the proportions of particles in these three categories must sum to 1.00. In one case (Total Nitrogen), the ANOVA detected a significant effect of site on soil nutrients, but the Scheffe F-test did not.

Zone	Habitat	Number of Soil Samples	pH	Total Nitrogen (mg/g)	Total Phosphorous (mg/g)
Zone 1	Terra Firme	3	5.09^{abc}(±0.72)	1.50^a(±1.14)	0.20^a(±0.10)
Zone 3	Terra Firme	3	4.22^{ab}(±0.62)	2.00^a(±0.35)	0.23^a(±0.06)
Zone Tachigali	Terra Firme	3	3.78^a(±0.10)	1.37^a(±0.06)	0.10^a(±0)
Zone 2	Floodplain	3	6.41^{cde}(±0.75)	3.57^a(±0.78)	0.83^b(0.06)
Zone 4	Floodplain	3	5.44^{bd}(±0.34)	3.37^a(±0.72)	0.70^b(±0)
Zone 7	Floodplain	3	7.74^c(±0.11)	2.33^a(±0.15)	0.77^b(±0.06)

Zone	Number of Soil Samples	Calcium (mg/100g)	Magnesium (mg/100g)	Sodium (mg/100g)	Potassium (mg/100g)
Zone 1	3	82.80^{ab}(±0.06)	10.23^{ab}(±8.03)	0.13(±0.06)	9.17^{ab}(±4.63)
Zone 3	3	9.60^a(±8.09)	4.97^a(±1.68)	0.50^a(±0)	15.17^{bc}(±4.94)
Zone Tachigali	3	5.30^a(±3.29)	1.77^a(±1.20)	0.50^a(±0)	5.77^a(±1.26)
Zone 2	3	400.67^{bc}(±122.87)	43.93^c(±6.70)	0.33^a(±0.15)	18.60bc(±2.66)
Zone 4	3	424.33^{bc}(±26.08)	39.73^{bc}(±2.57)	1.73^b(±0.42)	18.33^{bc}(±3.16)
Zone 7	3	492.33^c(±16.17)	43.23^c(±0.23)	0.37^a(±0.15)	26.13^c(±3.11)

Zone	Number of Soil Samples	Proportion Sand	Proportion Silt	Proportion Clay
Zone 1	3	0.68^d(±0.10)	0.25^a(±0.09)	0.07^a(±0.08)
Zone 3	3	0.47^{bc}(±0.05)	0.35^{ab}(±0.02)	0.18^{bc}(±0.04)
Zone Tachigali	3	0.59^{cd}(±0.04)	0.32^{ab}(±0.04)	0.10^{ab}(±0.02)
Zone 2	3	0.41^{abc}(±0.05)	0.48^b(±0.06)	0.11^{bcd}(±0.04)
Zone 4	3	0.31^{ab}(±0.01)	0.40ab(±0.04)	0.28de(±0.04)
Zone 7	3	0.21^a(±0.03)	0.65^c(±0.04)	0.14^{cd}(±0.03)

Laetia corymbulosa (Flacourtiaceae) is the most abundant tree species in this hectare, accounting for 31% of the inventoried individuals.

Zone 7: Approximately 6 km downriver from Pakitza, this site is the closest to the riverbank of all the sampled hectares. As such, it is subject to flooding in response to seasonal fluctuations in the river level, and potentially in response to short-term changes in the river level due to local rainstorms. Although this Zone has been inventoried, a detailed species list was not available; this plot is excluded from the floristic analyses described here. However, evidence of the unique

Table 2. Mean values (±std.dev.) of soil pH, nutrients, exchangeable cations, and texture for samples representing terrace and floodplain Zones. A Mann-Whitney U-test was conducted to detect significant differences between terrace and floodplain habitats with respect to each soil component. Within each soil character column, mean values with different superscripts are significantly different at the 0.05 level. The tests for significant effects of habitat type on the proportion of sand, silt and clay cannot truly be considered to be independent tests because the proportions of particles in these three categories must sum to 1.00. Nevertheless, these results show that terrace and floodplain sites show significant differences in soil particle composition.

Zones	Habitat	Number of Soil Samples	pH	Total Nitrogen (mg/g)	Total Phosphorous (mg/g)
Zones 1,3 & Tachigali	Terrace	9	4.36[b](±0.75)	1.62[a](±0.66)	0.18[a](±0.08)
Zones 2,4 & 7	Floodplain	9	6.53[a](±1.08)	3.09[b](±0.79)	0.77[b](±0.07)
Z statistic for Mann-Whitney U-test			-3.23	-3.05	-3.64
p-value			0.0012	0.0023	0.0003

Zone	Habitat	Calcium (mg/100g)	Magnesium (mg/100g)	Sodium (mg/100g)	Potassium (mg/100g)
Zones 1,3 & Tachigali	Terrace	32.57[a](±60.69)	5.66[a](±5.56)	0.38[a](±0.19)	10.03[a](±5.37)
Zones 2,4 & 7	Floodplain	439.11[b](±75.55)	42.30[b](±4.09)	0.81[a](±0.73)	21.02[b](±4.62)
Z statistic for Mann-Whitney U-test		-3.58	-3.58	-0.88	-3.18
p-value		0.0003	0.0003	0.3787	0.0015

Zone	Habitat	Proportion Sand	Proportion Silt	Proportion Clay
Zones 1,3 & Tachigali	Terrace	0.58[b](±0.11)	0.30[a](±0.07)	0.12[a](±0.07)
Zones 2, 4 & 7	Floodplain	0.31[a](±0.09)	0.51[b](±0.12)	0.18[a](±0.08)
Z statistic for Mann-Whitney U-test		-3.49	-3.49	-1.46
p-value		0.0005	0.0005	0.1443

environment provided by this site is the absence of the palm species so common in the other floodplain sites. *Guarea guidonia* (Meliaceae), *Sapium aereum* (Euphorbiaceae), *Sapium ixiamasense*, *Ficus insipida* (Moraceae), and *Guatteria* 'acutissima' (Annonaceae) are the dominant tree species in this hectare. Approximately 16 families, 29 species, and 435 individuals were inventoried on this plot (Erwin, 1990).

FLORISTIC ANALYSES

Species lists used in this study can be found in Dallmeier et al. (1993a and 1993b), and represent the results of a census conducted in 1991. Only trees recorded as living and greater than or equal to 10 cm dbh at the time of the 1991 census are included in the summaries provided here. In this chapter, "dominant" taxa are identified as those represented by the highest number of individuals. There are other legitimate criteria on which to base a definition of a taxon's relative or absolute dominance, such as the combined basal area of all individuals in the taxon. For the purposes of the current comparisons, however, dominance is assayed using the number of individuals > 10 cm dbh. One-hectare plots are compared with respect to the floristic composition, relative abundances, and absolute abundances of their 10 most dominant families and species.

Soil Quality

On October 21 - 25, 1990, three soil samples were collected from each of the six one-hectare plots. From Zones 1, 2, 3, 4, and Tachigali, one sample was removed from each of three central 20 x 20 meter quadrats (e.g., quadrats 12, 13, and 14). In Zone 2, these central quadrats correspond to quadrats 17, 18, and 19 of Plot 0213). From Zone 7, samples were obtained from the center of quadrats 22, 23, and 24 (Figure 2). Each soil sample consisted of a 3-inch diameter core that removed the top three inches of soil starting just below the litter layer. Samples were analyzed for the following qualities or components: pH, total nitrogen (mg/g), total phosphorous (mg/g), calcium (mg/100g), magnesium (mg/100g), sodium (mg/100g), potassium (mg/100g), and proportions of sand, silt, and clay. Methods of soil analysis can be found in Page *et al.* (1982).

One-way analyses of variance (ANOVA) were conducted to detect significant differences among one-hectare plots, and Mann-Whitney U-tests were conducted to detect significant differences between terra firme and floodplain habitats with respect to the mean values of each of the variables measured. pH and nutrient values were natural log-transformed and proportions of sand, silt, and clay were arcsin-transformed prior to analysis. Following the ANOVAS, Scheffe F-tests were conducted to detect significant differences between pairs of sites.

Litter Accumulation and Decomposition

In September 1988, litter-collecting "traps" were placed in Zone 1 (September 20 - 21), Zone 3 (September 23), Zone 2 (September 22), and Zone 7 (September 24). Each trap consisted of two 40-cm and two 50-cm pieces of 0.5-inch PVC tubing connected with PVC corner elbows to produce a 40 cm x 50 cm rectangle. Polyamide Nylon Fiber netting material (with square openings 0.3 mm on a side) was attached to the tubing to create a 0.20 m^2 trap. Each trap was secured to the ground at each corner with a 9-inch aluminum eye-peg. The traps were raised 1 - 6 cm above the surface of the soil (depending on local topography and the ease with which the pegs could be driven into the soil). These traps captured leaf, stem, and fruit and seed material; water and decomposed material less than 0.09 mm^2 in size passed through the mesh. Comparison of the total accumulated trap contents between sites provides a measure of the relative rate of litter accumulation; size particle distributions of the litter remaining in the traps provide a rough

Table 3.- Means of litter trap contents collected in 1991, after a -302-day period of accumulation. Traps are classified by Zone. Litter was air-dried and passed through a set of sieves to separate it into five size classes. Litter was weighed following oven-drying for three days at 105 degrees F.

ZONE 1 (Terra Firme):

Traps emptied November 30, 1990; contents collected September 28, 1991 (302 days accumulation)

Content Type	Mean of single trap (g)	Standard deviation	Number of traps
Leaves & Small Stems>4 mm	105.81	79.25	5
Fruit and seeds>4 mm	3.15	7.13	42
Litter material 2-4 mm	10.39	6.45	42
Litter material 1-2 mm	6.41	4.29	42
Litter material 0.3-1 mm	5.72	6.21	42
Total Trap contents	144.72	109.74	5
Proportion Leaves & Stems	0.74	0.063	5
Proportion Fruits & Seeds	0.02	0.017	5
Proportion Contents 2-4 mm	0.12	0.023	5
Proportion Contents 1-2 mm	0.07	0.020	5
Proportion Contents 0.3-1 mm	0.07	0.035	5

ZONE 3 (Terra Firme):

Traps emptied November 28, 1990; contents collected September 26-27, 1991 (303 days accumulation)

Content Type	Mean of single trap (g)	Standar deviation	Number of traps
Leaves & Small Stems>4mm	101.95	33.52	7
Fuit and seeds>4mm	2.07	3.30	56
Litter material 2-4 mm	12.69	9.26	56
Litter material 1-2 mm	6.13	2.86	56
Litter material 0.3-1 mm	5.72	3.85	56
Total Trap contents	126.87	40.07	7
Proportion Leaves & Stems	0.80	0.039	7
Proportion Fruits & Seeds	0.01	0.011	7
Proportion Contents 2-4 mm	0.09	0.032	7
Proportion Contents 1-2 mm	0.05	0.013	7
Proportion Contents 0.3-1 mm	0.05	0.011	7

ZONE TACHIGALI (High Terrace Plateau):

Traps emptied December 2, 1990; contents collected September 29,1991 (302 days accumulation)

Content Type	Mean of single trap (g)	Standard deviation	Number of traps
Leaves & Small Stems>4 mm	92.36	39.64	9
Fuit and seeds>4mm	5.59	18.73	45
Litter material 2-4 mm	10.72	3.67	45
Litter material 1-2 mm	6.38	2.41	45
Litter material 0.3-1 mm	8.10	5.10	45
Total Trap contents	123.51	49.67	9
Proportion Leaves & Stems	0.75	0.079	9
Proportion Fruits & Seeds	0.02	0.029	9
Proportion Contents 2-4 mm	0.09	0.020	9
Proportion Contents 1-2 mm	0.06	0.012	9
Proportion Contents 0.3-1 mm	0.08	0.030	9

ZONE 2 (*Occasionally inundated floodplain*):

Traps emptied December 1, 1990; contents collected September 28, 1991 (301 days accumulation)

Content Type	Mean of single trap (g)	Standard deviation	Number of traps
Leaves & Small Stems>4 mm	66.16	30.37	9
Fruit and seeds>4 mm	4.14	6.85	57
Litter material 2-4 mm	11.52	6.53	57
Litter material 1-2 mm	6.64	3.19	57
Litter material 0.3-1 mm	6.90	4.77	57
Total Trap contents	96.28	33.98	8
Proportion Leaves & Stems	0.75	0.050	8
Proportion Fruits & Seeds	0.02	0.017	8
Proportion Contents 2-4 mm	0.12	0.024	8
Proportion Contents 1-2 mm	0.06	0.014	8
Proportion Contents 0.3-1 mm	0.06	0.020	8

ZONE 4 (*Frequently inundated floodplain near old oxbow lake*):

Traps emptied December 1, 1990; contents collected September 30, 1991 (303 days accumulation)

Content type trap (g)	Mean of single of trap (g)	Standard deviation	Number
Leaves & Small Stems>4mm	78.58	26.91	9
Fruit and seeds>4 mm	1.61	5.06	57
Litter material>2-4 mm	20.52	11.32	57
Litter material>1-2 mm	9.92	5.20	57
Litter material 0.3-1 mm	8.83	5.82	57
Total Trap contents	116.27	35.28	9
Proportion Leaves & Stems	0.68	0.133	9
Proportion Fruits & Seeds	0.01	0.011	9
Proportion Contents 2-4 mm	0.18	0.091	9
Proportion Contents 1-2 mm	0.08	0.036	9
Proportion Contents 0.3-1 mm	0.06	0.021	9

ZONE 7 (*Regularly inundated floodplain*):

Traps emptied November 27, 1990; contents collected October 1, 1991 (308 days accumulation)

Content type trap (g)	Mean of single of trap (g)	Standard deviation	Number
Leaves & Small Stems>4 mm	70.04	17.43	5
Fruit and seeds>4 mm	0.44	0.48	24
Litter material 2-4 mm	13.78	5.86	24
Litter material 1-2 mm	10.14	3.37	24
Litter material 0.3-1 mm	16.95	10.77	24
Total trap contents	110.10	38.99	5
Proportion Leaves & Stems	0.61	0.095	5
Proportion Fruits & Seeds	0.01	0.007	5
Proportion Contents 2-4 mm	0.13	0.036	5
Proportion Contents 1-2 mm	0.10	0.010	5
Proportion Contents 0.3-1 mm	0.16	0.067	5

measure of the rate at which leaf and stem material break down from larger to smaller size classes.

In 1988, 45 traps were placed in each of Zones 1, 2, and 3 (five traps were placed in each of the central nine 20 x 20 meter quadrats of the inventoried hectares; see Figure 2 for locations and arrangements of traps). In Zone 7, 25 traps were arranged linearly through the center of the southeastern border of the hectare. Zone 7 was treated differently because severe flooding of the hectare near the river was considered possible during the rainy season, and inundation would have prevented measuring litter acccumulation during the intended one-year intervals.

In August - September 1989, all traps were located and their contents were removed, placed in plastic bags, and returned to Pakitza for immediate processing (Zone 1: contents removed September 7 - 8; Zone 2: August 30 - 31; Zone 3: September 4 - 6; Zone 7: September 9). During 1988 - 1989, the litter traps in each Zone therefore accumulated litter for a period of 342 - 352 days; the traps were left empty in September 1989 to begin a new cycle of collection.

The contents of each trap were placed in a fine nylon mesh bag (0.09 mm2 openings) to dry in the sun. Following drying, the litter was passed through four sieves of nylon netting (with holes 4 mm, 2 mm, 1 mm, and 0.30 mm on a side, respectively) to separate the contents into five size class categories: (a) Leaves and stems > 4.0 mm (the few woody stems that were greater than one centimeter in diameter were discarded); (b) Fruits and seeds > 4.0 mm; (c) material 2.0 - 4 .0 mm in size; (d) material 1.0 - 2.0 mm in size, and; (e) material 0.30 -1.0 mm in size. The leaf and small stem fraction was extremely bulky, so this fraction was retained for only nine traps per site (five traps from Zone 7). The center trap in each of the nine central 20 x 20 meter quadrats was used for this purpose. Once dried and separated by size class, samples were packed in plastic zip-lock bags and shipped to the University of California at Santa Barbara. Samples were oven-dried at 105 degreees Fahrenheit for three days (to reach a constant weight) and weighed to the nearest 0.1 mg.

In 1990, the traps were relocated and their contents collected on the following dates: Zone 1, October 4 - 6; Zone 2, October 8 - 12; Zone 3, October 2 - 4; Zone 7, October 18. During the 1989 - 1990 interval, each Zone therefore accumulated litter for 393 - 413 days. These samples were treated identically to those of the previous year.

From November 27 - December 2, 1990, all traps were emptied and additional traps were placed in Zones 2 and 3; an additional 16 traps per hectare were placed in the border quadrats (one trap at the center of each quadrat; Figure 3). At this time, traps were also placed in Zones 4 and Tachigali for the first time; 61 traps were placed in each hectare. The precise dates of trap placement in 1990 are listed in Table 3. The contents of all traps were collected for a final time between September 26 - October 1, 1991; during the 1990 - 1991 interval, each Zone therefore accumulated litter for 301 - 308 days (see Table 3). The accumulated litter in these traps was treated identically to that collected in 1989 and 1990.

The results presented below include a brief summary of the results of the 1988 - 1989 and the 1989 - 1990 sampling intervals, and a complete analysis of the 1990 - 1991 sampling interval. Trap components (the biomass representing each size class) were analyzed by one-way ANOVAS to detect significant differences among one-hectare plots and between habitat types with respect to the mean values of these components. Raw data for litter biomass were natural-log transformed prior to analysis. Data representing proportions of total biomass (e.g., Mass of leaves and stems/Mass of total trap contents) were arcsin transformed prior to analysis.

NUTRIENT QUALITY OF FINE LITTER

Fine litter (the 0.30 - 1.0 mm fraction) accumulated in the traps located in Zones 1, 2, 3, and 7 during the 1988 - 1989 interval was analyzed for nitrogen and phosphorous content. From each Zone, five samples were analyzed. Each Zone contributed one sample from the centrally located litter trap in each of five 20 x 20 meter quadrats (e.g., Zone 1 contributed samples from quadrats 8, 12, 13, 14, and 18; Figure 3). Methods of nutrient analysis can be found in Page *et al.* (1982). Mann-Whitney U-tests were conducted to detect significant differences between the fine litter accumulated in the terra firme and floodplain sites with respect to the mean levels of total nitrogen and phosphorous.

LEAF TRANSPLANT EXPERIMENT:

A field experiment to measure the rate of litter decomposition while controlling for the taxonomic composition of leaf litter, leaf-fall phenology, and site of decomposition

In the litter samples that accumulated in the litter "traps" described above, the relative abundance of dried litter material in each of the five size classes provides an indirect measure of the rate of litter decomposition: high rates of decomposition should be reflected in a relatively large proportion of material represented in the smallest size classes. However, there are two possible explanations for observed differences between sites in the distribution of accumulated litter among particle size classes. First, there may be phenological differences between sites with respect to leaf-fall. If the timing of leaf-fall differs between Zones, then the litter accumulated in some Zones may simply have had less time to decompose prior to litter collection than litter accumulated in other Zones. Differences among hectares or habitats in the timing of leaf-fall could account for differences among them in the proportion of litter in the smaller size classes observed several months after the placement of empty traps.

Second, the rate of decomposition (due to physical deterioration, microorganisms and/or arthropod detritivores) may truly differ among habitats or between sites within habitats. If the timing of leaf-fall does *not* differ between sites, then differences in the amount of litter represented in different size classes would

Table 4. Summary of one-way analyses of variance to detect statistically significant differences among Zones with respect to the biomass of litter accumulated in litter and seed traps during a -10 month period, December 1990- October 1991. This analysis includes Zones 1, 3, Tachigali, 2, 4, and 7. Raw data for litter biomass were natural-log transformed prior to analysis. Data representing proportions of total biomass (e.g. Mass of leaves and stems/Mass of total trap contents) were arcsin-transformed prior to analysis.

Biomass of litter material>4mm (primarily leaves, and some small stems)

Source of Variation	d.f.	Sum of Squares	F-test	p-value
Zone	5	1.063	0.813	0.5476
Error	38	9.934		
Total	43	10.997		

Biomass of fruits and seeds>4mm

Source of Variation	d.f.	Sum of Squares	F-test	p-value
Zone	5	40.779	3.453	0.0050
Error	237	559.854		
Total	242	600.633		

Biomass of material 2-4 mm

Source of Variation	d.f.	Sum of Squares	F-test	p-value
Zone	5	15.921	12.918	0.0001
Error	275	67.783		
Total	280	83.704		

Biomass of material 1-2 mm

Source of Variation	d.f.	Sum of Squares	F-test	p-value
Zone	5	12.434	10.018	0.0001
Error	275	68.262		
Total	280	80.696		

Biomass of material 0.3-1 mm

Source of Variation	d.f	Sum of Squares	F-test	p-value
Zone	5	29.020	13.245	0.0001
Error	275	120.504		
Total	280	149.524		

Biomass of total trap contents

Source of Variation	d.f.	Sum of Squares	F-test	p-value
Zone	5	.336	0.294	0.9131
Error	37	8.459		
Total	42	8.795		

Biomass of total trap contents excluding leaves and stems

Source of Variation	d.f.	Sum of Squares	F-test	p-value
Zone	5	10.816	7.528	0.0001
Error	275	79.022		
Total	280	89.838		

Mass of leaves & stems/Mass of total contents (Proportion Leaves & Stems)

Source of Variation	d.f.	Sum of Squares	F-test	p-value
Zone	5	.263	3.679	0.0084
Error	37	.53		
Total	42	.793		

Mass of Fruits & Seeds>4 mm/Mass of Total Contents (Proportion Fruits & Seeds)

Source of Variation	d.f.	Sum of Squares	F-test	p-value
Zone	5	.002	1.092	0.3812
Error	37	.012		
Total	42	.014		

Mass of Litter Material 2-4mm/Mass of Total Contents (Proportions Contents 2-4mm)

Source of Variation	d.f.	Sum of Squares	F-test	p-value
Zone	5	.044	3.560	0.0100
Error	37	.092		
Total	42	.136		

Mass of Litter Material 1-2mm/Mass of Total Contents (Proportion Contents 1-2 mm)

Source of Variation	d.f	Sum of Squares	F-test	p-value
Zone	5	.009	4.334	0.0033
Error	37	.016		
Total	42	.025		

Mass of Litter Material 0.3-1mm/Mass of Total Contents (Proportion Contents 0.3-1 mm)

Source of Variation	d.f.	Sum of Squares	F-test	p-value
Zone	5	.047	9.202	0.0001
Error	37	.038		
Total	42	.085		

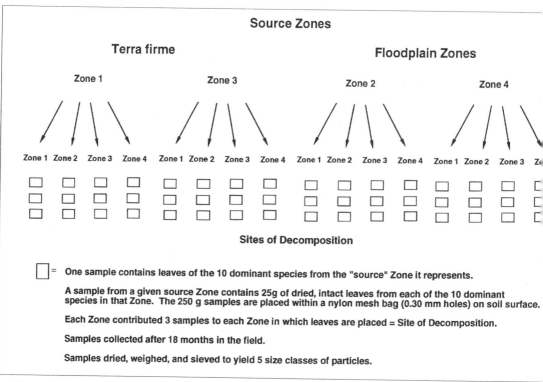

Fig. 4.– Design of reciprocal transplant experiment to detect the effects of the floristic composition of litter and the external environment on the rate of litter decomposition while controlling for potential effects of litter-fall phenology. Each small rectangle represents a fine mesh net bag containing 250 grams of dried leaf material from each "source" site: Zones 1,3,2,and 4. The 250 grams include 25 grams of dried leaf material from each of the 10 most numerous tree species from the source site (see Figures 6A-D for identification of these species). Three identical leaf samples from each zone were placed on soil in the home site and in each of the "foreign" sites. As all bags were placed in the field at the same time (October 1991), any potential effects of litter-fall phenology on the apparent rate of dedecomposition are controlled.

logically be the result of differences in the rate of decomposition. Such differences in the rate of decomposition, however, could have at least three direct or indirect causes (these are not mutually exclusive):

(a) *Differences between sites in the activity of microorganisms or arthoropod detritivores independent of soil quality.* If the terra firme sites support less dense or less metabolically active populations of litter-consuming microorganisms and/or arthropods than the floodplain sites, we would expect that litter decomposition would be slower in the former.

(b) *Differences between sites in the structure, thickness, chemical composition or size of the leaves or leaflets of the dominant taxa.* If some sites are dominated by plant taxa with leaves more resistant to decomposition than those of other sites, we would expect differences between sites in the proportion of accumulated litter represented by the smallest size classes.

(c) *Differences between sites in soil quality, which could play a role in determining the density, diversity and activity of soil microorganisms.* Differences among sites in

104

soil quality (e.g., quantities of nutrients) may reflect either a cause or a consequence of differences in microorganismal activity and litter decomposition rates. For example, if low-nutrient soils support only sparse populations of decomposers (relative to nutrient-rich soils), then soils with low nutrients may exhibit low rates of litter decomposition (in comparison to nutrient-rich soils). Alternatively, if microorganismal (or arthropod) activity differs among sites for reasons unrelated to initial soil quality (e.g., due to soil moisture or texture) but influences the rate of nutrient release from detritus, this may also yield a positive association between the population density of microorganisms, the rate of litter·decomposition, and measures of soil nutrients.

The results of the litter accumulation study described above do not permit one to identify with confidence the cause(s) of any observed differences among plots or habitats with respect to the frequency distribution of litter particle sizes. Phenological differences between sites, taxonomic differences in leaf structure or composition, or differences among sites in decomposer activity could all be responsible. In order to determine whether differences between sites in the proportions of litter material in different size classes are (at least in part) attributable to the taxonomic composition of the leaves produced in each site or to the environment in which leaves are decomposing, it is necessary to perform a reciprocal transplant experiment. In this type of experiment, leaves of the dominant taxa of each Zone are allowed to decompose both in their "home" Zone and in "foreign" Zones. In October 1991, this type of experiment was initiated; detailed results are reported elsewhere (Mazer, unpublished manuscript).

The experiment consisted of two steps (Figure 4):

(1) Approximately 500 grams of abscised leaves representing each of the 10 dominant species in Zones 1, 2, 3, and 4 were collected (see Results of Floristic Analysis, below). The leaves of each species were held in nylon mesh bags and sun-dried at Pakitza. Twenty-five grams of dried leaves from each of the 10 species were then placed in each of 12 nylon mesh bags (with openings of 0.09 mm2). Each of the 12 bags representing a Zone therefore contained 250 grams of dried leaves (25 grams/species). A total of 48 bags were prepared: 12 bags from each Zone, with each bag containing leaves from a total of 10 species.

(2) Three bags of leaves representing each of Zones 1, 2, 3, and 4 were placed at ground level in the central quadrat of the inventoried hectare in each of these four Zones in October 1991 and secured to the ground with aluminum stakes. This material could not be collected until June 1993. It was oven-dried, sieved, and weighed to determine the relative abundance of material in each size class.

Since this experiment controls for both taxonomic composition and the timing of leaf-fall, a between-site and between-habitat comparison of the relative abundances of different size classes can determine whether there are significant effects of site, habitat, or floristic composition of litter on the rate of litter decomposition. Because leaves from each Zone were permitted to decompose in every other Zone, and because all leaf material started out in the same dry condition, the results of this experiment indicate whether the physical environment (including temperature, humidity, and decomposer activity) or the floristic composition of the leaf litter is the primary determinant of the rate of leaf litter decomposition in a given environment. Moreover, because leaf samples were placed in bags with holes of only 0.09 mm² in size, excluding all but the smallest detritivores, differences among habitats in decomposition rate that are *independent* of the species composition of the leaf sample can be attributed to habitat-specific differences in decomposition rates induced by microorganisms (as opposed to larger arthropod detri-tivores).

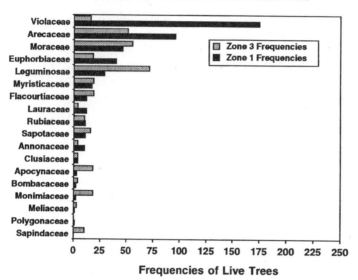

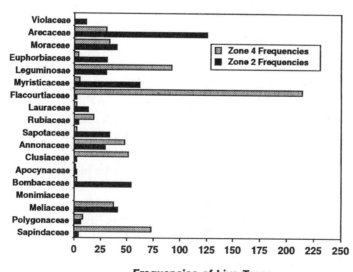

RESULTS
FLORISTIC
ANALYSIS
Family Level Comparisons

There are clear qualitative differences among Zones within habitat types and among habitat types with respect to the floristic composition and relative abundances of the 10 dominant families and species (Fig-

Fig. 5.– *Frequencies of trees (>10 cm dbh) in the dominant families in each of the inventoried terra firme and floodplain zones. Dominance is simply defined on the basis of the number of individual trees represented by each taxonomic family. Each of the families listed appeared as one of the 10 most numerous families in at least one of the zones, although most of the families were very rare in at least one zone. The Palmae, Moraceae, and Leguminosae were the only families that appeared as dominants in all of the zones.*

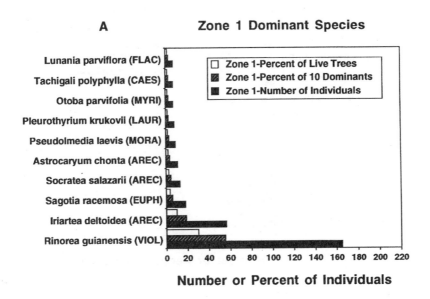

Fig. 6.– *Frequencies and percents of individuals in the 10 dominant species in the inventoried zones. The percent values are shown to indicate the percent of all live trees in 1991 accounted for by each of these dominant species (Percent of Live Trees) and the percent of all trees in the 10 dominant taxa accounted for by each of these species (Percent of Dominants). A. Zone 1 (terra firma). B. Zone 3 (terra firme). C. Zone 2 (floodplain). D. Zone 4 (floodplain).*

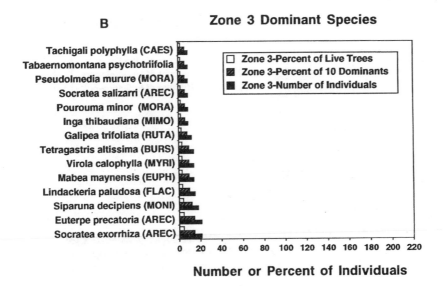

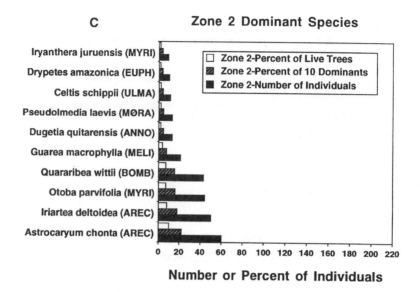

C Zone 2 Dominant Species

ures 5 - 6).

Zones 1 and 3 (terra firme) are qualitatively more similar to each other than are Zones 2 and 4 (floodplain) with respect to the identity of the 10 most abundant families (Figure 5). In both terra firme one-hectare plots, the Violaceae, Arecaceae (Palmae), Moraceae, Euphorbiaceae, Leguminosae, Myristicaceae, Flacourtiaceae, and Sapotaceae are among the 10 dominant families. Each of these

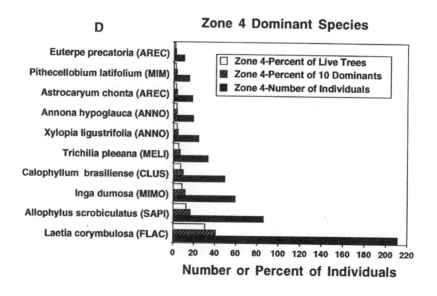

D Zone 4 Dominant Species

plots includes among its dominants only two families not dominant in the other Zone. Zone 1 includes the Rubiaceae and Lauraceae among its 10 dominant families, while Zone 3 supports the Monimiaceae and Apocynaceae among its 10 most abundant families.

In both floodplain plots, the Arecaceae, Moraceae, Leguminosae, Annonaceae, and Meliaceae are among the 10 most dominant families (Figure 5). Each of these Zones also supports five dominant families that are not dominant in the other. In Zone 2, the Euphorbiaceae, Myristicaceae, Lauraceae, Sapotaceae, and Bombacaceae are dominant families that are not dominant in Zone 4; in Zone 4, the Flacourtiaceae, Rubiaceae, Clusiaceae (Guttiferae), Sapindaceae, and Polygonaceae are dominant families that are not dominant in Zone 2.

In both floodplain sites, there are three dominant families that are also dominant in the terra firme Zones: the Arecaceae, Moraceae, and Leguminosae. Each habitat type, however, also supports at least one family not appearing among the dominant families in the other habitat type. For example, the Violaceae is a dominant family in both terra firme plots, but in neither of the floodplain plots. Similarly, the Meliaceae and Annonaceae are dominant families in both floodplain plots, but are not among the dominant families in either of the terra firme plots.

SPECIES LEVEL COMPARISONS

Three observations concern the frequency distributions of dominant species. First, there are strong differences between sites within habitat types with respect to the relative dominance of the two most abundant species (Figures 6A - 6D). In the inventoried hectare of Zone 1, *Rinorea guianensis* and *Iriartea deltoidea* together account for over 75% of the trees in the 10 dominant species and over 40% of all live trees in the hectare. In Zone 3, however, *Socratea exorrhiza* and *Euterpe precatoria* together account for about 30% of the live trees representing the 10 dominant species and about 10% of all live trees in the hectare. Similarly, in Zone 4, *Laetia corymbulosa* and *Allophylus scrobiculatus* account for more than 55% of the living individual trees in this plot's 10 dominant species (and over 40% of all live trees in the hectare). In contrast, in Zone 2, *Astrocaryum chonta* and *Iriartea deltoidea* account for only 40% of the living trees of this hectare's 10 dominant species, and less than 20% of all living trees in the hectare. Consequently, the shape of the frequency distribution of Zone 1 (terra firme) is more similar to that of Zone 4 (floodplain) than to that of Zone 3 (terra firme). Second, only five species are "generalists", appearing as dominant taxa in both terra firme and floodplain habitats: *Astrocaryum murumuru* (Arecaceae), *Euterpe precatoria* (Palmae), *Iriartea deltoidea* (Arecaceae), *Otoba parvifolia* (Lauraceae), and *Pseudolmedia laevis* (Moraceae). Third, the most numerous species of all — *Rinorea guianensis*, *Laetia corymbulosa*, and *Allophylus scrobiculatus* —appear to be quite specialized, each occuring as dominants in only one hectare.

Susan J. Mazer

Soil Quality
Differences Among All Six Sites

Table 1 reports mean values of soil pH, nutrients, exchangeable ions, and texture components for the three samples collected from each Zone. This table also reports statistically significant differences detected between Zones in soil quality.

The terra firme sites in general hold soil that is more acidic than the soils of the floodplain. Zone Tachigali has the most acidic soil (mean pH = 3.78), statistically significantly more acidic than Zone 2 (pH = 6.41), Zone 4 (pH = 5.44), and Zone 7 (pH = 7.74). The soil from both Zones 1 and 3 has a pH significantly lower than that of Zone 7 (floodplain).

Total nitrogen is lower in the terra firme than in the floodplain sites (results of one-way ANOVA on natural log-transformed values), although the Scheffe F-test did not detect significant differences among pairs of means. Total phosphorous is significantly lower in all of the terra firme sites than in any of the floodplain sites by over a factor of three (soil samples from Zone 2 have 8.3 times the phosphorous content as soil samples from Zone Tachigali). There are no significant differences between the terra firme hectares or between the floodplain hectqres with respect to nitrogen or phosphorous content.

More dramatically, the calcium content of the soil in each of the terra firme hectares is lower than that of any of the floodplain hectares by up to a factor of 90. Zone Tachigali (the most acidic) has the lowest levels of calcium (5.30 mg/100 g), while Zone 7 has the highest (492.33 mg/100 g). There are no significant differences between the terra firme Zones or between the floodplain Zones with respect to calcium concentration.

Zones 1, 3, and Tachigali (all terra firme) have significantly less magnesium in their soils than Zones 2 and 7 (floodplain); however, the level of magnesium in Zone 4 (floodplain) soil does not differ significantly from that of Zone 1 (although the mean of Zone 4 is nearly four times that of Zone 1). Again, Zone Tachigali has the lowest level of this element relative to all other terra firme zones, with a mean magnesium level of 1.77 mg/100 g, in comparison to 4.97 mg/100 g (Zone 3) and 10.23 mg/100 g (Zone 1).

Differences among hectares with respect to sodium and potassium are less clear. Zone 4 shows much higher sodium levels than any of the other Zones, regardless of habitat type. Potassium levels tend to be lower in the terra firme soils than in the floodplain soils, although there are several cases in which individual terra firme hectares do not differ significantly from floodplain hectares.

Soil texture differs among Zones in one important way. The terra firme sites are much sandier than those in the floodplain, which are in turn characterized by higher proportions of silt and clay.

Differences Between Habitats (Terra Firme vs. Floodplain)

In Table 2, Zones are pooled into terra firme and floodplain categories to show the distinct effects of site elevation on soil quality. It is clear that the terra firme Zones — characterized by a high degree of soil leeching without compensatory episodes of soil replenishment that presumably occur in the inundated floodplain sites — are more acidic and significantly lower in all nutrients (except for sodium) than are the floodplain sites. The terrace sites are also significantly sandier than the floodplain sites.

NUTRIENT QUALITY OF FINE LITTER: total nitrogen and phosphorous

Fine litter accumulating in different habitat types does not differ significantly with respect to the total nitrogen content of the finest litter particles (0.30 - 1 mm size class) ($Z = -0.907$, $p = 0.3643$, $N = 20$; Mann-Whitney U-test). There was no significant difference between terra firme (Zones 1 and 3) and floodplain (Zones 2 and 7) fine litter samples with respect to total nitrogen content (mean nitrogen content for terra firme fine litter = 23.31 mg/g, s.d. = 5.32 mg/g, N = 10; mean nitrogen content for floodplain fine litter samples = 21.10 mg/g, s.d. = 4.64 mg/g, N = 10).

The fine litter residing in traps in the terra firme Zones, however, contained significantly less total phosphorous than floodplain fine litter ($Z = -3.53$, $p = 0.0004$, $N = 20$; Mann-Whitney U-test). For terra firme fine litter, mean phosphorous content = 1.08 mg/g, s.d. = 0.26, N = 10; for floodplain fine litter, mean phosphorous content = 1.79 mg/g, s.d. = 0.36, N = 10. This observation is consistent with the suggestion that phosphorous is a limiting nutrient in tropical rainforests, particularly relative to nitrogen (Vitousek, 1984; Vogt, et al, 1986).

LITTER ACCUMULATION AND DECOMPOSITION

Mean total litter accumulation rates did not differ among Zones during any of the three sampling intervals (1988-1989, 1989-1990, and 1990-1991). However, the absolute and proportional amounts of litter in each of the size classes did differ significantly and consistently among Zones and habitat types.

Effects of Zone on Litter Accumulation 1988 - 1990: total and by size class

Figure 7 presents the mean total dried biomass of litter per trap for Zones 1, 3, and 2 sampled during the 1988 - 1989 and the 1989 - 1990 intervals. Zone 7 results are not reported here; traps were contaminated by flooding during the 1989 - 1990

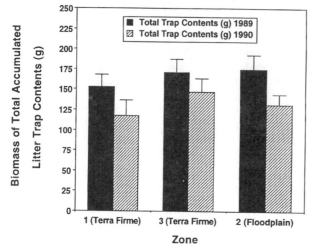

Mean Total Accumulated Litter Biomass (+ std. error)

By Zone (samples collected 1989 and 1990)

Fig. 7.– Mean (+std. error) total accumulated litter biomass per trap for litter traps collected in 1989 and in 1990 from Zones 2, 1 and 3. See text for precise dates of trap placement and collection. Among the means representing a given year (among black bars and among shaded bars), there are no significant differences among zones with respect to the quantity of accumulated litter. Biomass values represent dried litter.

interval. Within each approximately one-year interval (~347 days in 1988-89; ~403 days in 1989-90), there were no significant differences among Zones with respect to total litter accumulation.

Figure 8 presents, for the 1988 - 1989 sampling interval, the mean biomass per trap of litter contents separated into distinct size classes. The traps in the floodplain Zone contained significantly higher absolute amounts of litter in the 1 - 2 mm and 0.03 - 1 mm class than traps placed in either of the terra firme Zones. Moreover, the floodplain traps contained significantly more litter material in the 2 - 4 mm class than did the traps in Zone 1. Due to the relatively

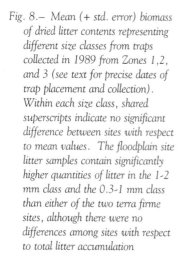

Fig. 8.– Mean (+ std. error) biomass of dried litter contents representing different size classes from traps collected in 1989 from Zones 1,2, and 3 (see text for precise dates of trap placement and collection). Within each size class, shared superscripts indicate no significant difference between sites with respect to mean values. The floodplain site litter samples contain significantly higher quantities of litter in the 1-2 mm class and the 0.3-1 mm class than either of the two terra firme sites, although there were no differences among sites with respect to total litter accumulation

high standard errors associated with mean levels of leaf material ("Leaves" re-

Traps Collected in 1989

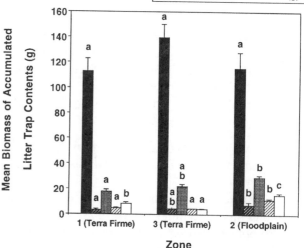

present leaf parts > 4 mm in size), there were no detectable significant differences among Zones with respect to the total amount of accumulated litter particles greater than 4 mm. The larger amount of litter material in the smaller size classes in Zone 2 traps suggests that the litter-fall in this floodplain habitat decomposed more rapidly than in the terra firme habitat.

This result is repeated among litter traps representing the 1989 - 1990 sampling interval (Figure 9). Zones did not differ significantly with respect to the amount of litter material greater than 4 mm in size; however, traps placed in the floodplain Zone contained significantly higher quantities of litter material in the 0.3 - 1 mm size class than traps in either of the terra firme Zones. Similar to the 1988 - 1989 interval, at the end of the 1989 - 1990 interval the floodplain traps contained significantly more material in the 2 - 4 mm range than Zone 1.

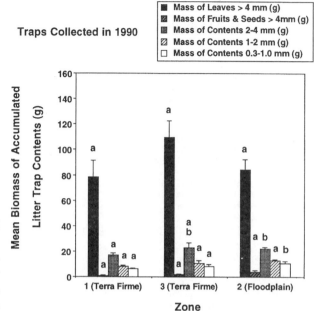

Traps Collected in 1990

Legend:
- ■ Mass of Leaves > 4 mm (g)
- ▨ Mass of Fruits & Seeds > 4mm (g)
- ▦ Mass of Contents 2-4 mm (g)
- ▨ Mass of Contents 1-2 mm (g)
- □ Mass of Contents 0.3-1.0 mm (g)

Fig. 9.— Mean (+ std. error) biomass of dried litter contents representing different size classes from traps collected in 1990 from Zones 2, 1 and 3 (see text for precise dates of trap placement and collection). Within each size class, shared superscripts indicate no significant difference between sites with respect to mean values. The floodplain site litter samples contain significantly higher quantities of litter in the 0.3-1 mm class than either of the two terra firme sites, and significantly higher quantities of litter in the 2-4 mm class than Zone 1, although there were no differences among sites with respect to total litter accumulation (Figure 7). There were no significant differences between Zones 1 and 3 with respect to the distribution of litter among size classes.

These results suggest a higher decomposition rate in the floodplain if the timing of litter-fall in the different zones does not differ significantly. If leaf litter in the floodplain does decompose more rapidly than the litter in Zones 1 and 3, then there must be a compensatory higher rate of litterfall into Zone 2 in order to maintain equal levels of total accumulated litter (as seen in Figure 7).

Effects of Zone on Litter Accumulation 1990 - 1991: total and by size class

The intensive sampling during the 1990 - 1991 interval (during which there were litter traps in a total of six Zones) allows an increased level of resolution. Figure 10 shows the mean total accumulated litter biomass per trap for each of the

Table 5. Means of litter trap contents collected in 1991. Traps are classified by Zone. Litter was air-dried in the field and passed through a set of sieves to separate it into five size/content categories. Litter was weighed following oven-drying for three days at 105 degrees Fahrenheit.

TERRA FIRME TRAPS POOLED (Zones 1,3, and Tachigali)

Content Type trap (g)	Mean of single of traps	Standard deviation	Number
Leaves & Small Stems>4mm	98.76	47.50	21
Fruit and seeds>4mm	3.50	11.39	143
Litter material>2-4mm	11.39	7.10	143
Litter material>1-2mm	6.29	3.21	143
Litter material 0.3-1mm	6.47	5.11	143
Total Trap contents	129.68	62.88	21
Proportion Leaves & Stems	0.76	0.067	21
Proportion Fruits & Seeds	0.02	0.022	21
Proportion Contents 2-4mm	0.10	0.026	21
Proportion Contents 1-2mm	0.06	0.015	21
Proportion Contents 0.2-1mm	0.07	0.029	21

FLOODPLAIN TRAPS POOLED (Zones 2, 4, and 7)

Content Type trap (g)	Meam of single of traps	Standard deviation	Number
Leaves & Small Stems>4mm	71.86	26.20	23
Fruit and seeds>4mm	2.45	5.65	138
Litter material 2-4mm	15.63	9.65	138
Litter material 1-2mm	8.60	4.46	138
Litter material 0.3-1mm	9.44	7.44	138
Total Trap contents	109.64	35.45	22
Proportion Leaves & Stems	0.69	0.111	22
Proportion Fruits & Seeds	0.01	0.013	22
Proportion Contents 2-4mm	0.15	0.066	22
Proportion Contents 1-2mm	0.08	0.028	22
Proportion Contents 0.3-1mm	0.08	0.055	22

sampled Zones. There were no significant differences among Zone means. The accumulated litter in each of the size classes (absolute quantities and proportions), however, did differ significantly among Zones (Figures 11 and 12).

Table 3 presents the means of all litter trap contents (absolute and proportional values represented by each size class). Table 4 presents the results of the analyses of variance conducted to detect significant differences among Zones with respect to mean litter accumulation (total and by size class) and proportional accumulation in each size class. All analyses indicate that there were significant effects of Zone on the total and proportional biomass of litter in each of the size classes smaller than 4 mm.

Although the mean mass of total trap contents and the mean mass of particles greater than 4 mm did not differ significantly among Zones (Figures 10 and 11), the floodplain sites appeared to have higher rates of litter decomposition than the terra firme sites (assuming that the timing of leaf-fall did not differ significantly among habitats). Zone 7 contained significantly higher quantities of litter material in the 0.3 - 1 mm and in the 1 - 2 mm range than all other Zones (except

for Zone 4; see Figure 11).
Over 15% of the total litter
in Zone 7 traps was in the
0.3 - 1 mm size class, as
compared with less than
9% in each of the other
Zones (Figure 12). Zone 4
contained significantly higher quantities of material
in the 2 - 4 mm size class
and the 1 - 2 mm size class
than Zones 1, 3, Tachigali,
and 2. Not all floodplain
Zones, however, differed
greatly from the terra firme
sites. For example, Zone 2
(floodplain) did not differ
significantly from Zones
Tachigali or Zone 1 (both
terra firme) with respect to
any of the size classes.

Mean Total Accumulated Litter Biomass (+ std. error)

By Zone (samples collected 1991)

Fig. 10.– *Mean (+ std. error) total accumulated litter biomass per trap for litter traps collected in 1991 from Zones 1,3, Tachigali, 2,4 and 7. See text for precise dates of trap placement and collection. There are no significant differences among sites with respect to the quantity of accumulated litter.*

Fig. 11.– *Mean (+ std. error) biomass of dried litter contents representing different size classes from traps collected in 1991 from Zones 1,3, Tachigali, 2,4 and 7. See text for precise dates of trap placement and collection. Within each size class, shared superscripts indicate no significant difference between sites with respect to mean values. The floodplain site litter samples (particularly Zones 4 and 7) generally contain significantly higher quantities of litter in the 1-2 mm and in the 0.3-1 mm classes than any of the terra firme sites, although there were no differences among sites with respect to total litter accumulation (Figure 10). There were significant differences between Zones within habitat types with respect to the distribution of litter among size classes.*

Mean Biomass (+ std. error) of Litter Trap Contents

by Size Class (collected 1991)

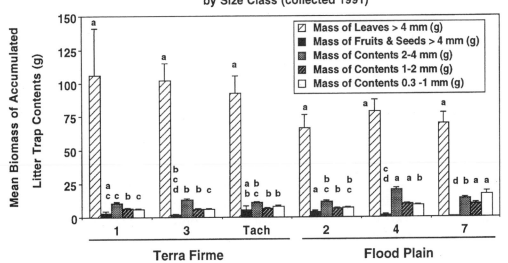

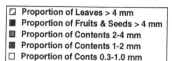

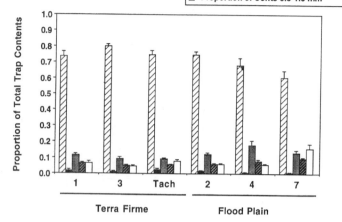

Fig. 12.– Mean (+ std. error) proportions (by mass) of dried litter contents in different size classes from traps collected in 1991 from Zones 1,3, Tachigali, 2,4 and 7. The floodplain site litter samples (particularly Zones 4 and 7) generally contain significantly higher proportions of litter in the 1-2 mm and 2-4 mm classes than the terra firme sites

Effects of Habitat on Litter Accumulation 1990 - 1991: total and by size class

When litter traps were classified according to habitat types (terra firme vs. floodplain), there was no significant difference between the terra firme and floodplain with respect to total litter accumulation per trap or the mass of litter particles greater than 4 mm in size (Figure 13; Tables 5 and 6). Strong effects of habitat on the quantity of litter found in the smaller size classes, however, were detected.

There were clear and consistent differences between habitats with respect to the quantity and proportion of litter material in the 0.3 - 4 mm range (Figures 14 and 15). For each of the litter particle size classes less than 4 mm, floodplain traps contained approximately 15 - 50% more material than terra firme traps (Table 5). Floodplain traps also appeared to contain a lower proportion of litter represented as detectable fruits and seeds than the terra firme traps, but it is not clear whether this is due to lower fruit production in the floodplain or to a higher rate of decay of reproductive structures. As in the 1988 - 1989 and the 1989 - 1990 sampling intervals, the rate at which leaf litter breaks down to the smallest size particles appears to be greater in the floodplain than in the terra firme Zones. The rate of fresh leaf-fall onto the floodplain floor may have to be higher than in the terra firme Zones in order to reconcile a relatively rapid rate of decomposition in the floodplain with the observation that traps in the two habitat types maintain similar total trap contents and a similar mass of particles greater than 4 mm.

116

Fig. 13.– Mean (+ std. error)
total accumulated litter biomass
per trap for litter traps collected
in1991 fromterra firme (Zones
1,3, and Tachigali pooled) and
floodplain (Zones 2,4, and 7
pooled)biomass of accumulated
litter.

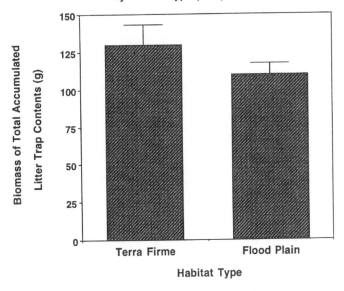

Mean Total Accumulated Litter Biomass (+ std. error)

by Habitat Type (samples collected 1991)

In all of the analyses summarized above, the relative abundances of litter particles among size classes suggest that the floodplain sites (Zones 2, 4 and 7) have higher rates of decomposition than the terra firme sites (Zones, 1, 3, and Tachigali). This result, together with the observation that the soils of the terra

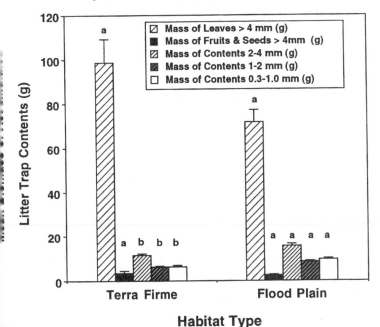

Mean Biomass (+ std. error) of Litter Trap Contents

by Size Class (samples collected 1991)

Legend:
- ☑ Mass of Leaves > 4 mm (g)
- ■ Mass of Fruits & Seeds > 4mm (g)
- ☑ Mass of Contents 2-4 mm (g)
- ▨ Mass of Contents 1-2 mm (g)
- ☐ Mass of Contents 0.3-1.0 mm (g)

Figure 14.- Mean (+std. error) biomass of dried litter contents representing different size classes from traps collected in 1991 from terra firme (Zones 1,3, and Tachigali pooled) and floodplain (Zones 2,4, and 7 pooled) sites. Within each size class, shared superscripts indicate no significant difference between mean values of litter biomass. The floodplain site litter samples contain significantly higher quantities of litter in the 2-4 mm, the 1-2 mm and the 0.3-1 mm classes than the terra firme samples, although there were no differences among habitats with respect to total litter accumulation (Figure 13).

117

firme plots are more acidic and lower in nutrients that the floodplain soils suggests that there may be lower levels of microorganismal (and/or arthropod detritivore) activity in the terra firme sites, accounting for the lower apparent rates of litter decomposition.

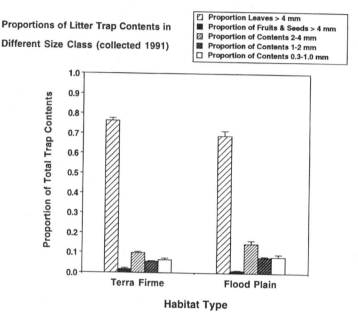

Proportions of Litter Trap Contents in Different Size Class (collected 1991)

☑ Proportion Leaves > 4 mm
■ Proportion of Fruits & Seeds > 4 mm
☑ Proportion of Contents 2-4 mm
▨ Proportion of Contents 1-2 mm
☐ Proportion of Contents 0.3-1.0 mm

Fig. 15.— Mean (+std. error) proportions (by mass) of dried litter contents in different size classes from traps collected in 1991 from terra firme and floodplain habitats. The floodplain site litter samples contain significantly higher proportions of litter in the 2-4 mm, the 1-2 mm, and the 0.3-1 mm classes than the terra firme samples.

A deeper understanding of the causes of the observed differences among habitats and Zones with respect to litter size class distributions awaits the detailed analysis of the reciprocal transplant experiment described above (Figure 4; Mazer, unpublished manuscript). Preliminary results (2-way ANOVAS), however, clearly show that the statistical effect of the site (Zone 1, 2, 3, or 4) in which leaves decompose is much, much stronger than the effect of the Zone from which leaves were sampled. The floristic composition of the leaves monitored in this experiment had little effect on the mass of leaf material (initially 250 grams of dried leaves) that was lost from the nylon mesh bags in which they decomposed. In contrast, the site of leaf decomposition had a strong effect on both the quantity of leaf material that did not pass through the 0.09 mm² mesh holes of these bags. The quantity of leaf material that was retained in the mesh bags was significantly higher in bags that were placed in the terra firme sites than in those that were placed in Zone 2 (floodplain). The quantity of litter lost, however, from Zone 4 was relatively low, due to a long period of inundation during the 1991 - 1993 interval, resulting in anaerobic conditions for the bags in this floodplain site.

DISCUSSION

The results of this study demonstrate that there are strong differences between the soil and litter environments of terra firme and floodplain sites. Moreover, even within terra firme and floodplain regions, there is significant variation among one-hectare sites with respect to some aspects of litter quality. If substrate quality imposes strong restrictions on the success of seed survival or seedling recruitment of certain taxa, then variation in substrate quality may contribute to the origin and maintenance of the floristic differences among sites. In this study, the association between floristic and substrate differences between sites is consistent with the hypothesis that the floristic composition of a site is strongly influenced by species' tolerances or preferences with respect to soil pH, nutrient levels, exchangeable ions, and texture. The current study, however, suggests an additional quality of a habitat's substrate that may differ significantly among zones and habitat types: the rate of decomposition of organic matter due to microorganismal and/or arthropod detritivores. This suggestion raises the intriguing possibility that habitats differ with respect to the risk of decomposition faced by a newly dispersed seed. This risk — if it is truly habitat-specific — potentially has a strong effect on the ecological ranges of different species, contributing to floristic differences among sites.

For each of three multiple-month sampling intervals (1988 -1991), there were no differences among habitats or sites with respect to total accumulated litter biomass. However, litter accumulating in the floodplain Zones appeared to decompose significantly and consistently more rapidly than litter accumulating in the terra firme. These differences between habitats exist despite the high degree of variation among hectares within habitat types with respect to the identity and relative abundance of their dominant species. If the rate of litter decomposition differs among habitats, and if the rate of decomposition is not due directly to the floristic composition of the litter (i.e., the biochemical resistance of certain species to microorganismal attack), then this implies that there are ecological attributes of distinct hectares and habitats that affect the rate of decay of organic matter. Such attributes are likely to include the activity levels of detritivores (and their predators) and other microorganisms.

The month-specific or week-specific rate of litter decomposition could not be measured in this study, due to my own time constraints and the limited accessibility of Manu National Park. Nevertheless, the three sampling intervals evaluated in this study provide "snap-shots" of litter composition that allow inferences to be made concerning the relative rate of leaf break-down within and among one-hectare sites. It must be emphasized that the rate of litter decomposition is only one of many environmental factors that may differ among sites and potentially influence the distribution and relative abundance of adult plants representing distinct taxa. Differences among sites in successional status, inundation, slope, aspect, light, humidity, seed predators, seedling herbivores and pathogens, seed

Table 6. Summary of one-way analyses of variance to detect statistically significant differences between habitat types (Terra Firme vs. Floodplain) with respect to the biomass of litter accumulated in litter and seed traps during a -10-month period, December 1990- October 1991. This analysis includes Zones 1,3, Tachigali, 2, 4, and 7.

Biomass of litter material>4mm (primarily leaves, and some small stems)

Source of Variation	d.f.	Sum of Squares	F-test	p-value
Habitat	1	.752	3.08	0.0865
Error	42	10.245		
Total	43	10.997		

Biomass of fruits and seeds>4mm

Source of Variation	d.f.	Sum of Squares	F-test	p-value
Habitat	1	2.029	0.82	0.3671
Error	241	598.605		
Total	242	600.633		

Biomass of material 2-4 mm

Source of Variation	d.f.	Sum of Squares	F-test	p-value
Habitat	1	5.904	21.17	0.0001
Error	279	77.8		
Total	280	83.704		

Biomass of material 1-2 mm

Source of Variation	d.f.	Sum of Squares	F-test	p-value
Habitat	1	6.827	25.79	0.0001
Error	279	73.869		
Total	280	80.696		

Biomass of material 0.3-1 mm

Source of Variation	d.f.	Sum of Squares	F-test	p-value
Habitat	1	9.1	18.08	0.0001
Error	279	140.424		
Total	280	149.524		

Biomass of total trap contents

Source of Variation	d.f.	Sum of Squares	F-test	p-value
Habitat	1	.095	0.45	0.5071
Error	41	8.700		
Total	42	8.795		

Biomass of total trap contents excluding leaves and stems

Source of Variation	d.f.	Sum of Squares	F-test	p-value
Habitat	1	5.848	19.43	0.0001
Error	279	83.990		
Total	280	89.838		

Mass of leaves & stems/Mass of total contents (Proportion Leaves & Stems)

Source of Variation	d.f.	Sum of Squares	F-test	p-value
Habitat	1	.117	7.09	0.011
Error	41	.676		
Total	42	.793		

Mass of Fruits & Seeds>4 mm/Mass of Total Contents (Proportion Fruits & Seeds)

Source of Variation	d.f.	Sum of Squares	F-test	p-value
Habitat	1	.001	2.54	0.1185
Error	41	.013		
Total	42	.014		

Mass of Litter Material 2-4 mm/Mass of Total Contents (Proportion Contents 2-4 mm)

Source of Variation	d.f.	Sum of Squares	F-test	p-value
Habitat	1	.026	9.79	0.0032
Error	41	.109		
Total	42	.136		

Mass of Litter Material 1-2 mm/Mass of Total Contents (Proportion Contents 1-2 mm)

Source of Variation	d.f.	Sum of Squares	F-test	p-value
Habitat	1	.004	8.22	0.0065
Error	41	.021		
Total	42	.025		

Mass of Litter Material 0.3-1 mm/Mass of Total Contents (Proportion Contents 0.3-1 mm)

Source of Variation	d.f.	Sum of Squares	F-test	p-value
Habitat	1	.002	1.19	0.2818
Error	41	.082		
Total	42	.085		

dispersal, frequency of light gaps, and other geographically variable biotic and abiotic factors were not measured in this study. Each of these factors, however, demand careful evaluation in order to determine their relative importance as correlates or causes of the floristic attributes of the plant communities inventoried here.

Susan J. Mazer

The Risk of Decomposition to Seeds and Seedlings and its Potential Influence on Plant Community Composition Through Species-Sorting and/or Natural Selection: speculations

Newly dispersed seeds and recently germinated seedlings are vulnerable to many sources of early mortality, including attack by fungi and other microorganisms (Augspurger, 1984; Kahn and Tripathi, 1991). If plant taxa differ in their abilities to withstand or to avoid decomposition by microorganisms, one would expect them to segregate among habitats according to their relative performance under different conditions. Alternatively, natural selection within habitats that differ in the rate of seed infection and seedling disease may result in the ecotypic divergence of geographically separated populations of a given species and the evolutionary convergence of sympatric unrelated species.

On an ecological time scale, habitats with high levels of microorganismal attack on seeds and seedlings may allow the successful invasion only of taxa possessing seed and seedling traits that can tolerate or avoid infection. On an evolutionary time scale, habitats with high levels of microorganismal pathogens should be characterized by strong natural selection favoring genotypes and local populations of taxa (or avatars, *sensu* Damuth, 1985) expressing these resistant seed and seedling traits. In sum, both ecological processes (i.e., species-sorting) and evolutionary processes (i.e., *in situ* natural selection) should result in the floristic divergence of distinct habitats in response to habitat-specific differences in the risk of seed and seedling decomposition.

The suggestions that distinct environments favor distinct sets of species with particular seed attributes and/or that distinct environments cause the evolution of specific seed traits are not novel. For example, several broad-scale comparative studies have detected significant differences among habitats in the mean seed mass of their component species (Salisbury, 1949, 1974; Baker, 1972; Foster and Janson, 1985; Mazer, 1989, and references within). However, the risk of decomposition *per se* has not (to my knowledge) been considered to be an ecological attribute that causes the differential recruitment of, or evolution of, taxa with seed and seedling traits adapted to cope with it.

While floristic divergence would be expected among habitats that impose different levels of seed and seedling mortality and different selective regimes on seed and seedling traits, the presence of floristic differences among habitats does not alone demonstrate that they are the result of these posited ecological differences. Two directions of empirical investigation are necessary to provide corroborative evidence. First, a study of the morphological and physiological attributes of the seeds and seedlings of the dominant taxa in distinct habitats might detect habitat-specific seed adaptations that have evolved in response to different levels of microorganismal activity. Seed traits that may enhance the tolerance or avoidance of pathogen attack may include seed coat thickness, long-distance dispersal mechanisms, powerful secondary chemical compounds, or the rate and timing of germination.

Second, reciprocal transplants of seeds or seedlings between habitats that differ (or appear to differ) in the abundance of microorganisms that attack live plant material could determine whether seeds or seedlings of species naturally dominant in habitats with low densities of such pathogens are particularly susceptible to attack in habitats with high densities of these predators or parasites. Conversely, one may find that the seeds of species that can tolerate (or may even require) habitats with high levels of microorganisms perform poorly (relative to their inter-specific competitors) in habitats with low levels of these "plant enemies". The inability of pathogen-tolerant taxa to recruit successfully into habitats with low levels of pathogen activity might result if there is a strong correlation among habitats between pathogen density and soil richness. To speculate wildly, some plant species may tolerate high levels of microorganismal activity but require nutrient-rich soils while other plant taxa may be highly subject to pathogen attack but can tolerate poor-quality soils. In other words, there may exist a trade-off among species with respect to their abilities to cope with low-nutrient soils and high rates of pathogen acitivity. Species may be specialized to cope with one or the other condition, but not both. Tropical rainforests, with their attendant variation among sites and habitats in soil quality, provide many opportunities to explore this idea.

ACKNOWLEDGEMENTS

This project could not have been done without the support of the Smithsonian's BIOLAT Program in Biodiversity. Terry Erwin, Don Wilson, Marsha Sitnik and Abelardo Sandoval provided much patience and good humor in response to last-minute requests for supplies and assistance; I greatly appreciate their efforts and support. Robin Foster (and subsequent teams from the Smithsonian Institution Biodiversity Program and the Museo de Historia Natural Javier Prado) provided most identifications of the tree species in the inventoried plots. George Venable provided the map on which Figure 1 is based; Robyn Burnham, Flor Chávez, Brian Farrell, Jerry Louton, Elsa Meza, George Middendorf, and Abelardo Sandoval provided greatly appreciated company and logistical support in the field; Rina Ramírez, Joaquina Albán, and Mirian Medina offered hospitality in Lima and at the Museo de Historia Natural Javier Prado; Severo Baldeón, Hamilton Beltrán, and Elsa Meza were tireless field and lab assistants without whom the collection and field-processing of leaf litter would not have been completed; at UCSB, Martin Doyle and Frank Setaro conducted much of the laboratory work; the National Science Foundation (BSR-9157270) provided support for laboratory assistance at UCSB. I also owe thanks to Scott Wing, sponsor of my 1987 - 1988 Smithsonian Postdoctoral Fellowship, for indulging my participation in BIOLAT

Susan J. Mazer

1987; and to John Damuth for field, lab, computer, and personal assistance. Finally, I would like to thank Robin Chazdon, Don Cipollini, Julie Denslow, Patricia Folgarait, Becky Ostertag, and Ed Veldkamp, who provided many crucial comments and criticisms concerning my interpretations of the processes underlying the patterns observed in this study.

LITERATURE CITED

Ashton, P. S. 1969. Speciation among tropical forest trees: some deductions in the light of recent evidence. Biol. J. Linn. Soc. 1: 155-196.

Augspurger, C. K. 1984. Seedling survival of tropical tree species: interactions of dispersal distance, light gaps, and pathogens. Ecology 65: 1705 - 1712.

Baker, H. G. 1972. Seed mass in relation to environmental conditions in California. Ecology 53: 997-1010.

Barik, S. K., H. N. Pandey, R. S. Tripathi, and P. Rao. 1992. Microenvironmental variability and species diversity in treefall gaps in a sub-tropical broadleaved forest. Vegetatio 103: 31 - 40.

Clark, D. A., and D. B. Clark. 1984. Spacing dynamics of a tropical rain forest tree: evaluation of the Janzen-Connell Model. American Naturalist 124: 769-788.

Condit, R. , S. P. Hubbell, and R. B. Foster. 1992. Recruitment near conspecific adults and the maintenance of tree and shrub diversity in a neotropical forest. American Naturalist 140: 261-286.

Connell, J. H. 1978. Diversity in tropical rain forests and coral reefs. Science 199: 1302-1310.

Connell, J. H., J. G. Tracey and L. J. Webb. 1984. Compensatory recruitment, growth, and mortality as factors maintaining rain forest tree diversity. Ecological Monographs 54: 141-164.

Dallmeier, F., R. Foster and J. Comiskey. 1993a. User's guide to the Manu Biosphere Reserve Biodiversity Plots, Peru. Zones 01 and 02. Smithsonian Institution, SI/MAB Program. Washington, D. C.

Dallmeier, F., R. Foster and J. Comiskey. 1993b. User's guide to the Manu Biosphere Reserve Biodiversity Plots, Peru. Zones 03 and 04. Smithsonian Institution, SI/MAB Program. Washington, D. C.

Damuth, J. D. 1985. Selection among "species": a formulation in terms of natural functional units. Evolution 39: 1132–1146.

Denslow, J. S. 1987. Tropical rain forest gaps and tree species diversity. Annual Reviews of Ecology and Systematics 18: 431-451.

Erwin, T. 1990. Natural history of the carabid beetles at the BIOLAT biological station, Rio Manu, Pakitza, Peru. Revista Peruana de Entomologia 33: 1-85.

Federov, A. A. 1966. The structure of the tropical rain forest and speciation in the humid tropics. Journal of Ecology 54: 1-11.

Foster, R. B. 1990. The floristic composition of the Rio Manu floodplain forest. pp 99-111, *In*, Gentry, A. H. (ed.) Four Neotropical Rainforests. Yale University Press, New Haven, Connecticut.

Foster, R. B., J. Arce B., and S. Wachter. 1986. Dispersal and sequential plant communities in Amazonian Peru floodplain. *In* Estrada, A. and Fleming, T. H. (eds.), Frugivores and seed dispersal. Dr. W. Junk Publishers, Dordrecht.

Foster, S. A. and C. H. Janson. 1985. The relationship between seed size and establishment conditions in tropical woody plants. Ecology 66: 773-780.

Gentry, A. H. 1981. Distributional patterns and an additional species of the *Passiflora vitifolia* complex: Amazonian species diversity due to edaphically differentiated

124

communities. Plant Systematics and Evolution 137: 95-105.

Gentry, A. H. 1982a. Phytogeographic patterns as evidence for a Choco refuge. pp. 112- 136, *In* Prance, G. T. (ed.) Biological diversification in the tropics. Proceedings of the Fifth International Symposium of the Association for Tropical Biology. Columbia University Press, New York.

Gentry, A. H. 1982b. Neotropical floristic diveristy: phytogeographical connections between Central and South America, Pleistocene climatic fluctuations, or an accident of the Andean orogeny? Annals of the Missouri Botanical Garden. 69: 557-593.

Gentry, A. H. 1986. Endemism in tropical versus temperate plant communities. pp. 153-181, *In* Soule, M. (ed.) Conservation Biology. Sinauer, Sunderland, Massachusetts.

Grubb, P. J. 1977. The maintenance of species richness in plant communities: the importance of the regeneration niche. Biological Reviews 52: 107-145.

Janzen, D. H. 1970. Herbivores and the number of tree species in tropical forests. American Naturalist 104: 501-528.

Khan, M. L. and R. S. Tripathi. 1991. Seedling survival and growth of early and late successional tree species as affected by insect herbivory and pathogen attack in sub-tropical humid forest stands of North-east India. Acta Oecologia - International Journal of Ecology. 12: 569 -579.

Mazer, S. J. 1989. Ecological, taxonomic and life history correlates of seed mass among Indiana Dune angiosperms. Ecological Monographs 59: 153-175.

Molofsky, J., and C. K. Augspurger. 1992. The effect of leaf litter on early seedling establishment in a tropical forest. Ecology 73: 68 - 77.

Page, A. L., R. H. Miller and D.R. Keeney. 1982. Methods of soil analysis. American Society of Agronomy, Inc., Soil Science Society of America, Inc., Madison, Wisconsin.

Prance, G. T. 1973. Phytogeographic support for the theory of Pleistocene forest reguges in the Amazon Basin, based on evidence from distribution patterns in Caryocaraceae, Chrysobalanaceae, Dichapetalaceae and Lecithydaceae. Acta Amazonia 3: 5 - 28.

Prance, G. T. 1982. Forest refuges: evidence from woody angiosperms. pp. 137-156, *In* Prance, G. T. (ed.) Biological diversification in the tropics. Proceedings of the Fifth International Symposium of the Association for Tropical Biology. Columbia University Press, New York.

Räsänen, M. E., J. S. Salo, and R. J. Kalliola. 1987. Fluvial perturbance in the Western Amazon basin: regulation by long-term sub-andean tectonics. Science 238: 1398 - 1401.

Salisbury, E. J. 1942. The Reproductive Capacity of Plants. Bell, London, England.

Salisbury, E. J. 1974. Seed size and mass in relation to environment. Proc. Roy. Soc. Lond. Series B: Biol. Sci. 186: 83-88.

Salo, J., R. Kalliola, I. Häkkinen, Y. Mäkinen, P. Niemelä, M. Puhakka, and P. D. Coley. 1986. River dynamics and the diversity of Amazon lowland forest. Nature 322: 254-258.

Salo, J. 1987. Pleistocene forest refuges in the Amazon: evaluation of the biostratigraphical, lithostratigraphical and geomorphological data. Ann. Zool. Fennici 24: 203-211.

Tripathi, R. S., and M. L. Khan. 1990. Effects of seed weight and microsite characteristics on germination and seedling fitness in two species of *Quercus* in a subtropical wet hill forest. Oikos. 57: 289 - 296.

Vitousek, P. M. 1984. Litterfall, nutrient cycling, and nutrient limitation in tropical forests. Ecology 65: 285 - 298.

Vogt, K. A., C. C. Grier, and D. J. Vogt. 1986. Production, turnover, and nutrient dynamics of above- and belowground detritus of world forests. Advances in Ecological Research 15: 303 - 377.

Diversity of Tropical Forest Leaf Litter from Pakitza, Perú

Robyn J. Burnham

Museum of Paleontology University of Michigan Ann Arbor, MI 48109-1079

ABSTRACT

Leaf litter samples from Pakitza Station, Manu National Park are compared to the composition, richness and diversity of their source trees ($\geq$ 10cm dbh) to determine the fidelity with which litter samples reflect these forest parameters. Leaf litter samples reflect the source forest heterogeneity, showing little evidence of redistribution following initial deposition on the forest floor. Both forest and litter show high species richness compared to other forests sampled by similar methods. Although litter samples (0.5 x 0.5m) poorly reflect total tree species richness of the surrounding hectare, a group of 13 litter samples from a central area of the forest include about 60% of the tree species richness of the surrounding half-hectare of forest and about 50% of the total tree species richness of the hectare of forest. Litter samples individually best reflect relatively small areas of forest, only about 700m^2, but incorporate many species that are not included in forest surveys, probably from climbers and saplings $\leq$10cm dbh. The importance of climbing plants (lianas and vines) in the litter samples reflects their apparent importance in the structure of the canopy, underlining the need for creative means for comparing biodiversity among source forests with differing structures.

INTRODUCTION

Numerous studies have addressed leaf litter in tropical areas over the past 25 years (Klinge and Rodrigues 1968; Cornforth 1970; Kunkel-Westphal and Kunkel 1979; Proctor et al. 1983; Proctor 1984; Songwe et al. 1988; Wright and Cornejo 1990). The great majority of these studies have investigated nutrient fluxes in relationship to litterfall in tropical areas, where nutrients are believed to be recycled rapidly once they are released to the forest floor from the standing

127

biomass. However, few researchers have investigated the species composition of forest litter as a component of the biological community that itself has several measurable parameters typically estimated in living communities, such as species richness and diversity, relative abundance of taxa, and geographic and temporal variation in floristic composition. Notable exceptions include the work of Kunkel-Westphal and Kunkel (1979) in Guatemala, Frangi and Lugo (1985) in Puerto Rico, and Songwe et al. in Cameroon (1988). These detailed studies were aimed at leaf phenology and litter turnover in tropical forests. Still, the degree to which species composition and distribution in the source forest are represented in litter has received almost no attention. The incredible species richness of tropical forests makes the identification of isolated leaves in forest litter a formidable task, so it is not a surprise to find such studies few in number. In addition, forest researchers have focused so intently on tree species of tropical forests, that it may have appeared redundant to determine species composition in the litter when the source trees could be measured and identified directly. Are the composition and structure of tropical forests mirrored in the litter produced by those forests?

The motivation for this study came from the need for paleobotanists to understand the relationship between a forest and the litter produced by that forest (Burnham 1989, Burnham et al. 1992). Many assemblages of fossil plants represent samples of litter produced by ancient forests. All processes leading from abscission of plant organs from the source tree to burial of organs in sediments affect the characteristics of a fossil deposit and often in highly predictable, and therefore interpretable ways. The process of fossilization begins with abscission and fall of plant organs to the forest floor; this step is reflected in the relationship between the forest floor litter and the structure and composition of the source forest. Subsequent processes may include transport of litter to a depositional site and degradation during or after burial by sediments. This contribution is one of a series of on-going investigations in modern forest communities from a variety of climatic zones for the purpose of clarifying the taphonomic processes commonly recurring during the origin of fossil leaf assemblages (Burnham et al. 1992, Burnham 1993; Burnham in press).

One of the notable features of the litter at Pakitza Station in Manu National Park when compared to sites in temperate areas is the high proportion of species present in the litter that are not trees, including epiphytes, hemiepiphytes, lianas, and vines. This may not come as a surprise to anyone who has walked through a tropical moist forest, but points out one of the major contributions that litter studies can make to the rapid assessment of biodiversity. By examining the species composition of the leaf litter, many other life forms can be added to the species list that otherwise would include only trees, given the current tradition of measuring stem diameters to $\geq$ 10cm diameter at breast height (dbh) in most tropical forests. In addition, although this measure is quite useful in estimating board-feet of wood present in the forest, it is the diameter of the conducting area of trees that has been shown to have a clear relationship to vegetative area (Waring 1983). Thus the measure is primarily a reflection of past productivity of trees, not necessarily reflective of present photosynthetic activity. Litter samples, in contrast, reflect the photosynthetic activity of the species in the forest over the past 6-48 months, regardless of the amount of wood present of each species (Coley 1988; Parker et al. 1989; Coley and Aide 1991). Therefore, the assessment of forest diversity and species importance from litter is an objective that is useful not only to paleoecologists, but also shows great promise for rapid assessment of biodiversity, species importance, and bioenergetics in tropical forests.

SAMPLING METHODOLOGY

TREE MAPPING, MEASUREMENT, IDENTIFICATION, AND IMPORTANCE VALUES

For the purposes of this contribution, only one forest hectare has been characterized in detail. The hectare is located within a 500 x 500m area that was chosen to represent Upper Floodplain Forest in a characterization of the habitats in the area of Pakitza Guard Station (Erwin 1991). The area of forest has been called "Zone 2" by local researchers, and the hectare included in this study is located at the center of Zone 2, approximately 400 meters from the Río Manu.

Trees were mapped, diameters measured, and identifications made by members of the Smithsonian Institution BIOLAT Field Course Team in 1988. The 660 mapped stems included only individuals larger than 10cm dbh, and of these 660 stems, 13 were unidentified woody vines. Tree identifications were made by Dr. Robin B. Foster of the Field Museum of Natural History (Chicago). Coordinate positions and diameters of stems were verified over three field seasons in the area by the author. Importance values were derived by calculating total cross-sectional area for each species.

LITTER SAMPLING, IDENTIFICATION AND IMPORTANCE VALUES

Litter was sampled at 13 sites, each 0.5 x 0.5m in area, located in the central 40 x 40 meter area of the hectare (Figure 1). Litter was sampled toward the end of the 3-month dry season during 1989 and 1990. The majority of the data presented here are derived from litter sampled on 27 September 1990, however the 1989 samples (collected 30 August 1989)are used for temporal comparison. All litter that had some probability of being identified was collected down to soil level.

Although woody flowering plants are often classified as either "deciduous" or "evergreen", virtually all woody flowering plants shed and renew their leaves on a cyclical basis. "Deciduous" plants generally shed all their leaves at one time and remain leafless from days to months, a behavior usually attributed to drought or cold weather. "Evergreen" plants are generally considered to be those plants that gradually shed their leaves and renew them at the same time. Many evergreen trees living under a seasonal climatic regime appear to shed the largest proportion of

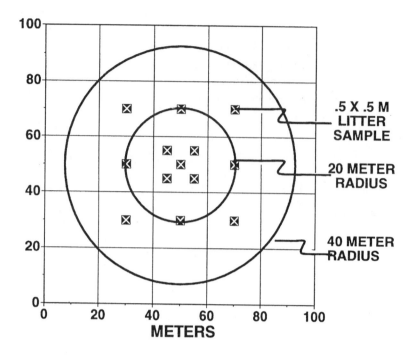

Fig. 1.– *Sampling pattern for 13 litter samples collected in Zone 2, Pakitza Guard Station, Manu National Park, Perú. Boxed X's mark litter sample site. Circles represent examples of forest areas to which litter samples are compared.*

their annually-renewed leaves during the same period of time that local deciduous trees are shedding leaves (Coley 1988; unpublished data from F.H. Cornejo and S.J. Wright in Panama, some exceptions noted in Wright and Cornejo 1990). In moist tropical forests, the presence of a two to three-month "less rainy season" appears to be the stimulus for both deciduous and evergreen trees to lose their leaves. Therefore, the mid to late dry season is the most appropriate time to sample litter of tropical forests if only a single series of samples can be made annually for logistical reasons. In Manu National Park, it has thus far not been possible to collect litter on a more regular basis throughout the year.

Litter was dried in the field in mesh bags or mesh-bottomed boxes and returned to the United States for identification. Litter was separated into twigs, flowers, fruits and leaves. All leaves and reproductive organs then were separated to species and identified using specimens collected directly from the source forest trees, climbers and shrubs. Each species was dried completely at 70° C to a stable dry weight, and weighed. Litter samples incorporated an average of 426 leaves or leaflets per sample. Litter samples included an average total dry weight of 161.7 grams (range 100.7 - 213.0g), including leaves, twigs and unidentifiable fragments, which can be extrapolated to about 6,500kg/hectare. These samples probably represent an accumulation of about 6 months, given the range of 6-12 mt/ha reported by numerous researchers in tropical moist forests (Brown 1980).

Species richness and litter importance values were determined on the basis of leaves alone. Importance values for each species in litter samples were defined as the total dry weight of leaves. All fruits and seeds from the samples were eliminated from consideration in calculating the importance values because of the intra-annually variable nature of fruit and seed production by different species in the forest.

RESULTS

SPECIES RICHNESS

The source forest includes 178 species of trees over 10 cm dbh. This number is approximate, due to remaining taxonomic revisions to be made in particularly large and difficult groups (i.e., *Inga*, as well as unidentified climbers). This species richness is comparable to values obtained from other forested Amazonian hectares (Fittkau and Klinge 1973; Prance et al. 1976; Balslev et al. 1987; Gentry 1988a,b, 1990; Pinedo-Vásquez et al. 1990). Total species richness of individual litter samples ranged from 25 to 48, with a mean value of 33.8. Total species richness of all 13 samples from the central 40 x 40 meters is 108. Comparison of these richness values for litter samples to forest richness may be slightly misleading if it is not made clear here that the litter richness reflects *all species* in the litter samples, not just tree species. When litter from species whose diameters are not known to exceed 10cm is excluded (i.e. climbers ,shrubs, herbs and indeterminate leaves), the tree species richness of individual samples ranges from 14 to 28 and tree species found in all 13 samples is 83. Taxa of indeterminate affinity in the litter ranged in number from 3-18 per sample, averaging 8 per sample. These indeterminate species are unrepresented among the source tree flora and from one-half to three-quarters very likely represent climbers, based on leaf morphology and some knowledge of the climbers in the source flora. The indeterminate forms were not entered into any subsequent analyses. Both forest and litter show high species richness, compared to other forests sampled by similar methods thus far (Burnham 1993).

SPECIES DIVERSITY

Species diversity has been defined by Pielou (1977) as a means for describing a community, however it stands as a statistical measure in which species richness and evenness in the sample are mingled indistinguishably. Such a measure may be difficult to interpret because so much community information has been entered into a single number. Here I have used the Shannon diversity index, which takes into account both species numbers and some measure of importance for each of the species. For litter samples, species importance values were defined as the total weight of a species in each sample; the importance value for source trees was defined as the total basal area represented by each species. Samples with high numbers of species and an even representation of importance of individuals among species will produce a high index value. Conversely, dominance of a sample by a single individual, or even just a low number of species per sample will produce a low index value. Shannon indices for litter samples and the source forest are reported in Table 1. Diversity values based on all species in individual litter samples range from 0.614 to 1.176 (Table 1, column 4). Combining all litter samples produces a diversity index of 1.353. The diversity index for the source forest is 1.554. If all non-trees are removed from the litter analysis, the combined samples have a diversity index of 1.285 (column 5).

AREA OF REPRESENTATION OF LITTER SAMPLES

A single $1/2$ m² sample of forest litter clearly is not sufficient to represent the species richness or diversity of an entire hectare of tropical forest. If an estimate of biodiversity is to be made using litter samples, it is important to know exactly what forest area is sampled by a litter sample of 0.5 x 0.5m. Therefore, comparisons were made between 1) tree species lists from circular forest areas with radii of 5, 10, 12.5, 15, 20, 25, 30, 35, and 40 meters and 2) species lists from 0.5x0.5m litter samples located at the center of these concentric sampling zones, including only those leaves derived from trees with dbh$\geq$ 10cm. Comparisons also were made between five litter samples in the central 14x14 area (figure 1) and the source forest, and all thirteen litter samples from the central 40x40m (Figure 1) and the source forest.

Table 1. Sample richness and diversity for 13 litter samples and one hectare of source forest from Zone 2, Pakitsa Station, Manu National Park, Perú.

SAMPLE NUMBER	SPECIES RICHNESS	TREE RICHNESS	SHANNON ALL IDENTIFIELD SPECIES	INDEX TREES ONLY
LITTER SAMPLES				
1	31	18	0.911	0.855
2	33	23	0.847	0.808
3	41	28	0.614	0.539
4	34	23	0.962	0.892
5	36	29	0.734	0.713
6	48	30	1.093	1.086
7	25	22	0.693	0.684
8	38	27	0.649	0.64
9	28	23	0.979	0.903
10	42	33	1.176	1.103
11	27	20	1.049	0.925
12	25	21	0.929	0.857
13	31	24	0.782	0.609
ALL SAMPLES	108	83	1.353	1.285
SOURCE FOREST				
source forest	Total Richness Unknown	~178 Tree Species	—	1.554

Similarity can be assessed most simply by comparing the total number of species in the litter samples with species richness of the forest areas. This comparison, however, may be misleading. The number of species in common between litter and forest samples is highly dependent on the total number of species in each sample, which in this case is limited in the 1/2m² samples. The raw-number comparisons are shown only for the combination of 5 and 13 litter samples in Figure 2.

A more informative means of comparing species composition in the forest and litter is with a similarity index in which sample size has an effect on the value of the index, such as Sorenson's Community Coefficient or a Simple Matching Coefficient. I have chosen to use Sorenson's Community Coefficient index (also known as Dice's index) because it emphasizes *shared* species, which is the informative portion of the species comparisons in this case, and does not count species that are *mutually absent* from both samples (as do simple matching coefficients). These comparisons using Sorenson's Coefficients are shown in Figure 3. Single samples best reflect a source area of about 700m² (15m radius). The

a.

FIVE LITTER SAMPLES COMPARED TO SURROUNDING 15 M RADIUS

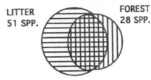

LITTER 51 SPP.   FOREST 28 SPP.

SPECIES IN COMMON = 21 (72% OF FOREST SPP.)
REPRESENT 92.2% OF STEM BIOMASS

b.

FIVE LITTER SAMPLES COMPARED TO SURROUNDING 20 M RADIUS

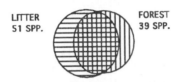

LITTER 51 SPP.   FOREST 39 SPP.

SPECIES IN COMMON = 27 (69% OF FOREST SPP.)
REPRESENT 89.3% OF STEM BIOMASS

c.

13 LITTER SAMPLES COMPARED TO SURROUNDING FOREST HECTARE

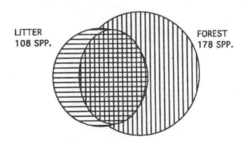

LITTER 108 SPP.   FOREST 178 SPP.

SPECIES IN COMMON = 76 (43% OF FOREST SPP.)
REPRESENT 81.2% OF STEM BIOMASS

Fig. 2.– *Comparisons of raw richness numbers of litter samles and source forest.*
a) *5 combined litter samples compared to a forest circle of 15m radius,*
b) *5 combined litter samples compared to a forest circle of 20m radius,*
c) *13 combined litter sampes compared to the hectare of surrounding source forest.*

Robyn J. Burnham

five combined samples from the central 14x14m area (196m²) show the greatest similarity to the forest composition of a 1250m² (20 meter radius). The combination of all thirteen samples, widely spaced in a 1600m² area shows the greatest similarity to a 5000 m² area, which is a forest circle of 40m radius, or one half hectare.

These combined samples, both the group of 5 and the group of 13, are not intended to serve as an independent means of testing the effect of increasing sample number. Rather, because single samples consistently show such limited spatial representation of the source forest, the combination of samples from a larger area is intended to determine the degree of improvement achieved by sampling over a larger area. Future studies may undertake an evaluation of the species composition in 5 contiguous samples, with species representing forest species in an area smaller than 1,250m².

SPECIES SIMILARITY: COMPARISON OF SINGLE AND COMBIN[ED] LITTER SAMPLES TO FOREST AREAS

(y-axis) SORENSON'S COEFFICIENT OF SIMILARITY

(x-axis) AREA OF FOREST COMPARED TO LITTER SAMPLES

Legend:
.... 13 SAMPLES COMBINED
– – – 5 SAMPLES COMBINED
——— SINGLE SAMPLES

Fig. 3. *Sorenson's Coefficient of Similarity derived by comparison between litter samples and specified forest area.*

LIFE-FORM REPRESENTATION IN LITTER

One of the notable differences between the data set derived from the source forest and that of the litter is the abundance of species of climbers (vines and lianas) in the litter samples. These species are all but absent from the source forest data set because climbers only occasionally have stem diameters of 10cm.

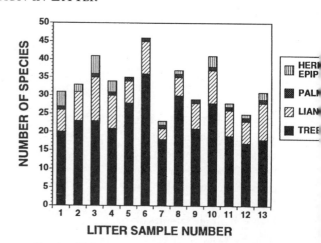

(y-axis) NUMBER OF SPECIES

(x-axis) LITTER SAMPLE NUMBER

Legend:
HER[B]
EPIP[HYTE]
PAL[M]
LIAN[A]
TREE

Fig. 4.– *Habit summary of species in litter samples from Zone 2, Pakitza Station, Manu National Park, Perú.*

134

Epiphytes, shrubs, and herbs also are not present in the source forest data because of their small stature. These life-forms however, rarely are present in litter. Figure 4 depicts the number of plant species of several life forms in each of the thirteen litter samples. Although some variation in the total number of climbers is evident, 13-32% of the species list from a litter sample represent climbers. Similar proportions of "epiphytes, vines, and herbs" are reported for a primary forest in Guatemala by Kunkel-Westphal and Kunkel (1979). These species are almost completely excluded from the source forest data at Pakitza, and indeed climbers are excluded from many tropical forest data sets, directly because of the diameter limits used, by explicit exclusion because of the known differences in hydraulic efficiencies between climbers and trees (Ewers et al. 1991), or because they lack obvious economic importance. There are presently little data that show the leaf life-times of climbers in comparison to trees (see Aide and Zimmerman 1990), yet these rates may influence the representation of climbers and trees in tropical litter.

Shrubs, herbs, and epiphytes are not well represented by the species lists from the litter samples. The leaves of shrubs, herbs and epiphytes, when combined contribute from 0 to 13% of the total species list, and most often represent less than 10% of total richness. These plants generally show some combination of three differences in their litter production when compared with tropical trees and climbers. First, they often bear leaves that abscise infrequently. This is particularly true of bromeliads and orchids, whose leaves are tough and probably are held on the plant for very long periods of time. Second, some plants do not abscise organs cleanly and quickly, leading to rotting of the plant organ while it is still attached to the source plant. This is carried to an extreme in annual herbs, in which the entire plant may die before any foliage abscission takes place. Third, the biomass produced yearly by shrubs, epiphytes and herbs is considerably less than that produced by trees, even for shrubs that may be relatively common in the understory of the forest.

Palms are an interesting case in this forest. Based on number of stems, two species of palms (*Iriartea deltoidea* and *Astrocaryum macrocalyx*) are the two most numerous species on the hectare. Even in terms of total basal area, these two species are among the ten most important species on the hectare. In contrast, palms are present in 12 of the 13 litter samples but generally occur in extremely low abundances, less than 1.5% of the total sample by weight. In only two cases were palms relatively important in the litter samples (>15% by weight), and in both of these cases, a whole palm frond had fallen directly over the sample site. Many pinnate-leaved palms, like *A. macrocalyx* and *I. deltoidea* bear few leaves at any one time (perhaps 15-30 leaves), their leaves are long-lived (1-7 years: Tomlinson 1990), and tend to disarticulate partially while still attached to the parent plant (Frangi and Lugo 1985). Very little material is available to the litter sites on average. An additional factor may be that due to the sheer bulk of palm leaves, they fall directly beneath the trunk of the tree, virtually slithering down the trunk after withering, and are not redistributed away from the trunk, thus rarely entering a litter sample.

135

Robyn J. Burnham

HETEROGENEITY IN SPECIES RICHNESS AND COMPOSITION

There is clearly a high degree of spatial heterogeneity in the distribution of species in a tropical forest and in the litter produced by those species. To allow a comparison of litter species heterogeneity among sites, Table 2 shows the Sorenson's Community Coefficient calculated among all pairs of litter samples. The index ranges from .15 to .65 among pairs of samples. With only one exception (sample 2 compared to sample 9), litter samples from the central 14x14m were the most similar to one another, with a minimal similarity of 0.53. In general, samples that were separated by the greatest distance were more dissimilar than those closer together. This result confirms the idea that, in general, the heterogeneity of the forest is reflected in the litter produced by the forest. That is, no strong homogenizing process is going on subsequent to leaf fall (such as redistribution by wind, water, etc.).

Table 2.- Sorenson's Coefficient of Similarity for all pairs of 13 samples from Zone 2, Pakitsa Station, Manu National Park, Perú, collected in 1990. The diagonal of this table represents similarity coefficients derived from comparing samples from a single site in the hectare collected in 1989 with those collected in 1990. Sorenson's Coefficient of Similarity=

$$\frac{2(\text{number of species in common between the two samples})}{[\# \text{ species in sample 1} + \# \text{species in sample 2}]}$$

	1	2	3	4	5	6	7	8	9	10	11	12	13
1	0.62												
2	0.31	0.67											
3	0.42	0.41	0.55										
4	0.41	0.49	0.50	0.58									
5	0.24	0.31	0.40	0.35	0.62								
6	0.31	0.38	0.32	0.42	0.44	0.65							
7	0.29	0.28	0.35	0.38	0.20	0.32	0.56						
8	0.51	0.46	0.39	0.47	0.37	0.47	0.31	0.70					
9	0.40	0.65	0.41	0.53	0.39	0.34	0.23	0.46	0.64				
10	0.42	0.52	0.49	0.60	0.40	0.53	0.31	0.57	0.56	0.68			
11	0.29	0.56	0.35	0.52	0.33	0.24	0.15	0.44	0.61	0.59	0.51		
12	0.37	0.55	0.38	0.47	0.28	0.35	0.29	0.48	0.64	0.62	0.59	0.70	
13	0.35	0.51	0.36	0.48	0.38	0.44	0.23	0.45	0.64	0.58	0.55	0.53	0.64

Temporal heterogeneity of litter samples may also affect an assessment of biodiversity from the litter. Litter samples in which leaves were identified to species were collected from Zone 2 at Pakitza twice over a two year period, during the same season each year. The late dry season was deemed to be the best single time to collect litter in a region of generally moist warm climate, if only one series of collections could be made per year. This choice was made because the maximum amount of leaf turnover, among both "deciduous" and "evergreen" trees, was expected at or just preceding this time. Observations by the author at Pakitza during the rainy season, and unpublished data of F.H. Cornejo and S.J. Wright from Panama support this assumption. Two consecutive yearly samples can only be suggestive of the temporal heterogeneity that might apply from year to year in the forest. Comparison of litter samples from 1989 with those of 1990 from the same site on the forest floor are presented here (diagonal of Table 2) only as a yardstick against which to gauge support for the hypothesis that the heterogeneity in the species composition of litter samples is strongest among sites, rather than between years. Sorenson's Coefficients for the similarity between 1989 and 1990 samples taken from the exact same site on the forest floor range from a low of 0.51 to a high of 0.70, considerably higher than the site to site variation from a single year. The lowest value was derived from a sample pair in which total species richness fell by one-third between the two years.

DISCUSSION

There are three major implications of the litter data presented above. First, it is clear that relative forest richness is adequately represented by litter accumulating under tropical forests. Single litter samples however represent from 8 to 16% of the total tree species richness of the hectare. A combination of 13 litter samples from a 40 x 40m area represent 46% of the total tree species richness of the hectare. Because the area of representation of the 13 combined samples is only about one half hectare (5000m^2), the species representation of that area is a more appropriate comparison for the 13 samples. Of the 117 tree species in the half hectare surrounding the 13 litter samples, 69, or 59% are represented in the litter samples. Thus, the combined litter samples reflect >50% of the source tree richness of the area they best represent. In addition these samples give excellent comparative data on other life forms that have been assessed rarely in tropical forest censuses. Confirmation of these patterns in other tropical forest types is necessary. It is clear, however, that a multiplication factor can be used to estimate total species richness, if richness is the measure required by the study. Rapid assessment of biodiversity and comparison among forests (relative biodiversity) would be gauged best by comparing numbers of all litter species from each forest plot, rather than comparing tree counts from one forest with litter counts from another forest.

Comparing tree species richness in litter to source tree is possible only if leaves are taxonomically identifiable, be they fossils or modern leaves. Thus, species counts of fossil leaf horizons will represent all life forms fossilized in the same way that modern litter counts represent all life forms in the litter. Paleobotanists and neobotanists must embrace the idea that tropical plant biodiversity includes life forms other than trees (Gentry and Dodson 1987). Assessment of leaf litter gives a general sense of biodiversity, even though direct comparison of numbers of leaves of each species to the source forests censused only for trees cannot be made until life-form classification has been made.

137

Second, single litter samples of the extent collected for this study from a tropical forest represent the species in a circle of about 15m radius. The best comparisons among species-rich forests, using a limited number of litter samples would be to compare areas of this size to one another, using presence and abundance of species in forest litter as the measure. Preliminary studies suggest that yearly variations in litter composition are far below site-to-site variation. Continuing sampling along the lines presented here is necessary to confirm some of the patterns seen, particularly the effect of sampling tropical forests at different times during the year to assess the importance of seasonality of litter fall on species richness.

Third, the most important implication of this study, as suggested above, is the abundance of life-forms other than trees in the litter of tropical forests. Litter samples reflect plants that abscise photosynthetic and reproductive organs on a continuous or periodic basis, not just those that are evident in terms of wood production. This implies that the forest litter is a good estimate of current structure, richness, diversity, and photosynthetic activity in tropical forests, perhaps far better than that estimated from studies limited by a minimum diameter for censused trees. In addition, the data from litter-based studies of species richness can add significantly to the interaction between paleobotanists/modern plant systematists and other disciplines whose major interest lies in the food resources, habitat diversity, and structural characteristics of tropical forests.

ACKNOWLEDGEMENTS

The encouragement and enthusiasm of Dr. Robin B. Foster was instrumental in this study. Assistance in the field with collections was generously provided by many individuals, particularly Flor Chavez Henderson, Severo Baldeón, and José Campos de la Cruz. Assistance with sample processing was provided enthusiastically by Jennifer Apple. S.J.Wright and F.H. Cornejo generously allowed access to unpublished litter data from Barro Colorado Island. I also thank the Ministerio de Agricultura, Dirección General Forestal y de Fauna del Perú for permission to work in Parque Nacional del Manu. Thorough and helpful reviews were provided by W.A. DiMichele, P. Acevedo-R., and an anonymous individual. Financial support was received from the Smithsonian Institution Biolat Program. This represents Biolat Contribution #93.

Aide, T.M. asnd J.K. Zimmerman 1990. Patterns of insect herbivory, growth, and survivorship in juveniles of a neotropical liana. Ecology 71(4):1412-1421.

Balslev, H., J. Luteyn, G. Oligaard, and L.B. Holm-Nielsen 1987. Composition and structure of adjacent unflooded and flood-plain forest in Amazonian Ecuador. Opera Botanica 92:37-57.

Brown, S. 1980. Rates of organic matter accumuation and litter production in tropical forest ecosystems. In : S. Brown, A.E. Lugo, and B. Liegel eds., The Role of Tropical Forests on the World Carbon Cycle. Center for Wetlands: Gainesville.

Burnham, R.J. 1993. Reconstructing richness in the plant fossil record. Palaios 8(4):376-384.

Burnham, R.J. 1989. Relationships between standing vegetation and leaf litter in a Paratropical Forest: Implications for Paleobotany. Review of Paleobotany and Palynology 58:5-32.

Burnham, R. J. in press. Stand characteristics and leaf litter composition of a dry forest hectare in Santa Rosa National Park, Costa Rica. Biotropica.

Burnham,R.J.,S.L. Wing and G.G.Parker. 1992. The reflection of deciduous forest communities in leaf litter: Implications for autochthonous litter assemblages from the fossil record. Paleobiology 18(1):34-53.

Coley, P.D. 1988. Effects of plant growth rate and leaf liftime on the amount and type of anti-herbivore defense. Oecologia 74:531-536.

Coley, P.D. and T.M. Aide. 1991. Comparison of herbivory and plant defenses in temperate and tropical borad-leaved forests. Pp 25-49 in P.W. Price, T.M. Lewinsohn, G.W. Fernandes and W.W. benson, eds. Plant-Animal Interactions: Evolutionary Ecology in Tropical and Temperate Regions, John Wiley.

Cornforth, I.S. 1970. Litterfall in a tropical rainforest. Journal of Applied Ecology 7:603-608.

Erwin. T. 1991. Carabidae de Pakitsa, Manu. Revista Peruana de Entomologia 33:2-83.

Ewers, F.W., J.B. Fisher, and K. Fichtner 1991. Water flux and xylem structure in vines. Pp 127-160 in F.E. Putz aand H.A. Mooney, eds.. The Biology of Vines. Cambridge University Press, Cambridge.

Fittkau, E.J. and J. Klinge. 1973. On biomass and trophic structure of the central Amazonian rain forest ecosystem. Biotropica 5(1):2-14.

Frangi, J.L. and A.E. Lugo. 1985. Ecosystem dynamics of a subtropical floodplain forest. Ecological Monographs 55(3):351-369.

Gentry, A.H. 1988a. Changes in plant community diversity and floristic composition on environmental and geographical gradients. Annals of the Missouri Botanical Garden 75:1-34.

Gentry, A.H. 1988b. Tree species richness of upper Amazonian forests. Procedings of the National Acad. Science 85:156-159.

Gentry, A.H. 1990. Floristic similarities and differences between southern Central America and upper and central Amazonia. Pp. 141-157 in A.H. Gentry, ed. Four Neotropical Rainforests. Yale University Press: New Haven.

Gentry, A.H. and C.H. Dodson. 1987. Contribution of non-trees to species richness of tropical rain forest. Biotropica 19:149-156.

Klinge, H. and W.A. Rodrigues. 1968. Litter production in an area of Amazonian Terra Firme forest. Part I. Litter-fall, organic carbon and total nitrogen contents of litter. Amazoniana 1:287-302.

Kunkel-Westphal, I. and P. Kunkel 1979. Litter fall in a Guatemalan primary forest, with details of leaf-shedding by some common tree species. Journal of Ecology 67:665-686.

Parker, G.G., J.P. O'Neill, and D. Higman 1989. Vertical profile and canopy organization in a mixed deciduous forest. Vegetatio 85:1-11.

Pielou, E.C. 1977. Mathematical Ecology. John Wiley and Sons: New York. 385p.

Pinedo-Vasquez, M.D. Zarin, P. Jipp, and J. Chota-Inuma. 1990. Use-values of tree species in a communal forest reserve in Northeast Peru. Conservation Biology 4(4):405-415.

Prance, G.T., W.A. Rodrigues, and M.F. da Silva 1976. Inventario de um hectare de mata de tierra firme, km 30 da Estrada Manaus-Itacoatiara. Acta Amazonica 6:9-35.

Proctor, J. 1984. Tropical forest litterfall II: the data set. Pp 83-113 in A.C. Chadwick and S.L. Sutton, eds. Tropical Rain-Forest: The Leeds Symposium.

Proctor, J., J.M. Anderson, S.C.L. Fogden, and H.W. Vallack. 1983. Ecological studies in four contrasting lowland rainforests in Gunung Mulu National Park, Sarawak, II. Litterfall, litter standing crop and preliminary observations on herbivory. Journal of Ecology 71:261-283.

Songwe, N.C, F.E. Fasehun, and D.U.U. Okali. 1988. Litterfall and productivity in a tropical raiin forest, Southern Bakundu Forest Reserve, Cameroon. Journal of Tropical Ecology 4:25-37.

Tomlinson, P.B. 1990. The Structural Biology of Palms. Clarendon Press: Oxford. 477p.

Waring, R.H. 1983. Estimating forest growth and efficiency in relation to canopy leaf area. Advances in Ecological Research 13:327-354.

Wright, S.J. and F. H. Cornejo. 1990. Seasonal drought and leaf all in a tropical forest. Ecology 71(3):1165-1175.

Estudio Preliminar de la Familia Arecaceae (Palmae) en el Parque Nacional del Manu (Pakitza y Cocha Cashu)

FLOR CHÁVEZ

The New York Botanical Garden Bronx, NY 10458.

RESUMEN.–

La flora de Palmeras de Pakitza se describe en base al trabajo de campo y consultas a herbarios realizados por el autor. La flora de palmeras presente en la zona de Pakitza es comparada con la diversidad de palmeras de Cocha Cashu, utilizando como referencia el Checklist de Plantas del Parque Nacional del Manu elaborado por Robin Foster (1987). Los resultados muestran 26 especies en 16 géneros para Pakitza y 25 especies para Cocha Cashu. También se describe la distribución geográfica, hábitat y usos más comunes de todas las especies de palmeras del PNM.

La familia Arecaceae cuenta con aproximadamente 2779 especies (Moore, 1973) que se encuentran distribuidas en todos los trópicos y subtrópicos. Para América, se calculan alrededor de 800 especies en 71 géneros, todos ellos endémicos, a excepción de *Elaeis* con una especie en Africa Occidental y *Raphia* con una especie en el Nuevo Mundo y otras en Africa (Henderson, 1990).

La flora de Arecaceas del Perú fue reactualizada (Kahn et al., 1992), los datos registran 2897 especímenes de herbario, pertenecientes a 35 géneros, de los cuales 33 son nativos y 2 introducidos. El 73% de éstos está identificado a nivel específico con un total de 152 especies. El 82% de las muestras proviene de departamentos amazónicos, mientras que los departamentos andinos circundantes a la Cuenca Amazónica han sido poco colectados.

La familia Arecaceae es la tercera familia con mayor representación dentro de los bosques de Cocha Cashu, PNM (Gentry, 1990). Alrededor de 35 especies, pertenecientes a 22 géneros, fueron colectadas en varios puntos del PNM, de las cuales poco más de 20 crecen en suelos aluviales de reciente formación (Foster, 1987,1990). Entre éstas se encuentran algunas especies de *Scheelea* y *Astrocaryum*, las cuales juegan un rol de gran importancia para la vida silvestre, como recurso alimenticio durante la época seca (Terborgh, 1983).

La información etnobotánica referente a esta familia todavía es desconocida para esta zona, a pesar de que la Institución AMETRA (Aplicación de Medicinas Tradicionales) trabajó con algunas comunidades nativas del PNM, la información obtenida por ellos todavía no está disponible.

Los objetivos del presente trabajo son los de calcular la diversidad florística y de proveer información general de la familia Arecaceae en la parte baja del PNM, en particular en las localidades de Pakitza y Cocha Cashu. Con esta finalidad se ha colectado material botánico y se han visitado los siguientes herbarios: Vargas Cusco (CUZ), New York Botanical Garden (NY), Universidad Mayor de San Marcos (USM), Museum of Natural History, Smithsonian Institution (US). También se ha recopilado información concerniente al uso de las plantas de esta familia.

ABSTRACT.–

The palm flora of Pakitza is described based on the author's field and herbarium work. This is compared with the palms of Cocha Cashu, using Foster's (1987) Checklist of Plants of Manu National Park. The results show that 26 species in 16 genera are present in Pakitza, and 25 species in Cocha Cashu. Geographical distribution, habitat and common uses of all species are described.

Tabla 1.—*Lista general de especies de la Familia Arecaceae (Palmae) en las localidades de Pakitza y Cocha Cashu - PNM (Madre de Dios 1990)*

Especies	Cocha Cashu	Pakitza
Chelyocarpus ulei Dammer	x	-
Mauritia flexuosa L. f.	x	x
Chamaedorea angustisecta Burret	x	x
Chamaedorea pauciflora Mart.	x	-
Chamaedorea pinnatifrons (Jacq.) Oerst.	-	x
Wendlandiella simplicifrons Burret	x	x
Iriartea deltoidea R. & P.	x	x
Socratea exorrhiza (Mart.) Wendl.	x	x
Socratea salazarii H. Moore	x	x
Euterpe precatoria Mart.	x	x
Oenocarpus balikii Kahn.	-	x
Oenocarpus bataua Mart.	x	x
Oenocarpus mapora Karst.	x	x
Hyospathe elegans Mart.	x	x
Attalea phalerata (Mart. ex Spreng.) Burret	x	x
Attalea tessmannii Burret	x	-
Attalea sp.	-	x
Aiphanes aculeata Willd.	x	x
Astrocaryum chonta Mart.	x	x
Desmoncus polyacanthos Mart.	x	x
Bactris concinna Mart.	x	x
Bactris monticola Barb.Rodr.	x	x
Bactris simplicifrons Mart.	x	-
Bactris sphaerocarpa Trail	-	x
Bactris sp.	-	x
Geonoma acaulis Mart.	x	x
Geonoma brongniartii Mart.	x	x
Geonoma deversa (Poit.) Kunth	x	x
Geonoma sp.	-	x
Phytelephas macrocarpa R. & P.	x	x

Clasificación filogenética establecida por Uhl & Dransfield (1987)

ÁREA DE ESTUDIO Y METODOLOGIA

La zona de trabajo está situada en la margen derecha del Río Manu (11°55'S y 71°15'W), a una altitud de 350 - 400 m. Las fases de campo se desarrollaron en los períodos de lluvia (febrero) y de secas (setiembre a octubre) de 1990.

La temperatura en esta región fluctúa entre 20°C y 30°C, llegando a superar en algunas ocasiones esta máxima entre los meses de agosto y octubre. La temperatura máxima registrada fue entre octubre y noviembre con una media máxima de 28.7°C y una media mínima de 20.6°C. La precipitación anual fue de 2,100 mm, con la estación seca entre junio y setiembre, variando entre 20 a 80 mm. La estación lluviosa es entre octubre y mayo, con precipitaciones entre 90 y 390 mm mensuales. Estos datos fueron registrados en la Estación Biológica de Cocha Cashu por J. Terborgh y estudiantes.

Las colecciones se realizaron en todas las parcelas y trochas diseñadas por el programa BIOLAT, utilizando la metodología tradicional de herborización. Las muestras en su mayoría están depositadas en el Herbario Vargas (CUZ).

Tabla 2.– Nombre local y partes más utilizadas de las Palmeras en la localidad de Pakitza-PNM (Madre de Dios, 1990)

Especie	Nombre local	Parte utilizada			
		Raíz	Tallo	Hoja	Fruto
Mauritia flexuosa	Aguaje	–	x*	x	x
C. angustisecta		–	–	–	–
C. pinnatifrons		–	–	–	–
Iriartea deltoidea	Huacrapona, Pona	x	x	x	–
Socratea exorrhiza	Cashapona, Pona	x	x	–	x
Socratea salazarii	Pona de altura	–	x	–	–
Euterpe precatoria	Huasaí	x	x	x	x
Oenocarpus bataua	Ungurahui	–	–	x	x
Oenocarpus balickii		–	–	–	–
Oenocarpus mapora	Sinami, Sinamillo	–	x	x	x
Hyospathe elegans	Palmiche	–	–	–	–
Attalea phalerata	Shapaja	–	–	x	x
Attalea sp.		–	–	–	–
Aiphanes aculeata	Shija-Shija	–	–	–	x
Astrocaryum chonta	Huicungo	–	x	x	–
Desmoncus polyacanthos		–	–	–	–
Bactris concinna	Ñeja, Ñejilla	–	–	–	x
Bactris monticola		–	–	–	–
Bactris sphaerocarpa		–	–	–	–
Bactris sp.		–	–	–	–
Geonoma acaulis	Palmiche	–	–	–	–
Geonoma brongniartii		–	–	–	–
Geonoma deversa	Palmiche	–	–	x	–
Geonoma sp.	«	–	–	–	–
Phytelephas macrocarpa	Yarina	–	–	x	x

* uso indirecto

TRATAMIENTO SISTEMÁTICO

Con la finalidad de facilitar la identificación de las palmeras en el campo, se han preparado claves para géneros y especies, utilizando los caracteres más sobresalientes.

Clave para los Géneros de Palmeras de Pakitza y Cocha Cashu

1. Hojas palmadas.
2. Tallo de hasta 25 m de altura, 23 - 50 cm diam; frutos cubiertos por escamas .... *Mauritia*
2. Tallo moderado hasta 8 m de alto, 4 - 7 cm diam; frutos no cubiertos por escamas .... *Chelyocarpus*
1. Hojas pinnadas o enteras con venación pinnada.
3. Tallo sostenido por una base de raíces fúlcreas altas; pinnas con ápice dentado.
4. Tallo de hasta 25 m de alto, usualmente con una dilatación en la parte alta; inflorescencia con (30 - 37) raquillas; bráctea cerrada en forma de cuerno; frutos globosos, glabros .... *Iriartea*

4. Tallo mediano, hasta 20 m de alto, generalmente menor, sin dilatación; inflorescencia pequeña con (12 - 17) raquillas; bráctea erecta no visible a simple vista; frutos elipsoides, glabros .... *Socratea*
3. Tallo no sostenido por una base de raíces fúlcreas; pinnas con ápice no dentado (a excepción del género *Aiphanes* que presenta espinas).
5. Espinas presentes, a veces circunscritas a los ápices de las hojas.
6. Tallo trepador; pinnas distales modificadas en garfios que le ayudan a trepar .... *Desmoncus*
6. Tallo no trepador; pinnas distales no modificadas en garfios.
7. Pinnas deltoideas dentadas .... *Aiphanes*
7. Pinnas no deltoideas o dentadas.
8. Envés de las pinnas con coloración plateada; inflorescencias usualmente con 1 - 3 flores pistiladas en la raquilla .... *Astrocaryum*
8. Envés de las pinnas sin coloración plateada; inflorescencias con flores pistiladas y estaminadas distribuidas a lo largo de la raquilla .... *Bactris*
5. Espinas ausentes.
9. Frutos cubiertos por proyecciones verrucosas cónicas, inflorescencia compacta ubicada a nivel del suelo .... *Phytelephas*
9. Frutos sin proyecciones verrucosas; inflorescencias no compactas no ubicadas a nivel del suelo.
10. Tallo de hasta 20 m de alto y 50 cm diam.
11. Inflorescencia infrafoliar; flores estaminadas y flores pistiladas en una misma inflorescencia; frutos pequeños (1 - 3 cm de largo, 1 - 2 cm diam), endocarpo delgado (1 - 2 mm de espesor).
12. Envés de las pinnas con coloración plateada; inflorescencia hipuriforme (forma de cola de caballo); frutos ovalados .... *Oenocarpus*
12. Envés de las pinnas sin coloración plateada; inflorescencia no hipuriforme; frutos globosos .... *Euterpe*
11. Inflorescencia interfoliar; flores estaminadas y flores pistiladas en inflorescencias separadas; frutos (3 - 8 cm de largo, 3 - 5 cm diam), endocarpo leñoso grueso (2 - 15 mm de espesor) .... *Attalea*
10. Palmeras de sotobosque alcanzan hasta 4 m de altura y 4 cm o menos diam.
13. Flores dispuestas en depresiones a lo largo de la raquilla .... *Geonoma*
13. Flores no dispuestas en depresiones a lo largo de la raquilla.
14. Hojas bífidas angostas (2 - 4 cm ancho) .... *Wendlandiella*
14. Hojas no bífidas.
15. Inflorescencia con 2 brácteas o cicatrices de éstas; flores estaminadas y flores pistiladas en una misma inflorescencia .... *Hyospathe*
15. Inflorescencia con 4 - 5 brácteas o cicatrices de éstas, flores estaminadas y flores pistiladas en diferentes individuos (dioicas) .... *Chamaedorea*

Los dieciséis géneros registrados son de amplia distribución en la amazonía tropical. A continuación se presentan las descripciones botánicas, utilizando un lenguaje simple, con el fin de que este documento sea útil a los profesionales de distintas especialidades que trabajan en esta zona. Se proporciona en primer lugar el tratamiento botánico de cada especie, se cita el nombre local, las características de campo más sobresalientes, el rango de distribución geográfica, el tipo de hábitat, las formas de uso más generalizados y finalmente se cita la lista de los especímenes examinados en los herbarios visitados. El orden de este tratamiento está basado en el sistema filogenético establecido por Uhl y Dransfield (1987).

CHELYOCARPUS *Dammer*

Palmeras de tamaño pequeño a moderado, monoicas. Tallo solitario o cespitoso, erecto o procumbente. Hojas palmadas, el limbo dividido en dos mitades, y cada una de ellas dividida en segmentos, el envés de color blanquecino. Inflorescencia interfoliar, de ramificación simple o doble, raquillas numerosas. Flores hermafroditas 2 - 4 sépalos, 2 - 4 pétalos, 5 - 9 estambres, 1 - 6 carpelos. Frutos globosos, residuo estigmático apical o sub apical. Eófilo bífido.

Distribución.–
Género de 4 especies, distribuidos en la amazonía, Brasil, Bolivia, Colombia y Perú. En la zona de estudio se registró una sola especie.

CHELYOCARPUS ulei Dammer

Palmera solitaria, erecta 1.2 - 8 m de altura, 4 - 7 cm diam. Hojas 10 - 15; vaina cubierta por un tomento lanoso, el limbo es circular dividido en 5 - 12 segmentos, a su vez cada segmento dividido apicalmente hasta en 4 segmentos libres. Inflorescencia interfoliar de ramificación simple. Flores de color amarillo-cremoso, sépalos 2, pétalos 2, estambres 5 - 8, gineceo con 2 carpelos libres. Fruto globoso-subgloboso, epicarpio corchoso al madurar. Eófilo bífido.

Distribución.–
Se encuentra en Brasil, Colombia y Ecuador; en el Perú está registrado para: Loreto, Madre de Dios, Pasco y San Martín.

Hábitat.–
Crece en terrenos bajos, áreas inundadas y también en bosques de tierra firme.
Especímenes examinados.
F. Kahn 2109 (USM); P. Núñez 6910 (CUZ).

MAURITIA *L.f.*

Palmeras altas, robustas, dioicas. Tallo solitario, erecto. Hojas numerosas, forman una corona muy amplia, costapalmadas, lámina circular dividida en numerosos segmentos. Inflorescencias interfoliares, raquillas con doble ramificación. Las flores estaminadas con 3 sépalos, 3 pétalos, 6 estambres, las flores pistiladas con 3 sépalos, 3 pétalos y 6 estaminodios. El fruto es globoso-elipsoide, cubierto por escamas imbricadas de color rojo-naranja a marrón-rojizo, mesocarpo carnoso de color naraja intenso, endocarpo delgado. Eófilo palmado.

Distribución.–
Género con 2 especies, de amplia distribución en la Cuenca Amazónica. En la zona de estudio se registró sólo una especie.

MAURITIA flexuosa L.f.

Nombre local.–

Aguaje; Palmera solitaria, alcanza hasta 25 m de altura. Tallo con 20 - 50 cm diam. Hojas costapalmadas, la lámina está dividida en segmentos de cerca 2 m de largo; ocasionalmente presenta pequeñas espinas en los márgenes; en los individuos jóvenes, las hojas secas persistentes. Inflorescencia de disposición interfoliar, alcanza entre 1 - 2 m de longitud. Frutos oblongo-elipsoides a oblongo-globosos, cubiertos por escamas marrón-rojizas, mesocarpo carnoso, de coloración anaranjada al madurar.

Distribución.–

De amplia distribución en la amazonía, se encuentra en Bolivia, Brasil, Colombia, Ecuador, Guyana, Surinam y Venezuela; en el Perú está registrado para Loreto, Madre de Dios, San Martín y Ucayali.

Hábitat.–

Crece en terrenos inundados y pantanos, donde cubre grandes extensiones que toman el nombre derivado del nombre local: Aguajales.

Usos.–

Las hojas jóvenes son colectadas para fabricar esteras. Los frutos son aprovechados para consumir el mesocarpo carnoso, una vez que éste ha sido suavizado por inmersión en agua caliente (no hervida); también se prepara una bebida conocida como "aguajina". Del interior del tronco se extraen larvas de coleópteros de la Familia Curculionidae *Rhynchophorus* spp., las cuales se comen fritas.

Especímenes examinados.–

F. Chávez 662 (CUZ); C. Vargas 16304 (CUZ); K. Young 49 (NY).

CHAMAEDOREA Willd.

Palmeras dioicas, de tamaño mediano. Tallo solitario o cespitoso, erecto, procumbente o rara vez trepador, color verde con nudos prominentes. Hojas enteras o pinnadas; pinnas en número variable, de forma linear o sigmoide, de disposición regular o irregular, las hojas enteras tienen los márgenes dentados. Inflorescencias interfoliares o infrafoliares, espigadas o ramificadas, solitarias o numerosas por nudo; raquillas pocas a numerosas; flores estaminadas con 3 sépalos, 3 pétalos, 6 estambres y un pequeño pistilodio, flores pistiladas con 3 sépalos, 3 pétalos, estaminodios pequeños o ausentes. Fruto globoso-elipsoide con residuo estigmático basal. Eófilo bífido o pinnado.

Distribución.–

Género con aproximadamente 100 especies, de amplia distribución, abarca desde México hasta Bolivia. En la zona de estudio, se registraron 3 especies.

Clave para especies de Chamaedorea

1. Hojas generalmente enteras .... *C. pauciflora*
1. Hojas pinnadas.
2. Pinnas (5 - 8 por lado), sigmoideas; inflorescencias estaminadas y pistiladas solitarias por nudo .... *C. pinnatifrons*
2. Varias pinnas (10 - 20 por lado), lineares; inflorescencias estaminadas hasta 7 por nudo, pistiladas solitarias por nudo .... *C. angustisecta*

CHAMAEDOREA Angustisecta Burret.

Palmera solitaria; tallo de 1 a 3 m de altura y de 2 a 2.5 cm diam. Hojas 5 - 8, pinnadas; pinnas lineares de disposición regular, extendidas en un mismo plano. Inflorescencias interfoliares, las estaminadas hasta 7 por nudo, ramificadas, las pistiladas solitarias. Frutos elipsoide-falcados, tienen una coloración negra al madurar.

Distribución.–

Se encuentra en Bolivia, Brasil; en el Perú está registrada para Ayacucho, Cusco, Junín, Madre de Dios y Ucayali.

Hábitat.–

Crece en zonas bajas, en bosques de tierra firme e inundables.

Especímenes examinados.–

F. Chávez 703 (CUZ); R. Foster 9655 (USM); P. Núñez 5551 (CUZ).

CHAMAEDOREA Pauciflora Mart.

Sinónimo.–

Chamaedorea integrifolia (Trail) Damm.

Palmera solitaria, alcanza hasta 2 m de altura. Tallo verde tenue, 2 - 4 cm diam. Hojas enteras, bífidas hasta un tercio de la lámina, haz de color verde obscuro, envés con líneas longitudinales de color amarillo. Inflorescencias interfoliares, las raquillas de color naranja intenso, las estaminadas hasta 7 por nudo, las pistiladas solitarias. Frutos elipsoides, de color negro al madurar.

Distribución.–

Se encuentra en Brasil, Colombia y Ecuador; en el Perú está registrada para Huánuco, Loreto, Madre de Dios, San Martín y Ucayali.

Hábitat.–

Crece en bosques de tierra firme, sobre suelos arenosos con buen drenaje.

Especímenes examinados.–

R. Foster et al. 11913 (USM); A. Gentry et al. 124 (NY); A. Gentry & N. Jaramillo 57528 (NY).

CHAMAEDOREA Pinnatifrons (Jacq.) Oerst.

Sinónimo.–
Chamaedorea lanceolata R & P.
Palmera solitaria. Tallo de 1 - 3 m de altura y de 1 -2.5 cm diam., verde tenue, nudoso. Hojas con una marcada línea amarilla en el envés, 4 - 6 pinnas por lado, sigmoides, dispuestas en forma alterna. Inflorescencias infrafoliares, estaminadas y pistiladas solitarias por nudo. Fruto globoso-elipsoide, adquiere una coloración negra al madurar.
Distribución.–
Se encuentra en Brasil, Bolivia, Colombia, Ecuador y Venezuela; en el Perú está registrada para Loreto, Madre de Dios y Ucayali.
Hábitat.–
Crece en tierras bajas, zonas inundables y adyacente a quebradas.
Especímenes examinados.–
C. Díaz & M. Alexiades 3130 (NY) F. Chávez 577 (CUZ, NY); F. Chávez 706 (CUZ); P. Núñez et al. 11409 (CUZ); L. Quiñónez s.n. (CUZ).

WENDLANDIELLA Dammer

Palmeras pequeñas de sotobosque, dioicas. Tallo cespitoso, por lo general reclinado. Hojas enteras o pinnadas. Inflorescencia interfoliar, de ramificación simple o doble, ocasionalmente espigada. Flores estaminadas con 3 sépalos, 3 pétalos, 6 estambres y un pistilodio; flores pistiladas con 3 sépalos, 3 pétalos, 6 estambres, 3 estaminodios. Fruto elipsoide con residuo estigmático basal. Semillas con endosperma homogéneo.
Distribución.–
Género con una sola especie, distribuida en la amazonía peruana y en el extremo oeste de Brasil y el norte de Bolivia.

WENDLANDIELLA simplicifrons Burret.

Palmera solitaria o cespitosa mide entre 0.5 - 1 m de altura. Tallo muy delgado (-1 cm). Hojas entre 4 y 11, con 1 - 2 pinnas por lado. Inflorescencia interfoliar, puede medir entre 2 y 10 cm de longitud. Frutos elipsoides adquieren una coloración naranja a rojiza al madurar.
Distribución.–
Se encuentra en Bolivia y Brasil; para el Perú está registrada para Huánuco, Junín, Loreto, Madre de Dios y Ucayali.
Hábitat.–
Crece en zonas de tierra firme y en lugares cercanos a cursos de agua y quebradas.

Especímenes examinados.–
F. Chávez 711 (CUZ, NY); A. Gentry 43276, 43421 (NY).

IRIARTEA *Ruíz & Pavón*

Palmera alta, robusta, monoica. Tallo solitario, cilíndrico, erecto, ensanchado en la parte alta; el fuste está sostenido por una base sólida de raíces fúlcreas, en forma de cono. Hojas pinnadas; vaina tubular formando un pseudocaule compacto; pinnas numerosas, ápice dentado y divididas en segmentos longitudinales, de disposición regular. Inflorescencia infrafoliar, péndula; bráctea cerrada en forma de cuerno; flores de ambos sexos en una misma inflorescencia, éstas dispuestas en triadas con una flor pistilada central y dos estaminadas laterales. Flor estaminada con 3 sépalos, 3 pétalos, 12 - 15 estambres; flores pistiladas con 3 sépalos, 3 pétalos, 10 - 13 estaminodios. Fruto globoso, amarillo-verdoso al madurar, con residuo estigmático apical o sub apical. Eófilo elíptico con margen dentado.

Distribución.–
Género con 1 especie ampliamente distribuida desde Nicaragua hasta el sur de Bolivia, incluyendo Brasil y Venezuela.

IRIARTEA deltoidea R.& P.

Sinónimo.–
Iriartea ventricosa Mart.
Nombre local.–
Pona; Palmera solitaria, erecta, alcanza hasta 25 m de altura. Tallo recto o a veces con una dilatación en la parte alta, 10 - 30 cm diam., en la parte recta y hasta 70 cm en la dilatación, en la base presenta raíces fúlcreas muy juntas que forman una base sólida en forma de cono de hasta 2 m de altura; las raíces nuevas son de coloración roja obscura a púrpura-obscura y están cubiertas por espinas cortas y romas. Las hojas presentan vainas foliares tubulares formando un pseudocaule, las pinnas deltoideas con margen dentado, cada pinna se encuentra dividida en 10 a 15 segmentos. Inflorescencia infrafoliar, la bráctea cerrada es elongada en forma de cuerno, puede medir hasta 1.20 m de longitud. Frutos globosos, adquieren una coloración amarillo-verdosa al madurar.

Distribución.–
Se encuentra en Nicaragua, Bolivia, Brasil y Venezuela; en el Perú está registrada para Amazonas, Cusco, Loreto, Madre de Dios, Pasco, San Martín y Ucayali.

Hábitat.–
Crece en bosque tropical húmedo, es abundante en la vertiente oriental de los Andes, confinada a áreas adyacentes a ríos y quebradas.

Usos.–
El tronco para "enponados" (entablado) de pisos, paredes, cercos, trochas, graderías; si es de tallo ventricoso, se aprovecha sólo la madera que está por debajo

de la dilatación que es más fuerte y duradera. Un tronco alto y de buen diámetro, después de "batido" (cortado en segmentos longitudinales) alcanza a cubrir una superficie de 9 m² aproximadamente.

Especímenes examinados.–

F. Chávez 647, 641, 681 (CUZ, NY); R. Foster et al. 9671 (USM); A. Gentry 57954 (NY); F. Kahn & J. Llosa 2175 (USM); K. Young 189 (NY).

SOCRATEA *Karst.*

Palmeras de tamaño moderado a alto, monoicas. Tallo solitario, erecto, cilíndrico soportado por raíces fúlcreas prominentes que forman un cono amplio y espaciado. Hojas pinnadas, vaina tubular formando un pseudocaule compacto; pinnas numerosas, dentadas, enteras o divididas en segmentos longitudinales, de disposición regular, extendidos en diferentes planos. Inflorescencia infrafoliar de ramificación simple; flores dispuestas en triadas, una flor pistilada central y dos flores estaminadas laterales. Flor estaminada con 3 sépalos, 3 pétalos y numerosos estambres 17 a 145; flor pistilada con 3 sépalos, 3 pétalos, sin estaminodios. Frutos ovoide-elípticos, de color amarillo-naranja al madurar con residuo estigmático apical. Eófilo bífido, praemorso.

Distribución.–

Género con 5 especies, de amplia distribución, desde Nicaragua hasta Bolivia, por el este desde Venezuela, las Guyanas y Brasil. En la zona de estudio se registraron 2 especies.

Clave para especies de Socratea

1. Base del tallo con raíces fúlcreas espaciadas, hasta 2 m de altura; pinnas divididas en segmentos; inflorescencia con 5 a 15 raquillas .... *S. exorrhiza*
1. Base del tallo con raíces fúlcreas unidas, hasta 1 m de altura; pinnas enteras; inflorescencias con 3 a 8 raquillas .... *S. salazarii*

SOCRATEA exorrhiza (Mart.) Wendl.

Nombre local.–

Cashapona; Palmera solitaria, alcanza hasta 20 m de altura. Tallo 10 - 20 cm diam., presenta raíces fúlcreas formando una base cónica abierta, éstas cubiertas por espinas, raíces nuevas de coloración marrón claro, la corona con alrededor de 7 a 8 hojas, las vainas forman un pseudocaule, pinnas alternas u opuestas, cada pinna se divide en aproximadamente 8 segmentos. Inflorescencia infrafoliar 5 a 15 raquillas, flores de color crema. Fruto ovoides, adquieren una coloración amarilla al madurar.

Distribución.–

Se encuentra desde Nicaragua hasta Bolivia, Brasil, Ecuador, Guyana, Surinam, Venezuela; en el Perú está registrada para Loreto, Madre de Dios y Ucayali.

Hábitat.–

Crece en áreas inundables adyacente a quebradas y ríos, también en bosques de tierra firme.

Usos.–

Las raíces espinosas son utilizadas como ralladores de yuca. El tronco se utiliza para entablar pisos, la madera es de buena calidad y durable.

Especímenes examinados.–

F. Chávez 678 (CUZ); F. Kahn & J. Llosa 2232 (USM).

SOCRATEA salazarii Moore.

Nombre local.–

Pona de altura; Palmera solitaria, mide entre 5 a 15 m de altura. Tallo 4 - 12 cm diam., con raíces fúlcreas que forman un cono más o menos cerrado de hasta 1 m de altura. Hojas 6 - 7, las vainas foliares unidas formando un pseudocaule; pinnas de disposición alterna o sub opuesta, las proximales tienen margen entero y las distales de margen dentado. Inflorescencia infrafoliar, erecta de 20 a 30 cm de longitud. Frutos, ovoide-elipsoides, no se observó frutos maduros.

Distribución.–

Se encuentra en Brasil, para el Perú está registrada para Amazonas, Loreto, Madre de Dios, Pasco, San Martín y Ucayali.

Hábitat.–

Crece en bosques de tierra firme entre los 300 a 700 m y en tierras bajas.

Usos.–

Es muy poco utilizada porque los tallos son delgados, algunas veces el tronco sirve como cerco de gallineros y paredes divisorias de habitaciones pequeñas.

Especímenes examinados.–

F. Chávez 638, 682 (CUZ); A. Gentry et al. 27100 (NY); Núñez et al. 11488 (CUZ, NY).

EUTERPE Mart.

Palmeras de tamaño moderado a alto, monoicas. Tallo solitario o cespitoso, erecto o ligeramente reclinado, ocasionalmente las raíces son visibles y forman un cono denso. Hojas pinnadas, la vaina tubular forma un pseudocaule compacto; pinnas lineares de disposición regular, extendidas en un mismo plano, sean éstas horizontales o péndulas. Inflorescencia infrafoliar, de ramificación simple; flores estaminadas y pistiladas en una misma inflorescencia, dispuestas en triadas. Flor estaminada con 3 sépalos, 3 pétalos, 6 estambres y un pistiloide trífido; flor pistilada con 3 sépalos, 3 pétalos, sin estaminodios. Frutos globoso-elipsoides, residuo estigmático sub apical o lateral. Eófilo bífido o pinnado.

Distribución.–

Género con 6 especies de amplia distribución en América Central, las Antillas y América del Sur. En la zona de estudio se registró sólo una especie.

EUTERPE precatoria Mart.

Nombre local.–

Huasaí; Palmera solitaria, erecta, 5 - 15 m de altura. Tallo 5 - 20 cm diam, con raíces epígeas formando una masa densa, entre 30 - 50 cm de alto; las raíces jóvenes de coloración rosada-rojiza. Hojas entre 8 -15; vaina foliar tubular, formando un pseudocaule de color verde intenso y con matiz amarillo, pinnas de disposición regular, extendidas en un mismo plano, lanceoladas, péndulas. Inflorescencia infrafoliar, las raquillas dispuestas sólo en la superficie inferior del raquis. Frutos globosos, de coloración morado-oscuro a negro al madurar.

Distribución.–

Se encuentra en América Central, Bolivia, Brasil, Colombia, Ecuador, Las Guyanas, Trinidad y Venezuela, en el Perú está registrada para Cusco, Huánuco, Loreto, Madre de Dios, Pasco, San Martín y Ucayali.

Hábitat.–

Crece en diversas áreas, preferentemente en zonas húmedas adyacente a quebradas y ríos.

Usos.–

El tronco es utilizado para sacar postes y "ripas" (piezas planas) para cubrir paredes exteriores, paredes divisorias y cercos, también para fabricar arcos y flechas. El "cogollo" (meristemo apical) es comestible usualmente en forma de ensaladas crudas o ligeramente cocidas "palmito". Los frutos son comestibles después de hervidos o se prepara una bebida refrescante; también de ellos se extrae un aceite para tonificar y fortalecer las raíces capilares.

Especímenes examinados.–

F. Chávez 675 (CUZ); R. Foster 9733 (NY).

OENOCARPUS Mart.

Palmeras de tamaño moderado a alto, monoicas. Tallo solitario o cespitoso, erecto o ligeramente reclinado. Hojas pinnadas, rara vez enteras; vainas parcial-mente abiertas formando un falso pseudocaule, márgenes fibrosos; pinnas lineares de disposición regular o agrupada, extendidas en uno o varios planos, envés blanco-plateado. Inflorescencia interfoliar, hipuriforme (en forma de cola de caballo), rara vez espigada, con flores de ambos sexos. Flor estaminada con 3 sépalos, 3 pétalos, 6 - 19 estambes y 1 pistilodio; flor pistilada con 3 sépalos, 3 pétalos, sin estaminodio. Fruto subgloboso, oblongo u ovovoide, con residuo estigmático apical. Eófilo entero, bífido o pinnado.

Distribución.–

Género con 9 especies, de amplia distribución, desde Costa Rica y Panamá hasta la región amazónica. En la zona de estudio se registraron 3 especies.

Nota.—Se incluye el género *Jessenia* como sinónimo, de acuerdo al tratamiento de Wessels Boer (1988).

Clave para especies de Oenocarpus

1. Tallo 7-20 m de altura, 15-30 cm diam., solitario; semillas con endosperma ruminado .... *O. bataua*
1. Tallo 5-13 m de altura, 4-15 cm diam, solitario o cespitoso; semilla con endosperma homogéneo.
2. Tallo solitario o cespitoso; pinnas de disposición más o menos regular y extendidas en un mismo plano .... *O. mapora*
2. Tallo solitario; pinnas de disposición irregular formando grupos, extendidas en varios planos .... *O. balickii*

OENOCARPUS balickii Kahn.

Palmera solitaria, 7 - 14 m de altura. Tallo 6 - 12 cm diam. Hojas 8 - 10; vaina cerrada formando un pseudocaule, cubierta por tomento marrón-rojizo; pinnas lineares dispuestas en grupos separados de 2 - 5, extendidas en diferentes planos. Inflorescencia infrafoliar, cubierta por tomento marrón-rojizo en la superficie inferior. Fruto globoso-elipsoide, morado obscuro al madurar.

Distribución.–

Se encuentra en Brasil, Colombia, Surinam y Venezuela; en el Perú está registrada para Loreto y Madre de Dios.

Hábitat.–

Crece en zonas de baja elevación, sobre bosques de tierra firme.

Especímenes examinados.–

F. Chávez (registro fotográfico); F. Kahn 2368 (USM).

OENOCARPUS bataua Mart.

Sinónimo.–

Jessenia bataua (Mart.) Burret

Nombre local.–

Ungurahui; Palmera solitaria, 7 - 20 m de altura. Tallo 15 - 30 cm diam, usualmente con raíces visibles hasta una altura de 1 m. Hojas erectas; pinnas de disposición regular y extendidas en un mismo plano, envés de coloración grisplateada. Inflorescencia infrafoliar. Frutos elipsoides 3 - 4 cm de largo, 2 - 2.5 cm diam, de coloración morado-obscura a negra al madurar; endosperma ruminado.

Distribución.–

Es de amplia distribución, desde el este de Panamá, hasta Bolivia, Brasil, las Guyanas, Trinidad y Venezuela; en el Perú está registrada para Loreto, Madre de Dios, San Martín y Ucayali.

Hábitat.–

Crece en áreas inundadas a lo largo de quebradas, en bosques de tierras bajas y a veces en bosques de tierra firme.

Usos.–

Los frutos son comestibles una vez hervidos, también de ellos se prepara una bebida refrescante conocida como "ungurahuina", y se extrae un aceite medicinal, que es utilizado para fortalecer las raíces del cabello y como fricciones para aliviar dolores musculares..

Especímenes examinados.–

F. Chávez 639, 680 (CUZ).

OENOCARPUS mapora Karst.

Nombre local.–

Sinami; Palmera cespitosa, ocasionalmente solitaria, 5 - 13 m de altura. Tallo 4 - 15 cm diam, con numerosas raíces epígeas. Hojas 5 - 10; pinnas lineares en disposición regular, más o menos extendidas en un mismo plano. Inflorescencia infrafoliar; raquillas cubiertas por tomento marrón-rojizo. Frutos globoso-elipsoides de coloración morado-obscura a negra al madurar.

Distribución.–

Se encuentra en Costa Rica, Bolivia, Brasil, Colombia y Ecuador; en el Perú está registrada para Loreto, Madre de Dios y San Martín.

Hábitat.–

Crece en bosques de tierras bajas, de tierra firme y terrenos inundables.

Usos.–

De los frutos se prepara una bebida refrescante.

Especímenes examinados.–

F. Chávez 673, 674 (CUZ); R. Foster et al. 9725 (NY); A. Gentry 57519 (NY); F. Kahn & Llosa 2130 (USM); P. Núñez 10673 (NY); P. Núñez 11408 (CUZ).

HYOSPATHE Mart.

Palmeras monoicas, de tamaño pequeño a mediano. Tallo solitario o cespitoso, erecto. Hojas pinnadas, ocasionalmente enteras; vainas tubulares formando un pseudocaule; pinnas de disposición regular o irregular, extendidas en un mismo plano. Inflorescencias infrafoliares, flores en triadas. Flor estaminada pedicelada, con 3 sépalos, 3 pétalos, 6 estambres y 1 pistilodio; flor pistilada sésil, con 3 sépalos, 3 pétalos y 6 estaminodios. Frutos elipsoides, con resíduo estigmático basal. Eófilo bífido.

Distribución.–
Género con 2 especies, distribuidas desde Costa Rica hasta el sur de Bolivia. En la zona de estudio se registró sólo una especie.

HYOSPATHE elegans Mart.

Nombre local.–
Palmiche; Palmera solitaria o cespitosa. Tallo 1 - 3 m de altura, 1 - 2.5 cm diam. Hojas 5 - 10, con vaina tubular formando un pseudocaule; lámina entera o pinnada; pinnas regulares extendidas en un mismo plano. Inflorescencia infrafoliar; raquillas numerosas. Frutos elipsoide-ovoides, de coloración negra al madurar.

Distribución.–
Se encuentra en Costa Rica, Bolivia, Brasil, Colombia, Ecuador y Venezuela; en el Perú está registrado para Huánuco, Junín, Loreto, Madre de Dios y Pasco.

Hábitat.–
Crece en bosques de baja elevación, sobre zonas inundables, ocasionalmente sobre tierra firme.

Especímenes examinados.–
F. Chávez 600, 644 (CUZ); R. Foster 3255 (NY).

ATTALEA Kunth

Palmeras pequeñas a grandes, monoicas. Tallo solitario o raramente cespitoso, aéreo o subterráneo. Hojas pinnadas; pinnas lineares, de disposición regular o agrupada, extendidas en uno o varios planos. Inflorescencia interfoliar, flores pistiladas y flores estaminadas en inflorescencias separadas o en una misma inflorescencia, estas modalidades se encuentran en un mismo individuo; bráctea peduncular leñosa, profundamente surcada en la superficie externa; flores dispuestas en triadas. Flor estaminada con 3 - 4 sépalos, 1 - 5 pétalos, 6 - 75 estambres y un pequeño pistilodio; flor pistilada con 3 sépalos, 3 pétalos y un anillo estaminodial. Frutos globosos, ovoides u oblongo-elipsoides, con residuo estigmático apical, endocarpo grueso y leñoso, con o sin fibras. Eófilo entero.

Distribución.–
Género con 27 especies, ampliamente distribuidas desde América Central hasta América del Sur, incluyendo Trinidad. Para la zona de estudio se han registrado 3 especies, una de las cuales no se ha podido identificar ya que fue recolectada en etapa juvenil.

*Nota.—*Se incluye los géneros *Scheelea* y *Maximiliana* como sinónimos, de acuerdo al tratamiento de Wessels Boer (1988).

Clave para especies de Attalea

1. Frutos 7 - 11 cm de largo, 3 - 5 cm diam; endocarpo con fibras agrupadas
.... *A. phalerata*
1. Frutos 12.5 - 13 cm de largo, 6.5 - 7 cm diam; endocarpo con fibras dispersas
.... *A. tessmannii*

ATTALEA phalerata Mart.

Sinónimo.–
Scheelea phalerata (Mart. ex Spreng.)Burret *Scheelea cephalotes* (Poepp. ex Mart.)Karsten
Nombre local.–
Shapaja; Palmera solitaria. Tallo erecto, procumbente o subterráneo, entre 2 - 8 m de altura, 25 - 40 cm diam, a menudo cubierto por vainas foliares persistentes. Hojas 10 -18; pinnas lineares en disposición irregular en grupos de 2 - 5, extendidas en diferentes planos. Inflorescencia interfoliar, bractea profundamente surcada en la superficie externa. Frutos oblongo-elipsoides, de coloración marrón-claro; semillas 2 - 3.
Distribución.–
Se encuentra en Bolivia, Brasil y Paraguay; en el Perú está registrada para Loreto, Madre de Dios y Ucayali.
Hábitat.–
Crece en regiones secas de baja elevación, áreas abiertas y bosques intensamente disturbados.
Usos.–
Las hojas son utilizadas para techar a pesar de que no son de buena calidad porque al secar tienden a arrugarse. También son utilizadas para la fabricación de cumbreras "cumbas". El fruto contiene un mesocarpo comestible.
Especímenes examinados.–
F. Chávez 679 (CUZ); A. Henderson & F. Chávez 1643 (CUZ, NY, USM); F. Kahn & J. Llosa 2148 (NY); O. Phillips & F. Chávez 632 (CUZ).

ATTALEA tessmannii Burret

Palmera alta, solitaria, 8 - 20 m de altura, 30 - 40 cm diam. Hojas 10 - 12; pinnas lineares, dispuestas en grupos de 3 - 6, extendidas en varios planos. Inflorescencias interfoliares; bráctea peduncular leñosa, profundamente surcada en la superficie externa; flores estaminadas y flores pistiladas en inflorescencias separadas. Frutos oblongo-elipsoides, de color marrón-tenue; endocarpo grueso y leñoso, con fibras dispersas.

Distribución.–
Se encuentra en el extremo occidental de la Cuenca Amazónica, Brasil; en el Perú está registrada para Loreto, Madre de Dios y Ucayali.

Hábitat.–
Crece en bosques de tierra firme y en zonas de baja elevación, es una especie poco común en la parte sur.

Especímenes examinados.–
R. Foster 11554 (USM); P. Núñez 14976 (CUZ).

ATTALEA sp.

Se colectó un ejemplar juvenil de 1.5 m de altura. Hojas 6, de 2 m de largo, dispuestas en forma espiralada; las pinnas lineares de 30 - 50 cm de largo, dispuestas irregularmente en grupos de 3 a 5 y extendidas en diferentes planos, la pinna apical dividida en la parte basal y unidas en el extremo distal, dejando aberturas a manera de ventanas.

Hábitat.–
Crece en bosques estacionalmente inundables, de suelo limoso.

Nota.—A juzgar por las características, es probable que se trate de un juvenil de *A. insignis* o *A. maripa.*

Espécimen examinado.–
F. Chávez 642 (CUZ).

AIPHANES Willd.

Palmeras de tamaño pequeño a moderado, monoica. Tallo solitario o cespitoso, espinoso, aéreo, erecto o subterráneo, algunas veces procumbente. Hojas pinnadas, rara vez enteras; pinnas lanceoladas a subtriangulares, el extremo distal ensanchado, dentado a praemorso, de disposición regular o irregular. Inflorescencia interfoliar, de ramificación simple, ocasionalmente espigada; flores dispuestas en triadas con una flor pistilada central y dos estaminadas laterales en la base de la raquilla, con sólo flores estaminadas en la parte apical. Flor estaminada con 3 sépalos, 3 pétalos, 6 estambres y un pequeño pistilodio; flor pistilada con 3 sépalos, 3 pétalos y un anillo estaminodial dentado. Frutos globosos con residuo estigmático apical, epicarpo usualmente liso, algunas veces espinoso. Eófilo bífido.

Distribución.–
Género con 22 especies, distribuidas en Panamá, Bolivia, Brasil, Colombia, Ecuador, Perú y Venezuela. En la zona de estudio se registró sólo una especie.

AIPHANES acualeata Willd.

Sinónimo.–
Aiphanes ernestii Burret
Nombre local.–
Shija-Shija; Palmera solitaria, 2 - 5 m de altura. Tallo 4 - 10 cm diam, espinoso. Hojas 6 - 15, pinnadas; pinnas ligeramente triangulares con el ápice praemorso, dispuestas en grupos de 2 a 5, extendidas en diferentes planos, con espinas en el envés. Inflorescencia interfoliar; bráctea peduncular persistente. Frutos globosos de color rojo-naranja al madurar.
Distribución.–
Se encuentra en Bolivia, Brasil, Colombia, Trinidad y Venezuela; en el Perú está registrada para Cusco, Huánuco y Madre de Dios.
Hábitat.–
Crece en zonas no inundables y en bosques de tierra firme.
Usos.–
Frutos comestibles.
Especímenes examinados.–
F. Chávez 713 (CUZ), R. Foster 9579 (USM); C. Vargas 17375, 18694 (CUZ).

BACTRIS Jacq. ex Scop.

Palmeras espinosas, monoicas, pequeñas a grandes. Tallo solitario o cespitoso. Hojas pinnadas o enteras con venación pinnada; pinnas regulares o irregulares, extendidas en un mismo o en varios planos. Inflorescencias usualmente interfoliares; flores generalmente dispuestas en triadas o pueden estar pareadas, a veces las flores estaminadas solitarias. Flor estaminada con 3 - 4 sépalos, 3 - 4 pétalos, 3 - 12 estambres y 1 pistilodio pequeño o ausente; flor pistilada en ocasiones posee estaminodios pequeños, formando un anillo estaminodial. Frutos globosos a globoso-comprimidos, ovoides a ovoide-comprimidos o elipsoides, con residuo estigmático apical. Eófilo bífido.
Distribución.–
Género con aproximadamente 60 especies, distribuidas a través del neotrópico. En la zona de estudio se registraron 5 especies, una de las cuales no ha sido identificada.

Clave para especies de Bactris

1. Palmas poco espinosas; espinas pequeñas y planas cubriendo moderadamente las superficies foliares.
2. Espinas casi ausentes, restringidas a los ápices de las hojas; inflorescencias con 1 - 5 raquillas .... *B. simplicifrons*

2. Espinas en los márgenes de las hojas; inflorescencia con raquilla simple
.... *B. sphaerocarpa*
1. Palmas muy espinosas; espinas grandes planas o cilíndricas, cubriendo profusamente el envés de las láminas foliares, las inflorescencias y los nudos del tallo.
3. Pinnas lineares, de disposición regular, extendidas en un mismo plano; inflorescencia con 1 - 3 raquillas .... *B. concinna*
3. Pinnas linear-sigmoides o sigmoides, de disposición regular o agrupada, extendidas en un mismo o varios planos.
4. Pinnas sigmoides de disposición regular, extendidas en un mismo plano, espinas planas; inflorescencia con 8 - 18 raquillas ....*B. monticola*
4. Pinnas linear-sigmoides, dispuestas en grupos de 3 - 4, extendidas en varios planos, espinas cilíndricas; inflorescencia con 1 - 2 raquillas .... *Bactris* sp.

BACTRIS concinna Mart.

Nombre local.–
Ñeja, Ñejilla; Palmera cespitosa, 2 - 5 m de altura, con 3 - 20 tallos, 1 - 4 cm diam, con espinas en los entrenudos. Hojas 3 - 10, pinnas lineares de disposición regular y extendidas en un mismo plano. Inflorescencia interfoliar con 1 - 2 raquillas. Frutos muy juntos, de color morado obscuro al madurar.

Distribución.–
Se encuentra en Bolivia, Brasil, Colombia y Ecuador; en el Perú está registrada para Loreto, Madre de Dios y Ucayali.

Hábitat.–
Crece en lugares de baja elevación, en áreas inundables, adyacente a quebradas y ríos, ocupando grandes extensiones.

Usos.–
Frutos comestibles.

Especímenes examinados.–
M. Alexiades 66 (NY); F. Chávez, 632, 707, 712 (CUZ); A. Henderson & F. Chávez 1630 (CUZ, NY); Núñez et al. 9832, 9974 (NY); M. Timaná 1334 (NY).

BACTRIS monticola Barb. Rodr.

Sinónimo.–
Bactris actioneura Drude & Trail
Palmera cespitosa, 2 - 5 m de altura, con 3 - 15 tallos de 2 - 4 cm diam, con espinas negras y planas en los entrenudos. Hojas 3 - 10, con abundantes espinas planas de color amarillo a lo largo la vaina, peciolo y raquis; pinnas sigmoides de disposición irregular, o extendidas en un mismo plano. Inflorescencia interfoliar, raquilla 8 - 17; bráctea peduncular cubierta por espinas planas. Frutos obovoides, morado-obscuros al madurar, cubiertos por diminutas espinas.

Distribución.–
Se encuentra en Bolivia, Brasil, Colombia, las Guyanas y Panamá; en el Perú está registrado para Amazonas, Loreto, Madre de Dios y Ucayali.

Hábitat.–

Crece en zonas bajas, en bosques de tierra firme, o a veces en zonas inundables.

Especímenes examinados.–

F. Chávez 617, 684 (CUZ, NY); F. Chávez 708, 714, 715, 716 (CUZ); K. Young 126 (NY).

BACTRIS simplicifrons Mart.

Palmera cespitosa, alcanza hasta 2 m de altura. Hojas 5 - 9; vaina y peciolo cubiertos por pequeñas espinas planas; pinnas lineares, linear-lanceoladas a sigmoides, 2 - 5 por lado, de disposición irregular, márgenes glabros, el haz ocasionalmente pubescente, el ápice con numerosas espinas. Inflorescencia infrafoliar, con 1 - 5 raquillas péndulas. Frutos globosos, glabros, de color rojo-naranja al madurar.

Distribución.–

Se encuentra en Bolivia, Brasil, Colombia, Ecuador, las Guyanas y Venezuela; en el Perú está registrada para Cusco, Loreto, Madre de Dios y San Martín.

Hábitat.–

Crece en zonas abiertas, en bosques de tierra firme.

Especímenes examinados.–

Foster et al. 11764 (NY); A. Henderson & F. Chávez 1639 (CUZ, NY).

BACTRIS sphaerocarpa Trail

Palmera cespitosa, 0.3 - 3 m de altura. Tallo 0.8 - 1.6 cm diam; con espinas en los entrenudos. Hojas 9 - 10; vaina, peciolo y raquis cubiertos por tomento marrón y algunas espinas planas de color amarillo o negro; pinnas sigmoides de disposición irregular, extendidas en varios planos, los ápices presentan pocas espinas. Inflorescencia interfoliar; raquilla simple; cáliz y corola tubulares. Frutos obovoides, mesocarpo jugoso, de color morado-obscuro al madurar, con residuo estigmático apical.

Distribución.–

Se encuentra en Brasil y Colombia; en el Perú está registrado para Loreto y Madre de Dios.

Hábitat.–

Crece en zonas bajas, en bosques de tierra firme.

Espécimen examinado.–

F. Chávez 694 (CUZ).

BACTRIS sp.

Palmera cespitosa, 0.5 - 2 m de altura, con 7 tallos de 2 cm diam, con abundantes espinas cilíndricas de color crema. Hojas 3 - 10; vaina, peciolo y raquis cubiertos por abundantes espinas de color amarillo-crema, pinnas linear-sigmoides de disposición irregular en grupos de 3 - 4, extendidas en varios planos. Inflorescencia interfoliar con 2 raquillas. No se observaron flores ni frutos.

Hábitat.–
Crece en zonas bajas, en bosques de tierra firme adyacente a quebradas y ríos.

*Nota.—*A juzgar por las características de la inflorescencia, es probable que se trate de una especie relacionada a *B. concinna*.

Espécimen examinado.–
F. Chávez 704 (CUZ, NY).

DESMONCUS Mart.

Palmeras pequeñas a grandes, monoicas. Tallo elongado, delgado, trepador, usualmente espinoso. Hojas pinnadas, dispuestas a lo largo del tallo; vainas tubulares; pinnas de disposición regular y extendidas en un mismo plano; las pinnas distales modificadas en garfios rectos o curvos. Inflorescencia interfoliar, flores dispuestas en triadas, una flor pistilada central y dos flores estaminadas laterales, hacia el ápice de la raquilla sólo hay flores estaminadas. Flor estaminada con 3 sépalos, 3 pétalos, 6 - 9 estambres y 1 pistilodio; flor pistilada con cáliz anular, corola anular tridentada y 6 estaminodios. Frutos globoso-elipsoides, ovoide u obovoide, con residuo estigmático apical.

Distribución.–
Género con aproximadamente 10 especies, ampliamente distribuido desde México hasta Brasil y Bolivia. En la zona de estudio se registró una sola especie.

DESMONCUS polyacanthos Mart.

Palmera trepadora, alcanza entre 2 - 15 m de largo. Tallos 3 - 5, con 1 - 2 cm diam. Hojas numerosas dispuestas a lo largo del tallo, raquis cubierto por espinas recurvadas; pinnas elíptico-lanceoladas, de disposición regular, extendidas en un mismo plano, las pinnas distales están modificadas en garfios rectos. Inflorescencia interfoliar; bráctea peduncular espinosa. Frutos sub globosos o elipsoides, de color rojo-naranja al madurar.

Distribución.–
Se encuentra en Brasil, Colombia, Ecuador, las Guyanas y Venezuela; en el Perú está registrada para Loreto y Madre de Dios.

Hábitat.–
Crece en zonas bajas, lugares abiertos adyacente a cursos de agua, quebradas y ríos.

Especímenes examinados.–
F. Chávez 626 (CUZ,NY); F. Chávez 683 (NY); A. Henderson & F. Chávez 1642 (CUZ, NY); P. Núñez 5534 (CUZ); P. Núñez 10015 (NY); A.C Smith 1392 (US).

ASTROCARYUM Meyer

Palmeras de tamaño moderado a grande, monoicas. Tallo solitario o cespitoso, corto, subterráneo o aéreo. Hojas pinnadas; vaina, peciolo y lámina cubiertas por espinas; pinnas lineares de disposición irregular en grupos, extendidas en varios planos, o de disposición regular, extendidas en un mismo plano; envés de un color blanco-grisáceo a plateado. Inflorescencia interfoliar. Flor estaminada con 3 sépalos, 3 pétalos, 3 - 12 estambres y un pequeño pistilodio; flor pistilada con cáliz y corola tubulares, estaminodios ausentes o presentes formando un anillo. Frutos globosos u obovoides, con residuo estigmático apical. Eófilo bífido.

Distribución.–
Género con aproximadamente 47 especies de amplia distribución, desde México, hasta Bolivia y Brasil. En la zona de estudio se registró una sola especie.

ASTROCARYUM chonta Mart.

Nombre local.–
Huicungo; Palmera solitaria de 3 a 10 m de altura. Tallo subterráneo o aéreo, 10 a 25 cm diam, recubierto por vainas foliares espinosas persistentes en su estado juvenil, cicatrices foliares bien marcadas. Hojas 6 - 15; vaina, peciolo y raquis cubiertos por espinas marrón oscuro; pinnas lineares con margen espinoso, de disposición regular y extendidas en un mismo plano, envés plateado. Inflorescencia interfoliar; flores estaminadas distribuidas a lo largo de las raquillas, las flores pistiladas sésiles en la base de la raquilla. Frutos ovoide-oblongos cubiertos densamente por espinas negras, mesocarpo fibroso, de color anaranjado al madurar.

Distribución.–
Se encuentra en la región sur de la Cuenca Amazónica, Bolivia y Brasil; en el Perú está registrada para Loreto, Madre de Dios y Ucayali.

Hábitat.–
Crece en terrenos inundables, ribera de ríos y quebradas.

Usos.–
El tronco es utilizado como poste en la construcción de casas porque es duro, fuerte y resistente al ataque de termitas.

Nota.—Esta especie fue identificada anteriormente como A. *macrocalyx* y A. *murumuru*, especies con las que está relacionada, y con las cuales se confunde. F. Kahn y B. Millan (1992) hicieron un tratamiento completo de este género.

Especímenes examinados.–
F. Chávez 627, 676 (CUZ); A. Gentry 26925 (USM).

GEONOMA Willd.

Palmeras monoicas, de tamaño pequeño a mediano. Tallo solitario o cespitoso. Hojas pinnadas u ocasionalmente enteras; pinnas de disposición regular o irregular, extendidas en un mismo plano. Inflorescencia interfoliar o infrafoliar; con raquillas simples, espigadas o ramificadas; flores dispuestas en triadas. Flor estaminada con 3 sépalos, 3 pétalos, éstos parcialmente unidos, 3 - 6 estambres y un pistilodio; flor pistilada con 3 sépalos libres, 3 pétalos parcialmente unidos y un tubo estaminodial crenado o ligeramente lobulado. Frutos globosos a elipsoides, con residuo estigmático basal. Eófilo bífido.

Distribución.—

Género con aproximadamente 80 especies, distribuidas en todo el neotrópico desde México hasta Bolivia, incluyendo las Antillas. Para la zona de estudio se han registrado 4 especies, una de las cuales aún no ha sido identificada.

Clave para especies de Geonoma

1. Tallo solitario, subterráneo pocas veces aéreo; raquilla simple.
2. Hendiduras que portan las flores dispuestas sobre líneas espiraladas muy unidas .... *G. acaulis*
2. Hendiduras que portan las flores dispuestas sobre líneas espiraladas separadas .... *G. brongniartii*
1. Tallo solitario o cespitoso, subterráneo o aéreo; raquilla con doble ramificación.
3. Tallo 1 - 2.5 m de altura y 0.5 - 2.5 cm diam; pinnas apicales alargadas, delgadas, de color verde obscuro .... *G. deversa*
3. Tallo hasta 1 - 3 m de altura y 1.5 - 3 cm diam; pinnas apicales más anchas que largas, de color verde tenue, lustroso .... *Geonoma* sp.

GEONOMA acaulis Mart.

Palmera pequeña. Tallo solitario, aéreo o subterráneo. Hojas 4 - 10, enteras o pinnadas; pinnas 3 - 10 por lado, sigmoideas. Inflorescencia interfoliar, la raquilla simple, con las hendiduras que portan a las flores muy juntas. Frutos globosos de color negro al madurar.

Distribución.—

Se encuentra en Bolivia, Brasil, Colombia, Ecuador y Venezuela; en el Perú está registrada para Loreto, Madre de Dios, Pasco y San Martín.

Hábitat.—

Crece en zonas bajas, en bosques de tierra firme y sobre suelos inundables.

Especímenes examinados.—

F. Chávez 652, 692, 756, 757 (CUZ); F. Chávez 688, 689, 695, 696, 698, 699, 710 (CUZ, NY); A. Gentry 43418 (NY); Quiñones s.n (CUZ).

GEONOMA brongniartii Mart.

Palmera pequeña, solitaria o cespitosa. Tallo aéreo o subterráneo, que alcanza hasta 1 m de altura y 2 cm diam. Hojas 7 - 8; pinnas regulares. Inflorescencia interfoliar, la raquilla simple con las hendiduras que alojan a las flores dispuestas en forma espiralada y espaciada. Frutos globoso-elipsoides, de color negro al madurar.

Distribución.–

Se encuentra en Bolivia, Brasil y Ecuador; en el Perú está registrada para Ayacucho, Junín, Loreto, Madre de Dios, Pasco, San Martín y Ucayali.

Hábitat.–

Crece en un amplio rango de hábitats, tanto en zonas inundables como en tierra firme.

Especímenes examinados.–

F. Chávez 705 (CUZ); F. Chávez 718, 745 (NY); A. Gentry & N. Jaramillo 57498 , 57500 (NY); Núñez 10590 (NY).

GEONOMA deversa (Poit.) Kunth

Nombre local.–

Palmiche; Palmera de sotobosque, cespitosa, crece hasta 2.5 m de altura. Tallo 0.5 - 2.5 cm diam. Hojas 5 - 17, lámina entera o pinnada; pinnas sigmoides. Inflorescencia infrafoliar, con ramificación simple o doble, hendiduras que alojan a las flores, dispuestas en filas espaciadas. Frutos globosos, morado-obscuros al madurar.

Distribución.–

Se encuentra en Costa Rica, Panamá, Bolivia, Brasil, Colombia, Ecuador, las Guyanas y Venezuela; en el Perú está registrada para Loreto, Madre de Dios y Junín.

Hábitat.–

Crece en zonas bajas, en bosques de tierra firme, adyacente a quebradas o áreas estacionalmente inundables.

Usos.–

Utilizada para techar. Para la fabricación de cada unidad llamada "paño de crisneja" se utilizan las hojas, las que son tejidas por la parte de los peciolos, utilizando como soporte horizontal una varilla recta de 3 m de largo, la cual se obtiene del raquis foliar de algunas palmeras arbóreas como *Oenocarpus bataua*, *Attalea maripa* o tallos de la Gramínea *Gynerium sagittatum* (Aubl.) Beauv. "cañabrava". Un paño tejido convencional mide 3 m de largo y 0.60 cm de ancho (longitud de la lámina foliar) y para su fabricación se requieren alrededor de 430 - 450 hojas.

Especímenes examinados.–

F. Chávez 643 (CUZ, NY); F. Chávez 693 (NY); V. Funk 8106, 8150 (US); A. Gentry & J. Revilla 1627 (NY); A. Henderson & F. Chávez 1632 (CUZ, NY); F. Kahn & J. Llosa 2116 (USM), F. Kahn & J. Llosa 2119 (NY); P. Núñez et.al. 9839 (NY); A.C. Smith 1318 (US).

GEONOMA sp.

Palmera cespitosa, 0.5 - 3 m de altura. Tallo 1 - 3 cm diam. Hojas 5 - 18, pinnadas o rara vez enteras; pinnas sigmoides, la pinna apical ensanchada. Inflorescencia infrafoliar, de ramificación doble, 10 - 30 cm de longitud, 10 - 25 raquillas. Frutos globosos, morado obscuro al madurar.

Hábitat.–
Crece en zonas bajas, sobre bosques de tierra firme, en suelos arcillosos de buen drenaje.

Nota.—Forma extensos manchales junto a *Geonoma deversa*, especie a la que posiblemente está relacionada.

Espécimen examinado.–
F. Chávez 685 (CUZ).

PHYTELEPHAS *Ruíz & Pavón*

Palmeras de tamaño moderado, dioicas. Tallo solitario o cespitoso, corto subterráneo o aéreo, procumbente o erecto. Hojas pinnadas, la vaina con abundante fibra marrón obscura; pinnas lineares de disposición regular y extendidas en un mismo plano. Inflorescencia con flores sésiles o pediceladas con perianto reducido, estambres 150 - 700. Inflorescencia pistilada al nivel del suelo, 4 - 10 flores por inflorescencia, tépalos 5, con numerosos estaminodios. Frutos de forma variada, epicarpo verrucoso, leñoso. Eófilo pinnado.

Distribución.–
Género con 5 especies, distribuidas desde Centro América hasta el sur de Bolivia. En la zona de estudio se registró sólo una especie.

PHYTELEPHAS macrocarpa R. & P.

Nombre local.–
Yarina.; Palmera solitaria o cespitosa. Tallo erecto, decumbente o subterráneo, alcanza hasta 4 m de altura y 8 - 12 cm diam. Hojas 10 - 30, erectas o semierectas; vaina cubierta con abundantes fibras marrón-obscuras, pinnas de disposición regular y extendidas en un mismo plano. Inflorescencia interfoliar; pedúnculo estaminado entre 25 -100 cm de largo, cubierto por grupos de flores; pedúnculo pistilado entre 15 - 30 cm de largo. Frutos cubiertos por verrugas piramidales. Semillas 4 - 5, con endosperma homogéneo.

Distribución.–
Se encuentra en Bolivia, Brasil y Colombia; en el Perú está registrada para Loreto, Madre de Dios, San Martín y Ucayali.

Hábitat.–
Crece en tierras bajas, sobre suelos estacionalmente o permanentemente inundados, cubre grandes extensiones.

Usos.–

Las hojas se utilizan para techar. Los frutos inmaduros, conocidos como "choclo", son comestibles; el endosperma líquido o "leche" es una bebida común, el cual adquiere una consistencia gelatinosa al ser cocido.

Espécimenes examinados.–

F. Chávez 672 (CUZ); O. Phillips & P. Núñez 156 (CUZ); A.C. Smith 2017 (USM).

RESULTADOS Y CONCLUSIONES

1.– La familia Arecaceae en Pakitza está representada por 26 especies en 16 géneros y Cocha Cashu por 25 especies en los mismos géneros (Tabla 1), 3 especies están identificadas hasta la categoría genérica por lo que se requiere mayor observación para una identificación acertada.

2.– La mayoría de las especies reportadas son de amplia distribución en el neotrópico; algunas pocas son de distribución más restringida, tal es el caso de *Chamaedorea angustisecta*, *Socratea salazarii*, *Oenocarpus balickii*, *Attalea tessmanni*, *Wendlandiella gracilis*.

3.– Las especies *Chelyocarpus ulei*, *Oenocarpus balickii*, *Bactris simplicifrons* y *Bactris sphaerocarpa* constituyen nuevos registros de distribución geográfica.

4.– A pesar de la proximidad de las dos zonas de estudio, ambas presentan hábitats exclusivos, la mayoría de las especies son comunes para ambas zonas, con algunas excepciones tales como *Chelyocarpus ulei*, *Chamaedorea pauciflora*, *Oenocarpus balickii*, *Attalea tessmanni*, *Bactris simplicifrons*, *Bactris sphaerocarpa*. Aunque esto no indica que no estén presentes en ambas zonas, es sólo una muestra más de la necesidad de intensificar las colecciones, en otros tipos de hábitats y en diferentes estaciones.

5.– Algunas especies crecen en un amplio rango de hábitats, desde bosques ribereños, hasta bosques de tierra firme, este es el caso de *Iriartea deltoidea*, *Euterpe precatoria* y *Astrocaryum chonta*, las cuales se colocan a veces entre las especies dominantes del bosque.

6.– Otras especies responden a patrones de distribución definidos, *Mauritia flexuosa*, *Chamaedorea pinnatifrons*, *Wendlandiella simplicifrons*, *Attalea phalerata*, *Phytelephas macrocarpa*, generalmente restringidos a bosques en zonas bajas y de relieve plano, estacional o permanentemente inundados.

7.– Las especies de sotobosque se encuentran agrupadas en cinco géneros, y su diversidad morfológica es muy amplia. Por ejemplo *Geonoma acaulis* tiene por lo menos cinco formas diferentes de hoja, variando en la longitud del peciolo, número de pinnas, tamaño del pedúnculo floral, tamaño de la raquilla; caracteres que difieren incluso entre individuos que ocupan el mismo área. En *Bactris concinna*, se pudo observar tres formas diferentes, con pinnas que varían en tamaño, forma (lanceoladas a sigmoides) y disposición (regular, irregular o agrupada); las raquillas de la inflorescencia con tamaño variable (4 - 12 cm de largo) y número (1 - 3) por inflorescencia.

8.- En términos generales, la diversidad de la flora de palmeras en esta parte de la amazonía es pobre si se toma como punto de comparación la diversidad registrada en otras zonas, por ejemplo F. Kahn (1992) registró 29 especies en 16 géneros en un área de 0.71 ha, aledaña a Jenaro Herrera en la Cuenca Baja del Río Ucayali; 34 especies en un área de 0.5 ha en la Cuenca Baja del Río Negro en Manaos (Brasil), estos inventarios fueron realizados en bosques de tierra firme. Los factores que influyen en la diversidad de palmeras todavía no están bien definidos.

9.- Los pocos datos referidos a los usos de estas palmeras se resumen en la Tabla 2, algunas de ellas, tales como *Euterpe precatoria*, *Astrocaryum chonta*, *Iriartea deltoidea*, *Socratea exorrhiza* son utilizadas casi en su totalidad. Sólo algunas especies de sotobosque son utilizadas, *Geonoma deversa* con hojas que proporcionan material para techar y ocasionalmente *Bactris concinna* cuyos frutos son consumidos; las otras especies aparentemente no son utilizadas. Si bien es cierto que las palmas de esta zona no tienen importancia preponderante desde el punto de vista económico, éstas son importantes dentro de la cultura tradicional de subsistencia del poblador ribereño y por lo tanto un estudio más profundo se hace necesario.

AGRADECIMIENTOS

La presente información es parte de mi trabajo de Tesis para optar al Título Profesional de Biólogo (Chávez, 1992). Agradezco al Programa BIOLAT por el apoyo financiero; a Pedro Acevedo y Andrew Henderson por la revisión del manuscrito y por sus sugerencias; a los herbarios consultados por las facilidades proporcionadas.

LITERATURA CITADA

Chávez, F. 1992. Arecaceas Arbóreas, Estudio Taxonómico y Usos en las Localidades de Pakitza-PNM y Tambopata- ZRTC. Tesis para optar al Título de Biólogo UNSAAC, Cusco.

Foster, R. 1987. Plantas del Perú, Checklist. Field Museum of Natural History, 1-27 p.

———. 1990. The Floristic Composition of the Rio Manu Floodplain Forest. Pages 99-111 in A. Gentry (ed.), Four Neotropical Rain Forests. Yale University Press, New Haven.

Gentry, A. 1990. Floristic similarieties and differences between Southern Central América and Upper and Central Amazonia. Pages 141-157 in A. Gentry (ed.), Four Neotropical Rain Forests. Yale University Press, New Haven.

Henderson, A. 1990. Arecaceae Part I. Introduction and the Iriarteinae. Flora Neotrópica, Monograph 53: 1-100.

Kahn, F., A. Henderson, L. Brako, M. Hoff and F. Moussa. 1992. Datos Preliminares a la actualización de la Flora de Palmae del Perú; Intensidad de Herborización y Riqueza de las Colecciones. Bull. Inst. fr. études andines 21 (2): 549-563.

—— and B. Millán. 1992. Astrocaryum (Palmae, Cocoeae, Bactridinae) in Amazonia. A preliminary treatment. Bull. Inst. fr. études andines. 21: 459-531.

Moore, H. Jr. 1973. Palms in the Tropical Forest Ecosystems of Africa and South América. Pages 63-68 in B. Meggers, E. Ayensu and W. Duckworth (eds.), Tropical Forest Ecosystems of Africa and South America: A comparative review. Smithsonian Institution Press, Washington, D.C.

Terborgh, J. 1983. Five New World Primates. A Study in Comparative Ecology. Monographs in Behavior and Ecology. Princeton University Press.

Uhl, N. and J. Dransfield. 1987. Genera Palmarum. A Classification of Palms based on the work of Harold Moore Jr. Bailey Hortorium and Allen Press, Lawrence, Kansas.

Wessels Boer, J. 1988. Palmas Indígenas de Venezuela. Pittiera 17: 1-332.

Inventario de los Bambúes de Pakitza: Anotaciones sobre su Diversidad

Ximena Londoño

Instituto Vallecaucano de Investigaciones Científicas,
A.A. 5660, Cali, Colombia

RESUMEN

Los bambúes (Poaceae: Bambusoideae) constituyen una de las plantas más diversas y económicamente más importantes del Nuevo Mundo. Presentan una amplia distribución, adaptándose a diversos tipos de hábitat, con una mayor concentración de especies en el trópico. En este trabajo se presenta la diversidad de bambúes en Pakitza; su adaptación a los diferentes microhábitats locales; y un análisis comparativo entre esta diversidad de Pakitza, y la de las estaciones biológicas La Selva en Costa Rica, la Isla de Barro Colorado en Panamá, y el Parque Nacional de Amacayacu en Colombia.

ABSTRACT

Bamboo (Poaceae: Bambusoideae) is one of the most diverse and economically important plants of the New World. It is widely distributed and adapted to a diverse range of habitats, and species richness is highly concentrated in the tropics. This study focuses on: 1) Bambusoideae diversity in Pakitza; 2) bamboo adaptation to various local microhabitats; and, 3) a comparative analysis of bamboo diversity at Pakitza, La Selva in Costa Rica, Barro Colorado Island in Panama, and Amacayacu in Colombia.

INTRODUCCIÓN

El Parque Nacional del Manu, localizado al suroriente del Perú, es considerado una de las regiones fitogeográficas con mayor diversidad biológica en el mundo (Foster, 1990; Gentry, 1990). La estación biológica Pakitza está localizada en la Zona Reservada de este parque a 11° 56' Sur, 71° 15' Oeste, y a 300-400 metros sobre el nivel del mar.

169

Los bambúes (Poaceae: Bambusoideae), componentes importantes de la flora de este parque, se encuentran representados por especies herbáceas, pequeñas y delicadas (Olyrodae) como *Piresia macrophylla* Soderstrom, y por especies leñosas (Bambusodae) como *Guadua weberbaueri* Pilger, que alcanzan a medir hasta 30 metros de altura. Esta subfamilia tiene un rango de distribución amplio en el neotrópico, desde los 46° de latitud norte hasta los 47° de latitud sur, y desde el nivel del mar hasta los 4000 metros de altura, donde ocupa diversos hábitats tales como sabanas, bosques húmedos cálidos, bosques montanos nublados y páramos (Soderstrom et al., 1988). La literatura actual reporta un total de 42 géneros y 515 especies para el Nuevo Mundo, lo que equivale a la mitad de la diversidad mundial que es de 90 géneros y aproximadamente 1100 especies. Se reconocen como áreas de referencia de alta diversidad en bambusoideas en América las siguientes: 1) la "mata littoranea" del sur de Bahía, Brasil, considerada el área con el máximo grado de endemismo y diversidad, con un total de 22 géneros (48%), de los cuales cinco son endémicos; 2) la parte norte y central de los Andes, centro de diversidad de bambúes leñosos, con siete géneros y aproximadamente 130 especies (Clark, 1993); 3) el rango latitudinal entre los 10°-15° de latitud tanto norte como sur, el cual reúne la mayor riqueza específica y el mayor grado de endemismo de bambúes herbáceos; y 4) la cuenca amazónica con aproximadamente 11 géneros herbáceos (48%) y 4 géneros leñosos (17%), siendo además, centro de diversificación de los géneros *Pariana* y *Olyra* (Soderstrom et al., 1988; Clark, 1990).

El área de Pakitza es reconocida como rica en diversidad de bambúes herbáceos. Los objetivos de esta investigación son: registrar las especies existentes en esta estación biológica; puntualizar su distribución en los diferentes microhábitats; y, estimar el grado de diversidad al compárársele con estaciones biológicas neotropicales tales como la Selva en Costa Rica (10° 25' N, 84° O), Barro Colorado en Panamá (9° 9' N, 79° 51' O), y el Parque Nacional de Amacayacu en Amazonas, Colombia (3° 49' S, 70° 16' O).

MÉTODO

Se recolectaron ejemplares de Bambusoideae en los meses de abril y mayo de 1991, buscando al azar las especies por las diferentes trochas de la estación biológica de Pakitza (Tachigali, Pacal, Castañal, Troncal Tachigali, Troncal Castañal, Aguajal, Radial 1, Radial 2, Radial 3 y Radial 4), equivalentes a 48 kilómetros de longitud. Una vez ubicada la mata de bambú, se procedió a la toma de datos y muestra de herbario siguiendo las recomendaciones de Soderstrom & Young (1983). Estas consisten en analizar por separado las diferentes estructuras morfológicas como culmos, hojas caulinares, ramas, follaje, inflorescencia si hubiere, y rizomas. Se colocaron en la prensa las partes que podían ser procesadas en papel periódico tales como follaje y hojas caulinares; los pedazos de culmo y rizomas se secaron y marcaron separadamente; se tomaron fotografías sobre detalles estructurales, hábitat y hábito de la planta, complementando así la muestra botánica. Para los estudios anatómicos y tambien morfológicos se preservaron en solución AFA (90% alcohol al 50% + 5% formalina + 5% acido acético glacial), pedazos de lámina foliar, yemas, frutos, raicillas, plántulas, porciones de culmo e inflorescencias, transfiriéndoles luego a alcohol al 70%. El material de herbario se secó al sol y se catalogó con el número de colecta del autor. La etiqueta que acompaña al especímen de herbario se redactó de la manera más concisa, con la mayor información posible, evitando incluir aquellos caracteres que son obviamente visibles en la muestra. Se obtuvieron de cada ejemplar entre 2 y 5 duplicados, los cuales fueron depositados en el herbario de la Universidad de San Marcos (USM) en Lima, y en el herbario Nacional de los Estados Unidos (US) en Washington, D.C. Para la identificación del material en el laboratorio se siguió el método de analizar comparativamente los caracteres morfológicos de los ejemplares de herbario, y se hicieron además cortes anatómicos transversales de la lámina foliar para algunos de ellos.

RESULTADOS Y DISCUSIÓN

GÉNEROS Y ESPECIES

Se registra un total de 7 géneros y 14 especies de Bambusoideae para Pakitza:
1. *Cryptochloa unispiculata* Soderstrom
2. *Olyra caudata* Trinius
3. *O. latifolia* L.
4. *Pariana aurita* Swallen
5. *P. bicolor* Tutin
6. *P. campestris* Aublet
7. *P. aff. ecuadorensis* Pilger
8. *P. gracilis* Doell
9. *P. aff. velutina* Swallen
10. *Pharus latifolius* L.
11. *P. virescens* Doell
12. *Piresia macrophylla* Soderstrom
13. *Elytrostachys* sp.
14. *Guadua weberbaueri* Pilger

Las doce primeras especies son bambúes herbáceos de las tribus Olyreae y Phareae (86%), y las dos últimas son bambúes leñosos de la tribu Bambuseae (14%). Unicamente dos de las especies anteriormente listadas fueron observadas fuera de Pakitza: *Pariana aurita* (Cocha Otorongo), y *P.* aff. *ecuadorensis* (Cocha Salvador). A continuación se presenta la descripción taxonómica de cada género, enfatizando el hábitat y distribución de las especies en Pakitza, y se incluye una clave genérica (Anexo I).

ANEXO I

CLAVE PARA LOS GÉNEROS DE BAMBUSOIDEAE DE PAKITZA

1 Plantas leñosas, entre 2 y 20 m de altura 2

 Plantas herbáceas, por debajo de 2 m de altura 3

2 Hoja caulinar con lámina angosta, atenuada y refleja provista de setas erectas y conspicuas en la boca de la vaina; ausencia de bandas blancas por encima y debajo de la línea nodal; sin espinas .... *Elytrostachys*

 Hoja caulinar con la vaina y la lámina continua o casi continua sin presencia de fimbrias en la boca de la vaina caulinar; banda de pelos blancos por encima y debajo de la línea nodal; con espinas .... *Guadua*

3 Setas orales presentes en la parte superior de la vaina foliar; inflorescencia en forma de espiga, desarticulada y desprendible en segmentos .... *Pariana*

 Setas orales ausentes en la parte superior de la vaina foliar; inflorescencia en panículas abiertas o contraídas 4

4 Nervadura lateral de la lámina foliar no paralela a la nervadura central; pecíolo largo y retorcido; raquis y ramas de la inflorescencia cubiertos por pelos uncinados .... *Pharus*

 Nervadura lateral de la lámina foliar paralela a la nervadura central; pecíolo corto y no retorcido; raquis y ramas de la inflorescencia pubescentes o glabros 5

5 Culmos dimórficos: culmos vegetativos erectos, culmos floríferos decumbentes desarrollándose debajo de la hojarasca .... *Piresia*
 Culmos no dimórficos: vegetativos y floríferos erectos 6

6 Espiguilla femenina con entrenudo presente entre las glumas y el flósculo; glumas no aristadas .... *Cryptochloa*

 Espiguilla femenina sin entrenudo presente entre las glumas y el flósculo; glumas aristadas .... *Olyra*

1. CRYPTOCHLOA SWALLEN

Bambú herbáceo del sotobosque de la selva, perenne, densamente cespitoso, de porte pequeño; entrenudos de la parte inferior del culmo muy elongados y sin follaje; follaje localizado en la parte superior; láminas conduplicadas, cerrándose por la noche. Inflorescencias varias por planta, poco conspicuas, con pocas flores. Espiguillas unisexuales. Espiguillas femeninas localizadas en la parte superior de la inflorescencia, comprimidas dorsalmente, lanceoladas, con glumas deciduas, membranosas, con un entrenudo entre las glumas y el flósculo; flósculo único, rígido, ovado, blanco marfil tornándose marmóreo pardusco cuando maduro, lema cubriendo la pálea, estigmas 3. Espiguillas masculinas más pequeñas que las femeninas, membranosas, sin glumas, rápidamente deciduas; estambres 3.

Este género incluye aproximadamente 15 especies, con distribución amplia en el neotrópico, desde el sur de México hasta las selvas chocoanas del noroeste de Suramérica y a través del Amazonas hasta el oriente del Brasil (Soderstrom, 1982). En Pakitza se registra una sola especie, *Cryptochloa unispiculata*, la cual se observa siempre asociada a suelos arenosos, tanto de la parte alta de la planicie inundable, como de los sitios de terrazas; también es frecuente encontrarle sobre el barranco, a orilla de las quebradas, en aquellos sitios que no alcanzan a ser afectados por las inundaciones. Forma matas cespitosas y pequeñas colonias, asociadas con *Piresia macrophylla*, y algunas especies de *Costus* y *Pariana*. Según Soderstrom (1982), en esta especie se observa una gran variación respecto a la forma y tamaño de la lámina foliar. En el material recolectado en Pakitza se observaron plantas de *C. unispiculata* con lámina foliar angosta y lanceolada, y plantas con lámina foliar ovoide y asimétrica, fáciles de distinguir vegetativamente, pero las diferencias no se traducen al nivel de la espiguilla floral. Es necesario realizar más colecciones de *Cryptochloa* en toda la cuenca amazónica para resolver la incógnita de que quizás exista más de una especie en este grupo de especímenes con una sola espiguilla femenina por inflorescencia. Para algunas de sus localidades específicas ver la Tabla 1.

2. OLYRA LINNAEUS

Bambú herbáceao, cespitoso, monoico, perenne; lámina foliar generalmente amplia. Inflorescencia en panículas, las espiguillas femeninas casi siempre se ubican hacia el extremo superior, y las masculinas hacia la base. Espiguillas femeninas con glumas desiguales, más grandes que el flósculo, frecuentemente aristadas, sin un entrenudo entre las glumas y el flósculo; lemas y páleas endurecidas, se desprenden por encima de las glumas. Espiguillas masculinas más pequeñas que las femeninas, membranosas, carecen de glumas, se desprenden fácilmente del pedicelo, lema trinervada; estambres 3.

Este es un género endémico del Nuevo Mundo, con una única especie, *Olyra latifolia*, naturalizada en Africa, Madagascar y en Fidji. Presenta un amplio rango

173

Tabla 1.— *Ubicación de las especies de Bambusoideae en Pakitza por trochas: Aquajal (A), Castañal (C), Cañabrava (CB); Pacal (P); Radial 2 (R2); Radial 3 (R3); Radial 4 (R4); Tachigali (T); Troncal Castañal (TC); y Troncal Tachigali (TT)*

ESPECIE	TROCHA
Cryptochloa unispiculata	C3, C29-31, P36, P54, R429-30, T140, R220
Elytrostachys sp.	R25-8, R220-21, R30-3, R35-7, R,13-17, R320-23, R325, R342, R346.5, R440, T23-64, T38, T73, T86, TC26-28, TT39,TT26-TT45
Guadua weberbaueri	A68-92, CB1-19, C0-9, C10-19, C20-29, C10-19, C40-49, C57-63, C66-68, C71, P1-28, P46-48, P58-60, R13-11, R211-13, R216-21, R223-28, R230, R347, R488, R444-45, R458-81, T1-23, T69, T71-72, T77-78, T93, T108, T123-124, TC1-7, TC11-25, TT6-14, TT18-20, TT22-26
Olyra caudata	T36, C7-8
O. latifolia	T4, T23, T26, T60, TT38
Pariana aurita	Cocha Otorongo
P. bicolor	A81-82, C3, C16, C56, P56, T142
P. campestris	C10, P14-15, P51, R312, T26-27, T42
P. aff. ecuadorensis	Cocha Salvador
P. gracilis	P36
P. aff. velutina	TT23
Pharus latifolius	CB16, P54, P56
P. virescens	P22, P36, P41, T142
Piresia macrophylla	P36, P54, T126, T142, R341

de distribución en el Nuevo Mundo, extendiéndose desde Florida (USA), México y las Antillas, hasta Argentina (Soderstrom & Zuloaga, 1989). Reúne un total de 23 especies, de las cuales solamente dos ocurren en Pakitza, *O. latifolia* y *O. caudata*. Estas especies son de porte alto, alcanzan excepcionalmente hasta 2-3 m de altura con culmos de 0.5 cm de diámetro; por su tamaño se les distingue fácilmente de las otras especies de Olyrodae en la estación. Crecen en el estrato inferior de los sitios de terrazas y prefieren los lugares en donde llegan directamente los rayos del sol, como los bordes de trochas y los claros de selva; son frecuentes colonizadoras de áreas recientemente abiertas o de bosques secundarios. Para algunas de sus localidades específicas ver la Tabla 1.

174

3. PARIANA AUBLET

Bambú herbáceo del sotobosque de la selva, rizomatoso o estolonífero, perenne. Culmos erectos o decumbentes, monomórficos o dimórficos; láminas foliares más bien anchas, con setas orales generalmente bien desarrolladas en la parte superior de la vaina. Inflorescencia nace en culmos separados, sin láminas foliares, terminal, en forma de espiga, con numerosos fascículos desarticulados y desprendibles en segmentos; fascículos compuestos por un verticilo de 4-6 espiguillas masculinas pediceladas, que rodean y cubren la única espiguilla femenina, sesil, y el segmento del raquis al cual está adherido. Espiguilla uniflora con 2-3 lodículas. Espiguillas femeninas con glumas membranosas, iguales, uninervadas; flósculo ligeramente más corto que las glumas, ovado, endurecido, glabro, estramineos; estigmas 2, plumosos; cariopsis raramente visto. Espiguillas masculinas con pedicelo amplio, endurecido, corchoso, aplanado, más corto, igual o mayor que el flósculo, connado con las espiguillas adyacentes; glumas iguales, erectas, desde angostas hasta ampliamente triangulares; flósculo desde ovado hasta angosto-elíptico, agudo u obtuso, membranoso; pálea más o menos similar a la lema; estambres 6-40 en número, filamentos connados basalmente; anteras amarillas y evidentes.

Este es un género endémico del neotrópico, con aproximadamente 30 especies. Se distribuye desde Costa Rica y sur de Trinidad hasta el norte de Bolivia, y la región de Bahía en Brasil, teniendo como centro de dispersión la Amazonía (Soderstrom et al., 1988). En Pakitza *Pariana* es el género de Bambusoideae más diverso (Figura 1) y el más abundante y frecuente de los bambúes herbáceos. Está representado por seis especies, *P. bicolor*, *P. campestris*, *P. gracilis*, *P. aff. velutina*, *P. aurita* y *P. aff. ecuadorensis*, de las cuales, las dos primeras son las más abundantes y frecuentes. *Pariana* habita preferencialmente los sitios de terrazas y

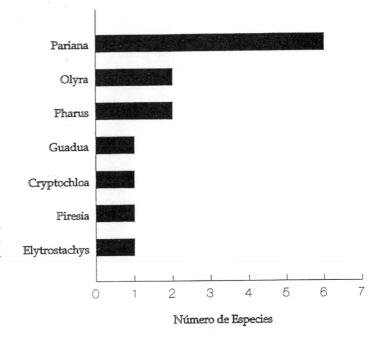

Fig. 1.– Géneros de Bambusoideae en Pakitza

Número de Especies

excepcionalmente las planicies inundables, donde forma colonias ligeramente extensas o matas individuales, que por lo general no sobrepasan los 40 cm de altura; se le encuentra siempre en el sotobosque de la selva, o de las poblaciones de paca (*Guadua weberbaueri*), y a orilla de las quebradas y de las trochas, asociado con aráceas, marantáceas, helechos y plántulas de palmas e ingas. De las especies anteriormente mencionadas, solamente *P. campestris* y *P. aurita* habitan también las planicies inundables y alcanzan a medir hasta 2 metros de altura. En la trocha Tachigali se detectó por su fragancia una planta de *P. campestris* totalmente florecida y siendo polinizada por cientos de abejas, con presencia de hormigas sobre la inflorescencia. Según Soderstrom y Calderón (1971), la cantidad, colorido y evidencia de las anteras son una adaptación para la polinización por insectos. Para algunas de sus localidades específicas ver la Tabla 1.

4. PHARUS BROWNE

Bambú herbáceo del sotobosque de la selva, monoico, cespitoso, perenne; culmos erectos o decumbentes; lámina foliar de linear a ovada, con las nervaduras laterales en dirección oblicua y divergentes con respecto a la nervadura central; pseudopecíolo prominente, retorcido 180° en la parte superior, invirtiendo la posición de la lámina. Inflorescencia en panícula abierta, con el raquis y las ramas cubiertos por pelos uncinados; ramas de la panícula desarticulándose del raquis fácilmente. Espiguillas unisexuales, unifloras. Espiguillas femeninas más grandes y alargadas que las masculinas, glumas subiguales, lanceoladas, persistentes, púrpuras o verdes, lemas más grandes que las glumas, desarticuladas y cubiertas por pelos uncinados; lodículas ausentes; estigmas 3, híspidos. Espiguillas masculinas membranáceas, elípticas, sobre pedicelos largos, alternando con las espiguillas femeninas, glumas desiguales, lemas ovadas, trinervadas, más grandes que la gluma; lodiculas 3, pequeñas; estambres 6, anteras blanquecinas.

Este es un género endémico del Nuevo Mundo con 7 especies que se distribuyen desde el centro-norte de Florida (USA) hasta Rochas, en el sur del Uruguay (Soderstrom et al., 1987).

Se reportan para Pakitza dos especies, *P. latifolius* y *P. virescens* que se caracterizan por tener pelos o setas en forma de ganchos sobre las lemas fértiles de las espiguillas femeninas y sobre las ramas de las inflorescencias. Esto permite que las estructuras reproductivas se adhieran a la piel o al pelo de mamíferos frecuentes y abundantes en esta selva como la paca (*Agouti paca*), el jabalí (*Tayassu pecari*), y la guangana (*Tayassu tajacu*), facilitando así su dispersión epizoocórica. Ambas especies crecen al borde del camino en los sitios de terrazas, con luz difusa, asociadas con heliconias, helechos, gramíneas y palmas. Solamente *P. latifolious* habita las planicies inundables, específicamente en la trocha Cañabrava, lo que sugiere una mayor adaptación de esta especie a las inundaciones estacionales. Se distingue *P. latifolius* fácilmente en el campo por sus inflorescencias de color marrón que se adhieren fuertemente a la piel o a la ropa, no forma colonias densas y alcanza un máximo de 1 m de altura; paralelamente *P. virescens* presenta inflorescencias de color verde claro, posee la misma capacidad de adherencia, forma colonias densas y extensas, y puede llegar a medir hasta 1.30 metros de altura. Judziewicz (1990) reporta polinización por insectos para este género. Se pudo confirmar este fenómeno en una población de *P. virescens* entre las estacas 41-42 de la trocha Pacal que estaba siendo polinizada por abejas. Para algunas de sus localidades específicas ver la Tabla 1.

5. PIRESIA SWALLEN

Bambú herbáceo del sotobosque de la selva, monoico, perenne, cespitoso. Culmos generalmente dimórficos; culmos vegetativos erectos, estériles, con nudos pronunciados, sosteniendo el complemento foliar en la porción superior; culmos floríferos decumbentes, con hojas reducidas, vainas sin hojas o láminas reflejas muy pequeñas. Inflorescencia racemiforme en todos los nudos del culmo. Espiguillas unifloras, las femeninas más grandes que las masculinas. Espiguilla femenina sobre pedicelos claviformes, glumas tan largas como la espiguilla, siempre de color púrpura; flósculo elíptico, endurecido, pubescente; estigmas 2. Cariopsis elíptico. Espiguilla masculina sobre pedicelos filiformes, tempranamente decíduos, transparentes, glumas generalmente ausentes, lemas delgadas, trinervadas, estambres 3.

Este es un género endémico del Nuevo Mundo, reúne 4 especies que se distribuyen en Trinidad, Norte de Suramérica, Amazonas y la región atlántica de Brasil (Soderstrom, 1982; Soderstrom et al., 1988). *Piresia macrophylla* es la única especie que ocurre en Pakitza; habita los suelos arenosos en los sitios de terrazas, siempre bajo sombra dentro del sotobosque y asociada con *C. unispiculata*, *Pariana* sp., helechos, commelinas, aráceas, marántaceas y plántulas de palmas. Para algunas de sus localidades específicas ver la Tabla 1.

6. ELYTROSTACHYS MCCLURE

Bambú leñoso, cespitoso, rizomas paquimorfos. Culmos en la porción inferior erectos o decumbentes, en la porción superior trepadores, apoyándose sobre la vegetación aledaña; entrenudos huecos, de pared delgada; yema solitaria con varias ramas subiguales por nudo; sin espinas; hojas caulinares con setas erectas, numerosas y conspicuas en la boca de la vaina, lámina caulinar angosta, atenuada y reflexa; varias ramas por complemento. Inflorescencia en las ramas laterales; espiguillas multibracteadas con 1-2 flósculos completos; 6 estambres; 2 estigmas.

Este género es endémico del neotrópico, crece en selvas húmedas de baja y mediana altitud, entre 300 y 1500 m.s.n.m. Reúne dos especies, *E. typica* y *E.*

clavigera, que ocurren solamente en Venezuela, Colombia y hasta Honduras en Centroamérica (McClure, 1973). La presencia de *Elytrostachys* en Pakitza amplía la distribución latitudinal y geográfica de este género en Suramérica hasta los 11° 56' (aprox. 12°) de latitud sur, Pakitza, Parque Nacional Manu, Perú.

Hay una sola especie de *Elytrostachys* en Pakitza y es nueva para la ciencia, sin embargo por falta de material florífero no se ha descrito; se distingue fácilmente de los otras dos especies por caracteres vegetativos, tales como tamaño y pubescencia de la lámina foliar, y color y pubescencia de los culmos y de las hojas caulinares. En Pakitza, *Elytrostachys* crece únicamente en los sitios de terrazas, no se observa en las planicies inundables, y es un buen indicador de tierra firme. Es frecuente observarle sobre las laderas ligeramente inclinadas, a orilla de caños o quebradas, y en los claros de la selva en donde constituye colonias dominantes o crece formando matas individuales asociada con palmas, aráceas, marantáceas, commelináceas, helechos, piperáceas y parianas. Se diferencia de *Guadua*, el otro bambú leñoso de la estación, por las fimbrias largas y conspicuas de la hoja caulinar, por la ausencia de espinas, y por la lámina caulinar angosta y en posición refleja. Se desconoce el nombre común y los usos de este bambú en Pakitza, sin embargo, la longitud de sus entrenudos y lo delgado de la pared del culmo son indicadores de que tiene potencial como fibra para fabricación de canastos y otros objetos artesanales. Para algunas de sus localidades específicas ver la Tabla 1.

7. GUADUA KUNTH

Bambú leñoso erecto o escandente; rizomas paquimorfos. Culmos huecos o sólidos, con una banda de pelos blancos por encima y debajo de la línea nodal; entrenudos de pared gruesa o delgada, acanalado cerca a la inserción de la yema o de la rama; yema típicamente solitaria, con una rama dominante por nudo; espinas por lo general presentes, particularmente en los nudos basales; hoja caulinar triangular, con los márgenes continuos o casi continuos. Lámina foliar de linear a ovada, pecíolada, con lígula interna y externa presentes; setas orales frecuentes. Inflorescencia en espiguillas precedidas por una bráctea subtendiente y un profilo, se localizan sobre los culmos y en las ramas con o sin follaje. Espiguillas multifloras, sésiles o pedunculadas; flósculos lanceolados a ovados, más de uno por espiguilla; lemas usualmente multinervadas, pálea usualmente más corta que la lema y con quillas aladas; lodículas 3; estambres 6; estigmas 2-3 híspidos a comúnmente plumosos.

Guadua reúne los bambúes económicamente más importantes del Nuevo Mundo, se extiende desde México por todos los países de Centroamérica y Sudamérica hasta Argentina, con excepción de Chile. Comprende aproximadamente 30 especies. La región amazónica y la orinoquía reúnen el 45% de las especies, y se postulan como el centro de radiación de este género (Londoño & Judziewicz, 1991).

178

Tabla 2.—Cuadro comparativo entre las especies de Bambusoideae de Pakitza, Amacayacu, La Selva, e Isla de Barro Colorado (IBC)

ESPECIES	PAKITZA	AMACAYACU	LA SELVA	I.B.C.
Chusquea simpliciflora	—	—	X	X
Cryptochloa concinna	—	—	X	—
Cryptochloa unispiculata	X	X	—	—
Elytrostachys clavigera	—	—	X	—
Elytrostachys sp.	X	—	—	—
Guadua glomerata	—	X	—	—
G. maclurei	—	—	—	X
G. superba	—	X	—	—
Guadua weberbaueri	X	X	—	—
Guadua sp.	—	X	—	—
Lithachne pauciflora	—	—	X	X
Olyra caudata	X	—	—	—
Olyra ecaudata	—	—	—	X
O. latifolia	X	X	X	X
O. loretensis	—	X	—	—
O. micrantha	—	X	—	—
Pariana aurita	X	—	—	—
P. bicolor	X	X	—	—
P. campestris	X	X	—	—
P. aff. ecuadorensis	X	—	—	—
P. gracilis	X	—	—	—
P. parvispica	—	—	X	—
P. aff. velutina	X	—	—	—
Pariana sp.	—	X	—	—
Pharus latifolius	X	—	X	X
P. parvifolius	—	—	—	X
P. virescens	X	X	X	X
P. vittatus	—	—	X	—
Piresia macrophylla	X	—	—	—
P. sympodica	—	X	—	—
Rhipidocladum racemiflorum	—	—	—	X
Streptochaeta sodiroana	—	—	X	X
S. spicata	—	—	—	X
Streptogyna americana	—	—	—	X

*Especies observadas en Cocha Otorongo y Cocha Salvador

TOTAL ESPECIES	14	13	10	12
TOTAL GENEROS	7	5	8	8
% Generos compartidos		100	62.5	37.5
% Especies compartidas		46	30	25

Guadua weberbaueri es el bambú leñoso más común en Pakitza donde se le ubica formando colonias densas conocidas como "pacales", o matas solitarias y dispersas, con 2-20 (-50) culmos/mata; habita las terrazas, las planicies inundables o pantanosas (aguajales), y crece tanto en suelos arenosos como arcillosos. Cuando forma "pacales", se puede observar que hay árboles que superan su dosel tales como cedros (Cedrela odorata), cecropias, palmas (Iriartea sp.) y Ficus; cuando forma matas solitarias y dispersas en el interior de la selva, se crea un amplio espacio entre su dosel y el dosel superior; sin embargo, algunos culmos logran ocupar parte de este espacio (20-30 metros), sin llegar a superar el dosel superior. Esta especie se caracteriza por tener rizomas paquimorfos cortos, de aproximadamente 20-30 cm de longitud, y rizomas alargados que pueden llegar a medir hasta 8 m de longitud, en donde el cuello del rizoma representa el 94% de su tamaño. Tal prolongación ocurre cuando la yema que se origina por debajo del cuello, en la parte media y superior del rizoma, y que da origen a un nuevo brote, se extiende en el subsuelo por varios metros, antes de emerger. Esta especie se diferencia fácilmente de los otros bambúes en la reserva por: a) la presencia de espinas sobre culmos y ramas, y, b) por sus culmos de color verde blanquecino, con entrenudos largos que alcanzan hasta 90 cm de longitud, frecuentemente conteniendo agua. Se le conoce localmente con el nombre de "paca" y sus culmos en esta región no tienen valor económico. Culturalmente se consume el agua de los entrenudos para calmar la sed, y además se dice que esta agua posee propiedades medicinales. Para algunas de sus localidades específicas ver la Tabla 1.

COMPARACIÓN FLORÍSTICA

Para el estudio comparativo de la diversidad de la flora de Bambusoideae en Pakitza, se han seleccionado tres estaciones biológicas en el neotrópico: La Selva en Costa Rica, la Isla de Barro Colorado (IBC), en Panamá, y Amacayacu en Colombia. Se excluyó de este análisis, la mata atlántica de Bahía, Brasil, debido al alto grado de diversidad y endemismo, con 22 géneros, 65 especies y aproximadamente 30 especies endémicas. Este alto registro numérico resulta difícil como parámetro comparativo para cualquier análisis en biodiversidad sobre Bambusoideae. El criterio de selección de estas estaciones biológicas se basó en la similitud del hábitat compartido, que se expresa en el tipo de formación vegetal (selva lluviosa baja), y en la altitud por debajo de los 500 metros. Los datos aquí empleados para La Selva e Isla de Barro Colorado se basan en investigaciones de material bibliográfico, y para Amacayacu, se basan en el trabajo de campo realizado por la autora (Tabla 2).

La diversidad de Bambusoideae en Amacayacu, al sur de Colombia en el Departamento del Amazonas, es de 13 especies en 5 géneros, compartiendo con Pakitza el 100% de sus géneros y el 46% de sus especies; la estación de La Selva reúne 10 especies en 8 géneros (Judziewicz y Pohl, 1984) y comparte con Pakitza el 62.5 % de sus géneros y el 30% de sus especies; y la Isla de Barro Colorado incluye 12 especies en 8 géneros (Croat, 1978; Judziewicz, com. per.), compartiendo con Pakitza el 37.5% de sus géneros y el 25% de sus especies (Tabla 2). Analizando el porcentaje de especies herbáceas y leñosas, se puede decir que Pakitza, con el 86% de los bambúes herbáceos (h) y el 14% de los bambúes leñosos (l), presenta una composición de Bambusoideae más afín con La Selva (80% h y 20% l) que con la Isla de Barro Colorado (75% h y 25% l) y que con Amacayacu (69% h y 31% l) (Figura 2). Las cuatro estaciones comparten únicamente dos especies de bambúes herbáceos: *Olyra latifolia* y *Pharus virescens* (Tabla 2). En el caso de los bambúes leñosos, no se presenta ninguna especie en común, ni siquiera a nivel de género; *Guadua* por ejemplo, es compartido por Pakitza, Amacayacu y la Isla de Barro Colorado, y el género *Elytrostachys* únicamente lo comparten Pakitza y La Selva (Tabla 2).

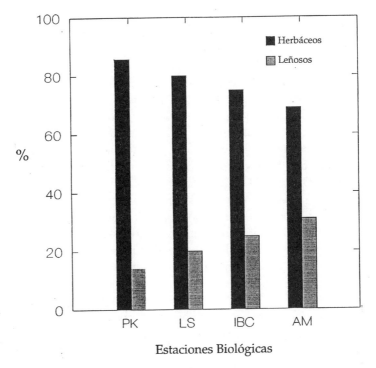

Fig. 2.– *Comparación de la subfamilia Bambusoideae según el porcentaje de Olyrodae (Herbáceos) y de Bambusodae (Leñoso) en Pakitza (PK), La Selva (LS), Isla Barro Colorado (IBC), y Amayacu (AM).*

CONCLUSIONES

La familia Poaceae, a la cual pertenecen los bambúes, es una de las familias menos numerosas y diversas en el Parque Nacional del Manu, según el estudio sobre la flora de las planicies inundables de este parque elaborado por Foster (1990). En Pakitza, sin embargo, la subfamilia Bambusoideae es un elemento abundante y frecuente. Un total de 14 especies en 7 géneros se registran para Pakitza, de las cuales el 86% son bambúes herbáceos de las tribus Olyreae y Phareae, y el 14% son bambúes leñosos de la tribu Bambuseae. Se considera a *Pariana* el género más diverso con un total de 6 especies, distribuídas en hábitats de terrazas y planicies inundables (Figura 1). Le siguen en grado de diversidad los géneros *Olyra* y *Pharus*, con dos especies cada uno (Figura 1). De todas las especies de Bambusoideae de Pakitza, *Guadua weberbaueri* es la más abundante y la que presenta una mayor capacidad de adaptación a los diferentes tipos de hábitat que existen en esta estación biológica; ocupa las planicies periódica y frecuentemente inundables, las terrazas planas y disectadas, y algunas áreas con deficiente drenaje como los aguajales, en donde durante la estación lluviosa puede soportar fluctuaciones de agua hasta de 1 metro por encima del nivel del suelo. Tanto en las planicies inundables como en las terrazas, G. *weberbaueri* puede constituir poblaciones densas ("pacales") o crecer en el sotobosque de la selva entremezclado con la vegetación, constituyendo matas bien definidas y distantes unas de otras. El carácter morfológico del rizoma paquiformo con cuello elongado, asociado a su rápido crecimiento vegetativo que alcanza hasta 72 cm/mes, (Tupayachi, común. pers.) explican: 1) la rápida colonización que esta especie hace de los claros de selva y, 2) la presencia de pequeñas matas dispersas pero interconectadas a través del sistema rizomático. De allí que se pueda concluir que la abundancia de esta especie y su fácil dispersión en Pakitza responde básicamente a caracteres intrínsecos de la especie y no a una dispersión por agentes externos como sí sucede con bambúes herbáceos como por ejemplo *Pharus latifolius* y *P. virescens*. Las poblaciones de G. *weberbaueri* pueden considerarse un ecosistema específico dentro de la reserva. Se sabe por ejemplo: a) que en Cocha Cashu hay 12 especies de aves que habitan estrictamente los bosques de bambú (Robinson y Terborgh, 1990), y que particularmente en Pakitza, los "pacales" albergan un alto porcentaje de aves (Servat, este volumen); b) que existe una comunidad de micos (*Saguinus fuscicollis*), que se observa siempre en las matas de bambú (Terborgh, 1983); c) que en los entrenudos de paca que contienen agua, existe una comunidad compleja de insectos (Louton, com. per.); y d) que las orugas de mariposas de la tribu *Pronophilini* se alimentan de las hojas de este bambú y depositan sus huevos sobre los brotes nuevos (D. Harvey, comun. pers.).

La calidad del suelo no parece ser un limitante en el crecimiento de G. *weberbaueri* pero sí en el de *Elytrostachys* sp., el cual se observa únicamente en los sitios de terrazas. Estas se caracterizan por tener suelos con un alto grado de hojarasca, significativamente más arenosos y ácidos que las planicies inundables, con bajo contenido en todos los nutrientes (N, P, K, Ca, y Mg) excepto en sodio (Mazer, este volumen). Se puede concluir, que *Elytrostachys* es un buen indicador de los sitios de terrazas planas o disectadas, que es menos abundante y frecuente que G. *weberbaueri*, y que difícilmente estas dos especies se encuentran compartiendo el mismo microhábitat. Esta especie de *Elytrostachys*, como señalé anteriormente, es nueva para la ciencia y su presencia en Pakitza amplía la distribución latitudinal del género en el hemisferio sur. Es probable que esta especie sea endémica del Parque Nacional de Manu, pero se hace necesario realizar más investigaciones botánicas en toda la cuenca amazónica a fin de incrementar colecciones que sustenten esta tesis.

Sobre la base de las observaciones en torno a los microhábitats que ocupan los bambúes en Pakitza, se puede concluir que el 100% de estas especies prefiere los suelos sueltos y arenosos de los sitios de terrazas, y que solamente el 29% de ellas puede adap-tarse también a las planicies inundables en donde los suelos son más arcillosos y con un nivel más alto de saturación.

El análisis de la composición de Bambusoideae de las cuatro estaciones biológicas sugiere que Pakitza registra la mayor diversidad específica mas no génerica (Figura 3); le sigue en diversidad Amacayacu, con 13 especies, la Isla de Barro Colorado con 12 especies, y por último, La Selva con 10 especies (Figura 3). La mayor diversidad génerica se registra en La Selva y en la Isla de Barro Colorado con 8 géneros, le sigue Pakitza con 7 géneros, y finalmente Amacayacu con 5 géneros (Figura 1). Al hacer el análisis comparativo del porcentaje de bambúes herbáceos y leñosos, es importante señalar el factor latitudinal. Se puede concluir de esta manera que Pakitza, ubicada a 12° de latitud sur, con el 86% de sus bambúes herbáceos y el 14% leñosos, tiene una composición de Bambusoideae más afín con La Selva, ubicada a 10° 25' de latitud norte, que con la Isla de Barro Colorado ubicada a 9° 9' de latitud norte, y finalmente con Amacayacu ubicada a 3° 49' de latitud sur (Figura 2). Esto refuerza la hipótesis que indica, que la mayor diversidad y el mayor grado de endemismo en cuanto a bambúes herbáceos se refiere, se da entre los 10°-15° de latitud norte y sur (Soderstrom et al., 1988). Consecuentemente, Amacayacu, localizado cerca a la línea ecuatorial, y con el menor porcentaje de bambúes herbáceos en su composición floral (69%), sustenta también esta hipótesis, en que a medida que nos acercamos al Ecuador, la diversidad de Olyrodae disminuye.

El predominio de los bambúes herbáceos en las cuatro estaciones (69%-86%), puede explicarse por el factor altitudinal; se conoce que altitudes por debajo de los 1000 metros son las preferidas por las Olyrodae, y es en este rango en donde se localiza la mayoría de las especies (Calderón & Soderstrom, 1980). En contraste, la baja diversidad de bambúes leñosos en las cuatro estaciones

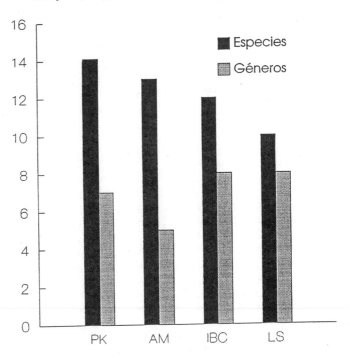

Fig. 3.– *Número de géneros y especies de Bambusoideae Pakitza (PK), Amayacu (AM), Isla de Barro Colorado y La Selva (LS).*

Estaciones Biológicas

(14%-31%) puede explicarse también desde una pespectiva altitudinal. Se sabe, por ejemplo, que estos bambúes presentan un incremento en su diversidad a medida que se asciende en los Andes, observándose una mayor concentración de especies entre los 2000-3000 metros sobre el nivel del mar (Clark, 1989; Londoño, 1990). Por debajo de los 1000 metros de altitud, esta diversidad tiende a disminuir, observándose sin embargo un mayor incremento en el número de individuos de cada especie. *Guadua weberbaueri* es un buen ejemplo para Pakitza, en donde se registra como especie dominante. Se concluye además de este análisis, que Pakitza comparte más especies con Amacayacu, en total seis, que con las otras dos estaciones biológicas (Tabla 2). Es probable que esto se deba a que Pakitza y Amacayacu se ubican en el ecosistema de la cuenca amazónica, donde comparten similares características edáficas, climáticas y de biomasa. Variaciones mínimas en estas características, como por ejemplo fertilidad del suelo (Pakitza), estimulan procesos de adaptación y competencia, que se expresan en este caso, en el mayor grado de diversidad y endemismo de Pakitza.

AGRADECIMIENTOS

Agradezco al programa BIOLAT del Smithsonian Institution por hacer posible esta investigación; a los curadores del herbario Nacional de los Estados Unidos (US) por permitirme utilizar la colección de Bambusoideae y realizar el trabajo de laboratorio; a los compañeros de la estación de campo en Pakitza, y del Museo de Historia Natural Javier Prado en Lima; a Alfredo Tupayachi por facilitarme información, y el acceso a las colecciones del herbario de la Universidad San Antonio Abad del Cuzco; a José Cuatrecasas por ayudarme a clarificar varios conceptos empleados en este trabajo; y especialmente a Abelardo Sandoval por su valiosa colaboración para la elaboración de este manuscrito.

LITERATURA CITADA

Calderón, C.E., & T.R. Soderstrom. 1980. The Genera of Bambusoideae (Poaceae) of the American Continent: Keys and Comments. Smithsonian Contrib. Bot. 44: 1-27.

Clark, L.G. 1989. Systematics of Chusquea Section Swallenochloa, Section Verticillatae, Section Serpentes, and Section Longifoliae (Poaceae: Bambusoideae). Syst. Bot. Monographs 27: 1-127.

Clark, L.G. 1990. Diversity and biogeography of Neotropical Bamboos (Poaceae:

Bambusoideae). Acta Bot. Bras. 4(1):125-132.

Clark, L.G. 1993. Diversity and distribution of the Andean Woody bamboos (Poaceae: Bambuseae). Proceedings of a Neotropical Montane Forests Symposium, The New York Botanical Garden, June 21-26.

Croat, T.B. 1978. Flora of Barro Colorado Island. Stanford Univ. Press, Stanford.

Foster, R.B. 1990. The Floristic Composition of the Rio Manu Floodplain Forest. Pp.

99-111, in Four Neotropical Rainforests (A.H. Gentry, ed.), Yale Univ. Press, New Haven and London, 1-627.

Gentry, A.H. 1990. Floristic Similarities and Differences between Southern Central America and Upper and Central Amazonia. Pp. 141-157, in Four Neotropical Rainforests (A.H. Gentry, ed.), Yale Univ. Press, New Haven and London, 1-627.

Judziewicz, E.J. 1990. Poaceae (Gramineae). Pp. 1-727, in A.R.A. Gorts-van Rijn (ed.), Flora of the Guianas, Koeltz Scientific Books, Germany, Series A: 8 (187):1-727.

Judziewicz, E.J. & R.W. Pohl. 1984. Grasses of La Selva, Costa Rica. Contr. Univ. of Wisconsin Herbarium 1(3): 1-86.

Londoño, X. 1990. Aspectos sobre la distribución y la ecología de los bambúes de Colombia (Poaceae: Bambusoideae). Caldasia 16 (77): 139-153.

Londoño, X. & E.J. Judziewicz. 1991. A new species of Guadua, Guadua calderoniana (Poaceae: Bambuseae), with notes on the genus in Bahia, Brazil. Novon 1: 27-32.

Mazer, S.J. (Este volumen). Floristic Composition, Soil Quality, Litter Accumulation, and Decomposition in Terra Firme and Floodplain Habitats in the vicinity of Pakitza, Peru.

McClure, F.A. 1973. Genera of bamboos native to the New World (Gramineae: Bambusoideae). Smithsonian Contrib. Bot. 9: 1-148.

Robinson, S.K. & J. Terborgh. 1990. Bird Communities of the Cocha Cashu Biological Station in Amazonian Peru. Pp. 199-216, in Four Neotropical Rainforests, (A.H. Gentry, ed.), Yale Univ. Press, New Haven and London, pp. 199-216.

Servat, G. 1996. An Annotated list of birds of the BIOLAT Biological Station at Pakitza, Peru. (Este volumen)

Soderstrom, T.R. 1982. New species of Cryptochloa and Piresia (Poaceae: Bambusoideae). Brittonia 34(2):199-209.

Soderstrom, T.R. & C.E. Calderón. 1971. Insect Pollination in Tropical Rain Forest Grasses. Biotropica 3(1): 1-16.

Soderstrom, T.R., R.P. Ellis, & E.J. Judziewicz. 1987. The Phareae and Streptogyneae (Poaceae) of Sri Lanka: A morphological-anatomical study. Smithsonian Contrib. Bot. 65: 1-27.

Soderstrom, T.R., E.J. Judziewicz, & L.G. Clark. 1988. Distribution patterns of neotropical bamboos. Pp. 121-157, in Proceedings of a Workshop on Neotropical Distribution Patterns (P.E. Vanzolini & R.E Heyer, eds.), Academia Brasileira de Ciencias, Rio de Janeiro.

Soderstrom, T.R. & S.M. Young. 1983. A Guide to Collecting Bamboos. Ann. Missouri Bot. Gard. 70: 128-136.

Soderstrom, T.R. & F. Zuloaga. 1989. A revision of the genus Olyra and the new segregate genus Parodiolyra (Poaceae: Bambusoideae: Olyreae). Smithsonian Contrib. Bot. 69: 1-79.

Terborgh, J. 1983. Five New World Primates: A Study in Comparative Ecology. Princeton Univ. Press, Princeton, N.J.

185

Estudio Preliminar sobre la Dinámica Poblacional de Guadua weberbaueri Pilger y Elytrostachys sp. (Poaceae: Bambusoideae) en Pakitza - Parque Nacional de Manu -Perú

Alfredo Tupayachi Herrera

Facultad de Ciencias Biológicas - Universidad Nacional de San Antonio Abad del Cusco. CUSCO - PERU

ABSTRACT:

Se presenta el resultado preliminar del estudio de la dinámica poblacional de *Guadua weberbaueri Pilger y Elytrostachys sp.* (Poaceae: Bambusoideae), en la Estación Biológica de Pakitza, Zona Reservada del Parque Nacional de Manu - Perú. La evaluación en dos estaciones del año, la dinámica de crecimiento, la relación existente con los árboles y arbustos, y las interacciones con la fauna asociada.

INTRODUCCIÓN

La subfamilia Bambusoideae es una de las más diversas y económicamente importantes subfamilias de las Gramineas. Los Bambúes del Nuevo Mundo son bastante diversos, incluyen un total de 43 géneros y de aproximadamente 440 - 460 especies; el Viejo Mundo reúne un total de 46 géneros y entre 400 - 510 especies (Londoño 1989).

En nuestro país y en especial en las regiones andinas, la *Guadua* (Bambú) contribuye eficazmente como material de construcción en sus diversas formas bajo la denominación de "Paca", así como en usos secundarios, tales como muebles y artesanías. A pesar de la importancia económica y social que estas Poaceas representan en el ámbito rural y urbano, hasta ahora no se ha realizado ningún estudio integral, de allí que no exista bibliografía especializada sobre su diversidad, distribución, usos tradicionales y actuales.

La Región Inka, que comprende a los departamentos de Cusco, Apurimac y Madre de Dios, cuenta con 44 zonas de vida natural de las 84 existentes para el Perú, la gran diversidad climática y fisiográfica en esta parte del territorio peruano, mantiene una relación directa con la diversidad florística y faunística acrecentada aún más con la presencia de la Cordillera Oriental que encierra hábitats importantes para el desarrollo de una alta diversidad. En este entendido, creemos que a ambos flancos de los andes existen bambúes, los que requieren ser explorados y estudiados botánica y ecológicamente.

MATERIALES Y MÉTODOS

TRABAJO DE CAMPO

En los meses de setiembre de 1989 y febrero de 1990, se realizó el trabajo de campo con el objetivo de conocer las estrategias de crecimiento de *Guadua* y *Elytrostachys*, cuál es el incremento poblacional en una hectárea y cuáles las interacciones de las comunidades de *Guadua* y *Elytrostachys* con la fauna asociada.

Utilizando el sistema de trochas (Troncales - radiales), recorrimos todo el área hasta entonces abarcada por el Programa BIOLAT, localizando las áreas pobladas por bambúes, tanto en las zonas demarcadas como fuera de ellas; se procedió a colectar las especies de bambúes leñosos siguiendo las recomendaciones de Soderstrom & Young (1987), los especímenes se depositaron en el Herbario Vargas (CUZ)_. Además se tomaron fotografías sobre el hábito y detalles de las estructuras morfológicas de las plantas con el fin de documentar la información de cada especie colectada.

Hecho el reconocimiento sobre las características de las ocho zonas de trabajo de BIOLAT, se eligió la zona III, por presentar poblaciones considerables de bambú, se trabajó en el plot 13 de una hectárea a la altura de las estacas 7 - 9 de la trocha "Castañal", en bosque de terraza plana; los cuadrantes de 400 m2 se subdividieron en parcelas rectangulares de 5 x 20 m (100 m^2) para una mayor confiabilidad en el censo, repitiéndose esta operación en los 25 cuadrantes del plot, para así conocer la dinámica poblacional.

Se evaluó así mismo en las dos temporadas (lluviosa y seca), los cuadrantes con mayor y menor densidad de bambúes y la relación con la presencia de árboles y arbustos. Fue localizada igualmente *Elytrostacys sp.* , bambú de altura en la trocha "Tachigalia" troncal, "Tachigalia" y las radiales "Jergón" "Escarabajo" y "Otorongo", ubicadas en pequeñas quebradas húmedas, procediéndose a marcarlas en cada núcleo (Ver mapa de distribución).

Para conocer el ritmo de crecimiento de los brotes de *Guadua* y *Elytrostachys* se procedió a marcar y medirlas en la temporada seca, para contrastarlas en la temporada lluviosa.

Referente a las estrategias de crecimiento del "clon" (Considerando al "clon" como un conjunto de individuos que supuestamente tienen un rizoma común, desarrollado y vigoroso, con numerosas yemas, generalmente ramificados y que originan anualmente a nuevos individuos en un núcleo o área determinada), éstas se delimitaron encerrándolas a través de cintas y marcando a cada individuo del clon para conocer sus variaciones en la temporada lluviosa, tanto en *Guadua* como en *Elytrostachys*.

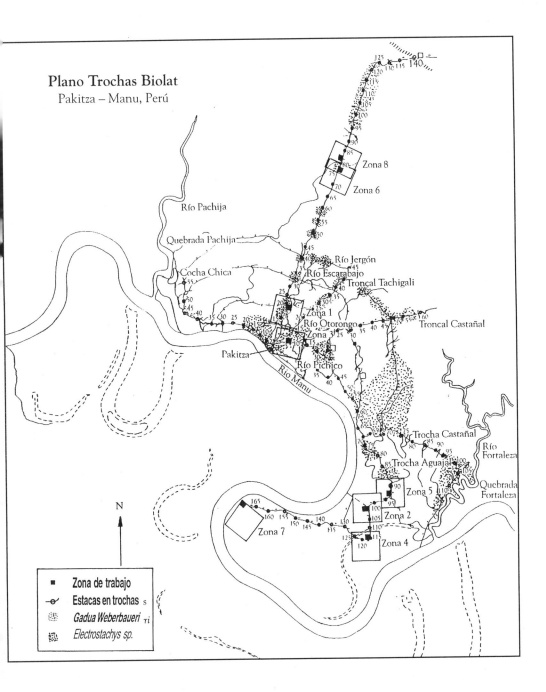

Plano Trochas Biolat
Pakitza – Manu, Perú

Río Pachija

Quebrada Pachija

Cocha Chica

Río Jergón

Río Escarabajo

Troncal Tachigali

Zona 8

Zona 6

Zona 1

Río Otorongo

Troncal Castañal

Zona 3

Pakitza

Río Pichico

Río Manu

Trocha Castañal

Río Fortaleza

Trocha Aguajal

Quebrada Fortaleza

Zona 5

Zona 2

Zona 4

N

Zona 7

- ■ **Zona de trabajo**
- ⊸ **Estacas en trochas**
- ░ *Gadua Weberbaueri*
- ▦ *Electrostachys sp.*

TRABAJO DE GABINETE

Para la determinación del material colectado se visitaron los Herbarios (USM) y Vargas (CUZ), también se envió al (MO), pero quien en definitiva determinó las dos especies de bambúes leñosos fue la especialista Dra. Ximena Londoño.

ÁREA DE ESTUDIO

Está ubicado en el Puesto de Control y Vigilancia de Pakitza, margen izquierda del Río Manu, entre las coordenadas Geográficas 70° 58' L.W. y 12° 07' L.S, a 350 m. sobre el nivel del mar, en el distrito de Fitzcarral, provincia de Manu y departamento de Madre de Dios. El área de operaciones abarca aproximadamente 8000 hectáreas y 47 km del sistema de trochas debidamente demarcadas, estacadas y numeradas en diferentes direcciones a partir del campamento base de la estación.

Según el Plan Maestro del Parque Nacional de Manu (1986), las características climáticas de la zona de vida para el área de trabajo son; Biotemperatura 18-24°c, precipitación de 2000-4000 mm. evapotranspiración de 1060.7 a 1414.3 mm, provincia de humedad. Per-húmedo, altitud aproximada 350 m, temperatura mínima 21.38°c, máxima de 26.71°c y una temperatura media anual de 24.05°c.

TAXONOMÍA DE LOS BAMBÚES

Las dos especies de bambúes estudiadas en Pakitza corresponden a *Guadua weberbaueri* Pilger, conocido en la región como "Ipa", "Paca" (Parodi, 1959). Es un bambú de 8-15 m de altura, que forma densas asociaciones denominadas "Ipales" o "Pacales", es estrictamente erecto en los primero 2-4 metros y luego arqueado en su extremo superior, las que se sostienen mediante ramas en la copa de los árboles y en los arbustos del bosque. El culmo es hueco de paredes delgadas, resistentes, entrenudos hasta de 80 cm de largo, diámetro de entrenudos de 4 a 6 cm. en promedio, contienen agua "Agua de paca" especialmente en la temporada lluviosa; hojas del culmo (brácteas), son triangulares desiduas de 20-40 cm de largo por 15 a 20 cm de ancho en su parte media. Presentan espinas en las ramas y en el culmo generalmente en número de cinco.

Elytrostachys sp. Conocido en Pakitza como "bambú carrizo" por los guardaparques, es una planta de 5 a 15 m de altura, los culmos son huecos de paredes delgadas, entrenudos de 40 cm de largo por 3 cm de diámetro. Hojas del culmo desiduas en forma triangular de 20 a 25 cm de largo por 10 a 15 cm de ancho, lámina caulinar desidua con fimbrias sobre la lígula; esta especie a diferencia de la anterior, no presenta espinas.

ECOLOGÍA

En Pakitza, **Guadua weberbaueri** Pilger crece en diversos hábitats, encontrándose asociado al bosque maduro, en la ribera de los ríos o formando asociaciones homogéneas "Manchales de pacas", en bosques de terraza y en bosques colinosos; mientras que *Elytrostachys sp.*, está localizado en pequeñas quebradas húmedas asociado a árboles y arbustos, que le sirven de apoyo; **Guadua** aprovecha espacios abiertos por la caída de grandes árboles o desplazamiento de suelos por derrumbes en bosques de altura, los que colonizan rápidamente, formando los ecosistemas llamados "Pacales" que ocupan considerables áreas.

RESULTADOS Y DISCUSIÓN

Como resultados preliminares del presente trabajo, se reporta para Pakitza dos especies de bambúes leñosos; *Guadua weberbaueri* Pilger y *Elytrostachys sp.*

Londoño (1990), refiere de *Elytrostachys* como un género endémico del Neotrópico con dos especies *E. tipica* y *E. clavigera;* la espacie *E. tipica* sólo para Venezuela y *E. clavigera* en Colombia y Centro América hasta Honduras en (MaClure, 1973). Por lo que este género es poco estudiado, no conociéndose nuevos reportes para el Perú. En cambio *Guadua* es un género americano endémico del Nuevo Mundo (Parodi, 1959), que se extiende desde México por todos los países de Centro y Sur América hasta Argentina con excepción de Chile; incluyendo aproximadamente 28 especies (Londoño, 1990).

El incremento poblacional de *Guadua weberbaueri* Pilger en una hectárea del Plot 13, evaluados entre setiembre de (1989) y febrero (1990), fue de 634 nuevos individuos,

CUADRO Nº 1: Incremento de individuos en Guadua weberbaueri Pilger durante los meses de setiembre (1989) a febrero (1990) en cuadrantes del Plot 13 - zona III.

Nº CUADRANTE	Nº INDIVIDUOS SETIEMB. 1989	Nº INDIVIDUOS FEBRERO 1990	INCRE- MENTO
1	02	04	02
2	34	47	13
3	74	97	23
4	55	78	23
5	27	49	22
6	13	24	11
7	37	52	15
8	33	47	14
9	44	69	25
10	32	49	17
11	07	15	08
12	25	44	19
13	56	65	09
14	28	34	06
15	21	33	12
16	29	40	11
17	53	86	33
18	76	156	80
19	107	158	51
20	55	94	39
21	51	59	08
22	77	119	42
23	82	153	71
24	65	116	51
25	80	109	29
TOTAL 25	1163	1797	634

variando desde 2 unidades hasta 71 y 80 nuevos individuos, en los cuadrantes 23 y 18 respectivamente (Cuadro Nº 1).

Esta diferencia por cuadrante posiblemente se deba a la relación de la mayor o menor área ocupada por los árboles marcados con placas y la concentración de arbolillos juveniles, con respecto a la presencia de bambúes; es así que en 5 cuadrantes seleccionados para cada caso (Cuadro 2a, 2b, 3a, 3b), nos demuestra que a mayor número de árboles y arbolillos, corresponde menor número de bambúes y viceversa, condicionados por la sombra de los árboles, la competencia por el espacio y la luz en este tipo de ecosistemas.

Al analizar la población clonal de *Guadua weberbaueri* Pilger, en 50 clones marcados al azar, se vio incrementada en 83 unidades, permaneciendo en algunos clones el número de individuos estacionario, mientras que en la mayoría se sumaron de 1 hasta 5 nuevas unidades (Cuadro Nª 4). En *Elytrostachys sp.*, el incremento en igual número de clones marcados en el sistema de trochas y radiales fue de 174 unidades, sumándose de 1 hasta 7 individuos (Cuadro Nª 5). La

RELACION Nº DE GUADUAS / AREA OCUPADA POR ARBOLES					
CUADRO Nº 2a :			CUADRO Nº 2b :		
MENOR DENSIDAD			MAYOR DENSIDAD		
NºCUAD.	Nº BAMBUC.	AREA m2	NºCUAD.	Nº BAMBUC.	AREA m2
01	02	2.227	18	76	0.477
11	07	1.259	19	107	0.587
06	13	1.738	22	77	0.339
15	21	0.581	23	82	0.655
12	25	1.391	25	80	0.582
5	68	7.196	5	422	2.640

diferencia en la población clonal creemos que es a las mejores condiciones del hábitat para *Elytrostachys*, por estar concentradas en pequeñas quebradas húmedas, no así *Guadua weberbaueri* Pilger, evaluados en el bosque de terraza plana.

Referente al índice de crecimiento en longitud muestreado en 50 individuos juveniles de *Guadua*, al mes de febrero, arrojó un incremento promedio de 0.72 m de altura (Cuadro Nª 6); mientras que en *Elytrostachys* en el sistema de trochas, el promedio de crecimiento fue de 0.52 m (Cuadro Nª 7), lo que nos demuestra que estas Bambusoideas logran su máximo crecimiento vegetativo, durante la

RELACION Nº DE GUADUAS Y Nº DE ARBOLILLOS POR CUADRANTES					
CUADRO Nº 3a :			CUADRO Nº 3b :		
MENOR DENSIDAD			MAYOR DENSIDAD		
NºCUAD.	Nº BAMBUC.	NºARBOLILLOS	NºCUAD.	Nº BAMBUC.	NºARBOLILLOS
01	02	128	18	76	46
11	07	130	22	77	59
06	13	151	25	80	86
15	21	118	23	82	68
12	25	109	19	107	62
5	68	636	5	422	321

CUADRO No.4.- INCREMENTO DE INDIVIDUOS DE *Guadua weberbaueri* Pilger EN 50 CLONES DURANTE LOS MESES DE SETIEMBRE (1989) Y FEBRERO (1990) EN CUADRANTES DEL PLOT 13 - ZONA III.

Nº CUADRANTE	Nº CLONES	Nº INDIV. SET.1989	Nº INDIV. FEB.1990	INCREMENTO
02	1	02	04	01
02	2	03	03	01
02	3	05	07	02
03	4	04	06	02
03	5	06	06	00
03	6	03	04	01
03	7	07	09	02
03	8	07	08	01
04	9	11	15	04
04	10	03	04	01
04	11	02	03	01
05	12	06	07	01
05	13	03	04	01
05	14	04	05	01
06	15	03	04	01
07	16	01	03	02
07	17	05	06	01
07	18	03	05	02
08	19	03	04	01
09	20	04	06	02
09	21	04	05	01
10	22	02	03	01
13	23	02	03	01
13	24	03	04	01
13	25	03	17	04
14	26	01	02	01
15	27	04	04	00
16	28	09	11	02
17	29	04	07	03
17	30	03	05	02
18	31	03	05	02
18	32	03	04	01
18	33	08	10	02
18	34	03	05	02
18	35	09	13	04
18	36	07	07	00
19	37	07	09	02
19	38	03	05	02
20	39	14	18	04
21	40	04	06	02
21	41	03	04	01
21	42	19	24	05
23	43	06	08	02
23	44	03	05	02
24	45	02	04	02
24	46	04	06	02
25	47	11	13	02
25	48	07	08	01
25	49	03	04	01
25	50	05	05	00
25	50	254	337	83

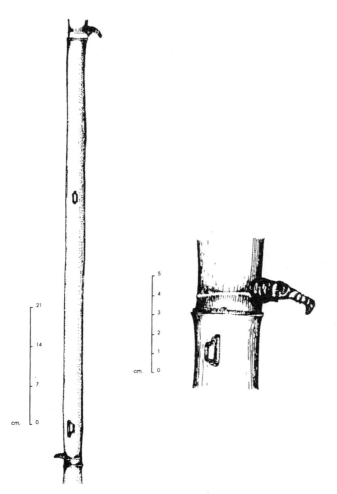

Graf. 1. *Entrenudos y nudos de Elytrostachys sp., mostrando orificios practicados por aves*

temporada lluviosa que corresponde a los meses de diciembre a marzo, cuando alcanzan su mayor altura y diámetro.

Resulta fácil diferenciar los nuevos individuos en el clon, por estar cubiertas de hojas bracteadas (caulinares), y su color verde intenso, con entrenudos sin pigmentaciones y nudos blanquecinos; mientras que los individuos de años anteriores se diferencian por ser más resistentes, con pigmentaciones por la presencia de líquenes y coloración opaca de los entrenudos.

INTERACCIONES CON LA FAUNA

Los "Bambusales" o "Pacales", constituyen ecosistemas importantes para especies de la fauna asociada tales como aves, anfibios, reptiles y mamíferos.

De los estudios realizados por Terborgh, Fitzpatrik y Emmons (1984), se desprende que las especies de aves residentes en los manchones de bambúes son: *Nannula rupicapilla* (Bucconidae), *Celeus Spectabilis* (Picidae), *Cercomarcra manu* (Furmicaridae), *Tryothorus genibarbis* (Troglodytidae), *Automalus melanopezus* (Fumariidae) y *Drymophyla devillei* (Furmicaridae).

Según Servat (1990), *Celeus spectabilis* (Picidae), es la especie que posiblemente practica las aberturas de contornos geométricos en los culmos de *Guadua weberbaueri* Pilger y *Elystrostachys* sp. (Graf. 1-2); indica igualmente que las especies de aves más conspicuas en los bambusales son: *Lophotriccus culophotes* (Tyrannidae), *Simoxonops ucayalae* (Furmariidae), *Ranphotrigon megacephala* (Tyrannidae), *Mechaeropterus pyrocephalus* (Pipridae), *Sporophila americana* (Fringillidae).

194

CUADRO No.5.- INCREMENTO DE INDIVIDUOS DE *Elystrostachys sp*. DURANTE LOS MESES DE SETIEMBRE (1989) Y FEBRERO (1990) EN EL SISTEMA DE TROCHAS.

TROCHAS ESTACAS	Nº CLONES	Nº .INDIV. SET.1989	Nº INDIV. FEB. 1990	INCREMENTO
T-II-4-35	1	04	06	02
	2	05	08	03
	3	06	08	02
37-38	4	09	11	03
	5	07	10	03
	6	10	13	03
	7	09	12	03
	8	21	24	03
	9	03	04	01
	10	13	15	02
39-40	11	12	14	02
	12	09	11	02
50-51	13	08	11	03
	14	05	06	01
	15	09	11	02
	16	10	13	03
54-55	17	17	22	05
	18	14	19	05
	19	05	07	02
	20	09	11	02
57-58	21	10	12	02
	22	13	17	04
87-88	23	06	09	03
	24	04	06	02
	25	10	16	06
	26	09	13	04
Trt-07-28	27	04	05	01
36-37	28	09	12	03
	29	· 06	08	02
39-40	30	26	32	06
	31	14	20	06
	32	18	25	07
	33	08	10	02
	34	12	17	05
R-3-20-21	35	07	09	02
R-4-1-2	36	07	09	02
2-3	37	22	28	06
6-8	38	05	07	02
	39	07	09	02
12-13	40	05	07	02
19-20	41	05	06	01
22-23	42	05	07	02
27-30	43	07	09	02
	44	05	07	02
	45	04	05	01
	46	07	09	02
	47	07	13	06
	48	12	15	03
	49	07	11	04
	50	06	10	04
	50	452	599	147

T = Trocha	TrT =	Troncal Tachigalia	
Tr = Troncal	R =	Radial	

Morales (1989), reporta para la Estación de Pakitza la especie *Dendrobates biolat*, encontrado en los culmos agujereados de *Guadua weberbaueri Pilger*, al parecer el anfibio, cumple su ciclo en los entrenudos cargados de agua y otros materiales en degradación.

Vivar (1990), al inventariar los roedores pequeños en Pakitza, identifica la "Rata del Bambú" *Dactylomys boliviensis Cabrera*, especie asociada a los bambúes, peculiar por sus hábitos nocturnos, que denotan su presencia a través de chillidos sostenidos.

Al evaluar las comunidades de *Guadua* y *Elytrostachys*, en las dos temporadas del año, hemos observado la presencia de numerosos ofidios entre las hojarascas, permaneciendo posiblemente en busca de alimento o de refugio en estos ecosistemas importantes del bosque húmedo tropical.

El presente trabajo, preliminar si bien considera algunos aspectos relacionados a la dinámica poblacional de dos especies leñosos de bambúes y las interacciones con la fauna circundante, sin embargo, requiere ser complementado con mayores estudios referentes a las tasas de incremento y mortalidad poblacional por hectárea/año; el comportamiento y la dinámica de los núcleos clonales, siendo necesario dedicar mayores esfuerzos a las investigaciones botánicas y ecológicas de las Bambusoideas leñosas y herbáceas en Pakitza.

AGRADECIMIENTOS

Al Programa BIOLAT, por darme la oportunidad de participar en los cursos de entrenamiento y financiar el presente trabajo.

Mi especial reconocimiento y gratitud a la Dra. Ximena Londoño por la difícil tarea en la determinación de las dos Bambusoideas leñosas de Pakitza, aporte de literatura especializada, revisión crítica del manuscrito y las invalorables orientaciones para el estudio de los bambúes.

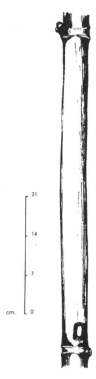

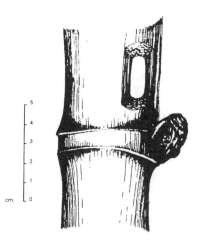

Gráf. 2 Entrenudo de Guadua weberbaueri mostrando orificios practicados por aves.

CUADRO No. 6.- INDICE DE CRECIMIENTO DE INDIVIDUOS DE *Guadua weberbaueri* Pilger EN CUADRANTES DEL PLOT 13 ZONA III Y TROCHAS.

No. PARCELA TROCHAS	MEDIDAS (M) (5Feb-1989)	MEDIDAS (m) (1 Mar-1990)	INCREMENTO (m) (25 DIAS)
5	1.82	2.60	0.78
9	0.62	2.60	0.98
14	1.90	2.84	0.95
19	1.97	2.50	0.53
20	2.96		(quebrado)
	3.80	4.40	0.60
24	2.80	3.70	0.90
	2.10	2.73	0.63
	1.30	1.87	0.57
25	0.90	2.40	0.50
	1.25	1.87	0.62
	0.65	1.20	0.55
	2.30	3.15	0.85
	1.40	2.10	0.70
T-11	1.60	2.52	0.92
	1.95	2.60	0.65
	1.40	1.98	0.58
	2.15	2.92	0.77
	3.00	3.84	0.84
	0.95	2.18	0.23
	2.23	3.05	0.85
	2.75	3.65	0.90
	2.37	2.87	0.52
	3.97	4.59	0.62
	1.32	1.95	0.63
	2.10	2.56	0.46
T-P	2.36	2.87	0.51
	1.21	1.93	0.72
	0.75	1.82	0.07
	3.17	3.79	0.62
	3.15	3.83	0.68
	4.05	4.76	0.71
	0.90	1.67	0.77
	2.46	3.05	0.59
	2.60	3.51	0.91
	1.83	2.69	0.86
	2.05	2.98	0.93
	0.87	1.67	0.80
	2.40	3.15	0.75
	1.18	2.96	0.78
	2.10	2.83	0.73
	3.24	3.78	0.54
	2.92	3.81	0.89
	3.00	4.79	0.79
	2.25	3.05	0.80
	1.33	1.95	0.62
	2.27	3.12	0.85
	2.50	3.34	0.84
	1.45	2.26	0.81
	1.57	2.29	0.72
			0.72

CUADRO No.7.- INDICE DE CRECIMIENTO DE INDIVIDUOS DE *Elystrostachys sp.* EN CUADRANTES DEL SISTEMA DE TROCHAS.

No.PARCELA TROCHAS	MEDIDAS (m) (5Feb-1989)	MEDIDAS (m) (1º Mar-1990)	INCREMENTO (m) (25 DIAS)
T-T-38-39	1.60	2.10	0.50
	1.85	2.48	0.60
	1.46	2.00	0.54
	1.27	2.10	0.83
	1.38	2.18	0.80
	0.00	0.69	0.69
	0.00	0.58	0.58
	1.19	2.20	1.01
	1.25	1.90	0.75
	0.00	0.87	0.87
	0.00	0.90	0.90
	1.10	1.40	0.30
	0.00	0.40	0.40
	1.19	1.54	0.35
	0.00	0.43	0.43
	0.00	0.65	0.65
	0.00	0.38	0.38
	0.00	0.96	0.96
	0.00	0.53	0.53
	1.95	2.55	0.60
	1.00	1.46	0.46
	1.59	2.08	0.46
	1.70	2.46	0.76
	1.62	2.17	0.55
	1.16	1.61	0.45
	2.12	2.94	0.82
	2.66	3.25	0.59
	1.75	2.90	1.15
	0.34	1.12	0.78
	2.28	2.46	0.18
	1.47	2.12	0.65
	0.33	0.69	0.36
	1.25	1.81	0.56
	1.43	1.59	0.16
R-4	2.90	3.70	0.80
	2.64	3.58	1.14
	0.40	1.20	0.80
	0.75	1.45	0.70
	0.98	1.60	0.62
TrT - 36-37	0.00	0.73	0.73
	0.30	1.10	0.80
	0.95	1.70	0.75
	0.40	1.15	0.75
39-40	0.00	0.95	0.95
	1.31	2.40	1.09
	0.85	1.30	0.45
	0.63	1.29	0.66
	1.25	2.10	0.85
	0.00	0.86	0.86
	0.54	1.18	0.64
			0.52

BIBLIOGRAFÍA

Londoño, X. 1989. Estudio Botánico, Ecológico, Silvicultural y Económico Industrial de la Bambusoideas de Colombia. Cespedesia, Vol. Nº 59-1990.

1990. Aspectos sobre la Distribución y la Ecología de los bambúes de Colombia (Poaceae; Bambusoideae: Bambuseae), Instituto Vallecaucano de Investigaciones Científicas. INCIVA. A.A. 5660 Cali, Colombia.

Morales, V. 1989. Resumen del IX Congreso Latinoamericano de Zoología, Cartagena-Colombia.

Parodi, L. 1959. Enciclopedia Argentina de Agricultura y Jardinería. Imprenta López. B.A. Argentina.

Servat, G. 1989. Comparación de la Abundancia y Riqueza de aves en cinco tipos de bosques en Pakitza.- Programa BIOLAT.

Soderstrom. T. & Young, S. 1987. Guía para Colectar bambúes.

Proyecto COLCIENCIAS. INCIVA 2108-07-009-85. Cali-Colombia.

Terborgh, J. Fitzpatrick & Emmons. 1984. Annotated Checklist of Bird and species Mammals of Cocha Cashu Biological Station. Manu National Park. Perú. Fieldiana Zoology New series Nº 21:1-27.

UNA/CEPID. 1986. Plan Maestro: Parque Nacional de Manu. Lima Perú.

Vivar, E. 1989. Inventario de Pequeños Roedores de Pakitza. Programa BIOLAT.

Weberbauer, A. 1945. El Mundo Vegetal de los Antiguos Peruanos. Estación Agrícola La Molina. Lima-Perú.

A Report on the Bryoflora of Perú

Noris Salazar Allen

Smithsonian Tropical Research Institute, Apartado 2072, Balboa,
Republic of Panama and Dept. de Botánica, Universidad de Panamá.

S. Robert Gradstein

Systematische Geobotanisches Institute
University of Göttingen Untere Karspüle[2] 73073 Göttingen Germany

ABSTRACT

Bryophytes are an important component of the tropical rainforests, contributing substantially to the hydric balance and the animal and plant diversity of these ecosystems, particularly in cloud forests. The varied topography and climatic zones in Peru are reflected in its very diverse bryoflora. Since the earliest bryophyte report in the XIX century, hundreds of botanists and collectors have visited Peru. Two of the most complete inventories of the bryoflora are those by the German BRYOTROP expedition to Northeastern Peru in 1982, and recently, 1990, Menzel's studies of semidesert, dry punas and subalpine regions of the Depts. of Arequipa, Moqueagua and Tacna, the inner Andean valleys around Cuzco and the moist eastern slopes of the southern Peruvian Andes to the lowlands of Río Madre de Dios. Today, the bryoflora includes a total of 889 species of mosses in 244 genera and 62 families and about 625 hepatics.

RESUMEN

Las briofitas son componentes importantes de los bosques tropicales contribuyendo, sustancialmente, al balance hídrico y a la diversidad de plantas y animales en estos ecosistemas, particularmente en las selvas nubosas. La variada topografía y zonas climáticas que caracterizan al Perú se reflejan en la alta diversidad de su brioflora. Desde el primer reporte de briofitas conocido, que data del siglo XIX, cientos de botánicos y colectores han visitado el Perú. De los inventarios florísticos de briofitas llevados a cabo, dos de los más completos son los de la expedición alemana BRYOTROP realizada en el noreste del Perú en 1982, y, recientemente, en 1990, los estudios de Menzel en las punas semidesérticas y secas y, las regiones subalpinas de los departamentos de Arequipa, Moquegua, y Tacna; los valles andinos internos alrededor de Cusco y las laderas húmedas del este, en la parte sur de los Andes peruanos hacia el Río Madre de Dios. Actualmente, la brioflora incluye un total de 889 especies de musgos en 244 géneros y 62 familias y, cerca de 625 hepáticas. Pakitza es una de las áreas menos exploradas en Perú. Estudios comparativos en otras selvas de tierras bajas en el norte de América del Sur y Panamá sugieren que la brioflora de Pakitza probablemente posea poca diversidad y fitomasa con relación a aquélla de selvas tropicales a mayores elevaciones. Se espera que la mayoría de las hepáticas foliosas sean miembros de las Lejeuneaceae y Plagiochilaceae. Es muy probable que los musgos corticícolas y pleurocárpicos predominen sobre los terrestres y acrocárpicos.

INTRODUCTION

Pakitza is one of the least surveyed areas in Peru. Comparative studies in other lowland forests in northern Southamerica and Panama suggests that the bryoflora of Pakitza will most probably have low diversity and phytomass when compared to those of other forests at higher elevations. The majority of the leafy liverworts are expected to be members of the Lejeuneaceae and Plagiochilaceae. Corticolous moss epiphytes and pleurocarps will most probably predominate over terrestrial mosses and acrocarps.

Traditionally, floristic inventories in the tropics cover almost exclusively the vascular vegetation and only few bryophytes (mosses and liverworts) and lichens are mentioned. Yet, bryophytes are an important component of tropical ecosystems, increasing in diversity (number of species) and phytomass in forests at middle to higher elevations. Mosses and hepatics are indicators of microclimatic conditions not usually shown by the vascular vegetation. They are important in the hydric balance of tropical forests particularly in cloud "mossy" forests where they act as rainfall interceptors (Pócs, 1982). Thus, they may reduce the negative effects of soil erosion caused by heavy rainfall. Bryophyte mats are moist sites suitable for the germination and establishment of small vascular plants (e.g., ferns, ericaceous herbs, bromeliads). A great number of microorganisms e.g., cyanobacteria, anhydrobiotic nematods, rotifers and tardigrades (Crowe, 1971) grow in association with bryophytes. The extent and biological significance of these symbiotic relationships are quite unknown in tropical forests. Organic substances, mainly terpenoids and lipophilic aromatic compounds contained in the oil bodies of many hepatics are related to antiherbivore activities, allelopathy, contact dermatitis and even to the isolation of active fragrant compounds with potential uses in cosmetics (Asakawa, 1990).

Very little is known today about community associations, population dynamics, phenology, species plasticity and the ecology of tropical bryophytes. Studies in Colombia (Churchill 1991a, 1991b; Churchill & Sastre-De Jesús, 1987; Gradstein et al., 1977; van Reenen & Gradstein, 1983), The Guyanas (Cornelissen & Gradstein, 1990; Florschütz-de Waard & Bekker, 1987) and in Northeastern Peru (Frahm, 1987a; Gradstein & Frahm, 1987) have pointed to the great diversity of the bryophyte flora of these areas. At the rate of deforestation of tropical rainforests, it will be difficult to establish the number of species lost, their importance and the impact their disappearance may cause. Pakitza offers a unique opportunity to address these issues as well as many others related to biodiversity and conservation.

The bryoflora of Peru is very rich and diverse. The first report of a moss specimen, *Pyrrhobryum spiniforme* (as *Hypnum spiniforme*) dates back to the early XIX century (Menzel, 1992). Between 1832 and 1834, A. Mathews, a British, made extensive collections that included the first samples of Andean mosses (Menzel, 1986). His 21 moss species from the Departamentos of Huanuco and Pasco were identified and published by Mitten in his "Musci Austro-Americani" (1869). R. Spruce made collecting trips that culminated in his "Hepaticae of the Amazon and the Andes of Peru and Ecuador" (1884-1885) as well as other publications and the "Exsiccata Musci Amazonici et Subandini". Sullivant (1859) published in the "United States Exploring Expedition" 1839, some records of mosses collected in the Department of Lima. Menzel (1986) cites three additional collectors Weddell (leg. anno 1847, 1851), Lechler (leg. anno 1852-54) and Hasskarl (leg. anno 1854) whose samples were identified by Hampe (1854, 1865), Mitten (1869) and Warnstorf (1891). E. Ule also collected in Peru during the years of 1902 and 1903 and, in the border areas of Brazil-Peru-Bolivia, from 1911 to 1912 (Vegter, 1988). His collections were identified by Brotherus (1906). From 1901 to 1905, A Weberbauer collected bryophytes in his trips through Moyobamba, Tarapoto and Yurimaguas. These were identified and published by Brotherus (1920). Menzel (1992) has recently published an excellent updated review of the bryological exploration in Peru.

The first compilation of the mosses reported for Peru was published by Soukup (1951) with 345 unrevised species. Hegewald & Hegewald (1975) published a second list in which they reported 568 species with their locality (by Departamentos) when known. At that time, no mosses were reported for eight (Ayacucho, Huancavelica, Ica, Lambayeque, Moquegua, Piura, Tacna and Tumbes) of the 23 Peruvian Departamentos. In 1977, Hegewald & Hegewald reported on their collecting trips to 13 Departments (98 collecting sites) in Peru in 1973. Mosses and liverworts were collected and a report was made of twenty percent of the collections determined. Fifty two mosses were reported as new to Peru and *Bryum alpinum* as new for South America. Five new species of hepatics were reported as new to Peru: *Jungermannia linguifolia* Gott., *J. ovato-trigona* (Steph.) Grolle, *J.sphaerocarpa* Hook., *Syzygiella grollei* Inoue (Paratype) and *Cylindrocolea rhizantha* (Mont.) Schust.

Frahm & Hegewald (1979) added 21 species of *Campylopus* (Musci: Dicranaceae) based on collections made by Hegewald & Hegewald in 1973. Hegewald & Hegewald (1985) reported from a collecting trip to 11 Departamentos, 115 species of mosses and 29 of hepatics as new to Peru. This raised the number of moss species from Peru to 834. Two years later, Menzel and Schultze-Motel (1987) recorded 903 species and discussed their distribution patterns.

In 1986, Menzel reported 83 species of mosses; 25 species and 3 genera were new for Peru. *Dicranowesia crispula* (Hedw.) Mild was reported new to South America.

A first catalogue of the hepatics of Peru was published by Menzel (1984). In all, 508 species had been reported until 1983. Most of the records are from the Departamentos Amazonas, Cajamarca, Cuzco, Huanuco, Junín, Lima, Loreto, Puno and San Martín.

An expedition of the National Science Museum, Tokyo, Japan from September to October 1984, gathered numerous bryophytes and other cryptogams in the Departamentos of Cuzco, Puno, Pasco and Junín. A report on this expedition (Inoue 1987) provided descriptions of 19 species of Grimmiaceae (mosses), including one species new to science and several new to the country, and of five new species of the hepatic family Plagiochilaceae. The report also provided numerous new data on oil bodies and chemical substances of miscellaneous hepatic species.

The BRYOTROP-PERU Expedition to northeastern Peru (in the areas around Leimebamba, Chachapoyas, Moyobamba, Yurimaguas and Tarapoto) from July to October 1982, rendered new additions to the bryoflora of this country. Most of these were published by Frahm, Gradstein, Menzel and Schultze-Motel in Frey (1987). Other reports on moss collections also appear in Menzel (1986). Eight genera and 56 species of mosses are reported as new to Peru (Schultze-Motel & Menzel, 1987a) and a new species of a pottiaceous moss *Tortella bryotropica* Zander is described as new to science. New combinations and synonyms are proposed and keys for the determination of Peruvian genera and some species are done for the first time. For the hepatics (Schultze-Motel & Menzel 1987b), seven genera and 119 species are reported as new to Peru. *Radula peruviana* Yamada, a new species is illustrated and described in detail. Like mosses, new synonyms and combinations are proposed and keys to Peruvian genera and species are provided.

Gradstein & Frahm (1987) made a determination of the altitudinal zonation of bryophytes in the BRYOTROP transect used for these studies. Four altitudinal zones were described using vegetation, physiognomical and floristic data. These are: Tropical Lowland (from sea level to 500m), Low Tropical Montane (from 500 to 1,900m), High Tropical Montane (from 1,900 to 3,200m) and Tropical Alpine (above 3,200m). This zonation correlates with results obtained by van Reenen & Gradstein (1983) in Colombia using an estimation of the abundance of bryphytes in relevees of the zonal vegetation. Also, Frahm (1987b, c) did studies on the phytomass of epiphytic bryophytes and determined light intensity, temperature and relative humidity of epiphyte habitats. He found that phytomass of the epiphytic bryophytes increases from the lowland to the forest line and is correlated with light intensity and humidity. Laboratory experiments on photosynthesis using various combinations of temperatures and light intensities indicated that high temperatures together with low light intensities as occurs in the tropical lowland forest, do not allow any net-photosynthesis.

Recently, Menzel (1992) did detailed studies of the semidesert, dry punas and subalpine regions of the Departments of Arequipa, Moqueagua and Tacna, the andean valleys around Cuzco and the moist eastern slopes of the Southern Andes to the lowlands of Río Madre de Dios. His study is still in progress and he will present the results at a later date,

The most updated checklist (Menzel 1992) which includes data on localities and altitudinal range of taxa with references on Type specimens and their location, reports a total of 889 species in 244 genera and 62 families. The total number of hepatics is about 625 (Gradstein pers.comm.).

Manu National Park of which Pakitza is a part, has a great diversity of habitats (Foster 1990a,b; Gentry & Terborgh, 1990). This part of the Peruvian Amazonia has areas that are quite pristine (Gentry & Terborgh, 1990) and thus ideal for floristic inventories and other botanical studies. In spite of important work on the bryophytes of Peru, vast areas remain poorly explored. Ten years ago, a bryological inventory of the Río Madre de Dios declared the area as priority for bryophyte research in Latin America (Griffin & Gradstein, 1982).

Comparative studies in other lowland forests of Peru (Frey 1987) and Panama (Gradstein & Salazar Allen, 1992; Salazar Allen et al., 1991) suggest that the bryoflora of Pakitza will most probably have low diversity and phytomass when compared to those of other forests at higher elevations. More mesic species will most probably be found in humid depressions and along banks of rivers and permanent creeks and at the bases of trees. The majority of leafy liverworts are expected to be members of the families Lejeuneaceae and Plagiochilaceae, most of which grow on bark except for some of the tiny Lejeuneaceae which are also epiphylls. Corticolous moss epiphytes and pleurocarpous taxa will most probably predominate over terrestrial mosses and acrocarps.

ACKNOWLEDGEMENTS

Floristic inventory of the bryoflora of Pakitza was made possible by BIOLAT grant to the senior author. Sincere acknowledgements to J.P. Frahm for useful comments on the original manuscript and for recent literature reports on the bryoflora of Peru.

LITERATURE CITED

Asakawa, Y. 1990. Terpenoid and aromatic compounds with pharmacological activity from bryophytes. Pp. 369-410, in Bryophytes their Chemistry and Chemical Taxonomy (H.D. Zinsmeister & R. Mues, eds.). Oxford Science Publications, Oxford, 470pp.

Brotherus, V. 1906. Musci amazonici et subandini Ulani. Hedwigia, 45:260-288.

Brotherus, V. 1920. Musci Weberbaueriani. Bot. Jahrb., 56:1-22.

Churchill, S. P. 1991a. Bryologia novo gratensis.V. Additional records for Colombia and Antioqhia, with a review of the distribution of *Hydropogon fontinaloides* in South America. The Bryologist, 94:44-48.

Churchill S. P. 1991b. The floristic composition and elevational distribution of Columbian moses. The Bryologist 94:157-167.

Churchill, S.P. & I.Sastre-De Jesús. 1987. Nuevos Registros para los Departamentos de Antioquia y Chocó, Colombia y una nueva especie del género *Trichosteleum*. The Bryologist, 90:246-250.

Cornelissen,J.H.C. & S. R. Gradstein. 1990. On the occurrence of bryophytes and macrolichens in different lowland rainforest types at Mabura Hill, Guyana. Tropical Bryology 3:29-35.

Crowe, J.H. 1971. Anhydrobiosis: An unsolved problem. American Naturalist, 105(946):563-573.

Florschütz-de Waard, J. & J.M. Bekker. 1987. A comparative study of the bryophyte flora of different forest types in West Surinam. Cryptogamie,Bryologie Lichénologie, 8:31-45.

Foster, R. 1990a. The floristic composition of the Río Manú floodplain forest. Pp. 99-111, in Four Neotropical Rainforests (A.H. Gentry, ed.). Yale University Press, New Haven, 627 pp.

Foster, R. 1990b. Long-term change in the successional forest community of the rio Manu floodplain. Pp. 565-572, in Four Neotropical Rainforest (A.H. Gentry, ed.). Yale University Press, New Haven, 627 pp.

Frahm, J.-P. 1987a. Zur bryologischen Erforschung des Untersuchungsgebietes. Pp. 7-8, in Moosflora und-vegetation in Regenwäldern NO-Perus. (W. Frey, ed.). J. Cramer, Berlin, 159 pp.

Frahm, J.-P. 1987b.Struktur und Zusammensetzung der epiphytischen Moosvegetation in Regenwäldern NO-Perus. Pp 115-141, in Moosflora und-vegetation in Regenwäldern NO-Perus (W. Frey, ed.). J. Cramer, Berlin, 159 pp.

Frahm, J.-P. 1987c. Okologische Studien über die epiphytische Moosvegetation in Regenwäldern NO-Perus, Pp 143-158, in Moosflora und-vegetation in Regenwäldern NO-Perus (W. Frey, ed.). J. Cramer, Berlin, 159 pp.

Frahm, J.-P. & E. Hegewald. 1979. Eine Moossammlung aus Peru II. *Campylopus* . Nova Hedwigia, 31:435-447.

Frey, W. (ed.), 1987. Moosflora und-vegetation in Regenwäldern NO-Perus. J. Cramer, Berlin, 159 pp.

Gentry, A. H. & Terborgh. 1990. Composition and dynamics of the Cocha Cashu "mature" floodplain forest. Pp. 542-564, in Four Neotropical Rainforests (A.H. Gentry, ed.). Yale University Press, New Haven, 627pp.

Gradstein, S.R., A.M. van Cleef & M.H. Fulford. 1977. Oilbody structure and ecological distribution of selected species of Tropical Andean Jungermanniales. Proc. K.Ned. Akad. Wet. Ser. C, 80:377-420.

Gradstein, S. R & J. - P. Frahm. 1987. Die floristische Höhengliederun der Moose entlang des BRYOTROP - Transekt in NO-Perú. Pp. 105-114, in Moosflora und vegetation in Regenwälden NO-Perú (w. Frey, ed.). J. Cramer, Berlin. 159 pp.

Gradstein, S. R. & N. Salazar Allen. 1992. Bryophyte diversity along an altitudinal gradient in Darian National Park. Tropical Bryology, 5:61-72.

Griffin III,D. & S. R. Gradstein. 1982. Bryological exploration in the Tropical Andes: current status. Beih.Nova Hedwigia, 71:513-521.

Hampe, E. 1854. Plantae quaedem Lechlerianae. Linnaea 27:553-556.

Hampe, E. 1865. Musci Novi, quos in Peruviae meridionalis orientalis provincia Carabaya legit Dr.J.K. Hasskarl. Flora 48:580-582.

Hegewald, P. & E.Hegewald. 1975. Verseichnis der Laubmoose von Peru nach Literaturangaben. J. Hattori Bot. Lab., 39:39-66.

Hegewald, E. & P. Hegewald. 1977. Eine Moossamlung aus Peru I. Nova Hedwigia, 28:731-758.

Hegewald, E. & P. Hegewald. 1985. Eine Moossammlung aus Peru. III. Nova Hedwigia, 41:219-271.

Inoue,H. (ed.) 1987. Studies on cryptogams in Southern Peru. Tokay University Press, Tokyo. 192pp.

Menzel, M. 1984. Katalog der Lebermoose von Peru. Willdenowia, 1:473-523.

Menzel, M. 1986. Beitrag zur andinen laubmoosflora von Peru. Willdenowia, 15:529-555.

Menzel, M. & W. Schultze-Motel. 1987. Studies on Peruvian bryophytes III. Phytogeographic analysis of the distribution patterns of Musci. Mem. New York Bot. Gard., 45:371-387.

Menzel, M. & W.Schultze-Motel. 1992. Preliminary checklist of the mosses of Peru. J. Hattori Bot. Lab., 71:175-254.

Mitten, W. 1869. Musci Austro-Americani. J. Linn. Soc., Bot., 12:1-659.

Pócs, T. 1982. Tropical forest bryophytes. Pp. 59-104, in Bryophyte Ecology (A.J.E. Smith, ed.). Chapman & Hall. London, 511 pp.

Reenen, G.B. A. van & S.R. Gradstein. 1983. Studies on Colombian Cryptogams XX. A transect analysis of the bryophyte vegetation along an altitudiinal gradient on the Sierra Nevada de Santa Marta, Colombia. Acta Bot. Neerl., 32(2):163-175.

Salazar Allen N., C. Arrocha y C. Chung. 1991. The Mosses of Barro Colorado Island. The Bryologist, 94:289-293.

Schultze-Motel, W. & M. Menzel. 1987a. Die Laubmoosflora im BRYOTROP-Transekt von Peru. Pp 9-59, in Moosflora und-vegetation in Regenwäldern NO-Perus. (W. Frey, ed.). J. Cramer, Berlin, 159 pp.

Schultze-Motel, W. & M. Menzel. 1987b. Die Lebermoosflora im BRYOTROP-Transekt von Peru. Pp. 61-104, in Moosflora und-vegetation in Regenwäldern NO-Perus. (W. Frey, ed.). J. Cramer, Berlin, 159 pp.

Soukup, J. 1951. Algunas diatomeas del Perú y lista de los musgos peruanos. Bol. Soc. Peruan. Bot.k 3:67-78.

Spruce, R. 1884-1885. Hepaticae of the Amazon and the Andes of Peru and Ecuador. Trans. & Proc. Bot. Soc. Edinburgh, reprinted Contri. New York Bot. Gard. 15:II-XII, [i-] vi-xi, 1-599[-589], Tabs. I-XXII, (1)-(14).

Sullivant, W.S. 1859.Cryptogamia of the United States Exploring Expedition, Musci. Phildelphia, 112 pp.

Vegter, H. I. 1988. Index Herbariorum Regnum Vegetabile 117, part II (7):1056-1057.

Warnstorf, C. 1891. Beiträge zur Kenntnis exotischer *Sphagna* IV. *Sphagna mucronata* . Hedwigia, 30:127-178.

Fauna

Invertebrates

Vertical Stratification of Flight by Ithomiine Butterflies (Lepidoptera: Nymphalidae) at Pakitza, Manu National Park, Perú

Mirian C. Medina

Robert K. Robbins, and Gerardo Lamas

Department of Zoology, University of Texas at Austin, Austin, TX 78712
Department of Entomology, National Museum of Natural History, Smithsonian Institution, Washington DC 20560
Departamento de Entomología, Museo de Historia Natural, UNMSM, Apartado 140434, Lima, Perú

ABSTRACT

In samples of ithomiine butterflies collected with insect nets, flying height was correlated with wing pattern and wing length, but not with sex or time of day. Wing pattern and length were also correlated with each other, so that larger, tiger patterned ithomiines tended to fly higher in the forest than did smaller, transparent patterned individuals. Since samples from traps showed the same correlation between wing pattern and size, this result was not likely to be a result of bias in sampling method. Vertical stratification by wing pattern has been previously explained in terms of predator-avoidance strategies. We suggest that stratification by wing length may be related to differences in flight behavior (e. g. flight distance, time aloft) at different strata.

INTRODUCTION

The height above the ground at which butterflies fly is statistically correlated with wing pattern (Poole, 1970, Papageorgis, 1974, 1975, DeVries, 1988). Poole reported such a correlation, primarily among ithomiine butterflies (Rancho Grande, Venezuela), and suggested that stratification was correlated with light intensity. Papageorgis identified five distinct wing pattern groups in Peruvian butterflies (three localities) and noted that individuals in each wing pattern group flew at different levels inside or above the forest. She suggested that patterns might be cryptic at lower light intensities, but aposematic at higher levels, a hypothesis that Brown (1988) supported. DeVries studied fruit-feeding adult nymphalid butterflies and showed that canopy species differ from understory species in size and color pattern.

Explanations for stratification of butterflies with similar wing patterns have focused on the predator-avoidance function of these patterns at different strata in and above the forest (Poole, 1970, Papageorgis, 1974, 1975, DeVries, 1988). The purpose of this study was to confirm the stratification of ithomiine butterflies in lowland rain forest and to determine whether other factors were also correlated with flying height.

METHODS

The study was conducted in upper flood plain forest, as characterized by Erwin, (1991), at Pakitza, Manu National Park, Madre de Dios, Perú (356 m). The site was 1.1 km in length and 50 m wide, crossed by the Caña Brava trail and situated between the rio Manu and a parallel stream (Erwin, 1991). The canopy was 25 - 30 m high with occasional breaks, so that patches of high light intensity were intermingled with shaded areas. Ithomiine butterflies were common at this site, which is the main reason why we chose it. Field sampling was done from 8-25 October 1990 during the transition from dry to wet season. Time of day and height above the ground were recorded for each individual in the field whereas wing length, wing pattern, and sex were scored later in the laboratory. Specimens were identified using the collection at the Museo de Historia Natural, Universidad Nacional Mayor de San Marcos, Lima, Perú, where all vouchers were deposited.

We collected ithomiines with insect-nets for the first 15 days of the study. Sighted butterflies were chased until captured or lost. Because it was harder to catch high-flying individuals, we set aside periods when only butterflies flying above 2 m were collected. Time of day was recorded using a wrist-watch, and height above the ground was measured using poles of known length. Wing length was measured in the laboratory as the distance from the base to the apex of the right forewing.

All sampling methods are biased because organisms are not randomly dispersed (Pielou, 1975). One way to assess bias is to use other sampling methods. Thus, we also collected ithomiines with standard butterfly traps baited with *Heliotropium indicum* L. (Boraginaceae) placed at different heights throughout the site for the final three days of the study (Beebe, 1955). According to our experience, this bait preferentially attracts males from all strata in the forest, but otherwise allowed us to see if the insect-net collected sample was biased with regard to wing length and wing pattern.

Using the terminology of Papageorgis, (1975), wing pattern was scored as "transparent," which included individuals with transparent, translucent and yellowish wings, or as "tiger," which included individuals with black stripes crossing a brownish-tan ground color. Other wing pattern groups recognized by Papageorgis were not represented in our samples. Flying height was classified as low (0-2 m above the ground), middle (2-4 m high) and high (> 4 m high). The reason for doing this was that the height above the ground at which a butterfly was flying varied between the time that it was sighted and collected. Grouping the data allowed us to score virtually all specimens unequivocally in a category. Also, previous results (Papageorgis, 1975) showed that butterflies with transparent wing patterns typically fly below 2 m while those with tiger patterns fly higher. We grouped time of day into early (0600 - 1000 hours), middle (1000 - 1400 hours), and late (1400 - 1800 hours).

Because a phylogeny of the Ithomiinae is lacking, we assessed (very preliminarily) the relative importance of phylogeny versus ecology as determinants of flying height by performing the same statistical test outlined below on *Napeogenes*. This genus was the only one in our sample which contained both tiger (two species) and transparent (three species) patterned adults and for which we collected enough individuals (99) to do statistical tests. If flying height is primarily determined by phylogeny, then all species of *Napeogenes* should fly in the same strata irrespective of their wing pattern. Alternately, if flying height is determined by wing pattern, then tiger patterned *Napeogenes* should fly in different strata than transparent individuals.

Analysis of Variance (ANOVA) was used to compare wing length with flying height while Chi-square Tests were used to compare discrete variables with flying height. A Tukey Multiple Comparison Test was used to compare differences between different categories of a discrete variable. Samples collected with insect-nets were compared with trap data using a t-Test or Chi-square Test, as was appropriate. We used STATISTIX PC DOS Version 2.0, Copyright (C) 1985, 1987, NH Analytical Software to perform statistical tests.

RESULTS AND DISCUSSION

We sampled 603 ithomiines of 47 species using insect-nets during the first 15 days of the study. Species were categorized by wing pattern (Table 1), which was significantly correlated with flying height above the ground (Chi = 34.82, $d.f.$ = 2, $p < 0.001$, Table 2). Butterflies with the transparent pattern tended to fly below 2 m while individuals with the tiger pattern flew above 2 m, confirming previous results (Papageorgis, 1975). Of 13 species with a tiger pattern, only *Mechanitis lysimnia* and *Napeogenes stella* were collected within 2 m of the ground.

Wing length was significantly correlated with height above the ground ($p < 0.001$, Table 3), and in a multiple comparisons test, larger butterflies (= longer wing length) flew significantly higher in the forest than did smaller butterflies ($p < 0.05$). Wing length was also significantly correlated with wing pattern ($p < 0.001$), which means that small, transparent patterned ithomiines flew near the ground while larger, tiger patterned butterflies flew higher in the forest. This result differs in one respect from fruit-feeding nymphalids (DeVries, 1988), for which wing length was negatively correlated with the height at which the butterflies flew. Neither sex nor time of day was significantly correlated with flying height ($p > 0.05$), which

213

Table 1: *Wing pattern, wing length (cm) and flying height of Ithomiinae collected with insect nets*

Species	Wing pattern	Wing length ($\mu \pm$ s.d., (N))	Flight height (0-2, 2-4, 4->)
Callithomia alexirrhoe thornax	Tiger	3.2,(1)	1,0,0
C. lenea zelie	Trans	3.1 ± 0.17, (11)	9,0,2
Ceratinia neso peruensis	Trans*	2.3 ± 0.14, (2)	1,1,0
Ceratiscada hymen hymen	Trans	2.1 ± 0.10, (3)	1,2,0
Episcada sulphurea sulphurea	Trans	2.1 ± 0.05, (11)	8,3,0
Forbestra olivencia aeneola	Tiger	3.1 ± 0.41, (18)	17,1,0
Godyris zavaleta ssp.n.	Trans	3.1 ± 0.10, (10)	9,1,0
Heterosais nephele nephele	Trans	2.7 ± 0.10, (30)	23,5,2
Hypoleria lavinia cajona	Trans	2.5 ± 0.09, (33)	31,2,0
H. virginia vitiosa	Trans	2.4 ± 0.09, (90)	86,4,0
"Hypoleria" aelia brevicula	Trans	2.1, (1)	1,0,0
"Hypoleria" orolina arzalia	Trans	2.1 ± 0.05, (5)	5,0,0
Hyposcada anchiala richardsi	Tiger	3.1 ± 0.20, (3)	1,2,0
H. illinissa dolabella	Trans	2.4, (1)	0,1,0
H. zarepha ssp.n.	Trans	2.2, (1)	1,0,0
Hypothyris euclea ssp.n.	Tiger	2.8 ± 0.06, (4)	4,0,0
H. ninonia ssp.n.	Tiger	3.1, collected only in traps	
H. semifulva ssp.n.	Tiger	3.0 ± 0.08, (9)	6,3,0
Ithomia arduinna arduinna	Trans	2.1 ± 0.05, (28)	28,0,0
I. lichyi neivai	Trans	2.3 ± 0.19, (5)	5,0,0
I. salapia ardea	Trans	2.3 ± 0.06, (3)	3,0,0
Mcclungia cymo salonina	Trans	2.2 ± 0.00, (3)	3,0,0
Mechanitis lysimnia menecles	Tiger	3.4 ± 0.12, (7)	7,0,0
Melinaea maelus lamasi	Tiger	4.0 ± 0.12, (5)	3,1,1
M. marsaeus clara	Tiger	4.1 ± 0.10, (3)	3,0,0
M. menophilus orestes	Tiger	4.1 ± 0.15, (15)	7,7,1
Methona confusa psamathe	Trans	3.9, 1	1,0,0
M. curvifascia	Trans	3.8, 1	1,0,0
M. grandior ssp.n.	Trans	4.6, 1	1,0,0
Napeogenes aethra deucalion	Tiger	2.9 ± 0.16, (44)	34,8,2
N. inachia patientia	Trans	2.2 ± 0.05, (17)	15,2,0
N. pharo pharo	Trans	2.3 ± 0.09, (11)	7,3,1
N. stella ssp.n.	Tiger	2.4 ± 0.12, (3)	3,0,0
N. sylphis sylphis	Trans	2.1 ± 0.08, (24)	19,5,0
Oleria didymaea didymaea	Trans	2.4 ± 0.11, (14)	14,0,0
O. gunilla ssp.n.	Trans	2.2 ± 0.21, (2)	2,0,0
O. onega lentita	Trans	2.3 ± 0.13, (80)	78,2,0
O. ramona calatha	Trans	2.2 ± 0.15, (18)	17,0,1
O. victorine victorine	Trans	2.3 ± 0.07, (13)	12,0,1
Paititia neglecta	Trans	4.3 ± 0.14, (2)	2,0,0
"Pseudoscada" florula ssp.n.	Trans	1.8, collected only in traps	
Pseudoscada timna ssp.n.	Trans	2.1 ± 0.20, (13)	13,0,0
Pteronymia antisao guntheri	Trans	2.3 ± 0.11, (5)	5,0,0
P. forsteri	Trans	2.0 ± 0.05, (8)	6,2,0
P. vestilla ucaya	Trans	1.9 ± 0.21, (3)	3,0,0
Rhodussa cantobrica pamina	Tiger	2.4 ± 0.06, (3)	3,0,0
Scada batesi batesi	Trans	1.8 ± 0.16, (8)	8,0,0
S. reckia labyrintha	Trans	1.7 ± 0.21, (5)	5,0,0
Tithorea harmonia brunnea	Tiger	3.9 ± 0.17, (25)	12,8,5

* The wing pattern of this species has elements of a tiger pattern, but even if it were categorized as tiger pattern, it would not significantly change statistical results.

Table 2: *Wing pattern versus flying height for Ithomiinae collected with insect nets*

Flying height	Observed	Transparent Expected	Chi	Observed	Tiger Expected	Chi
0-2m	422	401.37	1.06	103	123.63	3.44
2-4m	32	48.93	5.86	32	15.07	19.01
4->m	7	10.70	1.28	7	3.30	4.16
Total	461	461.00	8.20	142	142.00	26.61

Overall Chi square	34.82
P value 0.001	
Degrees of freedom	2

confirms Papageorgis's (1975) report that time of day is uncorrelated with flying height.

We trapped 203 individuals of 31 species during the final three days of the study. Only two of these species - each represented by one individual - had not been previously collected with insect-nets. Thus, insect-net collecting appeared to be a good way to sample virtually all ithomiine species present at that time. As expected, most trapped individuals (91.6%) were males, and wing pattern was uncorrelated with flying height, supporting the hypothesis that traps attracted butterflies from all strata in the forest.

Table 3: *ANOVA for wing length versus flying height (data in Table 1) for Ithomiinae collected with insect nets*

Source	SS	DF	Mean Sq	F Test
Between flying height	1.559	2	0.7797	20.97
Within flying height	22.310	600	0.3718	
Total	23.870	602		
				p<0.0001

Wing pattern and wing length in trap samples were correlated ($p < 0.001$), just as they were in the insect-net samples. Consequently, the conclusion that tiger patterned ithomiines are significantly larger than transparent patterned species is not the result of sampling bias. Compared with the insect-net samples, the trap samples contained significantly fewer large ($t = 3.21, d.f. = 804, p < 0.001$), tiger patterned (Chi = 7.54, $d.f. = 1$, $p < 0.01$) butterflies. We had concentrated on collecting high-flying ithomiines with insect-nets because of the difficulty of catching them. Assuming that the attraction of *Heliotropium* bait was independent of wing pattern or wing length, then it would appear that we over-sampled butterflies flying above 2 m in the insect-net samples.

The results of a similar analysis with *Napeogenes* , which contains both tiger and transparent patterned adults, were different. Flying height was statistically uncorrelated with either wing pattern (Chi = 0.51, p > 0.05) or wing length (F = 0.30, p > 0.05). Wing pattern changed at least once in this genus, but flying height did not. Thus, in this one case, phylogeny had more effect on flying height than did wing pattern or wing length.

It has not been previously noted that wing length of ithomiine butterflies is correlated with flying height. Since the distance between perches in the forest appears to be greater with increasing height, we tentatively suggest the testable hypothesis that ithomiine flying distance and time between alighting is positively correlated with both height above the ground and with wing length. An additional hypothesis (B. Drummond, pers. comm.) is that higher flying species employ patrolling courtship rather than display (perching) courtship.

ACKNOWLEDGEMENTS

We thank S. Mazer and M. Ryan for help with statistical analyses; Ryan for the use of computer facilities; W. Adams, F. S. Chew, P. DeVries, B. A. Drummond, R. Dudley, L. E. Gilbert and R. W. Poole for commenting on various drafts of the manuscript; and the Manu National Park authorities for permission to work at Pakitza. This research was supported by and is contribution number 87 from The Biological Diversity in Latin America (BIOLAT) Project, Smithsonian Institution.

LITERATURE CITED

Beebe, W. 1955. Two little-known selective insect attractants. Zoologica 40: 27-32.

Brown, K. S. Jr. 1988. Mimicry, aposematism and crypsis in Neotropical Lepidoptera: the importance of dual signals. Bull. Soc. Zool. Fr. 113: 83-119.

DeVries, P. J. 1988. Stratification of fruit feeding nymphalid butterflies in a Costa Rican rainforest. J. Res. Lepid. 26: 98-108.

Erwin, T. L. 1991. Natural history of the carabid beetles at the BIOLAT Biological Station, Rio Manu, Pakitza, Peru. Rev. Per. Entomol. 33: 1-85.

Papageorgis, C. 1974. The adaptative significance of wing coloration of mimetic Neotropical butterflies. Dissert. Princeton University, Princeton.

————. 1975. Mimicry in Neotropical butterflies. Amer. Scient. 63: 522-532.

Pielou, E. C. 1975. Ecological diversity. John Wiley & Sons, New York.

Poole, R. W. 1970. Habitat preferences of some species of a Mullerian-mimicry complex in Northern Venezuela, and their effects on evolution of mimic-wing pattern. J. N. Y. Entomol. Soc. 78: 121-129.

Taxonomic Composition and Ecological Structure of the Species-Rich Butterfly Community at Pakitza, Parque Nacional del Manu, Perú

Robert K. Robbins[1]

Gerardo Lamas[2]

Olaf H. H. Mielke[3]

Donald J. Harvey[1]

Mirna M. Casagrande[3]

[1]Department of Entomology, NHB Stop 127, National Museum of Natural History, Smithsonian Institution, Washington DC 20560

[2]Museo de Historia Natural, Universidad Nacional Mayor de San Marcos, Apartado 14-0434, Lima-14, Perú

[3]Departamento de Zoologia, Universidade Federal do Paraná, Caixa Postal 19020, 81531-970 Curitiba, Paraná, Brazil

ABSTRACT

1,300 butterfly species were sampled on five field-trips to Pakitza and are listed with their first dates of capture and whether they have been recorded at Tambopata, a reserve 235 km to the southeast. Approximately one-third of Pakitza's fauna are Hesperiidae, one-third Lycaenidae+Riodinidae, and one-third Nymphalidae+Papilionidae+Pieridae, which we suggest may be generally true for Neotropical butterfly communities. Slightly more than 10% of the species appear to be taxonomically undescribed. Almost 2% of the species have larvae that feed on plants other than angiosperms, and about 28% have larvae that eat monocotyledons. About one-third of the Riodinidae belong to tribes with larvae that are myrmecophilous. Adult butterflies were attracted to many substances, including wet sand, bird droppings, and flowers, but only about 10% of the fauna was attracted by decaying fruits, carrion, and excrement. Many of the most widespread, common Neotropical species, which are typical of disturbed habitats, were either unrecorded or rarely recorded at Pakitza. Butterflies that were "fogged" from the canopy by insecticide were mostly species of open areas and also were collected by other methods.

R. Robbins, G. Lamas, O. Mielke, D. Harvey and M. Casagrande

INTRODUCTION

Localities with the richest butterfly communities in the world occur in the lowland drainages of the Rio Solimões (Upper Amazon River) and Rio Madeira in Colombia, Ecuador, Perú, and Brazil (Brown, 1984; Emmel & Austin, 1990; Lamas et al., 1991; Robbins & Opler, 1996). More species may be found at 3,000-5,000 hectare sites in the Upper Amazon Basin than occur in most, if not all, African or Indo-Australian countries (Robbins, 1993). These communities are of great scientific interest because of their unusually high species richness, but they have not been been well-documented. The taxonomy of Amazonian Hesperiidae, Lycaenidae, and Riodinidae is poorly known, so specific identification has been difficult. Consequently, information on the taxonomic and ecological composition of these communities is scarce (but see Ebert, 1969; Drummond, 1976a; Hutchings, 1991).

The purpose of this paper is to provide basic information on the composition of the butterfly fauna of Pakitza, a biological station located in lowland rain forest (356 m elevation) on the east bank of the Rio Manu in the Reserved Zone of Parque Nacional Manu, Madre de Dios, Perú (11°56'47"S, 71°17'00"W). We list 1,300 identified species recorded on five field-trips, making Pakitza the richest documented site in the world for butterflies, and overview the taxonomic and ecological composition of Pakitza's fauna. We report on the diversity and dynamics of this community elsewhere.

STUDY SITE AND METHODS

Erwin (1991) mapped the trail system and many major streams at Pakitza. We sampled most of the forest types and other habitats that occur within 5 km of the base camp (Erwin, 1991), but concentrated our efforts along the banks of the Rio Manu and on the Tachigali, Castañal and Pacal trails. Consequently, the study site for our project was roughly a semi-circle of radius 5 km with an area of approximately 3,925 hectares. We usually collected within 10 m of trails in the forest, so 3,925 hectares is an upper limit of the actual area sampled.

Our field-work was limited to those short time-periods when the camp was open. Most field-work was done in September and October during the transition between the dry and wet seasons when lycaenid, riodinid, and hesperiid butterflies are usually most common and diverse. Consequently, our comments about seasonality are based primarily on Tambopata, a protected reserve 235 km to the southeast at similar elevation, where we collected at more different seasons than Pakitza (Lamas, 1981, 1983, 1985; Lamas et al., 1991).

Five field-trips were made: 8-23 September 1989, 2-21 October 1990, 27 October-16 November 1990, 19 April-14 May 1991, and 26 September-20

October 1991. There were two field-workers on each trip except 8-14 September 1989 (three people) and 26 September-20 October 1991 (four people). We recorded data on 97 days, totalling 247 person-days, and 1,311 person-hours. No data were taken on ten other days that were either too cold or rainy for butterfly activity.

A variety of collecting methods was used, including standard insect nets with pole extensions, baits, standard butterfly bait-traps, commercially obtained malaise traps, and "imitation" bird droppings (Austin et al., 1993; Lamas et al., 1993). Baits included rotting fish, decaying fruits, excrement, and withered *Heliotropium indicum* L. (Boraginaceae), a source of pyrrolizidine alkaloids (Beebe, 1955; Pliske, 1976). Besides the species that we collected as part of our project, we also recorded a few sightings of species which could be identified unambiguously. Additionally, other scientists at Pakitza gave us butterflies that they had trapped or collected.

It would be hard to overemphasize that specimen preparation and species identification were the most time-consuming and costly parts of this study. Responsibility for identification was apportioned as follows: Casagrande for Brassolinae; Lamas for other Nymphalidae, Pieridae, and Papilionidae; Mielke for Hesperiidae; Harvey for Riodinidae; and Robbins for Lycaenidae. Specimens were identified as well as possible using our taxonomic expertise, and the collections, type photographs, and literature of our respective institutions, where all specimens are being deposited. Even though we believe that our species list is the most authoritative one ever made for a South or Central American locality, some of the identifications are still provisional, and some are based only on males.

TAXONOMIC COMPOSITION

We list the 1,300 identified butterfly species (Appendix) that were collected at Pakitza (or positively identified by sight in 7 cases). There are 448 Hesperiidae, 25 Papilionidae, 31 Pieridae, 181 Lycaenidae, 246 Riodinidae, and 369 Nymphalidae. For each species, we note the first day on which it was sampled, the first day of capture during the fifth field-trip, and whether or not the species has been found at Tambopata, a protected reserve in Madre de Dios at a similar elevation (Lamas, 1981, 1983, 1985, 1994; Lamas et al., 1991), where 1,234 species have now been recorded. Although quantification of the sampling method and analysis of the resulting data are being published elsewhere, we present our data here so that they are available.

The taxonomic composition of the Pakitza sample (Table 1) is very close to one-third Hesperiidae (34.5%), one-third Lycaenidae + Riodinidae (32.8%), and one-third Papilionidae + Pieridae + Nymphalidae (32.7%). Similar partitions are also found (Table 1) at Tambopata (Lamas, 1994), Panama (Robbins, 1982), and Itatiaia, a park in Rio de Janeiro state (Zikán & Zikán, 1968). Although this 1:1:1 partition is not found in temperate North America (Miller & Brown, 1981) or in Serra do Japi in southern Brazil (Brown, 1992) (Table 1), primarily because

219

Table 1. For Pakitza, Tambopata (Lamas, 1994), Panama (Robbins and Small, 1981), Itatiaia (Zikán and Zikán, 1968), Serra do Japi (Brown, 1992), and North America (Miller and Brown, 1981), the percentage of true butterfly species (Papilionoidea) and of all butterflies (Papilionoidea + Hesperioidea) that belong to families Papilionidae, Pieridae, and Nymphalidae.

LOCALITY	% OF TRUE BUTTERFLIES	% OF ALL BUTTERFLIES
Pakitza	49.9%	32.7%
Tambopata	48.7%	31.4%
Panama	49.6%	----
Itatiaia	51.3%	32.3%
Serra do Japi	60.9%	38.0%
United States	65.6%	40.2%

riodinid diversity is low, we suspect that it is a robust "rule of thumb" for the taxonomic composition of lowland Neotropical butterfly communities.

Although we doubt that there is biological significance behind this non-phylogenetic partition of species richness, it may prove useful for species richness studies in the Neotropics. Given the taxonomic difficulties that we had in handling and identifying 1,300 species, future investigators who do not have a particular interest in Lycaenidae, Riodinidae, and Hesperiidae can focus on Papilionidae, Pieridae, and Nymphalidae and multiply by 3 to get an estimate for the entire fauna. For example, at least 204 Papilionidae, Pieridae, and Nymphalidae have been recorded from La Selva, a biological station in Costa Rica (DeVries, 1994). The other families have been largely unsampled, but we would estimate that at least 612 butterfly species occur at La Selva.

Of the 1,300 species in the Pakitza list, we could not identify 144 species (11%) that we believe are undescribed. These species belong to the Riodinidae (44), Hesperiidae (39), Lycaenidae (33), and to the nymphalid subfamilies Satyrinae (25), Brassolinae (2), and Nymphalinae (1). This result is further reason for limiting most diversity studies to Papilionidae, Pieridae, and Nymphalidae. Also, since the South American fauna is more poorly-known taxonomically than others, it is probably fair to conclude that at least 90% of the world's butterfly fauna is described.

COMMUNITY STRUCTURE

Although the purpose of this study was to assess the butterfly diversity of Pakitza, we also recorded incidental data on behavior and ecology. We present this information, even though it is incomplete, because we believe that it is the first attempt to look at the community structure of all butterflies at a Neotropical site.

Approximately 28% of the butterfly species at Pakitza feed as larvae on monocotyledons while most of the rest eat dicotyledons. The monocot feeders include 101 Satyrinae (excluding *Euptychia*), 22 Brassolinae, 225 Hesperiinae, and about 20 species in other subfamilies. A noteworthy feature of the Pakitza fauna is the 30 species of *Splendeuptychia* and *Caeruleuptychia*, nearly half of which are undescribed. Larvae of *Splendeuptychia* eat bamboo (Kendall, 1978; D. Murray, pers. comm.), which is very common at Pakitza (Erwin, 1991), while larvae of *Caeruleuptychia* eat palms (K. Brown, pers. comm.). Pakitza is one of the richest known sites for Ithomiinae (62 species), most of whose larvae feed on Solanaceae.

A small proportion of Pakitza's butterflies have larvae that do not eat angiosperms. Two species of *Eumaeus* (Lycaenidae) presumably feed on cycads (the foodplant of their sister species) (Robbins, in preparation); some species of *Calycopis* (Lycaenidae) and *Charis* (Riodinidae) appear to be detritivores (S. Johnson, 1985; Harvey, unpubl.); ten species of *Sarota* probably eat epiphylls (DeVries, 1988); and larvae of *Euptychia* (Nymphalidae) eat Selaginella or mosses (Singer et al., 1971, 1983, 1986). About 30 larvae and pupae of *Mimocastnia rothschildi* (Riodinidae) were found in an ant nest (*Cephalotes atratus*) in a dead branch. Larval feeding was not observed, but larvae may have been fed by ants (Harvey, in preparation). At least some species of *Setabis* (Riodinidae) have been reported as predaceous on Homoptera (Harvey, 1987).

Myrmecophily (symbiotic relationships between butterfly larvae and ants) is restricted, with few exceptions, in the Riodinidae to tribes Eurybiini, Lemoniini, and Nymphidiini (Harvey, 1987). Thus, a third of the riodinids at Pakitza (82 species) are expected to be myrmecophilous, which is a bit higher than most other Neotropical mainland areas, but less than Trinidad (Harvey, 1987). The distribution of myrmecophily in Lycaenidae is too poorly-known to allow similar estimates for them.

A conspicuous adult-feeding behavior at Pakitza was "puddling", in which males that appear to be freshly eclosed sip moisture in sunny spots from the dirt banks of the Rio Manu and some streams inside the forest. Most "puddlers" appear to be species of open areas, such as tree-fall gaps, river edges, and the upper canopy, and not, as a general rule, species restricted to undisturbed forest. Sodium in the soil attracts males, prolongs their feeding, and is transferred, in part, to females during mating (Arms et al., 1974; Adler & Pearson, 1982; Pivnick & McNeil, 1987; Lederhouse et al., 1990). Occasionally females also may "puddle", such as *Eunica* (Nymphalidae) in October 1991. Also, both sexes of *Ministrymon zilda* and *M. cleon* (Lycaenidae) regularly "puddle" in the late afternoon along the Rio Manu.

Perhaps the easiest way to summarize the extent of "puddling" behavior is to list those taxa in which it was not observed. They are *Parides* (*P. sesostris* puddles at other Amazonian sites, K. Brown, pers. comm.) (Papilionidae); *Dismorphia*, but not *Enantia* and *Pseudopieris* (Pieridae); all Lycaenidae except some *Ministrymon* and *Ocaria ocrisia*; most Riodinidae with *Lyropteryx*, *Rhetus*, *Ancyluris*, *Monethe*, *Parcella*, *Lasaia*, *Baeotis*, and *Melanis* being exceptions; Ithomiinae; Satyrinae; and Brassolinae. The phylogenetic incidence of "puddling" among Hesperiidae is not evident except that it occurs in all subfamilies at Pakitza.

Many Lycaenidae, particularly *Calycopis cerata* and *Celmia celmus*, congregate at drying stream beds at the end of the dry season. Individuals usually alight on vegetation, but also may land on moist dirt banks, where they sip moisture. In retrospect, it was our impression that this behavior occurred most often during the hottest part of the day and may have been a thermoregulatory behavior. It does not appear to be the same behavior as "puddling".

Many butterflies in primary Neotropical forest are associated with army ants (Zikán, 1929; Drummond, 1976b; Ray & Andrews, 1980; Lamas, 1983; Austin et al., 1993). These butterflies sip liquid from the ground or from bird droppings on leaves. Although *Agrias* (Charaxinae), Satyrinae, *Euselasia* (Riodinidae), and others were associated with army ants at Pakitza, Hesperiidae seemed to be the major butterfly participants, and "imitation" bird droppings attracted many more Hesperiidae than other butterflies (Lamas et al., 1993).

Few flowers at Pakitza attracted many butterflies, but we found adults feeding on other substances. As mentioned, many Hesperiidae and others eat bird "droppings", even when not associated with army ants (Lamas et al., 1993). About 10% of the species at Pakitza were attracted by decaying fruits, carrion, and excrement. Withered *Heliotropium indicum* L. (Boraginaceae) attracted many species of Ithomiinae in October 1990, but was less successful in other years.

Pakitza and Tambopata have a marked dry season from April-May to September-October. The abundance and diversity of most butterflies is highest during the transition between dry and wet seasons and lowest during the wet season. This pattern is particularly true for Lycaenidae and, to a lesser extent, for Riodinidae and Hesperiidae. However, adults of some species appear to fly only during the wet season, such as *Morpho menelaus* (Nymphalidae), or are most common at this time, such as *Saliana* (Hesperiidae). Most Nymphalinae and Limenitidinae (Nymphalidae) are conspicuous in the middle of the dry season, such as *Hamadryas* and *Eunica maja noerina*, and are often very worn by September, indicating that some of them may be in reproductive diapause.

Many of the most widespread, common, and weedy Neotropical butterflies, which are common in the vicinity of Puerto Maldonado, are absent or rare at Pakitza. *Danaus plexippus*, *D. gilippus* (Danainae), *Anartia jatrophae* (Nymphalinae), *Rekoa palegon*, *Strymon mulucha*, *Leptotes*, and *Hemiargus* (Lycaenidae) are unrecorded at Pakitza, and *Phoebis sennae* (Pieridae) was collected only twice. Consequently, sites in the Rio Madeira drainage that include a greater amount of disturbed habitat than at Pakitza would be expected to have more than 1,300 species. The biologically important question, though, is whether other sites have as many species of undisturbed habitats. These species are less able to survive in areas that have been modified by man and have more restricted distributions than species of disturbed habitats (Thomas, 1991; Spitzer et al., 1993).

Because butterflies in some groups fly primarily in one vertical stratum (Medina et al., 1996), a major question is whether our sampling methods missed a set of species restricted to the forest canopy. Fortunately, our colleagues, T. Erwin and M. Pogue, segregated butterflies that they "fogged" with insecticide from the forest canopy (Erwin 1983, 1990). Most of these species were widespread taxa of open areas, such as *Rekoa meton* (Lycaenidae), not species restricted to the canopy.

Further, we collected each of the "fogged" canopy species by other means. Although some species may live only in the upper strata of the forest, we have no evidence that such a fauna, if it exists, is very large.

ACKNOWLEDGEMENTS

We thank John MacDonald, William Rowe, and Nancy Clarke for participating in the project; field companions Mirian Medina, Christoph Häuser, Isabel Bohórquez, Terry Erwin, Michael Pogue, Jerry Louton, and Nancy Adams for providing specimens; Robert Lederhouse for providing references; Keith Brown and John Brown for reading and commenting on the manuscript, the staff of BIOLAT in Washington, Lima, and Pakitza, for arranging logistics and taking care of us; and the officials of the Peruvian Ministry of Agriculture who sanctioned our work at Pakitza. This paper is contribution number 92, Biological Diversity in Latin America (BIOLAT) Project, Smithsonian Institution, and contribution number 810 of the Department of Zoology, Universidade Federal do Paraná, Brazil.

LITERATURE CITED

Adler, P. H., and D. L. Pearson. 1982. Why do male butterflies visit mud puddles? Canad. J. Zool. 60: 322-325.

Arms, K., P. Feeny, and R. C. Lederhouse. 1974. Sodium: stimulus for puddling behavior by tiger swallowtail butterflies, *Papilio glaucus*. Science 185: 372-374.

Austin, G. T., J. P. Brock, and O. H. H. Mielke. 1993. Ants, birds, and skippers. Trop. Lepid. 4 (Suppl. 2): 1-11.

Beebe, W. 1955. Two little-known selective insect attractants. Zoologica 40: 27-32.

Brown Jr., K. S. 1984. Species diversity and abundance in Jaru, Rondonia (Brazil). News Lepid. Soc. 1984: 45-47.

Brown, K. S. Jr. 1992. Borboletas da Serra do Japi: diversidade, hábitats, recursos alimentares e variação temporal. Pp. 142-187 in L. P. C. Morellato, org. História natural da Serra do Japi: ecologia e preservação de uma área florestal no Sudeste do Brasil. Editora da UNICAMP/FAPESP, Campinas.

DeVries, P. J. 1988. The use of epiphylls as larval hostplants by the neotropical riodinid butterfly *Sarota gyas*. J. Nat. Hist. 22: 1447-1450.

DeVries, P. J. 1994. Patterns of butterfly diversity and promising topics in natural history and ecology. Pp. 187-194 in L. A. McDade, K. S. Bawa, H. S. Hespenheide, and G. S. Hartshorn, eds. La Selva, ecology and natural history of a neotropical rain forest. Univ. Chicago Press, Chicago.

Drummond III, B. A. 1976a. Comparative ecology and mimetic relationships of ithomiine butterflies in eastern Ecuador. Dissertation, University of Florida, Gainesville.

Drummond III, B. A. 1976b. Butterflies associated with an army ant swarm raid in Honduras. J. Lepid. Soc. 30: 237-238.

Ebert, H. 1969. On the frequency of butterflies in eastern Brazil, with a list of the butterfly fauna of Pocos de Caldas, Minas Gerais. J. Lepid. Soc. 23, Suppl. 3, 48 pp.

Eliot, J. N. 1973. The higher classification of the Lycaenidae (Lepidoptera): a tentative arrangement. Bull. Brit. Mus. (Nat. Hist.) Entomol. 28: 371-505.

Emmel, T. C. and G. T. Austin. 1990. The tropical rain forest butterfly fauna of Rondonia, Brazil: species diversity and conservation. Trop. Lepid. 1: 1-12.

Erwin, T. L. 1983. Tropical forest canopies: the last biotic frontier. Bull. Entomol. Soc. Amer. 29: 14-19.

Erwin, T. L. 1985. Tambopata Reserved Zone, Madre de Dios, Perú: history and description of the Reserve. Rev. Per. Entomol. 27: 1-8.

Erwin, T. L. 1990. Canopy arthropod biodiversity: a chronology of sampling techniques and results. Rev. Per. Entomol. 32: 71-77.

Erwin, T. L. 1991. Natural history of the carabid beetles at the BIOLAT biological Station, Rio Manu, Pakitza, Perú. Rev. Per. Entomol. 33: 1-85.

Evans, W. H. 1955. A catalogue of the American Hesperiidae indicating the classification and nomenclature adopted in the British Museum (Natural History). Part IV. Groups H-P, Hesperiinae and Megathyminae. British Museum, London, 499 pp., pls. 54-88.

Harvey, D.J. 1987. The higher classification of the Riodinidae (Lepidoptera). Ph. D. Dissertation, Univ. Texas, Austin, Texas, 216 pp.

Harvey, D. J. 1991. Higher classification of Nymphalidae. Appendix B. pp. 255-272 in Nijhout, H. F. 1991. The development and evolution of butterfly wing patterns. Smithsonian Inst. Press, Washington, D. C. xvi + 297 pp.

Hutchings H., R. W. 1991. Dinâmica de tres comunidades de Papilionoidea (Insecta: Lepidoptera) em fragmentos de floresta na Amazônia Central. Dissertacão de mestrado. Inst. Nac. Pesquisas Amazônia (INPA), Manaus.

Johnson, S. 1985. Culturing a detritivore, *Calycopis isobeon* (Butler & Druce). News Lepid. Soc. 1985: 41-42.

Kendall, R. O. 1978. Larval foodplant, life history notes and temporal distribution for *Splendeuptychia kendalli* (Satyridae) from Mexico. J. Lepid. Soc. 32: 86-87.

Klots, A. B. 1933. A generic revision of the Pieridae (Lepidoptera). Entomol. Amer. (new series) 12: 139-242.

Lamas, G. 1981. La fauna de mariposas de la Reserva de Tambopata, Madre de Dios, Perú (Lepidoptera, Papilionoidea y Hesperioidea). Rev. Soc. Mex. Lepid. 6: 23-40.

Lamas, G. 1983. Mariposas atraidas por hormigas legionarias en la Reserva de Tambopata, Perú. Rev. Soc. Mex. Lepid. 8: 49-51.

Lamas, G. 1985. Los Papilionoidea (Lepidoptera) de la Zona Reservada de Tambopata, Madre de Dios, Perú. I: Papilionidae, Pieridae y Nymphalidae (en parte). Rev. Per. Entomol. 27: 59-73.

Lamas, G. 1994. Butterflies of the Explorer's Inn Reserve. Pp. 62-63, 162-177 in R. B. Foster, J. L. Carr, and A. B. Forsyth, eds. The Tambopata Candamo Reserved Zone of Southeastern Perú: A. Biological Assessment. RAP Working Papers 6: 184 pp.

Lamas, G., O. H. H. Mielke, & R. K. Robbins. 1993. The Ahrenholz Technique for attracting tropical skippers (Hesperiidae). J. Lepid. Soc. 47: 80-82.

Lamas, G., R. K. Robbins, and D. J. Harvey. 1991. A preliminary butterfly fauna of Pakitza, Parque Nacional del Manu, Peru, with an estimate of its species richness. Publ. Mus. Hist. Nat. UNMSM (A) 40: 1-19.

Lederhouse, R. C., M. P. Ayres, and J. M. Scriber. 1990. Adult nutrition affects male virility in Papilio glaucus L. Funct. Ecol. 4: 743-751.

Medina, M., R. K. Robbins, and G. Lamas. 1996. Vertical stratification of flight by Ithomiinae butterflies (Lepidoptera: Nymphalidae) at Pakitza, Manu National Park, Perú. Pp. 211-216 (this volumen)

Miller, J. S. 1987. Phylogenetic studies in the Papilioninae (Lepidoptera: Papilionidae). Bull. Amer. Mus. Nat. Hist. 186: 365-512.

Miller, L. D. and F. M. Brown. 1981. A catalogue/checklist of the butterflies of America north of Mexico. Lepid. Soc. Mem. 2: 280 pp.

Pivnick, K. A. and J. N. McNeil. 1987. Puddling in butterflies: sodium affects reproductive success in *Thymelicus lineola*. Physiol. Entomol. 12: 461-472.

Pliske, T. E. 1976. Attraction of Lepidoptera to plants containing pyrrolizidine alkaloids. Environ. Entomol. 4: 455-473.

Ray, T. S. and C. C. Andrews. 1980. Antbutterflies: butterflies that follow army ants to feed on antbird droppings. Science 210: 1147-1148.

Robbins, R. K. 1982. How many butterfly species? News Lepid. Soc. 1982: 40-41.

Robbins, R. K. 1993. Comparison of butterfly diversity in the Neotropical and Oriental Regions. J. Lepid. Soc. 46: 298-300.

Robbins, R. K. and P. A. Opler. 1996. Butterfly diversity and a peliminary comparison with bird and mammal diversity. In Press in Biodiversity. National Academy of Sciences Press, Washington, DC. (D. E. Wilson, M. L. Reaka-Kudla, and E. O. Wilson, eds.).

Robbins, R. K. and G. B. Small. 1981. Wind dispersal of Panamanian hairstreak butterflies (Lepidoptera: Lycaenidae) and its evolutionary significance. Biotropica 13: 308-315.

Singer, M. C., P. R. Ehrlich, and L. E. Gilbert. 1971. Butterfly feeding on lycopsid. Science 172: 1341-1342.

Singer, M. C., P. J. DeVries, and P. R. Ehrlich. 1983. The *Cissia confusa* species group in Costa Rica and Trinidad. Zool. J. Linn. Soc. 79: 101-119.

Singer, M. C. and J. L. B. Mallet. 1986. Moss-feeding by a satyrine butterfly. J. Res. Lepid. 24: 392.

Spitzer, K., V. Novotny, M. Tonner, and J. Leps. 1993. Habitat preferences, distribution and seasonality of the butterflies (Lepidoptera, Papilionoidea) in a montane tropical rain forest, Vietnam. J. Biogeogr. 20: 109-121.

Thomas, C. D. 1991. Habitat use and geographic ranges of butterflies from the wet lowlands of Costa Rica. Biol. Conserv. 55: 269-281.

Zikán, J. F. 1929. Myrmekophilie bei Hesperiden? Entomol. Rundschau 46: 27-28.

Zikán, J. F. and W. Zikán. 1968. Inseto-fauna do Itatiaia e da Mantiqueira. III. Lepidoptera. Pesq. Agropec. Bras. 3: 45-109.

APPENDIX

Taxonomic list of the Pakitza butterflies. Species names with an asterisk (*) belong to groups in which only males were used for identification. Higher taxonomic categories follow Evans (1951-1955) for Hesperiidae, Miller (1987) for Papilionidae, Klots (1933) for Pieridae, Eliot (1973) for Lycaenidae, Harvey (1987) for Riodinidae, and Harvey (1991) for Nymphalidae.

The column "1st Day" lists the first day of capture for that species. If it was not collected as part of our project, we note whether it was a sight record (SR) or collected by another scientist (XX). The column "5th Trip" lists the first day of capture during the fifth field-trip or if it was not captured on this trip (NC). The column "Tambopata" notes whether or not the species was collected at Tambopata.

SPECIES	1ST DAY	5TH TRIP	TAMBO PATA
NYMPHALIDAE: HELICONIINAE			
1. Actinote pellenea hyalina Jordan, 1913	1	82	YES
2. A. thalia crassinia (Hopffer, 1874)	28	NC	NO
3. Philaethria dido (Linnaeus, 1763)	16	76	YES
4. Agraulis vanillae lucina C & R Felder, 1862	19	NC	YES
5. Dryas iulia alcionea (Cramer, 1779)	1	77	YES
6. Eueides aliphera aliphera (Godart, 1819)	16	77	YES
7. E. isabella hippolinus Butler, 1873	19	NC	YES
8. E. lybia lybia (Fabricius, 1775)	16	78	NO
9. E. tales tabernula Lamas, 1985	4	NC	YES
10. E. vibilia unifasciata Butler, 1873	28	77	YES
11. Laparus doris doris (Linnaeus, 1771)	12	77	YES
12. Neruda aoede manu (Lamas, 1976)	2	79	YES
13. Heliconius burneyi koenigi Neukirchen, 1995	1	83	YES
14. H. demeter tambopata Lamas, 1985	1	77	YES
15. H. elevatus lapis Lamas, 1976	2	80	YES
16. H. erato luscombei Lamas, 1976	1	75	YES
17. H. hecale sisyphus Salvin, 1871	4	75	YES
18. H. leucadia Bates, 1862	2	77	YES
19. H. melpomene schunkei Lamas, 1976	2	77	YES
20. H. numata lyrcaeus Weymer, 1891	1	75	YES
21. H. pardalinus maeon Weymer, 1891	16	NC	YES
22. H. sara thamar (Hübner, 1806)	1	75	YES
23. H. wallacei flavescens Weymer, 1891	76	76	YES
24. H. xanthocles quindecim Lamas, 1976	2	75	NO
NYMPHALIDAE: NYMPHALINAE			
25. Anartia amathea sticheli Fruhstorfer, 1907	40	NC	YES
26. Metamorpha elissa elissa Hübner, 1819	9	76	YES
27. Siproeta stelenes meridionalis (Fruhstorfer, 1909)	23	NC	YES
28. Junonia genoveva occidentalis C & R Felder, 1862	9	77	YES
29. Castilia angusta (Hewitson, 1868)	13	91	YES
30. C. perilla (Hewitson, 1852)	19	76	YES
31. Eresia clara clara Bates, 1864	22	78	YES
32. E. eunice eunice (Hübner, 1807)	4	81	YES
33. E. nauplius plagiata (Röber, 1913)	4	85	YES
34. Eresia sp. n.	89	89	NO
35. Ortilia gentina Higgins, 1981	16	80	YES
36. Tegosa claudina (Eschscholtz, 1821)	40	78	YES
37. Telenassa burchelli (Moulton, 1909)	8	76	YES
NYMPHALIDAE: LIMENITIDINAE			
38. Historis acheronta acheronta (Fabricius, 1775)	2	77	YES
39. H. odius dious Lamas, 1995	19	77	YES
40. Baeotus amazonicus (Riley, 1919)	8	76	YES

41. B. deucalion (C & R Felder, 1860)	4	76	YES
42. B. japetus (Staudinger, 1885)	13	85	YES
43. Smyrna blomfildia blomfildia (Fabricius, 1782)	19	NC	YES
44. Colobura dirce dirce (Linnaeus, 1758)	21	80	YES
45. Tigridia acesta tapajona (Butler, 1873)	16	75	YES
46. Biblis hyperia laticlavia (Thieme, 1904)	18	88	YES
47. Vila azeca azeca (Doubleday, 1848)	19	77	YES
48. V. emilia caecilia (C & R Felder, 1862)	2	75	YES
49. Myscelia capenas octomaculata (Butler, 1873)	2	77	YES
50. Catonephele acontius acontius (Linnaeus, 1771)	2	77	YES
51. C. antinoe (Godart, 1824)	28	97	YES
52. C. numilia numilia (Cramer, 1775)	6	75	YES
53. Nessaea hewitsonii boliviensis Jenkins, 1989	5	85	NO
54. N. obrina lesoudieri LeMoult, 1933	1	75	YES
55. Eunica alcmena flora C & R Felder, 1862	40	NC	NO
56. E. alpais alpais (Godart, 1824)	19	79	YES
57. E. amelia erroneata Oberthür, 1916	11	76	YES
58. E. bechina bechina (Hewitson, 1852)	15	97	NO
59. E. caelina alycia Fruhstorfer, 1909	6	88	YES
60. E. clytia (Hewitson, 1852)	5	82	YES
61. E. concordia (Hewitson, 1852)	16	77	YES
62. E. eurota eurota (Cramer, 1775)	5	77	YES
63. E. maja noerina Hall, 1935	48	92	YES
64. E. malvina malvina Bates, 1864	71	89	YES
65. E. margarita (Godart, 1824)	46	NC	NO
66. E. marsolia fasula Fruhstorfer, 1909	1	76	YES
67. E. mygdonia mygdonia (Godart, 1824)	2	76	YES
68. E. orphise (Cramer, 1775)	10	91	YES
69. E. sophonisba agele Seitz, 1915	53	75	YES
70. E. sydonia sydonia (Godart, 1824)	36	81	YES
71. Hamadryas amphinome amphinome (Linnaeus, 1767)	17	79	YES
72. H. arinome arinome (Lucas, 1853)	26	78	NO
73. H. chloe chloe (Stoll, 1787)	1	76	YES
74. H. iphthime iphthime (Bates, 1864)	82	82	YES
75. H. laodamia laodamia (Cramer, 1777)	83	83	YES
76. Ectima iona Doubleday, 1848	89	89	YES
77. E. lirides Staudinger, 1885	77	77	NO
78. E. thecla peruviana Bryk, 1953	21	93	YES
79. Panacea prola amazonica Fruhstorfer, 1915	1	77	YES
80. P. regina (Bates, 1864)	3	76	YES
81. Batesia hypochlora hypoxantha Salvin & Godman, 1868	1	76	NO
82. Asterope markii hewitsoni (Staudinger, 1886)	46	NC	YES
83. Pyrrhogyra crameri hagnodorus Fruhstorfer, 1908	2	75	YES
84. P. edocla cuparina Bates, 1865	16	77	YES
85. P. neaerea amphiro Bates, 1865	16	76	YES
86. P. otolais olivenca Fruhstorfer, 1908	1	77	YES
87. Temenis laothoe laothoe (Cramer, 1777)	2	76	YES
88. T. pulchra pallidior (Oberthür, 1901)	83	83	YES
89. Nica flavilla sylvestris Bates, 1864	53	76	YES
90. Peria lamis (Cramer, 1779)	6	78	YES
91. Dynamine aerata aerata (Butler, 1877)	19	76	YES

92. D. artemisia glauce (Bates, 1865)	76	76	YES
93. D. athemon barreiroi Fernández, 1928	19	76	YES
94. D. chryseis (Bates, 1865)	2	76	NO
95. D. coenus leucothea (Bates, 1865)	5	76	YES
96. D. gisella (Hewitson, 1857)	72	NC	NO
97. D. intermedia Talbot, 1932	53	NC	NO
98. D. paulina paulina (Bates, 1865)	2	NC	NO
99. D. smerdis smerdis Tessmann, 1928	16	77	NO
100. Haematera pyrame ssp. n.	32	NC	YES
101. Catacore kolyma pasithea (Hewitson, 1864)	45	78	YES
102. Diaethria clymena peruviana (Guenée, 1872)	18	76	YES
103. Paulogramma pyracmon peristera (Hewitson, 1853)	4	76	YES
104. Callicore astarte stratiotes (C & R Felder, 1861)	84	84	YES
105. C. cynosura cynosura (Doubleday, 1847)	2	76	YES
106. C. eunomia incarnata (Röber, 1915)	28	76	YES
107. C. hesperis (Guérin, 1844)	4	76	YES
108. C. hystaspes zelphanta (Hewitson, 1858)	30	80	YES
109. C. pygas cyllene (Doubleday, 1847)	36	NC	YES
110. C. texa maimuna (Hewitson, 1858)	18	76	NO
111. Adelpha aethalia davisii (Butler, 1877)	27	77	YES
112. A. attica (C & R Felder, 1867)	51	91	YES
113. A. boeotia fulica Fruhstorfer, 1915	79	79	NO
114. A. cocala urraca (C & R Felder, 1862)	4	NC	YES
115. A. cytherea lanilla Fruhstorfer, 1913	41	NC	YES
116. A. erotia erotia (Hewitson, 1847)	26	NC	NO
117. A. iphiclus iphiclus (Linnaeus, 1758)	2	76	YES
118. A. ixia pseudomessana Fruhstorfer, 1913	16	96	YES
119. A. jordani Fruhstorfer, 1913	16	79	YES
120. A. lerna lerna (Hewitson, 1847)	19	89	YES
121. A. mesentina chancha Staudinger, 1886	2	75	YES
122. A. naxia naxia (C & R Felder, 1867)	77	77	YES
123. A. phylaca juruana (Butler, 1877)	2	76	YES
124. A. plesaure phliassa (Godart, 1824)	2	75	YES
125. A. thesprotia delphicola Fruhstorfer, 1909	19	78	YES
126. A. uta Fruhstorfer, 1915	89	89	NO
127. A. zunilaces (?) ssp. n.	84	84	YES
128. Marpesia berania berania (Hewitson, 1852)	6	84	YES
129. M. chiron marius (Cramer, 1779)	2	76	YES
130. M. crethon (Fabricius, 1776)	32	77	YES
131. M. egina (Bates, 1865)	96	96	YES
132. M. furcula oechalia (Westwood, 1850)	2	78	YES
133. M. petreus petreus (Cramer, 1776)	16	81	YES
134. M. themistocles norica (Hewitson, 1852)	1	76	YES

NYMPHALIDAE: CHARAXINAE

135. Consul fabius divisus (Butler, 1874)	16	77	YES
136. Hypna clytemnestra negra C & R Felder, 1862	97	97	YES
137. Polygrapha xenocrates xenocrates (Westwood, 1850)	22	77	NO
138. Siderone galanthis thebais C & R Felder, 1862	79	79	YES
139. S. syntyche mars Bates, 1860	90	90	NO

140. Zaretis itys itys (Cramer, 1777)	6	75	YES
141. Fountainea ryphea ryphea (Cramer, 1775)	10	77	NO
142. Memphis basilia drucei (Staudinger, 1887)	1	75	YES
143. M. cambyses (Druce, 1877)	50	75	YES
144. M. glauce glauce (C & R Felder, 1862)	2	75	YES
145. M. memphis memphis (C & R Felder, 1867)	1	76	YES
146. M. phantes phantes (Hopffer, 1874)	21	NC	YES
147. M. moruus morpheus (Staudinger, 1886)	92	92	YES
148. M. philumena philumena (Doubleday, 1849)	35	77	YES
149. M. pithyusa (R. Felder, 1869)	19	88	NO
150. M. polycarmes (Fabricius, 1775)	4	75	YES
151. M. polyxo (Druce, 1874)	79	79	YES
152. M. praxias praxias (Hopffer, 1874)	46	96	NO
153. M. xenocles xenocles (Hewitson, 1850)	2	76	YES
154. Archaeoprepona amphimachus symaithus Fruhstorfer, 1916	18	77	YES
155. A. demophon muson (Fruhstorfer, 1905)	1	76	YES
156. A. demophoon andicola (Fruhstorfer, 1904)	16	93	YES
157. A. licomedes (Cramer, 1777)	30	81	YES
158. A. meander megabates Fruhstorfer, 1916	18	NC	YES
159. Prepona dexamenus dexamenus Hopffer, 1874	79	79	YES
160. P. laertes demodice (Godart, 1824)	65	75	YES
161. P. pheridamas (Cramer, 1777)	31	81	YES
162. Agrias claudina sardanapalus Bates, 1860	4	77	YES

NYMPHALIDAE: APATURINAE

163. Doxocopa agathina agathina (Cramer, 1777)	2	82	YES
164. D. laure griseldis (C & R Felder, 1862)	37	NC	YES
165. D. lavinia (Butler, 1866)	49	89	YES
166. D. linda linda (C & R Felder, 1862)	18	83	YES
167. D. pavon pavon (Latreille, 1809)	18	78	YES
168. D. zunilda floris (Fruhstorfer, 1907)	16	NC	YES

NYMPHALIDAE: MORPHINAE

169. Antirrhea hela C & R Felder, 1862	21	83	YES
170. A. philoctetes avernus Hopffer, 1874	3	78	YES
171. A. taygetina taygetina (Butler, 1868)	1	75	YES
172. Caerois chorinaeus protonoe Fruhstorfer, 1912	20	76	YES
173. Morpho achilles theodorus Fruhstorfer, 1907	1	75	YES
174. M. deidamia grambergi Weber, 1944	54	81	YES
175. M. eugenia ssp.	SR	NC	NO
176. M. menelaus alexandrovna Druce, 1874	SR	NC	YES
177. M. telemachus iphiclus C & R Felder, 1862	34	NC	YES

NYMPHALIDAE: BRASSOLINAE

178. Brassolis sophorae ardens Stichel, 1903	23	83	YES
179. Narope cyllabarus Westwood, 1851	20	76	YES
180. N. nesope Hewitson, 1869	91	91	YES
181. N. panniculus Stichel, 1904	94	94	YES

182. N. syllabus Staudinger, 1887	20	76	YES
183. Narope sp. n.	92	92	NO
184. Opsiphanes cassiae crameri C & R Felder, 1862	91	91	YES
185. O. invirae amplificatus Stichel, 1904	19	76	YES
186. O. quiteria quaestor Stichel, 1902	44	78	YES
187. Opoptera aorsa hilara Stichel, 1902	10	79	YES
188. Opoptera sp. n.	75	75	NO
189. Catoblepia berecynthia adjecta Stichel, 1906	1	76	YES
190. C. soranus (Westwood, 1851)	5	75	YES
191. C. xanthicles belisar Stichel, 1904	1	NC	YES
192. Selenophanes cassiope mapiriensis Bristow, 1982	2	77	YES
193. Eryphanis automedon tristis Staudinger, 1887	6	76	YES
194. Caligopsis seleucida seleucida (Hewitson, 1877)	26	76	YES
195. Caligo euphorbus euphorbus (C & R Felder, 1862)	XX	NC	YES
196. C. eurilochus livius Staudinger, 1886	20	78	YES
197. C. idomeneus idomenides Fruhstorfer, 1903	31	76	YES
198. C. placidianus Staudinger, 1887	21	NC	YES
199. C. teucer phorkys Fruhstorfer, 1912	32	NC	YES

NYMPHALIDAE: SATYRINAE

200. Cithaerias pireta ssp. n.	4	75	YES
201. Haetera piera ssp. n.	1	78	YES
202. Pierella hortona albofasciata Rosenberg & Talbot, 1914	1	75	YES
203. P. lamia chalybaea Godman, 1905	3	76	YES
204. P. lena brasiliensis (C & R Felder, 1862)	1	75	YES
205. Bia actorion rebeli Bryk, 1953	1	80	YES
206. Manataria hercyna hyrnethia Fruhstorfer, 1912	17	81	YES
207. Harjesia blanda (Möschler, 1877)	1	75	YES
208. H. obscura (Butler, 1867)	24	78	YES
209. H. oreba (Butler, 1870)	6	77	YES
210. Harjesia (?) sp. n.	1	NC	NO
211. Pseudodebis griseola (Weymer, 1911)	21	76	YES
212. P. marpessa (Hewitson, 1862)	78	78	YES
213. P. valentina (Cramer, 1779)	1	75	YES
214. Taygetis celia (Cramer, 1779)	1	76	NO
215. T. cleopatra C & R Felder, 1867	32	87	YES
216. T. echo koepckei Forster, 1964	83	83	YES
217. T. elegia Weymer, 1910	17	NC	NO
218. T. larua C & R Felder, 1867	1	75	YES
219. T. leuctra Butler, 1870	31	NC	NO
220. T. mermeria mermeria (Cramer, 1776)	4	76	YES
221. T. sosis Hopffer, 1874	6	87	YES
222. T. sylvia Bates, 1866	5	77	YES
223. T. thamyra (Cramer, 1779)	2	87	YES
224. T. virgilia (Cramer, 1776)	1	75	YES
225. Taygetis sp. n.	80	80	NO
226. Caeruleuptychia aegrota (Butler, 1867)	1	75	YES
227. C. brixius (Godart, 1824)	1	75	NO
228. C. cyanites (Butler, 1871)	20	NC	YES
229. C. glauca (Weymer, 1911)	21	81	NO

230. C. helios (Weymer, 1911)	19	81	YES
231. C. lobelia (Butler, 1870)	40	NC	YES
232. C. penicillata (Godman, 1905)	20	75	NO
233. C. scopulata (Godman, 1905)	1	75	YES
234. C. ziza (Butler, 1860)	1	78	YES
235. Caeruleuptychia sp. n. 1	1	NC	NO
236. Caeruleuptychia sp. n. 2	63	80	NO
237. Caeruleuptychia sp. n. 3	19	75	NO
238. Caeruleuptychia sp. n. 4	80	80	NO
239. Cepheuptychia cephus cephus (Fabricius, 1775)	39	93	YES
240. Cepheuptychia sp. n.	6	76	YES
241. Chloreuptychia arnaca (Fabricius, 1776)	2	76	YES
242. C. catharina (Staudinger, 1886)	28	NC	YES
243. C. chlorimene (Hübner, 1819)	1	78	NO
244. C. herseis (Godart, 1824)	1	78	YES
245. C. marica (Weymer, 1911)	1	95	NO
246. Chloreuptychia sp. n.	42	75	YES
247. Cissia myncea (Cramer, 1780)	2	85	YES
248. C. palladia (Butler, 1867)	61	95	YES
249. C. proba (Weymer, 1911)	4	83	YES
250. Erichthodes antonina (C & R Felder, 1867)	6	75	YES
251. Euptychia enyo Butler, 1867	21	83	YES
252. Euptychia sp. n.	89	89	NO
253. Hermeuptychia fallax (C & R Felder, 1862)	62	NC	NO
254. H. hermes (Fabricius, 1775)	1	75	YES
255. Magneuptychia analis (Godman, 1905)	1	81	NO
256. M. iris (C & R Felder, 1867)	1	87	YES
257. M. "helle" (Cramer, 1779) - homonym	18	77	YES
258. M. lea philippa (Butler, 1867)	27	75	YES
259. M. libye (Linnaeus, 1767)	2	NC	YES
260. M. moderata (Weymer, 1911)	5	75	YES
261. M. modesta (Butler, 1867)	1	88	YES
262. M. ocypete (Fabricius, 1776)	29	85	YES
263. M. segesta (Weymer, 1911)	19	79	NO
264. Magneuptychia sp. n. 1	17	87	NO
265. Magneuptychia sp. n. 2	18	87	YES
266. Magneuptychia sp. n. 3	44	83	YES
267. Magneuptychia sp. n. 4	21	77	YES
268. Magneuptychia sp. n. 5	6	77	NO
269. Magneuptychia sp. n. 6	20	83	NO
270. Megeuptychia antonoe (Cramer, 1775)	1	76	YES
271. Pareuptychia binocula binocula (Butler, 1869)	22	NC	YES
272. P. interjecta hesionides Forster, 1964	1	79	YES
273. P. ocirrhoe (Fabricius, 1776)	1	75	YES
274. P. summandosa (Gosse, 1880)	22	NC	YES
275. Pareuptychia sp. n.	10	77	NO
276. Paryphthimoides binalinea (Butler, 1867)	16	76	YES
277. Posttaygetis penelea penelea (Cramer, 1777)	6	80	YES
278. Rareuptychia clio (Weymer, 1911)	3	76	YES
279. Splendeuptychia ashna (Hewitson, 1869)	73	78	NO
280. S. aurigera (Weymer, 1911)	34	NC	NO

281. S. boliviensis Forster, 1964	13	75	YES
282. S. itonis (Hewitson, 1862)	1	75	YES
283. S. purusana (Aurivillius, 1929)	8	NC	YES
284. S. quadrina (Butler, 1869)	6	87	NO
285. S. triangula (Aurivillius, 1929)	3	76	YES
286. S. zischkai Forster, 1964	37	NC	NO
287. Splendeuptychia sp. n. 1	2	88	NO
288. Splendeuptychia sp. n. 2	3	76	NO
289. Splendeuptychia sp. n. 3	10	75	YES
290. Splendeuptychia sp. n. 4	34	81	NO
291. Splendeuptychia sp. n. 5	8	76	YES
292. Splendeuptychia sp. n. 6	1	76	YES
293. Splendeuptychia sp. n. 7	74	76	NO
294. Splendeuptychia sp. n. 8	19	85	NO
295. Splendeuptychia sp. n. 9	89	89	NO
296. Yphthimoides mythra (Weymer, 1911)	15	NC	YES
297. Y. renata (Stoll, 1780)	23	89	NO
298. Zischkaia amalda (Weymer, 1911)	4	75	YES
299. Z. saundersii (Butler, 1867)	28	84	NO
300. "Euptychia" ordinata (Weymer, 1911)	73	NC	YES
301. Amphidecta calliomma (C & R Felder, 1862)	34	81	YES
302. A. pignerator pignerator Butler, 1867	31	79	YES

NYMPHALIDAE: DANAINAE

303. Lycorea ilione phenarete (Doubleday, 1847)	16	96	YES
304. L. halia pales C & R Felder, 1862	3	80	YES
305. L. pasinuntia concolor Staudinger, 1885	XX	NC	NO
306. Danaus eresimus ssp. n.	18	NC	YES

NYMPHALIDAE: ITHOMIINAE

307. Athyrtis mechanitis salvini Srnka, 1884	4	75	YES
308. Tithorea harmonia brunnea Haensch, 1905	1	76	YES
309. Melinaea maelus lamasi Brown, 1977	4	75	YES
310. M. marsaeus clara Rosenberg & Talbot, 1914	1	87	YES
311. M. menophilus orestes Salvin, 1871	2	76	YES
312. M. mnasias romualdo Fox, 1965	24	NC	NO
313. Paititia neglecta Lamas, 1979	22	77	YES
314. Thyridia psidii ino C & R Felder, 1862	3	78	YES
315. Forbestra olivencia aeneola Fox, 1967	20	76	YES
316. Mechanitis lysimnia menecles Hewitson, 1860	9	76	YES
317. M. mazaeus mazaeus Hewitson, 1860	63	88	YES
318. M. polymnia angustifascia Talbot, 1928	22	NC	YES
319. Scada batesi batesi Haensch, 1903	2	76	NO
320. S. reckia labyrintha Lamas, 1985	1	76	YES
321. Aeria eurimedia negricola (C & R Felder, 1862)	18	75	NO
322. Methona confusa psamathe Godman & Salvin, 1898	1	75	YES
323. M. curvifascia Weymer, 1883	2	76	YES
324. M. grandior ssp. n.	1	78	NO

325. Rhodussa cantobrica pamina (Haensch, 1905)	5	75	YES
326. Napeogenes aethra deucalion Haensch, 1905	4	75	YES
327. N. inachia patientia Lamas, 1985	5	76	YES
328. N. pharo pharo (C & R Felder, 1862)	4	75	YES
329. N. stella ssp. n.	21	76	NO
330. N. sylphis sylphis (Guérin, 1844)	2	75	NO
331. Hypothyris euclea ssp. n.	18	76	YES
332. H. ninonia ssp. n.	22	83	NO
333. H. semifulva ssp. n.	17	75	NO
334. Hyposcada anchiala richardsi Fox, 1941	6	79	NO
335. H. illinissa dolabella (Hewitson, 1876)	XX	NC	NO
336. H. zarepha ssp. n.	43	NC	NO
337. Oleria alexina (Hewitson, 1859)	23	NC	NO
338. O. didymaea didymaea (Hewitson, 1876)	15	NC	YES
339. O. gunilla ssp. n.	XX	NC	NO
340. O. onega lentita Lamas, 1985	5	76	YES
341. O. ramona calatha Lamas, 1985	1	77	YES
342. O. victorine victorine (Guérin, 1844)	5	76	YES
343. Ithomia agnosia agnosia Hewitson, 1855	35	NC	YES
344. I. arduinna arduinna d'Almeida, 1952	4	76	YES
345. I. lagusa peruana Salvin, 1869	22	NC	NO
346. I. lichyi neivai d'Almeida, 1940	2	75	YES
347. I. salapia ardea Hewitson, 1855	41	78	YES
348. Callithomia alexirrhoe thornax Bates, 1862	54	NC	YES
349. C. lenea zelie (Guérin, 1844)	2	75	YES
350. Dircenna dero ssp. n.	19	NC	YES
351. D. loreta acreana d'Almeida, 1950	12	96	YES
352. Ceratinia neso peruensis (Haensch, 1905)	11	75	YES
353. C. tutia fuscens (Haensch, 1905)	33	NC	YES
354. Ceratiscada hymen hymen (Haensch, 1905)	18	76	YES
355. Episcada sulphurea sulphurea Haensch, 1905	19	76	NO
356. Episcada sp. n.	77	77	NO
357. Pteronymia antisao guntheri Lamas, 1985	11	76	YES
358. P. forsteri Baumann, 1985	4	76	YES
359. P. vestilla acaya Haensch, 1909	6	76	NO
360. Godyris zavaleta ssp. n.	17	76	NO
361. Hypoleria lavinia cajona Haensch, 1905	11	76	NO
362. H. virginia vitiosa Lamas, 1985	5	76	YES
363. "Hypoleria" aelia brevicula (d'Almeida, 1951)	30	90	NO
364. "H." orolina arzalia (Hewitson, 1876)	19	78	YES
365. Mcclungia cymo salonina (Hewitson, 1855)	7	76	NO
366. Pseudoscada timna ssp. n.	17	76	YES
367. Heterosais nephele nephele (Bates, 1862)	7	76	YES
368. "Pseudoscada" florula ssp. n.	16	83	NO

NYMPHALIDAE: LIBYTHEINAE

369. Libytheana carinenta carinenta (Cramer, 1777)	19	NC	YES

RIODINIDAE: EUSELASIINAE

370. Euselasia euboea euboea (Hewitson, 1853)	27	77	YES
371. E. pelor (Hewitson, 1853)*	16	77	NO
372. E. pellonia Stichel, 1919*	16	75	YES
373. E. mirania (Bates, 1868)*	26	NC	YES
374. E. toppini Sharpe, 1915	20	76	YES
375. E. euryone euryone (Hewitson, 1856)	28	75	YES
376. E. violetta (Bates, 1868)	24	NC	YES
377. E. arbas ssp.	16	87	YES
378. E. euoras (Hewitson, 1855)	51	NC	YES
379. E. eutychus (Hewitson, 1856)	19	85	YES
380. E. jugata Stichel, 1919	16	77	YES
381. E. euodias euodias (Hewitson, 1856)	16	77	YES
382. E. orba spectralis Stichel, 1919	XX	NC	YES
383. E. euriteus euriteus (Cramer, 1777)	15	76	YES
384. E. melaphaea condensa Stichel, 1927	19	77	YES
385. E. hygenius group, sp. 1*	21	NC	YES
386. E. hygenius group, sp. 2*	26	NC	YES
387. E. hygenius group, sp. 3*	18	83	YES
388. E. hygenius group, sp. 4*	19	75	YES
389. Euselasia aff. cafusa (Bates, 1868)	19	76	YES
390. E. alcmena (Druce, 1878)	5	75	NO
391. E. crinon Stichel, 1919	16	85	YES
392. E. fervida hahneli Staudinger, 1887	16	90	NO
393. E. gelanor erilis Stichel, 1919	21	84	YES
394. E. teleclus teleclus (Stoll, 1787)	20	83	YES
395. Euselasia sp., midas group	19	91	YES
396. E. eugeon (Hewitson, 1856)	26	79	YES
397. E. brevicauda Lathy, 1926	21	83	YES
398. E. uria angustifascia Lathy, 1926	19	77	YES
399. E. eubotes eubotes (Hewitson, 1856)	35	NC	YES
400. E. lysimachus Staudinger, 1888	5	83	NO
401. E. angulata (Bates, 1868)	21	83	YES
402. E. utica euphaes (Hewitson, 1855)	16	84	YES
403. Methone cecilia magnarea (Seitz, 1913)	26	85	NO

RIODINIDAE: RIODININAE

404. Perophthalma tullius tullius (Fabricius, 1787)	20	78	YES
405. Mesophthalma idotea ssp. (n.?)	1	76	YES
406. Leucochimona matatha chionea (Godman & Salvin, 1885)	5	75	YES
407. L. matisca (Hewitson, 1860)	66	90	YES
408. Semomesia croesus siccata Stichel, 1919	4	75	YES
409. S. macaris (Hewitson, 1859)	17	75	YES
410. S. tenella tenella Stichel, 1910	89	89	YES
411. Mesosemia aff. ephyne (Cramer, 1776)	20	81	YES
412. Mesosemia aff. metura Hewitson, 1873	18	83	YES
413. Mesosemia aff. gneris Westwood, 1851	43	88	NO
414. Mesosemia sp. 1	36	NC	NO
415. Mesosemia sp. 2	46	77	NO

416. Mesosemia aff. cyanira Stichel, 1909	25	NC	NO
417. M. cippus Hewitson, 1859	20	79	YES
418. M. ibycus Hewitson, 1859	10	83	YES
419. M. philocles thyestes Druce, 1878	12	75	YES
420. M. machaera ssp.	2	77	YES
421. M. materna Stichel, 1909	9	77	YES
422. Mesosemia aff. materna Stichel, 1909	2	76	YES
423. M. luperca Stichel, 1910	70	79	YES
424. Mesosemia sp. 3 (umbrosa ?)	2	81	NO
425. M. hedwigis Stichel, 1910	10	79	NO
426. M. naiadella naiadella Stichel, 1909	6	NC	YES
427. M. sirenia sirenia Stichel, 1909	8	75	YES
428. M. latissima Stichel, 1909	14	NC	NO
429. Mesosemia aff. evias Stichel, 1923	34	88	YES
430. M. menoetes paetula Stichel, 1915	8	77	YES
431. Mesosemia sp. 4 (nr. atroculis)	13	NC	NO
432. M. ulrica ulrica (Cramer, 1777)	27	82	YES
433. M. eumene furia Stichel, 1910	12	NC	NO
434. M. decolorata Lathy, 1932	1	NC	YES
435. M. macella Hewitson, 1859	95	95	NO
436. M. gigantea Stichel, 1915	22	81	NO
437. Eurybia nicaea ssp.	1	75	YES
438. E. caerulescens caerulescens Druce, 1904	8	81	YES
439. E. dardus franciscana C & R Felder, 1862	14	77	YES
440. E. promota Stichel, 1910 (?)	43	NC	YES
441. E. halimede halimede (Hübner, 1807)	4	75	YES
442. Alesa prema (Godart, 1824)	91	91	NO
443. Alesa aff. telephae (Boisduval, 1836)	3	91	NO
444. A. amesis (Cramer, 1777)	1	75	YES
445. A. hemiurga Bates, 1867	8	88	YES
446. Mimocastnia rothschildi Seitz, 1916	15	NC	NO
447. Hyphilaria parthenis tigrinella Stichel, 1909	3	NC	YES
448. Cremna actoris meleagris Hopffer, 1874	3	78	YES
449. C. thasus subrutila Stichel, 1910	8	NC	YES
450. Eunogyra satyrus Westwood, 1851	50	78	YES
451. Lyropteryx apollonia apollonia Westwood, 1851	20	88	YES
452. Cyrenia martia martia Westwood, 1851	75	75	YES
453. Ancyluris meliboeus meliboeus (Fabricius, 1776)	15	77	YES
454. A. etias melior Stichel, 1910	21	79	YES
455. A. aulestes eryxo (Saunders, 1859)	6	77	YES
456. Rhetus arcius huanus (Saunders, 1859)	49	76	YES
457. R. periander laonome (Morisse, 1838)	3	76	YES
458. Ithomeis lauronia Schaus, 1902	1	NC	YES
459. Isapis agyrtus sestus (Stichel, 1909)	3	75	YES
460. Themone poecila Bates, 1868	14	NC	NO
461. Notheme erota diadema Stichel, 1910	16	81	YES
462. Monethe albertus albertus C & R Felder, 1862	46	76	YES
463. Metacharis lucius (Fabricius, 1793)	9	75	YES
464. M. regalis regalis Butler, 1867	1	75	YES
465. Cariomothis erythromelas fulvus Lathy, 1932 (?)	5	96	YES
466. Syrmatia nyx (Hübner, 1817) (?)	14	92	NO

467. Chamaelimnas tircis iaeris Bates, 1868	44	91	YES
468. C. urbana Stichel, 1916	1	80	YES
469. Parcella amarynthina (C & R Felder, 1865)	4	77	YES
470. Charis anius (Cramer, 1776)	2	75	YES
471. Charis sp. n.	1	75	YES
472. C. gynaea zama Bates, 1868	1	76	YES
473. C. argyrea Bates, 1868	1	75	NO
474. Chalodeta theodora theodora (C & R Felder, 1862)	6	76	YES
475. C. lypera (Bates, 1868)	79	79	YES
476. C. chaonitis (Hewitson, 1866)	3	76	YES
477. Caria mantinea amazonica (Bates, 1868)	15	82	YES
478. C. trochilus arete (C & R Felder, 1861)	42	78	YES
479. C. "philema" Stichel, 1910	47	NC	NO
480. C. sponsa (Staudinger, 1887)	13	82	NO
481. Crocozona coecias coecias (Hewitson, 1866)	46	77	YES
482. Baeotis bacaenis bacaenita Schaus, 1902 (?)	9	78	YES
483. B. euprepes orthotaenia Seitz, 1916	2	76	NO
484. Lasaia agesilas agesilas (Latreille, 1809)	3	78	YES
485. L. arsis Staudinger, 1887	4	89	YES
486. L. pseudomeris Clench, 1972	19	90	YES
487. Amarynthis meneria (Cramer, 1776)	8	75	YES
488. Exoplisia cadmeis (Hewitson, 1866)	XX	NC	YES
489. Riodina lysippus lysias Stichel, 1910	29	78	YES
490. Melanis xarifa quadripunctata (Stichel, 1910)	21	79	YES
491. M. smithiae (Westwood, 1851)	18	76	NO
492. M. marathon stenotaenia (Röber, 1904)	76	76	YES
493. Mesene leucophrys Bates, 1868	1	75	YES
494. M. nola eupteryx Bates, 1868	8	83	YES
495. M. pyrrha Bates, 1868	19	77	YES
496. Mesene sp. 1	29	NC	NO
497. Mesene sp. 2	90	90	NO
498. Mesene monostigma (Erichson, 1848) (?)	83	83	YES
499. Mesene aff. silaris Godman & Salvin, 1878	77	77	NO
500. Symmachia rubina separata Lathy, 1932	23	NC	NO
501. S. accusatrix Westwood, 1851	84	84	NO
502. Symmachia sp. 1 (?cleonyma Hewitson, 1870)	79	79	YES
503. Symmachia sp. 2 (?probetor Stoll, 1782)	91	91	YES
504. S. asclepia asclepia Hewitson, 1870	32	83	YES
505. Phaenochitonia sophistes (Bates, 1868)	39	NC	YES
506. Sarota acantus (Stoll, 1781)	4	76	YES
507. Sarota sp. nr. acantus (Stoll, 1781)	8	76	YES
508. Sarota sp. 1	66	NC	NO
509. S. flavicincta (Lathy, 1932)	92	92	NO
510. Sarota aff. myrtea Godman & Salvin, 1886	14	NC	YES
511. Sarota sp. 2	53	81	NO
512. Sarota sp. 3	22	75	NO
513. Sarota sp. 4	93	93	NO
514. S. acanthoides spicata (Staudinger, 1888) (?)	20	NC	NO
515. S. chrysus chrysus (Stoll, 1781)	20	83	YES
516. Anteros formosus formosus (Cramer, 1777)	6	79	YES
517. A. bracteatus Hewitson, 1867	92	92	NO

518. A. renaldus renaldus (Stoll, 1790)	92	92	YES
519. Calydna caieta Hewitson, 1854	23	96	NO
520. C. punctata C & R Felder, 1861	6	76	YES
521. C. thersander (Stoll, 1780) (?)	76	76	NO
522. C. maculosa Bates, 1868	1	77	YES
523. C. hiria (Godart, 1824)	26	NC	NO
524. C. catana Hewitson, 1859	43	92	YES
525. C. carneia Hewitson, 1859	28	81	NO
526. C. cea Hewitson, 1859	91	91	NO
527. C. calyce Hewitson, 1859	29	NC	NO
528. Emesis lucinda lucinda (Cramer, 1775)	6	NC	NO
529. E. castigata castigata Stichel, 1910	4	76	YES
530. E. spreta Bates, 1868	20	75	NO
531. E. mandana mandana (Cramer, 1780)	34	81	YES
532. E. diogenia Prittwitz, 1865	4	77	NO
533. E. fatimella fatimella Westwood, 1851	76	76	YES
534. E. ocypore ocypore (Geyer, 1837)	82	82	YES
535. E. temesa emesina (Staudinger, 1887)	5	81	YES
536. E. progne (Godman, 1903)	21	NC	NO
537. Emesis sp. (?heteroclita Stichel, 1929)	78	78	NO
538. Argyrogrammana stilbe (Godart, 1824) (?) (holosticta?)	29	NC	NO
539. Argyrogrammana sp. 1 (trochilia rameli?)	6	NC	YES
540. Argyrogrammana sp. 2	25	NC	YES
541. Pachythone xanthe Bates, 1868	83	83	YES
542. Uraneis hyalina (Butler, 1867)	15	79	YES
543. Thisbe irenea ssp.	57	75	NO
544. Lemonias zygia ssp.	42	NC	NO
545. Juditha azan ssp. n.	2	75	YES
546. J. molpe molpe (Hübner, 1808)	2	75	YES
547. Synargis orestessa Hübner, 1819	3	76	YES
548. S. abaris (Cramer, 1776)	19	79	YES
549. S. gela gela (Hewitson, 1853)	2	80	YES
550. S. ochra ochra (Bates, 1868)	16	84	YES
551. S. phillone (Godart, 1824)	93	93	NO
552. Parnes nycteis Westwood, 1851	74	NC	YES
553. P. philotes Westwood, 1851	77	77	YES
554. Menander coruscans (Butler, 1867)	97	97	NO
555. M. pretus pretus (Cramer, 1777)	42	NC	NO
556. M. hebrus hebrus (Cramer, 1775)	3	NC	NO
557. Dysmathia portia Bates, 1868	85	85	NO
558. Dysmathia grosnyi Le Cerf, 1958	92	92	NO
559. Calospila lucianus lucianus (Fabricius, 1793)	9	83	YES
560. C. emylius emyliana (Stichel, 1911)	2	76	YES
561. C. rhodope amphis (Hewitson, 1870)	3	78	YES
562. C. parthaon (Dalman, 1823)	14	76	YES
563. C. zeanger pirene (Godman, 1903)	10	79	YES
564. Calospila sp. 1 (rhesa ssp.?)	23	84	YES
565. C. thara pulchra (Lathy, 1904)	6	80	NO
566. C. apotheta (Bates, 1868) (?)	92	92	NO
567. Calospila aff. hemileuca (Bates, 1868)	8	NC	NO
568. C. siaka siaka (Hewitson, 1858)	8	NC	NO

569. Calospila antonii Brévignon, 1995	79	79	NO
570. Adelotypa annulifera (Godman, 1903)	1	75	YES
571. A. densemaculata (Hewitson, 1870)	42	NC	NO
572. A. amasis (Hewitson, 1870)	6	NC	NO
573. A. epixanthe (Stichel, 1911)*	4	NC	YES
574. A. aminias aminias (Hewitson, 1863)*	13	76	YES
575. Adelotypa sp. 1*	4	75	NO
576. A. leucocyana (Geyer, 1837)*	1	75	YES
577. A. huebneri pauxilla (Stichel, 1911)*	1	76	YES
578. Adelotypa (aristus?)*	1	75	YES
579. A. mollis asemna Stichel, 1910	1	75	YES
580. A. trinitatis ssp.	16	76	NO
581. "Adelotypa" lampros (Bates, 1868)	4	NC	YES
582. Setabis epitus epiphanis (Stichel, 1910)	3	79	YES
583. S. velutina (Butler, 1867)	50	88	YES
584. S. pythioides (Butler, 1867)	13	75	YES
585. S. cruentata (Butler, 1867)	28	81	YES
586. S. flammula (Bates, 1868)	5	77	YES
587. Setabis sp. 1	2	NC	NO
588. Setabis sp. 2	XX	NC	NO
589. Theope eudocia eudocia Westwood, 1851	3	83	YES
590. T. hypoleuca Bates, 1868	11	77	NO
591. Theope sp. nr. hypoleuca Bates, 1868	89	89	YES
592. T. lycaenina Bates, 1868	4	85	NO
593. Theope sp.	15	NC	NO
594. T. pedias pedias Herrich-Schäffer, 1853	2	75	YES
595. T. excelsa Bates, 1868	14	85	YES
596. Theope aff. mundula Stichel, 1926	80	80	NO
597. Theope aff. theritas Hewitson, 1860	9	NC	NO
598. T. phaeo folia Godman & Salvin, 1886	14	90	NO
599. T. comosa Stichel, 1911	4	NC	NO
600. Theope aff. thootes Hewitson, 1860	10	85	YES
601. Theope aff. thestias Hewitson, 1860	79	79	YES
602. Calociasma pulcherrima comparata Stichel, 1911	1	75	NO
603. Nymphidium mantus (Cramer, 1775)	3	76	YES
604. N. fulminans fulminans Bates, 1868	3	75	YES
605. N. baeotia Hewitson, 1853	1	76	YES
606. N. minuta Druce, 1904	2	75	YES
607. N. azanoides amazonensis Callaghan, 1986	5	84	YES
608. N. omois Hewitson, 1865	22	NC	YES
609. N. ascolia augea Druce, 1904	2	75	YES
610. N. leucosia medusa Druce, 1904	1	75	YES
611. N. acherois erymanthus Ménétriès, 1855	1	75	YES
612. N. caricae parthenium Stichel, 1924	1	75	YES
613. N. lisimon lisimon (Stoll, 1790)	1	76	YES
614. Stalachtis calliope ssp. n.	10	83	YES
615. Setabis sp. n. 3	80	80	NO

LYCAENIDAE: THECLINAE

616. Eumaeus minijas (Hübner, 1809)	78	78	NO
617. E. toxana (Boisduval, 1870)	64	88	NO
618. Mithras nautes (Cramer, 1779)	19	75	YES
619. "Thecla" nr. orobia (Hewitson, 1867)	35	91	YES
620. "Thecla" cosmophila (Tessmann, 1928)	81	81	YES
621. "Thecla" maculata (Lathy, 1936)	20	81	YES
622. Thestius meridionalis (Draudt, 1920)	4	76	YES
623. "Thecla" ematheon (Cramer, 1777)	48	79	YES
624. Evenus gabriela (Cramer, 1775)	91	91	YES
625. E. batesii (Hewitson, 1865)	91	91	YES
626. E. floralia (Druce, 1907)	79	79	YES
627. E. satyroides (Hewitson, 1865)	SR	NC	YES
628. "Thecla" gibberosa (Hewitson, 1867)	10	97	NO
629. "Thecla" falerina (Hewitson, 1867)	4	75	YES
630. "Thecla" myrtea (Hewitson, 1867)	46	81	YES
631. "Thecla" myrtusa (Hewitson, 1867)	79	79	YES
632. Allosmaitia strophius (Godart, 1824)	95	95	NO
633. Arcas imperialis (Cramer, 1776)	3	75	YES
634. A. tuneta (Hewitson, 1865)	43	85	YES
635. Theritas mavors Hübner, 1818	80	80	YES
636. Denivia acontius (Goodson, 1945)	91	91	YES
637. D. phegeus (Hewitson, 1865)	14	79	YES
638. Denivia nr. viresco (Druce, 1907)	47	NC	NO
639. D. viresco (Druce, 1907)	10	89	YES
640. D. hemon (Cramer, 1775)	4	77	YES
641. D. lisus (Stoll, 1790)	91	91	NO
642. Atlides polybe (Linnaeus, 1763)	92	92	NO
643. A. atys (Cramer, 1779)	93	93	NO
644. Paiwarria telemus (Cramer, 1775)	26	83	YES
645. P. venulius (Cramer, 1779)	92	92	NO
646. "Thecla" ligurina (Hewitson, 1874)	96	96	YES
647. "Thecla" ergina (Hewitson, 1867)	48	92	YES
648. Thereus columbicola (Strand, 1916)	4	NC	YES
649. Arawacus separata (Lathy, 1926)	3	75	YES
650. Rekoa meton (Cramer, 1779)	80	80	NO
651. Ocaria ocrisia (Hewitson, 1868)	3	77	YES
652. Cyanophrys amyntor (Cramer, 1775)	9	NC	NO
653. Panthiades bitias (Cramer, 1777)	1	75	YES
654. P. aeolus (Fabricius, 1775)	79	79	YES
655. P. phaleros (Linnaeus, 1767)	2	78	YES
656. "Thecla" gemma (Druce, 1907)	4	84	YES
657. "Thecla" minyia (Hewitson, 1867)	93	93	YES
658. "Thecla" echelta (Hewitson, 1867)	14	NC	NO
659. Parrhasius polibetes (Stoll, 1781)	14	90	YES
660. P. orgia (Hewitson, 1867)	14	90	NO
661. Michaelus ira (Hewitson, 1867)	12	84	YES
662. M. vibidia (Hewitson, 1869)	14	90	YES
663. M. thordesa (Hewitson, 1867)	23	NC	YES
664. M. jebus (Godart, 1824)	89	89	NO

665. "Thecla" nr. gadira (Hewitson, 1867)	2	79	YES
666. "Thecla" norax (Godman & Salvin, 1887)	3	90	YES
667. "Thecla" levis (Druce, 1907)	89	89	NO
668. Olynthus obsoleta (Lathy, 1926)	10	84	YES
669. Olynthus essus (Herrich-Schäffer, 1853)	91	91	NO
670. O. nitor (Druce, 1907)	12	79	NO
671. Oenomaus ortygnus (Cramer, 1779)	14	NC	NO
672. Oenomaus nr. atena (Hewitson, 1867)	92	92	YES
673. Strymon cestri (Reakirt, 1867)	96	96	YES
674. S. ziba (Hewitson, 1868)	2	76	YES
675. S. megarus (Godart, 1824)	89	89	NO
676. Lamprospilus orcidia (Hewitson, 1874)	12	79	YES
677. Lamprospilus nr. picentia (Hewitson, 1868)	84	84	NO
678. L. netesca (Draudt, 1920)	14	79	NO
679. "Thecla" arza (Hewitson, 1874)	90	90	NO
680. "Thecla" taminella (Schaus, 1902)	14	79	YES
681. "Thecla" aruma (Hewitson, 1877)	2	76	YES
682. "Thecla" syllis (Godman & Salvin, 1877)	9	83	YES
683. Kisntam hesperitis (Butler & Druce, 1872)	2	76	YES
684. "Thecla" ceromia (Hewitson, 1877)	4	76	YES
685. "Thecla" vesper (Druce, 1909)	4	75	YES
686. Electrostrymon ecbatana (Hewitson, 1868)	14	84	NO
687. Symbiopsis "peruviana" (Lathy, 1936) - homonym	44	85	YES
688. S. aprica (Möschler, 1883)	1	79	NO
689. Calycopis calus (Godart, 1824)	6	79	YES
690. C. buphonia (Hewitson, 1868)	8	76	YES
691. C. demonassa (Hewitson, 1868)	1	77	YES
692. C. atnius (Herrich-Schäffer, 1853)*	1	76	YES
693. Calycopis nr. atnius (Herrich-Schäffer, 1853)*	3	84	NO
694. C. devia (Möschler, 1883)*	3	83	YES
695. C. centoripa (Hewitson, 1868)	2	75	YES
696. C. nicolayi Field, 1967 (?)	42	NC	YES
697. C. anfracta (Druce, 1907)*	3	79	YES
698. C. anastasia Field, 1967*	1	77	YES
699. C. vitruvia (Hewitson, 1877)	1	77	YES
700. C. caesaries (Druce, 1907)	1	83	YES
701. C. cerata (Hewitson, 1877)	6	76	YES
702. C. trebula (Hewitson, 1868)	12	76	YES
703. C. anapa (Field, 1967)	77	77	NO
704. C. orcilla (Hewitson, 1874)*	13	77	NO
705. C. naka (Field, 1967) (?)*	1	78	YES
706. Calycopis nr. vidulus (Druce, 1907)*	15	NC	YES
707. C. tifla (Field, 1967)*	81	81	NO
708. Calycopis nr. tifla (Field, 1967)*	3	81	YES
709. Calycopis nr. orcilla (Hewitson, 1874)*	15	75	YES
710. Calycopis nr. pisis (Godman & Salvin, 1887)*	24	NC	NO
711. C. barza (Field, 1967) (?)*	1	76	YES
712. Tmolus echion (Linnaeus, 1767)	2	75	YES
713. Tmolus nr. cydrara (Hewitson, 1868)	2	77	YES
714. T. cydrara (Hewitson, 1868)	6	79	YES
715. T. ufentina (Hewitson, 1868)	4	79	YES

716. Tmolus nr. ufentina (Hewitson, 1868)	3	79	YES
717. T. mutina (Hewitson, 1867)	2	75	YES
718. Tmolus nr. mutina (Hewitson, 1867)	91	91	NO
719. "Thecla" emessa (Hewitson, 1867)	10	84	YES
720. "Thecla" nr. opalia (Hewitson, 1868)	3	79	NO
721. "Thecla" nr. cupa (Druce, 1907)	76	76	NO
722. "Thecla" fabulla (Hewitson, 1868)	97	97	NO
723. "Thecla" nr. purpuriticus (Druce, 1907)	15	90	NO
724. "Thecla" tympania (Hewitson, 1869)*	6	75	YES
725. "Thecla" nr. tympania (Hewitson, 1869)*	6	76	YES
726. "Thecla" nr. empusa (Hewitson, 1867)*	12	75	NO
727. "Thecla" halciones (Butler & Druce, 1872)*	6	NC	NO
728. "Thecla" tarena (Hewitson, 1874)	28	81	YES
729. "Thecla" sospes (Draudt, 1920)	26	NC	NO
730. Siderus leucophaeus (Hübner, 1813)	19	87	YES
731. S. parvinotus Kaye, 1904	96	96	YES
732. Siderus nr. guapila (Schaus, 1913)	5	NC	NO
733. S. guayra (Jörgensen, 1935) (?)	1	82	NO
734. S. athymbra (Hewitson, 1867)	14	81	YES
735. S. metanira (Hewitson, 1867)	6	75	YES
736. S. viola (Draudt, 1920)	6	NC	NO
737. S. caninius (Druce, 1907)	84	84	NO
738. Siderus nr. panchaea (Hewitson, 1869)	77	77	NO
739. "Thecla" splendor (Johnson, 1991)	13	83	YES
740. Theclopsis lydus (Hübner, 1819)	3	77	YES
741. T. gargara (Hewitson, 1868)	3	75	YES
742. "Thecla" tephraeus (Geyer, 1837)	2	80	YES
743. "Thecla" nr. tephraeus (Geyer, 1837)	20	NC	YES
744. "T." sphinx (Fabricius, 1775)	13	79	YES
745. "T." phoster (Druce, 1907)	3	75	YES
746. "T." pulchritudo (Druce, 1907)	77	77	YES
747. "T." strephon (Fabricius, 1775)	16	77	YES
748. "Thecla" nr. strephon (Fabricius, 1775)	10	79	YES
749. "Thecla" perola (Hewitson, 1867)	8	76	NO
750. "T." parvipuncta (Lathy, 1926)	10	79	YES
751. "T." agrippa (Fabricius, 1793)	84	84	YES
752. "T." carteia (Hewitson, 1870)	4	76	YES
753. "Thecla" nr. carteia (Hewitson, 1870)	29	NC	YES
754. "T." tyriam (Druce, 1907)	4	75	YES
755. "Thecla" nr. tyriam (Druce, 1907)	20	90	YES
756. "Thecla" nr. malvania (Hewitson, 1867)	76	76	NO
757. "Thecla" nr. foyi (Schaus, 1902)	10	NC	NO
758. "Thecla" syedra (Hewitson, 1867)	15	91	YES
759. "Thecla" nr. syedra (Hewitson, 1867)	5	77	YES
760. "T." adela (Staudinger, 1888)	8	77	NO
761. "T." ambrax (Westwood, 1852)	85	85	NO
762. Ministrymon zilda (Hewitson, 1873)	6	76	YES
763. M. cruenta (Gosse, 1880)	5	85	YES
764. Ministrymon nr. cruenta (Gosse, 1880)	12	89	YES
765. M. cleon (Fabricius, 1775)	2	80	NO
766. "Thecla" terentia (Hewitson, 1868)	5	78	YES

767. "Thecla" lycabas (Cramer, 1777)	80	80	NO
768. Aubergina alda (Hewitson, 1868)	3	88	YES
769. Janthecla rocena (Hewitson, 1867)	6	84	YES
770. Janthecla nr. rocena (Hewitson, 1867)	26	83	NO
771. J. malvina (Hewitson, 1867)	91	91	YES
772. J. leea Venables & Robbins, 1991*	25	75	YES
773. J. sista (Hewitson, 1867)*	3	76	YES
774. Hypostrymon asa (Hewitson, 1873)	1	78	YES
775. Iaspis nr. talayra (Hewitson, 1868)	80	80	NO
776. I. thabena (Hewitson, 1868)	92	92	NO
777. Iaspis nr. beera (Hewitson, 1870)	5	NC	NO
778. I. temesa (Hewitson, 1868)	72	NC	YES
779. "Thecla" picus (Druce, 1907)	91	91	YES
780. Brangas teucria (Hewitson, 1868)	92	92	NO
781. B. getus (Fabricius, 1787)	75	75	YES
782. "Thecla" thespia (Hewitson, 1870)	90	90	NO
783. "Thecla" cupentus (Stoll, 1781)	10	84	YES
784. "Thecla" nr. biston (Möschler, 1877)	13	84	NO
785. Nesiostrymon celona (Hewitson, 1874)	79	79	YES
786. Erora oleris (Druce, 1907) (?)	32	NC	NO
787. E. phrosine (Druce, 1909)	41	NC	YES
788. E. carla (Schaus, 1902)	3	85	NO
789. Erora nr. opisena (Druce, 1912)	91	91	NO
790. E. badeta (Hewitson, 1873)	79	79	NO
791. "Thecla" tema (Hewitson, 1867)	1	75	YES
792. Caerofethra carnica (Hewitson, 1873)	43	84	YES
793. C. iambe (Godman & Salvin, 1887)	79	79	NO
794. Celmia celmus (Cramer, 1775)	1	75	YES
795. "Thecla" color (Druce, 1907)	46	85	YES
796. "Thecla" mecrida (Hewitson, 1867)	3	97	YES

PIERIDAE: DISMORPHIINAE

797. Pseudopieris nehemia melania Lamas, 1985	16	78	YES
798. Dismorphia amphione ssp. n.	26	78	NO
799. D. theucharila argochloe (Bates, 1861)	6	88	YES
800. Enantia lina galanthis (Bates, 1861)	11	76	YES
801. E. melite linealis (Prüffer, 1922)	19	77	YES
802. Moschoneura pinthous ssp. n.	1	81	NO
803. Patia orise denigrata (Rosenberg & Talbot, 1914)	12	NC	NO

PIERIDAE: PIERINAE

804. Anteos clorinde (Godart, 1824)	25	NC	NO
805. A. menippe (Hübner, 1818)	2	77	YES
806. Aphrissa fluminensis (d'Almeida, 1921)	4	78	YES
807. A. statira statira (Cramer, 1777)	2	77	YES
808. Phoebis argante larra (Fabricius, 1798)	2	NC	YES
809. P. philea philea (Linnaeus, 1763)	2	NC	YES
810. P. sennae marcellina (Cramer, 1777)	34	88	YES
811. Rhabdodryas trite trite (Linnaeus, 1758)	25	78	YES

812. Eurema agave agave (Cramer, 1775)	83	83	YES
813. E. albula espinosae (Fernández, 1928)	1	75	YES
814. E. arbela arbela Geyer, 1832	19	NC	NO
815. E. lirina (Bates, 1861)	22	NC	NO
816. E. paulina (Bates, 1861)	3	NC	YES
817. Pyrisitia leuce flavilla (Bates, 1861)	27	84	YES
818. P. nise ssp. n.	2	75	YES
819. Cunizza hirlanda ninguida (Fruhstorfer, 1907)	95	95	NO
820. Glutophrissa drusilla drusilla (Cramer, 1777)	2	76	YES
821. Ascia monuste automate (Burmeister, 1878)	25	NC	YES
822. Ganyra phaloe sublineata (Schaus, 1902)	18	78	YES
823. Itaballia demophile lucania (Fruhstorfer, 1907)	2	75	YES
824. I. pandosia pisonis (Hewitson, 1861)	1	75	YES
825. Pieriballia viardi rubecula (Fruhstorfer, 1907)	76	76	YES
826. Melete lycimnia peruviana (Lucas, 1852)	2	77	YES
827. Perrhybris pamela mazuka Lamas, 1981	16	80	YES

PAPILIONIDAE: PAPILIONINAE

828. Protographium agesilaus autosilaus (Bates, 1861)	2	78	YES
829. Eurytides dolicaon deileon (C & R Felder, 1865)	25	76	YES
830. Protesilaus glaucolaus leucas (Rothsch. & Jord., 1906)	2	82	YES
831. P. telesilaus telesilaus (C & R Felder, 1864)	18	76	YES
832. Mimoides ariarathes gayi (Lucas, 1852)	22	95	YES
833. M. pausanias pausanias (Hewitson, 1852)	2	78	YES
834. M. xynias xynias (Hewitson, 1875)	83	83	YES
835. Battus velus varus (Kollar, 1850)	78	78	YES
836. B. crassus crassus (Cramer, 1777)	SR	NC	YES
837. B. polydamas polydamas (Linnaeus, 1758)	41	NC	YES
838. Parides aeneas lamasi Racheli, 1988	20	76	YES
839. P. anchises drucei (Butler, 1874)	13	77	YES
840. P. echemon empistocles Küppers, 1975	XX	NC	NO
841. P. neophilus olivencius (Bates, 1861)	20	NC	YES
842. P. pizarro kuhlmanni (May, 1925)	19	76	YES
843. P. sesostris sesostris (Cramer, 1779)	10	75	YES
844. P. vertumnus astorius (Zikán, 1940)	17	91	YES
845. Pterourus zagreus zagreus (Doubleday, 1847)	88	88	NO
846. Heraclides anchisiades anchisiades (Esper, 1788)	26	80	YES
847. H. androgeus androgeus (Cramer, 1775)	95	95	YES
848. H. astyalus phanias (Rothschild & Jordan, 1906)	2	77	NO
849. H. chiansiades chiansiades (Westwood, 1872)	48	84	YES
850. H. garleppi interruptus (Staudinger, 1892)	40	78	NO
851. H. thoas cinyras (Ménétriès, 1857)	78	78	YES
852. H. torquatus torquatus (Cramer, 1777)	3	77	YES

HESPERIIDAE: PYRRHOPYGINAE

853. Pyrrhopyge pusca Evans, 1951	23	NC	NO
854. P. proculus draudti Bell, 1931	77	77	YES
855. P. rubricollis ssp. n.	90	90	NO
856. P. cometes ssp. n.	84	84	YES

857. Elbella intersecta intersecta (Herrich-Schäffer, 1869)	27	75	YES
858. E. merops (Bell, 1934)	84	84	YES
859. E. theseus (Bell, 1934)	77	77	NO
860. E. patrobas tingo Mielke, 1995	88	88	YES
861. E. blanda Evans, 1951	76	76	YES
862. E. azeta azeta (Hewitson, 1866)	76	76	YES
863. Elbella madeira Mielke, 1995	89	89	YES
864. E. etna Evans, 1951	3	76	NO
865. Protelbella alburna (Mabille, 1891)	88	88	NO
866. Parelbella ahira ahira (Hewitson, 1866)	92	92	NO
867. Nosphistia zonara (Hewitson, 1866)	37	97	YES
868. Jemadia hospita hospita (Butler, 1877)	77	77	YES
869. J. hewitsonii hewitsonii (Mabille, 1878)	2	85	YES
870. J. gnetus (Fabricius, 1782)	18	NC	YES
871. Mysoria sejanus ssp. n.	22	95	YES
872. Croniades pieria pieria (Hewitson, 1857)	16	96	NO
873. Myscelus nobilis (Cramer, 1777)	97	97	YES
874. M. amystis mysus Evans, 1951	88	88	YES
875. M. epimachia epimachia Herrich-Schäffer, 1869	76	76	NO
876. M. assaricus mapirica Strand, 1921	1	NC	NO
877. Passova passova styx (Möschler, 1879)	4	NC	YES
878. Aspitha agenoria sanies (Druce, 1908)	23	NC	YES

HESPERIIDAE: PYRGINAE

879. Phocides metrodorus metrodorus Bell, 1932	25	NC	YES
880. P. novalis Evans, 1952	90	90	YES
881. P. padrona Evans, 1952	91	91	YES
882. P. pigmalion hewitsonius (Mabille, 1883)	3	86	YES
883. Tarsoctenus corytus corba Evans, 1952	92	92	YES
884. T. praecia plutia (Hewitson, 1857)	81	81	YES
885. Phanus vitreus (Stoll, 1781)	3	75	YES
886. P. ecitonorum Austin, 1993	3	NC	YES
887. P. obscurior prestoni Miller, 1965	75	75	NO
888. P. marshalli (Kirby, 1880)	37	81	YES
889. Udranomia kikkawai (Weeks, 1906)	80	80	YES
890. Drephalys atinas (Mabille, 1888)	88	88	NO
891. D. eous (Hewitson, 1867)	2	NC	NO
892. D. hypargus (Mabille, 1891)	34	84	YES
893. Drephalys sp. n.	80	80	NO
894. Augiades crinisus (Cramer, 1780)	2	76	YES
895. Hyalothyrus leucomelas (Geyer, 1832)	42	75	YES
896. H. neleus neleus (Linnaeus, 1758)	4	93	NO
897. Phareas coeleste Westwood, 1852	51	NC	YES
898. Entheus eumelus ninyas Druce, 1912	16	90	YES
899. Entheus sp., gentius group	8	79	YES
900. Entheus sp., priassus group	1	79	YES
901. Cabirus procas junta Evans, 1952	18	76	NO
902. Proteides mercurius mercurius (Fabricius, 1787)	16	87	YES
903. Epargyreus socus sinus Evans, 1952	5	78	YES
904. E. exadeus exadeus (Cramer, 1779)	78	78	YES

905. E. spina spina Evans, 1952	89	89	NO
906. E. clavicornis clavicornis (Herrich-Schäffer, 1869)	18	78	YES
907. Polygonus manueli manueli Bell & Comstock, 1948	2	76	YES
908. Aguna sp. n.	4	83	YES
909. A. aurunce (Hewitson, 1867) (?)	10	84	YES
910. A. coelus (Stoll, 1782) (?)	15	97	YES
911. A. metophis (Latreille, 1824)	5	NC	NO
912. Aguna sp. n. 1	76	76	NO
913. Aguna sp. n. 2	84	84	NO
914. Aguna clina Evans, 1952	92	92	NO
915 Aguna sp. n. 3	81	81	NO
916 Polythrix octomaculata octomaculata (Sepp, 1844)	56	95	YES
917 P. minvanes (Williams, 1926)	75	75	YES
918 P. auginus (Hewitson, 1867) (?)	5	75	YES
919. P. metallescens (Mabille, 1888)	92	92	YES
920. Heronia labriaris (Butler, 1877)	76	76	YES
921. Chrysoplectrum pervivax (Hübner, 1819)	21	91	YES
922. C. perniciosus perniciosus (Herrich-Schäffer, 1869)	90	90	YES
923. Codatractus sp. n.	SR	NC	YES
924. Urbanus proteus proteus (Linnaeus, 1758)	30	NC	NO
925. U. pronta Evans, 1952	44	78	YES
926. U. esmeraldus (Butler, 1877)	16	NC	YES
927. U. esma Evans, 1952	28	87	NO
928. U. velinus (Plötz, 1880)(=acawoios Williams, 1926; n. syn.)	3	92	YES
929. U. teleus (Hübner, 1821)	20	77	YES
930. U. tanna Evans, 1952	78	78	NO
931. U. simplicius (Stoll, 1790)	82	82	YES
932. U. reductus (Riley, 1919)	32	NC	YES
933. U. doryssus doryssus (Swainson, 1831)	1	75	YES
934. U. virescens (Mabille, 1877)	82	82	YES
935. U. chalco (Hübner, 1823)	1	95	YES
936. Cephise cephise (Herrich-Schäffer, 1869) (?)	80	80	YES
937. Astraptes talus (Cramer, 1777)	80	80	YES
938. A. fulgerator fulgerator (Walch, 1775)	1	79	YES
939. A. aulus (Plötz, 1881)	28	83	YES
940. A. enotrus (Stoll, 1782)	75	75	YES
941. A. janeira (Schaus, 1902)	46	79	YES
942. A. alector hopfferi (Plötz, 1881)	9	75	YES
943. A. cretatus cretatus (Hayward, 1939)	3	79	YES
944. A. creteus creteus (Cramer, 1780)	6	89	YES
945. Narcosius hercules (Bell, 1956)	96	96	NO
946. N. narcosius narcosius (Stoll, 1790)	82	82	YES
947. N. samson (Evans, 1952)	92	92	NO
948. N. parisi parisi (Williams, 1927)	95	95	NO
949. N. nazaraeus Steinhauser, 1986	26	NC	NO
950. Calliades zeutus (Möschler, 1879)	51	NC	YES
951. Autochton neis (Geyer, 1832)	2	81	YES
952. A. longipennis (Plötz, 1882)	37	88	YES
953. A. zarex (Hübner, 1818)	1	76	YES
954. Bungalotis erythus (Cramer, 1775)	XX	NC	NO
955. B. astylos (Cramer, 1780)	37	NC	YES

956. Dyscophellus nicephorus (Hewitson, 1876)	25	NC	YES
957. D. marian Evans, 1952	36	85	NO
958. D. euribates euribates (Stoll, 1782)	37	80	YES
959. D. porcius porcius (C & R Felder, 1862)	14	80	NO
960. D. sebaldus (Stoll, 1781)	XX	NC	YES
961. Nascus phocus (Cramer, 1777)	25	NC	NO
962. N. paulliniae (Sepp, 1842)	23	95	YES
963. Porphyrogenes passalus passalus (Herrich-Schäffer, 1869)	79	79	NO
964. P. despecta despecta (Butler, 1870)	74	NC	NO
965. Oileides azines (Hewitson, 1867)	54	96	YES
966. Celaenorrhinus shema shema (Hewitson, 1877)	56	76	YES
967. C. disjunctus Bell, 1940	27	NC	YES
968. Celaenorrhinus sp. (similis group)	85	85	YES
969. C. syllius (C & R Felder, 1862)	8	91	YES
970. C. jao (Mabille, 1889)	12	80	YES
971. Spathilepia clonius (Cramer, 1775)	43	NC	NO
972. Telemiades delalande (Latreille, 1824)	1	77	YES
973. T. nicomedes nicomedes (Möschler, 1879)	91	91	NO
974. T. epicalus Hübner, 1819	9	84	YES
975. T. penidas (Hewitson, 1867)	92	92	YES
976. T. antiope tosca Evans, 1953	68	87	YES
977. T. amphion misitheus Mabille, 1888	1	79	YES
978. Pyrdalus corbulo corbulo (Stoll, 1781)	81	81	NO
979. Eracon clinias (Mabille, 1878)	26	77	NO
980. E. paulinus (Stoll, 1781)	23	NC	YES
981. Spioniades libethra (Hewitson, 1868)	83	83	YES
982. Mictris crispus (Herrich-Schäffer, 1870)	78	78	YES
983. Iliana purpurascens (Mabille & Boullet, 1912)	68	81	NO
984. Polyctor polyctor polyctor (Prittwitz, 1868)	35	77	YES
985. Nisoniades lata Steinhauser, 1989	78	78	NO
986. N. mimas (Cramer, 1775)	63	78	YES
987. N. ephora (Herrich-Schäffer, 1870)	16	NC	NO
988. N. evansi Steinhauser, 1989	78	78	YES
989. N. brunneata (Williams & Bell, 1939)	96	96	YES
990. N. macarius Herrich-Schäffer, 1870	8	81	YES
991. Pachyneuria l. lineatopunctata (Mab. & Boull., 1917)	70	83	YES
992. P. herophile (Hayward, 1940)	3	78	YES
993. Pellicia klugi Williams & Bell, 1939	14	78	YES
994. P. costimacula costimacula (Herrich-Schäffer, 1870)	76	76	YES
995. P. trax Evans, 1953	95	95	YES
996. P. dimidiata dimidiata Herrich-Schäffer, 1870	61	NC	NO
997. Pellicia sp. (n.?)	97	97	NO
998. Morvina morvus cyclopa Evans, 1953	32	75	NO
999. M. fissimacula rema Evans, 1953	2	92	YES
1000. M. falisca falia Evans, 1953	34	79	NO
1001. Myrinia binoculus (Möschler, 1877)	25	NC	NO
1002. M. myris (Mabille, 1898)	36	78	NO
1003. M. santa monka Evans, 1953	82	82	NO
1004. Xispia quadrata (Mabille, 1889)	78	78	NO
1005. Cyclosemia earina (Hewitson, 1878)	31	NC	YES
1006. Gorgopas trochilus (Hopffer, 1874)	41	78	YES

1007. Bolla mancoi (Lindsey, 1925)	65	NC	YES
1008. B. cupreiceps (Mabille, 1891)	32	95	YES
1009. B. morona morona (Bell, 1940)	32	97	YES
1010. B. zorilla (Plötz, 1886)	16	NC	NO
1011. Staphylus chlora Evans, 1953	66	NC	YES
1012. S. putumayo (Bell, 1937)	96	96	YES
1013. S. lizeri lizeri (Hayward, 1938)	8	NC	YES
1014. S. corumba (Williams & Bell, 1940)	20	NC	YES
1015. S. oeta (Plötz, 1884)	80	80	YES
1016. S. astra (Williams & Bell, 1940)	32	NC	YES
1017. S. minor minor Schaus, 1902	29	NC	NO
1018. Plumbago plumbago (Plötz, 1884)	28	75	YES
1019. Gorgythion begga pyralina (Möschler, 1877)	10	77	YES
1020. G. beggina escalophoides Evans, 1953	2	NC	YES
1021. Ouleus juxta juxta (Bell, 1934)	4	79	YES
1022. O. fatinitza (Plötz, 1884)	92	92	NO
1023. O. accedens noctis (Lindsey, 1925)	6	NC	YES
1024. Zera zera difficilis (Weeks, 1901)	78	78	NO
1025. Z. tetrastigma tetrastigma (Sepp, 1847)	79	79	NO
1026. Quadrus cerialis (Stoll, 1782)	6	77	YES
1027. Q. contubernalis contubernalis (Mabille, 1883)	13	75	YES
1028. Q. deyrollei porta Evans, 1953	1	NC	YES
1029. Pythonides jovianus fabricii Kirby, 1871	1	81	YES
1030. P. lerina (Hewitson, 1868)	2	76	YES
1031. P. grandis assecla Mabille, 1883	25	91	YES
1032. P. herennius herennius Geyer, 1838	66	75	YES
1033. P. eminus eminus Bell, 1934	72	NC	NO
1034. Pythonides maraca ssp. n.	16	76	YES
1035. Sostrata festiva (Erichson, 1848)	27	76	YES
1036. S. pusilla pusilla Godman & Salvin, 1895	2	84	YES
1037. Paches trifasciatus Lindsey, 1925	4	76	YES
1038. P. exosa (Butler, 1877)	71	NC	NO
1039. Haemactis sanguinalis (Westwood, 1852)	SR	NC	YES
1040. Milanion hemes ssp.	40	NC	YES
1041. M. pilumnus pilumnus Mabille & Boullet, 1917	6	75	YES
1042. Mylon ander ander Evans, 1953	89	89	YES
1043. M. menippus (Fabricius, 1776)	3	77	YES
1044. M. pelopidas (Fabricius, 1793)	45	NC	YES
1045. M. jason (Ehrmann, 1907)	3	77	YES
1046. Carrhenes fuscescens conia Evans, 1953	2	75	YES
1047. C. canescens leada (Butler, 1870)	16	NC	YES
1048. C. santes Bell, 1940	XX	NC	YES
1049. Clito clito (Fabricius, 1787)	77	77	YES
1050. C. zelotes (Hewitson, 1873)	82	82	NO
1051. Xenophanes tryxus (Stoll, 1780)	40	77	YES
1052. Antigonus nearchus (Latreille, 1817)	3	79	YES
1053. A. erosus (Hübner, 1812)	22	75	YES
1054. A. decens Butler, 1874	22	78	YES
1055. Anisochoria pedaliodina pedaliodina (Butler, 1870)	49	NC	YES
1056. Aethilla echina echina Hewitson, 1870	3	76	YES
1057. Achlyodes busirus heros Ehrmann, 1909	14	76	YES

1058. A. mithridates thraso (Hübner, 1807)	29	78	YES
1059. Grais stigmaticus stigmaticus (Mabille, 1883)	41	NC	NO
1060. Anastrus sempiternus simplicior (Möschler, 1877)	2	76	YES
1061. A. tolimus robigus (Plötz, 1884)	76	76	YES
1062. A. petius petius (Möschler, 1877)	26	77	YES
1063. A. meliboea bactra Evans, 1955	29	NC	YES
1064. A. obscurus narva Evans, 1955	32	77	YES
1065. Ebrietas infanda (Butler, 1877)	2	75	YES
1066. E. anacreon anacreon (Staudinger, 1876)	2	76	YES
1067. E. evanidus Mabille, 1898	6	75	YES
1068. Cycloglypha thrasibulus thrasibulus (Fabricius, 1793)	37	76	YES
1069. C. tisias (Godman & Salvin, 1896)	8	96	YES
1070. C. enega (Möschler, 1877)	8	76	NO
1071. Helias phalaenoides phalaenoides (Hübner, 1812)	10	NC	YES
1072. Camptopleura theramenes Mabille, 1877	85	85	YES
1073. C. auxo (Möschler, 1879)	2	76	YES
1074. Pyrgus oileus orcus (Stoll, 1780)	2	76	YES
1075. Heliopetes alana (Reakirt, 1868)	76	76	YES

HESPERIIDAE: HESPERIINAE

1076. Synapte silius (Latreille, 1824)	1	78	YES
1077. Lento sp. n. 1	25	75	YES
1078. L. ferrago (Plötz, 1884)	39	75	YES
1079. L. imerius (Plötz, 1884)	27	81	YES
1080. Lento sp. n. 2	46	75	YES
1081. Anthoptus epictetus (Fabricius, 1793)	81	81	YES
1082. A. insignis (Pl"ptz, 1882)	12	NC	YES
1083. Corticea corticea (Plötz, 1882)	78	78	YES
1084. Cantha calva Evans, 1955	16	75	YES
1085. Vinius sagitta (Mabille, 1889)	6	96	YES
1086. V. tryhana tryhana (Kaye, 1914)	1	77	YES
1087. Pheraeus fastus (Hayward, 1939)	68	NC	NO
1088. P. maria Steinhauser, 1991	19	75	YES
1089. Pheraeus sp. n. 1	15	75	YES
1090. Pheraeus sp. n. 2	9	77	YES
1091. Misius misius (Mabille, 1891)	5	NC	YES
1092. Molo mango (Guenée, 1865)	7	75	YES
1093. M. calcarea ssp. n.	2	81	YES
1094. Racta apella raza Evans, 1955	32	76	NO
1095. Apaustus gracilis smarti Evans, 1955	10	NC	NO
1096. Callimormus radiola radiola (Mabille, 1878)	34	NC	YES
1097. Eutocus matildae vinda Evans, 1955	29	87	YES
1098. E. quichua Lindsey, 1921	1	95	YES
1099. Ludens ludens (Mabille, 1891)	6	78	NO
1100. L. silvaticus (Hayward, 1940), nom. rev.	87	87	YES
1101. Methionopsis ina (Plötz, 1882)	4	77	YES
1102. M. dolor Evans, 1955	56	77	YES
1103. Artines sp.n.nr. aepitus (Geyer, 1832)	23	78	YES
1104. A. focus Evans, 1955	34	95	YES
1105. A. trogon Evans, 1955	17	75	YES

1106. Flaccilla aecas (Stoll, 1781)	91	91	YES
1107. Mnaseas bicolor inca Bell, 1930	34	77	YES
1108. Gallio sp. n.	78	78	YES
1109. Thargella caura caura (Plötz, 1882)	4	75	YES
1110. Venas evans (Butler, 1877)	8	85	YES
1111. V. caerulans (Mabille, 1878)	52	76	YES
1112. Phanes aletes (Geyer, 1832)	83	83	YES
1113. Phanes sp. n.	81	81	NO
1114. Vidius nappa Evans, 1955	30	NC	NO
1115. Vidius sp. n.	7	84	YES
1116. Cymaenes hazarma (Hewitson, 1877)	17	82	YES
1117. C. cavalla Evans, 1955	11	NC	YES
1118. C. laureolus loxa Evans, 1955	18	NC	NO
1119. C. uruba taberi (Weeks, 1901)	13	NC	YES
1120. Vehilius stictomenes stictomenes (Butler, 1877)	33	75	YES
1121. V. seriatus seriatus (Mabille, 1891)	55	79	NO
1122. V. danius ssp. n.	88	88	NO
1123. V. putus Bell, 1941	23	90	YES
1124. V. madius ssp. n.	1	77	YES
1125. Mnasilus allubita (Butler, 1877)	37	NC	YES
1126. Mnasitheus chrysophrys (Mabille, 1891)	89	89	YES
1127. M. gemignanii (Hayward, 1940)	25	NC	NO
1128. M. simplicissima (Herrich-Schäffer, 1870)	76	76	NO
1129. Mnasitheus sp. n.	80	80	NO
1130. Remella remus (Fabricius, 1798)	2	79	YES
1131. Moeris submetallescens (Hayward, 1940)	22	78	YES
1132. Parphorus storax storax (Mabille, 1891)	52	75	YES
1133. P. decora (Herrich-Schäffer, 1869)	16	82	YES
1134. P. prosper Evans, 1955	84	84	YES
1135. Parphorus sp. n. 1	31	83	NO
1136. Parphorus sp. n. 2	3	95	NO
1137. Parphorus sp. n. 3	81	81	YES
1138. Parphorus sp. n. 4	1	75	YES
1139. Papias phainis Godman, 1900	5	75	YES
1140. P. subcostulata subcostulata (Herrich-Schäffer, 1870)	3	NC	NO
1141. Propapias proximus (Bell, 1934)	1	75	YES
1142. Cobalopsis nero (Herrich-Schäffer, 1869)	4	75	YES
1143. Arita arita (Schaus, 1902)	23	75	YES
1144. Morys geisa geisa (Möschler, 1879)	16	81	YES
1145. Morys sp. n.	79	79	NO
1146. Psoralis chittara ssp. n.	8	NC	NO
1147. Psoralis sp. n. 1	16	77	YES
1148. Psoralis sp. n. 2	65	76	NO
1149. Tigasis fusca (Hayward, 1940)	51	NC	NO
1150. Tigasis sp. n. 1	77	77	YES
1151. Tigasis sp. n. 2	27	86	NO
1152. Vettius richardi (Weeks, 1906)	2	79	YES
1153. V. monacha (Plötz, 1882)	5	76	YES
1154. V. phyllus phyllus (Cramer, 1777)	10	75	YES
1155. V. marcus marcus (Fabricius, 1787)	6	75	YES
1156. V. artona (Hewitson, 1868)	20	84	YES

1157. V. arva Evans, 1955	1	75	NO
1158. V. fuldai (Bell, 1930)	75	75	YES
1159. Paracarystus hypargyra (Herrich-Schäffer, 1869)	65	81	YES
1160. P. menestries rona (Hewitson, 1866)	4	93	YES
1161. Turesis complanula (Herrich-Schäffer, 1869), nom. rev.	9	79	YES
1162. T. basta Evans, 1955	13	NC	YES
1163. Thoon canta Evans, 1955	8	79	YES
1164. T. modius (Mabille, 1889)	85	85	YES
1165. T. dubia (Bell, 1932)	32	79	YES
1166. T. taxes (Godman, 1900)	22	78	YES
1167. T. ponka Evans, 1955	72	95	YES
1168. T. ranka Evans, 1955	46	76	YES
1169. Thoon sp. n. 1	5	75	NO
1170. Thoon sp. n. 2 (nr. yesta Evans, 1955)	16	83	YES
1171. Justinia phaetusa phaetusa (Hewitson, 1866)	4	79	YES
1172. J. justinianus dappa Evans, 1955	51	83	YES
1173. J. maculata (Bell, 1930)	51	NC	NO
1174. Eutychide complana (Herrich-Schäffer, 1869)	13	78	YES
1175. E. subcordata subcordata (Herrich-Schäffer, 1869)	80	80	YES
1176. Onophas columbaria flossites (Butler, 1874)	96	96	YES
1177. Onophas sp. n.	23	80	NO
1178. Styriodes quadrinotata (Mabille, 1889)	42	77	NO
1179. S. badius (Bell, 1930)	1	75	YES
1180. S. quaka Evans, 1955	57	NC	YES
1181. Styriodes sp. n.	16	77	YES
1182. Enosis pruinosa pruinosa (Plötz, 1882)	31	84	YES
1183. E. iccius Evans, 1955	27	76	YES
1184. E. blotta Evans, 1955	42	87	YES
1185. E. immaculata demon Evans, 1955	21	89	YES
1186. Vertica verticalis ssp. n.	80	80	YES
1187. Ebusus ebusus ebusus (Cramer, 1780)	27	89	YES
1188. Evansiella cordela (Plötz, 1882)	80	80	NO
1189. Talides sinois sinois Hübner, 1819	19	NC	YES
1190. Tromba tromba Evans, 1955	84	84	YES
1191. Nyctus crinitus Mabille, 1891	90	90	NO
1192. Carystus periphas periphas Mabille, 1891	76	76	NO
1193. Tisias quadrata quadrata (Herrich-Schäffer, 1869)	23	80	YES
1194. T. rinda Evans, 1955	80	80	NO
1195. T. lesueur canna Evans, 1955	86	86	YES
1196. Moeros moeros (Möschler, 1877)	13	NC	YES
1197. Cobalus virbius virbius (Cramer, 1777)	4	NC	YES
1198. C. calvina (Hewitson, 1866)	69	81	YES
1199. Dubiella fiscella fiscella (Hewitson, 1877)	97	97	YES
1200. D. dubius (Stoll, 1781)	5	79	YES
1201. Carystina lysiteles (Mabille, 1891)	93	93	NO
1202. Tellona variegata (Hewitson, 1870)	89	89	YES
1203. Damas clavus (Herrich-Schäffer, 1869)	2	79	YES
1204. Orphe vatinius Godman, 1901	22	77	YES
1205. O. gerasa (Hewitson, 1867)	25	NC	YES
1206. Carystoides basoches (Latreille, 1824)	1	77	YES
1207. C. noseda (Hewitson, 1866)	25	80	YES

1208. C. sicania orbius (Godman, 1901)	14	80	YES
1209. C. maroma (Möschler, 1877)	30	79	NO
1210. C. cathaea (Hewitson, 1866)	57	93	YES
1211. Perichares philetes philetes (Gmelin, 1791)	20	76	YES
1212. P. lotus (Butler, 1870)	25	86	YES
1213. Orses cynisca (Swainson, 1821)	27	NC	YES
1214. Alera haworthiana (Swainson, 1821)	23	76	NO
1215. Alera sp. n	1	79	YES
1216. Lycas godart boisduvalii (Ehrmann, 1909)	26	75	YES
1217. L. argentea (Hewitson, 1866)	80	80	YES
1218. Saturnus saturnus saturnus (Fabricius, 1787)	36	75	YES
1219. S. metonidia (Schaus, 1902)	1	78	YES
1220. S. reticulata meton (Mabille, 1891)	8	NC	YES
1221. Phlebodes pertinax (Stoll, 1781)	6	76	YES
1222. P. campo sifax Evans, 1955	13	79	YES
1223. P. notex Evans, 1955	3	NC	YES
1224. P. virgo Evans, 1955 (?)	80	80	YES
1225. P. torax Evans, 1955	24	NC	YES
1226. P. eteocla (Plötz, 1882)	6	78	NO
1227. P. xanthobasis (Hayward, 1939)	26	NC	NO
1228. Phlebodes sp. n. (aff. torax Evans, 1955)	56	NC	NO
1229. Joanna boxi Evans, 1955	3	85	YES
1230. Quinta cannae (Herrich-Schäffer, 1869)	16	75	YES
1231. Cynea iquita (Bell, 1941)	29	NC	YES
1232. C. corisana (Möschler, 1883)	3	NC	YES
1233. C. popla Evans, 1955	2	79	YES
1234. C. megalops (Godman, 1900)	80	80	NO
1235. C. robba robba Evans, 1955	89	89	NO
1236. C. bistrigula (Herrich-Schäffer, 1869)	31	NC	YES
1237. C. diluta (Herrich-Schäffer, 1869)	83	83	YES
1238. Penicula bryanti (Weeks, 1906)	2	82	YES
1239. P. advena advena (Draudt, 1923)	6	81	YES
1240. P. crista Evans, 1955	19	75	YES
1241. Decinea decinea derisor (Mabille, 1891)	95	95	YES
1242. Decinea sp. n.	2	NC	NO
1243. D. dama (Herrich-Schäffer, 1869)	28	77	NO
1244. Cyclosma altama (Schaus, 1902)	30	77	NO
1245. Orthos orthos orthos (Godman, 1900)	2	77	YES
1246. O. trinka Evans, 1955	21	79	YES
1247. O. potesta (Bell, 1941) (?)	95	95	YES
1248. Orthos sp. n.	96	96	NO
1249. Hylephila phyleus phyleus (Drury, 1773)	16	NC	YES
1250. Pompeius pompeius (Latreille, 1824)	48	NC	YES
1251. Quasimellana angra Evans, 1955	76	76	NO
1252. Quasimellana pandora (Hayward, 1940)	50	90	YES
1253. Hansa devergens devergens (Draudt, 1923)	1	78	YES
1254. H. hyboma (Plötz, 1886)	27	92	NO
1255. Metron leucogaster ambrosei (Weeks, 1906)	19	90	YES
1256. M. schrottkyi hypochlora (Draudt, 1923)	19	76	NO
1257. Propertius propertius (Fabricius, 1793)	47	76	YES
1258. Phemiades pohli cidra Evans, 1955	91	91	YES

251

1259. P. milvius milor Evans, 1955	91	91	NO
1260. P. pseudophineus de Jong, 1983	3	93	NO
1261. Calpodes ethlius (Stoll, 1782)	10	83	YES
1262. Panoquina lucas (Fabricius, 1793)			
(=sylvicola Herrich-Schäffer, 1865; syn. n.), comb. nov.	3	84	NO
1263. P. fusina fusina (Hewitson, 1868)	3	76	YES
1264. P. evadnes (Stoll, 1781)	80	80	NO
1265. Panoquina sp. n.	XX	NC	NO
1266. Zenis jebus ssp. n.	22	91	YES
1267. Tirynthia conflua (Herrich-Schäffer, 1869)	9	75	NO
1268. Thespieus dalman (Latreille, 1824)	32	NC	NO
1269. Lindra simulius (Druce, 1876)	89	89	NO
1270. L. vanewrighti Mielke, 1978	91	91	NO
1271. L. boliviana Mielke, 1993	82	82	YES
1272. Oxynthes corusca (Herrich-Schäffer, 1869)	56	84	YES
1273. Niconiades xanthaphes Hübner, 1821	2	84	YES
1274. N. linga Evans, 1955	3	79	YES
1275. N. nabona Evans, 1955	87	87	NO
1276. N. centralis Mielke, 1967	84	84	NO
1277. Aides duma argyrina Cowan, 1970	6	80	YES
1278. A. brino (Stoll, 1781)	91	91	YES
1279. A. aegita (Hewitson, 1866)	22	80	YES
1280. Cravera laureata (Draudt, 1923)	91	91	NO
1281. Saliana triangularis (Kaye, 1914)	19	80	YES
1282. S. fusta Evans, 1955	92	92	YES
1283. S. fischer (Latreille, 1824)	59	79	YES
1284. S. nigel Evans, 1955	75	75	NO
1285. S. esperi Evans, 1955	96	96	YES
1286. S. longirostris (Sepp, 1840)	75	75	YES
1287. S. morsa Evans, 1955	22	NC	YES
1288. S. salius (Cramer, 1775)	61	77	YES
1289. S. saladin culta Evans, 1955	2	NC	YES
1290. Thracides cleanthes telmela (Hewitson, 1866)	76	76	YES
1291. T. thrasea (Hewitson, 1866)	86	86	YES
1292. Neoxeniades braesia braesia (Hewitson, 1867)	6	79	YES
1293. N. bajula ssp. n.	26	NC	NO
1294. Aroma aroma (Hewitson, 1867)	10	NC	YES
1295. Chloeria psittacina (C & R Felder, 1867)	SR	NC	YES
1296. Pyrrhopygopsis socrates orasus (Druce, 1876)	76	76	YES
1297. Unidentified 1 (Tigasis ?)	16	NC	NO
1298. Unidentified 2 (Eprius ?)	26	NC	NO
1299. Unidentified 3 (genus? - nr. Psoralis)	6	81	YES
1300. Unidentified 4 (genus?)	78	78	NO

Spiders of Pakitza (Madre de Dios, Perú):Species Richness and Notes on Community Structure

DIANA SILVA

Museo de Historia Natural
Apartado 14-0434
Lima 14, Peru

JONATHAN A. CODDINGTON

Dept. Entomology
National Museum of Natural History
Smithsonian Institution
Washington, DC 20560

RESUMEN

El muestreo cuantitativo realizado en Pakitza durante abril-mayo y setiembre-octubre de 1991 -sólo los ejemplares adultos (2616 arañas)- dio como resultado 498 especies de arañas distribuidas en 33 familias. El análisis de la estructura de la comunidad de arañas indica que el grupo de tejedoras de telas circulares es dominante en abundancia y diversidad de especies, seguido por el grupo de tejedoras de telas irregulares. Las familias numéricamente dominantes son Theridiidae y Araneidae, cada una representa el 28 % del total de ejemplares colectados; la tercera familia más abundante es Uloboridae (7.1 %). La mayoría de las especies colectadas (56 %) está representada sólo por uno o dos ejemplares, estas especies parecen tener una gran influencia en el estimado de la riqueza cuando se consideran las variaciones por estacionalidad o tipo de bosque -las diferencias no son significativas cuando se excluye las especies representadas sólo por un ejemplar. El mismo efecto se observa cuando los únicos se excluyen del estimado total de la riqueza de especies, el que es significativamente mayor a finales de la época seca. La araneofauna de la terraza aluvial antigua (OAT) parece ser más rica en especies que aquélla del bosque inundable alto (UFF), aunque puede ser un efecto del tamaño de la muestra. La evaluación de los métodos no-paramétricos utilizados para el estimado de la riqueza de especies demuestra que cada uno tiene sus ventajas y desventajas, aunque los intervalos de confianza superimponen. Quizá este rango de valores es suficiente para el estimado de la riqueza de especies. Cuando se compara los diferentes métodose usualmente se encuentra el siguiente orden, partiendo de aquéllos que proporcionan los estimados más bajos hasta aquéllos que indican los estimados más altos: lognormal, jackknife, Chao1, Chao2, y curva de acumulación de especies.

ABSTRACT

A quantitative sampling protocol conducted in Pakitza during early and late dry season (April-May and September-October, 1991) yielded 2616 adult spiders comprising 498 species and 33 families. For this sample, the orb weavers were the most abundant and diverse, followed by the sheet/line weavers. Species of Theridiidae and Araneidae were numerically dominant, each family accounting for approximately 28 % of the total collected specimens. The third most abundant family was Uloboridae comprising 7.1 % of the total collection. Most species (56%) were represented by only 1 or 2 individuals; these species strongly affect the richness estimate when variation due to season and type of forest are considered. There were more species in the late dry season than in the early dry season, but when the singletons (132 vs. 75) were excluded this effect disappears. The same effect is observed when all uniques were excluded from the total richness, which is substantially higher in the late dry season. The spider fauna of the old alluvial terrace forest (OAT) seems to be richer than that of the upper floodplain forest (UFF), although this may again be due to sample size. The assessment of non-parametric methods used to estimate the richness of spider species shows that each estimator has its strengths and weaknesses. Where available, the confidence intervals of all of the estimators overlap; perhaps this range of values is a sufficiently accurate estimate of species richness. Within any one comparison, the estimators often follow a set ranking from lowest to highest values: lognormal, jackknife, Chao1 and Chao2, species accumulation curve.

INTRODUCTION

Tropical forests, especially Neotropical forests, include some of the most species-rich ecosystems in the world. Exactly how rich is a matter of some debate, partly because methods to estimate species richness are themselves debatable and little understood. Although richness can be determined for long-lived sessile organisms like trees by exhaustively enumerating all individuals, it is time-consuming, laborious, and expensive (e.g. Hubbell and Foster, 1983). Exhaustive enumeration is not a practical option for many animal groups, because it is impossible to census all individuals. The species composition of the ecosystem is dynamic and will change during the period of the huge census effort required. Although censussing may work well for obvious, large, species-poor groups such as birds or perhaps larger terrestrial vertebrates, it is manifestly impractical for megadiverse groups such as terrestrial arthropods. The latter taxa are generally small in size, short-lived, and vagile. Estimating the species richness of such groups at a point in time is no small problem.

The current study arose from the first author's long-term interest in the patterns of distribution and abundance of Peruvian spiders, and the second author's interest in the possibility of estimating species richness by extrapolation from sample data. The inventory reported here was not ideal for either task, but it has taught us that Pakitza's spider fauna is so rich that adequate point samples or studies that encompass the entire fauna are probably beyond the reach of single investigators, though possibly attainable by larger groups of collaborating workers.

This study contributes to the larger effort of designing methods to estimate species richness of very diverse groups by applying several quantitative richness estimation methods to a series of samples collected in the same way among a series of forest types (Colwell and Coddington, 1994; Heyer et al., 1994; Longino 1994). It also provides a data set that others interested in the same problem can use (to obtain the full data set please write the second author). While the true richness of a given site at a given time for a given group may be nearly impossible to verify empirically, we anticipate that the various estimators may behave similarly when applied to different data. Even without knowing the "true" answer in any one case, we can learn something about the circumstances under which they are reliable and when they are likely to give very misleading results.

Available methods include the classic lognormal (Preston, 1948), the jackknife (Heltshe and Forrester, 1983, 1985), the two estimators here called Chao1 and Chao2 (Chao, 1984, 1987) and species accumulation curves, here fitted to the Michaelis-Menten equation, a hyperbolic function that seems to fit species accumulation curves rather well (Lamas et al., 1991; see Soberón and Llorente (1993) and Colwell and Coddington (1994) for a review). Other methods exist (Colwell and Coddington, 1994) but they are mainly variants of the above estimators and give comparable results. The Chao2 estimator was originally designed to estimate population size when probability of capture and recapture varied among individuals (Chao, 1987). This seems formally equivalent to the estimation of total species richness when species vary in relative abundance (and thus in probability of capture), and so it seems reasonable to apply it to the current problem. To the extent the data permitted, we applied these five estimators to our total data set, and partitions of it by forest type and season (early versus late dry season).

We also seek to inventory and characterize the dynamics of the spider fauna of Pakitza in at least a semi-quantitative way such that the resulting data will provide more than an annotated list of species and a museum collection to support tropical systematics, although both of those are worthwhile goals. Rusell-Smith and Stork (1994)briefly review spider diversity studies from other tropical areas. We particularly focus on differences and abundance of the spider fauna between early and late dry season, and between forest types. These questions were approached in two ways, by looking at the effect these variables have on the number of adults and number of species per hourly sample, and also by examining their effect on the inventory viewed as a whole. We assume that an environment with more spiders or species will be reflected in how much a collector can catch in a unit of effort. We were also interested to explore the effect that rare species have on such analyses (Gaston, 1994).

While data collection protocols are usually designed for a specific purpose (as ours have been to estimate richness), these data may also be useful to other investigators asking different questions (e. g. Huston, 1995; Rosenweig, 1995). The spider fauna of Pakitza is only known from one previous qualitative sampling by Coddington and Silva (unpubl. data). During a period of three weeks in September-October, 1987, we collected 237 species. As of 1991, six new species have already been described from that inventory (Baert, 1990a; Levi, 1991b; Millidge, 1991).

STUDY AREA

The study area is on the east side of the Manu River, among Pleistocene terraces up to 100 m above the present Manu river bed. The Biological Station of Pakitza, 11° 56'S/71° 17'W, at an elevation of 356 m, includes approximately 4000 ha of lowland rain forest with an extremely irregular topography. Erwin (1991) provides a detailed description for Pakitza.

Weather.- Data recorded in Cocha Cashu (approx. 21 km NE of Pakitza) for ten years shows two distinct seasons based upon annual mean fluctuation in rainfall and temperature (Erwin, 1991). Four complete years of data indicate an average rainfall of about 2000 mm, seasonally distributed, most of it falling between November and May. Dry season months (May-October) normally receive less than 100 mm, though year-to year variation in the intensity and duration of the dry season is considerable (Terborgh, 1990). Dry seasons are also characterized by very strong winds and short cold periods, at this time the temperature may drop to 10-15 °C (Erwin, pers. comm.)

*Vegetation.-*Rio Manu presents an undisturbed rainforest flora (Foster, 1990). Generally, there is a one or two layer canopy forest with numerous super-emergents and varied amounts of herbaceous or shrubby understory (Erwin, 1991). In the BIOLAT Station Erwin (1991) identified twelve forest types, but only seven were sampled during this study. We describe these seven forest types, with their acronyms as listed in Appendix 1, following Erwin (1991).

UPLAND SLOPE FOREST (USF).

This non-flooded forest type starts at stake 70 on Trail Tachigali and is found on reddish clay soil. There is no information on vegetation but according to Erwin (1991) the soil, drainage pattern, tree species, and associated microfauna are unique. The spiders were collected between stakes 80 and 100.

OLD ALLUVIAL TERRACE FOREST (OAT).

This non-flooded forest type is found on sandy surface soil overlaying red lateritic soil. These soils are rapidly drained. BIOLAT Zone 3 is on this type of forest. This zone is dominated by Leguminosae (16%), Moraceae (15.5%), and

Palmae (14.1%); lianas are essentially absent. Our samples were taken outside zone 3 along Castañal and Troncal Tachigali trails; however these are not pure OAT collections since there are patches of dissected alluvial terrace forest mixed along these trails. Collections from Pacal (roughly, between stakes 5 to 25) and Zúngaro trails were also included in this forest type.

DISSECTED ALLUVIAL TERRACE FOREST (DAT).

Well drained sandy surface soils characterize the non-flooded old alluvial terraces within 2 km of the Manu River. The dominant vegetation in this kind of forest are Violaceae (31.2%), Palmae (16.3 %), and Moraceae (10%). Samples are from Zone 1 and also along Tachigali trail, roughly between stakes 10 to 40. We may have mixed samples with a small patch of OAT.

LOWER FLOODPLAIN FOREST (LFF).

Two zones occupy the lower, seasonally-flooded floodplain and different communities of plants occur in each of these zones. The lower zone, which floods and drains many times during the year, is covered with grasses and willows. Only one sample was taken here. The upper zone, on the other hand, may only flood once or twice per year. This is characterized by a forest with fewer and smaller trees (10-20m) than in other parts of Pakitza. There are few palms and Zone 07 apparently is dominated by *Guarea* (29%) and *Sapium* (29%). The samples were taken inside this zone, and a few outside along Castañal trail.

UPPER FLOODPLAIN FOREST (UFF).

The seasonally-flooded recent floodplain is on the richest alluvial soils. Parts of this forest are subject to yearly inundation, while other large areas are inundated by the highest floods, which may only occur once a century (Foster, 1990). The dominant trees, 25-35m tall, belong to Myristicaceae (11%), Bombacaceae (8%), and Meliaceae (7%). There are also many palms (21%) growing in this forest. We worked along the trails around Zone 2 and Caña Brava trail.

CLOSED RIPARIAN VEGETATION (RVF).

A distinctive, seasonally-flooded streamside vegetation occupies certain stretches of the deeper stream courses along the main watersheds. This vegetation is overshadowed by the adjacent forest type. No surveys have been made to date. The samples were limited to Quebradas Picaflor, Trompetero, and Carpintero.

OXBOW LAKES (TGH).

Through a special collecting permit, since they are not in the BIOLAT station, it was possible to take a few samples from the seasonally-flooded lagoons (cochas) near Pakitza. The collections were made inside the forest, along the trails surrounding the oxbow lakes, and also from the aquatic herbs and shrubs in their exposed edges. The following information was taken from Ascorra et al. (1991): Cocha Juarez is on the east side of the Manu River, ca. 20 km river down from Pakitza. Cocha Otorongo is on the west side of the Manu River, between Salvador and Juarez lagoons. Cocha Salvador is also on the east side of Manu River, ca. 10 km river down to Pakitza. Cocha Totora is on the east side of Manu River, ca. 21 km NE Pakitza, in the Biological Station of Cocha Cashu.

METHODS

Sampling occurred during two periods in the dry season of 1991. The first period, from April 21 to May 13, coincided with the early dry season. The second one was from September 26 to October 19, during the late dry season. Although we collected spiders with both non-quantitative and quantitative methods, this paper presents only the quantitative data.

The sampling protocol used elements of that of Coddington et al. (1991), but differed in significant respects. First, sampling was almost entirely done by the first author. Second, the sampling focussed almost entirely on the shrub, tree-trunk, and aerial web-spinning fauna; methods that accessed other components of the fauna were de-emphasized. The inventory thus was not intended to be representative of the total fauna, but that is in some ways a virtue because the lack of breadth may be compensated by depth--it is probably the largest and most detailed quantitative local list of web and cursorial spiders of the shrub and tree trunk zones from a lowland Neotropical site in the literature. Each sample was classified by three factors. Forest type was as noted above. Time of day of collection was classified either as day (0900-1600) or night (2000 to 2400). Methods of collection were as described below. The basic sampling unit was one hour of constant searching for spiders. Juvenile specimens were not purposely collected, since only adults can be only reliably identified to species. The full database thus contains sample number, forest type, season, month, date, collector name, method, time of day, replicate (if the same method was used by the same person within one time period and place), BIOLAT plot number if applicable, species code, genus, and family.

The collecting methods employed were 1) searching and picking by hand from the aerial vegetation and other surfaces, colloquially known as "looking up"; 2) searching and picking by hand both up in the vegetation and on the ground, or "looking up and down"; 3) searching and picking by hand on the ground surfaces, leaf litter or under logs, or "looking down"; 4) use of a beating try on the understory vegetation or lower branches of trees; and 5) pitfall traps located inside BIOLAT plots. Pitfall collections have not been included in the present study.

As noted above, both the methods used and the allocation of sampling effort biased against the ground and litter fauna. The spider fauna inhabiting the leaf litter or ground crevices, represented in Neotropical forests mostly by anapids, oonopids and small gnaphosids (Höfer, 1990; pers. obs.), was mainly evaluated by non-quantitative methods during both periods of field work. Because these groups and their ecological equivalents were almost entirely missed by the methods employed, this inventory pertains mainly to patterns within aerial web builders or other spiders that inhabit the shrub, tree trunk, aerial web zone, or other such "non-forest floor" zones.

Terms of relative abundance, like commonness or rarity, are based upon the general impression of the spider fauna throughout the field work and by personal experience with other Peruvian lowland forests.

IDENTIFICATION

All specimens were sorted to morphospecies, but due to the scarcity of recent taxonomic revisions, many of the spiders can not be identified in a reasonable amount of time. Many Neotropical species are undescribed, and many of the known spider species were described without using modern taxonomic criteria, are based on juvenile specimens, or were described from only one sex.

We have gone to some lengths to include those taxonomic references most useful in identifying lowland Neotropical spiders. Ignorance of the literature is often a great obstacle to the study of spiders, and we hope that the bibliography presented here may help the beginning worker. Keyserling (1876-93), Pickard-Cambridge, F. O. (1897-1905), Pickard-Cambridge, O. (1889-1902), Simon (1892-1895, 1897-1903), Taczanowski (1872-79), in addition to papers by Baert and Maelfait (1986), Brignoli (1979), Bryant (1942, 1945), di Caporiacco (1947-1955), Chamberlin and Ivie (1942), Chickering (1937-1973), Jiménez (1988), Levi (1953-1993), Mello-Leitao (1939-1948), Nentwig (1993), Schenkel (1953), Schmidt (1971), Petrunkevitch (1925-1930), and Soares and Camargo (1955) are major works that describe Neotropical spiders and help to identify some species. However, only modern taxonomic revisions permit confident establishment of accurate names, and even then coverage is usually far from complete. References to genera that may occur in the Neotropics are cited under each family (Brignoli, 1983; Platnick, 1989, 1993). Families and genera are listed alphabetically, according to Platnick (1989), with a few exceptions.

Voucher specimens are deposited in the United States National Museum of Natural History, Smithsonian Institution. Duplicates and non-quantitative collections are kept in the Museo de Historia Natural de la Universidad Nacional Mayor de San Marcos, Lima (Peru).

ANALYSIS

Any statistical procedure assumes that the sample is a random selection from the universe being investigated. In the present case, the universe being investigated is that portion of the total spider fauna accessible by our collecting methods and present as adults in the seven forest types during the early and late dry season of 1991. "Accessible to the methods" is a crucially important qualifier. Obviously we can say very little about the portion of the spider community that exclusively abides in the canopy, burrows, or leaf litter because we made no concerted effort to collect them. How much of the spider community we thereby ignored is an interesting question. Judging from other studies (e.g. Young, 1992, Coddington unpubl. data), or virtually complete lists, e.g. Heimer and Nentwig, 1984; Kaston, 1948; Roberts, 1987), one may guess very roughly that the portion of the total fauna accessible to the methods applied here might be 50 - 85 % of the total. Litter inhabiting ground spiders such as erigonine linyphiids usually make up a large percentage of temperate communities, but they are unusually species-poor in the tropics. This taxon is replaced by groups like oonopids, pholcids, anapids, ochyroceratids, and other such cryptic forms. Typical values for the local richness of these tropical groups is at present unknown, although Höfer (1990) has presented some data for Amazonian terra firme forest. Another undercollected group is the Mygalomorphae, but these species constitute much less than 10% of the richness of a lowland tropical community. Presumably the largest omission is the canopy fauna. If current estimates of the low degree of overlap between canopy and subcanopy arthropod communities are correct, estimates based on subcanopy samples will be serious underestimated. In any case, if it is possible to estimate reliably the parametric value of the species richness of constrained samples, relationships such as the above can then be used to estimate the actual species richness.

We followed Magurran (1988) in fitting the data to a lognormal distribution. The area under the best-fit lognormal curve estimates the total species richness of the community. A shortcoming of the lognormal model is that no analytical formula for the confidence interval for the area under the curve exists and that the best method to fit discrete data to a continuous model is debatable (Colwell and Coddington, 1994; Ludwig and Reynolds, 1988; Pielou, 1975). However, it is the only model used here that permits a formal test of the fit of the data to the model.

Chao1, like the lognormal, does not require replicate samples and uses the relative abundance of species in the total sample to estimate richness (Chao, 1984). It works by augmenting the observed richness, S_0, by the square of the number of singletons n_1 divided by twice the number of doubletons, n_2, thus $S^* = S_0 + n_1^2 / 2n_2$. Algebraically this is the same formula as Chao2 (see below), and Chao (in litt.) has suggested that the formula developed for the variance of Chao2 may also be used for Chao1 (see below). Chao (1984) was careful to emphasize that this estimator is really a lower bound on S^*. It should work best if most of the information in the sample is concentrated in the lowest frequencies, e.g. singletons and doubletons should predominate in the sample. As that is often the case in tropical work, this estimator deserves careful consideration.

The remaining techniques all require a series of replicate samples. We used least squares techniques combined with non-linear curve fitting (Wilkerson, 1991) to find the asymptote of the Michaelis-Menten equation, $cum_n = S^* - (S^* * b) / (b + S_n)$, where cum_n = the number of species accumulated by the nth sample, S_n, S^* = total species richness, and b is a constant. To ascertain the effects of sample order on the asymptote, we randomized sample order 100 times, calculated an asymptote for each sample order, and computed the cumulative frequency distribution of these asymptotes. We then dropped the lowest and highest 2.5% of the cumulative distribution of asymptotes to approximate the interval within which 95% of asymptotes resulting from randomized sample orders should fall. This procedure is certainly not a technical 95% confidence interval on the species accumulation curve asymptote, but it does capture the variability in asymptotes due to sample order. We report the mean and the interval noted above as a measure of variability for the asymptote. Soberón and Llorente (1993) review the use of accumulation curves to estimate species richness. Of course, the accumulation curve technically reaches its asymptote only at infinity, but since decimal places in species richness estimates are biologically meaningless (we omit them throughout our results), the mathematical infinitude of an asymptote is not a serious objection to its practical use.

The jackknife estimator works by augmenting the observed number of species (S_0) by the number of species (k_1) unique to one sample, weighted by the number of samples, S (Heltshe and Forrester, 1983). Total species richness is $S^* = S_0 + k_1(S-1)/S$. In the limit in which all species occur in at least two samples, the jackknife accepts the observed number of species as the total richness. Its variance $var(S^*) = (S-1)/S[\Sigma j^2 f(j) - k_1^2 / n]$ is a function of the number of samples f(j) having j unique species. This is intuitively reasonable as well. If the unique species are distributed evenly across samples, the variance is low. If instead they are clumped in a few samples, their true total number is less certain, and the variance and confidence interval increase. Other higher order jackknife estimators also exist, but the results are largely the same as with the first order jackknife (Colwell and Coddington, 1994).

As noted above, Chao (1987) did not originally suggest Chao2 as an estimator of species richness, but rather to estimate population size when the capture probabilities vary among individuals. We trust that communities in which species differ in relative abundance is a formally equivalent problem. Chao2 works by augmenting observed richness, S_0, by the square of the number of unique species, k_1, divided by twice the number of species that occur in two samples only, k_2, thus $S^* = S_0 + k_1^2 / 2k_2$. The logic is in some senses "midway" between that of the jackknife, which also focusses on those species unique to particular samples, and Chao1, which is also sensitive to species that occur twice, albeit in abundance and not among samples. The variance of this estimator is $cvar = k_2 * (.25 * (k_1 / k_2)^4) + (k_1 / k_2)^3 + 0.5 * (k_1 / k_2)^2)$. Like Chao1, the estimator should work well if species occur in only one or two samples, and as this is common in tropical samples, it also deserves careful consideration.

Unlike the lognormal and species accumulation curves, the non-parametric methods (jackknife, Chao1, Chao2) all have upper limits on the estimate they can provide for a given sample. If all observed species are unique to various samples, the jackknife reaches its maximum value of just under twice the observed richness. The upper limit for the Chao1 and Chao2 estimators is much higher, about half the square of the number of singletons or uniques, respectively (Colwell and Coddington, 1994). In practice, this ought to mean that Chao1 and Chao2 ought to escape undersampling bias sooner than the jackknife. If they work well, they ought to be able to do so with less data. Like the jackknife, if all species are represented by at least two individuals (or in two samples), the richness estimated by Chao1 and Chao2 will equal the observed richness. We used SYSTAT ver. 5.02 (Wilkerson, 1991) for all statistical analyses.

RESULTS AND DISCUSSION

GENERAL

Table 1 summarizes the results of the inventory for the total catch as well as partitioning it by forest type, season, time of day and collector.

A total of 2616 adults and 498 species were collected in the 109 quantitative samples. Viewed as a whole, the sample contained 207 species (41.6%) represented by only one individual (singletons), an additional 17 species that also occurred in only one hourly sample (for a total of 224 "uniques"), and the most abundant species numbered only 106 individuals. The sample is typically tropical, with many rare and few common species. Sampling efforts focussed primarily on two forest types (OAT, UFF) and to a much lesser extent on a third (DAT). The distinction between DAT and OAT was not always clear, and, as noted above, some OAT samples may have contained spiders collected from DAT and visa versa. The remaining 4 forest types were sampled too sparsely (< 10 samples each) to permit conclusions; generally they have been omitted from the quantitative analyses of results. Sampling also concentrated on one very productive method, aerial hand-picking, or "looking up," and to a lesser extent on a mixture of this method with ground sampling, or "looking down." The total sample probably reflects the fauna of the herb and shrub layer as well as a single collector could access it, but is almost certainly biassed against the ground fauna, better sampled by "pure" looking down or trapping techniques (Höfer, 1990). Because of small sample size, this method and those involving beating were dropped from the analyses of the effects of seasonality, time of day, or forest type on composition of the samples. They have, however, been included in the estimate of overall species richness.

One simple measure of sampling completeness, density, or intensity is the ratio of individuals to species. The higher the ratio, the denser and more complete the

Table 4. Nºindividuals, samples, observed species, and mean and confidence interval (where available) the jackknife, Chao1 Chao2 and species accumulation richness estimators for three forest types, two seaso and the total data set.

			(1) JACKNIFE		(2) CHAO1		(3) CHAO2		(4) SPP.ACC.					
Partition	#Ind.	# Samp.	Obs	Est.	CL	Est.	CL	Est.	CL	Est.	CL	LOG. NORMAL	Mean 1-4	Mean- Obs.	Inventory Complet
FOREST															
DAT	218	12	108	185	26	271	115	316	136	505	119	122	319	211	0.34
UFF	797	32	250	389	31	456	99	499	116	484	195	304	457	207	0.55
OAT	1199	45	324	483	34	570	109	538	89	572	149	389	541	217	0.60
SEASON															
EARLY	1274	54	306	449	28	457	70	503	81	661	114	358	518	212	0.59
LATE	1342	55	368	560	37	649	113	661	114	668	150	459	635	267	0.58
TOTAL															
TOTAL	2616	109	498	720	41	788	108	812	113	747	99	612	767	269	0.65

be pooled to calculate overall relative abundance of species, the five independent estimates of richness mentioned in the introduction can be applied. Due to the small sample sizes for forests LFF, RVF, TGH and USF, some or all of the methods failed to provide reasonable answers, and so these results are omitted from Table 4 and Fig. 1.

Estimates based on the complete sample range from the lognormal (612) to Chao2 (812). The confidence limits of the estimators for the complete sample range from a minimum of 648 to a maximum of 896 species, but broadly overlap (Table 4, Fig. 1). This range of richness values could thus be considered a rough interval estimate of the parametric richness of the particular component of the Pakitza spider fauna sampled during that year. Nevertheless, it is still probably an underestimate (see below).

Although the fit of the total sample to the lognormal seems adequate graphically (Fig. 2), it can be rejected at the $p < 0.05$ level ($X^2 = 13.2$, df = 5, $0.2 < p < 0.05$). The data do not contain an observed mode, indicating that sample size may have been insufficient for a definitive test of the lognormal fit to the data. Insufficient sample size could also explain why the lognormal is consistently the lowest of the estimators for any given partition of the data (Table 4).

The lognormal clearly requires the

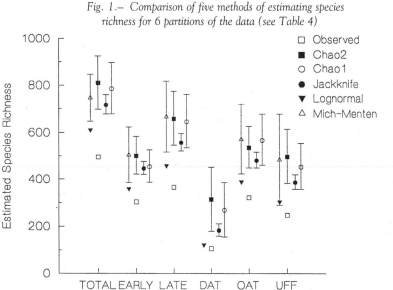

Fig. 1.– *Comparison of five methods of estimating species richness for 6 partitions of the data (see Table 4)*

□ Observed
■ Chao2
○ Chao1
● Jackknife
▼ Lognormal
△ Mich–Menten

Table 1: Summary statistics for Pakitza samples.

Data Partition	Tot Ind	S	Tot Spp	Sampling Intensity	Nº Singletons	Fraction of Total Singletons	Nº Uniques	Fraction of Total Uniques	In n
FOREST TYPE									
DAT	218	12	108	2.0	23	0.05	25	0.11	
LFF	133	7	82	1.6	10	0.02	10	0.04	
OAT	1199	45	324	3.7	90	0.18	95	0.42	
RVF	36	2	26	1.4	3	0.01	4	0.02	
TGH	167	6	99	1.7	20	0.04	22	0.10	
UFF	797	32	250	3.2	58	0.12	64	0.29	
USF	66	5	41	1.6	3	0.01	4	0.02	
SEASON									
EARLY	1274	54	306	4.2	75	0.15	84	0.38	
LATE	1342	55	368	3.7	132	0.27	140	0.63	
TIME OF DAY									
DAY	824	43	254	3.2	68	0.14	77	0.34	
NIGHT	1792	66	385	4.7	139	0.28	147	0.66	
METHOD									
AERIAL SEARCHING	1997	79	442	4.5	171	0.34	182	0.81	
AERIAL + GROUND SEARCHING	573	26	199	2.9	33	0.07	39	0.17	
3 HOUR BEATS	22	2	15	1.5	0	0.00	0	0.00	
1 HOUR BEATS	11	1	8	1.4	1	0.00	1	0.00	
GROUND SEARCHING	13	1	8	1.6	2	0.00	2	0.01	
TOTAL	2616	109	498	5.3	207	0.42	224	1.00	

sample. Sampling intensity (total ind./total spp.) for all of our samples together was 5.3, but when partitioned into samples from each of the forest types, sampling intensity ranged from 1.4 to 3.7. When partitioned by season, sampling intensity ranged from 3.7-4.2. In general, whenever a larger sample of a given sampling intensity is partitioned for analysis, sampling intensity drops and the ratio of rare to common species increases.

SAMPLE COMPOSITION.

Most of the available methods to estimate species richness require data structured as replicate samples. Two aspects of such samples are important, number of species and abundance within samples (e.g. presence/absence, singletons or not; uniques or not). For example, in this study, collectors averaged about 24 adult specimens per hour of work and about 17 species, both slightly higher than any of the three Bolivian sites reported by Coddington et al. (1991). Comparison of the Peruvian to the Bolivian data is not yet complete, but it is likely that the

...sample ...n (SD)	Spp./sample mean (SD)	Singletons portion of Partition Richness	Uniques portion of Partition Richness
.1 (8.1)	12 (4.8)	0.21	0.23
.0 (6.7)	15.7 (5.1)	0.12	0.12
▸ (12.7)	19.2 (7.4)	0.28	0.29
.0 (9.9)	13.1 (7.0)	0.12	0.15
.8 (8.5)	21.2 (5.6)	0.20	0.22
▪1 (2.1)	18.2 (7.4)	0.23	0.26
0 (2.4)	9.8 (4.6)	0.07	0.10
▸ (11.4)	16.4 (7.4)	0.25	0.27
▪ (11.1)	18.6 (7.1)	0.36	0.38
.6 (1.1)	12.7 (6.0)	0.27	0.30
.5 (1.3)	20.6 (6.4)	0.36	0.38
▪8 (1.2)	19.1 (6.9)	0.39	0.41
▪4 (2.7)	14.0 (7.0)	0.17	0.20
▪0 (5.0)	8.0 (4.2)	0.00	0.00
▪0 (na)	8 (na)	0.13	0.13
▪00 (na)	8 (na)	0.25	0.25
▪0 (1.1)	17.5 (7.3)	0.42	0.45

difference will be significant. It accords with the general impression that Peruvian forests are richer both in species and number of individuals than the more temperate Bolivian forests. It is appropriate to examine the structure of the data used to estimate richness as well as any influences the sampling protocol may have on number of animals or species per sample. It also provides an opportunity to ask if cumulative differences due to seasonality or forest type seen in the total sample are also reflected in the hourly samples.

Effect of Forest Type, Season, Method, Time of Day, and Collector

Viewing the data as replicate, hourly samples, forest type had a significant effect on richness but not on abundance within samples (Table 2). If the more poorly sampled forest types are included, the effect is less pronounced but generally the same. The dissected alluvial terraces (DAT forest) yielded significantly less rich hourly samples than either old alluvial terraces (OAT) or upland floodplains (UFF)(p< 0.005, p< 0.030, respectively, Tukey test). OAT and UFF were not different from each other. Although the difference between the forests may be real, it may also be due to low sample size from the DAT forest, which received only 12 hours of sampling. The number of adults or species per sample was not different between early and late dry season (Table 2).

Because so few methods were used to sample the fauna, and because the most frequently employed methods overlapped (aerial hand-picking versus aerial and ground hand-picking), method of collection was unlikely to affect significantly the richness or abundance of spiders within samples, and it did not (Table 3). Collecting method usually does have a significant effect (e.g. ground hand-picking versus beating; Coddington et al., 1991; Young, 1992). Beating had to be dropped from the analysis due to small sample size (Table 1). Note that even if some methods are less productive in terms of individuals or species, they still have a role in estimating richness if they access different components of the fauna.

Time of day, however, significantly affected both abundance and richness of the hourly samples (Table 3). Both more species and more individuals are collected at night. The interaction between time of day and method was also

Table 2. Analysis of variance in abundance and species richness per sample by season and forest type (for three forest types with sample size > 10).

ABUN   N: 88   MULTIPLE R: 0.276 SQUARED MULTIPLE R: 0.076

ANALYSIS OF VARIANCE

SOURCE	SUM-OF-SQUARES	DF	MEAN-SQUARE	F-RATIO	P
FOREST	717.809	2	358.905	2.468	0.091
SEASON	41.651	1	41.651	0.286	0.594
FOREST*SEASON	247.614	2	123.807	0.851	0.431
ERROR	11924.444	82	145.420		

NSP   N: 88   MULTIPLE R: 0.373 SQUARED MULTIPLE R: 0.139

ANALYSIS OF VARIANCE

SOURCE	SUM-OF-SQUARES	DF	MEAN-SQUARE	F-RATIO	P
FOREST	534.248	2	267.124	5.330	0.007*
SEASON	127.132	1	127.132	2.537	0.115
FOREST*SEASON	50.228	2	25.114	0.501	0.608
ERROR	4109.460	82	50.115		

significant. Hand-searching during the day is exceptionally unproductive, while hand-searching during the night is very productive. Collector identity had no significant effect on abundance or richness of the samples.

In summary, time of day strongly affected average richness of the hourly samples and to a lesser extent the average abundance of animals/sample. Forest type (DAT) affected richness, but not abundance (Table 2), perhaps due to differences in sampling effort.

SPECIES RICHNESS ESTIMATES

Because the data were taken as a series of smaller, replicate samples that can

Table 3: Analysis of variance in abundance and richness of samples by time of day (day vs. night) and method (Aerial searching versus aerial and ground searching).

ABUN   N: 88   MULTIPLE R: 0.422 SQUARED MULTIPLE R: 0.178

ANALYSIS OF VARIANCE

SOURCE	SUM-OF-SQUARES	DF	MEAN-SQUARE	F-RATIO	P
TIME OF DAY	629.655	1	629.655	4.985	0.028*
METHOD	7.049	1	7.049	0.056	0.814
TIME*METHOD	570.210	1	570.210	4.514	0.037*
ERROR	10609.770	84	126.307		

NSP   N: 88   MULTIPLE R: 0.617 SQUARED MULTIPLE R: 0.380

ANALYSIS OF VARIANCE

SOURCE	SUM-OF-SQUARES	DF	MEAN-SQUARE	F-RATIO	P
TIME OF DAY	754.626	1	754.626	21.424	0.000*
METHOD	2.523	1	2.523	0.072	0.790
TIME*METHOD	92.747	1	92.747	2.633	0.108
ERROR	2958.747	84	35.223		

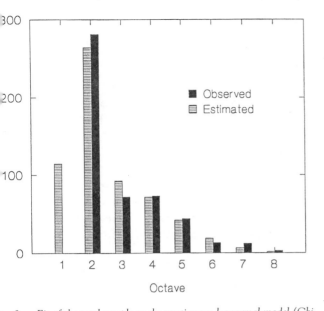

g. 2.– Fit of the total sample to the continuous lognormal model (Chi squared= 13.24, df=5, p<0.05)

most sampling effort to function well. Estimating the mean and variance of the normal distribution is chancy if the data lack an observed mode, but in large communities filled with rare species (=the tropics), "capturing the mode" requires a truly terrific sampling effort. Neither the complete sample nor any of its partitions contained a mode. The lognormal has the unique flaw that it depends to some extent on the full relative frequency distribution of the community, which in turn dictates that even common species must continue to be collected. Of course, rightward octaves could be truncated as well, but then the goodness of fit test (and the fit itself) will be based on even fewer degrees of freedom. It is hard to envisage fitting the lognormal to a tropical sample with an observed mode that contained fewer than five or six octaves, in which case the most abundant species would number in the 100's anyway. Relative abundance is notoriously difficult to measure accurately and therefore the lognormal may be doomed to fixate on artifacts caused by various kinds of sampling bias.

The jackknife estimates for all partitions are fairly low, and the confidence intervals are small (Table 4, Fig. 1). As noted above, it has the flaw that it cannot produce an estimate of more than twice the number of observed species. With the possible exception of the DAT forest partition, none of the jackknife estimates of richness in Table 4 are even close to double the observed value; perhaps this theoretical limit does not come

Fig. 3.– Plot of the minimum, maximum, and mean value (line) for 100 randomized samples orders for the total data set

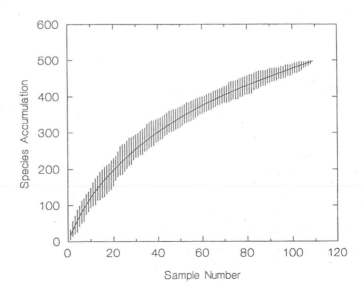

into play for these data. On the other hand, the behavior of the jackknife as this limit is approached is unknown. Perhaps high estimates are increasingly "difficult" to achieve as the limit is approached. The small confidence intervals given by the jackknife are probably explained by the high proportion of singletons (usually about 30-40% for any partition, Tables 1 and 4), which by definition are unique to a sample. For the total sample, 207 singletons must "fit" into 109 samples. The actual number of uniques was 224, meaning that 17 species with abundances greater than one were also unique to single samples. At an average of 17 or 18 species per sample (Table 1), the distribution of uniques across samples must be fairly uniform and must therefore result in a rather low variance, and, consequently, a fairly narrow confidence interval.

Chao (1984) carefully notes that Chao1 is a lower bound on the estimated richness, and further, that it should perform better in samples dominated by singletons and doubletons. For the complete Pakitza sample, 281 of 498 species, or 56%, were singletons or doubletons. Information on substantial numbers of species were thus discarded by this estimator, which depends crucially on the relative abundance of the two rarest classes of abundance. Whether accurate data on these frequency classes are the easiest or the most difficult to obtain is an interesting question. The ease of assessing presence versus absence, or nearly that, is confounded by stochastic errors and bias in sampling.

Chao2 utilizes the analogous number of species that occurred in just one or two samples, thus also discarding substantial amounts of information. Because Chao2 requires only presence-absence data and may be robust to undersampling bias (Colwell and Coddington, 1994) it may be the most practical richness estimator currently available. The estimates it provides (Table 4, Fig. 1), although typically high, may be closest to the true values. Both of Chao's estimators should work well on relatively sparsely sampled tropical faunas. Although the values given by each overlap quite closely, this is probably due to the high frequency of "rare" species in the sample (most uniques are singletons and visa versa).

The fit of the mean of 100 accumulation curves with randomized sample orders to the Michaelis-Menten model seems acceptable (Figs. 3, 4). It is disturbing, however, that the best fit curve ("Estimated" in Fig. 4) is more cupped and thus yields a lower asymptote than one might fit by eye to the observed curve. In many

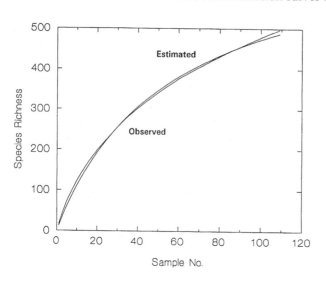

Fig. 4.– Plot of the least squares best fit curve against the mean curve for 100 randomized samples orders. The fit is good overall, but the Michaelis-Menten estimate is low at tails and high in the center of the sample range

of the 100 randomized accumulations the Mi-chaelis-Menten model also appeared to be low at the tails but high in the center of the curve. If systematic, this bias will deflate richness estimates. The behavior of the Michaelis-Menten model is also quite erratic for small data sets that represent sparse sampling. In Table 4, the DAT value is quite out of line from the others, undoubtedly because so few samples were available. An advantage of the method used here, i.e. taking the mean of a large number of asymptotes resulting from randomized sample orders rather than accepting the best fit asymptote to the mean of those curves, is that some of these biases may be reduced.

Species accumulation curves are in some ways the most attractive technique to estimate richness. They are straightforward and lend themselves to graphical evaluation. The chief problem is the lack of justification for the Michaelis-Menten equation compared to other possible hyperbolic functions. Soberón and Llorente (1993) discuss other possible models that may better represent the biological realities implicit in accumulation curves. However, the Michaelis-Menten function has been widely used in the past for this purpose, and it fits data reasonably well. Some more than merely analogical relationship among biological variables posed by the Michaelis-Menten equation needs to be demonstrated. The most fundamental problem with accumulation curves is that the curve is extrapolated well beyond the last sample. If the fit between the model and the data is systematically skewed, the skew grows along with the extrapolation. Probably any approach that assumes a biologically realistic model will encounter the same problem for many data sets, if only because biological reality is diverse. An alternative approach might be to find a hyperbolic function complex and flexible enough to fit any accumulation curve extremely closely. At least then the extrapolation would depend as closely as possible on whatever biological situation the observed data represented.

Good estimators of species richness should provide confidence intervals. At the very least, confidence intervals should engender a healthy skepticism of overly exact "numbers" of species, whether of a park or the entire Earth. As sampling effort or sample size increases, the confidence intervals should narrow, until finally the true value is specified. More efficient estimators of species richness should have all of these virtues, but achieve higher accuracy and precision on the basis of relatively fewer data (Coddington et al., 1991).

The estimators used here do not fulfill the above criteria in all respects. For example, the richness estimated for any of the data partitions in Table 4 correlates well with sample size. For Chao1, Chao2, and the jackknife the reason is clear; all these estimators work by augmenting the observed richness by some moiety, itself usually a function of the "rare" species, whether numerically rare (Chao1) or the very related notion of rarity in space or time (Chao2, the jackknife). If tropical faunas are so large that early in the sampling effort the accumulation of species, and mainly rare species, is essentially constant with increasing sampling effort (as it sometimes seems to in this case, see below), then the number of rare species and the observed richness increase in lock step. It is not until the rate of discovery of "new" species begins to drop, perhaps as evidenced by concavity in the accumulation curve, that any estimation procedure will begin to close in on the true value of richness.

For these data, the estimated richnesses for various data partitions correlate with total number of specimens or samples, observed richness, and number of singletons (compare Tables 1 and 4). Fig. 5 juxtaposes the observed richness against the mean of the "unobserved" moieties as estimated by the jackknife, Chao1, Chao2, and Michaelis-Menten function for various partitions of the data. Although for small samples sizes such as the DAT forest, the unobserved moiety nearly doubles the observed richness, for all other partitions it is remarkably constant, adding about 200-270 species to the observed total. In effect, the fraction added to the observed richness by the estimators increases less with sample size than does the observed richness. This behavior seems rather odd. If an estimator has the undesirable behavior of correlation with sample size (Colwell and Coddington, 1994), one might expect the unobserved moiety to correlate as much or more than the observed fraction, given its "extrapolative" origins. On

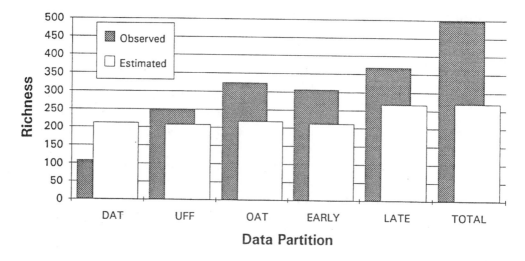

Fig. 5.– Histogram of the mean of the unobserved moieties for the jackknife, Chao1, Chao2, and Michaelis Menten model stimators, plotted against the observed richness for each of the 6 partitions of the total sample.

the other hand, if species richness estimators behave "correctly," one should see a compensatory decrease in the unobserved moiety with increasing sample size such that the total richness estimate remains constant over a wide range in sample size. Fig. 5 shows that the behavior of the unobserved moiety for these data and estimators is intermediate. It does not increase much with sample size, which is good, but it does not decrease either, and so the net effect is correlation with sample size. If one considers the ratio of observed to mean estimated richness for any given partition of the data (Table 4), the "degree of completion" of the inventory does rise with sample size. Perhaps the current data simply represent the relatively straight, early portion of the accumulation curve, but concavity is evident in Figs. 3 and 4. Given any reasonable frequency distribution, the estimators may have a practical upper bound that is a function of sampling effort. Until this upper bound exceeds the true parametric richness, procedures will always underestimate.

Within any one partition of the data, the estimators often have the same rank from low to high values: lognormal jackknife, Chao1, Chao2, Michaelis-Menten, although the rank of the latter is variable. Some of the reasons why this may be so in each case have been discussed above. Certainly the lognormal and the jackknife are usually lower, whereas the latter three are higher. The same pattern occurs in other data sets (Coddington, unpubl. data). As noted above, partitioning data into subsets tends to increase the numbers of rare species in the partitions compared to the whole dataset. If, as surmised above, Chao1 and Chao2 are more robust to undersampling bias than the jackknife or the lognormal, the disparity between the lower and higher estimators should be most obvious in the sparsest samples, and the effect should lessen as the sample approaches and then substantially surpasses half the total number of species.

Despite this expectation, the clusters of estimators for the six partitions of the data in Fig. 1 do not strongly support it. For the DAT forest, the lognormal and the jackknife are lower than Chao1 or Chao2, but this gap did not narrow greatly in the total data set. An alternative and highly possible explanation for this pattern is that even this sample, with 498 species comprising 2616 individuals, substantially undersamples the actual diversity at Pakitza and so that even the most liberal estimators are still largely constrained by undersampling bias.

In summary, each estimator used here has its strengths and weaknesses from both theoretical and pragmatic points of view. One interesting result is that a really informed guess of the number of species "as yet unseen" may require a variety of estimators subjected to a variety of analytical techniques. For example, the concavity seen in Figs. 3 and 4 provide real evidence that progress towards a complete inventory has been made. On the other hand, species accumulation curves may be more affected by undersampling bias that other estimators, and thus yield poorer estimates. Chao1 and Chao2 seem like useful and handy techniques, but they are closely similar to each other and don't really represent dramatically different approaches to the problem. The jackknife has a good statistical pedigree, and is quite conservative. Close agreement between it and other estimators may be the hallmark of a robust estimate. Ironically, the one estimator that seems almost useless is the lognormal. It requires an immense amount of data, is "murky" to fit, is clearly not independent of sample size, and provides no confidence interval. Its main virtue seems to be the immense interest lavished on it in the ecological literature (e.g. May, 1975), and hence its use as a bridge or benchmark to link the results of more capable estimators to past work.

Seasonality and Species Richness

Estimated species richness for the late dry season community is greater than for the early dry season (Table 4, Fig. 1). Among forests, OAT is richer than UFF or DAT (Table 4, Fig. 1). Species tend to be more abundant in the late dry season than in the early dry season (Appendix 1, $p < 0.033$, $n = 498$ species, Wilcoxon signed rank test), but if singletons are excluded, the effect disappears ($P < 0.623$, $n = 291$ species, Wilcoxon signed rank test). The total observed richness was also significantly higher in the late dry season (Table 1, $p < 0.000$, sign test), but again, when the 224 uniques are excluded, the effect disappears ($p < 0.139$).

Distribution of Singletons and Uniques

Because of the weight given to singleton or unique species by richness estimators, their distribution in the sample merits special attention. Despite roughly similar sample sizes, judged both by numbers of samples and individuals, the late dry season had more singletons and uniques than the early dry season (132 or 140 vs. 75 or 84, respectively, $p < 0.000$, sign test). Females predominated over males among singletons (135 vs. 72, $p < 0.000$, sign test), a result at odds with the common wisdom that webless, wandering males will appear more frequently as singletons than the sedentary, more conspicuous females. However, the sex ratio of the total sample was also highly biased towards females (1669 vs. 947, $p < 0.000$, t test). In contrast, raw numbers of singletons and uniques among forest types, time of day, and method correlates positively with sample size (Table 1), but when viewed as a fraction of the richness for that partition remain roughly constant at 20-30 % over a wide range in sample sizes (Table 1). Chi-square tests on the proportion of singletons in these cases, assuming an expected frequency proportional to number of hourly samples, are all insignificant. Apparently the probability of encountering singletons does not drop dramatically across this range of sample sizes. One might have expected singletons to comprise a smaller percentage of a sample if the sampling intensity is higher, but if anything, it is larger. In sum, the effect of rare species (whether as singletons or uniques) is dramatic on comparisons between partitions of the data.

Community Structure

It is clear that spiders are numerically abundant and represented by a large number of species in many kinds of microhabitats. It is also clear that spiders can provide clues to understand better the importance of habitat structure on the composition of terrestrial invertebrate communities. Apparently, the diversity of spider communities is positively correlated with microhabitat complexity (Uetz, 1991). However, the nature of interactions in Neotropical spider communities is relatively unknown, and, in general, information about the effects of physical variables such as microhabitat structure on the occurrence patterns of spiders is still scarce (Gertsch and Riechert, 1976; Post and Riechert, 1977; Uetz, 1990; Rypstra, 1983; Jocqué 1984; Döbel et al., 1990).

Our data shows that species composition, density and diversity may differ from one period of sampling to the other and also in different types of forest. Whether this effect is due to differences in sampling hours among forests, or seasons, or whether it reflects a natural phenomenon related to microhabitat qualities, will be clarified only with additional studies involving the phylogenetic history and ecological relationships within the whole community.

Our data suggest that spiders were more abundant and diverse in the late dry season than in the early dry season. The study presented by Lubin (1978), based on a year's census of web-building spiders on Barro Colorado Island, shows a sharp decrease in abundance of spiders throughout the dry season. Lubin found two population peaks, one in the late wet season and the second in the mid wet season; but a smaller increase in total numbers may occur after the first rains at the end of the dry season, followed by a decrease at the beginning of the wet season (Lubin, 1978).

Lubin has also shown a clear effect of forest type on the distribution of web-building spiders and she indicates that whereas the adults of some species are very restricted in time, the immatures can occur nearly year-round, defining two reproductive strategies: 1) a year-round emergence of immatures coupled with complete overlap of generations, and/or 2) the occurrence of long development periods of young, spanning seasons which are unfavorable for adults. These hypotheses may help to explain the existence of the large number of species represented by single adult specimens throughout a long period of sampling, and why they are overrepresented in the late dry season, especially when the great majority are web-building spiders.

Over 90% of the species in our sample occurred in the three Pakitza forests (DAT, OAT, and UFF) for which we have more than 10 hours of sampling (450 of 498 species, Table 1). Considering just the species from these three forest types, 370 were unique to one forest or another (Table 1), 23 were common to DAT

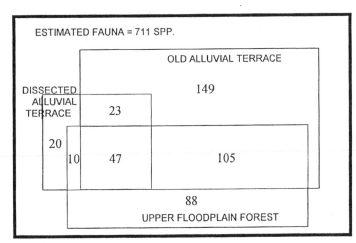

ESTIMATED FAUNA = 711 SPP.

OLD ALLUVIAL TERRACE

149

DISSECTED ALLUVIAL TERRACE

23

20

10 47 105

88

UPPER FLOODPLAIN FOREST

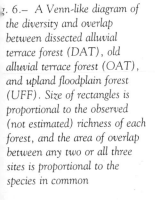

g. 6.– A Venn-like diagram of the diversity and overlap between dissected alluvial terrace forest (DAT), old alluvial terrace forest (OAT), and upland floodplain forest (UFF). Size of rectangles is proportional to the observed (not estimated) richness of each forest, and the area of overlap between any two or all three sites is proportional to the species in common and OAT, 10 were common to DAT and UFF, 105 were common to OAT and UFF, and 47 occurred in all three forests (Fig. 6). The question naturally arises of how dissimilar or distinct these forests are. Colwell and Coddington (1994) suggested "complementarity" as the distinctness or dissimilarity of two assemblages in any ecological dimension (e.g. species lists, host-parasite relations, pollinator-plant relationships, etc.), and proposed a simple statistic to measure it: the proportion of all members in two lists that occurs in only one or the other of them. Thus, the complementarity of two lists j and k is $C_{jk} = (S_j + S_k - V_{jk})/(S_j + S_k - 2*V_{jk})$, where S_j is the number of species from site j, S_k is the number from site k, and V_{jk} is the number in common. Using this statistic to compare the species lists from these three forest types, the DAT-OAT complementarity is 0.81, that of DAT-UFF is 0.85, and that of OAT-UFF is 0.64. Old alluvial forest is most distinct from upper floodplain forest, and not surprisingly, the alluvial terrace forests are quite similar.

In the following analysis we present an initial insight into the spider community of Pakitza. Apparently, in this community a highly heterogeneous environ-

Table 5.- Guild composition and abundance of the spider community at Pakitza.

Family	Spp. early	Spp. late	Spp. total	Ind. early	Ind. late	Ind. total	% spp.	% ind.
ORB-WEAVERS								
Anapidae	1	0	1	2	0	2	0.4	0.2
Araneidae	85	112	145	319	424	743	61.7	59.8
Deinopidae	1	2	2	2	5	7	0.9	0.6
Mysmenidae	9	1	9	33	3	36	3.8	2.9
Tetragnathidae	22	26	35	82	50	132	14.9	10.6
Theridiosomatidae	18	5	19	130	7	137	8.1	11.0
Uloboridae	16	21	24	77	108	185	10.2	14.9
SHEET-WEB WEAVERS								
Dictynidae	0	1	1	0	1	1	0.9	0.1
Linyphiidae	5	4	6	17	8	25	5.4	2.9
Pholcidae	11	8	12	56	28	84	10.8	9.6
Scytodidae	2	2	2	8	11	19	1.8	2.2
Theridiidae	63	65	90	400	347	747	81.1	85.3
CURSORIAL HUNTERS								
Anyphaenidae	6	9	13	13	16	29	15.3	11.1
Aphantochilidae	1	1	1	2	3	5	1.2	1.9
Caponiidae	1	0	1	1	0	1	1.2	0.4
Clubionidae	0	3	3	0	3	3	3.5	1.1
Corinnidae	5	11	13	9	17	26	15.3	10.0
Gnaphosidae	0	1	1	0	1	1	1.2	0.4
Lycosidae	5	3	6	17	5	22	7.1	8.4
Miturgidae	2	3	3	2	6	8	3.5	3.1
Oonopidae	2	3	3	2	4	6	3.5	2.3
Salticidae	18	35	41	33	127	160	48.2	61.3
AMBUSH PREDATORS								
Ctenidae	8	11	16	18	27	45	12.0	19.0
Hersiliidae	2	2	2	5	9	14	1.5	5.9
Heteropodidae	2	4	5	3	10	13	3.7	5.5
Mimetidae	6	10	11	14	45	59	8.2	24.9
Oxyopidae	3	6	8	5	24	29	6.0	12.2
Philodromidae	1	0	1	1	0	1	0.7	0.4
Pisauridae	1	3	3	4	23	27	2.2	11.4
Selenopidae	0	1	1	0	2	2	0.7	0.8
Senoculidae	2	4	4	4	14	18	3.0	7.6
Thomisidae	6	9	12	12	10	22	9.0	9.3
Trechaleidae	1	4	4	2	5	7	3.0	3.0

ment is causing the extreme temporal and spatial partitioning of microhabitats by the spiders. Although our data seem to support the hypothesis that guild formation tends to minimize competition (Post and Riechert, 1977) and that this high specialization may promote a greater species richness, there is not enough information about many other factors (Pielou, 1975) that may help to explain the high number of coexisting spider species in Pakitza.

We present this classification only as a first attempt that can be used in further comparisons with other spider communities to help understand species diversity patterns. Our guild categories primarily represent similarities in prey-capture strategy, although within any guild there is much variation in the details of prey capture. We recognized four guilds: orb-weavers, sheet/line weavers, ambush predators, and cursorial hunters (Table 5).

In Appendix 1 we present a complete list of species and their abundance in different forest types and seasons.

ORB WEAVERS

In Pakitza these comprise the richest (235 species) and most abundant (48 %) spider guild. Most species of this guild make an orb web, usually a two-dimensional structure, that captures mainly flying insects. Some species construct a highly modified structure, ranging from a three-dimensional web to only one silk line. Araneidae are the dominant spiders in this guild. In the following sections, useful taxonomic references are grouped at the end of each section.

ANAPIDAE, 1 SP (ANA)

These tiny spiders inhabit the leaf litter or fallen tree trunks of some tropical forests where they are relatively common (Höfer, 1990; pers. obs.). We collected two specimens of *Pseudanapis* in the early dry season. In spite of exhaustive searching for anapids, no additional specimens were found; however it is possible that during the dry season they seek refuge in inaccesible humid microhabitats. Only one other specimen was collected in 1987 (*Anapisona* sp.); we suspect that anapids are rare at Pakitza, although they may be present in the still unsorted canopy fogging samples, as is the case in other Peruvian lowland forests (pers. obs.). Balogh and Loksa (1968), Forster (1958), Forster and Platnick (1977), Georgescu (1987), Gertsch (1960), Müller (1987d), Platnick and Forster (1990), Platnick and Shadab (1978b, 1979a).

ARANEIDAE, 145 SPP (ARA)

In our samples araneids (the typical orb-weavers) were the richest and second most abundant family (743 ind.). These common spiders are found in a great variety of microhabitats from the ground up to the trees. *Eustala* was the richest (33 spp.) and most abundant genus (112 ind.). Most species (55 %) were represented by single specimens. Most individuals were taken in the late dry season and it appears that the dominant species have no preferences for forest types.

Some of the four species of *Mangora*, the second most abundant genus (106 ind.), were found only in certain types of forests. Species **1** (38 ind.) was dominant during the early season in OAT forest, while species **4**, the second most dominant araneid (51 ind.), was more or less equally distributed during the dry season in all forest types.

Micrathena is the second most diverse (18 spp.) araneid but most species are represented by few individuals.

Most specimens of *Cyclosa* (13 spp.), the third most abundant (74 ind.) araneid, were collected during the early dry season in OAT forest.

Parawixia kochi (Tacz.), species **94**, is the dominant araneid in Pakitza (53 ind.). It is broadly distributed in the Neotropics (Levi, 1992) and very abundant in Peruvian lowland forests; however, it was dominant only during the late dry season (47 ind.).

Alpaida delicata (Keys.), species **24**, is the third most common araneid in Pakitza (47 ind.). It is widely distributed in the Neotropics (Levi, 1988) and lowland forests in Peru. Most individuals (62 %) were collected in OAT forests.

Araneus venatrix (C.L. Koch), species **92**, is another common species with a very broad distribution throughout the Neotropics (Levi, 1991a). In Pakitza, most species were found during the late dry season (15 ind.) in UFF forests (61 %). Berman and Levi (1971), Bryant (1945), Chickering (1954, 1955), Gertsch (1955), Harrod et al. (1990), Levi (1968, 1970, 1972, 1980, 1985, 1986a, 1988, 1989, 1991-1993), Mello-Leitao (1945b).

DEINOPIDAE, 2 SPP. (DEI)

Most of these nocturnal spiders were found hanging from dry twigs. In the daytime they were collected by beating clusters of dry leaves, mainly during the late dry season. Coddington (1990).

MYSMENIDAE, 9 SPP. (MYS)

The peculiar three-dimensional web of these very tiny spiders (about 1 mm in size) is commonly found in the leaf litter, crevices of logs or tree trunks. Some species of *Mysmenopsis* are found as kleptoparasites of larger web spiders such as the araneid *Cyrtophora* or the diplurid *Linothele*. The dominant mysmenid, species **43**, was collected only during the early dry season. Baert (1990a), Baert and Maelfait (1983), Coyle and Meigs (1989), Georgescu (1987), Gertsch (1960), Levi (1956a), Müller (1987e), Platnick and Shadab (1978a).

TETRAGNATHIDAE, 35 SPP. (TET)

In terms of abundance this family ranked sixth (132 ind). Tetragnathids are frequently found in horizontal orb webs in various microhabitats from the ground layer up to the trees. *Glenognatha* and *Metabus*, the latter recorded from non-quantitative collections, are restricted to streams where they live in colonies. *Tetragnatha* are most common along streams but are also found inside the forest. The most abundant tetragnathid, *Leucauge* species **191**, was mainly collected in the early dry season. Baert (1987), Chickering (1957, 1962), Hormiga and Döbel (1990), Levi (1980, 1981, 1986b), Levi and Eickstedt (1989), Okuma (1992).

THERIDIOSOMATIDAE, 19 SPP. (THS)

It ranked fifth (137 ind.) in terms of abundance. The two or three-dimensional webs of these tiny spiders are found in a variety of microhabitats from the leaf litter up to the trees. Because they prefer wet microhabitats, dryness appears to have a strong effect on their richness and abundance.

Most species (95 %) were collected in the early dry season. *Epeirotypus* species **12**, numerically dominant (50 ind.), was collected in the early period from webs on spiny palm trunks; whereas the second most abundant theridiosomatid (31 ind.), *Theridiosoma* species **34**, was found during the same period in webs scarcely above the ground layer. Coddington (1986), Georgescu (1987).

ULOBORIDAE, 24 SPP. (ULO)

This family ranked third in terms of abundance (185 ind.). Solitary foragers may be found under leaves or very well camouflaged among the vegetation, others form colonies among shrubs, while others are kleptoparasites of various weaver spiders. Uloborids like *Miagrammopes* species have reduced the orb web to only one line. Most species are represented by few individuals. The two most common species, *Uloborus* **15** (50 ind.) and *Philoponella* **14** (41 ind.) do not exhibit major differences between early and late dry season; on the other hand, most individuals of one common species of *Miagrammopes* **214** (14 ind.) were collected only in the late dry season. Chickering (1968a), and Opell (1979, 1981, 1982, 1984, 1987).

SHEET/LINE WEAVERS

In this guild prey are detected by vibratory signals transmitted through sheet/line webs chiefly designed for walking arthropods. In terms of diversity (111 spp.) and abundance (34%) it ranked second in Pakitza. In this guild the dominant family is Theridiidae.

DICTYNIDAE, 1 SP (DIC)

These small spiders were collected under roughened bark of a large tree trunk during non-quantitative sampling and only one male was collected while looking up at night in an UFF forest. Dictynids are probably not this rare at Pakitza; we probably overlooked the appropriate microhabitat. Gertsch (1945, 1946).

LINYPHIIDAE, 6 SPP. (LIN)

Although these small spiders are commonly found in temperate zones, they are uncommon in lowland Neotropical forests. Linyphiids inhabit various microhabitats from the ground layer up to the trees. Most species are represented by few individuals. Baert (1987a, 1990b), Müller and Heimer (1991b), Millidge (1985, 1991).

PHOLCIDAE, 12 SPP. (PHO)

The conspicuous webs of these small spiders are found in different microhabitats from the ground layer up to the trees. This is the seventh most abundant family (84 ind.). Some species appear to prefer the early dry season; although the dominant species, no. 21, (33 ind.) does not show a major difference between the early and late dry season. Brignoli (1981), Gertsch (1939, 1982, 1986), Gertsch and Peck (1992), Kraus (1957), Mello-Leitao (1918, 1946-1947b).

SCYTODIDAE, 2 SPP. (SCY)

These spiders were associated with dry leaves suspended in various understory microhabitats. Most individuals were collected at night from spiny palm trunks in the late dry season. Mello-Leitao (1918), Valerio (1971, 1981).

THERIDIIDAE, 90 SPP. (THD)

These small to medium-sized spiders were the most abundant (747 ind.) and second most diverse family at Pakitza. Theridiids may be found as solitary foragers, in colonies, or as kleptoparasites of other weaver spiders, inhabiting various microhabitats from the ground layer up to the trees.

The dominant theridiid was *Episinus erythrophthalmus* (Simon), species **56**, (106 ind.), widely distributed throughout the Neotropics (Levi, 1964). It showed a preference for UFF forests in the early dry season.

Argyrodes amplifrons O.P.C., species **9**, is fairly common in lowland rainforests in Peru. It was the second most abundant theridiid (71 ind.) at Pakitza and was most common in the early dry season.

Thwaitesia bracteata (Exline), species **76**, the third most common theridiid in Pakitza (66 ind.) and broadly distributed in lowland forests of Peru, was collected mainly during the late dry season in UFF forests.

Argyrodes metaltissimus (S. & C.), species **75**, is another common spider in Pakitza (44 ind.). It is a kleptoparasite in the webs of the social theridiid *Anelosimus eximius* (Keys.), but solitary foragers may also be found underside leaves. This species is slightly more common in the late dry season. Archer (1950), Buckup and Marques (1991-1992), Exline and Levi (1962, 1965), Fowler and Levi (1979), Georgescu (1987), González (1991), Heimer and Müller (1991), Levi (1953-1955,

1956b-1957, 1959-1960, 1962-1967, 1968b), Levi and Levi (1962), Levi and Randolph (1975), Levi and Smith (1983), Marques and Buckup (1989, 1992), and Müller and Heimer (1990, 1991a).

CURSORIAL HUNTERS.

These spiders do not use webs for prey-capture and tend to move slowly (brief advances separated by long or short pauses) through the environment searching for prey. This guild ranked fourth in richness (85 spp.), although it is the third most abundant (10 %) in Pakitza. The dominant family is Salticidae (Table 5).

APHANTOCHILIDAE, 1 SP. (APH)

These ant-mimics spent most of their time on the vegetation or tree trunks searching for prey. Two genera (*Aphantochilus* and *Bucranium*) were collected in Pakitza, but only one is represented in our time based samples and more or less equally distributed in both early and late dry season. Gerschman and Pikelin (1964), Mello-Leitao (1946).

ANYPHAENIDAE, 13 SPP. (ANY)

These nocturnal spiders often seek refuge in the curled dry leaves of shrubs or suspended dry leaves clusters in the daytime. The two most common species are about as abundant in the early as in the late dry season. Brescovit (1991, 1992), Brescovit and Lise (1989), Gerschman and Schiapelli (1970), Platnick (1974).

CAPONIIDAE, 1 SP. (CAP)

These spiders are rare at Pakitza, but we expect to find more individuals in the canopy fogging samples, as is the case in other Peruvian lowland forests. A single male specimen was taken from the ground layer along a narrow stream of black water, near BIOLAT Zone 05 (early dry season). Alayón Garcia (1986), Birabén (1954a, 1951), Brignoli (1977), Chickering (1967), Platnick (1993b).

CLUBIONIDAE, 3 SPP. (CLU)

Three clubionid specimens were collected at night, all from the vegetation during the late dry season. Brescovit and Bonaldo (1992), Chickering (1937), Müller and Heimer (1988).

CORINNIDAE, 13 SPP. (COR)

Most corinnids are ant-mimics and are found searching for prey in various microhabitats from the ground layer up to the trees. Most species were collected in the late dry season. All species were uncommon. Chickering (1972), Reiskind (1969, 1971), Bauab Vianna (1979), Müller and Heimer (1989), Platnick and Shadab (1974), Platnick (1975b, 1979a).

GNAPHOSIDAE, 1 SP. (GNA)

A single female was collected from the vegetation in the early dry season. Baert and Maelfait (1986), Müller (1987a-c, 1988), Platnick (1975a, 1983a, 1983b), Platnick and Höfer (1990), Platnick and Shadab (1975-1976, 1979b-1988), Platnick and Murphy (1984).

LYCOSIDAE, 6 SPP. (LYC)

These diurnal spiders, which are often found wandering on the ground layer, occurred at low densities during the dry season at Pakitza. The dominant lycosid, species 17 (12 ind.), was collected in the early dry season. Capocasale (1982, 1990-91), and Dondale (1986), Maelfait and Baert (1986), Zimber (1963).

MITURGIDAE, 3 SPP. (MIT)

These uncommon spiders are found in the understory vegetation. Most individuals of these nocturnal spiders were found during the late dry season. Bonaldo (1992), Platnick and Shadab (1989), Platnick and Ramirez (1991).

SALTICIDAE, 41 SPP. (SAL)

The jumping spiders ranked fourth in terms of abundance (160 ind.) in Pakitza. They were found in all microhabitats, more often in the daytime. Most species were collected in the early dry season (71 %), but the two most abundant species (34 and 22 ind., respectively) were found in the late dry season. Another common salticid, species 23 (21 ind.), was collected in both early and late dry season. Bauab-Vianna (1979b, 1980, 1983), Bauab and Soares (1978, 1980, 1982-83), Cutler (1981, 1982, 1985, 1988), Cutler and Müller (1991), Galiano (1960-1991), Müller and Cutler (1989), Proszynski (1971).

AMBUSH PREDATORS.

The species in this guild tend to remain stationary for long periods of time waiting for prey. This group is represented by 134 species and they accounted for approximately 9 % of the total abundance. Ctenids are the most abundant (Table5).

CTENIDAE, 16 SPP. (CTE)

These typical nocturnal spiders live in various microhabitats from the ground layer up to the trees; they also occur on stream banks or near the water's edge of the river. Most species were uncommon and were collected in the late dry season. Bücherl et al. (1969), Chickering (1960), Eickstedt (1975, 1978, 1981, 1983), Eickstedt et al. (1969), Lachmuth et al. (1985), Mello-Leitao (1936), Peck (1981), Schiapelli and Gerschman (1972), Simo (1992).

HERSILIIDAE, 2 SPP. (HER)

These nocturnal spiders are found well camouflaged on the bark of large tree trunks. Few hersiliids were collected at Pakitza, mainly in the late dry season. No revisions for a Neotropical fauna.

HETEROPODIDAE, 5 SPP. (HET)

These nocturnal spiders were often found inside curled leaves in the daytime or sitting on the vegetation at night. All species were uncommon, and most of them were collected during the late dry season. Baert and Maelfait (1986).

MIMETIDAE, 11 SPP. (MIN)

These specialized predators of other spiders are commonly found on the underside of leaves or hanging from the vegetation at night. The dominant mimetid (23 ind.), species **96**, had higher densities in the late dry season. Archer (1950), Baert and Maelfait (1984), Chickering (1947, 1956), Mello-Leitao (1929), Platnick and Shadab (1993), Shear (1981).

OONOPIDAE, 3 SPP. (OON)

These very small spiders are frequently found in the leaf litter or under logs. Some specimens were collected at night in the late dry season from the vegetation. This is a family we expect to be more abundant in the canopy fogging samples, as it happens in Tambopata and Samiria forests (unpubl. data). Birabén (1954b), Brignoli (1978, 1979), Chickering (1951, 1968b-1970, 1972, 1973), Cooke (1972), Dumitrescu and Georgescu (1987).

OXYOPIDAE, 6 SPP. (OXY)

These spiders are known to be more active in the daytime when they are found in various microhabitats of the understory vegetation. The majority of our specimens were collected at night, from shrubs, in the late dry season. Brady (1964, 1969, 1970, 1975), Garcia-Neto (1989), Griswold (1983), Lourenço (1990), Mello-Leitao (1929).

PHILODROMIDAE, 1 SP. (PHI)

A single female was collected in Cocha Otorongo, from the vegetation (early dry season). Dondale and Redner (1969, 1976), Jiménez (1987), Sauer and Platnick (1972).

PISAURIDAE, 3 SPP. (PIS)

These diurnal spiders are found in various types of microhabitats of the understory vegetation. Some species may also occur in marshy environments. The dominant pisaurid (18 ind.), *Architis cymatilis* Carico, species **95**, was found only during the late dry season. Carico (1976, 1981, 1989, 1993a), Sierwald (1990).

SELENOPIDAE, 1 SP. (SEL)

Only two of these nocturnal spiders were collected from tree trunks (late dry season). Alayón Garcia (1992), Birabén (1953), Corronca (1990, 1991), Lins (1980), Muma (1953).

SENOCULIDAE, 4 SPP. (SEN)

These nocturnal spiders may be found in the daytime very well camouflaged in dry leaves or twigs. At night, they hang from the vegetation and resemble small pieces of dry leaves. Females with eggsacs were frequently seen in the late dry season. Our data indicate a slightly increase in the number of species and individuals in the late dry season. No recent revisions.

THOMISIDAE, 12 SPP. (THO)

Only few thomisids were collected from the vegetation, mainly in daytime. Birabén (1955), Chickering (1965), Dondale and Redner (1975) Garcia-Neto (1991), Jiménez (1992), Lise (1973, 1979, 1980a, 1980b, 1981), Mello-Leitao (1943), Rinaldi (1983, 1984, 1988).

TRECHALEIDAE, 4 SPP. (TRE)

These spiders, are mainly active in the daytime and occur in various microhabitats of the understory vegetation and also along the river, streams or marshy areas. Most species were collected in the late dry season. Carico (1993b), Carico et al. (1985), Sierwald (1990, 1993).

ACKNOWLEDGMENTS

We are indebted to the Peruvian camp helpers at Pakitza for their assistance. Special thanks are given to F. Coyle for his valuable comments on the manuscript, I. Bohorquez and M.E. Guevara for their assistance in the field work, C. Griswold, G. Hormiga, and S. Larcher, N. Scharff, for productive conversations and discussions on methods and taxonomy; they also supported this work in many other ways. Thanks also go to the Direccion General Forestal y Fauna for extending the collecting permits. L. Baert, J. E. Carico, H. W. Levi, A. F. Millidge, and P. Sierwald assisted with initial identifications. The study was funded by grants from the Scholarly Biological Diversity Studies and Neotropical Lowlands Research Programs of the Smithsonian Institution. This paper is contribution no. 54 from the Biological Diversity in Latin America Project (BIOLAT).

LITERATURE CITED

Archer, A. F. 1950. A study of theridiid and mimetid spiders with descriptions of new genera and species. Mus. Pap. Ala. nat. Hist., 30:1-40.

Alayón García, G. 1986. Descripción de una especie nueva de Nops MacLeay, 1839 (Arachnida: Araneae: Caponiidae). Poeyana, Cuba, 308:1-5

Alayón Garcia, G. 1992. La familia Selenopidae en República Dominicana. Poeyana, Cuba, 419:1-10.

Ascorra, C. E., D. E. Wilson, and M. Romo. 1991. Lista anotada de los quirópteros del Parque Nacional Manu, Perú. Publ. Mus. Hist. nat. UNMSM (A), 42:1-14.

Baert, L. 1987a. The genus *Brattia* Simon, 1894 in South America (Araneae, Linyphiidae). Bull. Ann. Soc. R. Belge Ent.,123:261-26.

Baert, L. 1987b. Spiders of the Galapagos Islands. Part IV. Miscellaneous families II. Bull. Inst. r. Sci. nat. Belg., 57:141-155.

Baert, L. 1990a. Mysmenidae (Araneae) from Peru. Bull. Inst. R. Sci. nat. Belg. (Ent.), 60:5-18.

Baert, L. 1990b. Spiders of the Galapagos. Part 5. Linyphiidae. Bull. Br. arachnol. Soc., 8(5):129-138.

Baert, L., and J. P. Maelfait. 1983. Spiders of the Galapagos Islands, I. Mysmenidae (Araneae). Bull. Br. arachnol. Soc., 6(3):102-108.

Baert, L., and J. P. Maelfait. 1984. Spiders from the Galapagos Islands, II. Mimetidae. Bull. Annls. Soc. r. belge Ent., 120(4-6):159-162.

Baert, L. and J. P. Maelfait. 1986a. A contribution to the knowledge of the spider fauna of Galapagos (Ecuador). Bull. Inst. r. Sci. nat. Belg. (Ent.), 56:93-123.

Baert, L. and J. P. Maelfait. 1986b. Spiders from the Galapagos Islands. III. Miscellaneous families. Bull. Br. arachnol. Soc., 7(2):52-56.

Balogh, J. I., and I. Loksa. 1968. The scientific results of the Hungarian soil zoological expedition to South America. 7. Arachnoidea. Description of Brazilian species of the families Symphytognathidae. Acta Zool., 14:287-294.

Bauab-Vianna, M. J. 1979a. Especie nova da Clubionidae do Brasil (Araneae). Revta. bras. Ent., 23(1):15-17.

Bauab-Vianna, M. J. 1979b. Descriçao de nova especie de *Sassacus* Peckham and Peckham, 1895 e a femea de *Beata albopilosa* Simon, 1903 (Araneae, Salticidae). Revta. bras. Ent., 23(4):193-196.

Bauab-Vianna, M. J. 1980. Duas novas especies Brasileiras de *Chirothecia* Taczanowski, 1878 (Araneae, Salticidae). Revta. bras. Biol., 40(3): 553-556.

Bauab-Vianna, M. J., and B. A. M. Soares. 1978a. Gênero e espécie novos de Salticidae do Brasil (Araneae). Revta. bras. Biol., 8(1):23-26.

Bauab-Vianna, M. J., and B. A. M. Soares. 1978b. Contribuiçao ao estudo dos Salticidae do Brasil (Araneae). Revta. bras. Biol., 38(1):19-22.

Bauab-Vianna, M. J., and B. A. M. Soares. 1978c. Contribuiçao ao estudo dos Salticidae do Brasil II. (Araneae). Revta. bras. Biol., 38(1):27-30.

283

Bauab-Vianna, M. J., and B. A. M. Soares. 1978d. Contribuiçao ao estudo dos Salticidae do Brasil, III. (Araneae). Revta. bras. Biol., 38(2):359-361.

Bauab-Vianna, M. J., and B. A. M. Soares. 1980a. Contribuiçao ao estudo dos Salticidae do Brasil, VIII (Araneae). Revta. bras. Biol., 40(4):697-699.

Bauab-Vianna, M. J., and B. A. M. Soares. 1980b. Contribuiçao ao estudo dos Salticidae (Araneae) do Brasil. Revta. bras. Ent., 24(1):1-6.

Bauab-Vianna, M. J., and B.A.M. Soares. 1980c. Duas novas espécies brasileiras de Chirothecia Taczanowski, 1878 (Araneae, Salticidae) Revta. bras. Biol., 40:553-556.

Bauab-Vianna, M. J., and B. A. M. Soares. 1982. Contribuiçao ao estudo dos Salticidae (Araneae) do Brasil. IX. Revta. bras. Ent., 26(1):87-91.

Bauab-Vianna, M. J., and B. A. M. Soares. 1983. Contribuiçao ao estudo dos Salticidae (Araneae) do Brasil. VII. Bolm. Zool., 6:47-51.

Bauab-Vianna, M. J., and B. A. M. Soares. 1983c. Descriçao do gênero Pensacolops, g. n. e de nova espécie de Chira Peckham, 1896 (Araneae, Salticidae). Bolm. Zool. Univ. S. Paulo, 7:1-6.

Berman, J. D., and H. W. Levi. 1971. The orb weaver genus Neoscona in North America (Araneae: Araneidae). Bull. Mus. Comp. Zool., 141(8):465-500.

Biraben, M. 1951. Dos especies nuevas del género Bruchnops Mello-Leitao (Araneae-Caponiidae). Rev. Soc. Entom. Arg., 15:57-64.

Birabén, M. 1953. Selenópidos argentinos. Misión de estudios de Patología Regional Argentina, 14(83-84):103-113.

Birabén, M. 1954a. Nueva especie de Nops. Neotropica, 1:43-44.

Birabén, M. 1954b. Nuevas Gamasomorphinae de la Argentina. Notas Mus. La Plata, 17:181-212.

Birabén, M. 1955. Dos tomisidos nuevos de Bolivia (Araneae). Misión de Estudios de Patología Regional Argentina, 26 (85-86): 73-77.

Bonaldo, A. B. 1992. Novas sinonimias no gênero Teminius Keyserling, 1887 (Araneae, Miturgidae). Iheringia (Zool.), 73: 113-115.

Brady, A. R. 1964. The lynx spiders of North America, North of Mexico (Araneae: Oxyopidae). Bull. Mus. Comp. Zool., 132:429-518.

Brady, A. R. 1969. A reconsideration of the Oxyopes apollo species group with descriptions of two new species (Araneae: Oxyopidae) Psyche (Camb.), 76:426-438.

Brady, A. R. 1970. The lynx spider genus Hamataliwa in Mexico and Central America (Araneae: Oxyopidae). Bull. Mus. Comp. Zool., 140(3):75-128.

Brady, A. R. 1975. The lynx spider genus Oxyopes in Mexico and Central America (Araneae: Oxyopidae). Psyche (Camb.), 82(2):189-243.

Brescovit, A. D. 1991a. Revalidaçao do gênero Isigonia Simon, con descriçao de uma espécie nova (Araneae, Anyphaenidae). Revta. bras. Ent., 35:721-727.

Brescovit, A. D. 1991b. Hibana, novo gênero de aranhas da família Anyphaenidae (Arachnida, Araneae). Revta. bras. Ent., 35:729-744.

Brescovit, A. D. 1991c. Descriçao da fêmea de Wulfila argentina (Araneae: Anyphaenidae). Revta. bras. Zool., 7:485-488.

Brescovit, A. D. 1992a. Revisao das aranhas do gênero Macrophyes O. Pickard-Cambridge, da Regiao Neotropical (Araneae: Anyphaenidae). Revta. bras. Entomol., 36(1):101-106.

Brescovit, A. D. 1992b. Revisao do grupo prospera do gênero Aysha Keyserling, 1891 na Regiao Neotropical (Araneae: Anyphaenidae). Iheringia (Zool.), 72:23-104.

Brescovit, A. D. 1992c. Descriçao do macho de Anyphaena inferens Chamberlin (Araneae: Anyphaenidae). Revta. bras. Entomol., 36 (1):107-109.

Brescovit, A. D., and A. B. Bonaldo. 1992. Genero Clubionoides Edwards, 1958 (Araneae, Clubionidae): combinaçoes novas e redescriçao de quatro especies neotropicais. Revta. bras. Entomol., 36(3):685-692.

Brescovit, A. D., and A. A. Lise. 1989. Redescription of *Anyphaena simonii* Becker, 1878 from *pectorosa* group (Araneae, Anyphaenidae). Iheringia (Zool.), 69:97-100.

Brignoli, P. M. 1977. Ragni del Brasile III. Note su *Bruchnops melloi* Biraben e sulla posizione sistematica dei Caponiidae (Arachnida, Araneae). Revue suisse Zool., 84:609-616.

Brignoli, P. M. 1978a. Spinnen aus Brasilien, 4. Zwei neue blinde Bodenspinnen aus Amazonien (Arachnida, Araneae). Beitr. naturk. Forsch. Südwestdtsch., 37:143-147.

Brignoli, P. M. 1979. Ragni del Brasile 5. Due nuovi generi e quattro nuove specie dello stato di Santa Catarina (Araneae). Revue Suisse Zool., 86(4):913-924.

Brignoli, P. M. 1981. Studies on the Pholcidae, 1. Notes on the genera *Artema* and *Physocyclus* (Araneae). Bull. Amer. Mus. Nat. Hist., 170(1):90-100.

Brignoli, P. M. 1983. *Catalogue of the Araneae described between 1940 and 1981.* Manchester Univ. Press. Manchester.

Bryant, E. B. 1942. Notes on the spiders of the Virgin Islands. Bull. Mus. Comp. Zool. Harvard, 89(7):315-363.

Bryant, E. B. 1945. The Argiopidae of Hispaniola. Bull. Mus. Comp. Zool., 140:359-418.

Bücherl, W. S., S. Lucas, and V. R. D. von Eickstedt. 1969. Spiders of the family Ctenidae, subfamily Phoneutriinae VI. Bibliographia phoneutriarum. Mems. Inst. Butantan, 34:47-66.

Buckup, E. H., and M. A. L. Marques. 1991. Aranhas Theridiidae da Ilha de Maracá, Roraima, Brasil. II. Gênero *Achaearanea* (Araneae). Iheringia (Zool.), 71:81-89.

Buckup, E. H., and M. A. L. Marques. 1992. Aranhas Theridiidae da Ilha de Maracá, Roraima, Brasil. III. Generos *Chrysso* e *Episinus* (Araneae). Iheringia (Zool.), 72:121-125.

Capocasale, R. M. 1982. Las especies del género *Porrimosa* Roewer, 1959 (Araneae, Hippasinae). J. Arachnol., 10(2):145-156.

Capocasale, R. M. 1990. Las especies de la subfamilia Hippasinae de América del Sur (Araneae, Lycosidae) J. Arachnol., 18:131-141.

Capocasale, R. M. 1991. Nuevos aportes al género *Porrimosa* Roewer (Araneae, Lycosidae). J. Arachnol., 19:93-96.

Caporiacco, L., di 1947. Diagnosi preliminari de specie nuove di aracnidi della Guiana Britannica raccolte dai professori Beccari e Romiti. Monitore Zool. Ital., 56:20-34.

Caporiacco, L., di 1948. Arachnida of British Guiana collected in 1931 and 1936 by Professors Beccari and Romiti. Proc. zool. Soc. London, 118(3):607-747.

Caporiacco, L., di 1954. Araignées de la Guyane Française du Museum d'Histoire Naturelle de Paris. Commentat. pontif. Acad. Scient., 16:45-193.

Caporiacco, L., di 1955. Estudios sobre los arácnidos de Venezuela, 2a parte: Araneae. Acta biol. Venez., 1(16):265-448.

Carico, J.E. 1976. The spider genus *Tinus* (Pisauridae). Psyche (Camb.), 83(1):63-78.

Carico, J. E. 1981. The neotropical spider genera *Architis* and *Staberius* (Pisauridae). Bull. Amer. Mus. Nat. Hist., 170(1):140-153.

Carico, J. E. 1989. Descriptions of two new species of the genus *Architis* (Araneae, Pisauridae) and the female of *A. vilhena* J. Arachnol., 17(2):221-224.

Carico, J. E. 1993a. Taxonomic notes on the genus *Architis* (Araneae, Pisauridae) and the status of the genus *Sisenna* Simon. J. Arachnol., 21(3):202-204.

Carico, J. E. 1993b. Revision of the genus *Trechalea* (Araneae, Trechaleidae) with a review of the taxonomy of the Trechaleidae and Pisauridae of the western hemisphere. J. Arachnol., 21(3):226-257.

Carico, J. E., J. Adis, and N. D. Penny. 1985. A new species of *Trechalea* (Pisauridae: Araneae) from central Amazonian inundation forests and notes on its natural history and ecology. Bull. Br. arachnol. Soc., 6(7):289-294.

Chamberlin, R. V., and W. Ivie. 1942. A hundred new species of American spiders. Bull. Univ. Utah, 32(13):1-117.

Chao, A. 1984. Nonparametric estimation of the number of classes in a population. Scand. J. Statist. 11:265-270.

Chao, A. 1987. Estimating the population size for capture-recapture data with unequal catchability. Biometrics 43:783-791.

Chickering, A. M. 1937. The Clubionidae of Barro Colorado Island, Panama. Trans. Am. Microscop. Soc. 56:1-47.

Chickering, A. M. 1947. The Mimetidae (Araneae) of Panama. Trans. Amer. Micros. Soc., 66:221-248.

Chickering, A. M. 1948. The genera of North American Dictynidae. Bull. Univ. Utah, 38(15):1-31.

Chickering, A. M. 1951. The Oonopidae of Panama. Bull. Mus. Comp. Zool., 106:207-245.

Chickering, A. M. 1954. The spider genus Mangora (Argiopidae) in Panama. Bull. Mus. Comp. Zool., 111:195-215.

Chickering, A. M. 1955. The genus Eustala in Central America. Bull. Mus. Comp. Zool., 112:391-518.

Chickering, A. M. 1956. Three new species of Mimetidae (Araneae) from Panama. Breviora, 57:1-14.

Chickering, A. M. 1957a. Notes on certain species of Tetragnatha in Central America and Mexico. Breviora, 67:1-4.

Chickering, A. M. 1957b. The genus Tetragnatha in Panama. Bull. Mus. Comp. Zool., 116:302-354.

Chickering, A. M. 1960. A new Acanthoctenus from Jamaica. Psyche (Camb.), 67:81-88.

Chickering, A.M. 1962. The genus Tetragnatha in Jamaica. Bull. Mus. Comp. Zool., 127:425-450.

Chickering, A. M. 1965. Panamanian spiders of the genus Tmarus. Bull. Mus. Comp. Zool., 133:337-368.

Chickering, A. M. 1965b. Five new species of the genus Tmarus from the West Indies. Psyche (Camb.), 72:229-240.

Chickering, A.M. 1967. The genus Nops (Araneae, Caponiidae) in Panama and the West Indies. Breviora, 274:1-19.

Chickering, A. M. 1968a. The genus Miagrammopes (Araneae, Uloboridae) in Panama and the West Indies. Breviora, 289:1-28.

Chickering, A. M. 1968b. The genus Dysderina (Araneae, Oonopidae) in Central America and the West Indies. Breviora, 296:1-37.

Chickering, A. M. 1968c. The genus Ischnothyreus (Araneae, Oonopidae) in Central America and the West Indies. Psyche (Camb.), 75(1):77-86.

Chickering, A. M. 1968d. The genus Scaphiella (Araneae, Oonopidae) in Central America and the West Indies. Psyche (Camb.), 75(2):135-156.

Chickering, A. M. 1969a. The genus Stenoonops (Araneae, Oonopidae) in Panama and the West Indies. Breviora, 339:1-35.

Chickering, A. M.,1969b. The family Oonopidae (Araneae) in Florida Psyche (Camb.), 76(2):144-162.

Chickering, A. M. 1969c. The genus Triaeris Simon (Araneae, Oonopidae) in Central America and the West Indies. Psyche (Camb.), 75(4):351-359.

Chickering, A. M. 1970. The genus Oonops (Araneae, Oonopidae) in Panama and the West Indies. Part. I. Psyche (Camb.), 77:487-512.

Chickering, A. M. 1972a. The genus Corinna (Araneae, Clubionidae) in Panama. Psyche (Camb.), 79(4):365-378.

Chickering, A. M. 1972b. The genus Oonops (Araneae: Oonopidae) in Panama and the West Indies. Part. II. Psyche (Camb.), 78(3):203-214.

Chickering, A. M. 1972c. The genus Oonops (Araneae, Oonopidae) in Panama and the West Indies. Part III. Psyche (Camb.), 78:104-115.

Chickering, A. M. 1973. Notes on Heteroonops and Triaeris (Araneae, Oonopidae). Psyche (Camb.), 80:227-229.

Coddington, J. A. 1986. The genera of the spider family Theridiosomatidae. Smithson. Contrib. Zool., 422:1-96.

Coddington, J. A. 1990. Ontogeny and homology in the male palpus of orb-weaving spiders and their relatives, with comments on phylogeny (Araneoclada: Araneoidea, Deinopoidea). Smithson. Contr. Zool., 496:1-52.

Coddington, J. A., C. E. Griswold, D. Silva, E. Peñaranda, and S. F. Larcher, 1991. Designing and testing sampling protocols to estimate biodiversity in tropical ecosystems. In: The Unity of Evolutionary Biology: Proceedings of the Fourth International Congress of Systematic and Evolutionary Biology. (E. C. Dudley, Ed.). Dioscorides Press, Pp.44-60.

Colwell, R. K. and J. A. Coddington. 1994. Estimating the extent of terrestrial biodiversity through extrapolation. Philosophical Transactions of the Royal Society (Series B), 345:101-118.

Cooke, J. A. L. 1972. A new genus and species of oonopid spider from Colombia. Bull. Br. arachnol. Soc., 2:90-92.

Corronca, J. A. 1990. Nota distribucional sobre *Selenops* Latreille (Araneae, Selenopidae) para la Argentina. Rev. Soc. Entomol. Argentina, 48(1-4):148.

Corronca, J. A. 1991. Aportes a la distribución de *Selenops spixi* (Perty, 1833) (Araneae, Selenopidae) en América del Sur. Rev. Soc. Entomol. Argentina, 49(1-4):150.

Coyle, F. A., and T. E. Meigs. 1989. Two new species of kleptoparasitic *Mysmenopsis* (Araneae, Mysmenidae) from Jamaica. J. Arachnol., 17:59-70.

Cutler, B. 1981a. On a collection of antlike jumping spiders from Bolivia (Araneae: Salticidae). Stud. neotr. Fauna Environm., 16(1):51-55.

Cutler, B. 1981b. A revision of the spider genus *Paradamoetas* (Araneae, Salticidae). Bull. Amer. Mus. Nat. Hist., 170(1): 207-215.

Cutler, B. 1982c. Description of a new species of *Paradamoetas* (Araneae: Salticidae), with a revised key to the genus. Great Lakes Entomol., 15(3):219-222.

Cutler, B. 1985. Taxonomic notes on neotropical species in the genus *Synemosyna* (Araneae: Salticidae). Stud. neotr. Fauna Environm., 20(2):83-91.

Cutler, B. 1988a. A revision of the American species of the antlike jumping spider genus *Synageles* (Araneae, Salticidae) J. Arachnol., 15(3):321-350.

Cutler, B. 1988b. Middle American *Synemosyna* (Araneae: Salticidae), a key and description of a new species. Stud. neotrop. Fauna Environm., 23:197-202.

Cutler, B., and H. G. Müller. 1991. The spider genus *Synemosina* in northern Colombia (Araneae: Salticidae). Stud. neotrop. Fauna Envir., 26:171-177.

Döbel, H. G., R. F. Denno and J. A. Coddington. 1990. Spider (Araneae) community structure in an intertidal salt marsh: effects of vegetation structure and tidal flooding. Environmental Entomology, 19(5): 1356-1370.

Dondale, C. D. 1986. The subfamilies of wolf spiders (Araneae: Lycosidae), in Actas X Congreso Internacional de Aracnología (Barrientos, J.A., ed.), Jaca, Spain, Instituto Pirenaico de Ecologia, 1:327-332.

Dondale, C. D., and J. H. Redner. 1969. The *infuscatus* and *dispar* groups of the spider genus *Philodromus* in North and Central America and the West Indies (Araneida: Thomisidae). Canad. Entomol., 101:921-954.

Dondale, C. D., and J. H. Redner. 1975. Revision of the spider genus *Apollophanes* (Araneidae: Thomisidae). Canad. Entomol., 107: 1175-1192.

Dondale, C. D., and J. H. Redner. 1976. A review of the spider genus *Philodromus* in the Americas (Araneida: Philodromidae). Canad. Ent., 108:127-157.

Dumitrescu, M., and M. Georgescu. 1987. Quelques representants de la famille Oonopidae (Araneae) du Venezuela, in Fauna hipogea y hemiedafica de Venezuela y de otros paises de America del Sur (V. Decu, T. Orghidan, D. Dancau, C. Bordon, O. Linares, F. Urbani, J. Tronchoni, C. Bosque, eds). Bucarest,Editura Academiei Republicii Socialiste Romania. Pp. 89-104.

Eickstedt, V. R. D. 1975. Aranhas coletadas nas grutas calcáreas de Iporanga, Sao Paulo, Brasil. Mems. Inst. Butantan, 39:61-71.

Eickstedt, V. R. D. 1978. Estudo sobre a sistemática de *Ctenus taeniatus* (Araneae; Labidognatha). Mems. Inst. Butantan, 40/41:211-219.

Eickstedt, V. R. D. 1981. Estudio sistemático de *Phoneutria nigriventer* (Keyserling, 1891) e *Phoneutria keyserlingi* (Pickard-Cambridge,

1897) (Araneae; Labidognatha; Ctenidae). Mems. Inst. Butantan, 42/43:95-126.

Eickstedt, V. R. D. 1983a. Aranhas do gênero Ctenus coletadas na foz do Rio Culuene, Xingu, Brasil: Descriçao de uma espécie nova e redescriçao de Ctenus villasboasi Mello-Leitao (Araneae; Ctenidae). Mems. Inst. Butantan, 44/45:161-169.

Eickstedt, V. R. D. 1983b. Redescriçao dos tipos de Ctenus similis, Ctenus albofasciatus e Ctenus minor (Araneae; Ctenidae). Mems. Inst. Butantan, 44/45:171-179.

Eickstedt, V. R. D. 1983c. Consideraçoes sobre a sistemática das espécies Amazônicas de Phoneutria (Araneae, Ctenidae). Revta. bras. Zool., 1:183-191.

Eickstedt, V. R. D., S. Lucas, and W. Bücherl. 1969. Aranhas da familia Ctenidae, subfamília Phoneutriinae VII. Contribuiçao ao estudo de Phoneutria fera Perty, 1833. Revalidaçao e sinonímias de Phoneutria rufibarbis Perty, 1838. Mems. Inst. Butantan, 34:67-74.

Erwin, T. L. 1991. Natural history of the carabid beetles at the BIOLAT Biological Station, Rio Manu, Pakitza, Peru. Rev. per. Entomol., 33:1-85.

Exline, H., and H. W. Levi. 1962. American spiders of the genus Argyrodes (Araneae Theridiidae). Bull. Mus. Comp. Zool., 127(2):75-202.

Exline, H., and H. W. Levi. 1965. The spider genus Synotaxus (Araneae: Theridiidae). Trans. Amer. Micros. Soc., 84:177-184.

Forster, R. R. 1958. Spiders of the family Symphytognathidae from North and South America. Amer. Mus. Novitates, 1885:1-14.

Forster, R. R., and N. I. Platnick. 1977. A review of the spider family Symphytognathidae (Arachnida: Araneae). Amer. Mus. Novitates, 2619:1-29.

Foster, R. B. 1990. The floristic composition of the Rio Manu floodplain forest, in Four Neotropical Rain Forests (A. L. Gentry, ed.). Yale Univ. Press. New Haven and London. Pp. 99-111.

Fowler, H. G., and H. W. Levi. 1979. A new quasisocial Anelosimus spider (Araneae, Theridiidae) from Paraguay. Psyche (Camb.), 86(1):11-18.

Galiano, M. E. 1960. Revisión del género Tylogonus. Rev. Soc. Ent. Argentina 22:93-103.

Galiano, M. E. 1961a. Un género de Salticidae nuevo para la Argentina: Alcimonotus. Physis B. Aires (C), 21:322-325.

Galiano, M. E. 1961b. Revisión del género Chira Peckham 1896. Comun. Mus. Argent. Cienc. Nat. "Bernardino Rivadavia", 3(6):159-188.

Galiano, M. E. 1962a. Los géneros Amphidraus Simon y Marma Simon. Acta zool. lilloana, 18:31-44.

Galiano, M. E. 1962b. Redescripción de especies del género Lyssomanes Hentz 1845. Acta zool. lilloana, 18:45-97.

Galiano, M. E. 1962c. Nota sobre el género Corythalia Koch. Physis B. Aires (C), 23:15-20.

Galiano, M. E. 1962d. Nota sobre el género Evophrys Koch. Physis B. Aires (C), 23:169-183.

Galiano, M. E. 1962e. Dos géneros de Salticidae nuevos para la Argentina. Physis B. Aires, 23:184.

Galiano, M. E. 1963a. Las especies americanas de arañas de la familia Salticidae descritas por Eugène Simon. Physis B. Aires (C), 23:273-470.

Galiano, M. E. 1963b. Nota sobre arañas del grupo Marpisseae. Rev. Soc. Ent. Argentina, 24:1-8.

Galiano, M. E. 1963c. Revisión del género Agelista Simon 1900 con notas sobre Titanattus notabilis (Mello-Leitao) comb.nov. Physis B. Aires (C), 24:29-34.

Galiano, M. E. 1963d. Género y especie de Salticidae nuevos para la Argentina. Rev. Soc. Ent. Argentina, 24:70.

Galiano, M. E. 1964a. Salticidae formiciformes. I. Revisión del género Martella Peckham 1892. Physis B. Aires (C), 24:353-363.

Galiano, M. E. 1964b. Salticidae formiciformes. II. Revisión del género Zuniga Peckham 1892. Acta zool. lilloana, 20:67-79.

Galiano, M. E. 1964c. Salticidae formiciformes. III. Revisión del género Simprulla Simon 1901. Physis B. Aires (C), 24:419-423.

Galiano, M. E. 1965a. Algunas especies de Salticidae nuevas para la Argentina. Physis B. Aires (C), 25:129-133.

Galiano, M. E. 1965b. Revisión del género *Sarinda* Peckham 1892. Rev. Mus. Arg. Cienc. Nat."Bernardino Rivadavia" (Ent.), 1:267-312.

Galiano, M. E. 1965c. Descripción de *Neonella minuta* n. sp. Rev. Soc. Ent. Argentina, 27:25-28.

Galiano, M. E. 1965d. Descripción de *Helvetia rioianensis* n. sp. y del alotipo macho de *Helvetia albovittata* Simon. Rev. Soc. Ent. Argentina, 27:47-50.

Galiano, M. E. 1966a. Salticidae formiciformes. V. Revisión del género *Synemosyna* Hentz 1846. Rev. Mus. Arg. Cienc. Nat. "Bernardino Rivadavia" (Ent.), 1:339-380.

Galiano, M. E. 1966b. Salticidae (Araneae) formiciformes VI. El género *Atomosphyrus* Simon, 1902. Physis B. Aires, Sec. C, 20(72):279-284.

Galiano, M. E. 1967a. Salticidae (Araneae) formiciformes VIII. Nuevas descripciones. Physis B. Aires (C), 27(72):27-39.

Galiano, M. E. 1967b. Dos nuevas especies del género *Amphidraus* Simon 1900 (Araneae, Salticidae). Physis B. Aires (C), 27(72):95-100.

Galiano, M. E. 1968c. Adiciones a la revision del género *Chira* Peckham, 1896 (Aran., Salticidae). Physis B. Aires (C), 27(75):349-366.

Galiano, M. E. 1968d. Revisión de los géneros *Acragas*, *Amycus*, *Encolpius*, *Hypaeus*, *Mago* y *Noegus* (Aran., Salticidae). Rev. Mus. Arg. Cienc. Nat. "Bernardino Rivadavia" (Ent.), 2(3):267-360.

Galiano, M. E. 1969a. Salticidae (Araneae) formiciformes IX. Adición a las revisiones de los géneros *Marella* y *Sarinda*. Physis B. Aires (C), 28(77):247-255.

Galiano, M. E. 1969d. Salticidae (Araneae) formiciformes VII. El género *Myrmarachne* MacLeay, 1839, en América. Rev. Mus. Arg. Cienc. nat. "Bernardino Rivadavia" (Ent.), 3(2):107-148.

Galiano, M. E. 1970a. Descripción de *Yepoella*, un nuevo género de Salticidae (Araneae). Rev. Mus. Arg. Cienc. nat. "Bernardino Rivadavia" (Zool.), 10(11):155-173.

Galiano, M. E. 1970b. Revisión del género *Tullgrenella* Mello-Leitao, 1941 (Araneae, Salticidae). Physis B. Aires (C), 29(79):323-355.

Galiano, M. E. 1971a. Salticidae (Araneae) formiciformes. Revisión del género *Fluda* Peckham, 1892. Physis B. Aires (C), 30(81): 573-599.

Galiano, M. E. 1971b. Salticidae (Araneae) formiciformes. XI. El género *Parafluda* Chickering, 1946. Rev. Soc. Ent. Argentina, 33(1-4):63-68.

Galiano, M. E. 1971c. Descripción del allotypus de *Synemosyna paraensis* Galiano, 1967. Salticidae formiciformes XII. Rev. Soc. Ent. Arg., 33(1-4):133-135.

Galiano, M. E. 1972a. Salticidae (Araneae) formiciformes. XIII. Revisión del género *Bellota* Peckham, 1892. Physis B. Aires (C), 31(83):463-484.

Galiano, M. E. 1972b. Revisión del género *Chirothecia* Taczanowski, 1878 (Araneae, Salticidae). Rev. Mus. Arg. Cienc. Nat. "Bernardino Rivadavia (Ent.), 4(1):1-42.

Galiano, M. E. 1974. Nuevos datos sobre tres especies de Salticidae (Araneae). Physis B. Aires (C), 33(86):1-12.

Galiano, M. E. 1975a. Salticidae (Araneae) formiciformes. XIV. Descripción de dos nuevas especies del género *Myrmarachne* MacLeay, 1839. Physis B. Aires (C), 33(87):221-230.

Galiano, M. E. 1975b. Salticidae (Araneae) formiciformes. XV. Descripción de *Corcovetella aemulatrix*, género y especie nuevos. Physis B. Aires (C), 34(88):33-39.

Galiano, M. E. 1976a. Revisión de los géneros *Hyetussa* y *Cerionesta* (Araneae, Salticidae). Primera parte. Physis B. Aires (C), 35(90):57-64.

Galiano, M. E. 1976b. Revisión de los géneros *Cerionesta* y *Hyetussa* (Araneae, Salticidae). Segunda Parte. Physis B. Aires (C), 35(91):231-242.

Galiano, M. E. 1976c. Dos nuevas especies del género *Helvetia* Peckham, 1894 (Araneae, Salticidae). Rev. Soc. Ent. Argentina, 35(1-4):51-56.

Galiano, M. E. 1976d. Descripción del alotipo hembra de *Amphidraus duckei* Galiano, 1967 (Araneae : Salticidae). Rev. Soc. Ent. Argentina, 35(1-4):57-58.

Galiano, M. E. 1977. Fauna desertico-costera peruana II. Dos nuevas especies de Salticidae (Araneae) de los tillandsiales de Lima. Rev. peruana Ent., 20(1):77-80.

Galiano, M. E. 1977(1978). Revisión del género *Phiale* C.L. Koch, 1846 (Araneae, Salticidae). I. Redescripción de *Phiale gratiosa, Phiale mimica* y *Phiale rufoguttata*. Physis B. Aires (C), 37(93):161-167.

Galiano, M. E. 1977b. Nota sobre los géneros *Cyllodania* y *Arachnomura* (Araneae: Salticidae). J. Arachnol., 3:137-150.

Galiano, M. E. 1978. Fauna desértico-costera peruana V. Dos Salticidae (Araneae) de Piura. Rev. per. Ent., 21(1):27-30.

Galiano, M. E. 1978(1979). Nuevos sinónimos en la familia Salticidae (Araneae). Rev. Soc. Ent. Argentina, 37(1-4):33-34.

Galiano, M. E. 1979b. Revisión del género *Eustiromastix* Simon, 1902 (Araneae, Salticidae). J. Arachnol., 7(3):169-186.

Galiano, M. E. 1979c. Revisión del género *Frigga* C. L. Koch, 1851. (Araneae, Salticidae). Acta zool. lilloana, 33(2):113-135.

Galiano, M. E. 1979d. Nota sobre *Phiale crocuta* (Taczanowski, 1879), su distribución y sus sinónimos (Araneae, Salticidae). Acta zool. lilloana, 35(2):689-696.

Galiano, M. E. 1979f. Revision of the genus *Phiale* C. L. Koch, 1846 (Araneae, Salticidae), 2. *Phiale guttata* (C. L. Koch, 1846) new combination. Bull. Br. arachnol. Soc., 4(8):345-348.

Galiano, M. E. 1980(1981). Algunos nuevos sinónimos en Salticidae (Araneae). Rev. Soc. Ent. Argentina, 39(3-4):283-286.

Galiano, M. E. 1980b. Revisión del género *Lyssomanes* Hentz 1845 (Araneae, Salticidae). Opera Lilloana, 30:1-104.

Galiano, M. E. 1980d. Catálogo de los especímenes típicos de Salticidae (Araneae) descriptos por Cándido F. de Mello-Leitao. Primera parte. Physis B. Aires (C), 39:31-40.

Galiano, M. E. 1981a. Algunos nuevos sinónimos en Salticidae (Araneae). Rev. Soc. Ent. Argentina, 39:283-285.

Galiano, M. E. 1981b. Revisión del género *Phiale* C. L. Koch, 1846 (Araneae, Salticidae) 3. Las especies polimórficas del grupo *mimica*. J. Arachnol., 9(1):61-85.

Galiano, M. E. 1981c. Revision of the genus *Phiale* C. L. Koch, 1846 (Araneae, Salticidae), 4. The polymorphic species of the *gratiosa* group. Bull. Br. arachnol. Soc., 5(5):205-216.

Galiano, M. E. 1981d. Three new species of Salticidae (Araneae). Bull. Amer. Mus. Nat. Hist., 170(1):216-218.

Galiano, M. E. 1981e. Revisión del género *Aphirape* C. L. Koch, 1851 (Araneae, Salticidae). Comun. Mus. Argent. Cienc. Nat. "Bernardino Rivadavia" (Ent.), 1(7):93-111.

Galiano, M. E. 1981f. Catálogo de los especímenes típicos de Salticidae (Araneae) descriptos por Cándido F. de Mello-Leitao. Segunda parte. Physis B. Aires (C), 39:11-17.

Galiano, M. E. 1982a. Revisión del género *Nycerella* (Araneae, Salticidae). Physis B. Aires (C), 41:53-63.

Galiano, M. E. 1982b. New combinations and synonymies in Salticidae (Araneae). Bull. Br. arachnol. Soc., 5(9):423-424.

Galiano, M. E. 1983. Descripción de *Sumampattus* nuevo género (Araneae, Salticidae). Physis B. Aires (C), 41:151-157.

Galiano, M. E. 1983(1984). Descripción de *Wedoquella* nuevo género (Araneae, Salticidae). J. Arachnol., 11(3):343-352.

Galiano, M. E. 1984a. New species of *Lyssomanes* Hentz, 1845 (Araneae, Salticidae). Bull. Br. arachnol. Soc., 6(6):268-276.

Galiano, M. E. 1984b. Revisión del género *Rudra* Peckham y Peckham (Araneae: Salticidae). Physis B. Aires(C), 42(103):63-72.

Galiano, M. E. 1985a. Tres nuevas especies de *Tylogonus* Simon, 1902 (Araneae, Salticidae). Hist.Nat.,Corrientes, 5(19):153-159.

Galiano, M. E. 1985(1987). Descripción de *Hisukattus* nuevo género (Araneae, Salticidae). Rev.Soc.Ent.Argentina, 44(2):137-148.

Galiano, M. E. 1985b. Two new species of *Semiopyla* with notes on *Semiopyla cataphracta* (Araneae: Salticidae). Revue suisse Zool., 92(2):281-290.

Galiano, M. E. 1985c. Revisión del género *Hurius* Simon, 1901 (Araneae, Salticidae). J. Arachnol., 13(1):9-18.

Galiano, M. E. 1986. Salticidae (Araneae) formiciformes. XVI. Especies nuevas o poco conocidas de *Simprulla, Fluda, Descanso* y *Peckhamia*. Physis B. Aires (C), 44:129-139.

Galiano, M. E. 1986(1989). Las especies de *Sitticus* del grupo *leucoproctus* (Araneae, Salticidae). Rev. Soc. Ent. Argentina, 45(1-4):257-267.

Galiano, M. E. 1987(1988). Revisión de los géneros del grupo Hurieae (Araneae, Salticidae). J. Arachnol., 15(3):285-301.

Galiano, M. E. 1987c. Description of *Aillutticus*, new genus (Araneae, Salticidae). Bull. Br. arachnol. Soc., 7:157-164.

Galiano, M. E. 1988. New species of *Neonella* Gertsch 1936 (Araneae:Salticidae). Revue suisse Zool., 95(2):439-448.

Galiano, M. E. 1989a. Note on the genera *Admestina* and *Akela* (Araneae, Salticidae). Bull. Br. arachnol. Soc., 8:49-50.

Galiano, M. E. 1991a. Las especies de *Sitticus* Simon del grupo *palpalis* (Araneae, Salticidae). Acta zool. lilloana, 40:59-68.

Galiano, M. E. 1991b. Revisión del género *Jollas* (Araneae, Salticidae). Physis B. Aires (C), 47:15-29.

Garcia-Neto, L. N. 1989. Uma especie nova de *Peucetia* Thorell, 1869, do Brasil. Iheringia (Zool.), 69:117-121.

Garcia-Neto, L. N. 1991. Descriçao do macho de *Tmarus albolineatus* Keyserling, 1880 (Araneae, Thomisidae). Bol. Mus. Nac., N. S., Zool, Rio de Janeiro, (345):1-6.

Gaston, K. J. 1994. Rarity. Chapman and Hall, London.

Georgescu, M. 1987. Araneae appartenant aux familles des Anapidae, Mysmenidae, Theridiosomatidae et Theridiidae, collectées par les membres de l'expédition biospeologique roumano-venezuelienne au Venezuela (Nov. - Dec. 1982), *in* Fauna hipogea y hemiedafica de Venezuela y de otros paises de America del Sur (V. Decu, T. Orghidan,

D. Dancau, C. Bordon, O. Linares, F. Urbani, J. Tronchoni, C. Bosque, eds.). Editura Academiei Republicii Socialiste Romania, Bucarest. Pp. 107-114.

Gerschman de Pikelin, B. S., and R. D. Schiapelli. 1970. El género *Monapia* Simon 1897 (Araneae: Anyphaenidae). Rev. Mus. Arg. Cienc. Nat. "Bernardino Rivadavia" (Zool.), 10(9):131-143.

Gertsch, W. J. 1939. A new genus in the Pholcidae. Am. Mus. Novitates. 1033:1-4.

Gertsch, W. J. 1945. Two interesting species of *Thallumetus*. Trans. Connecticut Acad. Arts and Sci., 36:191-197.

Gertsch, W. J. 1946. Notes on American spiders of the family Dictynidae. Am. Mus. Novitates, 1319:1-21.

Gertsch, W. J. 1955. The North American Bolas spiders of the genera *Mastophora* and *Agatostichus*. Bull. Amer. Mus. Nat. Hist. 106(4):225-254.

Gertsch, W. J. 1960. Descriptions of American spiders of the family Symphytognathidae. Amer. Mus. Novitates, 1981:1-40.

Gertsch, W. J. 1982. The spider genera *Pholcophora* and *Anopsicus* in North America, Central America and the West Indies. Tex. Mem. Mus. Bull., 28:95-144.

Gertsch, W. J. 1986. The spider genus *Metagonia* (Pholcidae) in North America, Central America and the West Indies. Texas Memorial Mus. Speological Monographs, 1:39-62.

Gertsch, W. J., and S. B. Peck. 1992. The pholcid spiders of the Galapagos Islands, Ecuador (Araneae, Pholcidae). Can. J. Zool., 70 (6):1185-1257.

Gertsch, W. J., and S. E. Riechert. 1976. The spatial and temporal partitioning of a desert spider community, with descriptions of new species. Amer. Mus. Novitates, 2604:1-25.

González, A. 1991. Cuatro nuevas especies del género *Euryopis* Menge, 1868 (Araneae, Theridiidae). Iheringia (Zool.), 71:59-66.

Griswold, C. E. 1983. *Tapinillus longipes* (Taczanowski), a web -building lynx spider from the American tropics (Araneae: Oxyopidae). J. Nat. Hist., 17:979-985.

Hammond, P. M. 1994. Practical approaches to the estimation of the extent of biodiversity of speciose groups. Phil. Trans. Royal. Soc. Lond. B 345:119-136

Harrod, J. C., H. W. Levi, and L. B. Leibensperger. 1990. The neotropical orbweavers of the genus *Larinia* (Araneae: Araneidae). Psyche (Camb.), 97:241-265.

Heimer, S., and H.G. Müller. 1991. *Styposis clausis* Levi, 1960 (Arachnida: Theridiidae) from the Sierra Nevada de Santa Marta (Colombia) and functional morphology of its copulatory organs. Revue suisse Zool., 98(1):159-163.

Heimer, S. and W. Nentwig. 1991. Spinnen Mitteleuropas. Ein Bestimmungsbuch. Paul Parey, Berlin and Hamburg.

Heltshe, J.F. and N.E. Forrester. 1983. Estimating species richness using the jacknife procedure. Biometrics 39: 1-11.

Heltshe, J.F. and N.E. Forrester. 1985. Statistical evaluation of the jackknife estimate of diversity when using quadrat samples. Ecology 66: 107-111.

Heyer, W.R., M.A. Donnelly, R.W. McDiarmid, L.C. Hayek, and M.S. Foster, (Eds.) 1994. Measuring and Monitoring Biological Diversity: Standard Methods for Amphibians. Smithsonian Institution Press, Washington, 1-364.

Höfer. H. 1990. The spider community (Araneae) of a Central Amazonian blackwater inundation forest (igapó). Acta Zool. Fennica 190:173-179.

Hormiga, G., and H. G. Döbel. 1990. A new *Glenognatha* (Araneae, Tetragnathidae) from New Jersey, with redescriptions of G. *centralis* and G. *minuta*. J. Arachnol., 18:195-204.

Hubbell, S. P. and R. B. Foster. 1983. Diversity of canopy trees in a neotropical forest and implications for conservation. Pp. 5-41, *in* Tropical Rain Forest: Ecology and Management (S. L. Sutton, T. C. Whitmore and A. C. Chadwick, eds.). Blackwell Scientific Publishing, Oxford.

huston, M. A. 1995. Biological Diversity: the Coexistence of species on Changing Landscapes. Cambridge Univ. Press, Cambridge, xix, 1-683.

Jiménez, M. L. 1987. Nuevas especies del género *Philodromus* (Araneae, Philodromidae) de la región del Cabo, B. C. S., México. J. Arachnol., 17:257-262.

Jiménez, M. L. 1988. Arañas de Baja California Sur, Mexico. Nuevos registros. Folia Entomol. Mex., (79):197-204.

Jiménez, M. L. 1992. New species of crab spiders from Baja California Sur (Araneae, Thomisidae). J. Arachnol., 20(1): 52-57.

Jocqué, R. 1984. Considérations concernant l'abondance relative des araignées errantes et des araignées à toile vivant au niveau du sol. Rev. Arachnol., 5(4):193-204.

Kaston, B. J. 1948. Spiders of Connecticut. Bull. Conn. geol. nat. Hist. Surv., 70:1-874.

Keyserling, E. 1876a. Über amerikanische Spinnenarten der Unterordnung Citigradae. Verh. zool.-bot. Ges. Wien, 26:609-708.

Keyserling, E. 1876b. Amerikanische Spinnenarten aus den Familien der Pholcidae, Scytodoidae und Dysderoidae. Verh. zool.-bot. Ges. Wien, 27:205-234.

Keyserling, E. 1878. Spinnen aus Uruguay und einigen anderen Gegenden Amerikas. Verh. zool.-bot. Ges. Wien, 27:571-624.

Keyserling, E. 1880a. Die Spinnen Amerikas, vol. 1. Laterigradae. Nürnberg. Pp. 1-283.

Keyserling, E. 1880b. Neue Spinnen aus Amerika. [I]. Verh. zool.-bot. Ges. Wien, 29:293-349.

Keyserling, E. 1881b. Neue Spinnen aus Amerika. II Folge. Verh. zool.-bot. Ges. Wien, 30:547-582.

Keyserling, E. 1882a. Neue Spinnen aus Amerika. III. Verh. zool.-bot. Ges. Wien, 31:269-314.

Keyserling, E. 1882b Neue Spinnen aus Amerika. IV. Verh. zool.-bot. Ges. Wien, 32:195-226.

Keyserling, E. 1884. Neue Spinnen aus America. V. Verh. zool.-bot. Ges. Wien, 33:649-684.

Keyserling, E. 1884b. Neue Spinnen aus America. VI. Verh. zool.-bot. Ges. Wien, 34:489-534.

Keyserling, E. 1884c. Die Spinnen Amerikas. Theridiidae, vol. 2, part 1. Nürnberg. Pp. 1-222.

Keyserling, E. 1886. Die Spinnen Amerikas. Theridiidae, part II. Nürnberg. Pp. 1-295.

Keyserling, E. 1887. Neue Spinnen aus America. VII. Verh. zool.-bot. Ges. Wien, 37:421-490.

Keyserling, E. 1891. Die Spinnen Amerikas. Brasilianische Spinnen. Nürnberg. Pp. 1-278.

Keyserling, E. 1892. Die Spinnen Amerikas. Epeiridae, part I. Nürnberg, 4(1):1-208.

Keyserling, E. 1893. Die Spinnen Amerikas. Epeiridae, part II. Nürnberg, 4(2):209-377.

Kraus, O. 1957. Araneenstudien. 1. Pholcidae (Smeringopodinae, Ninetinae). Senckenbergiana Biol., 38:217-243.

Lamas, G., R.K. Robbins, and D.J. Harvey. 1991. A preliminary survey of the butterfly fauna of Pakitza, Parque Nacional del Manu, Perú, with an estimate of its species richness. Publ. Mus. Hist. nat. UNMSM 40(A):1-19.

Lachmuth, U., M. Grasshoff, and F. G. Barth. 1985. Taxonomische Revision der Gattung *Cupiennius* Simon 1891 (Arachnida: Araneae: Ctenidae). Senckenberg. biol. 65:329-372.

Levi, H. W. 1953. New and rare *Dipoena* from Mexico and Central America. Amer. Mus. Novitates, 1639:1-11.

Levi, H. W. 1954a. Spiders of the genus *Euryopis* from North and Central America (Araneae, Theridiidae). Amer. Mus. Novitates 1666:1-48

Levi, H. W. 1954b. Spiders of the new genus *Theridiotis* (Araneae: Theridiidae). Trans. Am. Microscop. Soc., 73(2):177-189.

Levi, H. W. 1954c. The spider genera *Episinus* and *Spintharus* from North America, Central America and the West Indies (Araneae: Theridiidae). Jl. N.Y. Ent. Soc., 52:65-90.

Levi, H. W. 1954d. The spider genus *Theridula* in North and Central America and the West Indies (Araneae: Theridiidae). Trans. Amer. Micros. Soc., 73(4):331-343.

Levi, H. W. 1955a. The spider genera *Chrysso* and *Tidarren* in America (Araneae: Theridiidae). Jl. N.Y. ent. Soc., 63:59-81.

Levi, H. W. 1955b. The spider genera *Oronota* and *Stemmops* in North America, Central America and the West Indies (Araneae: Theridiidae). Ann. Ent. Soc. Amer., 48(5):333-342.

Levi, H. W. 1956a. The spider genus *Mysmena* in the Americas (Araneae, Theridiidae). Amer. Mus. Novitates, 1801:1-13.

Levi, H. W. 1956b. The spider genera *Neottiura* and *Anelosimus* in America (Araneae: Theridiidae). Trans. Amer. Micros. Soc. 74(4):407-422.

Levi, H. W. 1957a. The North American spider genera *Paratheridula*, *Tekellina*, *Pholcomma* and *Archerius* (Araneae: Theridiidae). Trans. Amer. Micros. Soc., 76(2):105-115.

Levi, H. W. 1957b. The spider genera *Enoplognatha*, *Theridion*, and *Paidisca* in America north of Mexico (Araneae, Theridiidae). Bull. Amer. Mus. Nat. Hist., 112(1):5-123.

Levi, H. W. 1957c. The spider genera *Crustulina* and *Steatoda* in North America, Central America, and the West Indies (Araneae: Theridiidae). Bull. Mus. Comp. Zool., 117:367-424.

Levi, H. W. 1959a. The spider genus *Latrodectus* (Araneae: Theridiidae). Trans. Amer. Micros. Soc., 78(1):7-43.

Levi, H. W. 1959b. The spider genus *Coleosoma* (Araneae: Theridiidae). Breviora, 110:1-8.

Levi, H. W. 1959c. The spider genera *Achaearanea*, *Theridion* and *Sphyrotinus* from Mexico, Central America and the West Indies (Araneae: Theridiidae). Bull. Mus. Comp. Zool., 121:57-163.

Levi, H. W. 1962a. The spider genera *Steatoda* and *Enoplognatha* in America (Araneae: Theridiidae). Psyche (Camb.), 69(1):11-36.

Levi, H. W. 1962b. More American spiders of the genus *Chrysso* (Araneae: Theridiidae). Psyche (Camb.), 69(4):209-237.

Levi, H. W. 1963a. American spiders of the genera *Audifia*, *Euryopis* and *Dipoena* (Araneae: Theridiidae). Bull. Mus. Comp. Zool., 129(2):121-185.

293

Levi, H. W. 1963b. American spiders of the genus *Achaearanea* and the new genus *Echinotheridion* (Araneae: Theridiidae). Bull. Mus. Comp. Zool., 129(3):187-240.

Levi, H. W. 1963c. American spiders of the genus *Theridion* (Araneae, Theridiidae). Bull. Mus. Comp. Zool., 129(10):481-589.

Levi, H. W. 1963d. The American spider genera *Spintharus* and *Thwaitesia* (Aranaea: Theridiidae). Psyche (Camb.), 70(4):223-234.

Levi, H. W. 1963e. The American spiders of the genus *Anelosimus* (Araneae: Theridiidae). Trans. Amer. Micros. Soc., 82:30-48.

Levi, H. W. 1963f. The spider genera *Cerocida, Hetschkia, Wirada* and *Craspedisia* (Araneae: Theridiidae). Psyche (Camb.), 70:170-179.

Levi, H. W. 1964a. The spider genus *Thymoites* in America (Araneae: Theridiidae). Bull. Mus. Comp. Zool., 130(7):445-471.

Levi, H. W. 1964b. American spiders of the genus *Phoroncidia* (Araneae: Theridiidae). Bull. Mus. Comp. Zool., 131:65-86.

Levi, H. W. 1964c. American spiders of the genus *Episinus* (Araneae: Theridiidae). Bull. Mus. Comp. Zool., 131:1-25.

Levi, H. W. 1964d. The spider genus *Helvibis* (Araneae: Theridiidae). Trans. Amer. Micros. Soc., 83:133-142.

Levi, H. W. 1964e. The American spiders of the genera *Styposis* and *Pholcomma* (Araneae: Theridiidae). Psyche (Camb.), 71:32-39.

Levi, H. W. 1964f. The spider genera *Stemmops, Chrosiothes,* and the new genus *Cabello* from America. Psyche (Camb.), 71:73-92.

Levi, H. W. 1965a. The spider genus *Synotaxus* (Theridiidae). Trans. Amer. Microscop. Soc., 84(2):177-184.

Levi, H. W. 1966. American spider genera *Theridula* and *Paratheridula* (Araneae, Theridiidae). Psyche (Camb.), 73(2):123-130.

Levi, H. W. 1967. Habitat observations, records and new South American Theridiid spiders (Araneae, Theridiidae). Bull. Mus. Comp. Zool., 136(2):21-37.

Levi, H. W. 1968. The spider genera *Gea* and *Argiope* in America (Araneae, Araneidae). Bull. Mus. Comp. Zool., 136(9):319-352.

Levi, H. W. 1968b. The spider family Hadrotarsidae and the genus *Hadrotarsus*. Trans. Amer. Micros. Soc., 87(2):141-145.

Levi, H. W. 1970. The *ravilla* group of the orbweaver genus *Eriophora* in North America (Araneae: Araneidae). Psyche (Camb.), 77(3):280-302.

Levi, H. W. 1972. The orb weaver genera *Singa* and *Hyposinga* in America (Araneae: Araneidae). Psyche (Camb.), 78(4):229-256.

Levi, H. W. 1980. The orb-weaver genus *Mecynogea*, the subfamily *Metinae* and the genera *Pachygnatha, Glenognatha* and *Azilia* of the subfamily Tetragnathinae north of Mexico (Araneae: Araneidae). Bull. Mus. Comp. Zool., 149(1):1-75.

Levi, H. W. 1981. The American orb-weaver genera *Dolichognatha* and *Tetragnatha* north of Mexico (Araneae: Araneida, Tetragnathinae). Bull. Mus. Comp. Zool., 149(5):271-318.

Levi, H. W. 1985. The spiny orb-weaver genera *Micrathena* and *Chaetacis* (Araneae: Araneidae). Bull. Mus. Comp. Zool. 150(8):429-618.

Levi, H. W. 1986a. The orb-weaver genus *Witica* (Araneae: Araneidae). Psyche (Camb.), 93:35-46.

Levi, H. W. 1986b. The neotropical orb-weaver genera *Chrysometa* and *Homalometa* (Araneae: Tetragnathidae). Bull. Mus. Comp. Zool., 151(3):91-215.

Levi, H. W. 1988. The orb-weaver genus *Alpaida* (Araneae: Araneidae). Bull. Mus. Comp. Zool., 151(7):365-487.

Levi, H. W. 1989. The neotropical orb-weaving genera *Epeiroides, Bertrana,* and *Amazonepeira* (Araneae: Araneidae). Psyche (Camb.), 96(1-2):75-100.

Levi, H. W. 1991a. The Neotropical and Mexican species of the orb-weaver genera *Araneus, Dubiepeira,* and *Aculepeira* (Araneae, Araneidae). Bull. Mus. Comp. Zool., 152:167-315.

Levi, H. W. 1991b. The Neotropical orb-weaver genera *Edricus* and *Wagneriana*

(Araneae: Araneidae). Bull. Mus. Comp. Zool., 152:363-415.

Levi, H. W. 1992a. Spiders of the orb-weaver genus *Parawixia* in America (Araneae: Araneidae). Bull. Mus. Comp. Zool., 153(1): 1-46.

Levi, H. W. 1992b. The American species of the orb-weaver genus *Carepalxis* and the new genus *Rubrepeira* (Araneae: Araneidae). Psyche (Camb.), 98(2-3):251-264.

Levi, H. W. 1993a. The orb-weaver genus *Kaira* (Araneae: Araneidae). J. Arachnol. 21:209-225.

Levi, H. W. 1993b. The Neotropical orb-weaving spiders of the genera *Wixia*, *Pozonia*, and *Ocrepeira* (Araneae: Araneidae). Bull. Mus. Comp. Zool., 153: 47-141.

Levi, H. W. 1993b. The new orb-weaver genus *Lewisepeira* (Araneae: Araneidae). Psyche (Camb.), 100(3-4):127-136.

Levi, H. W., and L. R. Levi. 1962. The genera of the spider family Theridiidae. Bull. Mus. Comp. Zool., 127(1):1-71.

Levi, H. W., and D. E. Randolph. 1975. A key and checklist of American spiders of the family Theridiidae north of Mexico (Araneae). J. Arachnol., 3:31-51.

Levi, H. W., and D. R. R. Smith. 1983. A new colonial *Anelosimus* spider from Surinam (Araneae: Theridiidae). Psyche (Camb.), 89: 275-278.

Levi, H. W., and V. R. D. von Eickstedt. 1989. The Nephilinae spiders of the Neotropics (Araneae: Tetragnathidae). Mems. Inst. Butantan, 51(2):43-56.

Lins D., P. F. 1980. Sobre uma coleçao de Selenopidae (Araneae) da Fundaçao Instituto Agronômico do Paraná. (Iapas). Revta. nordest. Biol., 3(especial):55-61.

Lise, A. A. 1973. Contribuiçao ao conhecimento do gênero *Sidyma* no Brasil, com descriçao de uma nova espécie (Araneae, Thomisidae). Iheringia (Zool.), 43:1-47.

Lise, A. A. 1979a. Tomisídeos neotropicais, 1: *Onoculus garruchus* sp. n. (Araneae - Thomisidae - Stephanopsinae). Iheringia (Zool.), 54:67-76.

Lise, A. A. 1979b. Tomisídeos neotropicais, 4: *Onocolus mitralis* sp. n. (Araneae, Thomisidae, Stephanopsinae). Revta. bras. Biol., 39(2):487-492.

Lise, A. A. 1980a. Tomisídeos neotropicais,2: *Onocolus eloaeus* sp. n. (Araneae-Thomisidae-Stephanopsinae). Iheringia (Zool.), 55:149-153.

Lise, A. A. 1980b. Tomisídeos neotropicais, 3: *Onocolus latiductus* sp. n. (Araneae-Thomisidae-Stephanopsinae). Iheringia (Zool.), 55:37-41.

Lise, A. A. 1981a. Tomisídeos neotropicais, 5: Revisao do género *Onocolus* Simon, 1895 (Araneae, Thomisidae, Stephanopsinae). Iheringia (Zool.), 57:3-97.

Lise, A. A. 1981b. Tomisídeos neotropicais, 6: *Sidyma kolpogaster* Lise, 1973 descriçao do macho e nova ocorrencia (Araneae, Thomisidae, Stephanopsinae). Iheringia (Zool.), 57:129-135.

Lourenço, W. R. 1990. A new species of *Peucetia* from Colombia. (Araneae, Oxyopidae). Caldasia, 16:193-195.

Longino, J. T. 1994. How to measure arthropod diversity in a tropical rainforest. Biology International 28: 3-13.

Lubin, Y. D. 1978. Seasonal abundance and diversity of web-building spiders in relation to habitat structure on Barro Colorado Island, Panama. J. Arachnol., 6(1):31-51.

Ludwig, J. A., and J. F. Reynolds. 1988. Statistical Ecology: A primer on methods and computing. Wiley Interscience, New York.

Maelfait, J. P., L. Baert. 1986. Observations sur les Lycosides des îles Galapagos. IXème Coll. Européen Arachnol. Bruxelles. Mém. Soc. r. ent. Belg., 33:139-142.

Magurran, A.E. 1988. Ecological Diversity and its Measurement. Princeton Univ. Press, Princeton.

Marques, M. A. L.. and E. H. Buckup. 1989. Duas novas espécies de Theridiidae (Araneae) dos gêneros *Cerocida* e *Echinotheridion* do Amazonas, Brasil. Iheringia (Zool.), 69:101-107.

Marques, M. A. L.. and E. H. Buckup. 1992. Aranhas Theridiidae da ilha de Maraca, Roraima, Brasil. Iheringia (Zool.), 73:55-58.

May, R. M. 1975. Patterns of species abundance and diversity. Pp. 81-120. *in* Ecology and Evolution of Communities (M. L. Cody and J. M. Diamond, eds.). Belknap Press, Cambridge, Massachusetts.

Mello-Leitao, C. F. 1918. Scytodidas e pholcidas do Brasil. Revta. Mus. Paulista, 10:83-144.

Mello-Leitao, C. F. 1929. Oxyopidos do Brasil. Revta. Mus. Paulista, 16:491-536.

Mello-Leitao, C. F. 1929. Mimetidos do Brasil. Revta. Mus. Paulista 16:539-568.

Mello-Leitao, C. F. 1936a. Essai monographique de la famille Acanthoctenidae. Ann. Acad. brasil. sci., 8:179-203.

Mello-Leitao, C. F. 1936b. Contribution a l'etude des Ctenides du Bresil Festschr. Strand, 1:1-31.

Mello-Leitao, C. F. 1939. Araignées américaines du Musée d'Histoire naturelle de Bâle. Revue Suisse de Zoologie, 46(2):43-93.

Mello-Leitao, C. F. 1943. Alguns pisauridas e tomisidas do Brasil. Revta. chil. Hist. nat., 45:164-172.

Mello-Leitao, C. F. 1944b. Algumas aranhas da regiao Amazonica. Bol. Mus. nac. Rio (n.s.), Zool., 25:1-12.

Mello-Leitao, C. F. 1945a. Some interesting new Brazilian spiders Trans. Conn. Acad. Arts Sci., 36:169-175.

Mello-Leitao, C. F. 1945b. Tres novas especies de Gasteracanthinae e notas sôbre a subfamilia. An. Acad. Bras. Cienc. Rio, 17(4): 261-267.

Mello-Leitao, C. F. 1945c. Arañas de Misiones, Corrientes y Entre Ríos. Rev. Mus. La Plata (n.s.), 4 Zool., 29:213-302.

Mello-Leitao, C. F. 1946. Notas sobre os Filistatidae e Pholcidae. Anais Acad. bras. Cienc., 18:39-83.

Mello-Leitao, C. F. 1947a. Aranhas do Paraná e Santa Catarina, das coleçoes do Museu Paranaense. Arq. Mus. Paranaense Curitiba, 6(6):231-304.

Mello-Leitao, C. F. 1947b. Some new Pholcids of the British Museum An. Acad. Bras. Cienc. Rio, 19(2):159-164.

Mello-Leitao, C. F. 1947c. Aranhas do Carmo do Rio Claro (Minas Gerais) coligidas pelo naturalista José C. M. Carvalho. Bol. Mus. Nac. Rio Janeiro Zool.,(80):1-34.

Mello-Leitao, C. F. 1947d. Algumas Aranhas novas de Pedra Açú e Paraná. Pap. Avulsos (Zool.), S. Paulo, 8(11):127-135.

Mello-Leitao, C. F. 1948. Contribuiçao ao conhecimento da fauna Araneológica da Guianas. An. Acad. Bras. Cienc. Rio, 20(2): 151-196.

Millidge, A. F. 1985. Some linyphiid spiders from South America (Araneae: Linyphiidae). Amer. Mus. Novitates, 2836:1-78.

Millidge, A. F. 1991. Further linyphiid spiders (Araneae) from South America. Bull. Am. Mus. Nat. Hist., 205:1-199.

Müller, H. G. 1987a. *Apodrassodes mono* n. sp. from Brasil (Araneida: Gnaphosidae). Bull. Br. arachnol. Soc., 7(5):145.

Müller, H. G. 1987b. Spiders from Colombia II. A new *Eilica* from the Santa Marta area, northern Colombia (Araneida: Gnaphosidae). Bull. Br. arachnol. Soc., 7:146.

Müller, H. G. 1987c. Drei neue Arten der Gattung *Camillina* Berland 1919 aus Brasilien (Arachnida: Araneae: Gnaphosidae). Senckenberg. biol., 68:187-190.

Müller, H. G. 1987d. Spiders from Colombia IV. *Anapis nevada* n. sp. and *Anapisona guerrai* n. sp. from the Sierra Nevada de Santa Marta (Araneida: Anapidae). Bull. Br. arachnol. Soc., 7:183-184.

Müller, H. G. 1987e. Spiders from Colombia V. A new *Mysmenopsis* from the Ciénaga Grande de Santa Marta, northern Colombia (Araneida: Mysmenidae). Bull. Br. arachnol. Soc., 7:185.

Müller, H. G. 1988. *Camillina samariensis* n. sp. aus dem Trockengebiet der region Santa Marta, n-Kolumbien. (Arachnida: Araneae: Gnaphosidae). Senckenberg. Biol., 68(4-6):397-399.

Müller, H. G., and B. Cutler. 1988(1989). The genus *Sarinda* Peckham 1892 in N-Colombia (Arachnida: Araneae: Salticidae). Senckenberg. biol., 69:73-76.

Müller, H. G., and S. Heimer. 1988. Spiders from Colombia, X. Redescription of

Corinna melloi (Schenkel, 1953) (=*falconia*) (Araneida: Clubionidae). Bull. Zool. Mus. Univ. Amst., 11(19):153-156.

Müller, H. G., and S. Heimer. 1990. Spiders from Colombia 12. The genera *Theridion* and *Thymoites*, with descriptions of five new species (Araneida: Theridiidae). Medio Ambiente, 10(2):136-144.

Müller, H. G., and S. Heimer. 1991a. Spiders from Colombia, XIII. The genera *Dipoena* Thorell 1869 and *Euryopis* Menge 1868 of the Santa Marta area, N-Colombia (Arachnida: Araneae:Theridiidae). Senckenberg. biol., 71:269-274.

Müller, H. G., and S. Heimer. 1991b. Spiders from Colombia XV. The linyphiid genus *Grammonota* Emerton, 1882. in northern Colombia, with descriptions of two new species (Arachnida: Araneida). Revue suisse Zool., 98:269-278.

Muma, M. H. 1953. A study of the spider family Selenopidae in North America, Central America, and the West Indies. Amer. Mus. Novitates, 1619:1-55.

Nentwig, W. 1993. Spiders of Panama. Biogeography, investigation, phenology, check list, key and bibliography of a tropical spider fauna. The Sandhill Crane Press, Gainesville, Florida.

Okuma, C. 1992. Notes on the Neotropical and Mexican species of *Tetragnatha* (Araneae, Tetragnathidae) with description of three new species. J. Fac. Agr. Kyushu Univ., 36(3-4):219-243.

Opell, B. D. 1979. Revision of the genera and tropical American species of the spider family Uloboridae. Bull. Mus. Comp. Zool., 148(10):443-549.

Opell, B. D. 1981. New Central and South American Uloboridae (Arachnida, Araneae). Bull. Amer. Mus. Nat. Hist., 170:219-228.

Opell, B. D. 1982. A new *Uloborus* Latreille species from Argentina (Arachnida: Araneae: Uloboridae). Proc. Biol. Soc. Washington, 95(3):554-556.

Opell, B. D. 1984. Phylogenetic review of the genus *Miagrammopes* (sensu lato) (Araneae, Uloboridae). J. Arachnol., 12(2):229-240.

Opell, B. D. 1987. The new species *Philoponella herediae* and its modified orb-web (Araneae, Uloboridae). J. Arachnol., 15(1):59-63.

Peck, W. B. 1981. The Ctenidae of Temperate zone North America. Bull. Am. Mus. Nat. Hist. 170:157-169

Petrunkevitch, A. 1925a. Descriptions of New or Inadequately-known American Spiders. Ann. ent. Soc. Amer., 18:313-322.

Petrunkevitch, A. 1925b Arachnida from Panama. Trans. Conn. Acad. Arts Sci., 27:51-248.

Petrunkevitch, A. 1926. Spiders from the Virgin Islands. Trans. Conn. Acad. Arts Sci., 28:71-78.

Petrunkevitch, A. 1929a. The Spider Fauna of Panama and its Central American Affiliation. Amer. Nat., 63:455-469.

Petrunkevitch, A. 1929b. Descriptions of New or Inadequately Known American Spiders (Second Paper). Ann. ent. Soc. Amer., 22:511-524.

Petrunkevitch, A. 1929c. The Spiders of Porto Rico. Part one. Trans. Conn. Acad. Arts Sci., 30:1-158.

Petrunkevitch, A. 1930. The Spiders of Porto Rico. Part two. Trans. Conn. Acad. Arts Sci., 30:159-355.

Petrunkevitch, A. 1930b. The Spiders of Porto Rico. Part three. Trans. Conn. Acad. Arts Sci., 30:1-191.

Pickard-Cambridge, O. 1889-1902. Arachnida, Araneida, 1:1-317, *in* Biologia Centrali Americana, Zool., London.

Pickard-Cambridge, F. O. 1897-1905. Arachnida - Araneida and Opiliones, 2:1-610, *in* Biologia Centrali Americana, Zool., London.

Pielou, E. C. 1975. *Ecological diversity*. Wiley Intersc., New York.

Platnick, N. I. 1974. The spider family Anyphaenidae in America, north of Mexico. Bull. Mus. Comp. Zool., 146(4):205-266.

Platnick, N. I. 1975a. A revision of the spider genus *Eilica* (Araneae, Gnaphosidae). Amer. Mus. Novitates, 2578:1-19.

297

Platnick, N. I. 1975b. A revision of the South American spider genus *Trachelopachys* (Araneae, Clubionidae). Amer. Mus. Novitates, 2589:1-25.

Platnick, N. I. 1979. A revision of the spider genus *Barrisca* (Araneae, Rhoicininae). J. Arachnol., 6:213-217.

Platnick, N. I. 1983a. A revision of the American spiders of the genus *Zelotes* (Araneae: Gnaphosidae). Bull. Amer. Mus. Nat. Hist., 174(2):97-191.

Platnick, N. I. 1983b. A review of the *chilensis* group of the spider genus *Echemoides* (Araneae, Gnaphosidae). Amer. Mus. Novitates, 2760:1-18.

Platnick, N. I. 1989. Advances in spider taxonomy 1981-1987. A supplement to Brignoli's A Catalogue of the Araneae described between 1940 and 1981. Manchester University Press.

Platnick, N. I. 1993a. Advances in spider taxonomy 1988-1991. With synonymies and transfers 1940-1980. New York Entomological Society and the American Museum of Natural History.

Platnick, N. I. 1993b. A new genus of the spider family Caponiidae (Araneae, Haplogynae) from California. Amer. Mus. Novitates, 3063:1-8.

Platnick, N. I., and Forster, R. R. 1990. On the spider family Anapidae (Araneae, Araneoidea) in the United States. Jl. N. Y. Entomol. Soc., 98(1):108-112.

Platnick, N. I., and Höfer, H. 1990. Systematics and ecology of ground spiders (Araneae, Gnaphosidae) from central Amazonian inundation forests. Amer. Mus. Novitates, 2971:1-16.

Platnick, N. I., and Murphy, J. A. 1984. A revision of the spider genera *Trachyzelotes* and *Urozelotes* (Araneae, Gnaphosidae). Amer. Mus. Novitates, 2792:1-30.

Platnick, N. I., and M. U. Shadab. 1974a. A revision of the *bispinosus* and *bicolor* groups of the spider genus *Trachelas* (Araneae, Clubionidae) in North and Central America and the West Indies. Amer. Mus. Novitates, 2560:1-34.

Platnick, N. I., and M. U. Shadab. 1974b. A revision of the *tranquillus* and *speciosus*

groups of the spider genus *Trachelas* (Araneae, Clubionidae) in North and Central America. Amer. Mus. Novitates, 2553:1-34.

Platnick, N. I., and M. U. Shadab. 1975. A revision of the spider genus *Gnaphosa* (Araneae, Gnaphosidae) in America. Bull. Amer. Mus. Nat. Hist., 155(1):1-66.

Platnick, N. I., M. U. Shadab. 1976. A revision of the spider genera *Lygromma* and *Neozimiris* (Araneae, Gnaphosidae). Amer. Mus. Novitates, 2598:1-23.

Platnick, N. I., and M. U. Shadab. 1976a. A revision of the neotropical spider genus *Zimiromus*, with notes on *Echemus* (Araneae, Gnaphosidae). Amer. Mus. Novitates, 2609:1-24.

Platnick, N. I., M. U. Shadab. 1978a. A review of the spider genus *Mysmenopsis* (Araneae, Mysmenidae). Amer. Mus. Novitates, 2661:1-22.

Platnick, N. I., and M. U. Shadab. 1978b. A review of the spider genus *Anapis* (Araneae, Anapidae), with a dual cladistic analysis. Amer. Mus. Novitates, 2663:1-23.

Platnick, N. I., and M. U. Shadab. 1979a. A review of the spider genera *Anapisona* and *Pseudanapis* (Araneae, Anapidae). Amer. Mus. Novitates, 2672:1-20.

Platnick, N. I., M. U. Shadab. 1979b. A revision of the neotropical spider genus *Echemoides*, with notes on other echemines (Araneae, Gnaphosidae). Amer. Mus. Novitates, 2669:1-22.

Platnick, N. I., and M. U. Shadab. 1980. Revision of the spider genus *Cesonia* (Araneae, Gnaphosidae). Bull. Amer. Mus. Nat. Hist., 165(4):337-385.

Platnick, N. I., M. U. Shadab. 1981a. A revision of the spider genus *Sergiolus* (Araneae, Gnaphosidae). Amer. Mus. Novitates, 2717:1-41.

Platnick, N. I., M. U. Shadab. 1981b. A new genus of the spider family Gnaphosidae (Arachnida, Araneae). Bull. Amer. Mus. Nat. Hist., 170(1):176-182.

Platnick, N. I., M. U. Shadab. 1981c. New species and records of neotropical Gnaphosidae (Arachnida, Araneae). Bull. Amer. Mus. Nat. Hist., 170(1):189-196.

Platnick, N. I., M. U. Shadab. 1981d. On the spider genus *Eilica* (Araneae, Gnaphosidae).Bull. Amer. Mus. Nat. Hist., 170 (1):183-188.

Platnick, N. I., M. U. Shadab. 1982a. A revision of the American spiders of the genus *Drassyllus* (Araneae, Gnaphosidae). Bull. Amer. Mus. Nat. Hist., 173(1):1-96.

Platnick, N. I., M. U. Shadab. 1982b. A revision of the American spiders of the genus *Camillina* (Araneae, Gnaphosidae). Amer. Mus. Novitates, 2748:1-38.

Platnick, N. I., M. U. Shadab. 1983a. A revision of the American spiders of the genus *Zelotes* (Araneae, Gnaphosidae). Bull. Amer. Mus. Nat. Hist., 174(2):99-191.

Platnick, N. I., M. U. Shadab. 1983b. A revision of the neotropical spider genus *Apodrassodes* (Araneae, Gnaphosidae). Amer. Mus. Novitates, 2763:1-14.

Platnick, N. I., M. U. Shadab. 1984. A revision of the Neotropical spiders of the new genus *Apophyllus* (Araneae, Gnaphosidae). Amer. Mus. Novitates, 2788:1-9.

Platnick, N. I., M. U. Shadab. 1988. A revision of the American spiders of the genus *Micaria* (Araneae, Gnaphosidae). Amer. Mus. Novitates, 2916:1-64.

Platnick, N. I., M. U. Shadab. 1989. A review of the spider genus *Teminius* (Araneae, Miturgidae). Amer. Mus. Novit., 2963:1-12.

Platnick, N. I., and M. U. Shadab. 1993. A review of the pirate spiders (Araneae, Mimetidae) of Chile. Amer. Mus. Novitates, 3074:1-30.

Platnick, N. I., and M. J. Ramirez. 1991. On South American *Teminius* (Araneae, Miturgidae). J. Arachnol., 19:1-3.

Post, W.M. and S.E. Riechert, 1977. Initial investigation into the structure of spider communities. J. Anim. Ecol., 46:729-749.

Preston, F.W. 1948. The commonness and rarity of species. Ecology 29: 254-283.

Prószynski, J. 1971. Catalogue of Salticidae (Aranei) specimens kept in major collections of the world. Annls. zool. Warsz., 28: 367-519.

Prószynski, J. 1971b. Redescription of type species of genera of Salticidae. VIII-X.

Revision of the subfamily Coccorchestinae. Annls. zool. Warsz., 28:153-204.

Prószynski, J. 1971c. Revision of the spider genus *Sitticus* Simon, 1901. II. *Sitticus saxicola* (C. L. Koch, 1848) and related forms. Annls. zool. Warsz. 28:183-204.

Reiskind, J. 1969. The spider subfamily Castianeirinae of North and Central America (Araneae, Clubionidae). Bull. Mus. Comp. Zool., 138(5):163-325.

Reiskind, J. 1971. The South American Castianeirinae I. The genus *Psellocoptus* (Araneae: Clubionidae). Psyche (Camb.), 78:193-202.

Rinaldi, I. M. P. 1983. Contribiuçao ao estudo das Misumeninae do Brasil (Araneae, Thomisidae). Revta. bras. Ent., 27(2):147-153.

Rinaldi, I. M. P. 1984. Contribuiçao ao estudo de *Acentroscellus* Simon, 1886 (*Acentroscelus*) (Araneae, Thomisidae, Misumeninae). Revta. bras. Ent., 28(1):109-114.

Rinaldi, I. M. P. 1988. *Misumenops* Cambridge and *Uraarachne* Keyserling (Araneae: Thomisidae: Thomisinae): synonyms, new combinations, and redescriptions. Revta. bras. Ent., 32(1):19-30.

Roberts, M.J. 1987. The spiders of great Britain and Ireland. Volume 2. Linyphiidae and checklist. Harley Books, Essex.

Rosenweig, M. L. 1995. Species Diversity in Space and Time. Cambridge Univ. Press, Cambridge, xxi, 1-436.

Russell-Smith, A. and Stork, N. E. 1994. Abundance and diversity of spiders from the canopy of tropical rainforests with particular references to Sulawesi, Indonesia. J. Tropical Ecology 10:545-558.

Rypstra, A. L. 1983. Web spiders in temperate and tropical forests: relative abundance and environmental correlates. Am. Mdl. Nat., 115:42-51.

Sauer, R. J., and N. I. Platnick. 1972. The crab spider genus *Ebo* (Araneida: Thomisidae) in the United States and Canada. Canad. Entomol., 104(1):35-60.

Schiapelli, R. D., and B. S. Gerschman de Pikelin. 1970. Consideraciones sobre el género *Ancylometes* Bertkau 1880 (Araneae: Pisauridae). Acta zool. lilloana, 27:155-179.

Schenkel, E. 1953. Bericht über einige Spinnentiere aus Venezuela. Verh. naturf. Ges. (Basel), 64:1-57.

Schmidt, G. E. W. 1971. Mit Bananen eingeschleppte Spinnen. Zool. Beitr. (N.F.), 17(2-3):387-433.

Shear, W. A. 1981. Structure of the male palpal organ in *Mimetus, Ero* and *Gelanor* (Araneoidea, Mimetidae). Bull. Amer. Mus. Nat. Hist., 170(1):257-262.

Sierwald, P. 1990. Morphology and homologous features in the male palpal organ in Pisauridae and other spider families, with notes on the taxonomy of Pisauridae. Nemouria, 35:1-59.

Sierwald, P. 1993. Revision of the spider genus *Paradossenus*, with notes on the family Trechaleidae and the subfamily Rhoicininae (Araneae, Lycosoidea). Rev. Arachnol. 10(3):53-74.

Simo, M. 1992. Variacion de los caracteres sexuales en *Asthenoctenus borelli* Simon, 1897 (Araneae, Ctenidae). Bol. Soc. Zool. Uruguay, 7:18-26.

Simon, E. 1892-1895. Histoire naturelle des Araignées. Paris, 1:1-1084.

Simon, E. 1897-1903. Histoire naturelle des Araignées. Paris, 2:1-1080.

Soares, B.A.M., and H. F. de Almeida Camargo. 1955. Algumas novas especies de aranhas brasileiras. Arq. Mus. Nac. Rio de Janeiro, 42:577-580.

Soberón M., J. and J. Llorente B. 1993. The use of species accumulation functions for the prediction of species richness. Conservation Biology 7(3): 480-488.

Taczanowski, L. 1872. Les Aranéides de la Guyane française. Horae Soc. ent. Ross., 8:32-132.

Taczanowski, L. 1873a. Les Aranéides de la Guyane française. Horae Soc. ent. Ross., 9:64-150, 261-286.

Taczanowski, L. 1873b. Les Aranéides de la Guyane française. Horae Soc. ent. Ross., 10:56-115.

Taczanowski, L. 1878a. Les Aranéides du Pérou. Famille des Attides Bull. Soc. imp. nat. Moscou, 53:278-374.

Taczanowski, L. 1878b. Les Aranéides du Pérou central. Horae Soc. ent. Ross., 14:140-175.

Taczanowski, L. 1879. Les Aranéides du Pérou central (suite). Horae Soc. ent. Ross., 15:102-136.

Terborgh, J. 1990. An overview of research at Cocha Cashu Biological Station, *in* Four Neotropical Rain Forests (A. L. Gentry, ed.). Yale Univ. Press. New Haven and London. Pp. 48-59.

Uetz, G. W. 1990. Influence of habitat and prey availability on spatial organization and behavior of colonial web-building spiders. Natl. Geogr. Res. 6(1):22-40.

Uetz, G. W. 1991. Habitat structure and spider foraging, *in* Habitat Structure (S. S. Bell, E. D. McCoy, and H. R. Mushinsky, eds.). Chapman and Hall. Pp. 325-348.

Uetz, G. W. 1992. Foraging strategies of spiders. Tree, 7: 155-159.

Valerio, C. E. 1971. The spider genus *Drymusa* in the new world (Araneae: Scytodidae). Florida Entomol., 54(2):193-200.

Valerio, C. E. 1981. Spitting spiders (Araneae, Scytodidae), *Scytodes* from Central America. Bull. Amer. Mus. Nat. Hist., 170(1):80-89.

Wilkerson, L. 1991. SYSTAT, ver. 5.02. SYSTAT Inc., Evanston, Illinois.

Young, L. H. 1992. Estimating Spider Species Richness in a southern appalachian cove hardwood forest. Master's Thesis, Western Carolina University.

Zimber, S. 1963. Estudos sôbre aranhas da familia Lycosidae. Cienc. Cult., S. Paulo, 15:19-24.

Appendix 1. Species list of spiders collected from Pakitza during 1991, partitioned by abundance within forest type and again within season.

AM	GENUS	SP	DAT	LFF	OAT	RVF	TGH	UFF	USF	Early	Late	TOTAL
NA	Pseudanapis	325	0	0	1	0	0	1	0	2	0	2
NY	Anyphaenid B	113	0	1	0	0	0	6	1	5	3	8
NY	Anyphaenid B	358	0	0	6	0	0	1	0	3	4	7
NY	Anyphaenid B	402	0	0	0	0	0	1	0	0	1	1
NY	Anyphaenid C	114	0	0	0	0	0	1	0	0	1	1
NY	Anyphaenid D	154	0	0	1	0	0	1	0	2	0	2
NY	Anyphaenid D	475	0	0	0	0	0	1	0	1	0	1
NY	Anyphaenid E	276	0	0	1	0	0	0	0	0	1	1
NY	Anyphaenid F	277	0	0	1	0	0	0	0	0	1	1
NY	Anyphaenid F	375	0	0	0	0	0	0	1	1	0	1
NY	Anyphaenid G	295	0	0	3	0	0	0	0	0	3	3
NY	Anyphaenid H	306	0	0	1	0	0	0	0	1	0	1
NY	Anyphaenid I	397	0	0	1	0	0	0	0	0	1	1
NY	Anyphaenid J	412	0	0	1	0	0	0	0	0	1	1
PH	Bucranium	371	0	2	2	0	0	1	0	2	3	5
ARA	Alpaida	467	0	0	0	0	0	2	0	2	0	2
ARA	Acacesia	149	0	0	3	0	0	0	0	1	2	3
ARA	Acacesia	152	1	1	4	0	2	3	0	5	6	11
ARA	Aculepeira	265	0	0	1	0	0	0	0	0	1	1
ARA	Alpaida	24	10	0	29	0	0	8	0	15	32	47
ARA	Alpaida	25	0	0	4	0	0	2	0	4	2	6
ARA	Alpaida	26	2	1	3	1	0	7	0	11	3	14
ARA	Alpaida	141	0	1	5	0	2	0	0	2	6	8
ARA	Alpaida	233	0	0	2	0	1	1	0	3	1	4
ARA	Alpaida	323	1	0	1	0	0	0	0	0	2	2
ARA	Alpaida	393	1	0	0	0	0	0	0	0	1	1
ARA	Alpaida	448	0	0	1	0	0	0	0	0	1	1
ARA	Alpaida	464	1	0	0	0	0	0	0	0	1	1
ARA	Alpaida	478	6	0	0	0	0	0	0	6	0	6
ARA	Araneinae K	33	0	0	1	0	0	0	0	1	0	1
ARA	Araneinae L	79	0	0	0	0	0	3	0	2	1	3
ARA	Araneinae M	209	2	1	0	0	0	2	1	2	4	6
ARA	Araneinae N	227	1	0	0	0	0	0	0	1	0	1
ARA	Araneinae O	275	0	0	2	0	0	0	0	0	2	2
ARA	Araneinae P	331	0	0	1	0	0	0	0	1	0	1
ARA	Araneinae Q	335	1	0	0	0	0	0	0	0	1	1
ARA	Araneinae R	392	1	0	0	0	0	1	0	0	2	2
ARA	Araneinae S	409	0	0	0	0	0	1	0	0	1	1
ARA	Araneinae T	437	0	0	1	0	0	1	0	0	2	2
ARA	Araneinae U	439	0	0	2	0	0	0	0	1	1	2
ARA	Araneinae V	477	0	0	1	0	0	0	0	0	1	1
ARA	Araneinae W	481	0	0	0	0	0	0	1	1	0	1
ARA	Araneinae X	487	0	0	1	0	0	0	0	1	0	1
ARA	Araneinae Y	498	1	0	0	0	0	0	0	0	1	1

FAM	GENUS	SP	DAT	LFF	OAT	RVF	TGH	UFF	USF	Early	Late	TOTAL
ARA	Araneus	92	0	4	0	0	3	11	0	3	15	18
ARA	Araneus	314	0	0	1	0	0	1	0	1	1	2
ARA	Araneus	494	1	0	0	0	0	0	0	1	0	1
ARA	Argiope	179	0	0	0	0	1	1	0	0	2	2
ARA	Aspidolasius	64	0	3	2	0	2	2	0	1	8	9
ARA	Bertrana	282	0	0	2	0	0	2	1	5	0	5
ARA	Chaetacis	5	2	1	8	0	1	0	1	10	3	13
ARA	Cyclosa	6	0	1	1	0	3	1	0	2	4	6
ARA	Cyclosa	29	1	0	6	0	0	2	0	7	2	9
ARA	Cyclosa	86	1	0	9	0	1	6	1	16	2	18
ARA	Cyclosa	100	0	0	11	0	0	1	0	7	5	12
ARA	Cyclosa	122	0	0	0	0	2	0	1	1	2	3
ARA	Cyclosa	170	0	0	0	0	1	0	0	0	1	1
ARA	Cyclosa	212	1	0	4	0	1	7	1	6	8	14
ARA	Cyclosa	220	0	1	0	0	1	0	0	0	2	2
ARA	Cyclosa	221	0	2	1	0	0	1	0	1	3	4
ARA	Cyclosa	297	0	0	0	0	0	1	0	0	1	1
ARA	Cyclosa	320	0	0	1	0	0	1	0	1	1	2
ARA	Cyclosa	385	0	0	0	0	0	1	0	0	1	1
ARA	Cyclosa	398	0	0	1	0	0	0	0	0	1	1
ARA	Cyrtophora	63	0	3	0	0	2	2	0	0	7	7
ARA	Cyrtophora	228	1	0	0	0	0	0	0	1	0	1
ARA	Cyrtophora	399	0	0	0	0	0	1	0	0	1	1
ARA	Dubiepeira	65	0	1	2	0	0	2	0	1	4	5
ARA	Dubiepeira	359	0	0	0	0	2	0	0	0	2	2
ARA	Enacrosoma	142	0	0	4	0	0	0	0	3	1	4
ARA	Enacrosoma	255	0	0	1	0	1	0	0	2	0	2
ARA	Enacrosoma	319	0	0	0	0	0	1	0	0	1	1
ARA	Eriophora	73	0	3	1	0	0	6	0	4	6	10
ARA	Eustala	355	0	0	0	0	0	2	0	0	2	2
ARA	Eustala	27	0	0	1	0	0	1	0	2	0	2
ARA	Eustala	28	0	0	1	0	0	0	0	1	0	1
ARA	Eustala	58	0	1	3	0	0	7	0	9	2	11
ARA	Eustala	68	0	1	0	0	0	0	0	0	1	1
ARA	Eustala	105	0	0	1	0	0	2	0	0	3	3
ARA	Eustala	106	0	0	15	0	1	17	3	14	22	36
ARA	Eustala	107	0	0	1	0	0	1	0	1	1	2
ARA	Eustala	140	0	0	1	0	0	0	0	1	0	1
ARA	Eustala	153	0	0	1	0	0	0	0	1	0	1
ARA	Eustala	251	0	0	1	0	0	0	0	0	1	1
ARA	Eustala	254	0	0	1	0	0	0	0	0	1	1
ARA	Eustala	268	1	0	0	0	0	0	0	0	1	1
ARA	Eustala	300	0	0	0	0	0	1	0	0	1	1
ARA	Eustala	312	1	0	4	0	0	0	0	2	3	5
ARA	Eustala	321	0	0	1	0	0	0	0	0	1	1
ARA	Eustala	338	0	0	2	0	0	1	0	3	0	3
ARA	Eustala	366	0	0	0	0	2	0	0	0	2	2
ARA	Eustala	401	0	0	0	0	0	1	0	0	1	1
ARA	Eustala	418	3	0	0	0	0	0	0	0	3	3

AM	GENUS	SP	DAT	LFF	OAT	RVF	TGH	UFF	USF	Early	Late	TOTAL
ARA	Eustala	421	0	0	0	0	1	0	0	1	0	1
ARA	Eustala	422	0	0	0	1	0	0	0	1	0	1
ARA	Eustala	426	0	0	0	0	1	0	0	0	1	1
ARA	Eustala	427	0	0	0	0	1	0	0	0	1	1
ARA	Eustala	431	0	0	1	0	0	0	0	0	1	1
ARA	Eustala	433	0	0	1	0	0	0	0	0	1	1
ARA	Eustala	434	0	0	1	0	0	0	0	1	0	1
ARA	Eustala	442	1	0	0	0	0	1	0	1	1	2
ARA	Eustala	443	0	0	0	0	0	1	0	1	0	1
ARA	Eustala	444	3	0	7	0	0	6	0	1	15	16
ARA	Eustala	461	0	0	1	0	4	0	0	0	5	5
ARA	Eustala	463	0	0	1	0	0	0	0	0	1	1
ARA	Eustala	465	1	0	0	0	0	0	0	0	1	1
ARA	Hypognatha	171	0	0	3	0	0	3	1	3	4	7
ARA	Kaira	479	0	0	0	0	0	1	0	1	0	1
ARA	Mangora	1	3	1	24	0	0	6	4	29	9	38
ARA	Mangora	4	5	2	22	1	1	20	0	23	28	51
ARA	Mangora	187	0	0	0	0	0	1	0	1	0	1
ARA	Mangora	192	0	0	2	0	0	0	0	0	2	2
ARA	Mangora	219	0	4	9	0	0	1	0	4	10	14
ARA	Mecynogea	3	4	3	5	0	0	2	1	5	10	15
ARA	Metazygia	115	0	0	2	0	0	3	0	2	3	5
ARA	Metazygia	330	0	0	3	0	0	1	0	1	3	4
ARA	Micrathena	2	0	0	0	0	0	0	2	2	0	2
ARA	Micrathena	7	2	0	8	0	0	2	0	8	4	12
ARA	Micrathena	55	0	0	4	0	0	3	0	6	1	7
ARA	Micrathena	67	0	1	1	0	0	7	0	8	1	9
ARA	Micrathena	74	1	0	0	0	0	2	0	2	1	3
ARA	Micrathena	78	0	0	3	0	0	3	0	4	2	6
ARA	Micrathena	162	0	1	2	0	1	3	0	5	2	7
ARA	Micrathena	180	0	0	1	0	3	2	0	2	4	6
ARA	Micrathena	186	0	0	1	0	0	0	0	1	0	1
ARA	Micrathena	193	0	0	2	0	0	0	0	0	2	2
ARA	Micrathena	230	0	0	0	0	1	0	0	1	0	1
ARA	Micrathena	246	0	0	0	0	0	1	0	1	0	1
ARA	Micrathena	267	0	0	1	0	0	0	0	0	1	1
ARA	Micrathena	270	0	0	2	0	0	1	0	0	3	3
ARA	Micrathena	286	0	0	0	0	0	1	0	1	0	1
ARA	Micrathena	364	0	0	0	0	1	0	0	0	1	1
ARA	Micrathena	417	0	0	2	0	0	0	0	0	2	2
ARA	Micrathena	484	0	0	1	0	0	0	0	1	0	1
ARA	Ocrepeira	80	0	0	0	0	0	1	0	1	0	1
ARA	Ocrepeira	104	0	0	8	0	0	10	0	10	8	18
ARA	Parawixia	94	5	5	23	0	3	17	0	6	47	53
ARA	Parawixia	110	0	0	3	0	0	2	0	1	4	5
ARA	Parawixia	287	0	0	0	0	1	0	0	0	1	1
ARA	Parawixia	302	1	0	1	0	0	0	0	0	2	2
ARA	Parawixia	389	0	0	0	0	0	1	0	0	1	1
ARA	Parawixia	449	0	0	1	0	0	0	0	0	1	1

FAM	GENUS	SP	DAT	LFF	OAT	RVF	TGH	UFF	USF	Early	Late	TOTAL
ARA	Pronous	483	0	0	1	0	0	0	0	1	0	1
ARA	Scoloderus	198	0	0	0	0	1	0	0	0	1	1
ARA	Spilasma	158	0	0	3	0	1	1	0	5	0	5
ARA	Testudinaria?	93	0	0	0	0	0	1	0	0	1	1
ARA	Testudinaria?	341	0	0	5	0	0	0	0	0	5	5
ARA	Testudinaria?	373	0	0	1	0	0	0	0	1	0	1
ARA	Verrucosa	382	0	0	0	0	0	1	0	0	1	1
ARA	Wagneriana	116	0	1	1	0	1	4	1	3	5	8
ARA	Wagneriana	156	0	0	1	0	0	0	0	1	0	1
ARA	Wagneriana	272	0	0	4	0	0	0	0	1	3	4
ARA	Wagneriana	311	0	0	3	0	0	1	0	3	1	4
ARA	Wagneriana	388	0	1	3	0	0	4	0	0	8	8
ARA	Wagneriana	406	0	0	0	0	0	1	0	0	1	1
ARA	Wagneriana	407	0	0	1	0	0	0	0	0	1	1
ARA	Wagneriana	413	0	0	1	0	0	0	0	0	1	1
ARA	Wagneriana	438	0	0	1	0	0	0	0	0	1	1
ARA	Xylethrus	139	0	1	3	0	0	1	0	3	2	5
ARA	Xylethrus	290	4	1	0	0	0	1	0	0	6	6
CAP	Nops?	125	0	0	0	1	0	0	0	1	0	1
CLU	Clubionid AA	259	0	0	1	0	0	0	0	0	1	1
CLU	Clubionid AA	471	0	0	0	0	0	1	0	0	1	1
CLU	Clubionid Z	395	0	0	1	0	0	0	0	0	1	1
COR	Castianeira	278	1	0	0	0	0	0	0	0	1	1
COR	Corinna?	88	0	0	2	0	0	1	0	0	3	3
COR	Corinna?	133	0	0	4	1	0	0	0	2	3	5
COR	Corinnid AB	159	0	0	1	0	0	2	0	2	1	3
COR	Corinnid AB	231	0	0	0	0	0	1	0	0	1	1
COR	Corinnid AC	269	0	0	1	0	0	0	0	0	1	1
COR	Corinnid AD	283	0	0	0	0	0	1	0	1	0	1
COR	Corinnid AE	344	0	0	1	0	0	0	0	1	0	1
COR	Myrmecium	210	1	0	0	0	0	1	0	0	2	2
COR	Myrmecotypus	298	1	0	0	0	0	0	0	0	1	1
COR	Sphecotypus	316	0	0	0	0	0	1	0	0	1	1
COR	Trachelas	235	0	0	1	0	0	0	0	0	1	1
COR	Trachelas	236	0	0	3	0	0	1	1	3	2	5
CTE	Acanthoctenus	488	0	0	1	0	0	1	0	2	0	2
CTE	Ancylometes	71	0	0	0	0	0	1	0	1	0	1
CTE	Ctenus	48	0	0	4	0	1	1	0	3	3	6
CTE	Ctenus	49	0	0	5	0	0	4	0	4	5	9
CTE	Ctenus	203	1	0	3	0	0	2	0	3	3	6
CTE	Ctenus	216	1	1	0	0	0	0	0	0	2	2
CTE	Ctenus	288	0	0	0	0	1	0	0	0	1	1
CTE	Ctenus	466	0	0	0	0	0	1	0	1	0	1
CTE	Ctenus?	47	0	0	1	0	0	0	0	1	0	1
CTE	Ctenus?	357	0	0	1	0	0	0	0	0	1	1
CTE	Ctenus?	451	0	0	0	0	0	1	0	0	1	1
CTE	Cupiennius	258	0	0	3	0	1	4	0	0	8	8
CTE	Enoploctenus	138	0	0	1	0	0	2	0	3	0	3
CTE	Isoctenus?	374	0	0	1	0	0	0	0	0	1	1

304

Spiders of Pakitza. Species Richness and Notes on Community Structure

FAM	GENUS	SP	DAT	LFF	OAT	RVF	TGH	UFF	USF	Early	Late	TOTAL
CTE	Phoneutria	148	0	0	1	0	0	0	0	0	1	1
CTE	Phymatoctenus?	410	0	0	1	0	0	0	0	0	1	1
DEI	Deinopis	322	1	0	3	0	0	0	0	0	4	4
DEI	Deinopis	356	0	0	0	0	0	3	0	2	1	3
DIC	Dictynid AF	453	0	0	0	0	0	1	0	0	1	1
GNA	Gnaphosid AG	491	0	0	1	0	0	0	0	1	0	1
HER	Tama	245	0	2	3	0	0	4	0	4	5	9
HER	Tama	339	0	0	3	0	0	2	0	1	4	5
HET	HeteropodidAH	242	0	1	0	0	0	1	0	0	2	2
HET	HeteropodidAI	347	0	0	0	0	0	1	0	0	1	1
HET	HeteropodidAJ	386	0	1	1	0	0	0	0	0	2	2
HET	Olios?	54	0	0	2	0	0	0	0	2	0	2
HET	Olios?	87	0	0	1	0	0	5	0	1	5	6
LIN	Meioneta	37	0	0	3	1	1	1	0	5	1	6
LIN	Meioneta	38	0	0	1	0	1	1	0	2	1	3
LIN	Meioneta	243	0	0	1	0	0	0	0	1	0	1
LIN	Meioneta	369	0	0	0	0	1	0	0	0	1	1
LIN	Meioneta?	472	3	0	5	0	0	0	0	8	0	8
LIN	Novafrontina	370	0	1	0	0	3	2	0	1	5	6
LYC	Lycosa?	17	1	0	9	0	0	1	1	12	0	12
LYC	Lycosid AM	131	0	0	0	1	0	0	0	1	0	1
LYC	Lycosid AM	132	0	0	0	2	0	0	0	2	0	2
LYC	Lycosid AN	457	0	0	0	0	1	0	0	0	1	1
LYC	Porrimosa	247	0	0	2	0	0	0	0	1	1	2
LYC	Schizocosa?	299	0	2	0	0	0	2	0	1	3	4
MIM	Ero	96	0	1	13	0	1	8	0	4	19	23
MIM	Ero	111	1	1	3	0	1	3	0	1	8	9
MIM	Ero	112	0	0	0	1	0	4	0	3	2	5
MIM	Ero	163	0	0	1	0	0	0	0	1	0	1
MIM	Ero	253	3	0	1	0	0	0	0	0	4	4
MIM	Ero	340	1	0	7	0	0	1	0	4	5	9
MIM	Ero	408	0	1	0	0	0	0	0	0	1	1
MIM	Ero	440	0	0	2	0	0	0	0	0	2	2
MIM	Ero	445	0	0	1	0	0	0	0	0	1	1
MIM	Gelanor	411	0	0	1	0	0	0	0	0	1	1
MIM	Mimetus	271	0	0	3	0	0	0	0	1	2	3
MIT	Eutichurus?	50	0	0	2	0	0	1	0	1	2	3
MIT	Miturgid AO	260	0	1	3	0	0	0	0	1	3	4
MIT	Miturgid AO	292	0	0	0	0	0	1	0	0	1	1
MYS	Maymena?	41	0	0	3	0	0	0	0	3	0	3
MYS	Mysmena	42	0	0	1	0	0	0	0	1	0	1
MYS	Mysmena	43	5	0	5	0	0	0	0	10	0	10
MYS	Mysmena	45	0	0	1	0	0	0	0	1	0	1
MYS	Mysmena	420	0	0	1	0	0	0	0	1	0	1
MYS	Mysmenopsis	18	4	0	2	0	0	0	0	6	0	6
MYS	Mysmenopsis	19	1	0	2	0	0	2	0	2	3	5
MYS	Mysmenopsis	249	2	0	4	0	0	0	0	6	0	6
MYS	Mysmenopsis	480	2	0	1	0	0	0	0	3	0	3
OON	Oonopid AP	160	1	0	3	0	0	0	0	1	3	4

FAM	GENUS	SP	DAT	LFF	OAT	RVF	TGH	UFF	USF	Early	Late	TOTAL
OON	Oonopid AQ	178	0	0	0	0	0	1	0	0	1	1
OON	Oonopid AQ	185	0	0	1	0	0	0	0	1	0	1
OXY	Oxyopes	256	2	5	5	0	0	4	0	2	14	16
OXY	Oxyopes	362	0	0	0	0	0	1	0	0	1	1
OXY	Oxyopes	492	0	0	5	0	0	0	0	0	5	5
OXY	Oxyopid AR	176	0	0	1	0	0	0	0	1	0	1
OXY	Oxyopid AR	415	0	1	0	0	0	0	0	0	1	1
OXY	Tapinillus	165	0	0	2	0	0	0	0	0	2	2
OXY	Tapinillus	223	0	0	1	0	0	0	0	0	1	1
OXY	Tapinillus	301	0	0	1	0	1	0	0	2	0	2
PHI	Ebo?	161	0	0	0	0	1	0	0	1	0	1
PHO	Metagonia?	90	0	0	4	0	0	4	0	5	3	8
PHO	Metagonia?	378	0	0	1	0	0	0	0	1	0	1
PHO	Micromerys	189	0	0	3	0	0	2	0	2	3	5
PHO	Modisimus?	22	1	0	3	2	0	1	0	7	0	7
PHO	Modisimus?	166	0	1	0	0	7	7	0	12	3	15
PHO	Physocyclus?	21	2	2	11	0	4	13	1	18	15	33
PHO	Physocyclus?	195	0	0	1	0	0	0	0	1	0	1
PHO	Physocyclus?	196	0	0	7	0	0	0	0	6	1	7
PHO	Physocyclus?	285	0	0	0	0	0	2	0	1	1	2
PHO	Physocyclus?	296	0	0	2	0	0	0	0	1	1	2
PHO	Physocyclus?	349	0	0	0	0	0	1	0	0	1	1
PHO	Physocyclus?	470	1	0	0	0	0	1	0	2	0	2
PIS	Architis	95	1	2	7	0	5	3	0	0	18	18
PIS	Dossenus	109	1	0	1	0	0	2	0	0	4	4
PIS	Thaumasia	130	0	0	2	2	0	1	0	4	1	5
SAL	Lyssomanes	119	6	2	11	0	1	2	0	0	22	22
SAL	Lyssomanes	199	3	6	18	0	1	6	0	0	34	34
SAL	Lyssomanes	313	0	0	0	0	0	6	0	0	6	6
SAL	Lyssomanes	400	0	0	0	0	0	1	0	0	1	1
SAL	Lyssomanes	441	0	0	1	0	0	0	0	0	1	1
SAL	Peckhamia	194	0	0	2	0	0	0	1	1	2	3
SAL	Salticid BL	16	1	0	0	0	0	0	0	1	0	1
SAL	Salticid BL	425	0	0	1	0	0	0	0	0	1	1
SAL	Salticid BM	20	0	2	1	0	0	0	0	1	2	3
SAL	Salticid BM	81	0	0	0	0	0	1	0	1	0	1
SAL	Salticid BM	303	0	0	1	0	0	0	0	0	1	1
SAL	Salticid BN	23	2	0	2	0	3	9	5	10	11	21
SAL	Salticid BO	82	0	0	2	0	0	1	0	3	0	3
SAL	Salticid BP	91	0	0	2	0	0	0	0	0	2	2
SAL	Salticid BQ	101	1	0	3	0	2	3	0	1	8	9
SAL	Salticid BQ	102	0	0	0	0	0	1	0	0	1	1
SAL	Salticid BR	126	0	1	1	0	0	1	0	0	3	3
SAL	Salticid BR	350	0	0	0	0	0	1	0	0	1	1
SAL	Salticid BS	134	0	0	0	1	0	1	0	1	1	2
SAL	Salticid BT	135	0	0	1	0	0	0	0	0	1	1
SAL	Salticid BT	208	1	0	1	1	1	3	0	3	4	7
SAL	Salticid BT	289	1	0	1	0	1	0	0	1	2	3
SAL	Salticid BU	147	0	0	1	0	0	0	0	1	0	1

FAM	GENUS	SP	DAT	LFF	OAT	RVF	TGH	UFF	USF	Early	Late	TOTAL
SAL	Salticid BU	167	0	0	0	0	2	0	0	1	1	2
SAL	Salticid BU	190	0	0	0	0	0	2	1	2	1	3
SAL	Salticid BV	168	0	0	0	0	1	0	0	1	0	1
SAL	Salticid BW	177	0	0	2	0	0	4	0	2	4	6
SAL	Salticid BW	205	0	0	1	0	0	0	1	1	1	2
SAL	Salticid BW	211	0	0	1	0	0	1	0	0	2	2
SAL	Salticid BX	206	0	0	3	0	0	0	0	0	3	3
SAL	Salticid BX	207	0	0	1	0	0	0	0	0	1	1
SAL	Salticid BX	213	0	1	0	0	0	0	0	0	1	1
SAL	Salticid BY	224	1	0	0	0	0	0	0	1	0	1
SAL	Salticid BZ	280	1	0	0	0	0	0	0	0	1	1
SAL	Salticid CA	351	0	0	0	0	0	1	0	0	1	1
SAL	Salticid CB	363	0	1	0	0	1	0	0	0	2	2
SAL	Salticid CC	368	0	0	0	0	1	0	0	0	1	1
SAL	Salticid CD	458	0	0	0	0	1	0	0	0	1	1
SAL	Salticid CE	459	1	0	0	0	1	0	0	1	1	2
SAL	Salticid CF	496	0	1	0	0	0	0	0	0	1	1
SAL	Synemosina	279	1	0	0	0	0	0	0	0	1	1
SCY	Scytodes	69	0	0	8	0	0	1	0	5	4	9
SCY	Scytodes	348	1	1	2	1	0	5	0	3	7	10
SEL	Selenops	294	0	0	2	0	0	0	0	0	2	2
SEN	Senoculus	108	0	1	3	0	0	3	0	2	5	7
SEN	Senoculus	151	0	0	5	0	0	1	0	2	4	6
SEN	Senoculus	334	1	0	0	0	0	0	0	0	1	1
SEN	Senoculus	436	0	0	4	0	0	0	0	0	4	4
TET	Dolichognatha	31	1	0	4	0	1	6	1	7	6	13
TET	Azilia	217	2	1	0	0	0	0	0	2	1	3
TET	Azilia	237	0	0	4	0	1	3	0	7	1	8
TET	Azilia	361	0	0	0	0	0	1	0	0	1	1
TET	Azilia?	66	0	2	0	0	0	0	0	0	2	2
TET	Chrysometa	30	2	0	3	0	0	0	0	2	3	5
TET	Chrysometa	70	0	1	0	0	0	0	0	0	1	1
TET	Chrysometa	261	0	1	2	0	0	1	0	0	4	4
TET	Chrysometa	308	0	0	2	0	0	0	0	2	0	2
TET	Chrysometa	403	0	0	0	0	0	1	0	0	1	1
TET	Chrysometa	430	0	0	1	0	0	0	1	1	1	2
TET	Dolichognatha	85	1	1	4	0	0	4	1	7	4	11
TET	Dolichognatha	345	0	0	2	0	0	1	0	1	2	3
TET	Dolichognatha	346	0	1	1	0	1	1	0	1	3	4
TET	Dolichognatha	352	1	0	0	0	1	1	0	0	3	3
TET	Glenognatha	129	0	0	1	2	0	0	0	3	0	3
TET	Homalometa?	324	0	0	0	0	0	2	0	1	1	2
TET	Leucauge	84	0	0	3	0	0	1	0	3	1	4
TET	Leucauge	127	0	0	0	3	5	1	0	9	0	9
TET	Leucauge	191	0	0	9	0	1	3	3	12	4	16
TET	Leucauge	326	0	0	1	0	0	1	1	3	0	3
TET	Leucauge	353	0	0	0	0	0	1	0	0	1	1
TET	Leucauge	365	0	0	0	0	2	0	0	0	2	2
TET	Leucauge	383	0	0	0	0	0	2	0	0	2	2

FAM	GENUS	SP	DAT	LFF	OAT	RVF	TGH	UFF	USF	Early	Late	TOTA
TET	Leucauge	394	0	0	1	0	0	0	0	0	1	1
TET	Leucauge	404	0	0	0	0	0	1	0	0	1	1
TET	Leucauge	423	0	0	1	0	0	2	0	3	0	3
TET	Leucauge	454	0	0	1	0	1	0	0	1	1	2
TET	Leucauge	455	0	0	0	0	1	0	0	0	1	1
TET	Leucauge	456	0	0	0	0	1	0	0	0	1	1
TET	Mecynometa	183	0	0	3	0	0	0	1	4	0	4
TET	Nephila	72	0	0	0	0	2	2	0	3	1	4
TET	Prionolaema?	181	0	0	3	2	0	0	0	5	0	5
TET	Tetragnatha	128	0	0	1	2	1	0	0	4	0	4
TET	Tetragnatha	473	0	0	0	0	0	1	0	1	0	1
THD	Achaearanea	8	3	0	1	0	1	2	1	8	0	8
THD	Achaearanea	62	0	0	1	0	0	0	0	1	0	1
THD	Achaearanea	146	3	1	7	0	0	6	1	12	6	18
THD	Achaearanea	175	0	0	6	0	0	6	0	7	5	12
THD	Achaearanea	182	0	1	3	0	0	1	0	2	3	5
THD	Achaearanea	337	0	0	3	0	0	1	0	4	0	4
THD	Achaearanea	342	0	0	1	0	0	0	0	0	1	1
THD	Achaearanea	493	0	0	1	0	0	0	0	0	1	1
THD	Achaearanea?	123	1	0	2	0	0	1	0	1	3	4
THD	Achaearanea?	155	0	1	3	0	0	3	0	1	6	7
THD	Achaearanea?	197	0	0	1	0	0	3	0	1	3	4
THD	Achaearanea?	201	0	0	1	0	0	0	0	1	0	1
THD	Achaearanea?	309	0	0	1	0	0	0	0	1	0	1
THD	Achaearanea?	310	0	0	2	0	0	1	0	2	1	3
THD	Achaearanea?	435	0	0	0	0	0	1	0	0	1	1
THD	Anelosimus	143	0	2	2	0	6	30	0	10	30	40
THD	Anelosimus	164	0	0	5	0	2	0	0	7	0	7
THD	Argyrodes	9	1	1	34	0	7	25	3	63	8	71
THD	Argyrodes	32	0	0	1	0	0	0	0	1	0	1
THD	Argyrodes	53	0	0	1	0	0	0	0	1	0	1
THD	Argyrodes	75	1	2	24	0	2	15	0	17	27	44
THD	Argyrodes	97	0	0	0	0	0	1	0	0	1	1
THD	Argyrodes	118	0	0	0	0	0	1	0	0	1	1
THD	Argyrodes	144	0	0	8	0	3	1	1	6	7	13
THD	Argyrodes	169	0	0	1	0	1	0	0	2	0	2
THD	Argyrodes	184	0	0	0	0	2	0	0	2	0	2
THD	Argyrodes	204	1	0	2	0	0	1	0	4	0	4
THD	Argyrodes	226	1	0	0	0	1	1	0	3	0	3
THD	Argyrodes	234	0	0	0	0	1	0	0	1	0	1
THD	Argyrodes	241	0	3	21	0	2	6	0	10	22	32
THD	Argyrodes	250	0	0	1	0	0	0	0	1	0	1
THD	Argyrodes	252	1	0	14	0	0	6	0	6	15	21
THD	Argyrodes	263	0	0	1	0	0	0	0	0	1	1
THD	Argyrodes	273	0	0	1	0	0	0	0	0	1	1
THD	Argyrodes	318	0	0	0	0	0	2	0	0	2	2
THD	Argyrodes	343	0	0	1	0	1	1	0	0	3	3
THD	Argyrodes	372	2	0	4	0	0	0	0	6	0	6
THD	Argyrodes	377	0	0	0	0	0	1	0	0	1	1

M	GENUS	SP	DAT	LFF	OAT	RVF	TGH	UFF	USF	Early	Late	TOTAL
HD	Argyrodes	391	1	0	1	0	0	0	0	1	1	2
HD	Argyrodes	424	0	0	1	0	0	0	0	0	1	1
HD	Argyrodes	469	0	0	0	0	0	7	0	0	7	7
HD	Chrosiothes	124	0	0	2	0	0	2	0	3	1	4
HD	Chrosiothes	248	0	1	0	0	0	0	0	0	1	1
HD	Chrosiothes	266	1	0	0	0	0	1	0	0	2	2
HD	Dipoena	11	0	0	11	0	0	3	0	8	6	14
HD	Dipoena	83	0	0	2	0	0	0	0	2	0	2
HD	Dipoena	145	0	0	6	0	0	3	0	2	7	9
HD	Dipoena	174	0	0	2	0	0	0	0	1	1	2
HD	Dipoena	264	0	0	8	0	0	2	0	1	9	10
HD	Dipoena	336	1	0	0	0	0	0	0	0	1	1
HD	Dipoena	354	0	0	0	0	0	1	0	0	1	1
HD	Dipoena	360	0	0	0	0	0	1	0	0	1	1
HD	Dipoena	379	0	0	1	0	0	0	0	0	1	1
HD	Dipoena	380	0	0	0	0	1	1	0	0	2	2
HD	Dipoena	381	0	0	0	0	0	1	0	0	1	1
HD	Dipoena	450	0	0	1	0	0	2	0	2	1	3
HD	Dipoena	462	0	0	1	0	0	0	0	0	1	1
HD	Dipoena	490	0	0	1	0	0	0	0	1	0	1
HD	Echinotheridion	315	0	0	2	0	0	1	0	2	1	3
HD	Episinus	56	0	4	39	2	0	61	0	66	40	106
HD	Episinus	57	0	0	15	0	0	1	0	14	2	16
HD	Episinus	150	1	0	6	0	0	5	0	6	6	12
HD	Episinus	240	0	0	2	0	0	4	0	4	2	6
HD	Episinus	489	0	0	1	0	0	1	0	2	0	2
HD	Helvibis	10	1	0	4	0	0	1	2	6	2	8
HD	Helvibis	103	1	1	9	1	0	12	2	11	15	26
HD	Helvibis	376	0	0	1	1	2	7	0	3	8	11
HD	Phoroncidia	274	0	0	2	0	0	0	0	1	1	2
HD	Phoroncidia	486	0	0	1	0	0	0	0	1	0	1
HD	Spintharus	51	0	0	10	0	0	6	0	10	6	16
HD	Synotaxus	52	0	1	11	0	0	9	0	18	3	21
HD	Theridiid AS	40	0	0	5	0	0	0	0	5	0	5
HD	Theridiid AT	157	1	0	2	0	1	1	0	2	3	5
HD	Theridiid AU	173	0	0	1	0	0	0	0	1	0	1
HD	Theridiid AV	218	1	0	1	0	0	0	0	0	2	2
HD	Theridiid AW	222	0	2	1	0	1	0	0	2	2	4
HD	Theridiid AX	262	0	0	1	0	0	0	0	0	1	1
HD	Theridiid AY	291	0	1	0	0	0	0	0	0	1	1
HD	Theridiid AZ	317	0	0	0	0	0	3	0	1	2	3
HD	Theridiid BA	332	0	0	1	0	0	0	0	1	0	1
HD	Theridiid BB	333	1	0	0	0	0	0	0	0	1	1
HD	Theridiid BC	384	0	0	0	0	0	1	0	0	1	1
HD	Theridiid BD	387	0	0	1	0	0	0	0	1	0	1
HD	Theridiid BE	460	0	0	1	0	1	0	0	1	1	2
HD	Theridiid BF	468	0	0	0	0	0	1	0	0	1	1
HD	Theridiid BG	497	1	0	0	0	0	0	0	1	0	1
HD	Thwaitesia	76	6	1	40	0	2	17	0	23	43	66

FAM	GENUS	SP	DAT	LFF	OAT	RVF	TGH	UFF	USF	Early	Late	TOT
THD	Thwaitesia	304	0	0	5	0	0	0	0	5	0	5
THD	Thymoites	61	0	0	5	2	0	0	0	6	1	7
THD	Tidarren	232	0	0	4	0	3	6	0	5	8	1
THO	Epicadus	396	0	0	1	0	0	1	0	0	2	2
THO	Epicadus?	293	0	1	0	0	0	0	0	0	1	1
THO	Onocolus	239	0	0	1	0	0	0	0	0	1	1
THO	Synaema?	419	0	0	3	0	0	1	1	4	1	5
THO	Thomisid BH	188	0	0	0	0	0	1	0	1	0	1
THO	Thomisid BI	329	0	0	1	0	0	0	1	2	0	2
THO	Thomisid BJ	452	0	0	0	0	0	1	0	0	1	1
THO	Tmarus	405	0	0	0	0	0	1	0	0	1	1
THO	Tmarus	428	0	0	1	0	0	0	0	0	1	1
THO	Tmarus	432	0	0	1	0	0	0	1	1	1	2
THO	Tmarus	474	0	0	0	0	0	1	0	1	0	1
THO	Tmarus	495	1	0	2	0	0	0	1	3	1	4
THS	Baalzebub	39	0	0	1	0	0	0	0	1	0	1
THS	Baalzebub	44	0	0	4	0	0	0	0	4	0	4
THS	Chthonos	98	0	0	0	0	0	1	0	0	1	1
THS	Chthonos	99	0	0	0	0	0	2	0	1	1	2
THS	Epeirotypus	12	20	0	20	0	0	0	10	49	1	50
THS	Naatlo	77	2	0	3	0	0	3	0	6	2	8
THS	Naatlo	485	0	0	5	0	0	0	0	5	0	5
THS	Ogulnius	13	1	0	0	0	0	0	0	1	0	1
THS	Ogulnius	46	1	0	2	0	0	0	0	3	0	3
THS	Ogulnius	281	3	0	6	0	0	0	0	7	2	9
THS	Plato	482	0	0	0	0	0	0	1	1	0	1
THS	Theridiosoma	34	2	0	29	0	0	0	0	31	0	31
THS	Theridiosoma	35	0	0	10	0	0	0	0	10	0	10
THS	Theridiosoma	36	0	0	1	0	0	0	0	1	0	1
THS	Theridiosoma	136	0	0	1	1	0	0	0	2	0	2
THS	Theridiosoma	137	0	0	4	1	0	0	0	5	0	5
THS	Theridiosoma	305	0	0	1	0	0	0	0	1	0	1
THS	Theridiosoma	416	0	0	0	0	1	0	0	1	0	1
THS	Theridiosoma	476	0	0	0	0	0	1	0	1	0	1
TRE	Hesydrus	89	0	0	0	0	0	3	0	2	1	3
TRE	Hesydrus	200	0	0	0	0	0	2	0	0	2	2
TRE	Rhoicinine A	429	0	0	1	0	0	0	0	0	1	1
TRE	Syntrechalea?	446	0	0	1	0	0	0	0	0	1	1
ULO	Miagrammopes	59	0	1	8	0	0	6	0	7	8	15
ULO	Miagrammopes	117	1	0	0	0	0	0	0	0	1	1
ULO	Miagrammopes	202	0	0	1	1	0	1	0	1	2	3
ULO	Miagrammopes	214	3	2	5	0	0	4	0	1	13	14
ULO	Miagrammopes	244	0	0	3	0	0	0	0	2	1	3
ULO	Miagrammopes	414	0	0	3	0	0	1	0	1	3	4
ULO	Philoponella	14	10	5	14	0	1	10	1	25	16	41
ULO	Philoponella	225	0	0	0	0	1	0	0	0	1	1
ULO	Philoponella	328	0	2	0	0	4	0	0	0	6	6
ULO	Uloborus	120	0	1	1	0	0	0	0	1	1	2
ULO	Uloborid BK	229	1	0	0	0	0	0	0	1	0	1

AM	GENUS	SP	DAT	LFF	OAT	RVF	TGH	UFF	USF	Early	Late	TOTAL
LO	Uloborus	15	2	1	30	0	1	16	0	22	28	50
LO	Uloborus	60	1	0	3	0	1	2	0	2	5	7
JLO	Uloborus	121	0	0	1	1	1	1	0	2	2	4
LO	Uloborus	215	3	0	1	0	0	0	0	0	4	4
LO	Uloborus	238	0	0	1	0	0	0	0	0	1	1
LO	Uloborus	257	0	1	0	0	0	0	0	0	1	1
LO	Uloborus	284	0	0	0	0	0	2	0	2	0	2
LO	Uloborus	307	0	0	4	0	0	4	0	2	6	8
LO	Uloborus	327	0	0	0	0	0	2	0	2	0	2
JLO	Uloborus	367	0	1	1	0	2	5	0	4	5	9
JLO	Uloborus	390	1	0	0	0	0	0	0	0	1	1
JLO	Uloborus	447	0	0	1	0	0	0	0	0	1	1
JLO	Zosis	172	0	1	1	0	1	1	0	2	2	4

Biodiversity of Cicadoidea (Homoptera) of Pakitza, Manu Reserved Zone and Tambopata Reserved Zone, Peru: A Faunal Comparison

Michael G. Pogue

Department of Entomology, MRC-169 Smithsonian Institution
Washington, D.C. 20560

ABSTRACT

At Pakitza, Manu Reserved Zone, Madre de Dios, Peru, during a total of 67 collecting days, 34 species of Cicadoidea (Homoptera) were collected. At Tambopata Reserved Zone, Madre de Dios, Peru, during a total of 70 collecting days, 41 species of Cicadoidea were collected. A total of 50 species was collected from both sites. Faunal similarity between these sites was 50%. Species accumulation was plotted against collecting days. Pakitza reached an asymptote, suggesting that few additional species will be added to the fauna during the months of September-November. An asymptote was not as clearly defined at Tambopata, suggesting that more species could be added to the fauna at that site. Tambopata is the most species rich site of any in the neotropics.

INTRODUCTION

Both study sites are part of the large drainage area of the Río Madre de Dios. Pakitza is a Vigilante Post that is associated with the BIOLAT Biological Station in the Reserved Zone of Manu, just outside Manu National Park, at 11° 56'47"S, 071° 17'00"W, on the Río Manu. Tambopata Reserved Zone is approximately 215 km SE of Pakitza on the Río Tambopata, a tributary of the Río Madre de Dios, at 12° 50'S, 069° 17'W (Fig. 1). Pakitza is higher in elevation at 356 m, than Tambopata at 290 m.

Cicadoidea, belonging to the Order Homoptera, comprises 6 families (Duffels and van der Laan 1985). Presently there are about 2300 species of Cicadoidea in the world with 378 species in the Neotropics, including the islands of the Caribbean. Two of these families, Cicadidae and Tibicinidae, are found at both

Pakitza and Tambopata. Tambopata has 41 species and Pakitza 34, with a total of 50 species, which is 13% of the Neotropical fauna. Tambopata is the most species rich site in the neotropics.

Taxonomic study of Neotropical Cicadoidea has been poor during the 20th century. No systematic revisions of neotropical genera have been completed. Faunal surveys were conducted for the Andean region (Jacobi 1907) and Ecuador (1925). The remaining studies have been descriptions of new species in various genera, but no major revision. This makes it extremely difficult to identify material without examining holotypes of all the species in all the genera represented here. I have included a checklist of the species that are represented at Pakitza and Tambopata, with as many identified with confidence that I could glean from the available literature (Tables 1 and 2). The purpose of this study is not a taxonomic one, but to show the tremendous species richness at these two sites. It is hoped that this data promotes comparison of species richness at other neotropical sites.

Table 1 Checklist of Cicadidae listing site occurance and months species were collected.

			Pakitza	Months	Tambopata	Months
Ariasa	sp. 1				X	Oct, Nov
Ariasa	sp. 2		X	Oct	X	Sep-Nov
Ariasa	sp. 3				X	Sep, Nov
Ariasa	sp. 4				X	Sep, Nov
Ariasa	sp. 5		X	Sep		
Ariasa	sp. 6		X	Sep, Oct		
Dorisiana	sp. 1		X	Sep, Oct	X	Sep-Nov
Fidicina	bogotana	Distant	X	Sep, Oct	X	Aug, Sep-Nov
Fidicina	mannifera	(Fabricius)	X	Sep, Oct	X	Sep-Nov
Fidicina	sp. 1		X	Sep		
Fidicina	sp. 2		X	Sep, Oct	X	Oct
Fidicina	sp. 3		X	Sep		
Fidicina	sp. 4				X	Sep, Oct
Fidicina	sp. 5		X	Oct	X	Sep, Oct
Fidicina	sp. 6		X	Sep		
Fidicina	sp. 7		X	Sep, Oct	X	Sep-Nov
Fidicina	sp. 8				X	nov
Fidicina	sp. 9				X	Oct
Fidicina	sp. 10		X	Sep, Oct		
Majeorona	bovilla	Distant	X	Sep, Oct	X	Sep, Oct
Orialella	boliviana	Distant	X	Sep, Oct	X	Aug-Oct
Proarna	guttulosa	(Wlker)	X	Sep, Oct	X	Oct, Nov
Proarna	sp. 1		X	Sep	X	Sep, Oct
Proarna	sp. 2		X	Sep, Oct	X	Sep
Proarna	sp. 3		X	Sep, Oct	X	Sep
Proarna	sp. 4		X	Sep, Oct		
Proarna	sp. 5		X	Sep, Nov	X	Sep-Nov
Proarna	sp. 6				X	Oct
Proarna	sp. 7		X	Sep, Oct	X	Oct, Nov
Proarna	sp. 8		X	Oct, Nov	X	Sep
Proarna	sp. 9		X	Oct		
Proarna	sp. 10		X	Sep, Oct	X	Sep, Oct
Quesada	gigas	Olivier	X	Sep, Oct	X	Oct
Genus A	sp.				X	Oct
Genus B	sp.		X	Oct		

Michael G. Pogue

SEASONALITY

Cicadas were collected at both sites primarily from September to November, which is the transition period between late dry to early wet seasons. The driest months are July and August, wettest are January and February (Erwin 1985, 1991b). September to mid-October can be considered the late dry season. At Pakitza, a distinct weather change signaling the beginning of the wet season occurred on October 16 in the years 1989-1991. From mid-October through November can be considered the early wet season. In Costa Rica cicadas exhibit seasonal adult emergence patterns (Young 1976, 1980a, 1980b, 1981). Due to the lack of collecting in the wet season at Pakitza and Tambopata little can be concluded about seasonality.

RESULTS

Biodiversity can be equated with species richness, that is the number of species, the habitat in which each species exists, and the evolution of a species lineage. Biodiversity is influenced through evolutionary processes, habitat availability, climate, latitude, and altitude. Species richness at a site is a readily observable index of the interactions among and between species and how these species are grouped as a living unit at that site. Species richness is a reasonable and knowable tool that can be used in setting policy and making decisions about biotic conservation and management (Erwin 1991a).

Species richness, number of species present at a site, will be the focus of the discussion on biodiversity of cicadas at Pakitza and Tambopata, and how this diversity compares with other organizational units (countries, sites) in the neotropics. Species richness, as shown in Fig. 2, compares the number of species present at Pakitza and Tambopata with other neotropical countries. The number of recorded cicada species in the neotropics ranges from 1 species present in Tobago to 100 species in Brazil. Compared with neoptropical countries, Pakitza and Tambopata are quite diverse, with 34 and 41 species respectively.

An index of faunal similarity will be used to compare the biodiversity of cicadas between organizational units. Faunal similarity (FS) was defined as C/(A+B)-C x 100 = % FS where A = number of species in area A, B = number of species in area B, and C = number of species shared between areas A and B.

Faunal similarity (FS), as shown in Fig. 3, compares the percentage of the shared species between the combined faunas of Peru and a neotropical country. This index is precise because it takes into account the entire fauna of both countries being compared. For two countries to have 100% FS, each country would have an identical fauna. If FS was defined as the percentage of the shared species

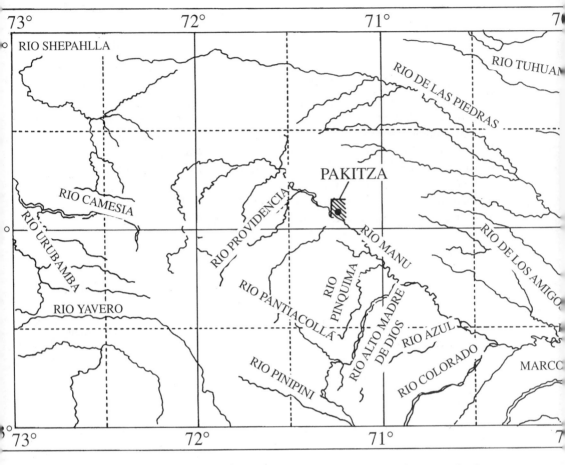

Fig. 1. – Map of Pakitza, Manu Reserved Zone, and Tambopata Reserved Zone, Madre de Dios, Perú.

METHODS

Several types of collecting methods were utilized. At Tambopata ultra-violet light was used with traps or by collecting from a sheet, at white light around the laboratory building, and from vegetation along trails. Similarly, at Pakitza specimens were collected with ultra-violet light traps or from a sheet, at white lights around buildings, by netting during the day, and by insecticidal fogging of tree canopies.

Collections from Tambopata were taken during November 1979, October-November 1982, August-October 1983, and September 1990. At Pakitza collections were made in September 1987-1988, September-early November 1990, and September-October 1991.

Data for determining species richness and faunal similarity of neotropical countries were obtained from the General Catalogue of the Homoptera, Fascicle VIII, Cicadoidea by Metcalf (1962, 1963), and Catalogue of the Cicadoidea (Homoptera, Auchenorhýncha) 1956-1980, by Duffels and Van der Laan (1985).

315

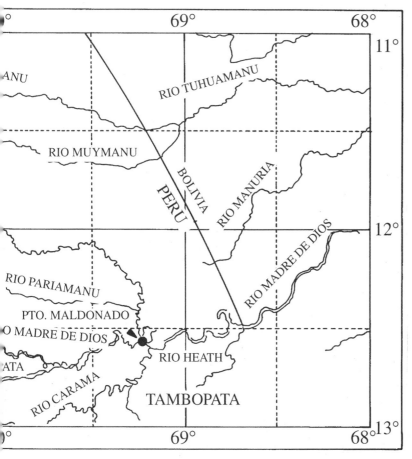

Twenty-six new species have been described from the neotropics since 1980 from French Guiana, Venezuela, Ecuador, and Brazil (Boulard 1982, 1985, 1986a, 1986b). The recorded cicada fauna of 16 islands in the Caribbean were combined and treated as a single faunal element.

A total of 1201 specimens were collected, 831 at Tambopata and 370 at Pakitza. All specimens collected for this study were given a unique number. Two types of numbered labels were used. Labels with the letters BIO-LAT/HOMO preceding the number refer to those specimens collected in association with the Biological Diversity Programs of the Smithsonian Institution. Other labels have the letters ADP preceding the number. All specimens were entered in a database using Microsoft Excel version 4.

HABITAT

Cicadas were associated with similar habitats at both study areas. These are typically non-flooded forests. Cicadas are not present in the seasonally-flooded forests at Pakitza (Zones 2 and 7). During 1988 and 1990, when cicada abundance was high in the upland forests of Pakitza, no adults, chorusing, or cast exuvia were found in seasonally flooded forests. Being subterranean during the nymphal stage probably limits these insects to non-flooded forests.

There are two types of non-flooded forests at Tambopata (Erwin 1985). Upland forest Type 1 occurs on the low undulating hills away from the river courses and lakes. The soil is reddish, clay-like, and drains poorly. This forest is of medium height (30-35 m) and averages 585 trees of 10 cm in diameter, or greater, at 1.37 m. Palms make up 22% of the trees with *Pourouma minor* (Moraceae) being the

TABLE 2. Checklist of Tibicinidae listing site ocurrance and months species were collected.

			Pakitza	Months	Tambopata	Months
Calyria	telifera	(Walker)			X	Nov
Carineta	cingenda	Distant			X	Oct,Nov
Carineta	illustris	Distant			X	Nov
Carineta	rufescens	(Fabricius)	X	Sep.Oct	X	Aug-Oct
Carineta	sp. 1		X	Sep,Oct	X	Oct,Nov
Carineta	sp. 2				X	Nov
Carineta	sp. 3		X	Oct	X	Sep-Nov
Carineta	sp. 4				X	Oct,Nov
Carineta	sp. 5		X	Feb,Mar,Sep-Nov	X	Oct,Nov
Carineta	sp. 6				X	Nov
Carineta	sp. 7		X	Nov	X	Feb,Oct,Nov
Taphura	hastifera	(Walker)	X	Sep-Nov	X	Sep-Nov
Taphura	nitida	(de Geer)	X	Sep-Nov	X	Oct,Nov
Taphura	sauliensis	Boulard			X	Nov
Selymbra	sp. 1				X	Sep-No

dominant hardwood. This forest type is typical around the clearing of the lodge and other buildings. Upland forest Type 2 is composed of ancient alluvial terraces that are high above the present river systems. The soil is sandy, reddish in color, and well drained. This forest is taller (35-40 m) and averages 583 trees of 10 cm in diameter, or greater, at 1.37 m. Palms only make up 3% of the tree species with *Iryanthera* (Myristicaceae) as the dominant hardwood.

Cicadas were sampled from two types of non-flooded forests at Pakitza (Erwin 1991b). The type of forest associated with the clearing and buildings of Pakitza is the old alluvial terrace forest with bamboo (Zone 3). The soil is sandy and beige or reddish in color and well drained. The hectare plot 13 in Zone 3 contains 538 individuals and approximately 94 species. The number of individual trees is dominated by Leguminosae (16%) with *Inga, Tachygali, Parkia,* and *Cedralinga.* Moraceae (15.5%) is represented by mostly *Pourouma* and *Pseudlomedia.* Palmae made up 14.4% of the individual trees with *Euterpe* and *Socratea* dominating. Families with the most species are Moraceae (15%), Leguminosae (13%), and Palmae (7%). Cicadas collected at UV light traps and sheets were associated with the dissected alluvial terrace forest (Zone 1). This forest type is characterized by old alluvial terraces that have been dissected by small streams on well drained sandy soils. The hectare plot 13 in Zone 1 contains 579 individuals and 140 species of trees. Individuals of Violaceae (31.2%), predominantly *Rinorea guianensis,* dominate, with Palmae (16.3%), mostly *Iriartea* and Moraceae (10%), generally *Pseudlomedia, Pourouma,* and *Cecropia sciadophylla* making up more than half of this forest type. Families with the most species are the Moraceae (15%), Euphorbiaceae (8.7%), Leguminosae (7%), and Palmae (7%).

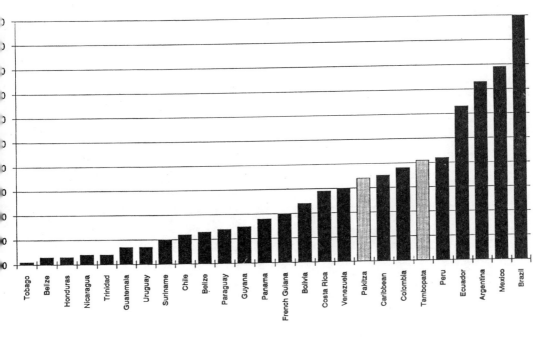

Fig. 2. – *Comparison of species richness between Pakitza and Tambopata with other Neotropical countries.*

between a neotropical country and Peru, faunal similarity between Tobago and Peru would be 100% because the single species recorded from Tobago also occurs in Peru. This way of expressing FS is misleading because the only species recorded from Tobago is a common widespread one, so Tobago would have 100% FS with most countries in Central and South America. By comparing the combined faunas a more realistic FS is achieved.

Faunal similarity to Peru was compared with all neotropical countries with cicadas recorded. The range of FS was from 0% with Uruguay and Honduras to 26.9% with Bolivia (Fig. 3). FS between Pakitza and Tambopata was 50%, with 25 species shared.

By arranging all specimens collected at both sites by date of capture, then recording all species collected on each day, accumulation curves were plotted against collecting days (Figs. 4-5). All collections were made during the transition period from late dry to early wet season, except for single specimens collected in February, 1984 at Tambopata and February, 1992 at Pakitza. The species accumulation curve for Pakitza is shown in Fig. 4. It is assumed that the asymptote of the curve begins to flatten when the maximum number of species for an area is reached. At Pakitza the curve has reached its asymptote at 34 species. However, the species accumulation curve for Tambopata has not flattened, but increased in 1990 (days 65-70) by 7 species for a total of 41 species (Fig. 5).

319

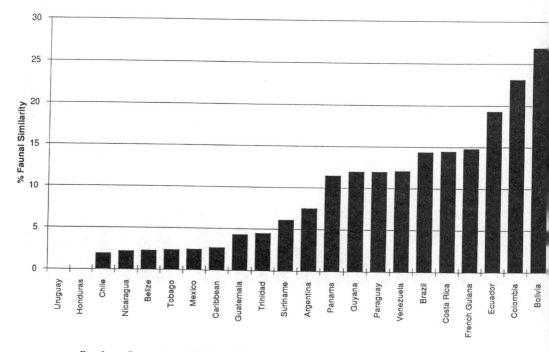

Fig. 3. – *Comparison of % Faunal Similarity between Peru and other Neoptropical countries.*

DISCUSSION

Two species that occur at both Pakitza and Tambopata, *Quesada gigas* and *Fidicina mannifera* are widespread throughout the neotropics. In Costa Rica these species are associated with trees in the family Leguminosae (Young 1980a, 1980b, 1981). These species may also be associated with Leguminosae at Pakitza and Tambopata as this family occurs in all upland forest types. Also, in Costa Rica *F. mannifera* is associated with palms of the genera *Geonoma*, *Iriartea*, *and Socratea* (Young 1973). Palmae is also represented in the upland forests of Pakitza and Tambopata.

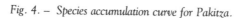

Fig. 4. – *Species accumulation curve for Pakitza.*

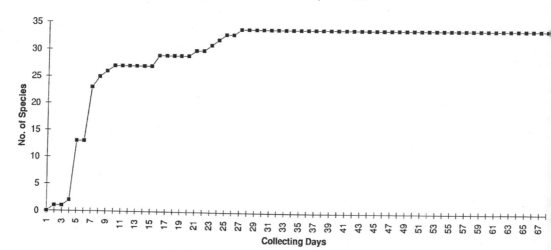

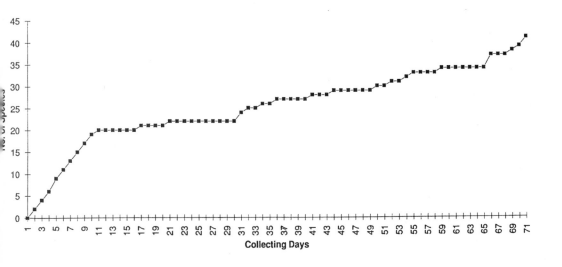

Fig. 5. – *Species accumulation curve for Tambopata.*

Several factors effect species richness, environmental, collecting activity, and human impact. Habitat and season influence species richness. Primary upland forest supports cicada species richness at Pakitza and Tambopata. Primary forest is also important in determining species richness at sites in Costa Rica (Young 1976). Little species richness data is available for specific sites in the neotropics. One lowland rain forest site in Costa Rica supports 12 cicada species. Pakitza and Tambopata support 3 to 3 1/2 times as many species. This is probably due to the influence of the great expanse of lowland rain forest in the Amazon basin compared to the small area of lowland rain forest in northeastern Costa Rica. As the rain forest is cut up into smaller and smaller packages continuity of related habitats is lost and overall biodiversity suffers. Different cicada species also emerge during different seasons of the year. In Costa Rica seasonal emergence patterns exist in both lowland rain forests and dry forests (Young 1976, 1980a, 1980b). The species richness at Pakitza and Tambopata represents a minimum number that should increase when collections can be made during the dry and wet seasons.

Of the two sites, Tambopata had the highest species richness of cicadas with 41 species, Pakitza had 34 species. Factors that may influence species richness at these sites are 1) climate, 2) life zone, and 3) forest flora. The wettest month at both Pakitza and Tambopata is January. Tambopata received an average of approximately 500 mm of rainfall during January of 1982-1983 (Erwin 1975). Pakitza received an average of 340 mm during January 1979, 1983-1990 (data actually from Cocha Cashu, 22 km NW of Pakitza) (Erwin 1991). The wet and dry seasons occur at the same time between the two sites. Tambopata is located at the boundary of Holdridge's Tropical and Subtropical Zones (Erwin 1975), whereas Pakitza is totally in the Tropical Zone (Erwin 1991). Tambopata may contain species that are more associated with the subtropical fauna. Cicadas were collected in two upland forest types at both sites. However, the floral makeup of these forests was somewhat different for the two sites. At Tambopata, Upland Forest Type 1, in terms of individual trees, contained 22% Palmae with *Pourouma minor* (Moraceae) the dominant hardwood. In Upland Forest Type 2, palms made

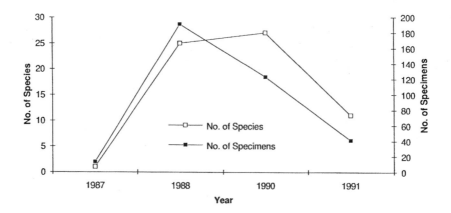

Fig. 6. - *Number of species and specimens collected per year at Pakitza.*

up only 3% of the individuals with *Iryanthera* (Myristicaceae) as the dominant hardwood. At Pakitza, the dissected alluvial terrace forest (Zone 1), in terms of individuals, contained 31.2% Violaceae, 16.3% Palmae, and 10% Moraceae. The old alluvial terrace forest (Zone 3) contained 16% Leguminosae, 16.3% Palmae, and 10% Moraceae.

Collecting activity influences species richness in the broader sense as depicted in Fig. 2. French Guiana is more diverse than Guyana and Suriname, because of recent collections (Boulard 1985, 1986a, 1986b). Ecuador owes its high species richness, in part, to a resident collector (Goding 1925). Goding increased Ecuador's fauna from 15 to 48 species. Torres collected extensively in Argentina and described many new species (Torres 1942, 1945, 1948a, 1948b, 1949, 1958a, 1958b, 1963, 1964). Cicadas of Costa Rica were studied by Young (1972, 1974, 1973, 1975, 1980a, 1980b, 1981). Distant treated Mexico and Central America (1881) documenting 47 species. Jacobi (1907) monographed 73 species of the Andean region which included Colombia, mountains of northern Venezuela, Ecuador, Peru, Bolivia, and Chile. As individual sites, Pakitza and Tambopata have a high degree of species richness. Only 4 countries, excluding Peru, have more cicadas than Tambopata, and 5 countries are more diverse than Pakitza. Both sites are more diverse than any Central American country.

Conclusions by Young (1976) indicate that human impact, such as clearing primary forest for agriculture can greatly influence species richness. At localities where some remnant primary forest is present, as along streams or on steep hillsides, the cicada fauna is rich. Areas that were cleared of primary forest and replaced by old secondary forest probably had large scale local extinction of the cicada fauna (Young 1976). Since there has been no human impact on Pakitza and Tambopata these sites can act as bench marks for understanding species richness as other sites in the neotropics are surveyed.

Faunal similarity (FS) between Pakitza and Tambopata was 50%. This is an index that can be used to compare faunas between sites. Fig. 3 compares the FS between Peru and other neotropical countries. The FS is highest with Bolivia. The majority of shared species with Bolivia are of Andean origin, as are the faunas of Colombia and Ecuador. In French Guiana and Brazil the shared fauna is Amazonian in origin. The Costa Rican shared fauna is generally lowland tropical with a few widespread species. Low FSs of Central America and Mexico indicate a different fauna than that of Peru and similar South American countries. The south temperate countries of Chile and Uruguay have a low FS.

Effort of collecting was quantified as number of collecting days. Different collectors were involved in collecting cicadas, so recording the collecting dates on the labels were not consistent. A total of 67 days were spent collecting at Pakitza and 70 days at Tambopata. When a species accumulation curve approaches its asymptote, it can be concluded that number of species at a site is reaching its maximum, and further collecting will have a negligible effect on species accumulation. In Fig. 4 the species accumulation curve for Pakitza has reached an asymptote for the transitional period between the dry and wet seasons. The 34 species at Pakitza can be considered a minimum number. In 1990 (days 65-70) 7

Fig. 7. - Number of species and specimens collected per year at Tambopata.

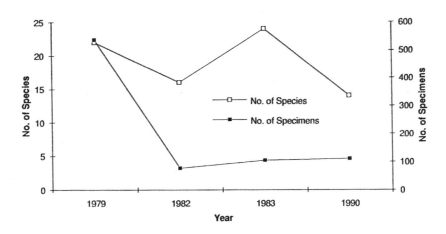

additional species were added to Tambopata's fauna. These additional species indicates that Tambopata has probably not quite reached its maximum species richness for this time of year. The 41 species at Tambopata can be considered a minimum number. These numbers will undoubtedly increase when these sites are collected in other seasons. Cicadas in Costa Rica show seasonality where some species only emerge during a particular season (Young 1976, 1980a, 1980b).

When collecting at Pakitza in 1987 and 1988-1991, it was noted that the even numbered years had more numbers and species of cicadas. The daytime chorusing was extremely loud and very noticeable. The opposite was true during the odd numbered years. Daytime chorusing was infrequent and fewer numbers and species of cicadas were collected (Fig. 6). However, at Tambopata (Fig. 7) it seems the opposite is true, more species were collected during the odd numbered years. This is a preliminary observation that needs to be confirmed by continued collecting at both sites.

Very little is known about cicada diversity at specific sites in the neotropics. Tambopata is probably the best known for insect diversity. Tambopata is the most species rich area in the world for the following taxonomic groups: 1). Spiders (Coddington et al. 1991), 2). Odonata (Paulson 1985), 3). Tiger beetles (Pearson 1985), 4). Asilidae (Fisher 1985), and 5). Tabanidae (Wilkerson and Fairchild 1985). The cicada data also support these findings.

ACKNOWLEDGEMENTS

I would like to thank Terry L. Erwin for suggesting this project and for field assistance. Many Peruvian students helped with collecting during 1988 and 1990. Funding was provided by the Smithsonian Institution's BIOLAT Program.

LITERATURE CITED

Boulard, M. 1982. Une nouvelle cigale néotropicale, halophile et crépusculaire (Homoptera, Cicadoidea). Revue fr. Ent. 4:108-112.

Boulard, M. 1985. Nouvelles cigales guyano-amazoniennes du genre *Carineta* (Homoptera, Tibicinidae). Nouv. Revue Ent. 2:415-429.

Boulard, M. 1986a. Une singulière évolution morphologique: Celle d'un appareil stridulant sur les genitalia des males de *Carineta*. Description de cinq espèces nouvelles (Hom. Tibicinidae). Annls Soc. ent. Fr. 22:191-204.

Boulard, M. 1986b. *Orialella aerizulae* n. sp., cigale nouvelle de la forêt guyanaise (Hom. Cicadoidea). L'Entomologiste. 42:345-347.

Coddington, J. A., C. E. Griswold, D. Silva Dávila, E. Peñaranda, and S. F. Larcher. 1991. Designing and testing sampling protocols to estimate biodiversity in tropical ecosystems. *In*, Dudley, E. C. (Ed.). The Unity of Evolutionary Biology: Proceedings of the Fourth International Congress of Systematic and Evolutionary Biology, pp. 44-60. Dioscorides Press, Portland, OR.

Distant, W. L. 1881. Biologia Centrali-Americana. Insecta. Rhyncota. Hemiptera-Homoptera. 1:1-21.

Duffels, J. P. and P. A. Van der Laan. 1985. Catalogue of the Cicadoidea (Homoptera, Auchenorhyncha) 1956-1980. Series Entomologica Volume 34. 414 pp. Dr. W. Junk Publishers, Dordrecht, The Netherlands.

Erwin, T. L. 1985. Tambopata Reserved Zone, Madre de Dios, Perú: History and description of the Reserve. Revista Peruana de Entomología 27:1-8.

Erwin, T. L. 1991a. An evolutionary basis for conservation strategies. Science 253:750-752.

Erwin, T. L. 1991b. Natural history of the carabid beetles at the BIOLAT Biological Station, Río Manu, Pakitza, Perú. Revista Peruana de Entomología 33:1-85.

Fisher, E. M. 1985. A preliminary list of the robber flies (Diptera: Asilidae) of the Tambopata Reserved Zone, Madre de Dios, Perú. Revista Peruana de Entomología 27:25-36.

Metcalf, Z. P. 1962. A bibliography of the Cicadoidea (Homptera: Auchenorhyncha). Contribution from the Entomology Department, North Carolina Agricultural Experiment Station, Paper No. 1373. 229 pp.

Metcalf, Z. P. 1963a. General Catalogue of the Homoptera. Fascicle VIII. Cicadoidea. Part 1, Cicadidae. Section I, Tibiceninae. Section II, Gaeaninae and Cicadinae. Contribution from the Entomology Department, North Carolina Agricultural Experiment Station, Paper No. 1502. 919 pp.

Metcalf, Z. P. 1963b. General Catalogue of the Homoptera. Fascicle VIII. Cicadoidea. Part 2, Tibicinidae. Contribution from the Entomology Department, North Carolina Agricultural Experiment Station, Paper No. 1564. 492 pp.

Paulson, D. R. 1985. Odonata of the Tambopata Reserved Zone, Madre de Dios, Perú. Revista Peruana de Entomologia 27:9-14.

Pearson, D. L. 1985. The tiger beetles (Coleoptera: Cicindelidae) of the Tambopata Reserved Zone, Madre de Dios, Perú. Revista Peruana de Entomologia 27:15-24.

Torres, B. A. 1942. Sobre un nuevo género y cuatro nuevas especies del género *Tettigades* Amy. et Serv. (Homoptera-Cicadidae). Notas Museo Plata 7:253-263.

Torres, B. A. 1945. Revisión de los géneros *Chonosia* Dist. *Mendozana* Dist. y *Derotettix* Berg y algunas interesantes notas cicadidologicas. (Homoptera-Cicadidae). Notas Museo Plata 10:55-82.

Torres, B. A. 1948a. Sobre seis nuevas especies del genero *Carineta* Amy. et Serv. (Homoptera-Cicadidae). Notas Museo Plata 13:113-127.

Torres, B. A. 1948b. *Tettigades blanchardi* nueva especie de cicadido. Notas Museo Plata 13:181-183.

Torres, B. A. 1949. Tres nuevas especies de cicadidos del genero *Tettigades.* Notas Museo Plata 14:181-190.

Torres, B. A. 1958a. Nuevos géneros *Acyroneura* y *Acuticephala, Guaranisaria bicolor* nueva especie (Homoptera-Cicadidae). Neotropica 4:17-26.

Torres, B. A. 1958b. Revisión del género "*Tettigades* " Amy. y Serv. (Homoptera-Cica-didae). Revista Museo La Plata (N.S.) Zoologia 7:51-106.

Torres, B. A. 1963. Desmembración en los géneros *Proarna* Stål y *Tympanoterpes* Stål. Creacion del nuevo genero: *Prasinosoma* (Homoptera, Cicadidae). Revista Societe Uruguay Entomología 5:13-23.

Torres, B. A. 1964. Estudio del genero *Guaranisaria* Distant, *Guaranisaria llanoi* una nueva especie (Homopter-Cicadidae). Anais II Congress of Latin-American Zoology. 1:143-152.

Wilkerson, R. C. and G. B. Fairchild. 1985. A checklist and generic key to the Tabanidae (Diptera) of Peru with special reference to the Tambopata Reserved Zone, Madre de Dios, Perú. Revista Peruana de Entomología 27:37-53.

Young, A. M. 1972. Cicada ecology in a Costa Rican tropical rain forest. Biotropica 4:152-159.

Young, A. M. 1973. Cicada populations on palms in tropical rain forest. Journal of the Palm Society 17:3-9.

Young, A. M. 1974. The population biology of neotropical cicadas. III. Behavioral natural history of *Pacarina* in Costa Rican grasslands. Entomological News 85:239-256.

Young, A. M. 1975. The population biology of neotropical cicadas. I. Emergences of *Procollina* and *Carineta* in Costa Rican montane forest. Biotropica 7:148-158.

Young, A. M. 1976. Notes on the faunistic complexity of cicadas (Homoptera; Cicadidae) in northern Costa Rica. Revista de Biologia Tropical 24:267-279.

Young, A. M. 1980a. Habitat and seasonal relationships of some cicadas (Homoptera:Cicadidae) in central Costa Rica. The American Midland Naturalist 103:155-166.

Young, A. M. 1980b. Seasonal adult emergences of cicadas (Homoptera:Cicadidae) in northwestern Costa Rica. Contributions in Biology and Geology, Milwaukee Public Museum, 40:1-29.

Young, A. M. 1981. Notes on the population ecology of cicadas (Homoptera:Cicadidae) in the Cuesta Angel forest ravine of northeastern Costa Rica. Psyche 8:175-195.

Contribución a la sistemática de las Mutílidas (Hymenoptera) del Perú, en especial las de la Estación Biológica BIOLAT, Río Manu, Pakitza

Diomedes Quintero A. y Roberto A. Cambra T.

Museo de Invertebrados G.B. Fairchild, Estafeta Universitaria, Universidad de Panamá, Panamá.

RESUMEN

La fauna de mutílidas del Perú ha sido una de las menos estudiadas en las Américas, teniendo reportadas sólo 41 especies y una subespecie, en 12 géneros. Mediante muestreos que llevamos a cabo en la Estación Biológica BIOLAT-Pakitza, en Puerto Maldonado, en Lima, y en tres estaciones de EXPLORAMA-Loreto, y con material examinado de museos, reconocemos ahora para el Perú 133 especies y dos subespecies, en 18 géneros, de las cuales 53 no han sido descritas.

Se reportan por primera vez para el Perú los siguientes dos subgéneros y cinco géneros de mutílidas: *Ephuta* (*Ephuseabra* Casal), NUEVO STATUS; *Ephuta* (*Ephutopsis* Ashmead), NUEVO STATUS; *Limaytilla* Casal; *Lomachaeta* Mickel; *Lophostigma* Mickel; *Pertyella* Mickel, y *Vianatilla* Casal. Sólo 8 especies de mutílidas del Perú se conocen por ambos sexos, 6.1% del total de especies reconocidas, muy bajo si se compara con el 43% de Panamá, y 77.5% de Virginia-Maryland, Estados Unidos. Se señalan tres especies, adicionales a las 8, cuyos sexos hemos reconocido han sido descritos como especies separadas; la sinonimia de uno de los dos sexos de esas tres especies se publicará posteriormente. Hemos descubierto recientemente machos de los siguientes cinco géneros, previamente conocidos sólo por hembras: *Calomutilla* Mickel; *Horcomutilla* Casal; *Lophostigma* Mickel; *Pertyella* Mickel, y *Vianatilla* Casal. Hemos incluido a los machos de estos géneros en la clave genérica de mutílidas del Perú. Se ha logrado la asociación sexual de *Lophomutilla* Mickel, 1952, género conocido sólo por hembras, con *Paramutilla* Mickel, 1973, conocido sólo por el holotipo macho, NUEVA SINONIMIA. Se colocan en sinonimia las dos siguientes especies: *Lophomutilla suarezi* Fritz y Pagliano, 1993 es *Lophomutilla denticulata* (Smith, 1855), NUEVA SINONIMIA, y *Xystromutilla tingoensis* Fritz, 1992 es *Xystromutilla mansueta* (Smith, 1879), NUEVA SINONIMIA. Hemos realizado las siguientes cinco NUEVAS COMBINACIONES: *Ephuta* (*Ephutopsis*) *vindex* (Smith, 1879) de *Mutilla v.; Lophomutilla halicta* (Mickel, 1973) de *Paramutilla h.; Pseudomethoca piura* (Casal, 1970) de *Sphinctopsis p.; Traumatomutilla simulatrix* (Smith, 1879) de *Mutilla simulatrix;* y *Xystromutilla mansueta* (Smith, 1879) de *Mutilla mansueta.* En Pakitza hemos encontrado 73 especies y dos subespecies, en 12 géneros y tres subgéneros. Estos records representan 54.1% de la fauna de mutílidas del Perú, lo que señala que esa región posee una gran riqueza de especies. Se ha preparado una clave genérica ilustrada para las mutílidas del Perú, incluyendo tres géneros que se sospecha puedan estar presentes pero que todavía no han sido encontrados: *Calomutilla, Horcomutilla* y *Tobantilla*.

Además, presentamos un listado de las especies de Mutillidae que reconocemos están presentes en el Perú. Algunas de las especies reportadas por primera vez para el Perú son también reportadas aquí por primera vez para otros países (ver Apéndice III, especies marcadas ++). Comparamos la riqueza de géneros y de especies de la fauna de mutílidas del Perú con la de Panamá y la región noreste de Estados Unidos (Maryland y Virginia).

ABSTRACT

The Peruvian mutillid fauna is one of the least known in the Americas; only 41 species and one subspecies, in 12 genera, have been reported. We have carried out field work at the following localities in Perú: Estación Biológica BIOLAT-Pakitza; Puerto Maldonado; Lima; and three EXPLORAMA field stations in Loreto, and we have examined Peruvian mutillids on loan from several museums.

We now recognize, as present in Perú, 133 species and three subspecies, in 18 genera, 53 of them not described. We report for the first time for Perú the following two mutillid subgenera and five genera: *Ephuta* (*Ephuseabra* Casal), NEW STATUS; *Ephuta* (*Ephutopsis* Ashmead), NEW STATUS; *Limaytilla* Casal; *Lomachaeta* Mickel; *Lophostigma* Mickel; *Pertyella* Mickel; and *Vianatilla* Casal. Only eight Peruvian mutillid species are known from both sexes, 6.1% of all Peruvian species we recognize. This percentage is distinctly lower than the 43% for Panamá, and the 77.5%for Virginia-Maryland, USA. We recognize here three species, in addition to the 8 mentioned above, whose sexes were described as separate species. One sex of each of these three species will be synonymyzed in a later publication. We recently discovered males for the following five genera, previously known only from females: *Calomutilla* Mickel, *Horcomutilla* Casal, *Lophostigma* Mickel, *Pertyella* Mickel, and *Vianatilla* Casal. We include these males in the generic key to Peruvian mutillids. We also associate *Paramutilla* Mickel, 1973, known from a single male, with *Lophomutilla* Mickel, 1952, know only from females, NEW SYNONYMY. We place in synonymy the following two species: *Lophomutilla suarezi* Fritz and Pagliano, 1993, as *Lophomutilla denticulata* (Smith, 1855), NEW SYNONYMY; and *Xystromutilla tingoensis* Fritz, 1992, as *Xystromutilla mansueta* (Smith, 1879), NEW SYNONYMY. The following five NEW COMBINATIONS are made: *Ephuta* (*Ephutopsis*) *vindex* (Smith, 1879), N. COMB. from *Mutilla v.; Lophomutilla halicta* (Mickel, 1973), N. COMB. from *Paramutilla h.; Pseudomethoca piura* (Casal, 1970), N. COMB. from *Sphinctopsis p.; Traumatomutilla simulatrix* (Smith, 1879), N. COMB. from *Mutilla simulatrix;* and *Xystromutilla mansueta* (Smith, 1879), N. COMB. from *Mutilla mansueta*. We report here for Pakitza 73 mutillid species and one subspecies, in 12 genera and three subgenera. These recods represent 56.5% of the mutillid fauna of Perú, indicating that the region has a high biodiversity. We provide an illustrated generic key for the mutillids of Perú, including the following three genera, suspected to be present but not found yet: *Calomutilla, Horcomutilla,* and *Tobantilla*. In addition, we present a list of all Peruvian mutillid taxa we currently recognize. We also present new distribution records for some of the species reported for the firt time for Perú (see Appendix III, species marked with ++). We compare the mutillid diversity of Perú with that of Panamá and northeastern United States (Maryland and Virginia).

INTRODUCCIÓN

La fauna de mutílidas del Perú ha sido una de las menos estudiadas en las Américas, teniendo reportados hasta el presente solamente unas 41 especies y una subespecie en 12 géneros. Este trabajo presenta una revisión preliminar de la fauna de mutílidas del Perú, nos hemos basado en colectas que hemos llevado a cabo en seis localidades del Perú, en una revisión bibliográfica, y en el estudio del material depositado en colecciones de referencia.

Para que la publicación sea lo más útil posible, con cierta reluctancia hemos incluido algunos cambios taxonómicos que habíamos reconocido y que hubiésemos preferido publicar posteriormente, en trabajos separados, de revisiones genéricas, pero esto podría haber tomado varios años adicionales de espera para dar a conocer esa información. Las asociaciones sexuales de los siguientes cinco géneros se han efectuado recientemente: *Calomutilla* Mickel (en una especie que no ha sido previamente descrita); *Horcomutilla* Casal (en *H. krombeini* Casal); *Lophostigma* Mickel (en *L. cincta* (du Buysson), ver Cambra y Quintero, en prensa); *Pertyella* Mickel (en *P. beata* (Cameron)), *Vianatilla* Casal (en una especie que no ha sido previamente descrita). Estos géneros eran conocidos únicamente por hembras, sus machos no descritos se describirán posteriormente, se han incluido en la clave genérica de la Mutillidae de Perú. Solamente consideramos válidos a 11 de los 12 géneros previamente reportados para el Perú. El género *Sphinctopsis* Mickel, con una especie reportada para el Perú, lo colocamos nuevamente en sinonimia bajo *Pseudomethoca*, como originalmente lo hizo Krombein (1951).

MATERIALES Y MÉTODOS

SITIOS DE ESTUDIO Y MÉTODOS DE COLECTA

Del 28 de octubre al 17 de noviembre de 1990 (finales de la estación seca) se efectuaron colectas en Lima y sus alrededores, y en las siguientes tres estaciones de EXPLORAMA, Dpto. de Loreto, Perú: Inn (40 km NE de Iquitos, en el Río Amazonas); Lodge (aproximadamente 50 km NE de Iquitos, en el Río Yanomono,

3°23'S, 72°52'O); Camp (unos 70 km NE de Iquitos, 3°10'S, 72°54'O, en el Río Sucusari). La región amazónica superior del Perú, donde se localizan las estaciones EXPLORAMA, ha sido caracterizada como selva tropical de tierras bajas inundables, cuyos niveles de agua fluctúan hasta 10 m por año (Harris y Davenport 1992). Dos viajes adicionales al Perú, con el grupo BIOLAT, del 13 de febrero al 13 de marzo de 1992 (estación lluviosa), y del 18 de junio al 10 de julio de 1993 (estación seca), nos permitieron efectuar colectas en el Dpto. Madre de Dios: Puerto Maldonado, y Pakitza: Río Manu [12°7'S, 70°58'O, detalles sobre la Zona de Reserva Manu y Pakitza en Erwin 1990]. En Panamá los datos básicos de muestreos de mutílidos se presentan en Cambra y Quintero (1992). En Estados Unidos los datos de los sitios donde se colocaron las trampas Malaise en Virginia y en Maryland aparecen en Smith (1991). Los muestreos en Pakitza se efectuaron manualmente (con pinzas y redes entomológicas), mediante cuatro trampas Malaise (Townes modificadas, de malla fina), 40 trampas amarillas (platos llenos hasta el borde con agua con pequeña cantidad de detergente), y 60 trampas "pitfall" llenas con glicol de etileno. Las trampas "pitfall" resultaron negativas para mutílidas pero en corto tiempo atrapaban gran cantidad de hormigas.

COLECCIONES DE REFERENCIA, ACRONIMIAS, ESPECÍMENES VOUCHER

A continuación se indica el nombre de los curadores y sus respectivas acronimias: Museo de Historia Natural, Universidad Nacional Mayor de San Marcos, Lima, Gerardo Lamas [MUNSM]; American Museum of Natural History, New York, J. G. Rozen [AMNH]; Natural History Museum of Los Angeles County, Los Angeles, Roy R. Snelling [NHMLA]; University of Minnesota Insect Collection, St. Paul, Philip J. Clausen [UMIC]; United States National Museum of Natural History, Smithsonian Institution, Washington D.C., Arnold S. Menke, USDA-Systematic Entomology Laboratory, y Karl V. Krombein, Department of Entomology [USNM]; Pontificia Universidad Católica del Ecuador, Giovanni Onore [PUCE]; Instituto de Zoología, Universidad Central de Venezuela, John E. Lattke [IZV]; The Natural History Museum, London, Tom Huddleston [BMNH]; Museo de Invertebrados G.B. Fairchild, Panamá, D. Quintero A. [MIUP]. Especímenes voucher de todas las especies serán depositados en el USNM, MIUP y MUNSM.

SISTEMÁTICA Y FORMATO DE PRESENTACIÓN

Se ha estudiado el material tipo de mutílidas descrito por Cameron y Smith, depositado en el BMNH, los tipos de mutílidas de Mickel en el UMIC y el USNM, y parte de los tipos de Casal depositados en el AMNH. La clasificación y terminología morfológica que hemos utilizado sigue las revisiones y descripciones taxonómicas de Mickel y Casal, y las categorías supragenéricas son las reconocidas por Brothers (1975). Los géneros se listan alfabéticamente dentro de cada una de las dos subfamilias de Mutillidae: Mutillinae y Sphaeropthalminae. A los miembros de la tribu Sphaeropthalmini se les indica en cual subtribu han sido clasificados mediante una de las dos siguientes abreviaciones: [S] = Sphaeropthalmina, [P] = Pseudomethocina. Para cada uno de los géneros que hemos encontrado en Perú, se les anota información sobre su número total de especies conocidas, distribución geográfica, número de especies previamente reportadas para el Perú y número de especies adicionales que hemos encontrado en Perú. Hemos incluido en este listado genérico alfabético a los tres géneros que consideramos pueden estar presentes en el Perú pero que todavía no se han colectado en ese país. Al número total de especies de cada género presentes en Perú, sigue el número de especies colectadas por ambos sexos (abreviado MH), o un sólo sexo (M, machos; H, hembras), y número de especies que no han sido previamente descritas. El material que se menciona como nuevo será descrito separadamente. Luego se indica el número de especies halladas en Pakitza, indicando entre paréntesis lo que representa en porcentaje (%) del número total de especies de ese género presentes en Perú. A continuación se presentan tres apéndices: 1. Clave Genérica de Mutillidae del Perú. 2. Cuadro comparativo de biodiversidad de mutílidas: géneros y especies del Perú, Panamá y la región noreste de Estados Unidos (Maryland-Virginia). 3. Listado de las especies de mutílidas del Perú. Para abreviar, no se le han incluido las fechas de colecta ni el nombre del colector a las nuevas colectas reportadas.

RESULTADOS Y DISCUSIÓN

GÉNEROS DE MUTILLINAE

Ephuta (*Ephuta* Say, 1836)

Ephuta es el género de Mutillidae del Nuevo Mundo con el mayor número de especies descritas, aproximadamente 211 especies, distribuidas desde Canadá hasta Argentina. El género *Ephuta* es objeto de revisión taxonómica por Quintero (en preparación), quien reconoce cuatro subgéneros, de los cuales tres se tratan en el presente trabajo. Solamente las tres siguientes especies del género *Ephuta* habían sido reportadas para el Perú: E. (*Ephuta*) *inca* Suárez, 1970, hembra, Sullana, Dpto. Piura; E (*Ephuta*) *peruviana* (André, 1905), macho, Vilcanota, Dpto. Cusco; E. (*Ephuta*) *viata* Casal, 1968, machos paratipos del Río Marañón, Dpto. Amazonas y Tingo María, Dpto. Huánuco, y de Bolivia. A la distribución de *E. trifida* (Gerstaecker, 1874), macho, reportada por Mickel en 1952 (Guyana, Venezuela y Brasil), Nonveiller (1990) añade al Perú, sin indicar datos de colecta. Reconocemos ahora que E. *trifida* está presente también en Panamá, Ecuador y Perú; hemos indicado los sitios de donde se han examinado nuevas colectas. Hemos encontrado en Perú 31 especies de *Ephuta*, adicionales a las cuatro

331

anteriormente mencionadas, reconociendo un total de 35 especies de *Ephuta* presentes en ese país (1 MH, 18 M, 16 H), de las cuales 15 especies (9M, 6H) no han sido previamente descritas. Se reportan por primera vez para el Perú las siguientes 11 especies de *Ephuta*, indicándose los países donde habían sido previamente reportadas: *E. abadia* (Cresson, 1902), macho, Brasil y Guyana; *E. argentula* (D. Torre, 1897), macho, Brasil; *E. birigua* Casal, 1969, hembra, Brasil; *E. cronopia* Casal, 1970, hembra, Brasil; *E. egeria* Mickel, 1952, hembra, Guyana; *E. elvina* Mickel, 1952, hembra, Guyana; *E. emarginata* Mickel, 1952, macho, Guyana, Trinidad; *E. erichto* Mickel, 1952, hembra, Guyana; *E. flavidens* Mickel, 1952, macho, Guyana, Brasil, Panamá; *E. fugax* (Smith, 1879), macho, Brasil, Guyana, Guiana Francesa; *E. indiscreta* Mickel, 1952, macho, Guyana. En Pakitza hemos hallado 25 especies de *Ephuta* (71.4% de las *Ephuta* del Perú).

A las hembras de *Ephuta* se les encuentra caminando preferentemente sobre la hojarasca húmeda en áreas de bosque con dosel. Presentan un comportamiento muy distintivo, que no se ha observado en otras hembras de mutílidas: elevan su abdomen, en posición casi perpendicular a la de su cuerpo y en esa forma caminan cortos trechos, manteniendo su tórax y cabeza alejados del substrato, con las patas estiradas como si fuesen zancos. Entonces reanudan su caminado normal (con "bobbing" del abdomen) por corto trecho, alternándolo luego con el anteriormente descrito. La posición perpendicular del abdomen, con cortas oscilaciones antero-posteriores, se sospecha que logra una elevación al máximo del área pigidial, que le facilita a la hembra la dispersión de moléculas feromonas en el aire para atraer a los machos, mecanismo más probable (comunicación química en vez de visual) para lograr la asociación de con-específicos previo al cortejo.

Al igual que en *Timulla* (ver Cambra y Quintero 1993), Deyrup y Manley (1986) reportan que en *Ephuta* hay transporte forético de la hembra áptera por el macho alado, fenómeno asociado con el apareamiento, aunque los detalles de la foresis en *Ephuta* no han sido todavía descritos. Las hembras de *Ephuta*, a diferencia de las de *Timulla*, parecen ser parasitoides con alta especificidad: solamente ectoparasitan pupas de pompílidas. Sin embargo, esta especificidad está pobremente sustentada por sólo cuatro reportes en la literatura.

Ephuta (*Ephuseabra* Casal, 1968) NUEVO STATUS

Los machos de este subgénero se caracterizan por presentar el hipopigio fuertemente convexo, con una profunda muesca en el borde caudal (Casal 1968); sus hembras son desconocidas. Casal (1968) incluye una especie, *E. morra morra* Casal, de Brasil y Argentina, con una subespecie de Brasil, *E. morra suava* Casal. El material tipo ha sido examinado; hemos colectado los siguientes 14 machos que reconocemos representan una subespecie no descrita de *E.* (*Ephuseabra*) *morra* : cuatro en Pakitza, y diez en Panamá (Cruce de Mono, Parque Nacional Darién). Se considera aquí a *Ephuseabra* como un subgénero de *Ephuta*.

Ephuta (*Ephutopsis* Ashmead, 1904) NUEVO STATUS

Este subgéneró se distingue por presentar machos con escutelo biespinoso, hipopigio con un diente en la porción mesal del borde caudal y valvas penianas con un par de dientes en el extremo caudal del borde ventral. Las hembras de *E. (Ephutopsis)* poseen una distintiva carena media longitudinal en el vértex, y con uno o ambos de los siguientes caracteres: una espinita cerca del margen posterior medio del hipopigio o una espina en la cara ventral distal de coxas anteriores. La presente información morfológica ha sido obtenida de asociaciones sexuales todavía no publicadas. La especie tipo de este subgénero es *E. (Ephutopsis) trinidadensis* (Ashmead, 1904). *Arcasina* Nagy, 1970, subgénero monotípico (*A. chendisa* Nagy, 1970, tipo en AMNH, examinado) consideramos que representa un sinónimo de *Ephuta* (*Ephutopsis*); la sinonimia formal se llevará a cabo como parte de la revisión genérica de *Ephuta* (en preparación). Al momento, D.Q.A. ha reconocido diez especies dentro de este subgénero y a cinco de ellas se les han asociado ambos sexos. Cuatro especies de este subgénero las hemos encontrado en Perú y las reportamos aquí por primera vez para ese país, indicándose los países donde habían sido previamente reportadas: *E.* (*Ephutopsis*) *championi* (Cameron, 1894), macho y hembra, Panamá; *E.* (*Ephutopsis*) *singularis* (Spinola, 1841), macho, Guiana Francesa, Brasil, Surinam, Guyana; *E.* (*Ephutopsis*) *solitaria* (Smith, 1879), hembra, Brasil, colectada también por nosotros en Panamá; *E. (Ephutopsis)vindex* (Smith, 1879), hembra (Holotipo 15.990, BMNH, examinado), Brasil, NUEVA COMBINACION de *Mutilla vindex*. Esta última especie es listada por Nonveiller (1990) como "Incertae sedis". Se colectaron cuatro hembras de *E.* (*E.*)*vindex* en Pakitza, dos durante la estación seca de 1993. Tres machos colectados en Pakitza, dos durante la estación seca y uno en la lluviosa, representan una especie no descrita cercana a *E. (Ephutopsis) forceps* Schuster, 1945 (especie de Costa Rica y Panamá), la cual consideramos muy probablemente sea del sexo opuesto de *E.* (*E.*) *vindex*.

Timulla Ashmead, 1899

Género considerado por Cambra y Quintero (1992) como el de mayor número de especies de Mutillidae en América. Actualmente reconocemos que *Ephuta* es el género de mutílidas de América con el mayor número de especies. *Timulla* incluye 172 especies y 3 subespecies neotropicales (Nonveiller 1990), distribuidas desde Mexico hasta Argentina. Solamente las siguientes cinco especies de *Timulla* habían sido reportadas para el Perú, indicando sus lugares de colecta: *T. cordillera* Mickel, 1938, macho, Pto. Bermúdez, Río Pichis, Dpto. Pasco; *T. hedone* Mickel, 1938, macho, Trujillo y Pacasmayo, Dpto. La Libertad, Lima; Dpto. Lima; *T. inca* Mickel, 1938, hembra, Lima, Dpto. Lima, y Ecuador; *T. manga* (Cresson, 1902), macho y hembra, Chanchamayo, Dpto. Junín, y Brasil; *T. mulfordi* Mickel, 1938, hembra, Pachitea, Dpto. Huánuco (hembra de *T. cordillera*, sinonimia en Cambra y Quintero, 1993). Consideramos que el macho de *T. inca* Mickel, colectado en

Lima y descrito por Giner (1944) con un signo de interrogación colocado después de *inca* (indicando que Giner no estaba seguro de su asociación sexual), es *T. hedone* Mickel porque su descripción y el tergo distal ilustrado (Giner 1944) son idénticos al del holotipo de *T. hedone*, examinado. La sinonimia formal *T. hedone* (nombre con precedencia en el número de página) con *T. inca*, se llevará a cabo en publicación separada. También, la descripción de 16 especímenes machos de *T. brancoensis*, especie cuyo macho no ha sido descrito. Hemos encontrado en el Perú las siguientes tres especies adicionales de *Timulla* : *T. brancoensis* Mickel, 1938, Brasil (Cambra y Quintero, 1993), y *T. sieberi* Mickel, 1938, Brasil (Cambra y Quintero, 1993), y el macho de una especie de *Timulla* que no ha sido previamente descrita, colectado en EXPLORAMA Camp, Dpto. Loreto. Del total de seis especies de *Timulla* que están presentes en el Perú (4MH, 1M, 1H) (reconociendo a *inca* y *hedone* como los dos sexos de una sola especie), dos especies (33.3%) están presentes en Pakitza.

Los machos de *Timulla* presentan un patrón generalizado de coloración "Batesian": abdomen con tegumento predominantemente naranja-rojizo, cabeza y tórax con tegumento negro. Esta coloración de los machos, de otra forma indefensos, la interpretamos como un mecanismo pasivo de defensa, mimetizando modelo aposemático de complejos Müllerianos exhibidos en una amplia zona geográfica de América por diversos grupos de himenópteros, con excelentes mecanismos defensivos: pompílidas y esfécidas.

Géneros de Sphaeropthalminae: Sphaeroptalmini

Atillum André, 1903 [P]

Género exclusivo de América del Sur, con 51 especies y una subespecie descritas, distribuidas entre 5° de latitud sur, en la seca región noreste del Brasil y 38°S, en Argentina (Mickel 1943). Solamente tres especies han sido previamente reportadas para el Perú: *A. blandulum* Mickel, 1943, *A. limbatum* Mickel, 1943 (probablemente la hembra de *blandulum*, según Mickel, ambos colectados en Sicuani, Dpto. Cusco), y *A. rubriceps* (Schrotky, 1902), hembra, Argentina y Brasil. Nonveiller (1990) omite a Brasil de la distribución conocida para *A. rubriceps* y le añade a Perú y Chile, sin localidades, distribución que necesita ser verificada. *Atillum optabile* Mickel, 1943, especie conocida solamente del holotipo macho, tiene datos de colecta muy imprecisos ("Hauté Plateaux" del Perú y Bolivia), y es probable que no haya sido colectada del Perú. El género *Atillum* aparentemente está ausente de la región amazónica (Mickel 1943), y no ha sido encontrado en Pakitza, donde es muy probable que no se localice, por ser una zona baja y húmeda. Si asumimos que *blandulum* y *limbatum* son los dos sexos de una misma especie, reconoceríamos a tres especies de *Atillum* (1MH, 1M, 1H) como presentes en el Perú.

Calomutilla Mickel, 1952 [P]

Género con cuatro especies descritas de Brasil y Guyana, cuyos machos se desconocían. El género *Calomutilla* no ha sido reportado para el Perú y tampoco lo hemos encontrado en ese país, pero sospechamos que pueda estar presente por lo que se ha incluido en la clave genérica de mutílidas del Perú. Recientemente hemos descubierto en Panamá al macho de una especie de *Calomutilla* que no ha sido descrita. También, hemos colectado en Sâo Luis, Maranhao, Brasil, el macho de otra especie de *Calomutilla* no descrita previamente. Estos descubrimientos nos permiten incluir al macho de *Calomutilla* en la clave genérica de mutílidas del Perú.

Dasymutilla Ashmead, 1899 [S]

Género con 53 especies y cuatro subespecies neotropicales; la mayoría de las especies de Dasymutilla han sido descritas del Hemisferio Norte. Algunos machos de los géneros *Dasymutilla* y *Traumatomutilla* poseen una fosa llena de pelos en el segundo esternito abdominal (Fig.7), siendo los únicos dos géneros en América que presentan esta característica. Solamente tres especies de *Dasymutilla* han sido reportadas para el Perú y ninguna de ellas ha sido encontrada en Pakitza. Su ausencia de Pakitza se explica porque las especies de *Dasymutilla* tienen marcada preferencia por habitats áridos y secos. Fácilmente se pueden colectar machos y hembras de *D. blattoserica* (Kohl, 1882) en Lima y en otros lugares del Departamento de Lima (Valle del Chillón, Chontay, Puruchuco y Atocongo). También hemos examinado especímenes de *D. blattoserica* colectados en San Pedro de Lloc, Dpto. La Libertad, 1H [MUNSM], y entre Jayanca-Motupe, Dpto. Lambayeque, 2H [MUNSM]. Si asumimos que *D. homochroma* Suárez, 1970, hembra, y *D. peruviana* Suárez, 1970, macho, son los dos sexos de una misma especie, entonces reconoceríamos sólo a dos especies de *Dasymutilla* (2MH) para el Perú. Suárez (1970) sugirió esta sinonimia basado en que los holotipos fueron colectados en San Miguel [de Cajamarca], en la misma fecha, y por el mismo colector.

Euspinolia Ashmead, 1903 [P]

Género con 14 especies descritas, con distribución limitada a Chile, Argentina y Perú. Dos especies, conocidas solamente por hembras, han sido reportadas para el Perú: *E. krombeini* Casal, 1964, Sullana, Dpto. Piura, y *E. rufula* Mickel, 1938, Verrugas, Dpto. Lima. Las especies de *Euspinolia* han sido colectadas de lugares secos por lo que no se espera que se encuentren en Pakitza.

Hoplocrates Mickel, 1937 [P]

Las 39 especies y tres subespecies de este género presentan una amplia distribución en América del Sur, con una sola especie presente en Panamá (Cambra y Quintero 1992). *Hoplocrates* y *Atillum* son los únicos géneros de

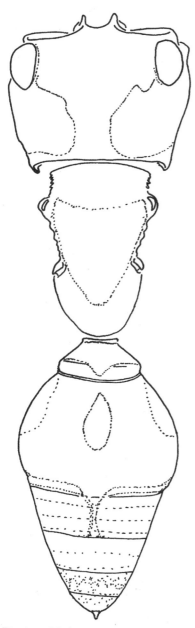

Fig. 1.– *Hoplocrates armata (Klug)*, hembra, habitus [Tachigali trail, Pakitza, Madre de Dios].

Diómedes Quintero A. y Roberto A. Cambra T.

Mutillidae de América cuyas hembras poseen 13 segmentos antenales (Mickel 1941). Ocho especies de *Hoplocrates* han sido reportadas del Perú (ver Apéndice III), todas conocidas por un sólo sexo. Nosotros hemos encontrado en Perú dos especies adicionales, cuyos machos se desconocen: *H. armata* (Klug, 1821), especie previamente conocida del Brasil y Bolivia; *H. oblectanea* Mickel, 1941, especie conocida únicamente por su material tipo del Brasil. Solamente una de las 10 especies de *Hoplocrates* del Perú (3M, 7H) está presente en Pakitza (10%).

Hoplomutilla Ashmead, 1899 [P]

Género con 93 especies y diez subespecies descritas, en su mayoría distribuidas en América del Sur. En Perú se han reportado previamente nueve especies y una subespecie de *Hoplomutilla* (ver Apéndice III). Nosotros hemos colectado las siguientes tres especies adicionales: *H. lanicia* Mickel, 1939, macho, conocida previamente sólo de Bolivia; *H. superba superba* (Gerstaecker, 1874), reportada previamente sólo de Colombia; *H. valeria* Casal, 1961, hembra, previamente conocida sólo del Amazonas, Brasil. Reconocemos ahora un total de doce especies y una subespecie (2M, 11H) de *Hoplomutilla* para el Perú, todas conocidas de un solo sexo. En Pakitza encontramos solamente tres especies y una subespecie de *Hoplomutilla* (30.8%).

Horcomutilla Casal, 1962 [P]

Género con doce especies descritas, todas en base a hembras, distribuidas desde Panamá (Cambra y Quintero 1992) hasta Argentina. Hasta el presente no ha sido reportado, ni hemos examinado especímenes de *Horcomutilla* del Perú. Sin embargo, consideramos que es muy probable que esté presente en el Perú. Las especies de *Horcomutilla* han sido colectadas tanto de áreas degradadas como de bosques tropicales húmedos. Recientemente hemos logrado asociar los dos sexos de *Horcomutilla krombeini* Casal, 1965, en Panamá, lo que nos ha permitido reconocer sus machos, previamente desconocidos (Cambra y Quintero 1992), y ubicarlos en la clave genérica de mutílidas del Perú. El macho de *H. krombeini*, cuya descripción completa se presenta en publicación separada, se distingue por ser el único macho de la Sphaeropthalminae en América que posee el ápice de los gonostilos bífidos. Asumimos que éste carácter debería estar presente en otros machos del mismo género. En efecto, se han encontrado gonostilos bífidos en machos de otra especie del mismo género, colectados en Venezuela. Por lo tanto, hemos establecido la validez de los gonostilos bífidos como carácter genérico de los machos de *Horcomutilla*.

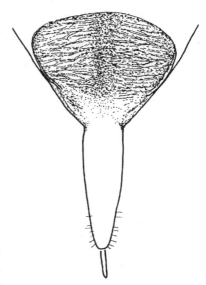

Limaytilla Casal, 1964 [S]

Género que incluye tres especies descritas de Argentina sobre la base de machos, las hembras son desconocidas. Son especies de hábitos crepusculares-nocturnos (Casal, 1964). Reportamos por primera vez a este género para el Perú, sobre la base del siguiente material de una especie que no ha sido descrita: un macho colectado 7km E. de Chaparra, 1450 m altura, Dpto. Arequipa.

Fig. 2.– *Área pigidial definida, Hoplomutilla sociata (Smith), hembra [Castañal trail, Pakitza, Madre de Dios]*

Lomachaeta Mickel, 1936 [S]

Hemos colectado en Pakitza, con trampa Malaise, a un específmen macho cuyas características distintivas son únicas, lo que nos permite ubicarlo en el género *Lomachaeta* Mickel. Las siguientes características de ese macho son diagnósticas: presencia de carena genal (es el único macho de la Shpaeropthalmina en América que la presenta; datos no publicados); forma del primer segmento abdominal; reticulado del tegumento de la cabeza y del tórax; la forma de la cabeza, pequeña y redondeada. Las hembras de este género han sido pobremente colectadas, especímenes son raros en museos; son muy pequeñas de largo corporal, miden menos de 5 mm. Las ocho especies del género *Lomachaeta* presentan una distribución discontinua en América: seis especies se conocen de Estados Unidos, dos de las cuales también están presentes en México, y dos especies de Argentina. Lamentablemente, las hembras de *Lomachaeta* todavía no las hemos podido colectar en Perú. El macho aquí reportado es el único de *Lomachaeta* que ha sido reportado para América del Sur hasta el presente.

Fig. 3.– *Área pigidial no definida, Lophomutilla mocajuba Casal, hembra [EXPLORAMA Lodge, Lake trail, Loreto]*

Lophomutilla Mickel, 1952 [S]

Género básicamente de América del Sur con 21 especies y dos subespecies descritas, cuyos machos se desconocían. Hemos llevado a cabo la asociación sexual

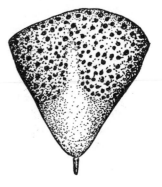

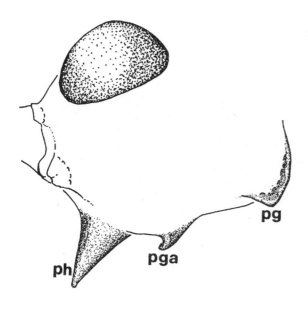

Fig. 4. *Cabeza de Hoplocrates admiranda Mickel, hembra, vista lateral; punturas tegumentarias no han sido dibujadas para destacar procesos; proceso genal (pg), proceso hipostomal (ph) y proceso genal anterior (pga) [EXPLORAMA Lodge, Lake trail, Loreto]*

de hembras de *Lophomutilla* con machos de *Paramutilla* Mickel, 1973, género monotípico descrito de Turrialba, Costa Rica, y reconocido sólo por el holotipo de *P. halicta* Mickel (macho criado de una celda de la abeja halíctida, *Augochlorella edentata* Michener). Hemos colectado la hembra de *P. halicta* en la localidad tipo, y es distintamente una *Lophomutilla, Lophomutilla halicta* (Mickel, 1973), NUEVA COMBI-NACIÓN, que será descrita separadamente. Adicionalmente, machos y hembras de una nueva especie de *Lophomutilla* han sido colectados y asociados sexualmente en Panamá. En la clave de géneros del Perú, las características genéricas del macho de *Lopomutilla* corresponden a las descritas por Mickel para *Paramutilla*, y son las características de machos que hemos colectado en EXPLORAMA Inn, Dpto. Loreto, en Panamá y Costa Rica, todos identificados como machos de *Paramutilla*, y asociados con hembras de *Lophomutilla*. Por lo tanto, *Paramutilla* Mickel se coloca en sinonimia bajo *Lophomutilla* Mickel, NUEVA SINONIMIA. Cambra está preparando una revisión formal de *Lophomutilla*, género que ahora reconocemos se distribuye desde Costa Rica hasta Argentina.

Tres especies de *Lophomutilla* han sido previamente descritas del Perú (Fritz 1990, Fritz y Pagliano 1993) (ver Apéndice III). Añadimos las siguientes cuatro especies de *Lophomutilla*, nuevas para el Perú: *L. bucki* Suárez, 1962, especie conocida sólo del holotipo colectado en Brasil; *L. denticulata* (Smith, 1855), especie conocida previamente sólo de Brasil; *L. mocajuba* Casal, 1961, conocida previamente sólo del holotipo de Brasil; *L. staphyloma* (Gerstaecker, 1874), especie conocida previamente sólo de Brasil. Casal (1969a) describe de Argentina cuatro nuevas especies de *Lophomutilla* y señala que una de ellas puede ser *L. staphyloma*. Nonveiller (1990) añade a Argentina a la distribución de *L. staphyloma*, sin detallar datos de colecta. No reconocemos como válida la subespecie creada por Mickel, *L. denticulata guianensis* Mickel, 1952, reportada como presente en Guyana y Surinam. Esta subespecie está basada en pequeñas diferencias de coloración tegumentaria de frente y gena, con respecto a la forma típica de Brasil. Hemos colectado en Pakitza especímenes con ambas coloraciones (10 con la coloración "guianensis" y dos con la coloración "denticulata" típica) por lo que consideramos que la variación de coloración tegumentaria no justifica diferenciación subespecífica. *Lophomutilla suarezi* Fritz y Pagliano, 1993 es *Lophomutilla denticulata* (Smith, 1855), NUEVA SINONIMIA. El tipo de Smith ha sido examinado y presenta la carena genal unida a la fosa periproboscidal; Fritz y

338

Pagliano erróneamente señalaron que no se unía. Por lo tanto, no tiene validez esta única supuesta diferencia entre *L. denticulata* y *L. suarezi* señalada por Fritz y Pagliano (1993). En Pakitza hemos colectado con Malaise, 13 machos de una especie no descrita de *Lophomutilla*, detrás del laboratorio del Campamento BIOLAT, Dpto. Madre de Dios, 1-9 marzo 1992 [MIUP]. De las siete especies de Lophomutilla [1 MH, 1M, 5H] que ahora reconocemos están presentes en Perú, 4 especies han sido colectadas en Pakitza (57.1%).

Lophostigma Mickel, 1952 [S]

Género que incluye a diez especies neotropicales (Cambra y Quintero 1992), cuyos machos eran desconocidos hasta el presente, se extiende desde México hasta Brasil (Cambra y Quintero, en prensa). Recientemente hemos asociado los dos sexos de *Lophostigma cincta* (du Buysson, 1892) en Panamá (Cambra y Quintero, en prensa), lo que nos ha permitido ubicar a machos del género *Lophostigma* en la clave genérica de mutílidas del Perú. Se reporta al género *Lophostigma* por primera vez para el Perú, donde hemos encontrado las siguientes tres especies, dos de las cuáles estan presentes en Pakitza (66.7%): *L. acanthophora* (Dalla Torre, 1897), especie conocida previamente sólo del holotipo de Pará, Brasil; *L. alopha* Mickel, 1952, especie conocida del material tipo de Guyana; *L. simoni* (du Buysson, 1892), especie conocida previamente sólo del holotipo de Corozal, Venezuela.

Pappognatha Mickel, 1939 [P]

Género con 13 especies descritas, distribuido desde Costa Rica hasta Bolivia (Nonveiller 1990). Es el único género de América que tiene hembras y machos con mandíbulas tomentosas, densamente cubiertas con pelos cortos. Se desconoce cuál pueda ser, si alguno, el significado funcional de esta peculiar pubescencia mandibular. Dos especies de *Pappognatha* han sido previamente reportadas para el Perú, sus machos se desconocen: *P. limes* Mickel, 1939, Pozuzo, Dpto. Pasco, y *P. speciosa* Mickel, 1939, Yurimaguas, Dpto. Loreto. Los machos de *Pappognatha* son extremadamente raros (Mickel 1939). Hemos colectado en Pakitza una hembra de *P. speciosa* Mickel y dos machos de una nueva especie de *Pappognatha*, cuya hembra no la pudimos colectar por asociación sexual. De las tres especies de *Pappognatha* que están presentes en Perú, dos especies han sido colec-tadas en Pakitza (66.7%).

Fig. 5.– *Cabeza de Sphaeropthalma (Photopsis) sp., hembra, vista lateral, carena genal ausente; ojos aplanados [Cerca Campus Uni. San Marcos, Lima]*

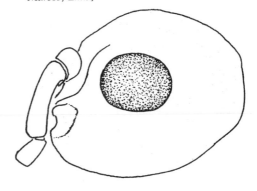

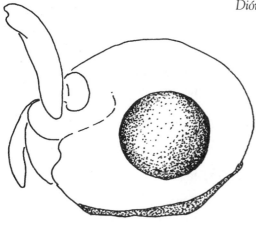

Fig. 6.– *Cabeza de Traumatomutilla weyrauchi* Mickel, hembra, vista lateral, carena genal presente; ojos hemisféricos [Tachigali trail, Pakitza, Loreto]

Pertyella Mickel, 1952 [P]

Género con 17 especies y una subespecie descritas, distribuido desde México hasta Argentina, todas basadas en hembras. Los machos de *Pertyella* no se conocían hasta el presente. Hemos logrado asociar los dos sexos de *P. beata* (Cameron, 1895) en Panamá, lo que nos ha permitido ubicar a los machos de *Pertyella* dentro de la clave genérica del Perú. Nosotros reportamos aquí por primera vez al género *Pertyella* para el Perú, donde reconocemos están presentes cinco especies que no han sido previamente descritas (2 M, 3 H), dos de las cuáles encontramos en Pakitza (40%). Los machos de *P. beata*, al igual que la nueva taxa de *Pertyella* del Perú, y de Panamá (Cambra y Quintero 1992), serán descritos separadamente.

Pseudomethoca Ashmead, 1896 [P]

Junto a *Dasymutilla*, son los dos géneros de *Sphaeropthalminae* con la más amplia distribución en América. Unas ochenta y dos especies de *Pseudomethoca* han sido descritas para el neotrópico, número de especies que incluye las nuevas combinaciones presentadas por Cambra y Quintero (1992), cuatro especies reconocidas como *Hoplognathoca* por Suárez (1963) [género sinónimo de *Pseudomethoca* al transferirse su especie tipo, *Pseudomethoca robinsonii* (Blake, 1871); sinonimia en Mickel 1964, Cambra y Quintero 1992], y otras especies que todavía no hemos transferido a *Pseudomethoca*, pero que reconocemos pertenecen a este género. *Pseudomethoca* es un género proteo, que necesita urgentemente ser revisado. Numerosas especies presentes en América del Sur, que fácilmente se identifican como *Pseudomethoca*, por lo vago de su definición genérica, fueron separadas por Casal en nuevos géneros, pobremente caracterizados y casi imposibles de reconocer y de separar de *Pseudomethoca*. Mickel (1937) transfirió la especie tipo de *Sphinctopsis* a *Pseudomethoca*, *P. melanocephala* (Perty, 1833), hembra. Krombein (1951) coloca a *Sphinctopsis* Mickel, 1928, en sinonimia bajo *Pseudomethoca* (en 1928, Mickel sólo ofrece un nuevo nombre para *Sphinctomutilla* André, nombre pre-ocupado). Hemos examinado material de Brasil determinado como *P. melanocephala* por Mickel y estamos de acuerdo que esta especie es una *Pseudomethoca*. Casal (1970, 1973) revalida a *Sphinctopsis*, y describe siete nuevas especies, sin presentar una justificación adecuada. Consideramos que no existen características genéricas válidas para mantener a *Sphinctopsis*, por lo que revalidamos la sinonimia de *Sphinctopsis* con *Pseudomethoca* propuesta por Krombein (1951).

Sólo una especie de *Pseudomethoca* ha sido previamente reportada para el Perú, *Pseudomethoca piura* (Casal, 1970), NUEVA COMBINACIÓN de *Sphinctopsis p.* Casal. Hemos colectado dos hembras adicionales de esta especie que era conocida solamente por el holotipo hembra, colectado en Piura, Dpto. Piura [USNM, examinado] (ver Apéndice III). Nosotros hemos reconocido la presencia de 16 especies adicionales de *Pseudomethoca* para el Perú, sólo una de ellas previamente descrita: *Pseudomethoca credula* (Cresson, 1902), especie anteriormente conocida sólo del Brasil; 28 hembras adicionales de *P. credula* fueron colectadas en tres localidades diferentes del Perú. En Pakitza hemos colectado 16 de las 19 especies (1MH, 5M, 11H) de *Pseudomethoca* del Perú (76.5%).

Sphaeropthalma (*Photopsis* Blake, 1886) [S]

Subgénero que en el continente americano presenta una curiosa distribución discontinua, que probablemente representa sólo un artefacto de colectas: la mayoría de sus especies se ha reportado de México y Estados Unidos, y unas diez especies de Chile, Argentina, Brasil, Perú y las Islas Galápagos. Las especies de *Photopsis* tienen actividades nocturnas (Ferguson 1962) y se han colectado en regiones áridas o de baja precipitación pluvial, por lo cual sospechamos que no se encuentren presentes en Pakitza. Solamente una especie del género *Sphaeropthalma* ha sido descrita del Perú: *S.* (*Photopsis*) *lenis* André, 1908, cuyo sintipo macho es de Brasil y de Vilcanota, Dpto. Cusco, Perú. Nonveiller (1990, página 89) considera que *lenis* André, junto con una subespecie de *lenis* del Brasil y otras dos especies de André, fue clasificada erróneamente en *Photopsis* por André y que su posición taxonómica necesita ser revisada, pero no da razones. Nosotros hemos encontrado una especie no descrita de *Photopsis* en el Perú, 8 machos y 6 hembras colectados en Lima y sus alrededores, la cual será descrita separadamente.

Traumatomutilla André, 1901 [S]

Género que incluye una 176 especies y 10 subespecies neotropicales (Nonveiller 1990, Cambra y Quintero 1992). Es el género de la Sphaeropthalminae más especioso de América, sin embargo, sólo el 2% de las especies de *Traumatomutilla* se co-

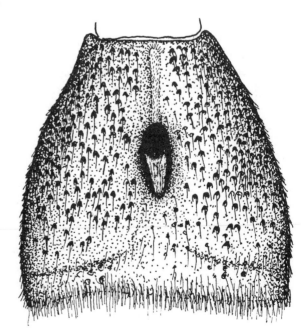

Fig. 7.– *Segundo esternito abdominal con fosa pubescente, Traumatomutilla vidua (Klug), macho [Estación Fontanilha, R. Humboldt, M.T., Brasil]*

Diómedes Quintero A. y Roberto A. Cambra T.

Fig. 8. Mandíbula de Pertyella sp., macho, vista frontal [Campamento BIOLAT, detrás de lab., Pakitza, Madre de Dios]

noce por ambos sexos. Las siguientes cinco especies de *Traumatomutilla* han sido reportadas para el Perú: *T. fascinata* (Smith, 1879), macho sin datos de colecta; *T. indicoides* Mickel, 1945, hembra, de Bolivia y Perú; *T. sodalicia* (Kohl, 1882), hembra, de Brasil, Bolivia, Perú, y Ecuador; *T. vitelligera* (Gerstaecker, 1874), hembra, de Perú, Ecuador, Venezuela, Brasil y Chile; *T. weyrauchi* Mickel, 1945, hembra, Oxapampa, Dpto. Pasco. Hemos examinado al paratipo de *T. weyrauchi*, una hembra de Bolivia, determinada por Mickel [USNM]. También, cinco hembras de esa especie colectadas en los departamentos de Loreto y Madre de Dios, Perú. Consideramos que *T. incerta* (Spinola, 1841), especie distribuida en la Guiana Francesa, Guyana y Brasil, no se puede distinguir de *T. weyrauchi*, y que ambas representan una sola especie, por lo que consideramos que *weyrauchi* deberá colocarse en sinonimia bajo *incerta*. En Perú hemos encontrado las siguientes diez especies adicionales de *Traumatomutilla*: *T. angustata* (André, 1906), hembra; *T. simulatrix* (Smith, 1879), hembra, ambas especies eran previamente conocidas sólo del Brasil, y ocho especies que no han sido descritas. El total de especies de *Traumatomutilla* para el Perú es 14 (3M, 11H). De ese total, siete especies (50%) están presentes en Pakitza.

Vianatilla Casal, 1962 [P]

Género con tres especies descritas para Brasil y Argentina (Nonveiller 1990), cuyos machos se desconocían. Reportamos aquí por primera vez al género *Vianatilla* para el Perú, con una nueva especie que será descrita posteriormente (dos hembras fueron colectadas en Pakitza), y cuya distribución se extiende hasta Panamá. Recientemente hemos descubierto en Panamá al macho de esa especie inédita de *Vianatilla*, completando su asociación sexual, lo que nos ha permitido incluirlo en la clave genérica de mutílidas del Perú.

Xystromutilla André, 1905 [S]

Género con ocho especies descritas, distribuidas desde Nicaragua hasta Argentina (Cambra y Quintero 1992). El macho de *X. turrialba* Casal, 1969b, única especie de *Xystromutilla* cuyo macho es conocido (Cambra y Quintero 1992), nos permite incluirlo en la clave genérica de las mutílidas del Perú. Las especies de *Xystromutilla* han sido colectadas de hábitats muy diversos, desde potreros a bosques húmedos tropicales, aunque parecen tener preferencia por hábitats abiertos, con vegetaciones secundarias o terciarias. El holotipo de *Mutilla mansueta*

Smith, 1879 (Ega, Brasil, Tipo N° 15.1025, BMNH), hembra, fue examinado por R.A.C. y es *Xystromutilla mansueta* (Smith), NUEVA COMBINACIÓN. Esta especie no fue incluida en las revisiones de *Xystromutilla* publicadas por Suárez (1960) y Casal (1969b), y ha sido listada por Nonveiller (1990) como "Incertae sedis". Hemos examinado dos especímenes adicionales de X. *mansueta* de Bolivia y Ecuador. No hemos encontrado diferencia alguna entre X. *mansueta* y la descripción de X. *tingoensis* Fritz, 1992, holotipo de Tingo María, Dpto. de Huánuco, Perú. Por lo tanto, colocamos a X. *tingoensis* Fritz como sinónimo de X. *mansueta* (Smith), NUEVA SINONIMIA. La segunda especie de *Xystromutilla*, que reconocemos está presente en Perú, es una especie que no ha sido previamente descrita. El único especimen hembra examinado fue criado de un nido abandonado de *Sceliphron* (Sphecidae), que había sido utilizado por una Eumenidae, Carretera Cusco-Abancay, Cruce de Cuya, departamento Apurímac, 1900 m, Perú. La celda parasitada fue colectada el 7 de agosto de 1971 por Colin Vardy, y la hembra *Xystromutilla* emergió el 6 de noviembre de ese año.

COMPARACIONES DE LA BIODIVERSIDAD DE LA FAUNA DE MUTÍLIDAS DEL PERÚ

Apenas podríamos decir que hemos logrado elevar los conocimientos sobre la biodiversidad de las mutílidas del Perú a un nivel "alfa". Hemos preparado la primera clave genérica de la Mutillidae de América del Sur en los últimos 40 años (la de Mickel, publicada en 1952 para la Guyana, en la actualidad ha quedado muy incompleta) y hemos reportado por primera vez para el Perú a cinco géneros, de los 18 géneros y dos subgéneros que ahora reconocemos están presentes en ese país, y señalamos a tres géneros adicionales que sospechamos puedan estar presentes pero que no han sido muestreados todavía del Perú. Areas extensas de la geografía del Perú no han sido muestreadas, y no se ha muestreado en forma sistemática la mayor parte del país. La taxa de mutílidas mejor colectada y estudiada es la de los animales de mayor tamaño (8 mm o más), con colores vistosos, y con hábitos poco secretivos. Dentro de éstos, en los géneros *Atillum, Hoplocrates, Hoplomutilla,* y *Dasymutilla* no hemos encontrado especies sin describir en el Perú.

Sospechamos que aproximadamente 30-35% de las especies de mutílidas del Perú todavía no han sido descritas. El número de asociaciones sexuales de la Mutillidae del Perú, al igual que para la mayor parte de

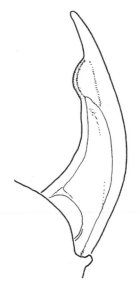

Fig. 9.– *Mandíbula de Pseudomethoca sp. 27, macho, vista frontal [Castañal trail, Pakitza, Madre de Dios]*

América del Sur, es decepcionantemente bajo. Sólo ocho especies de mutílidas del Perú se conocen por ambos sexos, siete de las cuales han sido asociadas por nosotros (las sinonimias de tres especies adicionales, cuyos sexos han sido descritos como especies separadas, se publicarán posteriormente). El conocimiento biológico de las mutílidas del Perú, especialmente sobre las relaciones de parasitismo, es prácticamente nulo. En vista de lo anterior, es extremadamente preliminar, aunque ciertamente muy instructivo, brindar comparaciones de faunas de Mutillidae de zonas con diferentes latitudes, como la que presentamos en el Apéndice II. Con métodos adicionales de colecta, trampas Malaise de malla fina y trampas amarillas, en dos años hemos encontrado en Panamá cinco géneros adicionales (Apéndice II) a los 13 que habíamos reportado (Cambra y Quintero 1992): *Huacotilla, Vianatilla, Lophomutilla, Calomutilla,* y *Protophotopsis.* Especies no descritas de estos cinco géneros fueron colectadas en potreros a orillas del río Perequeté, distrito Chorrera, provincia Panamá. En Pakitza hemos encontrado 73 especies y dos subespecies (54.1% del Perú) en 12 géneros y tres subgéneros (73.7% del Perú, lo que señala una gran riqueza de especies presentes en esa región. La biodiversidad es marcadamente menor en el norte (ver ApéndiceII). El número de individuos colectados de las poblaciones de cada especie es distintivamente menor en Pakitza que en las muestras Malaise de Virginia-Maryland. Esto indica que en las mutílidas de la región neotropical, los individuos viven más dispersos y que probablemente presentan poblaciones formadas por menos individuos. Pudimos observar marcados cambios estacionales en el número de individuos colectados en dos especies de mutílidas de Pakitza: *Timulla brancoensis* y *Pseudomethoca credula.* Durante la estación seca, se observó numerosas hembras de ambas especies caminando sobre el suelo arcilloso, duro, de las áreas abiertas del campamento BIOLAT, activamente inspeccionando sitios de anidación de esfécidas *Sphex* y abejas halíctidas. Durante la estación lluviosa, tanto las hembras como los machos de ambas especies son relativamente raros en Pakitza.

En el presente trabajo formulamos un "índice de asociación sexual" (IAS) para mutílidas, que consideramos servirá para estimar que cantidad de especies, del número total de especies descritas y conocidas sobre la base de un solo sexo en un género, tienen sexo opuesto que no ha sido previamente descrito. Este IAS se basa en las siguientes cifras de Cambra y Quintero (1993): de 25 especies de Timulla que sólo eran conocidas por un solo sexo (TUS), a las que nosotros les completamos sus asociaciones sexuales, únicamente en tres de esas especies el sexo opuesto no había sido previamente descrito. Once de las 22 restantes se colocaron en sinonimia. El IAS se calcula [3/25 x 100 = 12%] escogiendo de los dos sexos al que tiene el mayor número de especies descritas, y multiplicando ese número por 12% (TUS). El 50% del número de especies restantes, después que se substrae del TUS el IAS, se espera que caigan en sinonimia. Se asume que el porcentaje del IAS calculado para Timulla sea válido para otros géneros de mutílidas.

Sobre la base de las asociaciones sexuales de siete géneros que hemos llevado a cabo, podemos calcular el siguiente índice general de asociación sexual para los géneros de mutílidas: aproximadamente un 71.4% [5/7 x 100 = 71.4%] de los géneros cuyo sexo opuesto se desconoce, poseen el sexo opuesto que no ha sido previamente descrito. Es decir, aproximadamente la octava parte de los géneros cuyo sexo opuesto no se conoce, se espera sean colocados en sinonimia.

El coeficiente de similitud genérica (CSG=números de géneros en común/ número total de géneros presentes) de Pakitza con Panamá es muy alto, de un 86%, mientras que el CSG de Pakitza con el noreste de Estados Unidos (Virginia-Maryland) es de 21.4%.

Relaciones Filogenéticas de la Fauna de Mutillidae del Perú

Todavía no se ha llevado a cabo un análisis filogenético de ninguno de los grupos de la Mutillidae, y el conocimiento sobre la distribución de los grupos es muy incompleto. Por lo tanto, actualmente es muy difícil intentar reconstruir las relaciones filogenéticas de la fauna del Perú. Nosotros reconocemos que la fauna de mutílidas del Perú está básicamente compuesta de elementos gondwánicos que han diferenciado regionalmente (ninguno de los géneros de mutílidas de América está presente en otra parte del mundo), e integran tres principales componentes: 1) Elementos que se han diversificado exclusivamente en América del Sur, ejem. *Atillum, Euspinolia, Hoplocrates, Limaytilla* y *Xystromutilla*. Algunos elementos de este grupo parecen haber invadido recientemente el Istmo Centroamericano, ejem. *Xystromutilla turrialba* Casal, especie que se distribuye desde América del Sur hasta Nicaragua (Cambra y Quintero 1992), pero las restantes ocho especies de ese género (incluyendo la especie por describirse del Perú) son exclusivas de América del Sur. 2) Elementos que tienen sus centros de diversidad en América del Sur, y que han invadido y especiado en el Istmo Centroamericano, ejem. *Hoplomutilla, Lophomutilla* y *Pertyella*. 3) Elementos transzonales, que reconocemos como los más antiguos en toda América y los más ricos en especies por amplio margen, están distribuidos desde las regiones templadas Norte y Sur, y presentes en la cuenca amazónica, ejem. *Ephuta, Timulla, Pseudomethoca* y *Sphaeropthalma*. Son los elementos mejor representados en la fauna de mutílidas del Perú . En el Noreste de los Estados Unidos (Virginia y Maryland), esos cuatro géneros suman el 55.5% del total de especies de esa región, mientras que en Perú representan el 48% del total de especies aquí reconocidas.

AGRADECIMIENTO

Agradecemos al programa BIOLAT del Smithsonian Institution por pagar nuestros gastos durante las expediciones de 1992 y 1993 a Pakitza y a su personal por la gran ayuda que nos ha brindado. Nuestro agradecimiento a David R. Smith, USDA Systematic Entomology Laboratory, por separar, montar, etiquetar, y

Diómedes Quintero A. y Roberto A. Cambra T.

prontamente enviarnos por correo las mutílidas de las muestras Malaise capturadas en Pakitza por Brian V. Brown, actualmente en Natural History Museum of Los Angeles County, California. Le damos a Brian nuestras gracias por ayudarnos en las colectas en Pakitza y por poner a nuestra disposición el material de Mutillidae de sus Malaise. Nuestro agradecimiento al Instituto Nacional de Recursos Naturales Renovables, en particular a Roberto Arango e Indra Candanedo, quienes nos ayudaron con permisos y logística en el Parque Nacional Darién, Panamá. Nuestro agradecimiento a la Embajada Británica en Panamá, en particular al Embajador Dr. Thomas H. Malcomson, por financiar parte del viaje de R.A.C. a Inglaterra, y gracias al personal de The Natural History Museum, Londres, por su cooperación durante la visita. Los gastos de viajes al Parque Nacional Darién fueron financiados en parte por la Vicerrectoría de Investigación y Postgrado de la Universidad de Panamá, Fondo Nº 1-4500-91-12. Nuestro agradecimiento al Dr. Karl V. Krombein, Departamento de Entomología, USNM- Smithsonian Institution, y a Dr. Annette Aiello, Smithsonian Tropical Research Institute, quienes leyeron críticamente el manuscrito y ofrecieron valiosas sugerencias para mejorarlo. Agradecemos a todos los colegas peruanos que nos ayudaron en las colectas de Mutillidae en Pakitza. Les agradecemos a todos los curadores de museos que nos han permitido estudiar material de Mutillidae del Perú bajo su cuidado, y en especial a Philip J. Clausen, UMIC, Gerardo Lamas, MUNSM, Giovanni Onore, PUCE, por los préstamos que aquí reportamos. Nuestras gracias a David A. Nickle, USDA Systematic Entomology Laboratory, por permitirnos participar en su expedición a las estaciones de EXPLORAMA en 1990, y a los jóvenes australianos del grupo Earthwatch que nos acompañaron y ayudaron en las colectas. Todos nuestros gastos en ese viaje, y durante la visita de R.A.C. al BMNH, Londres, fueron sufragados por uno de nosotros (D.Q.A.). Gracias le da D.Q.A. a su colega y amigo, Félix Núñez, Universidad de Panamá, por asumir su carga docente cuando efectúa viajes de campo al exterior.

LITERATURA CITADA

Brothers, D.J. 1975. Phylogeny and classification of the aculeate Hymenoptera, with special reference to Mutillidae. Kansas Univ. Sci. Bull., 50:483-648.

Cambra T., R.A. y D. Quintero A. 1992. Velvet Ants of Panamá: Distribution and Systematics (Hymenoptera: Mutillidae). Pp. 459-478, *En* Insects of Panamá and Mesoamerica: Selected Studies (Quintero A.,D. y A. Aiello, eds.). Oxford University Press, Oxford, 720 pp.

____ .1993. Studies on *Timulla* Ashmead (Hymenoptera:Mutillidae): New distribution records and synonymies, and descriptions of previously unknown allotypes. Pan-Pacific Entomol., 69(4): 299-313.

____ . En prensa. The Mexican and Central American Species of Lophostigma Mickel, including a New Species, new distribution records, and taxonomic notes for the genus (Hymenoptera: Mutillidae). Pan-Pacific Entomol., 72..

Casal, O.H. 1964. Revisión de Limaytilla, nuevo género erémico y nocturno de Sphaeropthalmini (Hymenoptera, Mutillidae). Acta Zool. Lilloana, 20: 81-103.

____ . 1968. Aportaciones para el conocimiento de los Mutillidae de la República Argentina. II. Los machos de Ephutini Ashmead (Hymenoptera). Physis, 28(76): 77-93.

____ . 1969a. Sobre Lophomutilla Mickel, 1952 (Hymenoptera- Mutillidae). Rev. Soc. Entomol. Argentina, 31: 57-60.

____ . 1969b. Sobre Xystromutilla André, 1905 (Hymenoptera, Mutillidae). Physis, 29: 47-50.

____ . 1970. Algunas especies relacionadas con Sphinctopsis tucumana (André, 1908) (Hymenoptera, Mutillidae). Physis, 29 (79): 385-389.

____ . 1973. Especies argentinas relacionadas con Sphinctopsis pythagorea (Gerstaecker, 1874) (Hymenoptera, Mutillidae). Physis, 32 (84): 19-23.

Deyrup, M. y D. Manley. 1986. Sex-biased size variation in velvet ants (Hymenoptera: Mutillidae). Florida Entomol., 69 (2): 327-335.

Erwin, T.L. 1990 (1991). Natural History of the carabid beetles at the BIOLAT Biological Station, Río Manu, Pakitza, Perú. Rev. Peruana Entomol., 33: 1-85.

Ferguson, W.E. 1962. Biological Characteristics of the Mutillid subgenus Photopsis and their Systematic Value (Hymenoptera). Univ. California publ. Entomol., 27:1-92.

Fritz, M.A. 1990 (1989). Notas taxonómicas sobre los géneros *Lophomutilla* y *Pertyella* (Hymenoptera: Mutillidae). Revista Soc. Entomol. Argentina, 48(1-4): 129-142.

Fritz, M.A. 1992. Sobre mutílidos neotropicales nuevos y conocidos (Hymenoptera: Mutillidae). Gayana Zool. 56:13-19.

Fritz, M.A. y G. Pagliano. 1993. Sobre *Lophomutilla* Mickel y *Pertyella* Mickel (Hymenoptera Multillidae sic). Boll. Soc. entomol. ital., Genova, 124 (3): 209-220.

Giner, J. 1944. Algunos himenópteros del Museo de Barcelona (Fams): Sphecidae, Psammocharidae y Mutillidae (Him. acul.). Bol. Real Soc. Española Hist. Natur., 42: 345-369.

Harris, S.C. y L.J. Davenport. 1992. New species of microcaddisflies from the Amazon region, with special reference to Northeastern Perú (Trichoptera: Hydroptilidae). Proc. Entomol. Soc. Wash., 94 (4): 454-470.

Krombein, K.V. 1951. Mutillidae. *En* Hymenoptera of America north of Mexico, Synoptic Catalog (Muesebeck, C.F.W., K.V. Krombein y H.K. Townes, eds.). US Department of Agriculture, Monograph 2, 1420 pp.

Mickel, C.E. 1937. New World Mutillidae in the Spinola collection at Torino, Italy (Hymenoptera). Rev. de Entomol., Río de Janeiro, 7: 165-207.

___ . 1939. Monograph of the New Tropical Mutillid genus, Pappognatha (Hymenoptera: Mutillidae). Ann. Entomol. Soc. Amer., 32: 329-343.

___ . 1941. Monograph of the South American genus Hoplocrates Mickel (Hymenoptera: Mutillidae). Rev. Entomol. Río, 12: 341-414.

___ . 1943. The South American genus *Atillum* André (Hymenoptera: Mutillidae). Rev. Entomol. Río, 14:174-254.

___ . 1952. The Mutillidae (Wasps) of British Guiana. Zoologica, N.Y. Zool. Soc., 37 (3): 105-150.

___ . 1964. Synonymical notes on Neotropical Mutillidae (Hymenoptera). Proc. R. Entomol. Soc. London, 339 (9-10): 163-171.

Nonveiller, G. 1990. Catalogue of the Mutillidae, Myrmosidae and Bradynobaenidae of the Neotropical region including Mexico (Insecta: Hymenoptera). SPB Academic Publ. bv, Netherlands.

Smith, D.R. 1991. Flight records for twenty-eight species of *Macrophya* Dahlbom (Hymenoptera: Tenthredinidae) in Virginia, and an unusual specimen of *M. epinota* (Say). Proc. Entomol. Soc. Wash. 93 (3): 772-775.

Suárez, F.J. 1960. Datos sobre Mutílidos Neotropicales. 1. Nuevas especies de Sphaerophthalminae (Hymenoptera). Eos, 36:452-486.

___ . 1963. Datos sobre Mutílidos Neotropicales. V. Sinopsis del género Hoplognathoca Suárez (Hymenoptera-Mutillidae). Arch. Inst. Aclimatación, Almería, 12:55-66.

___ . 1970. Datos sobre Mutílidos Neotropicales. VII. Algunas especies del Perú representadas en las colecciones del Museo de Historia Natural de Basilea (Suiza) (Hymenoptera). Arch. Inst. Aclimatación, Almería, 15: 169-188.

APÉNDICE I

Clave genérica de Mutillidae del Perú

Para hacer la clave genérica lo más completa posible, se han incluido los siguientes tres géneros que se sospecha puedan estar presentes en el Perú (y también, en Pakitza), pero que hasta el presente todavía no han sido colectados en ese país: *Calomutilla, Horcomutilla,* y *Tobantilla*. Los géneros marcados con un asterisco (*) han sido colectados en Pakitza.

1. Hembras; individuos ápteros (Fig. 1); abdomen con seis segmentos abdominales visibles, con aguijón (Fig. 2) 2
-. Machos; formas aladas; abdomen con siete segmentos abdominales visibles, sin aguijón 21

2. Ojos fuertemente ovales; tórax rectangular, subrectangular u ovalado, anterior no es conspicuamente más ancho que posteriormente *(Mutillinae)* 3
-. Ojos circulares o subovales; tórax de formas variadas pero siempre conspicuamente más ancho anterior que posteriormente (Fig. 1) *(Sphaeropthalminae)* 4

3. Primer segmento abdominal completamente sésil con el segundo; tórax rectangular o subrectangular; líneas pubescentes en segundo tergito abdominal presentes .. *Timulla* *
-. Primer segmento abdominal distintivamente peciolado; tórax ovalado; líneas pubescentes en segundo tergito abdominal ausentes .... *Ephuta* *
a. Carena longitudinal media en vértex; con uno o ambos de los siguientes caracteres: espinita cerca del margen posterior medio del hipopigio, o espina en cara ventral distal de coxas anteriores .... *Ephuta (Ephutopsis)* *

b. Vértex sin carena longitudinal media; sin conjunto de caracteres anteriores .... *Ephuta* (*Ephuta*) *

4. Area pigidial bien definida, con carenas laterales y superficie generalmente esculturada (Fig. 2) 5
-. Area pigidial no definida, sin carenas laterales y con superficie no esculturada (Fig. 3) 14

5. Antena con 13 segmentos; cabeza con dos o cuatro procesos, un par en la gena y el otro al lado de la fosa proboscidal (Fig. 4) 6
-. Antena con 12 segmentos; cabeza generalmente sin procesos 7

6. Un par de procesos genales anteriores; primer segmento abdominal sésil con segundo; maculaciones compuestas de pelos gruesos; proceso metasternal bien desarrollado, proyectado entre metacoxas .... *Atillum*
-. Dos pares de procesos, un par genal anterior y el otro par en hipostoma (Fig. 4); primer segmento abdominal no sésil con segundo, de nodoso a forma de disco (Fig. 1); maculaciones pubescentes con pelos finos o moderadamente gruesos; sin proceso metasternal entre metacoxas .... *Hoplocrates* *

7. Pelos plumosos presentes; carena genal ausente (Fig. 5)
.... *Sphaeropthalma* (*Photopsis*)
-. Sin pelos plumosos, pelos simples solamente; carena genal ausente (en *Dasymutilla* y *Euspinolia*) o presente (Fig. 6) 8
8. Segundo tergito abdominal con distintivas carenas longitudinales; último segmento tarsal con proceso laminar generalmente cubriendo base de uñas tarsales, vistas dorsalmente .... *Hoplomutilla* *
-. Segundo tergito abdominal sin carenas longitudinales; último segmento tarsal sin proceso laminar sobre base de uñas tarsales (presente en pocas especies de *Traumatomutilla*) 9

9. Primer segmento abdominal distintivamente peciolado o nodoso, no sésil con el segundo; tórax piriforme o en forma de féretro; márgenes laterales del propodeo sin espinas 10
-. Primer segmento abdominal sésil con el segundo; tórax subpiriforme, en forma de violín, o trapezoidal; márgenes laterales del propodeo generalmente con espinas 12

10. Tegumento de cabeza y tórax reticulado; tórax en forma de féretro; carena genal presente; animales pequeños, 4-5 mm .... *Tobantilla*
-. Tegumento de cabeza y tórax con punturas o cubierto densamente con pelos decumbentes; tórax piriforme; carena genal presente o ausente; animales medianos, 7 mm o más 11

11. Carena genal ausente; calcaria negra; segundo tergito abdominal sin máculas tegumentarias; habitan áreas abiertas, de baja humedad [cuerpo cubierto de pubescencia decumbente] .... *Dasymutilla*
-. Carena genal presente; calcaria generalmente pálida; segundo tergito abdominal con dos o cuatro máculas tegumentarias; habitan generalmente selvas y lugares húmedos .... *Traumatomutilla* *

12. Carena genal ausente; mandíbulas edentadas distalmente .... *Euspinolia*
-. Carena genal presente; mandíbulas edentadas, bidentadas, o tridentadas distalmente 13
13. Cabeza con fuertes proyecciones suprantenales a manera de viseras; mandíbulas edentadas distalmente y con un enorme diente interno cerca de la mitad .... *Horcomutilla*

Diómedes Quintero A. y Roberto A. Cambra T.

-. Cabeza sin proyecciones suprantenales; mandíbulas bidentadas o tridentadas distalmente, sin un gran diente interno cerca de parte media .... *Pseudomethoca* *
Sphinctopsis Mickel: Sinonimia Krombein (1951)

14. Mandíbulas tomentosas, cubiertas densamente de pelos cortos, excepto área glabra de la punta; tórax piriforme; márgenes laterales del propodeo sin dientes; primer segmento abdominal en forma de disco, con hilera transversa de conspicuas espinas separando cara dorsal de la anterior .... *Pappognatha* *
-. Mandíbulas con pelos esparcidos, cortos y largos; tórax generalmente subpiriforme, en forma de violín; márgenes laterales del propodeo con o sin dientes; primer segmento abdominal cuando discoidal carece de hilera transversa de espinas separando caras anterior y dorsal 15

15. Tórax piriforme; márgenes laterales del propodeo sin espinas; con pelos plumosos o simples; carena genal presente o ausente 16
-. Tórax subpiriforme; márgenes laterales del propodeo con espinas; cuerpo con pelos sencillos; carena genal presente 17

16. Áreas pleurales del tórax con concavidades y áreas lisas; carena genal presente; cuerpo con pelos simples; tegumento del dorso de cabeza y tórax fuertemente reticulado; animales de 5 mm o menos de longitud corporal .... *Lomachaeta* *
-. Áreas pleurales del tórax totalmente punteadas, sin concavidades; carena genal ausente; cuerpo con pelos plumosos; tegumento dorso de la cabeza y del tórax no reticulado, con puntuaciones; animales de 6 mm o más de longitud corporal .... *Xystromutilla*

17. Cabeza grande y subcuadrada, distintivamente más ancha que el tórax; primer segmento abdominal en forma de disco o sésil con el segundo; carena genal no unida a fosa hipostomal por corta carena transversa; área antero-lateral del segundo tergito abdominal sin carenas ni crestas 18
-. Cabeza subglobosa, pequeña; primer segmento abdominal nodoso o discoidal, no sésil con el segundo; carena genal unida a fosa hipostomal por corta carena transversa; área antero-lateral del segundo tergito abdominal puede presentar conspicuas crestas con carenas interrumpidas 20

18. Carena genal no alcanza parte posterior del vértex; carena anterior de fosa hipostomal con corta proyección triangular en extremo lateral .... *Vianatilla**
-. Carena genal extendida hasta parte posterior del vértex; carena anterior de fosa hipostomal sin proyecciones 19

19. Mandíbulas con dos tercios proximales anchos y edentados, con tercio distal falcado, marcadamente angostado, y con inconspicuo diente en margen interno (Fig. 8); margen inferior del clípeo no dentado lateral a inserción de antenas .... *Pertyella* *
-. Mandíbulas delgadas, cerca de la base con un distintivo diente obtuso en margen interno; margen inferior del clípeo con un distintivo diente, o trituberculado, lateral a inserción de cada antena .... *Calomutilla*

20. Primer segmento abdominal nodoso; mandíbulas tridentadas distalmente
.... *Lophomutilla* *
-. Primer segmento abdominal en forma de disco; mandíbulas edentadas distalmente
.... *Lophostigma* *

21. Margen interno de ojos emarginado; tégula grande, conchiforme (Mutillinae) 22
-. Margen interno de ojos entero, sin emarginación; tégula pequeña, redondeada (Sphaeropthalminae) 23

22. Primer segmento abdominal sésil con el segundo; tergitos abdominales 3 al 7 sin carena longitudinal media; abdomen generalmente de tegumento predominantemente ferruginoso-naranja .... *Timulla* *

-. Primer segmento abdominal distintivamente peciolado; tergitos abdominales 3 al 7 con carena longitudinal media; abdomen generalmente de tegumento negro ...... *Ephuta* *

    a. Escutelo biespinoso; valvas penianas con un par de dientes en el extremo caudal del borde ventral .... *Ephuta* (*Ephutopsis*)*

    b. Escutelo normal.

    b1. Hipopigio fuertemente convexo, con una profunda emarginación mesal en borde caudal .... *Ephuta* (*Ephuseabra*)*

    b2. Hipopigio suavemente cóncavo o suavemente convexo o plano, sin profunda emarginación mesal en borde caudal .... *Ephuta* (*Ephuta*)*

23. Con pelos plumosos; líneas pubescentes presentes en segundo esternito abdominal; especies de hábitos nocturnos en su mayoría 24

-. Sin pelos plumosos, pelos simples solamente; líneas pubescentes ausentes en segundo esternito abdominal, excepto *Euspinolia* en que están presentes; especies de hábitos diurnos en su mayoría 26

24. Borde ventral de mandíbulas sin diente basal; tegumento negro; alas obscuras en parte; formas diurnas, con ojos y ocelos pequeños (distancia entre margen lateral del ojo a borde externo de un ocelo posterior aproximadamente 6 veces diámetro mayor del ocelo) .... *Xystromutilla*

-. Borde ventral de mandíbulas con conspicuo diente basal; tegumento rojizo pálido; alas transparentes; formas nocturnas, con ojos y ocelos grandes (distancia entre margen lateral del ojo a borde externo de un ocelo posterior aproximadamente 2 veces diámetro mayor del ocelo) 25

25. Último esternito con una escotadura mesal en borde caudal; tubérculos antenales con una expansión laminiforme en su cara interna .... *Limaytilla*

-. Último esternito abdominal sin una escotadura mesal en borde caudal; tubérculos antenales sin una expansión laminiforme en su cara interna .... *Sphaeropthalma* (*Photopsis*)

26. Mandíbulas tomentosas, cubiertas densamente con pelos cortos, excepto área glabra de la punta .... *Pappognatha* *

-. Mandíbulas con pelos esparcidos, cortos y largos 27

27. Carena genal presente 28

-. Carena genal ausente 30

28. Margen posterior del hipopigio bidentado; cabeza redondeada, pequeña, ligeramente más angosta que tórax; tegumento de cabeza y tórax reticulado; procesos espiniformes debajo de la cabeza ausentes; animales pequeños, menos de 6 mm ...... *Lomachaeta* *

-. Margen posterior del hipopigio sin dientes; cabeza cuadrada, grande, ligeramente más ancha que tórax; tegumento de cabeza y tórax con punturas; procesos espiniformes debajo de la cabeza presentes; animales grandes, más de 9 mm 29

29. Cabeza armada con dos pares de procesos, un par genal anterior y el otro lateral a fosa proboscidal .... *Hoplocrates* *

-. Cabeza armada con un par de procesos, cada uno en extremo anterior de carena genal .... *Atillum*

30. Último segmento tarsal con un proceso laminar sobre la base de las uñas tarsales; primer segmento abdominal sésil con el segundo .... *Hoplomutilla* *

-. Último segmento tarsal sin un proceso laminar sobre la base de las uñas tarsales; primer segmento abdominal sésil o peciolado 31

31. Primer segmento abdominal peciolado o nodoso, no sésil con el segundo; cabeza pequeña, casi redondeada 32
-. Primer segmento abdominal sésil con el segundo; cabeza grande y subcuadrada, o pequeña 35

32. Área pigidial definida lateralmente por carenas; superficie del pigidio generalmente esculturada con rugosidades o estrías; fovea pubescente generalmente presente en segundo esternito abdominal (Fig.7) 33
-. Área pigidial no definida, sin carenas laterales; superficie del pigidio lisa; segundo esternito abdominal carece de fovea pubescente 34

33. Cuerpo cubierto dorsalmente con densa pubescencia decumbente que oculta tegumento; calcarias negras; parte superior de mesopleura sin tubérculos o espinas; habitan áreas calientes, abiertas y de poca humedad .... *Dasymutilla*
-. Cuerpo cubierto con pelos esparcidos, dejando tegumento dorsal parcialmente visible; calcarias generalmente pálidas; parte superior de mesopleura con o sin tubérculos o espinas; habitan generalmente áreas selváticas húmedas .... *Traumatomutilla* *

34. Ángulos humerales del pronoto dentados; primer segmento abdominal peciolado, sin una cara plana posterior dorsal; mandíbulas edentadas distalmente; celda marginal redondeada distalmente .... *Lophomutilla* *
     Paramutilla Mickel NUEVA SINONIMIA
-. Ángulos humerales del pronoto redondeados, no dentados; primer segmento abdominal nodoso, con una distintiva cara plana posterior dorsal; mandíbulas bidentadas distalmente; celda marginal truncada distalmente .... *Lophostigma* *

35. Gonostilos de genitalia bífidos apicalmente .... *Horcomutilla*
-. Gonostilos de genitalia no bífidos apicalmente 36

36. Ojos pequeños y de poca convexidad, casi aplanados; líneas pubescentes en segundo esternito abdominal presentes; surcos parapsidales presentes, completos ... *Euspinolia*
-. Ojos grandes y globosos, fuertemente convexos; líneas pubescentes en segundo esternito abdominal ausentes; surcos parapsidales obsoletos 37

37. Dos procesos laminares presentes, laterales a región hipostomal; mandíbulas bidentadas distalmente .... *Vianatilla* *
-. Procesos laminares del área hipostomal ausentes (algunas especies de *Pseudomethoca* presentan machos con procesos cónicos, nunca laminares) 38

38. Margen anterior del clípeo sin diente anterior a la inserción de las antenas; cabeza generalmente pequeña, subredonda, raramente subcuadrada; mandíbulas no se angostan distalmente, bidentadas o tridentadas distalmente (Fig. 9) .... *Pseudomethoca* *
     Sphinctopsis Mickel: Sinonimia Krombein (1951)
-. Margen anterior del clípeo con un diente anterior a la inserción de cada una de las antenas (inconspicuo en *Pertyella*); cabeza grande, subcuadrada 39

39. Mandíbulas con tercio distal falcado y con inconspicuo diente en margen interno (Fig. 8), dos tercios proximales anchos y edentados .... *Pertyella* *
-. Mandíbulas distintivamente ensanchadas hacia el ápice, tridentadas distalmente .... *Calomutilla*

APÉNDICE II

Géneros	Número de especies y (subespecies) **			
	Perú	Pakitza	Panamá	VA-MD
Ephuta (Ephuta)	33	25	27	6
E. (Ephuseabra)	1(1)*	1(1)	1(1)*	
E. (Ephutopsis)	4	4	5	
Timulla	6	2	18	8(3)
Atillum	3			
Calomutilla			1*	
Dasymutilla	2		3	12
Euspinolia	2			
Hoplocrates	10	1	1	
Hoplomutilla	12(1)	4	4	
Horcomutilla			1	
Huacotilla			1*	
Limaytilla	1*			
Lomachaeta	1*	1		1*
Lophomutilla	7	4	8*	
Lophostigma	3*	2	2	
Myrmosa				4
Nanotopsis			1	
Pappognatha	3	2	2	
Pertyella	5*	2	6	
Photomorphus (Photomorphus)				3
Protophotopsis			1*	
Pseudomethoca	19	16	27	5(1)
Sphaerop. (Photopsis)	2			
S. (Sphaeropthalma)				1(1)
Traumatomutilla	14	7	7	
Vianatilla	1*	1	2*	
Xystromutilla	2		1	
TOTAL				
Géneros (subgéneros)	18(3)	12(3)	18(3)	8(4)
Especies (subespecies)	133(2)	73(1)	119	40(4)

* Géneros que se reportan por primera vez para esa región.
** Incluye números de especies reconocidas como nuevas, que serán descritas separadamente.

APÉNDICE III

Listado de las Especies de Mutílidas del Perú

Los géneros, y subgéneros que se reportan aquí por primera vez para el Perú se marcan con [◊]. A continuación del nombre genérico, número de especies que reconocemos presentes en Perú, número de especies conocidas por ambos sexos [MH], o por un sólo sexo: #M, #H. Las especies marcadas [+] son reportadas por primera vez para el Perú; [++] se reportan por primera vez en otro país; [*] macho será descrito en publicación separada. Después del nombre de la localidad, se anota el número de especímenes machos [M] y hembras [H] examinados de colectas nuestras o de préstamos que no han sido previamente reportados o que están en prensa. Aquella taxa que hemos reconocido como nueva, a describirse posteriormente, no ha sido listada. ** *Timulla mulfordi* Mickel, hembra, sinónimo de *T. cordillera* Mickel (Cambra & Quintero 1993).

MUTILLINAE
Ephuta (Ephuta) Say [35 spp: 1MH, 18M, 16H]
++ *E. (E.) abadia* (Cresson, 1902) .... Pakitza [5M]
    EXPLORAMA Lodge, Dpto. Loreto, MIUP [2M]
    PANAMÁ: Pavon Hill Road, Colón Prov., MIUP[1M]
        Cruce de Mono, Parque Nacional Darién, Darién Prov., MIUP [2M]
+ *E. (E.) argentula* (D. Torre, 1897) .... Pakitza [8M]
    Pucallpa, 200 m, Dpto. Ucayali, NHMLA [14M]
+ *E. (E.) birigua* Casal, 1969
    EXPLORAMA Lodge, Dpto. Loreto, MIUP [4H]
+ *E. (E.) cronopia* Casal, 1970 .... Pakitza [9H]
+ *E. (E.) egeria* Mickel, 1952 .... Pakitza [5H]
    EXPLORAMA Lodge, Dpto. Loreto, MIUP [4H]
+ *E. (E.) elvina* Mickel, 1952 .... Pakitza [5H]
+ *E. (E.) emarginata* Mickel, 1952
    Reserva Tambopata, Dpto. Madre de Dios, NHMLA [2M]
+ *E. (E.) erichtho* Mickel, 1952 .... Pakitza [1H]
+ *E. (E.) flavidens* Mickel, 1952 .... Pakitza [15M]
    Reserva Tambopata, Dpto. Madre de Dios, NHMLA [1M]
+ *E. (E.) fugax* (Smith, 1879) .... Pakitza [20M]
  E. (E.) inca Suárez, 1970
+ *E. (E.) indiscreta* Mickel, 1952 .... Pakitza [1M]
  E. (E.) peruviana (André, 1905)
++ *E. (E.) trifida* (Gerstaecker, 1874) .... Pakitza [28M, 20H]
    EXPLORAMA Lodge, Dpto. Loreto, MIUP [2M, 1H]
    PANAMÁ: Ampliamente distribuida: Provincias de Chiriquí, Darién, Colón, Panamá, MIUP [65M]
    ECUADOR: Limoncocha, Prov. Napo, Jun 1977, L. Vincent, USNM [3M]
  E. (E.) viata Casal, 1968

◊ **Ephuta (Ephuseabra)** Casal [1 sp: 1M] NUEVO ESTATUS
  E. (Ephuseabra) morra subespecie nueva .... Pakitza [4M]
◊ **Ephuta (Ephutopsis)** Ashmead [4 spp: 1MH, 1M, 2H] NUEVO ESTATUS
++ *E. (Ephutopsis) championi* (Cameron, 1894)
    Chanchamayo, Aug. 1948, J.M. Schunke, USNM [1M]
    Cord. Azul, Previsto [Dpto. Ucayali], 800 m, 25 May 1965, J.M.S., BMNH [1M]
    Fundo Shinchono, Dep. Huánuco, J.M. Schunke, USNM [1M]
    ECUADOR: Tena, Prov. Napo, 500 m, 11-28 Apr 1976, BMNH [2M]
    COLOMBIA: Río Barbacoas, 28 Mar 1974, M. Cooper, BMNH [1M]
        N de Sierra Nevada de Sta. Marta, Río Buritaca, 24 Nov 1974, M. Cooper, BMNH [1H]
    VENEZUELA: Los Ángeles del Tucuco, Zulia, 15-16 Apr 1981, USNM [1M]
++ *E. (Ephutopsis) singularis* (Spinola, 1841) .... Pakitza [1M]
    EXPLORAMA: Lodge, Dpto. Loreto, MIUP [1M]
    Yanayacu, Río Pachitea, Dpto. Huánuco, BMNH [1M]
    ECUADOR: Coca [Napo], May 1965, L.E. Peña, BMNH [1M]

+ *E.* (*Ephutopsis*) *solitaria* (Smith, 1879) .... Pakitza [1H]
+ *E.* (*Ephutopsis*) *vindex* (Smith, 1879) .... Pakitza [4H, 3M?]
    NUEVA COMBINACIÓN de Mutilla v. Smith
    Río Tambopata Res., 30 air km SW of Pto. Maldonado, 290m, Dpto. Madre de Dios, USNM [1M]

Timulla Ashmead [6 spp: 4MH, 1M, 1H]
T. brancoensis Mickel, 1938 .... Pakitza [25M*, 5H]
T. cordillera Mickel, 1938 .... Pakitza [19M, 54H**]
    Iparia, 320m, Dpto. Loreto, MUNSM [3M, 1H]
    Juanjuí, 400m, Río Huallaga, Dpto. San Martín, MUNSM [1H]
T. hedone Mickel, 1938
    Vista Alegre, Lima, Dpto. Lima, MUNSM [4M]
    Lurín, Dpto. Lima, MUNSM [1M]
T. inca Mickel, 1938
    Chosica, Dpto. Lima, MUNSM [1H]
    Cerca Univ. S. Marcos, Lima, Dpto. Lima, MUNSM [3H], MIUP [1H]
T. manga (Cresson, 1902)
T. sieberi Mickel, 1938

SPHAEROPTHALMINAE

Atillum André [4 spp: 2M, 2H]
A. blandulum Mickel, 1943
A. limbatum Mickel, 1943
A. optabile Mickel, 1943
A. rubriceps (Schrottky, 1902)

Dasymutilla Ashmead [3 spp: 1MH, 1M, 1H]
++*D. blattoserica* (Kohl, 1882)
    Desierto 4 hr antes de Tumbes, Dpto. Tumbes, IZV [3H]
    Entre Jayanca y Motupe, Dpto. Lambayeque, MUNSM [1H], MIUP [1H]
    San Pedro de Lloc, Dpto. La Libertad, MUNSM [1H]
    Lima, Chontay, Dpto. Lima [2H]
    Lima, Puruchuco, Dpto. Lima [1H]
    Lima, Valle del Chillón, 520m, Dpto. Lima, MUNSM [3M, 2H], MIUP [1M, 1H]
    Atocongo, MUNSM [1H]
    ECUADOR: El Empalme, Prov. Loja, PUCE [1H]
        Pto. Viejo, Prov. Manabi, MIUP [1H]
D. homochroma Suárez, 1970
    Desierto cerca de Tumbes, Dpto. Tumbes, MIUP [1H]
D. peruviana Suárez, 1970

Euspinolia Ashmead [2 spp: 2H]
Eus. krombeini Casal, 1964
Eus. rufula Mickel, 1938

Hoplocrates Mickel [10 spp: 3M, 7H]
H. admiranda Mickel, 1941
    EXPLORAMA Lodge, Dpto. Loreto, MIUP [4H]
    ECUADOR: Prov. Napo:
        Archidona, PUCE [2H]
        Coca, MIUP [1H]
        Vía Ollin-25, km 25, 1100 m, MIUP [1H]
+*H. armata* (Kulg, 1821) .... Pakitza [1H]
 H. buccata Mickel, 1941
    EXPLORAMA Lodge, Dpto. Loreto, MIUP [2M]
 H. centromaculata (Cresson, 1902)
    Juanjuí, Dpto. San Martín, MUNSM [1H]
 H. compar Mickel, 1945
    Tingo María, 2mi. E., roadside vegetation, 2000ft, Dpto. Huánuco, 4 Aug 1971, BMNH [1M]

Hoplocrates moneta (Gerstaecker, 1874)
  ECUADOR: Prov. Napo: Vía Ollín-25, km 25, 1100m, MIUP [1H]
+*H. oblectanea* Mickel, 1941
  EXPLORAMA Lodge, Dpto. Loreto, MIUP [12H]
H. rufonotata rufonotata (André, 1906)
H. spinigula Mickel, 1941
H. ucayalia Schuster, 1952

Hoplomutilla Ashmead [13 spp: 2M, 11H]
Hoplom. approximata approximata Mickel, 1939
  EXPLORAMA Camp, Dpto. Loreto, MIUP [1H]
Hoplom. approximata huallaga Schuster, 1951
Hoplom. conspecta Mickel, 1939
Hoplom. euryale euryale Mickel, 1939 ....Pakitza [3H]
+*Hoplom. lanicia* Mickel, 1939 .... Pakitza [1M]
Hoplom. patricialis (Gerstaecker, 1874)
  Especie reportada de Colombia y Brasil (Mickel 1939);presencia en Ecuador, Perú, y Bolivia
  (Nonveiller 1990, sin localidades), necesita ser verificada
Hoplom. peruviana (André, 1906) .... Pakitza [7M]
Hoplom. phorcys Mickel, 1939
  Tingo María, Dpto. Huánuco, MUNSM [1H]
Hoplom. rapax Mickel, 1939
  EXPLORAMA Camp, Dpto. Loreto, MIUP [1H]
  EXPLORAMA Lodge, Bushmaster trail, Dpto. Loreto, MIUP [3H]
Hoplom. rohweri Mickel, 1939
  Satipo, Dpto. Junín, 750m, MIUP [1H]
  San Luis de Shuaro, Chanchamayo, Dpto. Junín, MUNSM [1H]
  Iparia, Río Pachitea, Dpto. Loreto, MUNSM [1H]
  Juanjuí, Dpto. San Martín, MUNSM [1H]
  Perú, sin datos, MUNSM [2H]
Hoplom. sociata (Smith, 1879) .... Pakitza [4H]
+*Hoplom. superba superba* (Gerstaecker, 1874)
  Satipo, Dpto. Junín, MUNSM [1H], MIUP [1H]
  EXPLORAMA Camp, durmiendo 10 p.m. con mandíbulas sujetas a peciolo de hoja, Dpto. Loreto,
  MIUP [1H]
  EXPLORAMA Lodge, Dpto. Loreto, MIUP [3H]
  Pucallpa, Dpto. Loreto, MUNSM [1H]
+*Hoplom. valeria* Casal, 1961
  EXPLORAMA Lodge, Bushmaster trail, Dpto. Loreto, MIUP [1H]

◊*Limaytilla* Casal [1 sp: 1M]
  7 km E. de Chaparra, 1450m, Dpto. Arequipa, MIUP [1M]

◊*Lomachaeta* Mickel [1 sp: 1M]
  Lomachaeta sp .... Pakitza [1M]

Lophomutilla Mickel [7 spp: 1MH, 1M, 5H]
[=*Paramutilla* Mickel, macho, NUEVA SINONIMIA]
+*L. bucki* Suárez, 1962 .... Pakitza [9H]
+*L. denticulata* (Smith, 1855) ....Pakitza [12H]
  Tingo María, Dpto. Huánuco, ? [2H]
L. inca Fritz & Pagliano, 1993
  Dpto. Huánuco, 1000m, ? [1H]
+*L. mocajuba* Casal, 1961
  EXPLORAMA Lodge, Dpto. Loreto, MIUP [1H]
L. ophomuti Fritz, 1990
+*L. staphyloma* (Gerstaecker, 1874) ....Pakitza [5H]
  EXPLORAMA Inn, Dpto. Loreto, MIUP [4M, 6H]
◊*Lophostigma* Mickel [3 spp: 3H]
+*L. acantophora* (Dalla Torre, 1897) ....Pakitza [1H]
+*L. alopha* Mickel, 1952

EXPLORAMA Lodge, Dpto. Loreto, MIUP [1H]
+*L. simoni* (du Buysson, 1892) .... Pakitza [1H]

Pappognatha Mickel [3 spp: 1M, 2H]
P. limes Mickel, 1939
P. speciosa Mickel, 1939 .... Pakitza [1H]
    Tingo María, Dpto. Huánuco, roadside vegetation, 2000 ft, 10 Aug 1971, BMNH [1H]
    Parque Nacional Pacaya-Samiria, Dpto. Loreto, MUNSM [1H]

◊*Pertyella* Mickel [5 spp: 2M, 3H]

Pseudomethoca Ashmead [19 spp: 1MH, 5M, 13H]
=*Sphinctopsis* Mickel, SINONIMIA: Krombein 1951
+*Pseudomethoca credula* (Cresson, 1902) .... Pakitza [24H]
    EXPLORAMA Lodge, Dpto. Loreto, MIUP [2H]
    Puerto Maldonado, Dpto. Madre de Dios, MIUP [2H]
++*Pseudomethoca piura* (Casal, 1970) .... Pakitza [1H]
    NUEVA COMBINACIÓN de *Sphinctopsis p.* Casal
    EXPLORAMA Lodge, Lake trail, Dpto. Loreto, MIUP [1H]
    COLOMBIA: La Hormiga, near Mocoa, Putumayo, BMNH [1H]
    ECUADOR: Muyuma, 5 km W, of Tena, Napo, BMNH [1H]

Sphaeropthalma (*Photopsis* Blake) [2 spp: 1MH, 1M]
S. (P.) lenis André, 1908

Traumatomutilla André [14 spp: 3M, 11H]
+*T. angustata* (André, 1906) .... Pakitza [1H]
    EXPLORAMA Lodge, Lake trail, Yanamono R., Dpto. Loreto, 7 Nov 1990, MIUP [1H]
    Manu National Park, Colapa, near Cocha Cashu, on river bank, Dpto. Madre de Dios, 24 Dic 1992,
    MIUP [1H]
+*T. dubia albata* (Smith, 1879) .... Pakitza [6H]
T. fascinata (Smith, 1879)
Traumatomutilla incerta (Spinola, 1841) .... Pakitza [4H]
    T. weyrauchi Mickel, NUEVA SINONIMIA
    Pakitza, Malaise #3, USNM [1H]
    EXPLORAMA Lodge, Dpto. Loreto, MIUP [2H]
+*T. graphica* (Gerstaecker, 1874) .... Pakitza [1H]
T. indicoides Mickel, 1945
    Pucallpa, Dpto. Loreto, BMNH [1H]
+*Traumatomutilla simulatrix* (Smith, 1879) .... Pakitza [1H]
    NUEVA COMBINACIÓN de *Mutilla s.* Smith
    Pucallpa, Dpto. Loreto, BMNH [1H]
T. sodalicia (Kohl, 1882)
T. vitelligera (Gerstaecker, 1874)

◊*Vianatilla* Casal [1sp: 1H] .... Pakitza [2H]

Xystromutilla André [1 sp: 1H]
++*Xystromutilla mansueta* (Smith, 1879)
    NUEVA COMBINACIÓN de *Mutilla m.* Smith
    Tingo María, Dpto. Huánuco, ? [1H]
    BOLIVIA: Río Colorado, Bio Exp. 1921-2, W. Mann, USNM [1H]
    ECUADOR: Muyuna, 5 km Oeste de Tena, Prov. Napo, c. 550 m, 25-27 Ago 1979, M. Cooper,
    BMNH [1H]

Natural History of the Carabid Beetles at the BIOLAT Biological Station, Río Manu, Pakitza, Peru Supplement I. Additional records.

TERRY L. ERWIN

National Museum of Natural History, Smithsonian Institution,
Washington D.C. 20560

ABSTRACT

The occurrence and natural history of carabid beetles previously recorded at Pakitza are amplified with the addition of new tribal and generic records; additional keys and illustrations are provided for aid in identification of these. Six newly recorded generic-level taxa are presented in terms of number of species and their size ranges (overall length), microhabitats, food, season, and trail localities. New records include two new tribes: Pseudomorphini — *Pseudomorpha* (1 sp) and Paussini (Eohompterini) - - *Homopterus* (1 sp), *Eohomopterus* (1 sp); and new genera in previously recorded tribes, Ctenodactylini —*Amblycoleus* (2 spp) and Lebiini — *Cryptobatis* (1 sp) and a new genus and species treated here as *insertae sedis* (1 sp). A discussion of the measure of effort to acquire the Pakitza carabid inventory is presented in terms of scientific and conservation-oriented biodiversity assessment, survey, and inventory projects.
Key words: Coleoptera, Carabidae, Perú, Amazon Basin, Rio Manu, biodiversity, microhabitats, natural history, conservation.

INTRODUCTION

The BIOLAT Biological station at Pakitza is the richest local area ever recorded for this family of beetles; the number of species now totals over 600 species arrayed in 124 genera. This is nearly as many species as in all of New Guinea or Sri Lanka, but in only 4000 hectares. Since the publication of the first report on the area's carabid beetles (Erwin, 1991). I have sampled an additional 6 man-weeks with the aid of Felipe and Ejido Pfuño and Michael Pogue in September-October, 1991, July 1992, and June, 1993. Many new species were discovered and

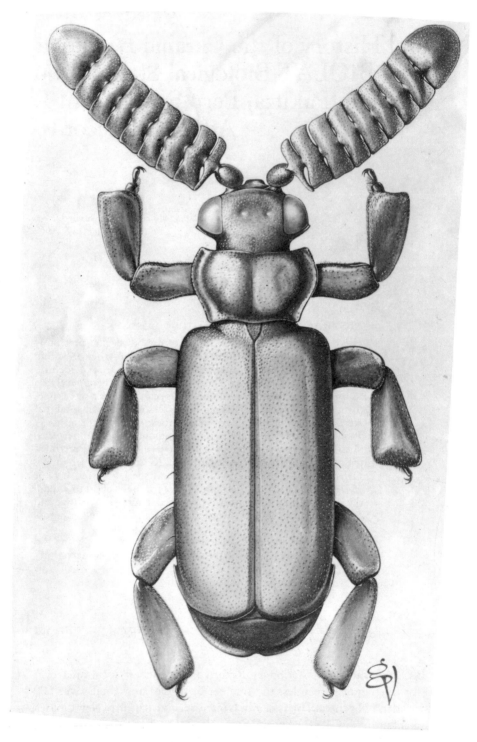

Fig. 1.– Habitus, dorsal aspect, *Homopterus subcordatus* Darlinton, Panamá

among these were new tribal and generic records. The latter are the subject of this paper; an account of the new species in previously recorded genera will be presented separately. Even with these many new records, however, the current knowledge of this family at Pakitza does not include those species restricted to nearby oxbow lakes which are not yet in the station's repertoire of habitats, nor has much sampling been done in the uplands 7 km north of Pakitza, at the end of the Tachigali Trail, nor in the deeply dissected upper stream valley of the Rio Fortaleza. Such inclusions would likely substantially raise the current inventory by scores of species, particularly in the intervalley ridgetop forest where two rare wingless species, indicating an unusual lowland fauna, were discovered and reported on previously.

NEW RECORDS OF CARABID BEETLES AT PAKITZA

SUPERTRIBE PSEUDOMORPHITAE

Pseudomorphini

Pseudomorpha, 1 sp (size range: 6.0mm to 7.0mm); these very blattoid-like carabids are among the more interesting of the family both in their form and habits. They live with ants and are modified accordingly in their external structure. The myrmecophilous larvae were described of a North American species (Erwin, 1981) and this was later amplified by Liebherr and Kavanaugh (1985) who showed that species of this genus have oviviparous young. Six specimens were found at P/24-25 (October, 1991) in dead fronds of *Astrocaryum macrocalyx* using insecticidal fog. The ants with cohabited which they have not yet been identified.

SUPERTRIBE PAUSSITAE

Paussini

Eohomopterus, 1 sp (size: 5.0mm); virtually nothing is known about this genus of beetles. The single specimen from Pakitza was collected by fogging bamboo (*Elytrostachys* sp.) near T/38. Undoubtedly they live with ants as do other members of the tribe, and are markedly modified in their external structure for this. The fact that their tarsal articles do not fold back into a tibial groove indicates that these beetles are far more primitive than those in the following genus.

Homopterus, 1 sp (size: 7.0mm); as in Fig. 1; these beetles have been reported from numerous localities, but most especially in Central America. Darlington (1950) reviewed what is known of them. The single specimen from Pakitza was collected at light in the clearing, as were those I got at Pacaya-Samiria National Reserve in northern Perú. They live with ants as do other members of the tribe, and are markedly modified in their external structure for this.

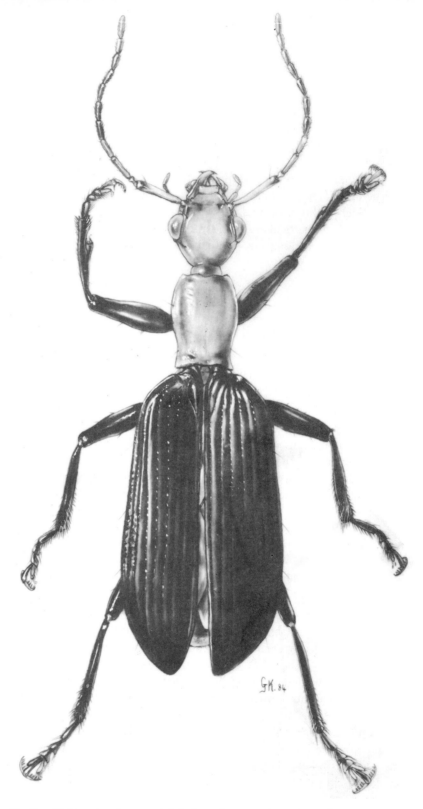

Fig. 2.– *Habitus, dorsal aspect. Askalaphium depressum* (Bates), Tambopata, Perú.

SUPERTRIBE CTENODACTYLITAE

Ctenodactylini

Askalaphium Liebke, Fig. 2. The illustration, loaned to me by Dr. Nigel Stork of The Natural History Museum in London, and drawn by Geffroy Kibby, was not available for my first report on the Pakitza carabids (Erwin 1991), so I have included it here.

Amblycoleus, 2 spp (size range: 6.5mm to 9.0mm); these beetles were collected with insecticidal fog blown into suspended dry leaves and dry leaves mixed with bamboo (*Guadua weberbaueri*) in old alluvial terrace forest both near the Manu and at T/47 in forest where there is no bamboo. Considering the large volume of dry leaves fogged in these areas between 1990 and 1993, and only 5 specimens of two species were collected, members of this genus must be quite rare.

SUPERTRIBE LEBIITAE

Lebiini

Cryptobatis, 1 sp (size range: 8.5 to 9.2mm); a single individual was collected by fogging suspended dry fronds of the palm, *Astrocaryum macrocalyx* , in upper floodplain forest near the Rio Manu. These beetles probably are associated with fungi on fallen logs, a microhabitat not yet well explored at Pakitza.

Insertae sedis, sp 1 (size range: 4.5mm to 6.0mm); this new species and genus has been found at Tambopata by fogging the crown of a leguminous tree and fogging the general canopy in both upper floodplain forest and terra firme forest. At Pakitza, they were fogged from the crown leaves of the bamboo *Guadua weberbaueri* . The lineage is related to *Hyboptera* and is under study by G. E. Ball and me.

DISCUSSION

In 23 man-weeks of collecting from 1987 to 1993, more than 600 species of carabid beetles were vouchered and their microhabitats recorded. No absolute measure of species accumulation versus effort expended was recorded, thus it is unknown whether the end of new records is in sight or not.

A measure of effort to acquire the Pakitza carabid inventory would have been desirable in terms of scientific and conservation-oriented biodiversity assessment, survey, and inventory projects, but I can say that now only in hindsight. However, I conclude that beetles, like some vertebrate and plant groups, are suitable for such projects in the future because a sound methodology has been developed for their rapid and efficient collecting, preparation, and interim identification. Thus, inclusion of beetles in conservation biology can provide a degree of resolution for environmental assessment and management not available from larger organisms because so many species can be inventoried in short order and their distribution across microhabitats known.

ACKNOWLEDGEMENTS

George Venable provided the illustration of *Homopterus cordatus* and Nigel Stork loaned me that of *Askalaphium depressum* ; Michael G. Pogue assisted in various stages of production and provided technical and field support. I heartily thank these folks for their efforts. Funding for these studies comes from the Biological Diversity Programs (Don Wilson, Director), Department of Entomology, National Museum of Natural History (Jonathan Coddington, Chairman), and Neotropical Lowlands Research Project (Ronald Heyer, Principal Investigator), all of the Smithsonian Institution. This paper # 91 in the BIOLAT Series.

LITERATURE CITED

Darlington, P.J. Jr. 1950. Paussid Beetles. Transactions of the American Entomological Society. 76(2):47-142.

Erwin, T. L. 1981. A synopsis of the immature stages of Pseudomorphini (Coleoptera: Carabidae) with notes on tribal affinities and behavior in relation to life with ants. Coleopterists Bulletin 35(1):53-68.

Erwin, T.L. 1991. Natural History of the Carabid Beetles at the BIOLAT Río Manu Biological Station, Pakitza, Peru. Revista Peruana de Entomología, Vol. 33, pp. 1-85.

Liebherr, J.K. and D.H. Kavanaugh. 1985. Ovoviviparity in carabid beetles of the genus Pseudomorpha (Insecta: Coleptera). Journal of Natural History. 19:1079-1086.

Nagel, P. 1987. Arealsystemanalyse afrikanischer Fühlerkäfer (Coleoptera, Carabidae, Paussinae): Ein Beitrag zur Rekonstruktion der Landschaftsgenese. Franz Steiner Verlag Wiesbaden GmbH, Stuttgart, Fe. Rep. Germany. 233p.

APPENDIX 1.

Revised keys to some genera of carabid tribes occurring at Pakitza, Peru.
Pseudomorpha, the only described genus of Pseudomorphini in tropical America,
was keyed in the Key to Tribes in Erwin (1991).

Paussini (Eohompterini, sensu Negal, 1987)

1   Tarsi not retractable into apex of tibia .... **Eohomopterus** Wassman
1'   Tarsi fully retractable into apex of tibia .... **Homopterus** Westwood

Ctenodactylini

1   Tarsal claws markedly denticulate; body markedly
     depressed or not 2
1'   Tarsal claws, at most, with one basal tooth or lobe; body
     not depressed 3
2   Body markedly depressed; elytra black, in contrast to rufous
     head and prothorax .... *Askalaphium* Liebke
2'   Body convex, elytra and forebody black .... *Ctenodactyla* Dejean
3   Fourth tarsomere bilobed, lobes connected throughout their length by a
     thin membrane, elytron apically obliquely truncate .... *Calophaena* Klug
3'   Fourth tarsomere bilobed, lobes separated; elytron apically rounded,
     or narrowly truncated in females. 4
4   Inner margin of eye with longitudinal carina 5
4'   Inner margin of eye without longitudinal carina 6
5   Head and pronotum smooth, shiny .... *Leptotrachelus* Liebke
5'   Head and pronotum densely punctate .... *Amblycoleus* Chaudoir
6   Mentum without a tooth .... *Pionycha* Chaudoir
6'   Mentum with a tooth .... *Teukrus* Liebke

Lebiini

1   Head ventrally without subortital setigerous punctures..................... 2
1'   Head ventrally with at least one pair of suborbital setigerous
     punctures. 18
2   Penultimate setigerous puncture of elytron umbilicate series
     displaced laterally .... *Apenes* LeConte
2'   Penultimate setigerous puncture of elytron umbilicate series not
     displaced laterally, **OR** displaced medially... 3
3   Posterior tibial spurs markedly unequal, margins serrate, inner spur al
     most as long as tarsomere 1; markedly narrowed, head pedunculate
     .... *Nemotarsus* LeConte
3'   Posterior tibial spurs subequal, their margins smooth; neck not markedly
     narrowed, head not pedunculate 4

4   Mandible widened near base, scrobe wide, lateral margin
     markedly rounded. 5
4'   Mandible not conspicuously widened near base, scrobe narrowed,
     lateral margin not markedly rounded 19
5   Head markedly narrowed and prolonged behind eyes; prothorax
     more or less tubular, without lateral flange at least at
     middle .... *Agra* Fabricius
5'   Head normal, not prolonged behind eyes; pronotum wider than
     long, or as wide as long, not narrowed anteriorly, not tubular, with
     lateral flange 6
6   Ultimate palpomere oval, not truncate at apex .... *Ogygium* Liebke
6'   Ultimate palpomere not oval; that of labial palpus more or less
     securiform 7
7   Mentum with tooth 8
7'   Mentum without tooth 15
8   Ligula with four apical setae; tarsomere 4 deeply emgarginate,
     but not bilobed 9
8'   Ligula with two apical setae 11
9   Tooth of mentum well developed .... *Plochionus* Latreille and Dejean
9'   Tooth of mentum a slight, but evident, emargination 10
10   Pronotum with base broadly lobed .... *Aspasiola* Chaudoir
10' Pronotum with base more or less straight 11
11   Anntennomere 2 only slightly shorter than 3, flagellar articles
     flattened and wide .... *Epikastea* Liebke
15   Tarsomeres dorsally sulcate 16
15' Tarsomeres dorsally smooth 18
16   Elytron with intervals 3 and 5 with 2 small setigerous pores at about
     the middle and at the apical third; intervals flat .... *Onota* Chaudoir
16' Elytron with intervals 3 and 5 with a series of large setae in setigerous
     pores that are somewhat tuberculate 17
17   Elytron with more or less flat interval, only the swollen setal bases
     obvious; side margin markedly reflexed throughout .... insertae sedis
17' Elytron with disc markedly uneven, setae on raised callouses; side
     marge broadly reflexed near middle only .... *Hyboptera* Chaudoir
18   Head and pronotum punctate .... *Cylindronotum* Putzeys
18' Head and pronotum smooth .... *Pseudotoglossa* Mateu
19   Penultimate setigerous puncture of elytron umbilicate series
     displaced medially; tarsomere broad, dilated, with tarsomere 4 bilobed ....
     .... *Lebia* Latreille
19' Penultimate setigerous puncture of elytron umbilicate series not
     displaced laterally, **OR** displaced medially .... *Negrea* Mateu
20   Labrum cordiform; elytral intervals 3, 5, 7 each with a series of long
     setae .... *Thoasia* Liebke

20' Labrum quadrate or rectangulate; elytral intervals 3, 5, 7 asetose ... **21**

21 Elytral apex obliquely truncate, lateral corner rounded; elytral surface finely and densely punctulate, almost imperceptibly costate; penultimate setigerous puncture of elytral umbilicate series displaced proximo-medially; tarsomere 4 of all legs deeply bilobed with fine spatulate setae beneath .... *Gallerucidia* Chaudoir

21' Combination of characteristics no as above **22**

22 Labrum normal, wider than long; penultimate setigerous puncture of elytron umbilicate series not displaced laterally .... *Euproctinus* Leng and Mutchler

22' Labrum narrow, as long or longer than wide, or markedly convex; penultimate setigerous puncture of elytron umbilicate series displaced laterally **23**

23 Body markedly depressed; integument brown .... *Hansus* Ball and Shpeley

23' Body not depressed; integument various, often with brassy sheen, or partly metallic, or pure black **24**

24 Labrum markedly convex, inflated .... *Eucheila** Dejean

24' Labrum flat...**25**

25 Elytral intervals densely and coarsely punctulate .... *Inna* Putzeys

25' Elytral intervals smooth... **26**

26 Mentum with tooth **27**

26' Mentum without tooth.. **28**

27 Hind tibia dorsally caniculate, the sulcus extended the length of the tibia .... *Catascopus* Kirby

27' Hind tibia not caniculate, surface smooth or strigulose .... *Stenognathus* Chaudoir

28 Mentum with lateral lobes subtruncate .... *Eurycoleus* Chaudoir

28' Mentum with lateral lobes pointed or narrowly rounded apically ... **29**

29 Pronotum lobed basally .... *Stenoglossa* Chaudoir

29' Pronotum straight basally .... *Coptodera* Dejean

The Trichoptera Collected on the Expeditions to Parque Manu, Madre de Dios, Peru.

Oliver. S. Flint, Jr.

Department of Entomology, National Museum of Natural History,
Smithsonian Institution Washington, DC 20560

ABSTRACT

The caddisflies (Trichoptera) are an order of holometabolous insects whose immature stages live in water. These insects (both adults and immature stages) were collected for one month in each of 1988 and 1989 at Pakitza (Dpto. Madre de Dios, Pcia. Manu) and en route to Pakitza between Paucartambo and Salvación (both Dpto. Cuzco, Pcia. Paucartambo), and for a few weeks in 1987 at Pakitza only. These collections have now been sorted to species, and those that have been described are named. The collections contain 14 families, 51 genera and 224 species. Of the 224 species, only 77 (34%) can be named with any degree of certainty, the remainder being undescribed or belonging to complexes needing further careful study to determine species limits. Pakitza and environs was the home to 114 (51%) species, 126 (56%) species were found in the montane sites, with only 16 (7%) species being common to both.

INTRODUCTION

The Trichoptera, or caddisflies, are an order of holometabolous insects, most of whose species pass their larval and pupal stages in fresh water. Their larvae are famous for constructing either tubular cases in which they live and carry around over the substrate, or fixed, silken retreats with attached nets by which they filter their food from the passing water. It is one of the smaller orders, estimates ranging from 10,000 species (Ross, 1967) to around 50,000 (Schmid, 1984) with 6,357 species described through 1970 (Higler, 1981; Spuris, 1991). The fauna of the Neotropical Realm, especially the tropical areas, is still very poorly known, and, lamentably, Peru is one of the most poorly known. Because of the paucity of data from this region, the invitation to join in this inventory was eagerly seized.

369

The first paper dealing with the Peruvian caddisflies was that of Martynov (1912), in which he presented a list of 24 species known from the country including 12 newly described species. Of these 24 species, 17 were described or recorded from "Callanga, 2-3000 m., Staudinger". The exact location of this site is still uncertain, but it appears to be somewhere in or near the Cosñipata Valley, into which the road from Paucartambo to Pilcopata descends. An interesting account of attempts to reach Callanga is given by Woytkowski (1978). Our collections along this route did rediscover several of the Martynov species for the first time since their descriptions. After the early work of Martynov, there have been very few, mostly small, studies devoted exclusively to the Peruvian fauna (Flint, 1975, 1980, Flint and Reyes, 1991). Reyes, in 1991, had compiled a list of 107 species known from Peru.

The material on which this paper is based was collected in 1987 by M.G. Pogue at Pakitza between 27 September and 4 October, in 1988 by O.S. Flint, Jr. and N.E Adams at several sites along the road on the eastern flanks of the Andes and at Pakitza between 2 and 22 September, and in 1989 by N.E. Adams along the same route between 28 August and 22 September. These collections of many thousand specimens have have now been determined, in so far as possible, and contain a total of 224 specific level taxa.

METHODS

The caddisflies were collected by a variety of methods. The first is simply with a "butterfly" net bumping or sweeping the vegetation along the margins of the watercourse and capturing the specimens as they fly out. Often careful observation of rock surfaces above the water, or wet, vertical rock faces, or the supporting piers and abutments of bridges will produce different species. Probably the most widely used and effective method for collecting caddisflies and other night active insects is the use of bright lights. If electricity can by provided (by battery, portable generator, or line) then an ultraviolet or mercury vapor bulb can be used; lacking electricity, a gasoline mantle lantern can be quite successful. The light can be used in conjunction with a variety of funnel type traps delivering everthing that arrives into alcohol or a killing jar. I prefer to place a white sheet (on which the insects rest after arrival) behind the light, because I can selectively pick off examples of all the different types, using a killing jar for a percentage of the material and dropping others into alcohol. This way I avoid collecting excessive numbers of insects. Another way to collect is with the use of the Malaise trap, which is a cage of open-mesh fabric baffles made in such a manner to direct entering insects into a killing chamber or jar of preservative. A trap of this nature placed across a stream where it will not be stolen or destroyed operates night and day and usually captures many species not collected by any other manner.

I normally pin a series of each apparent species, usually in the morning following a nights work. I try to select, in good light, a series, perhaps 10, of each

370

possibly different form for pinning. Additional specimens are put into the jar of alcohol with the rest of the catch. Many people prefer to have all their material in alcohol and this is easier and often safer in the field. However, I find the color pattern so valuable that pinning is worth the trouble.

Care of alcoholic material in the field is comparatively simple: make certain the fluid is not too diluted by changing it after a day if the specimens more than half fill the container. Secure the cap tightly so the jar does not leak. The care of pinned material can be more difficult. The specimens must dry promptly or they may mold: setting the box in the sun with the top slightly ajar (and taking it in at night) will usually suffice, but sometime it must be hung near the roof over the cookstove or fire. Ants are a constant danger to pinned material: roach and ant spray liberally applied to the outside of the pinning box usually is sufficient. Sometimes this will not work and the material must be stored (after drying) in a tight plastic bag with some moth flakes.

Returning from the field with the fresh material requires some care. All bottles of fluid are wrapped in tightly sealed plastic bags and usually shipped in the luggage. But the boxes of the more fragile pinned material are usually tied together and carried in hand onto the airplane and may then be placed in an overhead bin.

Once back to the laboratory the material is kept in place in the boxes until all the specimens are labelled, when they can finally be segregated as the specialist wishes. All labels should contain the basic data of locality (the inclusion of latitude and longitude is recommended and manditory for sites not found on readily available maps), date of collection and collector. Once the specimens have been labelled it is then possible to start sorting and identifying the collections.

In some cases valid identifications can be made on the basis of color pattern, but more frequently it will be necessary to examine the genitalia. It is often possible to see enough of the genital structure to make the identification directly from the pinned specimen. However, in many cases it is necessary to remove the abdomen and clear it by treatment in KOH. Although the abdomen will often separate easily from the metathorax by gently bending the abdomen back and forth, this method often results in the breakage of the specimen at some undesirable location. To prevent unwanted breakage place the specimen in a relaxing chamber overnight, and then cut the now soft abdomen away from the thorax. In order to remove the inner tissues and produce an undistorted specimen whose parts can be clearly seen it is necessary to treat the abdomen with KOH. The abdomen is left to soak in a solution of about 10% KOH is overnight. The following day the abdomen is moved to alcohol and the fragments of tissue can be easily expelled. If the KOH is heated to just below boiling and the abdomen placed in the warm solution, clearing is relatively quick and may take place in a few minutes. The cleared abdomen is now in condition for comparison with published figures of genitalia or with cleared genitalia from determined material.

LOCALITIES

The localities where collections were made in and around Pakitza were well defined and discussed with detailed maps by Erwin (1991), and will not be discussed further here. The sites where the aquatics group stopped and collected along the road from Cuzco, Puacartambo, Pilcopata, to Salvacion and on by boat to Boca Manu and Limonal, commonly referred to as "The Transect", are described both in the accompanying paper on the Odonata and here, as there are some differences in the sites sampled. The exact positions of these sites were difficult to ascertain in the 80's because: 1) no bus had a functioning odometer, 2) most kilometer posts along the road were missing, 3) although several altimeters were set to the known elevation of Cuzco on departure, they began to give different (often significantly) readings by the time Paucartambo was reached, and 4) accurate maps did not exist for most of the route (or at least were not available to us). Just in time to add the data to this paper, the June 1993 expedition over the same route was able to alleviate some of these problems. They had use of a Magellan Systems Corporation instrument to determine the exact latitude and longitude from the global positioning system. These figures are used herein. The bus in 1993 also had a working odometer and therefore exact road distances between sites were obtained. The elvations are still a problem as readings continued to vary and the instructions with the Magellan indicated that this feature was subject to considerable inaccuracy. As a result an average of all the readings made over the different years was obtained. This figure, rounded to the nearest 5 meters, is used in the following discussion. Thus, the following represents the best consensus values, presented in the order reached along the road regardless of the year.

Bridge with iron rails about 4 km after Paucartambo and before Abra Acanaco, 2870 m elevation, 13° 17.43' S, 71° 35.95' W. Clear; boulders, cobble a little sand; 5 m wide. 28 Aug 1989: a small collection in the puna, some agriculture.

Just beyond park entrance station at Abra Acanacu (at 13° 11.98' S, 71° 37.02' W), about km 106, 3420 m (highest collecting site). Spring seeps and small streams in cloud forest. 28 Aug 1989: a small, but valuable collection.

Three kilometers east of Buenos Aires, Puente Morro Leguia, km 135, 2200 m, 13° 07.44' S, 71° 43.37 W. Stream 5 m wide, 1/4—1/2 m deep, rocky, swift; in andean montane wet forest. Surber sample series taken in 1988 (2 Sep) and 1989; 2 nights spent (28—30 Aug) 1989, MV light collection at night '89.

Forty four kilometers west of Pilcopata, Puente San Pedro, km 152, 1450 m, 13° 03.30' S, 71° 32.78' W. Stream 5 m wide, 1/4 m deep, boulders to sand, swift; at transition between andean montane wet forest and upper andean tropical wet forest. Surber sample series taken in 1988 and 1989; 2 nights spent in both 1988 (2—3 Sep) and 1989 (30—31Aug), MV light collection at night in both years. In addition to the stream at the bridge, I walked down the road and collected, by net, along a slightly smaller stream a hundred meters or so down the road, and then further down the road, perhaps a kilometer, to where a small stream flowed down over a large rocky shelf just above the road.

Thirty two kilometers west of Pilcopata, Quitacalzón, km 164, 1050 m, 13° 01.57 S, 71° 29.97' W. Stream 3 m wide, 1/4 m deep, rock, gravel, sand, swift; upper andean tropical wet forest. Two nights (1—2 Sep) spent in 1989, MV light collection. In addition to the larger stream a second light collection was made at a second bridge about 50 meters away over a small stream.

Approximately midway between Pilcopata (km 196, at 12° 54.51' S, 71°24.20'W) and Atalaya (km 210, at 12° 53.34' S, 71° 21.55' W), 500 m. Roadside seeps and small streamlet, grassy vegetation, forest adjacent. Swept by net in day, on Sep 4 1988, while waiting for bus to negotiate deep holes and ruts.

Hostel Erika on Río Alto Madre de Dios, 400 m; across river from Salvación at near km 227. River 20—50 m wide, 1 or more m deep, rocks, bedrock, sand and silt. Three days in 1988 (Sep 4—6) and '89 (Sep 3—5); surber sample series taken in 1988 in a small stream entering river just above Hostel; MV light by river at night, net by day along stream behind Hostel (not good as stream badly scoured by floods). The following year the river carved a new channel nearer Salvación, leaving Erika about 2 km from the water!

"Limonal", a sandbar beside the river about 10 km up the Río Manu from Boca Manu (at 12° 15.96' S, 70° 55.42' W) and not many km below guard station "Romero"; overnight camp, about 200 m. River 20 m wide, 1 or more m deep; sand, silt, many downed trees in water. Night of Sep 7 1988; MV light by river (such swarms of insects at light it was virtually impossible to collect).

RESULTS AND DISCUSSION

The caddisfly collections made on the Pakitza expeditions have now been sorted to species, and those that have been described are named. The collections contain 14 families, 51 genera and 224 species. Of the 224 species, only 77 (34%) can be named with any degree of certainty, the remainder being undescribed or belonging to complexes needing further careful study to determine species limits. Pakitza and environs was the home to 114 (51%) species, 126 (56%) species were found in the montane sites, with only 16 (7%) species being common to both.

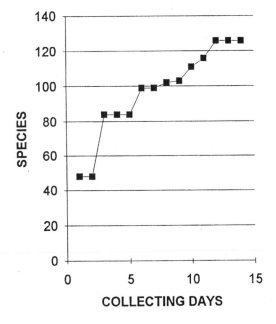

Fig. 1.– *Species accumulation curve for caddiflies collected on the montane transect.*

For the purposes of comparison, the sites have been divided into two series, one the montane the other the lowland. The montane series begins at the top of the pass, east of Paucartambo and includes the various stops descending the mountain - park Entrance Station, Puente Morro Leguia, Puente San Pedro, Quitacalzón - and finally the Hosteria Erika on the Upper Madre de Dios. The latter site is at

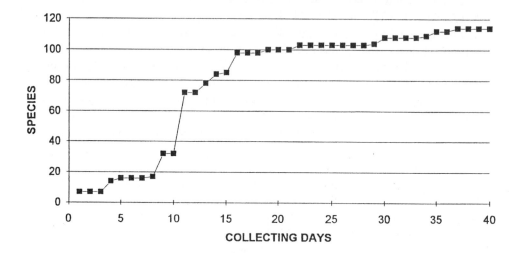

Fig. 2.– *Species accumulation curve for caddisflies collected in the lowlands, around Pakitza.*

the lowest elevation and on a large river, but the river is very fast with a rocky bottom, supporting a fauna more similar in general facies to the rest of the montane sites than to the lowland ones. This transect passes through a series of life zones: puna and elfin forest, upper montane forest and shrubland, andean montane wet forest, upper andean tropical wet forest, and humid andean foothills forest. All the lowland sites are on or near the Río Manu above Boca Manu and mostly around Pakitza in the tropical lowland forest zone. The 14 days effort on the mountain transect produced 126 species (56% of the total), while the 40 days effort at the lowland sites uncovered 114 species (51%). Only 16 species (7%) were found in both regions, with most overlap occurring between Erika and Pakitza.

Species accumulation curves (Figs. 1, 2) were prepared, but the data were not collected in a statistically rigorous manner so they can not be used predictively. Each day does not represent, necessarily, equal effort, or time. Collections made in the various years are strung together, which with the different collectors, are very unequal in technique (but each resulted in some species not taken in any other year). Another problem is due to the pooling with inclusive dates of collections made at the same site; all specimens from such a collection might have

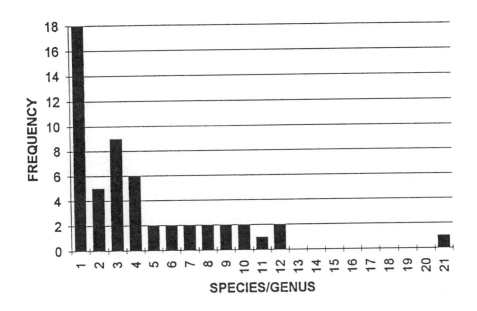

Fig. 3.– Frecuency of a given number of species in each genus or subgenus of caddisfly collected in this survey

a date of 9-14 Sep 1988, and all species first encountered in this lot would be credited to the first day. Nevertheless they are suggestive: the montane species list is still growing most rapidly, but perhaps leveling off a bit. The lowland list is now only very slowly growing, and would appear to be much closer to a maximum. I would predict that only the discovery of a different type of aquatic habitat, or perhaps a different season of the year, would increase the lowland fauna above 150 species. The montane fauna is still unpredictable in my estimation, with many habitat types still uncollected and techniques untried. The number of species here could well rise above 200.

For purposes of comparison with other insectan groups appearing in this volume, I counted the number of species in each genus or subgenus of caddisfly. The results are shown in figure 3. The curve is a fair approximation to the expected curve, especially considering only 54 genera were present.

TAXONOMIC LIST

The following list is a summary of the families, genera, and number of species found in each (with the number found at Pakitza and environs in parentheses).

Family Hydrobiosidae: *Atopsyche*, 10 species (0 Pakitza).
Family Glossosomatidae: *Mexitrichia*, 9 species (3 Pakitza).
                          Mortoniella, 4 species (0 Pakitza).

	Protoptila, 6 species (5 Pakitza).
	? *Antoptila*, 1 species (1 Pakitza).
Family Philopotamidae:	*Wormaldia*, 1 species (1 Pakitza).
	Chimarrhodella, 2 species (0 Pakitza).
	Chimarra, 13 species (2 Pakitza).
Family Ecnomidae:	*Austrotinodes*, 3 species (1 Pakitza).
Family Xiphocentronidae:	*Xiphocentron*, 2 species (2 Pakitza).
Family Polycentropodidae:	*Cernotina*, 3 species (3 Pakitza).
	Cyrnellus, 3 species (3 Pakitza).
	Nyctiophylax, 1 species (0 Pakitza).
	Polycentropus, 4 species (1 Pakitza).
	Polyplectropus, 3 species (2 Pakitza).
Family Hydroptilidae:	*Alisotrichia*, 1 species (1 Pakitza).
	"Flintiella", 1 species (1 Pakitza).
	Byrsopteryx, 1 species (0 Pakitza).
	Bredinia, 2 species (1 Pakitza).
	Ceratotrichia, 1 species (0 Pakitza).
	Anchitrichia, 1 species (0 Pakitza).
	Zumatrichia, 1 species (0 Pakitza).
	N. gen., 1 species (0 Pakitza).
	Acostatrichia, 1 species (1 Pakitza).
	Unknown gen., 2 species (1 Pakitza).
	Ochrotrichia, 14 species (10 Pakitza).
	Rhyacopsyche, 5 species (0 Pakitza).
	Hydroptila, 4 species (1 Pakitza).
	Oxyethira, 3 species (2 Pakitza).
	Neotrichia, 12 species (10 Pakitza).
Family Hydrosychidae:	*Smicridea*, 30 species (16 Pakitza).
	Leptonema, 12 species (7 Pakitza).
	Macronema, 4 species (3 Pakitza).
	Macrostemum, 3 species (3 Pakitza).
	Centromacronema, 3 species (0 Pakitza).
	Synoestropsis, 2 species (2 Pakitza).
Family Leptoceridae:	?N.gen., n.sp., 1 species (0 Pakitza).
	Atanatolica, 3 species (0 Pakitza).
	Grumichella, 1 species (0 Pakitza).
	Triplectides, 1 species (1 Pakitza).
	Achoropsyche, 1 species (1 Pakitza).
	Amphoropsyche, 1 species (0 Pakitza).
	Nectopsyche, 11 species (8 Pakitza).
	Oecetis, 10 species (9 Pakitza).
Family Atriplectidae:	N.gen., n.sp., 1 species (0 Pakitza).
Family Calamoceratidae:	*Banyllarga*, 4 species (1 Pakitza).
	Phylloicus, 7 species (5 Pakitza).

376

Family Odontoceridae: *Marilia*, 7 species (4 Pakitza).
Family Helicopsychidae: *Cochliopsyche*, 3 species (2 Pakitza).
                                     Helicopsyche, 4 species (1 Pakitza).
Family Anomalopsychidae: *Contulma*, 1 species (0 Pakitza).

KEY TO FAMILIES

The following key is to all the families of caddisflies known to occur in South America. Certain of the families are found only in the Chilean Subregion and no further mention of them is made - Stenopsychidae, Helicophidae, Kokiriidae, Tasimiidae, and Philorheithridae. Under each family heading is a key to the genera known from South America outside the Chilean Subregion (simply referred to as Chile in the distributions). I have tried to make the key simple by using easily seen, contrasting characteristics, but this has sometimes not been as clear-cut as desired.

1. Mesoscutellum composed of a triangular, flat area, with a vertical posterior margin; forewing length 1.5-4 mm .... Hydroptilidae
   Mesoscutellum evenly convex, without vertical posterior margin; length generally over 4 mm, rarely less than 2 mm 2
2. Ocelli present 3
   Ocelli absent 8
3. Maxillary palpus with fifth segment 2-3 times as long as fourth segment 4
   Maxillary palpus with either less than 5 segments or with fifth segment barely longer then fourth 5
4. Foreleg with a preapical spur .... Stenopsychidae
   Foreleg lacking a preapical spur .... Philopotamidae
5. Foreleg with 2 apical spurs (1 may be very small) 6
   Foreleg with 1 apical spur, or lacking all spurs 7
6. Midleg lacking preapical spurs; 1 apical spur of foreleg minute ....
   .... Anomalopsychidae
   Midleg with a pair of preapical spurs; both apical spurs of foreleg large
   Hydobiosidae
7. Foreleg with a single, well-developed apical spur; midleg with 1 or no preapical spurs .... Limnephilidae
   Foreleg lacking or with 1 hairlike apical spur; midleg with 2 preapical spurs (*Merionoptila* lacks them, but has wings reduced) .... Glossosomatidae
8. Maxillary palpus with terminal segment elongate and with suture-like cross striae, or palpi lacking 9
   Terminal segment subequal to preceeding segment, without cross striations
   12
9. Mesoscutum lacking setal warts .... Hydropsychidae
   Mesoscutum with distinct setal warts, or with a quadrangular anteromesal area delineated by sutures 10

377

10. Forewing with R$_1$ terminating in a fork .... Ecnomidae
    Forewing with R$_1$ entire to wing margin 11
11. Mesoscutum with a quadrangular anteromesal area delineated by sutures; no distinct setal warts .... Xiphocentronidae
    Mesoscutum without quadrangular area, but with distinct setal warts
    Polycentropodidae
12. Forewing with a distinct crossvein between anterior and posterior branches of M .... Calamoceratidae
    Forewing lacking this crossvein 13
13. Midtibia lacking preapical spur 14
    Midtibia with preapical spurs 17
14. Hindwing lacking conspicuously enlarged and/or hooked setae along entire anterior margin .... Sericostomatidae
    Hindwing with a row of conspicuously different setae along a part of the anterior margin 15
15. Hindwing with anterior margin lacking specialized setae for basal quarter or more before a row of hooked setae are present near midlength Leptoceridae.
    Hindwing with anterior margin bearing specialized setae from base for a variable distance apicad 16
16. Hindwing with specialized setae of anterior margin straight and elongate; maxillary palpi of ♂ of 5 subequal segments .... Helicophidae
    Hindwing with specialized setae of anterior margin curved or hooked and elongate; maxillary palpi of ♂ reduced to 2 or 3 segments .. Helicopsychidae
17. Head with mouth parts elongated into a rostrum from the end of which the palpi are borne .... Kokiriidae
    Head with mouth parts normal, palpi borne from venter of head 18
18. Wings with R$_{2+3}$ undivided .... Tasimiidae
    Forewings, at least, with R$_{2+3}$ forked 19
19. First segment of maxillary palpi short, with an apicomesal, setiferous, enlargement or lobe .... Philorheithridae
    First segment of maxillary palpi long, without any apicomesal enlargement
    20
20. Forewing with R$_1$ joining R$_2$ shortly before wing margin .... Odontoceridae
    Forewing with R$_1$ and R$_2$ extending freely to wing margin ...... Atriplectidae

FAMILY HYDROBIOSIDAE

This family is found over all of the Neotropical Realm, and enters the southwestern United States. It is also well represented in New Zealand, Australia and southeastern Asia. Twenty one genera are recognized in the New World, but only two are found outside the Chilean Subregion (the Peruvian *Dolochorema* is now considered a subgenus of *Atopsyche*).

KEY TO GENERA

1. Forewing with M_{1+2} and M_{3+4} forked at about half way to wing margin (Andes from Ecuador through Chile) .... *Cailloma*
   Forewing with M_{1+2} forked at about half way to wing margin, but M_{3+4} forked from near base (all Neotropics except Chile) .... *Atopsyche*

ATOPSYCHE ULMERI ROSS

This species was originally described from the Cosñipata Valley, Peru, and has since been recorded from the Yungas of La Paz, Bolivia.

Material Examined.— Puente San Pedro, 2—3 Sep 1988, MV light, 17♂, 14♀; same, but 30—31 Aug 1989, 5♂, 1♀. Stream 3 km E Puente San Pedro, 31 Aug 1989, MV light, 1♂. Quitacalzón, 1—2 Sep 1989, MV light, 15♂, 19♀. Streamlet 50 m E Quitacalzón, 2 Sep 1989, MV light, 1♂, 2♀.

ATOPSYCHE NEOTROPICALIS SCHMID

The species was recently described from Quincemil, Peru. This is the second recorded occurrence of the species.

Material Examined.— Puente San Pedro, 30—31 Aug 1989, MV light, 1♂, 1♀. Quitacalzón, 1—2 Sep 1989, MV light, 1♂, 4♀. Streamlet 50 m E Quitacalzón, 2 Sep 1989, MV light, 2♀. Hostel Erika, 4—6 Sep 1988, MV light, 13♀; same, but 3—5 Sep 1989, 1♂, 2♀.

ATOPSYCHE CALLOSA (NAVÁS)

This is one of the most widely distributed species of the genus, being known from Costa Rica south to Peru, and east across northern Venezuela.

Material Examined.— Puente San Pedro, 2—3 Sep 1988, MV light, 11♂, 21♀; same, but 30—31 Aug 1989, 2♀. Quitacalzón, 1—2 Sep 1989, MV light, 1♂, 7♀. Streamlet 50 m E Quitacalzón, 2 Sep 1989, MV light, 2♀. Hostel Erika, 4—6 Sep 1988, MV light, 9♀; same, but 3—5 Sep 1989, 5♀.

ATOPSYCHE VATUCRA ROSS

Another species described from the Cosñipata Valley, but not since recorded.

Material Examined.— Puente San Pedro, 2—3 Sep 1988, MV light, 3♂, 1♀. Quitacalzón, 1—2 Sep 1989, MV light, 1♂, 1♀. Streamlet 50 m E Quitacalzón, 2 Sep 1989, MV light, 1♀.

Oliver S. Flint, Jr.

ATOPSYCHE KINGI ROSS

Yet another species described from the Cosñipata Valley and not recorded afterwards.

Material Examined.— Puente San Pedro, 2—3 Sep 1988, MV light, 1♂, 1♀.

ATOPSYCHE PUHARCOCHA SCHMID

This species was recently described from several localities in La Paz and Cochabamba in Bolivia as well as Buenos Aires on our transect.

Material Examined.— Puente San Pedro, 2—3 Sep 1988, MV light, 2♂, 1♀.

ATOPSYCHE MANCOCAPAC SCHMID

This species was recently described from several localities around Puyo, Ecuador.

Material Examined.— Hostel Erika, 4—6 Sep 1988, MV light, 2♂, 1♀.

ATOPSYCHE LOBOSA ROSS AND KING

The species had been known only from Incachaca, Bolivia. Several males have recently been seen that were collected near the top of the transect; it is believed that the females are correctly associated.

Material Examined.— "Sueca", 1700 m, rain-forest, 23 Dec 1952, F. Woytkowski, 1♂ (INHS). Pillahuata, 2800 m, 14 Dec 1952, 1♂ (NMNH). "Pilco", side valley of river Paucartambo, 2800 m, 14—20 Jan 1953, 3♀ (INHS, NMNH). Puente Morro Leguia, 28—29 Aug 1989, MV light, 1♀.

ATOPSYCHE N. SP., NEAR MAJOR SCHMID

A single male metamorphotype of this species as taken at hight elevations.

Material Examined.— Near park entrance station, near km 106, 3420 m, 28 Aug 1989, 1♂ metamorphotype.

ATOPSYCHE SPECIES

The single adult female was also taken fairly high up, and is, in appearance, very much like females of A. unicolor or bicolor. It might possibly the female of the preceeding species, but is considered distinct for now.

Material Examined.— Puente Morro Leguia, 28—29 Aug 1989, MV light, 1♀.

FAMILY GLOSSOSOMATIDAE

Representatives of the family are found in all faunal regions of the world. All the South American genera are placed in the subfamily Protoptilinae. There are 7 other genera presently known only from Mexico, Central America, the West Indies or Chile that are not included in the key.

KEY TO GENERA

1. Wings, especially hind, reduced in size and venation (west-central Argentina)
   .... *Merionoptila*
   Wings not reduced 2
2. Two branches of M in forewing 3
   Three branches of M in forewing 4
3. Cu_1 branched apically in hindwing (Andes from Venezuela into Argentina)
   .... *Mortoniella*
   Cu_1 unbranched in hindwing (All Neotropics, except West Indies and Chile)
   .... *Mexitrichia*
4. R_{4+5} branching nearer forewing margin than R_{2+3} (southeastern Brazil)
   .... *Canoptila*
   R_{4+5} and R_{2+3} branching at nearly same level 5
5. Cu_1 in hindwing branched apically (central South America) .... *Antoptila*
   Cu_1 in hindwing simple (North, Central and South America, except Greater
   Antilles and Chile) .... *Protoptila*

MEXITRICHIA N. SP. 1

This species is distantly related to the Venezuelan M. *limona* Flint.

Material Examined.— Pakitza, trail 1, 1st stream (mkr. 14), 19—23 Sep 1989, Malaise trap, 1♂. Pakitza, trail 2, 1st stream, 14—23 Sep 1988, Malaise trap, 23♂, 7♀.

MEXITRICHIA N. SP. 2

This species is distantly related to the M. *simla* Flint, described from the island of Trinidad.

Material Examined.— Pakitza, trail 1, 1st stream (mkr. 14), 19—23 Sep 1989, Malaise trap, 4♂, 16♀. Pakitza, trail 2, 1st stream, 17—20 Sep 1988, UV light, 8♂, 28♀; same, but 14—23 Sep 1988, Malaise trap, 10♂, 25♀. Pakitza, trail 2, mkr. 18, 12—23 Sep 1989, Malaise trap, 1♀. Pakitza, kitchen stream, 18 Sep 1988, UV light, 1♂, 16♀.

Mexitrichia n. sp. 3

This species is very close to M. *macarenica* Flint, described from the Amazonian lowlands of Colombia. The forewing has the veins on the upperside, near the central region of the wing, bearing large, flattened scales.

Material Examined.— Hostel Erika, 4—6 Sep 1988, MV light, 35♂, 140♀; same, but 3—5 Sep 1989, 1♂; same, but 3 & 5 Sep 1989, R.A. Faitoute (colls. 20 & 26), 2♂, 5♀. Limonal (10 km N Boca Manu), Río Manu, 7 Sep 1988, MV light, 8♀. Manu River between Boca Manu & Romero, 6 Sep 1989, R.A. Faitoute (coll. 27), 2♀. Pakitza, 9 Sep 1988, 1♂.

Mexitrichia n. sp. 4

This species is close to M. *velasquezi* Flint, described from Antioquia in Colombia. The forewing has the veins on the upperside bearing scales, and the hindwing in the central region of the wing also covered with scales.

Material Examined.— Hostel Erika, 4—6 Sep 1988, MV light, 6♂, 37♀; same, but 3—5 Sep 1989, 1♂, 1♀; same, but 3 & 5 Sep 1989, R.A. Faitoute (colls. 20 & 26), 2♂, 4♀.

Mexitrichia atenuata Flint

This species was originaly described from Río Pichis, Puerto Bermudez, Peru and is here recorded for the second time. The forewing and hindwing are both densely covered on both surfaces with scales and hairs.

Material Examined.— Hostel Erika, 4—6 Sep 1988, MV light, 8♂, 21♀; same, but 3—5 Sep 1989, 8♂, 8♀; same, but 3 & 5 Sep 1989, R.A. Faitoute (colls. 20 & 26), 8♂, 6♀;

Mexitrichia n. sp. 5

This species in the form of the tenth tergum is reminiscent of M. *velasquezi*, but other parts of the genitalia make a true affinity doubtful. The wings are unmodified.

Material Examined.— Hostel Erika, 4—6 Sep 1988, MV light, 1♂, 11♀; same, but 3—5 Sep 1989, 2♂; same, but 3 & 5 Sep 1989, R.A. Faitoute (colls. 20 & 26), 2♂, 2♂.

Mexitrichia n. sp. 6

This species is also somewhat related to M. *macarenica* Flint, but differs strongly in the slender lateral processes of the phallus which are hooked apically. The wings are unmodified.

Material Examined.— Puente San Pedro, 2—3 Sep 1988, swept by net in daytime, 2♂.

MEXITRICHIA N. SP. 7

This is a very unusual species of no known close affinities. The wings are unmodified.

Material Examined.— Pilcopata to Atlaya, 4 Sep 1988, swept by net in daytime, 2♂.

MEXITRICHIA N. SP. 8

This is a very distinctive species, most similar to M. *atenuata*.

Material Examined.— Quitacalzón, 1—2 Sep 1989, MV light, 8♂. Streamlet 50 m E Quitacalzón, 2 Sep 1989, MV light, 1♂, 3♀.

MORTONIELLA N. SP. 1

This species is close to M. *angulata* Flint, described from Ecuador. I am not certain that the unassociated females belong to this one species, although they agree in coloration and in gross appearance of their genitalia.

Material Examined.— Puente San Pedro, 2—3 Sep 1988, MV light, 1♀. Quitacalzón, 1—2 Sep 1989, MV light, 1♀. Hostel Erika, 4—6 Sep 1988, MV light, 1♂, 1♀.

MORTONIELLA N. SP. 2

This species is very closely related to M. *enchrysa* Flint, described from Colombia, not only in coloration but also in structure of its genitalia.

Material Examined.— Puente San Pedro, 2—3 Sep 1988, MV light, 1♂. Quitacalzón, 1—2 Sep 1989, MV light, 1♀.

MORTONIELLA N. SP. 3

Another species of the *enchrysa* group, but abundantly distinct from its congeners in structure of its genitalia.

Material Examined.— Puente Morro Leguia, 28—29 Aug 1989, MV light, 1♂.

MORTONIELLA SP. 4

This is clearly a different species from any of the above, but, lacking males, its identity can not be ascertained. The forewings are uniformly fuscous, rather than bivittate or golden as are the other species.

Material Examined.— Puente Morro Leguia, 28—29 Aug 1989, MV light, 1♀.

PROTOPTILA N. SP. 1

The species is closely related to the Costa Rican P. *spirifera* Flint.

Material Examined.— Pakitza, trail 1, 1st stream (mkr. 14), 11 Sep 1988, UV light, 18♂, 9♀; same, but 9—14 Sep 1988, Malaise trap, 5♂, 9♀; same, but 19—23 Sep 1989, Malaise trap, 91♂, 52♀. Pakitza, trail 2, 1st stream, 17—20 Sep 1988, UV light, 60♂, 50♀; same, but 20 Sep 1988, M.G. Pogue, 1♂; same, but 14—23 Sep 1988, Malaise trap, 32♂, 77♀. Pakitza, trail 2, mkr 18, 12—23 Sep 1989, MV light, 2♂, 7♀. Pakitza, kitchen stream, 18 Sep 1988, UV light, 2♂, 3♀; same, but 12—18 Sep 1989, Malaise trap, 3♂, 3♀

PROTOPTILA N. SP. 2

The species is a member of the *dubitans* group, not clearly related to any other described species.

Material Examined.— Pakitza, 27 Sep 1987, UV trap, M.G. Pogue, 1♀. Pakitza, trail 1, 1st stream (mkr 14), 11 Sep 1988, UV light, 6♂, 23♀; same, but 19—23 Sep 1989, Malaise trap, 3♂, 1♀. Pakitza, trail 2, 1st stream, 17—20 Sep 1988, UV light, 4♂, 19♀; same, but 20 Sep 1988, M.G. Pogue, 5♂, 21♀; same, but 14—23 Sep 1988, Malaise trap, 1♂, 6♀. Pakitza, kitchen stream, 18 Sep 1988, UV light, 8♂, 76♀.

PROTOPTILA N. SP. 3

The species is very closely related to the Argentinian *P. misionensis* Flint, and, indeed, may be no more than a regional variation of it.

Material Examined.— Hostel Erika, 4—6 Sep 1988, MV light, 5♂, 16♀. Pakitza, trail 2, 1st stream, 17—20 Sep 1988, UV light, 1♂.

PROTOPTILA N. SP. 4

The species is another member of the *dubitans* group, but abundantly distinct from all other known species.

Material Examined.— Limonal (10 km N Boca Manu), Río Manu, 7 Sep 1988, MV light, 1♂, 12♀.

PROTOPTILA N. SP. 5

This is another species related to *spirifera*, but differs from it and other known species of group 1 in the sclerotized base of the lateral processes.

Material Examined.— Hostel Erika, 4—6 Sep 1988, MV light, 1♂, 25♀.

PROTOPTILA SP. 6

This is a very distinct species for which no males were found in the collection made on these expeditions.

Material Examined:— Hostel Erika, 4—6 Sep 1988, MV light, 1♀. Limonal (10 km N Boca Manu), Río Manu, 7 Sep 1988, MV light, 1♀.

? ANTOPTILA N. SP. 1

Although the genitalia of this species seem to be on the same plan as the other *Antoptila* species, the wings are much reduced with a consequent reduction in venation resulting in a pattern quite inconsistent with the type species of the genus.

Material Examined.— Pakitza, trail 2, 1st stream, 17—20 Sep 1988, UV light, 1♀; same, but 14—23 Sep 1988, Malaise trap, 12♂, 23♀.

FAMILY PHILOPOTAMIDAE

This family is widely distributed throughout the world and the entire Neotropics. *Wormaldia* and *Sortosa* are placed in the Philopotaminae, *Chimarrhodella* and *Chimarra* in the Chimarrinae. These four genera are all that are known from the Neotropical Realm.

KEY TO GENERA

1. Forewing with 3 branches to M 2
   Forewing with 4 branches to M 3
2. Foretibia with 1 small apical spur (all of the Neotropics except Chile)
   Chimarra ....
   Foretibia with 2 spurs, one almost twice as long as the other (Costa Rica south through the Andes into Bolivia) .... *Chimarrhodella*
3. Hindwing with 2A atrophied apically beyond a basal crossvein (all the Neotropics except Greater Antilles and Chile) .... *Wormaldia*
   Hindwing with 2A extending beyond crossvein, generally to wing margin (southeastern Brazil and Chile) .... *Sortosa*

WORMALDIA INSIGNIS MARTYNOV

The species was originally described from Callanga and its synonym, *ostina* Ross, was described from Santa Isabel, Cosñipata Valley. This record is still in the same general region.

Material Examined.— Pakitza, 30 Sep 1987, UV trap, M.G. Pogue, 1♂, 1♀.

CHIMARRHODELLA PERUVIANA (ROSS)

Originally described from the Cosñipata Vallley, it has since been recorded from Colombia and Venezuela.

Material Examined.— Puente San Pedro, 2—3 Sep 1988, by net in day, 3♂, 3♀. Stream, 3 km E Puente San Pedro, 31 Aug 1989, MV light, 1♂, 2♀. Quitacalzón, 1—2 Sep 1989, MV light, 2♂.

CHIMARRHODELLA ULMERI (ROSS)

Originally described from Aina, south Peru, it is very widespread from Bolivia to Venezuela, north to Costa Rica.

Material Examined.— Seeps E Buenos Aires, 29 Aug 1989, by net in day, 1♂, 1♀. Puente San Pedro, 2—3 Sep 1988, by net in day, 3♂, 1♀; same, but 30—31 Aug 1989, MV light, 1♂. Stream 3 km E Puente San Pedro, 31 Aug 1989, MV light and by net in day, 1♂, 1♀. Quitacalzón, 2 Sep 1989, by net in day, 1♀.

CHIMARRA (CURGIA) IMMACULATA (ULMER)

The species is widespread over the eastern Andes from Bolivia to Venezuela.

Material Examined.— Hostel Erika, 4—6 Sep 1988, MV light, 46♂, 46♀. Limonal (10 km N Boca Manu), Río Manu, 7 Sep 1988, MV light, 23♂, 25♀. Pakitza, Río Manu, 9—21 Sep 1988, MV light, 1♂, 1♀. Pakitza, trail 1, 1st stream, 11 Sep 1988, UV light, 19♂, 21♀. Pakitza, trail 1, mkr. 4, 8—22 Sep 1989, 1♂, 1♀. Pakitza, trail 2, 1st stream, 17—20 Sep 1988, UV light, 38♂, 34♀; same, but 14—23 Sep 1988, Malaise trap, 94♂, 82♀; same, but 20 Sep 1988, UV light, M. G. Pogue, 1♂. Pakitza, kitchen stream, 18 Sep 1988, UV light, 3♂, 13♀. Aguajal [ca. 5 km S Pakitza], 12 Sep 1988, M.G. Pogue, 2♂. Cocha Salvador, ca. 10 km S Pakitza, 13—14 Sep 1988, MV light, 1♂, 1♀.

CHIMARRA (CURGIA) CHRYSOSOMA, MS.

This and the following new species are members of the *margaritae* group. This species is also known from the Yungas of Bolivia.

Material Examined.— Puente Morro Leguia, 28—29 Aug 1989, MV light, 1♂. Puente San Pedro, 2—3 Sep 1988, MV light, 5♂. Quitacalzón, 1—2 Sep 1989, MV light, 9♂, 3♀. Streamlet 50 m E Quitacalzón, 2 Sep 1989, MV light, 4♂, 4♀.

CHIMARRA (CURGIA) ACULA, MS.

This and the preceding new species are members of the *margaritae* group.
Material Examined.— Puente San Pedro, 2—3 Sep 1988, MV light, 1♂, 3♀.

CHIMARRA (CURGIA) AVICEPS, MS.

This species is a member of the *distermina* group.
Material Examined.— Stream 3 km E Puente San Pedro, 31 Aug 1989, MV light, 2♂, 2♀.

CHIMARRA (CURGIA) ERECTILOBA, MS.

This and the following new species are closely related members of the *laguna* group. This species is only known from this region.

Material Examined.— Puente San Pedro, 2—3 Sep 1988, MV light, 7♂, 6♀; same, but 30—31 Aug 1989, 5♂, 5♀. Stream 3 km E Puente San Pedro, 31 Aug 1989, MV light, 1♂, 2♀. Quitacalzón, 1—2 Sep 1989, MV light, 3♂.

CHIMARRA (CURGIA) MYCTEROPHORA, MS.

This and the preceding new species are members of the *laguna* group. This species is also known from the Yungas of Bolivia.

Material Examined.— Puente San Pedro, 2—3 Sep 1988, MV light, 6♂, 10♀; same, but 30—31 Aug 1989, 2♂, 2♀.

CHIMARRA (CURGIA) PERUVIANA, MS.

This is another member of the *laguna* group. The species is also known northwardly to the Province of Napo in Ecuador.

Material Examined.— Quitacalzón, 1—2 Sep 1989, MV light, 5♂, 9♀. Streamlet 50 m E Quitacalzón, 2 Sep 1989, MV light, 4♀.

CHIMARRA (CURGIA) TAMBA, MS.

This is yet another member of the *laguna* group. This species is only known from this area.

Material Examined.— Puente San Pedro, 2—3 Sep 1988, MV light, 1♂.

CHIMARRA (CHIMARRA), POOLEI GRP. D, MS.

This is a new species of the *poolei* group, presently being revised. This species is known from as far east in the Amazon Basin as the Rio Xingu in Brazil.

Material Examined.— Hostel Erika, 4—6 Sep 88, MV light, 3♂. Pakitza, 9—23 Sep 1988, 6♀; same, but 30 Sep 1987, UV trap, M.G. Pogue, 1♂. Pakitza, Río Manu, 9—21 Sep 1989, MV light, 1♂. Pakitza, trail 1, 1st stream (mkr. 14), 11 Sep 1988, UV light, 1♂, 3♀; same, but 19—23 Sep 1989, Malaise trap, 2♂, 1♀. Pakitza, trail 1, mkr. 4, 8—22 Sep 1989, 1♂. Pakitza, trail 2, 1st stream, 17—20 Sep 1988, UV light, 8♂, 15♀; same, but 14—23 Sep 1988, Malaise trap, 7♂, 10♀. Pakitza, trail 2, mkr. 20, 17—20 Sep 1989, UV light, 6♂, 2♀. Pakitza, trail 2, mkr. 12, 16—22 Sep 1989, UV light, 7♂, 3♀.

CHIMARRA (CHIMARRA), POOLEI GRP. H, MS..

Another new species, apparently belonging to the *poolei* group. It is only known up to now from this region.

Material Examined.— Stream 3 km E Puente San Pedro, 31 Aug 1989, MV light, 1♂. Quitacalzón, 1—2 Sep 1989, MV light, 3♂, 7♀. Hostel Erika, 4—6 Sep 88, MV light, 5♂; same, but 3—5 Sep 89, 1♂, 2♀; same, but 3 & 5 Sep 1989, R.A. Faitoute (colls. 20 & 26), 1♂.

Chimarra (Chimarra), n. sp. D, ms.

This and the following species are distinctive new members of the *platyrhina* group. Both are known only from this one site.

Material Examined.— Hostel Erika, 4—6 Sep 88, MV light, 1♂; same, but 3— 5 Sep 89, 1♂; same, but 3 & 5 Sep 1989, R.A. Faitoute (colls. 20 & 26), 1♂.

Chimarra (Chimarra), n. sp. E, ms.

This species is closely related to the preceding species.

Material Examined.— Hostel Erika, 4—6 Sep 88, MV light, 1♂.

Chimarra (Chimarra) patosa Ross

This is a very distinctive species, the type of the *patosa* group, that probably will require a new subgenus when the genus is more fully analyzed. The original types were from the Cosñipata Valley and Callanga, Peru.

Material Examined.— Puente San Pedro, 30—31 Aug 1989, MV light, 1♂, 1♀. Quitacalzón, 1—2 Sep 1989, MV light, 1♀. Streamlet 50 m E Quitacalzón, 2 Sep 1989, MV light, 1♂.

Family Ecnomidae

The family is found over most of the world except the Nearctic Realm, but is no where generically diverse. Only this single genus is known from the Neotropics, where it is found in both the Brazilian and Chilean Subregions.

Austrotinodes n.sp.

This interesting species is quite closely related to the Chilean *talcana* (Navás), and thus the first known examples of the typical group of *Austrotinodes* to be found outside of the Chilean Subregion.

Material Examined.— Park Entrance Station, nr. km 106, seeps, 3420 m, 28 Aug 1989, 1♂.

Austrotinodes n. sp. 2

An interesting new species, apparently related to the Venezuelan *fuscomarginatus*, and thus a member of the second group of species. It is only known up to now from this region.

Material Examined.— Quitacalzón, at km 164, 1—2 Sep 1989, MV light, R. A. Faitoute (colls. 16 & 18), 1♂.

Austrotinodes sp.

These specimens are all female, and thus their identity is unknown; in fact, there may be two species represented in this material, one of which could be the opposite sex of the preceding one. They belong to the second group of species in the genus, that is widespread over the Neotropics outside the Chilean Region.

Material Examined.— Pakitza, trail 2, 1st stream, 17—20 Sep 1988, UV light, 2♀. Pakitza, trail 2, mkr. 12, 16—22 Sep 1989, MV light, 1♀.

FAMILY XIPHOCENTRONIDAE

Representatives of the family are found in tropical Africa, southeastern Asia and the American tropics. Three genera have been proposed for the New World species. Unfortunately the genera are defined only on characteristics of the male genitalia.

KEY TO GENERA

1. Claspers (inferior appendages) with a large lobe from posterior margin of basal segment, and ventrally with a dense band of long setae (Mexico south into Colombia) .... *Cnodocentron*
   Claspers without any such lobe or setae 2
2. Claspers with a bifid lobe covered with black, scabrous points at the junction of the two segments (Mexico to Venezuela .... *Machairocentron*
   Claspers lacking such a structure, but have a cluster of short, black setae in this general region (all the Neotropics except Chile) .... *Xiphocentron*

XIPHOCENTRON (ANTILLOTRICHIA) N. SP. 1

This is quite close to X. *mnestus* which is widespread in Venezuela and Colombia, at least. The forewing is fuscous with a slightly elongate, oblique, silver spot, with one end usually touching the anterior margin.

Material Examined.— Pakitza, trail 1, 1st stream (mkr. 14), 9—14 Sep 1988, Malaise trap, 1♀; same, but 19—23 Sep 1989, Malaise trap, 6♂, 4♀. Pakitza, trail 2, 1st stream, 14—23 Sep 1988, Malaise trap, 1♂. Pakitza, trail 2, mkr. 12, 16—22 Sep 1989, MV light, 1♂. Pakitza, kitchen stream 12—18 Sep 1989, Malaise trap, 2♀.

XIPHOCENTRON (ANTILLOTRICHIA) N. SP. 2

This is very distinctive species not clearly related to any other species. The forewing is fuscous with a round silver spot, centrally in the wing; the antennae of both sexes, basally, have dense fringes of hair, especially long on inner margin.

Material Examined.— Pakitza, trail 1, 1st stream (mkr. 14), 9—14 Sep 1988, Malaise trap, 1♂, 1♀; same, but 19—23 Sep 1989, Malaise trap, 1♂, 4♀.

Family Polycentropodidae

A family spread over all the regions of the world, it is well represented in the Neotropical Realm. The genus *Chilocentropus*, described from Chile, is presently unrecognized.

1. Foretibia with a preapical spur 2
   Foretibia lacking preapical spur (all New World except Chile) ..... *Cernotina*
2. Forewing with R_2 present 3
   Forewing with R_2 and R_3 fused to wing margin 4
3. Hindwing with R_2 present (all Neotropics) .... *Polycentropus*
   Hindwing with R_2 and R_3 fused to wing margin (all Neotropics, except Greater Antilles and Chile) .... *Polyplectropus*
4. Maxillary palpus with second segment long, third very slightly longer than second (all Neotropics, except West Indies and Chile) .... *Cyrnellus*
   Maxillary palpus with second segment short, third three times as long a second (all Neotropics, except West Indies and Chile) .... *Nyctiophylax*

Cernotina N. SP. 1

This is a very distinctive species without any obvious close relatives.

Material Examined.— Pakitza, trail 1, 1st stream (mkr. 14), 11 Sep 1988, UV light, 5♂, 33♀; same, but 9—14 Sep 1988, Malaise trap, 14♂, 5♀; same, but 19—23 Sep 1989, Malaise trap, 9♂. Pakitza, trail 2, 1st stream, 17—20 Sep 1988, UV light, 10♀; same, but 14—23 Sep 1988, Malaise trap, 16♂, 19♀; same, but 20 Sep 1988, light trap, M.G. Pogue, 4♂, 8♀. Pakitza, kitchen stream, 12—18 Sep 1989, Malaise trap, 2♂, 1♀.

Cernotina N. SP. 2

This is a distinctive species seeming to belong to the group of species related to *C. taeniata* Ross, in that the cerci have very long, incurved and darkened apices.

Material Examined.— Pakitza, trail 1, 1st stream (mkr. 14), 11 Sep 1988, UV light, 1♂; same, but 9—14 Sep 1988, Malaise trap, 1♂; same, but 19—23 Sep 1989, Malaise trap, 2♂. Pakitza, trail 2, 1st stream, 14—23 Sep 1988, Malaise trap, 1♂.

Cernotina N. SP. 3

This is another distinctive species seeming to belong to the group of species having the apex of the tenth tergum darkened and pointed, but without known close relatives beyond the group.

Material Examined.—Pakitza, trail 2, 1st stream, 20 Sep 1988, light trap, M.G. Pogue, 1♂.

CYRNELLUS MAMMILLATUS FLINT

This species is widespread over the Amazon Basin in Brazil and the Parana Basin in Argentina. These are the first published records from Peru.

Material Examined.— Pakitza, trail 1, 1st stream (mkr. 14), 11 Sep 1988, UV light, 2♂, 1♀; same, but 9—14 Sep 1988, Malaise trap, 7♂, 2♀; same, but 19—23 Sep 1989, Malaise trap, 2♂. Pakitza, trail 2, 1st stream, 20 Sep 1988, UV trap, M.G. Pogue, 3♂, 2♀; same, but 14—23 Sep 1988, Malaise trap, 1♂. Cocha Salvador, 10 km S Pakitza, 13—14 Sep 1988, MV light, 12♂, 23♀.

CYRNELLUS ULMERI FLINT

This species has a known distribution much like the preceding; Brazil and Argentina.

Material Examined.— Pakitza, trail 1, mkr. 8, 11—13 Sep 1989, MV light, 1♂.

CYRNELLUS COLLARIS FLINT

This is only the second recorded occurrence of the species which was described from the central Amazon Basin in Brazil.

Material Examined.— Pakitza, 9—23 Sep 1988, 1♂, 1♀. Pakitza, trail 1, mkr. 8, 11—13 Sep 1989, MV light, 1♂. Pakitza, trail 2, 1st stream, 20 Sep 1988, light trap, M.G. Pogue, 1♂, 3♀.

NYCTIOPHYLAX N. SP. 1

This is very close to *N. neotropicalis* which is widespread in South America. However, the male genitalia seem to offer several distinctions between the two species.

Material Examined.— Quitacalzón, 1—2 Sep 1989, MV light, 1♂.

POLYCENTROPUS CUSPIDATUS FLINT

This species was described from Puyo at the eastern foot of the Andes in central Ecuador; this is its second record.

Material Examined.— Pakitza, 9—23 Sep 1988, 1♂. Pakitza, trail 2, 1st stream, 14—23 Sep 1988, Malaise trap, 1♀. Pakitza, trail 2, mkr. 12, 16—22 Sep 1989, MV light, 1♂.

POLYCENTROPUS JOERGENSENI ULMER

This species is widespread in the Andean areas, being known from Argentina north to Venezuela; it has been previously recorded from the Department of La Libertad in Peru.

Material Examined.— Puente San Pedro, 2—3 Sep 1988, MV light, 1♂, 1♀; same, but 30—31 Aug 1989, 1♂. Stream 3 km E Puente San Pedro, 31 Aug 1989, MV light, 1♂. Quitacalzón, 1—2 Sep 1989, MV light, 2♀.

POLYCENTROPUS SP. 1

This species, which is only known from females, is, based on genitalia, clearly distinct from the females of both the preceding and following species.
Material Examined.— Quitacalzón, 1—2 Sep 1989, MV light, 3♀.

POLYCENTROPUS SP. 2

This species, also only known from a female is very distinctive.
Material Examined.— Puente Morro Leguia, 28—29 Aug 1989, MV light, 1♀.

POLYPLECTROPUS N. SP. 1

This is not clearly related to any other described species, and in fact it could possibly be better placed in *Polycentropus*.
Material Examined.— Quitacalzón, 1—2 Sep 1989, MV light, 1♂.

POLYPLECTROPUS N. SP. 2

This is very closely related to the Lesser Antillean species *P. bredini* Flint.
Material Examined.— Pakitza, 30 Sep 1987, UV trap, M.G. Pogue, 1♀. Pakitza, trail 1, 1st stream (mkr. 14), 11 Sep 1988, UV light, 5♂, 8♀; same, but 19—23 Sep 1989, Malaise trap, 1 ♂; same, but 20 Sep 1988, light trap, M.G. Pogue, 5♂, 1♀. Pakitza, trail 2, 1st stream, 17—20 Sep 1988, UV light, 3♀; same, but 14—23 Sep 1988, Malaise trap, 1♀. Pakitza, trail 2, mkr. 12, 16—22 Sep 1989, MV light, 1♂. Pakitza, trail 2, mkr. 18, 12—23 Sep 1989, MV light, 2♂, 1♀. Aguajal [ca. 5 km S Pakitza], 12 Sep 1988, UV trap, M.G. Pogue, 1♀.

POLYPLECTROPUS SP. 3

These specimens clearly represent a species different from the preceding, both on basis of coloration and genitalia. No males were taken which would have permitted a positive identification.
Material Examined.— Pakitza, Río Manu, 9—21 Sep 1988, MV light, 1♀. Cocha Salvador, 10 km S Pakitza, 13—14 Sep 1988, MV light, 1♀.

FAMILY HYDROPTILIDAE

The hydroptilids, commonly referred to as the micro-caddisflies, are found over the entire world, including many remote oceanic islands. The generic classification is difficult and frequently depends on characters of the male, including genitalia or modifications of the head, wings, or other appendages. In addition to those genera herein keyed, the following are known from the Neotropical Realm: *Celaenotrichia* and *Nothotrichia* from Chile, *Kumanskiella* from the Greater Antilles, *Ithytrichia* from Mexico, and *Diaulus* and *Peltopsyche* are known only as cases from Brazil.

KEY TO GENERA

1.   Ocelli present 5
    Ocelli absent 2
2.   Mesoscutum entire, without a transverse suture 3
    Mesoscutellum with a transverse suture running between lateral angles (Central and South America, except Chile and West Indies).. "Flintiella"
3.   Midleg lacking preapical spur (all of Neotropics except Chile)
    .... *Hydroptila*
    Midleg with preapical spur 4
4.   Male genitalia symmetrical; VII sternum with a long process (south central Venezuela) .... *Taraxitrichia*
    Genitalia, especially tenth tergum, markedly asymmetrical; seventh sternum lacking such a process (Central and northern South America and Greater Antilles) .... *Orthotrichia*
5.   Mesoscutellum lacking a transverse suture 6
    Mesoscutellum with a transverse suture between lateral angles 9
6.   Hindleg with only 1 preapical spur (all of Neotropics) .... *Neotrichia*
    Hindleg with 2 preapical spurs 7
7.   Midleg lacking preapical spurs (Central and northern South America)
    Mayatrichia
    Midleg with 1 preapical spur 8
8.   Anterior margin of segment IX in male convex or triangular in ventral view (all the Neotropics) .... *Oxyethira*
    Anterior margin of segment IX concave in ventral view (amazonian Brazil) .... *Tricholeiochiton*
9.   Metascutellum broad mesally, almost triangular in outine 11
    Metascutellum truncate laterally, usually narrow, thus narrowly rectangular in outline, rarely broader centrally, but still broadly truncate laterally.... 10
10.   Phallus ending in a central tube flanked by lateral processes, either a simple lobe or one that is more elongate and fimbriate; without internal spines and sclerites (Central and South America, Lesser Antilles) .... *Bredinia*
    Phallus variable, usually with no apical processes or these are everted spines, often with internal spines and other sclerites (Central and northern and western South America, West Indies) .... *Alisotrichia*

11. Phallus with a saddlelike midlength complex usually with a circular, lateral, windowlike structure and a basal loop 14
    Phallus with no such midlength complex 12
12. Foretibia with an apical spur 13
    Foretibia lacking an apical spur (all Neotropics except southeastern and southern South America) .... Ochrotrichia (Ochrotrichia)
13. Male genitalia with a rounded cercus, an elongate, narrow, hooked sclerite between tenth tergum and clasper, and phallus usually with 2 (uncommonly 1 or lacking), large, dark spines between midlength and apex (all Neotropics) .... Ochrotrichia (Metrichia)
    Genitalia lacking cercus and hooked sclerite, phallus without large hooks (All Neotropics except West Indies and Chile) .... Rhyacopsyche
14. Scape of male antenna greatly modified, often enlarged, bearing appendages and specialized setae 15
    Scape usually simple, rarely elongate or bean shaped and with some specialized setae mesally 16
15. Scape with very large lobes fitting into deep concavities in face and overlain by a large, pointed lobe from vertex (southeastern South America) .... Abtrichia
    Scape with a large frontal lobe covering half of face which is cupped, but not deeply so nor with lobe from vertex (Central and northern and western South America and Lesser Antilles) .... Zumatrichia
16. Male genitalia with lateral penis sheaths small, semimembranous; subgenital plate connected dorsally to tenth tergites, and produced ventrally to articulate apically with a sclerite lying in a dorsomesal grove of the approximate claspers (Central and northern South America, West Indies) .... Leucotrichia
    Lateral penis sheaths generally large, produced posteriad, sclerotized; subgenital plate generally lacking or of different structure; claspers widely separated 17
17. Ocelli 3 18
    Ocelli 2 20
18. Antenna of male with basal segment enlarged, globose and densely hairy (Peru) .... new genus
    Antenna with basal segment unmodified 19
19. Antenna of male generally with segments 3-9 broad and compressed, rarely unmodified; seventh sternum with a single, long apicomesal process (Central and northern South America) .... Costatrichia
    Antenna simple; seventh sternum with 2 elongate, pointed mesal processes (South America, except Chile) .... Acostatrichia
20. Antenna of male with middle flagellar segments enlarged and flattened, head with posterior warts large with many scale hairs projecting from beneath, basal portions of many longitudinal veins of forewing with rows of erect, enlarged hairs (Panama and northern and western South America) .... Ceratotrichia

Antenna simple, head either unmodified, or with an anteromesal plate and
other modifications, no veins or only R with specialized setae 21

21. Head of male with a reflexed, anteromesal plate and with a sac filled with
modified setae beneath it (Suriname south to Paraguay) .... *Anchitrichia*
Head of male unmodified (Central and South América, except Chile)
.... *Ascotrichia*

ALISOTRICHIA N. SP. 1

This is an interesting species of no obvious close affinities. It has an unmodified
head with only 2 ocelli, the antennal scape is slightly enlarged and bean shaped,
and a spur count of 0,2,4.

Material Examined.— Pakitza, kitchen stream, 12—18 Sep 1989, Malaise trap,
5♂.

"FLINTIELLA" N. SP. 1

Although clearly a member of this still undescribed genus, it seems to be
distinct from the other species that are known.

Material Examined.— Pakitza, trail 2, 1st stream, 14—23 Sep 1988, Malaise
trap, 4♂. Pakitza, kitchen stream, 12—18 Sep 1989, Malaise trap, 1♂.

BYRSOPTERYX N. SP. 1

This is an interesting species in a genus that is in the final stages of revision.
Until the publication appears the species relationships and identity are unknown.
The immature stages were taken in a small brook at the site and the adults were
found running over the rocks in bright sunlight at the same time.

Material Examined.— Hostel Erika, 3—5 Sep 1989, many larvae,
metamorphotypes, ♂ & ♀ adults.

BREDINIA N. SP. 1

This is a species in a moderate sized genus that is in the final stages of revision.
Until the publication appears, the relationships and identity of the species is
unknown.

Material Examined.— Pakitza, trail 1, 1st stream (mkr. 14), 9—14 Sep 1988,
Malaise trap, 9♂, 2♀; same, but 19—23 Sep 1989, Malaise trap, 1♂. Pakitza, trail
2, 1st stream, 14—23 Sep 1988, Malaise trap, 7♂, 1♀.

BREDINIA SP. 2.

A single female specimen of an unknown species of the genus was taken at
"Erika". Untill the genus is revised it is impossible to know if it the same as the
above species or yet another species.

Oliver S. Flint, Jr.

Material Examined.— Hostel Erika, 3 & 5 Sep 1989, MV light, R.A. Faitoute (colls. 20 & 26), 1♀.

CERATOTRICHIA FLAVICOMA FLINT

This species was recently described from Venezuela and Ecuador. This is the first record for Peru.
Material Examined.— Hostel Erika, 4—6 Sep 1988, MV light, 2♂, 1♀.

ANCHITRICHIA N. SP.

This species is most closely related to A. *duplifurcata* from Brazil and Paraguay.
Material Examined.— Hostel Erika, 4—6 Sep 1988, MV light, 4♂, 1♀.

ZUMATRICHIA N. SP.

This is the southernmost record of the genus. The species seems to be related to Z. *angula* from northern Panama.
Material Examined.— Hostel Erika, 4—6 Sep 1988, MV light, 2♂, 1♀.

LEUCOTRICHIINE, ? N. GEN., N. SP.

These specimens are unquestionably an undescribed species, but one without a clear-cut generic placement; probably a new genus will be established for the species when the tribe is studied in detail. The species has 3 ocelli, although the median ocellus is a bit reduced and placed in a shallow depression in the front of the head, the basal antennal segment is enlarged, globose and densely hairy, but the species seems to lack most other modifications of head, antennae and wings common in the tribe.
Material Examined.— Hostel Erika, 4—6 Sep 1988, MV light, 1♂, 3♀, same, but 3 & 5 Sep 1989, R.A. Faitoute (colls. 20 & 26), 1♂, 1♀.

ACOSTATRICHIA, N. SP.

The generic placement of this species is not absolutely certain, but it fits most closely into the concept of *Acostatrichia*: the head is unmodified, there are 3 ocelli, the antennae are simple, and the base of radius in the forewing is thickened. It is most similar to A. *spinifera*, but is clearly different.
Material Examined.— Pakitza, trail 1, 1st stream, 9—14 Sep 1988, Malaise trap, 1♂, 3♀. Pakitza, trail 2, 1st stream, 14—23 Sep 1988, Malaise trap, 36♂, 28♀.

LEUCOTRICHIINI, UNKNOWN GEN. AND SP., 1.

These large specimens clearly represent a species different from any of the above, but lacking an associated male, their identity can not be determined.

396

Material Examined.— Puente San Pedro, 2—3 Sep 1988, MV light, 10♀. Quitacalzón, 1—2 Sep 1989, MV light, 7♀.

LEUCOTRICHIINI, UNKNOWN GEN. AND SP., 2.

This is another large species clearly different from any of the above, but lacking an associated male, its identity can not be determined.

Material Examined.— Pakitza, 27 Sep 1987, UV trap, M.G. Pogue, 1♀.

RHYACOPSYCHE ANDINA FLINT

This species was recently described from examples taken in the highlands of the Andes in Colombia. This is the first record of the species in Peru.

Material Examined.— E. Buenos Aires, km. 135, 2150 m., 28—29 Aug 1989, MV light, 3♂, 1♀.

RHYACOPSYCHE N. SP. 1.

This species is closely related to the preceding, differing in details of the genitalia.

Material Examined.— Puente San Pedro, 2—3 Sep 1988, MV light, 1♂, 1♀; same, but 30—31 Aug 1989, 1♂, 2♀.

RHYACOPSYCHE N. SP. 2.

Another species in the same group as the two preceding, this species is quite different from them in details of the genitalia.

Material Examined.— Quitacalzón, 1—2 Sep 1989, MV light, 2♂, 1♀. Streamlet, 50 m E Quitacalzón, 2 Sep 1989, MV light, 1♂, 3♀.

RHYACOPSYCHE N. SP. 3.

This species belongs to the *turrialbae* group, and is most closely related to *R. jimena* from Colombia.

Material Examined.— Streamlet, 50 m E Quitacalzón, 2 Sep 1989, MV light, 4♂.

Rhyacopsyche n. sp. 4.

This is a species of obscure affinity, most likely belonging to the group of the first 3 species, but it is really very different from all.

Material Examined.— Hostel Erika, 3—5 Sep 1989, 1♂ metamorphotype, 1 empty pupal case.

Oliver S. Flint, Jr.

OCHROTRICHIA (O.) N. SP. 1.

This species is a member of the *tarsalis* group, most similar to O. *oblongata*, but abundantly different in details of the genitalia.

Material Examined.— Puente San Pedro, 2—3 Sep 1988, MV light, 1♂.

OCHROTRICHIA (O.) N. SP. 2.

This species is probably a member of the same group as the preceding, but very different in the structure of the genitalia.

Material Examined.— Puente San Pedro, 2—3 Sep 1988, MV light, 1♂; same, but 30—31 Aug 1989, 1♂. Stream 3 km E Puénte San Pedro, 31 Aug 1989, MV light, 1♂, 2♀.

OCHROTRICHIA (O.) N. SP. 3.

This species is a member of the *arranca* group, very close to O. *yanayacuana*.
Material Examined.— Puente San Pedro, 2—3 Sep 1988, MV light, 1♂, 2♀.

OCHROTRICHIA (O.) N. SP. 4.

This species is probably a member of the *xena* group, very close to O. *flagellata*.
Material Examined.— Pakitza, trail 1, 1st stream, 9—14 Sep 1988, Malaise trap, 5♂; same, but 19—23 Sep 1989, Malaise trap, 1♂.

OCHROTRICHIA (O.) N. SP. 5.

This species is also probably a member of the *xena* group, quite close to the preceding.

Material Examined.—Pakitza, trail 1, 1st stream, 19—23 Sep 1989, Malaise trap, 1♂. Pakitza, trail 2, 1st stream, 14—23 Sep 1988, Malaise trap, 7♂.

OCHROTRICHIA (O.) N. SP. 6.

This species is also probably a member of the *xena* group, but distinct from all the others.

Material Examined.— Pakitza, trail 2, 1st stream, 14—23 Sep 1988, Malaise trap, 1♂.

OCHROTRICHIA (O.) N. SP. 7.

This species is also probably a member of the *xena* group, also quite distinct from the others.

Material Examined.— Pakitza, trail 1, 1st stream (mkr. 14), 19—23 Sep 1989, Malaise trap, 1♂.

OCHROTRICHIA (O.) N. SP. 8.

This species is a member of the *tarsalis* group, quite close to new species 1.
Material Examined.— Pakitza, trail 2, 1st stream, 14—23 Sep 1988, Malaise trap, 5♂.

OCHROTRICHIA (M.) SP. 1.

This species is very close to *patagonica*, but the tip of the phallus appears broken off, and without this area certain specific identification is impossible.
Material Examined.— Stream 5 km N Paucartambo, 28 Aug 1989, 1♂.

OCHROTRICHIA (M.) N. SP. 2.

This species has tip of the phallus bearing two spines, one long the other short, the dorsal margin of the clasper is drawn out into a point, and the antennal segments are terete.
Material Examined.— Pakitza, trail 2, 1st stream, 14—23 Sep 1988, Malaise trap, 1♂.

OCHROTRICHIA (M.) N. SP. 3.

This species has tip of the phallus wholly enclosed in a sheath, and the ventral margin of the clasper is drawn out into a point.
Material Examined.— Pakitza, trail 2, 1st stream, 14—23 Sep 1988, Malaise trap, 1♂.

OCHROTRICHIA (M.) N. SP. 4.

This species is almost identical to species 2, but there are slight differences in the clasper, and the antennal segments are flatenned and very broad.
Material Examined.— Pakitza, trail 2, 1st stream, 14—23 Sep 1988, Malaise trap, 1♂. Pakitza, kitchen stream, 12—18 Sep 1989, Malaise trap, 3♂.

OCHROTRICHIA (M.) N. SP. 5.

This species has tip of the phallus braring two spines, both quite short, the clasper bears a small apicomesal point.
Material Examined.— Pakitza, trail 1, 1st stream, 9—14 Sep 1988, Malaise trap, 1♂.

OCHROTRICHIA (M.) N. SP. 6.

This species has tip of the phallus bearing two, quite long spines, and the dorsal surface of the abdominal segment 6 bears two large, lateral hair-tufts.

Material Examined.— Pakitza, kitchen stream, 12—18 Sep 1989, Malaise trap, 1♂.

HYDROPTILA N. SP. 1.

This is a species of obscure affinity, perhaps distantly related to *H. coscaroni*, but readily distinguished by the exceedingly long phallus with a very slender apical process.

Material Examined.— Puente San Pedro, 30—31 Aug 1989, MV light, 1♂.

HYDROPTILA N. SP. 2.

This is a species is very closely related to *H. venezuelensis*.

Material Examined.— Hostel Erika, 3—5 Sep 1989, MV light, 2♂.

HYDROPTILA N. SP. 3.

A very distinctive species of no obvious close relationships; the tenth tergites are long and very slender, as is the clasper which has its tip produced in a laterally produced single dark point, and the phallus with a single sclerotized apical process.

Material Examined.— Pakitza, 9 Sep 1988, 1♀. Pakitza, trail 1, 1st stream (mkr. 14), 11 Sep 1988, UV light, 1♂; same, but 19—23 Sep 1989, Malaise trap, 1♂, 4♀. Pakitza, trail 2, 1st stream, 14—23 Sep 1988, Malaise trap, 1♂; same, but 17—20 Sep 1988, UV light, 2♀.

HYDROPTILA SP. 4.

This female posseses a very distinctive genialia, but lacking associated males it is impossible to know what its relationships might be. It is unlikely that it is to be associated with either n. sp. 1 or 2.

Material Examined.— Hostel Erika, 3 & 5 Sep 1989, MV light, R.A. Faitoute (colls. 20 & 26), 1♀.

OXYETHIRA N. SP. 1.

The single male that is the basis for this species is very different in genitalic structure from all other New World species of the genus. The females placed here also posses very distinctive genialia, and are assumed to belong to this species, but this association is by no means certain.

Material Examined.— Puente San Pedro, 2—3 Sep 1988, MV light, 2♀. Hostel Erika, 4—6 Sep 1988, MV light, 1♀; same, but 3 & 5 Sep 1989, R.A. Faitoute (colls. 20 & 26), 1♂.

OXYETHIRA AZTECA MOSELY

This species, as currently defined, is widely distributed from Mexico (type locality) south to Pakitza, at least. The recent disentanglement of this species and *O. parce* has confused the exact distributions of the two species, at least until the old records are reconfirmed.

Material Examined.— Pakitza, 9 Sep 1988, 1♂. Pakitza, trail 1, 1st stream (mkr. 14), 11 Sep 1988, UV light, 17♂, 18♀; same, but 9—14 Sep 1988, Malaise trap, 1♂, 2♀; same, but 19—23 Sep 1989, Malaise trap, 15♂, 20♀. Pakitza, trail 2, 1st stream, 17—20 Sep 1988, UV light, 1♂, 2♀; same, but 14—23 Sep 1988, Malaise trap, 1♂, 2♀. Pakitza, kitchen stream, 18 Sep 1988, UV light, 8♂, 3♀; same, but 12—18 Sep 1989, Malaise trap, 3♀

OXYETHIRA N. SP. 2.

This very strange species is most similar to *rareza*, with which it shares a very asymmetrical male genitalia.

Material Examined.— Pakitza, trail 1, 1st stream (mkr. 14), 19—23 Sep 1989, Malaise trap, 1♂.

NEOTRICHIA N. SP. 1.

This species is a very typical member of the *corniculans* group, differing from the other described species by details of the male genitalia.

Material Examined.— Hostel Erika, 4—6 Sep 1988, MV light, 7♂, 3♀; same, but 3—5 Sep 1989, 1♂; same, but 3 & 5 Sep 1989, R.A. Faitoute (colls. 20 & 26), 11♂.

NEOTRICHIA N. SP. 2.

This species is a member of the "*Exitrichia*" group quite close to *colombiensis*, differing by details of the male genitalia.

Material Examined.— Hostel Erika, 3—5 Sep 1989, MV light, 3♂; same, but 3 & 5 Sep 1989, R.A. Faitoute (colls. 20 & 26), 3♂.

NEOTRICHIA N. SP. 3.

This species, also, is a member of the "*Exitrichia*" group most like *noteuna*, especially in the possesion of two long spines in the phallus.

Material Examined.— Limonal (10 km N Boca Manu), Río Manu, MV light, 7 Sep 1988, 1♂.

Oliver S. Flint, Jr.

NEOTRICHIA UNISPINA FLINT

This species is a member of the *"Exitrichia"* group, and was described from Suriname; this is only the second report for the species.

Material Examined.— Pakitza, 9 Sep 1988, 1♂.

NEOTRICHIA N. SP. 4.

This species is a member of the *"Exitrichia"* group, easily recognized by the darkened, twisted, apices of the claspers.

Material Examined.— Pakitza, trail 1, 1st stream (mkr. 14), 11 Sep 1988, UV light, 8♂; same, but 9—14 Sep 1988, Malaise trap, 1♂; same, but 19—23 Sep 1989, Malaise trap, 18♂. Pakitza, trail 2, 1st stream, 17—20 Sep 1988, UV light, 9♂; same, but 14—23 Sep 1988, Malaise trap, 53♂. Pakitza, kitchen stream, 18 Sep 1988, UV light 1♂; same, but 12—18 Sep 1989, Malaise trap, 1♂.

NEOTRICHIA N. SP. 5.

This species is a member of the *"Exitrichia"* group, and bears a pair of long spines from the dorsum of segment nine.

Material Examined.— Pakitza, trail 1, 1st stream (mkr. 14), 11 Sep 1988, UV light, 9♂; same, but 19—23 Sep 1989, Malaise trap, 12♂. Pakitza, trail 2, 1st stream, 17—20 Sep 1988, UV light, 1♂; same, but 14—23 Sep 1988, Malaise trap, 4♂. Pakitza, kitchen stream, 18 Sep 1988, UV light 2♂.

NEOTRICHIA N. SP. 6.

This species is a member of the *"Exitrichia"* group; its claspers are very short and darkened and the phallus does not bear heavy, darkened spines.

Material Examined.— Pakitza, trail 1, 1st stream (mkr. 14), 11 Sep 1988, UV light, 3♂; same, but 9—14 Sep 1988, Malaise trap, 1♂; same, but 19—23 Sep 1989, Malaise trap, 3♂.

NEOTRICHIA N. SP. 7.

This species is a member of the *"Lorotrichia"* group, similar in general pattern of its genitalia to the Mexican *xicana*.

Material Examined.— Pakitza, trail 1, 1st stream (mkr. 14), 11 Sep 1988, UV light, 2♂; same, but 9—14 Sep 1988, Malaise trap, 7♂; same, but 19—23 Sep 1989, Malaise trap, 28♂. Pakitza, trail 2, 1st stream, 17—20 Sep 1988, UV light, 2♂; same, but 14—23 Sep 1988, Malaise trap, 32♂.

NEOTRICHIA N. SP. 8.

This species is a member of the "*Exitrichia*" group; the phallus has 1 spine longer than the other and twisted at midlength with the shorter spine curled around the base of the longer spine.

Material Examined.— Pakitza, trail 1, 1st stream (mkr. 14), 11 Sep 1988, UV light, 2♂; same, but 19—23 Sep 1989, Malaise trap, 8♂. Pakitza, trail 2, 1st stream, 17—20 Sep 1988, UV light, 5♂; same, but 14—23 Sep 1988, Malaise trap, 30♂.

NEOTRICHIA N. SP. 9.

This species is a member of the "*Exitrichia*" group; it has rather abbreviated genitalia, with the phallus bearing a spine that is completely curled around its axis.

Material Examined.— Pakitza, trail 1, 1st stream, 11 Sep 1988, UV light, 2♂.

NEOTRICHIA N. SP. 10.

This species is a member of the "*Lorotrichia*" group, similar in general pattern of its genitalia to *cuernuda* from Venezuela.

Material Examined.— Pakitza, trail 1, 1st stream (mkr. 14), 9—14 Sep 1988, Malaise trap, 1♂; same, but 19—23 Sep 1989, Malaise trap, 6♂. Pakitza, trail 2, 1st stream, 14—23 Sep 1988, Malaise trap, 31♂. Pakitza, kitchen stream, 12—18 Sep 1989, Malaise trap, 1♂.

NEOTRICHIA N. SP. 11.

This species is an aberrant member of the "*Exitrichia*" group, bearing a pair of heavy, curved processes dorsolaterally from the ninth segment.

Material Examined.— Pakitza, trail 2, 1st stream, 14—23 Sep 1988, Malaise trap, 1♂. Pakitza, kitchen stream, 12—18 Sep 1989, Malaise trap, 2♂.

FAMILY HYDROPSYCHIDAE

This family, similarly to the preceeding, is widely distributed in all the regions of the world. In addition to the genera found in South America a number are known only from Mexico, Central America or the Greater Antilles: *Diplectrona*, *Cheumatopsyche*, *Hydropsyche*, *Calosopsyche*, *Mexipsyche* and *Plectropsyche*.

KEY TO GENERA

1. Antennae generally shorter than forewing; size smaller, forewing rarely exceeding 5 mm (all Neotropics) .... *Smicridea*
   Forewing 2 or 3 times as long as forewing; forewing usually over 7 mm 2
2. Palpi lacking (Central and South America, except West Indies and Chile)
   Synoestropsis
   Palpi present 3
3. Tibia of hindleg with 1 preapical spur; apex of forewing emarginate (Costa Rica south through lowland South America) .... *Plectromacronema*
   Hindtibia with 2 preapical spurs 4
4. Maxillary palpus with second segment 1 $1/_2$ -2 times as long as third (all Neotropics, except Chile) .... *Leptonema*
   Maxillary palpus with third segment as long or longer than second 5
5. Outer face of tip of foretibia elongated into a pointed process overlying basal tarsal segment (all Neotropics, except West Indies and Chile) ....
   .... *Centromacronema*
   Apex of foretibia without a process 6
6. Head middorsally with a longitudinal carina (reduced to posterior portion only in female); body densely hairy (lowland South America .... *Blepharopus*
   Head without such a carina; body sparsely hairy 7
7. Forewing without a crossvein between R_{2+3} and R_4; color of forewing pale with many anastamosing dark lines crossing it and a large spot over stigma (lowland South America) .... *Pseudomacronema*
   Forewing with a crossvein between R_{2+3} and R_4 or if lacking it, color a well-defined, yellow and brown pattern 8
8. Forewing color due mostly to scales, basal 2/3 usually green, bounded outwardly by a variably colored region, costal cell filled with silvery scales (all Neotropics, except Lesser Antlles and Chile) .... *Macronema*
   Forewing color due primarily to colors of the membrane and the pattern is widespread over the wings (all Neotropics, except West Indies and Chile) ..
   Macrostemum

SMICRIDEA (SMICRIDIA) CURVIPENIS FLINT

This species was recently described from examples collected in Colombia and Ecuador. These examples match perfectly as far as the male genitalia are concerned, yet have internal pheromone sacs much larger than the more northern examples.

Material Examined.— Puente San Pedro, 2—3 Sep 1988, MV light, 11♂; same, but 30—31 Aug 1989, 1♂. Quitacalzón, 1—2 Sep 1989, MV light, 1♂.

SMICRIDEA (SMICRIDEA) POLYFASCIATA MARTYNOV

This species was described from an example collected at 11°3'S, 75°17'W (near San Ramón, Junín), Peru, some 450 km NW of these examples. The species has recently been recorded from NW Bolivia north to central Colombia.

Material Examined.— Puente San Pedro, 2—3 Sep 1988, by net in day, 5♂.

SMICRIDEA (SMICRIDEA) BIDENTATA MARTYNOV

This species was described from an example collected at Callanga, Peru. This is the first time subsequent to its description that the species has been discovered.

Material Examined.— Pilcopata to Atlaya, 4 Sep 1988, by net in day, 1♂, 2♀. Pakitza, trail 2, mkr. 18, 12—23 Sep 1989, Malaise trap, 2♂.

SMICRIDEA (SMICRIDEA), PROBABLY NIGRICANS FLINT

This species was described from examples collected in Colombia and Ecuador. This example is a perfect match in size, color, and the bent down apex of the forewing, but lacking a male it is impossible to be certain.

Material Examined.— Puente San Pedro, 2—3 Sep 1988, by net in day, 1♀.

Smicridea (Smicridea) n. sp. 1

This species has been encountered quite frequently around Pakitza. It is most similar to *obliqua*, but is distinguished by small differences in the genitalia.

Material Examined.— Pakitza, Río Manu, 9—21 Sep 1988, MV light, 1♂, 4♀; same, but 17 Sep 1989, MV light, 1♂, 1♀. Pakitza, trail 1, 1st stream, 11 Sep 1988, UV light, 8♂, 13♀; same, but 9—14 Sep 1988, Malaise trap, 3♂, 2♀; same, but 19—23 Sep 1989, Malaise trap, 3♂, 9♀; same, but 8—9 Sep 1989, Gelhaus & Epstein, light trap, 1♂, 3♀. Pakitza, trail 2, 1st stream, 17—20 Sep 1988, UV light, 13♂, 14♀; same, but 20 Sep 1988, M. Pogue, light trap, 10♂, 12♀; same, but 14—23 Sep 1988, Malaise trap, 4♂, 3♀. Pakitza, kitchen stream, 18 Sep 1988, UV light, 3♂, 6♀; same, but 12—18 Sep 1989, Malaise trap, 4♂, 1♀. Aguajal [ca. 5 km S Pakitza], 12 Sep 1988, UV trap, M.G. Pogue, 1♂, 2♀.

SMICRIDEA (SMICRIDEA) N. SP. 2

This species is very close to *saucia*, differing only slight in the male genitalia.

Material Examined.— Quitacalzón, 1—2 Sep 1989, MV light, 1♂.

SMICRIDEA (SMICRIDEA) N. SP. 3

This species is very close to *bivittata*, differing only slightly in the shape of the apices of the claspers. The lone female is also assigned here, albeit with some doubts, because its genitalia are also very much like those of *bivittata*.

Material Examined.— Pakitza, trail 2, 1st stream, 20 Sep 1988, M. Pogue, light trap, 1♂. Aguajal [ca. 5 km S Pakitza], 12 Sep 1988, UV trap, M.G. Pogue, 1♀.

SMICRIDEA (SMICRIDEA) N. SP. 4

This species is a member of the *nigripennis* group, most similar to *reinerti*, but is distinguished by small differences in the genitalia.

Material Examined.— Pakitza, trail 1, 1st stream, 11 Sep 1988, UV light, 1♂, 2♀; same, but 9—14 Sep 1988, Malaise trap, 2♂, 2♀. Pakitza, trail 2, 1st stream, 17—20 Sep 1988, UV light, 1♂, 5♀; same, but 14—23 Sep 1988, Malaise trap, 2♂, 2♀. Pakitza, trail 2, marker 12, 16—22 Sep 1989, MV light, 5♂.

SMICRIDEA (SMICRIDEA) N. SP. 5

This is another member of the *nigripennis* quite close to the preceeding, but differing in the genitalia of both sexes.

Material Examined.— Pakitza, trail 1, 1st stream, 9—14 Sep 1988, Malaise trap, 1♀. Pakitza, trail 2, 1st stream, 14—23 Sep 1988, Malaise trap, 1♂, 1♀. Pakitza, kitchen stream, 12—18 Sep 1989, Malaise trap, 1♂, 2♀.

SMICRIDEA (RHYACOPHYLAX) PERUANA MARTYNOV

This species has been encountered quite frequently in Peru and northwestern Argentina. It was originally described from "Callanga", a site close to the present localities, although not precisely located at present.

Material Examined.— Puente San Pedro, 2—3 Sep 1988, MV light, 100♂♂ & ♀♀; same, but 30—31 Aug 1989, 35♂, 9♀; same, but 30 Aug 1989, R.A. Faitoute (coll. 9), 21♂, 9♀. Stream 3 km E Puente San Pedro, 31 Aug 1989, MV light, 11♂, 11♀. Quitacalzón, 1—2 Sep 1989, MV light, 14♂, 6♀. Streamlet 50 m E Quitacalzón, 2 Sep 1989, MV light, 10♂, 3♀.

SMICRIDEA (RHYACOPHYLAX) ANDICOLA FLINT

This species, a member of the *peruana* group, is widely distributed along the slopes of the Andes from Colombia through Ecuador, and now well south in Peru.

Material Examined.— Streamlet 50 m E Quitacalzón, 2 Sep 1989, MV light, 8♂, 6♀.

SMICRIDEA (RHYACOPHYLAX) ACUMINATA FLINT

This member of the *peruana* group, is widely distributed, being known previously from Costa Rica, Colombia and Peru.

Material Examined.— Quitacalzón, 1—2 Sep 1989, MV light, 2♂. Hostel Erika, 4—6 Sep 1988, MV light, 33♂, 21♀; same, but 3—5 Sep 1989, 1♂, 5♀; same, but 3 & 5 Sep 1989, R.A. Faitoute (colls. 20 & 26), 2♂, 2♀.

SMICRIDEA (RHYACOPHYLAX) N. SP. 1

This is a rather odd species in terms of the male genitalia, and does not have any obvious close relatives described at this time.

Material Examined.— Puente San Pedro, 2—3 Sep 1988, MV light, 34♂, 11♀; same, but 30—31 Aug 1989, 14♂, 2♀; same, but 30 Aug 1989, R.A. Faitoute (coll. 9), 17♂, 3♀. Stream 3 km E Puente San Pedro, 31 Aug 1989, MV light, 8♂, 13♀. Streamlet 50 m E Quitacalzón, 2 Sep 1989, MV light, 4♂, 1♀.

SMICRIDEA (RHYACOPHYLAX) N. SP. 2

This is one of largest species found in the genus up to now; it is the largest encountered in this study. The male genitalia are not similar to any other described species.

Material Examined.— Puente San Pedro, 2—3 Sep 1988, MV light, 13♂, 11♀; same, but 30—31 Aug 1989, 7♂, 13♀. Quitacalzón, 1—2 Sep 1989, MV light, 1♀. Streamlet 50 m E Quitacalzón, 2 Sep 1989, MV light, 1♀.

SMICRIDEA (RHYACOPHYLAX) N. SP. 6

This species is a member of the *peruana* group, distinguished by differences in the apex of the phallus.

Material Examined.— Streamlet 50 m E Quitacalzón, 2 Sep 1989, MV light, 1♂.

SMICRIDEA (RHYACOPHYLAX) MURINA MCLACHLAN

This is probably the most widespread species known in the subgenus. It is recorded Nicaragua in Central America, south along the western side of South America as far as central Chile.

Material Examined.— Puente San Pedro, 30 Aug 1989, MV light, R.A. Faitoute (coll. 9), 1♂. Streamlet 50 m E Quitacalzón, 2 Sep 1989, MV light, 1♂. Hostel Erika, 4—6 Sep 1988, MV light, 100♂♂ & ♀♀; same, but 3—5 Sep 1989, 50♂♂ &♀♀; same, but 3 & 5 Sep 1989, R.A. Faitoute (colls. 20 & 26), 50♂♂ & ♀♀. Limonal (10 km N Boca Manu), Río Manu, 7 Sep 1988, MV light, 9♂, 12♀. Between Boca Manu & Romero along Manu River, 6 Sep 1989, MV light, R.A. Faitoute (coll. 27), 1♂, 1♀.

SMICRIDEA (RHYACOPHYLAX) TITSCHKI FLINT

This species is known from a number of localities along the slopes of the Andes in Peru.

Material Examined.— Hostel Erika, 4—6 Sep 1988, MV light, 14♂, 4♀. Pakitza, Río Manu, 9—21 Sep 1988, MV light, 2♂.

SMICRIDEA (RHYACOPHYLAX) N. SP. 13

This species is not clearly a member of any known group. It is distinguished by the simple apex of the phallus, with only a membranous lobe and a curled internal sclerite.

Material Examined.— Hostel Erika, 3—5 Sep 1989, MV light, 1♂.

SMICRIDEA (RHYACOPHYLAX) PSEUDORADULA FLINT

This species is a member of the *radula* group, and was known only from Colombia and Ecuador. This record is a major range extension.

Material Examined.— Pakitza, trail 2, 1st stream, 20 Sep 1988, UV trap, M. Pogue, 2♂.

SMICRIDEA (RHYACOPHYLAX) N. SP. 3

This species is a member of the *radula* group, distinguished by the short, but very broad, dorsal lobe at the apex of the phallus.

Material Examined.— Hostel Erika, 4—6 Sep 1988, MV light, 2♂, 2♀; same, but 3—5 Sep 1989, 3♂; same, but 3 & 5 Sep 1989, R.A. Faitoute (colls. 20 & 26), 8♂, 8♀.

SMICRIDEA (RHYACOPHYLAX) N. SP. 5

This species is a member of the *radula* group, distinguished by the long dorsal lobe at the apex of the phallus.

Material Examined.— Streamlet 50 m E Quitacalzón, 2 Sep 1989, MV light, 2♂.

SMICRIDEA (RHYACOPHYLAX) BIDACTYLA FLINT

This recently described species, a member of the *signata* group, was known from Venezuela (questionably), Ecuador and the Department of Lambayeque in Peru. These records extend its known range considerably.

Material Examined.— Pakitza, 9—21 Sep 1988, MV light, 2♂, 1♀. Pakitza, trail 1, 1st stream, 11 Sep 1988, UV light, 1♂, 2♀. Pakitza, trail 2, 1st stream, 20 Sep 1988, UV trap, M. Pogue, 7♂, 9♀.

SMICRIDEA (RHYACOPHYLAX) N. SP. 4

This species is a member of the *signata* group, distinguished by widely separated and tapering apices of the tenth tergites and small differences in the apex of the phallus.

Material Examined.— Hostel Erika, 4—6 Sep 1988, MV light, 2♂, 1♀.

SMICRIDEA (RHYACOPHYLAX) N. SP. 7

This species is a member of the *signata* group, distinguished by the truncate and upturned apices of the tenth tergites and small differences in the apex of the phallus.

Material Examined.— Pakitza, Río Manu, 9—21 Sep 1988, MV light, 1♂. Pakitza, trail 1, 1st stream, 11 Sep 1988, UV light, 31♂, 22♀; same, but 9—14 Sep 1988, Malaise trap, 1♀. Pakitza, trail 2, 1st stream, 17—20 Sep 1988, UV light, 14♂, 11♀; same, but 14—23 Sep 1988, Malaise trap, 1♂, 6♀; same, but 20 Sep 1988, UV trap, M. Pogue, 50♂♂ & ♀♀. Pakitza, kitchen stream, 18 Sep 1988, UV light, 5♂, 6♀.

SMICRIDEA (RHYACOPHYLAX) N. SP. 8

This species is an unusual species with no apparent close affinities. It is distinguished by the two upturned spines from the apex of the phallus.

Material Examined.— Between Boca Manu and Romero, along Manu River, 6 Sep 1989, MV light, R.A. Faitoute (coll. 27), 2♂. Pakitza, Río Manu, 9—21 Sep 1988, MV light, 17♂, 2♀.

SMICRIDEA (RHYACOPHYLAX) VOLUTA FLINT

This distinctive species is widespread in the Amazon Basin in Brazil and almost as far south as Buenos Aires in Argentina. This record extends its known range into Peru.

Material Examined.— Pakitza, Río Manu, 9—21 Sep 1988, MV light, 1♂. Pakitza, trail 1, 1st stream, 11 Sep 1988, UV light, 1♂.

SMICRIDEA (RHYACOPHYLAX) N. SP. 12

This species is very similar to the preceeding, offering small differences in the tenth tergum, and in the apical structures of the phallus.

Material Examined.— Pakitza, trail 2, 1st stream, 20 Sep 1988, UV trap, M. Pogue, 1♂, 1♀.

SMICRIDEA (RHYACOPHYLAX) N. SP. 9

This is another odd species; it is distinguished by the dorsomesal spine from the apex of the phallus.

Material Examined.— Pakitza, trail 1, 1st stream, 11 Sep 1988, UV light, 8♂. Pakitza, trail 2, 1st stream, 20 Sep 1988, UV trap, M. Pogue, 2♂. Pakitza, kitchen stream, 18 Sep 1988, UV light, 2♂.

409

SMICRIDEA (RHYACOPHYLAX) N. SP. 10

This species seems to be a member of the *discalis* group, with which it shares the pair a small apicodorsal points at the tip of the phallus, but it differs from all other species in the group by also possesing lateral, spiculate pouches at the tip of the phallus.

Material Examined.— Limonal (10 km N Boca Manu), Río Manu, 7 Sep 1988, MV light, 100♂♂ & ♀♀. Between Boca Manu and Romero, along Manu river, 6 Sep 1989, MV light, R.A. Faitoute (coll. 27), 50♂♂ &♀♀. Pakitza, 17 Sep 1989, UV light, R.A. Faitoute (coll. 45), 50♂♂ & ♀♀. Pakitza, Río Manu, 9—21 Sep 1988, MV light, 100♂♂ & ♀♀; same, but 17 Sep 1989, 50♂♂ & ♀♀. Pakitza, trail 1, 1st stream (mkr. 14), 11 Sep 1988, UV light, 1♂; same, but 19 Sep 1989, R.A. Faitoute (coll. 47), 2♂. Pakitza, trail 1, mkr. 4, 8—22 Sep 1989, MV light, 75♂♂ & ♀♀. Pakitza, trail 2, mkr. 12, 16—22 Sep 1989, MV light, 1♂. Pakitza, trail 2, mkr. 18, 12—23 Sep 1989, Malaise trap, 1♂, 4♀; same, but 13 Sep 1989, R.A. Faitoute (coll. 39a), 2♂, 1♀. Pakitza, trail 2, mkr. 20, 17—20 Sep 1989, MV light, 3♂, 2♀. Pakitza, kitchen stream, 18 Sep 1988, UV light, 1♂, 2♀. Cocha Salvador, 10 km S Pakitza, 13—14 Sep 1988, MV light, 7♂, 1♀.

SMICRIDEA (RHYACOPHYLAX) N. SP. 11

This is a very distinctive species of the subgenus. It is easily recognized by being almost black with a distinct, transverse, subterminal, white band.

Material Examined.— Pakitza, Río Manu, 9—21 Sep 1988, MV light, 27♂, 8♀; same, but 17 Sep 1989, 4♂, 2♀. Pakitza, playa trail, 18 Sep 1989, MV light, 1♂. Pakitza, trail 1, mkr. 4, 8—22 Sep 1989, MV light, 7♂, 4♀. Pakitza, trail 1, mkr. 14, 19 Sep 1989, R.A. Faitoute (coll. 47), 1♂. Pakitza, trail 2, mkr. 20, 17—20 Sep 1989, MV light, 1♂. Pakitza, kitchen stream, 18 Sep 1988, UV light, 3♂, 2♀; same, but 12—18 Sep 1989, Malaise trap, 1♂. Cocha Salvador, 10 km S Pakitza, 13—14 Sep 1988, MV light, 3♂, 2♀.

CENTROMACRONEMA APICALE (WALKER)

The systematics of this, and almost all the other, species in *Centromacronema* is not very clear. What I am at this time calling species are defined mostly on gross appearance (size and coloration); the genitalia are very similar and specific differences have not yet been demonstrated. Within these broad limits, one finds noticeable differences in coloration within a species even at one site. At this time I consider these differences to be of intraspecific nature. Such is the case here with this species, there are two noticeably different forms. The species has been recorded from Costa Rica to Peru and east to Venezuela.

Material Examined.— Puente San Pedro, 2—3 Sep 1988, by net in day, 4♂; same, but 31 Aug 1989, 11♂, 2♀. Quitacalzón, 2 Sep 1989, 1♂.

CENTROMACRONEMA AURIPENNE (RAMBUR)

This species also is suject to considerable variation over its range, and shows both darker and paler forms here. It, or one of its many synonyms, has been recorded from Mexico to Brazil, including "Callanga" in Peru.

Material Examined.— E Buenos Aires, km. 135, 2150 m, 28—29 Aug 1989, 1♀. Puente San Pedro, 2—3 Sep 1988, net in daytime, 1♂; same, but 30—31 Aug 1989, 1♀.

CENTROMACRONEMA, PROBABLY OBSCURUM (ULMER)

I am using this name, with reservations as the type is now destroyed, for a species that is almost uniformly fuscous with a pale, transverse subterminal band on the forewing. I have seen this form from Honduras to Bolivia; it was described from Brazil.

Material Examined.— Puente San Pedro, 2—3 Sep 1988, by net in day, 13♂.

MACRONEMA FRATERNUM BANKS

This species is known from Costa Rica to Ecuador and east to Suriname; this is a major southerly range extension.

Material Examined.— Pakitza, 19 Sep 1989, J. Gelhaus (#445), 1♀. Pakitza, trail 2, mkr. 20, 17—20 Sep 1989, MV light, 1♂, 1♀. Pakitza, trail 2, mkr. 18, 12—23 Sep 1989, Malaise trap, 1♀.

MACRONEMA PERCITANS WALKER

This species is widespread in the Amazon Basin: known previously from Brazil and the Guianas, these records extend it known range considerably to the southwest.

Material Examined.— Pakitza, 27 Sep—5 Oct 1987, UV trap, M.G. Pogue, 5♂, 4♀. Pakitza, trail 1, 1st stream (mkr. 14), 11 Sep 1988, UV light, 1♀; same, but 19—23 Sep 1989, net collection, 1♂, 3♀. Pakitza, trail 1, mkr. 8, 11—13 Sep 1989, MV light, 1♂. Pakitza, trail 2, 1st stream, 17—20 Sep 1988, UV light, 1♂, 1♀; same, but 14—23 Sep 1988, Malaise trap, 1♂, 2♀. Pakitza, trail 2, mkr. 20, 17—20 Sep 1989, MV light, 3♂, 1♀. Pakitza, trail 2, mkr. 18, 12—23 Sep 1989, Malaise trap, 2♀. Pakitza, kitchen stream, 12—18 Sep 1989, Malaise trap, 1♂, 2♀.

MACRONEMA PERTYI BANKS

This species was known only from the central Amazonian region of Brazil; this adds considerable territory to the recorded range.

Material Examined.— Pakitza, trail 2, 1st stream, 14—23 Sep 1988, Malaise trap, 1♀. Pakitza, trail 1, mkr. 4, 8—22 Sep 1989, MV light, 1♀.

MACRONEMA, PROBABLY VARIIPENNE FLINT & BUENO

Because this record is based on females only, the specific identity can not be fully sustantiated. In appearance these examples match other specimens from Panama. The species has been recorded from Mexico to Ecuador, not including Peru.

Material Examined.— Quitacalzón, 2 Sep 1989, MV light, 4♂♀.

MACROSTEMUM ARCUATUM (ERICHSON)

This species has been reported previously only from the Guianas and central Amazonas of Brazil, this then, is a major extension of range.

Material Examined.— Pakitza, Río Manu, 9—21 Sep 1988, MV light, 1♀. Pakitza, trail 2, mkr. 20, 17—20 Sep 1989, MV light, 1♀.

MACROSTEMUM HYALINUM (PICTET)

Although only reported from the mountains of eastern Brazil previously it is much more widely distributed; I have examples from Colombia, Venezuela and Guyana.

Material Examined.— Pakitza, 1 Oct 1987, UV trap, M.G. Pogue, 1♂, 1♀. Pakitza, trail 2, mkr. 18, 12—23 Sep 1989, Malaise trap, 1♂, 1♀. Pakitza, trail 2, mkr. 20, 17—20 Sep 1989, MV light, 1♂.

MACROSTEMUM ULMERI (BANKS)

This species is widespread in the Neotropics: known previously from Honduras south to Peru and east to Suriname. It is frequently seen dancing in the sunshine over small forest streams around Pakitza.

Material Examined.— Puente San Pedro, 2—3 Sep 1988, MV light, 1♂. Pakitza, 1 Oct 1987, UV trap, M.G. Pogue, 1♂; same, but 9—23 Sep 1988, W.N. Mathis, 2♀. Pakitza, trail 1, 1st stream (mkr. 14), 9—14 Sep 1988, Malaise trap, 100♂♂ & ♀♀; same, but 19—23 Sep 1989, net collection, 11♂, 6♀. Pakitza, trail 1, mkr. 13 (Quebrada Claro), 8—9 Sep 1989, light trap, Gelhaus & Epstein, 1♀. Pakitza, trail 2, 1st stream (mkr. 15), 14—23 Sep 1988, Malaise trap, 100♂♂ & ♀♀; same, but 18 Sep 1989, by net, 6♂. Pakitza, trail 2, mkr. 12, 16—22 Sep 1989, MV light, 1♂. Pakitza, trail 2, mkr. 18, 12—23 Sep 1989, Malaise trap, 14♂, 8♀. Pakitza, kitchen stream, 12—18 Sep 1989, Malaise trap, 4♂, 15♀. Pakitza, Playa trail, 9 Sep 1989, Gelhaus & Epstein (#435), 1♂.

SYNOESTROPSIS GRISOLI NAVÁS

Widely reported from northern South America, it is here reported for the first time from Peru, although it had been expected there.

Material Examined.— Pakitza, Río Manu, 9—21 Sep 1988, MV light, 3♀. Pakitza, trail 1, mkr. 4, 8—22 Sep 1989, MV light, 3♀. Pakitza, trail 2, mkr. 20,

17—20 Sep 1989, MV light, 11♀. Pakitza, kitchen stream, 18 Sep 1988, UV light, 1♀.

SYNOESTROPSIS PUNCTIPENNIS ULMER

This species is also known from northern South America, but has been found through Central America as far north as Mexico. It is here reported for the first time from Peru.

Material Examined.— Pakitza, Río Manu, 17 Sep 1989, MV light, 1♀.

LEPTONEMA SPIRILLUM FLINT, MCALPINE & ROSS

The holotype of this species was from the Cosñipata Valley, with further records from Bolivia to Colombia and Venezuela. It is still quite common at torrential, small streams in the mountains.

Material Examined.— E Buenos Aires, km. 135, 2150 m, 28—29 Aug 1989, MV light, 2♀. Puente San Pedro, 2—3 Sep 1988, MV light, 50♂♂ & ♀♀; same, but 30—31 Aug 1989, 24♂♂ & ♀♀. Stream 3 km E Puente San Pedro, 31 Aug 1989, MV light, 5♂, 8♀. Quitacalzón, 1—2 Sep 1989, MV light, 93♂♂ &♀♀. Streamlet 50 m E Quitacalzón, 2 Sep 1989, MV light, 23♂♂ & ♀♀. Hostel Erika, 3—5 Sep 1989, MV light, 6♂.

LEPTONEMA N. SP. 1

This is a very distinctive species, tentatively placed in the *stigmosum* group. It is basically marked as the preceding species, also a member of the *stigmosum* group, but is a bit paler and smaller.

Material Examined.— Puente San Pedro, 2—3 Sep 1988, MV light, 1♂, 2♀.

LEPTONEMA INCA MOSELY

This species is found along the eastern slopes of the Andes from central Peru to Bolivia. It is one of the pale green species with a slight infuscation of the wing apices.

Material Examined.— Puente San Pedro, 2—3 Sep 1988, MV light, 4♂, 2♀. Stream 3 km E Puente San Pedro, 31 Aug 1989, MV light, 2♂. Quitacalzón, 1—2 Sep 1989, MV light, 13♂, 4♀.

LEPTONEMA TRIFIDUM FLINT, MCALPINE & ROSS

The holotype of this species was from Ecuador, but it is also known from the Cosñipata Valley. It is also a pale green species, virtually indistinguishable from the preceding on external characteristics.

Oliver S. Flint, Jr.

Material Examined.— Quitacalzón, 1—2 Sep 1989, MV light, 6♂, 3♀. Hostel Erika, 4—6 Sep 1988, MV light, 9♂; same, but 3—5 Sep 1989, 4♂.

LEPTONEMA ALCEATUM FLINT, MCALPINE & ROSS

This species was described from the Cosñipata Valley of Peru and the yungas of Bolivia. It is another pale green species, indistinguishable from the preceding ones on external characteristics.

Material Examined.— Hostel Erika, 4—6 Sep 1988, MV light, 1♂.

LEPTONEMA VIRIDIANUM NAVÁS

This species is very widely distributed in South America: the highlands of southeastern Brazil, Argentina and Paraguay, the eastern Andes from Bolivia to Colombia, and the Guianan Highlands of Venezuela and Guyana. It, too, is pale green in coloration.

Material Examined.— Hostel Erika, 4—6 Sep 1988, MV light, 2♂, 4♀; same, but 3—5 Sep 1989, 4♂. Pakitza, 27 Sep—4 Oct 1987, UV trap, M.G. Pogue, 37♂♂ & ♀♀; same, but 9—23 Sep 1988, 1♂, 15♀; same, but 8—20 Sep 1989, 2♂, 1♀. Pakitza, trail 1, mkr. 8, 11—13 Sep 1989, MV light, 1♂. Pakitza, trail 1, 1st stream (mkr. 14), 11 Sep 1988, UV light, 3♂, 2♀; same, but 9—14 Sep 1988, Malaise trap, 8♂, 4♀; same, but 19—23 Sep 1989, Malaise trap, 4♂, 3♀. Pakitza, trail 1, mkr. 13 (Quebrada Claro), 8—9 Sep 1989, light trap, Gelhaus & Epstein, 4♂. Pakitza, trail 2, 1st stream, 14—23 Sep 1988, Malaise trap, 75♂♂ & ♀♀; same, but 17—20 Sep 1988, UV light, 4♂, 3♀. Pakitza, trail 2, mkr. 12, 16—22 Sep 1989, MV light, 5♀. Pakitza, trail 2, mkr. 18, 12—23 Sep 1989, Malaise trap, 7♂, 4♀. Pakitza, trail 2, mkr. 20, 17—20 Sep 1989, MV light, 1♂, 2♀. Pakitza, kitchen stream, 18 Sep 1988, UV light, 4♂, 1♀. Pakitza, Playa trail, 18 Sep 1989, MV light, 1♂. Aguajal [ca. 5 km S. Pakitza], 12 Sep 1988, UV trap, M.G. Pogue, 1♂.

LEPTONEMA SPINULUM FLINT, MCALPINE & ROSS

The few records of this species are scattered over southeastern Brazil, the eastern Andes (including the Cosñipata Valley) and Guianan highlands. It is a pale green species, indistinguishable from the preceding ones on external characteristics.

Material Examined.— Pakitza, 30 Sep & 4 Oct 1987, UV trap, M.G. Pogue, 1♂, 1♀. Pakitza, trail 2, 1st stream, 17—20 Sep 1988, UV light, 1♂. Pakitza, trail 2, mkr. 12, 16—22 Sep 1989, MV light, 1♂, 1♀.

LEPTONEMA N. SP. 3

The genitalia of this species are very distinctive, and would seem to show a relationship with those of the *plicatum* group. It is a pale green species with wing apices infuscate, rather large, and generally indistinguishable from the preceding ones on external characteristics.

Material Examined.— Pakitza, 30 Sep & 1 Oct 1987, UV trap, M.G. Pogue, 8♂, 1♀. Pakitza, Río Manu, 9—21 Sep 1988, MV light, 1♀. Pakitza, trail 1, mkr. 4, 8—22 Sep 1989, MV light, 1♂, 1♀. Pakitza, trail 2, mkr. 12, 16—22 Sep 1989, MV light, 1♂. Pakitza, trail 2, mkr. 18, 12—23 Sep 1989, Malaise trap, 3♂, 1♀. Pakitza, trail 2, mkr. 20, 17—20 Sep 1989, MV light, 1♀.

Leptonema mandibulatum Flint, McAlpine & Ross

This species ranges along the eastern Andes from Bolivia to northern Ecuador. It is pale green when alive, rapidly fading to light brown when dead, with 2 dark spots at the base of the forewing in coloration.

Material Examined.— Hostel Erika, 4—6 Sep 1988, MV light, 9♂, 10♀; same, but 3—5 Sep 1989, 8♀. Limonal (10 km N Boca Manu), Río Manu, 7 Sep 1988, MV light, 6♀. Pakitza, Río Manu, 9—21 Sep 1988, MV light, 1♂, 9♀; same, but 17 Sep 1989, MV light, 3♂, 27♀. Pakitza, trail 1, mkr. 4, 8—22 Sep 1989, MV light, 1♂, 1♀; same, but 11 Sep 1989, light trap, Gelhaus & Epstein, 1♂. Pakitza, trail 2, mkr. 12, 16—22 Sep 1989, MV light, 1♂. Cocha Salvador, ca. 10 km S. Pakitza, 13—14 Sep 1988, MV light, 1♀.

Leptonema crassum Ulmer

This species is very wide ranging from southern Mexico south along the eastern Andes to southern Peru, and easterly across southeastern Brazil and Argentina. It is brown with 2 dark spots at the base of the forewing.

Material Examined.—Limonal (10 km. N Boca Manu), Río Manu, 7 Sep 1988, MV light, 1♀. Pakitza, Río Manu, 17 Sep 1989, MV light, 2♂.

Leptonema n. sp. 2

This species is another in the *crassum* group that had not been found previously. It is light brown, lacks the 2 dark spots at the base of the forewing, but has a fuscous stripe on the outer face of the basal antennal segments.

Material Examined.— Pakitza, Río Manu, 9—21 Sep 1988, MV light, 1♂, 2♀.

Leptonema sparsum (Ulmer)

This species is very wide ranging from Panama south across most of South America, including the Cosñipata Valley in Peru, as far as northern Argentina. It is brown with the forewing bearing dark, transverse bands.

Material Examined.— Pakitza, trail 2, 1st stream, 14—23 Sep 1988, Malaise trap, 1♂, 1♀. Pakitza, trail 2, mkr. 18, 12—23 Sep 1989, Malaise trap, 1♀. Aguajal [ca. 5 km S Pakitza], 12 Sep 1988, UV trap, M.G. Pogue, 1♂.

FAMILY LIMNEPHILIDAE

This is one of the dominant families in the north temperate zone, with three genera entering Mexico along the higher mountains, one of which even reaches central Costa Rica (*Clistoronia*, *Hesperophylax*, and *Limnephilus*). There is another cluster of genera common in the Chilean Subregion (*Antarctoecia*, *Austrocosmoecus*, *Magellomyia*, *Metacosmoecus*, *Monocosmoecus*, and *Platycosmoecus*, with *Chiloecia* and *Nostrafilla* presently unrecognized), with one outlier extending north along the high elevations of the Andes into southern Colombia (*Anomalocosmoecus*). Although not found in this survey, *Anomalocosmoecus illiesi* (Marlier), is widespread at higher elevations in Peru, and *A. blancasi* Schmid is found in Lake Titicaca.

FAMILY LEPTOCERIDAE

This family, found in all regions of the world, not only inhabits lotic sites, but many species are adapted to lentic habitats. A number of genera, found in the Neotropics, do not occur in the region treated: *Brachysetodes* and *Hudsonema* in Chile, and *Mystacides* in Mexico.

KEY TO GENERA

1. Hindwing with 3 apparent branches of M reaching wing margin 2
   Hindwing with only 2 branches of M reaching margin 6
2. Forewing thyridial cell very long and slender, almost twice as long as discal cell 3
   Forewing thyridial and discal cells subequal in length................................ 4
3. Hindwing crossveins *rs* and *r-m* in line (South America, except Chile) ....*Notalina*
   Hindwing crossvein *rs* apicad of *r-m* by at least its length (all Neotropics, except West Indies) .... *Triplectides*
4. Foretibia with an apical spur (Peru) .... new genus
   Foretibia lacking apical spurs 5
5. Dorsolateral setal wart of head long and narrow (South America, except Chile) ....*Grumichella*
   Dorsolateral wart broadly oval to trianguloid (Costa Rica, Lesser Antilles and South America, except Chile)..*Atanatolica*
6. Forewing with stem of M atrophied (Central and western South America) ....*Triaenodes*
   Forewing with M entire 7
7. Forewing with M apparently not branched (all Neotropics, except Chile) ... .*Oecetis*
   Forewing with M obviously branced apically 8

8. Hindwing with R, and M almost totally atrophied (all Neotropics) . *Nectopsyche*
   Basal portions of these veins clearly present 9
9. Forewing with thyridial cell twice as long as discal cell (Lesser Antilles, Andes
   of northern and western South America) .... *Amphoropsyche*
   Forewing with thyridial and discoidal cells subequal in length (lowlands of
   south America) .... *Achoropsyche*

PROBABLE NEW GENUS, N. SP.

This interesting specimen will probably require a new genus be established, as it seems very different from species in the other genera in the subfamily.

Material Examined.— Puente San Pedro, 2—3 Sep 1988, net in day, 1♂.

ATANATOLICA, SP. 1

This species is overall pale brown, with an infuscation along the hind margin of the forewings. It is probably undescribed, but lacking males it not possible to be certain.

Material Examined.— E Buenos Aires, km. 135, 2150 m, 28—29 Aug 1989, MV light, 80♀.

ATANATOLICA, N. SP. 2

This species is also basically pale brown, but the forewing has a longitudinal band of pale, golden hair anteriad of the posterior margin, which color hair then continues around the wing apex. The species is related closely to A. *zongo* Holzenthal.

Material Examined.— Puente San Pedro, 2—3 Sep 1988, MV light, 6 ♂♂ & ♀♀; same, but 30—31 Aug 1989, 10♂, 8♀.

ATANATOLICA, SP. 3

This species is pale brown basically, but the forewings show many small golden spots. It may be undescribed, but lacking males it not possible to be certain.

Material Examined.— Hostel Erika, 3—5 Sep 1989, MV light, 1♀.

GRUMICHELLA FLAVEOLA (ULMER)

This species is widely distributed along the Andes from northwestern Argentina to Colombia and Venezuela.

Material Examined.— E Buenos Aires, km. 135, 2150 m, 28—29 Aug 1989, MV light, 2♀. Puente San Pedro, 2—3 Sep 1988, MV light, 14♂♂ & ♀♀; same, but 30—31 Aug 1989, 22♂, 7♀. Stream 3 km E Puente San Pedro, 31 Aug 1989, MV light, 1♀. Quitacalzón, 1—2 Sep 1989, MV light, 1♀. Hostel Erika, 4—6 Sep 1988, MV light, 4♂♂ & ♀♀; same, but 3—5 Sep 1989, 12♂.

TRIPLECTIDES FLINTORUM HOLZENTHAL

In the recent revision of the genus, this species was separated from what had been considered to be a single, widespread, Neotropical species, T. *gracilis* (Burm.). The species is widespread, having been recorded from Mexico south to Ecuador; these records extend it known range much to the south.

Material Examined.— Pakitza, 27 Sep—4 Oct 1987, UV trap, M.G. Pogue, 5♂, 2♀; same, but 9—23 Sep 1988, 1♂; same, but 8—20 Sep 1989, 1♂; same, but 19 Sep 1989, J. Gelhaus, 1♂. Pakitza, trail 2, 1st stream (mkr. 15), 14—23 Sep 1988, Malaise trap, 1♂; same, but 18 Sep 1989, net collection, 1♀. Pakitza, trail 2, mkr. 12, 16—22 Sep 1989, Malaise trap, 1♀. Pakitza, trail 2, mkr. 18, 12—23 Sep 1989, net collection, 3♂, 1♂. Pakitza, trail 2, mkr. 20, 17—20 Sep 1989, MV and net collections, 2♂. Aguajal [ca. 5 km S. Pakitza], 18—19 Sep 1988, by net in day, 1♂.

AMPHOROPSYCHE SPINIFERA HOLZENTHAL

This species was recently described from the yungas of the northwestern corner of Bolivia. It is the first record of the species from Peru.

Material Examined.— Puente San Pedro, 2—3 Sep 1988, MV light, 1♂.

ACHOROPSYCHE DUODECIMPUNCTATA (NAVÁS)

This species has been reported from most countries of South America, from Colombia to Surinam south to Argentina, including Peru. It is generally found in lower elevations, often in the vicinity of large rivers, although most of these collections were taken at small streams in the forest.

Material Examined.— Pakitza, Río Manu, 17 Sep 1989, MV light, 1♂. Pakitza, trail 2, 1st stream, 14—23 Sep 1988, Malaise trap, 35♀; same, but 17—20 Sep 1988, UV light, 1♂, 6♀; same, but 20 Sep 1988, UV trap, M. Pogue, 9♀. Pakitza, trail 2, mkr. 18, 12—23 Sep 1989, MV light, 1♀. Pakitza, trail 2, mkr. 20, 17—20 Sep 1989, MV light, 2♂, 6♀. Pakitza, kitchen stream, 12—18 Sep 1989, Malaise trap, 1♀. Aguajal [ca. 5 km S. Pakitza], 12 Sep 1988, UV light, M.G. Pogue, 2♂.

NECTOPSYCHE SPLENDIDA (NAVÁS)

This species has been reported, as has the previous one, from most countries of South America, from Colombia to Guyana south to Argentina, including Peru. It too, is usually found in lower elevations, generally in the vicinity of large rivers.

Material Examined.— Pakitza, Río Manu, 9—21 Sep 1988, MV light, 12♂, 3♀; same, but 17 Sep 1989, 3♂. Pakitza, trail 1, mkr. 4, 8—22 Sep 1989, MV light, 1♂. Pakitza, kitchen stream, 18 Sep 1988, UV light, 1♂. Cocha Salvador, ca. 10 km S. Pakitza, 13—14 Sep 1988, MV light, 1♀.

NECTOPSYCHE QUATUORGUTTATA (NAVÁS)

Although this species has been reported only from Bolivia, Guyana and Suriname, it has a distribution and behaviour similar to the previous one.

Material Examined.— Pakitza, Río Manu, 9—21 Sep 1988, MV light, 10♂, 2♀.

NECTOPSYCHE TALEOLA FLINT

This species has been reported only from the original examples collected in Suriname. Its discovery in Peru indicates that it must range widely around the Amazon Basin.

Material Examined.— Pakitza, trail 2, 1st stream, 17—20 Sep 1988, UV light, 1♂; same, but 14—23 Sep 1988, Malaise trap, 2♀.

NECTOPSYCHE MACULIPENNIS FLINT

This species has been reported only from the orignal specimen collected in Paraguay. It must be widely distributed around the Amazon Basin as its discovery in Peru would indicate.

Material Examined.— Pakitza, trail 2, 1st stream, 17—20 Sep 1988, UV light, 6♂, 1♀; same, but 14—23 Sep 1988, Malaise trap, 2♀; same, but 20 Sep 1988, UV light, M.G. Pogue, 1♂.

NECTOPSYCHE, N. SP. 1

This species is very similar in appearance to *maculipennis*, and was at first though to be more of the same. It does differ slightly, but consistantly in details of the color pattern.

Material Examined.— Limonal (10 km N Boca Manu), Río Manu, 7 Sep 1988, MV light, 8♂. Pakitza, Río Manu, 9—21 Sep 1988, MV light, 19♂, 1♀; same, but 17 Sep 1989, 6♂, 2♀. Pakitza, Playa trail, 10 Sep 1989, J. Gelhaus, 1♂. Pakitza, trail 2, 1st stream, but 20 Sep 1988, UV light, M.G. Pogue, 1♂, 1♀. Pakitza, trail 2, mkr. 12, 16—22 Sep 1989, MV light, 8♂, 1♀. Pakitza, kitchen stream, 18 Sep 1988, UV light, 13♂, 5♀.

NECTOPSYCHE PUNCTATA (ULMER)

This species probably has the most widespread recorded distribution of any species in the genus. It is known from central Mexico south to Argentina. Although most frequently encounted in lowlands, it is also seen at much higher elevations, both near large rivers and small streams in forested sites.

Material Examined.— Hostal Erika, 4—6 Sep 1988, MV light, 12♂, 10♀; same, but 3—5 Sep 1989, 17♂. Limonal (10 km N Boca Manu), Río Manu, 7 Sep 1988, MV light, 3♂, 1♀. Pakitza, Río Manu, 9—21 Sep 1988, MV light, 8♂, 11♀; same, but 17 Sep 1989, 1♂, 1♀. Pakitza, Playa trail, 10 Sep 1989, J. Gelhaus, 1♂. Pakitza, trail 1, 1st stream, 11 Sep 1988, UV light, 1♀. Pakitza, trail 1, mkr. 4, 8—22 Sep 1989, MV light, 12♂. Pakitza, trail 1, mkr. 8, 11—13 Sep 1989, MV light, 8♂.

419

Pakitza, trail 2, 1st stream, 20 Sep 1988, UV light, M.G. Pogue, 1♂. Pakitza, trail 2, mkr. 12, 16—22 Sep 1989, MV light, 1♀. Aguajal [ca. 5 km S. Pakitza], 12 Sep 1988, UV trap, M.G. Pogue, 1♂.

NECTOPSYCHE MUHNI (NAVÁS)

This is another widespread, lowland species found throughout South America. It is known from Ecuador to Suriname and south to Argentina.

Material Examined.— Hostal Erika, 3—5 Sep 1989, MV light, 1♂. Pakitza, Río Manu, 9—21 Sep 1988, MV light, 6♂, 2♀; same, but 17 Sep 1989, 1♂. Pakitza, Playa trail, 18 Sep 1989, MV light, 1♂. Pakitza, trail 1, 1st stream (mkr. 14), 11 Sep 1988, UV light, 6♀; same, but 19—23 Sep 1989, Malaise trap, 1♂, 1♀. Pakitza, trail 1, mkr. 4, 8—22 Sep 1989, MV light, 1♂. Pakitza, trail 2, 1st stream, 17—20 Sep 1988, UV light, 4♀; same, but 14—23 Sep 1988, Malaise trap, 2♀; same, but 20 Sep 1988, UV light, M.G. Pogue, 3♂, 6♀. Pakitza, trail 2, mkr. 12, 16—22 Sep 1989, MV light, 1♀. Pakitza, trail 2, mkr. 18, 12—23 Sep 1989, MV light, 1♀. Pakitza, kitchen stream, 18 Sep 1988, UV light, 2♀.

NECTOPSYCHE, N. SP. 2

This species is a member of the *gemma* group, marked very much like *gemma* itself, but it has very different male genitalia.

Material Examined.— E Buenos Aires, km. 135, 2150 m, 28—29 Aug 1989, MV light, 16♂, 24♀.

NECTOPSYCHE, PROBABLY ARGENTATA FLINT

These examples are indistinguishable in coloration from typical *argentata*, however, there are enough differences in the male genitalia to cast some doubts on its identity. *N. argentata* was described from Colombia, Venezuela, and Costa Rica.

Material Examined.— Puente San Pedro, 2—3 Sep 1988, MV light, 13♂♂ & ♀♀. Quitacalzón, 1—2 Sep 1989, MV light, 9♂, 23♀; same, but 1—2 Sep 1989, R.A. Faitoute (colls. 16 & 18), 2♂, 6♀. Streamlet 50 m E Quitacalzón, 2 Sep 1989, MV light, 13♂, 17♀.

NECTOPSYCHE, N. SP. 3

These examples are another member of the *gemma* group, but very different in coloration. Instead of the forewing ground color being golden it is brown.

Material Examined.— Puente San Pedro, 2—3 Sep 1988, MV light, 3♂♂ & ♀♀; same, but 30—31 Aug 1989, 4♀. Quitacalzón, 1—2 Sep 1989, MV light, 1♀.

NECTOPSYCHE, PROBABLY GEMMOIDES FLINT

These examples are indistinguishable in coloration from typical *gemmoides*, however, as with *argentata*, there are enough differences in the male genitalia to cast some doubts on its identity. *N. gemmoides* is widely distributed from Mexico to Colombia and Trinidad South to Paraguay.

Material Examined.— Pakitza, Río Manu, 17 Sep 1989, MV light, 15♂, 2♀. Pakitza, Playa trail, 10 Sep 1989, J. Gelhaus, 1♂. Pakitza, trail 1, 1st stream (mkr. 14), 11 Sep 1988, UV light, 28 ♂♂ & ♀♀; same, but 19—23 Sep 1989, Malaise trap, 1♂. Pakitza, trail 1, mkr. 4, 8—22 Sep 1989, MV light, 5♂, 3♀. Pakitza, trail 2, mkr. 12, 16—22 Sep 1989, MV light, 1♀.

OECETIS PUNCTIPENNIS (ULMER)

This is another very widespread Neotropical species; records range from Nicaragua to Colombia and Suriname, south to Argentina.

Material Examined.— Limonal (10 km N Boca Manu), Río Manu, 7 Sep 1988, MV light, 1♀. Pakitza, Río Manu, 9—21 Sep 1988, MV light, 1♂. Pakitza, trail 1, 1st stream (mkr. 14), 11 Sep 1988, UV light, 1♂; same, but 19—23 Sep 1989, malaise trap, 1♀. Pakitza, trail 2, 1st stream, 17—20 Sep 1988, UV light, 4♂, 3♀; same, but 14—23 Sep 1988, Malaise trap, 3♀; same, but 20 Sep 1988, UV light, M.G. Pogue, 3♂, 3♀. Pakitza, trail 2, mkr. 18, 12—23 Sep 1989, MV light, 2♀. Pakitza, trail 2, mkr. 20, 17—20 Sep 1989, MV light, 1♂. Pakitza, kitchen stream, 18 Sep 1988, UV light, 2♂; same, but 12—18 Sep 1989, Malaise trap, 1♂.

OECETIS PARANENSIS FLINT

This species was only recorded from the original types from northern Argentina and Paraguay. This record, then, represents a major range extension.

Material Examined.— Cocha Salvador, 10 km S Pakitza, 13—14 Sep 1988, MV light, 3♂, 1♀.

OECETIS INCONSPICUA (WALKER)

This species is one of the most widespread new world species; Canada to the Amazon Basin, including the Greater Antilles. There have been attempts to divide the species on the basis of geography or male genital characters. Unfortunately, the latter attempt did not take into account the complex over its entire range, apparently resulting in incorrectly defined "species". What the correct species of this series is, is not certain at this time.

Material Examined.— Pakitza, Playa trail, 18 Sep 1989, MV light, 1♀. Aguajal [ca. 5 km S. Pakitza], 12 Sep 1988, UV light, M.G. Pogue, 1♀. Cocha Salvador, 10 km S Pakitza, 13—14 Sep 1988, MV light, 100♂♂ & ♀♀.

OECETIS, N. SP. 202 CHEN MS

This undescribed species is a member of the *falicia* group.

Material Examined.— Pakitza, trail 1, 1st stream, 9—14 Sep 1988, Malaise trap, 3♀. Pakitza, trail 2, 1st stream, 14—23 Sep 1988, Malaise trap, 1♂, 4♀. Pakitza, trail 2, mkr. 18, 12—23 Sep 1989, MV light, 1♂.

OECETIS, N. SP. 201 CHEN MS

This is another member of the *falicia* group, with distinctive male genitalia.

Material Examined.— Pakitza, trail 1, 1st stream (mkr.14), 9—14 Sep 1988, Malaise trap, 1♀; same, but 19—23 Sep 1989, 1♀. Pakitza, trail 2, 1st stream, 14—23 Sep 1988, Malaise trap, 3♂, 1♀.

OECETIS, N. SP. NEAR 201 CHEN MS

This is yet another member of the *falicia* group, quite different from the other two herein recorded.

Material Examined.— Pakitza, 9—23 Sep 1988, 1♀. Pakitza, trail 1, 1st stream (mkr.14), 9—14 Sep 1988, Malaise trap, 4♀; same, but 11 Sep 1988, UV light, 2♀; same, but 19—23 Sep 1989, Malaise trap, 12♀. Pakitza, trail 2, 1st stream, 14—23 Sep 1988, Malaise trap, 1♂.

OECETIS, N. SP. 4

This is a member of the *persimilis* group, quite different from the other known species. The abdominal terga 6—8 bear large, reticulate areas, and the anal angle of the hindwing a large hair pencil.

Material Examined.— Pakitza, trail 2, mkr. 20, 17—20 Sep 1989, MV light, 2♂.

OECETIS KNUTSONI FLINT

This is a member of the *punctata* group, known from localities scattered along the Andes from Venezuela and Colombia to Bolivia. This is the first record from Peru.

Material Examined.— Puente San Pedro, 2—3 Sep 1988, MV light, 19♂, 6♀; same, but 30—31 Aug 1989, 18♂, 4♀. Stream 3 km E Puente San Pedro, 31 Aug 1989, MV light, 1♂. Erika, 4—6 Sep 1988, MV light, 3♂. Aguajal [ca. 5 km S Pakitza], 12 Sep 1988, UV light, M.G. Pogue, 1♂, 2♀.

OECETIS, N. SP. 208 CHEN MS

This is a member of the *punctata* group, closest to *knutsoni*, but with male genitalia distinctly different from it.

Material Examined.— Erika, 4—6 Sep 1988, MV light, 4♂, 1♀; same, but 3 & 5 Sep 1989, R.A. Faitoute (colls. 20 & 26), 1♀. Pakitza, playa trail, 10 Sep 1989, light, Gelhaus & Epstein, 1♀. Pakitza, trail 1, 1st stream (mkr.14), 9—14 Sep 1988, Malaise trap, 2♀; same, but 11 Sep 1988, UV light, 1♂, 2♀. Pakitza, trail 2, 1st stream, 14—23 Sep 1988, Malaise trap, 2♀; same, but 17—20 Sep 1988, UV light, 1♀; same, but 20 Sep 1988, UV light, M.G. Pogue, 1♂.

OECETIS AVARA FLINT

This is a member of the *punctata* group, known from localities scattered along the Andes from Venezuela and Colombia to Bolivia. This is the first record from Peru.

Material Examined.— Erika, 3—5 Sep 1989, MV light, 1♂, 1♀.

FAMILY ATRIPLECTIDAE

This family was recently erected for a species known from Tasmania, and is readily distinguished by a very unusual larva. At virtually the same time the larva became known for a Seychellian species, indicating it too belonged in the family. A number of years ago Roback described a strange larva from Tingo María, Peru that we now recognize to be an atriplectid. In addition, I posses a single female from Bolivia that matches all the characteristics of the family, as well as a second larva (probably different from the Peruvian one) from southeastern Brazil.

PROBABLE N. GEN., N. SP.

The specimen here recorded is the first known male from the New World. Unfortunately it is teneral, and its forewings are crumpled just at the region of the chord, making this critical area of the venation undecipherable.

Material Examined.— Puente San Pedro, 30—31 Aug 1989, MV light, 1♂.

FAMILY CALAMOCERATIDAE

Although species and genera from all regions of the world have been placed in this family, nowhere does it seem very diverse nor abundant. In addition to the two genera found at Pakitza, a third, *Muriella*, is known from Costa Rica.

KEY TO GENERA

1. In fore- and hindwings, R_1 runs into R_2 before wing margin (all Neotropics)
....*Phylloicus*

   In wings, R1 runs free to wing margin (Mexico south to western Argentina)
....*Banyallarga*

BANYALLARGA YUNGENSIS FLINT

This species was recently described from northwestern Argentina and Peru. It was recorded from "Callanga", Peru by Martynov under the name *Ganonema vicarium*, a species which is not known from Peru.

Material Examined.— Puente Morro Leguía, 28—29 Aug 1989, MV light, 3♂, 6♀. Puente San Pedro, 2—3 Sep 1988, MV light, 1♂, 1♀; same, but 30—31 Aug 1989, 1♂. Stream 3 km E Puente San Pedro, 31 Aug 1989, MV light, 4♂, 2♀. Quitacalzón, 1—2 Sep 1989, MV light, 2♂.

BANYALLARGA LOXANUM (NAVÁS)

This species was described from southern Ecuador, and not recorded since. In addition to the type, I have seen examples from northwestern Argentina, Bolivia, Ecuador, and Peru.

Material Examined.— Puente Morro Leguía, 28—29 Aug 1989, MV light, 2♂, 8♀.

BANYALLARGA SP.

This species differs from the two recorded above by being pale brown. No males were taken so its identity is unknown at this time.

Material Examined.— Puente Morro Leguía, 28—29 Aug 1989, MV light, 1♀. Puente San Pedro, 30—31 Aug 1989, MV light, 1♀. Stream 3 km E Puente San Pedro, 31 Aug 1989, MV light, 1♀. Quitacalzón, 1—2 Sep 1989, MV light, 1♀.

BANYALLARGA N. SP. 1

This species is quite similar to the previous one in color, but is smaller and appears to have different genitalia.

Material Examined.— Pakitza, 27 Sep—1 Oct 1987, UV light, M.G. Pogue, 3♂, 1♀. Pakitza, trail 2, mkr. 18, 12—23 Sep 1989, MV light, 1♂. Pakitza, kitchen stream, 12—18 Sep 1989, Malaise trap, 1♂.

PHYLLOICUS N. SP. 1

This is a distinctively marked species; forewings fuscous with a unique banding of orange hair at their base and midlength.

Material Examined.— Puente San Pedro, 2—3 Sep 1988, MV light, 2♂, 1♀; same, but 30—31 Aug 1989, 2♂.

PHYLLOICUS ANGUSTIOR (ULMER)

This species was originally described from southeastern Brazil, but has since been recorded from Paraguay, Bolivia, Peru, Colombia, and Venezuela. It is thus one of the most widespread species of the genus.

Material Examined.— Puente San Pedro, 2—3 Sep 1988, MV light, 1♂. Streamlet 50 m Quitacalzón, MV light, 2 Sep 1989, MV light, 1♂.

PHYLLOICUS, PROBABLY *LITURATUS* BANKS

The type of *lituratus* was from Colombia, and it is known also from Costa Rica and Panama. These examples from Peru agree quite closely with the type in coloration and abdominal structures, but there are small differences in the male genitalia. Lacking examples from intermediate areas, it is difficult to assess the significance of these differences.

Material Examined.— Pakitza, 30 Sep & 2 Oct 1987, UV light, M.G. Pogue, 2♂. Pakitza, trail 1, 1st stream (mkr. 14), 11 Sep 1988, UV light, 2♂; same, but 19—23 Sep 1989, net collection, 1♂. Pakitza, trail 1, mkr. 4, 8—22 Sep 1989, MV light, 5♂. Pakitza, trail 2, 1st stream, 14—23 Sep 1988, Malaise trap, 1♂. Pakitza, trail 2, mkr. 18, 12—23 Sep 1989, Malaise trap, 3♂. Aguajal [ca. 5 km S Pakitza], 12 Sep 1988, UV trap, M.G. Pogue, 2♂.

PHYLLOICUS FENESTRATUS FLINT

This distinctively marked species was described from Suriname, but I have also seen it from the vicinity of Manaus, Brazil. This is the first record from the western end of the Amazon Basin.

Material Examined.— Pakitza, 4 Oct 1987, UV light, M.G. Pogue, 1♂. Pakitza, trail 1, mkr. 8, 11—13 Sep 1989, MV light, 1♂. Pakitza, trail 2, mkr. 18, 12—23 Sep 1989, Malaise trap, 1♂.

PHYLLOICUS N. SP. 2

This is a very colorful species: the forewings are basically fuscous with several broad, longitudinal bands of pinky-white hair, and the body ventrally and the leg bases are golden-yellow.

Material Examined.— Pakitza, 9—23 Sep 1988, 1♂; same, but 2 Oct 1987, UV light, M.G. Pogue, 1♂; same, but 19 Sep 1989, J. Gelhaus, 1♀. Pakitza, trail 1, 1st stream (mkr. 14), 9—14 Sep 1988, Malaise trap, 2♂, 1♀; same, but 11 Sep 1988, UV light, 1♂; same, but 19—23 Sep 1989, Malaise trap, 1♂, 2♀. Pakitza, trail 1, mkr. 8, 11—13 Sep 1989, MV light, 2♂. Pakitza, trail 2, 1st stream (mkr.15), 14—23 Sep 1988, Malaise trap, 27♂, 10♀; same, but 18 Sep 1989, net in day, 1♀. Pakitza, trail 2, mkr. 18, 12—23 Sep 1989, Malaise trap, 6♂. Pakitza, kitchen stream, 12—18 Sep 1989, Malaise trap, 7♂. Aguajal [ca. 5 km S. Pakitza], 12 Sep 1988, UV trap, M.G. Pogue, 1♀.

PHYLLOICUS N. SP. 3

This is smallest species taken in the area, and also the least colorful. The wings and body are uniformly pale brown.

Material Examined.— Pakitza, 30 Sep—1 Oct 1987, UV light, M.G. Pogue, 3♂, 3♀. Pakitza, trail 2, mkr. 18, 12—23 Sep 1989, Malaise trap, 3♂, 2♀. Pakitza, trail 2, mkr. 20, 17—20 Sep 1989, MV light, 2♂, 2♀.

Oliver S. Flint, Jr.

PHYLLOICUS N. SP. 4

This is large species, with orange body and orangish hairs to the basal two-thirds of the forewing, the apical third is fuscous as are the appendages. I also have a few examples from the Río Tambopata Reserve nearer Puerto Maldonado.

Material Examined.— Pakitza, trail 2, mkr. 18, 12—23 Sep 1989, Malaise trap, 1♀. Aguajal [ca, 5 km S. Pakitza], 12 Sep 1988, UV trap, M.G. Pogue, 1♂.

FAMILY ODONTOCERIDAE

The family is widespread in the northern Hemisphere, throughout the Neotropics and southeastern Asia south into Australia. It is nowhere very diverse generically, although specimens can be abundant at lights on occasion. The Brazilian genus, *Barypenthus*, is strikingly different from the majority of other genera in the family, and someday may be transferred to a new family.

KEY TO GENERA

1. Forewing narrow, 3-4 times as long as broad (all Neotropics, except Chile) .... *Marilia*
   Forewing very broad, barely more than twice as long as broad (southeastern Brazil) .... *Barypenthus*

MARILIA ELONGATA MARTYNOV

This is another of the species described by Martynov from Peru (only as 11°8's, 75°17'w), that has now been surely rediscovered. It is quite common near tumbling streams at lower elevations in the mountains.

Material Examined.— Puente San Pedro, 2—3 Sep 1988, MV light, 33♂, 8♀; same, but 30—31 Aug 1989, 33♂, 21♀. Quitacalzón, 1—2 Sep 1989, MV light, 7♀.

MARILIA FLEXUOSA ULMER

This species was described from females from Texas and Brazil and then recorded by Martynov from Callanga, Peru, and been further recorded from southern Ontario (Canada) to northwestern Argentina. It was taken both at lower elevations in the mountains and at Pakitza.

Material Examined.— Puente San Pedro, 2—3 Sep 1988, MV light, 3♂, 7♀; same, but 30—31 Aug 1989, 10♀. Stream 3 km E Puente San Pedro, 31 Aug 1989, MV light, 2♂, 4♀. Quitacalzón, 1—2 Sep 1989, MV light, 2♂, 61♀. Streamlet 50 m E Quitacalzón, 2 Sep 1989, MV light, 1♂, 20♀. Pakitza, trail 2, mkr. 20, 17—20 Sep 1989, MV light, 1♂.

MARILIA N. SP. 1

This specimen is very close to *elongata*, but offers several small differences in the male genitalia. Spurs:2,4,4; eyes large and contiguous.

Material Examined.— Pakitza, trail 2, mkr. 12, 16—22 Sep 1989, MV light, 1♂.

MARILIA N. SP. 2

These specimens are much like *infundibulum* from Argentina and Brazil, differing primarily in eye size and the shorter tenth tergum in the male genitalia. Spurs:2,4,2; eyes small and well separated.

Material Examined.— Pilcopata to Atlaya, 4 Sep 1988, by net, 1♂, 1♀.

MARILIA N. SP. 3

These specimens are much like *eleutheria* from Argentina, Paraguay, and Uruguay, differing primarily their space size and the shorter cerci of the male genitalia. Spurs:2,4,2; eyes large and contiguous. It is commonly taken along the Río Manu at and near Pakitza.

Material Examined.— Limonal (10 km N Boca Manu), Río Manu, 7 Sep 1988, MV light, 27♂, 22♀. Pakitza, Río Manu, 9—21 Sep 1988, MV light, 45♂, 18♀; same, but 17 Sep 1989, 13♂, 9♀. Pakitza, playa trail, 10 Sep 1989, light, 1♀. Cocha Salvador, 10 km S Pakitza, 13—14 Sep 1988, UV light, 4♀.

MARILIA N. SP. 4

This is a very distinctive species of the *fasiculata* group, and is common around the small streams in the vicinity of Pakitza. Spurs:2,4,4; eyes large and contiguous.

Material Examined.— Pakitza, 27 Sep—5 Oct 1987, UV light, M.G. Pogue, 1♂, 3♀. Pakitza, Playa trail, 10 Sep 1989, J. Gelhaus, 1♀. Pakitza, trail 1, 1st stream (mkr. 14), 9—14 Sep 1988, Malaise trap, 16♀; same, but 11 Sep 1988, UV light, 1♂, 1♀; same, but 19—23 Sep 1989, Malaise trap, 8♂, 31♀. Pakitza, trail 1, mkr. 8, 11—13 Sep 1989, MV light, 1♀. Pakitza, trail 2, 1st stream (mkr.15), 14—23 Sep 1988, Malaise trap, 4♂, 42♂; same, but 17—20 Sep 1988, UV light, 1♀. Pakitza, trail 2, mkr. 12, 16—22 Sep 1989, MV light, 1♂. Pakitza, trail 2, mkr. 18, 12—23 Sep 1989, Malaise trap, 1♂, 3♀. Pakitza, trail 2, mkr. 20, 17—20 Sep 1989, MV light, 5♂, 2♀. Pakitza, kitchen stream, 12—18 Sep 1989, Malaise trap, 1♀.

MARILIA N. SP. 5

This species is easily recognized by the very elongate cerci and tenth tergum of the male genitalia. Spurs:2,4,4; eyes small and widely separated.

Material Examined.— Puente Morro Leguia, 28—29 Aug 1989, MV light, 1♂.

427

Family Helicopsychidae

Members of this family are found throughout the New World, but are more restricted in the Old: southern Europe, Africa, southern Asia and south into Australia, New Zealand, and New Caledonia. All the New World species are placed in two genera, both of which are present in the Pakitza collections.

Key to genera

1. Antennae relatively short and stout, no more than $1^{1}/_{2}$ times length of forewing (all Neotropics) .... *Helicopsyche*
   Antennae very long and slender, 3-4 times length of forewing (Mexico south through South America, except Chile) .... *Cochliopsyche*

Cochliopsyche opalescens Flint

This is a very widespread species; it was described from northeastern Argentina, and recorded from Brazil, Ecuador, Guyana, Paraguay, Suriname, and Venezuela. This is the first published record from Peru.

Material Examined.—Limonal (10 km. N Boca Manu), Río Manu, 7 Sep 1988, MV light, 1♂, 1♀. Pakitza, Río Manu, 9—21 Sep 1988, MV light, 13♂, 15♀; same, but 17 Sep 1989, 2♂, 4♀. Pakitza, trail 2, mkr. 12, 16—22 Sep 1989, MV light, 7♂. Pakitza, trail 2, mkr. 20, 17—20 Sep 1989, MV light, 10♂, 2♀. Pakitza, stream near kitchen, 18 Sep 1988, UV light, 1♂.

Cochliopsyche n. sp. 1

A single male taken at Erika differs from the other few described species in this genus.

Material Examined.— Erika, 4—6 Sep 1988, MV light, 1♂.

Cochliopsyche n. sp. 2

This and the preceding species are larger and browner than *opalescens* and have distinctive male genitalia.

Material Examined.—Limonal (10 km. N Boca Manu), Río Manu, 7 Sep 1988, MV light, 7♀. Pakitza, Río Manu, 9—21 Sep 1988, MV light, 1♂, 2♀; same, but 17 Sep 1989, 2♂. Pakitza, trail 1, 1st stream, 11 Sep 1988, UV light, 1♂, 3♀. Pakitza, trail 2, 1st stream, 20 Sep 1988, UV trap, M.G. Pogue, 2♂, 2♀. Pakitza, trail 2, mkr. 20, 17—20 Sep 1989, MV light, 1♂, 2♀. Aguajal [ca 5 km S Pakitza], 12 Sep 1988, UV trap, M.G. Pogue, 1♀.

Helicopsyche woytkowskii Ross

This species was described from several specimens taken in the Cosñipata Valley, Peru. With *fistulata*, it shares an elongate tubule from the phallotremal sclerite of the phallus.

Material Examined.— Puente San Pedro, 2—3 Sep 1988, MV light, 4♂, 3♀; same, but 30—31 Aug 1989, 3♂.

HELICOPSYCHE N. SP. 1

In general appearance of the male clasper this species would appear to be close to *piroa*, but it differs significantly in the form of the tenth tergum.

Material Examined.— Puente San Pedro, 2—3 Sep 1988, MV light, 4♂; same, but 30—31 Aug 1989, 4♂. Quitacalzón, 1—2 Sep 1989, MV light, 3♂. Streamlet 50 m E Quitacalzón, 2 Sep 1989, MV light, 1♂.

HELICOPSYCHE EXTENSA ROSS

This is another species described from several specimens taken in the Cosñipata Valley, Peru. The clasper is very distinctive in this species.

Material Examined.— Erika, 4—6 Sep 1988, MV light, 1♂; same, but 3—5 Sep 1989, 1♂; same, but R.A. Faitoute (colls. 20 & 26), 1♂.

HELICOPSYCHE N. SP. 2

The general appearance of the male clasper of this species would seem to place it in the *vergelana* group; but it differs significantly from the others in the exceedingly long mesobasal lobe of the clasper.

Material Examined.— Pakitza, trail 1, 1st stream, 11 Sep 1988, UV light, 1♂, 1♀. Pakitza, trail 2, 1st stream, 14—23 Sep 1988, Malaise trap, 18♀. Pakitza, trail 2, mkr. 12, 16—22 Sep 1989, MV light, 1♂, 2♀. Pakitza, trail 2, mkr. 18, 12—23 Sep 1989, MV light, 1♀. Pakitza, trail 2, mkr. 20, 17—20 Sep 1989, MV light, 2♂. Pakitza, stream near kitchen, 18 Sep 1988, UV light, 1♂, 2♀; same, but 12—18 Sep 1989, Malaise trap, 2♀.

FAMILY ANOMALOPSYCHIDAE

The family was established for a single Chilean genus, with a second genus and species subsequently placed therein. More recently the second genus, *Contulma*, has been found to be widespread in the Neotropics.

CONTULMA ADAMSAE HOLZENTHAL AND FLINT

This is the first species of the family and genus found in Peru. It is not surprizing, however, as other species had been taken in Chile, Ecuador, Colombia, and Brazil. It was taken only at the highest elevation sampled on the survey.

Material Examined.— Near park entrance station, near km 106, 3420 m, 28 Aug 1989, 3♂, 1♀ metamorphotype, 2 larvae.

ACKNOWLEDGEMENTS

I am indebted to a number of friends and colleagues for their help in collecting caddisflies during the course of this study: Nancy E. Adams, Robin A. Faitoute, Amnon Freidberg, Jon Gelhaus, Jerry A. Louton, Wayne N. Mathis, Michael G. Pogue, and Luis Reyes A. Dr. Jerry A. Louton produced the graphs herein reproduced with his computer equipment and expertise. Dr. Robert K. Robbins provided valuable insight and counseling on the species accumulation curves.

LITERATURE CITED

Erwin, T.L. 1991 (for 1900). Natural History of the Carabid Beetles at the BIOLAT Biological Station, Rio Manu, Pakitza, Peru. Revista Peruana de Entomologia, 33:1-85.

Flint, O. S., Jr. 1975. Studies of neotropical caddisflies, XX: Trichoptera collected by the Hamburg South-Peruvian expedition. Entomologische Mitteilungen aus dem Zoologischen Museum Hamburg, 4:565-573.

———. 1980. VI. Trichoptera. Pp. 213-217, in The results of the Catherwood Foundation Bolivian-Peruvian Altiplano Expedition. Part I. Aquatic Insects except Diptera (S. S. Roback, ed.). Proc. Acad. Nat. Sci. Philadelphia, 132: 176-217.

Flint, O. S., Jr., and L. Reyes A. 1991. Studies of neotropical caddisflies, XLVI: The Trichoptera of the Río Moche basin, Department of La Libertad, Peru. Proc. Biol. Soc. Washington, 104:474-492.

Higler, L. W. G. 1981. Caddis fly systematics to 1960 and a review of the genera (Insecta:Trichoptera). Pp. 117-126, in Proceedings of the 3rd international symposium on Trichoptera (G. P. Moretti, ed.). Dr W. Junk, The Hague, Series Entomologia, 20:1-472.

Martynov, A. B. 1912. On two collections of Trichoptera from Peru. Annuaire de Musée Zoologique de l'Académie Impériale des Sciences de St. Pétersbourg, 17:1-40.

Ross, H. H. 1967. The evolution and past dispersal of the Trichoptera. Ann. Rev. Entomol., 12: 169-206.

Schmid, F. 1984. Essai d'evaluation de la faune mondiale des Trichoptères. P. 337, in Proceedings of the 4th international symposium on Trichoptera (J. C. Morse, ed.). Dr W. Junk, The Hague, Series Entomologia, 30:1-486.

Spuris, Z. 1991. New taxa of Trichoptera described in 1961-1970. Latvijas Entomologs, 34:54-95.

Woytkowski, F. 1978. Peru, my unpromised land. Translation, TT 76-54062, U.S. Dept. Commerce, Natl. Tech. Info. Serv. Springfield, VA, 22161, 231 pp, 6 charts.

The Odonata of Parque Nacional Manu, Madre de Dios, Peru; Natural History, Species Richness and Comparisons with Other Peruvian Sites

J.A. LOUTON,

National Museum of Natural History, Smithsonian Institution, Washington, DC, 20560, USA;

R.W. GARRISON,

Research Associate, Natural History Museum of Los Angeles County, 900 Exposition Boulevard, Los Angeles, CA 90007; and

O.S. FLINT,

National Museum of Natural History, Smithsonian Institution, Washington, DC, 20560, USA.

ABSTRACT

Collections of Odonata at Reserved Zone, Parque Nacional del Manu, were made during 1987-1989 in the vicinity of the park headquarters at Pakitza, at Cocha Salvador and along the road that follows the park boundary between Puente Morro Leguia (approx. 2200m) and Salvacion (approx. 550m). A few specimens collected along the Rio Alto Madre de Dios are included, although the area is outside the Reserved Zone boundary. The collections thus include material from Andean montane wet forest, mid-elevation transition zone, upper Andean tropical wet forest, humid Andean foothills forest and tropical lowland forest, although 85% of the material listed below is from tropical lowland forest at Pakitza or nearby. Specimens were hand-netted, taken by Malaise traps, mist nets, from larval rearings and from canopy-fogging collections. All collections were made during the transitional dry-to-wet season in late August through early October. The entire transect yielded 136 species with 117 species taken from the lowland study area around Pakitza. The data for the Pakitza collections were subjected to species richness estimation techniques and the results clustered around 130 species (probably a low estimate biased by lack of adequate collecting in standing-water habitats). Comparisons with a similar nearby site, the Tambopata Reserved Zone (250 km distant), and a site near Iquitos (1060 km distant) indicated that differences in collection emphasis or habitat diversity obscured comparisons, with Tambopata having highest overall species richness but with Pakitza having greater diversity among "non-weed" groups.Pakitza-Tambopata and Tambopata-Iquitos had similar beta-diversity while Pakitza-Iquitos had higher beta-diversity as measured by Jaccard's similarity coefficient and percent similarity.

431

J. A. Louton, R. W. Garrison, O. S. Flint.

INTRODUCTION

The Odonata (dragonflies and damselflies) are conspicuous components of tropical ecosystems because they are large day-flying insects frequently found in light gaps or open areas above water. Many have patterned bodies or wings that allow recognition in the field, even during flight. Both adults and larvae are important primary and secondary predators in their food chains and exhibit a broad array of predatory strategies. Adults generally take a wide variety of prey on the wing but some unusual specializations in feeding strategies exist such as spider predation in the giant helicopter damselflies (Pseudostigmatidae) (Calvert, 1923; Young, 1980; Fincke, 1992). Although adults are often generalists with regard to prey, they may be selective for patterns of flight activity by flying only in bright sunlight, deep shade, or at dusk. Larvae in various groups are phytotelmous (e.g. bromeliads, tree-holes or bamboo), rapid climbers on submerged vegetation, shallow burrowers in stream rapids or deep burrowers in river banks and lake bottoms. The systematic arrangement of the higher groups of Odonata is relatively stable, although relationships are yet to be examined using modern phylogenetic techniques. A world catalog of species has been produced (Bridges, 1993) making this small order (about 5,000 species worldwide) among the better documented insect groups. Although better studied than most other groups of insects, many new taxa from the Neotropical Region await discovery and description (perhaps 20%, judging from the results below). This is the first of two papers on the Odonata of P.N. Manu; the second, in preparation, will provide keys and descriptions of new species.

The collections reported herein were made for purposes of maximizing the information gained from our short periods of field time. We wanted to know what species were present and as much as possible about their natural history. That precluded field work based on quadrats, line-transects, or timed collecting since efficient collecting of these large strong-flying insects requires opportunism to collect most of the fauna in a few weeks of field time. Collections made as part of a rigorous sampling program are so limited that possible inferences about the total fauna based only on them are almost certainly inferior to inferences based on the raw list that results from intensive opportunistic collecting. In spite of this, we believe that we can make reasonable species richness estimates based on these collections by being selective in our methods and cautious in our interpretations. We have also made comparisons with collections from other locations that were also sampled opportunistically. A program of sampling based on hours of collecting effort as employed by Coddington et. al. (1991) for spiders has promise for Odonata as a reasonable compromise between "museum" versus "ecological" methods.

432

COLLECTING SITES

Descriptive terms used throughout for "forest types" are those used informally by tropical botanists who have worked in this area (R. Foster, pers. comm.). They were not necessarily used uniformly by all botanical workers and should not be rigidly applied, e.g. regarding elevational boundaries. Latitude-longitude are given for sites where available and are in the form of degrees and decimal minutes. This form is coming into wide use with the popularity of geopositioning systems (GPS) that use this default format to achieve finer resolution.

PUENTE MORRO LEGUÍA.

13° 07.44'S, 071° 43.37'W, 2200m elev. (GPS). This site is located at rd.km. 135 at the upper boundary of the Andean montane wet forest. Rio Morro Leguia is a clear stream three to five meters wide with waterfalls, rapids and small pools over a substrate of boulders and cobble with little fine gravel or sand. No agricultural disturbance or deforestation was noted.

PUENTE SAN PEDRO.

13° 03.30'S, 071° 32.78'W, 1450m elev. (GPS). This location is at rd.km. 152 at the transition between Andean montane wet forest and upper Andean tropical wet forest. Rio San Pedro is clear, three to five meters wide with small waterfalls, rapids and pools over a boulder and cobble substrate with a marked increase in fine gravel and sand in the pools. There was minor local clearing by a single family and patches of second growth forest indicate a more extensive previous clearing.

PUENTE QUITACALZÓN.

13° 01.57'S, 071° 29.97'W, 1050m elev. (GPS). This oddly named settlement consists of a small collection of buildings (1987-1991, nothing but a small shelter remained in 1993) at rd.km. 164. The stream was clear, with boulders, gravel and extensive patches of sand, with well-vegetated banks and little sign of rapid erosion. Local human activities included small clearings for banana and pineapples and lumbering. This was the lowest site on the transect with more or less continuously forested slopes.

PILCOPATA.

12° 54.51'S, 071° 24.20'W, 540 m elev. (GPS). A small collection was made at roadside seeps in the valley of the Rio Pilcopata between Pilcopata and Atalaya.

433

ATALAYA.

12° 53.34'S, 071° 21.55'W, 535m elev. (GPS). This small village at rd.km. 210 is at the head of navigation by large motorized canoes on the Rio Alto Madre de Dios.

ERIKA.

Lat.-long. not available. Erika Hostel is a small thatch and split palm hotel on the Rio Alto Madre de Dios across from Salvacion (prior to a change in river course in 1990) at rd.km 227 at approx. 500m. Collections were made at a stream adjacent to the Hostel that was clear, two to four meters wide, with a substrate of cobble, gravel, sand and fine silt from the red soil banks. Much of the immediate area is neglected banana, citrus, coffee and cacao groves returning to early second growth forest. The rugged, steep terrain behind the hostel is late second growth or selectively cut forests with a few small streams including one that supplies water for the hotel. Collections were mostly from areas of open sunlight along the larger stream and along the smaller spring-fed stream. *Epigomphus* and *Polythore* specimens were from partially shaded areas in dense second growth forest.

DIAMANTE.

12° 19.92'S, 070° 57.48'W, 275m elev. (GPS). Village between Salvacion and Boca Manu on the Rio Alto Madre de Dios. A single collection was made during a brief stop across from the village in a shallow, warm stream over sand and gravel; mostly in open areas in bright sunlight.

COCHA SALVADOR.

11° 59.85'S, 071° 13.96'W, 300m elev. (GPS). This is a large cocha (ox-bow lake) about 10 km SE of Pakitza. It appears early-successional because it is deep, the banks are steep and there is little filling except at the ends.

PAKITZA.

11° 56.65'S, 071° 16.98'W, 325m elev. (GPS). The study area is located on upper Amazon floodplain in an area that has a relatively high density of animals and rapid growth rate of trees due to high soil fertility and lack of significant recent human disturbance (Foster, 1990a; 1990b). The basecamp and park guard station is located on the NE side of the Rio Manu on a dissected Pleistocene terrace that stands up to 100m above the riverbed (Erwin, 1990). The relatively pristine forests nearby allowed us the opportunity to examine the fauna of essentially intact primary forests. The only logging operations known to exist in the area consisted of selective cutting that ended 40 years ago and did not extend upstream from Pakitza (R. Foster, pers. comm.). This area can only be reached by a two-day motorized canoe trip upstream from Pto. Maldonado or from Cuzco down to Salvacion by vehicle and then to Pakitza by a one and one-half day canoe trip. The study area around Pakitza is approximately 4,000 ha with a network of 36 km of trails (Erwin, 1990). There are several stream systems in the immediate vicinity of the basecamp, including three larger systems of 3-5 meters width and many seeps that form into 1-2 meter streams running under unbroken canopy. The cochas immediately across the river from Pakitza were off limits to us during the entire study due to the presence of a small group of recently contacted indians living there. The nearest accessible large cocha was Cocha Salvador. A small muddy cocha derived from one of the larger streams became available as a result of a new trail cut late in the study. In addition, we collected at a small-saw grass marsh and in a swamp developed on a filled cocha.

METHODS

Adults were collected mostly by hand-netting (approx. 1400 specimens), but additional material was obtained by Malaise trapping (3), from buildings (11), from mist nets (9) set for bats or birds and from canopy fogging operations (3). Larvae were collected by dip-netting or kick-netting in ox-bow lakes or streams and final instar larvae that appeared ready for emergence were kept alive in partially submerged rearing cages. Twenty-six individuals of 19 species were reared; four of these species were not collected by any other method. Collections were not made in any systematic way, e.g. quadrats, line transects, or timed collecting. However, a reasonable attempt was made to collect all specimens encountered (including common species) to develop a picture of relative abundance of species and because most collectors could not distinguish all (or in some cases, any) species in the field.

In spite of the "museum" collecting methods used, several techniques were employed to estimate the total number of species expected for Pakitza. Since quadrats were not employed, the measure of sampling effort used was either a collecting-day (date of capture) or simply the event of collection itself. A "collecting-day" in this context is a very crude approximation of collecting effort since weather conditions and the number of persons collecting on a given day fluctuated, causing daily production of specimens to vary (Figure 1). During the 1987 season, relatively little time was devoted to collecting Odonata. The 1988 and 1989 seasons of approximately 20 days each were devoted to the collection of Odonata and other aquatic insects. Several methods of species richness estimation were tried using SYSTAT script files developed by Coddington et. al. (1991 and pers. comm.). All methods assume an unbiased sample of species that are evenly accessible to the methods used and most were developed for use with

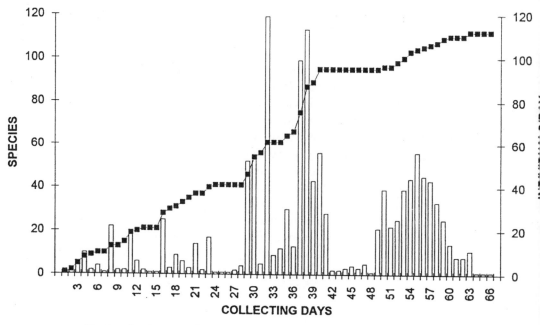

Fig. 1.– *Species accumulation curve with individuals collected / day for Pakitza, Perú*

quadrat samples. Chao's (1984, 1987) estimators were used and are recommended when the relative number of singletons and doubletons predominate in a collection. It does, however, have the additional assumption that sampled individuals are returned to a closed population. A poisson lognormal distribution was fit to our species abundance data by maximum likelihood. This method is described by Bulmer (1974) who suggested that this estimate gave somewhat low results for the data sets he studied. The data were also used to generate a species-accumulation curve whose asymptote was estimated based on the Michaelis-Menten model of enzyme kinetics similar to that employed by Lamas et al. (1991). The measure of sampling effort was accumulated number of individuals per collecting-day, with collecting time per day varying, instead of a precisely timed interval. A nonlinear as well as linear regression was fitted to determine the y-intercept (species estimate). Two non-parametric methods usually used for data acquired by quadrat sampling were tried as suggested by Coddington et. al. (1991) as a means of arriving at species estimates that have confidence intervals. The jackknife method (Heltsche and Forrester, 1983) estimates the number of species in a community as a function of the number of taxa that occur in only one quadrat (collecting-day for our data) and calculates the variance. This procedure assumes a random distribution of quadrats rather than a random distribution of individuals so that an obvious bias is introduced in substituting uneven collecting-days for quadrats. Boot-strapping was also applied to the data set to estimate the expected number of species. This estimator is based on species presence or absence in a series of "samples" that are randomly resampled with replacement. Calculation of the estimate of species richness for the resamples and overall variance are from the equations of Smith and van Belle (1984). Beta-diversity was calculated between Pakitza, Tambopata and Iquitos using Jaccard's Coefficient of similarity. It is derived from the ratio of the number of taxa shared relative to the total taxa in the comparison and neglects conjoint absences (Clifford and Stephenson, 1975). It was selected as a measure of beta-diversity because of its wide use and because it uses binary data, thus allowing comparisons with published taxa lists from other sites.

Material examined for this study is held in trust at the National Museum of Natural History, Smithsonian Institution for eventual repatriation of 50% to Peruvian institutions per agreements between BIOLAT and the Ministerio de Agricultura, Peru. Collections data are available in text or database form from the senior author or through the BIOLAT program.

The fauna of P.N. Manu

A total of 1536 specimens of 136 species were collected during the three field seasons in, or adjacent to, the P.N. Manu Reserved Zone (Table 1). Of these, 224 specimens in 52 species were collected along the elevational transect from Puente Morro Leguia (2200m) to Diamante (275m). Pakitza and nearby Cocha Salvador yielded 1318 specimens of 117 species. These represent conservative counts; all unidentified females that belonged to genera already represented in the sample

Table 1. Odonata species of P.N. Manu by locality and with brief habitat/ behavorial notes (numbers in parentheses refer to extended notes in appendix).

	Puente Morro Leguía, 2200m	Puente San Pedro, 1450m	Quitacalzón, 1050m	Pilcopata, 540m	Atalaya, 535m	Erika, 500m	Diamante, 275m	Cocha Salvador, 300m	Pakitza, 325m	Total	habitat/behavioral notes
Zygoptera											
Polythoridae											
Cora terminalis	1	0	0	0	0	0	0	0	0	1	small streams,high elev.
Polythore boliviana	0	3	2	0	0	4	0	0	0	9	butterfly mimic,at small streams,secondary forest
Polythore manua	0	0	0	0	0	4	0	0	116	120	butterfly mimic,small streams,primary forest (1)
Polythore sp.(undet.females)	0	0	1	0	0	1	0	0	0	2	
Dicteriadidae											
Heliocharis amazona	0	0	0	0	0	0	0	0	18	18	at streams in full sun (2)
Calopterygidae											
Hetaerina charca	0	0	0	0	0	11	0	0	0	11	at streams, secondary forests
Hetaerina rosea	0	0	0	0	0	31	0	0	4	35	reared from 3m stream, partial canopy
Hetaerina sanguinea	0	0	0	0	0	8	10	0	20	38	reared from 5m stream, open canopy
Mnesarete devillei	0	0	0	0	0	1	0	0	103	104	at streams, partial canopy
Mnesarete n.sp.A	0	0	0	0	0	0	0	0	81	81	at small streams, primary forest
Mnesarete n.sp.B	0	0	0	0	0	1	0	0	0	1	at stream, secondary forest
Perilestidae											
Perilestes kahli	0	0	0	0	0	0	0	0	10	10	along trails in dense forest

J. A. Louton, R. W. Garrison, O. S. Flint.

	Puente Morro Leguía, 2200m	Puente San Pedro, 1450m	Quitacalzón, 1050m	Pilcopata, 540m	Atalaya, 535m	Erika, 500m	Diamante, 275m	Cocha Salvador, 300m	Pakitza, 325m	Total	habitat/behavioral notes
Perissolestes sp.n. (nr.magdalenae)	0	0	0	0	0	0	0	0	2	2	along trails in dense forest
Perissolestes (?) sp.	0	0	0	0	0	0	0	0	1	1	along trails in dense forest
Megapodagrionidae											
Allopodagrion setigerum	0	2	0	0	0	0	0	0	0	2	at 5m stream, waterfalls, open canopy
Heteragrion aequatoriale?	0	0	0	0	0	4	0	0	0	4	at streams, secondary forest
Heteragrion inca (or near)	0	0	0	0	0	9	0	0	88	97	reared from seep under closed canopy
Philogenia boliviana	0	0	0	0	0	0	0	4	5	9	along trails, primary and secondary forests
Philogenia margarita	0	0	0	0	0	0	0	0	17	17	along trains, primary forest, dense canopy
Philogenia spp.(undet.females)	0	0	0	0	0	0	0	1	7	8	
Pseudostigmatidae											family of container-breeding spider predator
Mecistogaster jocaste	0	0	0	0	0	0	0	0	10	10	larvae in tree holes (Machado and Martinez
Mecistogaster linearis	0	0	0	0	0	2	0	0	19	21	larvae in tree holes (Fincke, 1984)
Mecistogaster n.sp.	0	0	0	0	0	0	0	0	2	2	larvae from bamboo internodes (3)
Mecistogaster undet.female A	0	0	0	0	0	0	0	0	1	1	
Mecistogaster undet.female B	0	0	0	0	0	0	0	0	1	1	
Microstigma rotundatum	0	0	0	0	0	0	0	0	2	2	larvae in fallen fruit husks (Santos,1981)
Protoneuridae											
Epipleoneura n.sp. (nr.peruviensis)	0	0	0	0	0	0	0	0	14	14	at small streams in primary forest, closed ca
Neoneura rubriventris	0	0	0	0	0	0	0	0	5	5	at small streams in primary forest, closed ca
Neoneura n.sp.A	0	0	0	0	0	0	0	0	2	2	at 5m stream, primary forest, open canopy
Neoneura n.sp.B	0	0	0	0	0	0	0	0	13	13	reared from 5m stream, primary forest, open
Protoneura amatoria	0	0	0	0	0	0	0	0	30	30	at streams along trails in primary forest
Protoneura paucinervis	0	0	0	0	0	0	0	13	0	13	at large ox-bow lake, primary forest (4)
Protoneura woytkowskii	0	0	0	0	0	0	0	0	8	8	at small streams, primary forest
Psaironeura tenuissima	0	0	0	0	0	0	0	0	11	11	at small streams, primary forest
Platystictidae											
Palaemnema sp.(undet. females)	0	0	0	0	0	1	0	0	1	2	along trails in primary and secondary forest
Coenagrionidae											mostly at standing water (except Argia)
Acanthagrion lancea	0	0	0	0	0	0	0	5	1	6	at ox-bow lakes, primary forest
Acanthagrion luteum	0	0	0	0	0	0	0	0	9	9	along trails in primary forest
Acanthagrion obsoletum	0	0	0	0	4	0	0	0	4	8	along trails in primary and secondary forests
Acanthagrion phallicornis	0	0	0	0	0	0	0	0	1	1	
Acanthagrion n.sp. (yungarum group)	0	0	0	0	0	8	0	0	0	8	secondary forest, partial canopy
Acanthagrion sp.	0	0	0	0	0	0	0	0	1	1	
Aeolagrion inca	0	0	0	0	0	0	0	0	2	2	along trails, primary forest
Argia adamsi	0	0	0	0	0	3	0	0	54	57	at streams, primary and secondary forests
Argia cuprea (Gloyd#43a)	0	0	0	0	0	0	0	0	76	76	reared from 1-3m streams, primary forest
Argia dificilis (Gloyd#35)	0	0	0	0	0	9	0	0	20	29	at streams, primary and secondary forests
Argia gerhardi	0	3	5	0	0	0	0	0	0	8	seeps and streams, partial canopy
Argia hamulata	0	0	0	0	0	0	0	0	8	8	along trails, primary forest
Argia indicatrix	0	0	0	0	0	0	0	0	2	2	sluggish streams/swamp in primary forest
Argia kokama	0	3	0	0	0	0	0	0	9	12	at streams, partial canopy, see elevation
Argia nigrior (or near)	0	0	0	2	0	0	0	0	14	16	at seeps and streams, partial or closed canopy
Argia thespis	0	0	0	0	0	0	0	0	45	45	at streams/swamp, primary forest, partial can
Argia variegata	0	0	0	1	0	0	0	0	0	1	roadside seeps
Argia sp.A	0	0	0	0	0	1	0	0	16	17	reared from 1-3m stream,primary and secondary fo
Argia sp.B	0	0	0	0	0	0	0	0	2	2	along trails, primary forest
Argia sp.C	0	0	0	0	0	0	0	0	6	6	at streams/swamp, primary forest
Argia sp.D	0	0	0	0	0	0	0	0	1	1	along trails, primary forest
Argia sp.E	0	0	0	0	0	0	2	0	0	2	at broad stream, open canopy
Argia sp.F	0	0	0	0	0	0	0	0	1	1	along trail, primary forest
Argia spp.(4-5 misc.spp.mostly female)	0	0	0	0	0	2	0	0	9	11	at streams
Leptobasis raineyi	0	0	0	0	0	0	0	0	1	1	at stream/swamp, primary forest
Leptobasis? sp.	0	0	0	0	0	0	0	0	2	2	along trails, primary forest
Metaleptobasis sp.A (sp.nov.)	0	0	0	0	0	0	0	0	20	20	along trails, primary forest
Metaleptobasis sp.B	0	0	0	0	0	0	0	0	6	6	along trails, primary forest

	Puente Morro Leguía, 2200m	Puente San Pedro, 1450m	Quitacalzón, 1050m	Pilcopata, 540m	Atalaya, 535m	Erika, 500m	Diamante, 275m	Cocha Salvador, 300m	Pakitza, 325m	Total	habitat/behavioral notes
etaleptobasis sp.C(sp.nov.)	0	0	0	0	0	0	0	0	3	3	along trails, primary forest
etaleptobasis sp.D(sp.nov.)	0	0	0	0	0	0	0	0	1	1	along trails, primary forest
etaleptobasis sp.E(sp.nov.)	0	0	0	0	0	0	0	0	6	6	along trails, primary forest
elebasis sp.nov.	0	0	0	0	0	0	0	0	20	20	along trails, primary forest
elebasis(?) sp.A	0	0	0	0	0	0	0	0	1	1	along trails, primary forest
elebasis(?) sp.A	0	0	0	0	0	0	0	0	2	2	along trails, primary forest
tera											
nidae											
eshna cornigera	0	1	0	0	0	0	0	0	0	1	
eshna marchali?	1	0	0	0	0	0	0	0	0	1	flying along road
ynacantha croceipennis	0	0	0	0	0	2	0	0	0	2	crepuscular, in clearings
ynacantha gracilis	0	0	0	0	0	0	0	0	9	9	crepuscular, in clearings
ynacantha interioris	0	0	0	0	0	2	0	0	2	4	crepuscular, in clearings
ynacantha membranalis	0	0	0	0	0	0	0	0	8	8	crepuscular, in clearings
ynacantha nervosa	0	0	0	0	0	0	0	0	2	2	crepuscular, in clearings
taurophlebia reticulata	0	0	0	0	0	2	0	0	0	2	along roads, clearings
riacanthagyna caribbea	0	0	0	0	0	0	0	0	1	1	crepuscular, in clearings
riacanthagyna satyrus (or near)	0	0	0	0	1	0	0	0	6	7	crepuscular, in clearings
nphidae											
agriogomphus sylvicola	0	0	0	0	0	0	0	0	9	9	reared from leaf packs in streams
Aphylla dentata?	0	0	0	0	0	0	0	0	8	8	from mist nets
Aphylla sp.	0	0	0	0	0	0	0	1	0	1	exuviae from ox-bow lake
Archaeogomphus furcatus	0	0	0	0	0	0	0	0	5	5	reared from trailing terrest. Vegetation in streams (5)
Archaeogomphus hamatus?	0	0	0	0	0	0	0	0	2	2	reared from trailing terrest. Vegetation in streams (5)
Epigomphus obtusus	0	0	1	0	0	1	0	0	16	18	at small streams,prim.&sec.forest,partial canopy
Peruvigomphus moyabambus	0	0	0	0	0	0	0	1	0	1	at ox-bow lake, primary forest
Phyllocycla sp.	0	0	0	0	0	0	0	1	0	1	exuviae from ox-bow lake, primary forest
Phyllogomphoides lieftincki	0	0	0	0	0	0	0	0	1	1	reared from 1-3m stream, partial canopy
Progomphus boliviensis?	0	0	0	0	0	0	0	0	2	2	reared from 1-3m partial canopy
Progomphus pygmaeus	0	0	0	0	0	0	0	0	3	3	reared from sand bars in broad, sandy streams
Progomphus sp.A(large female)	0	0	0	0	0	0	0	0	1	1	reared from 1-3m stream, partial canopy
Progomphus sp.B(large female)	0	1	0	0	0	0	0	0	0	1	at torrential stream, open canopy
rduliidae											
Gomphomacromia fallax	0	0	5	2	0	2	0	0	5	14	at seeps in forest (6)
ellulidae											
Anatya guttata	0	0	0	0	0	0	0	0	3	3	from canopy fogging ssamples only
Argyrothemis argentea	0	0	0	0	0	0	0	0	2	2	swamp, primary forest
Brachymesia herbida	0	0	0	0	0	1	0	0	0	1	
Brechmorhoga nubecula	0	0	0	0	0	1	0	0	1	2	reared from 2-4m stream,prim.& sec. forests
Cannaphila vibex	0	1	0	1	0	0	0	0	1	3	seepage areas
Dasythemis esmeralda	0	0	0	0	0	0	0	0	9	9	at seeps/swamp, primary forest
Dythemis multipunctata	0	0	0	0	0	1	0	0	5	6	reared from 1-3m streams, partial canopy
Elasmothemis cannacrioides	0	0	0	0	0	4	4	0	6	14	reared from sandy 5m streams, partial canopy
Erythrodiplax attenuata	0	0	0	0	0	0	0	0	15	15	at back-waters or small lagoons, open canopy
Erythrodiplax basalis	0	0	0	0	0	0	0	0	1	1	
Erythrodiplax castanea	0	0	0	0	0	0	0	0	7	7	at swamp, primary forest, partial canopy
Erythrodiplax fusca	0	0	0	0	0	1	0	0	1	2	at back-waters or small lagoons, open canopy
Erythrodiplax umbrata	0	0	0	0	0	0	0	0	2	2	
Erythrodiplax unimaculata	0	0	0	0	0	0	0	0	2	2	
Fylgia amazonica	0	0	0	0	0	0	0	0	1	1	at small swamp in dense forest (7)
Libellula herculea	0	0	0	0	1	0	0	0	0	1	
Macrothemis declivata	0	0	0	0	0	0	0	0	5	5	reared from 1-3m streams, primary forest, partial canopy
Macrothemis extensa	0	0	0	0	0	0	0	0	1	1	very cryptic, under canopy (8)
Macrothemis hemichlora	0	0	0	0	0	10	0	0	6	16	at small streams, primary and secondary forests
Macrothemis musiva	0	1	0	0	0	7	0	0	5	13	reared from 1-2m stream entering swamp

J. A. Louton, R. W. Garrison, O. S. Flint.

	Puente Morro Leguía, 2200m	Puente San Pedro, 1450m	Quitacalzón, 1050m	Pilcopata, 540m	Atalaya, 535m	Erika, 500m	Diamante, 275m	Cocha Salvador, 300m	Pakitza, 325m	Total	habitat/behavioral notes
Macrothemis sp.A (n.sp.nr.*tessellata*)	0	0	0	0	0	2	0	0	1	3	at clearings, primary and secondary forests
Macrothemis sp.B (n.sp.?)	0	0	0	0	0	0	0	0	2	2	at back-water or small lagoon, open canopy
Macrothemis sp.C	0	0	0	0	0	0	0	0	1	1	
Macrothemis D (didyma group)	0	0	0	0	0	0	0	0	1	1	
Macrothemis sp.E	0	0	0	0	0	9	0	0	4	13	at stream or small lagoon, open canopy
Micrathyria dictynna	0	0	0	0	0	0	0	0	6	6	along trails at stream crossings, partial canop
Micrathyria hippolyte	0	0	0	0	0	0	0	0	10	10	along trails at stream crossing, partial canop
Micrathyria spinifera	0	0	0	0	0	0	0	0	3	3	along trails at stream crossings, partial canop
Micrathyria sp.A(n.sp.near dictynna)	0	0	0	0	0	0	0	0	2	2	along trails at stream crossings, partial canop
Micrathyria sp.B	0	0	0	0	0	0	0	0	1	1	flew into dining tent
Misagria calverti	0	0	0	0	0	0	0	0	5	5	along trails at stream crossings,partial canop
Oligoclada pachystigma	0	0	0	0	0	0	0	6	0	6	at ox-bow lake, primary forest
Oligoclada walkeri	0	0	0	0	0	2	0	0	5	7	along trails, primary and secondary forests
Orthemis biolleyi	0	0	0	0	0	0	0	0	16	16	in mist nets, flying in camp clearing
Orthemis cultriformis	0	0	0	0	0	0	0	0	35	35	in mist nets, flying in camp clearing
Orthemis ferruginea	0	0	0	0	1	0	0	0	5	6	flies in openings in full sun
Pantala flavescens	0	0	0	0	1	0	0	0	1	2	long-distance flier, full sun
Perithemis bella	0	0	0	0	0	0	0	11	0	11	at ox-bow lake, primary forest
Perithemis cornelia	0	0	0	0	0	0	0	0	4	4	at sluggish streams,primary forest,partial canc
Perithemis electra	0	0	0	0	0	5	0	0	7	12	at sluggish streams,prim.&sec. forest, partial canop
Perithemis mooma	0	0	0	0	0	0	0	2	0	2	at ox-bow lake, primary forest
Perithemis parzefalli	0	0	0	0	0	4	0	1	9	14	at sluggish streams,prim.&sec. forest, partial canop
Perithemis thais	0	0	0	0	0	0	0	0	3	3	at sluggish streams,primary forest, partial can
Perithemis n.sp.A	0	0	0	0	0	0	0	0	5	5	at sluggish streams,primary forest, partial can
Sympetrun illotum gilvam	0	0	0	1	0	0	0	0	0	1	roadside seep
Uracis fastigiata	0	0	0	0	0	1	0	0	58	59	along trails under canopy
Uracis infumata	0	0	0	0	0	0	0	0	2	2	along trails under canopy
individuals	2	15	14	7	4	163	16	40	1273	1537	
species	2	8	3	3	4	33	3	11	110	136	

were dropped from the species tally. The list contains about 20 undescribed species in the genera Heteragrion, Mecistogaster, Epipleoneura, Neoneura, Acanthagrion, Argia, Metaleptobasis, Telebasis, Macrothemis, Micrathyria, Orthemis, and Perithemis. Species known only from Parque Manu include Polythore manua, Mecistogaster n.sp., Neoneura n.sp., Argia n.sp., Metaleptobasis n.sp., Telebasis n.sp., Macrothemis sp., and Perithemis n.sp.

Since the focus of BIOLAT collecting activity and research was at the facility at Pakitza, fewer collections were made along the elevational transect above Pakitza making among-site comparisons of diversity difficult. However, in 1988 a series of riffle samples (gravel substrate, depth about 10 cm, and current about .5 m/sec) were taken using a "square foot" Surber sampler at four sites on the transect at 2200m, 1450m, 500m, and 325m. Nine samples were taken per site yielding 2, 2, 6, and 115 total individuals per station respectively. Species per

440

station were 1, 2, 4 and 21 respectively indicating that both abundance and diversity are inversely related to elevation, at least for riffle-dwelling larvae of Odonata.

Species Richness estimates for Pakitza

The different estimators used show surprisingly congruent results in spite of the divergent methods of calculation and the diversity of assumptions associated with them. The following estimates assume that collectors will continue to collect in the same areas, using the same methods and with the same efficiency. However, as new trails are cut and additional areas opened to collecting the calculations will have to be redone. These estimates therefore only apply to the expected number of species in the areas already collected.

Several of the estimators gave expected values that clustered around 125 species. Chao's (1984, 1987) method indicated 127 species plus or minus 14. Although the population is not closed the sampling area is quite large, therefore we do not believe that the estimate is substantially changed by not returning captured individuals to the "population." The Poisson log-normal fit estimated 123 species plus or minus 15. This is lower than the results from most other methods and supports the suggestion of Bulmer (1974) that the method underestimates species richness. A linear fit to the Michaelis-Menten model yielded 121 species but the linear fit to the data appears poor. The highest estimate was from a non-linear fit to the Michaelis-Menton model with 162 species projected. When the data set was randomized to remove the collecting-order bias, the estimate dropped to 131 species (20 randomizations, more iterations would presumably have reduced the estimate further). The Jackknife estimate was for 137 species plus or minus 11. The Jackknife method is said to underestimate the number of species in communities with large numbers of rare species (Heltsche and Forrester, 1983), however, it gave the highest estimate of species richness for our data except for the non-linear Michaelis-Menten. The final estimates then, cluster around an expected value of 128 species, give or take a dozen or so, an estimate that seems reasonable to us, except that in subsequent seasons we will move into under-collected habitats (e.g. standing water) and these estimates will need to be recalculated to reflect that. In addition, we have no idea as to the robustness of the various estimation methods with regard to violation of their assumptions.

J. A. *Louton*, R. W. *Garrison*, O. S. *Flint*.

COMPARISON WITH TAMBOPATA
AND IQUITOS SITES

Comparisons between P.N. Manu, the Tambopata Reserved Zone and the Earth Watch Iquitos sites are not straightforward. The upper Rio Manu watershed (=PN Manu) includes an elevational gradient from 3300m at Tres Cruces to 350m at Pakitza. Except for the sparse collecting on the road transect along the eastern park boundary, survey activity was limited by prior agreement to the BIOLAT area at Pakitza of about 4,000 ha. with 36 km of trails. The Tambopata Reserve has an area of 5,500 ha, a trail system that appears from maps to be similar to that of Pakitza, many stream and cocha habitats and both black (acid) and white-water areas (Pearson, 1984). The BIOLAT study area at Pakitza, at 4,000 ha is somewhat smaller, has fewer accessible cochas and black water habitats were not seen. The Earthwatch sites in Iquitos, Loreto Province, Peru, are three ecotourist facilities: 1) the Explorama Inn (3o 42'S, 73° 12'W), 40 km downriver (NNW) of Iquitos; 2) the Explorama Lodge (3° 30'S, 73° 12'W), 80 km downriver; and 3) the Explornapo Camp (3° 25'S, 73° 05'W), 160 river km from Iquitos (down Rio Amazonas, up the Rio Napo then up the Rio Sucusari). A maximum of 20 km of trails were surveyed at all three sites (S. Dunkle, pers. comm.).

Table 2 summarizes species richness, species abundance and beta-diversity for the sites and Figure 2 graphs species richness for ease of comparisons across families and sites. Collection data from Tambopata suggests greater species richness than either Pakitza or Iquitos. However, if one examines the breakdown by families, it is apparent that much of Tambopata's richness is contributed by the libellulid, aeschnid and coenagrionid components, many members of which are primarily inhabitants of lentic (still water habitat) sites. We suspect that many representatives flourish in disturbed areas such as pasture ponds and irrigation ditches. Removal

Table 2. Alpha and beta diversity for sites at Pakitza, Tambopata and Iquitos, Peru.

| | Pakitza | | Tambopata | | Iquitos | | Jaccard's Coefficient (similarity) | | |
	species	indiv.	species	indiv.	species	indiv.	PAK-TAM	PAK-IQ	TAM-IQ
All Families	117	1318	142	1535	123	.	0.212	0.153	0.21
Polythoridae	1	116	1	22	3	.	.	.	.
Dicteriastidae	1	18	1	6	0	.	.	.	.
Calopterygidae	5	208	5	76	4	.	0.143	0.143	0
Lestidae	0	0	1	1	0	0	.	.	.
Perilestidae	3	13	2	4	3	.	.	.	.
Megapodagrionidae	4	122	1	31	6	.	.	.	.
Pseudostigmatidac	4	35	5	84	5	.	0.286	0.333	0.286
Protoneuridae	8	96	4	75	11	.	0.111	0.167	0
Platystictidae	1	1	0	0	0	.	.	.	.
Coenagrionidae	29	348	30	275	26	.	0.217	0.063	0.109
Aeshnidae	6	28	18	99	9	.	0.25	0.071	0.273
Gomphidae	10	49	6	12	8	.	0.067	0.133	0
Corduliidae	1	5	0	0	0	.	.	.	.
Libellulidae	44	279	68	850	48	.	0.274	0.25	0.357

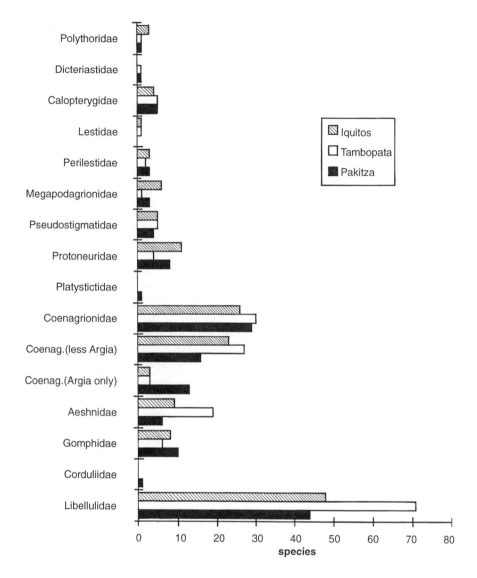

Fig. 2.– *Species/family for sites at Pakitza, Tambopata and Iquitos, Peru.*

of these three families (except for *Argia*, whose members are primarily lotic) results in 51 species for Pakitza, 29 for Tambopata and 43 for Iquitos among the remaining groups primarily inhabiting continuous primary forests with seeps and streams. Pakitza streams cut through gravel lenses providing gravel riffles favored by *Argia* species. T. Erwin (pers. comm.) states that this habitat is not present at Tambopata. Presence of gravel riffles alone may be sufficient to account for the difference (13 vs. 3 species of *Argia*, respectively).

Interpretation of beta-diversity may also reflect the presence of nearby disturbed areas. Jaccard's Coefficient of similarity (Table 2) indicated that Pakitza-Tambopata and Tambopata-Iquitos had virtually the same similarity quotients

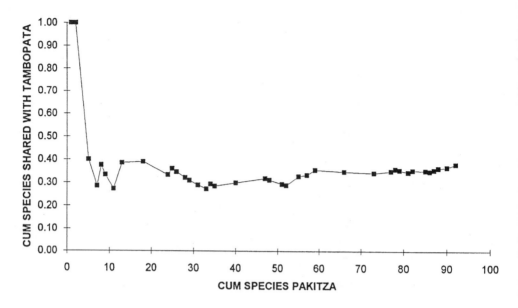

Fig. 3.– *Plot of cumulative species shared between Pakitza and Tambopata, Peru.*

(.21) while Pakitza-Iquitos were less similar (.15). Percent similarity (=number shared taxa/total taxa at both locations –number shared taxa) for Pakitza-Tambopata was 19%, Tambopata-Iquitos 23% and Pakitza-Iquitos 17%. Surprisingly, no distance effect is seen although the sites range from 250 to 1060 km apart. Beta-diversity at the family-level shows discordant patterns. The relatively high similarity of Libellulidae between Tambopata and Iquitos strengthens

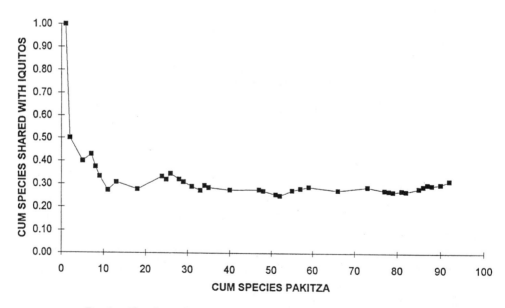

Fig. 4.– *Plot of cumulative species shared between Pakitza and Iquitos, Peru*

444

the suggestion that much of the overall alpha-diversity at these two sites is contributed by "weed species." The family with the highest coefficients between sites is the Pseudostigmatidae, not entirely unexpected since their container habitats are relatively disconnected from edaphic factors that probably play a role in controlling distribution in non-container species. The lowest similarity coefficients were for groups that are favored by under-canopy, flowing-water habitats such as Calopterygidae, Gomphidae, and Protoneuridae. Only fifteen species were present across all three sites and all but three of these were libellulid generalists. The non-libellulids were *Mecistogaster linearis* (Pseudostigmatidae), *Acanthagrion lancea* (Coenagrionidae), and *Gynacantha membranalis* (Aeshnidae). This suggests that uninformed comparisons based solely on these counts will obscure important differences if "weed" species (e.g. many coenagrionids and libellulids) get counted equally with species of primary forest habitats.

The determination of "weed" status is based on our collective experience and information queried from collectors who have undertaken field work in the Neotropics. Evidence for this is the occurrence at sites of human perturbation such as in towns or rural settlements, in areas of disturbance associated with agriculture (extensive clearings, drainage ditches, stock ponds), or in areas of obvious pollution from mining or industry. Species found in these areas are generally not found flying over streams or in small openings in primary forests and vice versa. Weed species are concentrated in the families Coenagrionidae, Aeschnidae, and especially the Libellulidae. Species indigenous to primary forests are concentrated in the families Polythoridae, Dicteriadidae, Calopterygidae, Lestidae, Perilestidae, Pseudostigmatidae, Protoneuridae, Platystictidae, *Argia* of the Coenagrionidae, and Gomphidae. These species are associated with undisturbed sites either at or near streams, in deep forest or in naturally occurring light gaps. Paulson (1984) pointed out the weed component of the fauna of the Tambopata Reserved Zone and Foster and Hubbell (1990c) pointed out similar problems in making floristic comparisons between neotropical forest sites where counts of plant species that included "weeds" swamped comparisons with relatively pristine sites.

As an attempt to predict the change in "cumulative similarity" to Tambopata with additional collecting at Pakitza, we plotted cumulative species collected at Pakitza against cumulative species shared between Pakitza and Tambopata (Fig. 3). A similar plot was made comparing Pakitza and Iquitos (Fig. 4). If commonly occurring species, presumably the first to be collected, tend to be shared the curve should fall and if rare species, presumably the last to be collected tend to be shared the curve should rise. The two plots are remarkably similar. After initial oscillations the lines remain more or less level. One possible explanation for this is that species abundant at one site are often rare or absent at the other and thus species abundant at both sites or rare at both sites are not the usual pattern. If this is typical it bodes well for comparison of species richness at incompletely collected sites but it does not bode well for extrapolating faunal lists for wide areas from a few sites. The slight upturn in similarity near the end of the accumulation curves was probably due to a spate of collecting in lentic habitats that favored

J. A. Louton, R. W. Garrison, O. S. Flint.

Coenagrionidae and Libellulidae, groups that we previously identified as "weeds" and among the groups with the greatest measured similarity between sites.

ACKNOWLEDGEMENTS

We thank the many collectors who helped during this study (N. Adams, R. Bouchard, T. Erwin, A. Freidberg, J. Gelhaus, D. Harvey, G. Lamas, M. Pogue, R. Robbins and G. Servat), and J. Coddington and R. Robbins for help with interpretation of data. G. Lamas provided critical information on butterfly models for polythorid mimics. We thank the former (T. Erwin) and present (D. Wilson) directors of the Biodiversity in Latin America (BIOLAT) program at the Smithsonian Institution for funding the field research.

REFERENCES

Bick, G. H. and J. C. Bick. 1990. *Polythore manua* spec. nov. from southern Peru (Zygoptera: Polythoridae). Odonatologica, 19(4):367-373.

Bridges, C.A. 1993. Catalogue of the family-group, genus-group and species-group names of the Odonata of the World (2d Ed.). Privately printed by the Author (502 W. Main St., #308, Urbana, Illinois, 61801, USA).

Bulmer, M.G. 1974. On fitting the poisson lognormal distribution to species-abundance data. Biometrics, 30:101-110.

Calvert, P.P. 1923. Studies on Costa Rican Odonata. X. *Megaloprepus*, its distribution, variation, habits and food. Entomol. News, 34(5):168-174.

Clifford, H.T. and W. Stephenson. 1975. An introduction to numerical classification. Academic Press, New York. 235pp.

Coddington, J.A., Griswold, C.E., Silva Dávila, D., Peñaranda, E. & Larcher, S.F. 1991, Disigning and testing sampling protocols to estimate biodiversity in tropical ecosystems. In: The unity of evolucionary biology: Proceeding of the Fourth International Congress of Systematic and Evolutionary Biology (ed. E.C. Dudley), pp. 44-60. Portland, Oregon: Dioscorides Press.

Dunkle, S. W. 1989a. Odonate collecting in the Peruvian Amazon. Argia, 1(1-4):5

Dunkle, S. W. 1989b. Odonata of the Explorama facilities near Iquitos, Loreto Department, Peru. Argia: Season Summary Supplement - 1989, 5-6.

Dunkle, S. W. 1990. Odonata (Dragonflies and Damselflies) of the Peruvian Amazon, a preliminary survey. Earthwatch Update. 2:13-15.

Dunkle, S. W. 1990. Dragonflies and Damselflies of the Explorama facilities. Earthwatch Update, 2:15-17.

Erwin, T. L. 1990. Natural history of the carabid beetles at the BIOLAT Biological Station, Rio Manu, Pakitza, Peru. Rev. Per. Entomol., 33:1-85

Fincke, O.M. 1984. Giant damselflies in a tropical forest: reproductive biology of *Megaloprepus coerulatus* with notes on *Mecistogaster* (Zygoptera: Pseudostigmatidae). Adv. Odonatol., 2:13-27.

Fincke, O.M. 1992. Behavioural ecology of the giant damselflies of Barro Colorado Island, Panama (Odonata: Zygoptera: Pseudostigmatidae). In: D.Quintero and A. Aiello (eds.), Insects of Panama and Mesoamerica. Oxford Univ. Press. Oxford, pp. 102-113.

Foster, R.B. 1990a. Long-term change in the successional forest community of the Rio Manu floodplain. In: A.H. Gentry (ed.), Four Neotropical Rainforests. Yale University Press, New Haven, pp. 565-572.

Foster, R.B. 1990b. The floristic composition of the Rio Manu floodplain forests. In: A.H. Gentry (ed.), Four Neotropical Rainforests. Yale University Press, New Haven, pp. 99-111.

Foster, R.B. 1990c. The floristic composition of the Barro Colorado forest. In: A.H. Gentry (ed.), Four Neotropical Rainforests. Yale University Press, New Haven, pp. 85-98.

Lamas, G.; R.K. Robbins and D.J. Harvey. 1991. A preliminary survey of the butterfly fauna of Pakitza, Parque Nacional del Manu, Peru, with an estimate of its species richness. Publ. Mus. Hist. Nat UNMSM (a), 40:1-19.

Louton, J.A.; J. Gelhaus and R.W. Bouchard. In Press [accepted, in revision]. The aquatic fauna of water-filled bamboo (Poaceae:Bambusoidea:Guadua) internodes in a Peruvian lowland tropical forest. Biotropica.

Machado, A.B.M. and A. Martinez. 1982. Oviposition by egg-throwing in a zygopteran, *Mecistogaster jocaste* (Pseudostigmatidae). Odonatologica, 11:15-22.

Marmels, J. 1982. The genus *Euthore* Selys in Venezuela, with special notes on *Euthore fasciata fasciata* (Hagen, 1853) (Zygoptera: Polythoridae). Adv. Odonatology 1:39-41.

Paulson, D. R. 1985. Odonata of the Tambopata Reserved Zone, Madre de Dios, Peru. Rev. Per. Entomol., 27:9-14.

Pearson, D.L. 1984. The tiger beetles (Coleoptera: Cicindelidae) of the Tambopata Reserved Zone, Madre de Dios, Peru. Rev. per. Ent., 27:15-24.

Young, A.M. 1980. Feeding and oviposition in the giant tropical damselfly *Megaloprepus coerulatus* [sic] (Drury) in Costa Rica. Biotropica, 12(3):237-239.

447

J. A. Louton, R. W. Garrison, O. S. Flint.

Appendix

Extended habitat/behavioral notes.

[1] Polythore manua, was recently described (Bick and Bick, 1990) from material collected at Erika and Pakitza and is not known elsewhere. It is locally abundant at Pakitza where it flies under closed canopy in dense forests along small streams and seeps. The wings of this species are orange and black, and with a distinctive white transverse band in each wing that is especially bright in tenerals. We collected *Polythore manua* flying in deep shade among ithomine butterflies with similar wing patterns. Twenty-one species of butterflies from three families (Papilionidae, Pieridae and Nymphalidae) have strikingly similar wing patterns (G.Lamas, pers. comm.) and eleven of those species occur at Pakitza (Lamas, et al., 1991). These are all members of Nymphalidae and include representatives from four subfamilies as follows: Danainae - *Lycorea halia pales*; Ithominae - *Athyrtis mechantis salvini, Tithorea harmonia brunnea, Melinaea maelus lamasi, M. marsaeus clara, M. menophilus orestes, Forbestra olivencia aeneola, Napogenes aethra deucalion*; Heliconiinae -*Heliconius hecale sisyphus, Heliconius numata lyrcaeus* and; Nymphalinae - *Eresia eunice* s.sp. (nr. *olivencia*). We believe that these damselflies are involved in the Batesian mimicry complex for which these butterflies are well known and that this may complicate schemes of polythorid species discrimination that rely heavily on wing patterns. For instance, *Polythore manua* may be a local variant displaying an ecotypic effect driven by the various mimicry models available throughout its range or, it may represent a rapidly coevolving species flock with many more species than previously understood. Inversely, non-lowland species of Polythoridae may tend to have relatively clear unmarked wings because of the lack of colorful toxic butterfly species that are less common at upper or mid elevation zones. Marmels (1982) reported that butterfly-damselfly mimicry also occurs for a lowland species of *Euthore* in Venezuela and RWG and E.Gonzalez (studies in progress) note that males of the endemic Middle American megapodagrionid *Paraphlebia zoe*, are strikingly dimorphic (dichromatic); one series of males have completely hyaline wings with a pruinose blue abdominal tip (as do their females); the other has a black wing tip with a chalky white band which makes them conspicuous in flight. These males are easily mistaken for the ithomine butterfly, *Episcada salvinia* which occur sympatrically with *Paraphlebia zoe*.

[2] *Heliocharis amazona* adults are large, strong-flying damselflies that perch on foliage with wings held horizontally; giving the impression of a slender gomphid dragonfly in action. Males defended perches aggressively, lifting wings and arching the abdomen upward as other males approached. Most captures were near sandy streams under broken canopy with substantial periods of sunlight.

[3] *Mecistogaster* n.sp. is a very small species probably conspecific with small larvae collected at Pakitza from water-filled bamboo internodes with lateral perforations (Louton, et al. in press).

[4] *Protoneura paucinervis* was found in primary forest near Cocha Salvador, a large ox-bow lake. Males and females were observed flying along the leaf margins of low-growing vegetation and capturing midges that were clinging to the undersides of the leaves. At intervals the search pattern was interrupted and small spider webs were searched and attempts were made to pull wrapped prey or bits of debris out of the webs. In addition, a male was observed hovering at a large orb-web, tugging at prey items in the web of the spider *Micrathena* sp. (Araneidae). This spider's abdomen has a central yellow spot and with two bright red dots at the bases of the large abdominal spines. Oddly, this pattern is repeated in arrangement and scale in the yellow dorsum of the thorax and bright red eyes of the damselfly leading us to suspect that some form of mimicry or common disruptive coloration may be at work. The feeding habits of this species may provide an analog to the preadaptation leading to exclusive spider-predation in the Pseudostigmatidae.

[5] *Gomphomacromia fallax* specimens were netted as they flew over seeps in forests in areas of 300-1000m elevation. Larvae that we guessed (by exclusion) to be *Gomphomacromia* were collected from seeps that formed a thin film of water over soft sediments in areas of deep shade. Larvae of Polythoridae were also present.

[6] Larvae of *Archaeogomphus furcatus* and *Archaeogomphus hamatus?* are bright green and somewhat transparent in life. They inhabited terrestrial vegetation that trailed in the water in contact with sand or mud. The unusually long slender claws of *Archaeogomphus* may be an adaptation to clinging to soft plant tissues.

[7] A single male of *Fylgia amazonica* was captured as it perched over water in a swamp in dense vegetation penetrated by spots of sunlight that vividly illuminated the white head and red abdomen.

[8] A single female of *Macrothemis extensa* was collected over a trickle in dense vegetation under closed canopy at 300m. It had odd, secretive habits; it flew in and perched on a thin horizontal stem upside-down with body parallel to the stem. This slender pale species with the suffused spot on its forewing was almost invisible in flight.

449

Fauna

VERTEBRATES

Ictiofauna del Parque Nacional Manu, Perú

HERNÁN ORTEGA

Departamento de Ictiología, Museo de Historia Natural,
Universidad Nacional Mayor de San Marcos. Apartado 14-0434, Lima-14, PERU.

ABSTRACT

The ichthyofauna of Parque Nacional Manu in Southeastern Peru is poorly known. From September 1987 to July 1993 eight ichthyological collecting expeditions were made to Parque Nacional Manu, Peru. The Park consists of approximately 1'000,000 ha, that includes areas in the departments of Madre de Dios and Cuzco. Fish samples and associated data were obtained from 26 different waterbodies, some in the Río Alto Madre de Dios basin but most in the Río Manu drainage. These collections include some 27,000 specimens of approximately 210 species, 148 genera, and 33 families in 10 orders. This fauna is compared with two other protected areas in Madre de Dios; some comments are made on the similarities and differences of the Madre de Dios ichthyofauna that of the upper Río Ucayali Basin.

RESUMEN

La ictiofauna del Parque Nacional Manu es poco conocida. De setiembre de 1987 a julio de 1993 se realizaron 8 expediciones de campo para la obtención de peces y datos relacionados en 26 cuerpos de agua en el Parque Nacional Manu, Perú. El Parque abarca una extensión aproximada de 1'000,000 ha, entre los departamentos de Madre de Dios y Cusco. En estas prospecciones se obtuvo aproximadamente 27,000 especímenes que permitieron la identificación preliminar de 210 especies, 148 géneros, 33 familias y 10 órdenes. Esta fauna es comparada con la encontrada en otras dos áreas protegidas en Madre de Dios y la presente en la cuenca del Alto Río Ucayali.

INTRODUCCIÓN

La ictiofauna del departamento de Madre de Dios es muy poco conocida, no existen antecedentes en la literatura respectiva. Las primeras expediciones ictiológicas importantes en el Perú (Cope, 1878) fueron efectuadas en el Alto Amazonas, incluyendo primordialmente los ríos Marañón, Ucayali, Huallaga y sus principales afluentes. Otras expediciones se realizaron a modo de transección, partiendo de la costa, incluyendo partes de la sierra, hasta llegar a la Amazonía (Eigenmann & Allen, 1942; Pearson, 1937; Fowler, 1940).

En 1982 se inician las primeras investigaciones sobre la ictiofauna de Madre de Dios, auspiciadas por Amazónica (Neotropical Lowland Forests Research Program) de la Institución Smithsoniana de Washington, D.C., realizándose estudios en la Reserva Natural de Tambopata y áreas vecinas a Puerto Maldonado.

En 1987, el Programa BIOLAT de la misma institución empieza el estudio de inventario sobre la ictiofauna del Parque Nacional Manu (PNM). La primera expedición (octubre 1987) incluyó zonas restringidas a las inmediaciones del Puesto de Vigilancia (P.V.) Pakitza en la margen izquierda del Río Manu. En la segunda, afluentes del Río Alto Madre de Dios, las quebradas San Pedro (Paucartambo, Cusco), Salvación y Diamante (Manu, Madre de Dios), y en el Río Manu, desde la zona de Cocha Salvador hasta la quebrada Panahua. En agosto de 1989 se repite gran parte de lo efectuado el año anterior. En abril y noviembre de 1990 se amplió el área de estudio en Pakitza, al abarcar mayor extensión y acceder a otros hábitats del parque. En los años 1991, 1992 y 1993 la cobertura fue mayor, incluyéndose ecosistemas acuáticos en la margen derecha del Río Manu y realizándose los trabajos de campo en distintos meses.

ÁREA DE ESTUDIO

Comprende parte de los departamentos de Cusco (provincia de Paucartambo) y Madre de Dios (provincia de Manu) incluyendo, en parte, las cuencas del Río Alto Madre de Dios y del Río Manu (Figs. 1 - 3), en especial en la Zona Reservada del Manu, entre las quebradas Fortaleza y Panahua.

LOCALIDADES DE MUESTREO

Se presenta una relación con las características generales de las localidades muestreadas:

01. QUEBRADA PICAFLOR - PAUJIL

Atraviesa el P.V. Pakitza de norte a sur. Agua clara en época seca (junio-setiembre, vaciante) y blanca en época lluviosa (diciembre-abril, creciente). Ancho y profundidad promedios: 5 y 0.8 m respectivamente. Fondo de arena, arcilla, y canto rodado; material vegetal (ramas y hojas) en descomposición en el bento de los remansos. Agua ligeramente ácida (pH 6.5) y temperatura 22-24°C.

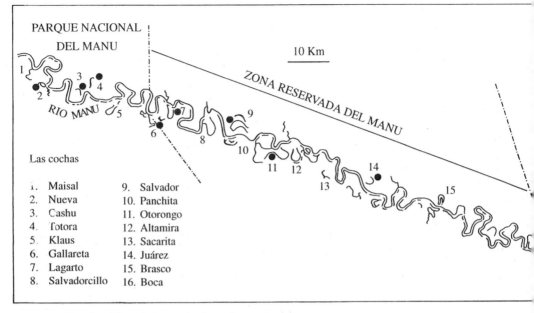

PARQUE NACIONAL
DEL MANU

10 Km

ZONA RESERVADA DEL MANU

RIO MANU

Las cochas

1. Maisal
2. Nueva
3. Cashu
4. Totora
5. Klaus
6. Gallareta
7. Lagarto
8. Salvadorcillo
9. Salvador
10. Panchita
11. Otorongo
12. Altamira
13. Sacarita
14. Juárez
15. Brasco
16. Boca

Fig. 3.– Mapa de los principales ambientes lénticos (cochas) estudiados (los círculos negros indican los lugares de colecta).

05. QUEBRADA FORTALEZA

Afluente del Río Manu en la margen izquierda. Agua clara en vaciante y blanca en creciente. Ancho y profundidad promedio: 15 y 1.2 m. En vaciante se alternan con frecuencia rápidos y remansos. Fondo arcillo-arenoso, canto rodado y vegetación sumergida indicadora de aguas alcalinas (Onagraceae), detritus orgánicos en el fondo de los remansos. Agua ligeramente alcalina (pH 7.4-7.8), con temperatura de 24-26°C.

06. QUEBRADA PACHIJA

Afluente del Río Manu en la margen izquierda, río arriba del P.V. Pakitza. Agua blanca la mayor parte del año; en vaciante, el caudal se reduce a una décima parte, dejando numerosos ambientes lénticos temporales en ambas márgenes. Ancho promedio: 10m, profundidad: 0.60m. Fondo areno-arcilloso. Vegetación ribereña con predominancia de gramíneas herbáceas y arbustos (Pennisetum sp. y Tessaria sp.).

07. QUEBRADA PANAHUA

Afluente del Río Manu en la margen derecha. Agua clara en vaciante y blanca la mayor parte del año, ancho promedio: 30 m y profundidad: 1.5 m. Fondo arcillo-arenoso, con detritus en las partes de aguas tranquilas, abundante limo en la unión con el Río Manu; vegetación ribereña alta, abundante y densa.

08. QUEBRADA CARPINTERO

Afluente de la Quebrada Fortaleza, agua clara-negra, atraviesa un bosque denso de vegetación variada y palmeras, ancho promedio: 1.8 m y profundidad: 0.45 m. Fondo areno-arcilloso con gran cantidad de material vegetal en descomposición y pH 5.8-6.1.

458

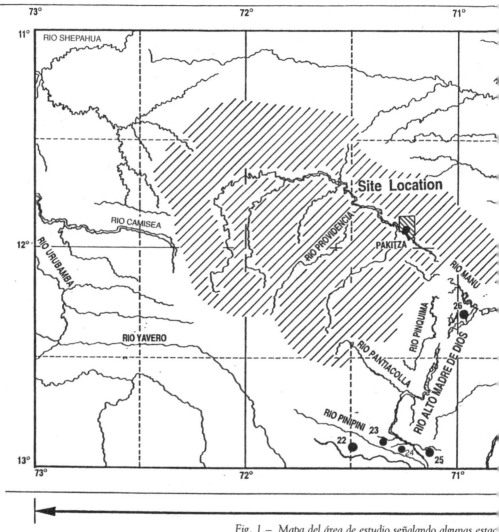

Fig. 1.– Mapa del área de estudio señalando algunas estac
(22. quebrada San Pedro, 23. quebrada Soga,24. quebra

02. QUEBRADA TROMPETERO

Recorre el P.V. Pakitza casi paralela al curso anterior, presenta una amplia red de drenaje del bosque alto. Agua clara-negra en la mayor parte del año y blanca en creciente. Ancho y profundidad promedios: 3 y 0.5 m. Fondo de arcilla, arena y canto rodado con remansos frecuentes que acumulan hojarasca en considerable cantidad, que le da un color té claro característico. Agua moderadamente ácida (pH 5.7).

03. QUEBRADA PAUCAR

Arroyuelo de corto recorrido, tributario de la quebrada Picaflor-Paujil, paralelo al P.V. Pakitza. Agua clara. Fondo de grava, arena y hojarasca. Ancho y profundidad promedio de 1.2 y 0.25 m respectivamente.

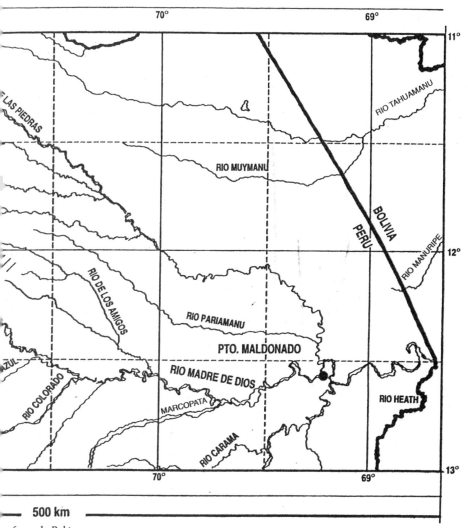

04. Río Manu

Principal ambiente lótico del PNM. Agua blanca, curso muy variable, ancho promedio: 60m, profundidad entre 0.7 y 4m en época de vaciante. Crece considerablemente en época de lluvias, aumentando el nivel en 3 m. Fondo areno-arcilloso y una capa renovable de limo, detritus y palizada. Vegetación ribereña con una típica sucesión vegetal (*Tessaria integrifolia, Gynerium sagittatum, Cecropia membranacea* y *Ochroma pyramidale*)(Kalliola *et al.*, 1987), que coloniza las nuevas playas. Los muestreos se efectuaron en sectores correspondientes a los ambientes y/o localidades asociados: Pakitza, Pachija, Panahua, Juárez, Cashu, Salvador y Romero.

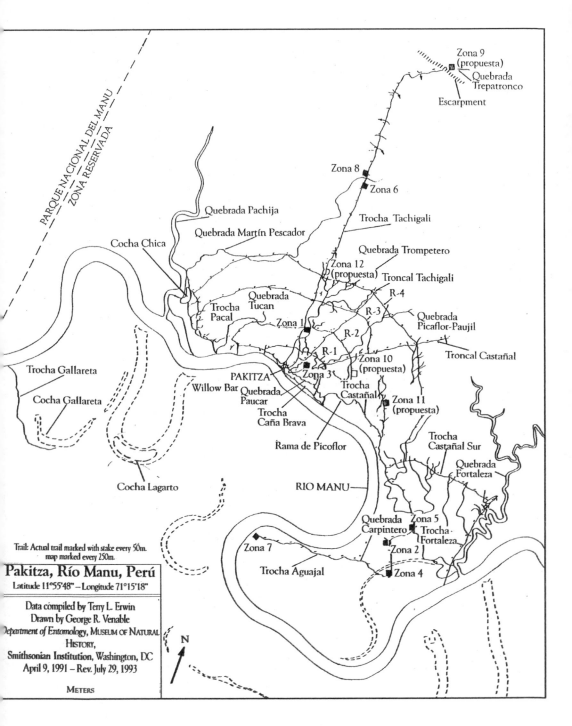

Zona 9
(propuesta)
Quebrada
Trepatronco
Escarpment

Zona 8
Zona 6

Trocha Tachigali

Quebrada Pachija

Quebrada Martín Pescador

Quebrada Trompetero

Cocha Chica

Zona 12
(propuesta)
Troncal Tachigali

Quebrada
Tucan
R-4

Trocha
Pacal
R-3

Zona 1
Quebrada
Picaflor-Paujil

R-2

Troncal Castañal

R-1

Trocha Gallareta
Zona 10
(propuesta)

PAKITZA
Zona 3

Cocha Gallareta
Willow Bar Quebrada
Paucar
Trocha
Castañal
Zona 11
(propuesta)

Trocha
Caña Brava

Trocha
Castañal Sur

Rama de Picoflor
Quebrada
Fortaleza

Cocha Lagarto

RIO MANU

Trail: Actual trail marked with stake every 50m.
map marked every 250m.

Quebrada
Carpintero
Zona 5
Trocha
Fortaleza

Pakitza, Río Manu, Perú
Latitude 11°55'48" – Longitude 71°15'18"

Zona 7
Zona 2

Trocha Aguajal
Zona 4

Data compiled by Terry L. Erwin
Drawn by George R. Venable
Department of Entomology, MUSEUM OF NATURAL
HISTORY,
Smithsonian Institution, Washington, DC
April 9, 1991 – Rev. July 29, 1993

METERS

N

PARQUE NACIONAL DEL MANU
ZONA RESERVADA

Fig. 2.– *Mapa de Pakitza mostrando los sistemas de trochas que dan acceso a los principale_
hábitats.*

457

09. Aguajal Pakitza

Ambiente léntico permanente, agua negra, aproximadamente de 3000 m² que se reduce a un 30% en vaciante. Profundidad promedio: 50 cm. Fondo arcilloso con abundante vegetación macrofítica en descomposición. Predominan *Mauritia flexuosa* y *Heliconia* spp. (pH 5.8).

10. Cocha Chica

Ambiente léntico temporal, agua blanca, ligado a la quebrada Pachija, superficie aproximada de 5000 m² en creciente, mientras en vaciante puede desaparecer. Fondo arcillo-arenoso y abundante limo. Vegetación predominante: *Pennisetum* sp. y *Tessaria* sp.

11. Quebrada Martín Pescador

Desemboca en la Quebrada Pachija. Agua clara, con abundante vegetación acuática sumergida y flotante, además de gramíneas en las riberas (*Gynerium* sp. y *Guadua* sp.). El ancho varía entre 4 y 7 m, profundidad promedio: 0.70 m. Fondo areno-arcilloso y con apreciable cantidad de detritus en los remansos. Temperatura del agua 24-28°C y pH 7.0-7.3.

12. Cocha Juárez

Laguna ubicada en la margen izquierda del Río Manu, en proceso de distrofia. Agua blanca-negra de color verdoso y turbia. Longitud aproximada de 1 km, ancho promedio: 70 m y profundidad: 0.8 m en vaciante. Fondo blando con abundante material orgánico, gramíneas y vegetación flotante (*Azolla* sp., *Lemna* sp. y *Pennisetum* sp.) formando extensas masas en ambas márgenes. Temperatura del agua 23-28°C y pH 6.3-6.8.

13. Cocha Otorongo

Laguna ubicada en la margen opuesta a Juárez. Agua negra, 1.8 km de longitud y 90 m de ancho, profundidad media de 2.5 m. Fondo arcilloso con abundante materia orgánica y vegetación ribereña; predominan gramíneas, herbáceas, *Heliconia* sp., y plantas flotantes, principalmente *Pistia* sp. Temperatura del agua 26-27°C y pH 6.0-6.5.

14. Cocha Salvador

Es la laguna de mayor extensión en el parque, ubicada en la margen izquierda del Río Manu. Mezcla de agua clara y blanca, de color claro-verdoso. Longitud aproximada: 3 km, ancho promedio: 120 m, profundidad promedio: 3 m. Ausencia de playas y orillares. Fondo arcilloso con abundante materia orgánica y vegetación arbustiva y arbórea densa en la ribera. Temperatura del agua 27-30°C y pH 6.6-7.0.

15. COCHA GALLARETA

Laguna ubicada en la margen derecha del Río Manu. Agua variable entre clara y negra, longitud: 900 m, ancho: 70 m y profundidad: 1.1 m (promedios). Transparencia de 50 cm. Abundancia de gramíneas herbáceas (*Pennisetum*) en las riberas formando masas flotantes. Fondo arcillo-arenoso con materia orgánica abundante. Temperatura del agua 28-29°C y pH 6.3-6.9.

16. COCHA PANAHUA

Ubicada entre la quebrada del mismo nombre y el Río Manu. Mezcla de agua blanca y clara, de color marrón-verdoso. Longitud: 700 m, ancho: 60 m y profundidad: 0.8 m. Con grandes masas de vegetación diversa flotante (principalmente *Azolla* sp.); áreas con *Heliconia* spp. en las riberas. Fondo blando con gruesa capa de materia orgánica. Temperatura del agua 26-28°C y pH 6.8-6.9.

17. COCHA CASHU

Laguna de agua blanca y negra, de color verdoso, debido a la proliferación de algas. Longitud aproximada de 1200 m, ancho y profundidad promedios: 70 y 1.8 m. Márgenes con profundidad media de 90 cm y los extremos más superficiales, lo que indica un proceso de acumulación de sólidos. Vegetación ribereña variada. Fondo arcillo-arenoso y abundante materia orgánica vegetal. Temperatura del agua 28-33°C y pH 5.9-6.4.

18. COCHA TOTORA

Laguna de agua negra en proceso de distrofia, incluida en la Estación Biológica Cocha Cashu. Longitud: 600 m, ancho: 50 m y profundidad promedio: 90 cm. Presenta disminución creciente de profundidad y área por acumulación de sedimentos e invasión marcada de vegetación enraizada; abundantes plantas flotantes (principalmente *Pistia* y *Pennisetum*) que ocupan casi dos tercios de la superficie. Temperatura del agua 28-33°C y pH 5.9-6.4.

19. COCHA NUEVA

Laguna de agua blanca, oligotrófica, ubicada en la margen derecha del Río Manu. Longitud 1.8 km, ancho: 70m y profundidad promedio: 1.5 m. Vegetación ribereña dominada por gramíneas, herbáceas y arbustos. Fondo arcillo-arenoso, con delgada capa de material vegetal en descomposición. Aislada del Río Manu desde aproximadamente 1986.

20. PANTANO CASHU

Ambiente léntico temporal. Agua negra, superficie aproximada de 2500m², profundidad promedio: 0.6m. Vegetación ribereña dominada por *Heliconia* sp. y masas de plantas flotantes con predominancia de *Pistia* sp.

21. COCHA LAGARTO

Ambiente léntico de agua negra, con superficie reducida (aproximadamente 3600 m^2), con plantas flotantes, bordeada por gramíneas y secundariamente por vegetación arbustiva y arbórea. Longitud 90, ancho 40 y profundidad media 0.8 m. Fondo arenoso con abundante material vegetal en descomposición, que al acumularse va reduciendo la profundidad, permitiendo el avance de las plantas enraizadas.

22. QUEBRADA SAN PEDRO

Arroyo de agua clara, torrentosa y fría (10°C). Afluente del Río Pilcopata (Paucartambo, Cusco), a 1000 m de altitud. Ancho variable entre 5 y 7 m, profundidad: 0.5-0.9 m. Curso con declive pronunciado. Fondo duro con grandes rocas, piedras, cantos rodados, arena y acumulación de detritus en remansos y bajo grandes piedras.

23. QUEBRADA CULLI

Situada frente a la localidad de Salvación, a 1 km del Hostal Erika. Agua clara, torrentosa, afluente del Río Alto Madre de Dios, ancho: 3-5 m, profundidad: 0.30-0.75 m. Márgenes con fuerte pendiente y el fondo compuesto de rocas, piedras, arena y detritus.

24. QUEBRADA SOGA

Arroyo de agua clara, torrentoso, afluente de la margen izquierda del Río Alto Madre de Dios, corre casi paralelamente al anterior y está ubicado frente a la desembocadura del Río Salvación. Ancho: 5 m, profundidad: 0.6 m. Fondo duro, rocas, canto rodado, arena y detritus.

25. RÍO SALVACIÓN

Afluente del Río Alto Madre de Dios en su margen derecha, con extensión amplia en la desembocadura. Agua clara-negra, transparencia total, declive moderado. Ancho: 5-12 m, profundidad: 0.5-1.2 m. Fondo arcillo-arenoso, con partes de canto rodado y detritus. Vegetación predominante herbácea y arbustiva en las riberas.

26. RÍO ALTO MADRE DE DIOS

Es el principal ambiente lótico de la provincia Manu. Agua clara en vaciante y blanca en creciente, ancho de 80 a 200m, profundidad que oscila entre 1 y 3m. Fondo de rocas, piedras, arena y detritus en los remansos. Frente a Diamante, en vaciante, se forman en ambas márgenes pequeñas lagunas temporales, con características físicas diferentes a las existentes en el canal principal. Ocurren bruscas fluctuaciones de niveles de acuerdo a la presencia de lluvias.

MATERIAL Y MÉTODOS

El material estudiado comprende unos 27,000 especímenes, colectados entre 1987 y 1993. Para la colecta se emplearon redes de arrastre de diferentes dimensiones: 2 x 1 m, 4 x 1.5 m, 6 x 1.8 m, 15 x 2.5 m, 30 x 1.8 m y con abertura de malla desde 2 hasta 30 mm. También se usaron aparejos individuales como atarrayas y redes de mano de malla fina y diferentes medidas.

Los datos de hábitat, relacionados con la calidad del agua, se tomaron al inicio de las colectas; los valores de pH son promedios de los registros en las épocas menos lluviosas.

Las capturas se realizaron principalmente entre las 0900 y 1800 horas, de manera exhaustiva hasta lograr muestras representativas. La fijación en formalina al 10% y la preservación en formalina al 5% o alcohol etílico al 70%. Se aplicó mayor esfuerzo en las localidades de la Zona Reservada, entre las quebradas Fortaleza y Panahua. Especímenes de tallas superiores a 350 mm fueron registrados, fotografiados y/o anotados como observaciones personales.

Los especímenes colectados están depositados en el Museo de Historia Natural, Universidad Nacional Mayor de San Marcos, Lima (MUSM) y en el National Museum of Natural History, Smithsonian Institution, Washington, D.C. (USNM).

Las especies se presentan como una lista anotada, siguiendo el orden evolutivo de acuerdo a listados recientes (Ortega & Vari, 1986; Ortega, 1991). Las especies son citadas con el autor y año de la descripción, seguido por las siglas de la colección, número de catalogación, localidad de procedencia y cantidad de ejemplares (entre paréntesis).

RESULTADOS

Lista Anotada de la Ictiofauna del Parque Nacional Manu, Madre de Dios, Perú.

Rajiformes

Potamotrygonidae
Paratrygon aieraba (Müller & Henle, 1841)
MUSM 3062 Loc. 04 (1)
Potamotrygon motoro (Natterer, 1841)
MUSM 3061 Loc. 05 (1)
Potamotrygon sp.
MUSM 3047 Loc. 04 (1)

Lepidosireniformes

Lepidosirenidae
Lepidosiren paradoxa Fitzinger, 1837
MUSM 3091 Loc. 14 (1)   MUSM 4153 Loc. 14 (1)
MUSM 4544 Loc. 12 (1)

CLUPEIFORMES

Clupeidae
Pellona altamazónica Cope, 1872
MUSM 3972 Loc. 14 (2)

Engraulididae
Anchoviella guianensis (Eigenmann, 1912)
MUSM 3802 Loc. 12 (177)
Anchoviella sp. A
USNM 302723 Loc. 04 (4)   USNM 302692 Loc. 05 (4)
USNM 302724 Loc. 14 (25)   MUSM 4960 Loc. 04 (4)
Anchoviella sp. B
USNM 302719 Loc. 04 (25)   USNM 302721 Loc. 07 (31)
MUSM 2257 Loc. 04 (8)   USNM 302718 Loc. 04 (42)
USNM 302717 Loc. 07 (14)

CHARACIFORMES

Acestrocephalus boehlkei Menezes, 1977
MUSM 3924 Loc. 06 (1)   MUSM 3957 Loc. 04 (1)
Acestrorhynchus altus Menezes, 1969
USNM 313477 Loc. 01 (1)
Acestrorhynchus lacustris (Reinhardt, 1874)
MUSM 3916 Loc. 10 (1)   MUSM 3946 Loc. 10 (2)
Acestrorhynchus sp.
MUSM 4963 Loc. 04 (3)
Aphyocharax alburnus (Günther, 1869)
MUSM 2800 Loc. 05 (2)   MUSM 3712 Loc. 04 (9)
Aphyocharax anisitsi Eigenmann & Kennedy, 1903
USNM 316558 Loc. 01 (4)
Aphyocharax avary Fowler, 1913
MUSM 3749 Loc. 04 (38)
Aphyocharax dentatus Eigenmann & Kennedy, 1903
USNM 302816 Loc 04 (9)   USNM 302815 Loc.04 (14)
USNM 316555 Loc. 04 (2)   USNM 316665 Loc. 04 (2)
Aphyocharax pappenheimi Ahl, 1923
USNM 316611 Loc. 14 (106)   USNM 302801 Loc. 04 (13)
USNM 303041 Loc. 04 (8)   USNM 316712 Loc. 06 (5)
USNM 316562 Loc. 07 (10)   USNM 303044 Loc. 14 (3)
Aphyocharax pusillus Günther, 1868
MUSM 3799 Loc. 04 (37)   USNM 302817 Loc. 07 (3)
MUSM 3748 Loc. 04 (88)
Astyanacinus multidens Pearson, 1924
MUSM 4565 Loc. 01 (3)   MUSM 4566 Loc. 17 (4)
MUSM 3709 Loc. 01 (4)   MUSM 3833 Loc. 26 (2)
MUSM 3800 Loc. 12 (1)   MUSM 3814 Loc. 23 (5)
MUSM 3754 Loc. 08 (1)   MUSM 4979 Loc. 11 (5)
MUSM 5006 Loc. 04 (100)   MUSM 4997 Loc. 02 (1)
Astyanax abramis (Jenyns, 1842)
USNM 302989 Loc. 05 (11)   USNM 295597 Loc. 01 (10)
MUSM 3107 Loc. 05 (1)   MUSM 4047 Loc. 04 (3)
Astyanax bimaculatus (Linnaeus, 1758)
USNM 302992 Loc. 07 (17)   MUSM 3838 Loc. 26 (1)
MUSM 3808 Loc. 04 (3)   MUSM 4998 Loc. 02 (1)

Astyanax fasciatus (Cuvier, 1819)
USNM 295563 Loc. 01 (7)   MUSM 2788 Loc. 08 (1)
MUSM 2437 Loc. 07 (1)

Astyanax maximus (Steindachner, 1875)
MUSM 3837 Loc. 26 (1)   MUSM 3823 Loc. 01 (3)
MUSM 3722 Loc 10 (10)   MUSM 2822 Loc. 01 (1)
MUSM 4999 Loc. 02 (4)

Astyanax zonatus Eigenmann, 1908
MUSM 3851 Loc. 02 (1)

Bario steindachneri (Eigenmann, 1893)
USNM 303062 Loc. 24 (6)   USNM 303063 Loc. 26 (3)
USNM 303061 Loc. 25 (2)   USNM 303060 Loc. 25 (1)

Brachychalcinus copei (Steindachner, 1882)
USNM 295577 Loc. 01 (1)   MUSM 4980 Loc. 11 (8)
MUSM 3899 Loc. 10 (2)   MUSM 4954 Loc. 04 (1)

Brycon erythropterum (Cope, 1872)
Loc. 26 (Ortega, obs. pers.)

Bryconacidnus ellisi (Pearson, 1924)
MUSM 3935 Loc. 25 (35)

Bryconamericus pectinatus Vari & Siebert, 1991
USNM 303442 Loc. 01 (8)   USNM 303441 Loc. 01 (5)
MUSM 2057 Loc. 01 HOLOTIPO
MUSM 2058 Loc. 01 (5 PARATIPOS)

Bryconamericus sp. A
USNM 302951 Loc. 22 (2)

Bryconamericus sp. B
USNM 302956 Loc. 24 (17)   USNM 302956 Loc. 24 (10)
USNM 302948 Loc. 24 (1)   USNM 303131 Loc. 24 (7)
USNM 302944 Loc. 24 (27)   USNM 302955 Loc. 24 (5)
USNM 302957 Loc. 24 (1)   USNM 302961 Loc. 24 (3)
USNM 303112 Loc. 24 (20)

Chalceus erythrurus Cope, 1870
MUSM 3756 Loc. 05 (1)   MUSM 3907 Loc. 04 (1)

Characidium zebra Eigenmann, 1909
MUSM 2823 Loc. 05 (1)   MUSM 2794 Loc. 08 (1)
MUSM 3832 Loc. 26 (1)

Characidium purpuratum Steindachner, 1882
USNM 302183 Loc. 24 (2)   USNM 302195 Loc. 24 (6)
MUSM 3815 Loc. 24 (2)

Characidium sp.
USNM 302194 Loc. 04 (9)   USNM 302196 Loc. 04 (12)
MUSM 4961 Loc. 04 (2)

Charax caudimaculatus Lucena, 1987
USNM 295596 Loc. 01 (4)   MUSM 4742 Loc. 06 (1)
MUSM 4977 Loc. 11 (3)

Charax tectifer Cope, 1870
MUSM 2791 Loc. 08 (1)   MUSM 3753 Loc. 08 (7)

Cheirodon piaba Lütken, 1874
MUSM 3965 Loc. 10 (8)   MUSM 3968 Loc. 19 (20)

Cheirodon drepanon (Fowler, 1913)
MUSM 2813 Loc. 05 (3)

Cheirodon fugitiva (Cope, 1870)
MUSM 3715 Loc. 04 (2)   MUSM 4986 Loc.11 (3)
USNM 302794 Loc. 07 (2)

Cheirodon notomelas Eigenmann, 1915
MUSM 4958 Loc. 04 (20)   MUSM 4063 Loc. 04 (1)

Cheirodon troemneri Fowler, 1942
MUSM 4962 Loc. 04 (3)

Cheirodon sp.
USNM 303121 Loc. 07 (200)   USNM 302793 Loc. 07 (25)
USNM 302969 Loc. 05 (25)   USNM 302795 Loc. 04 (16)
USNM 302796 Loc. 07 (25)

Cheirodon (Odontostilbe) sp.
USNM 302972 Loc. 05 (2)   USNM 302975 Loc. 07 (25)
USNM 302983 Loc. 04 (17)   USNM 302973 Loc. 01 (5)

Clupeacharax anchoveoides Pearson, 1924
USNM 302225 Loc. 04 (4)   USNM 295255 Loc. 04 (8)
MUSM 3897 Loc. 04 (8)   MUSM 3803 Loc. 04 (5)

Colossoma macropomum (Cuvier, 1818)
Loc. 04 (Ortega, obs. pers.)

Creagrutus anary Fowler, 1913
MUSM 3757 Loc. 25 (2)   USNM 302788 Loc. 24 (8)
USNM 303066 Loc. 25 (15)

Creagrutus beni Eigenmann, 1911
MUSM 2821 Loc. 05 (10)   MUSM 3807 Loc. 04 (3)
MUSM 3827 Loc 01 (1)

Creagrutus sp.
MUSM 4984 Loc. 01 (3)

Ctenobrycon hauxwellianus (Cope, 1870)
MUSM 3099 Loc. 05 (3)

Ctenobrycon spilurus (Cuvier & Valenciennes, 1849)
MUSM 3838 Loc 10 (3)   MUSM 4957 Loc. 04 (20)

Cynopotamus amazonus (Günther, 1868)
USNM 295594 Loc. 06 (5)

Deuterodon sp.
USNM 317756 Loc. 25 (2)

Engraulisoma taeniatum Castro, 1981
USNM 302227 Loc. 04 (25)   USNM 295569 Loc. 04 (12)
USNM 302266 Loc. 04 (3)   MUSM 3913 Loc. 05 (5)
MUSM 5004 Loc. 04 (4)   MUSM 3912 Loc. 04 (4)

Galeocharax gulo Cope, 1870
USNM 303144 Loc. 04 (1)   USNM 303145 Loc. 04 (1)
MUSM 3798 Loc. 04 (1)   MUSM 4976 Loc. 11 (3)
MUSM 4931 Loc. 04 (1)

Gephyrocharax sp.
USNM 302834 Loc 08 (4)   MUSM 3840 Loc. 26 (2)
MUSM 3841 Loc. 25 (2)   USNM 303051 Loc. 05 (1)
MUSM 4557 Loc. 03 (7)   USNM 303156 Loc. 09 (1)
MUSM 4975 Loc. 11 (15)

Gymnocorymbus thayeri Eigenmann, 1908
USNM 303155 Loc. 07 (5)   MUSM 3096 Loc. 10 (3)

Hemibrycon jabonero (Schultz, 1944)
MUSM 3824 Loc. 01 (2)   MUSM 3817 Loc. 25 (36)
MUSM 3759 Loc. 24 (25)   USNM 303056 Loc. 24 (25)
USNM 303134 Loc. 25 (4)

Hemigrammus sp.
USNM 303152 Loc. 25 (40)   USNM 303058 Loc. 26 (25)
USNM 303158 Loc. 05 (1)

Holoshestes heterodon Eigenmann, 1915
MUSM 3813 Loc. 26 (2)   MUSM 3834 Loc. 26 (3)
MUSM 3871 Loc. 08 (3)

Hyphessobrycon sp.
USNM 303153 Loc. 08 (30)   USNM 302765 Loc 05 (10)

Hysteronotus sp.
USNM 313485 Loc. 05 (2)

Knodus beta (Eigenmann, Henn & Wilson, 1914)
MUSM 3876 Loc. 01 (23)   MUSM 3714 Loc. 04 (56)
MUSM 4985 Loc. 01

Leptagoniates pi Vari, 1977
MUSM 2809 Loc. 05 (1)

Moenkhausia comma Eigenmann, 1908
MUSM 3880 Loc. 01 (2)

Moenkhausia dichroura (Kner, 1858)
USNM 295282 Loc. 01 (7)   MUSM 2811 Loc. 05 (4)
MUSM 4684 Loc. 16 (5)   MUSM 4678 Loc. 16 (18)

Moenkhausia oligolepis (Günther, 1864)
USNM 295564 Loc. 01 (12)   MUSM 1784 Loc. 09 (5)
USNM 302208 Loc. 05 (1)   MUSM 4959 Loc. 04 (1)
MUSM 4973 Loc. 11 (5)   MUSM 4927 Loc. 23 (6)

Moenkhausia sp.
USNM 302799 Loc. 07 (12)   USNM 302810 Loc. 07 (7)
USNM 302812 Loc. 14 (25)

Monotocheirodon pearsoni Pearson, 1924
USNM 302698 Loc. 26 (20)   USNM 303133 Loc. 04 (1)

Mylossoma duriventre (Cuvier, 1817)
MUSM 4688 Loc. 16 (1)

Othonocheirodus aff. *lethostigmus* (Gomes, 1947)
MUSM 3835 Loc. 26 (5)   MUSM 3810 Loc. 26 (3)
MUSM 3858 Loc. 25 (1)

Paragoniates alburnus Steindachner, 1876
USNM 303015 Loc. 04 (4)   MUSM 3092 Loc. 04 (3)
MUSM 3797 Loc. 04 (37)   USNM 302831 Loc. 05 (1)
USNM 302833 Loc. 04 (3)   USNM 303019 Loc. 04 (4)

Phenacogaster pectinatus (Cope, 1870)
MUSM 3869 Loc. 09 (2)

Phenacogaster sp.
USNM 313484 Loc. 04 (1)

Piabucus sp.
USNM 303020 Loc. 05 (1)
USNM 303021 Loc. 04 (1)

Piaractus brachypomus (Cuvier, 1818)
Loc. 04 (Ortega, obs. pers.)

Prionobrama filigera (Cope, 1870)
USNM 303016 Loc. 04 (3)   USNM 303149 Loc. 04 (5)
MUSM 2812 Loc. 05 (13)   USNM 303012 Loc. 07 (2)
USNM 303014 Loc. 04 (7)   USNM 303013 Loc. 04 (15)

Pristobrycon sp.
USNM 319654 Loc. 21 (1)   USNM 319299 Loc. 21 (1)

Prodontocharax melanotus Pearson, 1924
USNM 303157 Loc. 06 (20)   USNM 303149 Loc. 05 (3)
MUSM 2873 Loc. 01 (1)   USNM 302764 Loc. 04 (1)
USNM 303142 Loc. 25 (2)   USNM 303126 Loc. 07 (1)
USNM 325221 Loc. 04 (1)

Rhinobrycon negrensis Myers, 1944
MUSM 3934 Loc. 25 (4)   MUSM 4925 Loc. 23 (9)

Roeboides affinis (Günther, 1868)
MUSM 3101 Loc. 10 (3)

Roeboides myersi Gill, 1870
USNM 2956 Loc. 04 (4)

Salminus affinis Steindachner, 1880
USNM 319363 Loc. 01 (1)   USNM 319315 Loc. 04 (1)

Scopaeocharax sp.
MUSM 3910 Loc. 01 (46)   MUSM 4869 Loc. 11 (3)
USNM 317814 Loc. 11 (27)   USNM 317816 Loc. 01 (10)
USNM 317817 Loc. 11 (14)   USNM 317818 Loc. 01 (7)
USNM 317819 Loc. 01 (7)   USNM 317812 Loc. 06 (5)

Serrasalmus nattereri Kner, 1860
MUSM 3930 Loc. 04 (1)   MUSM 4942 Loc. 15 (7)

Serrasalmus rhombeus (Linnaeus, 1766)
USNM 314000 Loc. 14 (1)   MUSM 4951 Loc. 04 (2)
MUSM 3966 Loc. 10 (1)   MUSM 4866 Loc. 07 (1)

Serrasalmus spilopleura Kner, 1860
MUSM 3921 Loc. 05 (2)

Serrasalmus sp.
MUSM 4880 Loc. 14 (1)   MUSM 4949 Loc. 04 (1)

Tetragonopterus argenteus Cuvier, 1817
USNM 295256 Loc. 04 (1)   MUSM 4948 Loc. 04 (3)
MUSM 2808 Loc. 05 (1)   USNM 302272 Loc. 04 (1)

Triportheus albus (Cope, 1862)
MUSM 3963 Loc. 07 (2)

Triportheus angulatus (Spix, 1829)
USNM 302528 Loc. 14 (3)   MUSM 4955 Loc. 04 (20)
USNM 302210 Loc. 04 (1)   MUSM 3093 Loc. 10 (1)
MUSM 4875 Loc. 14 (6)

Triportheus elongatus (Günther, 1864)
USNM 295169 Loc. 04 (2)

Triportheus rotundatus (Schomburgk, 1841)
USNM 295166 Loc. 04 (9)

Tyttocharax tambopatensis Weitzman and Ortega, 1995
MUSM 3735 Loc. 08 (42)   USNM 317811 Loc. 02 (7)
USNM 317815 Loc. 08 (82)   USNM 323417 Loc. 02 (50)
USNM 317813 Loc. 02 (5)

Gasteropelecidae
Carnegiella myersi Fernández-Yépez, 1950
USNM 302823 Loc. 09 (25)   USNM 302827 Loc. 02 (18)
MUSM 2124 Loc. 09 (14)   MUSM 2793 Loc. 09 (1)
MUSM 4993 Loc. 02 (105)   MUSM 4926 Loc. 08 (62)

Carnegiella sp.
USNM 302825 Loc. 05 (16)   USNM 302826 Loc. 01 (2)
USNM 302822 Loc. 09 (4)

Thoracocharax stellatus (Kner, 1860)
USNM 302837 Loc. 14 (2)   USNM 302839 Loc. 04 (11)
MUSM 2820 Loc. 05 (1)   MUSM 3804 Loc. 04 (1)

Cynodontidae
Rhaphiodon vulpinus Spix, 1829
Loc. 04 (Ortega, obs. pers.)

Hemiodontidae
Anodus elongatus Spix, 1829
Loc. 14 (Ortega obs. pers.)

Erythrinidae
Erythrinus erythrinus (Schneider, 1801)
MUSM 4531 Loc. 03 (4)   MUSM 3127 Loc. 09 (1)
MUSM 4558 Loc. 03 (6)

Hoplerythrinus unitaeniatus (Spix, 1829)
USNM 295260 Loc. 01 (3)

Hoplias malabaricus (Bloch, 1794)
USNM 302347 Loc. 14 (3)   USNM 302172 Loc. 05 (2)
MUSM 2278 Loc. 01 (2)   MUSM 4879 Loc. 14 (4)
MUSM 4867 Loc. 07 (4)   MUSM 4964 Loc. 04 (4)
MUSM 4974 Loc. 11 (2)

Lebiasinidae
Pyrrhulina vittata Regan, 1912
USNM 302531 Loc. 08 (30)   USNM 302532 Loc. 08 (8)
MUSM 2120 Loc. 08 (27)   MUSM 2683 Loc. 08 (20)
MUSM 4676 Loc. 16 (1)   MUSM 4929 Loc. 08 (8)
MUSM 4923 Loc. 12 (7)

Parodontidae
Apareidon pongoense Allen, 1942
MUSM 3720 Loc. 04 (1)

Parodon buckleyi Boulenger, 1887
USNM 303024 Loc. 04 (20)   USNM 303025 Loc. 26 (1)
MUSM 3811 Loc. 24 (1)   MUSM 3818 Loc. 24 (1)
Parodon sp.
MUSM 4981 Loc. 11 (1)   MUSM 5003 Loc. 04 (200)

Prochilodontidae
Prochilodus nigricans Agassiz, 1829
USNM 302263 Loc. 07 (1)   MUSM 4874 Loc. 14 (8)
MUSM 3750 Loc. 04 (2)

Curimatidae
Potamorhina altamazonica (Cope, 1878)
USNM 32341 Loc. 14 (1)   MUSM 2090 Loc. 05 (1)
MUSM 3920 Loc. 10 (1)   MUSM 4313 Loc. 10 (1)
Psectrogaster rutiloides (Günther, 1864)
USNM 295278 Loc. 04 (1)   MUSM 2091 Loc. 05 (2)
Steindachnerina bimaculata (Steindachner, 1876)
USNM 302628 Loc. 14 (2)   MUSM 4950 Loc. 04 (20)
MUSM 4915 Loc. 17 (6)   MUSM 4887 Loc. 14 (20)
Steindachnerina binotata (Pearson, 1924)
USNM 295339 Loc. 04 (28)
Steindachnerina dobula (Günther, 1868)
USNM 302178 Loc. 07 (11)   USNM 302190 Loc. 06 (2)
MUSM 3619 Loc. 06 (1)   MUSM 3717 Loc. 01 (1)
MUSM 3718 Loc. 04 (1)   USNM 302182 Loc. 04 (2)

Steindachnerina guentheri (Eigenmann & Eigenmann, 1889)
USNM 302184 Loc. 07 (22) USNM 302192 Loc. 25 (24)
MUSM 2795 Loc. 09 (2) MUSM 3874 Loc. 01 (1)
USNM 302803 Loc. 07 (1) MUSM 4864 Loc. 07 (1)
MUSM 4978 Loc. 11 (5) MUSM 4947 Loc. 11 (2)

Steindachnerina hypostoma (Boulenger, 1887)
MUSM 3721 Loc. 07 (8) MUSM 4941 Loc. 04 (1)
MUSM 4946 Loc. 11 (4)

Anostomidae

Abramites hypselonotus (Günther, 1868)
USNM 319317 Loc. 01 (1)

Anostomus anostomus (Linnaeus, 1758)
MUSM 3890 Loc. 12 (1) MUSM 4691 Loc. 16 (1)

Leporellus vittatus (Valenciennes, 1849)
MUSM 3892 Loc. 12 (1)

Leporinus friderici (Bloch, 1794)
USNM 267223 Loc. 17 (2) MUSM 4969 Loc. 11 (1)
MUSM 3931 Loc. 04 (1) MUSM 4679 Loc. 16 (4)

Leporinus striatus Kner, 1859
USNM 295259 Loc. 01 (6) USNM 302533 Loc. 05 (1)
MUSM 2099 Loc. 05 (1) MUSM 2819 Loc. 05 (1)

Leporinus yophorus Eigenmann, 1922
MUSM 3893 Loc. 12 (1)

Schizodon fasciatus Spix, 1829
MUSM 3942 Loc. 12 (1)

GYMNOTIFORMES

Gymnotidae

Gymnotus carapo Linnaeus, 1758
USNM 295257 Loc. 01 (3) MUSM 4519 Loc. 08 (1)
MUSM 3855 Loc. 25 (3) MUSM 3949 Loc. 09 (1)
MUSM 4567 Loc. 08 (2)

Apteronotidae

Apteronotus albifrons (Linnaeus, 1776)
MUSM 4514 Loc. 06 (3)

Apteronotus bonaparti (Castelnau, 1855)
Loc, 04 (Hagedorn obs. pers.)

Sternarchorhynchus sp.
MUSM 4523 Loc. 04 (4) MUSM 4515 Loc. 06 (1)
MUSM 4553 Loc. 06 (2)

Sternopigidae

Eigenmannia virescens (Valenciennes, 1847)
MUSM 3948 Loc. 08 (1) MUSM 4521 Loc. 08 (2)
MUSM 4516 Loc. 08 (5)

Sternopygus macrurus (Bloch & Schneider, 1801)
USNM 295167 Loc. 04 (1) MUSM 4525 Loc. 04 (7)
USNM 302534 Loc. 26 (1) MUSM 2248 Loc. 06 (1)
MUSM 3964 loc. 16 (1)

Hypopomidae
Brachyhypopomus sp.
MUSM 1388 loc. 09 (1)
MUSM 3947 Loc. 09 (1)
MUSM 4524 Loc. 04 (4)
MUSM 4564 Loc. 02 (1)

MUSM 2470 Loc. 04 (1)
MUSM 4526 Loc. 04 (2)
MUSM 4520 Loc. 08 (8)

SILURIFORMES

Doradidae
Megalodoras sp.
Loc. 04 (Ortega, obs. pers.)
Trachydoras sp.
MUSM 4542 Loc. 04 (1)
Leptodoras sp.
MUSM 4551 Loc. 04 (2)

Auchenipteridae
Auchenipterus nuchalis (Spix, 1829)
MUSM 3919 Loc. 05 (2)   MUSM 3967 Loc. 05 (1)
Tatia sp.
MUSM 4535 Loc. 04 (1)

Aspredinidae
Bunocephalus bifidus (Eigenmann, 1942)
USNM 302707 Loc. 08 (1)   USNM 300984 Loc. 02 (1)
MUSM 2676 Loc. 26 (1)   MUSM 3738 Loc. 09 (1)
MUSM 4928 Loc. 08 (1)   MUSM 4917 Loc. 08 (1)
Ernstichthys megistus (Orcés, 1961)
USNM 303059 Loc. 26 (1)   MUSM 2675 Loc. 26 (1)
Ernstichthys sp.
MUSM 4527 Loc. 04 (4)

Pimelodidae
Brachyplatystoma filamentosum (Lichtenstein, 1819)
Loc. 04 (Ortega, obs. pers.)
Calophysus macropterus (Lichtenstein, 1819)
Loc. 04 (Ortega, obs. pers.)
Duopalatinus sp.
MUSM 4536 Loc. 04 (3)
Goslinia platynema (Boulenger, 1898)
Loc. 04 (Ortega, obs. pers.)
Hemisorubim platyrhynchos (Valenciennes, 1840)
Loc. 04 (Ortega, obs. pers.)
Heptapterus sp.
MUSM 02789 Loc. 08 (1)   MUSM 4939 Loc.04 (1)
Leiarius marmoratus Gill, 1870
Loc. 04 (Ortega, obs. pers.)
Microglanis sp.
USNM 302980 Loc. 02 (1)   MUSM 2796 Loc. 08 (1)
MUSM 3939 Loc. 07 (1)   MUSM 3937 Loc. 25 (1)

Nannorhamdia bolivianus (Pearson, 1924)
USNM 302701 Loc. 01 (1)   USNM 302691 Loc. 26 (4)
MUSM 2124 Loc. 05 (1)

Pimelodella hasemani Eigenmann, 1917
MUSM 2817 Loc. 05 (3)

Pimelodella sp.
USNM 302669 Loc. 04 (92)   MUSM 2818 Loc. 05 (2)

Pimelodus maculatus Lacépede, 1803
MUSM 3922 Loc. 05 (1)   MUSM 3923 Loc. 06 (1)

Pimelodus ornatus Kner, 1858
MUSM 3908 Loc. 06 (2)

Pimelodus pictus Steindachner, 1876
MUSM 2478 Loc. 04 (1)   MUSM 3719 Loc. 04 (1)
MUSM 3723 Loc. 04 (2)

Platysilurus barbatus Haseman, 1911
USNM 319351 Loc. 04 (1)   USNM 319339 Loc. 04 (1)
MUSM 3906 Loc. 05 (1)

Platystomatichthys sturio (Kner, 1857)
USNM 319341 Loc. 04 (1)

Phractocephalus hemioliopterus (Bloch & Schneider, 1801)
Loc. 04 (Ortega, obs. pers.)

Rhamdia sp.
USNM 300967 Loc. 01 (1)   MUSM 3762 Loc. 23 (1)
MUSM 4529 Loc. 03 (2)   MUSM 3740 Loc. 08 (1)

Sorubim lima (Schneider, 1801)
MUSM 5007 Loc. 04 (1)

Sorubimichthys planiceps (Agassiz, 1829)
Loc. 04 (Ortega obs. pers.)

Zungaro zungaro (Humboldt, 1833)
Loc. 04 (Ortega, obs. pers.)

Cetopsidae
Pseudocetopsis plumbeus (Steindachner, 1883)
MUSM 3247 Loc. 10 (1)

Trichomycteridae
Paravandellia sp.
MUSM 3917 Loc. 04 (4)

Homodiaetus maculatus (Steindachner, 1879)
MUSM 3917 Loc. 04 (1)   MUSM 3970 Loc. 19 (1)

Ituglanis amazonicus (Steindachner, 1883)
MUSM 2065 Loc. 08 (4)   MUSM 2787 Loc. 24 (1)
USNM 317738 Loc. 08 (5)

Pseudostegophilus nemurus (Günther, 1868)
MUSM 3895 Loc. 04 (1)   MUSM 3918 Loc. 10 (1)

Trichomycterus fassli (Steindachner, 1915)
MUSM 3932 Loc. 25 (1)   MUSM 3954 Loc. 24 (2)

Trichomycterus sp. A
USNM 302760 Loc. 22 (20)   UNSM 302756 Loc. 22 (3)
USNM 302689 Loc. 22 (6)   USNM 302670 Loc. 22 (6)

Trichomycterus sp. B
USNM 302727 Loc. 24 (1)   USNM 302759 Loc. 25 (1)
USNM 302757 Loc. 25 (4)   USNM 302758 Loc. 25 (2)
USNM 302755 Loc. 25 (3)   USNM 302727 Loc. 25 (1)

Vandellia plazaii Castelnau, 1855
USNM 302684 Loc. 07 (1)   USNM 302683 Loc. 07 (6)
MUSM 2014 Loc. 04 (1)   MUSM 4561 Loc. 04 (1)

Callichthyidae

Callichthys callichthys (Linnaeus, 1758)
MUSM 3887 Loc. 02 (5)   MUSM 3941 Loc. 09 (1)
MUSM 4528 Loc. 03 (3)   MUSM 5001 Loc. 02 (1)
MUSM 4559 Loc. 03 (1)

Corydoras aeneus (Gill, 1858)
USNM 324261 Loc. 08 (2)

Corydoras semiaquilus Weitzman, 1964
MUSM 2674 Loc. 25 (1)

Corydoras sodalis Nijssen & Isbrucker, 1986
MUSM 3889 Loc. 10 (1)   MUSM 4857 Loc. 10 (5)
USNM 300972 Loc. 01 (2)

Corydoras stenocephalus Eigenmann & Allen, 1942
USNM 302671 Loc. 08 (1)   MUSM 3846 Loc. 02 (1)

Corydoras trilineatus Cope, 1872
USNM 324270 Loc. 11 (4)

Hoplosternum sp.
USNM 300976 Loc. 01 (1)   MUSM 3940 Loc. 08 (3)

Loricariidae

Ancistrus cirrhosus (Valenciennes, 1840)
MUSM 3097 Loc. 10 (1)

Ancistrus sp.
USNM 302751 Loc. 02 (3)   MUSM 4859 Loc. 25 (6)
USNM 302730 Loc. 01 (11)   USNM 302746 Loc. 01 (3)

Aphanotorulus frankei Isbrucker & Nijssen, 1983
USNM 301646 Loc. 06 (16)   USNM 301642 Loc. 04 (20)
MUSM 3885 Loc. 07 (13)   MUSM 5005 Loc. 04 (5)

Chaetostoma sp.
USNM 302686 Loc. 25 (6)   USNM 302743 Loc. 24 (17)
MUSM 4872 Loc. 01 (1)   USNM 302744 Loc. 25 (3)
MUSM 4860 Loc. 25 (7)   MUSM 4996 Loc. 02 (2)

Crossoloricaria rhami Isbrucker & Nijssen, 1983
USNM 302702 Loc. 25 (3)   USNM 302735 Loc. 04 (1)

Farlowella sp.
USNM 302648 Loc. 04 (10)   USNM 301641 Loc. 02 (15)
MUSM 2429 Loc. 04 (8)   USNM 302649 Loc. 07 (1)

Hemiodontichthys acipenserinus (Kner, 1854)
USNM 302700 Loc. 07 (1)   MUSM 2455 Loc. 04 (2)
MUSM 3927 Loc. 05 (4)

Hypoptopoma sp.
USNM 302696 Loc. 14 (7)   MUSM 4856 Loc. 10 (2)
MUSM 2474 Loc. 14 (7)   MUSM 4873 Loc. 12 (1)
MUSM 4881 Loc. 14 (8)   MUSM 4890 Loc. 12 (1)
MUSM 4953 Loc. 04   MUSM 4554 Loc. 12 (1)

Hypostomus sp.
USNM 302647 Loc. 14 (7)   USNM 302761 Loc. 06 (25)
USNM 302688 Loc. 25 (1)   USNM 302728 Loc. 25 (1)
USNM 302732 Loc. 25 (1)   USNM 302762 Loc. 07 (4)
MUSM 4885 Loc. 14 (4)   USNM 302656 Loc. 04 (25)

MUSM 4885 Loc. 14 (4)   USNM 302656 Loc. 04 (25)

Lamontichthys filamentosus (La Monte, 1935)
MUSM 4534 Loc. 05 (2)   MUSM 4533 Loc. 04 (1)

Lasiancistrus sp.
USNM 302734 Loc. 25 (8)

Loricaria sp.
USNM 302644 Loc. 25 (25)   USNM 301648 Loc. 04 (14)
MUSM 2543 Loc. 05 (3)

Liposarcus disjunctivus Weber, 1991
MUSM 4876 Loc. 14 (1)

Loricarichthys sp.
MUSM 2450 Loc. 01 (1)   MUSM 4877 Loc. 14 (2)
MUSM 3909 Loc. 10 (1)   MUSM 3928 Loc. 04 (2)

Otocinclus sp.
USNM 301640 Loc. 01 (8)   MUSM 2033 Loc. 09 (8)
MUSM 2453 Loc. 04 (2)   MUSM 4870 Loc. 01 (1)

Planiloricaria cryptodon (Isbrucker, 1971)
MUSM 3925 Loc. 07 (1)   MUSM 4532 Loc. 04 (2)

Rineloricaria lanceolata (Günther, 1868)
MUSM 3045 Loc. 04 (3)   MUSM 4858 Loc. 25 (2)
MUSM 3745 Loc. 08 (2)

Rineloricaria sp.
USNM 301644 Loc. 01 (4)   USNM 302738 Loc. 08 (2)
MUSM 2463 Loc. 04 (1)   MUSM 3741 Loc. 08 (2)
USNM 302682 Loc. 25 (1)   MUSM 4919 Loc. 08 (1)
MUSM 4938 Loc. 12 (1)

Sturisoma sp.
USNM 302650 Loc. 06 (1)   USNM 302651 Loc. 04 (2)
MUSM 3894 Loc. 05 (1)   USNM 302650 Loc. 04 (2)

Astroblepidae

Astroblepus sp. A
MUSM 1692 Loc. 22 (14)   MUSM 2607 Loc. 22 (31)
USNM 302652 Loc. 22 (24)   USNM 302674 Loc. 22 (4)
USNM 302679 Loc. 22 (1)   USNM 302680 Loc. 22 (2)

Astroblepus sp. B
USNM 302675 Loc. 24 (5)   USNM 302678 Loc. 24 (5)
USNM 302677 Loc. 23 (1)   MUSM 3764 Loc. 23 (1)
USNM 302676 Loc. 23 (1)   MUSM 1692 Loc. 23 (10)
MUSM 2615 Loc. 24 (12)   MUSM 3827 Loc. 23 (1)

CYPRINODONTIFORMES

Belonidae
Pseudotylosurus angusticeps (Günther, 1866)
MUSM 3906 Loc. 05 (1)   MUSM 4540 Loc. 04 (1)

Rivulidae
Pterolebias sp.
MUSM 3120 Loc. 20 (10)   MUSM 3898 Loc. 17 (11)

Rivulus sp.
MUSM 4530 Loc. 03 (1)   MUSM 4543 Loc. 03 (3)

SYNBRANCHIFORMES

Synbranchidae
Synbranchus marmoratus Bloch, 1795
USNM 295277 Loc. 01 (1)   MUSM 3888 Loc. 14 (1)
MUSM 4469 Loc. 08 (1)   MUSM 4466 Loc. 14 (4)
MUSM 4563 Loc. 10 (1)

PERCIFORMES

Sciaenidae
Pachyurus schomburgkii Günther, 1860
USNM 302705 Loc. 04 (3)

Pachyurus sp.
MUSM 4868 Loc. 04 (1)

Plagioscion auratus (Castelnau, 1855)
MUSM 3969 Loc. 19 (1)

Cichlidae
Aequidens tetramerus (Heckel, 1840)
USNM 302658 Loc. 01 (14)   USNM 302659 Loc. 14 (5)
USNM 302660 Loc. 25 (37)   USNM 302720 Loc. 05 (9)
MUSM 2214 Loc. 14 (5)   MUSM 2816 Loc. 05 (2)
USNM 302663 Loc. 02 (1)   MUSM 4995 Loc. 02 (1)
MUSM 4970 Loc. 11 (1)

Apistogramma luelingi (Kullander,1976)
USNM 295353 Loc. 01 (21)   USNM 302704 Loc. 14 (7)
USNM 302729 Loc. 08 (5)   MUSM 1787 Loc. 09 (3)
MUSM 2119 Loc. 09 (7)   USNM 302703 Loc. 08 (3)

Apistogramma sp.
MUSM 4940 Loc. 12 (1)   MUSM 4937 Loc. 18 (1)
MUSM 4555 Loc. 02 (1)

Bujurquina eurhinus Kullander, 1986
USNM 295351 Loc. 01 (5)   USNM 298098 Loc. 05 (23)
MUSM 2136 Loc. 05 (3)   MUSM 2263 Loc. 06 (2)

Bujurquina sp.
MUSM 4971 Loc. 11 (1)   MUSM 4882 Loc. 14 (1)
MUSM 4921 Loc. 14 (2)

Cichlasoma boliviense Kullander, 1983
MUSM 4711 Loc. 06 (1)   MUSM 4861 Loc. 07 (6)
MUSM 4966 Loc. 04 (1)   MUSM 4943 Loc. 15 (5)
MUSM 4878 Loc. 14 (8)

Crenicichla semicincta Steindachner, 1892
MUSM 2100 Loc. 05 (3)   MUSM 4983 Loc. 01 (3)
MUSM 3104 Loc. 05 (2)   MUSM 4865 Loc. 07 (1)
MUSM 3905 Loc. 14 (2)

Satanoperca jurupari (Heckel, 1840)
Loc. 13 (Ortega, obs. pers.)

PLEURONECTIFORMES

Soleidae
Achirus achirus (Linnaeus, 1758)
MUSM 3791 Loc. 14 (2)

DISCUSIÓN

Este estudio permitió determinar la composición y riqueza de especies de peces en los ambientes acuáticos del Parque Nacional Manu y, en forma parcial, conocer la estructura de las comunidades de peces en los hábitats mejor estudiados de la Zona Reservada. Sobre la base de la información, la ictiofauna de Madre de Dios está más relacionada con las cuencas del Beni o Mamoré (Bolivia), que con las cuencas del Ucayali o Marañón en el Perú.

Haciendo una reseña de los cuerpos de agua estudiados, clasificándolos entre ambientes lóticos y lénticos y sus diversas formas, y relacionándolos a ciertos grupos de peces, tenemos:

I. *Lóticos:* **A)** Cursos de aguas torrentosas, frías (10°C), pendiente pronunciada y ubicadas a altitudes elevadas (600 -1000 m) y de fondo duro, que caracterizan el ambiente propio de peces reofílicos (*Astroblepus* sp., *Trichomycterus* sp. y *Chaetostoma* sp.). Es el caso de las quebradas San Pedro, Culli y Soga; **B)** Cursos de aguas tranquilas, cálidas (22° C), menor pendiente, ubicados en la llanura y de fondo variable. Incluyen un número diverso de ambientes que pueden separarse por el tipo de agua: 1) CURSOS DE AGUA CLARA, quebradas Picaflor, Martín Pescador y Río Salvación, que albergan peces de pequeño a mediano porte, como *Brachychalcinus*, *Moenkhausia* sp., *Charax* sp., *Astyanax*, *Scopaeocharax* y *Cichlasoma*, entre otros; 2) CURSOS DE AGUA BLANCA, comprendiendo la mayor extensión del Río Manu y afluentes, como Pachija y Panahua, que mantienen peces menudos de variadas especies (*Characidium*, *Aphyocharax*, *Parodon*, *Aphanotorulus*, *Pimelodella*, etc.) en sus orillas, especies de gran talla (*Sorubim*, *Brachyplatystoma*, *Pseudoplatystoma*, *Zungaro*, etc.) en el canal principal; 3) CURSOS DE AGUA NEGRA, que nacen y recorren el bosque adquiriendo esa coloración por la abundancia de detritus vegetal. En esta categoría están las Quebradas Trompetero y Carpintero, y en ellas ocurren: *Tyttocharax*, *Carnegiella*, *Pyrrhulina*, *Corydoras* y *Apistogramma*, entre otros.

II. *Lénticos:* Varían en forma, dimensión, duración, edad y tipo de agua, existiendo: **A)** Lagunas fluviales o «cochas» que varían en antigüedad; las más recientes, como Cocha Nueva, albergan una composición de peces similar a la existente en el Río Manu en la misma zona. Otras, de 20 o más años, como Salvador, Otorongo y Cashu, albergan considerable número de especies. Otro grupo de lagunas, las más antiguas, distróficas, como Totora y Juárez, están reduciéndose en superficie y profundidad por invasión de vegetación y acumulación de sedimentos; albergan comunidades diversas de peces y con poblaciones menores, la mayoría de talla menuda; **B)** Ambientes temporales, algunos conectados a ríos y/o quebradas, otros son depresiones dependientes de la acumulación de agua en creciente. Muy importantes por constituirse en refugios para un gran número de especies. Como en los frecuentes casos en las márgenes del río Manu, Pachija y en el interior de los bosques de Pakitza y Cashu, en el último caso fue posible ubicar dos poblaciones de peces anuales (*Pterolebias* sp.). **C)** Aguajal, ambiente léntico permanente con aguas negras, que está asociado a una comunidad vegetal donde predomina el «aguaje» (*Mauritia flexuosa*). Alberga diversas especies de pequeño porte, destacando caraciformes, siluriformes y cíclidos.

Los ambientes estudiados con mayor número de especies son el Río Manu, quebradas Fortaleza, Picaflor y Martín Pescador; presentando agua blanca el primero y clara-blanca los restantes. En los ambientes de agua negra, si bien no hay un gran número de especies, ocurren formas características, como characiformes y siluriformes de tallas menudas adaptados a los rápidos o dependientes del material alóctono de la vegetación ribereña. En los ambientes de altitudes superiores a 500m se aprecia un número de especies que corresponde principalmente a grupos adaptados a torrentes. Los peces que habitan las lagunas por lo general son formas que provienen del intercambio cíclico con el Río Manu, lo que se demuestra por la presencia de estadíos juveniles en los primeros meses del año y algunos son más representativos de aguas lénticas, caso de los cíclidos y formas que se reproducen más de una vez al año.

En la composición general de la ictiofauna destacan los Ostariophysi, representando más del 80% del total de especies (Characidae con el 42 %, Pimelodidae, 11% y Loricariidae con 10% del total).

En términos generales, la composición ictiofaunística por familias es más similar para el Parque Nacional Manu (PNM), como para la registrada en la Zona Reservada Tambopata-Candamo (ZRTC), y el Santuario Nacional Pampas del Heath (SNPH) que la presente en la cuenca del alto río Ucayali (entre Atalaya y Pucallpa). Comparando el PNM con la ZRTC, se nota la ausencia de los Helogenidae en el primero, con el SNPH la falta de Ageneiosidae. En cambio, con el Alto Ucayali, notamos entre los peces de gran talla la ausencia en el PNM de Osteoglossidae y Arapaimidae. Existe *Arapaima gigas* en la provincia de Tambopata (cuenca del río Madre de Dios), pero es una especie introducida desde Loreto. Es notoria la ausencia en la cuenca del río Madre de Dios de Ctenoluciidae, Chilodontidae, Batrachoididae, Nandidae y Tetraodontidae. En el PNM y en la ZRTC se registra en cambio Astroblepidae, entre los 600 y 1000 m. A nivel genérico, se aprecia solamente algunas diferencias y son mayores las similitudes, al comparar (Tabla 2) las composiciones de las áreas protegidas (PNM, ZRTC y SNPH). Por ejemplo, no se ha registrado hasta el momento en el PNM a *Helogenes*, *Megalonema*, y *Nannostomus*. En cambio, comparten alrededor del 60% de especies, principalmente carácidos, pimelódidos y loricáridos de tallas pequeñas a mediana (30 a 150 mm). Entre las formas menudas se observan muchas especializadas, que podrían ser consideradas indicadores de ciertos tipos de agua como *Tyttocharax* y *Scopaeocharax* que solamente se presentan en arroyos de agua negra o clara, respectivamente. Comparándola en géneros con la ictiofauna del río Ucayali, a nivel genérico es notoria la ausencia de representantes de *Caenotropus*, *Boulengerella*, *Platydoras*, *Brochis*, *Cichla*, *Astronotus*, *Chaetobranchus*, *Monocirrhus* y *Colomesus*, entre otros, en la primera.

El Parque Nacional del Manu mantiene en sus aguas una ictiofauna diversificada, asociada a los diferentes hábitats y a los factores climáticos regionales. En el presente estudio se ha identificado 210 especies, 148 géneros y 33 familias en 10 órdenes.

Probablemente el número de registros será mayor al intensificarse y aclararse dudas en la identificación del material reciente.

Se da a conocer nuevos registros para la ictiofauna de los peces continentales del Perú: *Aphyocharax anisitsi*, *A. avary*, *A. dentatus*, *A. pappenheimi*, *Astyanax zonatus*, *Characidium purpuratum*, *Cheirodon notomelas*, *C. troemneri*, *Ctenobrycon spilurus*, *Deuterodon sp.*, *Gephyrocharax sp.*, *Hemibrycon jabonero*, *Knodus beta*, *Monotocheiron pearsoni*, *Pristobrycon sp.*, *Goslinia platynema*, *Paravandellia sp.*, *Homodiaetus maculatus*, *Trichomycterus fassli* y *Liposarcus disjunctivus*.

Sin embargo, es importante señalar que en muchos casos las identificaciones son tentativas, y que el estado de la sistemática de los peces de agua dulce, especialmente en Characidae, es pobre (Böhlke et al., 1978), siendo necesarias revisiones taxonómicas como las realizadas en algunos Characiformes (Vari, 1983; Vari & Weitzman, 1990).

Tabla 1. Distribución de la ictiofauna en los principales hábitats del Parque Nacional Manu, PERU (Localidades: 01. quebrada Picaflor, 02. quebrada Trompetero, 04. río Manu, 05. quebrada Fortaleza, 06. quebrada Pachija, 08. quebrada Carpintero, 10. cocha Chica, 11. quebrada Martín Pescador, 12 cocha Juárez, 14. cocha Salvador, 24. quebrada Soga, 25. río Salvación, 26. río Alto Madre de Dios.

Especies / Localidades	01	02	04	05	06	08	10	11	12	14	24	25	26
Paratrygon aeiraba			x	x									
Potamotrygon motoro			x										
Potamotrygon sp.			x										
Lepidosiren paradoxa									x	x			
Pellona altamazónica										x			
Anchoviella guianensis									x				
Anchoviella sp. A			x	x									
Anchoviella sp. B			x										
Acestrocephalus boehlkei			x		x								
Acestrorhynchus altus	x						x	x					
A. lacustris							x						
Acestrorhynchus sp.			x					x					
Aphyocharax alburnus			x	x									
A. anitsis	x												
A. avary			x										
A. dentatus			x										
A. pappenheimi			x		x					x			
A. pusillus			x					x					
Astyanacinus multidens	x						x		x	x			
Astyanax abramis	x		x	x									
A. bimaculatus			x						x				
A. fasciatus	x				x				x				
A. maximus	x				x								x
A. zonatus		x											
Bario steindachneri										x	x	x	
Brachychalcinus copei	x							x	x				
Brycon erythropterum													x

477

Especies / Localidades	01	02	04	05	06	08	10	11	12	14	24	25	26
Bryconacidnus ellisi											x		
Bryconamericus pectinatus										x			
Bryconamericus sp. B													
Chalceus erythrurus	x		x	x									
Characidium zebra				x	x								
C. purpuratus											x		
Characidium sp.				x									
Charax caudimaculatus	x					x							
Ch. tectifer						x							
Cheirodon piaba							x						
Ch. drepanon				x									
Ch. fugitiva	x		x	x	x								
Ch. notomelas			x										
Ch. troemneri			x										
Cheirodon sp.				x									
Clupeacharax anchoveoides			x										
Colossoma macropomum			x										
Creagrutus anary	x		x	x						x	x		
C. beni	x		x	x									
Ctenobrycon hauxwellianus			x										
C. spilurus						x							
Cynopotamus amazonus			x		x								
Deuterodon sp.										x			
Engraulisoma taeniatum			x	x									
Galeocharax gulo			x				x						
Gephyrocharax sp.				x		x	x				x		x
Gymnocorymbus thayeri						x							
Hemibrycon jabonero	x									x	x		
Hemigrammus sp.				x							x		x
Holoshestes heterodon						x							x
Hyphessobrycon sp.				x		x							
Knodus aff. beta	x		x										
Leptagoniates pi			x										
Moenkhausia comma	x												
M. dichroura	x			x	x								
M. oligolepis	x			x			x						
Moenkhausia sp.									x				
Monotocheirodon pearsoni			x										x
Mylossoma duriventre						x							
Othonocheirodus aff. lethostigmus											x		x
Paragoniates alburnus			x	x									
Phenacogaster sp.			x										
Piabucus sp.			x	x									
Piaractus brachypomus			x										
Prionobrama filigera			x	x									
Prodontocharax melanotus	x		x	x	x						x		
Rhinobrycon negrensis											x		
Roeboides affinis							x						
R. myersi			x				x						
Salminus affinis	x		x										
Scopaeocharax sp.	x				x		x						
Serrasalmus nattereri			x										
S. rhombeus							x	x					
S. spilopleura				x									
Tetragonopterus argenteus			x	x									
Triportheus albus													
T. angulatus			x				x	x					

Especies / Localidades	01	02	04	05	06	08	10	11	12	14	24	25	26
T. elongatus			x										
T. rotundatus			x										
Tyttocharax tambopatensis		x			x								
Carnegiella myersi		x											
Carnegiella sp.	x			x				x					
Thoracocharax stellatus			x	x	x								
Rhaphiodon vulpinus			x							x			
Anodus elongantus			x										
Hoplerythrinus unitaeniatus					x								
Hoplias malabaricus	x			x	x			x		x			
Pyrrhulina vittata				x	x	x							
Apareidon pongoense			x										
Parodon buckleyi		x								x	x		
Prochilodus nigricans			x					x	x				
Potamorhina altamazonica				x				x			x		
Psectrogaster rutiloides			x	x									
Steindachnerina bimaculata			x		x								x
S. binotata			x										
S. dobula	x		x		x								
S. guentheri	x		x				x	x					
S. hypostoma			x										
Abramites hypselonotus	x												
Anostomus sp.										x			
Leporellus vittatus										x			
Leporinus friderici			x					x	x				
L. striatus	x			x									
L. yophorus									x				
Schizodon fasciatus				x					x				
Gymnotus carapo	x				x						x		
Apteronotus albifrons					x								
Apteronotus bonaparti				x									
Sternachorhynchus sp.			x		x								
Eigenmannia virescens					x								
Sternopygus macrurus			x		x								x
Brachyhypopomus sp.		x	x		x								
Megalodoras sp.			x										
Trachydoras sp.			x										
Leptodoras sp.			x										
Auchenipterus nuchalis				x									
Tatia sp.			x		x								
Bunocephalus bifidus		x					x						x
Ernstichthys megistus													x
Ernstichthys sp.			x										
Brachyplatystoma filamentosum			x										
Calophysus macropterus			x										
Duopalatinus sp.			x										
Goslinia platynema			x										
Hemisorubim platyrhynchos			x										
Heptapterus sp.			x		x								
Leiarius marmoratus			x										
Microglanis sp.		x			x							x	
Nannorhamdia bolivianus		x			x								x
Zungaro zungaro				x									
Phractocephalus hemioliopterus			x										
Pimelodella hasemani				x									
Pimelodella sp.			x	x									
Pimelodus maculatus			x	x	x								
P. ornatus					x								
P. pictus			x										
Platysilurus barbatus			x										

479

Especies / Localidades	01	02	04	05	06	08	10	11	12	14	24	25	26
Pseudotylosurus microps				x									
Platystomatichthys sturio			x										
Rhamdia sp.	x					x							
Sorubimichthys planiceps			x										
Sorubim lima			x										
Pseudocetopsis plumbeus							x						
Paravandellia sp.			x										
Homodiaetus maculatus			x										
Ituglanis amazonicus						x				x			
Pseudostegophilus nemurus			x				x						
Trichomycterus fassli										x	x		
Trichomycterus sp. B										x	x		
Vandellia plazaii			x										
Callichthys callichthys		x											
Corydoras aeneus					x								
C. semiaquilus													x
C. sodalis	x						x						
C. stenocephalus		x			x								
C. trilineatus									x				
Hoplosternum sp.	x				x								
Ancistrus cirrhosus						x							
Ancistrus sp.	x	x								x	x		
Aphanotorulus frankei		x			x								
Chaetostoma sp.		x	x							x	x	x	
Crossoloricaria rhami			x										
Farlowella sp.		x	x										
Hemiodontichthys acipenserinus			x	x									
Hypoptopoma sp.		x	x			x	x	x					
Hypostomus sp.	x		x		x						x		
Lamontichthys filamentosus		x	x										
Lasiancistrus sp.													x
Loricaria sp.		x	x	x									x
Loricarichthys sp.	x		x						x				
Lyposarcus disjunctivus									x				
Otocinclus sp.	x		x										
Planiloricaria cryptodon			x										
Rineloricaria lanceolata			x		x	x							
Rineloricaria sp.	x		x		x								
Sturisoma sp.		x	x	x									
Astroblepus sp. B										x			
Pseudotylosurus angusticeps			x	x									
Synbranchus marmoratus		x				x	x		x				
Pachyurus schomburgkii			x										
Pachyurus sp.			x										
Plagioscion auratus			x						x				
Aequidens tetramerus	x	x	x		x		x						x
Apistogramma luelingi	x												
Apistogramma sp.		x											
Bujurquina eurhinus	x		x	x				x	x				
Cichlasoma boliviense	x		x	x		x			x				
Crenicichla semicincta	x		x						x				
Crenicichla sp.									x				
Achirus achirus									x				
Totales	49	12	96	46	17	28	18	18	08	22	10	24	17

Tabla 2. Lista de familias y número de especies registradas en el Parque Nacional Manu (PNM), Zona Reservada Tambopata-Candamo (ZRTC) (Chang & Ortega, in prep.) y Santuario Nacional Pampas del Heath (SNPH) PERU (Ortega, 1994).

Familias	PNM	ZRTC	SNPH
	número de especies		
POTAMOTRYGONIDAE	03	01	00
LEPIDOSIRENIDAE	01	00	00
ARAPAIMIDAE	00	00	01
CLUPEIDAE	01	00	00
ENGRAULIDIIDAE	03	03	02
CHARACIDAE	86	84	48
GASTEROPELECIDAE	03	03	04
CYNODONTIDAE	01	00	01
HEMIODONTIDAE	01	00	01
ERYTHRINIDAE	03	03	02
LEBIASINIDAE	01	01	02
PARODONTIDAE	03	01	01
PROCHILODONTIDAE	01	01	01
CURIMATIDAE	07	06	04
ANOSTOMIDAE	07	04	03
GYMNOTIDAE	01	02	01
APTERONOTIDAE	03	00	00
STERNOPYGIDAE	02	02	03
HYPOPOMIDAE	01	03	01
RHAMPHICHTHYIDAE	00	01	00
DORADIDAE	03	01	00
AUCHENIPTERIDAE	02	01	01
ASPREDINIDAE	03	02	01
PIMELODIDAE	21	11	08
CETOPSIDAE	01	01	00
TRICHOMYCTERIDAE	08	06	03
HELOGENIDAE	00	01	01
CALLICHTHYIDAE	07	05	03
LORICARIIDAE	19	13	07
ASTROBLEPIDAE	02	01	00
BELONIDAE	01	00	01
RIVULIDAE	02	03	02
SYNBRANCHIDAE	01	01	00
SCIAENIDAE	03	02	00
CICHLIDAE	08	09	02
SOLEIDAE	01	00	01
Total 36	210	182	105
Esfuerzo (semanas)	31	8	3

AGRADECIMIENTOS

Mi reconocimiento a los Dres. Richard P. Vari, Stanley H. Weitzman, Darrel Siebert, Mary Rauchenberger y Carl Ferraris por la gentil colaboración. A los biólogos Guadalupe Contreras, Jaime Sarmiento, Iris Samanez, Fonchii Chang y María Guevara, a los Dres. Mary Hagedorn, Clifford Keller y Raymond Bouchard, por la significativa ayuda en los trabajos de campo y registro de datos limnológicos. En el trabajo de laboratorio, por su valioso apoyo a Fonchii Chang, y por la revisión del manuscrito a Fonchii Chang, Mary Hagedorn, Gerardo Lamas y Richard Vari.

LITERATURA CITADA

Böhlke, J.E., S.H. Weitzman & N.A. Menezes. 1978. Estado atual da sitemática de peixes de água doce da América do Sul. Acta Amazônica, 8(4): 57-677.

Cope, E. D. 1878. Synopsis of the Fishes of the Peruvian Amazon, obtained by Prof. James Orton during his Expeditions of 1873 and 1877. Proc. Amer. Philos. Soc. 17: 673-701.

Chang F. & H. Ortega. (In prep.). Ichthyofauna of the Tambopata-Candamo Reserved Zone, Southeastern Peru.

Eigenmann, C. H. & W. R. Allen. 1942. Fishes of Western South America. I: The Intercordilleran and Amazonian Lowland of Peru; II: The High Pampas, Bolivia, and Northern Chile, With a Revision of the Gymnotidae, and of the Genus Orestias 494 pages, plates 1-22. Lexington: The University of Kentucky

Fowler, H. W. 1940. A Collection of Fishes obtained by William C. Morrow in the Ucayali River Basin, Peru. Proc. Acad. Nat. Sci. Phila. 91: 219-289.

Kalliola, R., J. Salo & Y. Mäkinen. 1987. Regeneración Natural de las Selvas en la Amazonia Peruana 1: Dinámica Fluvial y Sucesión Ribereña. Mem. Mus. Hist. Nat. «Javier Prado» 19A: 1-102.

Mago - Leccia, F. 1994. Electric Fishes of the Continental Waters of America. Fundación para el Desarrollo de las Ciencias Físicas, Matemáticas y Naturales. (FUDECI). Biblioteca de la Academia de Ciencias Físicas, Matemáticas y Naturales Vol. XXIX. Caracas, Venezuela. 206 pages.

Ortega, H. 1994. Fish Fauna of the Pampas del Heath. In: The Tambopata-Candamo Reserved Zone of Sputheastern Perú: A Biological Assessment. RAP Working Papers 6:72-73 and 156-161.

Ortega, H. 1991. Adiciones y Correcciones a la Lista de Peces de Aguas Continentales del Perú. Publ. Mus. Hist. Nat. UNMSM (A) 39: 1-6.

Ortega, H. & R. P. Vari 1986. Annotated Checklist of the Freshwater Fishes of Peru. Smithsonian Contributions to Zoology 437: 1-25.

Pearson, N. 1937. The Fishes of the Atlantic and Pacific Slopes near Cajamarca, Peru. Proc. Calif. Acad. Sci. (4) 23: 87-98

Vari, R.P. 1983. Phylogenetics Relationships of the Families Curimatidae, Prochilodontidae, Anostomidae and Chilodontidae (Pisces: Characiformes). Smithsonian Contribution to Zoology, 378: 1-60.

Vari, R.P. & S.H. Weitzman. 1990. Review of the Phylogenetic Biogeography of the Freshwater Fishes of South America. In G. Peters and R. Hutterer, editors, Vertebrates in the Tropics, (Bonn, June 5-8, 1989), pages 381-393, 6 figures. Bonn: Alexander Koenig Zoological Research Institute and Zoological Museum.

Weitzman, S. H. & H. Ortega. 1995. A new species of Tyttocharax (Teleostei: Characidae: Glandulocaudinae: Xenurobryconidae from the Río Madre de Dios basin of Perú. Ichthyol. Explor. Freshwaters, Vol. 6, No. 2, pp. 129-148.

Species Diversity of Gymnotiform Fishes in Manu Bioreserve, Pakitza, Perú

MARY HAGEDORN

Department of Animal Health, National Zoological Park,
Washington, D.C. 20008

CLIFFORD KELLER

Institute of Neuroscience, University of Oregon,
Eugene, OR 97403

ABSTRACT

We have begun a long-term study of the biodiversity of the gymnotiform fishes of South America. The gymnotiform electric fish populations were assayed using electrical monitoring equipment in a relatively undisturbed environment, the Río Manu system at Pakitza, Peru. Within a 15 km² area near Pakitza, there are seven permanent rivers or streams containing at least 8 gymnotiform species. Six of these species emit wave-type electric organ discharges, the other 2 emit pulse-type discharges. The vast majority of the electric fish in the large, fast-flowing rivers were of the wave-type (94-99%), whereas the pulse-type species predominated in the smaller streams (78-93%). Within these streams, the number of electric fish increased with distance from the mouth of the Río Manu. All eight species differed in their distributions amongst the streams and microhabitats. Two of the eight species are currently undescribed. One of these undescribed species showed a marked sexual dimorphism in its electric organ discharge.

INTRODUCTION

Rapid destruction of tropical forests is a global event. Within the next 25 to 50 years, it is predicted that within these forest ecosystems there will be massive extinctions of species (for reviews, Raven, 1988; Janzen, 1988). Moreover, the growth of the human population in the tropics will fuel an increasing need for agricultural land making further forest destruction almost a certainty. These rather dire prospects have stimulated a recent upsurge in interest for understanding the extent and causes underlying the high biodiversity within tropical rainforest ecosystems. Until recently, many studies have focused on the diversity of terrestrial communities, and very little attention has been focused on their associated freshwater ecosystems. We are interested in some of the biological correlates of species diversity in neotropical river systems.

The Amazon is the largest river system in the world in terms of drainage area and the volume of freshwater released to the ocean (Goulding, 1980). The river and associated rainforest are a complex that create and maintain much of the weather within the Amazon basin. One group of freshwater fishes endemic to Central and South America are the gymnotiforms, commonly called electric fish. Worldwide, there are approximately 20,000 species of fish, and some estimates suggest that the gymnotiforms comprise about 0.5% of this total (Mago-Leccia, 1978; for a review, Wilson, 1988). Data from recent deep-water trawls in the Amazon and its larger tributaries indicated that gymnotiforms comprised 47-78 % of the catch in these deep-water areas (Barletta and Chao, 1993; Provenzano, 1993; Stewart and Ibarra, 1993). Thus, at least in some deep-water habitats of South America, gymnotiforms comprise a large proportion of the fish community.

The electric discharge emitted by these fish provides the field biologist with an easy and reliable means of assessing the density and diversity of this important group. Each electric fish constantly produces an electric organ discharge (EOD), thus providing an "electrical tag" that can be monitored remotely with a simple audio-amplifier, called a fish detector. The shapes of the EODs are species-specific, but are of two basic types: "pulse", having relatively long and variable intervals between discharges; and "wave", in which the EOD is sinusoidal and of a relatively constant frequency. Using fish detectors (and without actually ever seeing the fish), individual fish can be categorized as either pulse- or wave-type, and often identified to species as well. Except perhaps for the deep-water trawling, mentioned above, traditional methods of fishing severely underestimate the population density and diversity of gymnotiforms relative to other fish taxa (Ortega, 1996), because they do not adequately sample the daytime hiding places of these animals (i.e., submerged trees and vegetation). Using a fish detector to census the population, however, results in an underestimation of gymnotiform populations by only approximately 18% (Hagedorn, 1988) and thus provides a more reliable basis for comparisons between taxa.

Western Amazonas has some of the highest species diversity in the world for plants, some insect taxa and mammals (Gentry, 1988; Lamas et al., 1991). We have begun a quantitative, long-term study of the biodiversity and distributional patterns of gymnotiforms starting in a relatively undisturbed site within Western Amazonas at Pakitza, Peru. Our initial studies were performed during portions of a single wet (November, 1990) and dry (June, 1993) season in a variety of aquatic environments surrounding Pakitza, ranging from the large and fast-flowing Río Manu to smaller rainforest streams. Using fish detectors, we censused the density of gymnotiforms and described the distribution of wave- and pulse-type species within two or three 500 m transects in each stream. In addition, using hand-nets, we captured individuals from each species for positive identification, recorded their species-specific EODs, and took morphological measurements. This allowed us to note both morphological and electrical sexual dimorphisms. Each species was examined to estimate their state of gonadal maturation as an indicator of their readiness to breed. We also measured physico-chemical water parameters known to induce gonadal maturation in some species of gymnotiforms (Kirschbaum, 1979). Below, we also discuss some of the factors which may lead to local differences in the numbers of gymnotiform species.

METHODS

COLLECTION

Gymnotiforms are nocturnal, hiding in daytime refuges and moving into the open water to feed at night. During the day, these animals can be located easily by means of an audio-amplifier and then captured with a hand-net. Since EODs are species specific, a species description for electric fishes should include both morphological and electrical traits. Representative specimens from each species were collected and their EODs recorded in the laboratory. Once we determined the number of species around Pakitza and had sufficient samples, we located and identified animals by means of their EOD, but did not actually catch them. We discovered two undescribed species, *Sternarchorhynchus sp.* and a new hypopomid.

RECORDING AND ANALYSIS

Captured animals were brought into the laboratory to measure their electrical and physical characteristics. First, they were positioned near the center of a small aquarium (65 cm long; 5 cm wide; 12 cm deep) filled with water from their home stream. Their EOD was monitored with carbon electrodes placed 6-8 cm from the head and tail of the fish, with the head of the animal oriented towards the positive electrode. Their signals were then amplified differentially (Grass P-15; 10 x) and recorded with a Nagra III tape recorder on magnetic tape (Scotch 226; 38.1 cm/sec). EODs from each animal were transiently captured, digitized with 12 bit resolution (MacAdios; GW Instruments) at a sampling rate of 10 - 50 μs (depending on the species) and analyzed by Fourier analysis (Igor; Wavemetrics, Inc.) and then plotted. To test the accuracy of these recordings, fish were recorded in the small field-recording tank and also in a large 120 l aquarium. The small field-recording tank did not cause any distortion of the EOD signals, as the recorded EODs and power spectra were identical in both the large and the smaller tank. The frequencies which we report are uncorrected for temperature in the recording aquarium, however, these ranged from 27.6 - 32.0°C. We made measurements of the various EOD phases for some pulse-type fish from the graphed data (following the methods of Bratton and Kramer, 1988).

After the EOD was recorded, the animal was anesthetized with ethyl-m-aminobenzoate methanesulphonate (MS-222; ca. 1:15,000 in river water). Each animal was measured (head-to-tail length), weighed, identified with a tag, fixed

485

in 10% formalin in river water for two days, and then stored in 70 % ETOH. The gonads were inspected with a dissecting microscope at 120x, and their main axis was measured with a stage micrometer. If the gonads appeared mature, containing enlarged testes (3-7 mm) or mature ovaries (0.7-1.5 mm eggs), the fish was considered ready to breed.

DISTRIBUTION

The species distribution and density of gymnotiform fish were determined in five streams that represented the variety of stream types occurring in the permanent waters near to Pakitza. This represents an area of approximately 15 km². In each stream, we determined the distribution of gymnotiforms in relationship to the main river system, the Río Manu. At the mouth of each stream, a listening transect was made to determine whether there were any gymnotiforms present. Additionally, 500 m transects were mapped ca. 1 and 2-4 km upstream from the stream's mouth. Within these transects the width of the stream was measured at 50 m intervals and within each interval six to twelve depth soundings were made. All gymnotiforms in each transect were located by means of an audioamplifier and counted, and their locations were transferred to a map for comparisons of each species' distribution pattern.

LIMNOLOGY

In each stream, several physico-chemical water properties were measured. The temperature was measured ca. one meter above and below the surface of the water with a digital thermometer (Fisher). The pH was measured with both paper (colorpHast) and liquid (Merck) colorimetric tests that were each checked with a reference standard (Fisher; pH 7.0). Water flow at the surface was estimated by measuring the time it took a buoyant float to traverse 2 m. In the smaller streams, where stream flow varied considerably from pools to riffles, this measurement was taken in unobstructed riffles that were 10-15 cm in depth. The conductivity of the water was measured with an Orion 122 conductivity meter and water clarity was measured with a Secchi disk.

DESCRIPTION OF THE STUDY SITES

Pakitza is situated at approximately 300 m elevation, twelve degrees south of the equator and has discrete wet (November-April) and dry (April- November) seasons. We studied five of the seven permanent water systems around Pakitza (Fig. 1) in detail during two months, November 1990 and June 1993.

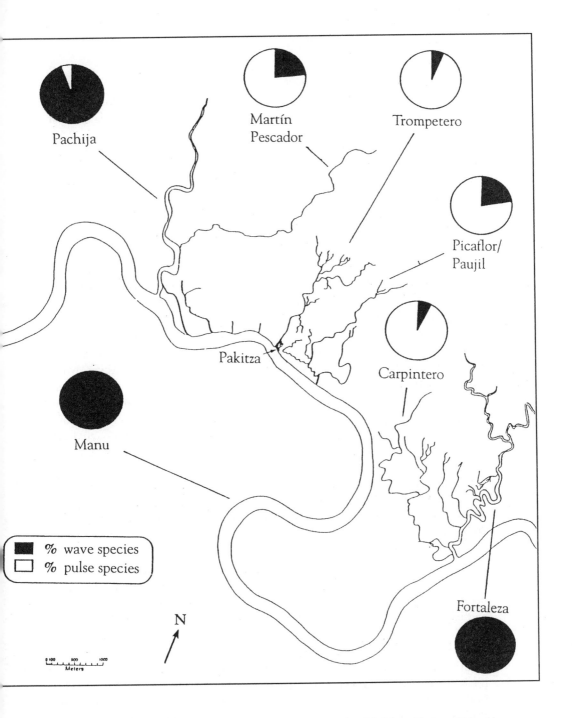

Fig. 1.– The permanent waters in the area around Pakitza, Peru (modified from Erwin and Venable, 1996). Pie-charts are used to represent the relative numbers of wave-(black shaded area) and pulse-type (white-shaded area) electric fishes in each stream. In the faster-flowing Río Manu and Quebradas Pachija and Fortaleza, 94 - 99% of the electric fish were wave-type species. In contrast, within the smaller and slower streams, Quebradas Martin Pescador, Picaflor/Paujil, Trompetero and Carpintero, the vast majority (78 - 93 %) of the electric fishes were pulse-type species.

Open-gallery, high-flow streams:

Quebrada Pachija flows into the Río Manu approximately 3 km upstream (west) of Pakitza (Fig. 1). Near its mouth, this stream is 40-50 m wide and fast-flowing within a stream bed composed of coarse sand. Within the lower 2 km, Pachija has a rather constant flow but wanders and shifts course greatly, continuously undercutting its banks and vegetation on the outer banks and depositing sandy bars to form new inner banks. The transitional shrub, *Tessaria*, rapidly colonizes these newly formed banks. The stream's sand and clay banks in this area rise ca. 2-4 m high. Upstream, the river's course is less wandering. Here, the river's sloping walls rise 4-6 m, consist mostly of clay, and are seldom undercut. The river bottom remains shifting sand. Approximately 4 km upstream from its mouth, the river bottom becomes structured with large clay rocks giving rise to small areas of more rapidly moving water. The river lies within, but is not covered by, a mature forest. In the rainy season, the river overflows its banks near the mouth and creates temporary (1-7 days) várzea forest.

Quebrada Fortaleza joins the Manu approximately 4 km downriver (southeast) from Pakitza (Fig. 1). Like Pachija, this is a wide sandy-bottom stream that is shallow in the dry season. There are areas of cobbled bottom, however, which allow formation of alternating pools and riffles. The surrounding forest is mature, but does not cover the stream. The banks of Quebrada Fortaleza rise to 6 - 10 m, thus preventing the river from overflowing its banks in the rainy season. The rainy season of 1992-3 left the lower 2 - 3 km of Quebrada Fortaleza deeply covered with mud, and all potential cover for gymnotiform fishes was gone.

Closed-gallery, low-flow streams:

We surveyed the five smaller streams near Pakitza: Quebrada Trompetero which joins the Río Manu about 200 m upstream from Pakitza; Quebrada Picaflor/Paujil which meets the Río Manu about 1 km downstream (east) of Pakitza; and Quebrada Carpintero which lies mainly atop a plateau ca. 3 km southeast of Pakitza and empties into Quebrada Fortaleza about 2 km upstream from its mouth (Fig. 1). In general, these are small, mud- and cobble-bottom streams alternating between rocky riffles and sandy pools. They are enclosed within a mature canopy and experience only relatively minor seasonal changes. Quebradas Trompetero and Picaflor/Paujil are often scoured by rains, but do not flood their banks, whereas Quebrada Carpintero forms long-term (weeks to months) várzea forest. The mouth and lowest 1 km of Quebrada Picaflor/Paujil is an area where no riffles and pools are formed. It has very steep clay banks (4 m) and is susceptible to flooding from the Río Manu as described below. Another small stream, Quebrada Martin Pescador, was discovered only recently, and although we made a listening survey of approximately 4 km of the stream, we did not consider it in our limnological analysis. Quebrada Martin Pescador empties into Quebrada Pachija about 1 km upstream from Quebrada Pachija's confluence with the Río Manu, or about 3 km northwest of Pakitza. In overall structure, it resembles Quebradas Trompetero and Picaflor/Paujil.

We observed little invasion by Río Manu waters into most of these streams. Quebradas Pachija and Fortaleza have high flow rates and, when the Río Manu rises, only a limited intrusion of Manu water into the mouths of these rivers occurs. Most often, the Río Manu simply blocks the quebrada's outflow, causing short-term fluctuations in the height (depth) of the lower sections of these quebradas. The smaller streams, Quebradas Carpintero and Trompetero, flow into the Río Manu with a relatively large elevational drop near their mouths. Thus the Río Manu's level has little impact on these streams. Quebrada Picaflor/Paujil was the stream most invaded by the Río Manu. When the Río Manu rises, a large intrusion of water flows into Picaflor/Paujil increasing its depth by up to 2 m.

RESULTS

The streams flowing into the Río Manu change rapidly both within and between seasons. Sandy rivers change course over a number of years, eroding banks, and drowning floating trees and other vegetation. This debris provides ideal habitat for many gymnotiforms but its transient nature has a profound effect on the associated gymnotiform communities. A portion of stream that had several hundred fish one day may have a substantial reduction in population after a heavy rain (up to 5 cm in a day). One example of these sorts of changes, occurred in Quebrada Fortaleza, where after the rainy season in 1993, the river mouth and ca. 2 km upstream was choked by clay sediment causing an almost complete loss of benthic organisms and the larger animals that feed on them. Similarly, the mouth of the Quebrada Pachija was in constant flux, changing many meters in size and position from one season to the next. Although we are presenting glimpses of a very dynamic system, some general trends can be seen.

LIMNOLOGY

Because successful breeding is the major factor involved in species diversity, we examined environmental variables known to strongly influence gonadal development in many species of gymnotiforms. These factors (temperature, conductivity, and pH) are summarized for all the streams in Table I. In general, open-gallery streams had higher daytime temperatures than closed-gallery streams, most streams had near neutral pH, and the higher-flow streams had the highest conductivity. The Secchi depth, and hence water clarity, was lowest in the Río Manu. The open gallery streams were wide, sometimes deep, and had high flow rates. Closed-gallery streams were narrower, had lower flow rates, and alternating areas of riffles and pools. Flow rates were estimated by multiplying average water velocity by the mean stream depth and width. This may overestimate the flows for closed-gallery streams in which the water velocity and stream depth varies from riffles to pools and our measured values are probably a bit high as affected by our choice of measurement sites (Table I). Never-the-less, a clear difference in flow rates is seen between the closed gallery and open gallery streams. An important variable that we were unable to measure is the variability of these flow rates from day to day and season to season.

Stream-type	Open-gallery			Closed-gallery		
Streams	Manu	Pachija	Fortaleza	Trompetero	Picaflor/Paujil	Carpintero
Temperature (°C)	23.5-24.4	24.4-26.8	26.2-29.4	23.7-26.2	23.4-25.6	21.8-23.0
pH	7.5	7.0-8.0	7.0-8.0	6.2-6.8	7.2-7.5	6.0-6.5
Conductivity (µS/cm)	163	195	272	26	104	17
Secchi Depth (cm)	13	43	104	>83	>130	78
Velocity (cm/s)	>200	74.8	36.3	27.3*	40.1*	18.8*
Mean Stream Depth(cm)		39.7±5.9	104.4±21.1	25.6±4.6	57.0±10.7	20.7±4.7
Mean Stream Wisth (m)		19.1±1.0	14.2±1.6	3.7±0.3	4.4±0.4	1.5±0.2
Flow (m³/sec)	>100	5.7	5.4	0.3	1.0	0.1

Table I : Limnology of the Streams

*velocity measured in riffles

SPECIES DIVERSITY

We have identified eight species of electric fish in the Pakitza area. These are *Apteronotus albifrons*, *A. bonapartii*, *Eigenmannia macrops*, *E. virescens*, *Gymnotus carapo*, *Sternopygus macrurus*, *Sternarchorhynchus sp.* and a new hypopmid species (Fig. 2). The last two species are new to the literature and undescribed.

Gymnotus carapo (Fig. 2a) was found in the low-flow rate streams, most commonly within the uppermost portions investigated, about 2-4 km above the mouth of the stream. The individuals ranged in size from 5.3-19.0 cm and in weight from 1.0-22.0 gm (n=13). No animals with mature gonads were found in either the wet or the dry season, and there were no signs of sexual dimorphism in morphology or EOD. Their EODs were triphasic pulse-type discharges with a peak-power frequency ranging from 1270 - 2832 Hz (mean = 1796 ± 159 SE) and a pulse duration of 1.0 - 1.5 ms.

The undescribed hypopomid (Fig. 2b) was found within the lower 1 - 2 km of the closed-gallery streams. They ranged in size from 4.0 - 14.2 cm and weighed 1.0 - 6.0 gm. Animals were gravid at the onset of the rainy season. The ovaries had a distribution of eggs in various states of maturation, the largest being golden colored and 0.75 - 1.2 mm in size, with immature eggs being whitish and smaller (0.3 - 0.45 mm). Testes of the mature males were 4.5 - 7.5 mm along their long

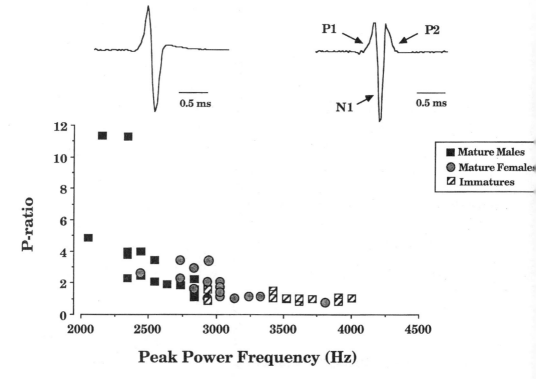

Fig. 3.– The hypopomid species has a sexually-dimorphic, triphasic EOD consisting of two positive phases (P1 and P2) and one negative phase (N1). The height of the two positive phases was measured and the ratio plotted as a function of the peak-power frequency and the animal's sex. Mature males have a P1/P2 ratio that is greater than 1.0 and a relatively low peak-power frequency. The inset at the left shows the EOD from a mature male. Note, that the third phase (P2) is almost absent. Immature animals and females have a P1/P2 ratio around 1.0 and a higher peak-power frequency. An EOD from an immature animal is shown in the inset at the right. Note P1 and P2 are almost equal in height.

frequency of adult animals but within the second harmonic of smaller, immature animals. Too few sexually mature specimens were captured to determine if a sexual dimorphism in the EOD was present.

Apteronotus albifrons (Fig. 2g) was found in open-gallery streams. Our specimens ranged from 7.7-19.3 cm in length and 2-34 gm in weight (n = 7). Two animals (one male and one female) were captured in breeding condition at the beginning of the rainy season. The ovaries had eggs in various states of maturation, the largest eggs were golden colored and 1.2 mm in size. The female's EOD had a higher fundamental frequency (1465 Hz) than did the male's (1289 Hz). Juvenile fish had a mean EOD frequency of 1240.3 ± 9.8 Hz SE (n = 3). During the dry season, all of the adults had regressed ovaries and both juvenile and immature animals had lower EOD frequencies (mean = 1074.5 ± 56.3 Hz SE; n = 4).

Two specimens of *A. bonapartii* (Fig. 2h) were found in the floating vegetation and debris in the Río Manu and did not have mature gonads during the dry season. These animals we-re dark gray with a black band at the margin of their anal fins. They were 11.5 and 11.7 cm long and weighed 5.0 and 6.9 gm, and had peak-power EOD frequencies of 2734.4 (the second harmonic, which had more power) and 1562.5 Hz (the first harmonic), respectively.

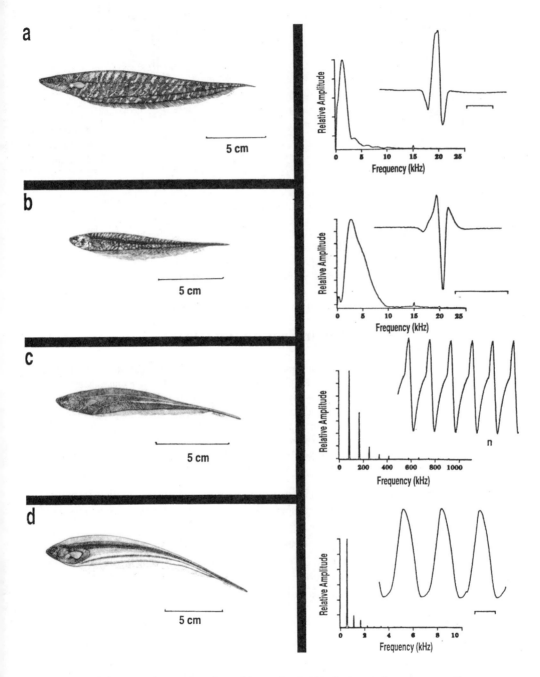

Fig. 2.– *Eight species of gymnotiform electric fish were found within the rivers and streams surrounding Pakitza, Peru. Drawings are on the left and representative EODs and power spectra are on the right. Bars = 1 ms.*

a) *Gymnotus carapo* is a pulse-type species with a triphasic EOD. This species is most commonly found in the slow-moving streams, ca. 2-4 km upstream.

b) The hypopomid species also has a triphasic pulse-type EOD, but its EOD is sexually dimorphic (see Fig. 3 for male and female EODs). This species is most commonly found in the slow-moving streams, ca. 1-2 km upstream. Bar = 1 ms.

c) *Sternopygus macrurus* is a wave-type species that is found in all of the rivers surrounding Pakitza.

d) *Eigenmannia virescens* is a wave-type species that is found in the slower-moving streams.

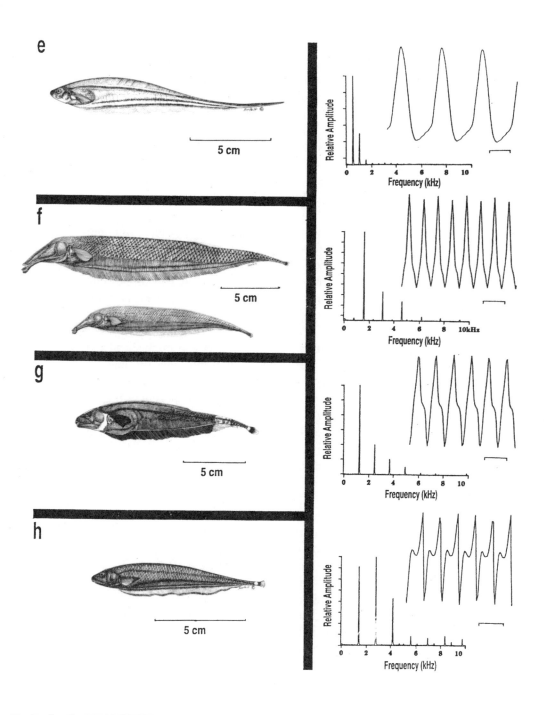

e) *Eigenmannia macrops* is a wave-type species found in the faster-moving streams.

f) *Sternarchorhynchus sp.* is a high-frequency wave-type species found in faster-moving streams. Upper drawing shows a mature male with large protruding teeth, while the lower drawing represents an immature with no protruding teeth.

g) *Apteronotus albifrons* is a high-frequency wave-type species also found in the faster-moving streams.

h) *Apteronotus bonapartii* is a wave species that is found in faster-moving streams.

axis. No external differences between the sexes were observed, but there was a sexual dimorphism in the wave-shape and peak-power frequency of the EOD. This species has a triphasic EOD with two positive phases (P1 and P2) and one negative phase (N1, Fig 3 inset). Mature males have a P1/P2 ratio greater than one and a relatively low peak-power frequency. Females and immatures, on the other hand, have a P1/P2 closer to 1 and a higher peak-power frequency (Fig. 3). Over-all, the peak-power frequency ranges from 2148-4004 Hz with a mean of 2978 ± 58 Hz (SE) and the duration of their pulses ranges from 0.6-1.25 ms with the mean for males = 0.93 ± 0.04 ms SE (n = 26) and that of females and juveniles = 0.79 ± 0.03 ms SE (n = 37).

Sternopygus macrurus (Fig 2c) was found in all streams. The specimens captured ranged from 5.7- 21.4 cm in length and weighed from 1-15 gm. Mature adults are difficult to capture, often residing in deeply undercut banks and were thus probably undersampled. None of the specimens we captured had mature gonads, possibly reflecting this sampling bias. *S. macrurus* is a wave-type fish and the peak-power frequency of the captured animals ranged from 50-195 Hz with a mean of 111.6 ± 11.5 Hz SE (n = 15).

In the Pakitza area, *Eigenmannia virescens* (Fig. 2d) is dark gray on the head and dorsal surface with distinctive black stripes at the mid-line and above the anal fin. This species is found predominantly in the closed-gallery streams and was in breeding condition at the beginning of the rainy season. Our specimens ranged from 11.8 - 18.7 cm in length and 5 - 9 gm in weight (n = 7). The ovaries of mature females contained eggs in various states of maturation, the largest being golden colored and 1.0 - 1.5 mm in size. The one mature male captured had a peak-power frequency of 351 Hz while the females ranged from 488-566 Hz with a mean of 510.6 ± 14.5 Hz SE (n = 6).

The second *Eigenmannia* species, *E. macrops* (Fig. 2e), had lighter body pigmentation and a distinctly larger eye, ca. twice the diameter of the eye of *E. virescens*. In further contrast to *E. virescens*, *E. macrops* was found only in the high flow-rate, open-gallery streams and had a range of EOD frequencies (507-781 Hz) slightly higher than *E. virescens*. Our specimens ranged from 10.2 - 17.2 cm in length and 3-10 gm in weight (n= 7). Not enough sexually mature specimens were captured to determine if there was any sexual dimorphism.

Sternarchorhynchus sp. (Fig. 2f) lived in the fastest flowing water sampled; most adult specimens were captured from a single rocky rapids within Quebrada Pachija. A large number of fry and small juveniles were found within the collected floating debris in fast water; along the edges of the Río Manu. Specimens in these combined samples ranged from 3.0 - 25.5 cm in length and from 2 - 38 gm in weight. Large, mature males have a protruding lower jaw with radiating (ca. 2 - 3 mm) spike-like teeth. Immatures and females have only small, recessed teeth on the lower jaw. These are high frequency, wave-type fish with peak-power EOD frequencies ranging from (977-2832 Hz) with a mean of 1608.5 ± 160.5 Hz SE (n= 14). A variety of EOD types were observed in this species (Fig. 4). Fourier spectra of these EODs showed that their peak power lies within the fundamental

DISTRIBUTION

The number of gymnotiform fish on a 500 m transect increased as a function of the distance from the mouth of the stream: at the mouth (0-1 fish /transect), 1 km upstream a mean of 74 ± 21 fish SE / 500 m , and at 2-4 km upstream a mean of 109 ± 17 fish SE/ 500 m (Fig. 5). Quebrada Carpintero had the highest number of fish / 500 m (293) but any gradient of densities above the mouth was not assessed because the stream was primarily a flat, flooded area (an Aguajal) without a clear upstream or downstream. The lowest density of fishes was found on the Quebrada Picaflor/Paujil with 33 fish / 500 m 1-2 km upstream and 76 fish / 500 m 4 km upstream. The remaining three streams (Quebradas Trompetero, Pachija, and Fortaleza) had in-termediate densi-ties that were all similar (ca. 75-140 / 500 m), even though these streams differed markedly in size and flow rates.

Fish densities with in the Río Manu and Quebrada Martin Pescador were asses-sed only with listening transects, because the Río Manu was difficult to work in and Quebrada Martin Pescador was only newly discovered. In the Río Manu, we made listening transects of 1 km along the edges (this included beach and submerged or floating vegetation) and within the central part of the river. A

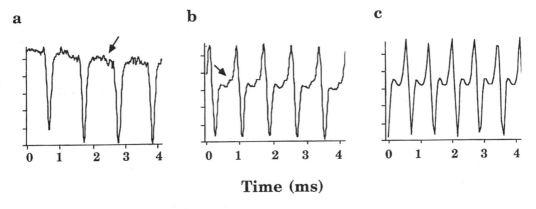

Fig. 4.– *The EODs of Sternarchorhynchus show a great deal of heterogeneity that may reflect changes with age, sex and/or activity pattern. a) A 3 cm fry has a somewhat 'noisy' (arrow) low frequency, sinusoidal EOD. b) The EOD of a young immature (10.4 cm) has a smoother pattern with a weak additional phase (arrow). c) The EOD of an 18 cm adult is smooth and regular and shows the additional phase more clearly. Another adult EOD, shown in Figure 2f, lacks the extra phase.*

morning transect identified the fishes' daytime refuge and an evening transect identified the area of the river used at night. Electric fish were found along the river's banks in floating and submerged vegetation during both transects and were never found to inhabit the central portion of the stream.

We found a strong correlation between the stream-type and the type of electric fish present (Fig. 1). Wave-type electric fish predominated in the high flow-rate,

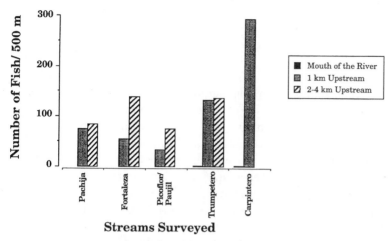

Fig. 5.– *The density of electric fish increases with distance from the stream's mouth. In each stream studied, the number of fish /500 m are shown. Averaging all streams, we found 0-1 fish /transect at the mouth, 74 ±21 (mean ± SE) at 1 km upstream, and 109 ± 17 at 2-4 km upstream.*

open-gallery streams (94-99.4%), whereas pulse-type fish predominated in the low flow-rate, closed-gallery streams (78-93%). This pattern was also maintained in Quebrada Martin Pescador, where we carried out only an informal listening transect, with the pulse-type fish comprising 77% of the population, and on the Río Manu, where a 1 km listening-transect yielded only 2 pulse-type fish out of more than 200 electric fish. Both of these pulse-type fish were found in shallower water close to the beach. Streams, such as Quebrada Picaflor/Paujil, that had direct access to the Río Manu, had fewer pulse-type fish (79% total fish / 500 m) within 1-2 km of their mouth, whereas streams that had no direct access to the Río Manu, such as Quebrada Carpintero, had a high density of pulse-type fish (93% fish / 500 m) throughout the stream.

Although almost every species could be found in each stream, there appeared to be microhabitat specializations by certain species. The pulse-type fish (G. *carapo* and the hypopomid) were found in the slower moving streams. This distribution was even further restricted, however, with the hypopomid predominating in areas 1-2 km from the stream's mouth and G. *carapo* dominating in areas above this. E. *virescens* inhabited slower-moving streams while E. *macrops* was found only in the faster-moving streams. Some species were found in only very limited areas. For example, adult *Sternarchorhynchus sp.* were captured from among boulders in only one section of rapids in the Quebrada Pachija. Young *Sternarchorhynchus* and our only two specimens of A. *bonapartii*, were found in floating debris that had collected in vegetation overhanging into the rapidly-flowing Río Manu.

DISCUSSION

Approximately 2,500-3,000 species of fish inhabit the Amazonian drainage (Goulding, 1980) of which 100 to 150 are gymnotiforms. We seek to understand and explain patterns of species distribution and diversity within the gymnotiforms that might also be useful for understanding larger issues of biodiversity in neotropical freshwaters. To this end, we have begun by documenting the electric fish species present in the permanent waters within a pristine middle elevation portion of the headwaters of the Amazon on the Río Manu. There are at least eight species of gymnotiform fish at Pakitza, Peru. Wave-type species, which emit a constant-frequency, wave-like electric signal dominate the larger streams, which are characterized by an open canopy, wider and deeper channels, and greater stream flows. Pulse-type species, produce variably timed pulsatile EODs and are found predominantly within the smaller streams, which have a closed canopy, lower flow rates, and are generally associated with alternating areas of pools and riffles.

Working over a five year period, Ortega (1996) attempted a complete inventory in the Manu Bioreserve and has found ca. 210 species of fishes. This represents a high level of species richness in a relatively small area when compared with studies carried out in other portions of the Amazon drainage. For example, with a deepwater trawling program, Barletta and Chao (1993) have found 70 species of fishes at the confluence of the Río Negro and Río Solimões in Brazil. Ibarra and Stewart (1989) sampled a 330 km stretch on each of two parallel headwater tributaries of the upper Amazon, the Río Napo and Río Aguarico. In sampling 19 separate sandy beach sites they found a total 208 species of fishes, 38 of which were rare species represented by single specimens. Finally, Stewart et al. (1987) summarized data on diverse habitats in the Río Napo, listing 473 species.

How does the species richness of gymnotiforms that we found near Pakitza compare with other sites? For such a comparison, we would prefer to compare similar fishing methods and use statistical techniques that would allow a conversion of catch/unit area into an index of diversity. Our data are qualitatively different from much of what has come before, however. Our work in assessing the local gymnotiform community was greatly facilitated by the use of fish-detectors to discover electric fish in otherwise difficult to sample habitats. Most traditional fishing techniques, in contrast, tend to undersample the smaller and the more cryptic gymnotiforms by concentrating their effort in the open water and in the daylight hours. For example, Ortega (unpublished data) captured only 20 gymnotiform specimens in Pakitza in two years of sampling with seines, gill nets, hand-nets and rotenone. It was relatively easy, however, with the use of a fish detector, to show large population numbers of gymnotiforms in the stationary debris along the edges of the same rivers. For this reason, our data is best compared with only a small number of other studies that have used special techniques to intensively study relatively small areas. A few studies that we might use for comparison, have employed specialized trawls that allow work in more confined areas and appear to preferentially sample smaller individuals. For example in deepwater habitats, Lopez-Rojas et al. (1984) used such a trawl extensively over a large area in the Orinoco River delta (elevation 20-30 m) and reported that gymnotiforms comprised 25 of the 59 (42%) species caught. Lasso and Castroviejo (1992) intensively trawled a 6 km stretch of the Caño Guaritico in the upper Apure drainage of Venezuela (elevation 50 m) characterized by a seasonally flooded, gallery forest. Their catch comprised 42 total species, 11 of which (26%) were gymnotiforms, second only to the siluriforms (61%). At the family level, the three most well-represented groups comprised the Loricariidae (10 spps.) and Pimelodidae (9 spps.) and the gymnotiform Apteronotidae (7 spps.). Perhaps due to the fact that they sampled only the main river, they found only one pulse-type species. In a more wide-ranging survey of the upper Apure drainage (elevation 30-50 m), Provenzano (1993) found 23 species of gymnotiforms.

Saul (1975) used a variety of traditional fishing techniques to intensively sample the fish community in an area of about 3 km² within the upper drainage of Ecuador's Río Aguarico (340m elevation). The area included much the same types of water systems as those we sampled at Pakitza, but only 3 out of 101 species were gymnotiforms. The catch from all areas was dominated by characoids except in the only lake sampled, where cichlids comprised 62% of the catch. The main river shared many of the same characteristics as the Río Manu, but only a single gymnotiform specimen was captured (an electric eel, *Electrophorus electricus*) out of a total of 53 species. One species of pulse-type fish, *G. carapo*, (vs. 37 species total) was found in limited numbers within a smaller river. *G. carapo* and a second pulse-type fish *Hypopomus* sp. (vs. 49 species total) were found in only slightly higher numbers in the pools and riffles of the smallest creeks. The same two species comprised 26% of the catch, however, within a swampy area (17 species total) where the muddy substrate was covered by a thick mat of decayed vegetation. It is likely that listening for gymnotiform EODs might reveal the presence of several wave-type species in these rivers and streams.

What biological factors might correlate with the number of gymnotiform species present? We briefly address several of these below: food resources, spawning and nursery areas, and predation.

Food Resources

The primary source of food for most electric fish is aquatic insects (Ellis, 1913, Saul 1975, Lundberg and Stager 1985). Although most gymnotiforms appear to be rather generalist consumers of aquatic insect larvae, some evidence for specialization that might allow niche-separation has been found. Ellis (1913) showed a correlation between the relative size of *G. carapo* and the types of food eaten; the smallest fish eat dipteran (chironomid) larvae, those between 10 and 24 cm eat mainly diptera and trichoptera and larger fish eat primarily shrimp and small fishes. Lundberg et al. (1987) and Lundberg and Mago-Leccia (1986) showed a high degree of specialization for zooplankton and small dipteran larvae by four species of the gymnotiform genus *Rhabdolichops*. A higher proportion of larger insect larvae were found in the diet of a fifth congener. One might thus hypothesize that a rich variety of aquatic food sources, be they zooplankton, insects, or fish, might favor a correspondingly rich diversity in the electric fish fauna. How do these factors relate to the Pakitza area? Ortega (1996) has demonstrated that the local fish fauna is highly diverse. Only one of eight gymnotiform species found at Pakitza (*Gymnotus*) is pisciverous, however, and thus the density of other fish may not play a large role in our study as prey items for gymnotiforms. A primary determinant of benthic invertebrate diversity is probably the richness in variety of hydrologic microzones (Statzner and Higler 1986). We have begun to characterize the hydrologic zones available to aquatic forms at Pakitza in the present report. How these relate to benthic invertebrate zonation near Pakitza is not yet known. Many aquatic invertebrates, however, are juvenile life stages of insects that emerge to breed terrestrially. The terrestrial insect community at Pakitza is extremely diverse and abundant (Erwin, pers. comm,) and thus, although the data is still quite incomplete, the aquatic larvae that serve as potential food sources are likely to be impressively diverse also.

SPAWNING AND NURSERY GROUNDS

The variety of breeding, spawning and nursery grounds, may also be important determining factors in electric fish diversity. In the lower reaches of the Amazon basin, the elevational gradient is quite small and seasonal flooding rises above the river banks producing vast expanses of várzea forest, swamps and areas rich in floating vegetation. These areas are ideal breeding and nursery grounds. Many species of electric fish breed during or at the onset of the rainy season when this flooded area provides an increase in food and protection for the young. The Río Manu is at a higher elevation (300-350 m), drains more rapidly and does not have large-scale seasonal flooding. During the rainy season, the Río Manu may rise 3-4 m in a few days causing the smaller rivers to rise and temporarily flood their banks, but this flooding is of limited spatial and temporal extent. Thus the only high quality, long-term breeding sites for gymnotiforms near Pakitza are the relatively small flooded areas such as Quebrada Carpintero, which, perhaps not coincidentally, had the highest density of gymnotiforms in our sample area. We found a relatively large number of fry and juvenile fish within the floating debris that was caught within the tangles of overhanging vegetation along the banks of the Río Manu.

PREDATION AND REFUGIA

Seasonal flooding and its associated habitat expansion provides many and diverse opportunities for adult gymnotiform fishes to find daytime cover. In the deeper rivers of the lower Amazon and Orinoco basins, such as the Ríos Apure, Negro, Solimões and Amazon, large numbers of gymnotiforms inhabit the central depths (Barletta and Chao, 1993; Provenzano, 1993). This is not true for the shallower Río Manu, however, where the population is probably limited, in part, to the edge vegetation and associated debris, and larger logs that temporarily provide cover in midstream. Thus in terms of daytime refugia, the Pakitza area may be more limited than areas of widespread flooding such as the Pantanal in Brazil, Pacaya Samiria in Peru or the Apure District in Venezuela where floating vegetation dominates the aquatic systems.

Predation may play an even more direct role in determining the distribution of electric fishes. Catfish are probably the most important predators on electric fish. They are both numerous and widely distributed, and, for at least several species of large catfish (e.g. *Zungaro*, *Pseudopimelodus*, *Pseudoplatystoma* and *Brachyplatystoma*), electric fish are an important part their diet (Reid, 1983, and C. Marrero, pers. comm.). Like the gymnotiforms, catfish are nocturnal. They are highly electrosensitive, using this sense as a primary means for prey localization (Kalmijn, 1974), and are able to locate and possibly eavesdrop on the EODs of electric fish. We hypothesize that these electrosensitive predators prey selectively on pulse-type gymnotiforms, thus to a large extent removing them from the larger rivers. In general, pulse-type EODs contain more low frequency components than do wave-type EODs (Fig. 2). Catfish are physiologically most sensitive to these low frequency electrical signals (Peters and Buwalda 1972; Kalmijn, 1974; Roth, 1975; DeWeille. 1983). Thus the low frequency component of the pulse-fish EODs would make these fish more susceptible to predation by large catfish resident in the large rivers.

If wave-type electric fish are less susceptible to predation than are pulse-type fish, why are there pulse-type fish at all? One hypothesis (Stoddard, pers. comm.) suggests that there is a high metabolic cost to producing a high frequency EOD. Pulse-type fish may lessen this cost by varying their discharge rate through the daily cycle, something wave-type fish do not do (Hagedorn and Heiligenberg, 1985). For example, *H. occidentalis* has an average daytime EOD frequency of 10-15 Hz , and an average nighttime EOD frequency of 100-150 Hz (measured during nighttime active periods; Hagedorn, unpublished data). Wave-type fish maintain a high EOD repetition rate, thus sampling their environment at a high rate, throughout the day-night cycle. The pulse-type fish may predominate in the smaller streams by avoiding large silurid predators and possibly by being better adapted physiologically to the more variable environments presented by smaller streams (Machado-Allison 1993). For example, *H. occidentalis* is a facultative air-breather (Hagedorn, unpublished data) and may survive in low flow regimes not conducive to survival of wave-type species.

What can and should be done to ensure high future levels of species richness? Erwin (1991) suggested that a cladistic approach to species diversity would allow identification of centers of radiation or "evolutionary fronts". These areas could be given higher priority for future protection. Centers of radiation may or may not coincide for various taxa, however. Pakitza is perhaps one of the world's richest areas for butterflies (Lamas et al. 1991), and has a high diversity of fish, but electric fish appear to be of only moderate diversity. A full cladistic treatment for these groups has not yet been undertaken, but these results suggest that when identifying centers of radiation, it is important to integrate information from many taxa and include both terrestrial and aquatic systems.

In a fully functional ecosystem reserve, both extinction and speciation will continue to play important roles. Therefore, beyond the listing of species and subsequent analysis using cladistics or other techniques, we seek to understand factors that support and even create species diversity. Only with this sort of information in hand, can we hope to properly identify and design future biological reserves.

ACKNOWLEDGEMENTS

We would like to thank several people for their help in the field and in the laboratory. Glenn Hagedorn suffered through an entire season of insect bites and parasites at Pakitza helping in all phases of the field work. Terry Takahashi, Randy Zelick, Walter Heiligenberg and Carl Hopkins generously lent us equipment for the field and Randy helped in the analysis of the data. We thank the reviewers for their time and thoughtful comments. Ellen Seefeldt created the beautiful biological drawings. Hernán Ortega showed us many field sites and helped in collecting the animals, as did Wilfredo Valles, Abelardo Sandoval, Eduardo Ticona and Eduardo Vega. Marsha Sitnik, Judy Sansbury, Don Wilson and Sally Keller organized equipment and managed the finances. The people of BIOLAT made the whole trip possible.

LITERATURE CITED

Barletta, M. and N.L. Chao. 1993. Benthic fishes of lower Río Negro and its confluence with Río Solimões-Amazonas, Central Amazonia, Brazil. Amer. Soc. of Ichthyol. and Herpetol. Abstr. 1993: 78.

Bratton, B. O. and B., Kramer. 1988. Intraspecific variability of the pulse-type discharges of the African electric fishes, *Pollimyrus isidori* and *Petrocephalus bovei* (Mormyridae, Teleostei), and their dependence upon water conductivity. Exp. Biol. 47: 227-238.

DeWeille, J.R. 1983. Electrosensory information processing by lateral line lobe neurons of catfish investigated by means of white noise cross-correlation. Comp. Biochem. Physiol. 74: 677-680.

Ellis, M.M. 1913. The gymnotid eels of tropical America. Mem. Carnegie Mus 6:109-145.

Erwin, T.L. 1991. An evolutionary basis for conservation strategies. Science 253 :750-752.

Gentry, A.H. 1988. Tree species richness of upper Amazonian forests. Proc. Natl. Acad. Sci. 85: 156-159.

Goulding, M.M. 1980. The fishes and the forest, explorations in Amazonian natural history. pp. 280, Univ. of Calif. Press: Berkeley.

Hagedorn, M. 1988. Ecology and behavior of a pulse-type electric fish, *Hypopomus occidentalis* (Gymnotiformes, Hypopomidae), in a fresh water stream in Panama. Copeia 2 :324-335.

Ibarra M. and D. J. Stewart. 1989. Longitudinal zonation of sandy beach fishes in the Napo river basin, eastern Ecuador. Copeia 1989(2):364-381.

Janzen, D.H. 1988. The most endangered tropical ecosystem. In: Biodiversity, E.O. Wilson and F. M. Peter (eds), pp.130-137, Washington: National Academy Press.

Kalmijn, A.J. 1974. The detection of electric fields from inanimate and animate sources other than electric organs. In: Handbook of Sensory

Physiology, Vol. III/3 (Ed. by A. Fessard), Springer, New York, pp. 147-200.

Kirschbaum, F. 1979. Reproduction of the weakly electric fish *Eigenmannia virescens* (Rhamphichthyidae, Teleostei) in captivity. I. Control of gonadal recrudescence and regression by environmental factors. Behav. Ecol. Sociobiol. 4 :331-355.

Lamas, G., R. K. Robbins, and D. J. Harvey. 1991. Preliminary survey of the butterfly fauna of Pakitza, Parque Nacional Del Manu, Peru, with an estimate of its species richness. Publ. Mus. Hist. Nat. UNMSM (A) 40:1-19.

Lasso, C., and J. Castroviejo 1992. Composition, abundance and biomass of the benthic fish fauna from the Guaritico river of a Venezuelan floodplain. Annals Limnol. 28(1):71-84.

Lopez-Rojas H., J.G. Lundberg, and E. Marsh. 1984. Design and operation of a small trawling apparatus for use with dugout canoes. N. Am. Jour. Fish. Manag. 4:331-334.

Lundberg, J.G. and F. Mago-Leccia. 1986. A review of R*habdolichops* (Gymnotiformes, Sternopygidae), a genus of South American freshwater fishes, with descriptions of four new species. Proc. Acad. Nat. Sci. Philadelphia. 138(1):53-85.

Lundberg, J.G., W.M. Lewis, J.F. Saunders, and F. Mago-Leccia. 1987. A major food web component in the Orinoco River channel: evidence from planktivorous electric fishes. Science 237: 81-83.

Mago-Leccia, F. 1978. Los peces de la familia Sternopygidae de Venezuela. Acta Científica Venezolana, 29 (1): 1-89.

Ortega, H. (1996) Ictiofauna del Parque Nacional Manu, Peru. In: Biodiversity of Pakitza, Manu Park, Peru, (This volume)

Peters, R.C., and R. J. A. Buwalda. 1972. Frequency response of the electroreceptors of the catfish, *Ictalurus nebulosus*. J. Comp. Physiol. 79: 29-38.

Provenzano, F. 1993. The benthic fish-fauna of the Apure River, Estado Apure, Venezuela. I.- Gymnotoidei and Loricariidae. Amer. Soc. of Ichthyol. and Herpetol. Abstr. 1993: 252

Raven, P.H. 1988. Our diminishing tropical forests. In: Biodiversity, E.O. Wilson and F. M. Peter (eds), pp.119-122, Washington: National Academy Press.

Reid, S. 1983. La biología de los bagres rayados *Pseudoplatystoma fasciatum* y *P. tigrinum* en la cuenca del rio Apure-Venezuela. Revista UNELLEZ de Cinecia y Technologia 1:13-41.

Roth, A. 1975. Electroreception in catfish: Temporal and spatial integration in receptors and central neurons. Exp. Brain Res. 23 (5):179.

Saul W. G. 1975. An ecological study of fishes at a site in upper amazonian Ecuador. Proc. Acad. Nat. Sci. Philadelphia 127(12):93-134.

Statzner, B. and B. Higler. 1986. Stream hydraulics as a major determinant of benthic invertebrate zonation patterns. Freshwater Biol. 16:127-139.

Stewart, D.J., R. Barriga and M. Ibarra. 1987. Ictiofauna de la cuenca del Río Napo, Ecuador oriental : Lista anotada de especies. Politécnica 12: 10-63.

Stewart, D.J. and M. Ibarra. 1993. Comparison of deep-river and adjacent sandy-beach assemblages in the lowlands of Eastern Ecuador. Amer. Soc. of Ichthyol. and Herpetol. Abstr.1993: 295.

Wilson, E.O. 1988. The current state of biological diversity. In: Biodiversity, E.O. Wilson and F. M. Peter (eds), pp.3-20, Washington: National Academy Press.

Annotated Checklist of the Amphibians and Reptiles of Pakitza, Manu National Park Reserve Zone, with Comments on the Herpetofauna of Madre de Dios, Peru

Víctor R. Morales

Departamento de Herpetología, Museo de Historia Natural, Universidad Nacional Mayor de San Marcos, Apartado 14-0434, Lima-14, Perú. Current Address: Calle B 135, Urb Humbolt, Lima-18, Perú.

Roy W. McDiarmid

National Biological Survey, Division of Amphibians and Reptiles, National Museum of Natural History, Washington, D.C. 20560, USA.

ABSTRACT

One hundred and twenty eight species of amphibians and reptiles were collected during the BIOLAT project at Pakitza, Manu National Park, Madre de Dios, Perú. The recorded herpetofauna includes the following species diversity: 1 salamander, 67 frogs, 5 turtles, 1 crocodilian, 1 amphisbaenian, 22 lizards, and 31 snakes. Of these, 10 species (7 frogs, 1 lizard and 2 snakes) are either new or unassignable to species. Species were recorded from 14 habitat types and 55% occur in dissected alluvial terrace forests, 47% in old alluvial terrace forests and 37% in upper floodplain flooded forests. Forest leaf litter was the most frequent of the 15 microhabitats used; 26% of the amphibian species and 42% of the reptile species were recorded in forest litter. Based on long-term sampling at four sites in Madre de Dios, the herpetofauna of that region consists of 113 species of amphibians and 118 species of reptiles. In a pair-wise comparison of faunas at all four sites, the Pakitza amphibian fauna was more similar to that from Cocha Cashu, while the Pakitza reptile fauna shared more species with that from Tambopata. Some of the between-site differences (especially for snakes) detected in this analysis are attributed to inadequate sampling; others apparently are the consequence of physiographic, ecological and historic differences between sites. Predictive tools developed from such studies facilitate decisions related to the conservation and maintenance of tropical diversity on both a regional and local scale.

RESUMEN

Ciento veinte y ocho especies de anfibios y reptiles fueron colec-tados en Pakitza, Parque Nacional de Manu, Madre de Dios, Perú a través del proyecto BIOLAT. El registro de la diversidad de la herpetofauna incluye las siguientes especies: 1 salamandra, 67 ranas, 5 tortugas, 1 cocodrilo, 1 anfisbaénido, 22 lagartijas, y 31 culebras. De éstas, 10 especies (7 ranas, 1 lagartija y 2 culebras) serían nuevas o aún no designadas. Las especies fueron registradas en 14 tipos de hábitat: el 55% ocurre en las bosques de terraza con quebradas, el 47% en los bosques de terraza aluvial viejo y el 37% en los bosques altamente inundables. La hojarasca en el bosque fue la más frecuentada por las especies de los 15 microhábitats; el 26% fue anfibios y el 42% reptiles. Basados en los muestros largos hechos en cuatro localidades de Madre de Dios, la herpetofauna de esa región consiste de 113 especies de anfibios y 118 especies de reptiles. En una comparacíon de la herpetofauna, a manera de pares de las cuatros localidades, la fauna de anfibios de Pakitza fue más similar a la de Cocha Cashu, mientras que la fauna de reptiles de Pakitza compartió más especies con Tambopata. Algunas diferencias entre las localidades (especialmente por las culebras), encontradas en este análisis, se atribuyeron al inadecuado muestreo. Otras diferencias entre los localidades, aparentemente son a consecuencia de la fisiografía, ecología e historia. Estos estudios pueden desarrollar ayudas predictivas para facilitar las decisiones relacionadas en la conservación y al mantenimiento de la diversidad tropical a escala regional y local.

INTRODUCTION

The amphibians and reptiles of the lowland wet forests of southeastern Peru became the focus of several independent investigations beginning in 1979. Studies have been done at four different localities in the department of Madre de Dios in Amazonian Peru. Two published surveys document the herpetofauna at Cocha Cashu in Manu National Park (Rodríguez and Cadle, 1990) and at Cuzco Amazónico (Duellman and Salas, 1991). Studies not yet published include a long-term study of the herpetofauna at the Tambopata Reserve by R. W. McDiarmid and R. B. Cocroft and one on species collected in the Pampas del Heath area by W. E. Duellman and V. R. Morales. As a result of these and a few other investigations many new species from this area have been described recently (e.g., *Hyla koecklini* and *H. allenorum* Duellman and Trueb, 1989; *Scinax chiquitana* de la Riva, 1990, *S. pedromedinae* Henle, 1991, and *S. icterica* by Duellman and Wiens, 1993; *Dendrobates biolat* Morales, 1992; *Epipedobates macero* Rodríquez and Myers, 1993) and we know of several others in preparation. As a result, the herpetofauna of lowland Madre de Dios, Peru may be better known than any comparable area in Amazonian South America. This is amazing as virtually nothing was know about the composition of the amphibian and reptile fauna in this region prior to 1980.

The Biological Diversity in Latin America Project (BIOLAT) began to work on the biodiversity of this region in the Reserve Zone adjacent to Manu National Park. Studies focused on the biota in about 4,000 hectares of lowland forest near a guard station on the east side of the Rio Manu (11° 56' 39" S latitude, 071° 16' 59" W longitude). The station, Pakitza, consists of a few wooden buildings in a cleared area on a dissected terrace at about 325 m elevation. High points on this terrace may be as much as 50 -- 75 m above the present river bed. Rainfall data are not available for the site but they probably are similar to those for Cocha Cashu (2,160 mm of rain a year, Erwin, 1991, Figure 3). Erwin (1991) and others (this volume) described the area in some detail. Herein, we summarize our work on the herpetofauna as part of the integrated study of the biodiversity of the Pakitza site.

METHODS AND MATERIALS

This report is based on amphibians and reptiles collected or observed by us or colleagues working with the BIOLAT program in the vicinity of Pakitza between 1987 and 1993. The BIOLAT project began an inventory of the biological diversity of Pakitza in September 1987. George Middendorf and VRM were with the first group to work at Pakitza and together they recorded 25 species of amphibians and 30 of reptiles during 28 days. VRM returned to Pakitza the following June. Because very little rain had fallen and conditions were quite dry, he collected only 11 species in a brief (12 day) period. VRM and RWM worked the site together in the dry season in September of 1988 and again in the wet season in January and February of 1989; together they collected 59 and 54 species on the respective trips. These additions brought the known fauna at Pakitza to 58 species of amphibians and 48 species of reptiles. The most diverse collection (62 species) was obtained during two weeks in the wet season in February, 1990 when VRM worked the site with Blga. María E. Guevara (Phycology). Another collection was made by Robert P. Reynolds and the BIOLAT group in February and March of 1992; they collected 56 species and added 4 frog and 3 snake species to the list. The final sample from the Pakitza area was made in early July, 1993 by Reynolds and another BIOLAT group; that trip recorded 25 species (not including larvae) of which 2 snakes were new to the site.

Collected materials were divided equally and are in the collections of the Museo de Historia Natural, Universidad Nacional Mayor de San Marcos (MHNSM) and the National Museum of Natural History (USNM). Tape-recorded calls of many of the frog species also are on file in the sound archives in the Division of Amphibians and Reptiles, National Museum of Natural History, Washington, D.C.

Some species of reptiles (e.g., *Podocnemis unifilis*, *Caiman crocodilus*) were frequently seen along the Rio Manu but, because they are protected by international agreements and relatively difficult to sample, the few representatives of these that were captured, were identified, marked and released. For most other species, we made an effort to sample representatives of each. With only a few exceptions (e.g., *Caiman crocodilus*), the species reported in this compilation are based on voucher specimens collected during the project.

Analyses comparing the amphibian and reptile faunas among the four Madre de Dios sites were done with programs SUDIST.BAS (distance indices for SU, sampling unit, resemblance) and CLUSTER.BAS (cluster analysis for classification of SUs) using an index of similarity (IS) = (2W/A+B), where W is the number of species shared between each locality, A is the number of species at locality A, and B is the number at locality B. The Index of Similarity we used was IS' = 1 - IS with values ranging from 0 -1. When SI' is equal to 0, all species are shared between sites; when SI' equals 1, there are no species known from both sites (i.e., totally different faunas). Details about these analyses were discussed by Ludwig and Reynolds (1988).

THE HERPETOFAUNA

The taxonomy and classification used in our compilation of the Pakitza herpetofauna follows the summaries by Frost (1985, and updated through 1993) and a recent monograph on *Leptodactylus* by Heyer (1994) for amphibians; the checklists and keys by Peters and Donoso-Barros (1970) for amphisbaenians and lizards, and by Peters and Orejas-Miranda for snakes (1970), as updated by Vanzolini (1986), Frost and Etheridge (1989) and Frost (1992); the checklist by King and Burke (1989) for crocodilians and turtles. A total of 68 species of amphibians and 60 species of reptiles were sampled at Pakitza on eight different occasions during the BIOLAT project; total field time amounted to about 21 weeks scattered across all months except August, November, and December (Table 1). John E. Cadle (see Rodríquez and Cadle, 1990) made a small collection of amphibians and reptiles at Pakitza in 1984. Other than a few poorly preserved specimens in bottles at the guard station at Pakitza, the Cadle material and our collections are the first records to our knowledge from this site. When species reported from Pakitza by Rodríquez and Cadle (1990), but not collected by us in our list, are added to the compilation, the known Pakitza herpetofauna includes 69 species of amphibians and 61 species of reptiles. This list does not included specimens collected from the areas surrounding Pakitza, even though we expect that many of them occur there.

As with most other projects designed to sample the entire herpetofauna at a site, considerable more time and effort must be put into the Pakitza area before the number of recorded species reaches the numeric diversity predicted from samples taken at comparable sites elsewhere in Madre de Dios. Nevertheless, our efforts have disclosed some species that are rare or previously unrecorded from the area (e.g., *Cochranella midas*, *Dendrophidion* sp., *Rhadinaea occipitalis*, *Bothrops brazili*, *Micrurus* sp.) and small samples of a few species (e.g., *Hyla*, *Eleutherodactylus*, *Chiasmocleis*) that apparently are new to science.

HABITAT USE

Erwin (1991) identified 12 distinct forest types distributed between seasonally flooded and non-flooded forests that were accessible by trail from the Pakitza station. Each was characterized by soil type, drainage, topography, and vegetation. Erwin also recognized several kinds of open habitats (e.g., tree falls, river margins, camp clearings, etc.) and a few specific habitats defined primarily by single plant species (e.g., caña brava along the river, bamboo thickets, etc.). These different forest types and associated open areas together with certain aquatic elements comprise the primary habitats at Pakitza. Erwin defined these habitats to aid in understanding carabid beetle diversity at Pakitza. While the habitat grain for vertebrate species often is quite different from that for insects and not well understood for most tropical species of amphibians and reptiles, we recognized many of the same habitats for our analysis at Pakitza.

TABLE 1. Number of species of amphibians and reptiles collected on eight visits to Pakitza, Madre de Dios, Perú.

Amphibians and Reptiles	Sampling Visits							
	1	2	3	4	5	6	7	8
AMPHIBIA								
Caudata				1	1	1		1
Anura	25	8	39	37	39	27	33	13
REPTILIA								
Testudines	2		1	3	1	2	2	1
Crocodilia	1		1					
Amphisbaenia	1							
Sauria	14	1	11	8	9	7	9	5
Serpentes	12	2	7	5	12	6	12	5
TOTAL	55	11	59	54	62	43	56	25

1 = 1-28 October 1987; George Middendorf and Víctor R. Morales.
2 = 18-28 June 1988; Víctor R. Morales.
3 = 5-24 September 1988; Víctor R. Morales and Roy W. McDiarmid.
4 = 22 Jan-1 Feb 1989; Víctor R. Morales and Roy W. McDiarmid.
5 = 4-28 February 1990; Víctor R. Morales and María E. Guevara.
6 = 19 April-13 May 1991; Víctor R. Morales and María E. Guevara.
7 = 13 February-10 March 1992; Robert P. Reynolds.
8 = 2-8 July 1993; Robert P. Reynolds.

For each specimen located during the survey, we recorded the habitat in which it was collected/observed. If we could not assign an individual to a specific habitat type, we referred it to the next larger unit, e.g., if we could not distinguish between old alluvial terrace forest and dissected alluvial terrace forest at the site where a specimen was collected, we recorded the specimen from alluvial terrace forest or simply upland forest accordingly. We used the following scheme and abbreviations to refer to habitat:

UPLAND, NON-FLOODED FOREST (UF)

Old alluvial terrace forest - rapidly drained upland forests; on sandy clay (reddish, beige or gray) over red lateritic clay; *UFo* without bamboo and *UFob* with bamboo.

Dissected alluvial terrace forest - upland forests on terraces dissected by streams with steep banks; surface soil sandy and well drained; *UFd*

SEASONALLY FLOODED FOREST (FF)

Upper floodplain forest - forests with periodic but not annual flooding; with recurrent deposition of alluvium; plant diversity and density high; *FFu*

Lower floodplain forest - forests along the Rio Manu subject to seasonal flooding; lower extent - bare sand, fine-grained alluvium over sand, or washed clay with grasses or willows; upper extent - short-stature forest of low diversity on gray leached alluvium; *FFl*

Oxbow palm swamp forest - internally drained, isolated swamp forests, often in old oxbow lakes; intermittent standing or slow moving, clear, acidic water; palms common; *OSFp*

Oxbow hardwood swamp forest - low forest of *Ficus* and *Laetia*, along old oxbows; soil of dense, fine gray clay; water up to meter deep during wet season; *OSFh*

Ridgetop hardwood swamp forest - depressions on flat-topped ridges with short forest on hummocks, bamboo in understory; internal drainage, water accumulating during wet season to 0.5 meters, dries each year; over gray clay; *RSF*

OPEN AREAS/CLEARINGS IN FOREST (OA)

Camp clearing - approximately two hectares of open area with several small, wooden buildings; vegetation of low weeds and grass, periodically cut; *OAc*

Mud/sand banks along river - shoreline along Rio Manu; *OAr*

Clearing edge/forest margin - *OAm*

AQUATIC HABITATS

Riverine - aquatic portions of Rio Manu; depth and width variable, seasonally flooded; mosaic of broad sandy/stony beaches, extensive silty shores, and steep clay banks; AR

Streams - smaller streams and quebradas that cut through the upland and seasonally flooded forests; substrate rock, cobble, sand, or silt; AS

Lagoon - permanent water lagoon, Cocha Chica, formed by a deep (former?) channel of the Quebrada Pachija; grassy belt around lagoon surrounded on three sides by forest; AL

The presence of species in the major habitats as represented in our samples is shown in Table 2. The distributions by habitat generally reflect the amount and kinds of each type at Pakitza, and their proximity to camp and access by trail. Review of these distributions allows the following generalizations: 55% of the species were found at least once in dissected alluvial terrace forests, 47% in old alluvial terrace forests, and 37% in upper floodplain flooded forest. About half of the Pakitza species have been recorded in more than one habitat. Only three of the 63 species known from single habitats are known from more than 10 specimens (i.e., common), and two of these (*Scinax rubra* and *Thecadactylus rapicauda*) are known only from open areas in and around camp. We suspect that many of the species that some might call "habitat specialists" will be shown to be more widely distributed as more material is collected. The majority (92%) of species (63) recorded from one habitat is known from 5 or fewer specimens. However, a few species (*Bufo guttatus*, *Cochranella midas*, some species of *Leptodactylus*, some microhylids, certain species of Teiidae, *Xenopholis scalaris*) may be restricted to specific habitats.

MICROHABITAT USE

Species of amphibians and reptiles seemingly occupy more distinct microhabitats in tropical compared to temperate forests. Whether this is primarily a consequence of the higher species diversity in tropical latitudes or actually reflects an increased complexity of tropical forests and a concomitant response on the part of species in the community (i.e., more specialists) remains to be demonstrated. In order to understand better the ecological distribution of amphibians and reptiles in this area, we attempted to assign each specimen observed or collected to a specific microhabitat. The microhabitats that we recognized for specimens sampled at Pakitza were: **aquatic** - actually in water **(aw)**, **on margin** of river, stream, or pond margin **(am)**, or on twigs or leaves **floating in water (af)**; **hole (h)** - in or near holes in ground or ones formed by roots of bushes and trees; **leaf litter** - in or on litter in **forest (fl)** or **camp clearing (cl)**; **low arboreal** - in bushes or low trees 0.5 to 2.0 m above ground **on leaf (lal)**, **on horizontal branch (lab)**, **on stem (las)**, or inside bamboo (lai); **high arboreal** - in bushes or trees 2.0 m above ground **on leaf (hal), on trunk (hat), or on branch (hab); open ground (og)** in camp area; **in or on buildings (b)** in camp. The ecological distribution of species by microhabitat in which individuals were collected is shown in Table 2.

TABLE 2. Amphibian and reptile species collected in the vicinity of Pakitza, Madre de Dios, by habitat and microhabitat. Activity (ACTIV) — N = Nocturnal, D = Diurnal; Relative Abundance (ABUND) — U = Uncommon, C = Common, A = Abundant. Macrohabitat (MACRO) — Upland Forest (UF) on old alluvial UFo, with bamboo UFob, or dissected alluvial UFd terrace; Flooded Forest (FF) on upper FFu or lower FFl floodplain; Oxbow Swamp Forest (OSF) with palms OSFp or hardwood OSFh; Ridgetop Swamp Forest (RSF); Open Areas in camp clearing (OAc), along river (OAr) or forest margin (OAm); Aquatic (A) riverine Ar, stream As, and lagoon Al habitats. Microhabitat (MICRO) — aquatic in water aw, along margins am, and on floating debris af; leaf litter in forest fl and in camp cl; low arboreal on leaf lal, on branch lab, inside bamboo lai, and on stem las; high arboreal on leaf hal, on branch hab, on trunk hat; hole in ground ho; building in camp b; open ground og.

TAXON	ACTIV	ABUND	MACRO	MICRO
AMPHIBIA - CAUDATA				
Plethodontidae				
Bolitoglossa altamazonica	N	C	FFu,UFd	lal,lai
AMPHIBIA - ANURA				
Bufonidae				
Bufo guttatus	N	U	OAr	og
Bufo marinus	N	C	FFu,OAc&r,UFd&o	fl,og
Bufo cf typhonius	D	U	FFl,UFo	fl
Dendrobatidae				
Colostethus trilineatus	D	C	FFu,UFd,UFo	fl
Colostethus sp.	D	C	FFu,UFd,UFo	fl
Dendrobates biolat	D	C	FFu,UFd,UFo	lai
Epipedobates femoralis	D	U	UFd,UFo	fl
Epipedobates pictus	D	C	OAm,UFd,UFo	fl
Epipedobates trivittatus	D	C	OAm,FFu,UFd&o	fl
Centrolenidae				
Cochranella midas	N	U	UFo	lal
Hylidae				
Hemiphractus scutatus	N	U	UFd	fl
Hyla acreana	N	U	OAm	lab
Hyla boans	N	U	FFu,OAm,UFd	hab,lab
Hyla calcarata	N	U	FFu	lab
Hyla fasciata	N	C	FFu,OSFp	lab
Hyla granosa	N	U	OSFp,RSF	lal
Hyla lanciformis	N	U	OAm,FFu,UFd	lab
Hyla leali	N	U	OSFh,OSFp,UFo	lal
Hyla leucophyllata	N	U	OSFp	lab

TAXON	ACTIV	ABUND	MACRO	MICRO
Hyla minuta	N	A	UFd,UFo	lal
Hyla parviceps	N	A	OAm,OSFh,UFd&o	lal
Hyla rhodopepla	N	A	RSF,UFd,UFo	lal
Hyla sarayacuensis	N	U	UFd	lal
Hyla "sp. A"	N	A	RSF,UFd	lal
Hyla "sp. B"	N	A	OAM,UFd	lal
Osteocephalus leprieurii	N	C	FFu,UFd,UFo	lab
Phrynohyas coriacea	N	U	OAm	lab
Phrynohyas venulosa	N	U	UFo	lab
Phyllomedusa atelopoides	N	U	UFd	fl
Phyllomedusa palliata	N	U	UFd,UFo	lab
Phyllomedusa tomopterna	N	U	OAm,UFd,UFo	hab
Phyllomedusa vaillanti	N	U	FFu,OSFp	lab
Phyllomedusa sp.	N	U	FFu,UFo	hab
Scarthyla ostinodactyla	D	U	OSFp	af,lal
Scinax chiquitana	N	C	UFd	lab
Scinax pedromedinai	D,N	U	UFd	lab
Scinax cf rubra	N	C	OAc	lab,lai
Leptodactylidae				
Adenomera andreae	N	C	OAc,UFo	cl
Ceratophrys cornuta	N	U	FFu,OSFp,UFd&o	fl
Edalorhina perezi	D	C	FFu,OSFp,UFd&o	ho
Eleutherodactylus altamazonicus	N	U	UFo	lal
Eleutherodactylus croceoinguinis	N	U	UFo	fl
Eleutherodactylus cruralis	D	U	UFo	fl
Eleutherodactylus diadematus	N	U	FFu	las
Eleutherodactylus fenestratus	N	C	FFu,OAc,UFd&o	cl
Eleutherodactylus ockendeni	N	U	UFd,UFo	lal
Eleutherodactylus peruvianus	N	A	FFu,OSFp,UFd,o,ob	fl,lab
Eleutherodactylus toftae	D	U	FFu,UFd,UFo	lab
Eleutherodactylus ventrimarmoratus	N	U	FFu,UFo	lab
Eleutherodactylus "sp. A"	N	U	OAc,UFo	hal
Eleutherodactylus "sp. B"	N	U	OSFp,UFo	lab
Ischnocnema quixensis	D	U	UFd	fl
Leptodactylus bolivianus	N	U	FFu,UFd,UFo	fl
Leptodactylus knudseni	N	U	UFd	fl
Leptodactylus leptodactyloides	N	U	FFu,UFd,UFo	fl,ho
Leptodactylus mystaceus	N	U	FFu	fl
Leptodactylus pentadactylus	N	C	FFu,OAm,UFd&o	ho
Leptodactylus petersi	N	U	OSFp	ho
Leptodactylus rhodomystax	N	C	FFu,UFd,UFo	fl
Leptodactylus rhodonotus	N	U	FFu,UFd,UFo	fl
Lithodytes lineatus	N	U	UFd,UFo	ho
Physalaemus petersi	N	U	FFu,UFd,UFo	fl
Phyllonastes myrmecoides	D	U	UFd	fl
Microhylidae				
Chiasmocleis ventrimaculata	N	U	UFd,UFo	af
Chismocleis sp.	N	U	UFo	am
Ctenophryne geayi	N	U	UFd	ho
Hamptophryne boliviana	N	A	OAm,OSFp,UFd&o	fl,am

REPTILIA - TESTUDINES
Chelidae

Phrynops geoffroanus	N	U	OAm,UFo	aw
Phrynops gibbus	N	U	UFd	aw
Platemys platycephala	N	U ·	OAm,RSF,UFd&o	aw

Pelomedusidae

Podocnemis unifilis	D	U	Ar,Al	aw

Testudinidae

Geochelone denticulata	D	U	OAm,UFd,UFo&od	fl

REPTILIA - CROCODILIA
Alligatoridae

Caiman crocodilus	N	U	Ar	aw

REPTILIA - AMPHISBAENIA
Amphisbaenidae

Amphisbaena fuliginosa	D	U	UFo	aw/fl?

REPTILIA - SAURIA
Gekkonidae

Gonatodes hasemani	D	U	OAc	b
Gonatodes humeralis	D	U	OAc,OSFp,UFd	b
Pseudogonatodes guianensis	D	U	FFu	fl
Thecadactylus rapicauda	N	C	OAc	b, lab

Hoplocercidae

Enyalioides palpebralis	D	U	UFd,UFo	lab,las

Polychridae

Anolis bombiceps	D	C	FFu,UFd,UFo	fl,lab,lat
Anolis fuscoauratus	D	C	FFu,UFd,UFo	fl,lab
Anolis punctatus	D	U	OAc,UFd,UFo	lab,hat

Scincidae

Mabuya bistriata	D	U	UFd	fl

Teiidae

Alopoglossus angulatus	D	U	UFd	fl
Ameiva ameiva	D	U	OAc	og
Bachia trisanale	D	U	UFo	fl
Kentropyx pelviceps	D	U	UFo	fl
Neusticurus ecpleopus	D	U	FFd	fl
Prionodactylus argulus	D	U	FFu,OAc,UFd&o	fl
Prionodactylus eigenmanni	D	U	FFu,UFd,UFo	fl
Tupinambis nigropunctatus	D	U	OAm	og

Tropiduridae

Stenocercus roseiventris	D	U	FFu	fl
Stenocercus sp.	D	U	FFu	fl
Tropidurus flaviceps	D	U	FFu	hab
Tropidurus plica	D	U	OAm	las
Tropidurus umbra	D	U	FFu	las

REPTILIA - SERPENTES
Boidae

Corallus hortulanus	N	U	OAm,OSFp	lab
Epicrates cenchria	N	U	OSFp	lab

Colubridae

Chironius exoletus	N?	U	UFd	las
Chironius fuscus	D	U	UFd	lab

Chironius scurrulus	D	U	FFu	fl
Clelia clelia	N	U	OAm,FFu,UFd	lab
Dendrophidion sp.	D	U	FFu	fl
Dipsas catesbyi	N	U	FFu,UFo	lab
Drepanoides anomalus	N	U	FFu	fl
Drymarchon corais	D	U	FFu	fl
Helicops angulatus	N	U	OAc,OAr,UFd	am
Helicops polylepis	N	U	OAr	am
Imantodes cenchoa	N	U	FFu,UFd,UFo	lab,las
Leptodeira annulata	N	U	FFu,UFd,UFo	fl,lab,lai
Liophis cobella	N	U	UFd	lab
Liophis typhlus	D	U	UFd	fl
Oxybelis fulgidus	D	U	UFd	lab
Oxyrhopus melanogenys	N	U	FFu,OAc,UFd	fl
Oxyrhopus petola	N	U	OAc	og
Rhadinaea brevirostris	D	U	UFd	fl
Rhadinaea occipitalis	D	U	UFd	fl
Tantilla melanocephala	N?	U	UFo	fl
Xenodon severus	D	U	FFl,FFu,UFd	fl
Xenopholis scalaris	N	U	UFd	fl
Elapidae				
Micrurus lemniscatus	N	U	UFo	og
Micrurus spixii	D	U	UFd	fl
Micrurus surinamensis	N	U	OAm,UFo	fl
Micrurus sp.	D,N	U	FFu,OAm	fl
Viperidae				
Bothriopsis bilineata	N	U	UFo	lab
Bothrops atrox	N	U	FFu,OAc,UFo	fl
Bothrops brazili	N	U	OAm	og

We recognize that our attempts to assign each specimen to a microhabitat (Table 2) may give a misleading impression of the ecology of the species, especially considering the relatively small sample sizes and inadequate sampling periods. For example, an individual frog may occur in several different microhabitats during its life. Adults of certain species of treefrogs spend most of their life in the forest canopy but periodically come to forest ponds to breed. Thus, during a relatively short period (e.g., 3 days) a single individual might move from the high canopy to a forest pond, call while floating in the water or from surrounding vegetation, sit on a branch in low vegetation, climb up the stem of a small forest tree and eventually return to the canopy. Depending on sampling method and timing, that individual might have been encountered in any of four or five distinct microhabitats, and if it were observed only at the breeding pond, we might be mislead into considering the species aquatic, when in fact it is arboreal. In spite of these concerns, we believe that only by noting the microhabitat for every observation will we begin to understand the ecology of poorly known species. Some specific examples will help to illustrate this point.

Two of the four species of microhylid frogs were almost exclusively found only at breeding sites. Each was recorded as aquatic, either floating (af) or at the margins (am) of the pond, but neither is an "aquatic" species in the sense of some of the turtles. The problem was that we seldom or never collected the species in microhabitats other than at the breeding ponds. Based on our experience with the species or related forms at other sites, we know that these frogs occur in leaf litter or in holes in the forest floor but we did not change the observation. How many other species were scored for a microhabitat in which they seldom or rarely occur, is unknown.

Early on, we decided to score the actual microhabitat for each observation unless there was clear evidence that the occurrence was not natural (i.e., specimen moved to a place to escape disturbance). The single specimen of *Tropidurus flaviceps* was found "swimming" in Quebrada Fortaleza, east of Zone 2 (Erwin, 1991). Apparently, the lizard had fallen or jumped from a overhanging limb of a large tree and landed in the water about the time that an ichthyological team was seining the stream. In this instance we recorded the specimen as hab (high arboreal branch), not aw (aquatic), based on experience with the species elsewhere and the assumption that it was in the water because it had been disturbed. Likewise, we also decided to record the microhabitat only for individuals that were active. Observations of snakes on a branch or leaf of tree at night were not scored as low arboreal for that individual unless there was clear evidence of activity. Sometimes this was difficult to determine but we made the decision on a case by case basis. The single specimen of *Chironius exoletus* appeared to be active when encountered at night but previous experience suggested that species of *Chironius* are diurnal and usually terrestrial. However, we could not rule out our observation, so we recorded it as N? and l as in Table 2. Because some species (e.g., many snakes) are rare or rarely encountered, gaining insight into their ecology and behavior will only be possible by combining observations derived from different studies at different sites. Thus, observations of activity and microhabitat use must be made carefully and described adequately when published. If these recommendations are followed, we eventually will come to understand the use of habitat by many tropical species.

ACTIVITY AND ABUNDANCE

We recorded the time of activity of each specimen collected and assigned each species to a nocturnal or diurnal category. Individuals had to be active when observed to be assigned to a category. We also attempted to assign each species to one of three categories of relative abundance based on the percentage of specimens of a species relative to the total Pakitza sample. The total number of adult specimens collected was about 1,117 specimens; for these calculations we did not include tadpoles or eggs in the total sample. We assigned relative abundances for species observed but not collected (e.g., riverine turtles and crocodilians) in the Reserve Zone near Pakitza based on our collective impressions of their relative abundances.

Calculated percentages of relative abundance based on our collections ranged from 0.1% to about 7.0%. We arbitrarily assigned a species to the uncommon (U) category if it comprised less than 1.0% of the total sample; examples of uncommon species include *Hemiphractus scutatus*, known from a single specimen collected in eight visits, and *Leptodactylus bolivianus*, represented by 10 collected specimens. A species was common (C) when its relative abundance was between 1.0 and 3.3% of the total sample; common species include *Anolis bombiceps* with 11 specimens collected and *Colostethus trilineatus* with 37 specimens. A species was abundant (A) when it contributed between 3.8 and 7.0% of the total sample. We considered *Hyla* "species A" with 43 specimens and *Hyla parviceps* with 78 specimens to be abundant.

We acknowledge that relative abundance values, as we have defined them, may not reflect adequately the abundance of species at Pakitza. For example, we did not sample equally across habitats or proportionally to the percentage that each habitat contributed to the total environment. Rather, we attempted to standardize our work during day and night sampling along trails radiating from the camp. Distant habitats (e.g., oxbow palm and hardwood swamp forests) were less frequently sampled, especially at night, and some were not accessible by foot during certain sampling periods (e.g., trails flooded during wet season). Other habitats (e.g., Cocha Chica lagoon, ridgetop hardwood swamp forests) were discovered late in the study and therefore not sampled proportional to habitats known and accessible by trail early in the study. Finally, vagaries of amphibian and reptile activity relative to wet and dry seasons on the Rio Manu also were reflected in our sampling. Many frogs were found only during the wet season and then located only by their calls. In contrast, lizard density and diversity seemed to be higher during the dry season. Although most sampling was by visual encounters along trails, we frequently used calls to find males of certain species (e.g., dendrobatids, *Eleutherodactylus*) and to locate breeding sites for others (e.g., hylids and microhylids). Even though we attempted to standardize our sampling procedures within habitats, estimates of abundance for some species may not be reflective of their relative abundance. For example, some abundant species (e.g., *Hyla* "sp. B") were collected in only one habitat and rarely outside of a large chorus, while other species were frequently heard but rarely (e.g., *Hyla lanciformis*) or never (*Phrynohyas* cf *resinifictrix*) collected. Because individuals (frogs and persons doing the sampling) are often attracted to a chorus from considerable distances, these temporary aggregations pose considerable problems for comparative analyses of relative densities. For example, we did not collect all specimens of all species from a chorus, and were selective as to how many specimens of each species were collected. In contrast, all specimens encountered along a trail were sampled and scored for a specific microhabitat within each habitat. In spite of these confounding problems, we think that the relative abundance data provide some knowledge about the activity, abundance, and diversity of the Pakitza herpetofauna.

SPECIES COMPOSITION

The herpetofauna of the Pakitza site includes 128 species of amphibians and reptiles. The microhabitats with the highest percentage of species are *forest leaf litter* with 26% of the amphibians (N=18) and 45% of the reptiles (N=27); *low arboreal on branch* with 28% (N=19) amphibians and 23% (N=14) reptiles; and *low arboreal on leaf* with 19% (N=13) amphibians and 3% (N=2) reptiles. Only about 4% of the herpetofauna (5 species of reptiles) occurs in the *aquatic* microhabitat.

Amphibians comprise about 53% of the total Pakitza herpetofauna and most of these are frogs (Table 2). One species of salamander (*Bolitoglossa altamazonica*) was found on four trips during both the wet and early dry seasons; most (17 of 19 specimens) were collected from the same stretch of trail in upper floodplain forest near the camp. A caecilian, *Oscaecilia bassleri* has been reported from Pakitza (Rodríquez and Cadle, 1990) based on a few specimens in the station collection that purportedly came from the immediate vicinity of the station. We did not include it on our list as no specimens were collected or positively known from Pakitza. We suspect that *Oscaecilia bassleri* and possibly other species of caecilian known from Madre de Dios (e.g., *Siphonops annulatus*) occur at Pakitza; their fossorial existence makes them unlikely candidates to be discovered during routine herpetofaunal sampling.

Of the 67 species of frogs in six families recorded from Pakitza, approximately 49% were taken in the *low arboreal* and 34% in *forest leaf litter* microhabitats. The remainder was distributed across five other microhabitats. The families with the highest species diversity are Hylidae (N=27) and Leptodactylidae (N=26). The greatest spread of microhabitats occupied was by species of the Leptodactylidae. Several species (e.g., *Bufo guttatus*, *Hemiphractus scutatus*, *Eleutherodactylus diadematus*, *E.* "species A" and *Phyllonastes myrmecoides*) were collected on only one visit and presumed to be rare. Their occurrence in the southern peruvian Amazon seemingly is rare too.

Cochranella midas was the only Centrolenidae recorded along the Rio Manu. Three adults were collect along a tiny forest stream near camp in October, 1987. In September, 1988 a single tadpole was found at the same spot in the stream where the adults had been collected the previous year. None has been taken since that time.

Three species of frogs were removed from the stomachs of snakes. Two *Ceratophrys cornuta* were inside an adult *Drymarchon corais*. A specimen of *Ctenophryne geayi* was removed from a *Helicops angulatus* and a specimen of *Scinax chiquitana* from inside a *Leptodeira annulata*.

The reptile fauna of Pakitza has 60 species, including 5 turtles, 1 crocodilian, 1 amphisbaenian, 22 lizards and 31 snakes. As with amphibians, reptiles were most common in *forest leaf litter* (50% of species) and *low arboreal* (32% of species) microhabitats. Most of the species (N=19) found in the low arboreal microhabitat were taken on branches.

516

The most common turtle, *Platemys platycephala*, was collected in small to moderate-sized pools in upland forest, ridgetop swamp forest, and at the edge of the camp clearing but only in the rainy season. Two small specimens of *Podocnemis unifilis* were "collected" by a local boatman (Trip 1) as food and given to us to eat. Although common in some stretches of the river, these two plus a large female with eggs (43 cm carapace length) from trip 8 were the only specimens of this species taken near Pakitza during our study.

The most common reptiles collected at Pakitza were the lizards *Thecadactylus rapicauda* - collected on every trip except September, 1988; *Anolis fuscoauratus* - collected on every trip except in the dry season (June) of 1988 and the wet season (February) of 1990; and *Ameiva ameiva* - absent in the wet season (January and February) of 1989. *Amphisbaena fuliginosa* and *Tropidurus flaviceps* were only collected once during the study. *Imantodes cenchoa* and *Leptodeira annulata* were the most common snake; specimens were collected at night in both flooded and non-flooded upland forests. In contrast, several other snake species are reported from Pakitza from single specimens, among which are two pit vipers, *Bothriopsis bilineata* and *Bothrops brazili*. Other interesting and seemingly rare snakes collected at Pakitza are *Dendrophidion* sp., *Rhadinaea occipitalis*, and *Xenopholis scalaris*. Four species of coral snakes occur at Pakitza; *Micrurus surinamensis* and M. sp. (similar to some specimens of M. *annellatus*) were found in the camp area near a small pond; the other species, M. *spixii* and M. *lemniscatus*, were found in the forest. It is likely that *Lachesis muta* occurs at Pakitza; this species has a wide distribution and has been reported from Cocha Cashu, 20 km to the northeast of Pakitza.

COMMENTS ON THE MADRE DE DIOS HERPETOFAUNA

The lowland herpetofauna of Madre de Dios, Peru, is known primarily from moderately extensive collections made at four sites in the department: Cocha Cashu, Pakitza, Tambopata, and Cuzco Amazónico. All four of these sites are in the Madre de Dios river drainage and separated by a maximum distance of about 300 km.

Cocha Cashu is in Manu National Park, northeast of Pakitza on the Rio Manu; according to Terborgh (1983, 1990) Cocha Cashu is at 350 — 400 m elevation and receives about 2,160 mm of rain a year (also see Erwin, 1991, Figure 3). The forests are of two major types: upland (high ground) mature forest and late successional, seasonally flooded forest; a large swamp forest dominated by *Ficus trigona* lies near the center of the site and three successional forest habitats parallel the river (Gentry and Terborgh 1990; Terborgh 1983). The herpetofauna of Cocha Cashu has been reported by Rodríquez and Cadle, 1990.

The Tambopata Reserve lies at an elevation of about 290 m and receives about 2,600 mm of rainfall annually. Erwin (1985) recognized seven major forest types that in many ways are similar to those reported from the other three sites. McDiarmid and Cocroft have been working on the amphibians and reptiles in the vicinity of Explorer's Inn since 1979 and currently are preparing a detailed account of the herpetofauna at Tambopata.

The Cusco Amazónico Reserve is slightly lower (200 m) and has an intermediate average annual rainfall (approximately 2,400 mm) compared to the other sites. The major habitats are on a flat, alluvial floodplain and include terra firma and seasonally inundated forests. Compared to the other three sites, much of the habitat at Cusco Amazónico has been disturbed by humans. Palms are common but bamboo has not been found; *Heliconia* swamps also are extensive in contrast to Tambopata and Pakitza. Duellman and Koechlin (1991) described the site and Duellman and Salas (1991) reported on the herpetofauna.

The total amphibian fauna of the four Madre de Dios localities approximates 113 species. Of these, 40 species (35%) occur at all four sites and 7 species (6%) are known only from Pakitza. A pair wise comparison of the amphibian faunas among the four sites is shown in Table 3; the values are Indices of Similarity (IS') and range from 0 (all species shared) to 1 (no species in common). Relatively small differences (0.28 to 0.36) separated the indices for the amphibian comparison among the four localities. In this analysis Pakitza was most similar to Cocha Cashu (0.28) followed closely by Cusco Amazónico (0.29) and then Tambopata (0.36). Essentially no differences in the similarity indices existed between Cuzco Amazónico and Tambopata and between Cusco Amazónico and Cocha Cashu (0.31). The degree of similarity between the amphibian faunas of Tambopata and Cocha Cashu was lower (0.33) but not as low as that between Pakitza and Tambopata (0.36). A clustering analysis ranks the Pakitza and Cocha Cashu faunas most similar with a value of 0.27, followed by Pakitza-Cocha Cashu and Cusco Amazónico at 0.36 and these three faunas plus Tambopata at 0.41.

The amphibian faunal comparisons produced some expected results. The amphibian faunas from the geographically closest localities (Pakitza and Cocha Cashu) were most similar. Even though Pakitza has less seasonally flooded forest and almost no large, cocha (= oxbow lake) habitat readily accessible for easy sampling, enough of this kind of habitat was available to offset any differences due to habitat availability. It also should be mentioned that the Cocha Cashu list (Rodríguez and Cadle, 1990, Table 22.1) included species not found specifically at the Cocha Cashu site; four amphibian species recorded only across the river from Cocha Cashu in habitat more similar to the upland dissected forest at Pakitza were included in our analysis but the three species known only from Pakitza, were not. Their inclusion tended to make the two sites more similar.

However, it is not intuitively obvious why the greatest difference was between the Pakitza and Tambopata faunas. Perhaps the lack of many good breeding sites, especially ponds and cochas, and the preponderance and proximity of drier upland forest at Pakitza compared to Tambopata account for part of the difference. Only

26 species of pond breeding hylids have been recorded at Pakitza, whereas 38 species have been recorded from Tambopata. Also, the Tambopata site has been worked more extensively and more frequently early in the wet season than Pakitza

Table 3.- A comparison of similarities for amphibian (to the right of the 0 line) and reptile (to the left of the 0 line) faunas among four sites in Madre de Dios, Perú. Values are Indices of Similarity (see text for explanation). PAKT = Pakitza; CUAM = Cuzco Amazónico; TMBO = Tambopata; COCH = Cocha Cashu.

	PAKT	CUAM	TMBO	COCH
PAKT	0	0.29	0.36	0.28
CUAM	0.41	0	0.31	0.31
TMBO	0.32	0.27	0	0.33
COCH	0.39	0.43	0.40	0

and this may account for some of the difference. About 66% of the amphibian species recorded from Pakitza are know from 11 or fewer individuals, and many of these (21 species) are known from five or fewer specimens.

The reptile fauna of the four Madre de Dios localities includes about 118 species, of which only 25 (21%) occur at all four sites. Six species (5%) of reptiles recorded in the Madre de Dios sample are known only from specimens collected at Pakitza. In contrast to amphibians, the patterns of faunal similarity among sites for reptiles are different (Table 3), and the indices have a broader spread (IS' = 0.27 to 0.43). The known reptile fauna of Pakitza is most similar to that at Tambopata (0.32), followed by Cocha Cashu (0.39) and Cusco Amazónico (0.41). Considering all sites, the greatest difference in reptile faunas is between Cusco Amazónico and Cocha Cashu (0.43) and the sites with the most shared species of reptiles are Cusco Amazónico and Tambopata (0.27). A cluster analysis ranked by decreasing similarity (fewer shared species) places Cusco Amazónico and Tambopata together (IS' = 0.32), followed by Cusco Amazónico-Tambopata plus Pakitza (0.36) and Cusco Amazónico-Tambopata-Pakitza plus Cocha Cashu (0.41).

That the patters of similarity among the four sites differ between amphibians and reptiles is interesting but may, in part, be an artifact of sampling. Most of the early sampling at Cocha Cashu was by Lily Rodríguez and focused more on amphibians than reptiles. We suspect that recent sampling at Cocha Cashu (John Terborgh, pers. comm.) will increase the known reptile diversity considerably. This amphibian bias also may have occurred at the other sites but, we believe, to a lesser extent. Another factor influencing the reptile comparisons has to do with the difficulty of sampling snakes in tropical forests. Experience has shown that with this kind of survey, the percentage of a snake fauna that is sampled is always considerably lower than that of amphibians given the same duration and intensity of study. The key to sampling snakes is the study duration and the sampling intensity (hours of searching). The species accumulation curve for amphibians is always steeper than for snakes, and unrecorded species of snakes are much lees likely the longer the study.

On the other hand, some of the differences may be real. Certainly the paucity of certain aquatic species (crocodilians, some turtles and snakes) reflects differences in available habitat; there are no large cochas or extensive swamps at Pakitza. Also, the seemingly lower density, and possibly lower diversity, of low arboreal and terrestrial (leaf litter) frogs at Pakitza, as compared to the other sites, may contribute to the apparently lower diversity and possibly lower density of terrestrial, frog-eating snakes.

In summary, we submit that our comparisons among the four sites have provided some interesting insights into understanding the diversity of amphibians and reptiles in Amazonian lowlands of southeastern Peru. The comparisons also have raised several intriguing questions about the herpetofaunal diversity in tropical lowland forests and the factors that influence that diversity. How many of the observed differences are real, i.e., due to differences in history, habitat heterogeneity, and ecology of the species, and how many are artifacts of inadequate sampling with non-standardized methodologies? As rigorous, standardized sampling methods become more routine and long-term studies of faunas at single sites across seasons and habitats are completed, the kind of information needed to answer these questions will become available. One goal of our studies is to develop some predictions about the expected diversity of amphibians and reptiles at one site as a function of geographic proximity and habitat comparability to known sites. With such predictive tools, we should be able to make better informed decisions regarding the conservation and management of large areas of lowland forest, and to identify more easily local sites that are in need of protection because of their unique habitats and included species diversity. Only through these and similar approaches can we begin to identify species diversity and takes steps to maintain it. Clearly, lots of work on the herpetofauna of the Amazonian Basin remains to be done and we need to get on with it in an efficient and expeditious manner.

ACKNOWLEDGEMENTS

The Dirección General Forestal y de Fauna, Ministerio de Agricultura, Lima, issued permits and offered facilities at the Pakitza station, and the Biological Diversity in Latin America Project (BIOLAT), Smithsonian Institution, Washington, D.C., supported our field work and investigations over the years. The Museo de Historia Natural de la Universidad Nacional Mayor de San Marcos

(Lima) and National Museum of Natural History (Washington) provided space and laboratory facilities and supported our work in several ways.

Many persons helped us during the field portions of this survey. Several BIOLAT students and other scientists brought in specimens or told us of their observations, and park guards, boat drivers, cooks, and other workers made our field stay at Pakitza easier and more enjoyable. Robert P. Reynolds and George Middendorf made important collections during the early and late stages of this study (Table 1) and added several species to the Pakitza herpetofauna. We especially want to thank Robyn Burnham who accompanied us into Pakitza in the wet season of 1989 and Maria Elena Guevara who worked with VRM in 1990 and 1991. Ronald Altig collaborated with us on the tadpole samples and Sandra Montalvo helped with the manuscript. To all the institutions and their staffs and our friends and colleagues that helped us with this study, we extend our sincere thanks.

LITERATURE CITED

de la Riva, I. 1990. Una especie nueva de *Ololygon* (Anura: Hylidae) procedente de Bolivia. Rev. Españ. Herp. 4:81-86.

Duellman, W. E. and J. E. Koechlin. 1991. The Reserva Cusco Amazónico, Peru: Biological investigation, conservation, and ecotourism. Occas. Pap. Mus. Nat. Hist. Univ. Kansas 142:1-38.

Duellman, W. E. and A. W. Salas. 1991. Annotated checklist of the amphibians and reptiles of Cusco Amazónico, Peru. Occas. Pap. Mus. Nat. Hist. Univ. Kansas 143:1-13.

Duellman, W. E. and L. Trueb. 1989. Two new treefrogs in the *Hyla parviceps* group from the Amazon Basin in southern Peru. Herpetologica 45:1-10.

Duellman, W. E. and J. J. Wiens. 1993. Hylid frogs of the genus *Scinax* Wagler, 1830, in Amazonian Ecuador and Peru. Occas. Pap. Mus. Nat. Hist. Univ. Kansas 153:1-57.

Erwin, T. L. 1985 [1984]. Tambopata Reserved Zone, Madre de Dios, Peru: History and description of the reserve. Rev. Peruana Entomol. 27:1-8.

Erwin, T. L. 1991 [1990]. Natural history of the carabid beetles at the BIOLAT Biological Station, Río Manu, Pakitza, Peru. Rev. Peruana Entomol. 33:1-85.

Frost, D. R. (ed.) 1985. Amphibian species of the world: A taxonomic and geographical reference. Allen Press, Inc. and Association of Systematics Collections, Lawrence, Kansas, v + 732 pp.

Frost, D. R. 1992. Phylogenetic analysis and taxonomy of the *Tropidurus* group of lizards (Iguania: Tropiduridae). Amer. Mus. Novitates (3033):1-68.

Frost, D. R. and R. Etheridge. 1989. A phylogenetic analysis and taxonomy of Iguanian lizards (Reptilia: Squamata). Misc. Publ. Mus. Nat. Hist. Univ. Kansas 81:1-65.

Gentry, A. H. and J. Terborgh. 1990. Composition and dynamic of the Cocha Cashu "Mature" floodplain forest, pp 542-564. *In* A. H. Gentry (ed.), Four Neotropical Rainforests. Yale University Press, 627 pp.

Henle, K. 1991. *Ololygon pedromedinae* sp. nov., ein neuer Knickzehenlaubfrosche (Hylidae) aus Peru. Salamandra 27:76-82.

Heyer, W. R. 1994. Variation within the *Leptodactylus podicipinus-wagneri* complex of frogs (Amphibia: Leptodactylidae). Smithsonian Contrib. Zool. (546):iv + 124pp.

King, F. W. and R. L. Burke (eds.) 1989. Crocodilian, Tuatara, and turtle species of the world: A taxonomic and geographic reference. Association of Systematics Collections, Washington, DC. xxii + 216 pp.

Ludwig, J. A. and J. F. Reynolds. 1988. Statistical Ecology. A primer on methods and computing. John Wiley & Sons, New York. 337 pp.

Morales, V. R. 1992. Dos especies nuevas de *Dendrobates* (Anura: Dendrobatidae) para Perú. Caribbean J. Sci. 28:191-199.

Peters, J. A. and R. Donoso-Barros. 1970. Catalogue of the neotropical Squamata: Part II. Lizards and amphisbaenians. Bull. U. S. Natl. Mus. 297:1-293.

Peters, J. A. and B. Orejas-Miranda. 1970. Catalogue of the neotropical Squamata: Part I. Snakes. Bull. U. S. Natl. Mus. 297:1-347.

Rodríguez, L. B. and J. E. Cadle. 1990. A preliminary overview of the herpetofauna of Cocha Cashu, Manu National Park, Peru, pp 410-425. *In* A. H. Gentry (ed.), Four Neotropical Rainforests. Yale University Press, 627 pp.

Rodríguez, L. B. and C. W. Myers. 1993. A new poison frog from Manu National Park, southeastern Peru (Dendrobatidae, *Epipedobates*). Amer. Mus. Novitates (3068):1-15.

Vanzolini, P. E. 1986. Addenda and corrigenda to the catalogue of neotropical Squamata. Smithsonian Herpetol. Inf. Ser. 70:1-25.

Diversidad Genética en Anfibios y Reptiles de Pakitza, Manu, Perú

JESÚS H. CÓRDOVA

Departamento de Herpetología, Museo de Historia Natural de la Universidad Nacional Mayor de San Marcos (UNMSM), Apartado 14-0434, Lima 14, Perú (JHC)

MARIO MONTEGHIRFO

Centro de Investigación de Bioquímica y Nutrición, CIBN-UNMSM / Apartado 1546, Lima 100, Perú (MM)

GUSTAVO YBAZETA.

Laboratorio de Genética Humana, Facultad de Ciencias Biológicas, UNMSM / Apartado 14-0010, Lima-14, Perú (GY)

RESUMEN

Se ha estudiado la diversidad genética de la herpetofauna de Pakitza por métodos citogenéticos y moleculares. Quince especies (10 de anfibios y 5 de reptiles) han sido caracterizadas cariotípicamente, obteniéndose además datos moleculares de cuatro de ellas. Cinco especies fueron genéticamente diversas (a nivel local y/o geográfico) y las restantes significaron reportes genéticos nuevos. *Bufo marinus* posee importante diversidad cromosómico-cariotípica y molecular, en Pakitza y en Perú. Existe probable diversidad cariotípica de tipo geográfico en una especie más de anuros (*Leptodactylus pentadactylus*) y en tres de reptiles (*Platemys platycephala, Thecadactylus rapicauda* y *Ameiva ameiva*). Estos resultados sugieren cambios en el tratamiento sistemático de algunos taxa, así como la conveniencia de proteger mejor el área de estudio que podría ser clave para la conservación tanto de la diversidad genética total de cada especie estudiada, como la de los ecosistemas que ocupan.

ABSTRACT

Cytogenetic and molecular studies have been performed on the genetic diversity of fifteen herpetofaunal species found in Pakitza. All 15 species (10 amphibians and five reptiles) have been karyotypically characterized and for four of them additional molecular data were obtained. Five species were genetically diverse and for the others their genetic data represent first reports. In *Bufo marinus* populations we found chromosomic-karyotypic and molecular diversity, within the same locality (Pakitza) and between differents localities in Peru. Very probably, geographical karyotypic diversity also occurs in one additional amphibians (*Leptodactylus pentadactylus*) and three reptiles (*Platemys platycephala, Thecadactylus rapicauda*, and *Ameiva ameiva*). These results suggest changes in the systematic treatment of some taxa, and the necessity to protect better the study area considered fundamental for the conservation of the total genetic diversity of the species studied and the ecosystems which they inhabit.

INTRODUCCIÓN

La Sistemática moderna reconoce que el criterio de especie se basa en la detección de discontinuidades más allá de las apreciables mediante el estudio de la morfología externa de los individuos. El hallazgo de especies sinmórficas mediante estudios genéticos (citogenéticos y/o electroforéticos, especialmente) ha demostrado su notable importancia para la solución de problemas taxonómicos allí donde la morfología clásica no tenía la resolución suficiente (Baverstock, 1983, 1986; Córdova, 1993; Fontdevila, 1987; Green, 1986; Reig, 1983; Reig y Useche, 1976, Reig et al., 1980; Ruiz y Fontdevila, 1982; Volobouev et al., 1987).

Problemas referentes a la identificación, clasificación, filogenia y distribución de especies vienen siendo superados gracias a los datos suministrados por los estudios de los cariotipos convencionales y/o bandeados, y/o de proteínas (Cei, 1985; Córdova y Descailleaux, 1995a, 1995b; Green, 1986; Hedges, 1986, 1989; Jotterand-Bellomo, 1984). Tales datos tienen la propiedad adicional de permitir apreciar la diversidad genética y hasta medirla, tanto a nivel inter como intraespecífica, en sus dimensiones vertical o local (en una misma área) y en la horizontal o comparada (entre distintas áreas) (Cothran y Smith, 1983; Nei, 1981; Rogers, 1972; D. M. Green, in litt.).

Entre los anfibios y reptiles existen conjuntos de especies cuya taxonomía es muy compleja, debido a la escasez o carencia de descriptores genéticos como los mencionados. Entre tales conjuntos destacan los géneros *Bufo, Hyla* y *Leptodactylus* en anfibios, y *Thecadactylus, Anolis, Ameiva* y *Platemys* en reptiles. Todos ellos tienen sus representantes en la localidad de Pakitza (Morales y McDiarmid, 1996), siendo el objetivo del presente trabajo entregar un avance del estado en que se encuentran los estudios en tales géneros de dicho lugar, basados en el análisis de sus cariotipos convencionales y/o bandeados, así como por el de las proteínas y péptidos de los venenos (de parotoides o piel) de anuros, mencionando datos adicionales que consideramos relevantes. Asimismo, se discuten éstos dentro de un contexto integral por especie para propósitos sistemáticos y se opina breve-mente sobre la importancia que podría tener el área de estudio como reservorio de diversidad genética.

MATERIALES Y MÉTODOS

Se analizó 88 ejemplares de 15 especies (10 de anfibios y cinco de reptiles), procedentes de la localidad de Pakitza, Manu, (departamento de Madre de Dios). Fueron identificados según las claves y descripciones de Caldwell (1991), Duellman (1978), Heyer (1972, 1979, 1994), Pritchart y Trebbau (1984), Vanzolini y Williams (1970) y Vellard (1959), y depositados en el National Museum of Natural History (Smithsonian Institution), U. S. A. y en el Museo de Historia Natural de la Universidad Nacional Mayor de San Marcos, Perú.

ESTUDIOS CROMOSÓMICOS

Especímenes

Se procesaron citogenéticamente 83 de los ejemplares de las 15 especies. Datos del autor principal sobre ejemplares de *Bufo marinus* (Linnaeus, 1758) de dos zonas cercanas a Pakitza y de cinco lejanas a ella se incorporaron para apreciar la diversidad cariotípica horizontal intraespecie (ver Tablas 1 y 2).

Preparación citológica, coloración y bandeo cromosómico

Los preparados cromosómicos se realizaron siguiendo el procedimiento descrito por Córdova (1993) y Córdova et al. (1987), a partir de muestras de médula ósea y testículos. Las coloraciones empleadas fueron: a) Convencional, con Giemsa al 2% en buffer fosfato pH. 6.8 por 6 min (Schmid, 1978) y b) CBG (Sumner, 1972), para visualizar las características generales y regiones de heterocromatina constitutiva (bandas C), respectivamente. En los casos en que se efectuaron ambas coloraciones en un mismo individuo, se hicieron por el procedimiento secuencial Convencional → CBG en la misma metafase, descrito en Córdova (1993).

Tabla 1- *Resumen de los estudios genéticos efectuados en herpetozoos de Pakitza para el presente trabajo.*

specie o subespecie	NEC	NTNE	NMES	NEB
MPHIBIA				
ufo marinus cf. marinus	60	387	52	4
sp. (grupo typhonius)	2	16	—	1
ptodactylus bolivianus	2	31	12	—
rhodomystax	3	48	36	1
rhodonotus	1	18	—	—
pentadactylus	2	19	—	—
leptodactyloides	1	7	—	—
yla fasciata	1	15	—	—
. lanciformis	2	23	—	1
inax rubra	1	12	—	—
EPTILIA				
hecadactylus rapicauda	3	38	—	—
nolis bombiceps	1	9	—	—
. fuscoauratus	1	15	—	—
meiva ameiva cf. petersii	2	18	—	—
atemys platycephala	1	8	—	—

EC = Número de ejemplares estudiados cariotípicamente.
TNE = Numero total de núcleos (metafases y/o diacinesis) analizadas.
MES = Número de metafases procesadas por coloraciones secuenciales (Convencional → CBG).
EB = Número de ejemplares estudiados bioquímicamente.

Análisis cromosómico

El análisis cromosómico fue hecho en base a 7-10 de las mejores metafases encontradas por individuo. Los cariotipos se construyeron mediante ampliaciones fotográficas obtenidas por un fotomicroscopio Leitz-ORTHOPLAN Orthomat, película Agfa-Ortho 25 y papel bromuro Kodak Polycontrast (grado 2 y 4). Se obtuvo el cariotipo ordenando los pares cromosómicos de manera descendente, empezando por los de mayor longitud y considerando la posición del centrómero. Luego de encontrar sus

Tabla 2.- *Procedencia de los* Bufo marinus *de diferentes lugares del Perú, cuyos datos genéticos se han tomado en el presente trabajo para fines comparativos.*

PROCEDENCIA				NECB	MC	B
Localidad	Latitud/ Longitud	Alt. msnm	Dpto.			
Aguas Verdes	03°28' S, 80°15' O	35	Tumbes	02	AV	—
Boca Colorado	12°24' S, 69°30' O	234	Madre de Dios	02	S	—
Jaén	05°42' S, 78°49' O	729	Cajamarca	01	N	01
La Merced	11°03' S, 75°18' O	751	Junín	—	—	01
Neshuya	08°27' S, 74°45' O	170	Ucayali	01	N/S	—
Pakitza	11°57' S, 71°17' O	356	Madre de Dios	60	S	04
Tambopata	12°50' S, 69°17' O	300	Madre de Dios	01	S	—
Tingo María	09°17' S, 76°00' O	649	Huánuco	18	N	—
Trujillo	08°07' S, 79°02' O	34	La Libertad	22	N	—
Tumbes	03°34' S, 80°28' O	7	Tumbes	—	—	01

Alt. msnm = Altitud en metros sobre el nivel del mar.
Dpto. = Departamento.
NECB = Número de ejemplares estudiados con bandas C.
MC = Morfo cariotípico según Córdova y Descailleaux 1996a.
AV = "Marinus-Aguas Verdes".
N = "Marinus-Norte".
S = "Marinus-Sur".
N/S = Híbrido entre "Marinus-Norte" y "Marinus-Sur".

valores cariométricos, se denominó a cada par según la nomenclatura dada por Levan et al. (1964), modificada por Green y Sessions (1991) y se elaboraron los idiogramas por especie.

Ensayos en Electroforesis de Proteínas

Especímenes

Se procesaron para este fin siete ejemplares pertenecientes a cuatro especies de anfibios procedentes de Pakitza (*Bufo marinus* [04 ejemplares], *B. sp.* (grupo "*typhonius*") (Linnaeus, 1758) [01], *Leptodactylus rhodomystax* Boulenger, 1883 [01] e *Hyla lanciformis* (Cope, 1871) [01]), adicionándose ejemplares de *Bufo* de localidades distantes (*B. marinus* y *B. limensis* Werner, 1901) (detalles en Fig. 1 y Tablas 1 y 2), a fin de apreciar su resolución para detectar diferencias interespecíficas y/o geográficas.

Procedimientos electroforéticos

Se obtuvieron muestras de veneno crudo desecado (para los *Bufo*) y de extracto de pieles preservadas en Metanol (restantes anfibios) siguiendo los procedimientos descritos por Meyer y Linde (1971) y J. E. Maggio (in litt.). Se liofilizaron los venenos individuo por individuo y se trabajaron por etapas con diferentes sistemas electroforéticos, a fin de encontrar aquél que brindara los mejores resultados.

Etapa I.-

En las primeras experiencias se utilizó la técnica de Giulian et al. (1985), aplicándose en *B. marinus* (de La Merced), *B. marinus* (de Tumbes) y *Leptodactylus rhodomystax* (de Pakitza) (Fig. 2 y Tabla 2).

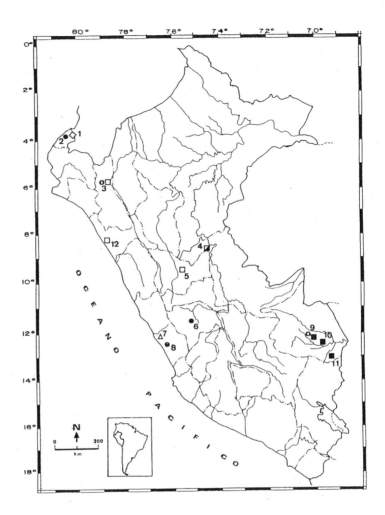

Fig. 1.– Mapa del Perú indicando las localidades de colecta de *Bufo marinus* y el tipo de información genética obtenido en cada una de éllas. *Bufo limensis* permite comparaciones interespecíficas. Localidades: 1 = Aguas Verdes; 2 = Tumbes: 3 = Jaén; 4 = Neshuya; 5 = Tingo María; 6 = La Merced; 7 = Lima; 8 = Cañete; 9 = Pakitza; 10 = Boca Colorado; 11 = Tambopata, y 12 = Trujillo. Datos Moleculares: círculo negro = Etapa I; círculo blanco = Etapa III; círculo blanco con franja transversal negra = Etapa III (*B. limensis*). Cariotipos: rombo = *B. marinus* "de Aguas Verdes"; cuadrado blanco = B. marinus "del Norte"; cuadrado negro = *B. marinus* " del Sur"; cuadrado blanco y negro por mitades = Híbrido *B. marinus* "del Norte" x B. marinus "del Sur"; triángulo = B. limensis.

Etapa II.-

Un segundo sistema fue ensayado, (Wiltfang et al. (1991), procesándose dos ejemplares de *B. marinus* de Pakitza. En este sistema se introdujeron dos modificaciones en la preparación de la muestra, con la finalidad de aumentar la visibilidad y resolución de las bandas. En la primera se centrifugó a 14,000 rpm por 5 min, luego se precipitaron las proteínas con acetona a –20°C por 25 min, se volvió a centrifugar a 5,400 rpm por 20 min, se eliminó el sobrenadante y se solubilizó el precipitado en el buffer de muestra. En la segunda modificación, el único cambio fue la ausencia de centrifugación a 14,000 rpm (Fig. 3).

Etapa III.-

Buscando optimizar nuestras técnicas, finalmente se trabajó con el protocolo de Fling and Gregerson (1986), en geles Laemmli con doble concentración de Tris en gradiente de 16% a 25% de poliacrilamida y muestras con cantidades diferentes (Fig. 4).

Métodos de coloración para los geles

Primero se usaron las coloraciones de Coomassie Blue R 250 y la de Coomassie Blue Coloidal, preparadas segun Wiltfang et al. (1991), y luego la coloración con nitrato de plata, según Morrissey (1981).

MÉTODOS DE MUESTREO

Dado que el objetivo principal del estudio era la caracterización y detección de diversidad genética de poblaciones y especies en Pakitza, el método de muestreo básico consistió en ubicar precozmente en cada expedición los lugares o puntos de mayor concentración de ejemplares por especie y, en lo posible, del mayor número de especies en cada punto. En ausencia o escasez de tales puntos, se optó por el método de muestreo por transectos, utilizando las trochas existentes en el área de trabajo. En la mayor parte de los casos, la captura de los especímenes se hizo manualmente. En otros se recurrió a redes y trampas de tipo "ratonera" o "tomahawk".

RESULTADOS

El análisis de 88 ejemplares de 15 de las especies más abundantes de Pakitza representa más del 31% (15/48) de las especies colectadas por el primer autor y del 12% (15/128) de las conocidas hasta la fecha para el lugar (Morales y McDiarmid, 1996). Son parte de una cuantiosa y diversa base de datos generada por las características de la investigación. Entre ellas destacan: a) el creciente número de taxa involucrados en función del tiempo y b) el incremento de y las mejoras en los procedimientos para obtener mayor información de tales taxa.

Los datos de *Bufo marinus* cubren un período de colectas que va desde la expedición de agosto de 1989 a la de febrero de 1992 (cinco expediciones de un mes cada una), con una época experimental en la de setiembre de 1988. Los referentes a las especies de las familias Hylidae, Leptodactylidae y restantes de la Bufonidae van de abril-1991 a febrero-1992 (tres expediciones), mientras que los de los reptiles, son casi exclusivos de la efectuada en febrero de 1992. Asimismo, los datos referentes a electroforesis de proteínas y péptidos de venenos de piel de anuros, recién empezaron con los especímenes colectados en octubre de 1991 y continuaron con los de febrero de 1992.

DATOS CROMOSÓMICO-CAROTÍPICOS

CLASE AMPHIBIA
Familia Bufonidae
Género *Bufo*
B. marinus cf. *marinus*
(Linnaeus, 1758)

La descripción detallada del cariotipo de los *marinus* de Pakitza se encuentra en Córdova y Descailleaux

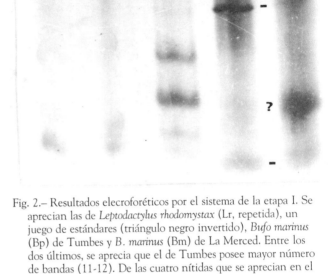

Fig. 2.– Resultados elecroforéticos por el sistema de la etapa I. Se aprecian las de *Leptodactylus rhodomystax* (Lr, repetida), un juego de estándares (triángulo negro invertido), *Bufo marinus* (Bp) de Tumbes y *B. marinus* (Bm) de La Merced. Entre los dos últimos, se aprecia que el de Tumbes posee mayor número de bandas (11-12). De las cuatro nítidas que se aprecian en el de la Merced, tres son compartidas con el de Tumbes (señaladas por un guión), mientras que su banda más notable (indicada por un signo de interrogación), no tiene su correspondiente entre las del de Tumbes.

(1995a), como "marinus-S" ("marinus del Sur"). Todos los *marinus* de Pakitza, poseen un número diploide 2n = 22 cromosomas (once pares). En coloración convencional forman tres grupos. El de los grandes, siendo los pares 1, 2, 3, y 5 metacéntricos (**m**), y el par 4 submetacéntrico (**sm**). El par 6 que es **m**, es el único de los medianos, mientras que cinco pares **m** (7-11) forman el grupo de los pequeños (fig. 2). Presenta constricciones secundarias en el brazo corto del par 7. En bandas C, todos los pares presentan bandas C positivas (C+) en las regiones centroméricas, en el telómero de 1p, en el tercio proximal de 3q, en la zona adyacente al telómero de 5q y en la adyacente al centrómero de 6q. Además, se encuentra en 1p, una banda de tonalidad menor (Cm), así como en la región distal del brazo largo (q) del par 3 (3q). El telómero del p del 11 y la región adyacente al cen-trómero de 8p se presentan en condición polimórfica para una banda C+ (Figs. 5a y 20d, y Tablas 1 y 2).

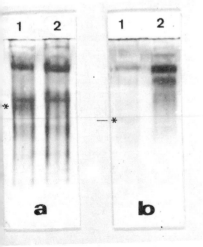

Fig. 3.– *Resultados electroforéticos de dos ejemplares (1 y 2) de marinus de Pakitza, según el sistema de la etapa II. En a) el patrón de bandas del ejemplar 1 presenta una banda extra respecto al del 2, y en b), donde se ha considerado una centrifugación menos, se revela otra banda extra entre estos mismos ejemplares. En ambos casos se encuentran señaladas por un guión y un asterisco.*

529

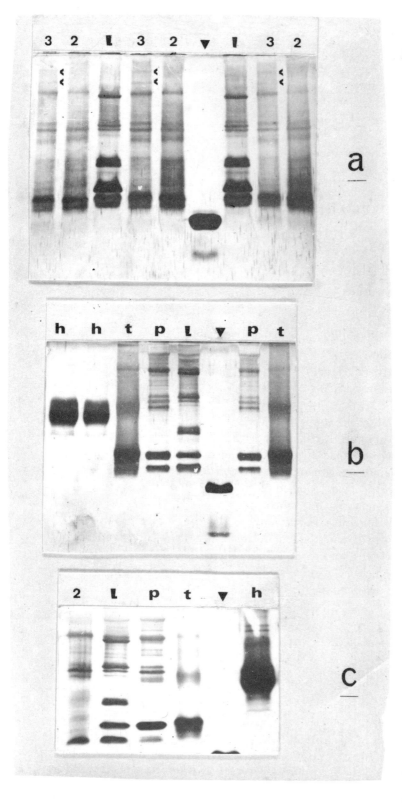

Fig. 4.– Resultados electroforéticos en el sistema de la etapa III. Se aprecian tres conjuntos de muestras (a-c) en geles. los tres (señalado por un triángulo negro invertido) se indica la corrida de nuestro estándar Insulina humana, cuya cadena ß se aprecia en todos los geles, mientras que cadena a no aparece en la parte c) de la presente figura. En a), se ve de izquierda a derecha, las corridas de dos especímenes de Pakitza (3 y repetidas tres veces), una muestra de B. limensis (L) (repetida dos veces) y el estándar. Obsérvese en los marinus que, dentro de un patrón de bandas mayoritaria mente compartido, el ejemplo 3 posee dos bandas (señaladas por cabezas de flecha) que están ausentes en el 2, además de tener otra banda (penúltima de abajo arriba) con una migración algo menor que su correspondiente en 2. En b) de izquierda a derecha se aprecian muestras repetidas de Hyla lanciformis (h) y Bufo sp. (grupo "typhonius") (t) Pakitza, y de B. marinus (p) de Jaén, una muestra de B. limensis (L) y del estándar. bien está sobreco-loreada la muestra del typhonius, se insinúa un patrón distintivo para cada especie. En c) se observan las muestras en cantidades iguales de concen traciones semejantes del género Bufo: B. marinus (Pakitza) (2), B. limensis (L), B. marinus (Jaén) (p) y B. sp. (grupo "typhonius") (t). Se aprecia mejor resolución de bandas y patrones específicos de especie o población. El estándar y una muestra de Hyla lanciformis mejor resuelta que en b), completan la figura

530

B. sp. (grupo *"typhonius"*) (Linnaeus, 1758)

El cariotipo de este *"typhonius"* tiene once pares de cromosomas (2n = 22) que pueden formar tres grupos segun su tamaño. Los pares del 1 al 4 forman el grupo de los grandes, siendo todos **m**, menos el 4 que es **sm**. El par 5 y el 6, que son **sm**, forman el de los medianos, mientras que los cinco pares restantes, el de los pequeños, son todos **m**, excepto el 9 y el 7 que son subtelocéntricos (**st**). Presenta constricciones secundarias en la region medial del brazo largo del 7, cuya descondensación puede incrementar la longitud de éste en más del doble (Figs. 8 y 21a, y Tablas 1 y 3).

Familia Leptodactylidae
Género *Leptodactylus*
L. bolivianus Boulenger, 1894

Posee un cariotipo con once pares cromosómicos (2n = 22). Un primer grupo conformado por cinco pares grandes. Los pares 1 y 5 son **m** , mientras que el 3 es **st** y el 2 y 4 **sm**. Dos pares son medianos, el 6 que es **m** y el 7 que es **sm**. El grupo de los pequeños está formado por cuatro pares que son **m** o **sm** (8-11), observándose en el brazo corto del 10 una constricción secundaria. Al bandeo C, todos sus pares tienen bandas C+ en la región centromérica. Adicionalmente presenta bandas C+ en las regiones adyacentes al centrómero de 1p, 2q, 3p, 3q, 4p, 5p, 5q, 7p, 8q, 10p y 11p, y en los telómeros de ambos brazos del 5. También presenta bandas Cm en los telómeros de ambos brazos del par 1, de 3p, 4p y 7p (Figs. 9 y 20a, y Tablas 1 y 2). En meiosis se observaron once bivalentes (Fig. 19a).

Fig. 5.– Homocariotipos a bandas C de *Bufo marinus*, a) "del Sur" (2n = 22). Nótese los telómeros de 1p positivamente marcados, además de una banda C+ en el tercio proximal al centrómero en 3q, b) "del Norte" (2n = 22). Nótese los telómeros de 1p negativamente marcados, y careciendo de la banda C+ en 3q. La barra horizontal en el extremo inferior de las figuras 5-19 equivale a 5μm.

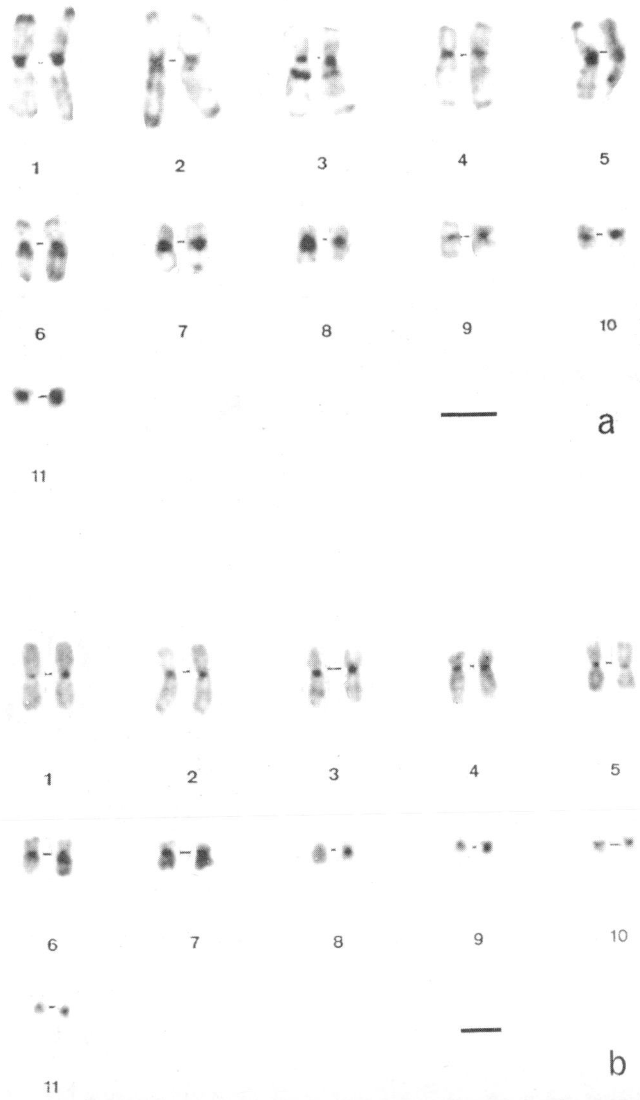

Tabla 3.- *Datos cariométricos de* Bufo marinus *cf.* marinus, *(BMM)*, B. sp. *(grupo*
"typhonius") (BTY), Hyla lanciformis *(HLA),* Sinax rubra *(SRU),* Leptodactylus bolivianus
(LBO), L. leptodactyloides *(LLE),* L. pentadactylus *(LPE),* L. rhodomystax *(LRD) y* L.
rhodonotus *(LRH) (Amphibia) de Pakitza.*

PC	BMM			BTY			HLA		
	LR	IC	TC	LR	IC	TC	LR	IC	TC
1	16.6	0.482	m	16.7	0.434	m	17.1	0.435	m
2	15.9	0.401	m	15.4	0.440	m	14.2	0.400	m
3	14.3	0.392	m	13.8	0.471	m	10.8	0.294	sm
4	12.3	0.343	sm	13.2	0.305	sm	10.8	0.176	st
5	11.0	0.471	m	10.0	0.298	sm	10.1	0.313	sm
6	8.2	0.452	m	8.8	0.342	sm	8.2	0.231	st
7	6.8	0.444	m	5.7	0.251	sm	6.3	0.407	m
8	4.7	0.418	m	4.9	0.419	m	6.3	0.325	sm
9	4.2	0.414	m	4.1	0.270	sm	5.7	0.444	m
10	3.3	0.467	m	4.1	0.435	m	5.4	0.353	sm
11	2.7	0.453	m	3.6	0.445	m	5.1	0.375	m

PC	SRU			LBO			LLE		
	LR	IC	TC	LR	IC	TC	LR	IC	TC
1	15.4	0.413	m	15.9	0.432	m	17.4	0.435	m
2	12.0	0.325	sm	13.6	0.368	sm	16.8	0.283	sm
3	10.5	0.279	sm	11.6	0.219	st	13.5	0.313	sm
4	9.6	0.357	sm	10.9	0.333	sm	12.3	0.273	sm
5	8.8	0.305	sm	8.7	0.469	m	10.6	0.263	sm
6	8.2	0.238	st	8.7	0.375	m	7.8	0.428	m
7	7.1	0.361	sm	7.3	0.300	sm	6.7	0.167	st
8	6.9	0.412	m	6.5	0.444	m	5.0	0.440	m
9	6.9	0.357	sm	5.8	0.438	m	3.9	0.120	t
10	6.1	0.359	sm	5.8	0.313	sm	3.6	0.125	t
11	4.3	0.456	m	5.1	0.357	sm	2.2	0.375	m
12	4.2	0.354	sm	———					

PC	LPE			LRD			LRH		
	LR	IC	TC	LR	IC	TC	LR	IC	TC
1	16.8	0.475	m	16.1	0.478	m	19.4	0.400	m
2	13.5	0.342	sm	14.0	0.333	sm	12.6	0.383	m
3	12.2	0.278	sm	12.0	0.235	st	12.5	0.267	sm
4	11.0	0.212	st	11.6	0.182	st	12.0	0.138	st
5	9.7	0.436	m	9.5	0.393	m	9.4	0.353	sm
6	9.3	0.387	m	8.4	0.375	m	7.5	0.365	sm
7	7.4	0.314	sm	7.2	0.300	sm	7.4	0.445	m
8	7.2	0.235	st	6.3	0.444	m	5.0	0.389	m
9	5.4	0.260	sm	5.6	0.375	m	4.7	0.354	sm
10	4.2	0.400	m	4.9	0.429	m	4.6	0.382	m
11	3.4	0.375	m	4.6	0.300	sm	4.5	0.365	sm

PC = Par cromosómico.
LR = Longitud relativa.
IC = Indice centromérico.
TC = Tipo cromosómico.
m = metacéntrico.
sm = submetacéntrico.
st = subtelocéntrico.

L. rhodomystax Boulenger, 1883

Tiene un cariotipo con once pares de cromosomas (2n = 22), en donde los cinco primeros son grandes, siendo el 1 y el 5 **m**, el 2 **sm**, mientras que el 3 y el 4 son **st**. Los siguientes son dos medianos, el 6 que es **m** y el 7 que es **sm**. Cuatro pares **m** o **sm** (8-11) forman el grupo de los pequeños. Las constricciones secundarias se encuentran en los telómeros del brazo largo del par 3. En bandas C, todos las regiones céntricas son C+, además bandas de este tipo se encuentran en medio de 4p, y en telómeros de 7p, 8p y 11p. Bandas Cm se encuentran en la región adyacente al centrómero de 1p y en los telómeros de 3p, 3q, 5p, 5q, 10p y 10q (Figs. 10 y 20b, y Tablas 1 y 3).

L. pentadactylus (Laurenti, 1768)

Su cariotipo consta de once pares de cromosomas (2n = 22), donde los cuatro primeros son grandes (el par 1 es **m**, 2 y 3 son **sm** y el 4 **st**). Los dos siguientes son medianos y **m**, mientras que cinco pares son pequeños (pares 7 y 9 son **sm**, el 8 es **st**, mientras que el 10 y el 11 son **m**). Las constricciones secundarias se hallaron en la región proximal al centrómero, sobre el brazo largo del par 8 (Figs. 11 y 21c, y Tablas 1 y 3).

L. rhodonotus (Gunther, 1868)

Posee un cariotipo con once pares cromosómicos (2n = 22), en donde los cinco primeros son grandes (pares 1 y 2 son **m**, 3, 4 y 5, **sm**). El grupo de los medianos está formado por los pares 6 y 7 que son **sm**, mientras que cinco pares (7-11) son pequeños y **m**. Constricciones secundarias se hallaron en la región medial del brazo corto del par 2 y en la región adyacente al centrómero, sobre el brazo corto de los pares 4, 6 y 8 (Figs. 12 y 21d, y Tablas 1 y 3).

L. leptodactyloides (Andersson, 1945)

Tiene un cariotipo con once pares de cromosomas (2n = 22), en el que los cinco primeros son grandes (el par 1 es **m**, y del 2 al 5 son **sm**). Dos son medianos, el 6 que es **m**, y el 7 que es **st**), mientras que los cuatro restantes son pequeños: 8 y 11 son **m**, en tanto que el 9 y 10 son **t**. Las constricciones secundarias parecen estar en el brazo corto del par 8 (Figs. 13 y 21b, y Tablas 1 y 3).

Familia Hylidae
Género *Hyla*
H. fasciata Gunther, 1859

Sólo se obtuvo cromosomas meióticos en células de testículos. En todas se encontraron doce bivalentes (n = 12), y al más pequeño (el 12), con una intensidad de coloración siempre menor a la de los restantes (Fig. 19b y Tabla 1).

H. lanciformis (Cope, 1871)

El cariotipo de esta especie consta de once pares cromosómicos (2n = 22). Los primeros cinco son grandes, siendo los pares 1 y 2 de tipo **m**, el 3 y el 5 son **sm** y el 4 **st**. Tiene un único par mediano (el 6) que es **st**, en tanto que el grupo de los pequeños está conformado por los pares 7, 9, y 11, que son **m**, y el 8 y 10 que son **sm**. No se ha podido detectar constricción secundaria alguna (Figs. 14 y 21e, y Tablas 1 y 3).

Género *Scinax*
S. rubra (Laurenti, 1768)

Su cariotipo posee doce pares de cromosomas (2n = 24). Los cinco primeros son grandes, siendo el par 1 **m** y los pares 2-5 de tipo **sm** y el 3 y el 5 **st**. Un par es mediano (el 6) y es **st**, mientras que los seis restantes son pequeños de tipo **m** (pares 8 y 11), y **sm** (pares 7, 9, 10 y 12). Se hallaron constricciones secundarias en la región adyacente al centrómero del brazo largo del par 11 (Figs. 15 y 21f, y Tablas 1 y 3).

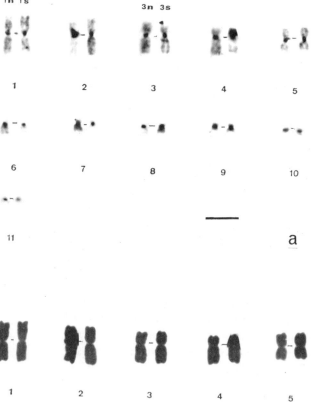

Fig. 6.– a) Heterocariotipo a bandas C de *Bufo marinus* "del Sur" / *B. marinus* "del Norte" (2n = 22). Obsérvese la presencia de los cromosomas marcadores de cada cariotipo (1s, 1n, 3s y 3n). b) Cariotipo a coloración convencional de la misma metafase vista en 3a. Obsérvese la incapacidad de esta técnica para evidenciar este cariotipo híbrido.

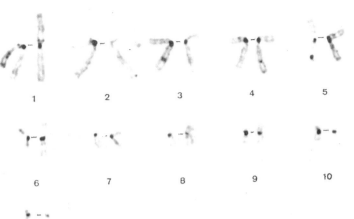

Fig. 7.– Homoca-riotipo a bandas C de *Bufo marinus* "de Aguas Verdes" (2n = 22). Nótese la forma más meta-céntrica del par 3 de este cariotipo, comparado con el de la Fig. 5, y la semejanza del par 1 con el de *B. marinus* "del Norte".

CLASE REPTILIA
Familia Chelidae
Género *Platemys*
P. platycephala Schneider, 1792

Sólo se obtuvo cromosomas de células de tejido testicular. Diacinesis y metafases I de meiosis mostraron 33 bivalentes (n = 33), pudiéndose distinguir once grandes, diez medianos y doce pequeños (Fig. 19f y Tablas 1 y 4).

Familia Gekkonidae
Género *Thecadactylus*
T. rapicauda (Houttuyn, 1782)

Posee un cariotipo que consta de 22 pares de cromosomas (2n = 44). El primer par es claramente mayor y de tipo **st**. El segundo par es casi el 30% menor que el primero y es tambien **st**. Luego vienen los 20 pares restantes que gradualmente van decreciendo en tamaño, siendo todos **st** o **t**. Existe un heteromorfismo en el par 7, atribuible por el momento a una pequeña constricción secundaria en su brazo corto. Otras constricciones secundarias se aprecian en el brazo corto del par 2 y en el telómero del brazo largo del 15 (Figs. 16, 22b y Tablas 1 y 4). En meiocitos se aprecian 22 bivalentes (n = 22) que también decrecen gradualmente en tamaño e intensidad de coloración, perdiendo algunos de los pequeños su pareamiento en diacinesis-metafase I (Fig. 19c).

Fig. 8.– Cariotipo de *Bufo sp.* (grupo "*typhonius*") (2n = 22). Obsérvese la notable constricción secundaria en la región media del brazo largo del par 7.

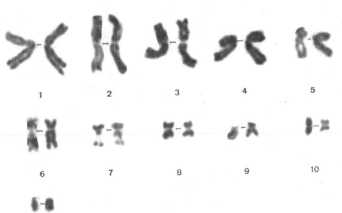

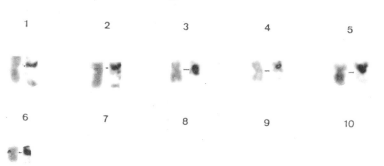

1	2	3	4	5

6	7	8	9	10

11

Fig. 9.– Hemicariotipos de *Leptodactylus bolivianus* (n = 11 y 2n = 22) por coloraciones secuenciales (convencional → CBG) en la misma metafase. Obsérvese el mayor número de bandas C+ del par 5 respecto al de los demás pares.

Familia Iguanidae

Género *Anolis*

A. *bombiceps* (Cope, 1876)

Tiene un cariotipo conformado por 14 pares cromosómicos (2n = 28). Los diez primeros se pueden considerar macrocromosomas y los cuatro restantes microcromosomas. Los macrocromosomas a su vez pueden formar tres subgrupos. Los cinco primeros pares (1-5) son grandes y de tipo **m**, excepto el 3 y 5 que son **sm**. Un único par (el 6) puede considerarse mediano y es también **m**, mientras que los cuatro restantes son pequeños, siendo el par 7 **sm** y los restantes **m** (8-10). El grupo de los microcromosomas está formado por cuatro pares (11-14) que decrecen gradualmente de tamaño (el 11 es **st** y 12-14, **sm**). Se ha podido detectar constricciones secundarias en la región medial del brazo corto del segundo par (Fig. 17, 22a y Tabla 1 y 4).

A. *fuscoauratus* D'Orbigny, 1837

Sólo se pudo obtener cromosomas meióticos a partir de testículos. En todas las diacinesis y metafases I observadas, se pudo apreciar 22 bivalentes (n = 22), diez grandes, tres medianos y nueve pequeños (Fig. 19e y Tabla 1).

Fig. 10.– Hemicariotipos de *Leptodactylus rhodomystax* (n = 11 y 2n = 22) por coloraciones secuenciales (convencional → CBG) en la misma metafase. Las constricciones secundarias se aprecian en la región telomérica del par 3.

1	2	3	4

6	7	8	9

11

536

Familia Teiidae
Género *Ameiva*
A. *ameiva* cf. *petersii* Cope, 1868

Tiene un cariotipo que consta de 24 pares cromosómicos (2n = 48), formándose dos grupos siguiendo a Gorman (1970): los macro y los microcromosomas (pares 1-12 y 13-24, respectivamente). Entre los primeros destacan el par 1, que es un largo **st**, así como el 2 y el 5 que son **sm**. los restantes son **st** o **t** (pares 3, 4 y 6-12). En el grupo de los microcromosomas (13-24), es difícil precisar la morfología de los pares, aun cuando decrecen gradualmente en tamaño (Figs. 18, 22c y Tablas 1 y 4). En meiosis se aprecian 24 bivalentes (n = 24), distinguiéndose 12 de mayor tamaño y 12 que son notoriamente menores (Fig. 19d).

Como información final debemos decir que no se han detectado concluyentemente heteromorfismos sexuales en las especies estudiadas.

ENSAYOS ELECTROFORÉTICOS

La Fig. 2 exhibe los resultados en el sistema de la etapa I. De izquierda a derecha se ven las corridas electroforéticas de las muestras de *Leptodactylus rhodomystax* (Lr) de la localidad de Pakitza, un juego de estándares de diferente peso molecular, Insulina, (cadena ß, 3.4 Kd), Aprotinina (6.5 Kd), Citocromo C (12.5 Kd) e Inhibidor de Tripsina (21.5 Kd), luego *Bufo marinus* (Bp) de Tumbes y *B. marinus* (Bm) de La Merced. En estos últimos, se aprecia una resolución adecuada en las bandas de mayor peso molecular al de los estándares, decreciendo aquélla cuanto menor es el peso de éstas. Las tres muestras exhiben patrones distintos, aun cuando los de *marinus* son los comparables por su origen similar (desecado de veneno crudo). El *marinus* de Tumbes revela hasta doce bandas (nueve de ellas de peso molecular mayor al de los estándares, una de peso similar al de éstos y una de menor peso), mientras que el de La Merced presenta cuatro bandas: dos tenues de mayor peso molecular, una principal o muy notable de peso molecular equivalente a uno de nuestros estándares (se aproxima a los 10 kd) y otra de menor peso molecular. Puede apreciarse también que de las cuatro bandas del *marinus* de La Merced, tres tienen sus correspondientes en el de Tumbes (son comunes a ambas poblaciones), no detectándose la banda principal del primero, en el segundo. En *L. rhodomystax*, se identifican en la parte superior dos bandas bien resueltas que co-

Fig. 11.– Cariotipo de *Leptodactylus pentadactylus* (2n = 22). Se observan constricciones secundarias en la región proximal al centrómero, en el par 8.

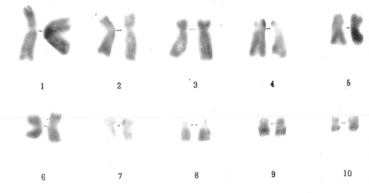

Tabla 4.— Datos cariométricos de *Ameiva ameiva cf. petersii* (AAP), *Anolis bombiceps* (ABO), y *Thecadactylus rapicauda* (TRA) (Reptilia) de Pakitza.

PC	AAP			ABO			TRA		
	LR	IC	TC	LR	IC	TC	LR	IC	TC
1	13.0	0.166	st	19.0	0.405	m	10.8	0.189	st
2	9.2	0.323	sm	14.1	0.385	sm	8.2	0.322	sm
3	7.9	0.191	st	12.8	0.369	sm	7.3	0.160	st
4	7.4	0.233	st	11.0	0.442	m	6.7	0.175	st
5	7.3	0.264	sm	10.0	0.337	sm	6.5	0.182	st
6	6.8	0.125	st	7.9	0.402	m	6.2	0.150	st
7	6.4	0.131	st	4.9	0.250	sm	5.6	0.155	st
8	5.5	0.154	st	4.3	0.393	m	5.3	0.165	st
9	5.1	0.169	st	4.0	0.381	m	5.0	0.113	t
10	4.7	0.182	st	3.4	0.409	m	4.6	0.187	st
11	4.3	0.167	st	2.8	0.225	st	4.1	0.143	st
12	3.4	0.240	st	2.4	0.250	sm	4.1	0.143	st
13	2.6	np	**	1.8	0.330	sm	3.8	0.155	st
14	2.1	np	**	1.7	0.365	sm	3.2	0.092	t
15	1.9	np	**	——			2.9	0.100	t
16	1.9	np	**	——			2.9	0.100	t
17	1.8	np	**	——			2.6	0.113	t
18	1.6	np	**	——			2.6	0.100	t
19	1.6	np	**	——			2.2	0.098	t
20	1.5	np	**	——			1.9	0.083	t
21	1.3	np	**	——			1.8	0.083	t
22	1.1	np	**	——			1.5	0.104	t
23	1.0	np	**	——			——		
24	0.9	np	**						

PC = Par cromosómico.
LR = Longitud relativa.
IC = Indice centromérico.
TC = Tipo cromosómico.
m = metacéntrico.
sm = submetacéntrico.
st = subtelocéntrico.
t = telocéntrico.
np = no precisable.
** = microcromosoma.

rresponden a péptidos de mayor peso molecular y una en la parte inferior de menor peso molecular al de los estándares.

En el sistema de la etapa II, la visualización de la migración electroforética de las muestras de dos ejemplares de *B. marinus* de Pakitza se vio inicialmente afectada por la presencia de contaminantes. Se asume sean mucopolisacáridos, dado que cuando se aplicó acetona a la muestra, se produjo un precipitado típico en ésta, desapareciendo el problema. Se pudo ver así en la Fig. 3a, que el patrón del especimen 1 exhibe una banda extra, por debajo de la banda principal que no se encuentra en el del 2 (señalada por un asterisco y guión). La Fig. 3b, que considera la supresión de una centrifugación, revela otra banda extra entre los mismos ejemplares.

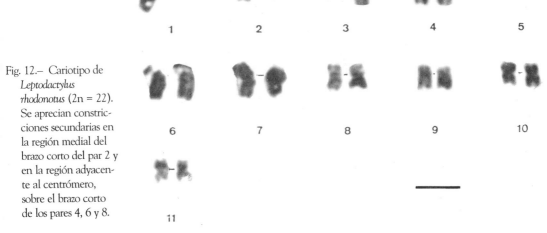

Fig. 12.– Cariotipo de *Leptodactylus rhodonotus* (2n = 22). Se aprecian constricciones secundarias en la región medial del brazo corto del par 2 y en la región adyacente al centrómero, sobre el brazo corto de los pares 4, 6 y 8.

La Fig. 4 presenta los resultados electroforéticos en el sistema de la etapa III, de tres conjuntos de corridas en geles con doble concentración de Tris y en gradiente de poliacrilamida (16%-25%). El tipo de concentración permitió obtener bandas con mayor separación, mientras que el gradiente mejoró la resolución de las mismas. En los tres geles, y señalado por un triángulo invertido, se indica la corrida de nuestro estándar, que fue la Insulina humana, cuya cadena ß es de 3.4 Kd y su cadena α es de 2.3 Kd (en Fig. 4c no se aprecia la cadena α).

En la Fig. 4a, vemos de izquierda a derecha las corridas de dos individuos de *B. marinus* de Pakitza (3 y 2), cada uno de ellos repetidos por tres veces y cada vez con diferente cantidad, una muestra de *B. limensis* (L) de Lima repetida dos veces también con diferentes cantidades, y el estándar. Los *marinus* (3 y 2), dentro de un patrón propio, revelan diferencias individuales. Así, la muestra 3 posee dos bandas de mayor peso molecular, que están ausentes en la 2, además de tener una banda de menor peso molecular (penúltima de abajo) con una migración ligeramente menor que la correspondiente en 2.

La Fig. 4b, permite visualizar de izquierda a derecha dos corridas con diferente cantidad de muestra de un mismo individuo de *Hyla lanciformis* (h) y *Bufo sp.* (grupo *"typhonius"*) (t) de Pakitza, así como de *B. marinus* (p) de Jaén y una sola muestra de *B. limensis* (L), de Lima, y el estándar. Se puede notar que cada especie presenta un patrón distintivo, aun cuando es menos nítido en *Bufo sp.* por el fondo sobre-coloreado, y en *Hyla*, en donde se encuentran reunidos los péptidos en la zona central, percibiéndose sólo un cambio de tonalidad dentro de la banda principal y la separación de una de menor peso molecular.

Figura 13. Hemicariotipo de *Leptodactylus leptodactyloides* (n = 11 y 2n = 22). Nótese el tamaño similar de los pares 1 y 2.

Finalmente, en la Fig. 4c se observan

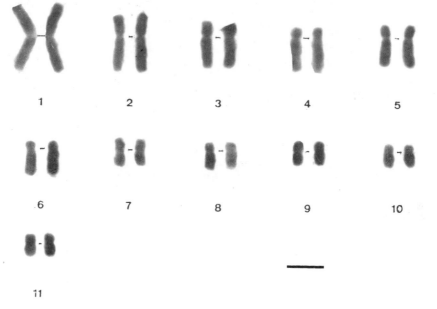

Fig. 14.– Cariotipo de *Hyla lanciformis* (2n = 22).

corridas de muestras en cantidades iguales de concentraciones semejantes del género *Bufo*, *B. marinus* (Pakitza), *B. limensis*, *B. marinus* (Jaén) y *B. sp.* (grupo "*typhonius*") (2, L, p, t, respectivamente), manifestándose en patrones con mejor separación y resolución de bandas, que posibilitan una comparación primaria intra e interespecífica. Completan la figura el estándar y una muestra de *Hyla lanciformis*, que exhibe también mayor separación de bandas respecto a lo visto en la Fig. 4b.

DISCUSIÓN

PROCEDIMIENTOS EMPLEADOS

La técnica citoge-nética seguida en los anfibios y reptiles de Pakitza, creemos, ha sido apropiada por los buenos resultados obtenidos en condiciones de campo. Los cariotipos representan el primer nivel de la caracterización genética de las poblaciones del área de estudio.

Los procedimientos moleculares en venenos de anfibios han sido efectuados con carácter experimental. Los resultados

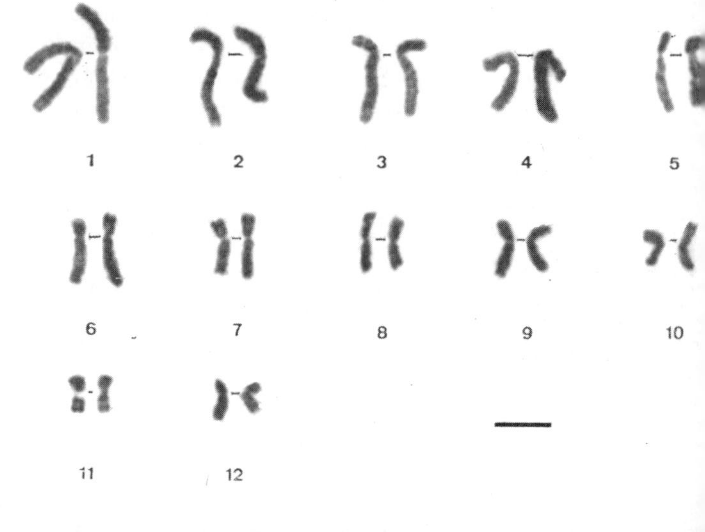

Fig. 15.– Cariotipo de *Scinax rubra* (2n = 24). Las constricciones secundarias se observan en la región adyacente al centrómero en el brazo largo del par 11.

540

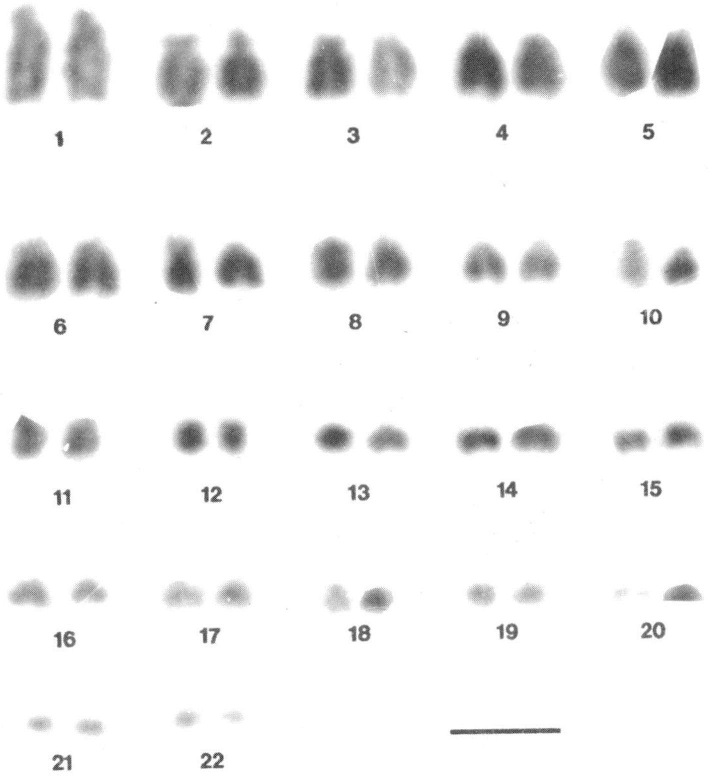

Fig. 16.– Cariotipo de *Thecadactylus rapicauda* (2n = 44). Las constricciones se observan en los brazos cortos de los pares 2 y 7, y en los telómeros del brazo largo del par 15. Nótese el sugerente heteromorfismo del par 7.

indican la conveniencia de utilizar en el futuro el sistema electroforético de la etapa III, por alcanzar mejor resolución de bandas. Tales procedimientos deben continuarse a fin de estudiar, conjuntamente con los datos cariotípicos, la diversidad genética y la sistemática de los anfibios. Autores tales como Baverstock et al. (1983, 1986), Bogart (1972, 1973, 1974), Cei (1985), Reig (1983), Reig y Useche (1976), Reig et al. (1980), Volobouev et al. (1987) y J. P. Bogart y S. B. Hedges (in litt) han demostrado la utilidad de este tipo de estudios.

Un enfoque sintético de los resultados de estas metodologías por taxa, sus implicancias sistemático-evolutivas y las referentes a la diversidad genética de las especies en el área de estudio, se hace necesario y lo ofrecemos a continuación.

TAXA GENÉTICAMENTE CARACTERIZADOS

Bufo marinus cf. marinus

El cariotipo a bandas C de los *marinus* de Pakitza resultó distinto a los encontrados en localidades distantes como Aguas Verdes, Jaén, Tingo María y Trujillo, e igual al de otras dos cercanas, Boca Colorado y Tambopata (Figs. 1, 5, 6, 7 y 20d, y Tabla 2). Esto prueba razonablemente la existencia de diversidad genética horizontal (o comparada) entre los *marinus* de Perú. En Córdova y Descailleaux (1996a) se describen formalmente los cariotipos de *marinus* que aquí se mencionan en sus rasgos más notables. En ese trabajo como en éste, se reconoce la condición polimórfica de una banda C+ en el brazo corto del par 11 de los *marinus* de Pakitza, que aparece débilmente asociada a los fenotipos "poeppigii" y "marinus" existentes en dicha localidad. En sólo cuatro casos se encontró correlación positiva (dos "poeppigii" fueron 11pC-/11pC- y dos "marinus" 11pC+/

11pC+), pero níngun híbrido (11pC+/11pC-) se pudo relacionar con los "fenotipos intermedios". Asimismo, en Córdova y Descailleaux (1996a), se discute ampliamente sobre la diversidad cariotípica de los *marinus* y su correspondencia con los morfo-taxa reconocidos para Perú. Además se concluye, y aquí lo confirmamos, que existen cariotipos que estarían ocupando áreas geográficas determinadas y que, cuando menos dos de ellos hibridizan en al menos un punto específico: Neshuya (Dpto. de Ucayali) (Fig. 1 y 6, y Tabla 2); también que existirían más cariotipos que morfo-taxa y que los *marinus* de Perú deben ser tratados como una especie con varias subespecies reconocibles por su cariotipo, precisando más lo propuesto por Zug y Zug (1979) en este sentido. Finalmente, que la morfología a bandas C del par 3 de los *marinus* de Pakitza constituye un estado intermedio o transicional (quizá relictual) entre otros dos existentes. Según este par, se forman dos grupos con los cariotipos de *Bufo* mundialmente conocidos, donde el morfo de Pakitza es el nexo genético entre tales cariotipos (vía el híbrido) y el lógico, para la cariosistemática del género (Córdova y Descailleaux, 1996a)

Los hallazgos electroforéticos en *marinus* de Perú presentados aquí son de carácter preliminar y muestran variantes que requieren de un análisis apropiado para su correcta interpretación. De los *marinus* de Pakitza se procesaron cuatro ejemplares (tres hembras y un macho) de expediciones distintas. Una de las hembras - cuya corrida electroforética no aparece en las figuras - fue colectada en octubre de 1991 y los especímenes restantes en febrero de 1992 (signados 1, 2 y 3 en Figs. 2, 3a y 4c). Los cuatro individuos en los distintos procedimientos electroforéticos exhibieron más regularidades que diferencias entre sus corridas. El especimen signado con el 2, corresponde en todos los casos al mismo ejemplar y se convirtió en el sistema de referencia que posibilitó la comparación entre los resultados de diferentes individuos. Se pudo apreciar que este ejemplar resultó casi idéntico al colectado en 1991 y acusó pocas diferencias (2-4 bandas) respecto a los especímenes 1 y 3, pero dentro de un patrón general (20-25 bandas) que puede ser tentativamente propuesto como representativo de las poblaciones de *marinus* de Pakitza (Fig. 4c).

Fig. 17.– Cariotipo de *Anolis bombiceps* (2n = 28). Se observan constricciones secundarias en la región media del brazo corto del par 2.

Los demás ejemplares de *Bufo* ensayados, teniendo en cuenta lo precedente y el que no acusan patologías evidentes en su morfología externa, creemos podrían representar razonablemente a sus respectivas especies o poblaciones, considerando las limitaciones de haber analizado un único ejemplar de cada uno de ellas. Alberts (1991) con las mismas limitaciones llegó a establecer relaciones adaptativas y filogenéticas en 16 especies de

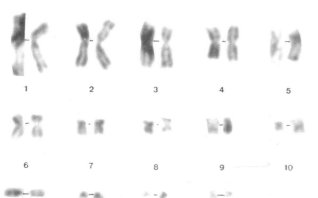

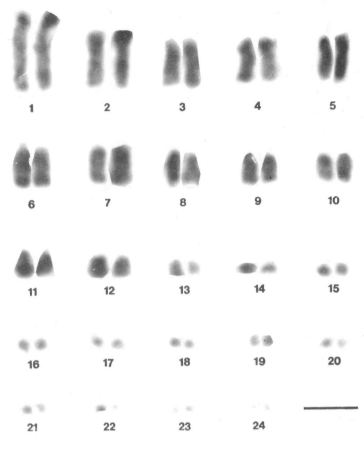

Fig. 18.– Cariotipo de *Ameiva ameiva cf. petersii* (2n = 48). Obsérvese los pares 2 y 5 que son submetacéntricos.

lagartijas. Así, las diferencias halladas entre los patrones electroforéticos de los *marinus* de localidades distantes (Figs. 1, 2, 4b y 4c) se corresponden con las de los cariotipos asignados para esas áreas. Una visión general de la Fig. 4c nos indica la muy probable existencia en el género *Bufo*, de un patrón electroforético específico de especie o población para proteínas y péptidos de venenos de parotoides, con bandas comunes y propias, susceptibles de ser evaluadas y de establecer relaciones de distancia o semejanza genética entre ellas, tales como las de Nei (1981) o Rogers (1972). Asimismo, y de *grosso* modo, podemos notar en la misma figura la semejanza de patrones entre B. *marinus* (Pakitza), B. *marinus* (Jaén) y B. *limensis* (2, p y L, respectivamente), diferenciables claramente del de B. sp. (grupo *"typhonius"*) (t).

En el estado del estudio, los resultados permiten afirmar que los *marinus* de Pakitza conforman poblaciones que poseen características singulares como el ser polifénicas, pues se componen de dos fenotipos básicos que intergradan ("marinus", "poeppigii" y sus "intermedios"), polimórficas (cromosómica y molecularmente), y con un cariotipo y patrón electroforético distinto a los hallados para los *marinus* de otras áreas de Perú. En lo sucesivo nos referiremos a los *marinus* de Pakitza como B. m. cf. *marinus* "del Sur" (BMM-S), resultando importante conservar su hábitat, por sus características genético-evolutivas quizá únicas, que podrían ser claves para el mantenimiento de la diversidad genética total de la especie.

Bufo sp. (grupo *"typhonius"*)

Parece ser el primer reporte del cariotipo (Figs. 8 y 21a, y Tabla 3) para esta especie del grupo *"typhonius"* de Pakitza. Segun Hoogmoed (1977, 1986, 1990), los *"typhonius"* del Perú están innominados y, si bien el ejemplar procesado concordó con la descripción que Caldwell (1991) hizo de B. *"typhonius"* de Brasil

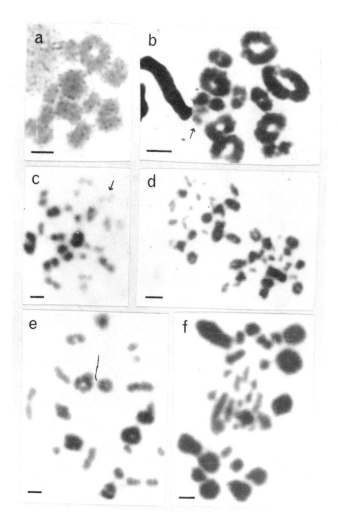

Fig. 19.– Configuraciones meióticas (diacinesis y metafases I) de anfibios y reptiles de Pakitza. La barra horizontal en el ángulo inferior izquierdo de cada vista indica 5 µm. Se observan los bivalentes de: a) *Leptodactylus bolivianus* (n = 11), b) *Hyla fasciata* (n = 12) (señalado por una flecha el menor de los bivalentes que en todas las vistas exhibió coloración atenuada), c) *Thecadactylus rapicauda* (n = 22) (con una flecha se señala un bivalente que ha perdido su pareamiento), d) *Ameiva ameiva* (se aprecia dos diacinesis cada una con n = 24), e) *Anolis fuscoauratus* (n = 22), f) *Platemys platycephala* (n = 33).

y con la fotografía de B. *margaritifera* (= B. *"typhonius"*), en Hoogmoed (1990), creemos prudente no atribuir este cariotipo a especie alguna, hasta tener mayores evidencias. Ningún miembro del grupo figura entre los cariotipos de *Bufo* reportados por Beçak *et al.* (1970), Bogart (1972), Brum-Zorrilla y Saez (1973), Benirschke y Hsu (1971, 1973, 1975), y Schmid (1978). Tampoco en listas o revisiones como las de King (1990), Morescalchi (1973) y Rabello (1970). Sólo Kuramoto (1990) reporta el número cromosómico (2n = 22) para *typhonius* y Bogart (1972) exhibe un cariotipo de B. *crucifer* [del grupo *"typhonius"* (Cei, 1972)], ambos coincidentes con el número cromosómico reportado aquí.

El patrón electroforético de B. sp. muestra tres conjuntos de proteínas y pép-tidos de mayor, medio y menor peso molecular que los estándares (Figs. 4b y 4c).

Leptodactylus bolivianus

Posiblemente este cariotipo (Fig. 9 y 20a, y Tabla 3) sea el primer reporte a nivel de bandas C para la especie. Figura entre los cariotipos a coloración convencional de los *Leptodactylus* reportados por Bogart (1974), bajo el nombre de L. *insularum* (Heyer y Diment, 1974) en un especimen de Colombia, no existiendo ningún dato publicado sobre bandeo cromosómico en esta especie según King (1990) y Kuramoto (1990). Las constricciones secundarias las tiene en el brazo corto del par 10, siendo un rasgo compartido con L. *natalensis* (Bogart, 1974), si bien éste lo tiene en el brazo largo.

544

Leptodactylus rhodomystax

Es muy probable que sea el primer reporte del cariotipo de esta especie (Figs. 10 y 20b, y Tabla 3), tanto en coloración convencional como para bandas C. No está entre los cariotipos convencionales publicados por Heyer (1972) y Bogart (1974) para *Leptodactylus*, ni en las listas de King (1990) y Kuramoto (1990). En este nivel de coloración es semejante al de *bolivianus* antes citado, tanto en el número de cromosomas, como en la morfología de la mayoría de sus pares, discrepando sólo en lo referente a la ubicación de las constricciones secundarias, que en *rhodomystax* se encuentra en el telómero del brazo largo del par 3. En donde se aprecian mayores diferencias es en bandas C. La distribución de la heterocromatina constitutiva entre estas especies es distinta, sobre todo en los pares 1, 3, 5, 8, 10 y 11.

El patrón electroforético (Fig. 2) presenta tres bandas, dos muy próximas de mayor peso molecular y la tercera que es de menor peso que los estándares.

Leptodactylus pentadactylus

El cariotipo convencional de esta especie (Figs. 11 y 21c, y Tabla 3) fue muy similar al reportado por Bogart (1974) para dos de sus poblaciones, una de Huánuco (Perú) y otra de Sao Paulo (Brasil). Coinciden en el número de cromosomas y en la morfología de casi todos los pares, incluso la localización de las constricciones secundarias (en el brazo corto del par 8). Existe una diferencia y está en los pares 4 y 5, que los ubicamos en el cariotipo en orden inverso respecto al de Bogart, por cuanto la longitud relativa lo determinó así. Probablemente exista algún reordenamiento cromosómico (p. ej. translocación recíproca) entre estos pares.

En este nivel de comparación, parece muy semejante a los cariotipos de *bolivianus* y *rhodomystax* tratados antes, así como al de *L. knudseni* reportado por Heyer (1972). Cabe esperar, como ocurrió con los dos primeros, que cuando se aplique la técnica de bandeo C se acentúen las diferencias.

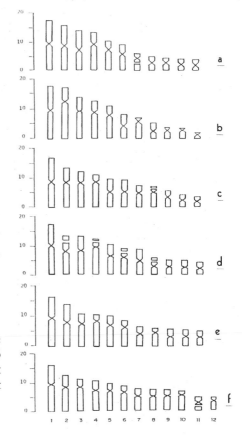

Fig. 20.– Ideogramas conteniendo el patrón de bandas C de: a) *Leptodactylus bolivianus*, b) *L. rhodomystax*, c) *Bufo marinus* "de Aguas Verdes", d) *B. marinus* "del Sur", y e) *B. marinus* "del Norte".

Leptodactylus rhodonotus

En coloración convencional, el cariotipo de esta especie (Figs. 12 y 21d, y Tabla 3) resultó semejante a los reportados para Perú por Bogart (1974) para la localidad de Huánuco, y Manya et al. (1985) para la de Tingo María (ambas en el Dpto. de Huánuco). Los tres poseen 22 cromosomas y diferencias respecto al de la última localidad, éstas se deben básicamente a la distinta forma de calificar a los tipos cromosómicos: cualitativa en Manya et al. (1985) y cuantitativa en el presente trabajo. La ubicación invertida de los pares 6 y 7 en el cariotipo y el uso de los términos "subtelocéntrico" y "telocéntrico" aquí, en vez del desusado "acrocéntrico", son las diferencias más notables, pudiendo decirse que a este nivel se trata del mismo cariotipo. Si la coloración de plata revela que las constricciones secundarias del par 2 portan las regiones organizadoras del nucleolo activas, concordarían plenamente.

Respecto al de Bogart (1974), las principales discrepancias están en el número de constricciones secundarias halladas. Bogart encontró dos pares como sus portadores (el 2 y el 7). Aquí hemos visto hasta cuatro, y están en los brazos cortos de los pares 2, 4, 6 y 8. El par 6 nuestro bien puede ser el 7 de Bogart, si se aplicasen los mismos criterios estadísticos para medir a los cromosomas portadores de constricciones secundarias.

Fig. 21.– Ideogramas convencionales de: a) *Bufo sp.* (grupo *"typhonius"*), b) *Leptodactylus leptodactyloides*, c) *L. pentadactylus*, d) *L. rhodonotus*, e) *Hyla lanciformis*, y f) *Sinax rubra*.

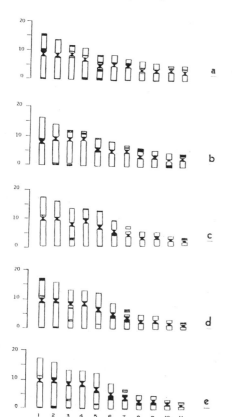

Leptodactylus leptodactyloides

Este cariotipo presentado aquí (2n = 22) puede considerarse el primer reporte para esta especie (Figs. 13 y 21b, y Tabla 3), cuya descripción coincide con la que Heyer (1994) dio para *Leptodactylus leptodactyloides*. Este autor afirma que pertenece al complejo *podicipinus-wagneri*, dentro del grupo *melanonotus*, y que se desconoce su cariotipo. No está en las listas de King (1990) y de Kuramoto (1990). Sólo se aprecia que coincide con el número cromosómico (2n = 22) reportado por Bogart (1974) para las especies del género.

Hyla fasciata

Carecemos de información sobre la morfología de los cromosomas somáticos de esta especie. El número diploide (2n = 24) fue reportado por Bogart y Bogart (1971), no contándose con más datos en la literatura según King (1990) y Kuramoto (1990). Puede ser éste el primer reporte en cuanto a la visualización de sus cromosomas meióticos y la determinación de su número haploide (n= 12, Fig. 19b). La morfología de sus cromosomas, según el tipo de bivalentes que forma, induce a creer que todos son meta o submetacéntricos. Quizá el más

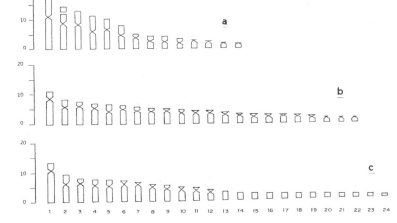

pequeño de los bivalentes sea el menos submetacéntrico del conjunto.

Hyla lanciformis

Presenta uno de los cariotipos atípicos para el género (2n = 22 cromosomas)

Fig. 22.– Ideogramas convencionales de: a) *Anolis bombiceps*, b) *Thecadactylus rapicauda* y c) *Ameiva ameiva* cf. *petersii*.

(Figs. 14 y 21e, y Tabla 3). Usualmente los *Hyla* se agrupan en los que poseen 24 cromosomas y los que tienen 30 (Anderson, 1991; Bogart, 1973; Schmid, 1978; Skuk y Langone, 1992). El segundo autor dice que sólo *H. albopunctata* y una población de *H. albofrenata* tienen este mismo número. No parece ser éste el primer reporte del cariotipo para la especie (R. O. de Sá, com. pers.), aun cuando no está entre las que cuentan con datos cromosómicos según King (1990) y Kuramoto (1990). El cariotipo convencional de los *lanciformis* de Pakitza resultó indistinguible del hallado por el primer autor (datos no publicados) en especímenes de Neshuya (Ucayali).

Scinax rubra

Un cariotipo de esta especie para Perú, pero sin indicar la localidad, fue reportado por Bogart (1973), bajo el nombre de *Hyla rubra*. Si bien ese cariotipo y el dado aquí (Figs. 15 y 21f, y Tabla 3) poseen el mismo número cromosómico (2n = 24 cromosomas), se apreciaron pequeñas diferencias en la longitud relativa de algunos de sus pares, que producen cambios en el orden asignado a cada uno dentro del cariotipo; así el 2 y el 3 nuestro están invertidos respecto al de Bogart. Dado que tales diferencias son muy pequeñas y las existentes entre los pares de un mismo cariotipo también lo son, debe tenerse mayores evidencias para pronunciarse sobre la posible causa de las mismas. En el *rubra* de Pakitza, encontramos las constricciones secundarias en el brazo largo del par 11, en la región adyacente al centrómero, dato que constituye un aporte respecto al trabajo de Bogart.

Platemys platycephala

El número haploide hallado (n = 33 bivalentes, Fig. 19f) en el único especimen procesado diferiría del reportado por Olmo (1986) [tomado de un cariotipo 2n = 64, Fig. 2a de Bickham (1984)] por tener un bivalente menos (n = 32). Desafortunadamente, no se indica la procedencia del material en esas publicaciones.

Ernst (1983), basado en criterios macromorfológicos, reportó variación geográfica en esta especie, tal que a una de sus poblaciones ubicada al noreste del Perú la ha reconocido como subespecie (*P. p. melanonota*). Importante será precisar si la diferencia encontrada en el número haploide se corresponde con el tipo de variación geográfica anotada o con alguna otra aún no precisada.

Thecadactylus rapicauda

El cariotipo de este gecónido dio como resultado 2n = 44 cromosomas y n = 22 bivalentes (Figs. 16, 19e, 22b y tabla 4), concordando en el número cromosómico con un reporte dado por Soma et al. (1975, citado por Olmo, 1986), en tanto que otro consignó 2n = 42 (McBee et al., 1984, citado por Olmo, 1986). No se ha podido hacer comparaciones mayores por cuanto aún no hemos visto sus cariotipos.

Llama la atención la semejanza existente entre el cariotipo convencional de *rapicauda* de Pakitza y el de dos especies de *Phyllodactylus* (Gekkonidae): *P. inaequalis* y *P. gerrhophygus*, reportados por Capetillo et al. (1992) para Chile. Todos los cromosomas en estas dos últimas son **t** o **st** como en *rapicauda*, estando las diferencias en el 2n (40 para los *Phyllodactylus* y 42 ó 44 para *Thecadactylus*) y en las dimensiones de los pares 1 y 2 de sus respectivos cariotipos. Son casi del mismo tamaño en los *Phylodactylus* (difieren en el orden del 0.02%), en tanto que en *Thecadactylus* la diferencia es notable (del orden de los 2.50%). Muy pocos reordenamientos cromosómicos explicarían estas diferencias, pero debe esperarse a tener información sobre sus cariotipos bandeados para hacer estimaciones más precisas. También deben obtenerse datos adicionales para conocer la naturaleza del heteromorfismo del par 7 aquí presentado. Bien podría tratarse de un heteromorfismo sexual del tipo XY reportado antes para otros gecónidos neotropicales (McBee et al. 1987).

Anolis bombiceps

El cariotipo de *bombiceps* de Pakitza (2n = 28) (Figs. 17, 22a y Tabla 4) parece ser el primer reporte para la especie, el de menor número para el grupo al que pertenece (*chrysolepis*) y uno de los menores del género (Blake, 1983; Gorman y Atkins, 1967 Gorman et al., 1983; Olmo, 1986; Vanzolini y Williams, 1970). Posee seis pares de macrocromosomas metacéntricos y no parece tener microcromosomas típicos. Si acaso se debiera calificar así a algunos, se limitaría a los pares 11-14. Los signados con los números 7-10 son, en efecto, cromosomas pequeños (**m** o **sm**), pero mucho mayores a los mencionados anteriormente.

Anolis fuscoauratus

El número cromosómico de esta especie es muy distinto al de la precedente. Sólo se obtuvo su número haploide (n = 22 bivalentes, Fig. 19e). El número diploide que se infiere es de 44 cromosomas, que estaría dentro del rango reportado para el género y cercano a su límite superior (Gorman *et al.* 1983, Olmo 1986). Se espera más información para establecer mayores comparaciones cariotípicas.

Ameiva ameiva cf. petersii

El cariotipo de esta probable subespecie (2n = 48) (Figs. 18, 19d, 22c y Tabla 4) resultó diferente, en cuanto al número cromosómico, de otros reportados para la especie y para el género: 2n = 50 (Gorman 1970, Schmid, 1988). Gorman menciona para dos subespecies de *Ameiva ameiva* (*ameiva* y *tobagona*), una fórmula cariotípica conformada por 26 macrocromosomas acrocéntricos (sic) (todos **st** o **t**) y 24 microcromosomas. El cariotipo dado aquí, tiene 24 macrocromosomas (22 **st** o **t** y 2 **sm**) y 24 microcromosomas. Una explicación de las diferencias podría ser que la morfología del par **sm** (el 2) en *petersii* se habría debido a una fusión de un cromosoma 2 de tipo *ameiva* o *tobagona*, con uno de los microcromosomas en el ancestro de *petersii*.

DIVERSIDAD GENÉTICA Y ÁREA DE ESTUDIO

Los aspectos descriptivos del valle del río Manu y la Zona Reservada del Manu, donde se ubica la Estación Biologica BIOLAT de Pakitza, se pueden encontrar en Erwin (1991). En esta parte trataremos sobre las relaciones entre el tipo y significado de la diversidad hallada en los herpetozoos de dicha zona.

La diversidad genética detectada en los anfibios pertenece a dos de los tres tipos fundamentales reconocidos: la de los genes estructurales o proteica y la cromosomico-cariotípica (el tercer tipo es la del ADN) (Solbrig 1991, Bawa et al. 1991). En reptiles sólo se trabajó sobre la segunda de las nombradas.

Las proteínas y péptidos de venenos tanto de la piel como de la especializada parotoides de anuros, son expresión directa del código genético (Cei, 1985; Low 1972), y las diferencias entre individuos coespecíficos o no son tratadas como diferencias entre estructuras homólogas (Cei, 1985; Huntsman, 1970; Low, 1972). Representan por ello una poderosa herramienta en la elucidación de problemas taxonómicos, adaptativos y evolutivos (Alberts, 1991; Cei, 1985; Low, 1972). Lo más importante aquí es la incorporación de un nuevo método para caracterizar, identificar y cuantificar de manera más precisa la diversidad genética intra e interespecífica de los anfibios de nuestra área de estudio.

La diversidad cromosomico-cariotípica de una especie es otra manera de conocer la diversidad genética de la misma, en razón de la usual dependencia evolutiva existente entre la primera y los genes estructurales (Cothran y Smith, 1983). Además, dado que las variantes cromosómicas por su naturaleza cambian las relaciones reproductivas entre sus portadores, promueven la modificación de las frecuencias de los genes que involucran y limitan la cohesión intraespecífica, es posible inferir acerca de la estructura poblacional de los taxa estudiados citogenéticamente (Fontdevila, 1987; Lewontin, 1979; White, 1978). En suma, caracterizar genéticamente a individuos, poblaciones y especies por métodos cariotípicos y moleculares brindará sólidas bases sistemático-evolutivas y para propósitos de su conservación.

Los *marinus* del Perú son claro ejemplo de las inferencias que permite tal caracterización. Los datos genéticos revelan diversidad molecular y cromosómica entre los *marinus* de Pakitza (diversidad vertical o local) y entre éstos, y los de las poblaciones que forman a ambos lados de los Andes en el Norte del Perú (diversidad horizontal o comparada). Tal hecho sugiere una diferenciación genética de tipo geográfico, siendo el paso inmediato profundizar sobre su estructura y dinámica poblacional para saber si responde o no - por ejemplo - al concepto de una metapoblación *sensu* Sinsch (1992), y delinear así la estrategia primaria de conservación de la especie.

Además, la existencia en Pakitza de poblaciones de otras especies cuyos cariotipos son diferentes de sus similares en otras áreas geográficas, como son *Leptodactylus pentadactylus, Platemys platycephala, Thecadactylus rapicauda* y *Ameiva ameiva*, estarían indicando la importancia del área de estudio como reservorio genético para la conservación de tales especies y, por ende, para el sostenimiento de su ecosistema. De la parte de la herpetofauna que son los anfibios, se sabe que su biomasa constituye una considerable fracción de numerosos ecosistemas y en algunos de éstos, son el grupo dominante de vertebrados (Anónimo, 1991).

Finalmente, deben estudiarse más taxa desde el punto de vista de su diversidad genética local y comparada, así como desde el filogenético y el biogeográfico, a fin de tener base para evaluar rigurosamente las áreas protegidas existentes y priorizar las que deban serlo en el futuro, dado que se cuenta ya con algunos estimadores que consideran tales estudios para este propósito (Morrone y Crisci 1992, Brooks et al. 1992).

AGRADECIMIENTOS

Los autores expresan su especial gratitud al Dr. Gerardo Lamas y a los revisores anónimos, por las críticas y sugerencias hechas al manuscrito. Asimismo, agradecen al Dr. Jaime Descailleaux por las facilidades brindadas como Jefe del Laboratorio de Genética Humana de la Universidad Nacional Mayor de San Marcos, a los Dres. Roy W. McDiarmid, Robert P. Reynolds, María L. Guevara y Ricardo Fujita, así como a los Sres. V. R. Morales, P. Baltazar, J. Icochea y A. Angulo, por su ayuda en diferentes partes del trabajo y el suministro de algunos ejemplares, y al Programa Biodiversidad en Latinoamérica (BIOLAT) de la Smithsonian Institution (USA), por el apoyo financiero al autor principal durante el vasto período de la investigación. También manifiestan su reconocimiento al Consejo Nacional de Ciencia y Tecnología (CONCYTEC) (Perú), a la International Foundation for Science (IFS) (Suecia), al Fondo Especial de Desarrollo Universitario de la Universidad Nacional Mayor de San Marcos (FEDU-UNMSM) (Perú) y al Dr. John A. Maggio, Harvard Medical School (USA), por la subvención parcial otorgada para estudios electroforéticos y/o expediciones a áreas distintas a las de Pakitza, que permitieron obtener información complementaria para el presente trabajo.

LITERATURA CITADA

Alberts, A. C. 1991. Phylogenetic and adaptative variation in lizards femoral gland secretions. Copeia, 1:69-79.

Anderson, K. 1991. Chromosome Evolution in Holartic *Hyla* treefrogs. Pp. 299-331, *in* Amphibian Cytogenetics and Evolution (D. M. Green and S. K. Sessions, eds.). Academic Press, Inc., New York, 456 pp.

Anónimo. 1991. Declining Amphibian Populations - a global phenomenon? Findings and recomendations. Alytes 9(2):33-42.

Baverstock, P. R., M. Adams and C. H. S. Watts. 1986. Biochemical differentiation among karyotypic forms of Australian *Rattus*. Genetica 71:11-22.

Baverstock, P. R., M. Adams, L. R. Maxson and T. H. Yosida. 1983. Genetic differentiation among Karyotypic forms of the Black Rat, *Rattus rattus*. Genetics, 105:969-983

Bawa, K., B. Schaal, O. T. Solbrig, S. Stearns, A. Templeton and G. Vidal. 1991. Biodiversity from the gene to the species. A. Pp. 15-36, *in* From genes to Ecosystems : A Research Agenda for Biodiversity (O. T. Solbrig, ed.). Published by The International Union of Biological Sciences, Paris, 123 pp.

Beçak, M. L., L. Denaro and W. Beçak 1970. Polyploidy and mechanisms of karyotype diversification in Amphibia. Cytogenetics, 9:225-238.

Benirschke, K. and T. C. Hsu. 1971. Chromosome Atlas: Fish, Amphibians, Reptiles and Birds. Vol. 1, Folios Am 1-11.

————. 1973. Chromosome Atlas: Fish, Amphibians, Reptiles and Birds. Vol. 2, Folios Am 12-23.

————. 1975. Chromosome Atlas: Fish, Amphibians, Reptiles and Birds. Vol. 3, Folios Am 24-36.

Bickham, J. W. 1984. Patterns and Modes of Chromosomal Evolution in Reptiles. Pp. 13-40, in Chromosomes in Evolution and Eucaryotic groups. (A. K. Sharma and A. Sharma, eds,). Vol. 2, CRC Press, Boca Raton, 447 pp.

Blake, J. A. 1983. Chromosomal C-banding in *Anolis grahani*. Pp. 621-625, *in* Advances in Herpetology and Evolutionary Biology (A. G. J. Rhodin and K. Miyata, eds.). Museum of Comparative Zoology, Cambridge, 725 pp.

Bogart, J. P. 1972. Karyotypes. Pp. 171-195, *in* Evolution in the Genus *Bufo* (W. F. Blair, ed). University of Texas Press, Austin, 459 pp.

————. 1973. Evolution of Anuran Karyotypes. Pp. 337-349, *in* Evolutionary Biology of the Anurans (J. L. Vial, ed.). University Missouri Press, Columbia, 470 pp.

————. 1974. A karyosystematic study of frogs in the genus *Leptodactylus* (Anura: Leptodactylidae). Copeia, 4:728-737.

Bogart, J. P. and J. E. Bogart. 1971. Genetic compatibility experiments between some South American anuran amphibians. Herpetologica, 27:225-235.

Brooks, D. R., R. L. Mayden and D. A. McLennan. 1992. Phylogeny and Biodiversity: Conserving our Evolutionary legacy. Trends in Ecology and Evolution, 7(2):55-59.

Brum-Zorrilla, N and F. A. Sáez. 1973. Chromosomes of South American Bufonidae (Amphibia: Anura). Caldasia, 11(52):51-61.

Caldwell, J. P. 1991. A new species of toad in the genus *Bufo* from Pará, Brazil, with an unusual breeding site. Papéis Avulsos de Zoologia, 37(26):289-400.

Capetillo, J., I. Northland y P. Iturra. 1992. Caracterización morfológica y cromosómica de *Phyllodactylus inaequalis* Cope y *P. gerrhopygus* (Wiegmann)(Gekkonidae). Nueva distribución geográfica en el Norte de Chile. Acta Zoológica Lilloana, 41:219—224.

Cei, J. M. 1972. *Bufo* of South America. Pp. 82-92, *in* Evolution in the Genus *Bufo* (W. F. Bair, ed.). University of Texas Press, Austin, 459 pp.

————. 1985. Taxonomic and Evolutionary Significance of Peptides in Amphibian Skins. Peptides, 6(3):13-16.

Córdova, J. H. 1993. Estudios cariotípicos y problemas taxonómicos en el grupo de *Bufo spinulosus* (Amphibia: Anura). Tesis para Título Profesional, Universidad Nacional Mayor de San Marcos, Lima, 55 pp.

Córdova J. H., y J. Descailleaux. 1996a. En revisión. Tres cariotipos diferentes y un híbrido en poblaciones naturales de *Bufo marinus* (L.) en Perú. Theorema.

————. 1996b. En revisión. Evolución cariotípica del género *Bufo* (Amphibia: Anura) en el Perú. Theorema .

Córdova, J. H., J. Descailleaux y W. Manya. 1987. Descripción del cariotipo de *Telmatobius arequipensis* (Anura: Leptodactylidae) y relaciones citogenéticas con otras especies del género. Revista Latinoamericana de Genética, 1(1):44-53.

Cothran E. G. and M. H. Smith. 1983. Chromosomal and genic divergence in Mammals. Systematic Zoology, 32:360-368.

Duellman, W. E. 1978. The biology of an equatorial herpetofauna in Amazonian Ecuador. Miscellaneous Publications, Museum of Natural History, University of Kansas, 65:1-352.

Ernst, C. M. 1983. Geographic Variation in Neotropical Turtle, *Platemys platycephala*. Journal of Herpetology, 17(4):345-355.

Erwin, T. L. 1991. Natural History of the carabid beetles at the BIOLAT Biological Station, Rio Manu, Pakitza, Peru. Revista Peruana de Entomología, 33:1-85.

Fling, P. S. and S. D. Gregerson. 1986. Peptide and protein molecular determination by electrophoresis using a High-Molarity tris Buffer System with Urea. Analytical Biochemistry, 155:83-88.

Fontdevila, A. 1987. Inestabilidad genética y estructura poblacional como factores del cambio transespecífico. Evolución Biológica 1:161-198.

Giulian, G. G., et al. 1985. Resolution of low molecular weight polypeptides in non urea sodium dodecyl sulfate polyacylamide gel system. Federal Proceedings. 44:686.

Gorman, G. C. 1970. Chromosomes and the Systematics of the family Teiidae (Sauria: Reptilia). Copeia, 2:230-245.

Gorman, G. C. and L. Atkins. 1967. The relationships of the *Anolis* of the *roquet* species group (Sauria:Iguanidae). II. Comparative chromosome cytology. Systematic Zoology, 16(2):137-143.

Gorman, G. C., D. Buth, M. Soulé and S. Y. Yang. 1983. The relationships of the Puerto Rican *Anolis*: Electrophoretic and Karyotypic studies. Pp. 626-642, *in* Advances in Herpetology and Evolutionary Biology (A. G. J. Rhodin and K. Miyata, eds.). Museum of Comparative Zoology, Cambridge, 725 pp.

Green, D. M. 1986. Systematics and Evolution of Western North American frogs allied to *Rana aurora* and *Rana boylii*: Karyological evidence. Systematic Zoology. 35(3):273-282.

Green, D. M. and S. K. Sessions. 1991. Nomenclature for Chromosomes. Pp. 431-432, *in* Amphibian Cytogenetics and Evolution (D. M. Green and S. K. Sessions, eds.). Academic Press, Inc. New York, 456 pp.

Hedges, S. B. 1986. An electrophoretic analysis of Holartic hylid frog evolution. Systematic Zoology, 35(1):1-21.

———. 1989. Evolution and Biogeography of West Indian Frogs of the genus *Eleutherodactylus*: Slow-evolving and the Major Groups. Pp. 305-370, *in*: Biogeography of the West Indies: Past, Present, and Future (C. Woods, ed.), Sandhill Crane Press, Gainesville, Florida. 623 pp.

Heyer, R. W. 1972. The status of *Leptodactylus pumilio* Boulenger (Amphibia, Leptodactylidae) and the description of a new species of *Leptodactylus* from Ecuador. Contributions in Science Los Angeles County Museum, 231:1-8.

———. 1979. Systematics of the *pentadactylus* Species Group of the Frog Genus *Leptodactylus* (Amphibia: Leptodactylidae). Smithsonian Contributions to Zoology, 301:1-43.

———. 1994. Variation within the *Leptodactylus podicipinus-wagneri* Complex of frogs (Amphibia:Leptodactylidae). Smithsonian Contributions to Zoology, 546:1-124.

Heyer, R. W. and M. J. Diment. 1974. The karyotype of *Vanzolinius discodactylus* and comments on usefulness of karyotype in determining relationships in the *Leptodactylus* complex (Amphibia, Leptodactylidae). Proceedings of the Biological Society of Washington, 87:327-335.

Hoogmoed, M. S. 1977 On the presence of *Bufo nasitus* Werner in Guiana, with a redescription of the species on the basis of recently collected material. Rijksmuseum van Natuurlijke Historie te Leiden, 51(16):265-275.

———. 1986. Biosystematic studies of the *Bufo "typhonius"* group. A preliminary progress report. Pp. 147-150, *in* Studies in Herpetology (Z. Rocek, ed.), Charles University, Prague, Czechoslovakia.

———. 1990. Biosystematics of South American Bufonidae, with special reference to the *Bufo "typhonius"* group. Pp. 113-123, *in* Vertebrates in the Tropics (G. Peters and R.

Hutterer, eds.). Museum Alexander Koenig, Bonn.

Huntsman, G. R. 1970. Disc Gel Electrophoresis blood sera and muscle extracts from some catostomid fishes. Copeia, 3: 457.

Jotterand-Bellomo, M. 1984. New developments in vertebrate cytotaxonomy VIII: Les Chromosomes des Rongeurs (Ordre Rodentia Bowdich, 1821). Genetica, 64:3-64.

King, M. 1990. Chordata 2. Amphibia. (Animal Cytogenetics, Vol. 4). Gebrüder Borntraeger, Berlin, 242 pp.

Kuramoto, M. 1990. A List of Chromosome numbers of Anuran amphibians. Bulletin of Furuoka University of Education, 39 (3):83-127.

Levan, A., K. Fredga and A. A. Sandberg. 1964. Nomenclature for centromeric positions on chromosomes. Hereditas, 52:201-220.

Lewontin, R. C. 1979. La base genética de la evolución. Ediciones Omega, Barcelona, 328 pp.

Low, B. S. 1972. Evidence from Parotoid-Gland Secretions. Pp. 244-264, in: Evolution in Genus *Bufo*. (W. F. Blair, ed.). University Texas Press, Austin, 459 pp.

Manya, W., J. H. Córdova y J. Descailleaux. 1985. Cariotipo y regiones organizadoras del nucleolo en *Leptodactylus rhodonotus* (Anura: Leptodactylidae). Boletín de la Facultad de Ciencias Biológicas de la Universidad "Ricardo Palma", 2:10-16.

McBee, K., J. W. Bickham, and J. R. Dixon. 1987. Male Heterogamety and Chromosomal Variation in Carribean Gekkos. Journal of Herpetology, 21(1):68-71.

Meyer, K. and H. Linde. 1971. Collection of Toad Venoms and Chemistry of the Toad Venoms Steroids. Pp. 521-556, in Venomous Animals and their Venoms (W. Bucherl and E. Buckley, eds.). Academic Press, New York, 37(2):1-687 pp.

Morales, V. R. y R. W. McDiarmid. 1996. Annotated Checklist of the amphibians and reptiles of Pakitza, Manu National Park Reserve Zone, with comments on the herpetofauna of Madre de Dios, Peru. In: Proceedings of the Symposium The Biodiversity of Pakitza and its environs. Biodiversity Programs. Smithsonian Institution (este volumen).

Morescalchi, A. 1973. Amphibia. Pp. 233-348, in Cytotaxonomy and Vertebrate Evolution

(A. B. Chiarelli y E. Capanna, eds.). Academic Press, London, 783 pp.

Morrisey, H. J. 1981. Silver Stain for protein in Polyacrylamide gels: A modified procedure with enhanced uniform sensitivity. Analytical Biochemistry, 177:307-310.

Morrone, J. J. y J. V. Crisci. 1992. Aplicación de métodos filogenéticos y panbiogeográficos en la conservación de la diversidad biológica. Evolución Biológica, 6:53-66.

Nei, M. 1981. Genetic distance and molecular taxonomy. (Problems in General Genetics, Vol.2). Proceedings of the XIV International Congress of Genetics. 2:7-22.

Olmo, E. 1986. Chordata 3 A. Reptilia. (Animal Cytogenetics, Vol 4). Gebrüder Borntraeger, Berlin, 100 pp.

Pritchard, P. C. H. and P. Trebbau. 1984. The Turtles of Venezuela. Publication of the Society for the study of Amphibians and Reptiles, Michigan, 414 pp.

Rabello, M. N. 1970. Chromosomal studies in Brasilian Anurans. Caryologia, 23(1):45-59.

Reig, O. A. 1983. Estado actual de la teoría de la formación de las especies animales. Informe Final IX Congreso Latinoamericano de Zoología: 37-57.

Reig, O. A. y M. Useche. 1976. Diversidad cariotípica y sistemática en poblaciones venezolanas de *Proechymis* (Rodentia, Echimidae), con datos adicionales sobre poblaciones de Perú y Colombia. Acta Científica Venezolana, 27:132-140.

Reig, O. A., M. Aguilera, M. A. Barros and M. Useche. 1980. Chromosomal Speciation in a Rassenkreis of Venezuelan spiny rats (Genus *Proechimys*, Rodentia, Echimidae). Genetica, 52/53:291-312.

Rogers, J. S. 1972. Measures of genetic similarity and genetic distance. Studies in Genetics VII, The University Texas Publication. 7213:145-153.

Ruiz, A. and A. Fontdevila. 1982. The Evolutionary History of *Drosophila buzzatii*. III. Cytogenetic relationships between two sibling species of the buzzatii cluster. Genetics, 101:503-518.

Schmid, M. 1978. Chromosome Banding in Amphibia. I. Constitutive Heterochromatin and Nucleolus Organizer Regions in *Bufo* and *Hyla*. Chromosama (Berl.), 63:361-388.

Schmid, M. and M. Guttembach 1988. Evolutionary diversity of reverse (R) fluorescent chromosome bands in vertebrates. Chromosoma (Berl.), 97:101-114.

Sinsch, U. 1992. Structure and dynamic of a natterjack toad metapopulation (*Bufo calamita*). Oecologia, 90:489-499.

Skuk, G. y J. A. Langone. 1992. Los cromosomas de cuatro especies del género *Hyla* (Anura: Hylidae) con número diploide 2n= 30. Acta Zoológica Lilloana, 41:165-171.

Solbrig, O. T. 1991. The IUBS-SCOPE-UNESCO Program of Research in Biodiversity. Pp. 5-14, *in* From Genes to Ecosystems: A Research Agenda for Biodiversity. (O. T. Solbrig, ed.). Published by The International Union of Biological Sciences, Paris, 123 pp.

Sumner, A. T. 1972. A simple technique for demostrating centromeric heterochromatin. Experimental Cell Research, 75:304-306.

Vanzolini, P. E. and E. E. Williams. 1970. I.- South American Anoles: The geographic differentiation and evolution of the *Anolis chrysolepis* species group (Sauria:Iguanidae).

Arquivos de Zoologia, Sao Paulo, 19 (1-2):1-124.

Vellard, J. 1959. Estudios sobre batracios andinos. V. El género *Bufo*. Memorias del Museo de Historia Natural. Imprenta de la Universidad Nacional Mayor de San Marcos. 8: 1-46 pp.

Volobouev, V. T., E. Viegas-Péguinot, F. Petter, B. Dutrillaux. 1987. Karyotypic diversity and taxonomic problems in the genus *Arvicanthis* (Rodentia, Muridae). Genetica, 72:147-150.

White, M. J. D. 1978. Modes of speciation. W. H. Freeman and Co. Edit., San Francisco, 455 pp.

Wiltfang, J., N. Arold and V. Neuhoff. 1991. A new multiphasic buffer system for sodium dodecyl sulfate-Polyacrylamide gel electrophoresis of proteins and peptides with molecular masses 100,000-1,000, and their detection with picomolar sensitivity. Electrophoresis, 12:352-366.

Zug, G. R. and P. B. Zug. 1979. The Marine Toad, *Bufo marinus*: A Natural History Resumé of Native Populations. Smithsonian Contributions to Zoology. 284:1-58 pp.

An Annotated List of Birds of the Biolat Biological Station at Pakitza, Perú.

GRACE P. SERVAT

Museo de Historia Natural, Universidad Nacional Mayor de San Marcos, Apartado 140434, Lima 14, Perú.[1]

ABSTRACT

The avifauna of Pakitza was periodically surveyed from 1987 to 1993 during both wet and dry seasons; 415 species of birds (76% of the lowland Manu National Park avifauna) are reported, with information on habitat and abundance. Vouchered evidence of occurrence is included for 47% of the species. Many of the species listed are from bamboo thickets, a dominant feature of the Pakitza landscape. Other species known to be associated with this habitat are predicted to occur at Pakitza, but their discovery awaits further fieldwork.

INTRODUCTION

Lowland tropical rainforests of the amazon basin have the richest and most diverse avifauna in the world (Haffer 1974). Despite the importance of these forests published records are scarce (Robbins et al. 1991). Lists of birds of these areas are important because they provide basic data for scientific research and conservation.

The BIOLAT Program of the National Museum of Natural History, Smithsonian Institution, initiated a long-term study of biological diversity at Pakitza, Peru in 1987 (Erwin 1991a). Although extensive bird studies have been conducted in Manu National Park, at Cocha Cashu Biological Station and surrounding areas, for some 16 years (Terborgh et al., 1984, Karr et al., 1990, Robinson and Terborgh, 1990), relatively little work has been done at Pakitza. As part of the BIOLAT program, I conducted a survey of the birds at this locality, from 1987 to 1993.

[1] *Current address: Department of Biology, University of Missouri at St. Louis, 8001 Natural Bridge Road, St. Louis, MO 63121.*

555

During nine field seasons, I was able to gather information on 415 species of birds and voucher 47% of them (Appendix). This list includes many birds associated with thickets of the bamboo species, *Guadua weberbauerii* and to a lesser extent *Elytrostachys* sp, both of which are abundant and extensive at Pakitza.

The present list, however, is likely far from being complete because at least 128 additional bird species might occur at this locality (excluding 11 species typically associated with lake margins and marshes), based on previous reports for Cocha Cashu and surrounding areas.

STUDY AREA

The BIOLAT Biological Station at the Pakitza Vigilance Post, Perú, lies on the east side of the Manu River, at 11°55'48"S, 71° 15'18"W, at an elevation of 350 m. Pakitza is about 10 km south of the boundary of the Reserve Zone of Manu National Park and 21 km south of Cocha Cashu Biological Station. The area encompasses approximately 4000 ha and has 36 km of maintained trails (for description, see Erwin (1991)).

Ancient (Pleistocene) terraces, running generally in a north-south direction, add some relief to the area. These terraces, up to 100 m above the present Manu River, are dissected by a system of small watersheds separated by narrow ridges and flat-topped hills. The mapped area has seven principal watersheds which drain into the Manu River (Fig. 1). The complex drainage system associated with the terraces accounts, in part, for the extremely high diversity of the area (Erwin 1991). The BIOLAT Station is in the Tropical Wet Forest Zone (Holdridge et al., 1971). The total rainfall is about 2.5 m per year, with wet (November-April) and dry (May-October) seasons.

The absence of lakes and marshes associated with the forest at Pakitza accounts for the few waterbirds reported from the station, compared to Cocha Cashu Biological Station. Only one small lake some 50 m across (rainy season), occurs within the BIOLAT area, and this size provides insufficient habitat to support lake species.

METHODS

Observations were made using binoculars while walking along the trail system. I recorded bird vocalizations with a Sony TCD 5M tape recorder and Sennheiser directional microphone. Extensive mist-net sampling (a total of 1008 net/hours) was made; 12 mist-nets (12-m, 4-shelf, 36-mm mesh) were used to sample secretive and quiet species from the understory in different seasons and habitats. Nets were placed mainly in the two types of bamboo thickets. Determination of habitat where the species occur was not based only in capture of birds in mist nets, but also by observations and recordings. Each net was operated for two days and then

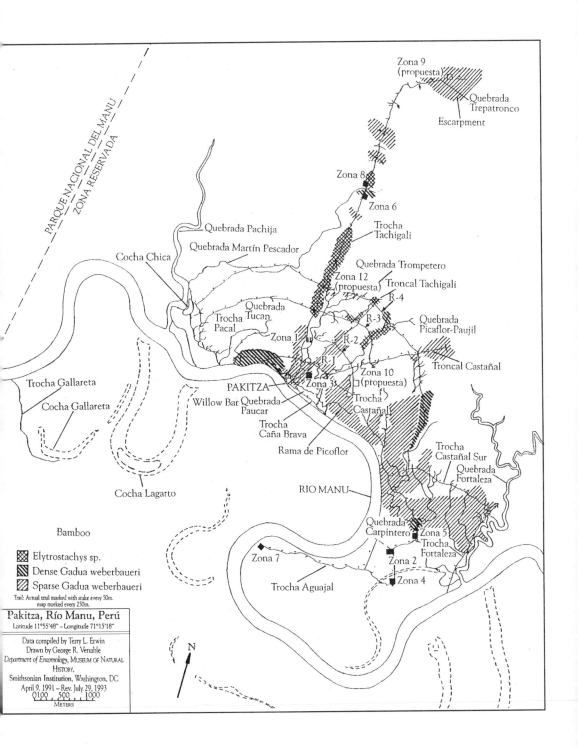

Fig. 1.– Map of the trail system, streams, and bamboo areas at Pakitza.

the position changed. Nets were open from dawn to approximately 1200 and from 1400 to 1700; captured birds were either photographed and released or collected and deposited as vouchers in the Museo de Historia Natural de la Universidad Nacional Mayor de San Marcos (MUSM). Specimen data includes museum catalog number, weight (in grams), gonadal measurements, soft part colors, molt, ossification as well as stomach content information; stomach contents were collected and stored in 70% alcohol (see also Servat 1993).

RESULTS AND DISCUSSION

HABITATS AT PAKITZA

Erwin (1991) gave a detailed account of the habitats at Pakitza with regard to beetles (Coleoptera). I adapted parts of this description, but placed the emphasis on how and where birds occur because birds use the environment in a more coarse-grained way than do beetles. The habitats are divided into three major categories: non-flooded forests, seasonally flooded forests, and open habitats.

NON-FLOODED FORESTS

1.- Terrace Forest (Tf).-

This forest, dominated by individuals of Leguminosae (*Inga, Tachigali, Parkia, Cedrelinga*), Moraceae (*Pourouma, Pseudolmedia*), and Palmae (*Euterpe, Socratea*), occurs on pleistocene terraces. These terraces are well drained and extend up to 7 km from the present riverbed of the Manu river. Also, included here are the dissected terrace forests of Erwin (1991). These forests are deeply dissected by small streams, some of which emanate from springs and are dominated by individuals of Violaceae (*Rinorea*), Palmae (*Iriartea*), and Moraceae (*Pseudolmedia, Pourouma, Cecropia*). Avifauna often seen in this type of forest at Pakitza includes: *Tinamus guttatus, Nyctibeus grandis, Baryphtengus martii, Microcerculus bambla, Tangara xanthogastra, Tangara gyrola,* and *Hylophilus thoracicus*.

2.- BAMBOO THICKETS

a.- Guadua Thickets (B1).-

Guadua weberbaueri Pilger, is common at Pakitza, growing in a variety of forest types. It forms dense thickets in some areas on the terraces; elsewhere it occurs as scattered individuals (Fig. 1). Many species of birds are closely associated with these bamboo thickets (Parker 1982, Terborgh et al. 1984). At Pakitza, the species of birds found only in this habitat are: *Nonnula ruficapilla, Picumnus rufiventris, Campylorhamphus trochilirostris, Simoxenops ucayalae, Automolus dorsalis, Automolus melanopezus, Cymbilaimus sanctaemariae, Myrmotherula ornata, Myrmotherula obscura, Microrhopias quixensis, Drymophila devillei, Cercomacra manu, Percnostola lophotes, Neopelma sulphureiventer, Leptopogon amaurocephalus, Hemitriccus flammulatus, Ramphotrigon megacephala,* and *Casiornis rufa* (although at Cocha Cashu occurs only in terra firme forest). *Lophotriccus eulophotes* and *Capsiempis flaveola* also were reported previously in this habitat at Pakitza (Servat and Pearson 1991, Servat 1993). Based on Robinson's list (in Karr et al. 1990), an additional two species exclusively associated with bamboo (*Celeus spectabilis, Poecilotriccus albifascies*) should also eventually be found at Pakitza. *Chlorostilbon mellisuga* and *Malacoptila semicincta* were found only in bamboo thickets at Pakitza although elsewhere occur in other types of forest.

My observations to date indicate that birds associated with bamboo only occur in G. *weberbauerii* thickets. Further studies are needed to compare bird faunas associated with bamboo thickets in other regions. Also, studies are needed on the natural history of bird species associated with this poorly known community.

b.- Elytrostachys Thickets (B2).-

The second bamboo species, *Elytrostachys* sp., is found in narrow patches on several trails (Fig. 1). In 1992, I worked in these areas to determine if this species of bamboo also supported an exclusive avifauna. Although none of the species found in *Guadua* thickets was present, I did add one species, *Myiobius barbatus*, to the Pakitza list. Some of the more common species observed in this bamboo habitat were: *Ancistrops strigilatus, Cercomacra serva, Gymnopithys salvini, Hylophilax poecilonota, Conopophaga peruviana, Onychorhynchus coronatus, Hemitriccus zosterops.* All occur in other types of habitat at Pakitza as well.

Seasonally-Flooded Forests

1.- Zabolo (Z).-

"Zabolo" is the pioneer vegetation along the Manu River that forms on banks not heavily affected by water action (terborg, et al. 1984). These banks accumulate a deep layer of silt and, when the river level is down, various grasses invade followed by *Tessaria integrifolia* (Compositae), and a 5 to 8 m wide band of *Gynerium sagittatum*, or "Caña Brava" (Gramineae). This dense stand of vegetation excludes nearly all other plants. Some of the bird species typically associated with this zabolo vegetation are: *Dolichonyx oryzivorus, Saltator coerulescens, Crypturellus cinereus, Claravis pretiosa, Todirostrum maculatum, Myiophobus fasciatus,* and *Todirostrum latirostre.*

2.- Lower Floodplain Forest (Lf).-

The area behind the zabolo zone may flood only once or twice per year and supports a well established forest standing on grey, leeched alluvium soil. This lower floodplain forest has fewer and smaller (10-20 m) trees than all other forest types at Pakitza. *Guariea* (Meliaceae) and *Sapium* (Euphorbiacea) are usually the two dominant genera; there are few, if any, palms. The most abundant tree species in the habitat are *Guatteria* sp. (Annonaceae), *Sapium aerum, S. ixiamasense*

(Euphorbiaceae), *Casearia decandra* (Flacourtiaceae), *Guarea quidonia, Cedrela odorata* (Meliaceae), *Cepropia menbranacea, Clarisia biflora, Ficus insipida* (Moraceae), *Zanthoxylum* sp. Some of the birds associated with this type of forest are: *Agamia agami, Columba cayennensis, Columba subvinacea, Glaucidium brasilianum, Aulacorhynchus prasinus, Celeus elegans, Veniliornis passerinus, Philydor rufus, Pitangus lictor* (although at Cocha Cashu this species occurs only at lakes), and *Myiodynastes maculatus.*

3.- Upper Floodplain Forest (Uf).-

Some areas along the Manu River are slightly higher than the forest described above. Only during very heavy rains, which may occur years or even decades apart, do flood waters invade this forest, creating a secondary floodplain above the primary one. Alluvium is accumulated during these episodic floods and, thus, the soil is richer than in upland forests. The dominant genus in this forest is the palm, *Iriartea*; dominant hardwoods are *Otoba* (Myristicaceae), *Quararibea* (Bombacaceae), *Guarea* and *Trichilia* (Meliaceae). Three species of birds are restricted to this habitat at Pakitza: *Crypturellus bartletti, Liosceles thoracicus,* and *Porphyrolaema porphyrolaema.*

4.- Oxbow Palm Swamp Forest (A).-

Palm swamp forests are found at low elevations near large river systems. Standing water occurs for over six months during the year in the lowest parts and more or less dries out in the dry season. Few species of trees tolerate the standing acidic water, but a palm, *Mauritia flexuosa*, specializes in the wettest part of the system. The understory is covered with *Heliconia* (Musaceae) and *Calathea* (Marantaceae).

Many species of hummingbirds gather in this habitat during the dry season, mainly because of the abundance of *Heliconia* flowers. Species typically found in this habitat include: *Phaethornis hispidus, Campylopterus largipennis, Glaucis hirsuta, Threnetes leucurus, Thalurania furcata,* and *Polyplancta aurescens*. These species are not, however, restricted to this habitat. During the dry season and when M. *flexuosa* is in fruit, *Ara ararauna, Ara macao,* and *Ara chloroptera* also occur here. *Hypocnemoides maculicauda* and *Chloroceryle aenea* are associated but not exclusive to this habitat. *Ara manilata, Myiozetetes luteiventris,* and *Berlepschia rikeri* also occur in this type of habitat at Cocha Cashu (S. Robinson pers. comm.), but were not observed at Pakitza.

OPEN HABITATS

1.- Beaches (S).-

Broad flat beaches occur along the Manu River. The lower beach zone, which floods many times during the year, has bare stretches of sand that, in some places, is covered by a fine-grained alluvium or washed clay. This eventually becomes covered with grasses and/or willows. Receding river levels expose the beaches and broad silty banks, attracting a variety of bird species including: *Ardea cocoi, Egretta thula, Philherodias pileatus, Tigrisoma lineatum, Casmerodius albus, Ajaia ajaja, Anhima cornuta, Neochen jubata, Haploxypterus cayanus, Charadrius collaris, Tringa solitaria, Bartramia longicauda, Actitis macularia, Calidris fuscicollis, Mycteria americana, Jabiru mycteria,* and *Rynchops nigra.*

2.- River Margin (Rm).-

The margins of Manu River are subject to flooding during the rainy season and during the dry season when mountain storms raise the river level dramatically, yet temporarily. During the rainy season, inundation will submerge plants growing along the edge of the river and leave trunks of half submerged dead trees exposed. Almost 90 species of birds are found in this habitat, as well as on beaches.

3.- Stream Margin (Sm).-

The margins of medium and large streams offer a particular topography that provides a unique habitat for certain birds that can only be found in these areas. A distinctive streamside vegetation occupies certain stretches of the deeper stream courses along the main watersheds. This vegetation is overshadowed by the adjacent forest type. Two of the birds typical of this type of habitat are *Butorides striatus* and *Basileuterus fulvicauda.*

4.- Lake Margin (Cocha Chica) (Lm).-

Since the 1970's, the mouth of Quebrada Pachija (Fig. 1) has been forming a broad delta of open sandy beach. About 0.5 km from its confluence with the Manu River, the Pachija River is channeled, separating a large island of primary and secondary floodplain forest from the Pakitza uplands. Near the beginning of the channel is a deep depression which retains water all year. This small lake, Cocha Chica, is surrounded by a broad grassy belt on one side and forest on three sides. A levee separates the lake from the Pachija River, at least during the dry season. The only record of *Opisthocomus hoazin* at Pakitza is from this area.

5.- Clearing (with buildings) (C).-

The Vigilance Post and BIOLAT headquarters occupy approximately 2 ha. Weeds and grasses are periodically cut; some fruit trees are present; and there are some isolated *Cecropia* trees. Common birds in this area are: *Cacicus cela, Contopus virens,* and *Piaya minuta.* Other occasional species include: *Chrysoptilus punctigula, Synallaxis albigularis, Troglodytes aedon,* and *Bubulcus ibis.*

6.- Overhead Space (O).-

The space that a bird crosses during flight can not be assigned to any particular type of habitat. Some birds have only been observed while flying, such as: *Sarcoramphus papa, Cathartes aura, Cathartes melambrotus, Pandion haliaetus, Elanoides forficatus, Ara severa,* and *Ara manilata.*

SPECIES LIST

The appendix provides a list of birds of Pakitza that includes 415 species known to occur at the BIOLAT Biological Station. The list provides information on the types of habitats in which the species occurs as well as the abundance. Abundance designations are: Common (C) for species recorded daily in preferred habitat; Uncommon (U) for species recorded every two days in preferred habitat; and, Rare (R) for species recorded fewer than five times. Designations refer to a subjective evaluation of the abundance of the species in the habitat(s) in which it occurs. The designations for evidence of occurrence at Pakitza (other than observations) are Photograph (p), Tape Recording (r), and Specimen (s). Most of the tape material has not yet been edited. Consequently, the species list likely will increase when additional vocalizations are identified. The percent of vouchered species also will increase. Species or habitats indicated by an asterisk corresponds to information provided by S. Robinson as a result of a visit to the area he made with J. Terborgh and C. Munn in October 1988.

ACKNOWLEDGEMENTS

I acknowledge Irma Franke, curator of birds of the Museo de Historia Natural de la Universidad Nacional Mayor de San Marcos for her support in this project. Many contributions to this list were made by T. L. Erwin and D. Pearson for which I thank them. J. Blake, D. Pearson and S. Robinson reviewed and made helpful comments on the manuscript. S. Robinson kindly provided additional information and allowed me to included here. I also thank the Dirección General de Forestal y de Fauna del Ministerio de Agricultura del Perú for providing permits to work at Pakitza and the personnel of Parque Nacional del Manu for their cooperation. Funds for this project were provided by the Biodiversity of Latin America Program (BIOLAT, Smithsonian Institution). This is contribution No. 43 in the BIOLAT series.

LITERATURE CITED

Erwin, T. L. 1991a. Establishing a tropical species co-occurrence database. Part 1. A plan for developing consistent biotic inventories in temperate and tropical habitats. Memorias del Museo de Historia Natural No. 20. Lima, Universidad Nacional Mayor de San Marcos. pp. 1-16

Erwin, T. L. 1991b. Natural history of the carabid beetles at the BIOLAT Biological Station, Rio Manu, Pakitza, Perú. Rev. Per. Ent. 33:1-85.

Haffer, J. 1974. Avian speciation in tropical South America, with a systematic survey of toucans (Ramphastidae) and jacamars (Galbulidae). Publication of the Nuttall Ornithological Club 14. 390 pp.

Holdridge, L. R., W. C. Wrenke, W. H. Hatheway, T. Liang, and J. A. Tossi, Jr. 1971.

Forest environments in tropical zones: a pilot study. Pergamon Press., New York, NY.

Karr, J. R., S. K. Robinson, J. G. Blake, and R. O. Bierregaard, Jr. 1990. Birds of four neotropical rainforests. Pp. 237-269 *in* Four Neotropical Rainforests (A. Gentry, ed.), Yale Univ. Press, New Haven, CT.

Parker, III, T. A. 1982. Observations of some unusual rainforest and marsh birds in southeastern Peru. Wilson Bull. 94:477-493.

Robbins, M. B., A. Capparella, R. S. Ridgely, S. W. Cardiff. 1991. Avifauna of the Río Manití and Quebrada Vainilla, Peru. Proc. Acad. Nat. Sci. Philadelphia 143:145-159.

Robinson, S. K., and J. W. Terborgh. 1990. Bird communities of the Cocha Cashu Biological Station in Amazonian Peru. Pp. 199-216 *in* Four Neotropical Rainforests (A. Gentry, ed.), Yale Univ. Press, New Haven, CT.

Servat, G. P., and D. L. Pearson. 1991. Natural history notes and records for seven poorly known bird species from Amazonian Peru. Bull. B. O. C. 111:92-95.

Servat, G. P. 1993. A new method of preparation to identify arthropods from stomach contents of birds. J. Field Ornithol., 64:49-54.

Servat, G. P. 1993. First records of the Yellow Tyrannulet (*Capsiempis flaveola*) in Perú. Wilson Bull. 105:534.

Terborgh, J. W., J. W. Fitzpatrick, and L. Emmons. 1984. Annotated checklist of bird and mammal species of Cocha Cashu Biological Station, Manu National Park, Peru. Fieldiana (Zool.) 21:1-29.

APPENDIX

THE LIST AND ITS CODES

FOREST TYPES
    NON-FLOODED FORESTS
        1.- TERRACE FOREST (Tf)
        2.- BAMBOO THICKETS
            a.- *Guadua* THICKETS (B1)
            b.- *Elytrostachys* THICKETS (B2)
    SEASONALLY-FLOODED FORESTS
        1.- ZABOLO (Z)
        2.- LOWER FLOODPLAIN FOREST (Lf)
        3.- UPPER FLOODPLAIN FOREST (Uf)
        4.- OXBOW PALM SWAMP FOREST (A)
    OPEN HABITATS
        1.- BEACH (S)
        2.- RIVER MARGIN (Rm)
        3.- STREAM MARGIN (Sm)
        4.- LAKE MARGIN (Lm)
        5.- OVERHEAD SPACE (O)
        6.- CLEARING (C)
ABUNDANCE
    COMMON (C)
    UNCOMMON (U)
    RARE (R)
EVIDENCE
    RECORDED (r)
    PHOTO (p)
    SPECIMEN (s)

LIST OF BIRDS OF PAKITZA (MANU NATIONAL PARK, PERU)

Species	Habitat	Abundance	Evidence
TINAMIDAE (8)			
Tinamus tao	Tf, Uf	R	
Tinamus major	Tf, Uf, Lf, B2	C	r
Tinamus guttatus	Tf	R	
Crypturellus cinereus	Tf, Uf, Lf	U	
Crypturellus soui	Tf, Lf, Z	U	
Crypturellus undulatus	Tf, Uf, Lf, Z	C	
Crypturellus bartletti	Uf	U	
Crypturellus variegatus	Tf, Uf	U	s

Species	Habitat	Abundance	Evidence
PHALACROCORACIDAE (1)			
Phalacrocorax olivaceus	Rm	C	p
ANHINGIDAE (1)			
Anhinga anhinga	Rm	U	p
ARDEIDAE (8)			
Ardea cocoi	Rm, S	C	p
Egretta thula	Rm, S	C	p
Agamia agami	Lf	U	
Philherodias pileatus	Rm, S	U	p
Tigrisoma lineatum	Rm, S	U	p
Bubulcus ibis	C	M	p
Casmerodius albus	Rm, S	C	p
Butorides striatus	Sm	U	
CICCONIDAE (2)			
Mycteria americana	S, O	U	p
Jabiru mycteria	S, O	U	p
THRESKIORNITHIDAE (2)			
Mesembrinibis cayennensis	Rm	R	
Ajaia ajaja	Rm, S	R	
ANHIMIDAE (1)			
Anhima cornuta	Rm, S	C	p
ANATIDAE (2)			
Neochen jubata	Rm, S	U	p
Cairina moschata	R	R	
CATHARTIDAE (4)			
Sarcoramphus papa	O	U	
Coragyps atratus	Rm, S, Z, O, C	C	p
Cathartes aura	O	R	
Cathartes melambrotus	O	U	
ACCIPITRIDAE (14)			
Elanoides forficatus	O	R	
Leptodon cayanensis	Tf, Uf, Lf	U	
Harpagus bidentatus	Tf, Uf, Lf	U	
Ictinia plumbea	Rm, O	C	
Buteo magnirostris	Rm, O, S, Z	C	p
Buteo brachyurus	Lf, C	R	
Leucopternis schistacea	Lf, Uf	U	
Busarellus nigricollis	Rm	U	p
Buteogallus urubitinga	Rm, Lf, Uf	U	
Morphnus guianensis	Tf, Uf, Lf, O	R	
Harpia harpyja	Tf, Uf, Lf, Rm, O	R	
Spizaetus ornatus	Tf, Uf, Lf, C	R	

Species	Habitat	Abundance	Evidence
Spizaetus tyrannus	Tf. Uf, Lf, C	R	
Rosthramus sociabilis	Rm	R	
PANDIONIDAE (1)			
Pandion haliaetus	O	R	
FALCONIDAE (7)			
Herpetotheres cachinnans	Uf, Lf	U	
Micrastur semitorquatus	Tf, Uf, Lf	R	
Micrastur ruficollis	Uf, Lf, O	U	
Micrastur gilvicollis	Tf, Uf, B1, O	U	p
Daptrius ater	Rm, C	C	s
Daptrius americanus	Tf, Uf, Lf, C	U	
Falco rufigularis	Tf, Uf, Lf, Rm	C	
CRACIDAE (4)			
Ortalis motmot	Lf, Rm, O	C	
Penelope jacquacu	Tf, Uf, Lf, Rm	U	
Aburria pipile	Tf, Uf, Lf	C	p
Crax mitu	Tf, Uf, Lf	U	p
PHASIANIDAE (1)			
Odontophorus stellatus	Tf, Uf, Lf	U	
OPISTHOCOMIDAE (1)			
Opisthocomus hoazin	Lm	U	p
PSOPHIIDAE (1)			
Psophia leucoptera	Tf, Uf, Lf	U	
RALLIDAE (1)			
Aramides cajanea	Tf, Uf, Lf	U	r
EURYPYGIDAE (1)			
Eurypyga helias	Tf, Uf, Rm	R	
CHARADRIIDAE (3)			
Haploxypterus cayanus	Rm, S	C	p
Charadrius collaris	Rm, S	C	
Pluvialis dominica*	Rm	V	
SCOLOPACIDAE (4)			
Tringa solitaria	Rm, S	C	p
Actitis macularia	S	C	
Calidris fuscicollis	S	R	
Bartramia longicauda	Rm, S	U	
LARIDAE (2)			
Phaethusa simplex	Rm, S, O	C	p
Sterna superciliaris	Rm, S, O	C	

Species	Habitat	Abundance	Evidence
RYNCHOPIDAE (1)			
Rynchops nigra	S, O	C	p
COLUMBIDAE (7)			
Columba cayennensis	Lf	C	
Columba subvinacea	Lf	U	
Columba plumbea	Rm, Sm, Tf, Uf, Lf	C	
Columbina picui		R	
Claravis pretiosa	Lf, Z	R	
Leptotila rufaxilla	Lf, C	C	
Geotrygon montana	Tf, Uf, Lf, Bl, Z	C	p
PSITTACIDAE (18)			
Ara ararauna	Tf, Uf, Lf, Rm, A, C, O	C	p
Ara macao	Tf, Uf, Lf, Rm, A, C, O	C	p
Ara chloroptera	Tf, Uf, Lf, Rm, A, C, O	C	
Ara severa	O	C	
Ara manilata	O ·	U	
Ara couloni	Lf, O	R	
Aratinga leucophthalmus	Tf, Uf, Lf	C	
Aratinga weddellii	Lf, O, C	C	
Pyrrhura picta	Uf, Lf, C	C	
Pyrrhura rupicola	Tf, Uf, Lf, C	C	
Forpus sclateri	Tf, Uf, Lf, O, C	R	
Brotogeris cyanoptera	Tf, Uf, Lf, O, C	C	
Brotogeris sanctithomae	Uf, Lf, C	C	
Pionites leucogaster	Tf, Uf, Lf, C	C	
Pionopsitta barrabandi	Tf, Uf, Lf, C	U	
Pionus menstruus	Tf, Uf, Lf, O	C	r
Amazona ochrocephala	Uf, Lf, C	C	
Amazona farinosa	Tf, Uf, C	C	
CUCULIDAE (6)			
Piaya cayana	Lf, Rm, C	C	p
Piaya melanogaster	Tf, Uf	R	
Piaya minuta	C	U	s
Crotophaga major	Rm, S	C	p
Crotophaga ani	Rm	C	
Dromococcyx pavoninus	Rm, Tf, Lf	R	
STRIGIDAE (8)			
Otus choliba	Tf?	R	
Otus watsonii	Tf, Uf, Lf, Bl	C	r
Lophostrix cristata	Tf, Uf, Lf, Bl	C	
Pulsatrix perspicillata	Tf, Uf	C	
Glaucidium minutissimun	Tf, Uf, Lf	C	
Glaucidium brasilianum	Lf	C	
Ciccaba huhula	Tf, Uf	R	r
Ciccaba virgata	Tf, Uf, Lf	C	

567

Grace P. Servat

Species	Habitat	Abundance	Evidence
NYCTIBIIDAE (2)			
Nyctibeus grandis	Tf	U	
Nyctibeus griseus	Tf, Rm	U	
CAPRIMULGIDAE (5)			
Lurocalis semitorquatus	Tf, Uf	U	
Chordeiles rupestris	Rm, S	C	p
Nyctidromus albicollis	Lf, Rm, S	C	p
Nyctiphrynus ocellatus	Tf, Uf	U	
Hydropsalis climacocerca	Rm	U	
APODIDAE (4)			
Streptoprogne zonaris	Rm, O	C	
Chaetura cinereiventris	Rm, O	C	
Chaetura brachyura	Rm, O	C	
Reinarda squamata	Rm, O	U	
TROCHILIDAE (13)			
Glaucis hirsuta	Tf, Uf, Lf, B1, A, C	C	p, s
Threnetes leucurus	Tf, Uf, Lf, B1, A, C	C	s
Phaethornis superciliosus	Tf, Uf, B1, B2, A, C	C	p, s
Phaethornis hispidus	B1, A, C	C	p, s
Phaethornis ruber	Tf, B1, B2, C	C	p, s
Campylopterus largipennis	Tf, B1, B2, A, C	C	s
Florisuga mellivora	Tf, Uf, Lf	U	
Thalurania furcata	Tf, Uf, Lf, B1, A, C	C	p, s
Hylocharis cyanus	Tf, Uf, Lf, C	R	
Chrysuronia oenone	Tf, Uf, Lf, B1	U	
Polyplancta aurescens	Uf, Lf, A	U	s
Heliothryx aurita	Tf, Uf, Sm	R	p, s
Chlorostilbon mellisuga	B1	R	s
TROGONIDAE (5)			
Trogon melanurus	Tf, Uf, Lf	C	
Trogon viridis	Tf, Uf, Lf	R	
Trogon collaris	Tf, Uf, Lf, B1	C	
Trogon curucui	Tf, Uf, Lf	C	p
Trogon violaceus	Tf, Uf, Lf	R	p
ALCEDINIDAE (5)			
Ceryle torquata	Rm, O	C	
Chloroceryle amazona	Rm, O	C	
Chloroceryle americana	Rm, Sm	C	p
Chloroceryle aenea	Tf, Uf, Lf, A	U	
Chloroceryle inda*	Tf		p, s
MOMOTIDAE (3)			
Electron platyrhynchum	Tf, Uf, Lf	C	p, s
Baryphtengus martii	Tf	R	
Momotus momota	Tf, Uf, Lf, B1	C	p, s

568

Species	Habitat	Abundance	Evidence
GALBULIDAE (3)			
Galbacyrhynchus purusianus	Lf, C	R	
Galbula cyanescens	Tf, Uf, Lf, Rm, B1, C	C	p, s
Jacamerops aurea	Tf, Uf	R	
BUCCONIDAE (8)			
Notharchus macrorhynchus	Tf, Uf, Lf	R	
Bucco capensis	Tf, Uf, Lf	R	
Nystalus striolatus	Tf, Uf, Lf	R	
Malacoptila semicincta	Tf*, B1	C	p, s
Nonnula ruficapilla	B1	C	p, s
Monasa nigrifrons	Tf, Uf, Lf, Rm, B1, C	C	r
Monasa morphoeus	Tf, Uf, B1, C	C	s
Chelidoptera tenebrosa	Rm, C	C	
CAPITONIDAE (2)			
Capito niger	Tf, Uf, Lf	C	
Eubucco richardsoni	Tf, Uf, Lf	U	
RAMPHASTIDAE (7)			
Aulacorhynchus prasinus	Lf	R	
Pteroglossus castanotis	Tf, Uf, Lf, Rm, C	C	r, s
Pteroglossus flavirostris	Tf, Uf, Lf	U	p
Pteroglossus beauharnaesii	Uf, Lf	U	
Selenidera reinwardtii	Tf, Uf, Lf	C	
Ramphastos culminatus	Tf, Uf, Lf	C	
Ramphastos cuvieri	Tf, Uf, Lf, C	C	p, r
PICIDAE (14)			
Picumnus rufiventris	B1	U	p, s
Chrysoptilus punctigula	C	R	r
Piculus leucolaemus	Tf, Uf, Lf	U	
Piculus chrysochloros	Tf, Uf, Lf	U	
Celeus elegans	Lf	U	
Celeus grammicus	Tf*, Uf, Lf	U	
Celeus flavus	Tf, Uf, Lf, B1, C	U	
Celeus torquatus	Tf, Uf	R	
Dryocopus lineatus	Lf, Rm	U	
Melanerpers cruentatus	Tf, Uf, Lf, C	C	
Veniliornis passerinus	Lf	U	
Veniliornis affinis	Uf, Lf	U	
Campephilus melanoleucus	Tf, Uf, Lf, C	C	
Campephilus rubricollis	Tf, Uf	U	
DENDROCOLAPTIDAE (16)			
Dendrocincla fuliginosa	Tf, Uf, Lf, B1, B2	C	s
Dendrocincla merula	Tf, Uf, Lf, B1	C	s
Deconychura longicauda	Tf, Uf, Lf	U	s
Sittasomus griseicapillus	Tf, B1	R	r?

Species	Habitat	Abundance	Evidence
Glyphorhynchus spirurus	Tf, Uf, Lf, A, B1	C	p, s
Nasica longirostris	Uf, Lf	U	p
Dendrexetastes rufigula	Tf, Uf, Lf	U	
Xiphocolaptes promeropirhynchus		Tf, Uf	U
Dendrocolaptes certhia	Tf, Uf, Lf	U	
Dendrocolaptes picumnus	Tf, Uf, Lf	U	
Xiphorhynchus picus	Rm, C	U	
Xiphorhynchus ocellatus	Tf, Lf, B1	C	p, s
Xiphorhynchus spixii	Tf, Uf, B1	C	s
Xiphorhynchus guttatus	Tf, Uf, Lf, A, B1, C	C	s
Lepidocolaptes albolineatus	Tf, Uf, Lf	U	s
Campylorhamphus trochilirostris	B1	U	p, s

FURNARIIDAE (22)

Species	Habitat	Abundance	Evidence
Furnarius leucopus	Uf, Lf, Rm, B1, C	C	p
Synallaxys albigularis	C	R	r
Synallaxis gujanensis	B1, C*	U	p
Cranioleuca gutturata	Tf, Uf	R	
Hyloctistes subulatus	Tf, Uf, B1	U	s
Ancistrops strigilatus	Tf, Uf, B1, B2	U	p, s
Simoxenops ucayalae	B1	U	p, s
Philydor erythrocercus	Tf, Uf, Lf	C	
Philydor pyrrhodes	Tf, Uf, Lf	U	
Philydor rufus	Lf	U	
Philydor erythropterus	Tf, Uf, Lf, B1	U	s
Philidor ruficaudatus	Tf, Uf, Lf,	C	s
Automolus infuscatus	Tf, Uf, B1	C	s
Automolus dorsalis	B1	R	
Automolus rubiginosus	Tf, B1	U	s
Automolus ochrolaemus	Tf, Lf, B1, B2	C	s
Automolus rufipileatus	Lf, B1	U	s
Automolus melanopezus	B1	R	s
Xenops rutilans	Tf, Uf, Lf	R	
Xenops minutus	Tf, Uf, Lf, B1, B2	C	p, s
Sclerurus mexicanus	Tf, Uf	R	
Sclerurus caudacutus	Tf, Uf, Lf	U	s

FORMICARIIDAE (49)

Species	Habitat	Abundance	Evidence
Cymbilaimus lineatus	Tf, Uf, Lf, B1, B2	C	s
Cymbilaimus sanctaemariae	B1	R	
Taraba major	Lf, C	U	p
Thamnophilus doliatus	B1, Rm	U	p, s
Thamnophilus aethiops	Tf, Uf, Lf	U	
Thamnophilus schistaceus	B1	U	s
Pygiptila stellaris	Tf, Uf, Lf	U	
Thamnomannes ardesiacus	Tf, Uf, Lf	C	s
Thamnomannes schistogynus	Tf, Uf, Lf, B1	C	p, s
Myrmotherula brachyura	Tf, Uf, Lf, C	C	
Myrmotherula sclateri	Tf, Uf, Lf	U	
Myrmotherula surinamensis	Rm	R	

Species	Habitat	Abundance	Evidence
Myrmotherula hauxwelli	Tf, Uf, Bl	C	s
Myrmotherula leucophthalma	Tf, Uf, Bl	C	s
Myrmotherula ornata	Bl	R	
Myrmotherula axillaris	Tf, Uf, Lf, Bl, A	C	s
Myrmotherula longipennis	Tf, Uf, Lf, Bl	C	s
Myrmotherula iheringi	Uf, Bl	U	s
Myrmotherula menetriessi	Tf, Uf, Lf, Bl	C	p, s
Myrmotherula obscura	Bl		s
Dichrozona cincta	Tf, Uf	U	
Microrhopias quixensis	Bl	U	r, s
Drymophila devillei	Bl	R	
Terenura humeralis	Tf, Uf, Lf	R	
Cercomacra cinerascens	Tf, Uf, Lf	U	
Cercomacra serva	Tf, Uf, Bl, B2	U	s
Cercomacra manu	Bl	R	r
Myrmoborus leucophrys	Tf, Uf, Lf, Bl, B2	C	s
Myrmoborus myotherinus	Tf, Uf, Lf, Bl, B2	C	p, s
Hypocnemis cantator	Lf, Bl	U	
Hypocnemoides maculicauda	Uf, A	U	
Percnostola lophotes	Bl	U	s
Sclateria naevia	Uf, A	U	s
Myrmeciza hemimelaena	Tf, Uf, Lf, Bl	C	s
Myrmeciza hyperythra	Tf, Uf, Lf, A	C	s
Myrmeciza goeldii	Tf, Uf, Lf, Bl	U	p, s
Myrmeciza fortis	Tf, Uf, Bl	U	s
Myrmeciza athrotorax	Lf, Z	C	s
Gymnopithys salvini	Tf, Uf, Bl, B2	U	s
Rhegmatorhina melanosticta	Tf, Uf, Lf, Bl	U	
Hylophilax naevia	Tf, Uf, Lf, Bl	C	p, s
Hylophilax poecilonota	Tf, Uf, Bl, B2	C	s
Phlegopsis nigromaculata	Tf, Uf, Lf, Bl, B2	C	p, s
Chamaeza nobilis	Tf, Uf	U	
Formicarius colma	Tf, Uf, A	U	p, s
Formicarius analis	Tf, Uf, Lf, Bl	C	s
Hylopezus berlepschi	Tf, Uf, Lf	R	
Myrmothera campanisoma	Tf, Uf, Lf	R	
Conopophaga peruviana	Tf, Uf, Bl, B2	U	s
RHINOCRYPTIDAE (1)			
Liosceles thoracicus	Uf	U	
TYRANNIDAE (51)			
Zimmerius gracilipes	Tf, Uf, Lf	U	
Ornithion inerme	Tf, Uf	U	
Tyrannulus elatus	Tf, Uf, Lf, C	U	
Myiopagis gaimardii	Tf, Uf, Lf	C	
Mionectes oleagineus	Tf, Uf, Lf, A, Bl, B2	C	p, s
Mionectes macconnelli	Tf, Lf, Bl	U	p, s
Leptopogon amaurocephalus	Bl	U	s
Corythopis torquata	Tf, Uf, Bl	C	s

Species	Habitat	Abundance	Evidence
Myiornis ecaudatus	Tf, Uf, Lf	U	p, s
Lophotriccus eulophotes	B1	U	p, s
Hemitriccus flammulatus	B1	U	s
Hemitriccus zosterops	Tf, Uf, B2	U	p, r?
Todirostrum latirostre	Lf, Z, B1	R	s
Todirostrum maculatum	Lf, Z	U	p
Todirostrum chrysocrotaphum	Tf, Uf, Lf	U	
Ramphotrigon megacephala	B1	R	s
Ramphotrigon ruficauda*	Tf		
Tolmomyas poliocephalus	Tf, Uf, Lf	C	
Tolmomyas assimilis*	Tf		
Platyrhynchus coronatus	Tf, Uf, B1	U	
Platyrhynchum platyrhynchos	Tf, Uf	U	s
Terenotriccus erythrurus	Tf, Uf, Lf, B1	C	p, s
Myiophobus fasciatus	Lf, Z	U	p
Myiobius barbatus	B2	R	s
Myiobius atricaudus*	Tf		
Contopus virens	Tf*, Lf, C	C	
Contopus cinereus	Z	V	
Empidonax euleri	Tf, Uf, Lf, A	U	s
Pyrocephalus rubinus	Rm, C	C	p
Ochthoeca littoralis	Rm, C	C	p
Muscisaxicola fluviatilis	Rm, C	C	
Attila bolivianus	Tf, Uf, Lf	U	
Attila spadiceus	Tf, Uf, Lf	U	p
Casiornis rufa	B1	R	p, s
Rhytipterna simplex	Tf, Uf, Lf	U	
Laniocera hypopyrra	Tf, Uf, B1	U	s
Syristes sibilator	Tf, Uf, C	U	
Onychorhynchus coronatus	Tf, Uf, B1, B2	U	p, s
Capsiempis flaveola	B1	R	s
Myiarchus tuberculifer	Tf, Uf, Lf, C	U	p
Myiarchus ferox	Lf, Z	C	s
Pitangus lictor	Lf	C	s
Pitangus sulphuratus	Lf, Rm, C	C	
Megarhynchus pitangua	Lf, Rm, C	U	p
Myiozetetes similis	Lf, Sm, C	C	p
Myiozetetes granadensis	Lf, Rm, C	C	
Myiodynastes maculatus	Lf	U	
Myiodynastes luteiventris	Lf	U	
Legatus leucophaius	Tf, Uf, Lf	C	
Empidonomus aurantiatrocristatus	Uf, Lf		R
Tyrannus melancholicus	Lf, Rm, Sm, C	C	s
PIPRIDAE (7)			
Schiffornis major	Uf, Lf	R	
Tyranneutes stolzmanni	Tf, Uf, B1	U	r, s
Neopelma sulphureiventer	B1	R	s
Pipra coronata	Tf, Uf, Lf, B1	C	p, s
Pipra fasciicauda	Tf, Uf, Lf, B1	C	p, s

Species	Habitat	Abundance	Evidence
Pipra chloromeros	Tf, Uf, Lf, B1, B2	C	s
Piprites chloris*	Tf		
COTINGIDAE (12)			
Pachyramphus marginatus	Tf, Uf	C	
Pachyramphus minor	Tf, Uf, Lf	C	
Tityra cayana	Tf, Uf, Lf, Rm	U	
Tityra semifasciata	Tf, Uf, Lf, Rm	U	
Tityra inquisitor	Lf, Rm	U	
Lipaugus vociferans	Tf	C	
Porphyrolaema porphyrolaema	Uf	R	
Cotinga maynana	Tf, Uf, Lf, Rm, C	U	
Cotinga cayana	Tf, Lf, Rm, C	U	
Conioptilon mcilhennyi	Tf*, Lf, Rm, C	R	r
Gymnoderus foetidus	Tf, Lf, O	C	
Querula purpurata	Tf, Uf, Lf,	C	
HIRUNDINIDAE (4)			
Tachycineta albiventer	Rm, O	C	p
Progne tapera	Rm, O	C	
Atticora fasciata	Rm, O, Sm	C	s
Stelgidopterix ruficollis	Rm, O, Sm	C	s
TROGLODYTIDAE (6)			
Campylorhynchus turdinus	Tf, Uf, Lf	R	
Thryothorus genibarbis	Tf, Lf, B1	U	p, s
Troglodytes aedon	C	U	
Microcerculus marginatus	Tf, Uf, Lf, B1	U	s
Microcerculus bambla	Tf	R	p, s
Cyphorhinus arada	Tf, Uf, Lf, B1	C	s
TURDINAE (5)			
Catharus ustulatus	Tf, Uf, Lf, B1	U	s
Turdus ignobilis	Tf, Lf	C	s
Turdus lawrencii	Tf, Uf, A, C	R	
Turdus albicollis	Tf, Uf, Lf, B1	U	p, s
Turdus hauxwelli	Tf, Uf, Lf	C	s
POLIOPTILINAE (2)			
Ramphocaenus melanurus	Lf, B1	R	s
Polioptila plumbea	Rm, Z	R	
EMBERIZINAE (8)			
Paroaria gularis	Rm	C	
Sporophila lineola	Rm, C	R	
Sporophila nigricollis	Rm	R	p, s
Sporophila caerulescens	Lf, Rm	U	p, s
Sporophila castaneiventris	Rm	R	
Oryzoborus angolensis	Rm	C	
Arremon taciturnus	Tf, Uf, Lf, B1, C	U	s

Species	Habitat	Abundance	Evidence
Ammodramus aurifrons	Lf, Rm	C	p, r
CARDINALINAE (4)			
Saltator maximus	Tf, Uf, Lf, Bl, C	U	p, s
Saltator coerulescens	Z	C	
Cyanocompsa cyanoides	Tf, Uf, Lf, Bl, C	C	r, s
Pitylus grossus	Tf, Bl, C	R	s
THRAUPINAE (30)			
Cissopis leveriana	Lf, C	C	p, r
Hemithraupis flavicollis	Tf, Uf	R	
Hemithraupis guira*	Tf		
Lanio versicolor	Tf, Uf, Lf, Bl	U	p, s
Tachyphonus rufiventer	Tf, Uf, Lf	U	
Tachyphonus luctuosus	Tf, Uf, Lf, Bl	U	
Habia rubica	Tf, Uf, Lf, Bl	C	p, s
Ramphocelus carbo	Lf, C	C	p, s
Ramphocelus nigrogularis	Lf, C	C	
Lamprospiza melanoleuca	Tf, Uf	U	
Thraupis episcopus	Lf, C	C	p, r, s
Thraupis palmarum	Lf, C	U	
Euphonia xanthogaster	Tf, Uf, Lf, C	U	p, r
Euphonia minuta	Tf, Uf, Lf	R	
Euphonia laniirostris	Lf, Rm	U	
Euphonia rufiventris	Tf, Uf, Lf, C	C	p
Euphonia chrysopastra	Tf, Uf, Lf, C	C	
Tangara velia	Tf, Uf, Lf, C	U	
Tangara callophrys	Tf, Uf, Lf	R	
Tangara chilensis	Tf, Uf, Lf, C	C	r
Tangara shrankii	Tf, Uf, Lf, C	C	p, s
Tangara xanthogastra	Tf	R	p, s
Tangara nigrocincta	Tf, Uf, Lf, C	R	
Tangara mexicana	Tf, Uf, Lf, C	C	
Tangara gyrola	Tf	R	
Dacnis cayana	Tf, Uf, Lf	C	
Dacnis lineata	Tf, Uf, Lf	C	
Dacnis flaviventer	Tf, Lf, C	R	
Chlorophanes spiza	Tf, Uf, Lf, C	U	p, s
Cyanerpes caeruleus	Tf, Uf, Lf, C	R	
TERSININAE (1)			
Tersina viridis	Tf, Lf, St, Rm	R	s
PARULIDAE (1)			
Basileuturus fulvicauda	Sm	R	s
VIREONIDAE (5)			
Vireo olivaceus	Tf, Uf, Lf, C	C	
Hylophilus thoracicus	Tf	R	
Hylophilus hypoxanthus	Tf, Uf, Lf,	U	

Species	Habitat	Abundance	Evidence
Hylophilus ochraceiceps	Tf, Uf, Lf, B1, B2	C	p, s
Vireolanius leucotis	Uf, Lf	C	
ICTERIDAE (10)			
Scaphidura oryzivora	Lf, Rm, C	C	
Clypicterus oseryi	Tf, Uf, Lf	R	
Psaracolius decumannus	Tf, Uf, Lf, Rm, C	U	
Psaracolius angustifrons	Tf, Uf, Lf, Rm, C	C	p
Gymnostinops yuracares	Tf, Uf, Lf, Rm, C	C	
Cacicus cela	Tf, Uf, Lf, Rm, Lm, C	C	p, s
Cacicus solitarius	Lf, Rm	U	
Icterus cayannensis	Tf, Uf, Lf, Rm	U	
Icterus icterus	Lf, Rm, Lm, C	U	
Dolichonyx oryzivorus	Rm, Z	R	
CORVIDAE (1)			
Cyanocorax violaceus	Lf, Rm	C	

Annotated Checklist of the Non–Flying Mammals at Pakitza, Manu Reserve Zone, Manu National Park, Perú

VÍCTOR PACHECO AND ELENA VIVAR

Departamento de Mastozoología, Museo de Historia Natural,
Universidad Nacional Mayor de San Marcos,
Apartado 14-0434, Lima-14, Perú.

ABSTRACT

We report 62 species of non-flying mammals from Pakitza Biological Station and nearby areas, belonging to 8 orders and 20 families, including 9 marsupials, 5 edentates, 11 primates, 9 carnivores, 1 tapir, 4 artiodactyls, 22 rodents, and 1 rabbit. Our record of *Neusticomys peruviensis* represents the second known specimen of this species. Our specimens of *Monodelphis brevicaudata* are the first reported from Peru, and those of *Marmosa murina, Marmosops parvidens, Gracilinanus agilis, Neacomys spinosus,* and an undescribed species of *Proechimys* are the first recorded from Manu National Park. In addition, we include systematic notes for some species, and discuss preliminary results on seasonal and habitat differences among diverse forest types. Finally, comments on the conservation status of the species are included.

RESUMEN

Reportamos 62 especies de mamíferos no-voladores para la Estación Biológica de Pakitza y alrededores, pertenecientes a 8 órdenes y 20 familias, incluyendo 9 marsupiales, 5 edentados, 11 primates, 9 carnívoros, 1 tapir, 4 artiodáctilos, 22 roedores y 1 conejo. Nuestro registro de *Neusticomys peruviensis* representa el segundo espécimen conocido de esta especie. Nuestros individuos de *Monodelphis brevicaudata* son los primeros reportados para el Perú; y los de *Marmosa murina, Marmosops parvidens, Gracilinanus agilis, Neacomys spinosus,* y una nueva especie de *Proechimys* son los primeros registrados en el Parque Nacional Manu. Además, se incluyen notas sistemáticas para algunas especies, y se discuten resultados preliminares acerca de diferencias estacionales y de hábitats encontrados entre diversos tipos de bosques. Finalmente, se comenta sobre el estado de conservación de las especies.

INTRODUCTION

Humid tropical forests are considered the most diverse ecosystem on earth, but are poorly known and in danger of disappearing because of heavy human impact. Detailed inventories of the mammalian fauna in specific sites of lowland tropical forests are scarce. Many long-term studies usually have focused on large-sized species; however, the small mammals, mostly bats and rodents, which represent almost 70% of the known species in Peru (Pacheco et al., 1995), are largely unknown in aspects of basic biology.

Pristine humid lowland forests are becoming increasingly scarce in the Neotropics. Manu National Park, established in 1973, is one of the few protected areas that remains virtually unaltered, a condition that has attracted numerous studies especially in the forests of Cocha Cashu Biological Station (Terborgh et al., 1984; Gentry, 1990). Grimwood (1969) commented on the diversity of mammals in Manu National Park. Terborgh et al. (op. cit.) reported a detailed inventory of birds and mammals of Cocha Cashu and nearby places. Janson and Emmons (1990) discussed the ecological structure of the community of mammals at Cocha Cashu and updated the Terborgh's list for non-volant mammals. The bats of Manu's lowland forests were treated in detail in Ascorra et al. (1991). Finally, a first comprehensive list of mammals of Manu Biosphere Reserve was presented by Pacheco et al. (1993). However, a detailed inventory of Manu and especially of Pakitza and Cocha Cashu Biological Stations, will require a longer and more intensive collection program. In this paper, we provide an annotated list of non-flying mammals from Pakitza, Reserved Zone of Manu Biosphere Reserve, include systematic notes for some species, discuss preliminary results on seasonal and habitat differences among diverse forest types, and comment on the conservation status of the species.

STUDY SITE AND METHODS

Pakitza Biological Station is located on the left bank of the Manu River (travelling downstream), near the eastern border of Manu Biosphere Reserve at 11°56'S, 71°17'W, at an elevation of 356 m, Departmento Madre de Dios, Peru (Fig. 1). Pakitza is placed about 10 km south of the Manu National Park border, and 21 km south of Cocha Cashu. The study area encompasses 4000 ha characterized by ancient terraces, up to 100 m above the Manu riverbed. These terraces are dissected by several quebradas forming a complex system of watersheds. Twelve forest types have been identified in the area (Zones of Erwin [1991]). A trail network system is already present in Pakitza study area, which includes several

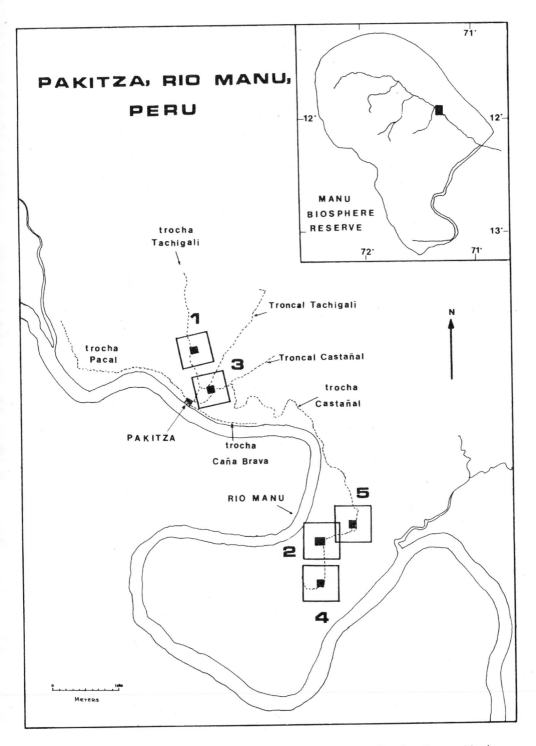

Fig. 1.– Map of Pakitza Biological Station, Madre de Dios, Peru; Manu Biosphere Reserve. Numbers refer to some of the BIOLAT permanent Zones (sensu Erwin, 1991).

main trails, radiating from Pakitza's camp to diverse points, each of them connected by trails (Fig. 1). The study site, the Zones, and the network of trails are described in detail by Erwin (1991).

We selected seven plots, representing four Zones and other habitats, to survey for small terrestrial mammals (Fig. 2). The first four plots correspond exactly to the first four Zones of Erwin (1991) to simplify comparisons. Plots were set primarily along the main trails, using the trail network system. A brief habitat description for the plots is provided in Table 1. The plots were systematically sampled by Vivar in September 1989; February and October 1990, and October 1991; and by Pacheco and Vivar in February 1992. September and October corresponded to the dry season, and February to the wet season. The severity and timing of the dry season is highly variable between years. October in some years might correspond to a wet or a dry season (Erwin, 1991; Terborgh, 1983). Although no measure of precipitation was taken, Octobers in 1990 and 1991 were exceptionally dry. Each year, an average of 4 weeks was devoted to trapping, using mostly Victor rattraps and Sherman live traps, for a total of 12,573 trapnights. Trap stations were placed at 12-15 m intervals along main trails. At each station, a minimum of two and a maximum of six traps were located, at least one pair on the ground and one on a tree, trying to combine a Victor and a Sherman trap, on the ground and on a tree. Traps located above ground were set mostly on vines, fallen trees, vertical trees, and other suitable places.

Plots were sampled from three to 12 days, mostly depending on the resulting trapping success. We were unable to sample the forest canopy extensively, but some traps (Victor and Sherman traps) were set 5 to 7 m high. Additionally, large and medium mammals were recorded by direct sightings of our team and other BIOLAT scientists since 1989.

Bait selection was difficult in Pakitza because the area is extremely rich in ants, cockroaches, orthoptera and other invertebrates, so that the baits were completely eaten in a couple of hours. After trying our standard bait, rolled oats mixed with peanut butter and vanilla, and several alternate baits including bananas, chestnut, corn, whole peanut and mandioca, we arrived to a bait consisting of pieces of mandioca or chestnut mixed with peanut butter and vanilla. This bait, although also eaten by ants, endured longer than the others.

Although our sampling efforts were not equally spread across all the plots, we analyze trap-success differences among the plots, and between the dry and wet season, when data is available. Some plots were not sampled either in wet or dry season because of logistic reasons. Estimates of relative abundance for small mammals are based on the absolute number of snap-trapnight captures (Tabla 2). Relative abundance is estimated for large and medium mammals based on sighting frequencies compiled from all records.

Stomachs of most of the capture species were analyzed to broadly indicate differences among species. We examine from 3 to 6 complete stomachs for abundant species, and 1 or 2 stomachs (when available) for the remaining species.

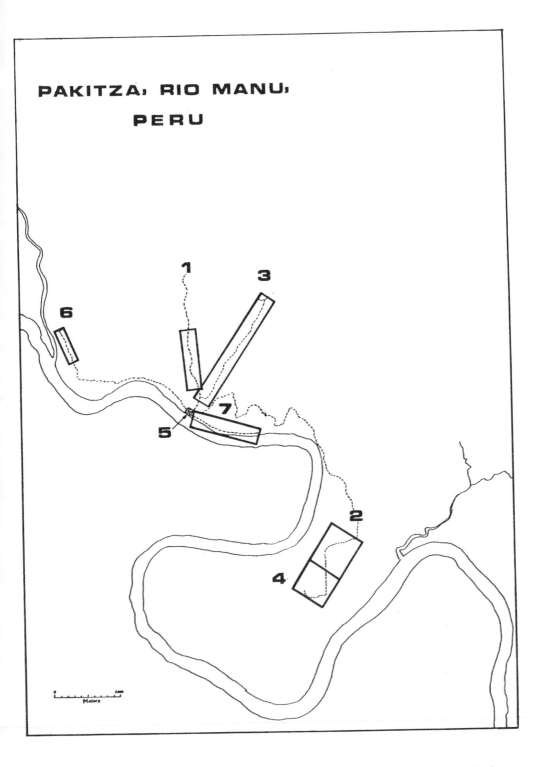

PAKITZA, RIO MANU, PERU

Fig. 2.– Map showing the seven sampling plots located in Pakitza Biological Station. Trapping was developed mainly along trails. Note that the first four plots are related to four BIOLAT permanent Zones.

We analyzed the data qualitatively, because of the greatly digested stomach contents of our few samples; and trophic status was defined by the presence of food items (e.g., fruits, ants, other invertebrates, seeds, plant remains and fungi) found in the stomachs. Diets of species only observed were not defined. Niche definition for these species can be found in Janson and Emmons (1990). Ecto- and endoparasites were collected from all specimens by R. Guerrero and will be treated separately elsewhere.

Table 1.— Brief description of habitats of the seven sampling plots carried out in Pakitza based on Erwin (1991). The first four plots correspond to the Zones (sensu Erwin, op. cit.), the other three plots represent other habitats. Plots are illustrated in Fig. 2.

Plots	Zones	Forest type description
1	1	Dissected alluvial terrace forest (Dat): old alluvial terraces that have been dissected by stream action. Have well drained sandy surface soils.
2	2	Upper floodplain forest (Uff): secondary floodpain subject to periodic inundation of rapidly moving water. It has greater amounts of soil nutrients.
3	3	Old alluvial terrace forest with bambu (OatB): On old high Pleistocene-age terrace left by the deep flowing rivers of the past. It is composed of a rapidly drained sandy surface soil. Spine bambu *Guadua weberbaueri* is abundant.
4	4	Oxbow hardwood swamp forest (Ohs): low forest on an ancient cocha. Water stands up to a meter deep during the rainy season, the clay is dry in the dry season.
5	-	Open areas (Oa): clearings occupied by buildings at Pakitza. It includes also nearby forests, where tents were frequently set.
6	-	Upper floodplain forest (Uff). It appears similar to plot 2.
7	-	Upper floodplain forest (Uff). It is similar to the plot 2 but much more altered by human activities.

Mammalian orders and families are arranged following Wilson and Reeder (1993); genera and species are listed alphabetically. The ordinal classification of marsupials follows Hershkovitz (1992). Subdivision of "*Marmosa* " (mouse opossums) into five genera follows Gardner and Creighton (1989). Generic classification of cats follows Wozencraft (1993).

The collected specimens were preserved as skins, skulls and skeletons, and some were preserved as alcoholic. These specimens are housed in the Museo de Historia Natural, Universidad Nacional Mayor de San Marcos (MUSM).

RESULTS AND DISCUSSION

ANALYSES OF SPECIES DIVERSITY

To date, 62 species of non-flying mammals belonging to eight orders and 20 families have been identified from Pakitza and nearby, including 9 marsupials, 5 edentates, 11 primates, 9 carnivores, 1 tapir, 4 artiodactyls, 22 rodents, and 1 rabbit (Table 2). This list will certainly increase with additional collections. Our specimen of *Neusticomys peruviensis* is the second specimen known for the species; the holotype and previously unique specimen was collected at Balta, Ucayali, Peru (Musser and Gardner, 1974), ca. 210 km north of Pakitza. Our specimens of *Monodelphis brevicaudata* are the first reported from Peru, and those of *Marmosa murina, Marmosops parvidens, Gracilinanus agilis, Neacomys spinosus,* and an undescribed species of *Proechimys* are the first recorded from Manu Biosphere Reserve.

Table 2.— Checklist of the non-flying mammalian species at Pakitza, Manu Reserved Zone, Manu National Park, Peru. Species indicated with a plot number are represented by specimens, and housed at the Museo de Historia Natural, University of San Marcos (MUSM)

Species	Plot	Trophic Status[a]	Canopy Height[b]	Abundance[c]	Macro habitat[d]
DIDELPHIMORPHIA (9 spp.)					
Didelphidae					
Didelphis marsupialis			T	U	
Gracilinanus agilis	7	P	U	R	Uff
Marmosa murina	2,5	I,P	T,U	U	OatB, Uff
Marmosops noctivagus	1,4,5,7	I,S	T,U	C	Dat,Uff,OatB,Ohs
Marmosops parvidens	3		U	R	OatB
Micoureus regina	1,2	A,I,Fr,P	T,U	R	Dat,Uff
Metachirus nudicaudatus	3,5,7	-	T	U	Rhs,Uff,OatB
Monodelphis brevicaudata	2,3	I,P	T	R	OatB,Uff
Philander opossum	7	-	T	R	Uff
EDENTATA (5 spp.)					
Myrmecophagidae					
Myrmecophaga tridactyla			T	U	
Tamandua tetradactyla			Sc	U	
Bradypodidae					
Bradypus sp.			Sc	R	
Megalonychidae					
Choloepus hoffmanni					
Dasypodidae					
Dasypus sp.			T	R	

Species	Plot	Trophic Status[a]	Canopy Height[b]	Abundance[c]	Macro habitat[d]
PRIMATES (11 spp.)					
Callitrichidae					
Cebuella pygmaea				R	
Saguinus fuscicollis			Ca	C	
Saguinus imperator			Ca	C	
Cebidae					
Alouatta seniculus			Ca	A	
Aotus nigriceps			Ca,Sc	C	
Ateles paniscus			Ca	A	
Callicebus brunneus			Ca	U	
Cebus albifrons			Ca	A	
Cebus apella			Ca	C	
Lagothrix lagotricha			Ca	R	
Saimiri boliviensis			Sc	A	
CARNIVORA (9 spp.)					
Procyonidae					
Nasua nasua			T,Sc	U	
Potos flavus			Sc	R	
Mustelidae					
Eira barbara			T,Sc	U	
Lutra longicaudis			W	U	
Pteronura brasiliensis			W	U	
Felidae					
Herpailurus yagouaroundi			T	U	
Leopardus pardalis			T	U	
Panthera onca			T,Sc	R	
Puma concolor			T	R	
PERISSODACTYLA (1 sp.)					
Tapiridae					
Tapirus terrestris			T	R	
ARTIODACTYLA (4 spp.)					
Tayassuidae					
Tayassu pecari			T	R	
Tayassu tajacu			T	C	
Cervidae					
Blastoceros dichotomus ?			T	R	
Mazama americana			T	U	
RODENTIA (22 spp.)					
Sciuridae					
Sciurus ignitus			Sc	C	
Sciurus spadiceus			Sc	C	
Muridae					
Neacomys spinosus	3,4,5		T	U	Rhs,OatB,Ohs

Species	Plot	Trophic Status[a]	Canopy Height[b]	Abundance[c]	Macro habitat[d]
Nectomys squamipes	2,3,5	I,P	W,T,C	U	Dat,Oa,Ohs
Neusticomys peruviensis	2	A	T	R	Uff
Oecomys bicolor	2,3,7	I,P	T	U	Oat,Rhs,Uff,OatB
Oecomys superans	7	Fu,P,S	T	R	Uff
Oligoryzomys microtis	5		C	A	Oa
Oryzomys capito	1,2,5 6,7	A,I,P,S	T	A	Uff,Dat,OatB Ops,Ohs
Oryzomys nitidus	1,2,3 4,5	A,I,P,S	T	A	Dat,OatB,Tgh, Rhs,Uff,Ohs
Rhipidomys couesi	5	I,P,S	C	R	OatB
Erethizontidae					
Coendou bicolor				R	
Agoutidae					
Agouti paca			T	U	
Dasyproctidae					
Dasyprocta variegata			T	C	
Myoprocta pratti			T	R	
Hydrochaeridae					
Hydrochaeris hydrochaeris			W	U	
Echimyidae					
Dactylomys dactylinus			Sc	C	
Mesomys hispidus	7	I,P	T	R	Uff
Proechimys brevicauda	5	P	T	R	Tgh, OatB
Proechimys simonsi	1,2,3 5,6	A,I,P,S	T	C	Uff,Dat,Tgh Oat,OatB
Proechimys steerei	2,4,5 6,7	A,I,P,S	T,C	A	Uff,OatB,Ohs
Proechimys sp.	2,3	A,I,Fu,P,S	T	U	Oat,Rhs,Uff
LAGOMORPHA (1 sp.)					
Leporidae					
Sylvilagus brasiliensis			T	U	

62 spp.

[a] Abbreviations are as follows:
  Fr= fruit pulp
  A = ants
  I = other invertebrates (mostly insects)
  P = plant remains (unidentified)
  S = seeds
  Fu = fungi
[b] Abbreviations are as follows:
  U = understory, ca. 5m high or less
  C = commensal with human habitations
  T = terrestrial
  W = aquatic or aquatic margin
  Sc = subcanopy
  Ca= canopy, ca 25 m or more
[c] Abbreviations are as follows:

A = abundant, often observed; small mammals represented by more than 15 captures.
C = common, frequently observed; from 9 to 15 captures.
U = uncommon, occasionally observed; from 3 to 8 captures.
R = rare, few sightings; less than 3 captures.
[d] Abbreviations follow Erwin (1991):
  Oat = Old alluvial terrace forest, w/o bamboo
  OatB = Old alluvial terrace forest, w bamboo
  Dat = Dissected alluvial terrace forest
  Uff = Upper floodplain forest
  Ops = Oxbow palm swamp forest
  Ohs = Oxbow hardwood swamp forest
  Rhs = Ridgetop hardwood swamp forest
  Tgh = Tall grass habitats: sedges and grasses

Janson and Emmons (1990) reported 70 species of non-flying mammals at Cocha Cashu or nearby, although for some species it is not clear whether the records are actually from Cocha Cashu or from other places along the Manu River. At least 16 species (marsupials *Caluromysiops irrupta*, *Caluromys lanatus*, and *Glironia* sp.; monkeys *Pithecia* sp., and *Callimico goeldii*; edentates *Cyclopes didactylus*, and *Priodontes maximus*; rodents *Sciurus sanborni*, *Oryzomys macconnelli*, *Oxymycterus* sp., *Dinomys branickii*, and *Echimys* sp.; carnivores *Procyon cancrivorus*, *Bassaricyon gabbii*, and *Galictis vittata*; and the deer *Mazama gouazoubira*), known to occur in Cocha Cashu (Janson and Emmons, op. cit.), have not yet been reported in Pakitza. Most of these species are medium or large size mammals, more likely to be recorded by sightings than by trapping. On the other hand, 4 marsupials, 3 rodents and 1 deer, not known in Cocha Cashu, are here reported for Pakitza. The larger species richness in Cocha Cashu appears to be better interpreted by the more intensive studies at Cocha Cashu than in Pakitza. Pakitza is only 21 km southeast of Cocha Cashu, in the same river drainage, and on the left side of the Manu river, such that both biological stations will be found to share the same mammalian fauna and that their inventory data can be combined for analysis. In this case, Cocha Cashu and Pakitza is extremely diverse, including at least 78 species of non-flying mammals, higher than that at Cusco Amazónico (58 spp., Woodman et al., 1991); Barro Colorado Island, Panama (39 spp., Glanz, 1990); La Selva, Costa Rica (46 spp., Wilson, 1990), and probably any other place in the Neotropics. Recently, *Monodelphis* sp. was collected and becomes one additional record for Cocha Cashu (C. Mitchell, pers. comm.).

Table 3.— Total of small mammal species and specimens snap-trapped in the 7 sampling plots, at wet and dry seasons, in Pakitza.

	Trapnights			Captures[a]		
Plots	Wet	Dry	Total	Wet	Dry	Total
1	1080			5 (7)		5 (7)
2	1458	1680	3138	9 (41)	5 (27)	11 (68)
3	618	1900	2418	1 (1)	7 (13)	7 (14)
4		1440			4 (24)	4 (24)
5	680			7 (10)		7 (10)
6	312			3 (3)		3 (3)
7	840	2665	3505	4 (6)	6 (17)	8 (23)

[a] Captures indicate species number. Number in parenthesis show the number of specimens captured.

Nine species of marsupials are known in Pakitza (Table 2). Among these, *Monodelphis brevicaudata* was represented by two specimens, one juvenile of age 2, and another of age 3 (*sensu* Pine et al., 1985). Here *Micoureus regina* is equivalent to *M. cinerea* of Janson and Emmons (1990). Currently, only *Philander opossum* is consider to inhabit the lowland forests of Madre de Dios (Emmons and Feer, 1990). Woodman et al. (1991) reported *P. andersoni* and not *opossum* from Cuzco Amazónico, but specimens in the Museo de Historia Natural (MUSM), from Pakitza and Cusco Amazónico clearly belong to *P. opossum* following Gardner and Patton (1972) and Hershkovitz (1992). The specimens of *Philander* from Cuzco Amazónico, housed at The University of Kansas Museum of Natural History (KU), have been also recently corrected to *P. opossum* (N. Woodman, pers. comm.).

Most of our specimens of marsupials were trapped on the ground, except for *Marmosops noctivagus* and *Micoureus regina*, that were also collected on trees. *Gracilinanus agilis* and *Marmosops parvidens* were caught by hand while the first was walking along the upper line of a mistnet, and the last climbing on a lower branch. Most marsupials were collected in Plot 2, an extremely rich forest that is periodically inundated with rapidly moving water (Table 1). One specimen of *Monodelphis brevicaudata* was collected in the Plot 2 and the other in the Plot 3, "pacal" habitat, both in Sherman traps.

Rodents were the most diverse group with 22 species. The great richness of native rodents is only comparable to that of Cocha Cashu (24 spp., Janson and Emmons, 1990) and Cuzco Amazónico (21 spp. [and not 24 spp.], Woodman et al., 1991). Our specimen of *Neusticomys peruviensis*, a young female of Tooth Wear Class 2 (TWC 2, sensu Voss, 1988), extends the known distribution of the species, and of the ichthyomyine rodents, almost 210 km south. Our specimen is grayish brown in dorsal pelage, with silvery gray on the sides becoming paler to the venter, and not buffy brown as in the type *peruviensis* (Musser and Gardner, 1974); the toes are white, the tail is short, black and conspicuously haired. The ears are small and black and not cream-colored. In skull and tooth characters, our specimen is like the holotype (TWC 4) except that, besides being younger and smaller (Greatest skull length, 25.77 vs. 28.1 mm), it has broader interorbital constriction (5.69 vs. 5.2 mm) and slightly longer maxillary toothrow (3.99 vs. 3.8 mm). More importantly, in our specimen the posterior edge of the inferior zygomatic root is located at level with the anterocone of M1; in the type *peruviensis* the posterior edge of the zygomatic root is located well anterior to the M1 anterocone (see Voss, 1988). These differences might indicate a specific distinction, but pending discovery of more adult specimens, we cannot yet judge the level of intraspecific or age variation. For this reason, our specimen is considered conspecific with *Neusticomys peruviensis*.

Neusticomys peruviensis was collected in Plot 2, in a Victor rat trap, using mandioca, peanut butter and vanilla as bait. The specimen was caught some 200m from the nearest water stream. Streams in this area are of clay bottom. Crabs of the family Trichodactylidae are known in these streams, which are likely to be preyed upon by *peruviensis*.

Our specimen of *Rhipidomys* is identical to those collected at Cuzco Amazónico and referred to *R. couesi*, and is considered conspecific. However, this taxon seems to represent an undescribed species being studied by C. Tribe (R.M. Timm, pers. comm.).

Our specimens of *Neacomys spinosus* are also identical to those collected at Cusco Amazónico. However, we were not able to collect *N. tenuipes*, also reported from Cusco Amazónico (Woodman et al., 1991). Specimens in the Museo de Historia Natural (MUSM) of *tenuipes*, from Cusco Amazónico, are actually juveniles (M3 not erupted) of *N. spinosus*. However, similar series housed at KU might indeed (or might not) correspond to *tenuipes*.

Edentates, carnivores, artiodactyls, and tapir include a group of large species that were seen rarely. Sightings of large size animals were only occasionally made by the authors and other colleagues working at Pakitza and nearby zones, so the species list reported here is still incomplete, compared to that for Cocha Cashu.

Mazama americana was often seen at Pakitza, and it is considered common. The brown brocket deer M. *gouazoubira* is also present in Manu National Park, but less common than *americana* (Grimwood, 1969). It was reported in Cocha Cashu (Janson and Emmons, 1990), and it is very likely to occur in Pakitza. An additional deer was observed at the border of Quebrada Picaflor, about 2 km SE of Pakitza's camp (G. Lamas, pers. comm.). Lamas' description of the deer agrees most likely with a female (no antlers) of *Blastoceros dichotomus*.

Primates are diverse and common in the forest of Pakitza, most of them show no fear of humans. A group of *Cebuella pygmaea* was observed and followed at Pakitza (Gazzo, 1985). *Callimico goeldii* and *Pithecia irrorata* are species rarely seen in Cocha Cashu (Terborgh, 1983), that might occur also in Pakitza. The single lagomorph, *Sylvilagus brasiliensis*, is absent in the forest but was often seen in open areas surrounding the camp.

CAPTURE ANALYSES AMONG PLOTS

In the analyses of snap-trapped mammals, we found differences in the diversity of species among plots; however, most of the comparisons are among plots 2, 3 and 7, where wet and dry season data and more trapnights are available. Plot 2 has the overall highest trapping success. We found more species diversity (11 spp.) and abundance (46% of all specimens) of small mammals in plot 2 than in others (Table 3). Plots 3 and 7, both with high trapnight efforts, have less diversity and specimens (e.g., 7 species [9% of captures] in plot 3, and 8 species [15% of captures] in plot 7). Less than 1500 trapnights were devoted to each of the other plots, nonetheless 7 species were taken in plot 5, and a good 16% of specimens were caught in plot 4. Plots 1, 5 and 6 yielded less than 1% of captures each, but were not extensively sampled. The relatively good species diversity of plot 5 might be due to the inclusion of captures from nearby forests.

We analyzed capture efficiency among plots in the wet season. Non-flooded forests of plot 1 were, at least compared to the periodically flooded forests of plot

2, poor in species number and abundance of small mammals (Table 3). Five species were collected in plot 1 (e.g., *Marmosops noctivagus*, *Micoureus regina*, *Oryzomys capito*, *O. nitidus*, and *Proechimys simonsi*) and nine species in plot 2 (e.g., *Marmosa murina*, *Micoureus regina*, *Monodelphis brevicaudata*, *Oryzomys capito*, *O. nitidus*, *Oecomys bicolor*, *Neusticomys peruviensis*, *Nectomys squamipes* and *Proechimys simonsi*). This supports Janson and Emmons (1990) who found in Cocha Cashu that most of the smaller terrestrial mammal species are limited largely to high-ground forests, which is also periodically flooded, so equivalent to plot 2. Unfortunately, high- terrace forests, as plot 1, are absent in Cocha Cashu study area, impeding further comparisons. The greater diversity and abundance of small mammals in plot 2 (Upper floodplain forests) might be explained by the high nutrient richness of the soil, especially if this is expressed in greater resources of invertebrates, seeds, and fruits for small mammals. Soils are richer in plot 2 because alluvium is periodically deposited after major floods, and it is not continuously leached as the upper forests (Erwin, 1991).

Four species of plot 1 are also known to occur in plot 2. The remaining species of plot 2 (except *Neusticomys peruviensis*) were also captured from other non-flooded forests. At this point, our data does not show some species preference for "high" or "low" forests as is currently occurring with carabid beetles (Erwin, 1991). However, differences may be occurring at the population density level and we urge further studies. In addition, a review of the degree to which species are affected by flooding is needed. Some of our captures were on fallen palm leaves surrounded by water, suggesting that few small rodents are limited by water. Pakitza is an ideal place for studies dealing with flooded and non-flooded forest comparisons, because of its more diverse topography and habitats.

The species diversity and relative abundance in plot 2 compares higher in the wet than in the dry season. 60% of the specimens, representing 9 species (see above), were collected in February 1992. Captures in the dry season (September, 1990) represented only 40% of total specimens in 5 species (*Marmosops noctivagus*, *O. capito*, *O. nitidus*, *Proechimys steerei* and *Proechimys* sp.). Only two species were common to both seasons, *Oryzomys capito* and *Oryzomys nitidus*, which were also the most abundant species in both seasons. However, higher captures were found in the dry seasons of plots 3 and 7, wich might be explained by the almost three times higher sampling devoted to the dry seasons. The dry season of plot 2 also compares higher than plot 3 and 7 in regard to captures, but not in species diversity.

A critical interpretation of the capture differences among the plots requires a more extensive knowledge of the habitats. Resource availability in Cocha Cashu is known to vary widely among different forest types (Janson and Emmons, 1990) and this factor might also explain the plot differences found in Pakitza. In addition, a more intensive and longer capture program is needed not only to document diversity, but to obtain more significant data among plots and between seasons. Capture efficiency in Pakitza is extremely low, which is not an unusual result for mammalogists currently working in the lowland tropical forests. However, we believe that capture methodology also needs to be improved in order to get more species, specimens and data, more appropriate for further ecological studies.

GENERAL DIET ANALYSES

Stomach content analyses of five marsupials showed that most are primarily insectivorous, feeding on ants and other insects. However, plant remains, fruits and seeds were also components of their diet (see Table 2). No fungi were found in the stomachs.

Trophic status of most small rodents are not precisely known in the habitats of Cocha Cashu (Janson and Emmons, 1990). We found that rodents were primarily omnivorous; but largely prefering ants, other insects, and plant remains. Fungi was found only in two species. Seeds were always small and complete, and apparently taken with sheaths and other fruits. These rodents are likely acting as seed dispersers, and this role should be further investigated.

CONSERVATION

The mammal populations at Pakitza appear to be in good condition. Hunting pressure in the Reserve Zone, appears negligible, except for the areas surrounding the small hamlet of Boca Manu, about 55 km straight line, southeast of Pakitza. Natives from the Manu River are allowed to hunt medium and large mammals for food, but only with native weapons, and their impact on the fauna appears to be minimal (C. Mitchell and Ráez, in litt.). Anthropogenic habitat disturbances are also absent on the middle and upper parts of Manu River, where most of the Park lies.

Long term studies of individual mammalian species produce refined data on ecological parameters such as energetics, habitat specificity and home range (Janson and Emmons, 1990), but it is not the best method to document species richness. Inventories, and associated collections in Pakitza have notably increased the number of species recorded in the lowland forests of Manu Biosphere Reserve, and surveys involving specimen collection should be supported as well as the long-term studies.

ACKNOWLEDGEMENTS

We thank the Dirección Forestal y Fauna of the Ministerio de Agricultura for permission to conduct fieldwork. Fieldwork at Pakitza was supported by the

Biological Diversity Program in Latin America (BIOLAT). The Office of Fellowships and Grants, Smithsonian Institution, is also acknowledged for supporting Pacheco's identification work at the National Museum of Natural History, Washington, D.C. Sergio Solari and Alfred L. Gardner confirmed identifications of some marsupials. We express our great appreciation to all BIOLAT colleagues who shared sightings of mammals. Louise H. Emmons and an anonymous reviewer provided valuable comments on the manuscript.

LITERATURE CITED

Ascorra, C. F., D. E. Wilson, and M. Romo. 1991. Lista anotada de los quirópteros del Parque Nacional Manu, Perú. Publicaciones del Museo de Historia Natural, Universidad Nacional Mayor de San Marcos, (A) 42:1-14.

Emmons, L. H., and F. Feer. 1990. Neotropical rainforest mammals. A field guide. The University of Chicago Press, 281 pp.

Erwin, T. L. 1991. Natural history of the carabid beetles at the BIOLAT Biological Station, Rio Manu, Pakitza, Peru. Revista Peruana de Entomología, 33:1-85.

Gardner, A. L., and G. K. Creighton. 1989. A new generic name for Tate's (1933) *microtarsus* group of South American mouse opossums (Marsupialia: Didelphidae). Proceedings of the Biological Society of Washington, 102:3-7.

Gardner, A. L., and J. L. Patton. 1972. New species of *Philander* (Marsupialia: Didelphidae) and *Mimon* (Chiroptera:Phyllostomidae) from Peru. Occasional Papers of the Museum of Zoology, Louisiana State University, 43:1-12.

Gazzo, C. 1985. Estudio sobre la bioecología de *Cebuella pygmaea* en el Parque Nacional Manu. Chapter 20:1-9, *in* Reporte Manu (M. A. Rios, ed.). Centro de Datos para la Conservación, Universidad Nacional Agraria La Molina.

Gentry, A. H. (ed.). 1990. Four neotropical rainforests. Yale University Press, New Haven, 627 pp.

Glanz, W. E. 1990. Neotropical mammal densities: How unusual is the community on Barro Colorado Island, Panama? Pp. 287-313, *in* Four neotropical forests (A. H. Gentry, ed.). Yale University Press, New Haven, 627 pp.

Grimwood, I. R. 1969. Notes on the distribution and status of some Peruvian mammals. American Commitee for International Wild Life Protection and New York Zoological Society, Special Publication, 21: 1-86.

Hershkovitz, P. 1992. The South American gracile mouse opossums, genus *Gracilinanus* Gardner and Creighton, 1989 (Marmosidae, Marsupialia): A taxonomic review with notes on general morphology and relationships. Fieldiana: Zoology, n.s., 70: 1-56.

Janson, C. H., and L. H. Emmons. 1990. Ecological structure of the nonflying mammal community at Cocha Cashu Biological Station, Manu National Park, Peru. Pp. 314-338, *in* Four neotropical forests (A. H. Gentry, ed.). Yale University Press, New Haven, 627 pp.

Musser, G. G., and A. L. Gardner. 1974. A new species of the ichthyomyine *Daptomys* from Peru. American Museum Novitates, 2537:1-23.

Pacheco, V., B. D. Patterson, J. L. Patton, L. H. Emmons, S. Solari, and C. F. Ascorra. 1993. List of mammal species known to occur in Manu Biosphere Reserve, Peru. Publicaciones del Museo de Historia Natural, Universidad Nacional Mayor de San Marcos, (A) 44:1-12.

Pacheco, V., H. de Macedo, E. Vivar, C. F. Ascorra, R. Arana-Cardó and S. Solari. 1995. Lista anotada de los mamíferos peruanos. Occasional Papers in Conservation Biology 2:1-35.

Pine, R. H., P. L. Dalby, and J. O. Matson. 1985. Ecology, postnatal development, morphometrics, and taxonomic status of the short-tailed opossum, *Monodelphis dimidiata*, an apparently semelparous annual marsupial. Annals of Carnegie Museum, 54(6):195-231.

Terborgh, J. W. 1983. Five new world primates. Monographs in Behavior and Ecology. Princeton University Press. Princeton, 260 pp.

Terborgh, J. W., J. W. Fitzpatrick, and L. H. Emmons. 1984. Annotated checklist of bird and mammal species of Cocha Cashu Biological Station, Manu National Park, Peru. Fieldiana: Zoology, n.s., 21:1-29.

Voss, R. S. 1988. Systematics and ecology of ichthyomyine rodents (Muroidea): Patterns of morphological evolution in a small adaptive radiation. Bulletin of the American Museum of Natural History, 188:259-493.

Wilson, D. E. 1990. Mammals of La Selva, Costa Rica. Pp. 273-286, *in* Four neotropical forests (A. H. Gentry, ed.). Yale Univ. Press, New Haven, 627 pp.

Wilson, D. E., and D. M. Reeder (eds.). 1993. Mammal species of the world, a taxonomic and geographic reference. Second ed. Smithsonian Institution Press, Washington, D.C.

Woodman N., R. M. Timm, R. Arana-Cardó, V. Pacheco, C. A. Schmidt, E. D. Hooper, and C. Pacheco-Acero. 1991. Annotated checklist of the mammals of Cuzco Amazonico, Peru. Occasional Papers of the Museum of Natural History, The University of Kansas, 145:1-12.

Wozencraft, W. C. 1993. Order Carnivora. Pp. 279-348, *in* Mammal species of the world, a taxonomic and geographic reference. Second ed. (D. E. Wilson and D. M. Reeder, eds.). Smithsonian Institution Press, Washington D.C.

Diversidad y Ecología de los Quirópteros en Pakitza

César F. Ascorra[1],

Sergio Solari T.[1]

Don E. Wilson[2]

[1]Departamento de Mastozoología, Museo de Historia Natural, Universidad Nacional Mayor de San Marcos, Ap. 140434, Lima 14, Perú (CFA, SS)
[2]Biodiversity Programs, National Museum of Natural History, Smithsonian Institution, Washington, DC 20560, USA (DEW)

RESUMEN

Reportamos 55 especies de quirópteros para la Estación Biológica de Pakitza, Zona Reservada, Parque Nacional Manu, Perú. Actualizamos el conocimiento de la distribución geográfica de cada especie, comentando aspectos de su biología y ecología como: abundancia, refugios, preferencias de hábitat, uso estratificado del bosque, actividad nocturna, condición reproductiva, y composición de la dieta.

ABSTRACT

We report 55 species of bats for the Pakitza Biological Station, Reserved Zone, Manu National Park, Perú. We update the geographical distribution of each and comment on their abundance, roosts, habitat preference, use of forest (understory, midstory, and canopy), nocturnal activity, female reproductive condition, and diet.

INTRODUCCION

Estudios previos sobre distribución geográfica de quirópteros en el Perú han estado basados en colecciones efectuadas en pocas localidades (Ascorra *et al.*, 1993; Gardner, 1976; Graham y Barkley, 1984; Koopman, 1978 y Tuttle, 1970), dejando grandes áreas sin muestreo de murciélagos. En el Parque Nacional Manu, los estudios en quirópteros se iniciaron en la Estación Biológica de Cocha Cashu (Terborgh *et al.*, 1984) y la Estación Biológica de Pakitza (Ascorra *et al.*, 1991) y recientemente Pacheco *et al.* (1993), reportaron el conocimiento actual de la mastofauna conocida para la Reserva de Biósfera del Manu. En este artículo reportamos las especies encontradas durante un estudio sobre la diversidad de quirópteros iniciado hace 6 años y actualizamos la información sobre la distribución geográfica en el Perú, biología y ecología de cada especie, comparando los resultados de nuestro estudio con lo reportado en la literatura.

ÁREA DE ESTUDIO

La Estación Biológica Pakitza (11° 56' 47"S, 71° 17' 00"W), es una estación científica operada por el Programa de Diversidad Biológica en Latino América (BIOLAT) del Smithsonian Institution, ubicada en la Zona Reservada del Parque Nacional Manu, aproximadamente a 65 km aguas arriba de la desembocadura del río Manu, en el río Madre de Dios, Provincia de Manu, Departamento de Madre de Dios, Región Inka, Perú.

Datos metereológicos tomados en la Estación Biológica Cocha Cashu, 21 km aguas arriba de Pakitza, indican una precipitación promedio anual de 2,080 mm, con una estación seca entre mayo y setiembre, y una temperatura media anual es de 24.1 °C. La vegetación de Bosque Húmedo Tropical del lugar ha sido definida como «bosque sempervirente estacional de baja altitud» (Kalliola *et al.*, 1987). La elevación de Pakitza es de 356 m. Aunque en toda la región ha habido algo de extracción selectiva de madera, antes de la creación del parque en 1970, el grado de intervención humana ha sido mínimo. Erwin (1991) describe con detalle los hábitats de Pakitza.

En el área de estudio muestreamos quirópteros en los siguientes ambientes:

1) Bosque de terraza: bosque no intervenido con un dosel forestal de 50 - 60 m, principalmente en trochas.

2) Quebradas del bosque: pequeños afluentes de curso lento y aproximadamente 5 - 10 m de ancho, parcialmente cubiertas por las copas de los árboles de las orillas.

3) Bordes de bosques: límites del claro de la estación biológica.

4) Bosque ribereño: vegetación de cañas (*Gynerium sagittatum*) y bambú (*Guadua* sp. y *Elytrostachys* sp.), 10 - 20 m a ambos lados de las orillas del río.

5) Orillas de río: playas arenosas a ambos lados del río Manu y Quebrada Pachija (tributario de la márgen noreste del Manu, ca. 5 km aguas arriba de Pakitza). Colocamos algunas redes en el cauce mismo de los ríos.

MÉTODOS

En Pakitza capturamos murciélagos en diferentes hábitats del 15 al 25 de octubre 1987, del 5 al 24 de setiembre 1988, del 31 de octubre al 15 de noviembre 1990 y del 13 de febrero al 9 de marzo 1992. El esfuerzo de captura en cada hábitat cada mes fue de 1 - 10 noches. Aunque en todos los muestreos empleamos redes de niebla colocadas en el sotobosque (0.5 - 5 m), en los meses de noviembre, y febrero - marzo utilizamos algunas redes ubicadas a niveles de subdosel forestal (5 - > 20 m). Algunos especímenes fueron obtenidos manualmente en refugios diurnos.

Las redes abiertas a las 17:30 h y cerradas a las 06:00 h eran revisadas cada 30 min. Los quirópteros capturados fueron mantenidos en bolsas individuales de lona, identificados y medidos (longitud del antebrazo y peso). La condición reproductiva de las hembras (preñada o lactando) fue determinada por examen externo.

Los especímenes de estudio de cada especie fueron preservados y depositados en las Colecciones del Museo de Historia Natural de la Universidad Nacional Mayor de San Marcos en Lima, Perú, y en el National Museum of Natural History de Washington, D.C., U.S.A.

Muestras fecales obtenidas durante los muestreos de noviembre, y febrero - marzo fueron extraídas de las bolsas de lona y colocadas en sobres de papel, secadas y guardadas hasta su análisis. En el laboratorio, estas muestras fueron rehidratadas y examinadas bajo un microscopio estereocospio, reconociendo restos de insectos, granos de polen, pulpa vegetal o semillas. Estas últimas eran separadas e identificadas por comparación con la Colección de Referencia del Proyecto Dispersión de Semillas del Centro de Investigacion «Jenaro Herrera», Instituto de Investigaciones de la Amazonía Peruana (IIAP), Iquitos, Perú.

Similarmente registramos la hora y hábitat de cada individuo capturado. En los muestreos de noviembre, y febrero- marzo se incluyeron además la altura de captura en la red.

Pruebas de x^2 (Sokal y Rohlf, 1969) fueron empleadas en el análisis de los datos de uso de hábitat, estratificación vertical y actividad nocturna de aquellas especies con más de 10 individuos capturados, a fin de discriminar distribuciones al azar.

RESULTADOS Y DISCUSIÓN

LISTA DE ESPECIES

En nuestro estudio se capturaron un total de 929 murciélagos pertenecientes a 55 especies ubicadas en 32 géneros y representando 7 familias. Indicamos la distribución previamente reportada en el Perú de cada especie, seguida de su distribución altitudinal y de nuestras observaciones en el campo. Ampliaciones del rango distribucional de algunas especies fueron hechas en base a nuestros especímenes reportados en Pacheco *et al.* (1993), y son detalladas aquí.

Nuestras observaciones referentes al uso de estratos verticales determinada por el muestreo con redes de niebla es resumida en la Tabla 1. La condición reproductiva de 377 individuos hembras pertenecientes a 47 especies es detallada en la Tabla 2. La Tabla 3 presenta resultados del análisis de dieta de 32 especies de quirópteros filostómidos, mientras que la Tabla 4 muestra los ítems vegetales encontrados en la dieta de murciélagos frugívoros.

Todas las especies listadas a continuación se encuentran representadas por especímenes de estudio depositados en las colecciones del Museo de Historia Natural, Universidad Nacional Mayor de San Marcos en Lima y el National Museum of Natural History en Washington D.C..

Tabla 1.– *Quirópteros registrados en diferentes estratos forestales* (N= *número*, h= *altura en metros*).

Especies	N	h				
		0-5	6-10	11-15	16-20	>20
Rhynchonycteris naso	2	2				
Saccopteryx bilineata	1	1	2			
Noctilio albiventris	61	51	10			
Noctilio leporinus	2	2				
Macrophyllum macrophyllum	3	3				
Micronycteris megalotis	4	3		1		
Micronycteris minuta	8	8				
Mimon crenulatum	2	2				
Phyllostomus elongatus	15	11	3	1		
Phyllostomus hastatus	19	12	3	2	1	1
Phyllostomus stenops	3	3				
Tonatia bidens	7	6			1	
Tonatia silvicola	7	7				
Trachops cirrhosus	9	8	1			
Anoura caudifera	3	3				
Choeroniscus minor	2	2				
Glossophaga commissarissi	5	5				
Glossophaga soricina	8	7	1			
Lonchophylla thomasi	4	3	1			
Carollia brevicauda	41	39	1	1		
Carollia castanea	75	71	2			1
Carollia perspicillata	50	44	5			1
Rhinophylla pumilio	4	4				
Dermanura anderseni	14	11	3			
Dermanura cinerea	2	2				
Dermanura gnoma	2	2				
Artibeus planirostris	60	48	10	1		1
Artibeus lituratus	36	17	14	4		1
Artibeus obscurus	59	53	3		1	2
Chiroderma trinitatum	1					1
Chiroderma villosum	1		1			
Platyrrhinus brachycephallus	14	10	3			1
Platyrrhinus helleri	8	7	1			
Platyrrhinus infuscus	1	1				
Sturnira lilium	14	14				

Uroderma bilobatum	9	6	1	2		
Uroderma magnirostrum	7	7				
Vampyressa bidens	1	1				
Vampyressa macconnelli	8	4	3			1
Vampyressa pusilla	2	2				
Vampyrodes caraccioli	2	1	1			
Diphylla ecaudata	2	2				
Furipterus horrens	1	1				
Thyroptera tricolor	1	1				
Lasiurus ega	1	1				
Myotis albescens	19	19				
Myotis nigricans	2	1	1			
Myotis riparius	9	9				
Myotis simus	3	3				
Molossus molossus	1		1			
TOTAL	**615**	**519**	**70**	**14**	**3**	**10**

Rhynchonycteris naso (Wied-Neuwied).Reportada anteriormente para Amazonas (Koopman, 1978), Cusco (Sanborn, 1951), Pasco (Tuttle, 1970), Loreto y Ucayali (Thomas, 1928a), y Madre de Dios (Ascorra *et al.*, 1991); entre los 200 y 700 m (Graham, 1983). Nuestros ejemplares provienen de quebradas y bordes de bosque.

Tabla 2. – Condición reproductiva observada en hembras de murciélago (N= *número de individuos examinados*, L= *en lactancia*, P= *preñadas*).

	Meses											
	Feb-Mar			Setiemb			Octubre			Noviemb		
Especies	N	L	P	N	L	P	N	L	P	N	L	P
Rhynchonycteris naso										1		
Saccopteryx bilineata										2		1
Noctilio albiventris	10	6	1	12	5					6		5
Macrophyllum macrophyllum										1		
Phyllostomus elongatus	4			4	2					4	1	
Phyllostomus hastatus	5	1	1	1	1					1		
Phyllostomus stenops				1								
Tonatia bidens										4	2	1
Tonatia brasiliensis				1								
Tonatia silvicola	1											
Trachops cirrhosus	2			3	1							
Anoura caudifera	1			1			1					
Choeroniscus minor				1								
Glossophaga commissarissi	1									2		1

César F. Ascorra. Sergio Solari y Don E. Wilson

Especies	Feb-Mar			Setiemb			Octubre			Noviemb		
	N	L	P	N	L	P	N	L	P	N	L	P
Glossophaga soricina	6	1					1			2		
Carollia brevicauda	7			16		6	1	1		3		1
Carollia castanea	29	2	3	10		4	1			12		4
Carollia perspicillata	11			6		3	1			7		5
Rhinophylla pumilio	3											
Dermanura anderseni	5		1							1		1
Dermanura cinerea										1		
Dermanura gnoma										1		1
Artibeus planirostris	29	2	7	17		9	1	1		9	1	2
Artibeus lituratus	21	5	1							7	1	2
Artibeus obscuru	6	1		4		2				5	1	
Chiroderma trinitatum										1		
Chiroderma villosum				1		1				1		
Platyrrhinus brachycephallus	8	5	1									
Platyrrhinus helleri	4	1								2	2	
Platyrrhinus infuscus				1								
Sturnira lilium	6	4	1									
Sturnira tildae							1					
Uroderma bilobatum	2	1		4		3	1			2	1	1
Uroderma magnirostrum	3		1	3		3				2	1	
Vampyressa bidens	1	1										
Vampyressa macconnelli	2	1		2		1	1					
Vampyressa nymphaea				1		1						
Vampyressa pusilla	1	1										
Vampyrodes caraccioli	2			3	1							
Desmodus rotundus				1								
Diphylla ecaudata	1											
Furipterus horrens	1											
Thyroptera tricolor	1	1		3		2				4		1
Lasiurus ega	1											
Myotis albescens	5	1		2		2				6		
Myotis nigricans	6	1		1		1						
Myotis simus	1		1									

Saccopteryx bilineata (Temminck).Anteriormente reportada para Tumbes, Huánuco, Ayacucho y Madre de Dios (Koopman, 1978), Pasco y Junín (Tuttle, 1970), Cusco (Sanborn, 1951), Loreto (Thomas, 1928a); entre los 200 y 900 m (Graham, 1983). Estos murciélagos los encontramos refugiándose entre «aletas» de árboles y al interior de un «tronco» hueco formado por la fusión de raíces adventicias de un ficus estrangulador; fueron colectados en bosque de terraza.

Noctilio albiventris Desmarest.Anteriormente reportada para Pasco y Cusco (Tuttle, 1970), Huánuco (Davis, 1976), San Martín (Koopman, 1978), Loreto (Tuttle, 1970), Ucayali (Sanborn, 1949) y Madre de Dios (Ascorra et al., 1991); entre los 200 y 700 m (Graham, 1983). Nuestros ejemplares provienen mayormente de muestreos en el río Manu, no obstante uno de ellos lo encontramos en bordes de bosque.

Noctilio leporinus (Linnaeus). Ha sido registrada anteriormente en Tumbes (Koopman, 1978), Pasco (Tuttle, 1970), Loreto (Thomas, 1928a) y Ucayali (Sanborn, 1949), y Madre de Dios (Pacheco *et al.*, 1993); entre los 200 y 700 m (Graham, 1983). Hallamos estos murciélagos bajo el follaje de la vegetación colgante en las riberas de erosión del río Manu. Observamos que *Noctilio leporinus* inicia su actividad 30 minutos antes que *N. albiventris* (alrededor de las 17:45 h), cuando aún hay buena visibilidad diurna.

Tabla 3.— *Composición de la dieta en Phyllostomidae* (N= *Número de muestras fecales positivas examinadas, i= insectos, ar= Araceae, Cu= Cucurbitaceae, gu= Guttiferae, hy= Hyppeicaceae, ma= Marcgraviaceae, ce= Cecropia spp., fi= Ficus spp., pi= Piperaceae, ni= taxa no identificados, pv= Pulpa Vegetal, po= Polen*).

	Número de muestras fecales positivas												
	N	i	ar	cu	gu	hy	ma	ce	fi	pi	ni	pv	po
Micronycteris megalotis	4	4											
Micronycteris minuta	5	5											
Mimon crenulatum	2	2											
Phyllostomus elongatus	28	28											
Phyllostomus hastatus	43	19			4			18				1	1
Phyllostomus stenops	3	2						1					
Tonatia bidens	6	6											
Tonatia silvicola	15	15											
Trachops cirrhosus	16	16											
Anoura caudifera	2											1	1
Glossophaga commissarissi	5	2											3
Glossophaga soricina	4									2			2
Lonchophylla thomasi	3	1											2
Carollia brevicauda	40	10			2	4	1			16	1	6	
Carollia castanea	49	9				1				34		4	1
Carollia perspicillata	57	21				4	1			23	1	6	1
Rhinophylla pumilio	2		2										
Dermanura anderseni	1								1				
Dermanura gnoma	1								1				
Artibeus planirostris	36	1						3	10		6	15	1
Artibeus lituratus	9							1	2			5	1
Artibeus obscurus	32							2	11	2	4	12	1
Platyrrhinus brachycephallus	5	2						3					
Platyrrhinus helleri	3							2	1				
Platyrrhinus infuscus	1			1									
Sturnira lilium	6									3	1		2
Uroderma bilobatum	5							3	1		1		
Uroderma magnirostrum	5								4		1		
Vampyressa bidens	1								1				
Vampyressa pusilla	1								1				
Vampyrodes caraccioli	2											1	1

Macrophyllum macrophyllum (Schinz). Encontrada en Amazonas y Pasco (Tuttle, 1970), Ucayali (Thomas, 1928a; Sanborn, 1949) y Madre de Dios (Ascorra *et al.*, 1991); entre los 200 y 400 m (Graham, 1983). La mayor parte de nuestros especímenes provienen de quebradas en el bosque; el análisis de muestras fecales confirman su dieta insectívora.

Micronycteris megalotis (Gray). Ha sido registrada para Tumbes y Piura (Koopman, 1978), Huánuco (Thomas, 1927a), Pasco y Junín (Tuttle, 1970), Cusco (Sanborn, 1951), Ucayali (Sanborn, 1949), y Madre de Dios (Ascorra *et al.*, 1991); entre los 200 y 2,900 m (Graham, 1983). Principalmente en bordes de bosque, pero también en quebradas y bosques de terraza. El análisis de muestras fecales reveló únicamente restos de insectos.

Micronycteris minuta (Gervais). Reportada para Pasco (Tuttle, 1970), Loreto y Cusco (Koopman, 1978), y Madre de Dios (Ascorra *et al.*, 1991); entre los 200 y 700 m (Graham,1983). Se los ubica principalmente en bosques de terraza. Al igual que la especie anterior, ésta es típicamente insectívora.

Mimon crenulatum (E. Geoffroy). Anteriormente reportada para San Martín (Thomas, 1927a), Pasco y Ucayali (Tuttle, 1970), Loreto (Thomas, 1928b) Madre de Dios (Ascorra *et al.*, 1991) y Cusco (Pacheco *et al.*, 1993); entre los 200 y 1400 m (Graham, 1983; Pacheco *et al.*, 1993). Fue únicamente colectado en bosques de terraza. El análisis de muestras fecales indica hábitos insectívoros.

Phyllostomus elongatus (E. Geoffroy). Encontrada en Pasco (Tuttle, 1970), Cusco (Sanborn, 1951), Loreto y Madre de Dios (Koopman,1978); entre los 200 y 1,180 m (Graham, 1983; Pacheco *et al.*, 1993). Hallamos esta especie principalmente en bosques de terraza, desde el sotobosque al subdosel.

Phyllostomus hastatus (Pallas). Anteriormente reportada para Tumbes, Amazonas, Huánuco, Junín, Ayacucho, Loreto y Madre de Dios (Koopman, 1978), San Martín y Pasco (Tuttle, 1970), Cusco (Sanborn, 1951); entre los 200 y 1,900 m (Graham,1983). Tanto en bordes de bosque como bosques de terraza, utilizando diferentes estratos verticales. No encontramos evidencia de hábitos carnívoros para esta especie, siendo más bien frugívoro.

Phyllostomus stenops (Peters). Previamente registrada en Ayacucho (Gardner, 1976), Madre de Dios (Ascorra *et al.*, 1991), Loreto (Ascorra *et al.*, 1993) y Cusco (Pacheco *et al.*, 1993); entre los 200 y 2700 m (Graham, 1983). Sólo se le ha encontrado en bosques de terraza.

Tonatia bidens (Spix). Reportada para Ucayali (Gardner, 1976), Pasco (Ascorra et al., 1989) y Madre de Dios (Ascorra *et al.*, 1991). En elevaciones de 350 a 1030 m (Pacheco *et al.*, 1993). A diferencia de los anteriores, hallamos esta especie principalmente en quebradas. En sus heces evidenciamos hábitos exclusivamente insectívoros.

Tonatia brasiliense (Peters). Reportada para Cusco (Koopman, 1978), Junín y Ucayali (Gardner, 1976) y Madre de Dios (Ascorra *et al.*, 1991); entre los 200 y 700 m (Graham, 1983). Capturado únicamente en quebradas y a nivel del suelo. Encontramos solamente restos de insectos en las muestras fecales.

Tonatia silvicola (D'Orbigny). Reportada para Piura, Junín y Madre de Dios (Koopman, 1978), Huánuco (Thomas, 1927b), Pasco (Tuttle, 1970), Cusco (Sanborn, 1951), Loreto (Thomas, 1928b), Ucayali (Gardner, 1976); entre los 200 y 1,500 m (Graham, 1983), aunque se le ha reportado hasta los 2000 m (Koopman, 1978). Está diferenciada de sus congenéricas en su preferencia por los bosques de terraza. Sólo hallamos evidencia de hábitos insectívoros en las muestras fecales.

Trachops cirrhosus (Spix). Registrada en Huánuco y Madre de Dios (Koopman, 1978), Pasco y Loreto (Tuttle, 1970) y Ucayali (Thomas, 1928a); entre los 200 y 1000 m (Graham, 1983; Pacheco *et al.*, 1993). Principalmente colectado en bosques de terraza. Los análisis de muestras fecales revelaron exclusivamente restos de insectos en su dieta.

Tabla 4. – *Semillas diseminadas por murciélagos frugívoros en Pakitza* (A= Febrero-Marzo 1992, B= Noviembre 1990; e= endozoochoria, s= synzoochoria).

FAMILIA Especie	Tipo	Número de muestras positivas	
		A	B
ARACEAE	e		2
CUCURBITACEAE			
Gurania sp.	e		4
GUTTIFERAE	e	2	1
HYPPERICACEAE			
Vismia spp.	e	2	8
MARCGRAVIACEAE	e		
MORACEAE			
Cecropia sciadophylla	e		1
Cecropia cf. ficifolia	e		19
Cecropia cf. membranaceae	e	3	9
Ficus insipida	e	5	1
Ficus sp.	e	17	9
PIPERACEAE			
Piper arboreum	e	9	14
Piper cf. aduncum	e	3	19
Piper spp.	e	6	39
NO IDENTIFICADA			
no identificadas	e/s	1/1	10/1

Anoura caudifera (E. Geoffroy). Previamente reportada para Junín (Sanborn, 1941), Cusco y Puno (Sanborn, 1951), Huánuco y Loreto (Koopman, 1978), y Madre de Dios (Ascorra *et al* 1991); entre los 300 y 2800 m (Graham, 1983). La hallamos circunscrita al sotobosque, tanto en quebradas como bosques de terraza y bordes de bosque.

Choeroniscus minor (Peters). En el Perú ha sido reportada para Huánuco y Pasco (Tuttle, 1970), Madre de Dios (Ascorra *et al.*, 1991) y Puno (Koopman, 1978); entre los 200 y 825 m (Graham, 1983; Pacheco *et al.*, 1993). Muestra su preferencia por las quebradas, pero también en bosques de terraza.

Glossophaga commissarisi Gardner. Reportada anteriormente para Loreto y Ucayali (Graham y Barkley, 1984), éstos son los primeros especímenes de Madre de Dios (Pacheco *et al.*, 1993). Se le localiza principalmente en bosques de terraza.

Glossophaga soricina (Pallas). Reportada anteriormente para Tumbes (Allen, 1908), Piura, La Libertad, Lima, Ica, Arequipa y Amazonas, (Ortiz de La Puente, 1951), Lambayeque, Ancash, San Martín, Huánuco y Madre de Dios (Koopman, 1978), Pasco y Junín (Tuttle, 1970), Loreto (Thomas, 1928b), Cusco (Thomas, 1920); entre los 200 y 1,900 m (Graham, 1983). Colectado en la mayoría de ambientes, excepto orillas de río.

Glossophaga sp. Dentro de los especímenes asignados a este género encontramos ejemplares que muestran caracteres intermedios entre G. *soricina* y G. *longirostris*. Nuestros ejemplares provienen de quebradas en bosques de terraza.

Lonchophylla thomasi J. Allen. Anteriormente reportada para Pasco (Koopman, 1978), Ucayali (Gardner, 1976) y Madre de Dios (Woodman *et al.*, 1991); entre los 200 y 1350 m (Graham, 1983; Pacheco *et al.*, 1993). Únicamente colectada en bosques de terraza. Las muestras fecales de la especie contenían restos de insectos y granos de polen.

Carollia brevicauda (Schinz). Previamente reportada para Huánuco, Junín, Puno y Madre de Dios (Pine, 1972), Pasco y Ayacucho (Koopman, 1978), Cusco (Tuttle, 1970), Loreto y Ucayali (Patton y Gardner, 1971); entre los 200 y 2300 m (Graham, 1983). Mayormente colectada en bosques de terraza y quebradas.

Carollia castanea H. Allen. Se le conoce en Huánuco (Pine, 1972), Pasco y Junín (Tuttle, 1970), Ayacucho y Cusco (Koopman, 1978), Loreto y Ucayali (Patton y Gardner, 1971) y Madre de Dios (Ascorra *et al.*, 1991), entre los 200 y 1100 m (Graham, 1983). Es la especie más abundante de Pakitza (Wilson *et al.*, este volumen), y la colectamos en todos los hábitats en proporciones muy similares, excepto en ríos.

Carollia perspicillata (Linnaeus). Previamente reportada en Tumbes, San Martín, Huánuco y Madre de Dios (Pine, 1972), Cajamarca, Amazonas, Ayacucho (Koopman, 1978), Pasco, Junín, Loreto (Tuttle, 1970), Puno (Sanborn, 1953); de 200 a 2250 m (Graham, 1983; Pacheco *et al.*, 1993). Esta es otra especie de amplia distribución en el bosque, prefiriendo los bosques de terraza.

Rhinophylla pumilio Peters. Fue anteriormente reportada para San Martín (Thomas, 1927a), Huánuco (Koopman, 1978), Pasco (Tuttle, 1970), Loreto y Ucayali (Carter, 1966) y Madre de Dios (Ascorra *et al.*, 1991); entre los 200 y 825 m (Graham, 1983; Pacheco *et al.*, 1993). Esta especie la encontramos principalmente en bosque ribereño; hallamos semillas de Araceae en las muestras fecales.

Artibeus lituratus (Olfers). Encontrada anteriormente en Tumbes, Cusco y Madre de Dios (Koopman, 1978), Cajamarca y Amazonas (Koopman, 1978), San Martín (Osgood, 1914; Thomas, 1927a), Huánuco (Sanborn, 1949), Pasco

(Tuttle, 1970), Loreto (Ascorra *et al.*, 1993; Davis, 1975) y Ucayali (Sanborn, 1949); entre los 200 y 1100 m (Graham, 1983). Fue colectado principalmente en bosques de terraza y bordes de bosque. El análisis de muestras fecales indica dieta estrictamente frugívora.

Artibeus obscurus (Schinz). Reportado anteriormente bajo el nombre de A. *fuliginosus* para Piura, Amazonas, Huánuco, Pasco, Junín, Cusco (Koopman, 1978), Loreto y Ucayali (Koepcke y Kraft, 1984) y Madre de Dios (Ascorra *et al.*, 1991). Se le localiza entre los 350 y 1030 m (Pacheco *et al.*, 1993). Se trata de otra de las especies más abundantes de Pakitza (Wilson *et al.*, este volumen), principalmente colectada en bosques de terraza y quebradas de bosque, con una mayor afinidad por el estrato de sotobosque. En sus heces se encontraron semillas de varias especies, así como pulpa y polen.

Artibeus planirostris (Spix). Anteriormente registrada, como A. *jamaicensis*, en Tumbes (Graham y Barkley, 1983), Cajamarca (Koopman, 1978), San Martín (Osgood, 1914; Thomas, 1927a), Huánuco, Ayacucho y Puno (Koopman, 1978), Pasco (Ascorra *et al.*, 1989), Junín y Madre de Dios (Koepcke y Kraft, 1984), Loreto (Thomas, 1928a y b), Ucayali (Sanborn, 1949) y Cusco (Pacheco *et al.*, 1993); entre los 200 y 1400 m (Graham, 1983). Comparte con sus congéneres la preferencia por los bosques de terraza. La única muestra fecal contenía exclusivamente arcilla, lo cual confirmaría la sospecha de que los murciélagos toman minerales en «colpas» o lamederos de sal, como otros animales (Ascorra y Wilson, 1991; Romo, comm. pers.).

Chiroderma trinitatum Goodwin. Anteriormente registrada en Huánuco, Cusco (Koopman, 1978), Pasco y Loreto (Davis, 1975; Tuttle, 1970), Ayacucho (Gardner, 1976) y Madre de Dios (Pacheco *et al.*, 1993); entre los 200 y 950 m (Graham, 1983, Pacheco *et al.*, 1993). Nuestro único ejemplar procede de la copa de los árboles en bosques de terraza.

Chiroderma villosum Peters. Reportado para San Martín (Thomas, 1927a), Junín y Cusco (Koopman, 1978), Pasco y Loreto (Thomas, 1927a; Tuttle, 1970), Ucayali (Thomas, 1928a) y Madre de Dios (Ascorra *et al.*, 1991), entre los 200 y 1000 m (Graham, 1983). Al igual que la especie anterior, ésta prefiere los bosques de terraza.

Dermanura anderseni (Osgood). Reportada para Huánuco, Pasco, Cusco, Loreto (Koopman, 1978) y Madre de Dios (Ascorra *et al.*, 1991); entre los 350 y 1030 m (Pacheco *et al.*, 1993). La colectamos mayormente en bordes de bosque, así como también en bosques de terraza. Hallamos semillas de *Ficus* sp. en las heces.

Dermanura cinerea (Gervais). Previamente registrada en Huánuco, Ayacucho, Cusco, Puno (Koopman, 1978), Junín (Thomas, 1924; Thomas, 1928a) y Madre de Dios (Ascorra *et al.*, 1991); entre los 200 y 700 m (Graham, 1983). Principalmente en quebradas, pero también en bosques de terraza.

Dermanura gnoma (Handley).Reportada para Loreto (Ascorra *et al.*, 1993), Ucayali (Handley, 1987) y Madre de Dios (Ascorra *et al.*, 1991); entre los 100 y 350 m (Handley, 1987; Pacheco *et al.*, 1993). La hallamos únicamente en el sotobosque de quebradas y bosques de terraza. Colectamos una hembra preñada en época de lluvias y hallamos semillas de *Ficus* sp. en las heces.

Mesophylla macconnelli Thomas. Se le reporta para Huánuco (Koopman, 1978), Pasco (Tuttle, 1970), Cusco (Sanborn, 1951), Loreto (Tuttle, 1970) y Madre de Dios (Ascorra *et al.*, 1991); entre los 200 y 1600 m (Graham, 1983). Principalmente colectado en bosques de terraza.

Platyrrhinus brachycephallus (Rouk Carter). Ha sido reportada para Huánuco, Ucayali (Gardner y Carter, 1972), Pasco, Cusco y Loreto (Koopman, 1978) y Madre de Dios (Ascorra *et al.*, 1991); entre los 100 y 900 m (Gardner y Carter, 1972; Pacheco *et al.*, 1993). Muestra una alta preferencia por los bordes de bosque.

Platyrrhinus helleri (Peters). Registrada anteriormente en Tumbes (Sanborn, 1951), Huánuco, Loreto y Ucayali (Gardner y Carter, 1972), Junín, Apurimac y Cusco (Koopman, 1978), y Madre de Dios (Pacheco *et al.*, 1993); entre los 200 y 1250 m (Graham, 1983; Pacheco *et al.*, 1993). Presenta una preferencia más notoria por los bordes de bosque que la especie anterior.

Platyrrhinus infuscus Peters. Reportada para Cusco, Junín y Madre de Dios (Koopman, 1978), Cajamarca, Huánuco, Ayacucho, Loreto y Ucayali (Gardner y Carter, 1972); entre los 200 y 1500 m (Graham, 1983). Es una de las especies más grandes dentro del género, y prefiere las quebradas. Hallamos semillas de Guttiferae en las heces.

Sturnira lilium (E. Geoffroy). Reportada anteriormente para Amazonas y Cajamarca (Pacheco y Patterson, 1991), Piura y Huánuco, Ayacucho (Koopman, 1978), Pasco y Junín, Cusco, Ucayali y Madre de Dios (Tuttle, 1970); de 200 a 1700 m (Graham, 1983). La hallamos principalmente en el sotobosque de bordes de bosque.

Sturnira tildae de la Torre. Encontrada en Huánuco (Koopman, 1978), Pasco (Tuttle, 1970), Loreto (Ascorra *et al.*, 1993), Ucayali (Pacheco y Patterson, 1991; Tuttle, 1970) y Madre de Dios (Ascorra *et al.*, 1991); entre los 200 y 780 m (Graham, 1983; Pacheco *et al.*, 1993). Sólo colectada en bosques de terraza.

Uroderma bilobatum Peters. Fue encontrada anteriormente en Tumbes, Pasco (Tuttle, 1970), La Libertad y Cajamarca, San Martín, Huánuco, Junín, Loreto y Ucayali (Davis, 1968), Amazonas y Ayacucho (Koopman, 1978), Cusco (Sanborn, 1951), y Madre de Dios (Ascorra *et al.*, 1991), entre los 200 y 1500 m (Graham, 1983). Distribuida en ambientes de bordes de bosque, bosques de terraza y quebradas. Nuestros resultados indican únicamente alimentación a base de frutos de *Cecropia*, *Ficus* y de otras plantas desconocidas.

Uroderma magnirostrum Davis. Reportada para Loreto y Ucayali (Davis, 1968) y Madre de Dios (Ascorra *et al.*, 1991). A elevaciones entre los 350 y 380 m (Pacheco *et al*, 1993). Esta especie también se encuentra en bosque ribereño, además de los mencionados para la especie anterior.

Vampyressa bidens (Dobson). Encontrada en Huánuco y Cusco (Koopman, 1978), Loreto y Ucayali (Sanborn, 1936; Tuttle, 1970) y Madre de Dios (Ascorra *et al.*, 1991); entre los 200 y 1050 m (Graham, 1983; Pacheco *et al.*, 1993). Se le localiza únicamente en bosques de terraza y quebradas.

Vampyressa pusilla (Wagner). Previamente registrada en Cusco (Sanborn, 1953), Loreto (Thomas, 1924) y Madre de Dios (Woodman *et al.*, 1991); entre los 300 y 1500 m (Graham, 1983). En Pakitza ha sido capturada muy cerca al piso, en bosques de terraza. Los reportes previos para el área de estudio de *V. pusilla* (Ascorra *et al.*, 1991) y *V. nymphaea* (Pacheco *et al.*, 1993, se basaron sobre un único ejemplar (cráneo con dentadura incompleta) recientemente reidentificado como *Artibeus gnomus*.

Vampyrodes caraccioli (Thomas). Encontrada en Pasco y Junín (Tuttle, 1970), Cusco (Koopman, 1978), Loreto y Ucayali (Thomas, 1924) y Madre de Dios (Pacheco *et al.*, 1993); entre los 200 y 1500 m (Graham, 1983). Prefiere las quebradas a los bosques de terraza. Hallamos polen en las muestras fecales.

Desmodus rotundus (E. Geoffroy). Esta especie ha sido reportada en Piura y La Libertad, Lima, Cajamarca, San Martín, Huánuco y Ayacucho, Cusco y Puno (Ortiz de la Puente, 1951), Ancash, Ica, Huancavelica y Apurímac (Koopman, 1978), Amazonas (Thomas y St. Leger, 1926), Pasco y Junín (Tuttle, 1970), Loreto (Ascorra *et al.*, 1993) y Madre de Dios (Ascorra *et al.*, 1991), entre los 200 y 2900 m (Graham, 1983). Sólo colectado en quebradas.

Diphylla ecaudata Spix. Reportada para Amazonas (Thomas, 1926; Thomas y St. Leger, 1926), San Martín (Thomas, 1927a), Pasco (Tuttle, 1970), Ucayali (Thomas, 1928a) y Madre de Dios (Pacheco *et al.*, 1993); entre los 200 y 1000 m (Graham, 1983). Sólo en bosques de terrazas.*Furipterus horrens* (F. Cuvier).

Previamente reportada para Loreto (Koopman, 1978), Ucayali (Tuttle, 1970) y Cusco y Madre de Dios (Pacheco *et al.*, 1993). Entre los 350 y 900 m (Pacheco *et al.*, 1993). Aunque con frecuencia observamos este delicado murciélago, volando en trochas y riberas del río Manu sombreadas por la vegetación, antes del crepúsculo, sólo capturamos un único individuo hembra, cerca al piso, en bosque ribereño y poco antes del amanecer.

Thyroptera tricolor Spix. Reportada para Huánuco (Koopman, 1978), Pasco (Tuttle, 1970), Cusco (Sanborn, 1951), Loreto (Ascorra *et al.*, 1993), Ucayali (Gardner, 1976) y Madre de Dios (Ascorra *et al.*, 1991), entre los 200 y 500 m (Graham, 1983). En la zona de estudio, pareciera refugiarse en hojas enrolladas solamente durante la época seca y principios de la época de lluvias. Los colectamos en sus refugios diurnos en un bosque de terraza, a excepción de un único individuo colectado con red de niebla.

Lasiurus ega (Gervais). Reportada para Ucayali (Gardner, 1976) y Madre de Dios (Pacheco *et al.*, 1993). Se refugia en el follaje (Timm et al., 1989). Capturamos un único ejemplar volando sobre el centro de una quebrada, suponemos cuando bebía agua.

Myotis albescens (E. Geoffroy). Reportada para Piura, Amazonas, Huánuco, Cusco, Loreto (La Val, 1973) y Madre de Dios (Ascorra et al., 1991), entre los 200 y 1500 m (Graham, 1983). Nuestras capturas provienen de orillas de río y quebradas, principalmente.

Myotis nigricans (Schinz). Reportada anteriormente para Piura, Lambayeque, Amazonas, Cajamarca, San Martín, Huánuco, Pasco, Junín, Cusco, Puno, Loreto y Madre de Dios (La Val, 1973), entre los 200 y 3300 m (Graham, 1983). Mayormente colectado en bosque de terraza.

Myotis riparius Handley. Reportada para Huánuco, Pasco, Cusco, Loreto (La Val, 1973) y Madre de Dios (Woodman et al., 1991), entre los 200 y 1380 m (Graham, 1983; Pacheco *et al.*, 1993). Colectado en bosques de terraza y bordes de bosque.

Myotis simus Thomas. Anteriormente registrada en Huánuco (La Val, 1973) y Madre de Dios (Pacheco *et al.*, 1993); entre los 200 y 700 m (Graham, 1983). Encontramos esta especie mayormente en bosque ribereño. Se alimenta de insectos.

Molossus molossus (Pallas). Reportada en Piura (Miller, 1913), Lambayeque, Pasco (Tuttle, 1970), Amazonas y Cajamarca, Junín (Koopman, 1978), San Martín (Osgood, 1914), Huánuco y Ayacucho (Warner et al., 1984), Cusco (Sanborn, 1951), Loreto (Thomas, 1928b) y Madre de Dios (Ascorra *et al.*, 1991), entre los 200 y 1500 m (Graham, 1983). Nuestro único ejemplar proviene de bordes de bosque.

Nyctinomops laticaudatus (E. Geoffroy). Conocida únicamente para Piura (Koopman, 1978) y Madre de Dios (Pacheco *et al.*, 1993), pero de amplia distribución. Alimentación insectívora. Nuestro único especimen fue encontrado muerto en un claro.

DISCUSIÓN

RIQUEZA DE ESPECIES

Del presente estudio se desprende que Pakitza, con 55 especies, es uno de los lugares con mayor riqueza faunística de quirópteros en el neotrópico. En el Centro de Investigaciones «Jenaro Herrera», Loreto, Perú, se han registrado 62 especies después de aproximadamente 3 años de intensivos muestreos mensuales, como parte de un estudio en regeneración natural (Ascorra *et al.*, 1993). En las cercanías del Cerro de la Neblina, Territorio Federal Amazonas, Venezuela, en un período de 2.5 años se han registrado 62 especies de murciélagos (Gardner, 1988). En la Estación Biológica «La Selva», Costa Rica, después de cerca de 20 años de estudios se han reportado 61 especies (Wilson, 1990). En Saint-Elie y Nourages, Guayana Francesa, en cerca de 10 años de investigación se han reportado 57 especies de quirópteros (Brosset y Charles-Dominique, 1990). Encontramos 32 géneros en Pakitza, comparados a los 33 de Jenaro Herrera, los 37 de la Selva y los 43 de la Guayana Francesa.

El mayor número de especies e individuos se encontró en la familia *Phyllostomidae*, la que por su gran radiación adaptiva es la más exitosa del neotrópico desplazando a otros taxa (Brosset y Charles-Dominique, 1990). Discusión sobre la estructura de la comunidad de quirópteros en Pakitza se halla en Wilson *et al.* (este volumen).

Preferencias de Hábitat

Cerca del 96% de las especies de murciélagos, a excepción de *Noctilio leporinus* y *Lasiurus ega*, fue obtenido tanto en trochas, quebradas y bordes de bosque de terraza en Pakitza. La ausencia de *N. leporinus* en el bosque se vincula a sus hábitos alimenticios, mientras que la presencia de *L. ega* en el centro de un cuerpo de agua se debería a su comportamiento para beber agua. En bosque ribereño encontramos el 30% de las especies. En este ambiente abundan principalmente los frugívoros de sotobosque (Carollinae), insectívoros de follaje (*M. megalotis*, *P. elongatus*), insectívoros aéreos (*M. simus*, *F. horrens*) y nectarívoros (*G. soricina*), a los que su morfología alar les permite un vuelo versátil entre la densa vegetación de cañas (*Gynerium sagitatum*) y bambú (*Guadua* y *Elytrostachys*). También se hallaron algunos frugívoros de dosel, los cuales, a excepción de *P. brachycephalus*, eran más frecuentes en bosque de terraza.

Aproximadamente el 60% de las especies frecuentaba quebradas en bosque de terraza. Probablemente muchas de ellas las utilizaban como vías de vuelo, a excepción de los insectívoros (*R. naso*, Phyllostominae, *Myotis* spp.) los cuales podrían estarse alimentando de insectos acuáticos o voladores. Cerca del 15% de las especies estaba presente en grandes cuerpos de agua. Entre ellas hallamos algunos frugívoros (*C. castanea*, *C. perspicillata* y *A. obscurus*). Al parecer estas tres especies prefieren usar pequeñas quebradas ocultas en el bosque como vías de vuelo, por lo que su presencia en el río Manu o Quebrada Pachija sería ocasional. La presencia de las restantes especies encontradas en este ambiente (*N. albiventris*, *N. leporinus*, *M. macrophyllum*, *L. ega*, *M. albescens* y *M. riparius*) se explica por sus hábitos insectívoros y/o piscívoros.

Uso de Estratos Forestales

Datos de altura de captura fueron tomados de 615 murciélagos de 50 especies (Tabla 1). Pruebas de x^2 efectuadas en especies con más de 10 capturas indican que la distribución vertical de los murciélagos durante la noche no ocurre al azar, confirmando observaciones similares en Guyana Francesa (Brosset y Charles-Dominique, 1990) y Brasil (Handley, 1967).

A excepción de los insectívoros aéreos *S. bilineata* y *M. molossus* y los frugívoros de dosel *Ch. trinitatum* y *Ch. villosum* que fueron encontrados a niveles del subdosel forestal, aproximadamente el 95%, fue encontrado en el sotobosque (Tabla 1). El 50% de las especies fue capturado únicamente en estratos inferiores, la mitad de ellas comprendía especies de insectívoros aéreos y del follaje y la otra mitad frugívoros y hematófagos. Mientras que el 40% de las especies empleaba tanto el sotobosque como el subdosel forestal. Probablemente el uso de los diferentes estratos del bosque por los murciélagos se relaciona a la disponibilidad de alimento y a la competencia inter-específica por el mismo.

ACTIVIDAD NOCTURNA

Se tomaron datos de las horas de captura de 607 individuos en 50 especies de murciélagos. Pruebas discriminatorias de x^2 efectuadas en aquellas especies con más de 10 capturas revelan que por lo menos el 40% de las especies presenta un patrón de actividad nocturna, coincidiendo con otras investigaciones (Brown, 1968; Charles-Dominique, 1991; Davis y Dixon, 1976; La Val, 1970; Márquez, 1986; Ramírez-Pulido y Armella, 1987).

Los insectívoros aéreos (*R. naso, S. bilineata, N. albiventris, F. horrens, T. tricolor, L. ega, Myotis* spp. y *M. molossus*) muestran un gran pico de actividad inmediatamente después del crepúsculo, el cual decrece en las siguientes horas, presentando otro segundo pico antes del amanecer. Este comportamiento coincide con los períodos de mayor densidad de insectos voladores diurnos y nocturnos (Brown, 1968). Por el contrario, los murciélagos que se alimentan de insectos posados en un sustrato (*M. macrophyllum, Micronycteris* spp., *M. crenulatum, P. elongatus, T. cirrhosus* y *Tonatia* spp.) parecen mostrar una distribución uniforme durante la noche, valiendo para ellos la explicación de Brown (1968) sobre el patrón de actividad de especies predatoras.

Las especies de frugívoros parecen tener patrones de actividad semejantes entre sí, siendo activos toda la noche con un pico de gran actividad en la primera parte de la noche.

REPRODUCCIÓN

Al examinar la condición reproductiva de 377 individuos hembras de 47 especies, encontramos 21 especies con hembras preñadas y 22 especies con hembras en lactancia (Tabla 2). A mediados de la época seca (setiembre), aproximadamente el 45% de las hembras se encontraba preñado y sólo el 1% en lactancia. Aunque el tamaño muestral es pequeño, a finales de la estación seca (Octubre), el 30% de las hembras se encontraba preñado y el 10% en lactancia. A inicios de la época de lluvias (noviembre), el 38% de las hembras se encontraba preñado y alrededor del 12% en lactancia. Para mediados de la época de lluvias (febrero - marzo), sólo el 10% de las hembras se hallaba preñado mientras que el 21% estaba lactando.

Aunque cada especie tiene patrones propios de reproducción, podemos afirmar de que el apareamiento en muchas de las especies en la zona de estudio ocurre a principios y mediados de la época seca, naciendo las crías durante la época de lluvias. Los períodos de alumbramiento probablemente coinciden con los de mayor disponibilidad de alimento (Wilson, 1979).

Composición de la Dieta

Analizamos 392 muestras fecales provenientes de 32 especies de Phyllostomidae, encontrando insectos como componente exclusivo de la dieta de los Phyllostominae *Micronycteris megalotis*, *M. minuta*, *Mimon crenulatum*, *Phyllostomus elongatus*, *Tonatia silvicola* y *Trachops cirrhosus* (Tabla 3). Igualmente hallamos insectos complementando en un 2 a 4% la dieta de los Glossophaginae, Carolliinae y Stenoderminae. Granos de polen constituían la dieta del 50 al 60% de los Glossophaginae y del 1 al 10% de los Stenoderminae.

En las muestras fecales, encontramos semillas de 25 especies de plantas pertenecientes a por lo menos 8 familias vegetales (Tabla 4). Más del 70% de muestras fecales con semillas pertenece a plantas pioneras, principalmente Piperaceae. Aunque sólo el 2% de las muestras contenía semillas diseminadas por synzoochoria, suponemos que muchas de las muestras conteniendo únicamente pulpa vegetal pertenecen a frutos de esta clase de plantas.

AGRADECIMIENTOS

Esta investigación fue financiada por el Programa de Diversidad Biológica en Latino America (BIOLAT), del National Museum of Natural History, Smithsonian Institution. Agradecemos a la Office of Fellowships and Grants de la Smithsonian Institution por subvencionar el trabajo de C. Ascorra en las colecciones del National Museum of Natural History. La identificación de semillas fue posible gracias a la subvención PSTC 7.228 del United States Agency for International Development (US-AID) a D. Gorchov, F. Cornejo y J. Terborgh. El análisis final de datos por computadora y edición del manuscrito fue posible gracias a la subvención 7564 del Biodiversity Support Program del United States World Wildlife Fund (US-WWF) a C. Ascorra y D. Wilson. Agradecemos al Instituto Nacional de Recursos Naturales (ex-Dirección General de Forestal y Fauna, y Programa de Parques Nacionales del Ministerio de Agricultura) por los permisos de colecta. Durante ciertos meses contamos con la valiosa colaboración de Francisco Dallmeier y María V. Tenicela en el trabajo de campo. Agradecemos a Alfred L. Gardner y Mónica Romo por la paciente revisión e importantes sugerencias y comentarios al manuscrito original. Elena Vivar gentilmente nos permitió reportar su ejemplar de *Nyctinomops laticaudatus*.

LITERATURA CITADA

Allen, G. M. 1908. Notes on Chiroptera. Bulletin of the Museum of Comparative Zoology, Harvard University, 52:25-63.

Ascorra, C. F. y D. E. Wilson. 1991. Bat frugivory and seed dispersal in the Amazon, Loreto, Peru. Publicaciones del Museo de Historia Natural, Universidad Nacional Mayor de San Marcos, Serie A, 43:1-6.

Ascorra, C. F., D. L. Gorchov y F. Cornejo. 1989. Observaciones en aves y murciélagos relacionadas a la dispersión de semillas en el Valle Palcazu, selva central del Perú. Boletín de Lima, 62:91-95.

————. 1993. The bats from Jenaro Herrera, Loreto, Peru. Mammalia 57:533-552.

Ascorra, C. F., D. E. Wilson y M. Romo. 1991. Lista anotada de los quirópteros del Parque Nacional Manu, Perú. Publicaciones del Museo de Historia Natural, Universidad Nacional Mayor de San Marcos, Serie A, 42:1-14.

Brosset, A. y P. Charles-Dominique. 1990. The bats from French Guyana: a taxonomic, faunistic and ecological approach. Mammalia, 54:509-560.

Brown, J. H. 1968. Activity patterns of some neotropical bats. Journal of Mammalogy, 49:754-757.

Carter, D. C. 1966. A new species of Rhinophylia (Mammalia, Chiroptera, Phyllotomatidae) from South America. Proceedings of the Biological Society of Washington, 79:235-238.

Charles-Dominique, P. 1991. Feeding strategy and actiity budget of the frugivorous bat Carollia perspicillata (Chiroptera: Phyllostomidae) in French Guiana. Journal of Tropical Ecology, 7:243-256.

Davis, W. B. 1968. A review of the genus Uroderma (Chiroptera). Journal of Mammalogy, 49:676-698.

Davis, W. B. 1975. Individual and sexual variation in Vampyressa bidens. Journal of Mammalogy, 56:262-265.

Davis, W. B. 1976. Geographic variation of the lesser Noctilio Noctilio albiventris (Chiroptera). Journal of Mammalogy, 57:687-707.

Davis, W. B. y J. R. Dixon. 1976. Activity of bats in a small village clearing near Iquitos, Peru. Journal of Mammalogy, 57:747-749.

Erwin, T. L. 1991. Natural History of the carabid beetles at the BIOLAT Biological Station, Rio Manu, Pakitza, Peru. Revista Peruana de Entomología, 33:1-85.

Gardner, A. L. 1976. The distributional status of some Peruvian Mammals. Occasional Papers of the Museum of Zoology, Louisiana State University, 48:1-18.

————. 1988. The mammals of Parque Nacional Serrania de la Neblina, Territorio Federal Amazonas, Venezuela. Pp. 695-765 in Cerro de la Neblina. Resultados de la Expedición 1983-1987. (C. Brewer-Carias, ed.). Editorial Sucre, Caracas. 922 p.

Gardner, A. L., y D. C. Carter. 1972. A review of the Peruvian species of Vampyrops (Chiroptera: Phyllostomatidae). Journal of Mammalogy, 53:72-82.

GraGraham, G. L. 1983. Changes in bat species diversity along an elevational gradient up the Peruvian Andes. Journal of Mammalogy, 64:559-571.

Graham, G. L. y L. J. Barkley. 1984. Noteworthy records of bats from Peru. Journal of Mammalogy, 65:709-711.

Handley, C. O. Jr., 1967. Bats of the canopy of an Amazonian forest. Atas do Simposio sobre a Biota Amazonica, 5(Zoologica):211-215.

Handley, C. O. Jr., 1987. New species of mammals from Northern South America; Fruit-eating bat, Genus Artibeus Leach. Fieldiana (Zoology) (New Series) 39:163-172.

Kalliola, R., J. Salo e Y. Makinen. 1987. Regeneración natural de selvas en la Amazonía Peruana 1: Dinámica fluvial y sucesión ribereña. Memorias del Museo de Historia Natural, Universidad Nacional Mayor de San Marcos, 18:1-102.

Koepcke, J. y R. Kraft. 1984. Cranial and external characters of the larger fruit bats of the genus *Artibeus* from Amazonian Peru. Spixiana 7:75-84.

Koopman, K. F. 1978. Zoogeography of Peruvian bats with special emphasis on the role of the Andes. American Museum Novitates, 2651:1-33.

La Val, R. K. 1970. Banding returns and activity periods of some Costa Rican bats. Southwestern Naturalist, 15:1-10.

————. 1973. A revision of the Neotropical bats genus *Myotis*. Contributions in Science, Natural History Museum of Los Angeles County, 15:1-54.

Márquez, S. A. 1986. Activity cycle, feeding and reproduction of *Molossus ater* (Chirptera: Molossidae) in Brazil. Boletim do Museu Paraense Emilio Goeldi, Zoologia, 2:159-179.

Miller, G. S. 1913. Notes on the bats of the genus *Molossus*. Proceedings of the United States National Museum, 46:85-92.

Ortiz de la Puente, J. 1951. Estudio monográfico de los quirópteros de Lima y alrededores. Publicaciones del Museo de Historia Natural «Javier Prado», Universidad Nacional Mayor de San Marcos, Zoología, 7: 1-48.

Osgood, W. H. 1914. Mammals of an expedition across northern Peru. Field Museum of Natural History, Zoological Series, 10:143-185.

Pacheco, V. y B. D. Patterson. 1991. Phylogeneteic relationships of the New World bat genus *Sturnira* (Chiroptera: Phyllostomidae). Pp. 101-121 *in* Contributions to Mammalogy i honor of Karl F. Koopman, (T. A. Griffiths y D. Klingener, eds.), Bulletin of the American Museum of Natural History, 206:1-432.

Pacheco, V., B. D. Patterson, J. L. Patton, L. H. Emmons, S. Solari y C. F. Ascorra. 1993. List of mammals species known to occur in Manu Biosphere Reserve, Peru. Publicaciones del Museo de Historia Natural, Universidad Nacional Mayor de San Marcos, Serie A, 44: 1-12.

Patton, J. L., y A. L. Gardner. 1971. Parallel evolution of multiple sex-chromosome systems in the phyllostomatid bats, *Carollia* and *Choeroniscus*. Experientia 27:105-106.

Pine, R. H. 1972. The bats of the genus *Carollia*. Technical Monography of the Texas Agriculture Experimental Station, Texas A and M University, 8:1-125.

Ramírez-Pulido, J. y M. A. Armella. 1987. Activity of neotropical bats (Chiroptera: Phyllostomidae) in Guerrero, Mexico. The Southwestern Naturalist, 32:363-370.

Sanborn, C. C., 1936. Records and measurements of Neotropical bats. Field Museum of Natural History, Zoology, 20:93-106.

Sanborn, C. C., 1949. Mammals from the Río Ucayali, Peru. Journal of Mammalogy, 30:277-288.

Sanborn, C. C. 1951. Mammals from Marcapata, southeastern Peru, Publicaciones del Museo de Historia Natural «Javier Prado», Universidad Nacional Mayor de San Marcos, Serie A, 6:1-26.

Sanborn, C. C. 1953. Mammals from the Departments of Cuzco and Puno, Peru. Publicaciones del Museo de Historia Natural «Javier Prado», Universidad Nacional Mayor de San Marcos, Serie A, 12:1-8.

Sokal, R. R. y F. J. Rohlf. 1969. Biometry: the principles and practice of statistics in biological research. W. H. Freeman and Company, San Francisco, 776 p.

Terborgh, J. W., J. W. Fitzpatrick, and L. H. Emmons. 1984. Annotated checklist of bird and mammal species of Cocha Cashu Biological Station, Manu National Park, Peru. Fieldiana (Zoology) (New Series) 21:1-29.

Thomas, O. 1920. Report on the mammalia collected by Mr. Edmund Heller during the Peruvian Expedition of 1915 under the auspices of Yale University and the National Geographic Society. Proceedings of the United States National Museum, 58:217-250.

Thomas, O. 1924. On a collection of mammals made by Mr. Latham Rutter in the Peruvian Amazonas. Annals and Magazine of Natural History, Serie 9, 13:530-538.

Thomas, O. 1926. The Godman-Thomas Expedition to Peru. III. On mammals collected

611

by Mr. R.W. Hendee in the Chachapoyas Region north of Peru. Annnals and Magazine of Natural History, Serie 9, 18:156-157.

Thomas, O. 1927a. The Godman-Thomas Expedition to Peru. V. On mammals collected by Mr. R.W. Hendee in the Province of San Martin, N. Peru, mostly at Yurac Yacu. Annnals and Magazine of Natural History. Serie 9, 19:361-375.

Thomas, O. 1927b. The Godman-Thomas Expedition to Peru. VI. On mammals from the Upper Huallaga and neighboring highlands. Annnals and Magazine of Natural History. Serie 9, 20:594-608.

Thomas, O. 1928a. The Godman-Thomas Expedition to Peru. VII. The mammals of the Rio Ucayali. Annnals and Magazine of Natural History, Serie 10, 2:249-265.

Thomas, O. 1928b. The Godman-Thomas Expedition to Peru. VIII. Annnals and Magazine of Natural History, Serie 10, 2:285-294.

Thomas, O. y J. St. Leger. 1926. The Godman-Thomas Expedition to Peru. IV. On mammals collected by Mr. R.W. Hendee of North Chachapoyas, Province of Amazonas, North Peru. Annnals and Magazine of Natural History, Serie 9, 18:345-349.

Timm, R. M., D. E. Wilson, B. L. Clauson, R. K. La Val y C. S. Vaughan.

1989. Mammals of the La Selva - Braulio Carrillo Complex, Costa Rica. U. S. Fish and Wildlife Service. North American Fauna, 75:1-162.

Tuttle, M. D. 1970. Distribution and zoogeography of Peruvian bats, with comments on natural history. The University of Kansas Science Bulletin, 49:45-8.

Warner, J. W., J. L. Patton, A. L. Gardner y R. J. Baker. 1984. Karyotypic analysis of twenty-one molossid bats (Molossidae: Chiroptera). Canadian Journal Of Cenetics and Citology, 16:165-176.

Wilson, D. E. 1979. Reproductive patterns. Pp. 317-378 *in*: Biology of Bats of the New World Family Phyllostomatidae. Part III (R. J. Baker, J. K. Jones, Jr., y D. C. Carter, eds.). Special Publications of the Museum Texas Tech University, 16:1-441.

————. 1990. Mammals of La Selva, Costa Rica. Pp. 273-286 *in*: Four Neotropical Rainforests (A. H. Gentry, ed.). Yale University Press, New Haven.

Woodman, N., R. M. Timm, R. Arana C., V. Pacheco, C. A. Schmidt, E. D., Hooper y C. Pacheco A. 1991. Annotated checklist of the mammals of Cuzco Amazonico, Peru. Occasional Papers of the Museum of Natural History, University of Kansas, 145:1-12.

Bats as Indicators of Habitat Disturbance

Don E. Wilson

Biodiversity Programs, National Museum of Natural History,
Smithsonian Institution, Washington, DC 20560, USA

Cesar F. Ascorra

Sergio Solari T.

Departamento de Mastozoologia, Museo de Historia Natural,
Universidad Nacional Mayor de San Marcos, Ap. 140434, Lima 14, PERU

ABSTRACT

Bat samples from six areas in Peru show that the relationship between those species that are routinely associated only with undisturbed, primary forested habitats, and those that are more normally associated with disturbed, secondary growth habitats, might be used to indicate the degree of disturbance of a given habitat.

INTRODUCTION

Various authors have noted the difference in composition of bat faunas from different regions and habitats (Findley and Wilson, 1984; Wilson, 1973). Although the relationship between bat species diversity and composition, and habitat diversity and composition has been noted by field scientists for years (Johns, et al., 1985), quantification of the relationship has been lacking. Comparisons of bat faunas from disturbed and undisturbed habitats in Mexico (Fenton et al., 1992), suggest a strong relationship between bats and their habitats.

With the current level of interest in identifying habitats that remain relatively undisturbed with a view towards practicing more appropriate conservation measures in the future, it would seem useful to document the relationship between those species of bats that are routinely associated only with undisturbed, primary-forest habitats, and those that are more normally associated with disturbed, second-growth habitats.

If the relationships can be established for a variety of species, it might be possible to use the density of certain species to indicate the disturbance degree in a given habitat. The converse should hold; obviously disturbed habitats can be

613

expected to contain a distinct subset of the species that might be available in undisturbed habitats.

With these hypotheses in mind, we compared data sets for six areas in Peru where we have assembled considerable knowledge of the bat faunas. Four of these represent areas with significant and different degrees of habitat disturbance, and the others are representative of undisturbed, primary lowland tropical rainforest.

STUDY SITES

SUCUSARI

The Amazon Center for Environmental Education and Research (ACEER) is a Scientific Station held by Conservacion de la Naturaleza Amazonica del Peru (CONAPAC) and ACEER Foundation, and located near the Sucusari, a white water tributary on the left bank of the Napo River, main tributary of the Amazon River, about 70 km NE Iquitos, Region of Loreto, Amazonian Peru (Figure 1). As in the following localities of Loreto the dry season lasts from June to September (Spichiger et al., 1989). We sampled bats in the following habitats:

Terrace forest.—
Undisturbed forest with a canopy of 35-40 m on well-drained slopes above the floodplain.

Forest edges.—
Borders of the scientific station clearing, surrounded by a small fringe of early secondary forest, regenerating from the station clearing.

YANAMONO

Yanamono (1° 16' S, 72° 54' W) is an ecotourism lodge operated by Exploraciones Amazonicas S.A., in the the Quebrada Yanamono, a white water tributary on the north bank of the Amazon River, and located 60 km NE Iquitos in the Region of Loreto, Amazonian Peru (Figure 1). At Yanamono we sampled in the following habitats:

Old secondary forest.—
A large patch of 20-year-old successional vegetation surrounded by continuous primary forest, pastures, and small familiar agricultural clearings.

Forest edges.—
Borders of the lodge clearing.

ISLA MUYUY

Isla Muyuy is an island 10 km long and 5 km wide, located in the Amazon River, about 20 km SE of Iquitos, Region of Loreto, Amazonian Peru (Figure 1). The water level on the island is regulated by the seasonal flooding of the Amazon River. During the inundation periods oxbow lakes, normally isolated from the main river, are connected to the river and many channels are found between the small portions of non-flooded forest. At Isla Muyuy we sampled bats in the following habitats:

Fig. 1.– Study sites, 1= Sucusari, 2= Yanamono, 3= Isla Muyuy, 4= Quebrada Blanco, 5= Jenaro Herrera and 6= Pakitza.

Non-flooded forest.–
Patches of undisturbed primary non-flooded forest surrounded by low flooded vegetation, agricultural clearings and different stages of secondary growth.
Agriculture clearings.–
Small agriculture clearings with fruit crops, between riparian flooded vegetation and secondary vegetation.

Quebrada Blanco

Quebrada Blanco is a white water tributary on the north bank of the black water Tahuayo River, in the Communal Reserve Tamshiyacu-Tahuayo, ca 70 km SSE of Iquitos, Region of Loreto, Amazonian Peru (Figure 1).

At Tamshiyacu, 40 km N, rainfall averages 2,337 mm per year (Bodmer, 1990). The vegetation of the area has been classified as upland, non flooded, terra firme forest (Bodmer, 1990).

At Quebrada Blanco we sampled bats in the following habitats:
Terrace forest.– Undisturbed forest with a canopy of 25 -30 m, on the steep right margin of the stream and undisturbed forest with a canopy 35 - 40 m on the flat left margin of the stream, about 17 km from its mouth in the Tahuayo River.
Secondary forest.– A four ha patch of regenerating forest within undisturbed and continuous primary forest close to the previous sampling site. This site was a fruit farm approximately 20 years ago.

615

Agriculture clearings.–

A >30, ha agricultural clearing with fruit crop farming, located about 8 km upstream from the mouth of the Tahuayo River.

Jenaro Herrera

The Centro de Investigaciones "Jenaro Herrera" (CIJH) (4° 55'S, 73° 45'W) is a field station held by the Instituto de Investigaciones de la Amazonia Peruana (IIAP), located aproximately 2.5 km east of the Ucayali River and 140 km SSW of Iquitos in the Region of Loreto, Amazonian Peru (Figure 1).

Rainfall averages 2,521 mm per year with a drier season that normally lasts from June to September (Spichiger et al., 1989); however, in each month of the year rainfall is variable, and several relatively dry months occurred in the rainy season during this study. Mean annual temperature is 26° C (Lopez-Parodi and Freitas, 1990). The average elevation is 130 m (Rios, J. unpublished thesis). The vegetation has been classified as low-terrace broadleaf tropical rain forest by Lopez-Parodi and Freitas (1990), who provided a detailed description of the various habitats available. At CIJH we sampled bats in the following habitats:

Terrace forest.–

Undisturbed or lightly disturbed forest with a canopy of 25 - 30 m, 1.3 - 1.5 km north of the CIJH station clearing.

Cleared strips.–

Two 30 m wide, 150 m long strips, cleared in May 1989 (Strip 1) and October 1989 (Strip 2), 140 m apart, inside primary forest at 1.3 km N of the station.

Secondary forest.–

Regeneration forest approximately 18 years old, along an abandoned timber extraction road, approximately 1 km east of the station.

Open areas.–

Forestry and agroforestry plantations within 1 km of the station and near buildings within the station clearing.

Pakitza

The BIOLAT Biological Station at Pakitza (11° 56'S, 71° 17'W), is a field station operated by the Smithsonian Institution's Biodiversity in Latin America Program (BIOLAT), located in the Reserved Zone of the Manu National Park, approximately 65 km upstream on the Manu River from its mouth at the Madre de Dios River, in the Province of Manu, Department of Madre de Dios, Inka Region, Peru (Figure 1).

At the Cocha Cashu Biological Station, 21 km upstream from Pakitza, rainfall averages 2080 mm, with a drier season that lasts from May to September. Mean annual temperature is 24.1 C. The elevation of Pakitza is 356 m. The vegetation has been classified as lowland evergreen tropical rain forest (Kalliola et al., 1987).

Although some selective timber extraction may have taken place in the general region prior to the creation of the park in 1970, the amount of disturbance was minimal. Erwin (1991) provided a detailed description of the various habitats available at Pakitza. At Pakitza we sampled bats in the following habitats:

Primary forest.–
Undisturbed forest with a canopy of 50 m N, and E of the station.
Forest edges.–
Borders of the biological station clearing.
Riparian forest.–
Vegetation of cane (*Gyneriumsagittatum*) and bamboo (*Guadua* and *Elytrosta-chys*), 10 - 20 m apart along stream banks.

River banks.–
Sandy beaches beside the Manu river. Some nets were placed acoss the stream.

METHODS

At Sucusari we mist-netted bats in June, 1991; July 1992; September, 1993; and December, 1993. Although nets were set mainly at ground level, about 1/10 of the effort was invested in canopy nets. In Yanamono, bats were mist-netted in March, 1991; July, 1992; December, 1992; and March 1993. At Isla Muyuy we sampled in August - September, 1992. At Quebrada Blanco we sampled bats in October - November, 1992. About 1/10 of the netting effort at this site was spent in canopy nets. All these sites were sampled as part of studies on bat-plant interactions and their role in the propagative success of useful amazonian plants in order to plan the sustainable use of the forest.

At Jenaro Herrera, we mist-netted bats in November -December 1988 and from May 1989 to October 1991, as part of a study of natural regeneration after strip clearing. Netting effort in each habitat each month consisted of 1 - 3 nights. Most nets placed at ground level (0.5 - 3 m), although in cleared strips about half the netting effort was at mid-story and subcanopy levels (5 - >20 m).

At Pakitza, we mist-netted bats in October 1987, September 1988, November 1990, and February - March 1992 as part of a study of the total biological diversity of the area. Netting effort at each habitat each month consisted of 1 - 10 nights. Most nets were placed at ground level (0.5 - 3 m), although 1/10 of the netting effort was at mid-story and sub-canopy levels (5 - >20 m).

Nets were checked for bats every 30 minutes. Netted bats were held in cloth bags, identified, and measured (forearm length and weight). Height of capture as well as habitat was recorded for each individual. Reproductive status (pregnant or lactating) was obtained from selected females by external examination.

Some voucher specimens of each species were saved and deposited in the Museo de Historia Natural, Universidad Nacional Mayor de San Marcos in Lima, Peru, and in the National Museum of Natural History in Washington, D.C., U.S.A. Otherwise, individuals were released at the end of each netting session.

The ratio of captures/netting session, was used to standardize the captures from each site.

Bat species composition in the different habitats was compared using the Index of Similarity I=2C/A+B where C equals the number of species shared between the two habitats and A and B are the numbers of species in each of the two sites (Krebs, 1985). This index ranges from 0 (no overlap) to 1.0 (complete overlap).

For determining the trophic structure of the communities, each species were segregated into one of the following trophic guilds:

Aerial Insectivores.–
Emballonuridae, Noctilionidae Thyropteridae, Furipteridae, Vespertilionidae, and Molossidae.

Foliage Gleaners.–
Phyllostominae (*Macrophyllum macrophyllum*, *Micronycteris* spp., *Mimon crenulatum*, *Tonatia* spp., and *Phyllostomus elongatus*).

Nectar Feeders.–
Glossophaginae and the Phyllostomine *Phyllostomus discolor*, which we often found dusted with pollen in Jenaro Herrera and Isla Muyuy.

Phyllostomine Frugivores.–
Phyllostomus hastatus and *P. stenops*. The first is usually considered an omnivore, but we found mainly seeds and occasional insect remains in their feces. Inspected day roosts at human dwellings only had seeds or fruit remains.

*Understory Frugivores.–*Carolliinae.

Canopy Frugivores.–Artibeus spp.

*Other Frugivores.–*The remaining Stenoderminae.

*Carnivores.–*Large Phyllostominae that feed on vertebrates (*Chrotopterus auritus* and *Trachops cirrhosus*).

*Vampires.–*Blood-feeding bats (*Desmodus rotundus* and *Diphylla ecaudata*)

RESULTS AND DISCUSSION

At Sucusari, we recorded 33 species in 20 netting sessions. At Yanamono, we registered 36 species in 24 netting sessions. On Isla Muyuy, we obtained 19 bat species in 7 netting sessions. At Quebrada Blanco, we recorded 30 species in 13 netting sessions. At Jenaro Herrera, we recorded 62 species in 103 netting sessions (Ascorra et al., 1993), and at Pakitza we record 57 species in 61 netting sessions (Ascorra et al., this volume) (Table 1).

Although the bias caused by the different netting effort at each site is corrected by the use of the ratio of Capture/netting effort, the differences in species diversity recorded at each site may be due to the unequal sampling efforts. In J. Herrera the almost continual inventory of species through time, and the significant effort spent in canopy and subcanopy mist-netting resulted in a more complete sample of the bat fauna (Table 1).

In all places the bat fauna seems to be represented by a few species with a large number of individuals and many with only a few captures (Figure 2).

Table 1.– Comparative structure of bat communities in the study sites using the ratio captures/netting effort (AI= aerial insectivores, GI= gleaner insectivores, CA= carnivores, NE= nectarivores, UF= understory frugivores, CF= canopy frugivores (*Artibeus* spp.), OF= other Stenoderminae, PF= Phyllostomine frugivores (*Phyllostomus hastatus, P. stenops*), VA= vampire).

Species	Guild	Sucusari	Yanamono	I. Muyuy	Q. Blanco	J.Herrera	Pakitza
Peropteryx kappleri	AI						0.001
Peropteryx leucoptera	AI	0.013					
Rhynchonycteris naso	AI	0.007	0.009				0.003
Saccopteryx bilineata	AI	0.020	0.017	0.006		0.004	0.004
Saccopteryx leptura	AI	0.003	0.007		0.006	0.002	
Noctilio albiventris	AI					0.001	0.013
Macrophyllum macrophyllum	GI						0.019
Micronycteris brachyotis	GI		0.002				
Micronycteris megalotis	GI	0.007			0.006	0.002	0.006
Micronycteris minuta	GI			0.006			0.012
Micronycteris nicefori	GI	0.003	0.004			0.024	0.001
Micronycteris schmidtorum	GI					0.000	
Mimon crenulatum	GI	0.010	0.026		0.102	0.011	0.004
Phyllostomus discolor	NE			0.105		0.002	
Phyllostomus elongatus	GI	0.020	0.028	0.025	0.042	0.007	0.035
Phyllostomus hastatus	PF	0.017	0.009	0.167	0.012	0.069	0.028
Phyllostomus stenops	PF					0.002	0.004
Tonatia bidens	GI	0.007	0.009			0.002	0.006
Tonatia brasiliensis	GI					0.001	0.001
Tonatia carrikeri	GI			0.006		0.001	
Trachops cirrhosus	CA	0.003	0.007	0.019	0.012	0.001	0.012
Tonatia silvicola	GI	0.003	0.002		0.012	0.004	0.013
Chrotopterus auritus	CA	0.007				0.002	
Vampyrum spectrum	CA					0.001	
Anoura caudifera	NE	0.003	0.002			0.001	0.008
Choeroniscus intermedius	NE					0.001	
Choeroniscus minor	NE						0.006

Species	Guild	Sucusari	Yanamono	I. Muyuy	Q. Blanco	J.Herrera	Pakitza
Glossophaga commissarisi	NE		0.009	0.025			0.006
Glossophaga soricina	NE		0.076	0.056	0.012	0.008	0.013
Lonchophylla mordax	NE				0.054	0.007	
Lonchophylla thomasi	NE		0.022		0.018	0.008	0.005
Carollia brevicauda	UF	0.113	0.107	0.142	0.102	0.158	0.080
Carollia castanea	UF	0.103	0.035		0.102	0.026	0.124
Carollia perspicillata	UF	0.046	0.396	0.265	0.036	0.273	0.092
Rhinophylla fischerae	UF	0.003			0.018	0.011	
Rhinophylla pumilio	UF	0.010	0.028		0.21	0.033	0.006
Artibeus anderseni	CF	0.020	0.063	0.105		0.002	0.023
Artibeus cinereus	CF				0.006		0.004
Artibeus concolor	CF					0.007	
Artibeus glaucus	CF				0.006		
Artibeus gnomus	CF				0.012	0.014	0.005
Artibeus hartii	CF					0.001	
Artibeus lituratus	CF	0.053	0.015	0.012	0.096	0.124	0.052
Artibeus obscurus	CF	0.053	0.004	0.025	0.054	0.031	0.119
Artibeus planirostris	CF	0.391	0.024		0.024	0.056	0.101
Chiroderma villosum	OF	0.003	0.004			0.002	0.004
Chiroderma trinitatum	OF	0.010				0.001	0.001
Platyrrhinus aurarius	OF		0.004				
Platyrrhinus brachycephalus	OF			0.006	0.006	0.001	0.017
Platyrrhinus helleri	OF	0.007	0.017			0.004	0.016
Platyrrhinus infuscus	OF						0.004
Stumira lilium	OF		0.015			0.010	0.018
Stumira luisi	OF			0.006			
Stumira magna	OF	0.003				0.004	
Stumira tildae	OF					0.005	0.003
Uroderma bilobatum	OF	0.010	0.020	0.012		0.015	0.021
Uroderma magnirostrum	OF		0.002			0.002	0.016
Vampyressa bidens	OF				0.006		0.003
Vampyressa brockii	OF					0.001	
Vampyressa macconnelli	OF				0.006	0.004	0.017
Vampyressa melissa	OF	0.003	0.002				
Vampyressa pusilla	OF	0.033	0.009			0.004	0.003
Vampyrodes caraccioli	OF	0.007					0.005
Desmodus rotundus	VA	0.003		0.006		0.045	0.003
Diphylla ecaudata	VA						0.003
Thyroptera discifera	AI					0.001	
Thyroptera tricolor	AI		0.002	0.006			
Furipterus horrens	AI					0.001	0.001
Lasiurus ega	AI						0.001
Eptesicus brasiliensis	AI					0.001	
Eumops hansae	AI				0.006		
Myotis albescens	AI		0.004				0.041
Myotis nigricans	AI	0.007	0.004		0.006	0.007	0.004
Myotis riparius	AI		0.013		0.012	0.004	0.012
Myotis simus	AI				0.006	0.003	0.004
Molossus ater	AI					0.001	
Molossus molossus	AI				0.006	0.005	0.001
Molossus sinaloe	AI		0.002				
Molossoops neglectus	AI					0.002	
Promops centralis	AI					0.009	
INDIVIDUALS (Total)		302	460	162	167	2229	772
NET SESSIONS (Total)		20	24	7	13	103	61

The similarity in bat species between Isla Muyuy and any other site was very low (<0.44), while the other sites proved similar in bat species composition (I>.05) (Table 2). The highest values of similarity were found between Yanamono and Sucusari (I=0.73) and the lowest (I=0.31) between Sucusari and Isla Muyuy (Table 2).

Aerial insectivores are more abundant at Sucusari, Ya-namono, and Pakitza (>0.05 captures/netting session), sites with closed and con-tinuous forest. Isla Muyuy, Quebrada Blanco, and Jenaro Herrera, with less than 0.04 captures/netting session, are areas with only forest patches, or large farms close to forest, or large pastures, and agricultural clearings respectively (Table 1 and Figure 3).

Foliage Gleaners are more abundant in Sucusari, Yanamono, Quebrada Blanco, and Pakitza (>0.05 captures/netting session), where there is tall and continuous forest, than in Isla Muyuy and Jenaro Herrera (<0.04 captures/netting session), where the forest is patchy or disturbed with forestry plantations (Table 1 and Figure 3).

Carnivores and vampires seem be rare and less abundant everywhere (Table 1 and Figure 3), although the latter are more abundant in Jenaro Herrera (Table 1) than in the other sites.

Nectarivores reach the highest values in sites with fruit crops close to the forest such as Yanamono, Isla Muyuy, and Quebrada Blanco, where they account for

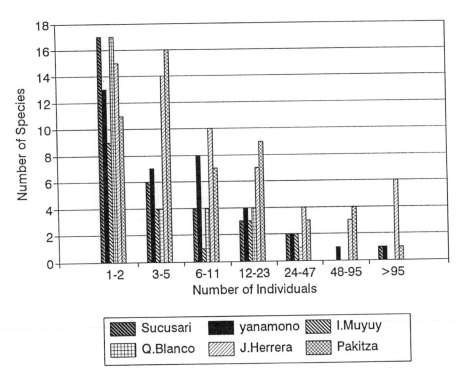

Fig. 2.– *Number of individuals per species of bats captured in the study sites.*

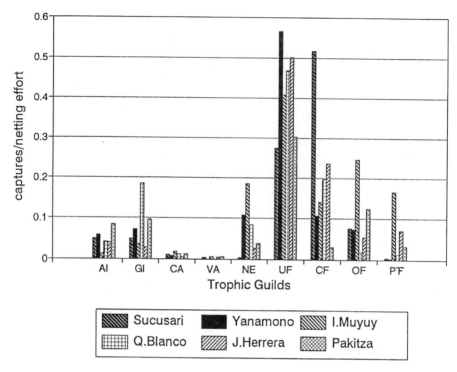

Fig. 3.– *Abundance of bat species at study sites by trophic guilds. A. Predators (AI= aerial insectivors, GI= foliage gleaners, CA= carnivores, VA= vampires, PF= Phyllostomine frugivores, UF= understory frugivores, CF= canopy frugivores, OF= other stenodermine frugivores, NE= nectarivores).*

>0.08 captures/netting session (Table 1 and Figure 3). Understory frugivores reach the lowest values (<0.3 captures/netting session) in undisturbed areas such as Sucusari and Pakitza, while the converse is found in areas with nearby and considerable secondary growth (>0.4 captures/netting session) such as Yanamono, Isla Muyuy, Quebrada Blanco, and Jenaro Herrerea (Table 1 and Figure 3).

Canopy frugivores in the genus *Artibeus* are more abundant at Sucusari (0.5 captures/netting session) (Table 1 and Figure 3). The presence of some salt licks in the area and the drinking behavior sugested by Ascorra and Wilson (1992), might be affecting the representation of these bats in samples. The remarkable abundance of other stenodermine frugivores in Jenaro Herrera (>0.2 captures/netting session) might be a result of the higher netting effort spent in the canopy in this area (Table 1 and Figure 3).

In the six sites, frugivores are the domi-nant group, but Understory Frugivores (Ca-rolliinae) are more a-bundant at Yana-mono, Isla Muyuy, Quebrada Blanco and Jena-ro Herre-ra, proba-bly due to the high avai-lability of their main food source (pioneer and second growth plant species), than at Sucusari and Pakitza where mature forest vegetation is predominant.

Other differences between sites appear for the other groups of bats (Figure 3). Insectivores are more abundant in non-disturbed areas and this is probably due to

Table 2.—*Number of bat species netted in each site and index of similarity between habitats*

Similarity with: Site	N	Yanamono	I.Muyuy	Q.Blanco	J.Herrera	Pakitza
Sucusari	33	0.73	0.31	0.54	0.61	0.58
Yanamono	36		0.44	0.55	0.57	0.62
I. Muyuy	19			0.37	0.37	0.32
Q. Blanco	30				0.57	0.53
J. Herrera	62					0.64
Pakitza	57					

the high plant diversity that also supports high diversity of insects. In highly disturbed areas the lower plant diversity and abundance of a few pioneer second-growth plant species might be affecting the quantity or quality of the insect resource. However, it may also be easier for insectivorous species, with their highly developed echolocation system, to detect the mist nets in more open areas. The well-developed echolocation systems of most insectivorous bats makes it very difficult to sample them in any unbiased way using mist nets.

The phyllostomine frugivore *Phyllostomus hastatus* (Table 1), most abundant in disturbed areas, might be indicating the abundance of its food source in this kind of habitat. Fecal sample analysis showed the preference of this species for fruits of *Cecropia* spp., all of which are pioneer species, as well as for the local fruit crop *Pourouma cecropiaefolia*. Pollen grains of *Musa paradisiaca* and *Ochroma pyramidale* have been re-covered from dusted faces and fur of this bat.

The abundance of vampires at Jenaro Herrera is obviously due to cattle density in the area, whereas domestic livestock is totally lacking at Pakitza. Other groups such as nectarivores, more common in secondary forest or agricultural habitats, might be reflecting the abundance of their food sources in such habitats.

Comparative analysis of species composition and abundance between the study sites (Table 1), shows a noteworthy relationship between the abundance (or scarcity) of certain species and the degree of disturbance (or non-disturbance) of the habitat. Species such as *Carollia perspicillata*, *Phyllostomus hastatus*, and *Desmodus rotundus* are more abundant in highly disturbed habitats. We suggest that the abundance of these species might be used as an indication of high habitat disturbance. Taxa such as Emballonuridae, insectivorous Phyllostominae, Thyropteridae, Furipteridae, and Vespertilionidae (Table 1) are more abundant in undisturbed than in disturbed habitats and the abundance of these species might be used as indication of little or no habitat disturbance.

Although many bat species seem to be abundant at any site, they probably are using microhabitats differentially at each site. For many sites, more intensive inventory work is needed to completely assess species composition.

In general, we would suggest that an abundance of members of the subfamily Carolliinae is a good indication of disturbed habitats, and an abundance of phyllostomine insectivores indicates undisturbed forest. Perhaps the best single indicator of disturbance is the common vampire bat, *Desmodus rotundus*, which is abundant only in areas that have been modified to support domestic livestock. It is more difficult to single out any particular species as being uniformly good indicators of undisturbed forest, as all such species naturally occur at low

Don E. Wilson, César F. Ascorra and Sergio Solari

population densities. However, our data clearly show that, with the exception of *Phyllostomus hastatus*, members of the subfamily Phyllostominae are far more likely to occur in undisturbed forest habitats.

RESUMEN

Muestreos de murciélagos en seis areas de la amazonía peruana demuestran que la relación entre las especies asociadas con bosques primarios, no intervenidos, y aquéllas otras asociadas con ambientes intervenidos y formaciones secundarias podría ser usada para indicar el grado de intervención de un hábitat determinado.

ACKNOWLEDGEMENTS

The research at Sucusari and Yanamono was supported by CONAPAC and ACEER Foundation, Grant to C. Ascorra. Special thanks to Peter Jenson of Exploraciones Amazonicas for research facilities at his sites. The research at Isla Muyuy and Quebrada Blanco, and the final data analysis and computer work was funded by World Wildlife Fund's Biodiversity Support Program Grant No. 7564 to C. Ascorra and D. Wilson. We thank the Instituto Veterinario de Investigaciones Tropicales y de Altura (CI-IVITA) of the Universidad Nacional Mayor de San Marcos for permits and facilities at Isla Muyuy and Quebrada Blanco Biological Stations. The research at Jenaro Herrera was supported under Grant No. 7.228, Program in Science and Technology Cooperation, Office of Science Advisor, U.S. Agency for International Development to D. Gorchov, F. Cornejo, and J. Terborgh. Research at Pakitza was supported by the Smithsonian Institution's Biodiversity in Latin America Programs (BIOLAT) Grant to C. Ascorra. We thank the Office of Fellowship and Grants of the Smithsonian Institution for supporting Ascorra's work in the National Museum of Natural History Collections. We thank the Instituto Nacional de Recursos Naturales - INRENA (ex-Direccion General de Forestal y Fauna and the Programa de Parques Nacionales of the Ministerio de Agricultura) and the Direccion Regional de Recusos Naturales y Medio Ambiente of the Gobierno Regional de Loreto, for collecting permits. We thank the Instituto de Investigaciones de la Amazonia Peruana (IIAP) and J. Lopez-Parodi and M. Isuiza for use and facilities of the Centro de Investigaciones "Jenaro Herrera". We thank Juan F. Loja-Aleman, S. Sevick, and E. Studier for their valuable assistance in the field work at Sucusari and Yanamono. Local farmers Gonzalo Torres and Juan Huanaquiri gave us valuable field assistance on Isla Muyuy and Quebrada Blanco respectively. R. Arana-Cardo, D.L. Gorchov, V. Pacheco, and J. Palmeirim helped with the field work during certain months at Jenaro Herrera. F. Dallmeier and M.V. Tenicela gave valuable help with field work during certain months at Pakitza. We especially thank James Penn Jr. and the local Community of Chino in the Communal Reserve Tamshiyacu-Tahuayo for their involvement in our research and for applying some of our results in the management of their comunal reserve. We thank F. Encarnacion, M.B. Fenton, D.L. Gorchov, and an anonymous reviewer for their comments and suggestions that improved this paper. This is Contribution No. 44 of the Smithsonian Institution's Biodiversity in Latin America Programs (BIOLAT) and Contribution No. 2 of the Programa de Evaluacion Permanente de la Biodiversidad Amazonica (BIOAMAZ).

LITERATURE CITED

Ascorra, C. F., and D. E. Wilson. 1992. Bat frugivory and seed dispersal in the Amazon, Loreto, Peru. Publicaciones del Museo de Historia Natural de la Universidad Nacional Mayor de San Marcos, Serie A, 43:1-6.

Ascorra, C. F., D. E. Wilson, and M. Romo. 1991. Lista anotada de los Quirópteros del Parque Nacional Manu, Peru. Publicaciones del Museo de Historia Natural, Universidad Nacional Mayor de San Marcos, Serie A, 42:1-14.

Ascorra, C. F., D. L. Gorchov, and F. Cornejo. 1993. The bats from Jenaro Herrera, Loreto, Peru. Mammalia, 57:533-552.

Bodmer, R. E. 1990. Responses of ungulates to seasonal inundations in the Amazonian floodplain. Journal of Tropical Ecology, 6:191-201.

Erwin, T. L. 1991. Natural history of the carabid beetles at the BIOLAT Biological Station, Rio Manu, Pakitza, Peru. Revista Peruana de Entomologia, 33:1-85.

Fenton, M. B., L. Acharya, D. Audet, M.B.C. Hickey, C. Merriman, M.K. Obrist, and D.M. Syme. 1992. Phyllostomid bats (Chiroptera: Phyllostomidae) as indicators of habitat disruption in the Neotropics. Biotropica, 24: 440-446.

Findley, J. S., and D. E. Wilson. 1984 Are bats rare in tropical Africa?. Biotropica, 15:299-303

Johns, A. D., R. H. Pine, and D. E. Wilson. 1985. Rain forest bats–an uncertain future. Bat News, Fauna and Flora Preservation Society, London, 5:4-5.

Kalliola, R. J. Salo, and Yrjo Makinen. 1987. Regeneración natural de Selvas en la Amazonia Peruana 1: Dinamica fluvial y sucesion riberena. Memorias del Museo de Historia Natural, Universidad Nacional Mayor de san Marcos, 18:1-102.

Krebs, C.J. 1985. Ecology: the experimental analysis of distribution and abundance. 3rd. ed. Harper and Row, New York.

Lopez-Parodi, J. & D. Freitas. 1990. Geographical aspects of forested wetlands in the lower Ucayali, Peruvian Amazon. Forest Ecology and Management, 33/34:157-168.

Spichiger, L., J. Meroz, P.A. Loizeau, & L. Stutz de Ortega. 1989. Contribucion a la Flora de la Amazonia Peruana. Los Arboles del Arboretum Jenaro Herrera. Vol. 1. Conservatoire et Jardin Botaniques de Geneve, Switzerland.

Wilson, D. E. 1973. Bat faunas: A trophic comparison. Systematic Zoology, 22:14-29.

Streblidae (Díptera: Pupipara) Parásitos de los Murciélagos de Pakitza, Parque Nacional Manu (Perú)

Ricardo Guerrero

Instituto de Zoología Tropical, Facultad de Ciencias,
Universidad Central de Venezuela, Apartado 47058,
Caracas 1041A, Venezuela

RESUMEN

En la estación lluviosa de 1992, se colectaron 425 murciélagos de 40 especies, de ellos el 48.5% resultó parasitado por un total de 1338 *Streblidae* pertenecientes a 33 especies, de las que 10 resultaron nuevas para el Perú. La relación parásito-hospedador es analizada para las distintas especies, tanto a nivel de población como de comunidad y de su distribución dentro del área estudiada.

INTRODUCCIÓN

Los *Streblidae* son un grupo de dípteros exclusivamente parásitos de murciélagos de distribución pantropical, aunque pueden penetrar hasta las zonas más cálidas de las regiones templadas y en las zonas montañosas más frías de los trópicos. Actualmente se conocen unas 223 especies repartidas en 5 subfamilias; 3 de las subfamilias son exclusivas del Nuevo Mundo y contienen 147 especies (Guerrero, 1992a); la mayoría son neotropicales con distribuciones bien definidas, aunque algunas pueden presentar una distribución disyunta, encontrándose en el sur de Estados Unidos y en el norte de Sudamérica, pero no en Centroamérica (Wenzel, 1976). En Perú los *Streblidae* son conocidos desde que Townsend (1913) describió a *Synthesiostrebla amorphochili*, endémico del Perú, redescrito por Jobling (1947), pero que no ha podido ser reexaminado recientemente (Guerrero, 1993c); posteriormente no se encuentra ninguna publicación dedicada exclusivamente a Perú hasta que Koepcke (1987) en su tesis doctoral sobre las comunidades de murciélagos, en la estación de Panguana en Huánuco, incluye un pequeño capítulo sobre los Streblidae colectados por ella.

La Ecología y los principales aspectos de la relación parásito-hospedador, en los *Streblidae* del Nuevo Mundo, son relativamente poco conocidos y en la mayoría de los casos sólo se conocen algunos datos sobre la autoecología de las especies más abundantes (Ross, 1961; Kunz, 1976; Overal, 1980; Marshall, 1982 y Fritz, 1983) encontrándose muy pocos trabajos sobre la estructura de las comunidades (Gómez, 1984; Guerrero, 1990).

En el presente trabajo, además de la lista de especies encontradas, trataremos de explicar algunos de los aspectos más importantes de la relación parásito-hospedador, en la región estudiada.

MATERIALES Y MÉTODOS

El material aquí estudiado fue colectado entre el 14 de febrero y el 8 de marzo de 1992, es decir en plena estación lluviosa, en los alrededores de la estación biológica de Pakitza.

Los murciélagos fueron capturados con mallas de neblina, colocadas en 7 zonas en los alrededores de la estación de Pakitza. La identificación de los murciélagos se hizo según Ascorra et. al. (1991). La toponimia corresponde a la usada por Erwin (1990). Las zonas son:

1.- Campamento Base: en la periferia de las edificaciones de los guardaparque y por lo tanto altamente intervenida.

2.- Río Manu: mallas colocadas en medio del Río Manu, en la desembocadura de la quebrada de Pacal, a unos 200 metros al NW de la localidad anterior.

3.- Orilla opuesta: mallas en un bosque húmedo tropical primario, en el lado opuesto al Campamento Base.

4.- Caña Brava: zona situada, en promedio, a unos 500 metros al SE del Campamento Base y con abundantes palmas.

5.- Castañal: trocha de penetración en el bosque primario, situada al NE del Campamento Base.

6.- Tachigali: trocha de penetración en el bosque primario, situada al N del Campamento Base.

7.- Pachija: mallas colocadas sobre la quebrada del mismo nombre, situada a más de 2 km al NW del Campamento Base.

Una vez capturados, los murciélagos eran sacrificados e inmediatamente guardados individualmente en bolsas plásticas herméticamente cerradas hasta el día siguiente; otros murciélagos cuyas heces eran necesarias para estudiar su dieta, fueron guardados vivos individualmente en bolsas de tela, siendo sacrificados al día siguiente. En ambos casos los murciélagos, fueron revisados para ectoparásitos, los cuales se guardaron en viales con etanol 70º para su posterior identificación.

Para la Taxonomía y la Sistemática del grupo seguiremos los esquemas usados anteriormente (Guerrero 1990, 1992a, 1992b, 1993a, 1993b, 1993c y 1993d).

La relación parásito-hospedador fue establecida según los parámetros propuestos por Kisielewska (1970a) y Guerrero (1979) para comunidades de helmintos endoparásitos y modificados para ectoparásitos por Guerrero (1990) puesto que parecen ser, ecológicamente, más correctos que los propuestos por Margolis et.al. (1982). Los parámetros son calculados de la siguiente manera:

Siendo **P** el número de parásitos colectados

$\quad\quad$ **Hi** el número de hospedadores parasitados

$\quad\quad$ **Ht** el número total de hospedadores revisados

Extensidad o Prevalencia (**E**)

$\quad\quad$ $E = (Hi \, / \, Ht) \times 100$

Densidad relativa o Intensidad (**Dr**)

$\quad\quad$ $Dr = P \, / \, Hi$

Densidad absoluta o Intensividad (**Da**)

$\quad\quad$ $Da = P \, / \, Ht$

Índice de infección (**ii**)

$\quad\quad$ $ii = Da \times (E \, / \, 100)$

El índice de infección permite determinar el papel ecológico (**ER**) que cumple cada especie dentro de la comunidad y que viene expresado en tres categorías, cuyos intervalos se separan fácilmente por valores de varios logaritmos (ver tabla 2). estas categorías se denominan:

$\quad\quad$ **D** $\quad$ = especie(s) dominante(s)

$\quad\quad$ **SD** = especie(s) subdominante(s)

$\quad\quad$ **A** $\quad$ = especie(s) accesoria (s)

Encontrándose:

Los índices utilizados para determinar la diversidad de la comunidad de parásitos, esto es, la comunidad de parásitos en una población o especie de hospedadores son los de Shannon, Pielou, Simpson y Hill debido a las características que reúnen entre todos ellos y calculados según Magurran (1988).

La comparación en la composición de especies de las distintas localidades se realizó usando el índice Jacard, según lo establece Pielou (1979).

Para determinar la especificidad de la supracomunidad, esto es, la comunidad de parásitos en la comunidad de los hospedadores, usaremos la estimación de ancho y superposición de nicho propuesta por Pielou (1972, 1975), ya anteriormente utilizada en supracomunidades de Streblidae (Guerrero, 1990), de forma que el ancho (**W**) y la superposición (**L**) son calculados por las medidas estandarizadas (Ver Guerrero en este volumen):

$$W = \frac{H_{A(B)}}{H_{(B)}} \quad\quad y \quad\quad H = \frac{H_{B(A)}}{H_{(A)}}$$

Tabla 1.- Hospedadores colectados en las diferentes zonas de muestreo.

especie de murciélago[1]	zonas de muestreo[2]							Abr.[4]
	1[3]	2	3	4	5	6	7	
Rhynchonycteris naso	0/1							R. nas
Noctilio albiventris	1/1	40/40					14/14	N.alb
Micronycteris megalotis	1/1							M.meg
Micronycteris minuta	1/2							M.min
Macrophyllum macrophyllum	0/1							M.mac
Tonatia silvicola	0/2			1/2	3/3			T. sil
Phyllostomus elongatus	2/3		4/5		1/1		1/1	P. elo
Phyllostomus hastatus	11/11			1/1	3/3	1/1		P. has
Trachops cirrhosus	4/4		1/1		2/2			T.Cir
Glossophaga commissarisi	2/2				1/1			G.com
Glossophaga soricina	1/2			0/2	0/2			G. Sor
Lonchophylla thomasi					2/4			L.tho
Anoura caudifer					0/1			A.cau
Choeroniscus minor	0/1							C. min
Carollia brevicauda	10/15		5/6	2/3	6/10		1/1	C.bre
Carollia castanea	11/31	0/1	1/2	0/1	4/10			C.cas
Carollia perspicillata	10/18		0/2	0/1	9/12		2/2	C.per
Rhinophylla pumilio	0/3			0/1	0/1			R.pum
Sturnira lilium	5/10			0/1	2/2			S.lil
Uroderma bilobatum	1/3				2/2			U.bil
Uroderma magnirostrum	0/3							U.mag
Platyrrhinus brachycephalus	0/6			0/1	0/1	0/1		P.bra
Platyrrhinus helleri	0/10			0/2				P.hel
Platyrrhinus infuscus							0/1	P.inf
Vampyrodes caraccioli						0/2		V.car
Vampyressa bidens						0/1		V.bid
Vampyressa pusilla	0/1				0/1			V.pus
Mesophylla macconnelli	0/3				0/1			V.mac
Artibeus anderseni	0/11							A.and
Artibeus jamaicensis	3/8			7/10	6/15	0/1		A.jam
Artibeus lituratus	1/10				6/11			A.lit
Artibeus obscurus	5/19			2/8	3/11	0/1		A.obs
Diphylla ecaudata					2/2			D.eca
Furipterus horrens	0/1							F.hor
Thyroptera tricolor	0/1							T.tri
Lasiurus ega							0/1	L.ega
Myotis 3 spp	0/4	0/1	0/1		0/9		0/7	M.spp
Molossus molossus	0/1							M.mol

1   Organizadas según Ascorra et. al., 1991
2   Según se indican en Materiales y Métodos
3   Parasitados por Streblidae/total revisados
4   Abreviaturas usadas

siendo

$H_{(A)}$ La diversidad de parásitos de la colección
$H_{(B)}$ La diversidad de hospedadores
$H_{B(A)}$ La diversidad promedio de los parásitos
$H_{A(B)}$ La diversidad promedio de los hospedadores

Todos los cálculos han sido realizados en una computadora personal modelo IBM PS-2 50, con un programa en TURBASIC desarrollado por el autor.

RESULTADOS Y DISCUSIÓN

HOSPEDADORES

Se recogieron un total de 425 murciélagos de 40 especies en las 7 zonas de colección (tabla 1). De esta tabla se observa que 206 murciélagos, el 48.5%, estaba parasitado, existiendo en algunos casos diferencias según la zona donde fueron colectados. En el caso de *Tonatia silvicola* tenemos que ninguno de los ejemplares colectados en el Campamento Base estaban parasitados, mientras que todos los colectados en Castañal sí lo estaban. Koepcke (1987) en una zona similar, encontró un valor un poco menor, pues de 659 murciélagos sólo 276, el 41.9%, estaba parasitado.

De las 40 especies de murciélagos colectadas, 19 (47.5%) resultaron parasitadas con Streblidae, siendo la mayoría de ellas de la familia Phyllostomidae que son los hospedadores más frecuentes (Wenzel et.al., 1966; Guerrero 1990). Koepcke (1987) reporta valores un poco mayores, ya que de 52 especies el 59.6%, es decir 31, estaba parasitado.

TAXONOMÍA

Las especies colectadas son:

Trichobius uniformis Curran, 1935
Material colectado: 1 macho y 1 hembra ex 2 *Glossophaga commissarisi*
Comentarios: Es la primera vez que se encuentra en esta especie de hospedador.

Trichobius lonchophyllae Wenzel, 1966
Material colectado: 1 macho ex *Lonchophylla thomasi*
Comentarios: Es la primera vez que se encuentra esta especie en Perú y en este hospedador.

Trichobius longipes (Rudow, 1871)
Material colectado: 21 machos y 14 hembras ex 8 *Phyllostomus elongatus* y 8 machos, 8 hembras y 1 sexo ? ex 10 *P. hastatus*

Trichobius dugesii Townsend, 1891
Material colectado: 1 macho ex *Glossophaga soricina*.

Trichobius joblingi Wenzel, 1966
Material colectado: 18 machos, 5 hembras y 1 sexo ? ex *Carollia brevicauda*; 11 machos y 6 hembras ex 14 *C. castanea*; 16 machos y 5 hembras ex 15 *C. perspicillata* y 2 machos y 7 hembras ex 4 *Phyllostomus elongatus*.
Comentarios: El material proveniente de *C. castanea*, posiblemente pertenece a una nueva especie.

Trichobius handleyi Wenzel, 1976
Material colectado: 1 macho ex *Micronycteris megalotis*
Comentarios: Esta es la primera vez que se colecta esta especie fuera de Venezuela, de donde fue descrita originalmente.

Trichobius dugesioides Wenzel, 1966
Material colectado: 25 machos y 8 hembras ex 6 *Trachops cirrhosus* y 3 machos ex 2 *Carollia perspicillata*.

Trichobius diphyllae Wenzel, 1966
Material colectado: 16 machos y 8 hembras ex 2 *Diphylla ecaudata*.
Comentarios: El material es tentativamente asignado a esta especie (Guerrero, 1993a), ya que difiere notablemente del material centroamericano.

Xenotrichobius sp
Material colectado: 1 hembra ex *Noctilio albiventris*.
Comentarios: Esta hembra no corresponde con la descripción de la especie tipo y posiblemente sea la hembra de una especie nueva (Guerrero en prep.) y mal identificada por Koepcke (1988) como *X. noctilionis* Wenzel, 1976.

Spreiseria ambigua Kessel, 1925
Material estudiado: 4 machos y 2 hembras ex 6 *Carollia perspicillata*; 2 machos y 2 hembras ex 3 *C. breviacauda* y 1 macho ex *Trachops cirrhosus*.

Speiseria peytonae Wenzel, 1976
Material estudiado: 5 machos y 3 hembras ex 7 *Carollia brevicauda*.
Comentarios: La especie se señala por primera vez en Perú.

Speiseria magnioculus Wenzel, 1976
Material estudiado: 1 macho ex *Diphylla ecaudata*
Comentarios: Esta especie es un parásito típico de *Trachops cirrhosus* (Guerrero, 1993b), sin embargo en nuestra colección no la encontramos en ese hospedador.

Parastrebla handleyi Wenzel, 1966
Material estudiado: 1 hembra ex *Micronycteris megalotis*.
Comentarios: Esta rara especie no había sido colectada anteriormente en Perú.

Pseudostrebla riberori Costa Lima, 1921
Material estudiado: 1 macho ex *Tonatia silvicola*.

Paratrichobius longicrus (Miranda Ribeiro, 1907)
Material estudiado: 7 machos y 2 sexo ? ex 7 *Artibeus lituratus*.

Paratrichobius dunni (Curran, 1935)
Material estudiado: 1 macho y 1 hembra ex 2 *Uroderma bilobatum*.

Neotrichobius bisetosus Wenzel, 1976
Material estudiado: 12 machos y 8 hembras ex 9 *Artibeus obscurus* y 1 hembra ex *A. jamaicensis*.

Megistopoda aranea (Coquillett, 1899)
Material estudiado: 4 machos y 8 hembras ex 7 *Artibeus jamaicensis* y 1 hembra ex *Uroderma bilobatum*.

Megistopoda proxima (Séguy, 1926)
Material estudiado: 6 machos y 4 hembras ex 6 *Sturnira lilium*.

Aspidoptera phyllostomatis (Perty, 1833)
Material estudiado: 7 machos y 3 hembras ex 7 *Artibeus jamaicensis* y 1 macho y 1 hembra ex 1 *A. obscurus*.

Aspidoptera falcata Wenzel, 1976
Material estudiado: 3 hembras ex 2 *Sturnira lilium*.
Comentarios: Koepcke (1988) señala a *Aspidoptera delatorrei* como el parásito más abundante en *S. lilium*, sin embargo esta especie sólo se encuentra entre Panamá y el Noroeste de Venezuela y no en la Amazonía (Guerrero, 1993c).

Mastoptera minuta (Costa Lima, 1921)
Material estudiado: 41 machos, 36 hembras y 2 sexo ? ex 13 *Phyllostomus hastatus*; 2 machos y 2 hembras ex 2 *P. elongatus* 5 machos y 2 hembras ex 3 *Tonatia silvicola* y 1 hembra ex *Carollia brevicauda*.

Noctiliostrebla maai Wenzel, 1966
Material estudiado: 204 machos y 185 hembras ex 52 *Noctilio albiventris*.

Paradyschiria parvula Falcoz, 1931
Material estudiado: 243 machos, 217 hembras y 1 sexo ? ex 55 *Noctilio albiventris*.

Strebla mirabilis (Waterhouse, 1879)
Material estudiado: 5 machos y 2 hembras ex 5 *Trachops cirrhosus* y 1 macho ex *Phyllostomus elongatus*.

Strebla guajiro (García y Casal, 1965)
Material estudiado: 7 machos ex 7 *Carollia brevicauda*; 6 machos y 3 hembras ex 8 *C. brevicauda* y 4 machos y 1 hembra ex 5 *C. perspicillata*.

Strebla consocia Wenzel, 1966
Material estudiado: 18 machos, 13 hembras y 10 sexo ? ex 8 *Phyllostomus hastatus* y 17 machos y 8 hembras ex 6 *P. elongatus*.

Strebla machadoi Wenzel, 1966
Material estudiado: 3 machos y 1 hembra ex 1 *Micronycteris minuta*.
Comentarios: Esta especie se señala por primera vez en Perú.

Strebla diphyllae Wenzel, 1966
Material estudiado: 3 machos ex 2 *Diphylla ecaudata*.
Comentarios: Esta especie se señala por primera vez en Perú.

Strebla kohlsi Wenzel, 1966
Material estudiado: 1 macho ex *Tonatia silvicola* y 1 hembra ex *Phylloderma stenops*.
Comentarios: Esta especie se señala por primera vez en Perú.

Strebla alvarezi Wenzel, 1966
Material estudiado: 1 hembra ex *Lonchophylla thomasi*.
Comentarios: Esta especie se señala por primera vez en Perú.

Strebla curvata Wenzel, 1976
Material estudiado: 2 machos ex 2 *Glossophaga commissarisi*.
Comentarios: Esta especie se señala por primera vez en este hospedador y en Perú.

Metelasmus pseudopterus Coquillett, 1907
Material estudiado: 5 machos y 1 hembra ex 5 *Artibeus jamaicensis*

RELACIÓN PARÁSITO-HOSPEDADOR

Prevalencia y densidad
En la tabla 2, se presenta un resumen de los valores correspondientes al número de murciélagos parasitados por cada una de las especies de parásitos y las densidades alcanzadas por éstos, así como una idea del papel ecológico que juega cada especie, dentro de la comunidad parasitaria en cada especie de murciélago. En dicha tabla se observa que en la gran mayoría de los casos, el 71%, la densidad absoluta de los parásitos no supera el valor de un parásito por hospedador, lo que indica la baja carga parasitaria típica del grupo.

Con respecto a la densidad relativa, es decir el número de parásitos por hospedador infectado, también se observa que solamente en el 25% de los casos se supera el número de 2 parásitos por hospedador.

Es de resaltar que *Noctilio albiventris*, la especie de murciélago más colectada, presenta un comportamiento similar para sus especies de parásitos dominantes, *P. parvula* y *N. maai*, al señalado por Koepcke (1987); sin embargo Guerrero (1990) en base al análisis de material proveniente de más de 24.500 murciélagos de Venezuela, observa que ambas especies presentan una frecuencia de infección y unas densidades mucho menores a las encontradas en Pakitza.

Tabla 2.- *Parámetros poblacionales de las especies de Streblidae en cada especie de hospedador*

Streblidae	Hospedador [1]	Hi [2]	P	E	Dr	Da	ii	ER
Par. parvula	N.alb	55	461	98.2	8.38	8.23	8.085140	D
Noc. maai	"	52	389	92.9	7.48	6.95	6.450255	D
Xenotrichobius sp	"	1	1	1.8	1.00	0.02	0.000319	A
Tri. handleyi	M.meg	1	1	100.0	1.00	1.00	1.000000	–
Par. handleyi	"	1	1	100.0	1.00	1.00	1.000000	–
Str. macadoi	M.min	1	4	50.0	4.00	2.00	1.000000	D
Tri. handleyi	"	1	1	50.0	1.00	0.50	0.250000	SD
Mas. minuta	T.sil	3	7	42.9	2.33	1.00	0.428571	D
Str. kohlsi	"	1	1	14.3	1.00	0.14	0.020408	A
Pse. riberoi	"	1	1	14.3	1.00	0.14	0.020408	A
Tri. longipes	P.elo	8	35	80.0	4.38	3.50	2.800000	D
Str. consocia	"	6	25	60.0	4.17	2.50	1.500000	D
Tri. joblingi	"	4	9	40.0	2.25	0.90	0.360000	SD
Mas. minuta	"	2	4	20.0	2.00	0.40	0.800000	A
Str. mirabilis	"	1	1	10.0	1.00	0.10	0.010000	A
Mas. minuta	P.has	13	79	81.3	6.08	4.94	4.011719	D
Str. consocia	"	8	43	50.0	5.38	2.69	1.343750	SD
Tri. longipes	"	10	17	62.5	1.70	1.06	0.664063	A
Tri. dugesioides	T.cir	6	33	85.7	5.50	4.71	4.040816	D
Str. mirabilis	"	5	7	71.4	1.40	1.00	0.714286	SD
Spe. ambigua	"	1	1	14.3	1.00	0.14	0.020408	A
Tri. uniformis	G.com	2	2	66.7	1.00	0.67	0.444444	D
Str. curvata	"	2	2	66.7	1.00	0.67	0.444444	D
Tri. dugesti	G.sor	1	1	16.6	1.00	0.16	0.026560	–
Tri. lonchopyllae	L.tho	1	1	25.0	1.00	0.25	0.062500	–
Str. alvarezi	"	1	1	25.0	1.00	0.25	0.062500	–
Tri. joblingi	C.bre	15	24	42.9	1.60	0.69	0.293878	D
Spe. paytonae	"	7	8	20.0	1.14	0.23	0.045714	SD
Str. guajiro	"	7	7	20.0	1.00	0.20	0.040000	SD
Spe. ambigua	"	3	4	8.6	1.33	0.11	0.009796	A
Mas. minuta	"	1	1	2.9	1.00	0.03	0.000816	A
Tri. joblingi	C.cas	14	17	31.1	1.21	0.38	0.117531	D
Str. guajiro	"	8	9	17.8	1.13	0.20	0.035556	SD
Tri. joblingi	C.per	15	21	42.9	1.40	0.60	0.257143	D
Spe. ambigua	"	6	6	17.1	1.00	0.17	0.029388	SD
Str. guajiro	"	5	5	14.3	1.00	0.14	0.020408	SD
Tri. dugesioides	"	2	3	5.7	1.50	0.09	0.004898	A
Meg. proxima	S.lil	6	10	46.2	1.67	0.77	0.355030	D
Asp. falcata	"	2	3	15.4	1.50	0.23	0.035503	SD
Par. dunni	U.bil	2	2	40.0	1.00	0.40	0.160000	D
Meg. aranea	"	1	1	20.0	1.00	0.20	0.400000	SD
Meg. aranea	A.jam	7	12	20.6	1.71	0.35	0.072664	D
Asp. phyllostomatis	"	7	10	20.6	1.43	0.29	0.060554	D
Met. pseudpterus	"	5	6	14.7	1.20	0.18	0.025952	SD
Neo. bisetosus	"	1	1	2.9	1.00	0.03	0.000865	A
Par. longicrus	A.lit	7	10	47.6	1.43	0.48	0.22848	–
Neo. bisetosus	A.obs	9	20	23.1	2.22	0.51	0.118343	D
Asp. phyllostomatis	"	1	2	2.6	2.00	0.05	0.001315	A
Tri. diphyllae	D.eca	2	24	100.0	12.00	12.00	12.000000	D
Str. diphyllae	"	2	3	100.0	1.50	1.50	1.500000	SD
Spe. magnioculus	"	1	1	50.0	1.00	0.50	0.250000	A

1   Ver tabla 1
2   Abreviaturas según Materiales y métodos

Existen notables diferencias entre los resultados aquí encontrados en las especies de *Phyllostomus*, con respecto a los resultados de Koepcke (1987), en particular *Mastoptera minuta* que, de acuerdo a nuestros resultados, es la especie dominante en *P. hastatus* y casi no aparece en el material de Koepcke (loc. cit.), esta situación puede tratarse de un artefacto en los resultados de dicha autora, ya que los miembros del género *Mastoptera* son muy pequeños y muchas veces no se colectan o se confunden con ácaros de la familia Spinturnicidae.

También debe resaltarse el hecho de que Koepke (1987) encuentra valores mucho mayores en la pevalencia y en las densidades de *A. phyllostomatis* y *M. aranea* provenientes de *A. jamaicensis* (identificado co-

hospedadores	Para1	Hi2	P	E	Dr	Da	ii
Noc. albiventris	3	56	851	100.0	15.20	15.20	15.196428
Mic. megalotis	2	1	2	100.0	2.00	2.00	2.000000
Mic. minuta	2	1	5	50.0	5.00	2.50	1.250000
Ton. silvicola	3	4	9	57.1	2.25	1.29	0.734694
Phy. elongatus	5	8	74	80.0	9.25	7.40	5.920000
Phy. hastatus	3	16	139	100.0	8.69	8.69	8.687500
Tra. cirrhosus	3	7	41	100.0	5.86	5.86	5.857143
Glo. commissarisi	2	3	4	100.0	1.33	1.33	1.333333
Glo. soricina	1	1	1	16.6	1.00	0.16	0.026560
Lon. thomasi	2	2	2	50.0	1.00	0.50	0.250000
Car. brevicauda	5	24	44	68.6	1.83	1.26	0.862041
Car. castanea	2	17	26	37.8	1.53	0.58	0.218272
Car. perspicillata	4	21	35	60.0	1.67	1.00	0.600000
Stu. lilium	2	7	13	53.8	1.86	1.00	0.538462
Uro. bilobatum	2	3	3	60.0	1.00	0.60	0.360000
Art. jamaicensis	4	16	29	47.1	1.81	0.85	0.401384
Art. lituratus	1	7	10	47.6	1.43	0.48	0.228480
Art. obscurus	2	10	22	25.6	2.20	0.56	0.144642
Dip. ecaudata	2	2	28	100.0	14.00	14.00	14.000000

Tabla 3.- Parámetros poblacionales totales en cada especie de hospedador

[1] especies de parásitos
[2] abreviaturas según Materiales y Métodos

mo *Artibeus planirostris* por Koepke), los valores encontrados aquí corresponden a los indicados por Guerrero (1990) para material venezolano.

En la tabla 3, se encuentran resumidos los parámetros poblacionales totales por especie de hospedador, en ellos se puede observar la misma concordancia señalada por Guerrero (1990) entre el contenido energético de la alimentación y el número de parásitos encontrados; así tenemos que aquellas especies con dieta fundamentalmente carnívora soportan un número mayor de parásitos que las especies frugívoras.

Proporción sexual

Con respecto a la proporción sexual tenemos que sólo el 45.4% de los 324 lotes de parásitos colectados, entendiéndose por lote el conjunto de parásitos encontrados en cada murciélago, resultó contener individuos de ambos sexos. Guerrero

(1990) encuentra un promedio de 47.82% de infecciones bisexuales luego, ésta situación es común entre los Streblidae.

Marshall (1981a) señala que entre los insectos ectoparásitos el 53.3% de las especies presenta una proporción sexual de 1:1, presentándose en la mayoría de los casos en que esta relación no se cumple, una dominancia de las hembras debido a su longevidad. En los Streblidae la proporción de casos en que la relación es diferente de 1:1, es del 42.4% según Marshall (1981b) y 39.7% según Guerrero (1990), pero la gran mayoría de las veces el número de machos es mayor que el de hembras. De acuerdo con Marshall (1982) esto es un artefacto debido a que las hembras descienden del hospedador, pero Overal (1980) y Fritz (1983) demuestran la baja sobrevivencia que presentan estos parásitos al encontrarse fuera del hospedador. Por lo tanto el problema de la desproporción sexual del grupo no está aclarado aún.

Diversidad y Biodiversidad

En la tabla 4 tenemos los valores de los índices de diversidad calculados para las especies hospedadoras con más de una especie de parásito y el número de especies de Streblidae encontrados en cada especie de hospedador, como estimador de la biodiversidad.

Los valores de diversidad son, aproximadamente, coincidentes con los indicados anteriormente por Guerrero (1990) para estas especies de murciélagos, con la única excepción de N. *albiventris* en el que se observa una mayor equitatividad en la suprapoblación de Pakitza al ser comparada con los resultados de Venezuela (Guerrero loc. cit.) en donde los resultados obtenidos al sumar los datos provenientes de varias suprapoblaciones, siempre se observa que hay una clara dominancia de las especies del género *Paradyschiria* sobre las de *Noctiliostrebla*, pero en Pakitza las especies de ambos géneros tienen casi el mismo papel ecológico (tabla 2).

Aunque muchos autores asocian directamente la diversidad con la biodiversidad, lo hacen de manera intuitiva y son pocos los que tratan de establecer una relación entre estas dos variables. Los cambios en la biodiversidad son asociados a la desaparición total o regional de alguna(s) especie(s) y sus consecuencias dentro del ecosistema a nivel de las cadenas tróficas (Reid y Miller, 1989) pero no se evalúan en función de la diversidad ecológica ya que ésta, generalmente, se mide dentro de un solo estrato trófico o funcional (Kisielewska, 1970a, 1970b) y no dentro de todo el ecosistema. En nuestro caso observamos que la diversidad es inversa a la biodiversidad. Así, hay una correlación positiva estadísticamente significativa entre el valor del índice de Shannon y el número de especies de parásitos, lo cual significa que a medida de que se incorporan más especies de Streblidae a la comunidad de parásitos, alguna de ellas se hace más dominante o, por el contrario, estas especies que tratan de establecerse en la población de hospedadores sólo lo hacen de una manera marginal.

Localidades y Supracomunidades

Al igual que el término población, la definición de comunidad, al ser referido a parásitos, plantea una serie de inconvenientes ampliamente debatidos por

Tabla 5.- Valores de la especificidad comunitaria

localidad	W	L	div P	div H
Panguana 1	0.138	0.258	2.833	2.439
Pakitza (Total)	0.178	0.303	2.600	2.203
Pakitza (Loc.1)	0.232	0.291	2.317	2.137
Pakitza (Loc.2)	0.167	0.523	1.543	0.884
Pakitza (Loc.4)	0.113	0.397	1.451	0.987
Pakitza (Loc.5)	0.145	0.206	2.425	2.252
Pakitza (Loc.7)	0.054	0.535	1.224	0.601

1   Calculados de los datos de Koepcke (1987)

diferentes autores (Macko, 1981; Holmes y Price, 1986; Esch et. al., 1990). En nuestro caso entendemos por supracomunidad al conjunto de todos los parásitos encontrados en una comunidad de hospedadores localizada en un punto geográfico definido, es decir los parásitos de Pakitza o de la localidad 1 de Pakitza.

La caracterización de una supracomunidad, con el fin de compararla con otras, se hace por medio de lo que hemos llamado Especificidad Comunitaria, la cual da una idea de cuánto es el intercambio de parásitos entre las diferentes especies de hospedadores en una localidad dada y estimado por el ancho y la superposición del nicho, trófico o espacial, de las distintas especies de parásitos. Otra forma de comparar las supracomunidades, ya más relacionada a la biodiversidad, es simplemente determinar la relación entre las especies comunes y no comunes a las dos localidades a comparar.

En la tabla 5 tenemos los valores del ancho y superposición de nicho, así como la diversidad de parásitos y de hospedadores. Dicha tabla nos indica que los valores de Pakitza son similares a los obtenidos por Koepcke (1987) para Panguana y que la localidad 7 es aquella donde hay menor intercambio de parásitos entre las diferentes especies de hospedadores. Guerrero (1990) demostró que la Especificidad Comunitaria tiene cierta relación con el tipo de ambiente donde se hace el estudio y por lo tanto con el grado de humedad y la altura. Los resultados aquí obtenidos se asemejan más a los de un bosque húmedo tropical que a los de un bosque muy húmedo tropical (sensu Handley, 1976).

La tabla 6 muestra los valores del índice de Jacard para las especies de parásitos y de hospedadores. Aunque pudiera suponerse que la una es función de la otra si

Tabla 6.- Valores del índice comparativo de Jacard para las poblaciones de parásitos y de hospedadores

parásitos		hospedadores						
		1	2	3	4	5	6	7
localidad	1[1]	———	0.100	0.200	0.400	0.543	0.133	0.156
localidad	2	0.087	———	0.222	0.063	0.074	0.074	0.200
localidad	3	0.348	0.000	———	0.200	0.250	0.000	0.444
localidad	4	0.348	0.000	0.333	———	0.440	0.333	0.055
localidad	5	0.437	0.000	0.292	0.240	———	0.167	0.148
localidad	6	0.130	0.000	0.375	0.222	0.130	———	0.000
localidad	7	0.292	0.250	0.333	0.067	0.148	0.100	———

1   ver Materiales y Métodos

hay una alta especificidad. Guerrero (1990) demostró que no hay correspondencia filogenética, en la especificidad, de los Streblidae neotropicales y sus murciélagos hospedadores. En nuestros resultados se observa que el coeficiente de correlación entre el valor del índice de Jacard de los parásitos y el de los hospedadores es 0.608636, es decir, hay correspondencia pero poca. El valor más alto observado para los parásitos, corresponde al comparar las localidades 1 y 5 (.437), posiblemente debido a su proximidad. Sin embargo este valor es similar al obtenido al comparar Pakitza con los resultados de Koecpcke (1987) en Panguana (0.429); entre los hospedadores la mayor similaridad es igualmente entre las localidades 1 y 5.

AGRADECIMIENTOS

El autor agradece a Don E. Wilson, director del Programa BIOLAT, por la oportunidad de realizar este trabajo. A Abelardo Sandoval por la excelente labor logística que permitió maximizar el trabajo de campo. A César F. Ascorra y su grupo por colectar e identificar la gran mayoría de los murciélagos usados en este trabajo. A Fiedrich Reiss y Juliane Koepcke-Diller del Zoologische Staatssammlung de Munich por permitirme revisar el material colectado en Panguana.

LITERATURA CITADA

Ascorra, C. F., D. E. Wilson y M. Romo. 1991. Lista anotada de los quirópteros del Parque Nacional Manu, Perú. Publicaciones del Museo de Historia Natural. Serie A Zoología 42:1-14.

Erwin, T. 1990. Natural history of the carabid beetles at the BIOLAT Biological Station, Rio Manu, Pakitza, Peru. Revista Peruana de Entomología 33:1-85

Esch, G. W., A. W. Shostak, D. J. Marcogliese y T. M. Goater. 1990 . Patterns and processes in helminth parasite communities: an overview . Pp. 1-19, *in* Parasite Communities: Patterns and Processes (G. W. Esch , A. O. Bush y J. M. Aho, eds.). Chapman and Hall , New York , 335 pp.

Fritz, G. N. 1983. Biology and ecology of bat filies (Diptera : Streblidae) on bats in the genus *Carollia* . Journal of Medical Entomology 20: 1-10

Gómez, J. 1984. Análisis de las Comunidades de Ectoparásitos de murciélagos en un ecosistema de Selva Húmeda. Premontana. Tesis de Licenciatura, Facultad de Ciencias, Universidad Central de Venezuela, Caracas, 108 pp.

Guerrero, R. 1979. The structure of the endoparasite helminth communities of rodents in an urbangradient. Ph. D. thesis, Polish Academy of Sciences, Warszawa , 148 pp.

Guerrero, R. 1990 Streblidae (Diptera: Pupipara) parásitos de murciélagos de Venezuela (Sistemática, Ecología y Evolución). Trabajo de Ascenso, Universidad Central de Venezuela, Caracas, 370 pp.

Guerrero, R. 1992a. Catálogo de los Streblidae (Diptera: Pupipara) parásitos de murciélagos (Mammalia: Chiroptera) del Nuevo Mundo. I. Clave para los géneros y

Nycterophiliinae. Acta Biológica Venezuelica. *en prensa*

Guerrero, R. 1992b. Catálogo de los Streblidae (Diptera: Pupipara) parásitos de murciélagos (Mammalia: Chiroptera) del Nuevo Mundo. II. Los grupos: pallidus, caecus, major, uniformis y longipes del género *Trichobius* Gervais, 1844. Acta Biológica Venezuelica *en prensa*

Guerrero, R. 1993a. Catálogo de los Streblidae (Diptera: Pupipara) parásitos de murciélagos (Mammalia: Chiroptera) del Nuevo Mundo. III. Los grupos: dugesii, dunni y phyllostomae del género *Trichobius* Gervais, 1844. Acta Biologica Venezuelica *en prensa*

Guerrero, R. 1993b. Catálogo de los Streblidae (Diptera: Pupipara) parásitos de murciélagos (Mammalia: Chiroptera) del Nuevo Mundo. IV. Trichobiinae con alas desarrolladas. Boletín Venezolano de Entomología. *en prensa*

Guerrero, R. 1993c. Catálogo de los Streblidae (Diptera: Pupipara) parásitos de murciélagos (Mammalia: Chiroptera) del Nuevo Mundo. V. Trichobiinae con alas reducidas o ausentes y miscelaneos. Boletín Venezolano de Entomología. *en prensa*

Guerrero, R. 1993d. Catálogo de los Streblidae (Diptera: Pupipara) parásitos de murciélagos (Mammalia: Chiroptera) del Nuevo Mundo. VI. Streblinae. Acta Biológica Venezuelica. *en prensa*

Handley, C. O. 1976. Mammals of the Smithsonian Venezuelan Project. Brigham Young University Science Bulletin, Biological Series 20:1-91

Holmes, J. C. y P. W. PRICE. 1986 Communities of Parasites. Pp. 187-213, *in* Community Ecology: Pattern and Process (D. J. Anderson y J. Kikkawa eds.). Blackwell Scientific Publications, Oxford, 342 pp.

Jobling, B. 1947. On Speiseria ambigua Kessel and Synthesiostrebla amorphochili Townsend , with redescription of the latter (Diptera, Streblidae). Proceedings of the Royal Entomological Society of London (B) 16:39-42

Kisielewska, K. 1970a. On the Theoretical foundations of Parasitosinecology. Bulletin de la Academie Polonaise des Sciences, Serie C, 18:103-106

Kisielewska, K. 1970b. Ecological organization of intestinal helminth grouping in *Clethrionomys glareolus* (Schreb.) (Rodentia). I. Structure and seasonal dynamics of helminth groupings in a host population in the Bialowieza National Park. Acta Parasitologica Pololica 18:121-147

Koepcke, J. 1987. Okologische studien an einer Fledermaus-artengemeinschaft im tropischen Regenwald von Peru. Ph. D. thesis, Ludwig-Maximilians-Universität, München, 439 pp.

Kunz, T. H. 1976. Observations on the winter ecology of the batfly *Trichobius corynorhini* Cockerell (Diptera: Streblidae). Journal of Medical Entomology 12:631-636

Macko, J. K. 1981b. On the peculiarity of most common intraspecific communities in animal in general, and with special regard to helminths. Folia Parasitolica (Praha) 28:3 19-326

Magurran, A. L. 1988. Ecological Diversity and its Measuring. Princent on University Press, New Jersey, 179 pp.

Margolis, L., R. Anderson y J. Holmes. 1982. The use of ecological terms in Parasitology. (Report of an Ad-Hoc Commitee of the American Society of Parasitologists). Journal of Parasitology, 68:131-133

Marshall, A. G. 1981a. The Ecology of Ectoparasitic Insects. Academic Press, London, 459 pp.

Marshall, A. G. 1981b. The sex ratio in ectoparasitic insects. Ecological Entomology 6:155-174

Marshall, A. G. 1982 Ecology of Insects Ectoparasitic on Bats. Pp. 369-401 *in* Ecology of Bats (T. H. Kunz ed.). Plenum Press, New York, 432 pp.

Overal, W. L. 1980 Host-relations of the Batfly *Megistopoda aranea* (Diptera: Streblidae) in Panamá. University of Kansas, Science Bulletin 52:1-20

Pielou, E. C. 1972. Niche width and niche overlap: a method for measuring them. Ecology 53:687-692

Pielou, E. C. 1975. Ecological Diversity. John Wiley & Sons, New York, 385 pp.

Pielou, E. C. 1979. Biogeography. John Wiley & Sons, New York 351 pp.

Reid W. V. y K. R. Miller. 1989. Keeping options alive. The Scientific Basis for Conserving Biodiversity. World Resources Institute, Washington, 128 pp.

Ross, A. 1961. Biological studies on bat ectoparasites of the genus *Trichobius* (Diptera: Streblidae) in North America, north of Mexico. Wasmann Journal of biology, 19:229-246

Townsend, C. H. T. 1913. A new genus of Streblidae. Proceedings of the Entomological Society of Washington 15:98-99

Wenzel, R. L., V. Tipton y A. Kiewlicz. 1966 The streblid batflies of Panamá (Diptera Calypterae: Streblidae). Pp. 405-675, *in* Ectoparasites of Panamá (R. L. Wenzel and V. Tipton eds.). Field Museum of Natural History, Chicago Illinois, 861 pp.

Wenzel, R. L. 1976. The streblid batflies of Venezuela (Diptera: Streblidae). Brigham Young University Science Bulletin, Biological Series 20:1-177

Estudio preliminar de los ectoparásitos de los murciélagos de Pakitza, Parque Nacional Manu (Perú)

RICARDO GUERRERO

Instituto de Zoología Tropical
Facultad de Ciencias - Universidad Central de Venezuela,
Apdo. 47058, Caracas 1041A, Venezuela

RESUMEN

En la estación lluviosa de 1992, se colectaron 425 murciélagos de 41 especies, de ellos el 83.0 % resultó parasitado por un total de 1361 dípteros pertenecientes a 2 familias y 6679 ácaros de 8 familias. La relación parásito-hospedador es analizada para los diferentes grupos, calculándose la cantidad de hospedadores infectados por cada grupo, sus densidades y diversidad, estableciéndose las relaciones de competencia y facilitación entre los distintos tipos de ectoparásitos y las características y similaridades entre las diferentes localidades del área estudiada.

INTRODUCCIÓN

Los murciélagos son un grupo de mamíferos caracterizados por contener una parasitofauna muy rica, tanto de endoparásitos como de ectoparásitos, éstos últimos están representados por numerosos grupos, generalmente de artrópodos, cuya adaptación al parasitismo es claramente de origen polifilético. Así se encuentran parásitos pertenecientes a varios órdenes de insectos y a numerosas familias de ácaros (Anciaux de Faveaux,1971-1976; Webb y Loomis,1977; Marshall 1981,1982; Nutting,1985) haciéndolos un grupo particularmente interesante para estudios de biodiversidad o de diversidad ecológica, aunque los estudios faunísticos de una región particular, como el caso de los trabajos realizados en Cuba, Panamá, Venezuela o Suriname, arrojan tal cantidad de especies nuevas que se hipertrofia la parte sistemática y se descuida la parte ecológica.

Hasta el momento en Perú no se ha realizado un trabajo intensivo y sistematizado sobre los ectoparásitos de los murciélagos, de forma que el poco conocimiento que se tiene de los mismos se debe a pequeños trabajos circunstanciales generalmente realizados para describir algunas especies nuevas (Kohls et.al., 1969; Radovsky y Furman,1969; Brennan,1970; etc.) y hay un gran vacío de información en grupos de parásitos muy conspicuos y exclusivos de los murciélagos como son los Polyctenidae (Ueshima,1972) y los Labidocarpidae (Guerrero,1992).

Trataremos de aclarar algunos aspectos de la relación parásito-hospedador en murciélagos del bosque húmedo tropical del Parque Nacional Manu, tratados en esta primera aproximación a nivel de familia, debido a la serie de especies nuevas colectadas y que deben ser descritas. Los Streblidae, uno de los grupos cuya sistemática es bien conocida, son tratados en detalle en otro trabajo de este mismo volumen.

MATERIALES Y MÉTODOS

El material fue colectado entre el 14 de febrero y el 8 de marzo de 1992, es decir en la estación lluviosa. Los murciélagos, identificados siguiendo a Ascorra et. al. (1991), se capturaron con mallas de neblina colocadas en 7 zonas, en los alrededores de la estación de Pakitza, con el fin de cubrir la mayor variedad de hábitats posibles. La toponimia está según Erwin (1990). Las zonas son:

1.- Campamento Base: en la periferia de las edificaciones de los guardaparques y por lo tanto altamente intervenida.

2.- Río Manu: mallas colocadas en medio del río Manu, en la desembocadura de la quebrada de Pacal, a unos 200 metros al NO de la localidad anterior.

3.- Orilla opuesta: mallas en un bosque humedo tropical primario, en el lado opuesto al Campamento Base.

4.- Caña Brava: zona situada, en promedio, a unos 500 metros al SE del Campamento Base y con abundantes palmas.

5.- Castañal: trocha de penetración, en el bosque primario, situada al ENE del Campamento Base.

6.- Tachigali: trocha de penetración, en el bosque primario, situada al N del Campamento Base.

7.- Pachija: mallas colocadas sobre la quebrada del mismo nombre, situada a más de 2 km al NW del Campamento Base.

Una vez capturados, los murciélagos eran sacrificados e inmediatamente guardados, individualmente en bolsas plásticas herméticamente cerradas, hasta el día siguiente; otros murciélagos, cuyas heces eran necesarias para estudiar su dieta, eran guardados vivos, individualmente en bolsas de tela, hasta el día siguiente cuando eran sacrificados. En ambos casos, los murciélagos eran extraídos y al igual que las bolsas en donde habían sido guardados, se revisaban bajo un microscópio estereoscópico y los ectoparásitos se recogían guardándose en viales con alcohol 70° para su posterior identificación.

La relación parasito-hospedador fue establecida según los parámetros propuestos por Kisielewska (1970) y Guerrero (1979) para comunidades de helmintos endoparásitos y modificados para ectoparásitos por Guerrero (1990), según se explica en este mismo volumen. Los parámetros usados se calculan de la siguiente manera:

siendo **P** el número de parásitos colectados

Hi el número de hospedadores parasitados

Ht el número total de hospedadores revisados

Extensidad o Prevalencia (**E**)

$$E = \{Hi \ / \ Ht\} \times 100$$

Densidad relativa o Intensidad (**Dr**)

$$Dr = P \ / \ Hi$$

Densidad absoluta o Intensividad (**Da**)

$$Da = P \ / \ Ht$$

Indice de infección (**ii**)

$$ii = Da \times \{E \ / \ 100\}$$

El índice de infección permite determinar el papel ecológico (**ER**) que cumple cada especie dentro de la comunidad y que viene expresado en tres categorías:

D	=	especie(s) dominante(s)
SD	=	especie(s) subdominante(s)
A	=	especie(s) accesoria(s)

Los índices utilizados para determinar la diversidad de la comunidad de parásitos, esto es la comunidad de parásitos en una población o especie de hospedadores, son los de Shannon, Pielou, Simpson y Hill debido a las características que reúnen entre todos ellos y calculados según Magurran (1988).

El grado de asociación o de competencia entre los diferentes grupos de parásitos se determinó usando el índice Jacard, según lo establece Pielou (1979), y calculado de la siguiente manera:

$$J = \frac{AB}{AB + A + B}$$

en donde

A es el número de hospedadores parasitados sólo por la familia 1.

B es el número de hospedadores parasitados sólo por la familia 2.

y   **AB** es el número de hospedadores parasitados, al mismo tiempo, por las familias 1 y 2.

Ricardo Guerrero

Esta relación, en sus casos extremos, nos indica una máxima competencia con un valor de **J = 0** es decir, ningún hospedador es parasitado por ambas familias y cuando **J = 1** todos los hospedadores, parasitados, lo están por ambas especies. Sin embargo este valor sólo señala una idea de la simultaneidad en la aparición de ambas especies, por lo que se calculó una relación más cuantitativa, que indica si realmente hay una facilitación de un parásito por otro al aumentar la densidad de los parásitos cuando están ambas familias, con respecto a cuando está presente sólo una de ellas.

Para esto, modificamos el índice de Jacard de la siguiente manera:

$$Jm = \frac{\overline{AB}}{\overline{A} + \overline{B}}$$

En donde

$\overline{AB}$ es el promedio del número de parásitos, de las familias 1 y 2, cuando ambas están presentes en el mismo hospedador.

$\overline{A}$ es el promedio del número de parásitos, de la familia 1, cuando ésta aparece sola.

y $\overline{B}$ es el promedio del número de parásitos, de la familia 2, cuando ésta aparece sola.

Para el cálculo de la especificidad de la supracomunidad, esto es la comunidad de parásitos en la comunidad de los hospedadores, usaremos la estimación de ancho y superposición de nicho propuesta por Pielou (1972,1975), ya ampliamente usada por nosotros en supracomunidades (Guerrero 1979, 1990 y en este mismo volumen). El ancho (**W**) y la superposición (**L**) son calculados por la medidas estandarizadas.

$$W = \frac{H_{A(B)}}{H_{(B)}} \qquad y \qquad H = \frac{H_{B(A)}}{H_{(A)}}$$

siendo:

$$H_{(A)} = \frac{1}{N} \log \frac{N!}{\prod_i n_i{*}!} = \quad$$ La diversidad de parásitos de la colección observada en las N ocurrencias.

646

$$H_{(B)} = \frac{1}{N} \log \frac{N!}{\prod_j n_{*j}!} =$$

La diversidad de hospedadores en la colección de ocurrencias.

$$H_{B(A)} = \sum_j \frac{n_{*j}}{N} \left\{ \frac{1}{n_{*j}!} \log \frac{n_{*j}!}{\prod_i n_{ij}!} \right\} =$$

La diversidad promedio de los parásitos en una especie de hospedador, promediada sobre todas las especies de hospedadores.

$$H_{A(B)} = \sum_j \frac{n_{i*}!}{N} \left\{ \frac{1}{n_{i*}} \log \frac{n_{i*}!}{\prod_j n_{ij}!} \right\} =$$

La diversidad promedio de las ocurrencias en los hospedadores de una especie de parásito promediada sobre todas las especies de parásitos.

y en donde

n_{ij} es el número de ocurrencias del parásito *i* en la especie de hospedador *j*

$n_{i*} = \sum_j n_{ij}$ es el número de ocurrencias del parásito *i* en todas las especies de hospedador

$n_{i*} = \sum_i n_{ij}$ es el número de ocurrencias de cualquier parásito en la especie de hospedador *j*

$N = \sum_i \sum_j n_{ij}$ es el número total de ocurrencias de todos los parásitos en todas las especies de hospedador, teniendo en cuenta que por ocurrencia se refiere a la presencia de una especie de parásito en un hospedador, sin importar el número de parásitos.

Todos los cálculos han sido realizados en una computadora personal modelo IBM PS-2 50, con un programa en TURBASIC desarrollado por el autor.

RESULTADOS Y DISCUSIÓN

HOSPEDADORES

Se recogieron un total de 424 murciélagos de 41 especies en las 7 zonas de colección (tabla 1). De esta tabla, se observa que 352 murciélagos, el 83.0 %, estaban parasitados; no existiendo, aparentemente, diferencias cuantitativas entre las zonas en donde fueron colectados.

Sólo 5 especies, *Rhychonycteris naso*, *Macrophyllum macrophyllum*, *Furipterus horrens*, *Thyroptera tricolor* y *Lasiurus ega*, todas ellas escasas en la zona (Ascorra et.al., 1991), generalmente con refugios en partes abiertas y en la mayoría de los casos representadas por un solo ejemplar, resultaron sin parásitos. Esto indica que el 87.8 % de las especies de murciélagos resultaron ser hospedadoras de alguna especie de parásitos.

PARÁSITOS

Se colectaron un gran total de 8,040 ectoparásitos (tabla 2) distribuidos de la siguiente forma:

Diptera pupipara

Streblidae Kolenati,1863. (STR). Esta familia, formada por individuos exclusivamente parásitos de murciélagos, generalmente Phyllostomidae, es la mejor representada entre los dípteros, de ella se colectaron 1332 individuos y es bien conocida de Perú (Wenzel,1970, Koepcke,1987).

Nycteribiidae Samouelle,1819. (NYC). Este grupo de dípteros, tan adaptados a la vida parasitaria, es más frecuentemente encontrado en Vespertilionidae y siempre son más escasos que los Streblidae, en nuestro caso solamente colectamos 29 individuos en *Myotis* spp. El grupo es conocido de Perú desde la revisión de Guimaraes y D'Andretta (1956).

Acarina: Mesostigmata

Macronyssidae Oudemans,1936. (MAC). Este grupo de parásitos se encuentra sobre todos los vertebrados terrestres, sin embargo algunos géneros, con gran biodiversidad, son exclusivos de los murciélagos (Radovski 1967,1985) en donde son relativamente abundantes, aunque difíciles de recolectar en muestreos de rutina al punto que ni Fonseca (1948) ni (Radovski op.cit.) en sus revisiones mencionan material de Perú. En Pakitza se encontraron 1137 ejemplares en una gran variedad de hospedadores.

Spinturnicidae Oudemans,1902. (SPI). Esta familia, exclusiva de murciélagos, está bien representada en la mayoría de las colecciones, 882 ejemplares en la muestra, sin embargo tampoco aparece señalada para Perú en ninguna de las revisiones del grupo (Rudnick,1960; Webb y Loomis,1977).

Familia indeterminada. (ACA). Se colectaron 9 hembras, sobre 7 *Noctilio albiventris*, de una especie de ácaro mesostigmatido que no ha podido ser asignada a ninguna de las familias de ácaros parásitos de mamíferos y que parece ser un Uropodido.

Tabla 1.—*Hospedadores colectados en las diferentes zonas de muestreo.*

Especie de murciélago	zonas de muestreo[1]						
	1[2]	2	3	4	5	6	7
Rhynchonycteris naso	0/1						
Noctilio albiventris	1/1	40/40					14/14
Micronycteris megalotis	1/1						
Micronycteris minuta	2/2						
Macrophyllum macrophyllum		0/1					
Tonatia silvicola	1/2			2/2	3/3		
Phyllostomus elongatus	2/3		5/5		1/1		1/1
Phyllostomus hastatus	11/11			1/1	3/3	1/1	
Phylloderma stenops	1/1		1/1		1/1		
Trachops cirrhosus	4/4		1/1		2/2		
Glossophaga commissarisi	2/2				1/1		
Glossophaga soricina	1/2			1/2	0/2		
Lonchophylla thomasi					2/4		
Anoura caudifer					1/1		
Choeroniscus minor	1/1						
Carollia brevicauda	12/15		6/6	2/3	9/10		1/1
Carollia castanea	27/31	0/1	2/2	0/1	9/10		
Carollia perspicillata	18/18		1/2	1/1	12/12		2/2
Rhinophylla pumilio	3/3			1/1	1/1		
Sturnira lilium	6/10			0/1	2/2		
Uroderma bilobatum	1/3				2/2		
Uroderma magnirostrum	1/3						
Platyrrhinus brachycephalus	6/6			1/1	1/1	1/1	
Platyrrhinus helleri	9/10			2/2			
Platyrrhinus infuscus							1/1
Vampyrodes caraccioli					2/2		
Vampyressa bidens					1/1		
Vampyressa pusilla	1/1				1/1		
Mesophylla macconnelli	2/3				0/1		
Artibeus anderseni	5/11						
Artibeus jamaicensis	7/8			9/10	13/15	1/1	
Artibeus lituratus	9/10				10/11		
Artibeus obscurus	8/19			2/8	7/11	1/1	
Diphylla ecaudata					2/2		
Furipterus horrens	0/1						
Thyroptera tricolor	0/1						
Lasiurus ega							0/1
Myotis 3 spp	4/4	1/1	1/1		8/9		7/7
Molossus molossus	1/1						

[1] Según se indican en Materiales y Métodos
[2] parasitados / total revisados

Acarina: Ixodides

Argasidae Canestrini,1890. (ARG). Las garrapatas suaves son comúnmente encontradas, en forma larval, en murciélagos que viven en colonias bien establecidas y en donde hay gran intercambio de parásitos entre sus miembros. Nuestra colección contiene 300 ejemplares, casi todos sobre *Noctilio albiventris*, el cual normalmente está parasitado por especies del género *Ornithodoros*.

Tabla 2.—N£mero de parásitos colectados en cada especie de hospedador.

Hospedador	STR	NYC	TRO	MAC	LAB	SPI	ARG	SAR	MYO	ACA
			Parásitos[1]							
N. albiventris	849		1		426		299	2		9
M. megalotis	2	5		6		1				
M. minuta	5		3	18	9	1				
T. silvicola	9		259	14	4	21				
P. elongatus	74		70	35	72	91				
P. hastatus	139		2	248	715	374			43	
P. stenops	1		46	1	141	1				
T. cirrhosus	36		168	117		53				
G. commissarisi	4		1			3				
G. soricina	1					4				
L. thomasi	2									
A. caudifer			5							
C. minor			9		6				1	
C. brevicauda	44		221	65				4		
C. castanea	26		365	2		5		260		
C. perspicillata	34		423	17	222			29		
R. pumilio			20	13		9		2		
S. lilium	13			19	37	3				
U. bilobatum	3									
U. magnirostrum					38					
P. brachycephalus				1	39	15		1	1	
P. helleri				3	64	27		1		
P. infuscus				1		4				
V. caraccioli				13	20	9				
V. bidens					3					
V. pusilla					4	6				
M. macconnelli						4				
A. anderseni				2	9					
A. jamaicensis	29		166	112	76	139		18	1	
A. lituratus	10		47	41		78		9		
A. obscurus	22		2	7	134	12	1			
D. ecaudata	28		18							
Myotis 3 spp		29	1	362	49	24		3		
M. molossus			1	7	76				1	
TOTAL	1332	29	1825	1137	2154	882	300	327	45	9
Da	3.14	0.07	4.30	2.68	5.00	2.08	0.71	0.77	0.11	0.02
Dr	6.43	2.42	15.2	11.2	30.3	8.32	50.0	8.39	5.00	1.29

[1] Abreviaturas según Resultados

Acarina: Prostigmata

Myobiidae Megnin,1877. (MYO). Este escaso grupo de parásitos está representado en nuestra colección por 45 ejemplares del género *Eudusbabekia*.

Trombiculidae Ewing,1944. (TRO). Esta familia constituye uno de los grupos de parásitos más abundantes en los vertebrados en general y de los mamíferos en particular. En Pakitza resultaron ser el segundo grupo en importancia, despues de Labidocarpidae, con 1825 ejemplares colectados.

Acarina: Astigmata

Labidocarpidae Gunther,1942 (LAB). Esta es otra familia que solamente se encuentra como ectoparásitos de murciélagos; resultan particularmente frecuentes, como lo demuestran los 2154 ejemplares de Pakitza, sin embargo son raramente colectados y existen muchas más especies de las señaladas hasta ahora en la literatura. En la última revisión sobre el grupo, Guerrero (1992) no señala la familia en Perú.

Sarcoptidae Murray,1877. (SAR). Al igual que los Labidocarpidae, los Sarcoptidae de murciélagos son un grupo muy frecuente y abundante pero poco colectado, debido a su pequeño tamaño, como lo demuestran los 327 ejemplares que forman nuestra colección.

RELACIÓN PARÁSITO-HOSPEDADOR

El análisis comparativo, a nivel de comunidad o supracomunidad *sensu* Esch et.al. (1990), en ectoparásitos resulta muy difícil de realizar, especialmente en los ecosistemas tropicales. Existen trabajos faunísticos muy completos, como los realizados en Panamá y Venezuela bajo la dirección de R. L. Wenzel y V. Tipton (Wenzel y Tipton,1966; Handley,1976) o en Africa al sur del Sahara coordinados por F. Zumpt (Zumpt, 1961), pero éstos son, fundamentalmente, de carácter cualitativo y no cuantitativo, produciendo sólo listas de especies y cuando se cuantifica la relación parásito-hospe-dador ésta se realiza en un solo grupo taxonómico, como por ejemplo en los Spinturnicidae (Herrin y Tipton,1976), pero no se hace a nivel de la comunidad total de ectoparásitos. Esta falta de análisis a nivel comunitario, derivada de la complejidad taxonómica, es tan evidente que Marshall (1981), en uno de los trabajos más completos sobre la ecología de los insectos ectoparásitos, casi no menciona la palabra comunidad (faunula en Marshall op.cit.).

A nivel de comunidad, los resultados del material colectado en Pakitza se encuentran resumidos en las tablas 3 y 4.

En la tabla 3 se observa que de las 36 especies de murciélagos en las que se encontraron parásitos, el 47.2 % de ellas, es decir en 17, todos los individuos estaban parasitados y sólo en 4 el número de individuos parasitados es inferior al 50 %. Las densidades presentan valores elevados, con la absoluta entre 0.50 y 95.06 y una media de 18.13 parásitos por hospedador, valor muy alto resultado de las altas cargas parasitarias encontradas en los ácaros de las familias Spinturnicidae, Trombiculidae, Macronyssidae y Labidocarpidae y en dípteros Streblidae.

Con respecto a la diversidad biológica se observa en la tabla 3 que el número de unidades taxonómicas, familias en nuestro caso, no depende del tamaño de la muestra ya que el valor del coeficiente de regresión, entre el número de familias y el número de hospedadores infectados de cada especies, es 0.6021.

La diversidad ecológica está representada en la tabla 4, en la que se observan valores muy altos de diversidad, en especial en la especies del género *Phyllostomus* y en los *Artibeus* grandes, en los cuales hay varias especies con valores poblacionales muy parecidos, lo cual indicaría poca competencia entre los distintos tipos de parásitos o una facilitación entre los distintos grupos.

La competencia entre diferentes grupos está bien documentada entre los endoparásitos pero es menos conocida en ectoparásitos, refiriéndose en general a comparaciones intragrupo o sólo entre pares de grupos taxonómicos, encontrándose casos de exclusión entre malófagos y anopluros (Hopkins,1949; Mohr y Stumpf,1964), de facilitación entre especies de malófagos (Ward, 1957) y de competencia o facilitación entre especies de pulgas, dependiendo de la especie del hospedador (Evans y Freeman,1950). La complejidad del fenómeno competencia-facilitación en el parasitismo se debe a dos factores que diferencian

Tabla 3.—*Parámetros poblacionales totales en cada especie de hospedador*

Hospedadores	para[1]	Hi[2]	P	E	Dr	Da	ii
Noc. albiventris	6	56	1586	100.0	28.32	28.32	28.321428
Mic. megalotis	4	1	14	100.0	14.00	14.00	14.000000
Mic. minuta	5	2	36	100.0	18.00	18.00	18.000000
Ton. silvicola	5	6	307	85.7	51.17	43.86	37.591839
Phy. elongatus	5	9	342	90.0	38.00	34.20	30.780001
Phy. hastatus	6	16	1521	100.0	95.06	95.06	95.062500
Phy. stenops	5	3	190	100.0	63.33	63.33	63.333332
Tra. cirrhosus	4	7	374	100.0	53.43	53.43	53.428570
Glo. commissarisi	3	3	8	100.0	2.67	2.67	2.666667
Glo. soricina	2	2	5	33.3	2.50	0.83	0.277778
Lon. thomasi	1	2	2	50.0	1.00	0.50	0.250000
Ano. caudifer	1	1	5	100.0	5.00	5.00	5.000000
Cho. minor	3	1	16	100.0	16.00	16.00	16.000000
Car. brevicauda	4	29	334	82.9	11.52	9.54	7.908660
Car. castanea	4	38	653	84.4	17.18	14.51	12.253827
Car. perspicillata	5	33	725	94.3	21.97	20.71	19.530611
Rhi. pumilio	4	5	44	100.0	8.80	8.80	8.800000
Stu. lilium	4	8	72	61.5	9.00	5.54	3.408284
Uro. bilobatum	1	3	3	60.0	1.00	0.60	0.360000
Uro. magnirostrum	1	1	38	33.3	38.00	12.67	4.221780
Pla. brachycephalus	5	9	57	100.0	6.33	6.33	6.333333
Pla. helleri	4	11	96	91.7	8.73	8.00	7.333333
Pla. infuscus	2	1	5	100.0	5.00	5.00	5.000000
Vam. caraccioli	3	2	42	100.0	21.00	21.00	21.000000
Vam. bidens	1	1	3	100.0	3.00	3.00	3.000000
Vam. pusilla	2	2	10	100.0	5.00	5.00	5.000000
Mes. macconnelli	1	2	10	50.0	5.00	2.50	1.250000
Art. anderseni	2	5	11	45.5	2.20	1.00	0.454545
Art. jamaicensis	7	29	541	85.3	18.66	15.91	13.571230
Art. lituratus	5	19	185	90.5	9.74	8.81	7.970521
Art. obscurus	6	18	178	46.2	9.89	4.56	2.106509
Dip. ecaudata	2	2	46	100.0	23.00	23.00	23.000000
Myotis 3 spp	6	21	468	95.5	22.29	21.27	20.305786
Mol. molossus	4	1	85	100.0	85.00	85.00	85.000000

[1] familias de parásitos
[2] abreviaturas según Materiales y Métodos

Tabla 4.—*Índices de diversidad para cada especie de hospedador*

hospedadores	shannon	pielou	simpson	hill[1]
Noc. albiventris	1.045	0.583	0.394	0.892
Mic. megalotis	1.197	0.864	0.337	0.897
Mic. minuta	1.274	0.792	0.340	0.824
Ton. silvicola	0.628	0.390	0.720	0.742
Phy. elongatus	1.569	0.975	0.214	0.971
Phy. hastatus	1.324	0.739	0.317	0.839
Phy. stenops	0.648	0.402	0.609	0.859
Tra. cirrhosus	1.225	0.884	0.329	0.893
Glo. commissarisi	0.974	0.887	0.406	0.929
Glo. soricina	0.500	0.722	0.680	0.892
Cho. minor	0.865	0.787	0.461	0.914
Car. brevicauda	0.912	0.658	0.493	0.815
Car. castanea	0.838	0.604	0.473	0.915
Car. perspicillata	1.037	0.644	0.433	0.808
Rhi. pumilio	1.184	0.854	0.338	0.906
Stu. lilium	1.135	0.819	0.368	0.873
Pla. brachycephalus	0.824	0.512	0.538	0.815
Pla. helleri	0.816	0.589	0.525	0.842
Pla. infuscus	0.500	0.722	0.680	0.892
Vam. caraccioli	1.046	0.952	0.368	0.953
Vam. pusilla	0.673	0.971	0.520	0.981
Art. anderseni	0.474	0.684	0.702	0.886
Art. jamaicensis	1.595	0.820	0.227	0.895
Art. lituratus	1.351	0.839	0.297	0.873
Art. obscurus	0.861	0.480	0.588	0.719
Dip. ecaudata	0.669	0.966	0.524	0.978
Myotis 3 spp	0.805	0.449	0.616	0.726
Mol. molossus	0.410	0.296	0.807	0.823

los parásitos de los organismos de vida libre, por una parte no hay competencia entre parásitos por el recurso alimento ya que entre ectoparásitos, siendo la mayoría hematófagos, debe existir el recurso en cantidad suficiente, de forma que la competencia que se establece es por el uso del espacio. Así encontramos que hay una total separación espacial que minimiza la competencia, los dípteros se mueven libremente por el cuerpo del murciélago, pero en especial entre el pelo, los Trombiculidae y los Argasidae se encuentran fijados en la piel de las alas o el uropatagio, los Spinturnicidae se encuentran libres también en la piel de las alas y menos en el uropatagio, los Macronyssidae se encuentran libres en todo el cuerpo, los Labidocarpidae están fijos en los pelos modificados de la cara, patas, genitales y patagio, los Myobiidae fijos en las zonas desnudas de la cara, los Sarcoptidae fijos en los bordes de las alas y los ácaros no determinados estaban fijados en la base de las uñas de las patas.

Tabla 5.—*Valores promedios del índice de Jacard (bajo la diagonal) y de su modificación (sobre la diagonal).*

famls.	familias									
	STR	NYC	TRO	MAC	LAB	SPI	ARG	SAR	MYO	ACA
STRE	—	n.a[1]	1.4	5.1	4.9	4.0	2.3	2.3	3.3	1.2
NYC	n.a	—	0.0	3.0	0.6	0.0	n.a	3.0	n.a	n.a
TRO	0.29	0.0	—	1.5	0.6	3.3	4.6	0.6	0.0	0.0
MAC	0.41	0.52	0.20	—	1.2	1.6	0.0	1.1	0.3	n.a
LAB	0.24	0.07	0.06	0.20	—	2.2	0.0	0.3	0.5	0.9
SPI	0.54	0.0	0.28	0.33	0.20	—	0.0	1.0	0.6	n.a
ARG	0.05	n.a	0.50	0.0	0.0	0.0	—	0.0	n.a	0.0
SAR	0.16	0.17	0.12	0.02	0.01	0.15	0.0	—	2.1	0.0
MYO	0.19	n.a	0.0	0.09	0.23	0.10	n.a	0.13	—	n.a
ACA	0.13	n.a	0.0	n.a	0.05	n.a	0.0	0.0	n.a	—

[1] no aplicable, es decir ambas familias no se encuentran al mismo tiempo

Tabla 6.—*Valores de la especificidad comunitaria*

localidad	W	L	div P	div H
Pakitza (Total)	0.749	0.605	1.830	2.303
Pakitza (Loc.1)[1]	0.737	0.633	1.640	2.284
Pakitza (Loc.2)	0.000	0.934	1.025	0.067
Pakitza (Loc.3)	0.566	0.581	1.425	1.379
Pakitza (Loc.4)	0.561	0.565	1.495	1.485
Pakitza (Loc.5)	0.433	0.550	1.123	0.893
Pakitza (Loc.7)	0.417	0.487	1.373	1.207

[1] ver Materiales y Métodos

El otro factor que interviene en la vida parasitaria es la facilitación, es decir puede darse el caso que por la calidad o cantidad de un parásito, éste incide sobre la calidad y cantidad de defensas del hospedador, haciéndolo más suceptible a ser colonizado más facilmente por más individuos de la misma especie o de otras especies de parásitos. En la tabla 5 están los valores promedios del índice de Jacard y se puede observar que los Macronyssidae y los Spinturnicidae aparecen frecuentemente junto a los dípteros, es decir los grupos con alta movilidad parecen no molestarse al igual que los Trombiculidae y los Argasidae, que si bien están fijos en las mismas partes del cuerpo. En ambos casos se trata de estados larvales que tienen una parte de su ciclo de vida fuera del hospedador y de ahí su movilidad. Además esta similaridad, en su comportamiento, pareciera incidir sobre el estado fisiológico y etológico de su hospedador, hasta observarse cómo aumenta su número al encontrarse simultáneamente ambos grupos, sobre el mismo hospedador, como lo revela el valor del índice de Jacard modificado. Igualmente, grupos como los Streblidae parecieran facilitar el establecimiento de grupos fijos como Sarcoptidae y Myobiidae.

LOCALIDADES Y SUPRACOMUNIDADES

Tabla 7.—*Valores del índice comparativo de Jacard para las familias de parásitos y las especies de hospedadores.*

parásitos	hospedadores						
	1	2	3	4	5	6	7
localidad 1[1]	——	0.111	0.229	0.444	0.625	0.148	0.179
localidad 2	0.500	——	0.250	0.071	0.077	0.000	0.286
localidad 3	0.875	0.555	——	0.188	0.280	0.000	0.300
localidad 4	0.875	0.400	0.750	——	0.423	0.333	0.125
localidad 5	0.888	0.600	0.777	0.777	——	0.160	0.148
localidad 6	0.555	0.250	0.500	0.714	0.55	——	0.000
localidad 7	0.750	0.555	0.750	0.750	0.777	0.500	——

[1] ver Materiales y Métodos

La supracomunidad de parásitos, es decir todos los parásitos encontrados en todos los hospedadores revisados de una localidad determinada, puede ser analizada siguiendo dos criterios: a) la especificidad parasitaria, estimada con los índices de ancho y superposición del nicho ecológico propuestos por Pielou (1972,1975) o b) la similaridad, entre la composición cualitativa de especies, estimada por el índice de Jacard. Los resultados de ambas están expresados en las tablas 6 y 7.

En la tabla 6 se observa que hay poca especificidad parasitaria intralocalidad como resultado directo del nivel taxonómico en que se está trabajando, familias.

Aún así debe resaltarse que en ningún caso hay una identidad total, es decir no todas las especies de murciélagos comparten los mismos tipos de parásitos, ni siquiera en los sitios donde la muestra es menor, como es el caso de la localidad 2 que siendo la representada por el menor número de hospedadores, éstos no comparten ninguna familia de parásitos.

Los resultados obtenidos al comparar cualitativamente 2 localidades entre sí, expresados en la tabla 7, nos indican que no hay ninguna pareja de localidades que presenten identidad cualitativa y aunque las especies de parásitos encontradas deben depender de las especies de murciélagos y por lo tanto a una mayor similitud entre las comunidades de hospedadores le debe corresponder una mayor similitud de las comunidades de parásitos, el coeficiente de correlación entre los valores del índice de Jacard para hospedadores y para los parásitos es relativamente bajo, 0.720, luego es posible que en las zonas de muestreo haya poblaciones de murciélagos diferentes caracterizadas por distintas parasitofaunas, como ya se ha demostrado en otras localidades (Guerrero en prep.).

AGRADECIMIENTOS

El autor agradece a Don E. Wilson, director del Programa BIOLAT, por la oportunidad de realizar este trabajo. A Abelardo Sandoval por la excelente labor logística que permitió maximizar el trabajo de campo. A César F. Ascorra y su grupo por colectar e identificar la gran mayoría de los murciélagos usados en este trabajo.

LITERATURA CITADA

Anciaux de Faveaux, M. 1971-1976. Catalogue des acariens parasites et commensaux des chiropteres. Documents de Travail Institut Royal des Sciences Naturelles de Belgique. 7:1-637 (7 partes)

Ascorra, C. F., D. E. Wilson y M. Romo. 1991. Lista anotada de los quirópteros del Parque Nacional Manu, Perú. Publicaciones del Museo de Historia Natural. Serie A Zoología 42:1-14

Brennan, J. M. 1970. *Colicus*, a new neotropical genus with descriptions of two new species and a key to included species. Journal of Medical Entomology 7:271-273

Esch, G. W., A. W. Shostak, D. J. Marcogliese y T. M. Goater. 1990. Patterns and processes in helminth parasite communities: an overview. Pp. 1-19, *in* Parasite Communities: Patterns and Processes (G. W. Esch, A. O. Bush y J. M. Aho, eds.). Chapman and Hall, New York, 335

Erwin, T. L. 1990. Natural history of the carabid beetles at the BIOLAT Biological Station, Rio Manu, Pakitza, Peru. Revista Peruana de Entomología 33:1-85

Evans, F. C. y R. B. Freeman. 1950. On the relationship of some mammal fleas to their hosts. Annals of the Entomological Society of America 43:320-333

Fonseca, Flavio da. 1948. A monograph of the genera and species of Macronyssidae

Oudemans,1936 (synom.: Liponissidae Vitzthum,1931) (Acari). Proceeding of the Zoological Society of London 118:249-334

Guerrero, R. 1979. The structure of the endoparasite helminth communities of rodents in an urban gradient. Ph.D. thesis, Polish Academy of Sciences, Warszawa, 148 pp.

Guerrero, R. 1990 Streblidae (Diptera:Pupipara) parásitos de murciélagos de Venezuela (Sistemática, Ecología y Evolución). Trabajo de Ascenso, Universidad Central de Venezuela, Caracas, 370 pp.

Guerrero, R. 1992. Catálogo de los Labidocarpidae (Acarina, Listrophoroidea) parásitos de los murciélagos (Mammalia, Chiroptera) neotropicales. Studies on Neotropical Fauna and Environment 27:19-41

Guimaraes, L. R. y M. A. V. D'Andretta. 1956. Sinopse dos Nycteribiidae (Diptera) do Novo Mundo. Arquivos de Zoologia do Estado de Sao Paulo 10:1-184

Handley, C. O. 1976. Mammals of the Smithsonian Venezuelan Project. Brigham Young University Science Bulletin, Biological Series 20(5):1-91

Herrin, C. S. y V. J. Tipton. 1976. Spinturnicid mites of Venezuela (Acarina:Spinturnicidae). Brigham Young University Science Bulletin, Biological Series 20:(2)1-72

Hopkins, G. H. E. 1949. The host-associations of the lice of mammals. Proceedings of the Zoological Society of London 119:387-604

Kisielewska, K. 1970a. On the Theoretical foundations of Parasitosinecology. Bulletin de la Academie Polonaisedes Sciences, Serie C, 18:103-106

Koepcke, J. 1987. Ökologische studien an einer Fledermaus-artengemeinschaft im tropischen Regenwald von Peru. Ph.D. thesis, Ludwig-Maximilians-Universität, München,439 pp.

Kohls, G. M.; C. M. Clifford y E. K. Jones. 1969. The systematics of the subfamily Ornithodorinae (Argasidae).IV.- Eight new species of Ornithodoros from the Western Hemisphere. Annals of the Entomoligical Society of America 62:1035-1043

Magurran, A. L. 1988. Ecological Diversity and its Measuring.Princenton University Press, New Jersey, 179 pp.

Marshall, A. G. 1981. The Ecology of Ectoparasitic Insects. Academic Press, London, 459 pp.

Marshall, A. G. 1982 Ecology of Insects Ectoparasitic on Bats. Pp. 369-401 in Ecology of Bats (T. H. Kunz ed.).Plenum Press, New York, 432 pp.

Mohr, C. O. y W. A. Stumpf. 1964. Louse and chigger infestations as related to host size and home ranges of small mammals. Transations 29th North American Wildlife Natural Research Conference Pp. 181-195

Nutting, W. B. 1985. Prostigmata -Mammalia. Validation of Coevolutionary Phylogenies. Pp. 569-640 in Coevolution of Parasitic Arthropods and Mammals (K. C. Kim ed.). John Wiley and Sons, New York, 800 pp.

Pielou, E. C. 1972. Niche width and niche overlap: a methodfor measuring them. Ecology 53:687-692

Pielou, E. C. 1975. Ecological Diversity. John Wiley & Sons,New York, 385 pp.

Pielou, E. C. 1979. Biogeography. John Wiley & Sons, New York 351 pp.

Radovsky, F. J. 1967. The Macronyssidae and Laelapidae (Acarina:Mesostigmata) parasitic on bats. University of California Publications in Entomology 46:1-288

Radovsky, F. J. 1985. Evolution of Mammalian Mesostigmate mites. Pp. 441-504 in Coevolution of Parasitic Arthropods and Mammals (K. C. Kim ed.). John Wiley and Sons, New York, 800 pp.

Radovsky, F. J. y D. P. Furman. 1969. An unusual new genus and species of Macronyssidae parasitic on a disc-wingedbat. Journal of Medical Entomology 6:385-393

Rudnick, A. 1960. A revision of the mites of the family Spinturnicidae (Acarina). University of CaliforniaPublications in Entomology 17:157-284

Ueshima, N. 1972. New World Polyctenidae (Hemiptera), with special reference to Venezuelan species. Brigham Young University Science Bulletin, Biological Series 17:13-21

Ward, R. A. 1957. A study of the host distribution and some relationships of biting lice (Mallophaga) parasitic on birds of the order Tinamifirmes. Part II. Annals of the Entomological Society of America 50:452-459

Webb, J. P. y R. B. Loomis. 1977. Ectoparasites Pp.57-119 *in* Biology of the bats of the New World Family Phyllostomatidae. (R. J. Baker, J. K. Jones y D. C. Carter eds.). Part II. Special Publications of Museum of the Texas Tech University

Wenzel, R. L. 1970. A catalogue of the Diptera of the Americas south of the United States. Museu de Zoologia, Universidade de Sao Paulo 100:1-25

Wenzel, R. L. y V. J. Tipton (editores). 1966. Ectoparasites of Panama. Field Museum of Natural History, Chicago, 861 pp.

Zumpt, F. 1961. The Arthropods Parasites of Vertebrates in Africa South of the Sahara (Ethiopian Region). (Vol. I) (Chelicerata). South African Institute for Medical Research, Johanesburg, 457 pp.

Amblyopinodes amazonicus new species (Coleoptera:Staphyliniidae) a parasite of rodents from Pakitza, Perú

Ricardo Guerrero

Instituto de Zoología Tropical
Facultad de Ciencias – U.C.V.
Apdo. 47058, Caracas 1041A, Venezuela

ABSTRACT

Amblyopinus amazonicus n.sp., a parasite of *Oryzomys* spp from Pakitza, Perú is describrd. The species is related with the *piceus* group based on the sclerotized movable piece, and differs from it in lacking claviform setae in sternum VI; also is distinguishable from *A. major* in the reduced number of teeth on ventral margin of parameres.

INTRODUCTION

Amblyopinodes Seevers, 1955 contains aproximately 15 morphotypes, species and subspecies, (Barrera & Machado-Allison, 1965; Machado-Allison & Barrera, 1972) mostly parasites in cricetids from Southern South America (Argentina, Southern Brazil, Paraguay and Uruguay), peruvian Andes, Guyana Highlands in Venezuela and Northeast Brazil, consequently the group is found in montane habitats and temperate or even cold climates (Machado-Allison y Barrera, 1972). Searching for parasites of small mammals in Pakitza, peruvian Amazonas, some Amblyopinini were found, the first in the amazonas region which belong to a new species described as follows.

The material is deposited in the Colección de Parasitología, Museo de Biología, Universidad Central de Venezuela, Caracas (CP-MBUCV), Departamento de Entomología, Museo de Historia Natural, Universidad Nacional Mayor de San Marcos, Lima (MUSM), and National Museum of Natural History, Smithsonian Institution, Washington, (USNM).

Ricardo Guerrero

DESCRIPTIONS

Amblyopinodes amazonicus new species

Males: 7.7-8.7 mm
Female: 7.7 mm

Description: Male: Head: Labrum small, arcuated, with 8-10 short but strong setae on each side, 2 longer. Eyes small, with facetation hardly distinguishable; ocular margin with 4-5 stout setae, one longer. Antennae relatively long, with first segment 40% longer than second; antennnal groove wide, deep, without setae on ventral margin. Submenton large, wide, with anterior margin very slightly concave, and 3-5 small setae on each side, and 2 innermost larger than others. Gula long with pair of macrosetae, close to each other, about 6-12 setae on each side of anterior half of which anterior-interior pair longer than others. *Thorax:* Pronotum wide, large, with protruding anterior angles; posterior margin slightly concave in middle, with 4 macrosetae on each side, outermost in angle. Total length of pronotum approximately one-half distance between posterior angles and equal to distance between anterior angles. Elytra covered by uniformly long setae and wider than long. Prosternum with anterior margin concave, 2 characteristic macrosetae, and 20-30 small setae on each side. Mesosternum with apex slightly

		Left side				Right side			
		H1	P1	P2	A	H	P1	P2	A
T	II	2	2	2	2	2	2	2	2
E	III	2	2	2	3	2	2	2	2
R	IV	1	2	2	2	1	1	2	2
G	V	1	1	2	2	2	1	2	2
I	VI	1	1	2	2	2	1	2+1	2
T	VII	2+12	1+1	2+1	2+1	1+1	1	2+1	2+1
E	VIII	3	2	4	—	3	3	2	—
S									
T	III³	9	8	10	11	7	7	9	11
E	IV³	5	4	5	6	6	3	6	6
R	V³	2	2	2	1	2	2	2	1
N	VI	1+1	2+1	3+1	4+2	2+1	3+1	3+1	4+2
I	VII	2+1	3+1	4+2	4+2	1+1	3+2	4+2	4+2
T	VIII	6	7	7	7	6	8	7	8
E									

Table 1.- Abdomen chaetotaxy

1. H = Holotype
    P1 = Paratype ex *O. capito*
    P2 = Paratype ex *O. niditus*
    A = Alotype
2. marginal + submarginal setae
3. claviform setae

projected between coxae; chaetotaxy consisting of 5 long and 10-12 shorter setae. Metasternum with sinus deep and long setae limited to basal two-thirds. *Legs:* Prothoracic legs as in other species of genus; V tarsal segment of mesothoracic legs with three pairs of strong setae, V tarsal segment of metathoracic legs with four pairs of stout setae, plus three spiniform setae. *Abdomen:* Tergites II and III with 2 macrosetae on each side; IV, V, and IV with 1-2 rarely 3; VII 1-2 marginal and 1 submarginal; VIII with 1 marginal and 2-4 submarginals on each side. Sternites III to V with 7-10, 3-6, and 2 claviform setae respectively. Sternite VI with 1-3 marginal and 1 submarginal macro; VII with 1-4 marginals, and 1-2 submarginal macrosetae; VIII with 6-8 macrosetae on each side and sinus wide and deep as in A. *adae* and A. *guimaraesi* (individual variations on table 1). *Modified segments and genitalia:* Tergite IX subtriangular, protruding posterior margin with 1 long seta on each angle. Sternite IX long with straight posterior margin, cover by small setae. Cerci strong, with long mostly marginal setae. Phallic organ with long, flat,

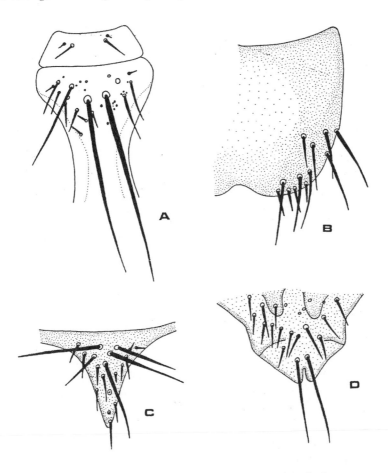

Fig. 1.– *Amblyopinodes amazonicus*, new species: A, *gula and submentum*; B, *male sternite VIII, omitting surface setae*; C, *Mesosternum*; D, *Metasternum*.

Fig. 2.– *Amblyopinodes*
amazonicus, new species:
A, *Phallic organ*; B,
Apex of parameres.

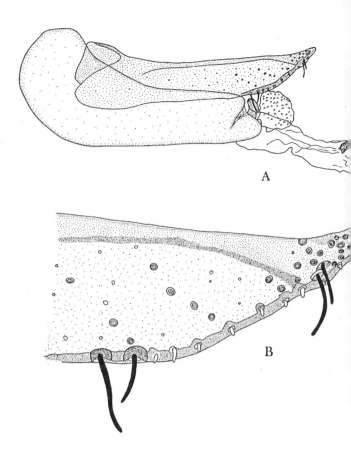

A

B

sclerotized parameres; apex rounded and elevated. Ventral setae of parameres short, distal pair close to apex. Ventral margin with 5-11 marginal teeth. Movable sclerotized piece large, with apical margin striated, almost parallel margins as in *A. piceus.*

Female: Stronger than male. Chaetotaxy of tergites and sternites in Table 1. Cerci slender. Coxites slender, long, and surpassing apex of cerci, with two long and two shorter apical

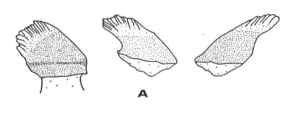

A

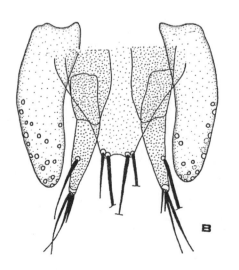

B

macrosetae in each one. Tergite IX slightly concave with 2 apical setae of different length on each corner.

Holotype: Male ex *Oryzomys capito* (Rodentia: Cricetidae), Pakitza, Madre de Dios, PERU, February 1993 (MUSM).

Alotype: Female, same data as holotype.

Paratype: Male same data as holotype but in CP-MBUCV.

Paratype: Male same data as holotype but ex *Oryzomys nitidus*, in USNM.

Fig. 3.– *Amblyopinodes amazonicus, new*
species: A, *Sclerotized movable piece,*
holotype, paratype ex O. capito, and
paratype ex O. nitidus; B, *Female tergite IX,*
coxites, and cerci.

Etymology.- Latin, "from Amazonas", the species constitutes the first record of the genus for the amazonian basin.

Remarks.- Machado-Allison (1963) in his paper established 4 groups of species, among these the group I containing *Amblyopinodes piceus piceus* (Brethés, 1926) and *A. p. distinctus* Machado-Allison, 1962, characterized by having claviform setae in four sternites, III to VI, the other species have only three by the absence of claviform setae on sternite VI. Later Machado-Allison and Barrera (1972) described *Amblyopinodes major*, with the movable sclerotized piece similar to *piceus*, but having claviform setae in sternites III to V. *A. amazonicus* n. sp. is related to *A. piceus* group, *A. major* and *A. adae* Machado-Allison, 1962; by the shape of the movable sclerotized piece but distinguishable of *A. p. piceus* and *A. p. distinctus* by the absence of claviform setae on sternite VI; *A. major* is bigger, the phallic organ less massive, parameres have 23 marginal and submarginal teeth (5-11 in **amazonicus**) and the apex of parameres has a couple of macrosetae well separated but in *amazonicus* the macrosetae are close; *A. adae* differs by chaetotaxy of meso and metasternal processes and the shape of parameres.

ACKNOWLEDGEMENTS

Field work in Peru was funded by BIOLAT program of the National Museum of Natural History, Smithsonian Institution. This is the contribution No. 85 of the Smithsonian Institution's Biological Diversity in Latin America (BIOLAT) Program.

LITERATURE CITED

Barrera, A. & C.E. Machado-Allison, 1965. *Coleópteros ectoparásitos de mamíferos.* Ciencia (México) 23:201-208.

Machado-Allisons, C.E. 1962. *Nuevos estafilinídeos parásitos de roedores y clave para las especies del género Amblyopinodes Seevers, 1955* (Col. Staphylinidae). —Papéis Avulsos do Departamento de Zoollogia. Sao Paulo 15:81-90.

Machado-Allison, C.E., 1963. Revisión del Género Amblyopinodes Seevers, 1955 (Coleoptera, Staphylinidae).— Acta Biológica Venezuelica 3:371-416.

Machado-Allison, C.E., & Alfredo Barrera. 1972. *Venezuelan Amblyopinini (Insecta: Coleoptera, Staphylinidae).*— Brigham Young University Science Bulletin, Biological Series 17:1-14.

The *Basilia junquiensis* Species-Group (Diptera: Nycteribiidae) with Description of a New Species from Pakitza, Perú

RICARDO GUERRERO

Instituto de Zoología Tropical. Facultad de Ciencias - U.C.V.
Apdo. 47058, Caracas 1041A, Venezuela

ABSTRACT

Basilia manu, a new species of nycteribiid batfly is described from Pakitza, Southeastern Peru. *Basilia anceps* is redescribed on basis of Venezuelan material. The host and geographic distribution of the *Basilia junquiensis* species-group is analyzed, and the males and females of the group are characterized.

INTRODUCTION

The group *junquiensis* was established by Guimaraes & D'Andretta (1956) as group IV, characterized for its «ausência do 3° tergito visível e pelo grande desenvolvimento das placas que formanm o 5° esternito, com o desaparecimento concomitante de um dos esternitos anteriores...», containing 2 species: B. *junquiensis* Guimaraes, 1946 and B. *anceps* Guimaraes & D'Andretta (1956). However, Theodor (1967) included them within the the group *speiseri*, remarking these 2 species are very closely related between them, and could form a subdivision within the *speiseri* group.

In the present work, B. *anceps* is redescribed on the basis of material from Southern Venezuela, and a new species of the Peruvian Amazonia is described, justifying the revalidation of the group as it was originally established.

Morphological nomenclature is the same used by Theodor (1967). Measurements are expressed in microns or any if indication is given, mean values followed by maximum and minimum values, total length from the anterior thorax margin to the abdomen end; number of setae is given by mode and its minimum and maximum values. The material is deposited in the Colección de Parasitología, Museo de Biología, Universidad Central de Venezuela, Caracas (CP-MBUCV), Departamento de Entomología, Museo de Historia Natural, Universidad Nacional Mayor de San Marcos, Lima (MUSM), and National Museum of Natural History, Smithsonian Institution, Washington, (USNM).

DESCRIPTION

Basilia manu n. sp.

Basilia sp (b) Guimaraes & D'Andretta, 1956:125

Females: 1.98 (1.80-2.16) mm

Males: 1.83 (1.66-1.98) mm

Description: Head:

Weakly laterally compressed; anterior dorsum with an oblique series of 3 setae on each side, hindmost pair shorter and slightly behind the level of eyes; anterior margin of each gena with 3 (1-4) short setae on surface and 3 (2-4) longer setae lower; postgena with 7 (4-9) setae on each side. Palpi with a long apical seta, 2/5 as long as its terminal bristle, and 8 (7-10) lateroventral setae. Eyes with 3 facets, but only 2 full developed (Fig. 1-A), on a pigmented common basis, as in *B. nana*. Theca subquadrate, longer than wide, about 3/5 as long as labella.

Thorax:

Wider than long, measuring 720 (660-740) long, 850 (800-920) of maximum width in females and 660 (630-690) and 780 (760-800), respectively, in males. Mesonotum slightly broadening before posterior margin, which is weakly reflexed dorsally but without the median digitiform process; with 7 (6-8) notopleural setae. Thoracic ctenidium with 18 (16-19) spines. Posterior margin of sternal plate concave, fringed with setae of varied length and robustness, 3 or 4 pairs of which longer; mesosternal setae shorter than metasternal setae.

Legs:

Long and slightly laterally compressed; lengths of femora and tibiae I-III of female: 705 (663-725), 832 (780-881), 805 (764-858) and 552 (523-593), 608 (577-632), 601 (569-632), respectively, and of male: 654 (601-725), 763 (725-780), 754 (725-780) and 551 (530-577), 599 (569-624), 579 (538-624). Tibiae with 3 rows of ventral bristles. Basitarsus III about 2.34 (2.21-2.56) times as long as three consecutive tarsomeres in females and 2.17 (2.00-2.29) in males.

Abdomen (Female):

First tergite half as long as tergal plate II, margin rounded, fringed by 22-29 setae, mostly medium to long length in middle, irregularly interspersed with few short, strong ones; 5-13 submarginal short setae; discal setae short, two patches; median suture rather evident. Tergal plate II twice as long as wide, with lateral margins nearly straight, posterior margin slightly rounded; hind margin fringed with 6 (4-7) long strong setae interspersed with 1 or 2 spinelike setae; bare surface, except for a group on the anterior lateral corner of 8 (4-8) medium-sized light setae, measuring 101-211 long, and 7 (6-12) short setae, 27-101 long, near the midline. Anal segment slightly conical, with long posterior setae and short lateral setae. Lateral connexivum (i.e. area between abdominal spiracles III and VII) with very

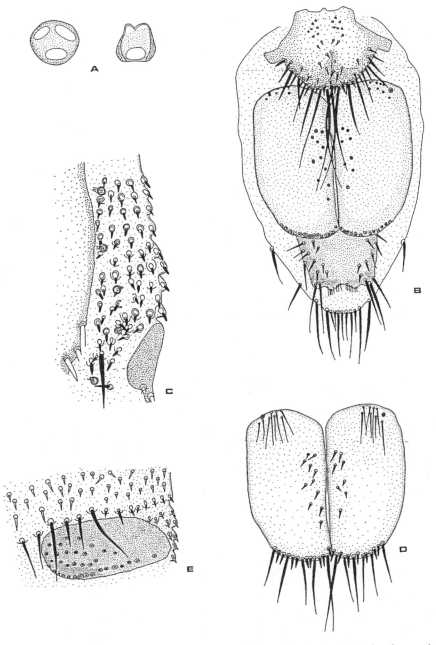

Fig. 1.– *Basilia manu*, new species, female: A, *eye, apical and lateral view*; B, *dorsal view of abdomen (omitting setae of tergal plate II)*; C, *lateral connexivum*; D, *tergal plate II*; E, *anterior part of abdomen, ventral view (omitting setae of sternite V)*.

short, spinelike postulate setae. Sternite I+II 784 (764-796) long (including spines of ctenidium); ctenidium of posterior margin with 51-66 spines. Sternites III and IV are not separable, represented by 4-5 rows of spinelike postulate setae and a median posterior row of 10 (8-11) long setae. Sternites V and VI sclerotized and divided on midline, each one thus with two lateral sclerites; each plate of sternite V with 3-4 rows of shorter setae on the midline and a row of long setae on hind margin. Each sclerite of sternite VI with 1 (1-3) setae close to midline and posterior margin fringed with 4-5 long setae interspersed with 1 short seta. Terminal sternite conical, with few discal setae. Adanal plate arcuated with 3 long and 2-3 short setae on distal end. Anal sclerite small with 2-6 setae. Genital plate with 3-4 setae, the external pair long.

Abdomen (Male):

Tergite I shorter than wide; surface with 15-17 small discal setae forming two patches, fringe of posterior margin interrupted medially, composed of 14-18 moderatelly long setae in two patches. Surface of tergites II-VI always bare; tergite II-IV with short and long setae arranged alternatively on the hind margin; posterior fringes of tergite V-VI complete with 1 pair of outstandingly long bristles; Dorsal length of anal segment slightly longer than its width at base, setose posterolaterally and posterior fringes stronger. Sternite I+II 377 (367-398) long; ctenidium of posterior margin with 52-61 spines; sternite III with 2-3 rows, and sternite IV with 1-2 rows of preapical short setae; sternite V longer, with 1-2 rows of longer setae and 11 (11-13) spines, 39-62 long, on the median region of the hind border. Ventral surface of anal segment setose. Clasper long and slender, straight with 8 (6-8) strong setae ventrally, apex pointed, darkened and distinctly decurved. Genitalia rather similar to that of *Basilia* sp (b) of Guimaraes and D'Andretta,1956; aedeagus long and slender, 289 (274-306) long, nearly parallelsided, serrated on dorsal margin with some minute teeth, apex narrowing but pointless; Paramere forked distally, 208 (195-218) long, aedeagal apodeme 389 (336-432) long; Basal arc with very broad, pointed lateral arms; deckplate longer than wide narrowing posteriorly.

Holotype:
Female ex *Myotis riparius* (Chiroptera: Vespertilionidae), Pakitza, Madre de Dios, PERU, February, 1993 (MUSM)

Alotype:
Male, same data as holotype

Paratypes:
4 males and 12 females, same data as holotype (in MUSM, USNM, and CP-MBUCV); 5 males and 2 females, same data as holotype but ex *Myotis simus* (in MUSM, USNM, and CP-MBUCV); 1 male and 1 female, same data as holotype but ex *Myotis nigricans* (MUSM); 1 male, same data as holotype but ex *Myotis albescens* (MUSM).

Etymology.--
Derived directly from the type locality, which is the Manu Reserved Zone, a big park of tropical forest in southeastern Perú.

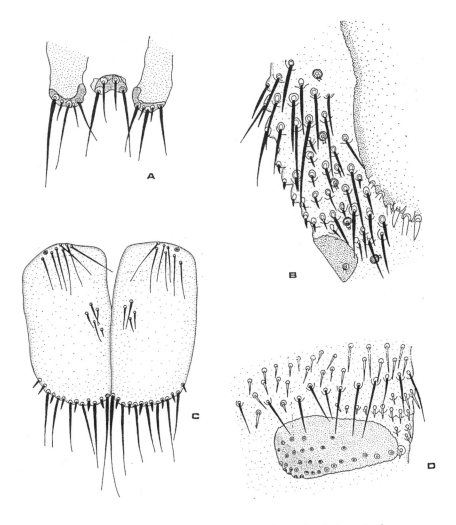

Fig. 2.– Basilia manu, new species, female: A,postgenital and adanal plates. Basilia anceps, female: B,lateral connexivum; C, tergal plate II; D, anterior part of abdomen, ventral view (omitting setae of sternite V).

Remarks.--

Our material resembles that of the species Basilia junquiensis Guimaraes,1946 and B. anceps Guimaraes & D'Andretta,1956, but is differentiated by the abdominal lateral conexivum setae very short, spinelike, while in B. junquiensis all setae are long, and in B. anceps all are short extending farther to spiracle IV; in these species, the row of setae that represents the margin of sternum IV are of the same size and much longer than the anterior setae, while in B. manu only the 8-11 median setae are long and the lateral setae are as short as the anterior setae; furthermore, in our species, each sclerite of sternum VI presents 1-2 anterior setae to the row of the hind margin, while the two cited species have no setae on the surface of sternum VI. Males are known only for B. anceps, its description have no figures (Guimaraes,1966) and is too general to be compared with our specimen, however, Guimaraes (op. cit.) reported 8 spines on the margin of sternite V (IV in his nomenclature), while in our specimen there are more than 11. Guimaraes and D'Andretta (1956) described 1 male, from *Myotis nigricans* of Cusco, Peru, named *Basilia* sp (b), and they pointed out that it is completely different to the males of the other known species, specially by the parameres forked distally and the aedeagus long and slender; our material shows the same characteristics and, moreover, following the scale of drawings of the authors, the aedeagus is approximately 289 µ long and parameres 206 µ long, measurements that are also coincident with our specimen; this considerations, together with the fact that the material came from *Myotis* of the Cusco zone, and the location of our material is at the slope of the Cusco mountains, allows us to assume that *Basila manu* y *Basila* sp (b) of Guimaraes and D'Andretta are the same species.

Basilia anceps Guimaraes & D'Andretta, 1956

Basilia anceps Guimaraes & D'Andretta, 1956:113

Females: 1.68 (1.54-1.80) mm
Males: 1.46 (1.40-1.54) mm

Description: Head:

Weakly compressed laterally; Antero-dorsally with an oblique series of 3 (2-3) setae on each side, hindmost pair shorter and slightly behind the level of eyes; anterior margin of each gena with 3 (2-4) short setae on surface and 3 (3-4) long setae below; postgena with 6 (4-9) setae on each side. Palpi with a long apical seta, 2/5 as long as its terminal bristle, and 8 (7-9) lateroventral setae. Theca subquadrate, longer than wide, about 3/5 as long as labella.

Thorax:

Wider than long, measuring 650 (610-670) long, by a maximum width of 770 (730-800) in females and 630 (610-670)and 720 (690-750), respectively, in males. Mesonotum widening slightly after middle, posterior margin weakly reflexed dorsally but without the median digitiform process; with 7 (6-8) notopleural setae. Thoracic ctenidium with 17 (15-18) spines. Posterior margin of sternal plate deeply concave in middle, fringed with setae of varied length and robustness,of wich 3 or 4 pairs are long; mesosternal setae finer and shorter than metasternal setae.

Legs:

Long and little laterally compressed; lengths of femora and tibiae I-III: 646 (606-694), 762 (741-780), 766 (741-780) and 491 (429-530), 554 (491-593), 624 (476-562), respectively in female; 627 (593-694), 733 (694-796), 730 (694-796) and 496 (468-530), 543 (523-562), 526 (484-570), respectively in male. Tibiae

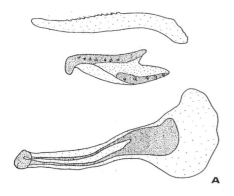

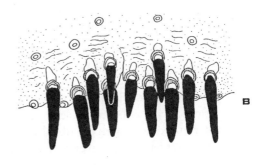

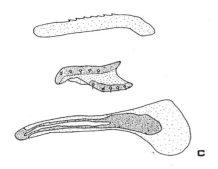

Fig. 3.– *Basilia manu, new species, male:* A, *genitalia;* B, *espiniform setae of fifth sternite (omitting other setae).Basilia anceps, male:* C, *genitalia;* D, *espiniform setae of fifth sternite (omitting other setae).*

with 3 rows of ventral bristles. Basitarsus III about 2.27 (2.18-2.47) times as long as three sucessive tarsomeres in females and 2.26 (2.11-2.46) in males.

Abdomen (Female):

First tergite half as long as tergal plate II, margin rounded, fringed by 18-21 setae, mostly medium to long length in middle, irregularly interspersed with few short, strong setae; short discal setae, forming two patches; median suture rather evident. Tergal plate II twice as long as wide, with lateral margins straight, posterior margin slightly rounded; hind margin fringed with 6-7 long strong setae interspersed with 1, rarely 2 spinelike setae; bare surface, except for a group of 7 (6-10) setae of medium size, measuring 78-195 long, light setae on the anterior lateral corner and 4 (3-6) short setae, lengths 93-141, sometimes 1 seta measuring 23 long near the midline in a patch. Anal segment slightly conical, with long posterior setae and short dorsal setae Lateral connexivum with long setae on upper half, and short, spinelike setae behind spiracle IV, there are also long setae forming a row between spiracles and tergal plate II, and in a patch anterior to spiracle VII.

671

Sternite I+II 714 (686-741) long (including spines of ctenidium); ctenidium of posterior margin with 52-63 spines. Sternites III and IV not separable, represented by 4-5 rows of short setae and a posterior row of very long setae (Fig. 2-D). Sternites V and VI sclerotized and divided on midline, thus each one with two lateral sclerites; each plate of sternite V with 3 rows of short setae on the midline and a row of long setae on hind margin. Sclerites of sternite VI with posterior margin fringed with 3-4 long setae irregularly interspersed with short setae. Terminal sternite conical, with few discal setae. Adanal plate arcuated, with 3-4 longer and 2 shorter setae on distal end. Anal sclerite small, with 2-5 setae. Genital plate with 3-4 setae, the external pair longer.

Abdomen (Male):

Tergite I slightly shorter than wide; surface with 12-14 small discal setae in two patches, fringe of posterior margin interrupted medianly, composed of 14-18 moderately long setae in two patches. Surface of tergites II-VI always bare; tergite II-IV with short and long setae, arranged alternately on the hind margin; posterior fringes of tergite V complete, with 1-2 pairs of outstandingly long bristles, and of tergite VI with 3-4 pairs; dorsum of anal segment slightly longer than wide at base, posterolaterally setose, posterior fringes stronger. Sternite I+II 362 (343-406) long; ctenidium of posterior margin with 48-50 spines; sternite III with 2-3 rows, and sternite IV with 1-2 rows of preapical short setae; sternite V more long, with 2 rows of long setae and 7 (6-9) spines, 19-36 long, on median zone of the hind border. Ventral surface of anal segment setose. Clasper long, slender and straight, with 8 (7-8) strong setae ventrally, apex pointed, darkened and distinctly decurved. Aedeagus 225 (215-236) long, nearly parallel sided, serrated on dorsal margin with few minute teeth, apex pointless; Paramere forked distally, 160 (154-166) long, aedeagal apodeme 335 (328-342) long; Basal arc with very broad, pointed lateral arms; deck plate longer than wide narrowing posteriorly.

Material examined.--

Venezuela: AMAZONAS, 3 females and 1 male ex *Myotis riparius*, Culebra, Rio Cunucunuma, 16.III.85 (CP-MBUCV 0495); 3 females and 2 males, same host and locality, 11.X.1988 (CP-MBUCV 3293); BOLIVAR, 1 male ex *Myotis nigricans*, El Paují, 70 Km W. Sta. Elena, 3.VIII.1985 (CP-MBUCV 1176); 1 female and 1 male ex *M. riparius*, same locality, 17.VIII.1984 (CP-MBUCV 4578).

Remarks.--

Neither in original description nor in original figures of this species (Guimaraes and D'Andretta, 1956), appeared the long setae between spiracles and tergum I and surrounding spiracle VII, observed in our specimen; however, we do not think that the presence or absence of these setae are indicative of a different species.

Discussion.--

The *junquiensis* group (group IV), was one of the 7 groups established by Guimaraes and D'Andretta (1956) to clust the *Basilia* species already known for the New World; however, Theodor (1967) reduced the groups of species to 4, arguing that the characters used by Guimaraes and D'Andretta (op. cit.) were useful at species level, but not for supraspecies ranks; so, Theodor joined up the *junquiensis* and the *speiseri* (group III of Guimaraes and D'Andretta) groups, and defined *Basilia anceps* as subspecies of *B. junquiensis*. However, these changes were not accepted by Guimaraes (1972). This situation have two problems: or the above mentioned morphotypes are subspecies or full species, forming a natural and independent group, or they are part of the *speiseri* group. We will try to clarify both questions as follows.

Guimaraes and D'Andretta (1956), describing *B. anceps*, suggested that it could be just a subspecies of *B. junquiensis*. Theodor (1967), without any comment about it, defined *anceps* as subspecies of *junquiensis*, probably by its great similarity; with the same criteria *manu* should be also a subspecies. Later, Guimaraes (1972) mantained *anceps* as species. *B.junquiensis* was known by a female holotype collected from *Myotis nigricans* of Sao Paulo, Brazil (Guimaraes, 1946), and by 3 females from *M. nigricans* and *M. riparius* of Western Venezuela (Guimaraes, 1972). *B. anceps* was described with 3 females from *M. nigricans* of Caquetá, Colombia, and 1 female from the same host of Huanuco, Peru (Guimaraes and D'Andretta, 1956); lately, another 3 males and 2 females were found in *M. nigricans*, and 2 females in *M. simus*, both of Panamá (Guimaraes, 1966), but Handley (1966), in the same volume, identified it as *Myotis simus riparius*, being really *Myotis riparius* (LaVal, 1973); Guerrero (1989), reported 1 male and 3 females from *M. nigricans* of Southern Venezuela, totaling 4 males and 5 females from the same host, and 1 male and 2 females form *M. riparius*, also from Southern Venezuela; finally, 19 specimens of *B. manu* are known from *M. riparius*, 7 from *M. simus*, 3 from *M. nigricans*, and 1 from *M. albescens*, all of Peru. Literally a puzzle as Guimaraes (1972) points out, since apparently there is not any correspondence among the 3 morphotypes, their hosts and geographic distribution, that allows one to assign a clearly determined region or a host species for each morphotype, which means a subspecific taxonomic rank associated to a geographical zone or to a host species; instead, there is an overlapping of hosts and distribution ranges, as was observed in Peru, where 2 morphotypes were found at relatively near locations. For these reasons, I think that the morphotypes are full species.

The main character used to separate *juquiensis* and *anceps* from the other species of *Basilia* of the New World, was the absence of sternite IV (III in original nomenclature), due to the big size of the sclerites of the sternites V y VI and sternite I+II, also particularlly long. The condition of only 2 sternites both divided into 2 sclerites, and sternite I+II, is unique within the *Basilia* genus and in the *junquiensis*, *anceps* and *manu* species. When Guimaraes and D'Andretta (1956) described the male named *Basilia* sp b, pointed out that its parameres are completely different to the other species of the genus, forked in its anterior part, the same as *anceps*. For these reasons, I think that the *junquiensis* group must be considered as a natural supraspecific unit, characterized by :

Female with only two tergites before the anal segment, tergum II twice longer than wide with the posterior margin slightly rounded, sternum III not individualized, sternum IV absent, and sternum V and VI divided in 2 sclerites. Male with aedeagus long and slender, with part of the anterior margin serrated, short and strong parameres with forked terminal end.

Species grouped:

> Basilia junquiensis Guimaraes,1946
> Basilia anceps Guimaraes & D'Andretta,1956
> Basilia manu n. sp.
> > Basilia sp (b) Guimaraes & D'Andretta,1956

ACKNOWLEDGMENTS

Field work in Peru was funded by BIOLAT program of the National Museum of Natural History, Smithsonian Institution. I am grateful to Fundación Terramar for provide field support in the Venezuelan Amazonas. The Peruvian bats were collected and identified by César Ascorra, to whom I extend my gratitude. This is the contribution no. 84 of the Smithsonian Institution's Biological Diversity in Latin America (BIOLAT) Program.

LITERATURE CITED

Guerrero, R. 1989. Lista de los parásitos de mamíferos del cerro Marahuaca, Territorio Federal Amazonas, Venezuela. Acta Terramaris 1:85-96.

Guimaraes, L. R. 1946. Revisao das espécies sulamericanas do gènero Basilia (Diptera, Nycteribiidae). Arquivos de Zoologia do Estado de Sao Paulo 5:1-88.

------. 1966. Nycteribiid batflies from Panama (Diptera, Nycteribiidae). Pp. 393-404 in R. L. Wenzel & V. J. Tipton, eds., Ectoparasites of Panama. Chicago.

------. 1972. Venezuelan Nycteribiid batflies (Diptera, Nycteribiidae).--Brigham Young University Science Bulletin, Biological Series 17 (1):1-11.

------, & M. A. D'Andretta. 1956. Sinopse dos Nycteribiidae (Diptera) do Novo Mundo. Arquivos de Zoologia do Estado de Sao Paulo 10:1-184.

Handley, C. O. 1966. Checklist of the Mammals of Panama. Pp. 753-793 in R. L. Wenzel & V. J. Tipton, eds., Ectoparasites of Panama. Chicago.

LaVal, R. K. 1973. A revision of the Neotropical bats of the genus Myotis. National History Museum of Los Angeles County Sience Bulletin 15:1-54.

Theodor, O. 1967. An illustrated catalogue of the Rothschild collection of Nycteribiidae (Diptera) in the British Museum (Natural History) with keys and short descriptions for the identification of subfamilies, genera, species and subspecies. British Museum (Natural History) Publication 655:1-506.

Instituto de Zoología Tropical, Facultad de Ciencias, Universidad Central de Venezuela, Apartado 47058, Caracas 1041A, Venezuela.

Contributors

César Ascorra G.
UNIVERSIDAD NACIONAL MAYOR DE SAN MARCOS
Museo de Historia Natural
Casilla 14-0434
Lima 14, PERU

Robyn J. Burnham
UNIVERSITY OF MICHIGAN
Museum of Paleontology
Ann Arbor, MI 48109-1079
USA

Roberto A. Cambra T.
UNIVERSITARIA DE PANAMÁ
UNIVERSIDAD DE PANAMÁ, PANAMÁ
Museo de Invertebrados
G.B. Fairchild, Estafeta

Mirna Casagrande
UNIVERSIDAD FEDERAL DO PARANA
Dept. de Entomologia
C.P. 19020
81531-970 Curitiba, Parana
BRAZIL

Flor Chávez
NEW YORK BOTANICAL GARDEN
Palm Flora of the Amazon Project
Bronx, NY 10458
USA

Jonathan A. Coddington
SMITHSONIAN INSTITUTION, NMNH
Department of Entomology, MRC 105
10th & Constitution Ave., N.W.
Washington, D.C. 20560
USA

James A. Comiskey
SMITHSONIAN INSTITUTION, QUAD
MAB/Man & The Biosphere Biological Diversity
1100 Jefferson Drive, S.W., MRC 705
Washington, D.C. 20560
USA

Jesús H. Córdova
UNIVERSIDAD NACIONAL MAYOR DE SAN MARCOS
Museo de Historia Natural
Casilla 14-0434
Lima 14, PERU

Francisco Dallmeier
SMITHSONIAN INSTITUTION, QUAD
MAB/Man & The Biosphere Biological Diversity
1100 Jefferson Drive, S.W., MRC 705
Washington, D.C. 20560
USA

Terry L. Erwin
SMITHSONIAN INSTITUTION, NMNH
Department of Entomology, MRC 169
10th & Constitution Ave., N.W.
Washington, D.C. 20560
USA

Oliver S. Flint, Jr.
SMITHSONIAN INSTITUTION, NMNH
Department of Entomology, MRC 105
10th & Constitution Ave., N.W.
Washington, D.C. 20560
USA

Robin B. Foster
SMITHSONIAN TROPICAL RESEARCH INSTITUTE
**Apartado 2072, Balboa Panamá and Botany
Deparment**, Field Museum Chicago
IL, 60605-2496

Rossen W. Garrison
RESEARCH ASSOCIATE,
Natural History Museum of Los Angeles
County, 900 Expositum Boulevard,
Los Angeles, C.A. 90007

Ricardo Guerrero
UNIVERSIDAD CENTRAL DE VENEZUELA
Instituto de Zoología Tropical
Apartado 47058

Caracas 1041A, VENEZUELA

Mary Hagedorn
SMITHSONIAN INSTITUTION
National Zoological Park, MRC 551
Department of Animal Health
3000 Connecticut Ave., N.W.
Washington, D.C. 20008
USA

Donald J. Harvey
SMITHSONIAN INSTITUTION, NMNH
Department of Entomology, MRC 127
10th & Constitution Ave., N.W.
Washington, D.C. 20560
USA

Margo Kabel
SMITHSONIAN INSTITUTION
National Portrait Gallery, MRC 213
8th & F Streets, N.W.
Washington, D.C. 20560
USA

Clifford H. Keller
UNIVERSITY OF OREGON
Institute of Neuroscience
222 Huestis Hall
Eugene, OR 97403
USA

Gerardo Lamas M.
UNIVERSIDAD NACIONAL MAYOR DE SAN MARCOS
Museo de Historia Natural
Casilla 14-0434
Lima 14, PERU

Ximena Londoño P.
INSTITUTO VALLECAUCANO DE INVESTIGACIO-
NES CIENTÍFICAS - INCIVA
Apartado Aéreo 5660
Cali, COLOMBIA

Jerry A. Louton
SMITHSONIAN INSTITUTION, NMNH
Department of Entomology, MRC 165
10th & Constitution Ave., N.W.
Washington, D.C. 20560
USA

Roy W. McDiarmid
NATIONAL BIOLOGICAL SURVEY
**División of Amphibians and
Reptiles, NMNH**
Washington, D.C. 20560
USA

Mirian C. Medina
UNIVERSITY OF TEXAS AT AUSTIN
Department of Zoology
Austin, TX 78712
USA

Olaf Mielke
UNIVERSIDADE FEDERAL DO PARANÁ
Dept. de Zoologia
C.P. 19020
81531-970 - Curitiba, Paraná
BRAZIL

Mario Monteghirfo
UNIVERSIDAD NACIONAL MAYOR DE SAN MARCOS
**Centro de Investigación de Bioquímica y
Nutrición. C/BN - UNMSM**
Apartado 1546
Lima 100, PERU

Víctor R. Morales M.
UNIVERSIDAD NACIONAL MAYOR DE SAN MARCOS
Museo de Historia Natural
Apartado 14-0434
Lima 14 - PERU

Hernán Ortega
UNIVERSIDAD NACIONAL MAYOR DE SAN MARCOS
Museo de Historia Natural
Casilla 14-0434
Lima 14, PERU

Víctor Pacheco
UNIVERSIDAD NACIONAL MAYOR DE SAN MARCOS
Museo de Historia Natural
Casilla 14-0434
Lima 14, PERU